THE GLOBAL SKI

Editorial Office:
8 St. Albans Grove, London W8 5PN
Fax: 0171 937 1595 Tel.0171 937 1595

Australian Distributors
Bookwise International
54 Crittenden Road
Findon 5023, S. Australia.
Tel: 08 268 8222
Fax: 08 268 8704

Published by:
Skier's Holiday Guide Club
in association with SkiNetica, a division of Netica plc
8 St. Albans Grove, London W8 5PN
Fax: 0171 937 1595 Tel: 0171 937 1595
Printed and bound in Great Britain by R. R. Donnelly-Pindar, Feltham, Middlesex

North American Distributors
Hunter Publishing Inc
239 South Beach Road
Hobe Sound, FL 33455
Tel: 407 546 7986
Fax: 407 546 8040

Whilst every care has been taken with the preparation of this Guide, over a period of several months, we cannot be held responsible for any inaccuracies or omissions. All prices should be taken as a guide and re-checked at the time of making reservations.

ISBN 0 9517481 5 7

RESORT INDEX

RESORT INDEX

GENERAL INDEX

EDITOR'S COMMENT

This 24th edition of Britain's longest running Ski Guide embraces some 400 resorts in 23 countries and has, therefore, been appropriately renamed 'The Global Ski Guide'.

SkiNetica: We are particularly happy to announce the partnership with Netica plc, whose skiing division, Ski Netica, will be sponsoring The Global Ski Guide for the next five years and will incorporate the Guide into its on-line ski information service on the Internet. As well as detailed information on resort facilities, SkiNetica's web site will eventually provide updated information on local weather, snow conditions, hotel availability and so on.

Another interesting feature of the service is the alliance between SkiNetica and the International Ski Federation (FIS) whereby SkiNetica will calculate and publish the World Cup ski rankings after every event. It will be fascinating to see how this new medium for ski information develops. The SkiNetica web site is available at www.SkiNetica.com.

Saving Money: Unfortunately skiing is not the cheapest type of holiday, particularly for the family where prices are multiplied several times. In this respect we try to help and refer readers to the Skier's Holiday Guide Club, pages 6 - 11. It will be seen that apart from discounts on holidays booked via the Club, 213 sports shops in the U.K. and the resorts offer discounts to members on hire and/or purchases.

Car Skiing Holidays: The cheapest form of ski holiday for a group of 3 - 4 persons is to travel by car. One only has to look at the prices in pages 9 and 10 to appreciate this fact.

Snowboarding: Our charts in pages 266-267 show resorts which have fun parks and half pipes for this fast growing sport, along with prices for instruction and equipment hire. It should be noted that 162 resort sports shops allow discounts on hire and some on purchases, whilst the 51 in the UK discounts on purchases.

North America: Claire Walter, our North American editor has done a thorough update on the resorts, pages 14 - 43, including brief reports on six new ones. She points out in her introduction that many resorts are now combining to offer multi resort lift passes. Under Park City, page 34, she mentions that one of the biggest developments is taking place in the Canyons area with the construction of an eight seater gondolaway, a restaurant and beginners area at the top and five new four seater chair-lifts - total cost 18.2 million dollars! For those who are interested in Heli-Skiing her article in page 12 will be particularly helpful. We again thank Claire for her efforts.

Around the World: In pages 255-264 we briefly feature some 60 resorts or heli-ski operations in eight distant countries. Not the places one would go for a weekend but at some stage you may be visiting relatives or business associates nearby. Failing this it is hoped that you will enjoy reading through the section.

In publishing the above mentioned resorts we would like to thank Sasha St. Clair for all his hard work. As many readers will remember Sasha was editor and publisher of the excellent full colour Skier's Atlas of Australia and New Zealand. He is at present in the USA furthering his knowledge of ski resorts in all parts of the world.

Impressions: We also publish some of our Correspondents' impressions on skiing at some of these far distant resorts. Kay Anderson, Robert Harrison and Adrian Essex, do so on North American resorts, page 13, whilst Judy Skeats does so on Australia and New Zealand, page 265.

The Global Ski Guide - Ski Hotline: For snow reports and weather conditions members will again have their own Ski Hotline covering some 180 resorts in Europe and North America. See page 8 and also the membership card. It will be seen that reports can be obtained by telephone or fax.

Membership Card: Your membership card will be found in the back of this Guide. You may have all your equipment and clothing but suggest that you should always take this with you on holiday. Things do go wrong, e.g. a few years ago a large party lost all their equipment in transit and had to hire at the resort. The party leader produced his membership card which saved him well over £100.

French School Holidays: For the 1998 season French school holidays will be staggered in four zones, starting 4th February and terminating 25th March.

Resort Facilities Charts, North America: It is regretted that much of the updated information for this section came in too late to be included. SkiNetica will be able to show the full updating of this section, alternatively it can be obtained by telephoning the editorial office, 0171 937 1595.

Appreciation: We again thank the directors of the resort tourist office and their staff for their assistance; and the owners of sports shops in the U.K. resort sports shops and artificial ski slopes who have allowed discounts for Club members. Grateful thanks to our editors, assistant editors and correspondents listed in the title page and last but not least SkiNetica for their sponsorship of this Guide.

Wishing all members a successful and enjoyable holiday.

SKIER'S HOLIDAY GUIDE CLUB

8 St. Albans Grove, London W8 5PN

Tel & Fax: 0171 937 1595

FREE MEMBERSHIP

The purchase of the Guide automatically entitles UK or Overseas readers to one year's membership of the Club from 1st October 1997, so one is not simply buying a publication but a valuable service in addition to the various concessions for members, listed, which can more than pay for the cost of the Guide! A **membership card** is contained at the back of the Guide and **discount vouchers** will be found in page 296. Service to members is as follows:

* A comprehensive free advisory service based on 51 years' experience, and not simply confined to providing resort and hotel information but an assessment of values on the holiday packages as a whole.
* Discounts on purchases of clothing and equipment and equipment hire at 162 resort sports shops.
* Discounts on purchases of clothing and equipment and equipment hire at 51 sports shops in the UK.
* Discounts at 11 artificial ski slopes in the UK.
* A discount of **£20 per car** on 'Car Skiing' & Self-Catering holidays.
* A discount of **£5 per member** on Self-Catering holidays by air or rail.
* A discount of **£10 per member** for holidays based on hotel accommodation or staffed chalets with travel by air or rail.
* A discount of **10%** on car snow chains.

  A discount of **10%** on car roof boxes.
* Booking service for rail travel.
* Booking service for air travel.
* Booking service for Chalets and apartments with Interhome.
* Booking service with selected hotels and tour operators.
* Comprehensive Winter Sports Insurance service.

CONCESSIONS FOR MEMBERS AT SPORTS SHOPS IN THE RESORTS

See pages 278-279

Country/Resort	Name of Sports Shop	Percentage Discount to Members On Hire	On Purchases
ANDORRA			
Arsinal	Sports Rossel	20	5
La Massana	Sports Rossel	20	5
Pal	Sports Rossel	20	5
Pas de la Casa	Ski Calbo	20	5
Soldeu	Ski Calbo	20	5
AUSTRIA			
Fieberbrunn	Widmann Sport	10	–
Gargellen	Madrisa–Skiverleih	10	–
Hochgurgl	Intersport Riml	10	5
Lermoos	Sport Mader	10	–
Obergurgl	Intersport Riml	10	–
Obertauern	Sporthaus Gloria	10	5
St. Anton	Sport Pangratz	10	5
Seefeld	Sport Christian	15	–
Söll	Ski Centre Stoll Söll	15	10
Steinach	Sport Messner	10	10
Westendorf	Dieter's Sport Shop	15++	10++
Zell am Ziller	Schuh u Sport Pendl	5	5

++Cash

Country/Resort	Name of Sports Shop	Percentage Discount to Members On Hire	On Purchases
FRANCE			
Alpe D'Huez	Henri Sports (Les Bergers)	20	5
	Henri Sports (Chamois d'Or)	20	5
	Man Sport (Les Bergers)	20	5
Argentière	Les Grands Montets Sports	20	5
Avoriaz	Superski (Place Central)	20	5
	Mir-Famose (Place Central)	20	5
	Skiland (Falaise)	20	5
	SkiFun (Falaise)	20	5
	Sport Espace (Falaise)	20	5
Chamonix	Ogier Sports	20	5
Chatel	Inter-Sport	15	10
	Francis Sport (Les Névés)	20	5
	Francis Sport (Chamois d'Or)	20	5
	Le Linga	20	5
Courchevel 1650	Serge Sport (Ourse Bleue)	20	5
Courchevel 1850	Ski Service (Club Hotel)	20	5
	Ski Service (Chabichou)	20	5
	Ski Service (Chamois)	20	5
	Ski Service (Tovets)	20	5
	Ski Service (New Solarium)	20	5
	Ski Service (Bellecôte)	20	5

CONCESSIONS FOR MEMBERS AT SPORTS SHOPS IN THE RESORTS

See pages 278-279

Country/Resort	Name of Sports Shop	Percentage Discount to Members On Hire	On Purchases
FRANCE			
Flaine	Flaine Sport (Forêt)	20	5
	Général Sport (Hameau)	20	5
	La Boutique (Forum)	20	5
Isola 200	Morisset Sport	20	5
La Clusaz	Guy Perillat Shop (Le Portillo)	20	5
Belle Plagne	Belle Plan Sports	20	5
Plagne Centre	Allais Ski Service	20	5
Plagne Bellecôte	Skiteam	20	5
Plagne 1800	Plagne 1800 Sports	20	5
Champagny	In'Sport	20	5
Aime 200	Skiteam	20	5
Montabert	Sport Passion	20	5
Les Coches	La Godille	20	5
La Rosière	Ski Boutique La Poudre	20	5
La Tania	Ski Wave	20	5
Le Corbier	Noel Sports	20	5
Les Arcs	Ski Shop (Arc 1600)	20	5
	Ski Shop (Arc 1800)	20	5
	Ski Shop (Arc 2000)	20	5
Les Carroz	Ski 2000	20	5
Les Coches	La Poudreuse	20	5
Les Deux Alpes	Brun Sport (Centre)	20	5
	Hibernatus (Vénosc)	20	5
	J M Sports	20	5
	La Datcha	20	5
Les Menuires	Léo Lacroix Sports (La Croisette)	20	5
	Léo Lacroix Sports (Reberty)	20	5
	Skiloc CC Sports (Preyerand)	20	5
Mégève	Duvillard et Lafforgue	20	5
Méribel	Sport Boutique (Les Carlines)	20	5
	Sport Boutique (Centre)	20	5
	Germain Sport (Centre)	20	5
	Sport Tecnik (La Chaudanne)	20	5
	Chamois Sports (1600)	15	10
Méribel Mottaret	Ski Espace (Res. Olympia)	20	5
	Superski (Res. Le Pralin)	20	5
	Surf Machine (Res. Plan du Lac)	20	5
	Sport Boutique (Hameau)	20	5
Morzine	La Caribou Sports	20	5
Risoul	Evasion Sport (Front de Neige)	20	5
	Evasion Sport (Res. Mélèzes A)	20	5
	Free Ride (Mélèzes)	20	5
St Lary	Rodriguez Sport (Pla d'Adet)	20	5
Serre Chevalier	Régis Sport (1350)	20	5
	Régis Sport (1400)	20	5
	Régis Sport (1400)	20	5
Tignes	Point Service Ski (Val Claret)	20	5
	Point Service Ski (Lavachet)	20	5
	Point Service Ski (Le Borsat)	20	5
	Point Service Ski (Chalet Club)	20	5
	Point Service Ski (Rd Point Pistes)	20	5
	Point Service Ski (Le Lac)	20	5
	Sport Glisse (Val Claret)	20	10
Val Cenis	Sports Vanoise	20	5
	La Poudre	20	5
Val d'Isére	Skiset (La Daille)	20	5
	Point Service Ski (Centre)	20	5
Valfréjus	Ski Pro	20	5
Valloire	Val d'Auréa Sport	20	5
Valmorel	Claude Sport	20	5
Val Thorens	Goitschel Sports (Péclet)	20	5
	Goitschel Sports (Caron)	20	5
	Goitschel Sports (Espace Goitschel)	20	5
	Skiloc CC Sports (Altineige)	20	5
Vaujany	Sami Ski	20	5
Villars de Lans	Nouvelles Glisses	20	5

Country/Resort	Name of Sports Shop	Percentage Discount to Members On Hire	On Purchases
ITALY			
Foppolo	Mode Sport F. Berera	5	10
Limone	Bottero Ski	10	10
Macugnaga	Rabogliatti Sport	10	10
NORWAY			
Nordseter	Aktivitets & Skisenter	10	–
Wadahl	Wadahl Sports	10	10
SPAIN			
Sierra Nevada	Veleta Ski	10	10
SWEDEN			
Duved	Duveds Skiduthyrning	10	10
SWITZERLAND			
Adelboden	Hari Sport	10	–
Andermatt	Meyer's Sporthaus	10	10
	Alpina Sport	10	–
Anzere	Jacky Sports	10	–
	Crazy Corner Sports	10	–
Arosa	Carmenna Sport	10	–
	Bananas Snowboard Centre	10	–
Bettmeralp	Mattig Sport	10	–
Braunwald	Kessler Sport	10	–
Celerina	Testa Sport	10	10
Champery	Berra Sports	10	10*
	Borgeat Sports	10	–
Crans-Montana	Galeries Bouby Sports	10	–
Davos-Dorf	Ettinger Sport	10	5
	PaarSenn Sport	10	–
Davos-Platz	Ettinger Sport	10	5
	Grischetta Sport	10	–
Disentis	Bergbahnen Disentis AG	10	–
Engelberg	Quattro Sport	10	–
	Titlis-Sport	10	10
Flims-Dorf	Bundi Sport	10	–
Flims-Waldhaus	Bundi Sport	10	–
Flumserberg	Gubser Sport	10	
Grindelwald	Graf Sport	10	–
Gstaad	Hermenjat Sports	10	–
	Hermenjat Boutiques	10	–
Klosters	Gotschna Sport	10	–
	Albeina Sport	10	–
Laax	Meini Sport Mode	10	–
Lenzerheide	Pesco Sport	10	–
Les Diablerets	Jacky Sports	10	–
Leysin	Hefti Sports	10	–
Morgins	Morgins-Sports	10	–
Riederalp	Krüger Sport	10	–
Rougemont	Duperrex Sport	10++	10++
Saas-Fee	Anthamatten Sport	10	–
Samnaun	Hangl Sport	10	–
Samedan	Luthi Sport	10	–
Savognin	Wasescha Sport AG	10	–
Schönreid	Frautschi Sports AG	10	–
Scuol	Hanin Conradin Sport	10	–
Silvaplana	Skiservice Corvatsch	10	–
St. Moritz-Bad	Corviglia Sport Shop	10	–
St. Moritz	Corviglia Sport Shop	10	–
Verbier	Danni Sports	20	10
	La Vallée Sport	10	–
	Ski Service SA	10	–
Villars	Dåtwyler Sport	10	–
Wildhaus	Steiner Sport	10	–
Zermatt	Bayard Sport	10	–
Zuoz	Willy Sport	10	–

* Over SF 100 ++ Cash –

CONCESSIONS FOR MEMBERS AT SPORTS SHOPS IN THE U.K

See pages 286-293

City Town	Name of Sports Shop	Percentage Discount to Members On Hire	On Purchases
Aberdeen	Ann Robb Sports Studio	–	10
Aviemore	Ski Road Skis	15	10
	Speyside Sports	10	10
Barnet	John Pollock	–	5
Bedford	Two Seasons	10	10
Bicester	Beans	–	10
Blackpool	Alpine Centre	–	10
Bowness-on-Windermere	Ski Treks/Lakeland Leisure	10	12
Brighton	Eurosport Ltd	10	10
Bristol	Ellis Brigham	5	–
Broughton-in-Furness	Mountain Centre	–	10
Burnley	Sportak Ltd	–	10++****
Buxton	Jo Royle	–	10
Canterbury	Captain's Cabin Ld.	10***	10***
Catterick	Ski Slope Shop	10	10
Chatham	Captain's Cabin	10***	10***
Chelmsford	Ski Plus	–	10
Cheltenham	Horace Barton & Son	–	10
Chester	Sail & Ski	–	10
Eastbourne	Outdoor Life	–	10+
Elland	BAC Ski Shop	10	10
Esher	Europa Ski Lodge	–	5
Gloucester	Horace Barton	–	10
Grantown-on-Spey	Speyside Sports	10	10****
Hanley	Mountain Fever	–	10
Harlow	John Pollock	–	5
Havant	Filarinskis	5	10
Hemel Hempstead	Snowcap	–	5
Kingston Upon Thames	Snowbusiness Ltd	10***	10***
Leeds	Severn Sports	–	10
Leicester	Roger Turner Mountain Sports	–	10
Liverpool	Ellis Brigham	10	–
London	Don Farrell	–	10***
Loughton	John Pollock	–	5
Milton Keynes	The Outdoor Shop	–	20
Newcastle-upon-Tyne	LD Mountain Centre	–	10
Northampton	Two Seasons	10	10
Norwich	R. G. Pilch	–	10***
Nottingham	Roger Turner Mountain Sports	–	10
Oldham	Paul Braithwaite	10	10
Oxford	Westsports	–	10
Peterborough	Hereward Ski & Walk	–	20****
Pontefract	Crossley Tordoff	–	10
Portsmouth	Peter Anderson Sports	–	10
Reading	Pro Activ	5	5
Richmond	Snowball Ski Company	–	Varies
Stockport	Alpenstock	–	10
	Base Camp	–	10
Sunderland	Reynolds Outdoor Centre	–	5
Swindon	Westsports Ski Shop	–	10
Yeadon (Leeds)	The Great Outdoors	–	10

*** Credit Cards 5%   ****Not on special offers

+On purchases of £100 or over   ++Cash/Cheque sales only

CONCESSIONS FOR MEMBERS AT ARTIFICIAL SKI SLOPES IN THE U.K

See pages 284-285

City Town	Name of Slope	Percentage Discount to Members
Aldershot	Alpine Ski Centre	10++
Churchill	Avon Ski Centre	10*
Edinburgh	Hillend Ski Centre	10++
Halifax	Halifax Ski Centre	10
Hemel Hempstead	Hemel Ski Centre	5++
London	Crystal Palace Ski School	10
Newmilns	Newmilns Ski Slope	10
Tallington	Ski & Snowboard Centre	10
Tunbridge Wells	Bowls Ski Centre	10*
Uxbridge	Hillingdon Ski & Snowboard Centre	10
Welwyn Garden City	Gosling Ski Centre	10++

*On Ski Lessons   ++ Recreational skiing

WINTER SPORTS INSURANCE

Car Breakdown Insurance: All our Car skiing holidays include breakdown insurance for your car. A brief summary of the cover is as follows:-

Immobilisation or theft prior to travel	£1,000
Roadside Assistance	Unlimited
Vehicle Repatriation	Unlimited
Loss of Vehicle use	Unlimited
Alternative snowchains and/or ski rack	£250

Personal Accident Insurance: As mentioned in page 294 it is essential that you take out personal cover. We can arrange this for you at the following premiums:-

	Skiing	Non Skiing
Up to 5 days	£24.00	£8.00
Up to 10 days	£28.00	£10.00
Up to 17 days	£30.00	£12.00
Up to 24 days	£32.00	£14.00

A brief summary of cover is as follows:-

Personal Accident	£25,000
Medical Expenses	£5,000,000
Baggage and Personal Effects	£1,500
Personal Money/Ski Pass cash limit	£300
Personal Liability	£1,000,000
Winter Sports Equipment	£500

Full details will be sent with your confirmation of booking.

GLOBAL SKI GUIDE

SKI HOTLINE

Latest reports for 180+ ski resorts throughout Europe and North America. For full details of snow and weather conditions by voice or fax dial:

0891 654 625

For a voice forecast

0897 500 625

For a fax forecast

Please ensure you use a fax handset if accessing a fax report. Calls cost 50p/min at all times (as at 8/97). SKI Hotline is a product of Newstel Information Ltd, 203 Pentagon Centre, Glasgow G3 8AZ. Helpline: 0990 133 345

CLUB HOLIDAYS 1997/98 SEASON

By Car via Channel Ferries or Channel Tunnel: We list a series of 'Car Skiing' holidays to 33 resorts in Austria, France, Italy and Switzerland. This type of holiday based on self-catering accommodation has three main advantages:- (1) The most economical form of holiday. (2) No luggage or carriage of skis problems – load up at home and off-load at the resort. (3) A car can be useful for visiting nearby resorts and particularly if snow conditions are not good at the resort of your choice.

By Air, Rail or Coach: For tour operators' package holidays by air, rail or coach based on hotel or staffed chalet accommodation, we have appointed Gemini Travel, an IATA and ABTA agency, as the Club's official agents. This means that members can select any holidays from a major tour operator's brochure and make reservations via the Club.

Prices in the following tables are in £ sterling per person and include:

* Return cross channel fares for car (any length) and for the number of persons stated, by ferry or Le Shuttle.
* Vehicle Insurance
* Self-Catering accommodation in the number of rooms as stated for a period of 7 nights. All apartments are fully equipped with bathroom/shower, wc, kitchen/kitchenette and in most cases balcony or terrace. We would be pleased to give quotations for 14 nights or longer in the resort.

Notes: Local Charges: These are shown below each resort, LT = Local tax; BL = Hire of bed linen and towels; these however, can be taken if preferred.

Returnable Deposits: Normally between £100-£150 in local currency, Eurocheque or credit card.

Arrival & Departure: It does not matter when you leave the U.K. but reservations are normally from Saturday to Saturday. Arrival time between 1600-1900 hours and vacating the premises by 1000 hours on the day of departure.
Quotations can be given for resorts not shown in these tables.

As with all holidays our advisory service is available and we welcome the opportunity of discussing, on the telephone, the most suitable resort and accommodation for your particular requirement.

'CAR SKIING' HOLIDAYS 1997-98 SEASON

7 Nights Self-Catering Accommodation. **For reservations ring 0171 937 1595**

Country	**AUSTRIA**											
Resort	**Badgastein**		**Bad Hofgastein**		**Kirchberg**		**Kitzbühel**		**Saalbach**		**Zell am See**	
Apartment	22B	70B	1D	110C	T22	300A	100C	200C	20C	1C	T22	200C
Ref. No.	2 rooms	3 rooms	1 room	2 rooms	2 rooms	2 rooms	2 rooms	2 rooms	1 room	2 rooms	2 rooms	4 rooms
No. of Persons	4	6	4	5	5	5	4	4	4	4	4	6
Arrival Dates												
20 Dec.	104	101	93	84	130	112	139	122	134	157	113	117
27 Dec.	127	110	113	91	148	126	162	143	151	181	134	129
3 Jan.	110	74	98	88	134	115	174	127	138	163	119	120
10,17,24 Jan.	86	73	78	84	117	101	121	106	121	140	98	108
31 Jan,7,14,21 Feb	127	110	113	87	148	112	162	133	141	171	134	122
28 Feb-11 Apr.	111	89	95	84	117	112	121	106	130	140	109	108
Local charges	LT	BL	LT	BL	LT	BL	LT	BL	LT	BL	LT	BL

Country	**FRANCE**									
Resort	**Alpe d'Huez**		**Les Arcs**		**Chamonix**		**Chatel**		**Flaine**	
Ref. No.	T14	T24	T14	T24	T14	T22	T22	T32	T12	T22
Apartment	Studio	2 rooms	Studio	2 rooms	Studio	2 rooms	2 rooms	3 rooms	Studio	2 rooms
No. Persons	4	6	4	6	4	4	4	6	4	4
Arrival Dates										
20 Dec.	110	98	116	109	95	106	94	79	131	150
27 Dec.	124	117	134	129	131	148	129	101	151	182
3,10 Jan.	85	69	91	83	85	93	94	79	90	105
17,24,31 Jan.	85	69	91	83	85	93	94	79	97	112
7 Feb.	130	117	134	129	114	148	147	117	131	150
14,21 Feb.	130	117	134	129	114	148	147	117	151	182
28 Feb.	107	98	116	109	95	106	103	85	115	131
7 Mar.	107	98	116	109	95	106	103	85	104	121
14 Mar.	85	69	91	83	85	93	94	79	104	121
21,28 Mar.	85	69	91	83	85	93	94	79	115	131
4,11 Apr.	85	69	76	67	85	93	94	79	89	131
Local charges	LT	BL	LT	BL	LT	BL	BL	LT	LT	BL

'CAR SKIING' HOLIDAYS

Country	**FRANCE**									
Resort	**La Clusaz**		**Les Deux Alpes**			**Les Menuires**			**Méribel & Les Allues**	
Ref. No.	T22	T32	T14	T22	T32	T12	T22	T24	T24	10B
Apartment	2 rooms	3 rooms	Studio	2 rooms	3 rooms	Studio	2 rooms	2 rooms	2 rooms	4 rooms
No. of persons	4	6	4	4	6	4	4	6	6	7
Arrival Dates										
20 Dec.	71	54	116	125	92	96	126	91	131	85
27 Dec.	116	83	136	147	109	124	160	119	173	85
3,10,17 Jan.	71	54	86	91	67	75	90	66	101	85
24,31 Jan.	71	54	86	91	67	75	90	66	131	85
7 Feb.	137	100	136	147	109	124	160	119	173	92
14,21 Feb.	137	100	136	147	109	124	160	119	191	92
28 Feb.	116	83	86	91	75	96	126	91	131	85
7 Mar.	116	83	86	91	75	96	126	91	120	85
14 Mar.-4 Apr.	71	54	86	91	75	96	126	91	120	85
11 Apr.	71	54	86	91	75	96	90	66	101	80
Local charges	LT	BL	LT	BL	BL	LT	BL	BL	LT	BL

Country	**FRANCE**							**ITALY***		
Resort	**Risoul**		**Tignes**			**Val Thorens**		**Livigno**	**Sestriere**	
Ref. No.	T12	T22	T12	T22	T32	T12	T24	57B	T23	T14
Apartment	Studio	2 rooms	Studio	2 rooms	3 rooms	Studio	2 rooms	3 rooms	2 rooms	Studio
No. of persons	4	4	4	4	6	4	6	4	5	4
Arrival Dates										
20 Dec.	95	114	122	144	120	105	101	109	104	120
27 Dec.	95	114	147	176	149	134	129	155	134	147
3 Jan.	76	88	91	104	83	85	75	109	71	81
10-31 Jan.	76	88	91	104	83	85	75	109	71	124
7,14,21 Feb.	116	140	147	176	149	134	129	119	110	124
28 Feb.-7 Mar.	95	114	122	144	120	105	101	119	110	124
14 Mar.-4 Apr.	76	88	122	144	120	105	101	119	110	124
11 Apr.	69	79	91	104	83	85	75	119	110	124
Local charges	LT	BL	LT	BL	BL	LT	BL	Inc.	BL	BL

***Italy:** We can give quotations for the following Italian resorts:- Aprica, Bormio, Canazei, Corvara, La Thuile, Macugnaga, Madonna di Campiglio, Pila, San Martino di Castrozza & Valtournenche.

Country	**SWITZERLAND**									
Resort	**Andermatt**	**Crans/Montana**		**Davos**		**Engelberg**	**Flims/Laax**	**Grindelwald**		**Grächen**
Ref. No.	100C	T23	T33	T20	T21	T22	T22	200A	130C	25E
Apartment	2 rooms	2 rooms	3 rooms	2 rooms	2 rooms	2 rooms	2 rooms	2 rooms	3 rooms	3 rooms
No. of persons	4	4	6	4	4	4	4	4	5	4
Arrival Dates										
20 Dec.	117	107	103	207	196	114	126	90	128	129
27 Dec.	145	148	148	207	196	134	167	106	144	150
3 Jan.	133	125	122	180	171	123	144	87	132	135
10,17 Jan.	117	94	88	144	138	107	114	78	116	114
24,31 Jan.	117	94	88	201	191	107	114	78	116	114
7,14,21,28 Feb.	128	148	148	201	191	134	154	99	144	136
7,14,21,28 Mar.	117	94	88	163	126	107	114	99	144	150
4,11 Apr.	128	130	130	163	126	116	131	99	144	150
Local charges	LT	LT	BL	LT	LT	LT	LT	LT	LT	LT

Country	**SWITZERLAND**											
Resort	**Haute Nendaz**		**Saas Fee**		**St. Moritz**	**Verbier**		**Villars**		**Zermatt**		
Ref. No.	T23	T32	T22	T33	120H	T12	T33	T23	T33	T23	T22	T32
Apartment	2 rooms	3 rooms	2 rooms	3 rooms	2 rooms	Studio	3 rooms	2 rooms	3 rooms	2 rooms	2 rooms	3 rooms
No. of persons	4	6	4	6	4	4	6	4	6	4	4	6
Arrival Dates												
20 Dec.	106	90	146	97	231	142	126	128	122	176	163	**155**
27 Dec.	122	103	146	97	268	165	150	153	139	216	199	181
3 Jan.	110	93	123	82	240	133	115	134	126	180	191	164
10,17,24 Jan.	94	80	123	82	203	90	69	109	109	190	181	140
31 Jan.	94	80	123	82	252	90	69	109	109	190	181	140
7,14,21,28 Feb.	122	103	146	97	252	148	131	153	139	199	199	158
7,14,21,28 Mar.	94	80	146	97	252	116	100	109	109	199	199	158
4 Apr.	106	92	146	97	252	148	131	109	109	199	199	158
11 Apr.	106	92	146	82	252	148	131	109	109	199	199	158
Local charges	LT	BL	LT	LT	LT,BL	LT	BL	LT	BL	LT	BL	BL

HOTEL HOLIDAYS BY AIR 1997/98 SEASON

In association with JAC Travel International Ltd

For advice and reservations ring 0171 937 1595

If skiers wish to save a considerable amount of money on holidays based on hotel accommodation then the low season periods should be selected. The holidays listed below are for departures in early January when hoteliers and tour operators produce their lowest rates. During this period the resorts are uncrowded and under normal conditions the snow is good.

The prices include return air travel, transfers from airport to resort and vice versa; 7 nights accommodation in twin bedded room with bath or shower and wc; meal arrangements half board; service charges and taxes. Prices are per person.

SAVE £10 PER PERSON: Members booking this type of holiday via the Club/JAC Travel International receive a discount of £10 per person on high or low season holidays. It also applies to Staffed Chalet Holidays. Vouchers will be found in page 296.

Resort/Hotel	Star Rating	7 Nights From £
AUSTRIA		
Alpbach		
Alpbacherhof	****	351
Böglerhof	****	498
Bad Hofgastein		
Krone	***	323
Filzmoos		
Alpenkrone	****	309
Hinterglemm		
Glemmtalerhof	****	47[illegible]
Hochleiten	***	357
Ischgl		
Albona	****	452
Kitzbühel		
Tyrol	***	320
Schweizerhof	****	410
Weisses Rössl	****	470
Mayrhofen		
Kramerwirt	****	321
Strass	****	420
Niederau		
Staffler	***	267
Austria	****	343
Obergurgl		
Josl	***	363
Jenewein	****	477
Wiesental	***	424
Obertauern		
Latschenhof	****	475
Taurach	***	425
Saalbach		
Kristall	****	446
Alpenhotel	****	455
St. Anton		
Alpenhof	***	415
Arlberg	****	459
Seefeld		
Haymon	***	385
Hiltpolt	****	444
Sölden		
Tyrol	**	435
Bergland	****	525
Söll		
Eggerwirt	***	315
Tyrol	****	415
Westendorf		
Theresiana	***	291
Post	***	333
Zell am See		
Seehof	***	315
St. Georg	****	477
FRANCE		
Alpe d'Huez		
Grandes Rousses	***	392
Belle Plagne		
Eldorador	**	417

Resort/Hotel	Star Rating	7 Nights From £
Chamonix		
Richmond	**	315
Mont Blanc	****	564
Chatel		
Fleur de Neige	***	379
Courchevel 1650		
Le Floride	***	461
Du Golf	***	485
Courchevel 1850		
Ducs de Savoi	****	698
La Potinière	**	419
Courcheneige	***	582
Flaine		
Aujon	**	289
Le Totem	***	395
Les Deux Alpes		
La Farandole	****	438
Mounier	***	519
Les Menuires		
L'Ours Blanc	***	472
Méribel		
L'Eterlou	***	498
Méribel Mottaret		
La Tarentaise	***	499
Morzine		
Le Tremplin	***	359
Serre Chevalier		
Le Christiana	***	415
Tignes		
Terril Blanc	***	429
Val d'Isère		
Le Kern	**	415
Grand Paradis	***	553
Tsanteleina	***	555
Val Thorens		
Le Sherpa	***	461
Le Val Thorens	***	421
ITALY		
Bormio		
Posta	****	344
Girasole	***	320
Cervinia		
Astoria	***	383
Punta Maquinaz	****	514
Cristallo	****	507
Cortina		
Italia	**	349
Parc Victoria	****	485
Courmayeur		
Edelweiss	**	381
Livigno		
Sporting	**	269
Europa	***	344
Madesimo		
Andossi	***	335
Emet	****	359

Resort/Hotel	Star Rating	7 Nights From £
ITALY		
Madonna		
Milano	***	415
Savoia Palace	****	425
Sauze d'Oulx		
Stella Alpina	**	310
Holiday Debili	***	349
Selva Val Gardena		
Alpino Plan	***	445
Gran Baita	****	614
Sestriere		
Hermitage	***	379
SPAIN		
Formigal		
Nieve Sol	***	229
Sierra Nevada		
Melia Sierra Nevada	****	345
SWITZERLAND		
Adelboden		
Adler	***	375
Steinmattle	****	390
Arosa		
Bellevue	****	496
Crans		
National	***	316
Astor	****	351
Davos		
Cresta	***	390
National	****	453
Grindelwald		
Eiger	****	388
Lenzerheide		
Alpina	****	430
Sun Star	****	524
Montana		
De la Forête	***	341
National	***	316
Mürren		
Jungfrau	***	370
Eiger	****	505
Saas Fee		
Marmotte	***	357
Walliserhof	****	557
St. Moritz		
Monopol	****	521
Steffani	****	657
Verbier		
Auberge	**	385
De la Poste	***	405
De Verbier	***	439
Wengen		
Brunner	***	385
Falken	***	344
Regina	****	395
Zermatt		
Dom	***	385
Park Beau Site	****	440
Alex	****	617

Note: Air supplements are applicable for travel from provincial airports

STAFFED CHALET HOLIDAYS: For members interested in this type of holiday in France, Italy or Switzerland at prices per person from £293 for 7 nights, we shall be pleased to give special quotations. Ring 0171 937 1595.

AIR TICKETS: We can also provide air tickets to European and North American airports from London and provincial airports at competitive prices.

HELI-SKIING IN NORTH AMERICA

by Claire Walter

Some skiers come to North America just for the heli-skiing, arguable the most exciting, energizing, thrilling and, yes, expensive types of ski vacation there is. It started in Canada and is still thriving there, where both multi-day (normally one-week) and one-day programs exist. Canada's best-known heli-skiing companies are Canadian Mountain Holidays and Mike Wiegele Heli-Skiing, both of which fly in the British Columbian Rockies, outside national park boundaries.

One-week programs normally include simple yet comfortable accommodations in backcountry lodges, three meals a day, the services of a guide and use of an avalanche transceiver. Two- or three-day programs may instead include lodging in the valley, with daily flights to ski.

Less known are the widely scattered U.S. operations, which struggle harder against environmental restrictions and other restraints. More than in Canada, U.S. operators design shorter programs to dovetail into resort-based vacations. An ideal way to test heli-skiing's frozen waters is on such a one-day program, which includes guide services, lunch, snacks, guide and transceiver. Once you know whether your temperament is suited to heli-skiing's deliberate pace and whether you have backcountry stamina, you can decide if a week-long trip is for you.

Whether you go for one day or several, you'll find that heli-skiing is at once thrilling and extremely controlled. Before you take off, you'll be drilled in how to use an avalanche transceiver (always supplied) and how to help in a rescue should a slide occur. Pay attention.

Once you are skiing, the guide is the czar – benevolent and charming perhaps, but the absolute dictator with the last and only word on where clients may go. If your guide says, "Ski one at a time. Stay to the left of that stand of trees. And don't go any farther than that big rock," that's what you'd better do. The best conditions are in the rugged backcountry, in new powder and on medium to steep terrain. While operators are ultra-cautious, nature cannot be controlled or predicted with ironclad assurance, and avalanches remain a possibility. The guide knows how to read the snow and is familiar with the terrain, and only a fool doesn't listen to his instructions.

You need to be a strong, high intermediate or better skier or rider to get the most out of a heli-day – with the emphasis on strong. Fat skis, snowboards and sometimes tele-boards are the favored gear in the helicopter-served backcountry. Fat skis surf over the snow and require, and many outfitters either include them in the price or rent them. When you book, check on the availability of these soft-snow wonders – and arrange to rent elsewhere if you can't get them from the operator. The services of a trained guided are mandatory, and lunches are always included in full-day programs.

Heli-skiing isn't for everyone. Helicopters are frighteningly expensive to operate, and the small guide-to-client ratio makes it dear as well. Even the least expensive programs cost a bundle. Say you've budgeted $500 for skiing. Ten thousand vertical feet is a good day's heli-skiing which costs roughly $500. That sum would buy you ten $50 lift tickets on a major mountain studded with high-speed lifts where a 15,000-vertical-foot day is easy to attain – and you're your own boss in where you ski.

One week programs run to several thousands of dollars. And in all, if your group elects "extra runs" beyond the contracted-for number, you must pay additionally/ You have to judge how you want to spend those big bucks. However, aficionados will tell you that the excitement of laying new tracks run after run in the pristine backcountry, even for a day, is worth a dozen on a crowded mountain.

Here are the heli-skiing operations in the western portion of the continental United States and Canada (with phone numbers including area code). One-week programs have extremely limited capacity and are normally booked far, far in advance. One-day programs are easier to book and can be reserved along with your vacation. In any event, capacity for all is extremely limited, so phoning in as far as possible in advance is recommended.

Mike Wiegle Heli-skiing, British Columbia (Canadian Tourism Commission)

HELI-SKIING BY THE DAY

High Mountain Heli-Skiing out of Jackson Hole, Wyoming, (307) 733-3274
Sun Valley Heli-Ski Guides, Sun Valley, Idaho, (800) 872-3108.
Telluride Heli-Trax , Telluride, Colorado, (970) 728-4904.
Timberline Heli-Skiing, Deer Valley, Utah, (801) 753-7628.
Wasatch Powderbird Guides, Snowbird, Utah, (801) 742-2800.

ONE- TO THREE-PACKAGES

Assiniboine Heli Tours, Canmore, Alberta, (403) 678-5600.
Canadian Helicopters, Canmore, Alberta, (403) 678-2207.
Canmore Helicopters, Canmore, Alberta, (403) 678-4802.
Kootenay Helicopter Skiing, Nakusp, British Columbia, (250) 265-3121.
Mountain Wings, Canmore, Alberta, (403) 678-4251.
North Cascade Heli-Skiing, Okanogan National Forest, Washington, (800) 494-HELI (494-4354) or (509) 996-3272.
Purcell Heli-Ski, Golden, British Columbia, (250) 344-5410.
Robson Heli-Magic, Valemount, British Columbia, (250) 566-4333.
R.K. Heli-Ski Panorama, Panorama, British Columbia, (250) 342-3889.
Ruby Mountain Helicopter Skiing, Nevada, (702) 753-7628.
Selkirk Tangiers Heli-Skiing, Golden, British Columbia, (250) 344-5016.
Tyax Heli-Skiing, Whistler, British Columbia, (250) 952-4105.
Whistler Heli-Skiing, Whistler, British Columbia, (250) 932-4105.

ONE-WEEK PACKAGES

CMH Heli-Skiing, nine areas and several backcountry lodges; office in Banff, Alberta, (403) 762-7100.
Mike Wiegele Helicopter Skiing, Blue River, British Columbia; office in Banff, Alberta, (403) 762-5548.

IMPRESSIONS ON NORTH AMERICA

In the last two editions of this Guide we have published reports from our regular correspondents who visited North America for their skiing holidays. Three further correspondents who crossed the Atlantic give their impressions in this page.

The first report comes from Robert Harrison, who with his wife, visited Squaw Valley during March. He writes as follows:-

I would like to report, somewhat belatedly, upon my visit to Squaw Valley in March this year.

In fact, upon reading the entry, I was surprised at the extent and accuracy of the report; we were staying in the Resort at Squaw Creek which already has a generous and accurate entry. Moreover, the report for this resort as a whole in all aspects, under all headings, remains accurate, with no additions. The same can be said for the lift and piste system.

I was unable to visit the Squaw Valley Ski Corporation HQ until the end of our stay, but at that time I handed over a copy of the 1996 guide, which was gratefully received.

I would just like to endorse the comments within the 1996 guide "Impressions on North America" which again in particularly good in drawing a distinction between the facilities available in North America compared, I would say less favourable, with a more charming village and après ski atmosphere in most of the traditional European resorts.

Whilst we were in the Lake Tahoe region, we briefly visited Alpine Meadows, which is equally briefly reported upon in the guide. From all the US resorts that I have visited, this one most closely resembled European "Alpine" conditions both in terms of the terrain, and one particular mountain hut. The resort probably does not merit a larger report than that included within the 1996 guide, in view of the fact that, at present at least, Alpine Meadows is a ski field, with no apparent accommodation other than that offered in nearby resorts and towns such as Truckee and Tahoe, with the rather more distant airport and casino city of Reno.

If I can be of any further help and assistance in these entries or for the forthcoming season, please do not hesitate to contact me.

The second report comes from Kay Anderson who visited Killington, in Vermont, from 31 March to 14 April.

Having skied in Europe for a number of years, it was time to experience the runs of North America.

In the state of Vermont, Killington is approximately a three hour coach journey from Boston. Killington itself has no real centre; the majority of shops and restaurants are situated along the Killington Road, which is 3-4 miles long. Many of the lodges offer a courtesy bus service to the slopes and a ski bus service operates from Killington Village lodging facilities to the Snowshed Base Lodge – timings however were unpredictable. A car is recommended.

The resort itself is very quiet during the week and is made up of six mountains – Snowshed, Rams Head, Bear, Skyeship and Sunrise. The runs are a mixture of grades particularly good for beginners, with challenging double blacks for the good intermediate skier. The grading of some runs were, however, inconsistent.

The area has vast snow making facilities enabling skiing from November to June. Conditions were mixed and included a metre of snow, rain and sunshine all in the same week! Mountain restaurants are situated at all of the base lodges, offering a wide range of reasonably priced food.

The ski school did not reach the standard of European ski schools. Those in the party taking lessons received little instruction and on one occasion a group of beginners were left at the mountain summit top ski unaccompanied to the base lodge.

Whilst resort staff were friendly, the operation of the resort was quite outdated. The lift system itself is adequate, but less efficient than many of its European counterparts. The lift pass prices were comparable with Europe, however the lift pass system is antiquated.

For après ski, there is a good choice of restaurants offering a variety of foods – Italian, seafood and Chinese included. Prices on average ranged from £10 upwards for a main course and drinks. Killington has a night club, bowling alley and numerous bars for evening entertainment.

Lasting impressions – a good holiday with some excellent skiing; not however the efficient American resort originally anticipated. I would not necessarily return to the east coast but look forward to experiencing west coast American skiing sometime in the future!

The third report comes from Adrian Essex, who with his wife and three daughters aged 16, 12 and 7 visited Banff.

We decided to take our annual skiing holiday somewhere further afield than the purpose-built French resorts we have enjoyed for 14 years. Attracted by high quality powder, favourable exchange rates, friendly people and a change of scenery we chose Banff.

Overall – the holiday was a success, everyone enjoyed it, no-one wanted to leave, and difficult moments were few. We took pleasure from every part of it, so that even the flight included lessons on great circles and sightings of Iceland, Greenland and ice floes.

High quality powder – the snow conditions were the best I have experienced. The sensation of schussing on snow rather than ice is rare an wonderful. Our 7-year-old definitely benefited from being able to tackle her first black run on real powdery snow.

A favourable exchange rate – for once I over-estimated the amount of cash needed! Meals were very reasonable compared to the gold-plated fare served in French resorts. Some ski-hire was pre-paid but local prices would have been cheaper. The kit was the best and newest we have hired and gave no cause for complaint.

Friendly people – they are genuinely friendly and seemed to want to see us again Children get an especially warm welcome and were allowed to relax the prohibition on talking to strangers for a week. Some of the friendliness is pre-programmed and pavlovian but much of it is genuine and combined with a naive charm.

A change of scenery – the Rockies are different to the Alps with long flat approach roads and trees right up to the peaks. The National Park restrictions are enforced so most building is well away from the beauty spots. The shopping centre has enough that is familiar (Macdonalds, Benetton, Body Shop, etc.) to make one feel at home but enough that is special to the area (leather goods, Indian and Eskimo artefacts and clothing, work by local artists and an RCM shop) to create a unique feel.

Plus points – the snow, the people, value for money, elk outside the hotel room, no dogs in restaurants, well behaved lift queues, staff who want to serve you, the giant hot tub.

Disappointments – daily bus rides to smallish skiing areas, an antiquated (but soon to be replaced) ticketing system requiring a visit to the office every day.

NORTH AMERICA

by CLAIRE WALTER

North America's hundreds of ski resorts stretch across the massive northern tier of the United States and southern Canada. In this *Global Ski Guide 1998* section on North America we've selected just a handful for full writeups and 20 more for brief reports, but they are all the kind of destination worth crossing an ocean for – in terms of superlative skiing and also for enjoyable après ski and non-ski possibilities.

The resorts have been selected with an eye towards variety. Some are old mining or ranching towns (Aspen and Jackson Hole, respectively) with a new, or at least additional, incarnation as destination resorts. Others (Sun Valley in the 1930s, Vail in the 1960s, Snowbird in the 1970s and Beaver Creek in the 1980s) were built as ski resorts. All but five (Sun Valley, Telluride, Crested Butte, Steamboat and Jackson Hole) are near enough to major population centres to attract large weekend crowds. And several (Heavenly Resort, Aspen, Vail and Breckenridge) are as known for night-life as for days on the slopes. Environmental concerns have halted new resort construction (Deer Valley was the last significant built-from-scratch resort), and now the concentration is on retrofitting, rebuilding and sometimes renaming older ski areas (the former Tod Mountain now Sun Peaks and the old Mont Tremblant is now Tremblant, and both have been upgraded from simple ski areas into complete resorts).

Skiing in North America is neither 'better' nor 'worse' than skiing the Alps. The two are vastly different. Rocky Mountain resorts offer reliable snow conditions, state-of-the-art lift networks which minimise queues and maximise skiing time and people who are genuinely happy to welcome skiers from abroad. Many resorts offer free guided orientation tours of the mountain or station congenial hosts to answer questions.

East or West, life is more casual in North American ski resorts than in European ones. Friendships tend to be formed on lifts, in ski class and at après-ski watering holes. North American skiers tend to be open, friendly and polite in liftlines, even at peak periods. Since guests rarely take their meals in their hotels, there is an abundance of fine restaurants featuring a staggering variety of cuisines in most resorts, but many skiers like to economise by staying in spacious condominium apartments and preparing some of their own meals.

All the resorts here have substantial lift capacity and enough terrain to keep a skier happy for a week or more without retracing his or her ski tracks too often. All have excellent ski schools in which to learn or to improve. All offer rental equipment that is modern and has been properly safety-checked. All have excellent trained ski patrols which offer free rescue and first-aid service, and avalanche control is part of everyday operations where necessary.

Eastern resorts have the benefit of being closer to the U.K., and they also combine well with sightseeing in New York, Washington, Boston, Montreal and Quebec City, but if you are going for the skiing and the skiing alone, the West is best. In the East, you'll find reliable snowmaking, excellent midweek prices (for the ski resorts cater to weekenders from all of these metropolitan areas and are uncrowded midweek) and the quaint charm of North America's most traditional regions are appealing. In New England and eastern Canada, where elevations are lower and natural snow less generous, base-to-summit snowmaking is the rule. Machine-made snow, which is denser than natural snow, provides excellent and reliable ski conditions. Snowmaking operations take place any time the temperature is below freezing. Compared to the West, temperatures tend to be lower, and the humidity higher, but since the slopes are all far below the treeline, many runs are relatively sheltered. January can be cold, but spring skiing is especially pleasant, since machine-made snow corns up very well into a comfortably but not overly heavy skiing surface.

Each of the Western areas selected has a record of high annual snow accumulations, and even these are often supplemented by snowmaking. U.S. Rockies resorts are generally at higher elevations than their counterparts in the Alps. This means the towns as well as the mountains get plenty of sun through the day. The timberline in the Colorado Rockies is at about 11,000 feet, but lower in the northern United States and Canada. The trails are often wide, and almost-treeless bowls are not uncommon in major Western resorts. Days are usually sunny. Even in mid-winter when daytime Fahrenheit temperatures might stay in the teens or twenties, it is comfortable because of the low humidity. Snowmaking, once an added insurance in case of a lean snow year, is common to ensure early-season skiing as well as to guarantee good skiing – regardless of natural snowfall or the wear and tear of skier traffic – all season long American snowmaking is far more sophisticated and efficient than snowmaking in the Alps. The Rockies in general and Utah's Wasatch Range in particular are renowned for prodigious quantities of natural powder snow. The Sierra of California and Coast Mountains of British Columbia get the quantity, but the powder isn't as fluffy. Western ski schools specialise in teaching skiers how to handle powder. Wide skis, nicknamed "fat skis", are available in rental shops and make skiing fresh powder or chopped-up crud a breeze. In addition, many trails – particularly those marked novice or intermediate – are packed and groomed so well that they seem to be manicured.

North American skiers like the comfort of chair-lifts, so the few drag-lifts that exist are generally relegated to real beginners' slopes or, more commonly, isolated expert runs. State-of-the-art lifts are found all over North America. The current infatuation is with high-speed quad chair-lifts which zoom up the mountain at twice the speed of conventional lifts. Vail has ten of these queue-eating monsters. Americans don't believe that a ski holiday ought to be spent in line, so waits of more than 15 minutes are rare, even at peak holiday periods.

Canadian mountains are likely to have more surface lifts than their U.S. counterparts. Half-day, all-day and multi-day tickets which are affixed to skiers' clothing are the rule although electronic ticketing is gaining a toehold. In some resorts, multi-day passes consist of coupons which are exchanged for individual tickets. Lift queues are orderly. Everyone waits his or her turn, and no one shoves, elbows or steps on other people's skis just to worm into line.

Ski school carries many benefits. Ski classes (not just private lessons) usually have liftline-cutting privileges. Classes are small (eight is usual, ten is rare), and everyone speaks English. Tuition is given in a relaxed, friendly manner. Skiers are encouraged to learn how to feel the slopes, not simply to ski in the exact wake of an instructor. Specialty "workshops" or "clinics" for women, recreational racers, or would-be mogul or powder skiers proliferate and are very worthwhile. Other than at the beginner level, most Americans tend to avoid ski school, resulting in top classes that are often so small that they resemble privates.

Getting to U.S. resorts is easier than ever. Skiers from the U.K. and Europe have several routine choices. There is limited non-stop service from to North America's major ski gateways, and most skiers fly transatlantic to New York, Chicago, Los Angeles and other cities and transfer to a second flight. Denver is the most used gateway to the Colorado resorts (with connections to Wyoming and New Mexico). Salt Lake City is the airport for all Utah resorts and for connections to Idaho, and San Francisco or Reno are suitable for the Sierra destinations. Calgary is the gateway for Banff and Lake Louise, while Vancouver is the one for Whistler. From Denver, there is frequent van service to most Colorado resorts. Aspen, Vail, Crested Butte, Telluride, Steamboat, Jackson Hole, Sun Valley and others have small airports nearby with non-stop service from cities like Chicago, Dallas/Fort Worth, New York and Los Angeles; as well as connecting flights from Denver or Salt Lake City.

Canada offers all the hearty hospitality and fine snow of the United States – with a few bonuses. The exchange rate for this Commonwealth partner's dollar is currently about one-third more favourable than the U.S. dollar, making Canada a real bargain. In western Canada, the summit elevations and the timberline are lower than in Western U.S. mountains, but the more northern latitude makes for a climatic trade-off in terms of cold versus oxygen. In addition, the resorts in Quebec have a distinct Gaelic flavour that appeals to skiers who enjoy going to France – but with North American concepts of spacious accommodation and friendliness. The main gateways are Montreal, Toronto, Calgary and Vancouver.

Standard vacation packages include lodging and lifts. Meals, transfers, lessons and rental equipment are usually extra, though U.K. tour operators usually include some of these components. Major resorts usually offer free shuttle bus service. In large ski towns, these buses operate all evening long for dinner and après-ski convenience. Nevertheless, for those who prefer, car hire can be arranged at all gateway airports and at some resorts. In most, a car is not necessary, and in some it's a downright nuisance. Since New England-bound skiers might want to combine a ski holiday with sightseeing in New York, Boston or even Washington, a car would be useful. Highways are excellent and well marked, and the East has no complicated high-mountain passes to navigate.

Multi-area tickets are proliferating. The Ski The Summit Pass has traditionally been used for Arapahoe Basin, Breckenridge, Copper Mountain and Keystone, but with massive realignments in resort ownership (see below), it's future is uncertain for the 1997-98 ski season. The same goes for the Premier Passport, which has been good at Aspen Mountain, Aspen Highlands, Snowmass, Buttermilk, Beaver Creek and Vail and includes van transfer between the Aspen and Vail areas. Ski Utah offers a ticket valid at Alta, Brighton, Deer Valley, Park City, Wolf Mountain, Snowbird and Solitude. Ski Lake Tahoe's deal is for skiing at Alpine Meadows, Heavenly Valley, Kirkwood, Northstar, Sierra-at-Tahoe and Squaw Valley. Norquay, Ski Louise and Sunshine share a lift pass, while Blackcomb and Whistler boast a fully interchangeable ticket.

The most significant changes in North American skiing has the rapid consolidation of several resorts under each of several owners. As this issue of *The Global Ski Guide 1998* was being prepared, the extent of multi-day, multi-area lift passes was not yet known. What we do know is that Colorado's Vail, Beaver Creek, Breckenridge and Arapahoe Basin are now all owned by Vail Resorts Inc. and will offer a totally interchangeable lift ticket (much as the three Aspen areas do). There will also be luxury bus service at a modest cost between Vail and Beaver Creek on the west side of Vail Pass with Breckenridge and Keystone on the east side.

IntraWest, the Vancouver-based giant which put

Whistler on the map, now owns both Whistler and Blackcomb Mountains, as well as Panorama, all in British Columbia, plus Colorado's Copper Mountain, Quebec's Tremblant, Vermont's Stratton and Snowshoe, West Virginia. The American Skiing Company, based in Maine, operates half-a-dozen resorts in New England which offer multi-day, multi-area tickets for peripatetic skiers. These are Sunday River and Sugarloaf, Maine; Sugarbush, Killington and Mt. Snow, Vermont; and Attitash/Beaver Peak, New Hampshire. In addition, the firm has purchased Wolf Mountain (formerly ParkWest, Utah), in Park City, and may rename it.

George Gillett, a former owner of Vail, formed a company called Booth Creek investments and bought a scattershot group of ski areas across the U.S., and how it plans to mesh them and operate them is a still unanswered question. At this writing, Booth Creek owns Cranmore and Waterville, New Hampshire; Grand Targhee, Wyoming; four ski areas around Snoqualmie Pass, Washington, and Bear Mountain, Northstar-at-Tahoe and Sierra-at-Tahoe, California. The Kircher family of Michigan owns two areas there, as well as Big Sky, Montana; Brighton, Utah, and Crystal Mountain, Washington. And Charlie Locke's Locke, Stock & Barrel owns Lake Louise, Fortress Mountain, Nakiska (site of the Alpine events during the 1988 Winter Olympics) and, newly, Fernie Snow Valley, all in the Canadian Rockies.

No matter who owns them, North American resorts are ideal for families. All have full-day nursery care for small children (in many cases, starting with infants just a few months old), and programmes consisting of both ski lessons and indoor play for ages three and up. Children from age six or seven love action-packed classes, where learning to ski is fun. Some resorts also have special classes for fast-moving teenagers. Youngsters have lunch with their instructors and classmates, and are kept entertained all day. Some resorts also have discreetly supervised teen centers and/or dinner and evening entertainment for children so that parents can occasionally go out by themselves.

But best of all, many resorts have attractive kids-free arrangements all or part of the season. Under such offers, children ski free, often stay free and may even get free rental equipment on a one-to-one basis with parents for part or all of the season (usually excepting Christmas), even in top resorts. In case Grandma and Grandpa wish to come along, many American ski areas offer free skiing to seniors 70 and older any time.

Hotels and lodges are less formal than their Alpine counterparts. Hotel rooms are huge. Many are configured as "double-doubles" – two double beds which can accommodate a family. All have private baths and colour televisions, which get dozens of cable channels 24 hours a day. Many also offer movie channels with pay-per-view showings of cinema hits. Hotel and restaurant service might not always be slickly professional, but it is generally prompt and nearly always cheerful.

Many North American skiers prefer condominium apartment accommodation. Arrangements include studio, one-bedroom and multi-bedroom suites and are especially price-worthy for groups or families. Many have at least one telly for each bedroom and all have kitchen facilities. It can be economically smart to make breakfast daily and some other meals through the week. Markets and delis are at all areas, and they are open evenings and weekends for the convenience of skiers. (This is also true, incidentally, of shops at North American ski resorts. No store closes during the noon hour or on weekends, and most are open for several hours after the lifts close.)

A winter vacation in North America is more than a ski vacation. It is a visit to the brash and brassy former colonies. And there's no language barrier to skiing the U.S. or Canada.

SNOWBIRD

Height of Resort: 8,100 ft.
Bottom of Lowest Lift: 7,760 ft.
Height of Top Station: 11,000 ft.
Nearest Major Airport: Salt Lake City
Route by Car: Take Interstate Highway 80 east from Salt Lake City to Interstate 15 south. Turn east on Highway 215 into Little Cottonwood Canyon. Driving time is 45 minutes.
Resort Facilities Charts: See page 216

In the United States, the Rocky Mountains are famous for their powder snow. In the Rockies, Utah's Wasatch Range for its powder snow. In Utah, Little Cottonwood Canyon is famous for its powder. And there waits Snowbird, a sparkling ski area with challenging terrain and an intimate resort atmosphere.

Snowbird: Snowbird's 125-passenger aerial tramway leaves the Plaza, which is the hub of all resort activity, and heads straight for the sky and some of the best tough skiing in America. Powder lovers head for Primrose Path, Silver Fox, Peruvian Cirque, Little Cloud and Regulator Johnson, steep tracks down the faces of bowls sculpted into the top of the mountain. Intermediates can take Chip's Run off the top, but generally it's experts only up there. A double chair-lift on Little Cloud offers above-the-timberline skiing, including Regulator Johnson Bowl, a vast snowfield.

Intermediates usually start the day by skiing downhill a short way from the Plaza to the Wilbere Ridge chair or the Gad I chair. Wilbere offers a handful of mildly challenging runs down the sheltered face of a protected ridge and is also popular during inclement weather or for warming up. Gad I, which has now been upgraded to the resort's first high-speed quad, leads to the Mid-Gad restaurant and gives experts the steep upper portion of a slope called Big Emma to tackle and access to the mid-mountain Gad II chair. Gad II serves the upper portion of massive Gad Valley, terrain full of gullies and couloirs, dips and trails, all geared for intermediate and advanced skiers. This section is for skiers only; no snowboards permitted. The Mid-Gad double chair parallels Gad I, but terminates at the restaurant well below the top station of Gad I. There are shortcuts through the woods, powder-holding glades and serpentine runs that offer wonderful variety. Lower Bassackwards is a long intermediate run feeding into Lower Big Emma, one of the widest, tamest novice slopes imaginable.

A mountain guide programme specialises in off-trail skiing, and Utah Powderbirds offer helicopter skiing by the day from an excellent new facility directly at the base of the resort; the company also maintains an office in the Cliff Lodge. Snowbird offers a complementary guide service at 9 and 10 am. and at 1 p.m. daily to help newcomers of all ability levels to get acquainted with the mountain. Fun Run is a top-to-bottom piste marked with orange-topped posts designating one of the easier ways down the mountain. It changes daily, depending on grooming and snow conditions.

Rank beginners and youngsters finally have more territory to work with on the main mountain. The Baby Thunder double chairlift serves a dozen novice and intermediate runs. Beginners still will find comfort on the Chickadee chair and two extremely mild slopes right near the lodges. The ski school finds it gets a lot of business from accomplished skiers who come out expressly to learn how to handle the powder, which is the lightest and driest of any American ski region, since Utah's clouds build up over the desert. Little Cottonwood Canyon averages double or triple the snowfall of many other major Rocky Mountain resorts. Some years, the ski season stretches to the end of June! Snowbird is one of the participants in the Ski Utah group, whose coupon book is also good at Alta, Brighton, Deer Valley, Park City, Wolf Mountain and Solitude. The Interconnect is full-day, guided backcountry-plus-lift excursion all the way to Park City.

Alta: One of the unheralded pleasures of vacationing at Snowbird is that it is a chance for a day trip up the canyon to Alta, one of America's classic old ski resorts and the one that started the powder cult in Utah. Alta's accommodations are few (though excellent) but its skiing is exceptional as befits the grande dame of Little Cottonwood Canyon. (See "Other U.S. and Canadian Resorts," page 42).

In a Few Words: Gorgeous scenery, the fluffiest snow in skidom and superb runs for intermediate and expert skiers are the hallmarks of Snowbird.

Après Ski: The Forklift is always popular right after skiing. It offers a large selection of snacks and two large-screen televisions. The Aerie at the Cliff Lodge has a lounge, café, fine dining and mellow music - usually jazz. The Atrium serves breakfast, lunch and après ski, while The Summit adjacent to the spa and pool serves healthy snacks, sandwiches, smoothies and pizza.

The Lodge Club has good après ski and a refined dinner menu with a Medterranean influence. The Steak Pit is known for hearty portions of steaks, seafood and chicken. The Keyhole specialises in food and drink from south of the border. The Birdfeeder is fine for hot dogs and other snacks, while the Forklift is popular for burgers, quiche and other light fare. The Plaza has self-service breakfast and lunch. Royce's Restaurant, downvalley at the racquet club, is another option for fine dining but in a sporty setting – and with a piano bar.

Some people come to Snowbird just for the Cliff Spa, a two-story health and beauty center atop the Cliff Lodge. Exercise, massage, beauty treatments and spa cuisine in a casual café are available in conjunction with, or instead of, a day on the slopes. Its outdoor rooftop swimming pool and huge hot tub feature a fabulous view of the mountains. Since the entire spa facility is now for adults only, families and youngsters use the ground-level outdoor pool. This year Snowbird is expanding its evening recrational options with a fine new outdoor pool and hot tub complex at the base of the Chickadee slope, which is lighted for skiing, snowboarding and recreational lugeing. The resort also operates the Canyon Racquet Club and offers tennis privileges on 10 indoor courts to resort guests.

It is easy to combine skiing at Snowbird with a day of sightseeing in Salt Lake City, a brief bus ride away. Tabernacle Square, centre of Mormon worship with historical displays, is the leading attraction. Trolley Square is an exciting shopping mall retrieved from a decayed street-car barn, while conventionally situated. Two department stores and smaller shops about in the city and in outlying shopping malls and interesting craft shops are the best bet.

Lodging: There are just four lodges with a total of fewer than 1,200 beds at Snowbird, which is one reason that vacationers manage a lot of skiing there. Children 12 and under stay free in their parents' room and ski free all winter long. The crowds build on weekends and school vacation weeks, when it seems everyone from Salt Lake City is there too, just for the day, of course.

All of the lodges – The Lodge at Snowbird, The Inn, the Cliff Lodge and the Iron Blosam Lodge - are quasi-highrise, sturdily built and tastefully decorated structures. All feature mix of studios, bedrooms and suites. The new wing of the Cliff Lodge has the poshest accommodations, which are now being marketed as timeshares that are available for rent when they are not occupied. And four lodges all offer such amenities as saunas, elevators, some sort of lounge, heated swimming pool and so on. In addition to the types of accommodation standard in Snowbird's luxurious lexicon, there are still a few dormitory rooms appropriate for economy-minded young skiers.

Other bargain-seekers might consider a motel in Salt Lake City. The room rates would be lower, but a rental car or public bus would be necessary for the commute. Alta also offers half a dozen lodges, the best of which are Alta Lodge and the Rustler, but these are not bargains. Several condominiums are available between the two ski resorts.Remember that free skiing for children 12 and under is available all season long regardless of whether a family stays at Snowbird.

JACKSON HOLE

Height of Resort: 6,311 ft.
Height of Top Station: 10,450 ft.
Airport: Jackson, Wyoming
Route by Car: Drive east from Salt Lake City on Interstate Highway 80 to Evanston, Wyoming, to 189 north to Jackson. Driving time is five to six hours. To reach the resort of Teton Village, go two miles west on State Highway 22 to Highway 390 north. Jackson's own airport is 10 miles from town or 22 miles from Teton Village.
Resort Facilities Charts: See page 211

The wildest of the Wild West ski resorts, both in terms of challenging skiing and ambience in the nearby town of Jackson. Located in the incredibly beautiful Teton Range, Jackson Hole is a uniquely American place to ski.

Jackson Hole: It's easy to run out of superlatives when describing massive Rendezvous Mountain, for it offers America's greatest continuous vertical (nearly 4,200 vertical feet from summit to base) and remains one of its toughest. More than half of Jackson Hole's slopes are recommended for the advanced or expert skier, and most of these are on Rendezvous. The main access from Teton Village to the summit is via 63-passenger tramway. You can reserve a place in advance for one of the three or four hourly departures, so you won't have to wait in line. There's also an airline-like standby queue.

Once at the top, you don't get a chance to take an easy warm-up run. The only sane route from the summit is via black-diamond Rendezvous Bowl, a wide, steep section that is graced with the yellow warning triangle mainly because of the traffic comprised of wobbly-legged newcomers to Jackson Hole. The insane way is Corbett's Couloir, one of the toughest of the tough chutes which gives super-experts a short cut avoiding the crowd of merely competent skiers working their way through the bowl. Corbett's requires a leap-for-life followed by a landing in a narrow, rock-walled chute. Few try it, but more come to watch—either from the top or the bottom.

Rendezvous Peak is a truly large mountain, deeply etched with bowls (five on the upper mountain alone) and canyons (lower down) There are relatively easy road-like routes linking various mountain sectors, and even a sturdy intermediate can snake down the whole vertical. But by and large, the mountain remains the playground of better skiers. From the summit, there are two options: Rendezvous Trail off to the right and Gros Ventre Traverse, which offers upper intermediates something they can finally handle in relaxed fashion, namely a run simply called the Grand to the bottom of the Thunder chair. Rendezvous Trail leads to glorious open ridge skiing known as the Hobacks, never crowded and a favourite among powder hours. The Hobacks are tough, but they are the challenging glory of the lower mountain. However, the best snow is often higher up. The Upper Sublette Ridge quad chair (1,630 vertical feet) enable skiers to stay on the top half of the mountain, but that top half, alone, exceeds many other total ski areas in terms of vertical and challenge.

The Thunder Chair, a fixed-grip quad, parallel to the third quarter of the tramway is another lift serving a huge chunk of medium-level to awesomely steep terrain on the north side of Rendezvous. From the Thunder area, it is possible to ski back down to Teton Village via several intermediate routes or to take the long tra-verse to Casper Bowl terrain. Casper Bowl, served by one chairlift, is a deep cleft between Rendezvous and Après Vous. It is the best bet for intermediate and advanced skiers either warming up for or cooling off from the rigours of Rendezvous Mountain. Peppered with blue squares and red rectangles, Casper Bowl's turf includes a respectable 1,046 feet of vertical. There is good tree skiing and an assortment of wide runs. The trail called Beaver Tooth and the two best routes down Moran Face, Wide Open and Sleeping Indian, are genuine Jackson Hole black diamonds amid the intermediate runs of Casper Bowl. This segment of the area, incidentally, is relatively sheltered on the blusteriest mid-winter days.

The latest addition to Jackson Hole is the Bridger gondola, serving Rendezvous Peak's new northern runs. This new network of mostly intermediate trails and the lift itself are more sheltered from the wind than is the high-towered tram. The gondola has been designed to remain running even when weather halts tram operations. More important, it changes the complexion of Jackson Hole in general into a more balanced resort with a true range of something for everyone—but without compromising the exceptional challenge of mighty Rendezvous peak.

Anywhere else, Apres Vous, a 2,100-vertical foot mountain served by three double chairlifts and cut with four novice runs, four long intermediate trails and a web of expert runs off to one side would be a respectable ski hill all by itself. At Jackson Hole, however, this is what Americans call the bunny hill – the beginners' hill, the ski school slope. It contains the few runs genuinely within the reach of the less-than-intermediate skier.

Two chairlifts, Eagle's Rest and Teewinot, provide access to the area's easiest runs. From the top ofTeewinot, a high-speed quad, the long Après Vous chair leads to Moran, which serves as the recreational. racing trail and funnels to the Solitude Traverse back to the bottom of the Casper Bowl chair. Secret Slope, a small network of truly expert runs, nestles on upper Apres Vous near the boundary of Jackson Hole's patrolled ski terrain.

Apres Vous is also the starting point for the Teton Village cross-country trail, a fairly short, sheltered track that is quite lovely. Many skiers enjoy a break from the big mountain by taking half-day or full-day guided cross-country tours, the latter in Grand Teton National Park and including lunch. No fewer than 10 guide services offer cross-country excursions along the river, through the canyons and into the vast beauty of the winter parklands around Jackson Hole. Helicopter excursions with guides into the untracked backcountry are possible from February through June with High Mountain Helicopter Skiing.

Jackson is a place for good skiers who want to extend their limits. The ski school's programmes include various speciality clinics for skiers and snowboarders, including those for women, snowboarders and skiing or snowboarding the steeps. The children's facilities, both for non-skiers and skiers, are now relocated in expanded space in the MountinPlaza Building and also deserve mention.

In a Few Words: Jackson Hole describes itself as a 'skier's mountain', and so it is. Management is so confident that vacationers can set their own personal records for vertical feet skied in a week that they provide a log for visitors to fill in and give weekly awards for anyone documenting 100,000 or 150,000 vertical feet. Gold-plated belt buckles are awarded to skiers who have respectively logged 300,000, 500,000 and 1 million vertical feet.

Jackson Hole Ski Three: An excellent program offers interchangeable coupon book for Jackson Hole, Snow King and Grand Targhee. At mighty Jackson Hole, it includes just the skiing—and that's enough. At Snow King, a small, steep mountain right in the town of Jackson, you get skiing and dinner. This mighty midget offers doorstep skiing for guests of the Snow King Resort and is also great for anyone who wishes to combine a half day of skiing with shopping, sightseeing or just relaxing. There is also night skiing for those who just can't get enough. In addition to the challenging runs on the main mountain, Snow King offers a fine, gentle nursery slope for beginners and small children. Ski Three is also valid for skiing at Grand Targhee and for bus transportation to get there or a group ski lesson for those with their own transportation. The Targhee Express bus makes daily pickups starting at 7.30 a.m. from various points in Jackson For more information on Grand Targhee, see "Other U.S. and Canadian Resorts," page 43.

Après Ski: In addition to giving skiers some of North America's most challenging terrain, Jackson Hole offers really unique activities that mean a well-spent day off the slopes. The most famous of these are trips into the Old Faithful area of nearby Yellowstone National Park. America's best-known geyser spews forth dramatically every hour around the clock throughout the year. While summer visitors form a throng, winter visitors view this splendid natural spectacle in comparative isolation. It is possible to drive yourself in via rented snowmobile, and daily snowcoach tours are also offered for those who prefer to be driven. In addition to day trips, overnight stays can be arranged at Old Faithful Lodge, and the cross-country skiing in America's oldest national park is also outstanding. Other popular excursions are full-day snowmobile or dogsled trips into Granite Hot Springs, where there's swimming at 8,000 feet in a 105° natural pool and sleigh rides into the National Elk Refuge, where a 10,000-head herd spends the winter. Ice skating on the indoor rink at Snow King or night skiing on the hill are popular family diversions.

Nightlife, dining and lodging are divided into two main locations, the old town of Jackson and Teton Village at the base of the lifts. They are 12 miles apart, and shuttle buses connect the two. Après ski starts at Teton Village when the lifts close with live entertainment at several bars, including at the famous Mangy Moose, Sojourner's Renezvous Lounge and in the bars in each of the handful of other lodges. Half a dozen Teton Village restaurants offer a variety of styles of cooking. The Mangy Moose, the resort's oldest and most picturesque watering hole, has two eateries: Mangy Moose Restaurant and Rocky Mountain Oyster. The Inn at Jackson Hole has two, the Inn Restaurant and Jenny Leigh's Dining Room. The Alpenhof Dining Room is an award-winning restaurant with Continental cuisine, while The Range is an intimate American restaurant. Nearby, en route to the town of Jackson, Calico Pizza Parlor is good for light eating, and Stiegler's, between town and mountain, for formal dining.

Whether you are staying at the resort, on town or in between, no Jackson Hole vacation is complete without an evening on the town in Jackson. Its Wild West atmosphere is unique, and it has become a notable Western art centre. The most popular bars are the J.J.'s the Silver Dollar Bar in the Wort Hotel, the Million Dollar Cowboy Bar around the corner, and The Virginian nearby. Bar stools made of saddles and a bar top embedded with real silver dollars are the stuff of which their atmosphere is made.

Downtown dining choices range from down-home fare at Bubba's Bar-B-Que to trendy restaurants specialising in new American cuisine. In fact, for a town where, until recently, gourmet dining meant a big slab of beef at the a place like the Million Dollar Cowboy Steakhouse, the change has been dramatic. The Cadillac Grille, with its dramatic art deco look and an eclectic menu, is one of the oldest of the new restaurants. More recent additions to Jackson's culinary scene include the Snake River Grille, Off Broadway and Gouloff's. Sweetwater Restaurant serves light lunches and more elaborate dinners. Elegant dining with sesnational views is at The Granary at Spring Creek Resort.

While a car is useful for making the scene at Jackson Hole, it's not necessary. START (the acronym for Southern Teton Area Rapid Transit) offers low-cost shuttle service between Jackson and Teton Village from early morning until after midnight. Aspens Shuttle runs between the Aspens and Teton Village, and the free Teton Village Shuttle make the village circuit.

Lodging: Teton Village has traditionally been known more for convenience than for charm, but the resort is undergoing a dramatic facelift which will add atmosphere to the matchless slopeside location. The village will never grow too large, and the choice of

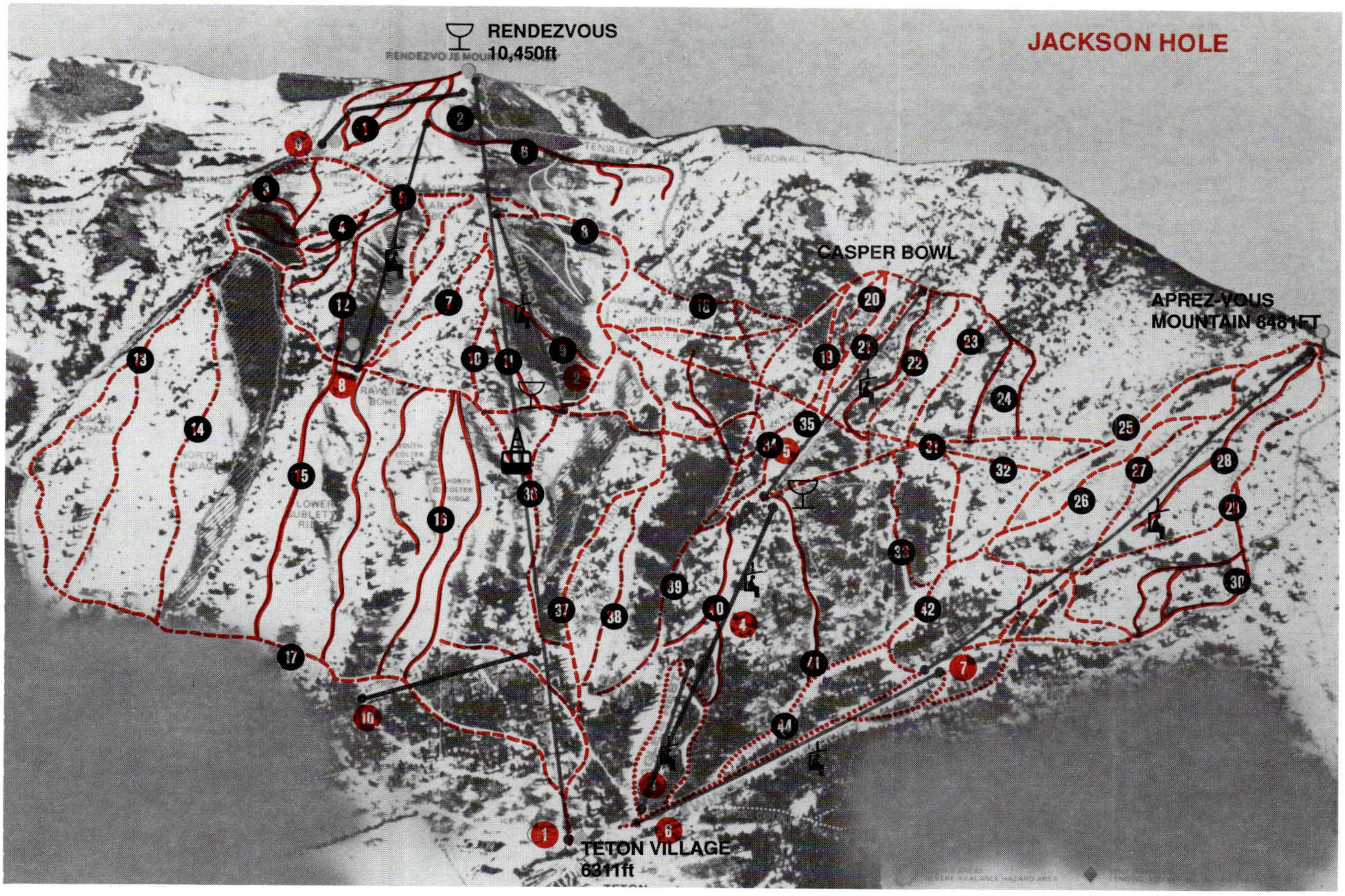

Mountain railways | Cableways | Gondolaways | Chair-lifts | Drag-lifts | ...... Easy runs | ------- Medium runs | ——— Difficult runs | Mountain restaurants

Jackson Hole: Runs: 1 Rendezvous Bowl; 2 Corbett's Couloir; 3 Rendezvous Trail; 4 Bird in the Hand; 5 Grosvenor Traverse; 6 East Ridge Traverse; 7 Grand; 8 Gros Ventre; 9 Thunder; 10 Gannett; 11 Riverton; 12 Pen's Run; 13 South Hoback; 14 North Hoback; 15 Lower Sublette Ridge; 16 Buffalo Bowl; 17 Union Pass Traverse; 18 Perce Traverse; 19 Camp Ground; 20 Timbered Island; 21 Lift Line; 22 Sleeping Indian; 23 Wide Open; 24 Moran Face; 25 Moran Nastar; 26 Werner; 27 Teewinot Gully; 28 Teewinot; 29 St. Johns; 30 Secret Slope; 31 Togwotee Pass Traverse; Lower Teewinot; 44 Lower Werner; a further 20 runs not shown on this map.
Lift Numbers: 1 cableway (tram); 2 Thunder (4 seater chair); 3 Eagles Rest (dc); 4 Crystal Springs (dc); 5 Casper Bowl (3 seater chair); 6 Teewinot (dc); 7 Après Vous (dc); 8 Upper Sublette Ridge (4 seater chair); 9 Rendezvous Bowl (drag); 10 Union Pass (drag)
Runs: •••••••••••••••••••••••• Easy - - - - - - - - - - - - - - - - Medium - • - • - • - • - • - • - • - Medium Difficult ———————— Difficult

lodging will remain limited in quantity but not in quality. In addition to several condominium complexes at the base of the lifts, there are half-a-dozen hostelries. They range from the elegant Alpenhof Lodge to the Hostel, an economical lodge that spares no comfort but helps skiers hoard dollars. The Alpenhof, closest to the lifts, is a popular after-ski and dinner spot as well as a fine lodge. Nearby are the Sojourner Inn, the Crystal Springs Inn, and the Best Western Inn at Jackson Hole.

In town, the choice is greater. The Wort Hotel is the classic hotel of downtown Jackson. The leader in size and comfort, however, is the spacious Snow King Resort, which has 204 rooms and suites and a wealth of diversions, including an outdoor swimming pool, skating rink, dining facilities and its own small, challenging ski area. The Cowboy Village Resort is a fairly new Western-style complex close to the Town Square with 57 log cabins but many modern comforts. The Lodge at Jackson Hole is an all-suite hotel with 100 rooms Other in-town properties are mostly moderately priced motels. As the southern gateway to Yellowstone National Park, Jackson offers abundant summer accommodations, and many properties view winter as their off-peak season.

Two of the most luxurious properties are found between the town and the resort. Spring Creek Resort is a development of exquisite hotel rooms and condominiums atop a private mountain, while the Jackson Hole Racquet Club Resort features deluxe condominiums and an excellent athletic club, indoor tennis and cross-country skiing at the door. Also on the shuttle route between town and mountain resort is The Virginian, with 158 spacious rooms and several on-site services. The region now also features several romantic bed-and-breakfast inns with distinctive atmosphere. The Alpine House, The Huff House, The Painted Porch, the Teton Tree House Bed & Breakfast and the Teton View all are charming and provide an unusual option for enjoying the splendours of Jackson Hole.

SUN VALLEY

Height of Resort: 6,010 ft. (Sun Valley village)
Bottom of lowest lift: 5,750 ft.
Height of Top Station: 9,150 ft.
Nearest Airports: Hailey, Idaho (12 miles)
Nearest Major Airport: Boise (82 miles)
Regional Airport: Twin Falls (154 miles)
Route by Car: Drive Interstate Highway 84 east from Boise to U.S. 20 east to Rte. 75 north, which leads to Ketchum and Sun Valley. From Twin Falls, proceed north on Rte. 75.
Driving time is about three hours from Boise and $1^1/_2$ hours from Twin Falls.
Resort Facilities Charts: See page 212.

The oldest of America's glamour resorts, Sun Valley was in business when Aspen was just a mining ghost town and Vail a sheep meadow. It has more than kept up with the times, in terms of lifts, lodging, snowmaking, mountain restaurants and other amenities – on the slopes and off – expected by the demanding skier and vacationer.

Bald Mountain: Baldy soars 3,400 feet above the surrounding valley, dominating not only the landscape, but also the minds and hearts of some of the continent's best and best-heeled skiers. It's a huge and complex mountain, one of the few that can be skied in almost all directions. Yet Sun Valley is remote, averaging just 3,500 skiers per day on the mountain. Coupled with 13 chair-lifts, including seven high-speed detachable quads, this makes for the just about greatest uphill capacity per skier of any major resort on the continent. Baldy is also renowned as a challenging ski area with huge open bowls, ultra-long cruising runs for fast giant slalom-style turns and a few of the most famous mogul runs in America.

The best-known of Baldy's renowned expert terrain is on the eastern side, known as River Run, which is becoming a significant gateway to the ski terrain with a new day lodge and a true base development. It is here that strong expert skiers put their leg muscles and resilience to the test on Exhibition, a slope with steep moguls and a chairlift carrying skiers overhead to watch the 'performance' on the snows beneath. Actually, Exhibition is just the toughest and best known of half a dozen canyons reachable via Ridge Run from the summit. Some are as challenging, if not as visible, as Exhibition, but several are fine for intermediate skiers too. A long novice trail winds down from the top, while the right side of River Run gives powder skiers the glorious open powder fields known as the College South slopes to play on and Frenchman's Gulch offers fine medium-standard runs.

College South is small-time bowl skiing compared

to The Bowls on Baldy's sunny south flank. Mayday, Lefty, Farout, Lookout, Easter and Christmas are their names, and spectacular wide-open skiing is the game. With the exception of some tougher glade runs between the patrolled pistes and the Inhibition and Cold Spring routes, The Bowls are negotiable by sturdy intermediate skiers, especially when conditions are favourable The Roundhouse is Bowl skiers' favourite slopeside eatery. If North American skiing has a corner that mimics the look and flavour of the Alps, Baldy's bowls are the place.

Seattle Ridge is laced with a group of wide upper novice through intermediate runs. Gretchen's Gold and Christin's Silver were named after two local women who won Olympic medals 40 years apart – Gretchen Fraser in 1948 and Christin Cooper in 1988. (Picabo's Street, elsewhere on the mountain, honours the 1994 Olympic medalist and 1995 and 1996 World Cup downhill champion.) Another rather new express quad now serves this popular section. The three-year-old Seattle Ridge Lodge is a splendid mountain restaurant that provides perhaps the best views. Sun Valley has a reputation for excellent slope grooming, and nowhere is this practised more conscientiously than on Seattle Ridge's wide runs.

The most extensive snowmaking, the first two high-speed lifts installed at the resort and a gorgeous restaurant, cafeteria and day lodge are on the Warm Springs side. The Warm Springs terrain on Baldy's snow-holding north side provides skiing for everyone, in one case, on the same trail. Upper Greyhawk is as steep a trail as an expert could want. There's a small midsection that tapers off into intermediate turf, while below the intersection with a meandering novice trail, it smoothes and flattens for less accomplished skiers. Elsewhere at Warm Springs, experts tackle the Flying Maid, Upper Limelight and the run recently renamed Picabo's Street after Sun Valley's speed queen, 1995 World Cup downhill champion Picabo Street. Novices delight on Middle Warm Springs and the wide and handsome Lower Warm Springs run. Frenchman's Ridge, between Warm Springs and River Run, is a beautiful bowl which, though unpatrolled, has its own enthusiasts.

Sun Valley pioneered so much in American skiing life that it is difficult to overstate its importance for over half a century. Not only was it the first planned ski resort in America, but it launched trends, major and minor. It was the first with a large, heated outdoor pool for après ski soaking and one of the pioneers in snow grooming. And the Roundhouse was America's first true mountain restaurant. There is a self- service buffet section and a sit-down restaurant called Averell's. With enormous lift capacity and a small town, Sun Valley is never crowded, not even in high season, but the resort tries to boost theme weeks for singles, ski clubs, seniors and families.

Dollar Mountain: Dollar Mountain is Sun Valley's novice hill, albeit one with wide open-slope skiing rarely found right at resort village altitude. Sun Valley's renowned ski school, one of America's first to embark on wholesale importation of European instructors, is headquartered at Dollar, where beginners' classes are held. Actually, even intermediate skiers will find Dollar a comfortable place to adjust to the clime before embarking on the upper reaches of big Baldy.

Elkhorn Mountain: Interconnected with Dollar is one-lift Elkhorn Mountain, a convenience added for residents of the Elkhorn village complex. Four slopes, two each ranked for novice and intermediate skiers, comprise the terrain.

Sun Valley Heli-Ski runs full-day tours, as well as shorter two- and three-hour programmes for those who just want a taste of heli-skiing. The Sun Valley area has become well known among cross-country skiers too. Some 175 kilometers of Nordic tracks are groomed as immaculately as mountain trails, and backcountry opportunities abound as well.

In a Few Words: Skiing at Sun Valley has to be described in 'something for everyone' terms, from the rawest first-timer to the most demanding expert, and fat skis for powder and crud are included in the rates. For those who aren't satisfied with acres of snow and dozens of slopes on Baldy, helicopter skiing in the outback can be booked. Sun Valley Heli-Ski offers excellent helicopter skiing options to several nearby mountain ranges.

Après Ski: Sun Valley life actually revolves around several centres. Technically, Sun Valley is the resort development around the famous Sun Valley Lodge, the nearby Sun Valley Inn and the small commercial strip known as The Mall between them. It also extends to the town of Ketchum, which was a ranching centre before there was ever skiing in the Sawtooth Range, and to the newer development as the base of Warm Springs. Ketchum is now an artsy town with fine shops and galleries. Just 12 miles away, and site of the nearest airport, is Hailey, a town being infused with energy because Bruce Willis and Melanie Griffith, Hollywood celebrity actors, have bought and restored a number of buildings there. The Mint is a fine restaurant and nightpot that has been book fairly big name acts, thereby also drawing the Ketchum crowd.

From last-run time when the outdoor terraces and watering holes at Warm Springs fill up, until "last call" is announced at Whiskey Jacques in town, the after-ski scene is one of liveliness and variety. The places around The Mall (spoken to rhyme with "all", not "shall") are matchless for experiencing the true Sun Valley ambiance. Après ski starts when hungry skiers descend on The Konditorei for European-style pastries. It hits its zenith at the Sun Valley Lodge, which was patronised by Hollywood celebrities some 60 years ago, where the Duchin Room offers sophisticated après ski and dancing, elegantly presented, in a luxurious setting. In the Ram Bar at the nearby Inn, Michael Murphy does hilarious, bawdy one-man shows every night. Elegant French service, fine food and music for dancing make the Lodge Dining Room unique in the overall casual realm of North American skiing.

Downtown, the Galleria Wine and Espresso Bar, Java on Fourth, and the Pony Espresso Café draw after-ski crowds. the Sun Valley Wine Company is an excellent wine bar and casual restaurant with crisp and varied, yet simple, food. The Olympic Bar features a good atmosphere and ski racing memorabilia. Other popular spots for food and drink include the Pioneer, a long-time favourite for steak, prime rib and good drinks, and Baldy's Bistro, a newer spot which serves from early breakfast to late-night snacks. At Warm Springs, the Apple's Bar & Grill and The Baldy Base Club have light food. casual ambiance and often live entertainment.

Sun Valley and Ketchum are known for excellent cuisine, with outposts of various countries' fare in greater Sun Valley. Michel's Christiania Restaurant offers well-prepared French and Continental cuisine in a pleasant glass-walled chalet. Felix Restarant is an Austrian retaurant in the Knob Hill Inn, and China Pepper downtown does all sorts of Oriental dishes. Desperado's, Teuqila Joe's and Mam Inez are good Mexican eating places. But the dominant cuisine is contemporary American, with a little fusion from other culinary trends. The Buffalo Cafe, The Cafeat the Brewery, Chandler's Restaurant, A Hungarian Radish, Ketchum Grill, The Awtooth Club and Something Special all fit into that category.

It would be a pity to ski Sun Valley without an evening at Trail Creek Cabin, where Ernest Hemingway, who made Ketchum his home, went when he wanted to celebrate. Horse-drawn sleighs leave the Sun Valley Inn four times an evening for a half-hour ride to a large cabin that harkens back to the area's mining and sheep ranching days. Hearty American fare dominates the menu: barbecued spare ribs, Idaho mountain trout, barbecued chicken, sirloin steak. An accordionist entertains, and dancing is also on the agenda. A Winter's Feast is a ski-in, snowshoe-in or sleighride to a yurt for an excellent dinner.

Another special experience is to step into cross-country skis and glide an easy mile to a Mongol-style yurt at the foot of the Boulder Mountains. Five-course dinners, including exotic specialties from Mongolia, China, the Americas and Europe, are served in one of the most unusual experiences anywhere in the realm of Rocky Mountain skiing.

Ketchum also is something of a north-coountry cultural mecca. Its art galleries put on a gallery evening one Friday each month when all are open, and there are often music, dance, film and concert programmes too.

Lodging: Ketchum is the real town close to Sun Valley, but there is also a purpose-built resort village that was started as the same time as the first ski terrain and remains the spiritual center for skiers and other winter pilgrims. The Sun Valley Lodge is a living landmark in American skiing—and American celebrity, for Sun Valley was put on the map by Hollywood stars of yesterday who skied there. The nearby Sun Valley Inn is more casual, and the Lodge Apartments are spacious condominiums within an easy walk of The Mall.

Other condominiums found at Warm Springs, around Ketchum and in Elkhorn, a separate village-style development on the other side of Dollar Mountain, now comprise the bulk of the resort's bed capacity. They range from luxury properties such as Cottonwoods to such modest ones as Ateliers. The River Street Inn is an elegant bed-and-breakfast inn featuring Japanese soaking tubs, while the Idaho Country Inn has just 10 cozy and luxurious rooms, each decorated on a different theme drawn from Idaho history. The Knob Hill Inn combines Austrian charm with American efficiency. For the real budget-minded, there are also economy motels in Ketchum and Hailey, which is just 12 miles away.

Free buses connect Sun Valley, Elkhorn and Ketchum with one another and with the lifts on Baldy and Dollar Mountain. Children's classes were relocated two years ago from Dollar to Baldy, so that most parents and most children are skiing on the same mountain. For pre-skiers, there are five child-care facilities in Sun Valley and Ketchum, but the best news for families is that youngsters to age 17 may stay free and ski free with their parents during all but Christmas/New Year and peak season in late February and early March.

HEAVENLY SKI RESORT

Height of Resort: 6,200 ft.
Bottom of Lowest Lift: 6,540 ft.
Height of Top Station: 10,167 ft.
Nearest Airport:South Lake Tahoe Airport
Nearest Major Airports: San Francisco and Reno
Route by Car: From San Francisco, Interstate Highway 80 east to U.S. Highway 50 east South Lake Tahoe. From Reno, Interstate 395 south to Highway 50 west.
Driving times are $3^1/_2$ and $1^1/_4$ hours respectively.
Resort Facilities Charts: See page 211

Heavenly's attractions are unique even among the West's varied ski areas. Fantastic high-mountain ski terrain straddles the border between two states. The ski area's 3,500-foot vertical drop is the greatest around Lake Tahoe. With 4,800 acres of patrolled terrain, Heavenly is one of North America's largest ski areas, which also offers awesome variety in ambiance and even scenery. The setting above a deep blue lake is among the most spectacular in skidom, and the après ski is lively with big-name entertainers and casino gambling headlining the attractions.

Heavenly West: This is the California side, and it provides the greatest lift capacity up the mountain, with an aerial tram and two parallel chairs from the base, and contains just over half of the area's most difficult runs and the lion's share of its easiest. It is there, in and around a large day lodge, that the main ski school meeting place, ski shop, ski rental and other facilities are headquartered. Some skiers are happy on the lower slopes of the California side all the time. Roundabout is a sinuous trail that snakes its

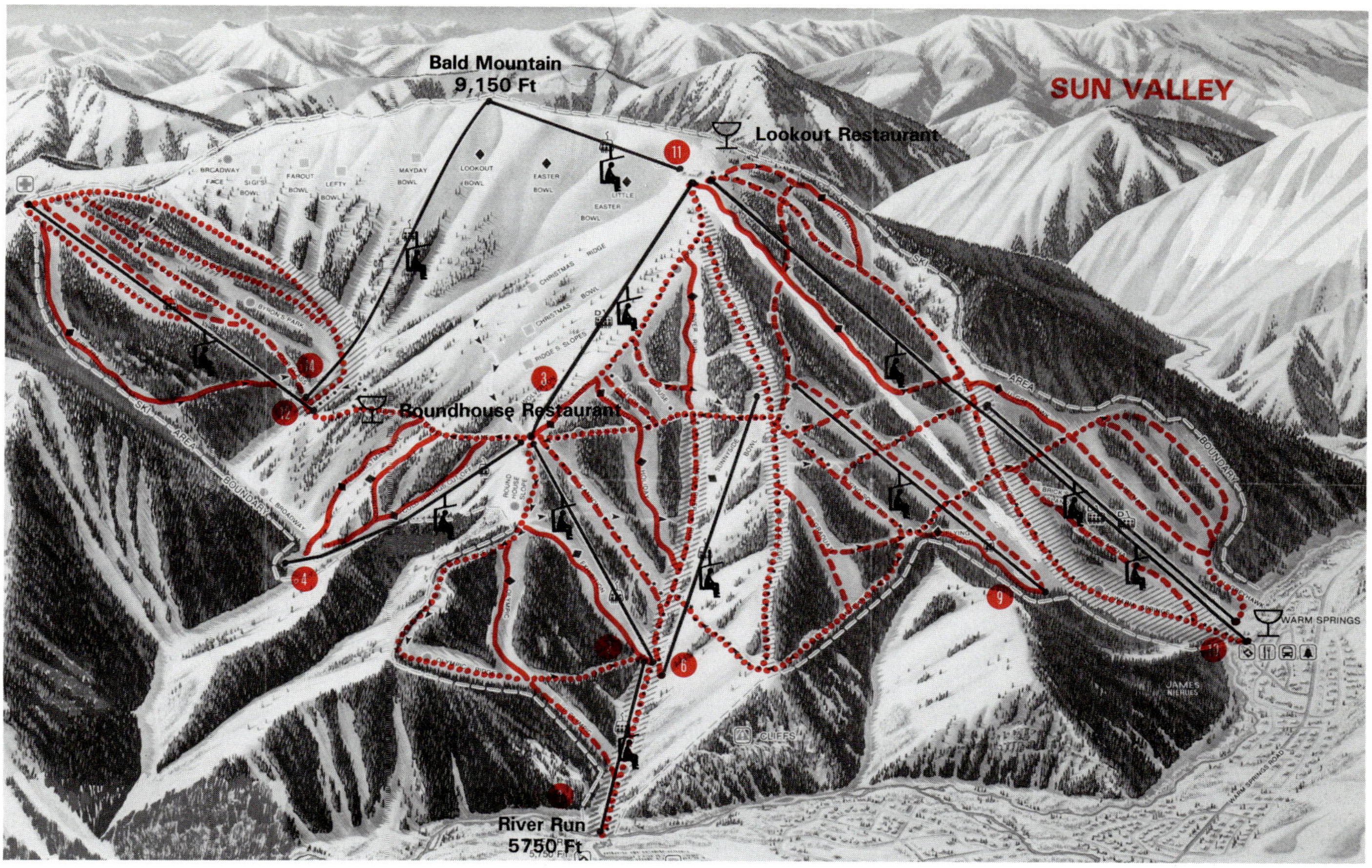

Sun Valley Lift Numbers: 1 River Run, 3 Christmas, 7 Greyhawk, 10 Challenger, 12 Seattle Ridge are all high speed 4 seater chair-lifts; 2 Exhibition, 6 Sunnyside, 11 Lookout, 12 Seattle Ridge, 14 Mayday are all 3 seater chair-lifts; 4 Cold Springs, 9 Flying Squirrel are double chair-lifts.

Runs: · · · · · · · · · · · · · · · · · · Easy - Medium ———————— Difficult

---

Dollar/Elkhorn Runs: 48 Hidden Valley, 49 Graduation, 50 Half Dollar Bowl, 51 Cabin Practice, 52 Half Dollar's Worth, 53 Old Bowl, 54 New Bowl, 55 Face of Dollar, 56 Poverty Flats, 57 Quarter Dollar Bowl, 58 Sheepherder, 59 Joint Venture, 60 Arrowhead Way, 61 Elkhorn Face, 62 Elkhorn Bowl.

Lift Numbers: 13 Dollar, 14 Half Dollar, 15 Quarter Dollar, 16 Elkhorn.

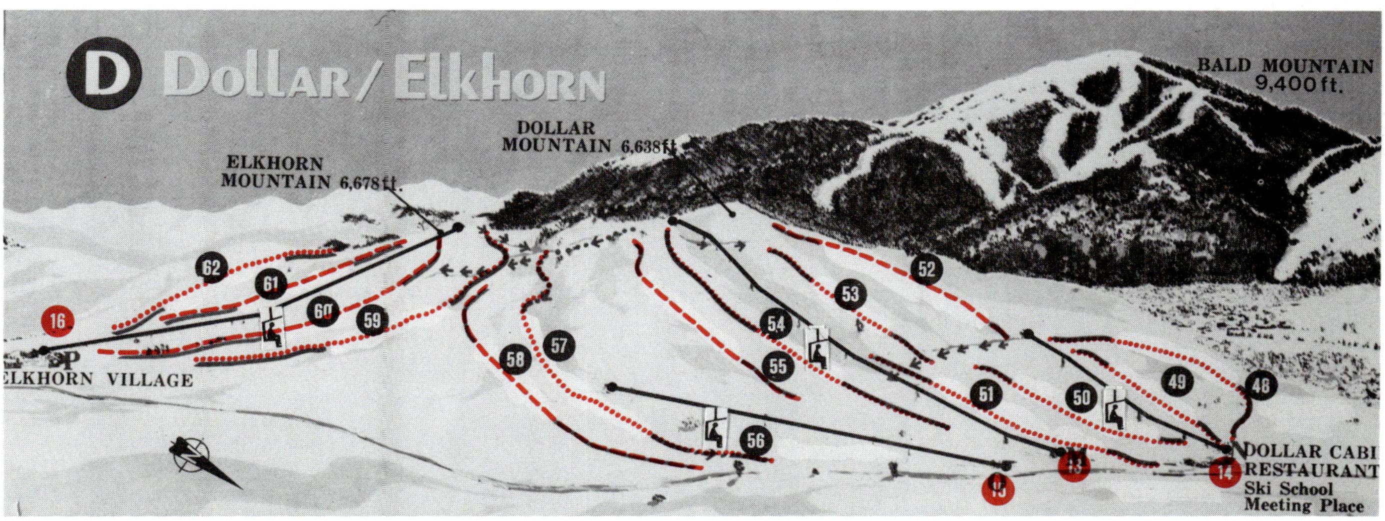

Mountain railways | Cableways | Gondolaways | Chair-lifts | Drag-lifts | ...... Easy runs | ------- Medium runs | ——— Difficult runs | Mountain restaurants

way down the steep mountain face so cleverly that even novices negotiate it easily. But the true delights of Heavenly West are in the bowls about the upper tram terminal. From there, where another restaurant and ski school meeting place are located, lifts scatter off in all directions.

The Powder Bowl chair services lovely Alpine-like terrain for novice and intermediate skiers. Ridge and Sky chairs open long intermediate trails, including Skyline which has fine skiing, spectacular views and access to the Nevada side. Experts enjoy the challenges of such steep and often mogully runs as South Fork Skiway, Ellie's, North Fork Skiway and Waterfall, a short but hair-raising pitch. A complex web of lifts of all sorts, including every known permutation of chairlift except a one-passenger chair, seves acres and acres of undulating slopes and fine trails on Heavenly West. An elaborate master plan for the redevelopment of this side of the ski area was working its way through regulatory commissions at this writing. The first of the new lifts, which will hopefull be in operation in 1997-98, is a six-passenger chairlift called the Tamarack Express, from mid-mountain on the California side to near the top of the Dipper Express on the Nevada side. Eventually, the area hopes to install an eight-passenger gondola, seven other lifts and two on-mountain restaurants, as well as renovate the base facilities.

If you want to understand Heavenly's natural setting, join a free Ski With A Ranger mountain tour at 10:30 and 1:30 daily from the top of the aerial tram. The Monument Peak Restaurant at the Top-of-the-Tram Lodge offers filling lunches with a view, and there is also a self-service cafeteria and a popular outdoor deck. Sky Meadows, a mid-mountain eating spot at the base of the Sky Express chair, is more casual and includes a grill-it-yourself barbecue terrace. There have long been plans to build a gondola from town to the slopes.

Heavenly North: It is possible to ski to the Nevada side from the Sky Chair or Ridge Chair via the Skyline Trail, or one can take the Stagecoach or Boulder lifts into the heart of the Nevada terrain. To ski the upper mountain, several choices present themselves, including the Comet, Heavenly's first high-speed quad, or Dipper, a high-speed quad, or on the network of varied terrain lower on the mountain. This is primarily intermediates' paradise. Glorious bowls, challenging glades and wide slopes abound. The lower reaches of the Nevada side offer a variety of novice and intermediate runs. North Bowl Ski Way and West Perimeter are two options for experts. Mott Canyon and adjacent Killebrew Canyon wear two black diamonds, while Milky Way Bowl, a single black bowl above, is easily accessed from the Skyline Trail.

There are lodges with food service at the bottom stations of both the Stagecoach and Boulder chairlifts, but the most congenial lunch spot is on a plateau known as East Peak. Located near the top stations of three lifts and the bottom stations of two more, this spacious lodge and terrace resembles the Piccadilly Circus of Heavenly's Nevada terrain. One of the biggest changes at Heavenly over the last few years is an enhanced commitment to families, investing half a million dollars in junior ski school improvements and adding programmes for pre-skiers, as well as young skiers and snowboarders. Uneasy parents or those with a very young child in the nursery may borrow a pager for a modest day fee.

In addition to skiing at Heavenly, the multi-day Ski Lake Tahoe pass is usable also at Alpine Meadows, Kirkwood, Northstar-at-Tahoe, Sierra-at-Tahoe or Squaw Valley, site of the 1960 Winter Olympics. Even without a car, you can take the Tahoe Casino Express from Reno-Tahoe International Airport or Greyhound from San Francisco, and transportation between ski resorts is also offered daily.

In a Few Words: Heavenly offers a real range of terrain, so that skiers of varying abilities can ride lifts and eat together, separating only for the run of their choice. Both the scenery and the lift and trail configuration are reminiscent of Alpine landscapes and ski circus layouts.

Après Ski: Traditional after-ski activities include stopping for a drink at the California Bar in the main lodge on the California side (live entertainment every afternoon), at the Monument Mountain Lounge at the top of the tram, with an unsurpassed view of the blue waters of the lake below, or at the Black Diamond Mexican Cantina at the Boulder Lodge on the Nevada side.

But traditional after-ski entertainment is only a part of the picture at Heavenly, one resort where people come as much for the après ski and instead-of-ski as for the excellent slopes and heavy snow. That's because Nevada is the only state in the U.S. that

Heavenly Valley West Side Lift Numbers: 1 Aerial Tram, 2 Gunbarrel, 3 West Bowl, 4 Powder Bowl, 5 Waterfall, 6 Pioneer Bowl, 7 Sky, 8 Ridge, 9 Dipper, 11 Groove, 12 Patsy's, 13 Mitey Mites (Beginners' lifts), 14 Pioneer, 15 World Cup

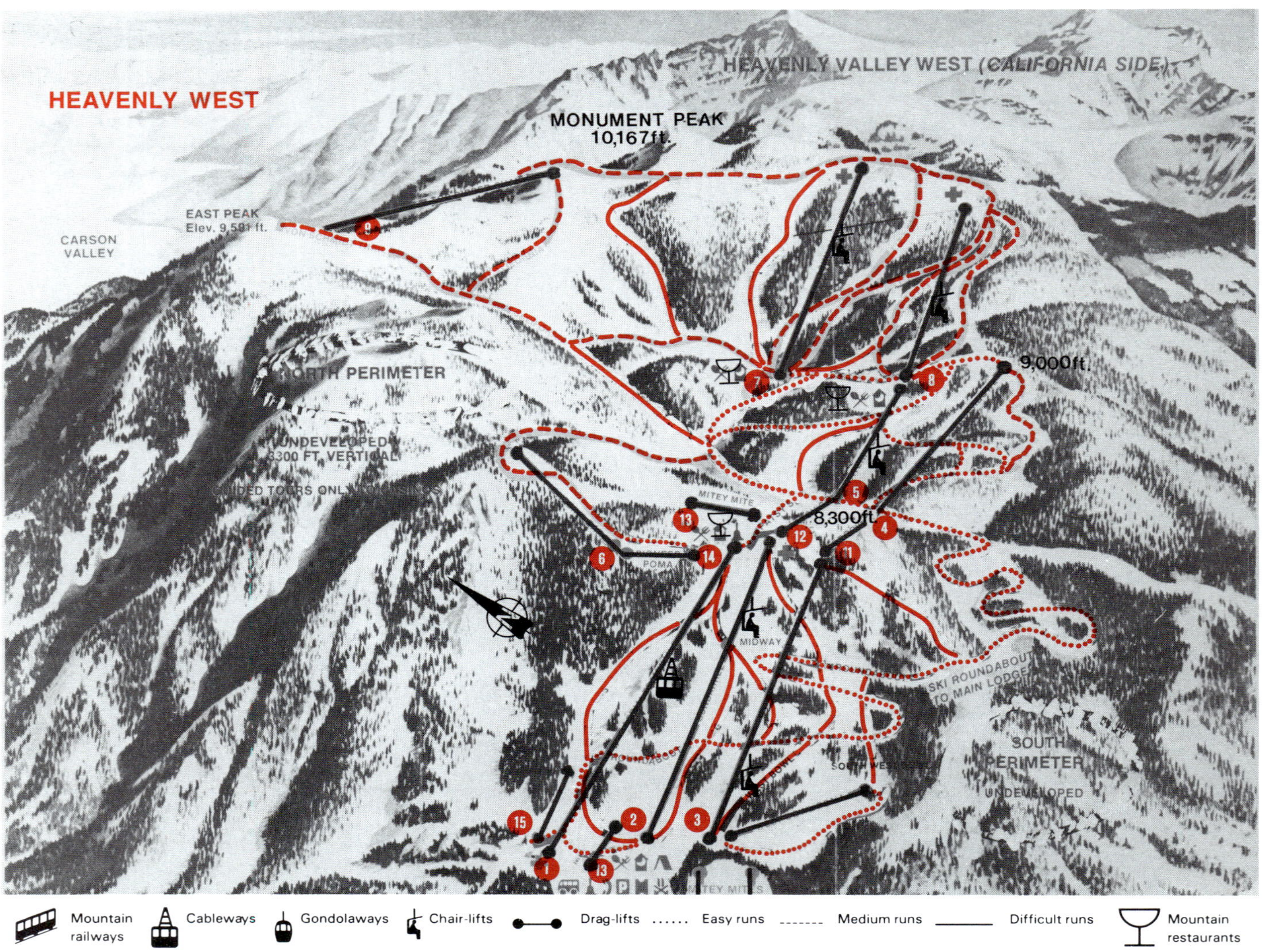

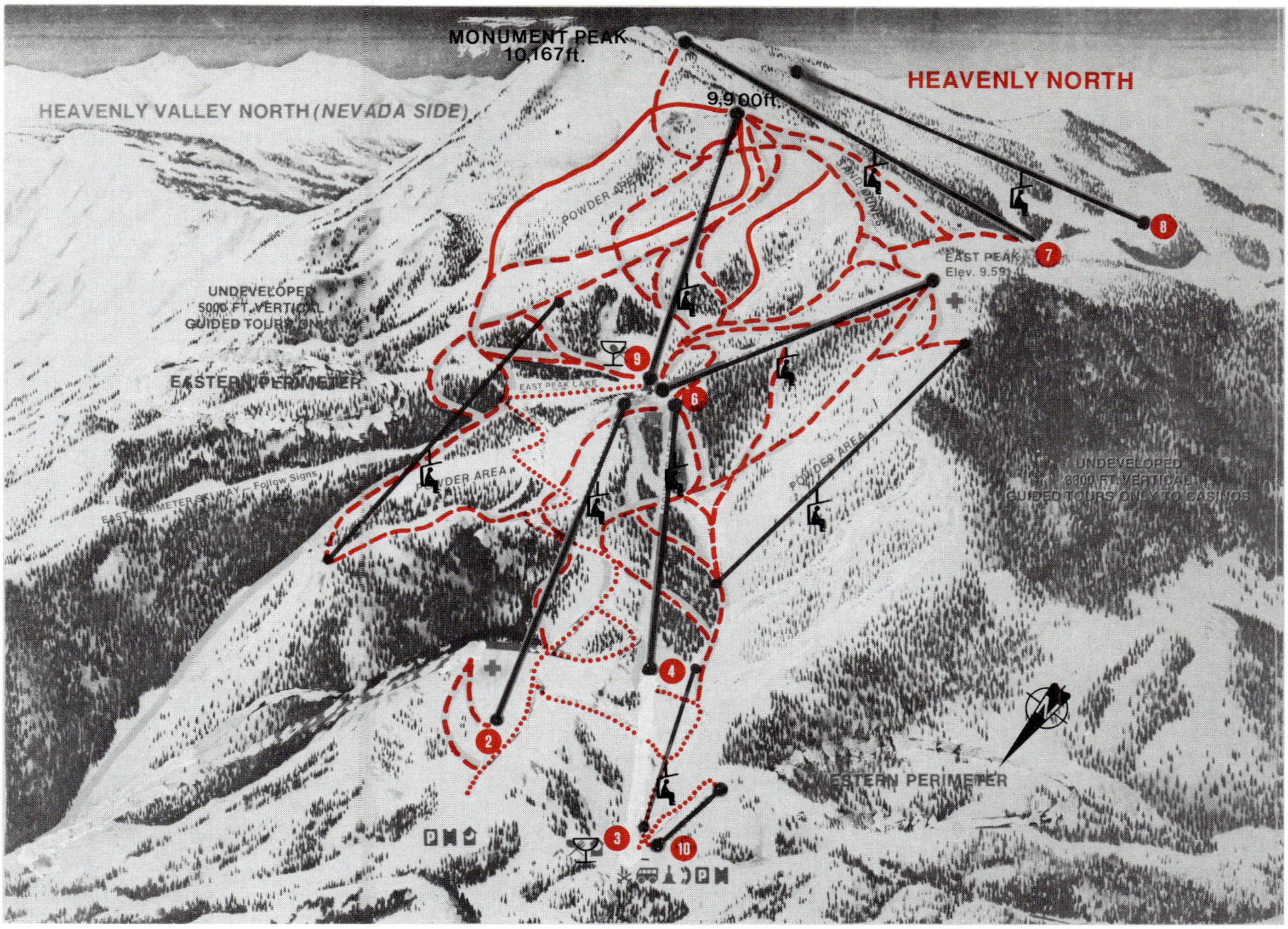

Heavenly Valley North Side Lift Numbers: 1 Galaxy, 2 Stage Coach, 3 Boulder, 4 North Bowl, 6 Comet and 9 Dipper (high speed 4 seater chair-lifts), 7 Sky, 8 Ridge, 9 Dipper, 10 Mitey Mite, 11 Olympic

Runs: • • • • • • • • • • • • • • • • • • • Easy - - - - - - - - - - - - - - - - - - - Medium ———————————— Difficult

offers big-time, round-the-clock gambling. At the Stateline casinos, there's 24-hour-a-day action at the tables and at the ubiquitous slot machines just a mile away from the ski area at such Las Vegas-type casino-hotels as Harrah's, Harvey's, Caesar's and High Sierra. In addition to gambling, these large hotels offer topflight nightclub entertainment, fine dining and dancing, as well as luxurious guestrooms.

Heavenly's après ski and dining scene actually spreads from Stateline, ablaze with Nevada neon, to the quieter, more restrained precincts of adjacent South Lake Tahoe on the California side of the border. Stateline feels like a casino town. South Lake Tahoe feels like a lakeside resort and has undergone an ambitious development plan which to make it less congested and more upscale. Heavenly provides an Alpine framework for them both, and when the gondola is in, that context will be solidified.

Stateline's casino-hotels all offer many dining options, including lavish, reasonably priced all-you-can-eat buffets. Elsewhere, the region's interesting continental cuisine, Cantina Los Tres Hombres and El Vaquero (Mexican), Petrello's, Celeste's and Scooza (Italian), Dixie's (Cajun and Creole), the Chart House (seafood and steaks), Swiss Chalet (Swiss), Dory's Oar (New England-style seafood transplanted westward) and Evan's (contemporary American cuisine). All serve dinner and some serve lunch. And this just scratches the surface of Lake Tahoe dining options.

One can soak away tired muscles – and sometimes inhibitions – in a private redwood tub filled with circulating hot water at Shingle Creek Hot Tubs or Nephele's Hot Tubs. Turtle's is a plush disco and nightclub in the Embassy Suites, and Wild West has three dance floors and an astonishing sound system playing country-and-western music. Nero's 2000 at Caesar's is the top casino dance club.

This South Lake Tahoe area is excellent for non-skiers and casual skiers too. Snowmobile, cross-country and snowshoe opportunities abound for those who want a non-Alpine outdoor experience in the splendid Sierra Nevada Range. Lake Tahoe itself, the deepest mountain lake in America, never freezes over, and wonderful paddlewheel sightseeing cruises are scheduled all winter long.

It is also possible to take the "Tahoe Queen" to the North Shore for skiing at Alpine, Northstar or Squaw, but these are also served by bus, as are Heavenly, Kirkwood and Sierra-at-Tahoe, the other South Shore ski area which participates in the Ski Lake Tahoe lift pass.

Lodging: Dozens of hotels, motels and condominiums line the lake and offer vacationers vast options in price, layout, location and degree of luxury. Free buses make three loops along the California accommodations neighbourhoods, and the Lake Lapper is an inexpensive shuttle along Lake Tahoe's east and west shores.

Just as the big casino-hotels are the *ne plus ultra* of local night life, they are the flossiest places to stay. The ski crowd mixes amicably with the gaming crowd. In addition, there are dozens of hotels, motels, inns, lodges and condominiums with a total of 11,500 beds. Many of these are on the California side of the state line, yet several are within walking distance of the casinos. The Embassy Suites Resort combines the advantages of hotel and condo lodging and includes free full breakfast, morning newspaper and apres ski reception every evening. The Inn by the Lake is well-run and has water views, an outdoor heated pool and complimentary continental breakfast. Ridge Tahoe are luxurious townhouses with hotel services, while the Bavarian Village is comprised of economical condos on a quiet street. Bell Court is set amid the towering pines and offers free ski shuttle. The Fantasy Inn boasts "theme rooms" that are a good choice for romantic couples. The nearest accommodations to the Heavenly North lifts is Tahoe Seasons, an all-suite property, and the nearest to Heavenly West lifts are Heavenly Valley Townhouses and other condominium developments.

BRECKENRIDGE

Height of Resort: 9,610 ft.
Height of Top Station: 12,213 ft.
Nearest Major Airport: Denver
Route by Car: Interstate 70 west from Denver to Frisco, then Colorado Route 9 south to Breckenridge.
Driving time is about two hours.
Resort Facilities Charts: See page 210

Breckenridge is the name of a ski area comprising three substantial mountains that rise above a historic town of the same name. The ski area is now under the same ownership as Vail, Beaver Creek and Keystone, and fully interchangeable lift passes and inter-resort transportation are available. Breckenridge has typically attracted great numbers of U.K. skiers, who will find an entire new skiing experience. Eighteen million dollars, the greatest single-year investment in Breckenridge's 36-year skiing history, has bought two new high-speed quad chairlifts (for a total of six), a 50 percent increase in snowmaking, additional on-mountain food-service and retail establishments and the much-needed renovation of the Bergenhof

Breckenridge: Most people who ski Breckenridge ski three adjacent lift-served mountains, each with its own lift and trail network and interconnected at strategic spots by cross-over trails. No one of these mountains has vast vertical drop by Rockies standards, but taken together they provide sufficient terrain for a week's skiing and with the addition of the four-resort ticket, they offer far more than that. In addition, hard-core experts go off-piste on a fourth mountain, which has no lifts but is avalanche-controlled and patrolled.

Peak 8 is the oldest, highest, largest and northernmost of Breckenridge's three inter-connected ski mountains. From a base area that still has a slightly rustic feel, lifts rise up in a semi-circle to a hug complex network of interwoven runs. The lower lifts serve the easiest slopes, while the Colorado SuperChair, one of Breckenridge's six high-speed quads, climbs to a high plateau where the Vista Haus is found. Below is a dense web of trails for all ability levels. Those on the main face of the mountain are mostly for novice and intermediate skiers. Those on the south-eastern wall of the upper mountain are for experts. Mach I is one of America's top mogul slopes, and its neighbours are equally challenging.

Above the restaurant is one of the area's two new high-speed qauds as well as a T-bar that accesses Breckenridge's high bowls, both in altitude and in the level of skill they require. Contest and Horseshoe Bowls, especially the latter, have been luring powderhounds to steep, tree-free snowfields for years. Breckenridge also gives those fit skiers who are willing to hike in another playground, Imperial Bowl. Entry is by hiking up a ridge 12,213 feet above sea level, and when there are a few feet of snow on top of that, Breckenridge is able to claim the only skiing in America above 13,000 feet.

When the snowpack suffices, skiers hike from the top of the Peak 8 T-bar to ski the ungroomed steeps of Peak 7. Because it has no direct lift service, this terrain has a challenging backcountry air. Most of the terrain is above the treeline, and most of it is very steep.

Peak 9 is the centre of Breckenridge's skiing is on this mountain, whose bottom station is closest to town and which has the most slopeside lodging. The Quicksilver was America's first detachable quad, and though its speed is not up to newer models, it still keeps queues to a minimum and feeds skiers into the heart of Breckenridge's terrain. The lower slopes, served by the quad and a mid-mountain chair, are outstanding gentle novice terrain, offering gentle pitch and generous width. The Mercury SuperChair angles off from the base of Peak 9 to provide a shortcut to Peak 8, while a second new high-speed quad accesses real medium-standard trails. Higher up on 9 is a fine web of mostly medium runs with pleasant detours through the trees for glade lovers. Like Peak 8, Peak 9 challenges experts who tackle the high-expert terrain on the backside.

Peak 10 is Breckenridge's powdery outback. It is a statistical midget, but a giant in terms of challenge. There's just one lift, but it is another queue-gobbling detachable quad called the Falcon SuperChair. The 1,389-foot vertical is half of Peak 8's, and the 16 trails just over a quarter of what the oldest mountain now offers. But this terrain consists of chutes, headwalls, glades and other parcels of paradise for good skiers seeking thrills.

There are no base facilities at Peak 10, but both 8 and 9 offer child care, ski school, ski rental and dining facilities. The Peak 8 nursery takes babies from 2 months and its FantaSki Kingdom has terrain and a new surface lift for the littlest beginners. The Peak 9 children's centre is part of the Beaver Run complex.

There is a lovely, rustic touring centre on the Peak 8 access road with 22 km. of groomed trails, classes for beginners and a mountain guide service for day trips into the backcountry. Additional loipes are found at the Frisco Nordic Center, just down the road, which is operated by the same family.

In a Few Words: Mighty, massive Breckenridge is one of the leading Rockies destinations for British skiers. Little wonder. There's convenience to Denver, outstanding skiing on three mountains and a lively, very American town nearby.

Après Ski: The après ski action is as important in Breckenridge as a day on the slopes. Breckenridge, a large resort town with pillows for 23,000 guests, is a 19th century mining boomtown with a picturesque Western-style Victorian Main Street and a wealth of new construction surrounding it. Not surprisingly, it serves as the après ski and shopping capital of Summit County. It has long had the image of drawing a young active crowd, but with scores of bars, restaurants and shops, there is now an abundance of after-ski styles for all.

As soon as the lifts close, the indoor taverns and outdoor decks begin to rock, presumably including the new version of the Bergenhof at the base of Peak 8. At the base of Peak 9, notable spots are Tiffany's at Beaver Run, Breck's at the Breckenridge Hilton, Maggie and Jake T. Pounder's, both at the Village at Breckenridge. The latter claims to be the only place in town owned by a dog. Adam's Street Grill, Downstairs at Eric's and the Salt Creek Saloon get good happy-hour crowds. Later, there's dancing at Breck's Lounge, Tiffany's, Joshua's, Meach's Mogul and Remington's. The Breckenridge Brewery & Pub is popular with connoisseurs of "boutique brews", conviviality and filling food.

Breckenridge offers a splendid variety of restaurants, both in style and in cuisine. Spencer's Steaks &

Breckenridge Lifts: Numbers 1 Colorado, 2 Quicksilver, 3 Falcon & 6 Mercury are high speed 4 seater chair-lifts; the remainder consist of one triple and 9 double chair-lifts plus 2 drag-lifts.

Runs: • Easy - - - - - - - - - - - - - - - - Medium ———————— Difficult

Please note: This is not the official trail map for the Breckenridge Ski Corporation. Please pick up an official trail map when you arrive in the area.

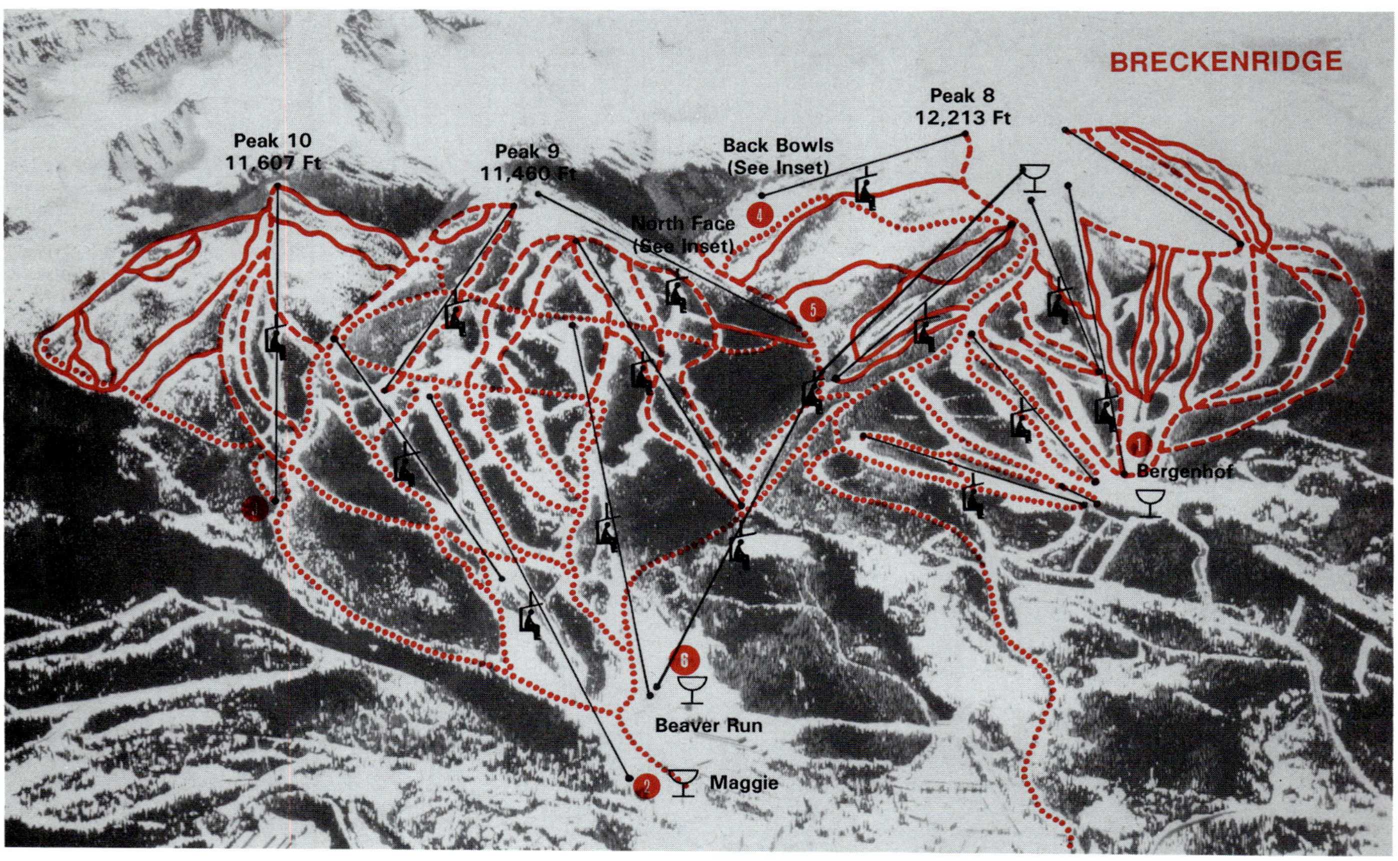

Spirits at Beaver Run serves seafood and steaks and has a great salad bar. Fine dining places Pierre's for French cuisine, the restaurant at the St. Bernard Inn for northern Italian specialties and the Wellington Inn's restaurant for central European favorites. For steaks and other American specialties served in an old Western ambiance, the Briar Rose Restaurant and the Brown Hotel shine. You'll find good natural foods at the Blue Moose and Cafe Three Eleven. Poirrier's serves Cajun specialties while the Pasta Jay's has a southern Italian accent. the Top of the World at the Lodge at Breckenridge offers fine food and views to match. It's worth a short ride from town.

Lower on the price scale, the Gold Pan dishes up large portions of Mexican food in a casual 19th century building, while Mi Casa is Mexican with a glossier overlay. Pizza is found at Fatty's Chicago Pizza, Jake T. Pounder's and Domino's, a fast-food chain. Wendy's, a burger chain, and Baskin & Robbins, known for 31 ice cream flavours, also have outlets in Breckenridge.

One of the most popular non-ski diversions at Breckenridge is to spend a day at Tiger Run, America's largest snowmobile centre with guided drive-yourself excursions and a popular evening ride in a heated snowcat for dinner in an old bar in a historic mining camp called Dry Gulch. Nordic Dinner Sleighrides operating out of the Breckenridge Nordic Center do a great sleighride, featuring steak dinner and Scott Joplin-style ragtime entertainment.

Lodging: Most of Breckenridge's accommodations are modern and well appointed. The Breckenridge Hilton, which is extremely popular with British tour operators, is a full-service hotel with easy access to Peak 9. The nearby Breckenridge Mountain Lodge is also convenient but has a more rustic atmosphere. Beaver Run, Breckenridge's largest property, and the newly renovated Village at Breckenridge, a complex of four standards of accommodations under one management, are slopeside at Peak 9. Both have condominium-style units but hotel services. Beaver Run is especially lavishly equipped, with an excellent indoor/outdoor pool, the world's largest indoor mini-golf setup and a large video game arcade. Also nearby, the Chateaux is known for spacious, luxuriously furnished units.

Breckenridge has literally hundreds of condominium units, and since the addition of a three-seater chairlift between Peaks 8 and 9 in 1996, many more are now truly ski-in, ski-out. Bed-and-breakfast inns, from economy to deluxe, tend to foster Breckenridge's old mining ambiance, but with all the modern comforts. The free Town Trolley operates day and night to shuttle guests along Main Street, accommodations and Peak 9.

KEYSTONE

Height of Resort: 9,300 ft. (Keystone Mountain)
Height of Top Station: 11,980 ft. (The Outback)
Nearest Major Airport: Denver
Route by Car: Take Interstate 70 west from Denver to Dillon. Follow U.S. Route 6 east to Keystone.
Driving time is under two hours.
Resort Facilities Charts: See page 211

Keystone, one of Colorado's prettiest resorts, is also one of its fastest-changing. The face of the resort has gotten a complete makeover with the addition of an attractive new village directly at the base of the gondola in 1996, and in 1997, it became part of Vail Resort, Inc., which provided an infusion of capital for mountain and lodging improvements, as well as joint lift passes with Breckenridge, Vail and Beaver Creek. Keystone itself comprises three interconnected mountains.

Keystone Mountain: Keystone's development was one of the first designs intended to provide a lot of ski runs with as little intrusion as possible on the ecology of the mountain. The ski terrain is a graceful web of narrow runs snaking through the trees, served by one six-passenger gondola, chairlifts of all sorts and two drag-lifts for beginners. Keystone was one of the last areas in North America to prohibit snowboarding, but since the ban was lifted, the resort has embraced the sport with great enthusiasm. An excellent snowboard park was installed high on the mountain at Packsaddle Bowl – and even lighted for light skiing. Snowboarding facilities are again being improved and expanded, and Keystone is adding a tubing hill for added off-skis diversion.

The center of this part of the base area is the Mountain House, which is now actually an attractive complex of buildings with rental shop, ski and other retail shops, food service, ski school and day care. Capping Keystone is the spacious Summit House, which serves soups, hot and cold sandwiches, beer, wine and non-potent beverages. In order to give skiers of all ability levels equal access to this attractive facility, there are trails for all from the top. Beginners can choose Spring Dipper or Schoolmarm and intermediates have a choice of many routes from the summit, but advanced skiers have to suffer a short stretch on easy terrain before hitting ëtheir' trails. Most of the relatively advanced slopes are grouped below the novice area called Packsaddle Bowl and all seem to be called Go Devil. This plus Last Hoot and Lower Jackwhacker are the only somewhat expert runs on the lower mountain, the remainder of Keystone by Night

The east side of Keystone's terrain is known as River Run, which – with the development of a village of the same name – has become more and more important. The main access is via the six-passenger Skyway gondola, which zips up the 2,340 vertical feet in just 10 minutes. When this gondola was opened, it enabled Keystone to put in lights for night skiing, and for anyone who has never skied under the stars (well, under the arc lights which are under the stars), it is a special treat. Keystone is a meticulously groomed mountain, and somehow, when the snow underfoot is smooth, the lights put a magical glow on the trails while the surrounding woods and inky-black and other skiers appear as eerie figures, skiers seem to ski more confidently than ever. The lifts at Keystone run continuously from 8.30 a.m. until 9 p.m. daily, and any lift ticket valid at Keystone is good for night skiing too. A new high-speed quad supplements the gondola and a new egress trail spreads the traffic, both welcome on this increasingly popular part of the mountain..

North Peak: Adjacent to Keystone Mountain, and accessible from summit via a second six-passenger gondola, is North Peak, with 12 high-intermediate and expert bump runs on a 1,620-foot vertical. This terrain boosted the Keystone complex's reputation from one of primarily intermediate skiing to one where experts would also be happy. Starfire is often groomed, but most of North Peak's dozen runs are dotted with moguls. The gondola connecting the top of Keystone Mountain to the top of North Peak provides quicker access to the resort's more difficult skiing, while a second mountaintop restaurant called the Outpost crowns North Peak. It is a stylish spot, offering excellent food, both self-service and sitdown.

The Outback: The Outback, Keystone's third contiguous mountain, is tucked in behind North Peak, with terrain that extends the vertical with a crown of above-the-treeline skiing and enhances the experience. It consists of open glades and wide, fall-line runs, a mix designed for the strong intermediate and advanced skier. By walking up the ridge above the Outback Express lift, skiers reach the Outback Bowls – tree-free on top, heavily gladed below and challenging all the way.

Keystone's outstanding cross-country centre has more than 20 miles of groomed, track-set trails both in the valley and at the top of the mountain (the latter with gondola access). With a top-rated children's programme, a children's learning centre for tiny beginning skiers, a mining-theme ski park called Gold Rush Alley for on-mountain fun and the cool snowboarding centre, Keystone is a good family choice.

In a Few Words: The team of Keystone's three contiguous mountains plus Breckenridge, Vail and Beaver Creek provides a variety of skiing experiences plus a fabulous luxury resort and matchless proximity to Denver.

Après Ski: Keystone is a rather subdued and relatively elegant resort built around a small, sparkling lake. While there is not a massive number of drinking, dining and dancing spots in the village, what exists has been specifically spread across the spectrum of styles and prices. Night skiing and apres ski melt into one, with Keysters at the River Run base and Gassy's and the Last Lift Bar in the Mountain House at the main Keystone base among the spots getting the early crowds. Later, the music music- and dance-loving crowd tend to head for The Last Lift Bar for noise and merriment. In addition to live entertainment, there are pool tables (an inelegant relative of billiards) and video games, as well as a supersized 10-foot television screen for anyone wishing to strike up an acquaintance with American spectator sports. Keysters at the River Run base has karaoke nightly. Teens have their own nightspot, a discreetly supervised, alcohol-free club called MonteZuma's.

Keystone has become something of a fine-food mecca, even offering a culinary institute for professional cooks, cooking classes for enthusiastic amateurs and special chefs' tasting dinner. At the Keystone Lodge, the Garden Room is the fanciest restaurant, specializing in steak, lamb, salmon and Continental specialties, some cooked at tableside, and its wine list is impressive. For a more casual, more rugged atmosphere and more beef, The Bighorn fits the bill. It also has an impressive salad bar. The casual Edgewater Café nearby offers moderately priced breakfast, luncheon and dinner selections. Ida Belle's Bar & Grill features Mexican food, big burgers, sandwiches, shuffleboard and a juke box. The Village at River Run has several new places to eat, ranging from the casual Kickapoo Tavern which offers large portions of home-style American fare and the Great Northern, a brew pub and chop house.

Because of night skiing, the Summit House remains open late. But the real treat is to take two gondolas to The Outpost atop North Peak, which offers two spectacular dining options, a fondue dinner with live entertainment is a delicious Euro-treat in Der Fondue Chessel and the Alpenglow Stube for elegant dinners are served at in a gorgeous setting.

Away from the ski facilities, the Keystone Ranch is an elegantly refurbished old log house which serves exacting, exciting, unusual meals in a gracious setting. On the other wide of the resort, Ski Tip Lodge is a quaint bed-and-breakfast inn but is best known for its delicious dinners in a charming country setting. Keystone also puts on dinner sleighrides to a rustic cabin on the back ranch where a hearty down-home meal like prime ribs or barbecued chicken is featured, along with lively singalongs.

The Snake River Saloon, on U.S. 6 near the resort proper, is the closest off-campus option, with live music and dancing nightly. It boasts about having been the birthplace of rock-and-roll in the Keystone area, and it also serves good beef and fish. Nearby, in The Inn, is RazzBerry's, a recently refurbished, contemporary bar and restaurant specializing in fine, modern American cuisine. There are other options in nearby Silverthorne and Dillon. The Ristorante Al Lago specialises in northern Italian cuisine in a chalet-style setting, and Antonia's is also known for excellent pasta, seafood and a fine wine list comprised mainly of top California vintages. For a different culinary tradition, there's Silverheels Southwest Grill, a Spanish-American hacienda where steaks and seafood are cooked on a red-hot tabletop granite slab. Pug Ryan's Steakhouse dishes up just the kind of dishes you'd expect. The Old Dillon Inn is a noisy classic for Tex-Mex food and loud music.

Anyone with a yen for made-in-the-U.S.A. fast food

need go no further than the busy Dillon exit off Interstate 70, where assorted fast-food chains are found. The money saved can be disposed of nicely in the nearby Silverthorne Outlet Mall, where name brand clothing and other items can be purchased at bargain prices. Summit Stages provide free shuttle-bus service to the Dillon/Silverthorne area, as well as elsewhere in the county.

Keystone is not only a ski resort but a four-seasons sports resort. In winter, this means there are a lot of activities to participate in and watch. The skating centre on Keystone Lake offers instruction and rentals in figure skating and general skating too. The Keystone Tennis Club has indoor courts, while Keystone Lodge and several condominiums offer heated outdoor pools and some fitness facilities.

Lodging: The original Keystone resort development is centered around Keystone Lake, with low-rise condominiums at water's edge and also tucked into the surrounding woods. In addition, there are other condominium lodgings along U.S. 6 and also near Lake Dillon, as well as motels closer to the Interstate. Keystone's own frequent free bus system connects all of the resort's lodging.

The resort's top hotel is the Keystone Lodge. Half of the rooms in this modern, award-winning full-service hotel centrally located adjacent to Keystone Plaza are being renovated this year, and the rest will be completed in 1998-99. The lodge offers fine, large rooms, a cocktail lounge, three of Keystone's restaurants and the most convenient access to everything going on in the village.

The other luxury property is the Chateaux d'Mont, just 15 ultra-luxury apartment villas steps from the Mountain House. The resort's other, older condominiums range from spacious, deluxe three-bedroom units to smaller, simpler, more economical apartments. Nothing in Keystone Village is really inconvenient, for even the farthest afield is within a quick walk of the Plaza. The base area of the ski mountain itself is a free shuttle bus ride away. If you prefer to walk to the lifts, you'll prefer the Village at River Run, which right at the base of the Skyway gondola. It offers Keystone's newest, most stylish units – though not necessarily the most spacious. All are extremely attractive and comfortable, and each complex has a pool, an outdoor hot tub or similar amenity on site too. Ski Tip Lodge, in addition to being an appealing dining spot, accommodates up to 50 overnighters in its charming quarters on a bed-and-breakfast plan. Children 12 and under may stay free when sharing their parents' quarters in all resort accommodations.

COPPER MOUNTAIN

Height of Resort: 9,600 ft.
Height of Top Station: 12,360 ft.
Nearest Major Airport: Denver
Route by Car: Take Interstate 70 west from Denver to the junction of Route 91, where Copper Mountain is located.
Driving time is about two hours.
Resort Facilities Charts: See page 210

Copper is a well-designed contemporary resort development, known for its logical mountain layout. Nearly two-thirds of the spacious terrain is geared to intermediate skiers, many of whom come in family or club groups. Recently bought by IntraWest, the Vancouver-based resort developer which put Whistler on the map, Copper Mountain next season promises to be a whole new place from Copper Mountain this season.

Copper Mountain: When Copper Mountain, just off the main east-west highway through Colorado, was developed and management had a choice of concentrating the heaviest initial investment in base and village facilities or in facilities on the mountain, they chose the latter course – a course which, naturally, will change as soon as IntraWest applies its development muscle, philosophy and budget to Copper. This meant that from opening day, Copper had big-mountain skiing, even though the trappings of resorthood have taken a little longer in coming.

Copper Mountain, in a sense, is like an open book which you can 'read' from left to right. The most difficult terrain is on the left as you face the hill. The enormous census of intermediate trails fills the centre of the mountain. The easier terrain is on the right, near the spacious base lodge and away from the down-rushing traffic from the more challenging slopes. Skiing around the mountain is a pleasure, and funnelling back to the base lodges is easy. Only at the very top of the mountain, where the most recent terrain expansions have taken place, are the runs nearly uniformly black. Serving the impressive lacework of trails, crowned by open bowls and snowfields, are 20 lifts including three high-speed quads (two from the main base area) to zip skiers from the bottom station to high points in the terrain in 10 minutes or less.

Union Creek is Copper's novice terrain, which is as tame as can be, with long, wide reassuring runs to make even new skiers feel like champions. Even the names are soothing: Scooter, Easy Feeling, Fairway and Loverly, all on the western end of the trail system, tucked on the distant side of one of the long ridges and on a smallish slope on the other side of one of the terrain's natural drainages.

Of the detachable quads, American Flyer, is the main lift up the primary ridge of Union Peak. It leads to a fine group of mid-mountain intermediate trails and also accesses the gentle upper runs of Union Park and the ungentle ones of Union Bowl near the summit. This is a small bowl that skis big, with steeps, chutes, cornices and glades on a relatively modest 773-foot vertical. A small warming hut and snack bar is found at the top of American Flyer. American Eagle, another high-speed quad, is the main lift from the village to the terrain on Copper Peak. The runs directly off American Eagle are wide mid-range cruisers. A third high-speed four-seater, still unnamed at press time, was added in 1994, replacing a pair of doubles. It is also the gateway to another 500 acres of bowl skiing, to be developed soon off Union Park. Everything to the east climbs the difficulty scale, as does everything above the top station of the quad. Brennan's Grin, Murphy's Law and Mine Dump are narrow mogul chutes. Resolution Bowl starts with a steep headwall, gentles deceivingly into a quartet of mellow-looking trails and then plunges again into a steep slope which is notable for tough mogul terrain. Serviced by its own chair, this is an isolated sector for good, strong skiers.

Copper Bowl is Copper Mountain's trump card for good skiers. This grandiose parcel tucked in behind Copper and Union Peaks was long a little-kept secret that required considerable off-piste expertise. Steep faces, open glades, and fine powder fields characterise the skiing embraced by two long ridges now served by two double chairlifts. A long, fairly easy road snakes down one side of the bowl, which is doable even by intermediate skiers who want to get a look at this magnificent cirque. But off-piste still prevails, with open snowfields, glades and even some chutes that require a long traverse,

Copper has an outstanding children's programme, starting with Belly Button Babies and Belly Button Bakery for small pre-skiers, through a top ski school programme for all ability and energy levels. Ski school for adults is equally well regarded. For cross-country skiers, Copper offers 25 km. of marked, groomed trails.

In a Few Words: Copper is a special place for beginners wishing to learn and for intermediate and advanced skiers, particularly those who want to improve their skiing in a pleasant, caring atmosphere and on a fine mountain.

Après Ski: Copper Mountain, with its small village right at the base of the lifts, is ideal for families or for self-contained groups who enjoy each other's companionship and help create their own amusement. Après ski with live entertainment starts on the main level of the Copper Commons day lodge building at the base of the two quads. The Pub, downstairs, features a club-like atmosphere and English ale for the homesick. Farley's, a popular soup/sandwich/beer dispensary at the bottom of E Lift, B-Lift Pub and O'Shea's also offer after-ski, as well as informal food.

For dinner, Pesce Fresco has a breezy, contemporary atmosphere and a menu of international specialties on the light side. Rackets in the athletic club has Southwestern American cuisine and a huge salad bar. Farley's does steaks, burgers and the ubiquitous Mexican specialties. The Steak-Out in the centre of the village serves beef and seafood. The nearby Imperial Palace is known for reasonably priced Chinese food.

Much after-ski life involves relaxing in front of a fire, concentrating over a backgammon board and the like. Although shops are few, there is a market at Snowbridge Square for those who would like to save money by preparing meals in their condominium kitchen facilities.

The outstanding Copper Mountain Racquet & Athletic Club also has an outstanding health and racquet club, and admission is free to resort guests. It features a 25-yard lap pull in a landscaped hall, Nautilus and free weights, indoor tennis and racquetball courts, aerobics, tanning beds, steamrooms, saunas, hot tubs and nursery.

Lodging: Condominium apartments really are the name of the Copper Mountain accommodations game and are likely to remain so, even after IntraWest performs its magic. Everything is within easy walking distances of the lifts. Since Copper Mountain is new, so is all its lodging and the entire resort has been honoured with four diamonds from the American Automobile Association, which rates accommodations nationwide. Apartment units range from studios appropriate for singles or two people to massive four-bedroom-plus-loft apartments housing up to 10 people. Most complexes offer a range of apartment sizes. Every one of Copper's more than one dozen condominium complexes features units with kitchens, fireplaces, telephones and colour television in each unit and washing machines and dryers on the premises so no-one has to go home with a bagful of dirty laundry. Additional luxuries abound. Anaconda and Togwotee have Jacuzzi whirlpools while Snowbridge, Summit House East and Wheeler House have saunas. There are heated swimming pools at Timber Creek and Copper Valley. Copper Bridge, Copper Junction and Snowflake have lounges on the premises.

Copper Mountain is also the site of the only Club Med ski village in North America. Located at the western end of the resort, near the base of the American Flyer quad, it offers all of the international flavour and well-known all-inclusive formula within the context of an all-American ski resort. It is very international, as expected, yet English is used more than at Club Meds that you might know from the Alps. The Foxpine Inn is Copper Mountain's first hotel-type lodging. It features 55 well-appointed rooms, pool and restaurant on the premises. Additional accommodations are available at nearby Dillon and Frisco with free Summit Stages shuttle bus service to Copper.

BIG SKY

Height of Resort: 7,500 ft.
Bottom of Lowest Lift: 6,970 ft.
Top of Highest Lift: 11,150 ft.
Nearest Airport: Bozeman
Route by Car: Take Route 191 south for 43 miles to the seven-mile-long resort access road.
Resort Facilities Charts: See page 210.

Beautiful scenery, a secluded setting and proximity to the winter wonders of Yellowstone National Park characterize this beguiling resort.

Lone Mountain: Lone Mountain is to Big Sky what the Matterhorn is to Zermatt, a landmark peak and a defining element. Its newest development, a cableway to the summit of Lone Peak, was the most exciting news in the Rockies last year, because it

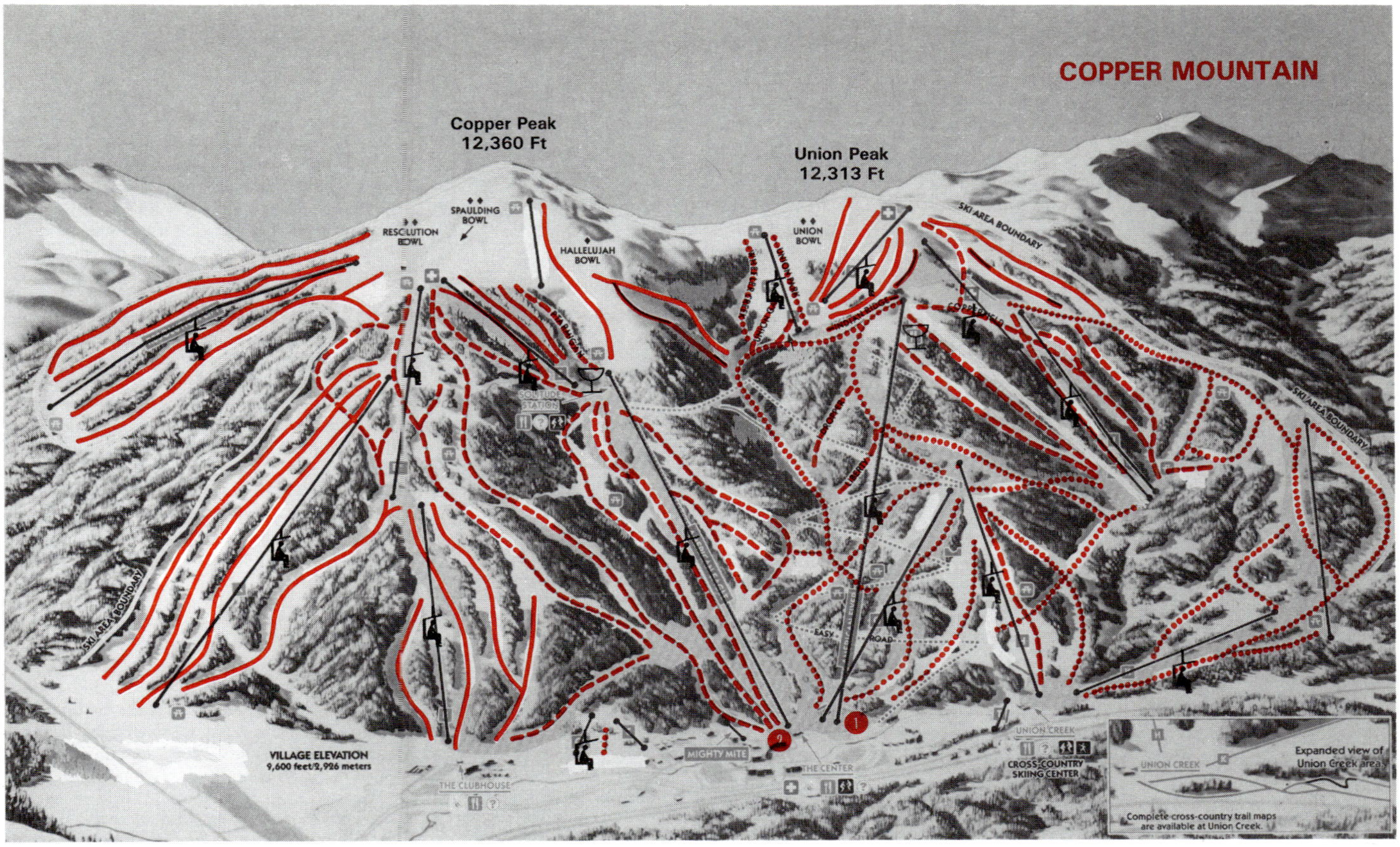

Copper Mountain Lifts: This area is served by 18 lifts. Numbers 1 (American Flyer), 2 (American Eagle) and 3 are high speed 4-seater chair-lifts. There are 6 triple and 7 double chair-lifts, plus 4 drag-lifts.

Runs: · · · · · · · · · · · · · · · · · · Easy - - - - - - - - - - - - - - - - - - Medium ———————————— Difficult

increased the area's vertical to 4,180 ft. – for one season the most in the U.S. It also offers an astonishing variety of ski terrain. The lower portion, served by a four-passenger gondola, a chair-lift and one drag lift, is primarily novice and intermediate terrain. Runs like Calamity Jane, Huntley Hollow, Crazy Horse and Mr. K undulated enchantingly through the woods. High above, with access by the Lone Peak triple chair, is a steep white basin known as The Bowl. With new powder – a common occurrence at this area with an average annual snowfall of 400 inches – it provides unsurpassed deep-snow skiing for strong intermediate and advanced skiers. After doubling its uphill capacity with new high-speed chair-lifts in the last seven years, Big Sky made its biggest commitment with the installation of a 15-passenger tram to the summit of Lone Mountain. The capacity is intentionally low, which essentially retains a similar backcountry feel to that experienced by skiers who previously had to hike up to the extreme, high-expert terrain at the top. In addition to accessing heart-stopping steeps, the new tram and the upper reaches of the European-style south-facing slopes afford awesome views as far as the Tetons and the Yellowstone National Park caldera. The Shed Horn double chair-lift opens additional intermediate terrain on Lone Mountain's lower slopes. Experts also make their way to the Challenger double chair-lift and the Country Club tow to access Big Sky's most extreme lift- served terrain. Big and Little Rock Tongues, Midnight Basin and Kurt's Glade each proudly wear a black diamond or two.

Andesite Mountain: At virtually a right angle from Lone Mountain's gondola is the Ram Charger high-speed quad chairlift, which leads to the top of gentler Andesite Mountain. All wooded with skiing off a total of three lifts and on a total of three sides, Andesite has a follow-the-sun option is unusual on North American mountains. The Southern Comfort trails are gentle enough for new skiers. Those served by the Mad Wolf quad, new this season to replace a conventional-speed double chair-lift, are somewhat more challenging. When set up for racing, Big Horn is a noteworthy downhill trail. When recreational skiers do it, it is an exceptional intermediate cruiser.

The other runs off Mad Wolf are all steeper and usually bumpier too. The front side of Andesite, near the Ram Charger lift, also has excellent mid-level runs.

A ski vacation at Big Sky has special appeal for families, not just because the resort is so compact and congenial, but also because it offers free lift tickets for children. As many as two youngsters up to age 10 per paying adult ski free every day of the ski season, including Christmas and February/March holidays. There is also a separate children's terrain garden with kiddie bumps, cartoon figure obstacles and other variations to help youngsters learn and have fun.

In A Few Words: Big Sky skiing encompasses the real range from nursery-slope children to hotshot cliff-jumping, chute-shooting experts – and everyone between.

Après-Ski: The base village was totally redone and expanded for 1996-97, giving a harmonious "resort" feeling that Big Sky previously lacked. Chet's Bar in the Huntley Lodge, Scissorbill's Bar & Grill, M.R. Hummer's, The Caboose, a renovated Whiskey Jack and Buckskin Charlie's, all at or near the base of the lifts, provide après-ski refreshments, sometimes music and often dinner as well. Montana permits limited coin-operated gambling, and several machines are found in nightspots around the resort.

The dining rooms of two major properties are also good dinner choices. The Huntley Lodge Dining Room serves Continental cuisine, has a good wine list and a puts on a knockout Sunday brunch. Lone Mountain Ranch Dining Room is a spectacular restaurant with traditional and creative American cuisine. The ranch also runs a sleighride dinner to its North Fork Cabin. Elsewhere at the resort, choices include Twin Panda serving oriental dishes, the Edelweiss for Austrian and German cuisine, the First Place Restaurant for atmosphere and fine food, Scissorbill's for good food and a terrific wine and champagne list and Whiskey Jack for moderate prices and popular dishes.

Lone Mountain ranch, part-way down the mountain, is charming, hospitable and all-American in ambiance – and good, ample meals are served too. Some nights, the ranch also offers a hearty and fun dinner sleighride to a back cabin. At the bottom of the access road (and accessed by a complimentary shuttle to and from the resort), Buck's T-4 Dining Room serves Western specialties such as steak, game and seafood. The 320 Ranch serves dinners both in the rustic dining room and in conjunction with an evening sleighride.

No Big Sky holiday is complete without a trip 47 miles south into Yellowstone National Park. Although Old Faithful is at the other end of the park, less renowned thermal features are included in the snowmobile and snowcoach tours available from the village of West Yellowstone. Big Sky can book these tours. Lone Mountain Ranch offers excellent cross-country skiing on meticulously groomed runs, and there are also abundant Nordic opportunities in the backcountry.

Lodging: Big Sky's major lodging property is the combined Huntley Lodge/Shoshone Condominium complex. Joined to each other and to the largest conference center at a northern Rockies resort, they offer hotel room and apartment accommodations, an indoor/outdoor pool, fitness centre and dining, entertainment and shopping. Nearby condominiums include Arrowhead, BeaverHead, Hill Condominiums, Skycrest and Stillwater.

Part-way down the mountain is Lone Mountain Ranch, a dude ranch capable of offering a combined ski trip and authentic Western vacation. Accommodations are in quaint cabins, with common areas for dining, entertainment and socializing in separate buildings. Complete packages including three meals a day are offered, and the ranch also is the site of Big Sky's exceptional Nordic facility with 50 miles of groomed cross-country ski trails.

More condominiums and private homes, some available for short-term rental, are spread across what is referred to Meadow Village. This area is the summer golf course, so the vistas are as wide as the accommodations are spacious. River Rock Lodge is a fairly new European-style hotel seven miles from the lifts.Down in the Gallatin River Valley, Best Western Buck's T-4 Lodge, Rainbow Ranch Lodge and the 320 Ranch are atmospheric lodging options.

ASPEN

Height of Resort: 7,930 ft.
Height of Top Station: 11,212 ft. (Aspen Mountain), 11,800 ft. (Aspen Highlands), 9,840 ft. (Buttermilk)
Nearest Airport: Aspen
Nearest Major Airport: Denver
Route by Car: Follow Interstate 70 westward from Denver to Rte. 82 east to Aspen (Snowmass turnoff is reached before Aspen). Driving time is four to five hours from Denver, depending on weather.
Resort Facilities Chart: See Page 210

To American skiers, Aspen is like Mecca to Moslems – a place to visit, at least once. In many ways, this sparkling resort remains the standard by which all other resorts are ultimately judged. Now a sprawling town with four massive mountains, Aspen is Aspen Mountain, Aspen Highlands and Buttermilk, in or near Aspen, and also at Snowmass, 12 miles from town.

Aspen Mountain: Rising straight over downtown Aspen, this granddaddy of Colorado ski mountains looms nearly 3,330 feet above the town. It is one of America's classic mountains for good skiers – and for good *skiers* only, for it is the only ski area in Colorado, and one of the few in North America, where snowboarding is prohibited..

Aspen mountain is configured somewhat like a wedding cake scored by deep ridges. The six-passenger Silver Queen gondola takes just 13 minutes to reach the summit. Auxiliary feeder chairs (one on Little Nell, the other on Dipsey Doodle) lead to a second tier of two more chairlifts (on renowned Ruthie's Run and Bell Mountain Ridge) providing access to two more chairs that meet at the summit. The Ridge of Bell, right under the gondola, comprises much of Aspen Mountain's most challenging skiing. Steep powder-holding trails are cut down both faces of the ridge, spilling strong skiers into gulches that funnel them back to the bottom of the chair for another try.

From the gondola top station, skiers reach a sizable high-mountain cirque which garners most of Aspen Mountain's traffic. One high-speed quad and a short double chairlift access medium-steep and very steep runs that feed back into this bowl. There are groomed cruising runs, enticing mogul fields and plenty of off-piste glades in what must be considered the heart of the mountain. A fixed-grip quad to the west and an old double chair to the east serve lots of long runs, some of which are groomed on given days and some which are not. One of the mountain's famous show-off run is Ruthie's Run, where downhill races are held, and in Aspen terms, is rated an intermediate trail, and there's no question that strong intermediates can handle it. However, it tends to get mogulled which brings out the hotshots. Along the way are three slopeside restaurants, the Sundeck up on top, the popular Bonnie's at Midway and La Baita beside Ruthie's Run. From the top, the view of the Maroon Bell range is spectacular even by Colorado standards. Spar Gulch and Dago Cut Road, both of which feed into Kleenex Corner, are the most popular, most crowded routes down at the end of the day, and though they tend to ice up despite the area's best grooming efforts, few Aspen skiers would be seen riding the gondola back down.

Free mountain daily tours help skiers orient themselves on Aspen Mountain, and guided snowcat skiing of 1,200 acres of open slopes and bowls in the Little Annie area on Aspen Mountain's back side are a powder skier's dream come true.

Buttermilk: This two-mountain complex on the outskirts of town remains unique to Aspen, because it has just two expert trails. Basically, it is over 2,000 vertical feet of glorious skiing for novices and low intermediates, as well as one of America's premier teaching hills for skiing and snowboarding. In fact, it has become something of a snowboarding mecca within the overall Aspen meccas, because that is where Kevin and Brian Delaney established their Delaney Adult Snowboarding Camps, which offer the no-longer-young a quick, effective immersion into a young, youthful diversion. Still, even advanced skiers and snowboarders who are acclimated to Aspen's altitude often warm up with a day at Buttermilk and adjacent Tiehack, and it is a sneak-away favourite for locals after a storm, when the powder lingers in Tiehack's trees.

The bottom of the complex is known as Main Buttermilk. It features a baby T-bar, a tow and a high-speed quad to the summit, where a restaurant and ski school meeting place are situated. This lift opens long trails gentle enough for novice skiers. Parallel to the top of the quad is the Savio double chairlift which gives access to such popular medium difficult runs as Upper Savio, Ptarmigan and Sterner Buttermilk's.
Off on the complex's right flank is Buttermilk West, a novice and intermediate area served by the long Larkspur chair-lift and graced by a casual eating spot called Café West. The left flank is the Tiehack area, which contains the mountain's handful of expert slopes, Anneliese's Restaurant and a slalom practice hill. All three sectors are interconnected.

Aspen Highlands: The mountain is configured much like a contorted pyramid, and it offers an unusual mix of sizable terrain for novices and advanced skiers with less for intermediates. Two high-speed quads cut the base-to-summit ride from what was once nearly an hour to just 20 minutes. Loges Peak, known for its fabulous views and the cascade of super-steep double blacks down either side plus grandiose bowl skiing, are Highlands' crowning glory.

The rest of the mountain is an odd but interesting place. Runs of all standards interlace one another, and the lifts go off in odd directions too. The Exhibition quad goes to a plateau, site of the Merry-Go-Round Restaurant, a simply furnished self-service place known for outstanding food and a topnotch desserts. Above that is the Cloud 9 Chair, which services Highland's densest concentration of medium runs, though some bumps into a good approximation of expert turn. Finally the Loges Peak quad climbs to the scenic summit. There are supplementary lifts on either side of this uphill lift chain.

Beginners essentially are relegated to the nursery slope at the bottom of the mountain, where not much is happening, and to a few long roads which serpentine down the mountain. Novices with a little skiing experience enjoy the green runs under Exhibition II. Intermediates have a strange assortment of runs – at least one off each chair. Free mountain tours are given daily.

In a Few Words: Any one of Aspen's four mountains, with the exception of Buttermilk, would

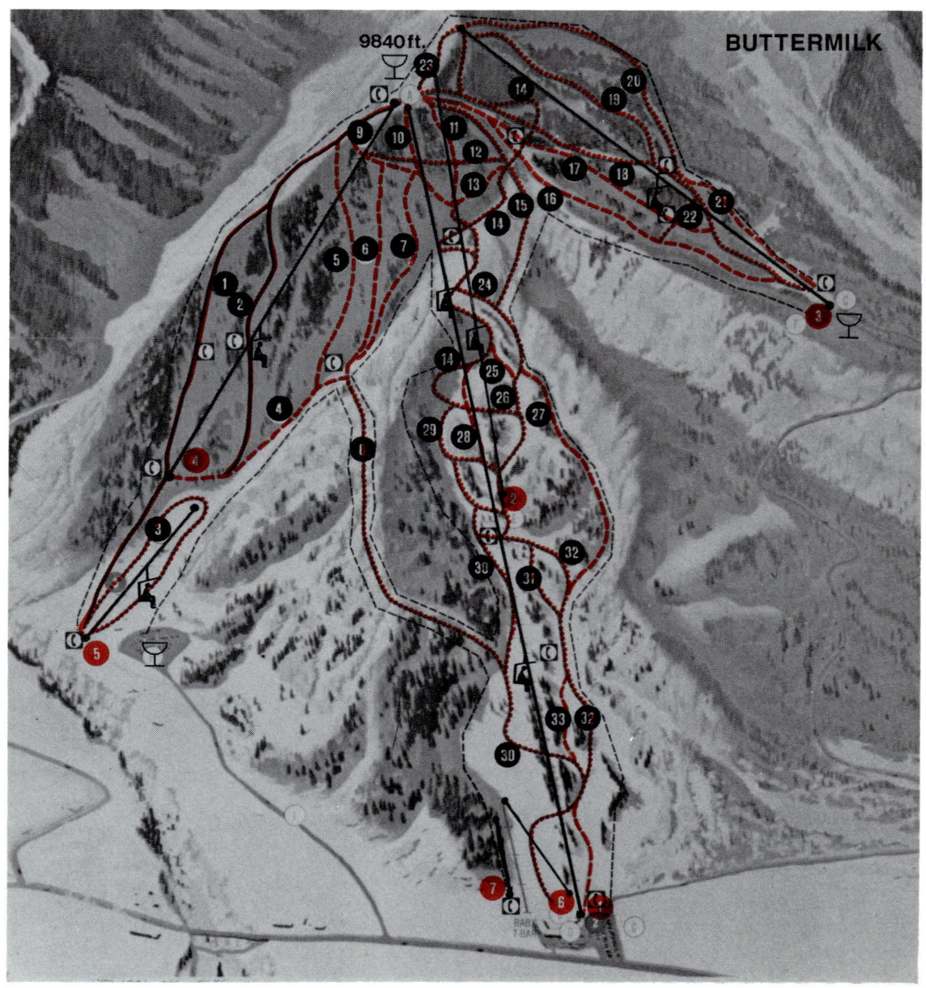

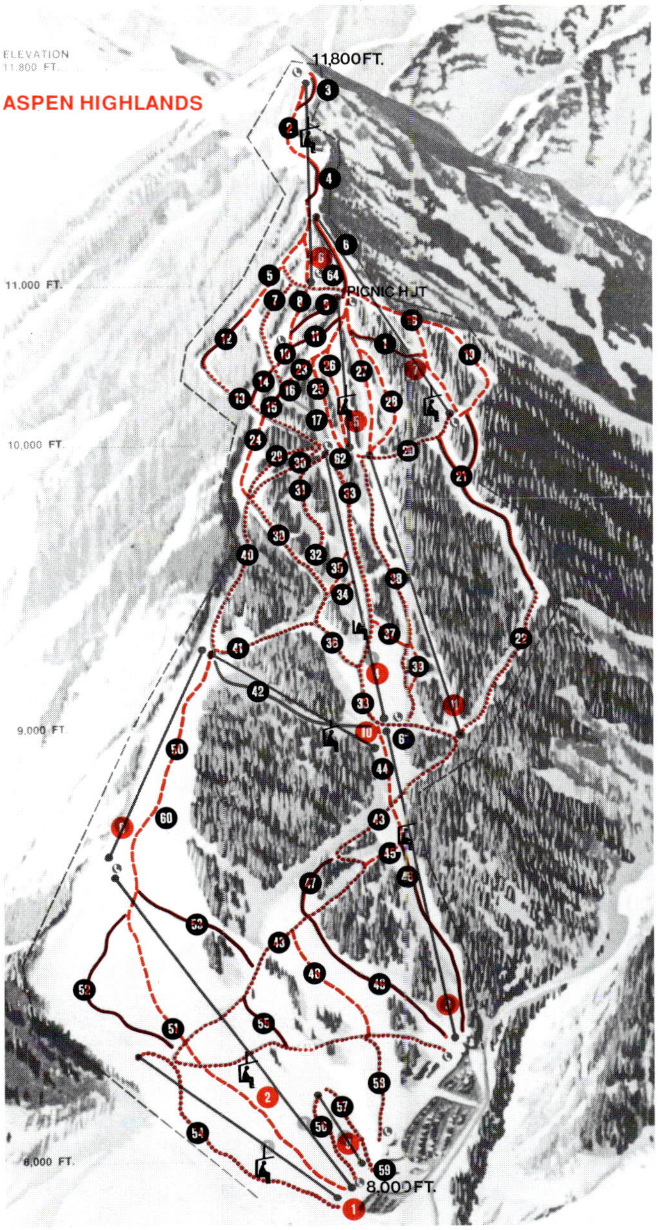

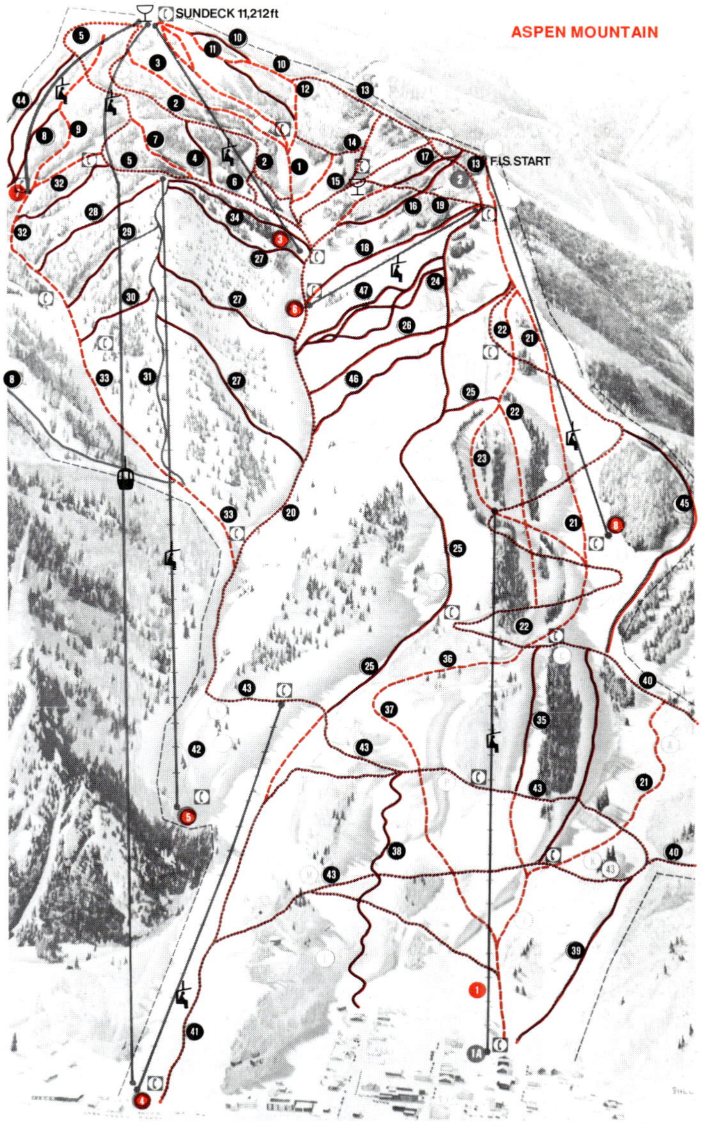

Runs: . . . . Easy - Medium ———————————— Difficult

Buttermilk Runs:

1 Javelin
2 Tiehack
3 Ego Hill
4 Sterner Gulch
5 Sterner
6 Ptarmigan
7 Buckskin
8 Sterner Catwalk
9 Clinic Hill
10 Upper Savio
11 Friedl's
13 Overpass
14 Homestead Road
15 Ridge Trail
16 Teaser
17 Camp Bird
33 Government
18 Homestead
19 Upper Larkspur
20 Red's Run
21 Lower Larkspur
22 Catwalk
23 Tom's Thumb
24 Lover's Lane
25 Upper By-Pass
26 Lower By-Pass
27 Jacob's Ladder
28 Lower Savio
29 Bear Trail
30 Columbine
31 Baby Doe
32 Spruce

Aspen Highlands Runs:

1 Jug's Hill; 2 Broadway; 3 Mousetrap; 4 Loges; 5 Hayden; 6 Olympic; 7 Meadows; 8 Kandahar; 9 Alps; 10 Meadows Cut-Off; 11 The Wall; 12 Boomerang; 13 Coachlight Catwalk; 14 Interstate 70; 15 Le Chamonix; 16 Easy Street Catwalk; 17 Andrew's; 18 Grand Prix; 19 Pyramid Park; 20 Phone 4 Catwalk; 21 Moment of Truth; 22 Phone 5 Catwalk; 23 Wine Ridge; 24 Drop-Off; 25 Heather-bedlam; 26 Floradora; 27 Gunbarrel; 28 Deane's; 29 Treva's; 30 Prospector; 31 Norway; 32 Lower Norway; 33 Exhibition; 34 Tower 25 Cut-Off; 35 Christy Canyon; 36 Nugget; 37 Prospector Gulch; 38 Red Onion; 39 Lower Red Onion; 40 T-Lazy-7; 41 Cakewalk; 42 Upper Stein; 43 Park Avenue; 44 Golden Barrel; 45 Arthur's; 46 Lower Stein; 47 Upper Jerome; 48 Jerome Park; 49 Jerome Bowl; 50 Golden Horn; 51 Thunderbowl; 52 Powderbowl; 53 Epicure; 54 Smuggler; 55 Limelight; 56 Mother's; 57 Apple Pie; 58 Half-Inch.

Aspen Mountain Runs:

1 Dipsy Doodle
2 Silver Bell
3 Pussy Foot
4 Blondies
5 One and Two Leaf
6 Deer Park
7 Silver Dip
8 Gentleman's Ridge
9 Copper Cut-Off
10 Buckhorn
11 Buckhorn Cut-Off
12 Midnight Cut-Off
13 Midway Road
14 North American
15 Tourtelotte Park
16 Red's Run
17 Little Percy
18 F.I.S. Trail
19 Nervous Traverse
20 Spar Gulch
21 Ruthie's Run
22 Roch Run
23 Kreuzeck
24 International
25 Silver Queen
26 Short Snort
27 Face of Bell
28 Back of Bell 1
29 Back of Bell 2
30 Back of Bell 3
31 Bell Mountain Ridge
32 Copper Trail
33 Copper Bowl
34 Sunset
35 Corkscrew
36 Magnificio Cut-Off
37 Magnificio
38 F.I.S. Slalom Hill
39 Norway Slope
40 Dago Cut Road
41 Little Nell
42 Bingo Slot
43 Catwalk
44 North Star
45 Aztec
46 Zaugg Dump
47 No Name Glade

Buttermilk Lift Numbers: Served by five chair-lifts, including one express chair, and two drag-lifts. 1 Main Buttermilk 4 seater, 2 Savio, 3 Buttermilk West, 4 Upper Tiehack,
5 Lower Tiehack, and drag-lifts, 6 Pendi Peak, 7 ski school lift.

Aspen Highlands Lift Numbers: Served by 9 chair-lifts and 2 drag-lifts, 1 Smuggler, 2 Thunder Bowl, 3 & 4 Exhibition (3 is a 4-seater), 5 Cloud 9, Loges Peak (4-seater), 7 Olympic, 8 Golden Horn (drag-lift). 9 SkiWee, 10 Nugget (drag-lift), 11 Grand Prix

Aspen Mountain Lift Numbers: Silver Queen (gondola) supplemented by 7 chair-lifts, 1A, 3 super chair-lift (4-seater), 4 Little Nell, 5 Bell Mountain, 6 chair-lift, 7 Gents Ridge, 8 Ruthie's

be a worthy vacation destination. To have them all accessible at once is riches beyond a skier's belief. The caveat must be that a single ski week offers time barely to test out each mountain, but not nearly enough to get to know them all.

Après Ski: In addition to exceptional skiing, Aspen is renowned for exceptional après skiing. In fact, it has become the glamorous après ski leader of the Rockies. Imagine an American-style cast and resemblances on this side of the Atlantic to a winter version of the habitués of the Riviera, and you get a notion of après ski at Aspen. There are the beautiful people and their predilection for swinging spots, who love (and often live in) America's most famous ski town. It is a place for celebrities and for regular American skiers who want to be where winter things are happening. The hot spots where celebrities and millionaires dine may change with whim and fashion, but overall, the eating in Aspen is exceptional by any reckoning. Incredibly, there are now more than 100 restaurants and bars in Aspen and at nearby Snowmass. To name and describe them all would be a chapter unto itself. Most small cities – and even large ones – don't offer the variety of restaurants found in this Rocky Mountain town.

Immediately after the lifts close, the Ajax Tavern at the base of Little Nell buzzes. Now part of a complex that includes the Little Nell Hotel , its big outdoor deck is always busy and positively thronged on sunny afternoons. The Hotel Jerome's bar, nicknamed the J-Bar, is popular through the evening, as are the lounges of the Little Nell and Ritz-Carlton hotels. The Tippler, The Red Onion and the Smuggler Land Office have been drawing evening crowds forever. Shooters Saloon is a country-and-Western spot, while the Flying Dog Brew Pub is the first micro-brewery to open in Aspen in the 20th century. Aspen's Crystal Palace is an opulent dinner cabaret which combines wicked wit and good food.

Aspen by now is no small town. It has international-calibre shops offering everything from fresh pastries to fresh flowers. The shopping is good and includes an array of stores specialising in one-of-a-kind and custom made clothing, artwork and crafts. There are such diverse amusements as duplicate bridge, concerts, flying and gliding lessons, hot air ballooning, cinemas, name entertainment in the historic Wheeler Opera House, a museum, health clubs, tennis and even Mass at a nearby monastery. . The Winterskol Carnival takes place each January. The local youth centre, which videos, pool, darts and a low-cost snackbar, invites visiting teens to join locals.

Aspen is known as a culinary center, with top American chefs installed at the Little Nell Restaurant, the Ritz-Carlton Dining Room, Pinons, Ajax Tavern and others. The hotel restaurants are elegant, pricey and excellent. Renaissance has a French-accented contemporary menu, with a fancy restaurant downstairs and a more casual bistro upstairs. The Ajax Tavern at the base of the gondola serves breakfast, but the Mediterranean-style lunches and dinners created by its award-winning chef are among Aspen's best. Poons shines with contemporary creativity. Other restaurants are well-regarded too. Carnivale and Mezzaluna are contemporary Italian. while Cache Cache is nouvelle franÂais. Syzygy is casual and contemporary – and costly.

There are less prepossessing (and less expensive) eating places too. Motherlode is home-style Italian. Nick-N-Willie's prepares "designer pizza" to be cooked at home. La Cocina and La Cantina serve Mexican. The Hard Rock Cafe has burgers, a retro-rock atmosphere and similar youthful appeal. Planet Hollywood is a new hotspot whose investors are big-time show business names. The Pine Creek Cookhouse at Ashcroft, which incidentally is one of America's premier ski touring centres, serves Hungarian and other continental specialties in a rustic setting. Boogie's Diner has a funky '50s atmosphere, filling portions and less-than-astronomical prices.

Eating is one of Aspenites' favourite pastimes, but that doesn't mean drinking and dancing aren't popular too. Numerous nightspots, good bars attached to good restaurants and the requisite census of dance emporiums are features of Aspen's abundant night life. Aspen swings loud and long.

Lodging: As Aspen's four mountains have room for thousands of skiers, the scores of hotels, motels, lodges, apartment buildings, condominiums, dorms and chalets at Aspen and environs have pillows for thousands of weary heads.

The expensive and elegant Little Nell Hotel at the base of Aspen Mountain is designed for high-powered executives who happen to be skiers – or skiers who happen to be high-powered executives, who treasure a refined ambiance, excellent services and convenient location. For those who cannot leave work behind, there are business services beyond those offered at most resort hotels. You can stay in an elegant landmark, the century-old Hotel Jerome. There is no better way to step into an incredibly luxurious version of the Old West than to pass through the Jerome's portals. The luxurious rooms, both in the old hotel and in a new wing, are spacious and charming. Most recently, the deluxe Ritz Carlton Aspen debuted with attractive accommodations, fine amenities, excellent cuisine and outstanding

Snowmass Lift Numbers: 1 Fanny Hill, 2 Burlingame, 3 Sam's Knob, 4 Big Burn, 5 Campground, 6 Assay Hill, 7 Funnel, 8 Alpine Springs, 9 Sheer Bliss, 10 Elk Camp, 11 Wood Run, 12 High Alpine, 13 Coney Glade, 15 Naked Lady.
Lift numbers 1, 4, 8, 10, 12 and 13 are high speed 4 seater chair-lifts.

Runs: . . . . Easy - - - - - - - - - - - - - - - - - - Medium ———————— Difficult

Please note: Extensive runs for experts only and reached from the top stations of High Alpine, 11,775 ft., and Big Burn, 11,835 ft., are not shown on this map.

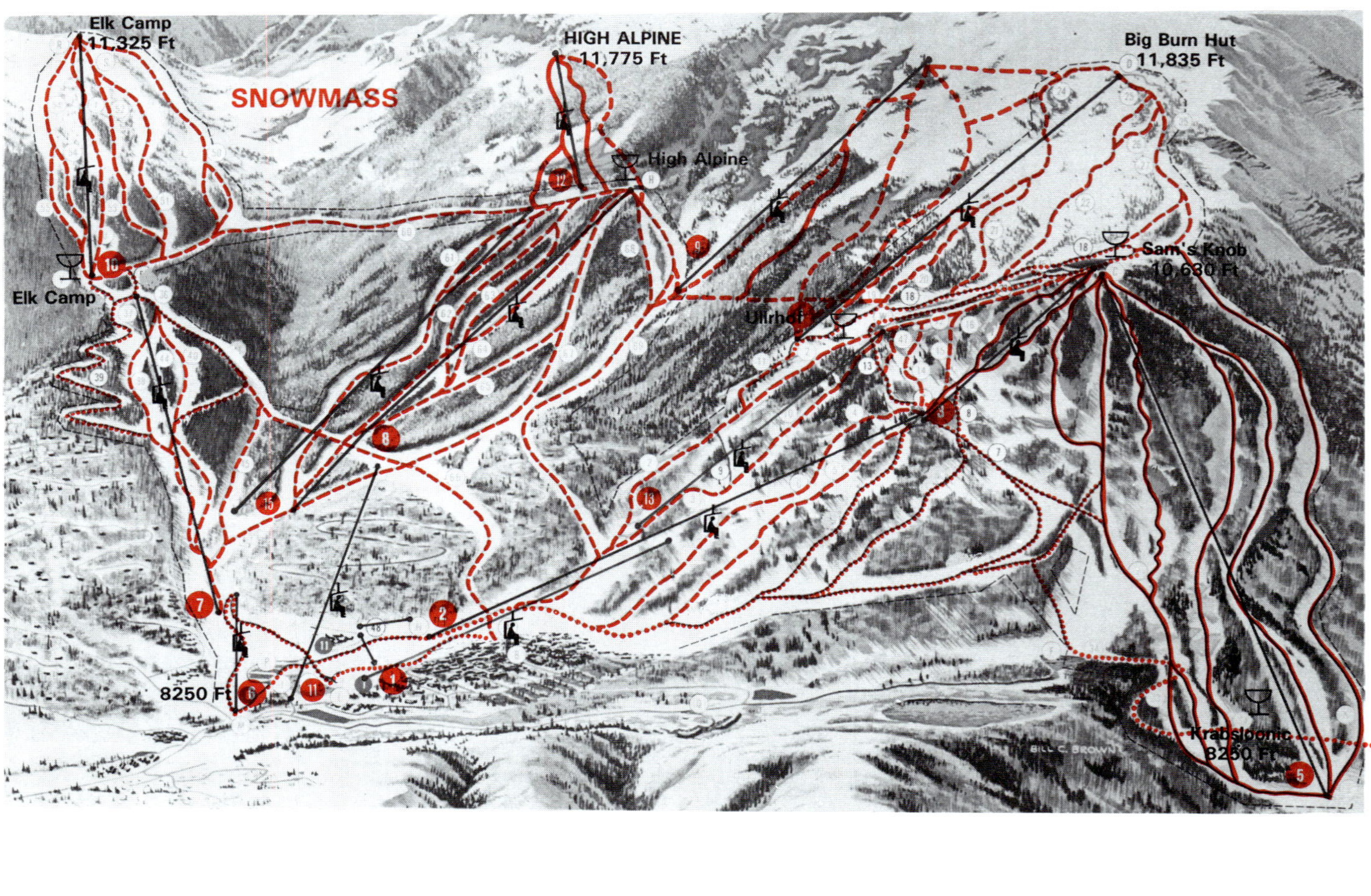

service. It is a short walk (or free ride) from the slopes and rivals The Little Nell in terms of personal and business services. Aspen Meadows, home of the prestigious Aspen Institute for Humanistic Studies, is now winterized. It is a tranquil campus-like complex.

Other noteworthy lodgings all over town, include the recently renovated Aspen Club Lodge, which offers guest privileges at the Aspen Club Health and Fitness Centre. The Aspen Country Inn has also been renovated, with new bathrooms and fireplaces in many rooms. It is at the base of Buttermilk and has free shuttle service to Aspen's down-town and all ski areas. The Heatherbed, a more casual lodge, has also been recently redone. The Hotel Lenado and Independence Square Hotels are both distinctively decorated and offer roof-top tubs with sensational views. The Sardy House is a splendid Victorian inn. Among the condominium selections, the standouts include The Gant, which has two swimming pools and three hot tubs, and The Brand, which consists of just six pricey and exquisite units. There are also moderately priced condominiums, some – like the Alpenblick, Chateau Aspen, Dolomite Villa and Fifth Avenue Condominiums – within walking distance of the lifts. On the lower end of the scale, amenities may vary from unit to unit and do not tend to have the luxury or flair one associates with a resort such as Aspen.

Except for the dearth of infant care, child care options abound, ranging from nurseries for wee ones to excellent children's ski instruction. The Max the Moose bus transports children from the lodgings to ski school and back, which is an excellent amenity for families where parents want to ski a different mountain from where their children are. In addition to the lodges that have their own courtesy vans, Roaring Fork Transportation Authority buses make low-cost runs all over the Aspen-Snowmass area and as far up Route 82 as Glenwood Springs from early morning until past midnight. Free ski buses run continually during the morning and afternoon peak hours between the two resorts and all four mountains.

SNOWMASS

Height of Bottom Station: 8,104 ft.
Height of Top Station: 12,310 ft.
Nearest Airport: Aspen
Nearest Major Airport: Denver
Route by Car: Follow Interstate 70 west to Rte. 82 east to the Snowmass turnoff. Driving time is four to five hours from Denver, depending on weather.
Resort Facilities Charts: See page 211

Snowmass, a scant 12 miles from Aspen, is a contemporary resort town which offers comfort and respite from Aspen's frenetic pace,FS as well as doorstep skiing on the largest, most complex of the Aspen areas four mountains, which are all skiable on one lift pass.

Snowmass: When this vast mountain complex was first developed in the late 1960's, the Aspen Skiing Corporation was concerned that its contemporary slopeside lodging, vast then underutilised terrain and empty lifts would not have enough appeal on their own. So to emphasise the tie with the main town and let a little glamour rub off, Snowmass was intentionally called Snowmass-at-Aspen. Today, Snowmass needs no such identification, for it stands on its own, and skiers quartered in Aspen often make the reverse commute to Snowmass's wide trails, farflung area stretching across three peaks and spectacular intermediate and advanced ski terrain. Snowmass stands on its own as the most popular of the region's four mountains, now featuring seven high-speed quad chairlifts.

Snowmass was the first purpose-built resort and ski development with ski-in, ski-out lodging and an emphasis on long medium-standard runs. The terrain is a spread across a broad massif which is so sprawling that moving between the two most distant points in the trail system would take the better part of a morning or afternoon – even with five high-speed chair-lifts along the way.

The traditional port of entry for most skiers is via the Snowmass Mall, a slope-side pedestrian village core, where novice skiers have a choice of over half-a-dozen gentle novice runs. The best -known is the nursery slop known as Fanny Hill, served by a high-speed quad chair-lift, while Funnel, at over a mile, is the longest. Now, Two Creeks has become the second gatway to the trail system After years of frequently revised plans, Two Creeks has developed as Snowmass' second base. With a mass transit centre providing the quickest access into Snowmass' trail system and the second lift bottom station, skiers commuting from Aspen via a new express shuttle experience far fewer traffic delays and even shorter lift queues than in the past. It features a spacious new day, a high-speed four-place chair-lift, a handful of mostly intermediate trails. The Two Creeks lift feeds into the Elk Camp chairlift was converted to a high-speed four-seater, with the result that skiers can reach the summit from the newest base in under 20 minutes.

From the lifts leading up from the original Snowmass Mall/Fanny Hill approach, the trail system widens out toward Sam's Knob to the right. Crowned by a namesake restaurant with splendid views and offering another eating option at Ullrhof below, Sam's Knob provides its share of wide cruising runs on one side and steeper ones off another. Those steeps are the gateway to Campground whose four black runs are rarely groomed, though a mid-level one often is. The bottom station of the Campground chair is at the lowest elevation of Snowmass's system.

To the left of the main trails, skiers have dozens of blue, blue/black and solid black choices. Near the centre of the trail system are Alpine Springs and Naked Lady, parallel chairs interlaced with lush runs between heavy stands of trees. Farther up is the High Alpine chair, with fine mogul runs down the headwall and super-steep glades and bowls in Hanging Valley and the Cirque, which this year gets a drag lift, extending the area's vertical and making its most challenging terrain more accessible – at least from February to April, when it is expected to operate. During these months, when the summit winds typically die down and the snowpack builds up, Snowmass will boast the country's highest vertical – 4,405 feet – measured from the top of the Cirque to the bottom of Two Creeks.

Gwyn's High Alpine Restaurant, near the bottom station of the chairlift of the same name, is one of the best on the mountain. Off on one side are the awesome Hanging Valley Glades, among the foremost high-expert terrain at Snowmass. Elk Camp occupies the far left point of the fan. Café Suzanne is located at the base of the Elk Camp chair and a further half-dozen splendid intermediate runs which inspire confidence and invite speed.

In the fashion of saving the best for last, special attention must go to Big Burn, perhaps the finest single cruising slope in the land. Half a dozen of Snowmass's finest, widest runs are spectacularly meshed into the Big Burn. Served by a high-speed quad chair on terrain that was cleared by an ancient forest fire, the Big Burn is essentially one vast intermediate slope half a mile wide that is the quintessential something-for-everyone run. Novices can traverse it safely, width giving them ample opportunity to turn. Intermediates can savour fabulous ego skiing that encourages a right-feeling rhythm and gives their skiing a lift they've never enjoyed. Even Aspen's fussy experts flock to the Big Burn after a good snowfall, for its powder is rated tops. They enjoy slaloming around the old stumps and new growth poking through the snow, though admittedly some of the "new growth" is maturing into tall trees.

Snowmass is a complex and wonderful place, and the Snowmass' genial ski ambassadors offer a free $1^1/_2$-hour guided tour each Sunday morning to help newcomers get acquainted with it all. The total figures come out to 17 chairlifts (seven of them high-speed quads) with a capacity of nearly 24,000 skiers an hour. There are 2,575 acres of ski terrain on a 3,615-foot vertical and a noteworthy racing programme for serious amateur and pure recreational racers alike. Most recently, Snowmass added North America's first recreational speed-skiing course, which enables skiers to don a helmet, take some training and go flat out, straight downhill, as much as skill and courage permit.

Snowmass is also an exemplary family skiing mountain, with top children's programmes, Snow Cubs is the nursery for the littlest vacationers (with skiing from age three but outdoor play for younger tots as well) and Big Burn Bears for skiers from age three and up. There is even a separate programme for fast-moving teenagers, one of the few for those who are no longer children but not yet adults. (There are evening programmes as well, enabling parents to enjoy adult dinners and entertainment while the youngsters have a good time in supervised programmes too.)

Après Ski: In contast to Aspen, Snowmass is subdued. Sno'Beach, where the Snowmass Village pedestrian mall meets the slopes, is the top sport after skiing.The Tower has been drawing after-skiers forever, thanks to the wonderful bartenders who also perform magic tricks. The.Brothers Grille in the Silvertree Hotel is popular for casual dining. Cowboys starts cranking at lunch, shifts into overdrive after skiing and keeps going through the dinner hours with food, drink and Western-style ambiance. The Stew Pot is perfect for moderately priced dinners. La Bohème and La Brasserie are pleasant adjacent French dining spots. Arguably the best restaurant at Snowmass is Sage, in the Snowmass Club & Lodge. Burlingame Cabin Dinner Sleighrides also offer Western decor, Western-style cooking and an entertaining evening. You get to the cabin by snowcat-pulled sleigh. The dogs do the work at Krabloonik, Snowmass' sled dog kennels which offers dogsled rides and also has a fine restaurant. Many Snowmass guests flee to Aspen for evening entertainment, at least some evenings. RFTA buses, which run free ski shuttles, charge a modest fee for the Snowmass-Aspen evening runs.

Lodging: The best bet for guests who like a short stroll to the lifts and a ski-back at the end of the day are at Snowmass. Snowmass Village lodging includes two fine hotels (the Silvertree and the Stonebridge Inn, both the both renovated and expanded not long ago) and a slew of spacious condominium developments, most right at slopeside. An exception to slopeside is the Snowmass Club, a luxury hotel and condominium development with its own and health spa and indoor tennis centre. Located near the golf course, it is a short (free) shuttle-bus ride from the lifts.

STOWE

Height of Resort: 1,559 ft.
Bottom of Lowest Lift: 2,343 ft.
Height of Top Station: 4,393 ft.
Nearest Airport: Burlington
Nearest Major Airport: Boston
Route by Car: From Burlington, take Interstate 89 south to Waterbury and follow Route 100 north into Stowe. From, Boston, take Interstate 93 north to Interstate 89 north. Exit at Waterbury and follow Route 100 north eight miles to Stowe centre at the intersection with Route 108. Driving time is 45 minutes from Burlington, four hours from Boston.
Resort Facilities Charts: See page 212

Stowe is the village, Mt. Mansfield is the major peak, and Stowe Mountain Resort is the ski complex's official name, but everyone calls them Stowe. Together, they have long earned the nickname of 'Ski capital of the East.'

Mt. Mansfield: One of the oldest, biggest and most respected ski mountains in the United States, skiing began on Mt. Mansfield in the '30s and really got going with the erection of a single chairlift in 1940. It was the first chairlift in the eastern U.S. and was for years the highest and longest in the country. Stowe – indeed the entire ski sport – has never been the same. In recent years, upgrading and retrofitting has been a priority at this classical mountain. New lifts, enhanced traffic flow, trail reconfiguration, a careful attention to snow grooming and, most important, snowmaking on nearly three quarters of the area make venerable Stowe an up-to-date ski destination.

'The Mountain', as regulars regularly call it, has half-a-dozen of the steepest, most challenging ski runs in the world. Goat, Starr, National, International, Liftline and portions of Nosedive begin with narrow pitches of 35 degrees or better and take their just place beside the toughest that St. Anton, St. Moritz, Val d'Isère and Jackson Hole have to offer. They are each one to two miles of twisting, mogully vertical walls that spawned the truism, 'If you can ski Stowe you can ski anywhere.'

There is still ample challenge for purists, but there is also tender loving care administered to much of the mountain by snowmaking and grooming crews. The thrills and chills and spills of Mt. Mansfield are still there, accessible via a high-speed quad chairlift. The Octagon, a cafeteria at the top, provides warmth, refreshment and unparalleled views, for Mt. Mansfield's summit is the highest point in the State of Vermont. It is one of the few states in America where you can actually ski on the highest mountain.

Mt. Mansfield's mellowing includes ample terrain for intermediate and even fairly new skiers, all accessible by a double chairlift. Lord, Lower Nosedive, North Slope, Lower Hayride, Skimeister, Standard and Upper Tyro are skiable by sturdy intermediates, although at many mountains some of these would be ranked as the most difficult trails. Toll Road, Lullaby Lane and Lower Tyro are genuinely navigable by novices who want to share the thrill of skiing The Mountain. Other recent lift improvements at Mt. Mansfield included the installation of a double chair on the Toll House, Stowe's legendary nursery ski slope which is as good a place as ever for new skiers to practise their first turns.

Gondola Area: Interconnected with Mt. Mansfield's slopes are those served by a high-speed, eight-passenger gondola, said to be the world's fastest, reaching the top in just six minutes. More sheltered than Mt. Mansfield yet sufficiently interesting even for advanced skiers, this complex consists of medium-difficult Gondolier, Perry Merrill and Switchback which weave in and out of one another and tougher Chin Clip off by itself. The gondola area drops below the 'chin' created by the profile of the Mt. Mansfield ridge, which explains how both Chin Clip and Nosedive got their names. The gondola area's trails were recontoured and equipped with enhanced snowmaking. The gondola base has its own parking lot and day lodge, and there is also a dramatic restaurant called The Midway Lodge, which is known for excellent seafood and sandwiches. There is night skiing here and a drag lift too. To ski to the gondola from Mt. Mansfield, take Rimrock from the Octagon and bear left. For the return trip, follow Cliff Trail from the gondola unloading station and bear right.

Spruce Peak: Spruce Peak is known for wide open skiing. It is a four-lift network designed for novice and intermediate skiers and is the only trail system not interconnected with the others, although all are skiable on one ticket and the construction of a transfer-lift has been approved. The three Little Spruce double chairlifts and drag-lift rise from beside the Spruce base lodge, while the Big Spruce chair starts higher up on the mountain. Novices dismount at the mid-station, for the wide, winning delights of West Slope, East Slope and Rick's Run. Excellent intermediate skiing off the top terminal of the Little Spruce chair includes Upper West Run, Lower Smugglers' and Ridge Run. The latter leads into Main Street and from there to the base of the Big Spruce lift. This slow old double chair serves some of the kindest, least crowded intermediate terrain around. Sterling, Main Street, Whirlaway and Upper Smugglers offer fine skiing.

Spruce Peak is also the headquarters for Stowe's highly respected Children's Adventure Center, which includes day care for infants as young as two months, as well as ski and snowboarding instruction. For smaller children, the 1,200-square-foot outdoor snowplay area is one of the best in the East. Parents of children in day care can carry beepers so that the can be contacted anywhere at the resort in case of need.

When natural snowfall permits, it is a delightful day excursion to ski from the Look Out atop Big Spruce over the mountain to a small resort called Smugglers' Notch. This connection has now been formalized with marked trails and a multi-day ticket called Stowe Vacation Card, which Smugglers for a day's skiing (as well as a number of other discounts and free offers).

Nordic Skiing: At Stowe, cross-country skiing receives equal billing with downhill, and the resort is ideal for families and groups that include both kinds of skiers. Two hundred miles of interconnected loipes link four dedicated cross-country centres: Stowe Mountain Resort X-C, Trapp Family Lodge, Edson Hill Manor and Topnotch, and even the Stowe Recreation Path built for summer bicycling, jogging and walking. This system is the greatest in New England and one of the most extensive in all of North America.

In a Few Words: Mt. Mansfield's most rigorous slopes have given Stowe its reputation throughout the ski world but there are other fine possibilities for beginning and intermediate skiers, as well as cross-country enthusiasts. The resort is so confident of visitors' satisfaction that it offers a guarantee on skiing, ski school, Stowe Mountain Resort lodging and dining.

Après Ski: Après_ski action starts right at the mountain, both at the bar in the Mansfield Base Lodge and the Midway Bar in the Midway Lodge. The Broken Ski Tavern at the Inn at the Mountain is cozy. The Matterhorn near the mountain has live entertainment and a hearty après_ski scene. British skiers with a touch of homesickness will want to check out Ye Olde England Inne. The Biloboong is an Aussie-accented pub.

Stowe has some of the country's best ski-resort restaurants. Many pride themselves on their outstanding kitchens, unique menus and fine wine cellars. Topnotch, Stowehof, Œle de France, Hob Knob, L.P.s, Ten Acres, the Cliff House at the top of the gondola and the Inn on the Mountain serve Continental-style dishes at various price levels and with varying degrees of formality. The Trapp Family Lodge is elegant Austrian, while the Salzburg Inn is less formal Austrian and lower in price. Charlie B's Pub at the Stoweflake, Blue Moon Cafe, Green Mountain Inn and Partridge Inn specialise in New England dishes. Foxfire has an Italianate menu, while the Trattoria la Festa is very Italiano. The Shed has a microbrewery and serves light meals. Also, Town & Country's Carriage Room, Depot Street Malt Shoppe, McCarthy's, and Whiskers offer light meals at moderate prices. Ye Olde New England Inne and Charlie B's have live music. The Cactus Cafe and Miguel's Stowe Away reflect New England's new infatuation with Mexican food.

It's roughly seven miles between Stowe centre and the Mt. Mansfield lifts, and the restaurants and after-ski watering hotels range along the distance. A free trolley-style shuttle operates during the day and until 10.30 p.m. Downtown Stowe is a typically charming small New England village with a picturesque white frame church at it heart. There are a number of nice little shops, and the shopping – like the dining and après skiing – spreads up the Mountain Road for miles. There are several small shopping centres, one of which has a cinema. Stowe also has a skating rink, indoor tennis, ice fishing and sledding. The biggest event on Stowe's winter calendar is the annual winter carnival, which runs for 10 days each January. It's a week full of such merriment as races (including a dog-sled race), snow-sculpture contest, dances (among them, U.S. country-style square dance and a fancy ball) and entertainment.

Lodging: In terms of location, Stowe has everything from slopeside lodgings close to the lifts to accommodations in the heart of the village. In terms of style, the range runs from small family-run inns that service simple meals family-style (take your portion from the serving dishes and pass the rest) to elegant four-star accommodations with caring service and first-rate dining rooms.

The Inn at the Mountain at the Toll House base, the Stoweflake, Topnotch at Stowe and the Trapp Family Lodge are four of the best. Topnotch is a complete and first-rate resort hotel with lovely rooms, a full fitness centre, whirlpool, sauna, massage, quiet bar and fine dining. The Golden Eagle is a top family hotel.

Stowe boasts many charming country inns, which offer a traditional New England ambiance and a memorable holiday experience. In the centre of the village are the Green Mountain Inn and The Inn at the Brass Lantern. The Stowe Inn at Little River is an exquisite, recently renovated inn. The Grey Fox has recently been totally renovated and expanded, and Ye Olde England Inn has townhouse lodging. The Mountain Road Resort has been steadily upgraded to a high standard.

There are numerous motels, most with access directly to the outdoors from each room. Some have bedrooms with bathrooms only, others have suites that include living rooms and kitchenettes. Other motel-type lodging includes the Peacock Motel. Town & Country, Buccaneer, Hob Knob, Snowdrift, Sunset Motor-Inn, Stowe Motel, Golden Kitz, Sun & Ski, Mountaineer, and Innsbruck Motor Inn. Meal plans generally are no meals or breakfast only, although some have breakfast/dinner packages.

There are relatively few classic New England ski lodges left, but a number of those still in existence are in and around Stowe. This is the way American skiers used to live 30 or so years back. Many are converted farmhouses. Shared baths and small, functional rooms are common. When included in the rate, dining is family-style, and after-ski entertainment means going out or making your own entertainment around the fireplace of a big, cosy living room. The details differ, but the basic format remains in such places as Nichols, Logwood, Walkabout Creek Lodge, Ski Inn, Fiddler's Green, Anderse's and Siebeness, Stowe Bound is an informal lodge whose organically grown food comes largely from its own gardens. The Round Hearth is a large inexpensive dorm catering mainly to groups. There is also a bargain basement ski dorm. Some motels and inns have private cottages for rent on the premises. Condominium apartments are available through the Mt. Mansfield Town Houses and other complexes.

VAIL

Height of Resort: 8,200 ft.
Height of Top Station: 11,250 ft.
Nearest Airport: Eagle County (40 miles)
Nearest Major Airport: Denver (110 miles)
Route by Car: Drive west from Denver on Interstate Highway 70 along which Vail is located. From Eagle, take I-70 east to Vail.
Driving time about two hours from Denver.
Resort Facilities Charts: See page 212

Vail is one of America's biggest and overall best ski resorts for all grades of skiers. It combines quality and quantity as well as accessibility in a matchless manner. Vail Resorts, which developed and operates Vail and Beaver Creek, has purchased Keystone Resort and the Breckenridge ski area. This winter, a fully interchangeable lift pass will be introduced for these four enormous, varied ski areas.

Vail Mountain: In less than 40 years, this mountain has become America's number one ski area by most measures. Its 27 lifts, including ten high-speed quad chairs can ferry 43,470 skiers an hour to 3,687 acres of skiable terrain within a permit area of more than

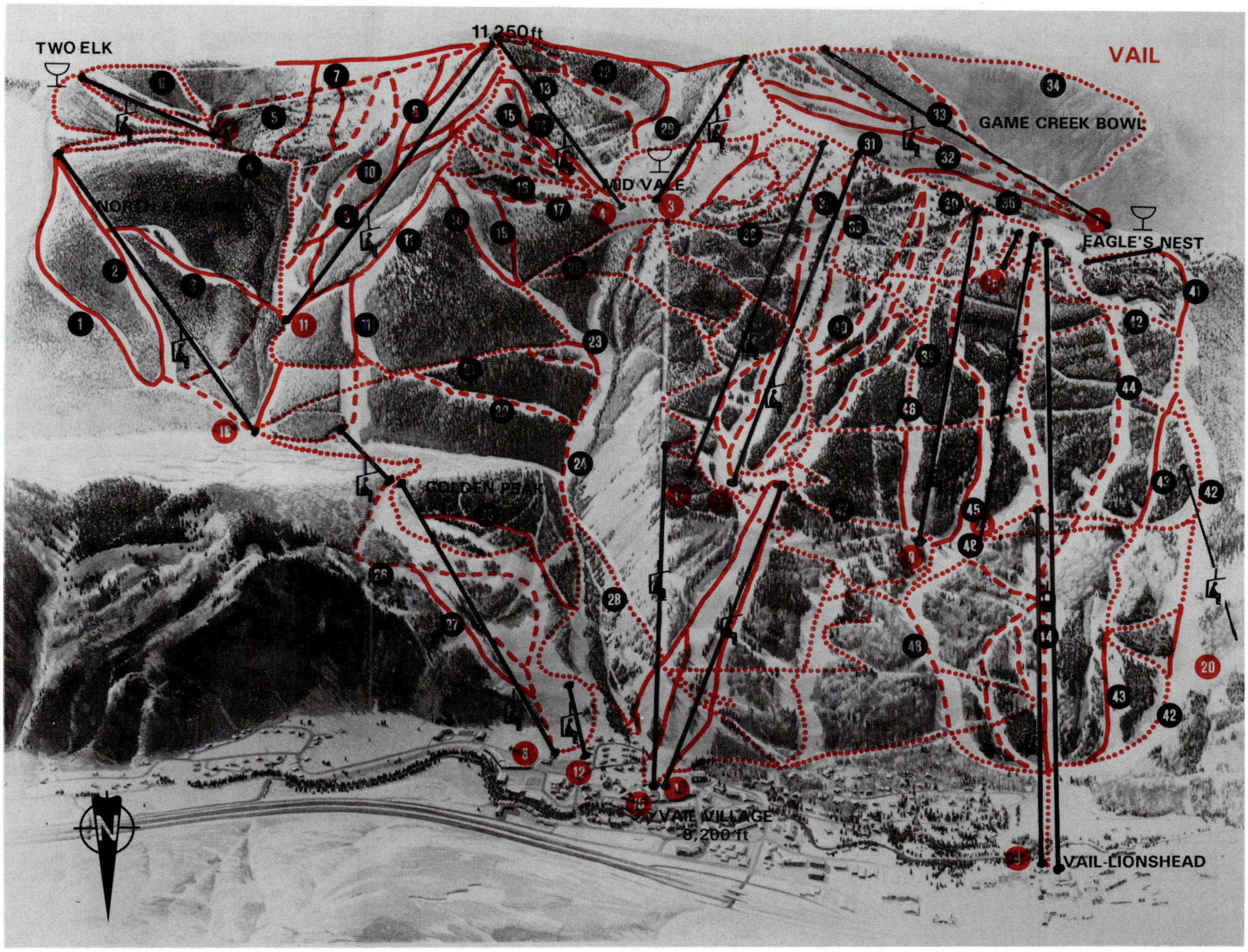

Vail Lifts: The area is served by 25 lifts, 20 on the front (north) side and 5 in the Back Bowls. Lift numbers 2, 3, 4, 7, 8, 11, 16, 26 and number 21 in Back Bowls are high speed 4 seater chair-lifts; Cascade Village is a conventional speed quad.

Lift Numbers North Side: 1 Giant Steps, 2 Avanti Express, 3 Hunky Dory, 4 Mountain Top Express, 6 Golden Peak, 7 Game Creek Express. 8 Born Free Express, 9 Minnie's, 10 Highline, 11 Northwoods Express, 12 Gopher Hill, 14 Sourdough, 15 Little Eagle, 16 Vista Bahn Express. 18 Eagles Nest (drag-lift), 19 Lionshead Gondolaway, 20 Cascade Village; 26 Pride Express.

Back Bowls: 5 High Noon, 21 Orient Express, 22 Mongolia (drag-lift), 23 Sun Up, 24 West Wall (drag-lift), 25 Wapiti (tow). These lifts are not shown on the above map.

Vail North Side: Main Runs: 1 Blue Ox; 2 Highline; 3 Roger's Run; 4 Flap Jack; 5 Timber Line Catwalk; Whisky Jack; 7 Headwall Ridge; 8 First Step; 9 Gandy Dancer; 10 North Star; 11 Prima; 12 Minturn Mile; 13 Ramshorn; 14 Zot; 15 Whistle Pig; 16 Swingsville; 17 Christmas; 18 Riva Ridge; 19 Riva Glade; 20 Gitalong Road; 21 Skid Road; 22 North Face Catwalk; 23 Tourist Trap; 24 Mill Creek; 25 Aspen Alley; 26 Boo Boo; 27 After Thought; 28 Mill Creek Road; 29 The Skipper; 30 Eagles Nest Ridge; 31 Faro; 32 Showboat; 33 The Woods; 34 Lost Boy; 35 Ouzo; 36 Mid Vail Express; 37 Avanti; 38 Pickeroon; 39 Surrender; 40 The Berries; 41 Racers Sima; 42 Simba; 43 Safari; 44 Bwana; 45 Minnie's Mile; 46 Ledges; 47 Lion's Way; 48 Born Free.

Runs: • Easy - Medium ———————————— Difficult

12,500 acres. The 3,250-foot vertical is one of America's leaders. The east-to-west stretch, from the far corner of the China Bowl area to the lift and trail developed exclusively to service the satellite called Cascade Village, is over seven miles. More than a million and a half skier visits a year are tallied here – a combination of vacationers from all over the world and day-trip skiers from Denver, a two-hour drive to the east.

The heavily wooded front side of the mountain has over 100 American-style trails carved through the forest, with nearly an equal division between novice, intermediates and advanced terrain, while the back side features Alpine-style pistes groomed on a series side-by-side bowls. There are four lift entrances to Vail Mountain. Golden Peak, the traditional teaching hill, leads to the eastern area of the vast mountain, which has been totally redone in the last two years, with a new base lodge, kindergarten, rental shop and high-speed quad chairlift. The new chair makes Golden Peak the easiest port of entry to the high-expert mogul runs of Northeast Bowl, the mountain-top novice terrain off Chair 14 or the sensational spread known as China Bowl.

Even with the upgrades on Golden Peak, the main entry into Vail's vast terrain is via the VistaBahn Express from the core of Vail Village. The VistaBahn is a high-speed lift also covered with a Plexiglas shield to protect riders from the wind and snow. It unloads at Mid-Vail, a high plateau at the base of a cirque which is practically an area within an area. Mid-Vail is a main meeting spot and popular lunch stop with both indoor dining and a huge south-facing deck. There are few steep sections at Mid-Vail, but essentially, this is intermediate paradise, comprised of wide sun-kissed trails with two chair-lifts. Two of these are super-speed quads. The Mountaintop Express is the gateway to the upper intermediate and expert sector called Northwoods, while the Hunky Dory quad accesssing original Back Bowls is now a high-speed lift.

Lionshead, with a year-old 12-passenger gondola and yet two more high-speed quads as an alternate, is the favourite playground of skiers who love long runs which alternate steepish pitches and terraces – but never flats that require poling. The entire upper mountain, between Lionshead and the top of Chair 3 to Mid-Vail, brackets a large network of mostly easy to medium-standard trails. There are a few steep headwalls to challenge incipient experts, but all are easily avoided by less skilled skiers. The ridge top between Chair 3 and Lionshead is also the entry into Game Creek Bowl, a steepish west-facing cirque served by another high-speed chair-lift. The westernmost chairlift from the base and thus the fourth entry point is a shortcut into the Lionshead sector for guests of the Cascade Hotel and Club, a luxurious hotel which keynotes a satellite development called Cascade Village.

All of Vail's sprawling front side – from the tame three-mile Run called Gitalong Road to the vertiginous bumped-up steeps of Highline, Blue Ox and Prima – pale in comparison with the Back Bowls scooped out of the mountain's sunny south side.

The Bowls – all seven of them – define the Vail uniqueness. They look European with packed pistes bracketed by ungroomed cover, but the snow is uniquely American Western powder. The original bowls, Sun Up and Sun Down, are steep and steeper. Vail's "Far East" is usually referred to as China Bowl, which is served by a high-speed quad. Tea Cup, Sun Up's nearest neighbour, is the steepest of the new quintet, while China Bowl and Siberia Bowl are middling, while adjuncts Inner and Outer Mongolia are gentler, have longer runouts and are so remote that they feel like the essence of off-piste skiing. Though there are now three chair-lifts and two drag-lifts in these Back Bowls, the acreage is more than double that of the front – and all of it demands a degree of strength and skill.

In addition to easy access to the in-town restaurants and shops both at Vail Village and at Lionshead, there are nine on-mountain eating facilities. In addition to the normal American self-service cafeteria, these range from rather fancy table service options at Eagles Nest and Mid-Vail to several new ski-up snack bars at high-traffic points, including one serving frankfurters and one serving Chinese food (at Far East, of course). The most popular is the Two Elk, a stylish self-service restaurant with fine fine food and exceptional views.

Vail and its sister resort Beaver Creek, 10 miles to the west as well as Keystone and Breckenridge to the east, are skiable on fully interchangeable lift tickets. Vail's prestigious ski school is the largest in America, and its children's programmes for three-year-olds and up have won particular acclaim for their creativity and caring. Both at Vail and at Beaver Creek, on-mountain theme areas have been established for youngsters to have fun as they learn. Children ski through terrain gardens created in around a Western-style fort, Indian burial ground, mine or other theme.

In a Few Words: All other ski areas in the American West are dwarfed by the quantity and quality of Vail, which was demonstrated eloquently during the 1989 World Alpine Ski Championships which were so well organised that the F.I.S. has selected Vail to play a reprise in 1999.

Après Ski: Vail's watchwords are variety, quality and money when it comes to après ski life. As can be expected in a town with a guest capacity of 25,000, Vail's better than 100 restaurants and bars cover a range of styles and cuisines. A caveat: there are few bargains. One bargain that appeals to all ages is the skis-on Hot Winter Nights extravaganza performed weekly through much of the season at Golden Peak. It's free.

Vail Village is still the big draw for après ski strolling and night life. Vail's après ski scene is one of the liveliest in the Rockies. It starts early at spots near the lifts and winds down in the wee hours.The Red Lion Inn, which opened in time for Vail's inaugural season, is still an enormously popular après ski watering hole. So is Pepi's Bar at the Gasthof Gramshammer. In spring, the open-air patios of both places are crowded as well. Other hot spots are Mickey Poag's at the Lodge at Vail (named for the entertainer who is a fixture there), the Hong Kong Cafe, Trail's End at Lionshead (a favourite of ski instructors and other locals) and the Cascade Hotel's Lobby Bar (for mellow sophisticated sounds).

Fine dining abounds at Vail, where talented chefs, both creative and classic, preside over excellent restaurants. The St. Moritz, Ambrosia, the Alpenrose, Sweet Basil, the Left Bank, Eaglewood at the Vail Athletic Club, the Wildflower in the Lodge at Vail and Ludwig's, Lancelot and the Stuberl, all in the Sonnenalp, round up the selection of commendable continental restaurants. The Antlers dining room at the Gasthof Gramshammer elegantly offers Continental specialities, heavy on those of Austro-Hungarian origin. Steaks and chops are good at the elegant Lord Gore at Manor Vail overlooking Golden PeakThis fine restaurant also specialises in exotic game such as buffalo steak, medallions of antelope and elk roast. The Ore House, the Red Lion Inn, Bart and Yeti's and the Bully Ranch in the Sonnenalp specialise in such solid fare as steak, prime rib, barbecued spareribs and crab.

Later in the evening, there's dancing at Nick's and The Club, Of these, Nick's gets the younger crowd. At Lionshead, the Bart and Yeti's and Grill are popular. And for those who like nightlife from the past, The Daily Grind is a coffee shop of an updated '60s type which serves excellent espresso and cappuccino and poetry readings in the evening.

It is astonishing how many people keep busy at Vail without ever skiing. As well as numerous fine shops and art galleries, non-ski sports abound. Four top-rated health and fitness centres, an indoor ice skating rink, indoor tennis and racquetball courts, bowling lanes, dozens of swimming pools indoors and out and Vail Nature Centre's 'interpretative' cross-country and snowshoe trails are among the off-slope activities. Nearby Pirey Ranch also has cross-country skiing and other winter options. Vail operates America's first and longest natural recreational bobrun.

Not only does Vail care for youngsters too young to ski and those in ski classes, but the resort also has an outstanding junior après ski programme. Kids Night Out Goes Western is a supervised dinner and entertainment option for youngsters aged five through 12.

Lodging: Vail's top properties are world-class and centrally located. The Lodge at Vail, the opulent Sonnenalp Resort, the Vail Athletic Club, Gasthof Gramshammer, the Cascade Hotel & Club and L'0stello are luxurious and convenient to lifts, shopping and entertainment. Most of these are centrally located, but the Cascade Hotel is noteworthy because it is almost-urban hotel in the new development called Cascade Village, which features a splendid health spa, cinema and access directly to Lionshead via the never-crowded Cascade Village chairlift. These top lodgings are all expensive, but they are on a par with the leading hotels in the leading Alpine resorts—but without the snobbery or overblown formality.

Some of the outlying accommodations compensate in relative economy for what they lack in central location (though Vail's outstanding free bus system means that nothing is really out of the way). However, some standout properties are in "the suburbs". The Vail Racquet Club condominiums are four miles east of Vail Village. These luxurious units are convenient to one of the resort's premier health and racquet-sports facilities. Marriott's Streamside, two miles west of Lionshead, features luxuriously appointed condominium apartments in a quiet, secluded setting. The complex has a guest lounge, indoor/outdoor heated swimming pools and hot tub, sauna and steamroom.

BEAVER CREEK

Height of Resort: 8,100 ft.
Height of Lowest Lift: 7,400 ft.
Height of Top Station: 11,440 ft.
Nearest Airport: Eagle County (30 miles)
Nearest Major Airport: Denver
Route by Car: Beaver Creek is located 10 miles west of Vail; take Interstate-70 west from Denver or east from Eagle and exit at Avon. Drive south to Beaver Creek's gated entrance.
Resort Facilities Charts: See page 210

Beaver Creek is one of the newest and most luxurious ski resorts in America, combining excellent skiing with luxurious lodging. Last season, it was interlinked with Arrowhead, down in the Eagle River Vail, and this year, it offers interchangeable skiing not only with Vail but also with Keystone and Breckenridge.

Beaver Creek: The elegant confines of Beaver Creek Village remain the heart the ski terrain. The main runs are accessed by the Centennial SuperChair, one of Beaver Creek's six high-speed quad chairlifts. At the top of the lift is Spruce Saddle, an elegant mountain restaurant. To the east is Rose Bowl, to the west the Birds of Prey and Larkspur Bowl, above at the gentle summit slopes and across the valley in the sector called McCoy Park. Between Birds of Prey and Larkspur is Grouse Mountain, with intermediate and expert runs, with a high-speed quad and super-steep runs. It is known for steep, narrow mogul runs on top, widening and becoming gentler at the bottom.

Arrowhead, originally a small ski area originally built as amenity to a resort development, has one high-speed quad chair-lift and a drag-lift for beginners. The runs are long and elegant; there simply aren't a lot of them, but as a new gateway into Beaver Creek, Arrowhead has really come into its own. Bachelor Gulch was developed in 1996-97 as a connector between Beaver Creek Village and Arrowhead. The BachelorBahn high-speed quad and a web of lovely cruising trails make this newest mountain sector congenial as well as connective.

Some of Beaver Creek's sectors seem geared primarily for one ability level or another. There are some excellent nursery slopes and an outstanding children's terrain garden at the very bottom of the mountain, while the front face in and around the Centennial chairlift is predominantly intermediate. The gentle summit runs are ultra-wide, super gentle and meticulously groomed. The Birds of Prey and Grouse Mountain are steep and narrow double-black runs which build up bumps to challenge even experts.

Other terrain is an unusual intertwining of terrain of different standards. Rose Bowl contains one section of Cinch, ultra-easy path from the summit to Spruce Saddle, as well as the lush and lovely intermediate slope called Stone Creek meadows and three short, tricky steeps. Similarly, Larkspur Bowl consists of one wide cirque which is a dream under a foot of fresh powder, several medium-steep runs studded with stands of trees and three short mogul pitches. McCoy Park has just a handful of intermediate trails, including the four-miler called Buckskin to the village, plus a mountain-top ski-touring centre.

At peak periods when it seems as if the world is at Vail and on weekends when all of Denver appears to be there too, Beaver Creek offers a perpetually less crowded alternative to Vail. With booming second-home development and much recent development geared toward making these elegant and expensive vacation homes ski-in, ski-out, you can also tour around the slopes and have a glance at some of the most splendid mountain homes in North America.

In a Few Words: Originally planned as a satellite to take the pressure of Vail, Beaver Creek in less than a decade has become a mature, elegant, self-contained resort with the additional benefit of being skiable on a fully interchangeable lift ticket with Vail and two Summit County resorts.

Après Ski: After-ski life is refined and quiet. All of the accommodations are close to the lifts, and many lounges provide relaxing spots for a congenial drink. The Crooked Hearth, in the Hyatt, serves 12 specialty wines by the glass and the hotel's Lobby Bar is a civilised oasis. Many skiers prefer simply to stop at Village Hall, the classy carpeted base chalet, after skiing.

One of the greatest evening treats in the Rockies is a snowcat-towed sleighride to Beano's Cabin for dinner. Beano's, an elegantly rustic luncheon club, is open for members only during the skiing day, but in the evening, it serves good dinners and has live entertainment. Other dinner options for fine dining in elegant settings are Patina in the Hyatt, Legends in the Poste Montane, the Black Diamond at the Inn at Beaver Creek and the First Season in the Charter. The Golden Eagle and Coyote Café are less formal. Especially fine for those dining with children is the new prix fixe dinner, family-style policy at McCoy's on Village Hall.

Mirabelle at the base of Beaver Creek specialises in the cuisine of the South of France in a renovated 80-year-old pioneer homestead. The Restaurant Picasso in the Lodge at Cordillera in nearby Edwards offers another option for excellent continental meals, while several spots in Avon can be counted on for less expensive, more casual dinners. Among them are the Hole in the Wall, Chicago Pizza Factory, Tijuana Express and the Iron Horse. For a down-home, all-American evening, there are several super casual places in nearby Minturn which serve huge portions both of food and merriment. Among them are the Minturn Country Club for steaks and seafood, Chili-Willy's for spicy Tex-Mex and the Saloon also for Tex-Mex but with a rowdier Western atmosphere.

Lodging: Beaver Creek is a limited-access aerie to which only overnight guests may bring their automobiles. Day skiers park in lots at the bottom of a long access road and take a free bus up to the resort village, which in consequently very quiet and compact cause it does not have to accommodate traffic. It is also an architecturally harmonious development with tasteful buildings that are a real retreat rather than giving the sense of an active, bustling village. Since the ski area is just a decade old and all of the accommodations are even newer, all conform to the highest standards of luxury.

All of the hotels and condominiums are extremely luxurious. The leader is the acclaimed Hyatt Regency Beaver Creek, this deluxe chain's first property in a mountain resort. This large, well appointed hotel approaches the toniest five-star properties in the Alps in terms of food and services and exceeds most of them in room size and opulent custom furnishings. There is a fitness centre and complex of several slopeside outdoor heated swimming pools and hot tubs.

Nearby are other excellent hotels and condominiums, all either ski-in, ski-out or within easy walking distance of the lifts. These include The Charter at Beaver Creek, The Chateau, Park Plaza, Strawberry Park, the Inn at Beaver Creek, the Pines, St. James Place, Saddle Ridge at Beaver Creek and the Beaver Creek Inn – luxury spots all.

At the bottom of the broad valley lies Avon, a less prepossessing, less expensive alternative to overnighting in Beaver Creek. The Comfort Inn is a mid-range hotel which offers a good value, and condominium developments abound. Free buses make the rounds in Avon and ferry skiers up the mountain to Beaver Creek, and inexpensive buses connect both Beaver Creek and Avon with Vail.

STEAMBOAT

Height of Resort: 6,900 ft,
Height of Top Station: 10,500 ft.
Nearest Airport: Steamboat Springs (3 miles)
Regional airport: Hayden (20 miles)
Nearest Major Airport: Denver (160 miles).
Route by Car: From Hayden, follow U.S. 40 east to Steamboat Springs. From Denver, take Interstate 70 west from Denver. Just west of Idaho Springs, follow U.S. 40 west over Berthoud and Rabbit Ears Passes to Steamboat. As an option, continue west on I-to through the Eisenhower Tunnel to the Dillon/Silverthorne exit. Follow Colorado Rte. 9 north to Kremmling, then U.S. 40 west to Steamboat.
Driving time is 3½ to 4 hours from Denver, depending on weather.
Resort Facilities Chart: See page 211

Steamboat is the most determinedly cowboy-flavoured of all U.S. ski resorts, combining the special ambiance of the Old West with up-to-date facilities on a remarkable mountain known for its fluffy 'champagne powder'.

Steamboat: A look at the web-like Steamboat trail system on a map reflects the problem of trying to project an undulating four-peak mountain onto a flat sheet of paper. Steamboat knows how bewildering this first glance can be, however so it dispatches 1970 world champion Billy Kidd to ski with guests every afternoon and show them around. He meets skiers at the top of the gondola at 1 p.m. every afternoon; there is no charge for skiing with this congenial champ. In addition to Billy's itinerary, mountain hosts do free tours too. What Billy and the mountain hosts show – and what skiers can find for themselves – is a complex mountain that unfolds surprise after surprise as one rides skyward on lift after lift. The face of Steamboat is Mount Werner and is ever changing, with a speedy eight-passenger gondola and a total of 17 chairlifts.

The skiable terrain spreads across three peaks, Mount Werner, Storm Peak and Sunshine Peak. They loom above the lower mountain called Christie. Rising directly over Steamboat Village, Christie contains the lion's share of the area's beginners' terrain and a goodly portion of the intermediate runs as well. A few expert slopes – Voodoo, See Me, Vertigo and Oops – are also cut through the trees. In addition to the chair-lifts that serve this terrain, Steamboat's major feeder lift, North America's first eight-passenger gondola, rises 2,200 feet from the village to the Thunderhead restaurant with a convenient mid-mountain location.

From Thunderhead, it is possible to ski down to the Burgess Creek area in one direction or the Priest Creek area in the other. Both are known for fine expert slopes and excellent intermediate trails, nicely interwoven so that middling skiers can courageously take a difficult run and advanced skiers can relax on a somewhat easier one without breaking pace.

The wide and gladed Storm Peak slopes are exceptionally delightful intermediate terrain. Big Meadows and Buddy's Run are two of the best. Shadows, Twilight and lower High Noon are the best known of the expert runs from the Priest Creek chair on Sunshine Peak. Much of this terrain, too, is gladed. Since these wide-spaced trees tend to hold the snow and protect it from the sun's harshest glare, this upper terrain has Steamboat's fluffiest powder as well as some of its prettiest scenery. In 1996-97, Steamboat opened 179 acres of intermediate and advanced terrain called Morningside Park, with an additional 770 acres on Pioneer Ridge, north of the existing ski area, on the docket next.

The Thunderhead is an outstanding mountain restaurant, with food options ranging from a huge barbecue Sundeck to Hazie's, a classy sit-down restaurant. The Rendezvous Saddle Restaurant at Priest Creek also has a cafeteria and an excellent restaurant, Ragnar's, plus a large deck. There's a new snack bar with sundeck at the top of the Four Points chair-lift.

The resort has always been popular with families, but that popularity skyrocketed with the introduction of America's first large-scale Kids Ski Free programme, which offers free lodging, lifts and even rental equipment during the entire ski season save Christmas/New Year when accommodations are at a participating hotel or condominium (and most are). Children's ski lessons, however, remain additional. Steamboat's teen ticket category for ages 12 to 15 accommodates families with older youngsters.

In addition to an outstanding children's programme, Steamboat offers a galaxy of specialised seminars, clinics, and workshops to help skiers enhance their skills. The Billy Kidd Center for Performance Skiing is a standout, offering racing camps for recreational skiers who want to run gates better, Nelson Carmichael Bump Camps for skiers who want to improve their mogul skiing, and the Billy Kidd Challenge for advanced skiers seeking challenges from gates to moguls, steeps to glades.

One of the country's best snowcat operations is Steamboat Powder Cats, which operates on 15 square miles of backcountry terrain at Buffalo Pass. It's a great one- or two-day adventure for strong skiers.

In a Few Words: Steamboat coined the phrase "champagne powder". In January 1996, a single-month record 259° inches of snow fell on the mountain, and the area measured a seasonlong total of 529° inches.

Après Ski: There are two components to the Steamboat resort experience. One is the modern development at the base of the mountain centered around Gondola Square and Ski Time Square. The other is the original community of Steamboat Springs, three miles from the mountain, with a strong Old West accent. The immediate après ski action centres around the Grubstake, a busy, lively bar at Gondola Square and Buddy's in the Sheraton. Later, it moves to such places as the Tugboat Saloon, which is lively and a bit rowdy and Heavenly Daze Brew Pub, a favourite in Ski Time Square with microbrewed beers, light food and music. Steamboat Brewery and Tavern is the in-town microbrewery. The Saloon between town and mountain has Western dancing.

Steamboat Springs' reputation as an après ski town, complete with real cowpokes and ranchers, has been diluted somewhat with the resort development at the

Steamboat Lifts: This area is served by 21 lifts, one eight-passenger gondola, 2 high-speed quads, 1 four-seater, 6 triple and 8 double chair-lifts plus 3 drag-lifts and 1 Magic Carpet lift for children.
Lift Numbers: 1 Silver Bullet, 2 Southface, 3 Headwall, 4 Preview, 5 Christie Two, 6 Christie Three, 7 Bashor, 8 Thunderhead, 9 Arrowhead, 10 Burgess Creek, 11 Storm Peak Express, 12 Four Points, 13 WJW, 14 Bar UE (-UE), 15 Elkhead, 16 Priest Creek, 17 Sundown Express, 18 Sunshine, 19 South Peak, 20 Rough Rider.
Runs: • • • • • • • • • Easy - - - - - - - - - Medium ———— Difficult

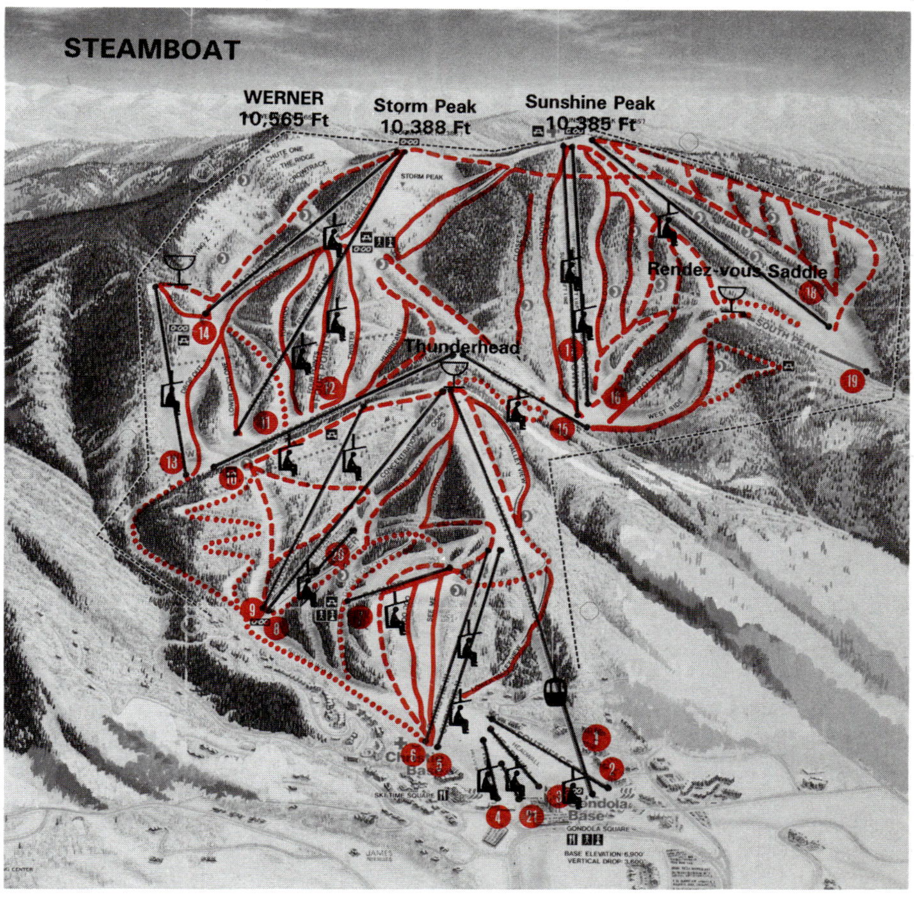

ski mountain. The fallout of tourist-orientated restaurants and shops has, of course, smoothed the roughest edges off the community. Yet visitors can rub elbows with newly arrived or born-and-bred locals, including real cowboys, over whiskey neat or draught beer as well as sample food from the corners of the world. Western wear for visiting dudes (and tack for their horses) can be purchased at F.M. Light & Sons and Soda Creek Outfitters.

Dining options abound – on, near and away from the mountain. The gondola operates the five nights a week when Hazie's in the Thunderhead Lodge is open for fine dining with a splendid view of the lights of the Yampa Valley. Ragnar's also serves Scandinavian dinners five nights a week. Travel between the gondola top station and the Rendezvous Saddle Restaurant is by sleigh.

Good restaurants at the mountain resort include the Grubstake (basic American food and burgers), Mattie Silk's (Continental cuisine), the Butcher Shop (steaks) and Cipriani's (excellent northern Italian). Dos Amigos and La Montana serve Mexican food. One of the best steak spots is The Ore House at the Pine Grove, an atmospheric restaurant in the renovated barn of the century-old ranch which predated the skis resort. Downtown, the Old West Steakhouse is recommended, and the Chart House (steak and seafood) between the mountain and town is the Steamboat outpost of a popular chain. Elsewhere in town, L'Apogee has Steamboat Springs' most noteworthy fine dining. Giovanni's has "Brooklyn-style" red-sauce Italian specialities, and Mazzola's serves basic, moderately priced pasta and pizza.

Howelson Hill offers night skiing, ski jumping and ice skating, as well as lighted cross-country loipes. The Steamboat Springs Health & Recreation Assn. has three naturally heated pools and water slides. Strawberry Hot Springs, seven miles from town, has outdoor hot pools for day and night soaking. Tennis players book the clay courts at the Tennis Center at Steamboat. The Kids' Vacation Center also has evening entertainment for children five nights a week, and there's a new evening programme for teens called Night Owls.

Steamboat Springs at its most Western shows itself the first full week in February, when the annual Winter Carnival takes place. A variety of home-grown competitions, ranging from ski jumping at Howelson Hill to various horseback contests down Main Street, attracting residents of all ages who vie for prizes. Mostly, however, it's the fun and not the prizes that appeal to visitors and residents alike.

Lodging: Steamboat has much housing at the base of the lifts. The Sheraton Steamboat is the most convenient and luxurious hotel. It is hard to miss, for it is the tallest building in the village. Each room has two queen-size beds, colour TV and balcony. Condominiums include Storm Meadows, Thunderhead Lodge and Ski Time Square.

A variety of hotels, motels and lodges are located in Steamboat Springs and environs. The degree of luxury ranges from 'very' to not-at-all, from dorm-style to complete with sauna and swimming pool and private colour TV. Noteworthy is the Rabbit Ears Motel for its location directly across from a natural hot-springs pool. The Holiday Inn, Super 8 and West Western Ptarmigan Inn are archetypal American motels. Rainbow cottages for accessibility to shuttle transportation for the car-less. The Harbor Hotel, Alpine Rose, Clermont Inn, Mariposa, Oak Street Bed and Breakfast and the Steamboat Bed and Breakfast hold all the aces for charm.

Steamboat Springs Transit (SST) buses run every 30 minutes between town, most lodges and the mountain between 6.30 am and 12.30 the next morning.

PARK CITY

Height of Resort: 6,900 ft.
Height of Top Station: 10,000 ft. (Park City)
Bottom of Lowest Lift: 7,200 ft. (Deer Valley)
Height of Top Station: 9,400 ft. (Deer Valley)
Bottom of Lowest Lift: 6,800 ft. (The Canyons)
Height of Top Station: 9,400 ft. (The Canyons)
Nearest Major Airport: Salt Lake City
Route by Car: Follow Interstate 80, 20 miles east from Salt Lake City to the Park City exit. Follow Route 224 south for six miles to resort.
Driving time is about 40 minutes.
Resort Facilities Charts: See page 211

Park City's is a true Cinderella story, the tale of a town grown from a decaying mining community into a ski resort of extraordinary variety and quality with three Alpine ski areas, plus North America's newest venue for ski jumping and bobsledding, built for the 2002 Winter Olympics.

Park City Mountain Resort: The ski area which shares the same name as the town is a statistical giant that lays claim to being Utah's largest. This year, it boasts three high-speed six-place chairlifts, more than any other North American resort. It stands to reason that all this uphill capacity (23,000 skiers an hour) leads to ample terrain, including 83 runs and 650 acres of bowls.

The lower portion of the mountain is served by four chairs, PayDay (now a six-seater), Ski Team, First Time and Three Kings. The former two have a few short pitches to lure experts as well as a profusion for novice and intermediate skiers, while the latter two serve sheltered beginners' terrain. This area is lit until 10 p.m. nightly for skiing under the stars. The Ski Team runs, where America's Opening World Cup or pro races are often held, has a chairlift and two additional runs.

Another new six-place chairlift, called Bonanza, whisks skiers and snowboarders to the Summit area from the top of PayDay. The mid-upper portion of Park City's terrain is known for long, sweeping runs, heavily canted toward the intermediate, especially off the King Consolidated and the Prospector high-speed quad chair-lifts. Even novices can ski the top, namely the Meadow and Claim Jumper and navigate an easy route to the bottom again.

Experts gravitate toward Blueslip Bowl, Silver Skis, the Shaft and Thaynes, skiable off the chairs that unload at or near the Summit House mountain restaurant. But the Summit is at a false summit, not at the true one which is 700 feet higher. A double chairlift reaches Park City's highest point atop Jupiter Bowl. Swooping below it in a wide arc, these 650 powdery acres of steep snowfields, bowls and chutes are the best Park City has to offer experts.

For visitors staying in town rather than near the resort base or in outlying lodging served by free shuttle bus, the easiest access into the ski area is by a triple known as the Town Chair, which ferries skiers directly from the outskirts of town into the heart of the expansive ski terrain. The best of the three mountain restaurants is the Mid-Mountain Restaurant, a landmark mining building moved from its original site and refurbished as a fine self-service restaurant with atmosphere and entertainment.

Park City is skiable on a multi-area Ski Utah lift pass, which also includes Deer Valley and ParkWest (or whatever it will be called) located up and down the road respectively, Brighton and Solitude in the next valley which is called Big Cottonwood Canyon and Alta and Snowbird two valleys over in Little Cottonwood Canyon. One of North America's rare off-piste adventures is the guided Utah Interconnect, a ski and lift route along all three valleys. Strong intermediate and better skiers may join the Interconnect, a day-long guided tour from Park City to Big (and sometimes Little) Cottonwood or the reverse.

For those who want a backcountry, off-piste adventure, Park City Snowcat Cruises accesses backcountry powder at a lower price than heli-skiing. The White Pines Touring Center also runs full-day and multi-day backcountry trips.

Deer Valley: North America's only competitor to Beaver Creek in the ultra-luxury category is this exclusive ski area and resort development two miles above Park City. From Snow Park Lodge, at 7,200 ft., a pair of lifts, including a high-speed four-seater, climb to Silver Lake Lodge, which is the jumping off point for most of the skiing. There are many more options for intermediate and advanced skiers using four chairlifts on Bald Mountain, with a summit elevation of 9,400 ft. The Mayflower and Sultan lift areas, on the far reaches of Flagstaff Mountain, features a small bowl, some excellent steep trails and fine tree skiing as well. These It is the services and the pampering that draw skiers to this meticulous mountain.

Yet Deer Valley offers adventure skiing as well. There is currently pay-per-ride snowcat service into Empire Canyon, a huge basin comprised snowfields, glades and very steep chutes that is slated for eventual lift service. Stein Eriksen, the ageless hero of the 1952 Winter Olympics, is Deer Valley's director of skiing and a symbol of the resort's class and maintains a very public presence. Deer Valley, which has earned a reputation in the American skiing world for exceptional food in its mountain restaurants and for flawless slope grooming, is often referred to as the Rolls Royce of American skiing – more a luxury ride of extreme smoothness than an unpredictable, sporty adventure.

The Canyons: The Canyons is graduating from being the most understated to the hottest ski area in the valley. An investment of $18.2 million is being a new eight passenger gondolaway with a restaurant and a new beginner area on top, and five new four-seater chairlifts, three of them high-speed express lifts.* The area is three miles down-valley from Park City and has been the antithesis to Deer Valley. From the base area, you see just a wide, appealing novice slope. Hidden from view are two deep, steep-sides ridges. There are medium-standard routes along the ridge tops and in the valleys between them, but the runs down the sides range from moderately steep to practically vertical. Seven double chairs which ASC bought along with the mountain are old workhorses. Some will eventually be replaced. In some ways, this Utah area will be linked with its Eastern kin with joint ticketing programmes, but with the exception of Saturdays, when many hot young Salt Lake City skiers are skimming the snow and jumping the bumps, this area has never been crowded, and when Utah gets its fabled snowfalls, the powder lasts and lasts.

Utah Winter Sports Park: This facility, which was built for the ski jumping, bobsled, and luge events for the 2002 Winter Olympics, is unique in the world. Not only is it a year-round training facility for jumpers and freestyle skiers, but it offers anyone a chance to learn the fundamentals of ski jumping. Every skier can learn the basics to be Eddie "the Eagle" Edwards for a day. The complex, nicknamed "Park City's fourth ski area," features eight jumps ranging from 18 to 90 meters. The big ramps are used for serious competitive jumping, which is a thrilling sport to watch, while the small ones are used for teaching beginners. The park also has a small lodge with a snack bar and a slow chairlift for those who don't want to walk all the way up the big jumping hill.

**Due to the late arrival of the above information on The Canyons, we regret that we are unable to show these lifts on the map.*

Park City Lifts: This area is served by 15 lifts, (one gondola, three 4-seater, 6 triple and 5 double chair-lifts).

Lift Numbers:

1	4- seater gondola
2	Prospector, high speed 4-seater chair-lift
3	Crescent, 4-seater chair-lift
4	Payday
5	Motherlode
6	King Consolidated, high-speed 4-seater chair-lift
7	Pioneer
8	Town Lift
9	First Time, 3-seater chair-lift
10	Three Kings
11	Ski Team
12	Lost Prospector
13	Thaynes
14	Jupiter
15	Eagle

Park City Lower Map: This shows the run served by the triple chair-lift, Pioneer, which are not shown on the top map.

Runs: • • • • • • • • • • • Easy
--- Medium
——————————— Difficult

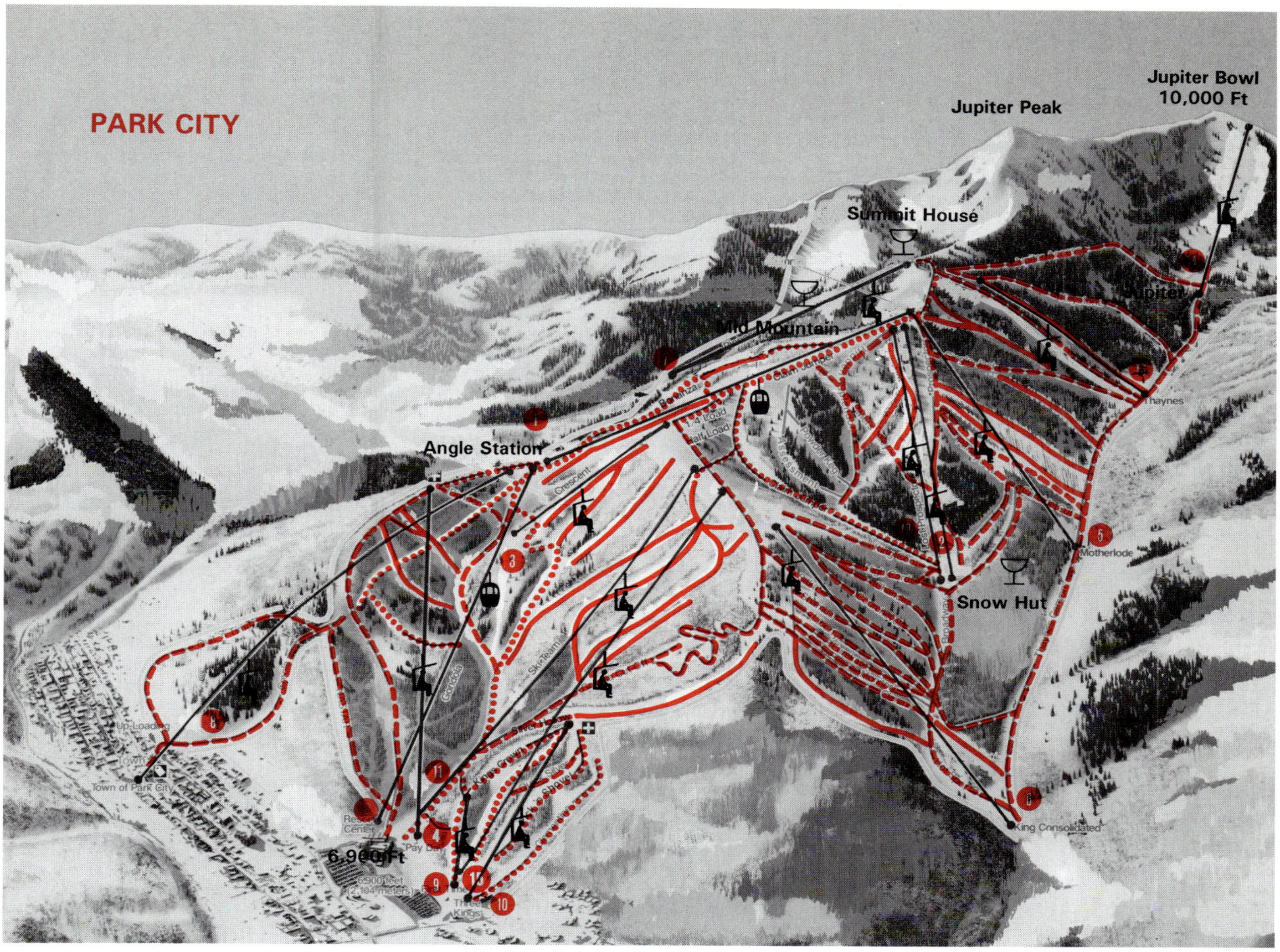
PARK CITY
Jupiter Peak
Jupiter Bowl
10,000 Ft
Summit House
Jupiter
Mid Mountain
Angle Station
Crescent
Bonanza
Thaynes
Motherlode
Snow Hut
King Consolidated
Town of Park City
6,900 Ft

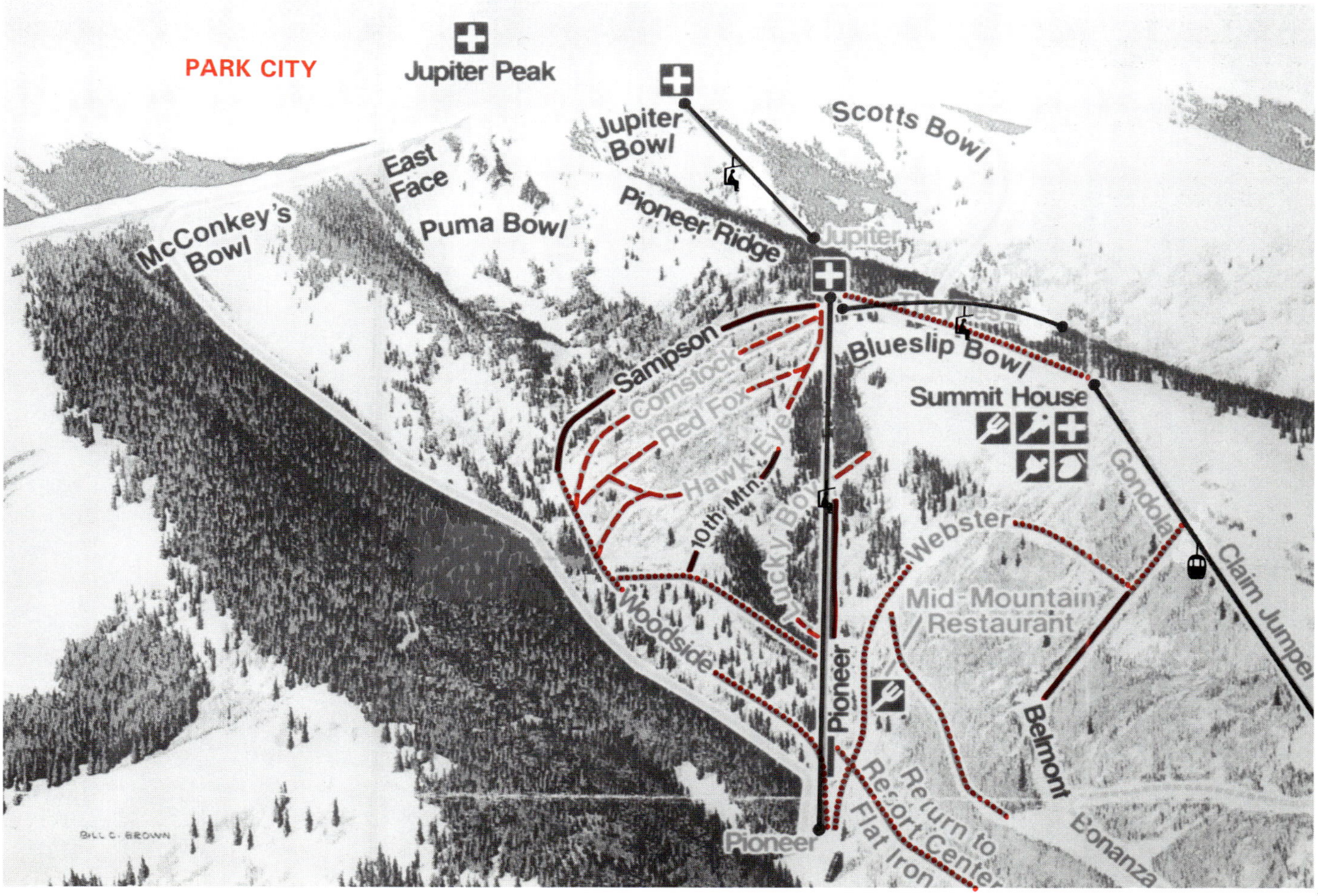
PARK CITY
Jupiter Peak
Jupiter Bowl
Scotts Bowl
East Face
McConkey's Bowl
Puma Bowl
Pioneer Ridge
Jupiter
Thaynes
Sampson
Comstock
Red Fox
Hawk Eye
10th Mtn.
Lucky Boy
Blueslip Bowl
Summit House
Gondola
Claim Jumper
Webster
Mid-Mountain Restaurant
Woodside
Pioneer
Belmont
Pioneer
Return to Resort Center
Flat Iron
Bonanza
BILL C. BROWN

In a Few Words: Vast and varied terrain for all abilities is the watchword of Park City skiing – much of it blessed with the fluffy powder for which Utah is renowned. The proximity of Deer Valley and ParkWest and the easy accessibility of four other worthwhile ski areas make Park City a fine resort choice.

Après Ski: Park City is big, so after-ski life comes in the variety and quantity that befit a sizeable ski town. Lodging, dining and accommodations are split between the new resort development at the base of the mountain and the old mining town of Park City. You can get a real taste of that heritage by visiting the Park City Mine Adventure, which is a tour, guided by a retired miner, of the Ontario silver mine whose lode contributed so heavily to the town's lusty boom years. You'll ride 1,500 ft. into the heart of the mine on a multi-storeyed elevator, ride a mine train and see informative above-ground exhibits.

Après ski starts after Park City's lifts close both at lively places at the Resort Center at the main lift base and in town. At the mountain, the top spots are Steeps, Baja Cantina and Ziggy's. In town, the Club and the Alamo are nextdoor neighbours on Main Street, and Cisero's up the street all start early and run late. The Wasatch Brew Pub at the top of Main Street serves at least four freshly brewed beers and ales each evening and also have dinner service, both light meals and more substantial ones. In addition, Deer Valley is isolated and tranquil, yet is also part of the greater Park City scene.

The restaurant roster in Park City is impressive; in fact many claim it is now on a culinary par with the top North American ski resorts. There are eating places of all kinds. For elegant, Continental-style singing, there are Adolph's near the Nordic center and the Glitretind at the Stein Eriksen Lodge. Grappa and Mileti's serve authentic Italian cuisine. Hearty steaks and simple prepared seafood specialities are offered at Claimjumper, Grubsteak and Brand X Cattle Co. Bistro 7000 is a spacious and modern slopeside restaurant serving a variety of cuisine. For light meals, sandwiches and burgers, Park City has Main Street Deli and Burgie's. Davanzas serves casual food with an Italian accent. For Mexican fare, try the Irish Camel, Borderline, Nacho Mama's or the Baja Cantina. Ichiban is known for its sushi and other Japanese offerings, while Nonna Maria does things Mediterranean with a flair. Try the Morning Ray Café for fresh baked goods at breakfast and lunch. Zoom Roadhouse Grill is one of the newest hotsports in town. Run by Sundance, which in turn is owned by actor Robert Redford, it serves "refreshed" American cuisine—as trendy as it is attractive. Some people go to Deer Valley to ski. Others go to dine. The Seafood Buffet in Snow Park Lodge and the elegant Mariposa in Silver Lake Lodge are worth the ride. High Country Snowmobile Tours does lunch and dinner rides, while The Homestead, a 20-minute drive from Park City, is a classic American Inn serving classic American fare.

Lodging: As with dining and entertainment, the Park City accommodations picture is drawn in plenitude. Condominium developments ring the town, which itself has hotels, lodges, dorms and even renovated mining buildings. Condominium complexes aplenty offer apartments in all sizes, from studios on up. Property management firms frequently handle more than one complex, all of which are relatively new.

At the Resort Center base are such convenient choices as the Resort Center Lodge & Inn, Silver King, Snow Flower and Shadow Ridge. Motherlode are quasi-Victorian-style condos, with all modern conveniences but an adaptive traditional style, close to Main Street and the Town Lift. Park Station is a condo-hotel adjacent to the Town Lift. The Blue Church Lodge has condos in a historic old church. Farther afield are such complexes as the Inn at Prospector Square, Powder Wood and Park City Village – the last being most convenient to Wolf Mountain.

Hotels include the Yarrow, the Radisson Inn Park City and the Park City Olympia Hotel. Chateau Après is an informal budget lodge with both rooms with private baths and dorm rooms for youthful budget-watchers. The Homestead is a large and lovely classic country inn 16 miles from Park City, a substantial commute but worthwhile just for the atmosphere. Ambiance plus convenient Park City locations are found in a growing group of charming bed-and-breakfast inns, including the Old Miner's Lodge, Snowed Inn, and the Washington School Inn. Sheer luxury is found at the Stein Eriksen Lodge in Deer Valley, as well as in adjacent condominiums. Another Deer Valley option is the Goldener Hirsch, an offshoot of the Austrian landmark. On the bargain side of the scale are motels down in Salt Lake City, with easy bus transfers for skiing.

TELLURIDE

Height of Resort: 8,745 feet
Height of Top Station: 11,890 feet
Nearest Airport: Telluride
Regional Airport: Montrose (57 miles)
Nearest Major Airports: Grand Junction (120 miles), Denver (320 miles)
Route by Car: From Grand Junction, U.S. Route 50 east to Montrose, U.S. Route 550 south to Ridgway, Colorado Routes 62 and Route 145. Driving time is 2½ hours. From Denver, U.S. Route 285 south to Poncha Springs, U.S. Route 50 west to Montrose, U.S. 550 south to Ridgway, Colorado Routes 62 and 145. Driving time is about seven hours, depending on the weather.
Resort Facilities Chart: See page 212

Telluride is a charming and historic mining town at the base of one of Colorado's finest ski mountains, in the midst of which the elegant, purpose-built resort called Telluride Mountain Village has taken shape. Bonuses are abundant snowfall, a spectacular setting in the soaring San Juan Mountains and uncrowded slopes.

Telluride: The standard entrance to the ski terrain is via the Oak Street and Coonskin chairlifts directly at the edge of town. They access the so-called Front Face, which consists of several super-steep mogul runs such as The Plunge and Spiral Stairs, and they also are the gateway to the milder, mellower terrain cupped into an enormous mountain cirque. This area is called Gorrono Basin, and it contains the lion's

Telluride Lifts: One high speed quad,2 triple & 6 double chair-lifts **Runs: .... Easy ---------- Medium ———— Difficult**

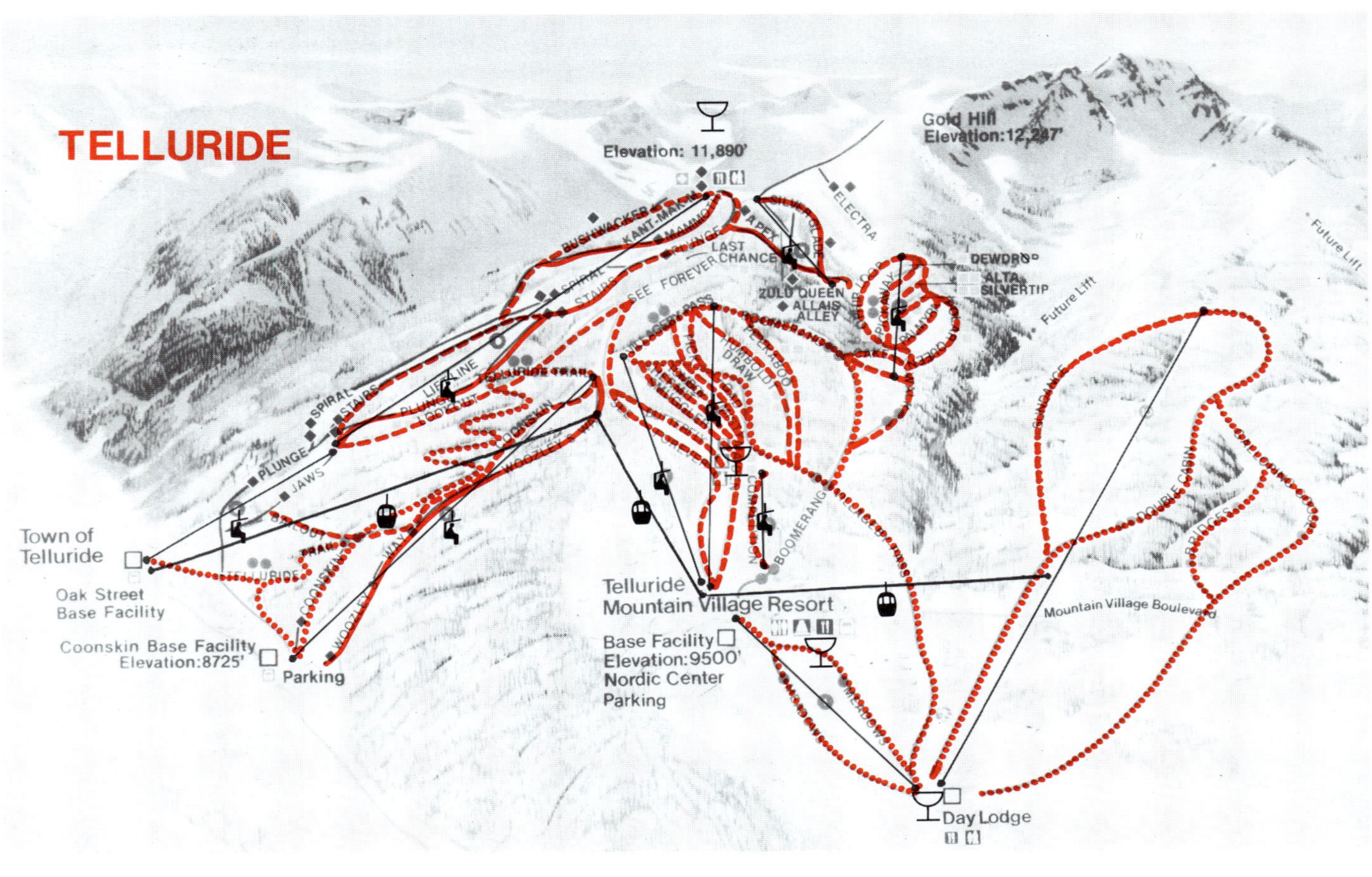

share of Tellurides green-circle and blue-square runs. In this midst of this normal skiers' paradise is Gorrono Ranch, a mountain dining restaurant imbued with authentic Western charm and flavour.

The new entrance to the ski terrain is from Telluride Mountain Village at the base of the Gorrono lifts. This glossy, flossy development – on a par with Beaver Creek – offers exceptional slope-side lodging and several good lunch-time eating places. There is 100-acre nursery slope at the village level slope served by the Chondola, a unique lift that has both four-place chairlift seats and gondola cars, so that it can be used both as transportation and as a conventional ski lift. On the other side of this nascent resort development, the Sunshine Express, said to be the world's longest high-speed quad chair-lift, leads to the dozen novice and intermediate runs of Sunshine Peak. This lift never has queues, so moderate skiers can get in as many runs a day as their legs can handle.

Arranged in a semi-circle above Gorrono are more expert runs. Silverglade, Electra and Apex are among these steep parcels, which are shorter than the Front Face runs but usually get more sun and more powder snow as well. Giuseppi's at the top of Lift 9 is a small mountain restaurant (in Europe, it would be called a hut) with casual food and fabulous views of the San Juan Mountains. A steep hike-in area called Gold Peak requires a 15-minute uphill walk to gain an additional 350 vertical feet to ski the ungroomed powder fields, chutes and glades arranged on a small part of a huge cirque that eventually will see lift service.

In December 1996, Telluride ushered in a new era with the opening of a long-awaited transit gondola to ferry guests between the town side and Mountain Village side of the ski slopes. It can be used as a ski lift to a high point on the ridge, but it really is designed as a key to transportation ease. It gives guests staying at either side a shortcut to skiing or dining or shopping anywhere they wish, saving seven tedious miles on often slick roads.

In a Few Words: Telluride has skiing for all levels of ability, but its splendid reputation as a true skier's mountain rests on its steepest slopes, its abundant powder and its absence of crowds.

Après Ski: Bierstube is an old favorite and Border House, a newer Tex-Mex places, catch the immediate après ski crowd heading for old Telluride from the Coonskin side. Telluride Mountain Village is just sorting itself out, but the Village Bar & Grill appears to be the best bet there. Later, various Western-style saloons downtown show the greatest liveliness. These include the Fly Me to the Moon Saloon, Last Dollar Saloon, O'Bannon's and the bar in the New Sheridan Hotel. La Biota is Telluride's sophisticated side. Downstairs at Swede-Finn Hall offers pool and conviviality. Cafe Kokopelli has jazz and other entertainment. One World Cafe has music and dancing. The House, located in an old home, is for games and drinks. Station One is a slick brew pub and restaurant located in a restored railroad depot, and there is also a brew pub in the back section of Baked in Telluride.

Fine restaurants abound. In town, kudos go to 221 South Oak and Swede-Finn Hall, which both have fine eclectic American cuisine, the Cactus Cafe serving Southwestern fare, Campagna for Italian country cuisine in a historic house and La Marmotte for more classic French dishes. The Cosmopolitan in the new Hotel Columbia is Telluride's culinary hotspot. Less formal meals may be enjoyed at the Excelsior Cafe, Floradora Saloon, the Telluride Country Club and Sofio's Mexican Cafe. Hungry diners flock to Leimgruber's for satiating German dinners. At Telluride Mountain Village, The Legends of the Peaks is sophisticated yet informal.

Lodging: Much of the in-town lodging is in condominiums, most within an easy walk of the Oak Street and/or Coonskin lifts – although at Telluride's altitude, some visitors find any walk a bit strenuous. Among the best-located complexes are the Cimmaron Lodge, Etta Place, Lulu City, Manitou Riverhouses and Viking Suites Hotel. The Ice House Lodge has spacious, modern rooms with refrigerators and private balconies. The San Sophia is the most opulent of Telluride's downtown bed-and-breakfast inns. The historic New Sheridan Hotel has been renovated with style and charm. Other charmers include the lovely new Hotel Columbia, Alpine Inn, the Johnstone Inn and the Manitou Hotel Bed and Breakfast. The Best Western Tomboy Inn is a motel-style lodge.

The centerpiece of Telluride Mountain Village is the five-year-old, 177-room Peaks at Telluride, a luxurious contemporary landmark which combines exceptional service, attractive decor and an outstanding fitness and beauty spa. Aspen Ridge Townhomes and Kenyata Legend House are two of the deluxe ski-out, ski-in condo complexes at the resort, while the long-planned Franz Klammer Lodge is premiered in 1996-97, an instant oasis of luxury, spaciousness and service. Pennington's is a gorgeous and charming B&B near the Mountain Village entrance. Early-season free skiing offers are made in co-operation with several lodging properties.

SQUAW VALLEY USA

Height of Resort: 6,200 ft.
Height of Top Station: 9,050 ft.
Nearest Airports: Reno, San Francisco
Route by car: From Reno, take Interstate I-80 west to Route 89 south.
From the San Francisco Bay Area, take Interstate 80 east to Route 89 south.
Driving times are about one and four hours respectively.
Resort Facilities Charts: See page 211.

The site of the 1960 Winter Olympic Games was long left to fallow. But in recent years, this huge mountain complex near Lake Tahoe has been upgraded and brought up to contemporary standards for ski facilities. A slopeside village development is in the works, and combined with lodging options at the lake and skiing at nearby North Lake Tahoe resorts as well, Squaw offers a varied holiday experience.

Squaw Valley: The mega-ski area is spread across six peaks in the craggy Sierra Nevada Range, giving the skiing a real Alpine look and feel. These peaks and the slopes cascading from their summits form one of North America's grandest ski amphitheatres with scores of European- style pistes etched onto the snowfields. Many of the runs, especially those threading through the high cliffs known as the Palisades, are steep and draw some of America's most daring skiers. What most differentiates the skiing from that found in the Alps is the snowfall.

Most years, Squaw and its neighbours are blanketed with Sierra snowfalls – normally as much as 450 inches in a normal year and often more than 500 inches. It's not generally the light powder of the Rockies but a wetter snow nicknamed "Sierra Cement", which nevertheless packs down beautifully to create a good skiing surface. Squaw is skiable on the Ski Lake Tahoe interchangeable pass with Alpine (its nearest neighbour), Heavenly, Kirkwood,

Northstar and Sierra-at-Tahoe. It is also a participant in the Ski Tahoe North Ticket (available only from the Tahoe North Convention & Visitors Bureau), good at such large mountains as Squaw, Alpine, Northstar and Sugar Bowl, plus four smaller ones, Boreal Ridge, Diamond Peak, Homewood and Mt. Rose.

At the fringe of the huge parking lots and cluster of commercial buildings comprising Olympic House & Plaza rise a dozen of Squaw Valley's nearly three dozen lifts. Some serve just the nursery slopes, but two are European-style feeder lifts to two mid-mountain complexes, both at 8,200 ft. – and designating a level of the mountain by its elevation is also more a European than an American custom. The six-passenger gondola and two long supplementary chairlifts, one a triple and one a high-speed quad, rise to Gold Coast. A 150- passenger cable car leads to High Camp. A new pulse lift now connects High Camp and Gold Coast, adding to the resort's European appearance..

The gondola reaches the middle of Squaw's vast terrain, with Gold Coast, a huge three-level lodge with three restaurants, several bars and huge sundecks, as the centrepiece. It is surrounded by eight chairlifts, mostly leading to great white boulevards on the flanks of 8,700-ft. Emigrant Peak geared for mid-level skiers. Four chairlifts of various configurations lead to the inspired intermediate terrain of Emigrant Peak. A long ridge connects it with Squaw Peak, at 8,900 ft. the highest of the resort's summits and also the steepest. The Headwall triple and Cornice II double chairlifts hoist experts to the big bowls, high chutes and steep faces cascading off Squaw Peak. Tucked behind Emigrant Peak is Granite Chief Peak, 350 ft. higher and somewhat more challenging but still nowhere near Squaw Peak for difficulty. The slopes leading to the drainage between these two peaks are among the most popular at Squaw.

High Camp is also a good area from which to ski the Emigrant/Granite Chief sector. It offers exceptional facilities, including some found nowhere else in North American skiing. several food service establishments, bars, an exceptional amount of sundecking and the High Camp Bath & Tennis Club's pools, spas and two tennis courts playable from mid-March on. Although Squaw Valley's rink from the 1960 Olympics is history, the Olympic Ice Pavilion at High Camp provides the opportunity to skate at this rarified altitude from 11 a.m. until 9 p.m. daily in a covered ice rink. The bungee tower nearby offers a thrilling yet safe, controlled jump. There is also limited night skiing on week-ends and holidays.

From the busy gondola/tram base, two long chairlifts skew off to the left. Exhibition primarily serves the racing hill, but KT-22 accesses some of the most spectacular expert skiing in the West. This formidable mountain was so named because one of Squaw Valley's pioneers Sandy Poulsen needed to make 22 kick turns to get to the bottom the first time she skied it. This is 2,000 ft. of relentless black- diamond challenge. Even on weekends when the rest of Squaw is crowded there is rarely a queue for the KT-22 chair, which is now an express four-seater. Beyond, the Red Dog triple leads to more intermediate and advanced terrain. Unlike the sparsely forested slopes above 6,200 ft., these runs are a combination of paths through the trees and open slopes which are also fringed with trees – all good choices for snowy days. Big Red leads to the top of Snow King Peak, and the Squaw Creek triple comes up the other side from the new Resort at Squaw Creek.

Squaw Valley, known for its commitment to family skiing, has expanded its children's ski school facility, now called Children's World. Available for youngsters from three to twelve, there are now three pony tows and a platterpull for the expanded terrain garden from very small skiers and beginners. Ten Little Indians is the slopeside nursery for ages six months to two years.

In a Few Words: Squaw Valley is an awesome mountain group with an complex, high-capacity lift system and wide-ranging skiing, including exceptional high-expert terrain.

Après Ski: The tram operates until 10 p.m. nightly so that much of the après-skiing takes place up on the mountain at High Camp, in the Terrace Bar & Restaurant, Alexander's Bar & Grill and The Poolside Cafe. The Oyster Bar has micro-brewed beers, sashimi and sometimes live music. At the base, several options present themselves, including The Beer Garden, the Olympic Bar & Grill, the Clocktower Cafe and Sierra Scoops for ice cream. The Headwall Cafe features an indoor climbing wall as unique entertainment. Slopes at the Squaw Valley Inn is a fun-filled après-ski bar with big-screen sports TV and music. At the Resort at Squaw Creek at the other end of Squaw Valley, the fun is at the Hardscramble Creek Bar & Grill with a large ski-in deck serving light food and providing entertainment, and Bullwacker's Pub for drinks and games such as pool, shuffleboard and darts. For dining, the best options at and near Squaw Valley include the Benton's (innovative continental and American) and, at the Resort at Squaw Creek, Glissandes (fancy French), Cascades (American regional specialties) and Sweet Potatoes (gourmet deli).

Many skiers stay in the mountain town of Truckee or the lakeside resort of Tahoe City. For dining, Truckee's Left Bank serves French cuisine, O.B.'s has a huge menu and prime rib cuts to match, the Truckee Trattoria (contemporary California cuisine with an Italian accent) and The Passage specialises in seafood. High above Truckee, Cottonwood has wonderful views and fine food, especially steak and seafood. Tahoe City offers more options. Among the popular spots are Yama for sushi, Jake's On The Lake for seafood and steaks, Wolfdale's for Japanese-California cuisine, Lake House Pizza with a fine weekday happy hour and good informal fare, Grazi! for "progressive Italian" creations, Christy Hill for California specialties, Rosie's Cafe, a very popular spot for casual food. and the Eggschange for huge gourmet breakfasts to fuel skiers through the day. In Tahoe Vista, six miles to the north, Captain John's for seafood done in a country French manner. The Black Bear Tavern on the West Shore serves New England dishes and private-label beers.

Tahoe City has several spots for music and dancing. Humpty's for all sorts of entertainment including big-screen TV sports and dancing nightly. Rosie's has dancing, a friendly atmosphere, and many special evenings and attracts lots of locals. The Sunnyside Resort has live music in the lounge several evenings a week. The Pierce Street Annex has music and dancing nightly. Rosie's has dancing to a live band on Tuesday nights. The Captain's Alpenhaus on the West Shore does a fun-filled singalong Basque dinner to live accordion music on Wednesday nights.

Even livelier evenings can be found across the Nevada border, where the Cal-Neva Lodge, Crystal Bay Club, Hyatt Regency Lake Tahoe and the Tahoe Biltmore offer gambling, music, dancing and entertainment. Even the bright lights of Reno with all its big, brassy casino-hotels are but an hour away.

Lodging: The luxury leader not just of Squaw Valley but of the Sierra ski areas (with the arguable exception of some of the better casino-hotels) is the Resort at Squaw Creek. The convenience of a three-seater chairlift from and a ski run back to the hotel simply can't be beat. In addition, as a self-contained resort property, it includes luxurious accommodations, fine and casual dining, entertainment, shops, skating rink, fitness centre and dynamite outdoor swimming pool.

Other properties are also located directly at Squaw Valley USA. The Squaw Valley Lodge at the base of the Squaw Peak Express lift features deluxe studios and suites furnished in a contemporary style, plus hot tubs, sauna, steamroom, Nautilus workout centre and Reno Airport shuttle. The Squaw Valley Inn adjacent to the cable car, done in a California adaptation of "English manor" decor, has comfortable rooms, restaurant, lounge and outdoor hot tubs. The Squaw Tahoe Resort at the base of the Big Red chair-lift and the Olympic Village Inn a short walk from the lifts both have studio and one-bedroom units, all with kitchenettes, plus outdoor hot tubs and saunas. The inn also has a bar, a fireplace lobby and a free ski shuttle if even the short walk is too long. The Hostel at Squaw Valley is a dorm-style accommodation for budget-minded skiers equipped with sleeping bags. The Christy Inn, half a mile from the lifts, is a cozy lodge with excellent views. Nearby condo complexes include Christy Hill, Squaw Meadows and Valley View. All have two bedrooms and full kitchens.

Granlibakken is the congenial but oddly named resort which actually has its own tiny ski hill. Certainly not worth crossing an ocean for, it nevertheless provides an economical lodging base for Squaw and the other Tahoe areas. Its "condo and breakfast" package also includes complimentary shuttle to Squaw Valley, six miles away.

Slightly farther afield are accommodations in Truckee (the River Ranch is a noteworthy charmer) and Tahoe City (the Sunnyside Resort is a charming lake-front B&B). The Hyatt Regency Lake Tahoe is a large, well-run casino-hotel in Incline Village, 25 miles from Squaw Valley. Recently renovated with a forest decorating theme, it includes accommodations in hotel rooms or lake-front cottages, a casino, entertainment, three restaurants, shops, fitness centre, heated swimming pool, tennis courts and a fine children's programme called Camp Hyatt. The nearby Cal-Neva Resort Hotel is a full-service resort hotel with a casino, entertainment, pool, a European-style health spa and lake views. The less opulent Tahoe Biltmore in Crystal Bay is on the ski shuttle route.

CRESTED BUTTE

Height of Resort: 9,375 feet
Bottom of Lowest Lift: 9,100 feet
Height of Top Station: 12,162 feet
Nearest airport: Gunnison
Nearest major airport: Denver (230 miles)
Regional Airport: Gunnison (28 miles)
Route by Car: From Denver, U.S. 285 south to U.S. 50 west to Gunnison, then Colorado Route 135 north to Crested Butte. Driving time is $4^1/_2$ hours from Denver and half an hour from Gunnison.
Resort Facilities Chart: See Page 210

Crested Butte is a very Western-style resort, located in the midst of the ranching country of south-central Colorado, which is rapidly developing into a resort area. It combines a charming, historic village with a purpose-built resort at the base of a fine, uncrowded ski mountain.

Crested Butte: The ski terrain wraps around a landmark pinnacle called Crested Butte, which gave the old town, and the mountain its name. The Silver Queen Express high-speed quad chairlift leads directly to primarily advanced terrain but also provides a faster way to the remainder of the mountain. The Keystone, now upgraded from a triple chair to a second high-speed quad, leads mostly to novice runs on the lower mountain and is an alternate to the quad. In addition, wide open slopes of various pitches offers everything from nursery slopes to racing hills at the bottom of the

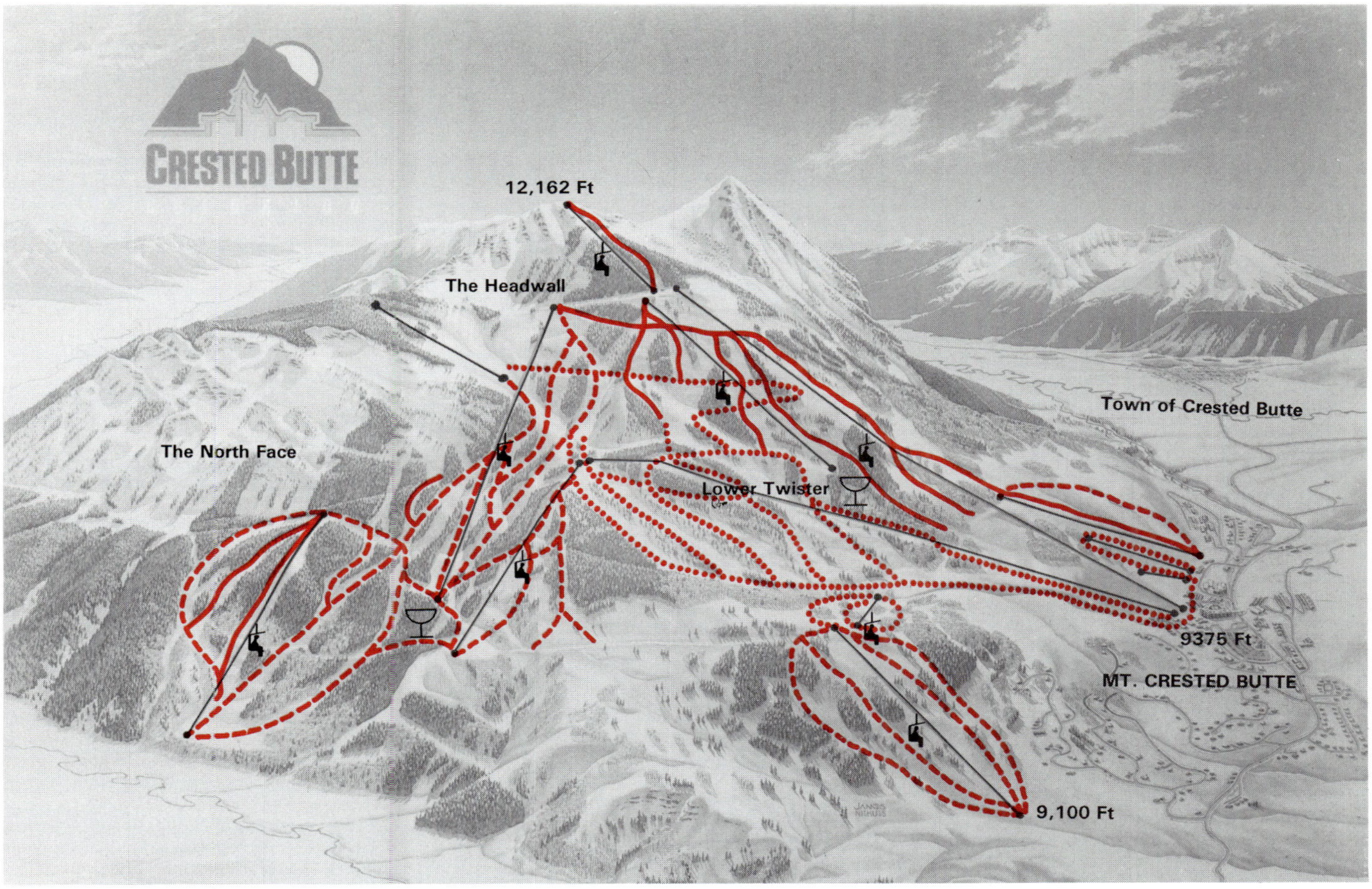

Crested Butte Lifts: Two super quads, 3 triples, 4 double chair-lifts and 4 drag-lifts

Runs: ....Easy --------Medium ———— Difficult

mountain, with several lifts to service them. Also in this area, near the Silver Queen Express bottom station, is the Butteopia Children's Center, with day care and instruction both for non-skiers and young skiers.

The Twister chairlift above the quad is used mainly by mogul mashers who stay on such steep bump runs as Crystal, Twister and Upper Jokerville. Crested Butte's ample intermediate terrain is around the corner from the frontside of the mountain, and its three chairlifts – Teocalli, Paradise and East River – offer a great variety of medium-standard skiing. The Paradise Warming Hut at the bottom of the Paradise lift is a congenial mid-day stopping place with a large sundeck and friendly atmosphere. Continuing in that direction from lift to lift and run to run eventually leads to Easy River. Served by a triple chairlift, the terrain offers both Paradise-style cruising and advanced terrain for skiers and snowboarders coming off the North Face (see below).

In recent years, Crested Butte elevated itself into the ranks of America's most rigorous skiing mountains with the addition of two super-steep parcels of never-groomed terrain. The North Face, accessed by drag lift near the top of the Paradise chair, offers 400 acres of truly challenging chutes, headwalls and tight glades. The U.S. Extreme Skiing Championships are regularly held on these formidable high-expert slopes. The High Lift, a T-bar, whose loading area is a short walk up from the top of the Silver Queen quad, leads to more extreme terrain, notably steep walls, narrow chutes and vertiginous chutes. It is also possible to hoist skis upon shoulders and hike 600 vertical feet to ski down the pristine snowfields from Crested Butte's summit.

Not an expensive resort to begin with, Crested Butte has an unsurpassed low-season offer. During a period from late November until shortly before Christmas, Crested Butte has been offering free skiing and free beginner ski lessons. Normally, early snows just begin to dust the ground and snowmaking is necessary to launch the season for the Thanksgiving holiday, traditionally the start of the ski season, but November and early December both in 1991 and 1992 comprised the snowiest such periods on record. Bargain-hunting skiers got champagne skiing on a beer budget. Ski Free's exact dates change, but it normally appears on the calendar before Christmas and again in early April.

In a Few Words: Crested Butte offers excellent skiing and a friendly resort atmosphere, along with some of America's best bargains.

Après Ski: The merriment starts at Crested Butte Mountain Resort, when Rafters in the Gothic Building starts rocking. Other spots with good drinks and sometimes entertainment are Harry Harper's in the Plaza, Casey's and the Dugout Sports Bar in the Grande Butte Hotel's lounge. Later, the action moves to town, notably to Kochevar's, the Wooden Nickel and Talk of the Town.

Several dining options are available at the resort. The Artichoke specializes in steak and prime rib, while Harry Harper's is a casual pizza spot. Gionanni's Grande Cafe in the Grande Butte Hotel is stylish. In town, Soupcon and Le Bousquet are charming and French. Donita's Cantina puts out huge portions of Tex-Mex specialties, while The Bistro and Cafe Lobo are casual and reasonably priced. The best bargain for hungry eaters is Slogar Bar and Restaurant, which offers huge portions of home-style American favorites such as skillet-friend chicken and steaks, accompanied by literal heaps of mashed potatoes, creamed corn and biscuits.

Lodging: The most convenient location is in Mt. Crested Butte, but not all accommodations are ski-out, ski-in. Leading those which are is the Crested Butte Marriott Resort (formerly called the Grande Butte Hotel). It has been completely refurbished and refurnished for 1997-98. The Sheraton Hotel at Crested Butte (formerly the Mountainlair) has also been completely redone, including a new indoor/outdoor pool, fitness center, restaurant, bar, deli and retail shops. Nearby condominiums include The Gateway (deluxe and ski-in, ski-out), Paradise Condominiums(walking distance to the T-bar) and the Plaza, which combines condo layout with hotel services. Snowcrest Condominiums are across the pedestrian bridge from the lifts. The Manor Lodge is unpretentious and located a short walk from the lifts, while the nearby Nordic Inn combines a touch of European ambiance with American friendliness.

In town, the luxury leader is the gorgeous Crested Butte Club, which offers just seven fireplace suites, a full athletic club and direct access to the cross-country skiing centre. The Claimjumper is a fun-filled B&B with humorous theme rooms in an inimitable American style. The Elk Mountain Lodge is a former miners' hotel which offers simple, moderately priced rooms. The Irwin Lodge, located outside of town in the Silvergate Recreational Area, is a charming inn in a pristine setting which is now under new ownership and has also been totally rehabilitated. Though not convenient for lift-served skiing, it is a private powder paradise, with near-private snowcat skiing on 2,400 ungroomed acres.

CANADA

BANFF & LAKE LOUISE

Height of Resort: 4,280 ft.
Height of Base of Lifts: 5,450 ft. (Lake Louise); 5,700 ft. (Mt. Norquay); 5,440 ft. (bottom of Sunshine gondola) and 7,200 ft. (Sunshine Village).
Height of Top Stations: 8,765 ft. (Lake Louise); 7,005 ft. (Mt. Norquay) 8,954 ft. (Sunshine Village)
Nearest Major Airport: Calgary
Route by Car: TransCanada Highway (Route 1) west directly to Banff.
Driving time is about 2 hours.
Resort Facilities Charts: See page 212

Located in the heart of Banff National Park, the town of Banff is one interesting resort with three nearby ski areas, two of which have their own villages at the base. One lift pass is valid for all three areas and includes free motorcoach shuttles to all three areas. For those who prefer to ski in a group, Banff Club Ski is an all-inclusive skiing programme which moves around suiting the class's ability and the snow conditions.

Lake Louise: This is one of Canada's largest ski areas, spread across three mountains (Whitehorn, Temple and Larch). The vertical drop of 3,325 ft. is the third highest in Canada, well served by lifts and restaurants with sun terraces, and the scenery is among the best in the Rockies. Lake Louise counts over 70 runs in its census, but again, that is somehow being conservative, given the vast number of possible routes across these two peaks, especially considering the expansive bowls embraced between them. Mt. Whitehorn is he main mountain, with skiing on three sides. The upper slopes are tree-free steeps and bowls, with a few easy roads contouring across the most harrowing pitches, mid-mountain provides glade skiing, and the lower slopes are thickly forested with trails cut through them.

There are runs for skiers of all ability levels, ranging from rank beginner to impressive expert. Lift service has undergone steady improvement. There are now two high-speed quads, two triples, four doubles and two drag-lifts. The high-speed quad chair that speeds the ride from the recently redeveloped base area to Whitehorn Lodge, a mountain restaurant which has become the core of Louise skiing. From there the Top of the World Express, another quad, provides access to the back-side bowls. An older alternative is to take the steep drag-lift to the summit, accessing some of North America's most impressive perpendicular pitches on the front of the mountain and, more important, to the glorious bowls and snow-holding glades on the back side. The Larch area, on a mountainside across a small, high valley, offers a small network of wide, scenic trails and sensational glades, plus some awesome hike-to, off-piste steeps above. Long chair-lifts open an array of sweeping intermediate trails, interlaced with enough runs for novices to keep everyone up on the mountain.

Banff/Mount Norquay: This is one of western Canada's most venerable ski areas, and it remains a small, low-altitude oasis committed to family skiing, recreational racing and low-key fun. Norquay, which installed Canada's first chair-lift in 1948, remains an old- mode ski area. When it was developed, it had (and still has) a front face comprised of only very gentle and very steep terrain. The addition of a section called Mystic Ridge on a second mountain was a successful attempt to raise the venerable place from being a largely local area whose major advantage was proximity to town to being a small, bright star in the Banff galaxy. Mystic Ridge provides much-needed intermediate terrain, now totalling nearly half of the 25 runs.

There are still fine, rather flat slopes for new skiers and stunning steeps for experts, as well as excellent facilities for snowboarders, but the newer intermediate terrain is a potent lure for vacationers, especially those who want to ski for half a day and shop or sightsee the other half. Lift upgrades have been dramatic too. This smallest of the three Banff areas now has a high-speed quad, a conventional four-seater, two older double chairlifts and a drag-lift on a 1,350-ft. vertical. Norquay attracts visitors who want to combine half a day on the slopes with half a day of shopping or museum-going in town, snowboarders and high-speed hotshots, who aim to join Club 35,000, an honorary society whose gold pin signifies 27 runs (35,000 ft.) off the number 1 chairlift. Twenty-three runs earn a silver and 19 are needed for a bronze.

Sunshine Village: To many Banff area regulars, this is the most enchanting of the three areas – and also the one with the reputation for the best snow, with no snowmaking needed for a season that stretches from November to May. A six-passenger gondola climbs to a high bowl, with lifts and trails going off in every direction. Sunshine is Canada's highest resort, boasting vistas and a 360-degree-skiing layout that are more like a parcel of the Alps than anyplace else in the Rockies. Lookout Mountain, topping off at 8,954 ft., offers some true above-the-timberline skiing. In European fashion, pistes have been marked across the face of this sizeable treeless mountain. There are a couple of routes for experts, more for intermediates and even one for the less skilled. As you ride the Great Divide Chair to Lookout's uppermost terrain, you cross the Continental Divide and therefore pass from Alberta into British Columbia.

Mount Standish, topping out at 7,875 ft., features a treacherously challenging headwall and acres of tamer slopes above. Below, Waterfall again will tax the advanced skier. Seven chairlifts (including a high-speed quad, a triple and four doubles), three T-bars and two tows serve all the widespread terrain. Sunshine's slopes are easy to ski around, following the sun from one lift and face to another. The newest sector is Goat's Eye Mountain, opened two years ago with the first of three lifts, reputed to be the fastest high-speed quad in the world, and exceptional high terrain. It combines sensational, high-mountain scenery with challenging runs, the easiest of which are demanding blues and the toughest of which are formidable indeed. It has been described as "helicopter-like skiing" – and that's an apt description.

Sunshine village is a carless settlement linked to the world below by the gondola. Sunshine Inn is a full-service hotel with comfortable rooms as well as dorm accommodations for economisers. Chalet accommodations are condo-like units. The community is ideal for families with small children, since there is no traffic, and cribs, pre-schoolers' classes and free daytime baby-sitting are available.

The cross-country opportunities in the Banff/Lake Louise area are virtually limitless. Prepared loipes and marked but ungroomed routes abound, especially around Lake Louise but, in truth, all over. A great trip takes you from the fringes of the Lake Louise ski area to Skoki Lodge, a historic and charming backcountry hut for lunch, afternoon tea or an overnight stay.

In a Few Words: Banff/Mt. Norquay is recommended for skiers wanting to stay close by town. Sunshine Village is a compact, friendly and very snow-sure place especially appealing to families. Lake Louise ski area's slopes go on for ever and provide plenty of variety. The best part of Banff skiing is that all are accessible by shuttle bus and one ski pass.
Après Ski: It's probably fair to say that Banff offers as great a variety of after-ski activities as any resort in North America. A favourite relaxation immediately after the slopes is a plunge into the natural hot springs which initially helped make the resort renowned, and the two-year-old health and beauty spa at the Banff Springs Hotel is world-class. Day, multi-day and ski-spa combinations are available. Thus refreshed, visitors can decide whether to shop in a selection of stores of all kinds that line Banff Avenue and some of the side streets, go gallery hopping, attend a concert or theatrical performance, go dancing, take in a movie or just decide where to eat dinner. No fewer than 10 lounges offer entertainment and/or dancing, ranging from mellow folk or nostalgic pop to thumping rock and ear-pounding disco.

Shopping is a fine art in Banff, mainly from the massive summer trade. Several boutiques offer interesting selections. Souvenirs can range from pseudo-Indian trinkets to exquisite native folk arts and craft. There are several interesting gift shops, but most might not interest U.K. skiers since they specialise in selling the biggest collection of bone china this side of Shannon Airport to American visitors. The champion shoppers in recent years seem to be the Japanese, however, who now comprise over 10 per cent of Banff's winter guests. They buy fine furs and good jewellery.

Banff is in the province of Alberta, so it stands to reason that the succulent cuts of famed Alberta beef are specialities at many local restaurants. Bumper's Beef House, Melissa's Missteak and the Caboose Co. Ltd., specialise in beef entrées, although several also feature sometimes surprising ethnic cuisine from one country or another and perhaps seafood as well. Toro, for example, boasts of a Grecian influence, while the Athena, whose name would indicate a Greek orientation, serves pizza and spaghetti, as does T.J.'s. Pizza & Pasta.

The best Italian food in town is available at Ticino, a venerable Italian-Swiss restaurant with a fine eclectic menu. Giorgio's Trattoria is pure Italian, and the Waldhaus at the Banff Springs Hotel does fondues. The dining room at the Banff Springs Hotel is baronial. Joshua's and Silver City Food & Beverage Co. serve eclectic menus in nostalgically Western surroundings. The Sukiyaki serve Japanese fare. Rundle Restaurant claims Chinese and Western specialities while the Silver Dragon is pure Chinese. Smitty's Pancake House and Phil's Restaurant serve light, moderately priced dishes at various times of day. The Chinook is the Banff Park Lodge's moderately priced family restaurant, also open to non-hotel guests. Once or twice a week, a night-time sleighride and barbecue is organised for a special entertainment.

Each of the three ski areas has its own slopeside after-ski spot. Later, to combine an elegant, traditional atmosphere, fine food and dancing, there's the Rob Roy Dining Room, the biggest and most historic of the restaurants in the Banff Springs Hotel. Music and often dancing are found at The Works and Whiskey Creek Saloon, both at the Banff Springs Hotel, as well as Tommy's Neighbourhood Pub, Magpie and Stump, Wild Bill's Legendary Saloon and Silver City. The Buffalo Paddock has drinks, video games, pool, darts and other entertainment. The Rose & Crown is an English-style pub. In Lake Louise Village,

Lodging: The Banff Springs Hotel, which overlooks the entire town like a castle, is the resort's real reason for being. It is one of the massive, turreted hotels built early in the century by the Canadian Pacific Railroad to spur travel all over this vast country, especially in what was then western wilderness. This enormous hostelry, with its Kafka-esque halls and massive public rooms, has undergone a major rehabilitation to increase the comfort without harming the ambiance. Rooms range from basic, through comfortable, to antique-filled suites. A shopping arcade, Olympic-size pool, gymnasium, on-premises ski shop and an array of dining and dancing choices are among the facilities. But best of all is Solstice, a 35,000-square-foot spa of such tranquility, luxury, beauty and service that it is rarely rivaled and certainly unsurpassed in North America's ski country.

The Rimrock Resort Hotel is an elegant aerie perched high on Sulphur Mountain with 291 luxurious rooms and 54 suites (11 with fireplaces). It boasts two restaurants, two lounges, full health club with indoor pool, video game room, day-care facilities and free shuttle to Banff. Much smaller but almost as fine is the new Rundlestone Lodge, with rooms and suites (some with kitchenettes, lofts, Jacuzzis, and/or fireplaces), which operates on the bed-and-breakfast format. The Banff Caribou Lodge, the most modest of the three, has 200 comfortable rooms, a health club with three whirlpools and one restaurant. The elegant Banff Park Lodge, near the centre of the town, is a stylish hotel, dramatically conceived and well executed - as contemporary as the Banff Springs Hotel is traditional. Charlton's has two award-winning properties, Cedar Court and Evergreen Court. The Mount Royal Hotel has the most central location, and the Bow View Lodge offers a glimpse of the creek which runs through Banff. Driftwood, Red Carpet, Irwin's. Charlton's Cedar Court, the Banff Motel, the Alpine Motel, the Voyager Inn and the Big Horn Motel form a chain stretching from the outskirts of the downtown district in the direction of the Trans Canada Highway. The Timberline Hotel is on the Mount Norquay access road and there are accommodations at Lake Louise and Sunshine Village.

Lake Louise is one of western Canada's most popular summer destinations, for there is a magnificent lake as well as a ski area with that name. Owing to the growing popularity of skiing, more and more of these accommodations are open for the winter, including the renovated Chateau Lake Louise Hotel, which almost rivals the Banff Springs for grandeur and scale and actually surpasses it for scenic location and convenience to skiing. Both are run by CP Hotels, a mark of Canadian quality. The nearby Deer Lodge is a smaller, more casual, place, and the Lake Louise Inn offers kitchen and economy units close to the ski area. Free ski buses connect all hotels with the base of the Lake Louise lifts. The Emerald Lake Lodge, deep in Banff National Park, offers deluxe cottage-style accommodations in a secluded and beautiful setting and on-site cross-country skiing. It is still an easy commute to Lake Louise, but you will want a car of your own.

WHISTLER/BLACKCOMB

Height of resort: 2,214 ft.
Height of top station: 7,494 ft. (Blackcomb Mountain), 7,160 ft. (Whistler Mountain)
Nearest airport: Vancouver
Route by Car: Take Highway 89 north from Vancouver to Whistler, 75 miles and about two hours.
Resort Facilities Charts: See page 212

Whistler Village is nestled between the two mountains which boast North America's greatest vertical drops (more than 5,000 ft. each between base and summit), over 200 runs, six bowls and two glaciers, all served by 27 of the most up-to-date lifts. They are skiable on a fully interchangeable lift ticket, which now reflects the recent corporate merger of the two mountains rather than just a business arrangement. This means that the C$31 million invested in the two areas in 1997-98 is driven by synergy instead of competition.

Whistler Mountain: Whistler is a complicated mountain, with major sectors that would each comprise a good-size ski area. There are two points of entry into the mountain's vast terrain system, from Whistler Creek via two high-speed quads, the Quicksilver Express whose chairs are covered with Plexiglas domes and then the Redline Express, or from Whistler Village via 10-passenger gondola called the Whistler Express. Both of these approaches culminate on a high plateau called the Roundhouse, where a restaurant and the top stations of several shorter lifts are also found. It creates the aura of Picadilly Circus in the sky – a place of high traffic and high energy.

From the Roundhouse, it is possible to ski back toward Whistler Creek, an sector that is gaining appeal as it is beginning a redevelopment and upgrade. Most skiers stick to the mostly easy to intermediate runs served by the Redline Express and the Orange Chair, but when the snow is good all the way to the base, an 4,300-vertical-ft. cruise down Franz's is one of downhill skiing's super marathons.

On the Whistler Village side, the delightful intermediate and advanced runs served by the Green Express, the Black Chair, and the Olympic Chair (and the broadly spaced trees between them) are long and varied. There's tremendous variety in terms of width, pitch and overall feeling to these runs. they range from steep twisters to broad boulevards, from popular runs which always attract a crowd to hidden glades which seem like private powder stashes.

Whistler's crowning glory, accessed by the Peak Chair, are five bowls from big to bigger to bigger still to bigger yet and finally to awesomely huge. When the snow is fresh, the visibility good and the ski patrol has done all its avalanche control, one of Whistler's few remaining bottlenecks is the queue for advanced and expert skiers waiting for this conventional-speed three-seater. The wait is worthwhile. Glacier Bowl and Whistler Bowl are steep and straightforward. With access close to the Peak Chair's top-station (there's also a mid-station unload to avoid the hairiest drop-ins), they lend themselves to yoyo skiing and showing off as well. West Bowl is slightly tamer, but it funnels into a drainage farther down and requires a return via the Redline Express or Orange Chair. The biggest and "bestest" bowl is Harmony plastered against the back side of the mountain. They are vast in dimension, with pistes packed down the middle and vast ungroomed acreage on all sides. The Harmony Express eliminates the need to traverse back to the lifts. Although the bowls are primarily an expert's paradise, intermediate skiers desiring the experience and the view can take Highway 86, a blue-square road along the back.

Blackcomb Mountain: The bottom station of Blackcomb's gondola is just steps from the bottom station of Whistler's gondola, giving skiers staying in the village an easy choice of which mountain to ski – and an easy way to change their minds. Whereas Whistler is a complicated mountain with interwoven trails that scatter across the mountain's complex topography, Blackcomb is straightforward with long, sinuous runs right down the fall line. There are a couple of lifts for the nursery slopes at the bottom, but the main access up the mountain is via the Wizard Express and then the Solar Coaster Express. The latter lets off at the Rendezvous Restaurant, which is Blackcomb's equivalent of the Roundhouse across the valley.

The Solar Coaster, plus the Stoker Chair and the Catskinner Chair on either side of it, access a web of popular runs for cruising or mogul skiing. The Jersey Cream Express, which angles up from the left side, offers a similar mix, whilst the Crystal Ridge Chair still farther off to the left is used less as a ski lift than as transportation to the Crystal Hut, a small mountain restaurant with a big-time view. From the hut's deck, it is possible to look up to the mountain summit and down to Blackcomb Village – exactly one mile vertical.

From the Rendezvous area, a long traverse leads to the Seventh Heaven Express, a high-speed four-seater which both serves the base open snowfields called Seventh Heaven and ferries skiers to the very summit. Here is Blackcomb's series of single- and double-diamond chutes that challenge the most skilled and courageous skiers: Pakalolo, Purple Haze, Cougar Chute, the fabled Saudan Couloir and more than a dozen others.

Blackcomb's backside, the land of glacier skiing, offers thrills of a less intimidating sort. This landscape is so rugged that it was used to mimic the Himalayas in the mountaineering sequences for the film <ital>K2<ital>, yet the snow surface is manageable by strong intermediates with more of a liking for wild scenery than wild skiing. Horstman Glacier, nestled between two steep ridges, has two T-bars and is the site of Blackcomb's summer skiing (a rarity in North America). It is possible to shuttle up and down this smooth (except where the bumps are aloud to build) steady glacier all day. A traverse away is the longer, steeper run down Blackcomb Glacier. It's a long trip, requiring a ski-out via a long road and a ride out on the Jersey Cream Express.

In a Few Words: In addition to grandiose terrain, a fully interchangeable lift ticket and excellent children's facilities on both mountains, Whistler and Blackcomb skiers may join Ski Esprit's lively classes – more fun than a traditional ski school, more helpful than a plain guide service to get the most out of skiing both mountains.

Après Ski: The big bar at the Carleton Lodge, smack between the two mountains, is where after-skiing starts in Whistler Village and at The Lodge at Blackcomb's main base. (Day- skiing Vancouverites also like the Boot Pub at the Whistler Creek base for live bands, pool, big-screen TV and well- priced food.) Because it is a pedestrian village inspired by the most enchanting towns in the Alps, it is easy to amble from spot to spot. Buffalo Bill's and Garfinkel's rock and roll in the old style. The Savage Beagle has currently popular recorded hits. Tommy Africa's Club is for pure, hip rock till the wee hours. Mellower after-ski is found at the bars of the elegant Chateau Whistler.

Dining options abound. Because Yanks and Canadians have eclectic tastes and the Japanese, who comprise 20 percent of Whistler's visitors, also like a hint of home, there is a fine mix of Western and Oriental restaurants. As an example, the Whistler and Blackcomb bases among them offer Rim Rock Cafe & Oyster Bar (seafood, creatively prepared), Monk's Grill (traditional seafood), Val d'Isere (Alsatian cuisine), Ristorante Araxi (Spanish, Provençale, northern Italian), Umberto's (unadulterated Italian), Sushi Village and Irori (fine Japanese), Ingrid's Village Cafe and Cafe Presto (both for light meals), Chez Joel (Franco-Swiss), Teppan Village (Japanese steakhouse), Planter's (domestic steak and seafood), Wainwright's (elegant atmosphere and Canadian specialties) and Twigs (award-winning Pacific Northwest cuisine).

Lodging: Whistler Village and the Blackcomb base are connected by shuttle bus and paved walkway. Whistler Creek is "around the corner" and requires transportation to the main action centers. Most accommodations in all three locations are within an easy walk of the lifts. Because the developments are all relatively new, underground parking, pools, saunas and hot tubs abound in Whistler Village.

In Whistler Village, the new Pan Pacific Hotel is located right between the bottom stations of the two mountains' gondolas, which might just be the best location at the resort. Units in the nearby Mountainside Lodge have private Jacuzzis and fireplaces. The Listel Whistler is more casual and economical. Most of the other accommodations are condominium-style with full or efficiency kitchens, though some also have hotel-type front desks and other services. Among them are the Carleton Lodge across from the Pan Pacific, Hearthstone Lodge and the Delta Mountain Inn. Radisson Blackcomb Suites at Whistler Resort is an umbrella designation for five condominium properties.

The most luxurious property at Whistler (and one of the finest in North America) is the Chateau Whistler, opened four years ago by the prestigious CP Hotel group at the base of the Blackcomb lifts. Excellent dining and entertainment, luxurious rooms, health club, indoor/outdoor swimming pool and fine shops are found in this baronial hotel. Nearby are such luxury complexes as the Glacier Lodge, Blackcomb Lodge, Le Chamois and The Marquise. The Greystone Lodge is comfortable but not as fancy.

NORTH AMERICAN RESORTS

BRIEF REPORTS

CANADA

JASPER/MARMOT BASIN, Alberta: What the resort town of Banff is to Banff National Park, the resort town of Jasper is to its northern neighbor, Jasper National Park. The town is a busy tourist centre in summer, but in winter, it is a low-key, low-cost ski destination. It is also a place where wild Canada is at your doorstep. Elk graze all around town and on the Jasper Park Lodge golf course, and you're likely to spot other wildlife too. Smaller and farther north than Banff, Jasper offers skiing on one mountain, Marmot Basin, instead of three. The ski area, which is the northernmost in the Canadian Rockies, offers magnificent scenery, excellent snow and an outstanding variety of terrain, including snowfields and steep bowls above the treeline, offering the sort of off-piste possibilities that skiers normally find more in the Alps. This mid-size area encompasses an astonishing variety of terrain, including wide, gentle beginner slopes, intermediate cruising runs and truly steep options, above and below the trees on a 2,300-foot vertical. With no crowds, lift queues for the high-speed quad are virtually non-existent, Marmot's single downside can be plunging mid-winter temperatures, requiring a warm-up now and then – making the spacious three-year-old mid-mountain restaurant is especially welcome.

MONT STE.-ANNE, Quebec: This energetic resort in the heart of French Canada provides an unusual multi-cultural skiing holiday, combining distinctly Gallic and Anglo flavours in one appealing dish. The south-facing mountain is a giant by Eastern standards, looming 2,050 vertical feet above the St. Lawrence River. The ski area has some 50 trails on three sides of the mountain. The ski area has invested millions of dollars in upgrading its lifts (among them, an eight-passenger gondola and two high-speed quad chairs), snowmaking and grooming equipment which works on as many as half of the runs every night. Speaking of night, Mont Ste.-Anne also boasts a huge night-skiing operation for those who simply can't get enough. A modern purpose-built resort has taken shape at the base of the mountains, and nearby is one of North America's best and most comprehensive cross-country centres. Quebec City, the only walled city remaining in North America and a true piece of Europe transplanted across the ocean, is just half-an-hour to the west. A number of hotels offer ski/lodging packages, and the city also is a popular option for a dinner and entertainment.

PANORAMA, British Columbia: Panorama is a western Canadian giant, whose 4,300-foot vertical is the third-greatest in North America (after Whistler and Blackcomb and greater than anything in the United States). The terrain is set back like a tiered cake, with the easiest skiing near the village, the most sublime cruising in the middle and the most challenging chutes and mogul runs just below the small summit. In addition to the excellent trail system, Panorama is the home base for R.K. Heli-Skiing, whose heliport is right at the foot of the mountain. that makes it a good bet for The small village is tucked into the hillside below the ski lifts. Small and quiet, it is a relaxing retreat.

SILVER STAR, British Columbia: The resort sits in a high basin above the Okanagan Valley in central British Columbia Purely and simply, this is one of the best family resorts around. It is a cheerful new village built in an Old West style with lifts and ski slopes on all sides. In addition to just enough nightlife for adults, there's swimming, night skiing, ice skating and tubing for youngsters. The main mountain, accessed from the snowy head of Main Street, offers abundant beginner and intermediate terrain, night skiing and some distant runs for advanced skiers. The next mountain over, Putnam Creek, offers true expert steeps—both mogul runs and tight, powder-holding glades. In addition to the Alpine slopes' terrific variety, Silver Star offers interconnected Nordic trails with the Sovereign Lake Cross-Country Ski Area, one of Canada's best.

TREMBLANT, Quebec: This is North America's newest old (or oldest new) resort. The continent's first rope tow was installed at nearby Shawbridge in 1933, and Mont Tremblant was developed in 1938. It is a big beefy mountain which a commendable vertical, but for years, it bounced back and forth among different owners, and improvements were few. In 1992, the venerable resort was purchased by IntraWest, the company that put Whistler/Blackcomb on the international skiing map. IntraWest invested a fortune in an entire new village built in the style of old Quebec, new lifts, new terrain, upgraded snowmaking enhanced grooming and, added for 1997-98, a spectacular new indoor recreation and fitness centre called AquaClub. There are now 1,000 hotel rooms, suites and apartments at the base of the mountain, including the Chateau Tremblant, a luxurious new hotel. The mountain has two base areas. The village nestles against the bottom of the South Side, while day skiers from nearby Montreal access the trails from the North Side base. The vertical rise is over 2,100 feet, which is significant in the East. The 74 named runs range from easy beginner slopes to narrow corkscrews of considerable challenge, and the combination of North American efficiency, Gallic charm and moderate Canadian prices can't be beat.

UNITED STATES

ALTA, Utah: This one of the most traditional resorts in America and one of the country's powder capitals as well. It maintains a reputation for purity. There are no high-speed lifts, no snowboards permitted and minimal grooming. It is lift-served, off-piste skiing at its very best. Alta's scenery is dramatic, and its ambiance unrivaled – as long as you are not looking for rollicking nightlife, shopping or a town of any sort. The approach to Alta is terrifying. Two snowy cliffs loom over the narrow valley. Occasionally, a skier can be seen picking a route through mountainous moguls. It is tempting to turn around and go home. But wait. That view Alf's High Rustler, if not the steepest slope in America these days, still its most intimidating, blocks the view of a gigantic hidden back bowl which offers cruising for intermediates, some respectable pitches for experts and spectacular scenery for all. A good novice area is down near the base, near a small huddle of lodges that are popular with regular guests – European-style – who return every year.

ALPINE MEADOWS, California: Located on Lake Tahoe's North shore, Alpine Meadows is known for varied and sprawling ski terrain on two mountain sectors, one a broad ridge called Ward's Peak (with a top station at 8,440 ft.) and a smaller, more conical mountain called Scott's The totality of the terrain bespeaks variety, and some hidden runs offer a true off-piste feeling. The area has one high-speed detachable quad chair-lift, two triples, eight doubles and two drag-lifts. Skiers who know Alpine well treasure its steep chutes, grandiose snowfields and long medium-standard runs. They also appreciate the nearly 400 inches of annual snowfall which gives Alpine the longest season in the Tahoe area. There are no accommodations right at the mountain, but some development is nearby, and Truckee and Tahoe City also offer lodging. Alpine is a reasonable commute from Reno, which has the closest major airport and a lively casino-hotel option. Alpine is part of the quintet that offers the Ski Tahoe lift pass, good also at nearby Northstar and Squaw Valley, as well as at Sierra-at-Tahoe, Heavenly Ski Resort and Kirkwood on the South Shore, and also on the Ski Tahoe North Lift Ticket valid at eight large and small North Shore ski areas.

THE BIG MOUNTAIN, Montana: Not to be confused with Big Sky,which is in southwestern Montana, this hideaway resort in northwestern Montana is just being discovered by vacationers.This is a large, complex ski area with everything from cruising runs to demanding glades and bowls facing in several compass directions. The 50 slopes and trails spread over 4,000 acres are usually uncrowded, and the view from the summit is 6,770 ft. summit toward Flathead Lake is no less than spectacular. The high-speed quad operates both day and night, the latter both for skiing and dining in the mountaintop restaurant. Limited lodging is available at the base, and other accommodations are found in nearby Whitefish, where Amtrak's daily train between Minneapolis and Seattle stops. The ride is exceptionally scenic and can be combined with a skiing holiday, as can ski-touring in Glacier National Park, one of America's western wonders.

GRAND TARGHEE, Wyoming: This is a small ski resort and huge ski mountain on the Wyoming/Idaho border. It is known for its exceptional powder skiing and minimal lift queues. Two new quad chairlifts, one a high-speed model, have speeded the ride up to the high ridge that enfolds the ski area. Below are two large basins that offer groomed pistes, nearly treeless bowls above and excellent tree skiing below. The area gets an average of more than 500 inches of snow a year, and with guests of the very small base village and a few commuters from Jackson, the powder never gets tracked out from one storm to the next. If you want to hog even more first tracks than the uncrowded slopes permit, consider snowcat skiing. Targhee also operates snowcat skiing on an adjacent mountain.

A day of snowcat skiing is similar to helicopter skiing but for less money and no chance of being grounded by weather.

HUNTER MOUNTAIN, New York: For anyone who wants a few days of U.S. skiing perhaps mixed with a winter sightseeing holiday, Hunter Mountain is a good bet. With 33 miles of trails of all ability levels and 17 lifts wedged onto a 1,600 ft. vertical, it contains some of the gentlest slopes in skidom; K-27, one of the most perpendicular pitches in North America; and everything in between. Snowmaking and grooming provide a season that lasts from November to May. There are accommodations aplenty near Hunter, and a growing development right at the base. The skiing is much better on weekdays, when the weekend mobs from New York City are absent, but night life is far more frenetic on weekend and holiday periods.

SUGARBUSH, Vermont: Sugarbush South is a glossy resort development with complex skiing on a huge mountain, abundant lodging at slopeside (or nearly so) and a neat little village. Sugarbush North is a high mountain known for outstanding cruising terrain and good snow conditions. The two started as separate areas, then merged under one ownership and now are physically connected by a two-mile-long chairlift. Outstanding terrain for all levels of skier. Sugarbush is so complex that it offers specific sectors for particular kinds of skiers. For instance, families virtually have the Gate House area with its own day lodge, gentle trails and lifts to themselves, and high experts have the steep twisty Castle Rock terrain as their challenging playground. In addition to abundant lodging right at the resort, quaint country inns abound in nearby Warren, Waitsfied and the surrounding area.

KILLINGTON, Vermont: The New England ski season usually starts and ends on Killington's timetable, for this massive six-peak complex in central Vermont cranks up its snowmaking earlier and shuts down its last chair later than nearly any other Eastern ski mountain. It has one of America's largest and best snowmaking systems. One of America's leading ski areas for comprehensive lift-and-lesson packages, Killington finds favour with beginners anxious for fine instruction, intermediates hoping to improve and true experts who love Killington's steepest slopes and largest moguls. Killington has 107 slopes and trails, a 3,060 ft. vertical and a galaxy of lifts including America's longest and fastest gondola, 5 double chair-lifts, 4 triples and 7 quads. A hotel and ample condominium lodging are located at the base of the area and a 5-mile access road is also lined with places to sleep and dine.

LAKE PLACID, New York: Lake Placid, having twice hosted the Winter Games, is a charter member of that illustrious fraternity of Olympic sites. There were no Alpine ski events in 1932, but the next Olympics slalom, giant slalom and downhill were run on Whiteface Mountain, a challenging classic Northeastern mountain which underwent a multi-million dollar facelift for 1980. Whiteface has a 3,216 ft. vertical, the greatest in the East, served by 9 chair-lifts and covered by an excellent snowmaking system over 93 per cent of the terrain. The village of Lake Placid is situated attractively beside Mirror Lake. There are fine cross-country trails, ski jumps, speed skating oval and bobsled run operating all winter long. It is an Olympic training site now too. Many lodging, dining and après ski opportunities are found in Lake Placid, which is actually closer to Montreal than to New York City.

MAMMOTH MOUNTAIN, California: On weekends this huge mountain, one of America's biggest, is mobbed with Los Angeles skiers. During the week, vacationers have to themselves an astonishing 3,100 ft. vertical mountain which contains more than 150 trails, open slopes and bowls above the timberline. This vast mountain is served by two 6-passenger gondolas, 14 double chair-lifts; 7 triples, 5 quads and 2 drag-lifts. The total lift capacity – 53,000 skiers per hour – is America's greatest. With an average snowfall exceeding 330 inches, a new high capacity snowmaking system as a supplement and a calendar-girdling season that runs from November to July, Mammoth is a massive and sunny ski destination too often overlooked by vacationers. Mammoth also owns June Mountain, half-an-hour's drive. Both are skiable on the same lift ticket. June is best for novice and intermediate skiers, while Mammoth appeals even to high experts. There are two lodges at the mountain and 30,000 additional beds in hotels and condominiums in the nearby town of Mammoth Lakes.

NORTHSTAR, California: One of the mid-size resorts in the Lake Tahoe galaxy, Northstar nevertheless shines as one of the most service-oriented and family-friendliest resorts in the land. The skiing on 2,280 vertical ft. is heavily canted toward novice and intermediate skiers, but lift lines are rarely a serious problem (there's also an electronically controlled, preferred ticketing system called Club Vertical to cure that) and the children's facilities are excellent. The skiing is on two faces, the front side of the mountain with the lion's share of the easiest terrain, and the newer, more demanding backside runs known as Schaffer Camp. A self-contained condominium village – complete with limited but quality restaurants, shops and entertainment—nestles at the base. Northstar accepts the Ski Lake Tahoe lift pass which is also good at Alpine Meadows, Heavenly, Kirkwood and Squaw Valley.

PURGATORY, Colorado: Located in south-western Colorado, north of Durango, this is a casual, low-key, moderately priced resort mainly for intermediate skiers who want a friendly atmosphere and basically undemanding skiing. Purgatory installed its first high-speed four-seater for 1995-96. There is a small, convenient village at the bottom of the mountain which has condominiums, a handful of shops and a place or two to eat and drink. A complete resort complex called Tamarron appeals to people who want a true hotel, while a number of inexpensive to moderately-priced hotels and motels are in Durango, half-an-hour away and linked by free shuttle buses into the evening. It is also possible to visit Mesa Verde National Park, site of the mysterious Cliff Dwellings built by the Anasazis, a sophisticated pre-Columbian tribe which simply vanished centuries ago.

SUGARLOAF, Maine: From the 4,237 ft. summit of Maine's second-highest peak, skiers find 80 trails for all skiing ability levels topped by the only above-the-treeline snowfield is the East. Sugarloaf has a reputation as a demanding mountain, but in reality, improved grooming and snowmaking have tamed much of this giant. There is even a children's adventure trail called Moose Alley. A large slopeside hotel, a smaller inn and more than 800 condominium units offer convenient lodging but rarely crowds, for the area gears up mostly when weekending Bostonians come to ride the 14 lifts, including one gondola and two quad chairlifts.

SUNDAY RIVER, Maine: No American ski destination has come so far, so fast as Sunday River, developing in little more than a decade from a medium-size, mostly local mountain to one of New England's top ski resorts. With a steadily increasing lift-and-trail network now totalling a dozen lifts with a 24,000-skier-per-hour uphill capacity and 78 runs, including White Heat which is billed as the "steepest, longest, widest" run in the East. Sunday River's snowmaking has quickly become legendary. The lodging is mostly family- and group-pleasing condominium style, but the Summit Hotel and Conference Center, by far Sunday River's most luxurious property, provides lodging alternatives. The Snow Cap Lodge is designed for economy-minded ski groups.

TAOS, New Mexico: One of America's earliest, and finest self-contained ski resorts, Taos Ski Valley is the fulfilment of the vision of its Swiss-born ski pioneer wedded to the mountains of northern New Mexico. Where else can one ski on a two-mountain 2,612 vertical ft. ski area, 65% of whose runs are for advanced and expert skiers, live and eat in a slopeside hotel with a decidedly European ambience and make a day trip to a nearby Indian pueblo, America's oldest continuously inhabited settlement- to sightsee or shop? There's no place else with the magic of Taos Ski Valley, a combination prized by skiers who want warm, sunny extraordinary challenging skiing by day and pampered living after the lifts close at night. While Taos Ski Valley feels like a mountain hideaway, the town of Taos, 35 minutes down the road, is typically Southwestern. It has become a notable art centre, and it offers a choice of accommodations and restaurants not available in the tight ski valley. The nearest major airport is Albuquerque, and a trip to Taos is easily combinable with time in the art and culinary mecca of Santa Fe, and those with more holiday time can also visit the Grand Canyon in neighbouring Arizona too.

WINTER PARK, Colorado: Starting as a day-trip area on the Front Range of the Rockies for lucky Denverites, Winter Park blossomed into first a weekend area and more recently as a destination resort too. There are 22 chair-lifts, plus skiing on the sprawling 3,000 vertical ft. mountain which encompasses 1,305 acres with trail, glade and bowl skiing. Mary Jane has moderately to extremely challenging skiing on two mountain faces, while the Vasquez area is more moderate. The Parsenn Bowl area consists of above the timber-line bowls and glade skiing below. Also, the Lodge at Sunspot is the classy new summit restaurant. Winter Park dedicates itself to new skiers with two lifts and a 20-acre beginners' area called Learn to Ski Park. Winter Park's most notable contribution is as a pioneering area in teaching the handicapped how to ski. Instruction is offered to those afflicted with a variety of handicaps, specialised equipment is available at nominal cost, and the base lodge is barrier-free. The 1990 World Disabled Ski Championships were held here, as were the '91 World Masters Championships. There is no village as such, but many condo complexes, inns and lodges and a gaggle of shops, restaurants and night spots stretch along Route 40 near the ski area.

AUSTRIA

BRAND

Height of Resort: 3,412 ft.
Height of Top Station: 6,297 ft.
Nearest International Airport: Zurich
Map Reference: 1D See page 237
Route by Car: See pages 236-237
Resort Facilities Charts: See page 212
Hotel Reference Charts: See page 227

The village of Brand stretches for almost 2km. along a wide and open valley close to the Swiss border amidst a beautiful landscape. There is a well arranged interlinking lift system. The pistes are wide, and some run through wooded mountainside. On the eastern or lower side of the village the two-stage double Niggenkopfbahn chair-lift takes one first to Eggen, 4,127ft., and then to Niggenkopf, 5,200ft. The Gulma drag-lift continues the ascent from this point to a height of 5,850ft. At the western and upper end of the village the Palüdbahn double chair-lift goes up to Melkboden, 5,167ft., and leads to the long Palüdlift rising to 6,297ft., the highest station of the resort. There is a wonderful view of the surrounding mountains from here, and a variety of descents to either end of the village or to the intermediate stations. Some of the steep north-facing, unpisted slopes offer good powder snow skiing. One enjoyable run is from the top of the Palüdlift, beginning steeply through the Lorenzital valley and then more gently for another 5km. or so to the eastern side of the village. This can be interrupted halfway to return to the main ski area by way of the Tannlegerlift. The run through the Lorenzital valley is sometimes closed due to avalanche danger and this has the effect of splitting the mountain into two sections. To overcome this another piste has been built running from the top of the Palüdlift back to the Niggenkopf and the Gulma drag-lift. The skiing is not really difficult on any of the runs and the pistes are wide and maintained. The extensive slopes on the south-west side of the village, with a drag-lift, are suitable for beginners. A shuttle bus between Niggenkopf and Palüdbahn is included in the lift pass. Attractive mountain restaurants with large sun terraces underline demi pension arrangements for this resort. There are two prepared Nordic skiing (langlauf) tracks, one in the village area of 21km. and the other which starts from the top of the Niggenkopf chair-lift 6km. in length. There are good bed and breakfast facilities and most rooms have private bath or shower, and a wide selection of restaurants. The nearby village of Bürserberg, 5km. away, is connected by post bus fares included with lift pass – has two double chair-lifts and two drag-lifts which are included in the Brandnertal abonnement (see separate report).

For those who want a child-free day in the mountains, Brand has an excellent ski school for children from the age of 4 upwards. The Hotel Lagant operates a nursery for children under 4 years, a daily service which includes lunch.

In a Few Words: Excellent for beginners and average skiers; a good value abonnement; a fine centre for the family; excellent ski school; langlauf; 4 indoor tennis courts; an indoor hotel pool at the Sporting Club Lagant and Hotel Colrosa open to non-residents; a skating rink, floodlit at night; riding; ski races for guests every Thursday evening; a popular resort with British skiers.

Après Ski: Mostly informal and lively. The attractive Scesa Taverna is the centre for tea dance sessions and has a good disco in the evenings. There one can sample a different Austrian speciality every day, accompanied by excellent draught beer. Some delicacy can always be found here late at night, and the Scesa's Alpler Kaffee is strongly recommended for those who like Irish coffee. The Brandnerhof, Jägerheim and Valbona have very nice restaurants. The two-lane bowling alley opposite the Niggenkopf chair-lift is very popular. The Britannia Pub is a favourite meeting place at all hours. There are supermarkets, sports and souvenir shops, a hairdresser, and Sport Spycher is particularly recommended for its selection of attractive clothes. Other activities include an indoor riding school; climbing school; ski tours; ski-safaris and para-gliding courses.

Recommended Hotels:

Sporthotel Beck: Owned by Werner and Christi Beck. Pleasant hotel with 68 beds, all rooms with bath, 16 hotel apartments, lounge with open fire, stüble, heated indoor swimming pool sun terrace, aperitive bar, sauna, Turkish steam-bath, solarium, fitness room and massage. Close to nursery slopes and popular with families. Riding hall 40 metres away.

Hotel Colrosa: An attractive modern hotel near village centre. Bedrooms nicely furnished, all with private bath, elegant dining room, sitting room, bar and heated indoor swimming pool, sauna and massage.

Hotel Garni-Gulma: A comfortable small modern hotel in centre of village, bed and breakfast only. Attractive bedrooms, all with bath, breakfast room and sitting room.

Hotel Hämmerle: One of Brand's old established hotels, modernised and extended. Situated 200m. from the Niggenkopf chair-lift. Attractive and spacious reception rooms and comfortably furnished good size bedrooms.

Hotel Lagant: Next to the Niggenkopf chair-lift, all bedrooms of good size with bath, furnished in modern style and every room with a balcony. Well laid out dining room approached through comfortable small reception room and bar. Small indoor swimming pool. Sauna, solarium, whirlpool, nursery and conference room.

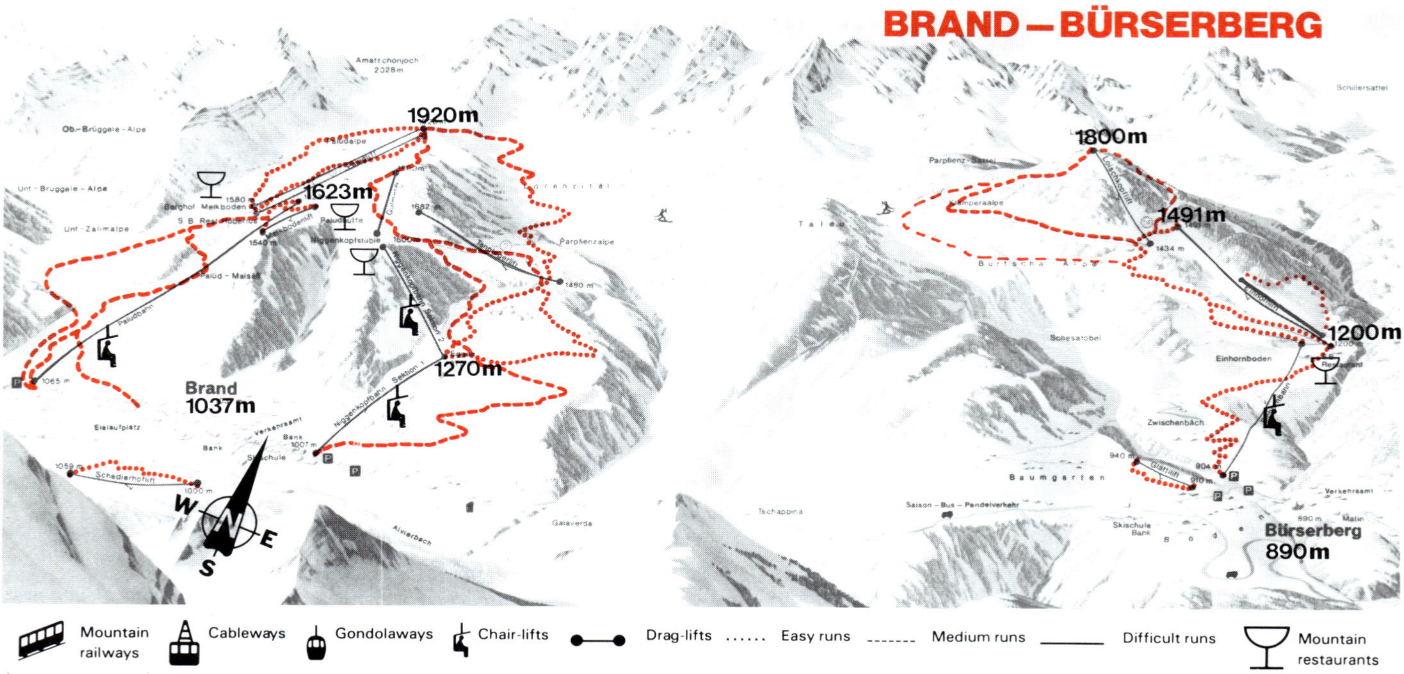

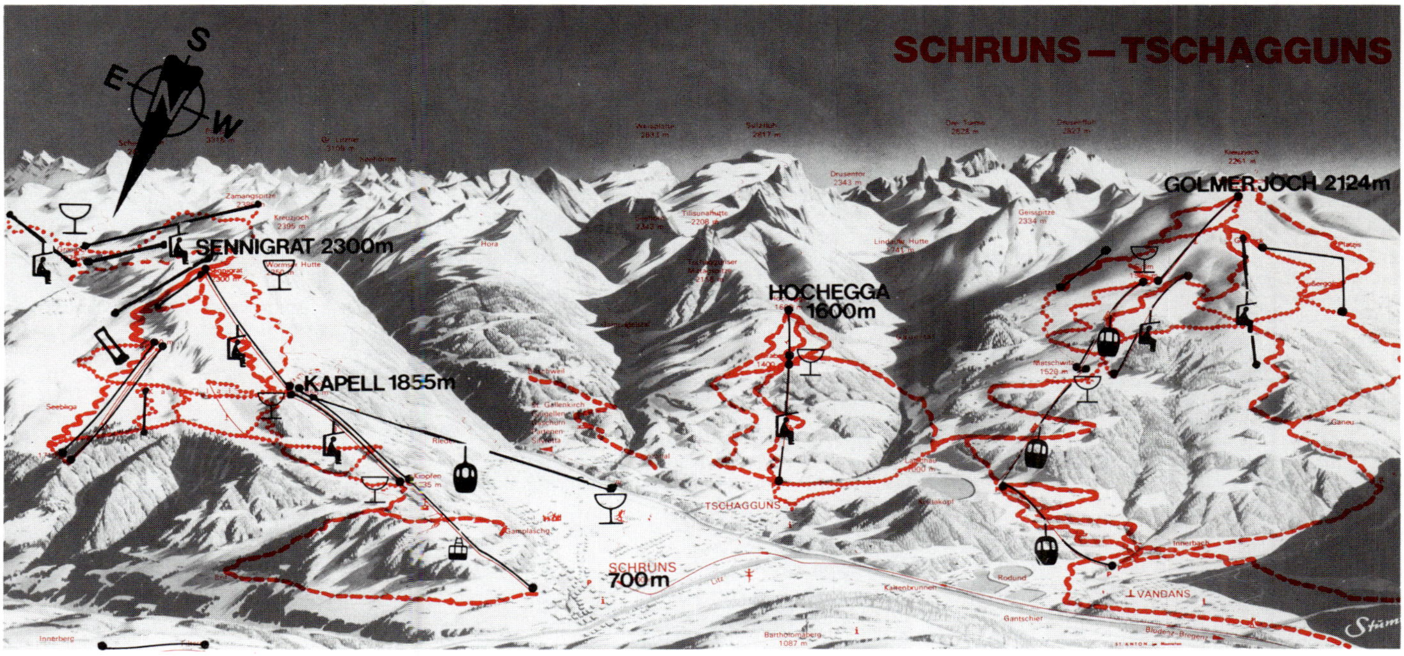

Mountain railways | Cableways | Gondolaways | Chair-lifts | Drag-lifts | ...... Easy runs | ------- Medium runs | ——— Difficult runs | Mountain restaurants

Hotel Scesaplana: An Alpine style hotel situated in the centre of the village, efficiently run by Helmut and Ruth Schwärzler, who also own the Lagant. Good sized bedrooms all with private bath, including family suites. All rooms have colour TV, telephone, bar and safe. Spacious dining room, which always has a centre table of various salads and sweets for guests to help themselves. in addition to the excellent table d'hôte, an à la carte menu is available and 3 dinner dances are held each week. Comfortable reception room and bar, large Scesa Taverna night club and good indoor swimming pool, whirlpool, sauna and steam-bath, solarium, massage, plus conference facilities for up to 50 persons.

Hotel Walliserhof: A very pleasant modern hotel near the Scesaplana, a lovely spacious and light dining room, L-shaped reception room and bar tastefully furnished bedrooms with large windows, all with private bath and balcony, swimming pool with glass sliding doors opening to a terrace. Sauna and massage.

BÜRSERBERG

Height of Resort: 2,919 ft.
Height of Top Station: 5,904 ft.
Nearest International Airport: Zurich
Map Reference: 1D See page 237
Route by Car: See pages 236-237
Resort Facilities Charts: See page 213
Hotel Reference Charts: See page 227

Soon after leaving Bludenz one comes across the small resort of Bürserberg, on the north-west side of the road leading to Brand, which is 5km. further on. The two resorts are not linked but a good bus service operates at fairly regular intervals between the two. Although small, Bürserberg is widely spread, and on the lower road one finds the ski school. The first station, Einhornboden, lies at 3,608ft., which can be reached by chair-lift from the village or by a good road. Here there is a car park, restaurants and a ski kindergarten. From this point the run back to the village is on fairly open south-west facing slopes. From Einhornboden two lifts rise in a north-westerly direction, almost in line ahead. The first, the Einhorn lift, which terminates on the summit of the mountain of the same name at 5,904ft., where one has a magnificent view of the surrounding area. There are runs down both sides of the mountain through wide wooded glades, joining the main run back to Einhornboden just below the Loischkopf lift. The ski area is small and compact and suitable for beginners to intermediates, and for those who require greater variety, the Bürserberg lift pass includes the free use of the local connecting bus and all the ski-lifts in the neighbouring resort of Brand. Nordic skiing (langlauf) is also catered for, and the 16km langlauf trail is situated near the top station of the Einhorn chair-lift.

There is also a 6km. toboggan run. For parents with young children there is an excellent ski kindergarten, high season only, taking children from three years old.

In a Few Words: Quiet picturesque resort, small but well spread out. Good for beginners to intermediate skiers. Good ski kindergarten. Long toboggan run; Nordic skiing; 30km. of cleared walks, ski safaris, guided tours.

Après Ski: Most of the evening entertainment takes place in the hotels. Although the resort is small and quiet, Brand being only 5km. away means that après ski facilities of the neighbouring resort can also be utilised when required. Supermarket, souvenir shop, bars and discos.

Recommended Hotels:

Hotel Burftchahof: Situated near to the top station of the Einhorn chair-lift. Pleasant dining room with bar. Rooms of medium size, comfortably furnished and all have private bath or shower and w.c. Each room has a balcony giving panoramic mountain views.

Hotel Taleu: Situated near to the ski-lifts, the Taleu is a modern building. The rooms are of large size, well planned and have private bathroom, w.c., telephone, safe and TV. All the rooms have either a balcony or access to terraces giving superb views along the valley. Pleasant reception area includes lounge plus a bar, dining area adjacent. There is a discothèque, good indoor swimming pool, sauna and solarium. Ski school and ski hire based at the hotel. There is also a 6km toboggan run.

SCHRUNS & TSCHAGGUNS

Height of Resort: 2,275 ft.
Height of Top Station: 7,544 ft.
Nearest International Airport: Zurich
Map Reference: ID See page 237
Route by Car: See pages 236-237
Resort Facilities Charts: See page 215
Hotel Reference Charts: See page 228

SCHRUNS

The small town of Schruns centres round the attractive Kirchplatz and a warm, cheerful and busy atmosphere pervades the air. Schruns spreads across the widest part of the Montafon valley on the sunny side and is also well known as a health resort.

A two-section cable, the Hochjoch, travels to Kapell, 6,029ft., the entry point to the Grasjoch ski area on the Sennigrat mountain. Here the Kapell restaurant is one of the largest and best mountain restaurants to be found anywhere, with an enormous sun terrace. The self-service section caters for 650, the serviced section 350 and, as all the skiing revolves round this area, skiers normally remain at Kapell at midday rather than return to the town unless they plan to continue their day's skiing at Tschagguns. An alternative means of reaching Kapell is via the Zamang gondolaway which starts about 1 km. south of the village centre. A chairlift operates from Kapell up to Sennigrat, 7,544ft., and from this point two difficult runs and one medium across the wide open north and north-west facing slopes. The 'Hochjoch taxi', a further lift, takes one from Sennigrat to Kreuzjoch.

From this point there are some easy runs down to Grasjoch-Hütte restaurant. Further easy runs are to be found in this area served by two chair-lifts and a drag-lift. Two long drag-lifts run parallel from a height of 5,557ft. to the north-east of the Kapell restaurant up to 6,852ft. and there is a further shorter drag-lift to the right. Here the skiing is above the treeline and on north to north-west facing slopes, apart from the run to the middle station of the cableway. From here one can return to Kapell by chair-lift. Two wide pisted runs of about 6km. through wooded slopes lead down from Kapell to Schruns. The recent construction of the Ski tunnel, 470 metres long and 6 metres wide, reputed to be one of the longest in the world, has opened up a delightful run from the top station to Schruns via Kapell, some 12 km in length with a v ertical descent of 5,200ft.

In a Few Words: A small town with lots of activities; compact lift system on upper slopes; within easy reach of 55 further lifts in the valley; prices reasonable and good value.

TSCHAGGUNS

Just across the Ill river from Schruns is the smaller resort of Tschagguns with its two ski areas. From the south-east of the village a chair-lift goes up to Grabs, 4,550ft., where there is a restaurant, from which point a drag-lift continues to Hochegga, 5,200ft. Two medium grade runs of about 4km. lead back to the bottom station over north facing slopes, open to begin with and becoming wooded in places further down but forming no obstacles to skiers. On the west side of the Grabs lower terminal there is a beginners' drag-lift.

3km. above Tschagguns on the edge of two reservoirs is the small village of Latschau, linked to Schruns and Tschagguns by post bus. At this point the first stage of the gondolaway, with cabins for 8 persons, comes up from Vandans. The second stage continues from Latschau to Matschwitz, 4,940ft., where there is a restaurant, thence rising to Grüneck Panorama restaurant and the Berghof Golm, 6,233ft., situated in the heart of the Golm ski area. The restaurant has a large sun terrace and live music is played there at weekends. The third stage of the gondolaway is supplemented by a quad chair-lift terminating in roughly the same area. A trainer lift is situated to the east of the restaurant and to the west a chair-lift and drag-lift.. A surmounting drag-lift covers the last stage up to Golmer Joch, 6,968ft., the highest point. From here there is a good selection of medium runs down north or north-west facing slopes and up to 10 km. in length. The Aussergolm drag-lift with a rise of 623ft. extends the variety of skiing on these superb slopes.

The upper pistes are over open country and the lower, through broad wooded glades. The difference in height from the top to the bottom station is 3,653ft., or to Vandans, 4,758ft. The top station of both lift systems gives access to the marvellous Rhätikon and Silvretta touring areas.

In a Few Words: A small but lively village, given added scope by its proximity to Schruns; also within easy reach of Gaschurn and Gargellen; medium price and good value.

Après Ski, Schruns and Tschagguns: The two resorts are within a stone's throw, only kept apart by the river Ill, so that visitors can enjoy the facilities of both resorts using either as a base. There is a great variety of bars, night clubs and restaurants. A good place to call at on the way back from a day's skiing in Schruns is the delightful 200-year-old Taube Hotel, with its large stüberl always crammed full at this time of day. Food is also available. The Cresta has a large selection of food until 9 p.m. and a smaller menu up till midnight. The Löwen Hotel has a live band in its Löwen-grube night club and an agreeable variety of food is available in the Löwen-Grill until midnight.

In Schruns, dancing to live music is available at the Zimba-Keller, Löwengrube and a lively disco at Paperla pub. There is a floodlit toboggan run from the top of the Vandans gondolaway. There are loads of good eating places in both villages and those staying on a bed and breakfast basis can have the fun of trying them out. During high season it is essential to book tables in advance. Prices medium.

Recommended Hotels:

Schruns:

Hotel Alpenrose: A low chalet-style hotel on four floors, 5 minutes' walk from the centre. Attractive dining room with nearby stüberl. Second dining room mostly for hotel guests. Small sitting room and open fire and bar. Bedrooms of good size, all with bath or shower and many with balconies.

Hotel Chesa Platina: A modern hotel, built in 1971, about 5 minutes' walk from the centre. Small and attractive dining room with wood panelled walls, bar, TV room and sitting room. Good sized bedrooms fully carpeted, nicely furnished and all with very fine bathrooms, telephone, radio and TV; wide corridors divide the rooms, sauna, solarium and fitness room.

Pension Irma: In a quiet position about 5 minutes' walk from the centre. Small, only 15 beds, very nicely furnished. Rooms with private bath. Bed and breakfast or demi-pension.

Tschagguns:

Chalet Alpila: Situated 5 minutes' walk from the centre of the village, this is a small and charming family hotel. all rooms with bath or shower, and nearly all with balcony; cosy receptions rooms and and rustic keller bar. Large sun terrace.

Hotel Cresta: A delightful hotel in a central position. Large reception hall, lounge-bar and spacious bright dining room with part wood panelled ceiling, TV room and sun terrace. Good size bedrooms attractively furnished, many with bath or shower and balcony. Large and very nicely decorated Tavern.

GARGELLEN

Height of Resort: 4,628 ft.
Height of Top Station: 7,600 ft.
Nearest International Airport: Zurich
Map Reference: IE See page 237
Route by Car: See pages 236-237
Resort Facilities Charts: See page 213
Hotel Reference Charts: See page 227

Gargellen is regarded by its many regular holiday visitors as one of the finest small ski resorts in Austria, offering a delightfully friendly atmosphere, traditional village architecture and a small but varied selection of hotels catering for every taste. Situated at the head of the Montafon valley, its position and height ensure good snow conditions throughout the season and one can ski to the door of most hotels. The kindergarten and nursery slopes are situated in the centre of the village and small children can be left in charge of the friendly instructors and/or nurses for the whole day. There are two drag-lifts serving the nursery slopes, one by the Madrisa Hotel, another by the Alpenhotel Vergalden, where beginners can perfect the lessons of the day. An efficient double stage chair-lift whisks one out of the village to the Schafberg Station where most ski school groups meet each morning and afternoon. A new panorama mountain restaurant serves traditional food which can be eaten on the large sun terrace. Refreshment may also be obtained from popular mountain huts – the Obwaldhütte reached via the Schnapfenwald run and the Kesselhütte reached via the Täli run or a short walk from the middle station.

From the Schafberg the main slopes are served by 4 drag-lifts from which one can choose a variety of runs to suit one's ability and requirements be they the tough, steep black mogul field of the 'Standard'; the deep snow of the Madrisa-Steilhang and Nidla which retain snow qualities for an exceptional time after snow falls, or the long, knee jarring Schnapfenwald Red which runs from the top of the highest drag-lift, the Gargellner Köpfe, 7,600ft, right down to the village. Beginners and intermediates might prefer the gentle slopes of Tali or the Schwefeltobel, whilst the long blue run from the top of the Schafberg drag-lift down to the village requires plenty of stamina but not courage.

Day tours, covered by the ski pass, can be arranged and most upper intermediate classes manage a trip to Klosters in Switzerland which is over the mountain ridge.

In a Few Words: A first class small resort, with a friendly atmosphere and efficient organisation, suitable for beginners to medium standard skiers and ideal for families. Ski touring available for all standards. High standard hotels. Good kindergarten. Snow conditions dependable.

Après Ski: There is a good and varied selection although Gargellen is fairly small. On the way down from the slopes, below the Schnapfenwald lift, tucked away in the trees, is Obwald Hütte, a popular stop before returning home. Hot drinks, soup, sausages and wine are available at lunchtime. The Kessel-Hütte on Gargellen Alpe is well worth the walk from the middle station. Barga, another cosy mountain restaurant, situated beside the piste, serves pizzas in all shapes and sizes. Many ski classes end their day at the cosy Stübli 'Tiaja' for drinks and a warm up before dinner. Delicious teas can be obtained at the Hotel Edelweiss and in the Hotel Das Meine. The 'Montafoner Stube' in the Hotel Madrisa, with its traditional stone oven and centuries old wooden panelling from the original house, is a very popular restaurant and its cellarbar, 'Chaverna-Disco' is one of the most frequented spots in the village. The bar at the Das Kleine Hotel is popular with locals and guests. A further favourite meeting point for young and old is the rustic 'Schmalzberg-Schöpfle' with its curling rink situated in front of the Hotel Heimspitze. In the village a Kinder menu offers good value for children's lunch. Other entertainment is organised and the very efficient Tourist Office will always provide details.

Recommended Hotels:

Hotel Bachmann: Situated in a sunny position with a lovely view, spacious dining room, lounge with open log fire. Bedrooms large and comfortably furnished. Swimming pool and sauna free for guests.

Hotel Feriengut Gargellenhof: Popular with English guests. A small, cosy hotel with Austrian atmosphere. Children's playroom.

Hotel Madrisa: Major reconstruction work in the once old-style hotel has taken place during 1970 and 1980 and the old gabled wing is the only reminder of the past apart from much of the traditional woodwork and panelling which has been re-used in the reconstruction. The hotel has beautifully furnished bedrooms with bath, w.c., balcony, radio, telephone and living area, in addition to family rooms and apartments. Very attractive dining room, reception area with open fireplace and bar; the Montafon parlour; cellar bar with dancing; lovely indoor swimming pool of rustic design, sauna, vapour bath, massage room and solarium; gymnasium; children's playroom; films and ski hire and repair centre. The hotel is efficiently run by its owners, Mr. and Mrs. Rhomberg.

Hotel Silvretta: A modern hotel with pleasant dining room cum lounge, bedrooms, comfortable, many with balcony and shower. Attractive bar overlooking swimming pool. Fitness room.

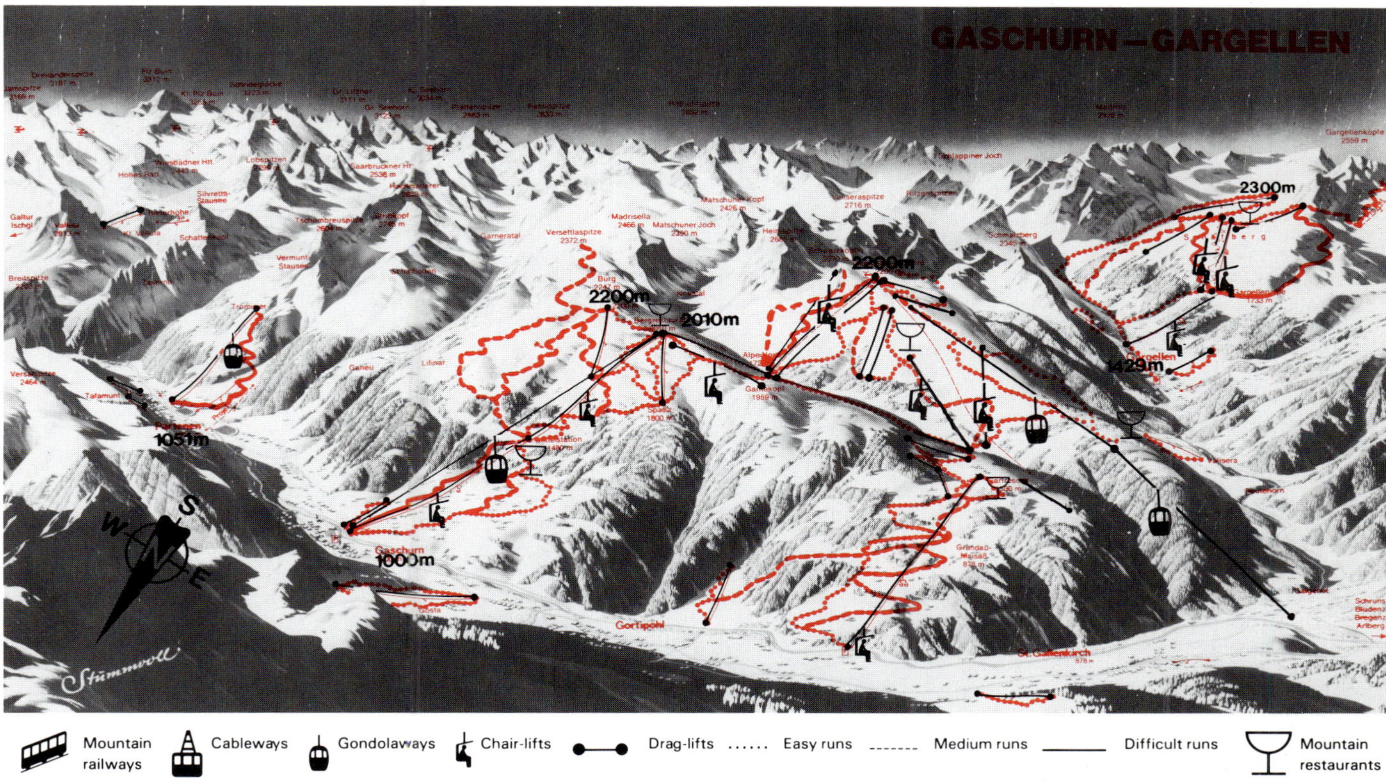

GASCHURN-PARTENEN

Height of Resort: 3,280 ft.
Height of Top Station: 7,546 ft.
Nearest International Airport: Zurich
Map Reference: 1E See page 237
Route by Car: See page 236-237
Resort Facilities Charts: See page 214
Hotel Reference Charts: See page 227

Gaschurn and Partenen lie in the sheltered part of a wide open, sunny valley in the Montafon. The picturesque village stretches along the valley and is dominated by its high-spired church in the centre. Like its neighbour, Gargellen, its friendly atmosphere is immediately apparent. Partenen, nearby, is also attractive as a village and provides good ski touring, with reliable snow because of its north-facing runs. The main skiing area is the Silvretta-Nova. A double section six seater gondola, two minutes' walk from the village, provides access to this area, whose top station is 6,595ft. The ascent of 3,313ft. takes 10 minutes. The Bella Nova Restaurant with à la carte menu, large sun terrace and indoor and outdoor bars, is situated at this top station. The runs are varied and interesting – up to 6km. down to the village, on north and north-east facing slopes. The runs are partly wooded but the pistes are wide, and it is usually possible to ski right down to the village until the end of March, sometimes until mid-April. The 'Zutl Brez'n' restaurant is at the middle station of the gondolaway and also the start of the toboggan run down to the village.

There are extensive nursery slopes on the south side of the village using the Gosta lift. Around the top station of the Versettla area the ski slopes are open and normally the snow is excellent throughout the season. The lift system is well interlinked. The Burg drag-lift runs from below the top station almost up to Burg, 7,218ft., and running parallel on the other side of the gondolaway the Spatla drag-lift starts at 5,905ft., rising to meet the top station of the gondolaway. From here there are some good north-west facing runs, some fairly difficult, down the valley to Alpe Nova, 5,643ft., from which one can either take the Nova chair-lift or drag-lift back to the top station, or move into the Silvretta Nova area as below.

Silvretta Nova Area: From Alpe Nova the new Schwarzköpfle 6 seater chair-lift and triple chair-lift rise to Gampabinger Berg, 7,546ft., and introduce one to the excellent Silvretta-Nova skiing. This area can also be reached via the St. Gallenkirch two-stage chair-lift 3km. north-west of the village, which connects with nearby twin drag-lifts; these two lifts also serve the runs on the crest. Sporadically wooded runs of about 4km. down the north-east facing slopes to the lowest station are of medium grade. The two areas are compactly interlinked and in addition, a bus service operates between Gaschurn and St. Gallenkirch to complete the circuit. The longest run is about 8km., with 4,500ft. difference in height.

Partenen: A shuttle bus travels between Gaschurn and Partenen where one finds on the left of the valley two drag-lifts serving the nursery slopes. To the right the gondolaway rises to Trominier, 5,675ft., the entry point to the famous Silvretta touring area. A minibus takes one through the tunnels to the Silvrettasee where many high level tours of all grades begin. Here one can stay at the Alpengasthaus where the food is reputed to be good and the daily charge for demi-pension ranges from 420-570 A.S. per day. The gondolaway is included in the lift pass but there is a charge for the minibus.

In a Few Words: A delightful small resort; compact lift system serving 100km of prepared runs; reliable snow; ideal for families. Suitable for beginners, intermediate standard and beyond; three nearby resorts for keen piste skiers; entry point for wonderful ski touring; average prices and good value.

Après Ski: The Hotel Silvretta Nova has dancing and an indoor pool with sauna, massage and facials (residents only). In the Heuboda disco, other facilities include Pub Purzelbaum and Weinstube 'Zum Weinbauern'. The Hotel Sonnblick, Posthotel Rössle, Landhotel Älpili, Hotel Verwall, Aparthotel Tschanun and Hotel Daneu all have indoor pools (residents only). The 'Nachtschwärmer' and Mein Liebes Montafon in St. Gallenkirch are also worth a visit. A meal at the Alt-Montafon is a must and it's essential to reserve a table as it's practically always full. The restaurant is modern, built in traditional Montafon style, with two dining areas. Most skiers go to the Kiosk with its intimate and lively atmosphere and delicious cakes, open till 8 p.m. Another après ski venue is the Hut, near the Hotel Versettla, which is open every day, and the hotel is very popular as you can ski down to it from the Versettla piste. If the weather doesn't favour skiing, you may like to take advantage of the indoor tennis hall, which has three courts and four training machines. A visit is recommended to the Berggasthof Garfrescha-Hüsle, at the top of the St. Gallenkirch for lunch and a swim in the panoramic pool before skiing back to Gaschurn. Children are well catered for at the Schikindergarten Gaschurn, open from 0830 to 1630 and providing four hours' ski instruction a day plus a hot lunch. There are three small supermarkets and a few other shops and also a sanatorium specialising in dieting.

Recommended Hotels:

Posthotel Rössle: A comfortable Montafon-style hotel, one larger wing built in 1985. The dining room and stüberl leading off it both have much carved wood panelling. All bedrooms have bath or shower, wc, TV; are bright and good size and most have balcony. Attractive sitting room with open fire. indoor swimming pool extending outside as well, two lane bowling, sauna. Central position.

Hotel Sonnblick: A modern hotel built in 1972 next to the pension, with the same lovely views. Very attractive bedrooms with wooden decor, heavy carved doors, all with bathrooms and most with balcony. Open fire in the entrance hall, agreeable reception rooms. À la carte restaurant. Heated indoor pool, sauna and solarium. turkish bath, billiards and table tennis.

Hotel Verwall: This hotel, 8 minutes from the centre, was recently completely reconstructed. All bedrooms have bath or shower. Pleasant dining room, sitting room and bar. Heated indoor swimming pool, sun terrace and sauna.

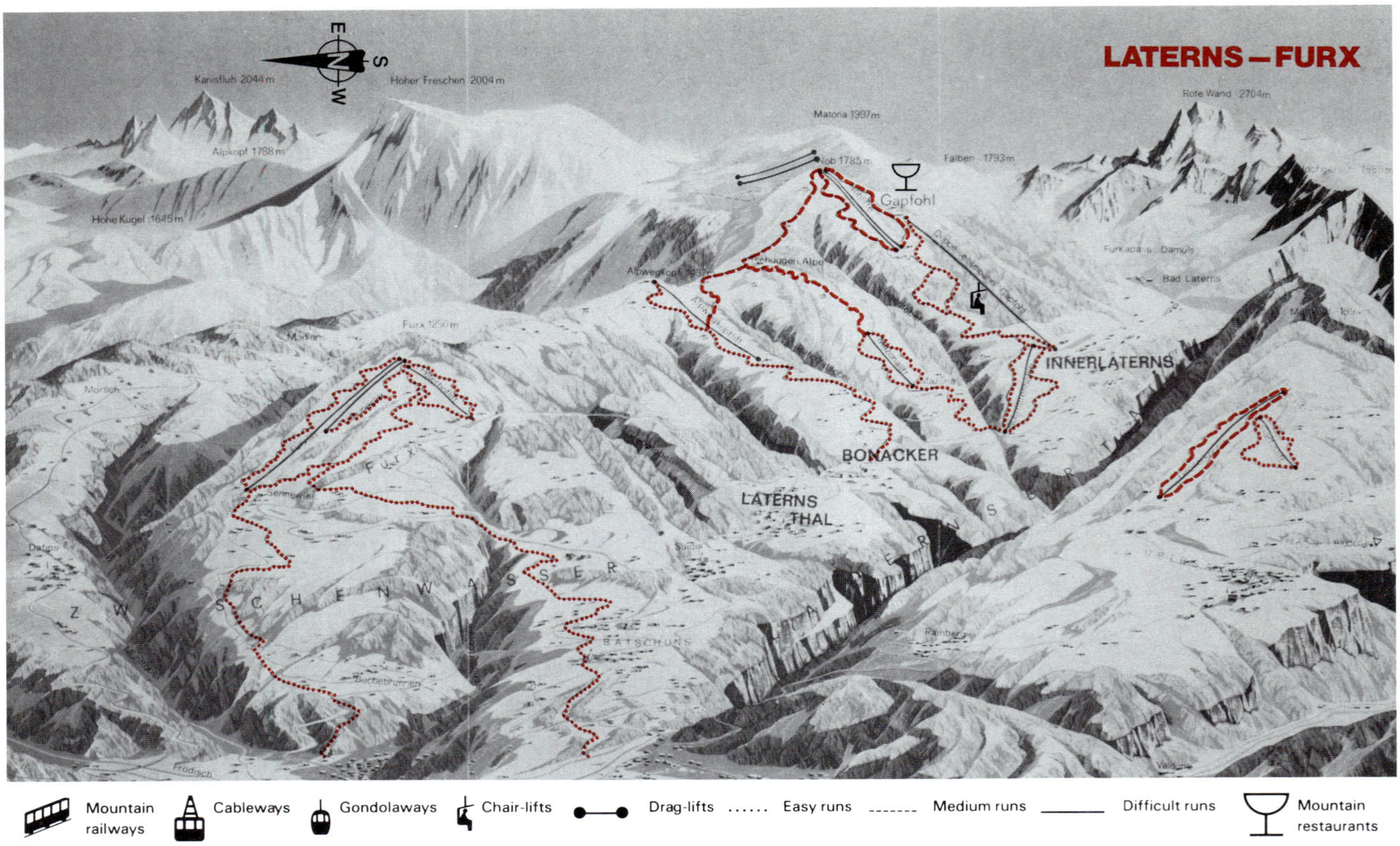

GURTIS

Height of Resort. 2,952 ft.
Height of Top Station: 4,5,22 ft.
Nearest International Airport: Zurich
Map Reference: ID See page 237
Route by Car: See pages 236-237
Resort Facilities Charts: See page 214
Hotel Reference Charts: See page 227

Reached by an excellent approach road of 8 km. the small picturesque resort of Gurtis is spread over a fairly wide area across the meadows and wooded slopes which lie below the Gampberg.

Facing north gives it the advantage of a fairly long season for a resort of its height, with snow normally guaranteed to the end of March. This also has the disadvantage of short sunshine hours in the village area during the months of December and January, which makes February and March more popular.

Accommodation in common with a lot of small resorts, is limited. There are four gasthofs and pensions and a number of flats and chalets, giving a total of 290 beds. More beds are available at Nenzing and Frastanz, which lie in the main valley, below Gurtis. Although there are a few shops in Gurtis, guests will find it necessary to go to Nenzing (7km.) or Feldkirch (8km.) in order to get a wider choice of goods. The same applies to après ski; whilst the hotels are very pleasant and have cosy bars, there are no night clubs as such. The ski area is to the northwest of the village, where the main lift rises to a height of 3,509ft. From the top there are runs down either side, or one can cross to a further drag-lift which rises to a height of 4,592ft. This lift is in the parish of Frastanz and serves longer and more difficult runs. A drag-lift in the centre of the village serves one of the nursery slopes.

In a Few Words: An excellent resort for beginners and second year skiers. If travelling by car the more experienced skiers can find greater variety at the nearby resorts of Brand, Schruns, Tschagguns, Gargellen and Gaschurn.

Après Ski: A small quiet village of few shops, but with real charm. Walks along pleasant sunny paths are available with frequent stops for a drink at some of the attractive gasthofs or chalets. The Alpenrose has live music each Wednesday evening.

Gasthof Leni: Situated on the south-eastern edge of Gurtis, has the advantage of being in the sunniest spot in the village. It is approximately 350 metres from the centre, off a quiet private road that runs along the foot of the nursery slopes. There is a small sitting room and a very attractive dining room, decorated in traditional style, serving excellent food, overlooking the valley with magnificent views through the panoramic windows. A bar in the keller is the nearest thing to après ski. Small and friendly with drinks very reasonably priced. The bedrooms are pleasant, most with their own balcony, but none with private bath, Ideally situated with a warm friendly atmosphere.

LATERNS AND FURX

Height of Resort: 2,952 ft.
Height of Top Station: 5,854 ft.
Nearest International Airport: Zurich
Map Reference: ID See page 237
Route by Car: See page 236-237
Resort Facilities Charts: See page 214
Hotel Reference Charts: See page 228

LATERNS

Situated in the Laternsertal is the unspoilt resort of Laterns. It is slightly unusual in that the resort itself is spread out and comprises of five small villages with two main skiing areas at either end. Furx and Innerlaterns.

The valley is sunny and attractive and runs east from the main town of Rankweil situated at the head of the valley approximately 10 kms from Innerlaterns. The Laterns villages are reached by a good, well-surfaced pass 7km. long. Still relatively undeveloped, there is insufficient accommodation for the facilities offered. There are 3 hotels providing 245 beds and pensions adding a further 350 beds.

There is a modern network of eight lifts which service a number of well-marked pistes, natural and man-made. It is certainly to the skier's advantage that there are not more beds in the immediate villages, as it means little or no queueing. The pistes also tend to remain in good condition. Laterns is popular amongst those lucky enough to live nearby and so tends to get a little crowded at weekends, but even then it is probably less crowded than the average larger resort. Innerlaterns provides the main lift which is a 4 seater chair-lift, 2000 metres long, rising to 5,084ft. At the bottom is a 3 star hotel with sports shop and ski school and at the top, a mountain Inn. Both have large, south-facing restaurants and attractive sun terraces. From the top station there is a choice of skiing through woods to the bottom by way of a very wide piste, which then separates to give a choice of three runs, or skiing down to a double drag-lift 1,000 metres long and rising to a height of 5,854ft. There is a further choice of three runs from here, all of varying standards. Two of the runs finish at the mountain restaurant and the other, a very easy and very beautiful piste, crosses to the Alpwegkopf chalet. Here you can enjoy a drink or a meal. The chalet offers accommodation for parties, but this would probably be unsuitable for most people as it is a little rough and ready, although a party of thirty or so who were prepared to make their own entertainment etc. would probably have tremendous fun. From here an attractive wooded piste winds down to Furx, the other skiing area.

FURX

Furx is approximately twenty minutes by car from Innerlaterns. It consists of a few houses and a most attractive gasthof. There are two drag-lifts, the longest being 1,100 metres rising to a height of 3,939ft. The pistes are simple, but do not offer enough variety to the more experienced skier.

However, this is ideal for the beginner or a family with young children.

In a Few Words: An attractive skiing area but not for those looking for a lively night life. Uncrowded runs, mostly south-west and south facing. Skiing ideal for beginners to intermediates; 1 langlauf trail; toboggan run.

Recommended Hotels:

Laterns:

GasthofBergfrieden: Situated between Bonacker and Innerlaterns. 38 bedrooms, all with showers, most facing south with balcony, comfortable and furnished in the Tyrolean style. There is a large dining room, sitting room, and bar.

Berghof Gapfohl: Situated at the top of the double chair-lift, with a large, pleasant self-service restaurant providing good meals or snacks. An attractive, sheltered sun terrace. Rustic-styled dormitory accommodation ranging from 2-bedded to 10-bedded rooms, making it ideal for parties. There is a night club in the basement.

Hotel Kühboden (Innerlaterns): Pleasantly furnished, with 29 double bedrooms all with shower, most with south-facing balconies. Situated at the foot of the 4 seater chair-lift leading to Gapfohl, which is convenient for the skiing but some way out from the centre. Restaurant, bar, self-service restaurant; large sitting room; fitness centre with sauna.

Furx:

Berggasthof Peterhof: Ideally situated at the foot of the nursery slope, this gasthof has a total of thirty beds. None of the rooms have shower or bath, but most have a balcony and are comfortable. Guests can enjoy a good meal in the traditionally furnished dining room. Peterhof is clean, attractive and typical of a pleasant family gasthof.

RAGGAL

Height of Resort: 3,332 ft.
Height of Top Station: 4,264 ft.
Nearest International Airport: Zurich
Map Reference: 1D See page 237
Route by Car.- See pages 236-237
Resort Facilities Charts: See page 215
Hotel Reference Charts: See page 228

Raggal, the only village actually on the north-facing side of the Grosses Walsertal, stands at an altitude of 3,332ft. It is reached by a good road from Ludesch, a small town at the head of the valley. Like most of the Grosses Walsertal villages, Raggal is not at the bottom of the valley, but sits comfortably part of the way up on a wide meadow beneath the wooded slopes of the Hoher Frassen. A charming picturesque village spreads out over a fairly wide area.

From all parts of the village one has magnificent views across and to either end of the valley. The 1100 beds in the village are made up from two hotels, five gasthofs and a number of chalets, apartments and pensions. There are several shops of various kinds. As it is on a north-facing side, it is pleasantly surprising how much sun actually gets into the village, although in December and January there is very little. The season tends to be restricted from February to April for this reason. Skiing is centred round a very gradual nursery slope with three drag-lifts. It is here that the ski school meets and, according to demand, up to fifteen instructors are available. The owner of the ski school was the Swedish Olympic team instructor, so a high standard of tuition can be expected. Raggal is especially suitable for the beginner with easy progression from the small drag lift on the nursery slope to the main drag-lift, which rises 853ft. over a length of 800 metres. There are several pistes from the top with a choice of either skiing down or across to the only other lift in the village.

This lift takes one up to the highest point, 4,264ft. Again there is a choice of several pistes down. Whilst Raggal would not satisfy the advanced skier, the beginner and less experienced skiers would have a lot of fun here. There are also the slopes at nearby Marul served by a chair-lift and drag-lift.

In Few Words: An attractive small resort, ideal for beginners, second and third year skiers and families. North and north-west facing slopes so snow is normally good.

Hotel Nova: This is the main hotel in the village, conveniently positioned two minutes' walk from the ski school meeting place. The reception rooms lead off an impressive hall. 20 of the 33 bedrooms have private bathrooms and some have their own balcony. The rooms are modern but traditionally furnished. This hotel provides most of the après ski in the village, with general entertainment including Austrian evenings, fondue parties etc. every night. The music is provided by a live band and disco

SONNTAG/STEIN

Height of Resort: 3,700/4,264 ft.
Height of Top Station: 5,741 ft.
Nearest International Airport: Zurich
Map Reference: ID See page 237
Route by Car: See pages 236-237

This resort is mentioned as it is both unusual and attractive, although very small. Sonntag lies half-way up the south-facing side of the Grosses Walsertal. There are seven gasthofs in the village and a few private houses.

The reason this resort is unusual is because all the skiing takes place on the opposite side of the valley, at a place called Stein. The only way to get to Stein is by way of a cable car. It departs from the centre of Sonntag and takes approximately four minutes to cross the 1,600 metres.

There are no cars in Stein and everything has to come on the cableway. Stein lies on the west-facing side of the valley, 4,264 ft. up. There is a chair-lift which rises to a height of 5,741ft. At the top there is a choice of two pistes, one more or less following the lift down, the other a wide piste that winds its way through woods. The skiing, although very limited, is most enjoyable and easy with the season lasting until early April. There are three restaurants at the top station of the cableway and a snow bar. Restaurant Berghaus Wiesa is run by the Familie Eugen Burtscher. Whilst it cannot be said to be smart, there is an unmistakable character about the place and prices are very reasonable. There are four chalets in Stein with a total of 66 beds, which can be booked by writing to the Tourist Office, A6731 Sonntag, Gr. Walsertal. It must be realised that Stein is very small. It has only two lifts and the cableway closes down at 8.00 p.m., which cuts out any evening visits to surrounding villages. On the other hand, it is the perfect place for a party of up to thirty young people or children, or indeed a ski club who are prepared to make their own entertainment, and prepared to rough it a little.

A lift pass covers nearby resorts and includes a free ski bus service. For Nordic skiers there is also a 15km. trail.

FONTANELLA/FASCHINA

Height of Resort: 3,774/4,920 ft.
Height of Top Station: 6,560 ft.
Nearest International Airport: Zurich
Map Reference: ID See page 237
Route by Car: See pages 236-237
Resort Facilities Charts: See page 213
Hotel Reference Charts: See page 227

Resorts for the enthusiast: that is the best way of describing Fontanella and Faschina which are 4km. apart.

Faschina, high up at the end of the Grosses Walsertal, is a small village consisting of three hotels, three gasthofs, a few houses and a shop. Nearly all the skiing is in the Faschina area and the valley in which it lies runs up from the south. It therefore enjoys long hours of sunshine but is high enough and has sufficient snow to enable one to ski up to the end of April in a good season. Driving to the car park in Faschina one can see the main chair-lift rising up the Guggernulli to the left which is 1,780 metres long, with the top station at 6,019ft. From the top there is a magnificent view across the two valleys and to the right, the end of the Laternsertal and the village of Damüls; to the left, Fontanella and Grosses Walsertal. By taking the piste to the right, one soon finds oneself in deep powder snow, which continues round the mountain until reaching the south-east facing slope. A fairly steep piste runs directly below the chair-lift. By taking the narrow piste to the left, one comes across a wide, sunny, bowl shaped valley. Up the centre of this area a 4 seater chair-lift rises to a height of 6,560ft. Skiing here is excellent, with runs both simple for the inexperienced and difficult enough to keep the more advanced skier happy. From this point it is also possible to ski down to Fontanella, which is not a marked piste. A further drag-lift rises from the southern perimeter of the village and goes half-way up the Guggernulli, to finish under the chair-lift. This is popular with those not sufficiently confident to manage the run from the top of the chair-lift. The lift pass also covers Damüls and Sonntag/Stein (see separate reports), reached by a free ski-bus service.

In a Few Words: For a small resort it has a good ski area; ideal for families; reliable snow; interesting off-piste skiing; ideal for beginners and those up to intermediate standard whose main object is skiing.

Après Ski: There are a surprising number of facilities for.a small resort, such as three heated indoor swimming pools, six saunas; solarium; bowling alley. Night life is on the quiet side but there is dancing to live music in a number of hotels several nights a week and a disco every evening.

Recommended Hotels:

Alpengasthof Rössle: A very pleasant gasthof run and owned by the Schafer family. It is smarter than the average gasthof with a single, pleasantly furnished room doubling as a dining room and sitting room. A door leading from the dining room gives access to a south-facing terrace, where drinks are served before a meal. Rössle is the last house in the village with the front door, like all the hotels in the resort, leading straight onto the ski slopes. There are 15 rooms, 9 of which have a private shower, and a few their own balcony. The rooms are spacious and comfortably furnished. The dining room tends to get crowded at lunch, which is not exactly surprising, as the food is both appetizing and plentiful. Also, attached to the gasthof is the only shop, which is run by father and son. This is principally a sports shop where ski equipment can be hired, but it is also a general shop where souvenirs can be purchased.

DAMÜLS

Height of Resort:4,680 ft.
Height of Top Station: 6,585 ft.
Nearest International Airport: Zurich
Map Reference : ID See page 237
Route by Car: See pages 236-237
Winter Sports Facilities Chart: See page 213
Hotel Facilities Chart: See page 227

As far as base heights for Austrian resorts are concerned Damüls, standing at 4,680ft., is one of the highest. This small resort situated at the head of a valley is really divided into two sections by a shallow wooded gully with the interlinking ski areas on each side in both areas. Located in the Bregenzerwald of the Vorarlberg the resort of Damüls has much charm and character.

On the western side the 1400m. Oberdamüls double chair-lift rises north-westwards and converges on the same ridge as the Sunnegg chair-lift which climbs up from the eastern side of the village. Runs back to the base of the former lift from both top stations are easy and intermediate over south-east facing slopes, whilst the direct run back to the base of the chair-lift is difficult with mogul and wooded terrain. One can however, gain access to the eastern area by continuing the run from the foot of the drag-lift turning left near the church and finishing near the Uga lift, see below. On the eastern side one finds a trainer lift and nearby the 1,600m. long Uga double chair-lift which reaches the shoulder of the Mittagspitze mountain. From this point via a short easy run to the west one picks up the double chair-lift from which there are beautiful views of the surrounding area. From the top of both these lifts there are easy runs back to the village and intermediate runs over south west facing slopes to the foot of the Sunnegg chair-lift, the link with the western area. Alternatively one can take the adjoining Waligsaden drag-lift and from the top return on an easy run to the village or the Hasenbühel chair-lift for an off piste run down to the foot of the Sunnegg chair-lift. On the south side the Furka chair-lift serves three runs for beginners and intermediates and also provides access to some good off-piste skiing.

There is plenty of scope for the off-piste enthusiast and a circuit for nordic skiers.

The resort has one supermarkets, post office, bank, kindergarten, sports shop and a few cafés. The lift pass also covers Fontanella-Faschina and Sonntag/Stein (see separate reports), reached by a free ski-bus service.

In a Few Words: A delightful small village, but not compact. An excellent interlinking ski area, ideal for beginners to intermediates; mostly open terrain and good off-piste opportunities.

Après Ski: Mostly in the hotels and several organised weekly programmes of events including disco evenings. There are cosy bars and cafés for a quiet drink.

Recommended Hotels:

Hotel Damülserhof: An excellently run family hotel situated close to the Oberdamüls lift. Furnished in traditional style with the emphasis on comfort. All rooms with bath/shower and w.c. and direct dialling telephones. Very attractive restaurant where a large buffet breakfast is served each morning. Tastefully furnished lounge, smaller sitting area with open fire, stüberl and bar with disco. A large indoor swimming pool and sauna. The Inge family, the owners, create a good atmosphere.

Hotel Madlener: A long established hotel with a new wing. All rooms in the new wing have private bath and w.c., also some of those in the older section. A small but comfortable lounge is to be found on the first floor; there is a charming wood panelled stüberl and beneath the dining room a keller bar and disco where candlelight zither evenings are often held – it is also the venue for fondue and glühwein parties. The hotel is situated 5 minutes' walk from the Uga chair-lift and it is well run by the Madlener family.

KLÖSTERLE

Height of Resort: 3,608 ft.
Height of Top Station: 7,166 ft.
Nearest International Airport: Zurich
Map Reference: ID See page 237
Route by Car: See pages 236-237
Resort Facilities Chart: See page 214
Hotel Reference Charts: See page 228

Situated in the central part of Klostertal valley, away from the by-pass for heavy traffic; the village is on the southern side of the valley so it catches the sun. It consists of 35 hotels and pensions providing some 700 beds. The skiing in this part of the valley is reached by a modern gondolaway, installed for the 1997/98 season, each cabin holding 8 persons. It is situated midway between Klösterle and Wald. It is 2,150 metres long and rises in a southerly direction to 6,051ft. where there is a self-service restaurant and sun terrace with magnificent views to all points of the compass.

Nearby drag-lifts serve the excellent nursery slopes. The Obermuri 4-seater chair-lift, 1,950 metres long, rises in an easterly direction to 7,166ft., vertical rise 1,115ft. From this point there are runs, west facing, down to the restaurant suitable for all grades; or one can bypass the restaurant, a few metres before reaching it, and take the north facing run back to the bottom of the gondolaway. On the eastern side, two further drag-lifts serve intermediate open north-east facing slopes to the restaurant and north facing runs back to the village. Nordic skiing and.curling is catered for and there is a free bus service connecting with the lifts.

In a Few Words: A good snow area and its mainly north facing slopes mean a long season. Five smaller resorts in the area also provide skiing whilst the larger resorts such as Lech, Zürs, Stuben and St. Anton are almost on the doorstep. 15 instructors form the very good ski school. Excellent for families with young children.

Après Ski: A quaint village which appears quiet during the day, due to the skiing being a little outside the village, fairly lively at night. There are two discothèques and several attractive bars, one is a converted monastery, run by Fam. Salzgeber.

Recommended Hotels:

Klösterle-Ferienheim Albona: A Tyrolean styled pension with 20 beds in single, twin and 3 bedded rooms and 2 apartments with bedroom, sitting room, bath & wc. Most rooms have balcony and some are with shower. Pleasant dining and sitting rooms. Underneath is a supermarket and the original Keller Bar with dancing.

STUBEN

Height of Resort: 4,592 ft.
Height of Top Station: 7,872 ft.
Nearest International Airport: Zurich
Map Reference: 2D See page 237
Route by Car: See pages 236-237
Resort Facilities Charts: See page 216
Hotel Reference Charts: See page 229

Stuben is situated at the end, and in the widest part of the valley immediately beneath the Arlberg Pass, which takes the traffic on to Lech, Zürs and St. Anton. The village itself is situated to the right of the main road and includes a few shops and about six hotels and pensions with a total of 630 beds. The houses and hotels are all huddled very closely together, making the central street appear both steep and narrow. The village is quaint and has a character of its own. It is fairly expensive.

The most important development for Stuben was the installation of a triple chair lift in 1980, from Rauz to the Ulmer Hütte area, thus providing skiers from Stuben access to the Valluga skiing in St. Anton where two additional lifts were completed at the same time. Rauz is reached from Stuben by taking the chair-lift to the first station on the Albona which serves an easy run down to Rauz.

Stuben's immediate skiing is in two principal areas. The first, for beginners, is situated on the opposite side of the road, a sunny nursery slope served by two drag-lifts. The second area is catered for by a two stage chair-lift rising to a height of 7,872ft., on the Albona mountain. From the top there are fine views across to Zürs in one direction and St. Anton in the other. This area is a paradise for the experienced skier and the south side provides sunny skiing in the months of December and January. Beginners and less experienced skiers can ski on this side by taking the chair-lift to the middle station, where there is a small restaurant. There are several grades of piste down the Albona, the most difficult more or less follows the line of the chair-lift. By taking the main piste to the left one quickly come upon a second beautiful valley with a drag-lift running up the centre. From the top of the drag-lift is an alternative route down the Albona. From here one can ski to the half-way station or straight down to the bottom. Whichever run is taken, all offer the same good conditions. The snow on the Albona, as well as in the village, tends to be deeper than the surrounding districts. There is no logical explanation for this, but as a result the skiing is generally good until late spring.

In a Few Words: Always masses of snow, a good area for medium to good skiers. Though beginners catered for, not the most suitable resort for them and not practical for young children. Stuben's north and north-west facing slopes provide excellent skiing into late season. The link with St. Anton opens up this vast ski area and with Zürs and Lech circuit almost next door, what more could one ask for!

Après Ski: This is mainly a hard and fast skiing village, with the usual amenities, two indoor swimming pools and four sauna baths. Night life is good and thoroughly enjoyable.

Recommended Hotel:

Hotel Albona: A very comfortable 'B' class hotel, situated in the centre of town, 2 minutes walk from the chair-lift. All rooms have private bath or shower and are very comfortably furnished. There is a good bar and sitting room. The dining room is traditionally furnished and good food is served by helpful and willing waiters. In the Keller a disco plays every night. The night club seems very popular and everyone appears to enjoy themselves in the attractive decor and cosy atmosphere.

LECH am ARLBERG

Height of Resort: 4,712 ft.
Height of Top Station: 8,099 ft.
Nearest International Airport: Zurich
Map Reference: 2D See page 237
Route by Car: See pages 236-237
Resort Facilities Charts: See page 214
Hotel Reference Charts: See page 228

This international resort is 15km. from Langen on the main railway line and enjoys great popularity. Its altitude is comparatively high as Austrian resorts go and good snow conditions therefore normally prevail throughout the season. The village is open and sunny and popular with families. It soon becomes heavily booked so it is advisable to book early. The traditional style hotels are well designed and comfortable and provide a variety of evening entertainment. In addition to its own extensive skiing area, Lech is interlinked with Zürs and the hamlets of Oberlech and Zug, with a great variety of lifts giving access to some magnificent downhill runs. This forms part of the Arlberg ski area with 85 lifts serving 260km. of prepared runs under one pass. The old drag-lift at Rotschrofen has been removed and a 2 seater chair-lift installed. The upper station is at a higher level and the run down is much more attractive and varied. The bottleneck at Steinmäder has been relieved by the installation of a 4 seater chair-lift which increases the capacity from 1385 to 2880 persons per hour. The two Rüfikopf cablecars (capacity 1300 per hour), rise from the centre of the village to Rüfikopf, 7,637ft., with a restaurant at the top. Here one enters the Zürs ski area and the 5km. run to Zürs can be enjoyed by skiers of most standards. The two runs back to Lech from Rüfikopf are however much more difficult and for the experienced only. A further run from Zürs, taking the chair-lift to Seekopf and descending to Lech via Madloch is recommended for average to higher standard skiers. There are a great number of lifts on the western side of the village covering the Lech/Oberlech area,

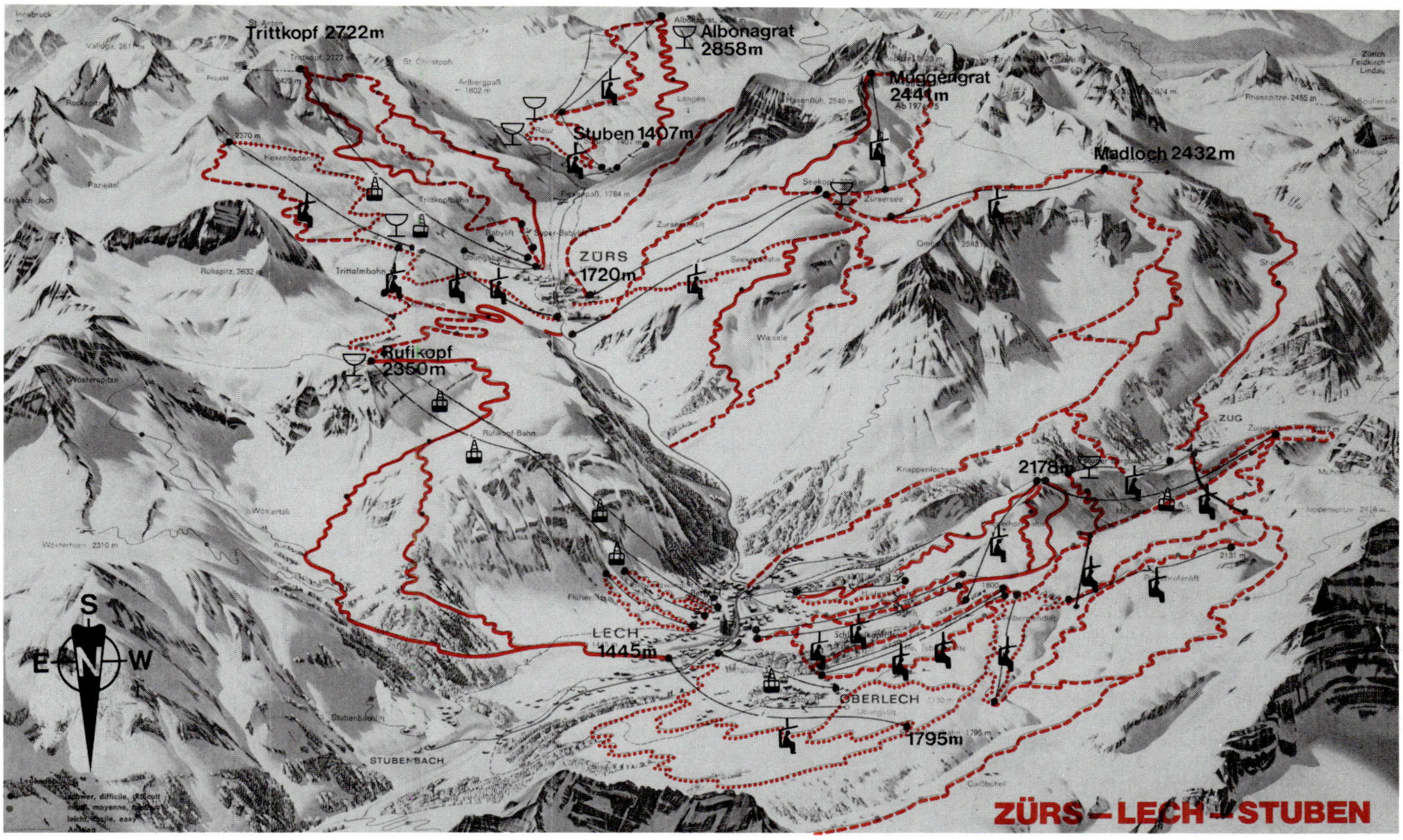

Mountain railways | Cableways | Gondolaways | Chair-lifts | Drag-lifts | ...... Easy runs | ------- Medium runs | ______ Difficult runs | Mountain restaurants

including a cable-car and chair-lifts enabling the less experienced skier to take advantage of these runs. The installation of two chair-lifts, one 2-seater and one 4, at Schlegelkopf has improved the flow in this area. From the top of the Schlegelkopf lift a short run leads to the Kriegerhorn chair-lift, with a top station of 7,078ft., where there is a choice of runs back to Lech or to Zug. From Zug the chair-lift returns to the Kriegerhorn and the location of the popular Palmenalpe Restaurant, from which one can then ski to Oberlech or Lech. Further lifts extend the range of this area, which provides the opportunity for all standards of skiers to enjoy a wide variety of runs.

The Short schuss speed recorded run near the Weibermahd chair-lift is very popular. Electronic light barriers record one's speed, which is displayed at the finishing line in kilometres per hour. There is also a pleasant Nordic ski trail which follows the line of the river from Lech to a point past Zug.

Beginners and Children: There are two very good nursery slopes, the Schwarzwand and the Flühen, both served by button lifts with a vertical rise of 262ft. These are situated close to the Berghof Hotel, who have installed an extended rope baby lift at the base of the Schwarzwand nursery slope.

In a Few Words: Sunny, well organised resort. Well planned lift system; excellent hotels; night life fun; suitable for families; kindergarten; interesting walks for non skiers; skating rink; curling; toboggan run; langlauf; ski schools also offer instruction in carving, Telemark, snowboarding and paragliding; indoor tennis and squash courts; expensive.

Après Ski: The entertainment scene is very lively: several restaurants, one hotel with band and several discothèques. Popular night venues include Pub Pfefforkörndl, the disco Sidestep in the Hotel Krone and the disco Klausur in the hotel Almhof Schneider. Also fairly crowded is the après ski club discothèque. Tea dancing takes place at the Tannbergerhof as well as in the evening. The Tannbergerhof is right in the centre of the village and a favourite meeting place. A visit to the Berghof restaurant is recommended, and so is it to that of the Hotel Post. The Madlochblick has a very pleasant restaurant decorated in traditional Austrian style; Café Charly provides Italian dishes; or, under a fine night sky, take a sleigh ride to the Gasthof Rote Wand in Zug, which specialises in fondues, for a quite different and lovely evening. There are bars outside when it's sunny, which add to the party mood. The shops are good but expensive. There is a kindergarten open Sunday to Friday, and many lovely walks.

Recommended Hotels:

Hotel Berghof: In a sunny position near the Rüfikopf cableway and run by the friendly Burger family, this hotel is tastefully designed and decorated and provides a high standard of comfort. Excellent cuisine. Bar with open fire.

Haus Rudboden: Very nice small bed and breakfast, with meals next door at the Madlockblick Hotel. Very reasonable in price. 15 beds, some rooms with bath or shower, some with balcony, 5 minutes from centre.

Hotel Tannbergerhof: One of Lech's leading hotels centrally situated and efficiently run by Hilde Jochum. Attractive reception rooms furnished in Tyrolean style. Award winning restaurant. All bedrooms with bath/shower, wc, telephone, radio and TV. Cosy disco and bar with tea dancing and again in the evening. There is a swimming pool and whirl pool for hotel guests in Chalet Hilde, 8 minutes from the hotel.

ZÜRS am ARLBERG

Height of Resort: 5,590 ft,
Height of Top Station: 8,036 ft.
Nearest International Airport: Zurich
Map Reference: 2D See page 237
Route by Car: See pages 236-237
Resort Facilities Charts: See page 216
Hotel Reference Charts: See page 229

Zürs is a small, international resort of 24 hotels and pensions, with a few shops, 8km. from Langen on the main railway, and 5km. by road from Lech. Easily reached by rail, bus or car from Zurich, the main visitors being Austrian and German business and professional people together with a number of North American, Australian, a few British and other European nationalities. All facilities and hotels being of the highest standard, thoroughly recommended to those seeking the ultimate in skiing and good living, without the hustle and bustle of larger busy resorts, but not for those seeking diversions such as shops and other activities.

Zürs lies in a sunny valley well above the tree line enjoying a long season. Lifts direct from the village cover the slopes on both sides of the valley. Runs end back at the village, all bottom stations can be skied to from any of the top stations.

To the east, a two stage triple chair-lift, with restaurant at the middle station, leads to Hexenboden, 7,702ft., medium and difficult runs lead down to Zürs. Parallel to this lift, from the other end of the village, a cableway rises to Trittkopf, 7,874ft., runs from here are of advanced standard. On the western side, a detachable, high speed, quadruple chair-lift, new in 1987, and a long drag-lift from the village centre, lead to Seekopf, 7,176ft., with restaurant overlooking the frozen lake, Zürsersee. From here a two-seater chair-lift leads to Muggengrat, 8,038ft., and provides access to north and north west facing slopes with short, medium and steep runs back to the Seekopf, or an initially steep, then fairly easy run direct to the village via the Flexen Pass. Also from Seekopf, the Madloch chair-lift rises to 7,904ft., with easy runs back to Zürs, alternatively, medium standard, or above skiers, can embark on the beautiful run to Lech, returning to Zürs by way of the twin Rüfikopf cableways.

There is considerable scope in the Zürs area for 'off' piste skiing, both near to and away from the piste with everything from extreme to easy. A point of some interest is the extensive skiing area available without the slopes being cluttered with uphill transport installations. Piste machines seldom work during skiing, a practice some other resorts could follow to advantage. Even when many resorts suffer from the lack of snow the meticulous attention to detail by the piste machine crews ensures that the pistes are kept in the best possible condition.

Discounted period lift passes help to reduce the number of day visitors. The high standard of behaviour of skiers at the lifts and on the slopes was of particular note. The completely connected, extensive skiing of Zürs and Lech can be greatly increased, nearby St. Christof, Stuben and St. Anton, being on the same ski pass, but require a bus (not on ski pass) or taxi connection.

The ski school maintains a very high standard; classes are well balanced and not too large.

Three small lifts near to the village provide beginner slopes. A slalom course near to the Trittkopf cableway and a giant slalom course near the middle drag-lift have free timing facilities for general use.

In a Few Words: Built specifically as a ski resort, with excellent snow conditions, high standard hotels and ski school. Snow-surfing, paragliding, and helicopter skiing service. Demand for accommodation exceeds supply, a recent survey showing some 80% of visitors having visited Zürs at least five times. Expensive but good value.

Après Ski: For lunch or after skiing, the Hirlanda or Mathies are popular and excellent. Après ski is generally sophisticated with a choice of bars and nightclubs mainly in hotels. The younger set go for the Zürserl at the Edelweiss; and the Hotel Alpenrose is very popular; the Vernissage Galerie Bar is one of the late night drinking spots. There are also discothèques in the luxurious Hotel Zürserhof and the Zürsersee.

Recommended Hotels:

Hotel Alpenrose Post: One of Austria's largest winter sports hotels and modernised throughout, spacious reception, rooms attractively furnished, comfortable bedrooms, swimming pool and sauna.

Hotel Edelweiss: In the centre of the village, a popular hotel with a warm and friendly atmosphere. Bedrooms particularly attractive, all with private bath or shower; apartments; large comfortable lounge and elegant dining room, restaurant Chesa Verde. Dancing in the evenings, discothèque Zürserl.

Hotel Lorünser: An extremely attractive and well designed hotel with traditional Tyrolean decor. There are 4 dining rooms, elegant and beautifully furnished, 3 comfortable sitting rooms and a bar. Bedrooms are of a good size and tastefully furnished. 2 whirlpools, sauna, solarium, massage and fitness room.

Haus Mathies: Entirely rebuilt in 1981. Exceptionally attractive, charming and popular stüberl, dining room, sitting room and bar. All the 23 rooms have a private bath.

Hotel Zürserhof: A large luxury hotel with 190 beds, attractive bedrooms all with private bath, apartments with open fireplace, TV, ice box etc. Elegant and beautifully furnished reception rooms, bar, sauna, solarium, dancing in the evenings in the 'Galaxy' disco. Many sports facilities, including a tennis hall, bowling, billiards, and golf driving range. Children's playroom.

ST. ANTON am ARLBERG

Height of Resort: 4,210 ft.
Height of Top Station: 9,222 ft.
Nearest International Airport: Zurich
Map Reference: 2D See page 237
Route by Car: See pages 236-237
Resort Facilities Charts: See page 215
Hotel Reference Charts: See page 228

An international resort stretching out along each side of the main street which runs parallel to the main railway line. Famous for its excellent ski school, St. Anton's four main ski areas plus the direct link with the Stuben area provides a great variety of skiing favouring the intermediate to advanced skiers.

Furthermore, its proximity to the resorts of Lech and Zürs adds to the enormous selection of runs. In common with a number of resorts, St. Anton is leading the way with snow machines. Some 59 machines are strategically placed between the village and Galzig and the Rendl ski areas thus ensuring good snow on the runs down from these stations.

Galzig Area: A fast cable-car goes up to Galzig, 6,860ft., where there is a large self-service and à la carte restaurant. Various short runs lead to the bottom and 2 drag-lifts plus two 4 seater chair-lifts return to Galzig. From here too there is an enjoyable run to St. Christoph, which can be followed by a journey by a 4 seater chair-lift back to Galzig. Most of these runs are of medium standard, the steeper ones to the village being more difficult. A 4 seater chair-lift allows skiers from the Galzig area to reach Gampen without coming back to the village.

Valluga Area: The cable-car journey from Galzig to Vallugagrat, 8,750ft., is fairly spectacular, in some places 700ft. from the ground. It is worth taking this trip and also visiting the peak of the Valluga, 9,222ft., with its all round view of the mountain tops of the surrounding countries. The three main runs down depart eastward from Vallugagrat, near the top of the Vallugalift, via Walfagehrjoch-Ulmerhütte, Mattunjoch, or Schindlerkar, all medium difficult to very difficult in standard. These runs are all popular and to avoid long queueing for the cable-car a system of stamping one's skis with the number of the cable-car one will travel on, allows one to ski elsewhere whilst waiting for the Valluga cable-car. The opening of the two 3 seater chair-lifts, one from Rauz to Ulmerhütte, and the other from below Ulmerhütte to Schindlergrat has reduced queueing considerably.

Gampen-Kapall: A mountain railway and parallel, a 4-seater chair-lift take one from the village to Gampen, 6,100ft., with its self-service restaurant, sun terrace and good nursery slopes. From here there are varied runs back to the village. Two surmounting chair-lifts rise from Gampen to Kapall, where there is a further restaurant and drag-lift. Here there is a choice of skiing back to Gampen or over the top to join the Valluga/Mattun run or the fairly difficult St. Jakob/Nasserein run.

Rendl Area: The construction of two double chair-lifts opened up a huge deep snow skiing area on the Rendl. The lower station is situated 10 minutes from the village and a ski shuttle bus operates throughout the day from the level crossing. The skiing is reached by gondolaway taking some 15 minutes to reach Brandkreuz, 6,888ft., where there is a large self-service restaurant and sun terrace. Below this the Gampberg lift rises to Gampberg, 7,872ft. In addition there are two drag-lifts, one of these a long one from Upper Moostal to Brandkreuz. The slopes in this area face in westerly to northerly direction, improving the range of St. Anton's skiing. There are two main routes back to the village, one via Brandkreuz and lower Moostal over varied, open, mogul and wooded slopes, medium to difficult in standard, or the direct route to St. Anton from Gampberg, with excellent powder snow on the higher slopes. This is a very steep and difficult run, particularly where it is wooded, and inadvisable without a guide because of the cliffs and danger of avalanching. A slalom course with starting gates has been set up in this area.

Stuben Link: The installation of a triple chair-lift from Rauz to the Ulmer Hütte means that skiers from St. Anton can enjoy the very fine skiing on Stuben's Albona mountain (for details see Stuben). It should also be mentioned that a bus service runs between Rauz and Zürs making the former a very important junction point. There is a 'fun' run from the Ulmer Hütte down and across the road continuing along an empty river valley to Stuben.

Arlberg Ski Pass: There is now only one ski pass which covers all areas – Lech, Zürs, Stuben, St. Christoph, St. Anton and the Sonnenkopf Ski area in the Klostertal. The Post bus runs frequently during the day between St. Anton and Lech/Zürs.

Nordic skiing (langlauf) is well catered for, with 40km. of prepared tracks and also a langlauf ski school at Nasserein with equipment hire.

In a Few Words: An international resort, the experienced skier will benefit from it most although beginners are well catered for; excellent ski schools with some 250 ski instructors. In the main expensive but one can enjoy a reasonably priced holiday at the less popular restaurants and bars.

Après Ski: Plenty of variety, though not cheap, and mostly fairly crowded. There is a wide choice of cafés serving delicious hot chocolate and cream cakes, and draught beer is often available. The nightclubs include discos at the Postkeller, Amadeus, and a small nightclub with accordionist at the Hotel Alpenhof.Two spots under the Sport Hotel are the Stanton and the more expensive 'Drop In' discothèque. Pub 37 is small with a friendly atmosphere providing draft lager and beer. The Krazy Kangaruh situated above the village has long been popular with its disco dancing, whilst one can enjoy a good meal in the restaurant: it also serves cheap drinks during the 'Happy hour' 3-4p.m. The Piccadilly, next to the Hotel Post has a large bar with draft beer, loud music, but a good atmosphere. The Nassereinhof offers excellent food at very reasonable prices and Rodelhütte above Nasserein is popular and here food is cooked on the spot. One can enjoy a relaxing evening in the comfortable bar and disco at the Hotel Alte Post where prices are reasonable, whilst the Montjola is the place for excellent fondues cooked in wine. Other activities include bowling, an indoor hotel swimming pool, sauna, and a skating rink. indoor tennis hall with 3 courts and a squash court.

Recommended Hotels:

Hotel Arlberg: Large hotel 10 minutes from village centre. Large modern dining room, attractively furnished in Tyrolean style. Comfortable lounge and bar, à la carte restaurant, stüberl, indoor swimming pool, sauna, Turkish bath and solarium.

Haus Bergheim: This is an excellent bed and breakfast pension run by Walter Tscholl, and is situated next to the cableway terminal. Friendly and efficient service.

Hotel Post: This well-known hotel with 120 beds is in the centre of the village, within 3 minutes walk from the lifts. All rooms with bath or shower. There are 2 dining rooms and a large comfortable lounge, 2 bars, 'Postkeller', with live music and Pub Piccadilly. Relax area with sauna, steambath, jacuzzi and solarium.

Hotel Rosanna Stüberl: A first-class small hotel, built on the old Rosannastüberl site. All bedrooms with bath or shower. Pension arrangements half board or full board. À la carte restaurant and bar.

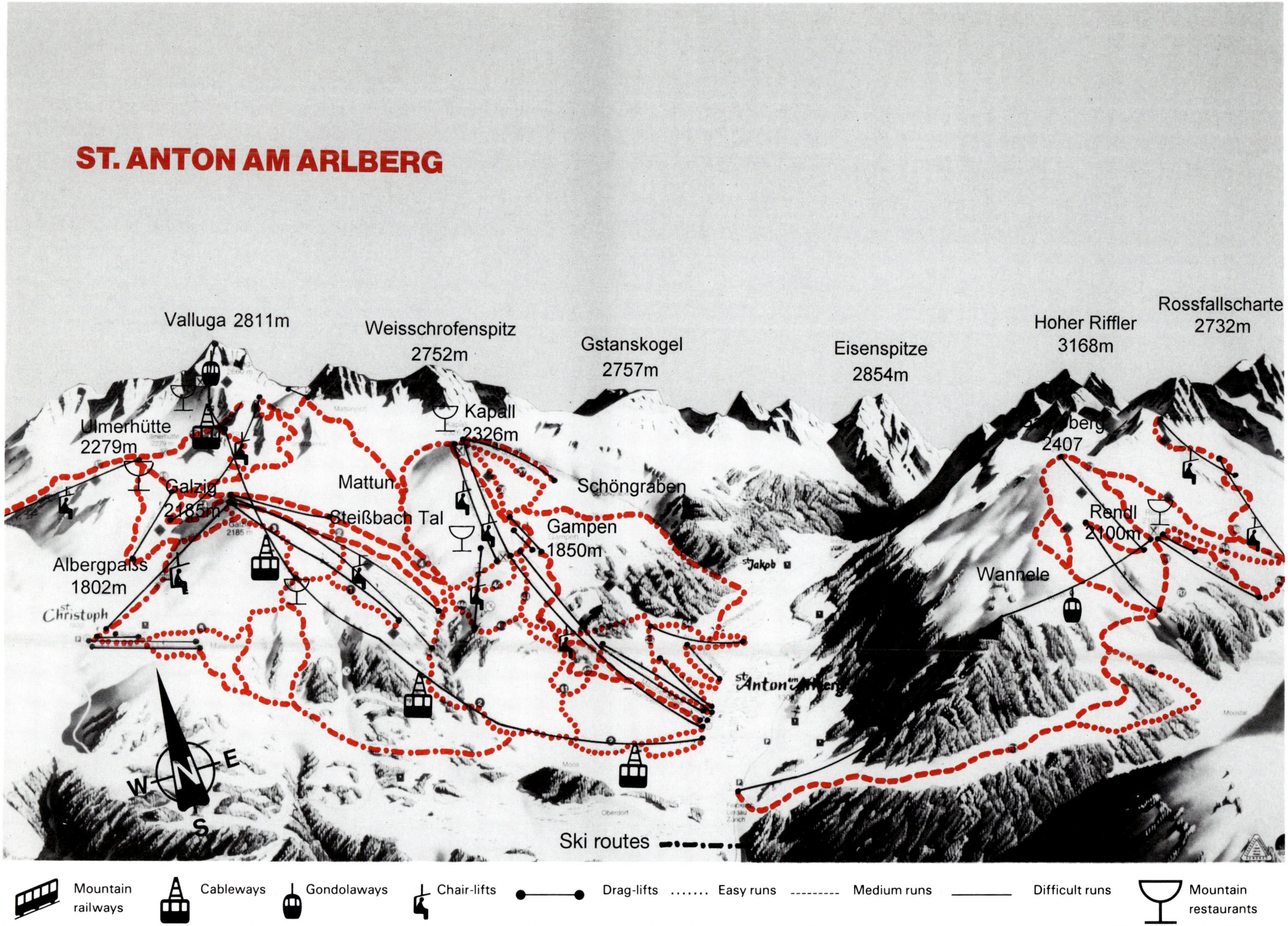
ST. ANTON AM ARLBERG
Valluga 2811m
Weisschrofenspitz 2752m
Gstanskogel 2757m
Eisenspitze 2854m
Hoher Riffler 3168m
Rossfallscharte 2732m
Ulmerhütte 2279m
Kapall 2326m
Galzig 2185m
Mattun
Steißbach Tal
Schöngraben
Gampen 1850m
Albergpaß 1802m
St. Christoph
St. Jakob
St. Anton am Arlberg
Wannele
Rendl 2100m
2407
W
N
E
S
Ski routes
Mountain railways
Cableways
Gondolaways
Chair-lifts
Drag-lifts
Easy runs
Medium runs
Difficult runs
Mountain restaurants

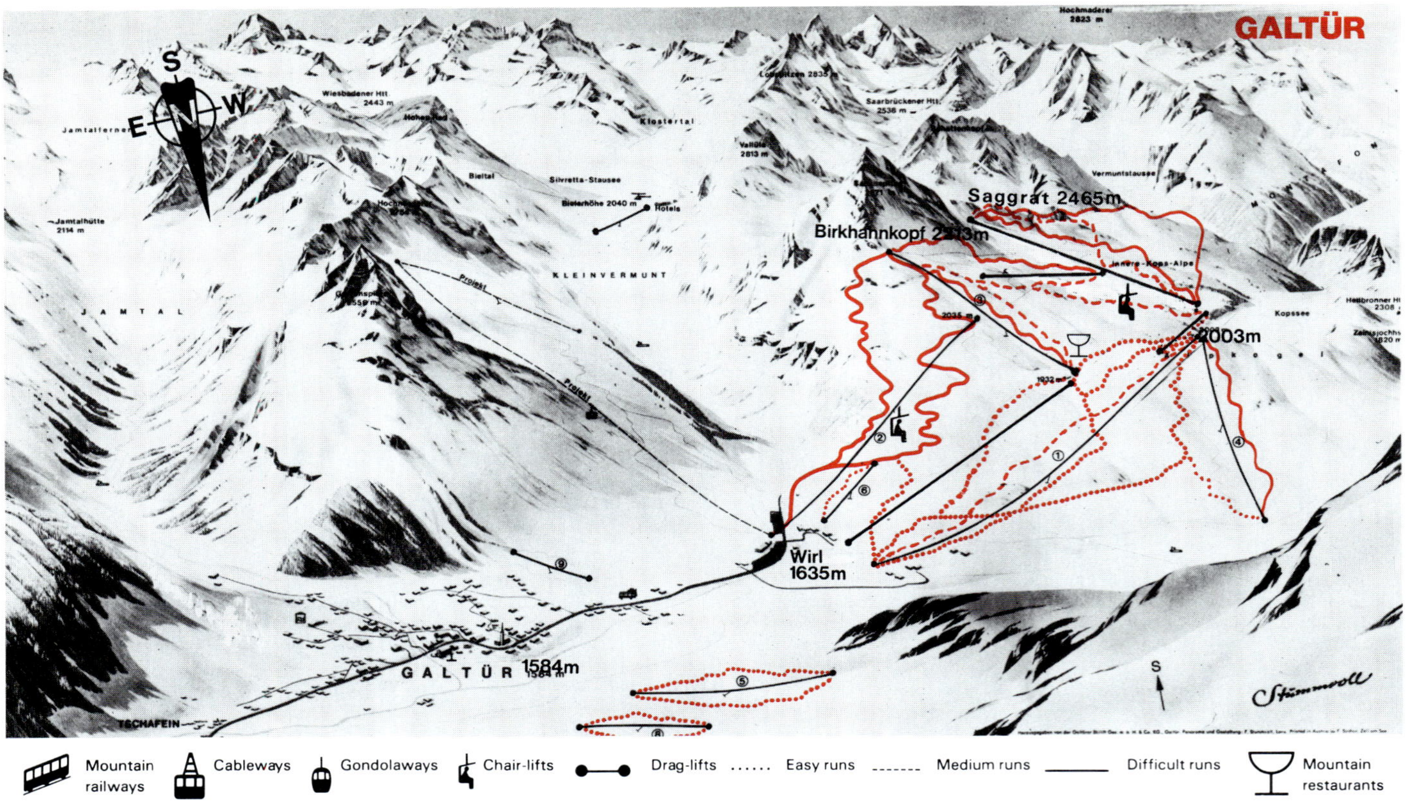

Hotel Schwarzer Adler: An extremely well-run hotel in a central position. The dining room is very attractive, in two sections, with excellent food and service. Pleasant lounge with open fire. Comfortable bedrooms, apartments and studios. All rooms with bath/shower, wc, TV and radio. A pleasant annexe immediately opposite, above Café Tschol, a popular meeting place under the same management. Sauna, steambath, whirlpool and solarium.

Hotel Valluga: Standing back off the main street, 10 minutes walk from the village centre and near the Tyrol, this is an attractive chalet style hotel with a Tyrolean atmosphere. Bedrooms are comfortable and the reception rooms tastefully decorated and furnished.

GALTÜR

Height of Resort: 5,796 ft.
Height of Top Station: 7,544 ft.
Nearest International Airport: Munich
***Map Reference:* 6D See page 237**
***Route by Car:* See pages 236-237**
***Resort Facilities Charts:* See page 213**
***Hotel Reference Charts:* See page 227**

Galtür lies at the top of the Paznaun valley at the foot of the Silvretta Pass (closed in winter) and is close to the Swiss border. It is 40km. from Landeck and about 15 minutes' journey from Ischgl. Its height of 5,796ft. and predominately north-east facing slopes virtually ensure snow from December till May. Long famed as a ski-mountaineering and touring centre, Galtür has more recently developed its ski-lift system to cater for downhill skiing. Most of the hotels and facilities are in the central village of Galtür. The main ski area however is 2km. away, at Wirl with buses running quite frequently until about 7 p.m. There is a choice of two chair-lifts and two drag-lifts, which link with seven further drag-lifts, the highest station being the Breitspitzbahn, 7,544ft.

These slopes are mainly north-east facing, and there are three charming mountain restaurants in this area. Most runs are suitable for beginners to intermediate skiers, with 3 black runs for the more expert; the longest being 3.2km. long. Galtür is a suitable centre for all grades of skiers, even the most expert, as the Silvretta ski pass offers unlimited use of all Ischgl lifts (10km. distant with bus service) as well as the other valley resorts of Kappl and See, totalling 68 lifts.

Most ski instructors are also mountain guides and classes are organised for off-piste day tours as an alternative to normal piste instruction. This is one aspect that makes Galtür different from the average resort. Examples of the many easy popular day tours which can either be undertaken by climbing on skins or by Snocat are those to the Bielerhohe Hut on the Silvretta Staussee, 6,707ft., or the Jamtalhütte, 6,900ft. It should be mentioned that Galtür is an excellent resort for langlauf, with 45km. of trails. The ski school has several langlauf instructors and special courses are arranged.

In a Few Words: Charming, peaceful and unspoilt mountain resort, until more recently principally a centre for ski touring, for which it is ideally placed. Good for groups and families of different standards, with activities for non-skiers. Although good for family groups, the resort can be rather cold early season, so for families with young children it is better to take a holiday from mid to late season. Abonnement for Ischgl considerably increases its scope.

Après Ski: For such a small resort, the choice of nightlife is surprisingly varied. You can dance away the evening to records on a pocket handkerchief floor or you can choose between bands and discos and more room to manoeuvre; one of the largest dancing places seats up to 230 people. There is a lively and packed thé dansant at the Wirlerhof, the Almhof, the Weiberhimml and the Iglu, where skiers straight from the slopes and en route to Galtür, crowd into the cafés for hot drinks and slices of cake. As the thé dansant fast seems to be dying out, the noise and warmth of the Wirlerhof, the Almhof and Iglu from 4 to 6 is really rather a cheering sight. The Hotel Post disco, La Tschuetta Bar, is popular, and so is the Iglu. A small skating rink in the middle of the village with typical skating tunes lend a happy touch and continues, floodlit, during the evening. The indoor swimming pool, one of the first in the Austrian Alps to be purified with ozone, is well worth a visit and is included in the abonnement. Also indoor tennis courts, squash court, skittle alley, tobogganing, tandem flights and kindergarten.

Recommended Hotels:

Gasthof Alpina: A small and simple gasthof owned by ski teacher Herbert Walter, a gentle climb of some 200m. from the village centre. A charming wine stübli in the centre with dancing to records, reasonably priced and very popular with the locals.

Alpenhotel-Tirol: A delightful small hotel, beautifully furnished in traditional style, with great attention to detail and personal interest by the owners. Attractive dining room with good food, sauna and very agreeable pine kellerbar open four evenings a week.

Hotel Post: Most attractive hotel, very old in parts, particularly the Stübli (it was Galtür's original inn), with modern wing. Very well designed bedrooms, all with bath, radio and telephone, some with refrigerators. Solarium, fitness room, sauna, massage, table tennis, children's playroom, TV room. 'La Tschuetta' intimate bar with band or disco 2 nights a week.

ISCHGL

Height of Resort: 4,600 ft.
Height of Top Station: 9,394 ft.
Nearest International Airport: Munich/Zurich
Map Reference: 6D See page 237
Route by Car: See pages 236-237
Resort Facilities Charts: See page 214
Hotel Reference Charts: See page 228

To the south-west of Austria, close to the Swiss border and in the heart of the beautiful Silvretta mountains lies the small and charming village of Ischgl. It is thirty minutes by road from the main line station of Landeck, along the Paznaun valley. Ischgl has grown rapidly, and caters for beginners with its nursery slopes actually in the village, and on top of the Idalp, reached by gondolaway. It is however, also good for more advanced skiers, who will find excellent skiing above the village, both on and off-piste. The uphill transport to this area has been improved considerably. A 6 person gondolaway has replaced the old cableway to Idalp, whilst the Fimba gondolaway starts from the north-east side of the village terminating just above Idalp and a third leaving the village from the same area arrives at Pardatschgrat. The total transportation from the valley to the upper ski slopes is 6,000 an hour. All three top stations are between 7,580ft. and 8,606ft., and on the way up one travels over some of the most beautiful scenery in the Alps. From all three points a magnificent vista spreads out before one, a broad sun-filled bowl surrounded by towering mountain peaks. This area is equipped with a well laid-out lift system, and from the top of the Idjoch triple and 4 seater chair-lifts one can cross over to Alp Trida and Samnaun and here there are 8 drag-lifts, 3 chair-lifts and a new cableway, serving delightful easy and medium runs and a wide variety of off-piste skiing. The skiing on the Ischgl side is easy to medium, on open slopes, mostly facing west, north, and north-west. The snow therefore remains good in this area until late season. There is a tremendous range of touring in the Silvretta mountains and some very enjoyable runs for the medium skier. There are a number of runs down to Ischgl, approaching the village through wooded slopes. This is also a very good area for cross-country (langlauf), having 45 km. of prepared trails.

In a Few Words: Lively and charming village with delightful atmosphere; main ski area is speedily reached from the village; suitable for second year to medium skiers rather than beginners; ski touring for all grades; well maintained pistes.

Après Ski: Several excellent night clubs with dancing till the early hours, the Wunderbar (Hotel Madlein) Trofana-Tenne, the Trofana-Alm, Niki's Stadl and Seespitzkeller. The Wunderbar is recommended for its friendly atmosphere, good music with plenty of room for dancing. The daily tea dance at theAlte Löbli is very popular, as is the Café Marend, near the gondola terminals. Tea dances are also held at Kitzloch, Trofana-Alm, Seespitzkeller and Niki's Stadl. The Salnerhof is a popular venue and reasonable in price. There are a number of good places to eat – the Piz Tasna, Silvretta Hotel, Ischglerhof, Goldener Adler and the Gasthof Sonne with live music, which has become very popular with British visitors. The cheapest beer can be found at the Konditorei Salner, which is always crowded after skiing. The Silvretta Leisure Centre has a large swimming pool with rocks and waves, sauna, solarium, table tennis and billiards. The Silvretta tennis centre has 4 indoor courts.

Recommended Hotels:

Hotel Madleine: This very fine family run hotel is situated in a central position. Its three buildings are linked internally, comfortable bedrooms all with bath, wc, telephone, radio and balcony. Large wood panelled lounge with open fire and bar; heated indoor swimming pool; sauna; turkish bath and solarium. Dancing to live music in the Wunderbar.

Hotel Post: A very attractive hotel with an old and new section. Large, modern dining room, spacious and comfortable lounge. Bedrooms in the new section are well designed and attractive, many with bath or shower. Indoor swimming pool.

Hotel Sonne: An old inn, in the centre of the village. Excellent à la carte menu and pension guests also eat well. Bedrooms all with bath/shower, wc, radio and telephone; reception-lounge area; fitness centre, whirlpool, turkish bath, sauna, solarium and Wippas Stüberl.

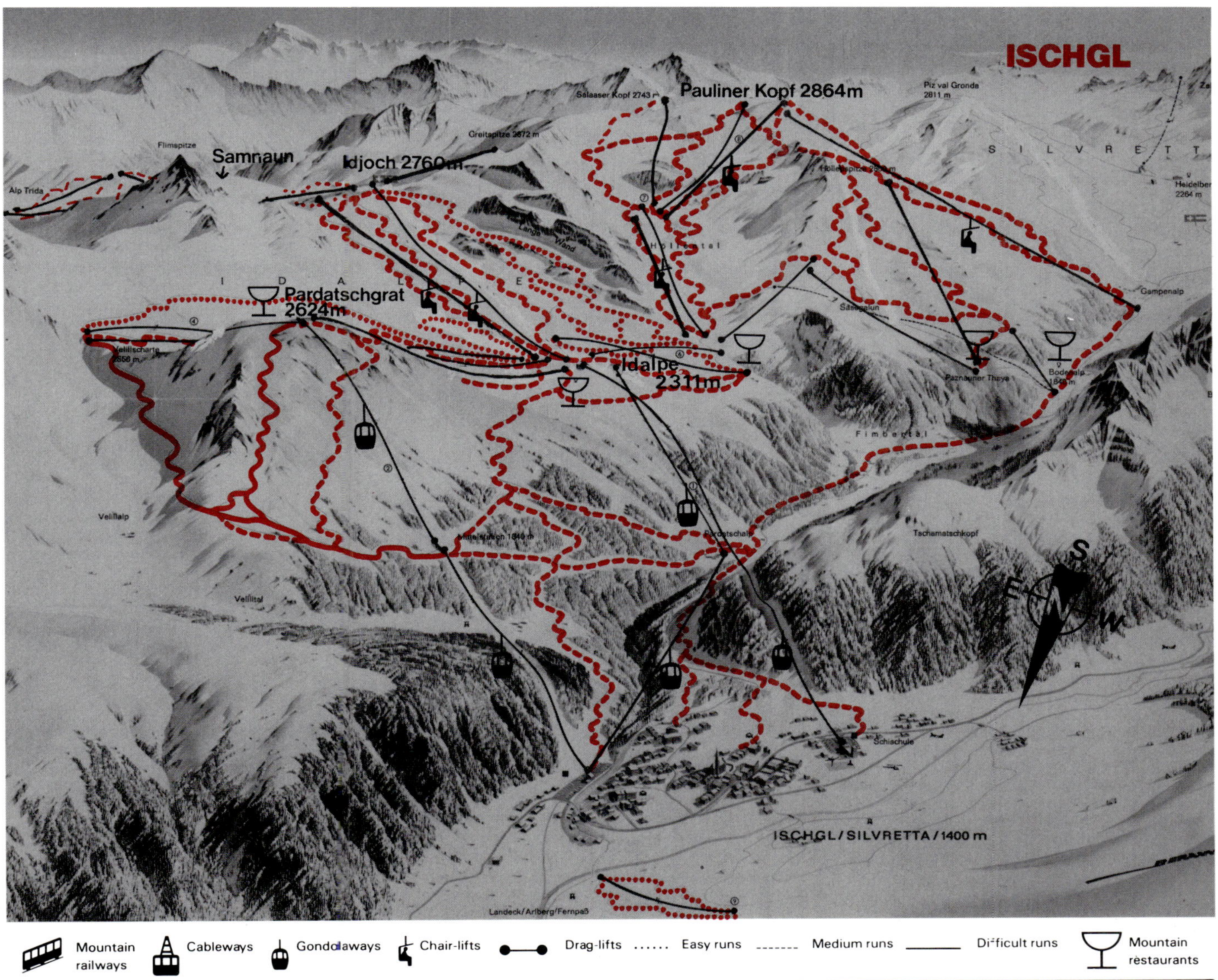

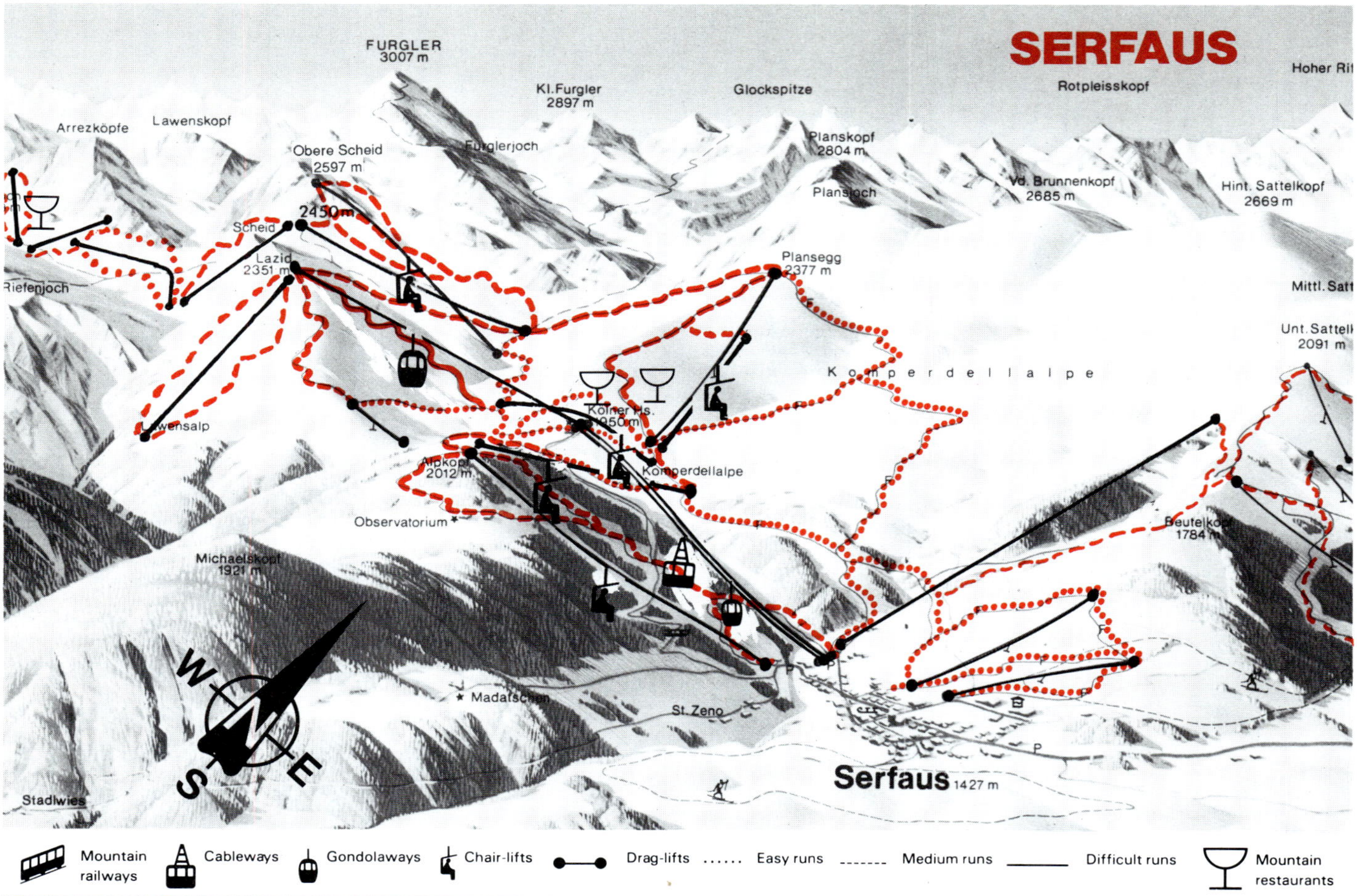

Hotel Tyrol: Opposite the cableway terminal, this is an older hotel but sections have been modernised. The dining room is particularly attractive; a large modern extension has been added with new bars, sitting rooms and reception area; and one will find a happy and relaxed atmosphere in the Stüberl.

SERFAUS

Height of Resort: 4,682 ft.
Height of Top Station: 8,858 ft.
Nearest International Airport: Munich
Map Reference: 2D See page 237
Route by Car: See pages 236-237
Resort Facilities Charts: See page 215
Hotel Reference Charts: See page 228

A farming village which has been developed as a ski resort without losing its traditional character and charm, Serfaus lies in a south-east facing position above the Inn valley with a background of towering snow-covered mountain peaks. The village is medium to large - 15 minutes' walk from one end of the main street to the other and there is no through-traffic. To cut down the number of cars in the resort, day visitors have to leave their cars in the car park on the outskirts and take the underground railway. This is propelled by cables and lifted clear with air-jets so it is virtually noiseless. Passengers can de-train in the centre of the village or continue to the western side terminating at the bottom stations of the Komperdell gondolaway and cableway where there are ski-lockers. Visitors travelling by car with hotel reservations can enter the village and are able to park their cars outside the hotels. The proposed link by chair-lift with the neighbouring resort of Fiss will extend the skiing to 130km. of prepared pistes, served by 36 lifts with a total capacity of 35,000 persons per hour. At present there is a lift pass covering the two resorts.

The Serfaus skiing is compact with a well planned lift system. The gentle south facing slopes to the north of the village, with their 2 drag-lifts, are excellent for beginners. There are two main lifts approaching the general ski area from the western side of the village. A six seater gondolaway, carrying 2,400 persons per hour, and a small cableway which runs approximately parallel, both converging on the Kölner Haus, 6,792 ft. This is the hub of the ski area where one finds a large self-service restaurant with open fires, sun terrace and good food. Two further restaurants, Sport Alm and Lazid are situated just below. The slopes surrounding this area, now served by a 4 seater chair-lift, provide excellent facilities for the ski school which operates until late season. From here a drag-lift rises to Alpkopf, 6539 ft., which serves an intermediate run to base. From this top station one has a marvellous view of the huge snow bowl surrounded by distant peaks.

The gondolaway now continues from Kölner Haus to Lazid, 7,641ft., giving access to a selection of runs of up to 3km. to Kölner Haus or from 5-6km. down to the village, all easy to medium on north-east facing slopes. A drag-lift between Lawensalp and Lazid serves intermediate runs over south-facing slopes.. Two long drag-lifts rise to Plansegg, 7,800ft., leading to various south-east facing runs back to Kölner Haus or to the village. On these upper slopes the skiing is open but protected from strong winds by the high mountains surrounding. A great improvement to this was the opening up of the Masner valley to the west, which is also protected from strong winds by the high mountains beyond. A long drag-lift from the foot of the Scheid lift travels westward and connects with two further drag-lifts rising west and north, the highest-reaching 8,858ft. The recently installed 4 seater chair-lift to Obere Scheid, 8,520ft., provides a good east facing run to base, and from the top one has a wonderful panoramic view of the area. This area is ideal for intermediates and those with limited experience. There are very lovely views down the Masner valley.

Children: There are excellent facilities for children. Those from 2-3 years are well cared for at the Kindergarten in the village whilst the 3-4 year olds are accommodated in the Kinder-Schneealm. This is a well designed play area above the village and children are collected at the valley station and looked after from 1015 -1530 hours. The daily rate is about 285 AS which includes meals and beverages. There is also a children's ski school and full information for all of the above can be obtained from the Tourist Office.

Lift Passes: In addition to the pass for Serfaus area there is a second pass covering 7 areas:- Serfaus, Fiss/Ladis, Venetregion/Landeck, Nauders, Hochzeiger/Pitztal, Fendels and Gletcher Kaunertal. A ski bus connects Serfaus with Fiss/Ladis.

In a Few Words: A very appealing resort with excellent skiing for beginners to medium skiers, with compact ski area and lifts well arranged; recommended for families; kindergarten; good touring in surrounding area; atmosphere friendly and lively; medium price and good value.

Après Ski: Plenty of activity for a resort of this size, mostly organised between the hotels. Tea and evening dancing at the popular Serfauserhof café/bar; live groups with dancing at the Hotels Post, Serfauserhof and Schmiede. The Noldi-Bar with its live group always attracts a good following. Also very popular is the Patschi-Pub, the Hasenstall Pub and the Filou at the Astoria Sportcafé with dancing to live group or discothèque, and the Pub Café am Platz with its cosy atmosphere. Attractive walks, swimming, etc.

Recommended Hotels:

Hotel Alpenhof: Situated adjacent to the nursery lift and overlooking the village, the Alpenhof is a well run comfortable hotel furnished in traditional style, the large windows taking full advantage of the splendid scenery. All rooms with private bath.

Hotel Cervosa: Situated on high ground to the south of the village, 5 minutes' walk from the centre, this is an extremely nice hotel. Large reception hall/ sitting room, 2 attractive dining rooms and further comfortable, colourful and well designed sitting rooms a very lovely swimming pool, sauna, bar, large sun terrace and Keller Bar with good group. Bedrooms tastefully furnished, most with bath or shower, and a large number with south facing balconies. Squash, fitness centre, bowling and curling.

Pension Edelweiss: A high standard small modern pension centrally situated, providing comfortable accommodation. Attractive dining room with large windows, giving magnificent views. Good atmosphere.

Hotel Post: Situated in the village centre and directly opposite an underground railway station for easy access to ski lifts. Large comfortable rooms, all with private facilities, including a number of family suites for up to six people. Lounge with open fireplace, and the outside ice bar is a popular meeting place. Large dining room with a choice of excellent food. Sauna, steam bath, whirlpools and children's play room.

Hotel Schwarzer Adler: A nice chalet style hotel on the entrance side of the village. Large bright dining room, small lounge with open fire, bar, large sun terrace. Modern bedrooms pleasantly furnished, all with bath or shower. Good atmosphere.

NAUDERS

Height of Resort: 4,590 ft.
Height of Top Station: 9,002 ft.
Nearest International Airport: Munich
Map Reference: 2E See page 237
Route by Car: See pages 236-237
Resort Facilities Charts: See page 215
Hotel Reference Charts: See page 228

The small and pretty village of Nauders, with its narrow streets and mixture of old and new buildings, is very close to the Austrian/Swiss/Italian borders. By road, the journey from Landeck passes through the lovely valley of the blue-green Inn river, rising gently for the last 9km. up a winding road, through small tunnels, to a point where there is a breath-taking view of the sun-filled valley spreading out below, surrounded on the east by the imposing Ötztalen Range and on the west by the magnificent Silvretta mountains. Nauders is compactly set in the centre of this valley and offers two separate areas for skiing.

To reach the area on the south-east side of the village one takes the Bergkastel gondolaway and from the top ski down on an intermediate run to the Goldseehütte. Here a 2,200 metres long chair-lift rises northwards to Tscheyek, 8,858ft., with an easy and intermediate run back to base. Alternatively one can break the journey about 400 metres down and take the drag-lift up to Gueser Kopf, 9,022ft., now the highest station in the resort, which serves a difficult run until it joins the reasy run to the Goldseehütte. From this point one can ski down to the lower station of the Geissloch drag-lift rising southeastward to 7,546ft., which serves northwest facing intermediate runs or one can continue southwestward from the base of the lift to the lower station of the Bergkastel gondolaway (see below).

To the west of the village the Mutzkopf double chair-lift runs north-south to Riatsch, 6,080ft. Here there is a restaurant with a large sun terrace and a beautiful view over towering mountain ranges stretching far into the distance. From the top, two north facing runs lead back to the village, the Familienabfahrt, a medium standard run edged by trees but broad, and the wooded Toni Seelos Abfahrt is a more difficult run.

A 2,750m. long gondolaway, the Bergkastel, with 6-seater cabins, rises 2,624ft. from the Reschen area up to the edge of the tree line, and there is a self-service restaurant here. This area can also be reached from the village by the Lärchenhang double chair-lift and surmounting drag-lift. Nearby the 1,300m. long Zirm parallel drag-lifts run in the direction of the Bergkastelspitze summit, with an ascent of 1,148ft. to the top station, 8,530ft. Near the restaurant and trainer lift a further drag-lift operates. The Almlift, catering particularly for good skiers, completes the ski areas at Bergkastel. This area offers north and northwest facing runs. The Zirm drag-lift serves an open terrain whereas the runs from the top of the gondolaway lead through wide, wooded slopes.

Six mobile snow-making machines operate in this area. A free bus service links this area to the village, though it is possible to ski back across the fields. Nauders is a good centre for ski touring and in the spring the ski school arranges frequent tours.

Extensive nursery slopes are to be found in the village area and also at Bergkastel.

In a Few Words: The increase in range of skiing available has given this resort a new dimension. Set amid beautiful scenery, it is an attractive village with good atmosphere. Nursery slopes extensive; skiing suitable for beginners to advanced intermediates; an 8km toboggan run; good value.

Après Ski: This is informal but lively. In the Tennisstüberl there is live music in the afternoons and evenings and disco music in the 'Traktor Tenna'. Another favourite haunt is the disco-café 'Relax' with its cosy atmosphere, normally in full swing until 3 a.m. The restaurant Stadlwirt has zither music and Tiroler Abends. Very popular and cheap drinking venues are the bowling alley, the Chess Pub and Maxi Pub, open till 1 a.m., whilst there are plenty of bars and attractive hotel restaurants to visit.

Recommended Hotels:

Hotel Almhof: A modern chalet style hotel very well run by the charming Herr Kröll. All rooms with bath/shower, balcony and telephone. Apartments available. Large lounge/bar, with open fire, for residents. Separate bar/restaurant with open fire, TV room, children's playroom, swimming pool, underwater massage, sauna, solarium, fitness room. American style breakfast served up until 1000 hrs which is very popular with skiers and a full dinner with choice of menu.

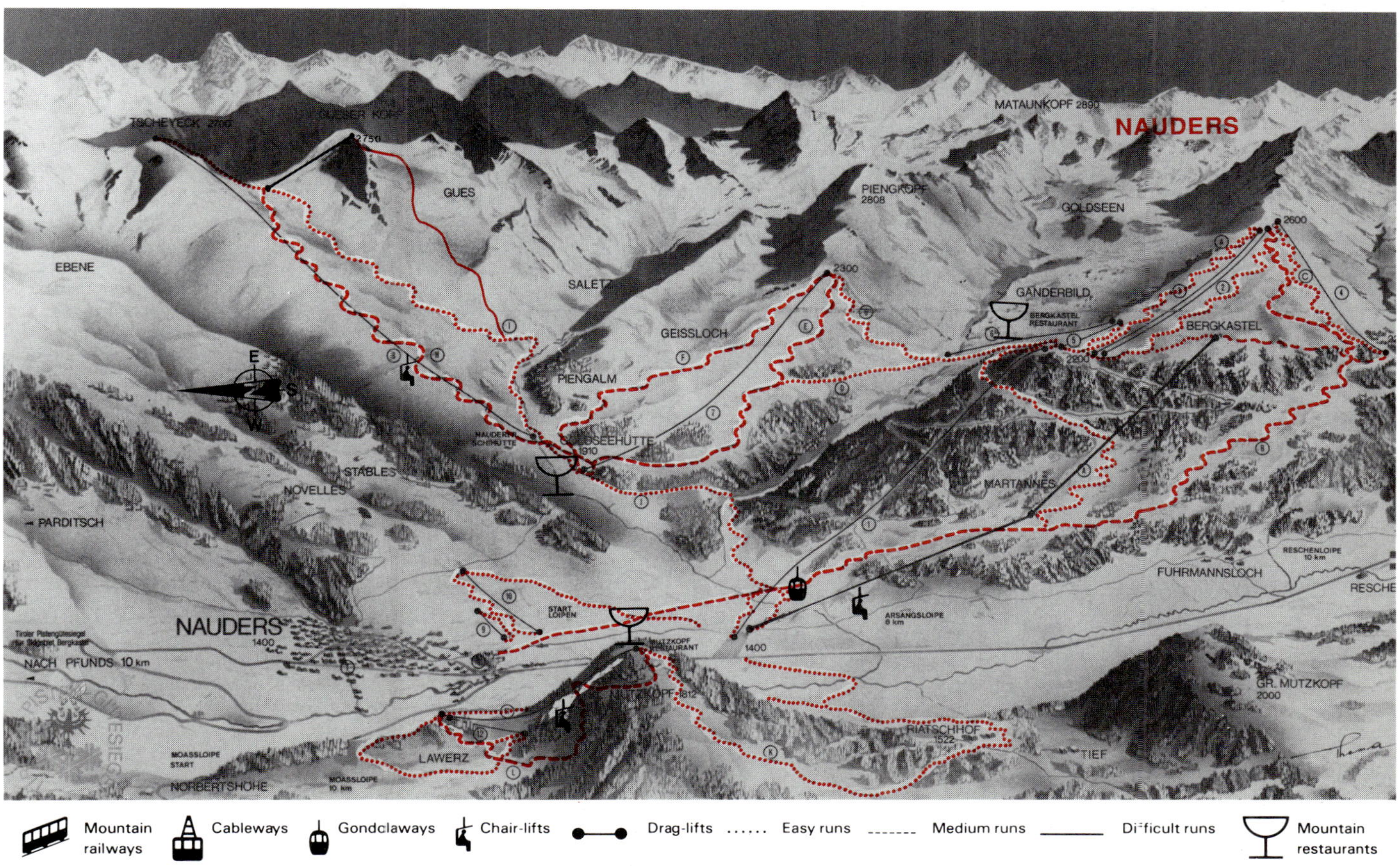

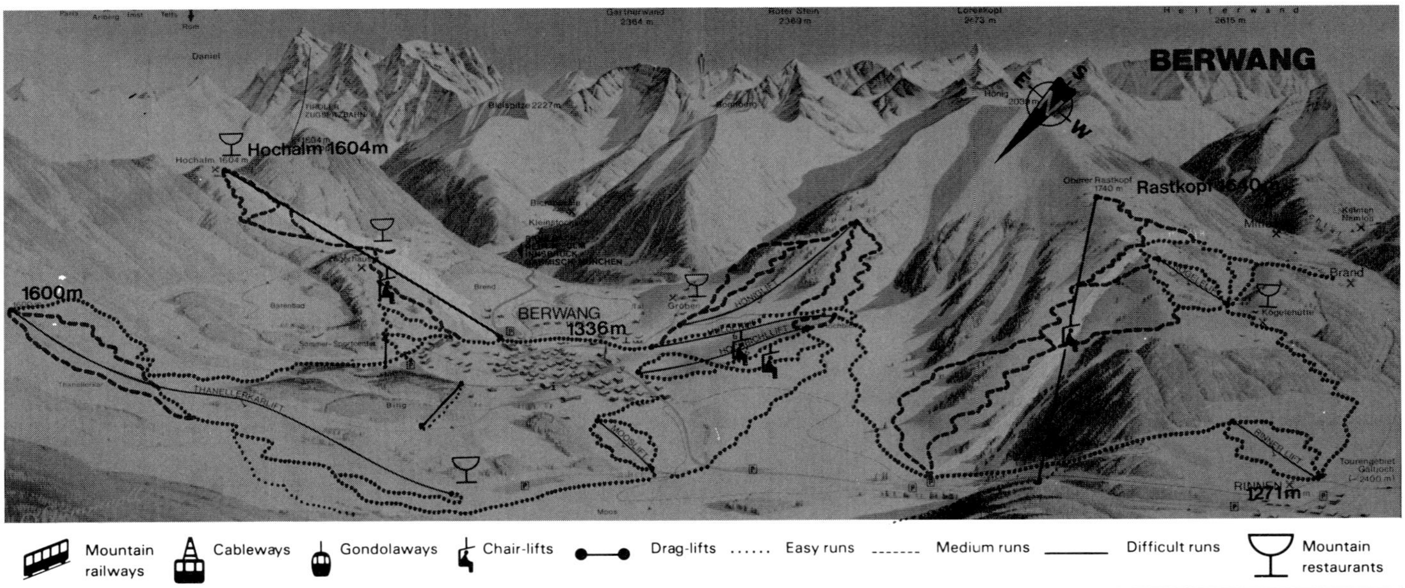

Chalet Alpina: A chalet style pension one minute from centre. Cosy bedrooms nicely furnished with built-in cupboards, fitted carpets and balconies. All rooms with bath or shower. Attractive Tyrolean breakfast room. Sauna and solarium.

Hotels Maultasch & Tyrolerhof: Known as the Sporthotel but they have now reverted to their original names though still linked by underground tunnel. The lower parts of both hotels have been completely rebuilt. Each hotel has an attractive and comfortable dining room and lounge-bar, separate à la carte restaurants. Piano music in both lounges during afternoon and evening. Bedrooms of good size most with bath/shower. Large indoor swimming pool serving both hotels.

BERWANG

Height of Resort: 4,398 ft.
Height of Top Station: 5,395 ft.
Nearest International Airport: Munich
Map Reference: 2C See page 237
Route by Car: See pages 236-237
Resort Facilities Charts: See page 212
Hotel Reference Charts: See page 227

Berwang is situated in the northernmost part of the Tirol, in the Zugspitzgebiet, which is the salient north of the Fernpass close to Garmisch and the German border. This area also contains the Austrian resorts of Reutte, Lermoos and Ehrwald. Berwang stands in a picturesque snow bowl surrounded by fir-clad mountains 4km. up a valley from Bichlbach, the latter lying on the main road from Reutte to Lermoos. Its neighbouring resort, Rinnen, 2km. away, is linked by chair-lift, and the prices are more moderate. Travelling by car via the Belgian and German autobahns and striking south by Ulm, Berwang is one of the first Austrian resorts one meets, and fairly easily reached in one full day's driving from the Channel ports.

Berwang has remained a small unspoilt village with 21 hotels and pensions, 110 holiday apartments and many bed and breakfast boarding houses. It is built on a hill with a lower and upper village, but the lifts are so arranged that wherever one stays one can put on one's skis close to the hotel and return on skis to its vicinity. It enjoys long hours of sunshine from February onwards but the village itself (not the south facing slopes) is restricted to 4 and 5 hours per day respectively in December and January. Besides skiing there is a small natural ice rink, curling, cleared walking tracks and an 800 metres illuminated toboggan run from the Jägerhaus restaurant, reached by road. There is a Mini Club, a type of kindergarten for playing rather than skiing, for children up to the age of 5 years, which is open every weekday from 1330-1630 hours.

More pisted slopes, blue and red, have been opened and these are served by 4 chair-lifts and 6 drag-lifts. Three of these serve south facing slopes, 4 north facing and the remainder west facing. From the eastern side of the village a fast 4 seater chair-lift reaches Hochalm restaurant, 5,262ft., replacing the two old surmounting chair-lifts. A double chair-lift with its base near the neighbouring village of Bichlbach links with the Berwang ski area at the Hochalm restaurant. Most runs are relatively short, approximately 3.5km., and favour beginner to early intermediate standard, although the direct runs down from, the Honig lift and from the Rastkopf double chair-lift, 5,708ft., are steep and more challenging for better skiers. Both these north facing slopes give good powder, snow off-piste variations.

From Rastkopf there are also easy runs of some 3km. down to the small neighbouring resort of Rinnen; lifts are on the same abonnenent. A feature of Berwang is that all the lifts have been strategically sited and if tackled in a clockwise direction each one links with the next to form a full skiing circle round the whole Berwang bowl – a little walking is needed at certain points in the circuit, although new runs cut through the trees in 1993 has improved this situation considerably. An intermediate skier can easily manage the full circuit in a day, whilst better skiers can fit in all the marked runs. The choice of beginner slopes is well above average. The Berwang ski pass also covers the nearby resorts of Lermoos, Ehrwald, Biberwier, Garmisch, Seefeld and Mittenwald; therefore a car is an asset.

Nordic skiing is popular, with 3 circuits of 1.5, 5 and 5.5km., respectively. A rather novel attraction is the free tractor-driven 'train' operating several times a day between Rinnen and Berwang. Pony sleigh rides are organised 3 days a week and on one evening; and husky sleigh rides on request.

In a Few Words: An unspoilt and pretty Tyrolean village. Lift capacity more than sufficient to cope with its guests even in high season and virtually no queueing. An excellent choice for beginners and early intermediates. Although there are two steep runs with powder snow possibilities, not really enough variety for good skiers in Berwang alone but with a car,other resorts are within easy reach. Generally sunny and relaxed atmosphere, without the hurly burly atmosphere of the large ski resort. Not sufficiently high for good skiing after March.

Après Ski: An amazingly large and varied choice of entertainment. The Hotel Berwangerhof has a daily thé dansant and in the evenings a range of live music There are several popular cafés where skiers crowd in to devour mouthwatering cakes at teatime. The heated swimming pool in the Berwangerhof is open to non-residents. In a fortnight's holiday it would be quite possible to do something different every evening, the only necessary ingredient being money of which you'll need quite a bit.

The Tourist Office issues a weekly list of events with the minimum of overlapping, thus allowing the visitor an opportunity to sample everything. A French culinary evening, a Balkan 'skewer' evening, a Tiroler evening, a draught beer evening, a fondue evening, a harmonium evening, a fiddler evening, a guest-cabaret evening (terrifying!), a curling evening (weather permitting), a cold buffet evening, a pork and sing-song evening, a candlelight dancing evening and a lovers-dancing-to-dream-music evening . . . all this, incredibly, was available to us during one week's stay! As well there is the basic nightly dancing in hotels and stüberls, skating by floodlight, disco, drinking in kellers and bars, torchlight processions on skis and the weekly prize-giving following the guests' ski races. During Christmas and the New Year period Berwang puts on its own ski show for two weeks.

Recommended Hotels:

Gasthof Edelweiss: A family run gasthof since 1924, where the proprietor does the cooking. Situated at the bottom of the village conveniently near the Sonnen and Mulden lifts. The outside is Exceptionally inviting, decorated in typical Tyrolean painted style. Small stube and bar also charmingly Tyrolean.

Bedrooms modernised with local-style painted furniture, all with private showers. Whirl-pool. Underground garage for 17 cars.

LERMOOS

Height of Resort: 3,263 ft.
Height of Top Station: 7,215 ft.
Nearest International Airport: Munich
Map Reference: 3D See page 237
Route by Car: See pages 236-237
Resort Facilities Charts: See page 215
Hotel Reference Charts: See page 228

12km. from the German border of Austria is Lermoos, a long north facing village, open and sunny, which lies at the foot of the Grubigstein. 2km. to the south east is a minor resort, Biberwier, whilst across the Moos, or plain, beneath the Zugspitze massif, equidistant from Lermoos is a further resort, Ehrwald. All are quickly and easily accessible by a bus service, every 30 minutes in high season – free for holders of ski passes and guest cards. The train service between Ehrwald and Vils is also included - although the lifts do not interlink.

At Lermoos, from the south-western side of the village, a single chair-lift, Hochmoos, rises westwards and from the north-western end a new gondolaway, Grubigstein, travels northwards, with both lifts converging at the middle station, 4,380ft. Here there is a mountain restaurant and natural meeting place. Adjacent to the restaurant is a drag-lift serving fairly easy slopes in the area. From this middle station a selection of wide easy to medium runs, some off-piste, return to the wide nursery slopes or the village. Here there is a drag-lift serving the beginners area. From the middle station, the Grubigstein single chair-lift continues to 7,215ft. and another restaurant. There is a natural ski arena here which is also served by a double chair-lift, the Grubigläcke, a high speed 4 seater chair-lift, Grubigalm, and a further 2 seater chair-lift, Schihütte. A selection of runs, often edged by woods but with plenty of space provide an interesting variation for medium to advanced skiers.

At Biberwier, two surmounting chair-lifts and two surmounting drag-lifts rise to 6,142ft. and offer two main runs, with variations, which converge and return the skier to the village. A gondolaway, 8 drag-lifts and a double chair-lift cover a selection of interesting, and in one case difficult, runs at Ehrwald. This latter enables advanced skiers to return across the face of the mountain to the village. A special feature of the region is available to enterprising, but advanced skiers. This entails a combined ski-tour and trek across the Zugspitze eventually emerging above the Ehrwalder Alm before descending to the village, a total distance of approximately 20km. This run has to be taken with a ski instructor and mountain guide and is dependent on local weather conditions. It can be arranged through the Lermoos Ski School (Herr Pechtl). Ski passes cover the Lermoos and Biberwier area. The 'Happy-Ski-Card' from 3 up to 21 days includes Lermoos - Ehrwald (Zugspitze) - Biberwier - Bichlbach - Berwang - Heiterwang - Seefeld - Leutasch - Reith - Mittenwald and Garmisch-Partenkirchen. An additional feature of this delightful valley is the tremendous facility for cross-country skiing. There are 75 miles of interconnecting tracks, all specially prepared. Ski instruction is available as is equipment hire.

In a Few Words: Beginers to intermediates will be at home here, although the combined facilities of the neighbouring resorts provide a great variety of runs for more advanced skiers. One of the best areas for Nordic skiing. Cheerful atmosphere and reasonably priced. Good for young families and parties.

Après Ski: Very casual. Dancing at several hotels. Swimming pools, toboganning, sleigh rides, curling, skating, all in the village. There are Tyrolean evenings at the Hotel Edelweiss. The Simon Conditorei has wonderful cakes, pastries, hot chocolate and glühhwein which can be enjoyed before a magnificent view of the Zugspitze and Sonnenspitze. Non-skiers can take advantage of various walks and visits to Garmisch Partenkirchen or the amazing castles of Ludwig II – Neuschwanstein, Hohenschwangau and Linderhof. Excursions further afield are also available.

Recommended Hotels:

Gasthof Alpenrose: A modern chalet-style pension about 300m. from the Grubig chair-lift. Attractively furnished in Tyrolean style, bright dining room. Good atmosphere. Run by Fritz Petz, ski instructor.

Hotel Edelweiss: An attractive Tyrolean style hotel situated near the Grubig chair-lift in quiet sunny position. Pleasant dining room, café cum lounge-bar, comfortable bedrooms, many with balcony, swimming pool.

SEEFELD

Height of Resort: 3,872 ft.
Height of Top Station: 6,890 ft.
Nearest International Airport: Munich
Map Reference: 3D See page 237
Route by Car: See pages 236-237
Resort Facilities Charts: See page 215
Hotel Reference Charts: See page 228

Although Seefeld does not have a wide variety of skiing compared with some resorts, its claim in having a great variety of sporting activities must rank high amongst Alpine resorts. To start with it has 40 indoor and one outdoor heated swimming pools, 52 sauna baths, 40 Alpine curling rinks, natural and artificial skating rinks, riding, 8 tennis and 2 squash courts, bowling alley, a casino, cinema, 6 night clubs with bands and 3 discothèques. Its cross-country skiing facilities are excellent, having prepared and marked tracks totalling 200km., along with a service station containing changing rooms, locker rooms, showers, etc. The Alpine ski area is served by 21 lifts, with total capacity of 16,000 persons per hour. 70% of the ski area is covered by snow cannons. For the non-skier there are 60km. of cleared walks. The village itself is spread over an open, sunny plateau above the Inn valley, surrounded by gentle slopes with the higher mountains beyond.

The pedestrian zone in the village centre has many shops, bars and restaurants.

Seefeld has a good sunshine record, and with its great variety of activities is ideal for families and parties with skiers and non-skiers.

The skiing is divided into two areas with a free bus service linking both.

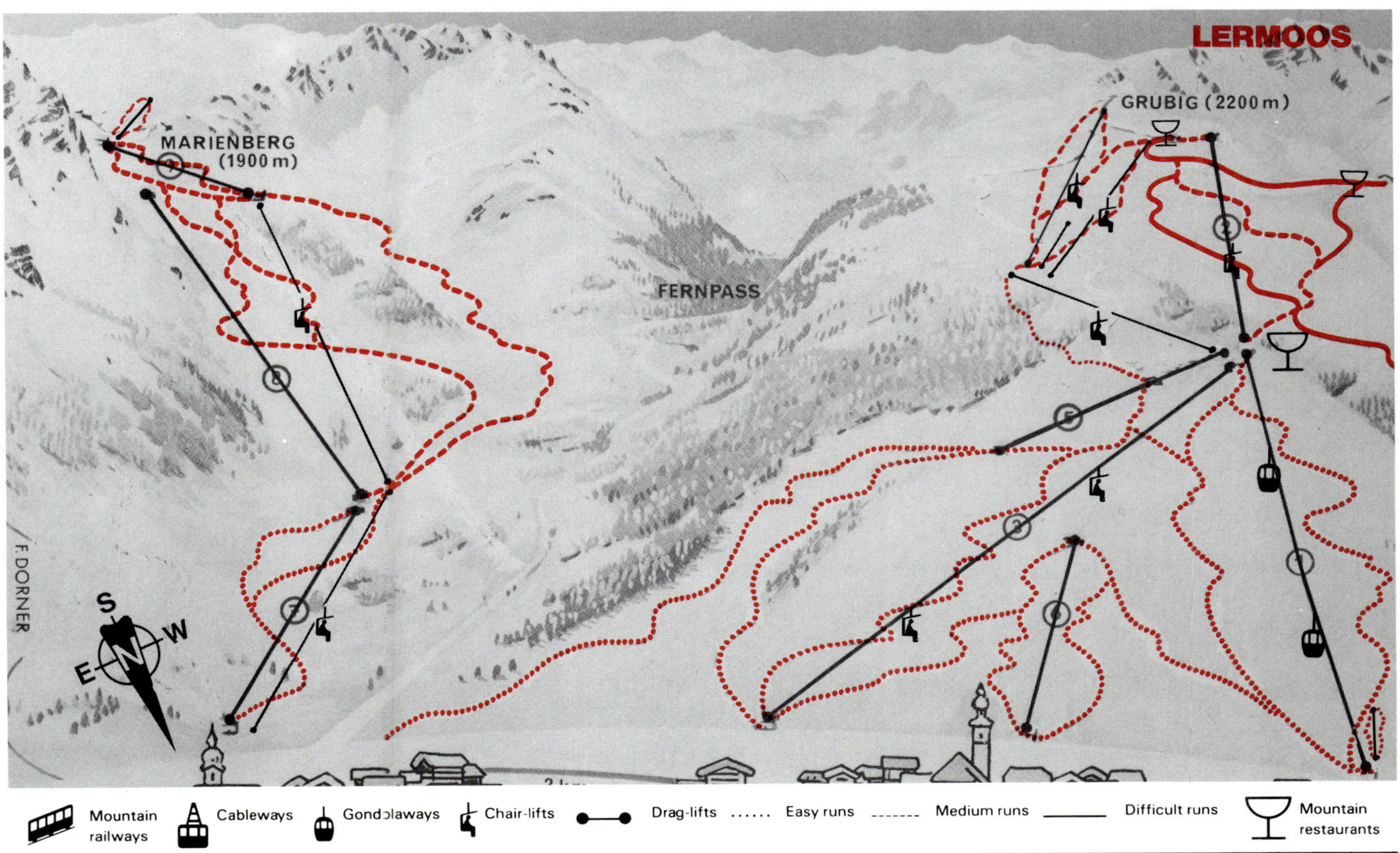

Gschwandtkopf Area: On the south-western side of the village a 4-seater chair-lift rises to Gschwandtkopf, 4,920ft. Two surmounting drag-lifts on the right also reach the top station, where there are two restaurants. There are also two drag-lifts to the left of this main system, and another chair-lift rising from Reith serving an east facing run. All runs are easy and over north facing slopes, ideal for beginners and second-year skiers and served with snowmaking machines. Two chair-lifts running from the Mösern side up to Gschwandtkofp, serving easy to medium runs, were opened for the 1995/96 season.

Rosshütte Area: On the north-eastern side of the village a mountain railway rises to Rosshütte, 5,749ft., where there is a restaurant and to the right, a new double chair-lift leads up from the Hermannstal to Rosashütte. From the restaurant a cableway rises south-eastwards to Seefelder Joch, 6,780ft., with a drag-lift running parallel almost to the top station serving a medium grade run, whilst a second cableway swings up south-westward to Harmelekopf, 6,890ft. The north-west facing, medium run from the top divides about a third of the way down; to the right it continues medium through wide, wooded glades; whilst to the left the piste is steeper, fairly closely wooded and difficult. The runs from Rosshütte back to the village, which follow the line of the mountain railway, are easy, whilst the run via Hermannstal is intermediate. Snow making machines cover the pistes from Seefelder Joch down to the village. Four further nursery drag-lifts are to be found on the north-west side of the village centre.

The 'Happy Ski Card' is also available covering the Seefeld area and the resorts of Mittenwald, Garmisch, Ehrwald, Lermoos, Biberwier, Bichlbach, Berwang and Heiterang.

In a Few Words: Excellent facilities for beginners; one of the best resorts for cross-country skiing; sunny and ideal for families - kindergarten; plenty of variety for the non-skier; good night life.

Après Ski: An abundance of night clubs, keller bars to suit all tastes and pockets. in addition there is a casino, 40 indoor and one heated outdoor swimming pools (including a radioactive one to soothe all those aches!) saunas, riding, sleigh rides, ski bobbing, snow-speed-rafting, curling, skating, tennis, bowling, indoor golf, miles of cleared walking paths and excursions to other towns.

Recommended Hotels:

Pension Hiltpot: Situated in the centre of the pedestrian zone of the village, a modern hotel with attractive bedrooms, all with bath/shower and balcony. Lounge and TV rooms; sauna and solarium on the first floor and restaurant on the ground floor. The café is a popular meeting place.

Hotel Karwendelhof: An elegant luxury hotel, one of its attractive features wooden panelled and beamed ceilings throughout, set against white walls and colourful furniture. Guests' main dining room is particularly beautiful with wooden pillars and alcoves. There are several lounges, grill room, keller bar. Well furnished bedrooms, many with private bath and balcony; also apartments. Sauna, steam grotto, whirlpool, solarium, massage and small congress room.

Hotel Philipp: A hotel of high standard and very well run. Attractive Tyrolean style decor; pleasant dining room and lounges. The proprietor skis with clients.

Hotel Post: A hotel of first class category in a central position. Attractive dining room, comfortable lounges, bar with taped music for dancing. The hotel also runs a very popular pub. The bedrooms are pleasant and well furnished, most with private bath and balconies. À la carte restaurant; sauna and solarium.

SÖLDEN & HOCHSÖLDEN Ötztal Arena

Height of Resort: 4,518 ft.
Height of Top Station: 10,030 ft.
Nearest International Airport: Munich
Map Reference: 3E See page 237
Route by Car: See pages 236-237
Resort Facilities Charts: See page 216
Hotel Reference Charts: See page 229

Whilst these two villages are quite different and are separated by a height of some 2,339ft., the skiing forms one large area with its interlinked lift system. Sölden stretches along the road leading from Ötz to Obergurgl and is a fair-sized village, whereas Hochsölden is small and compact, set on a sunny ledge. Hochsölden has the advantage, because of its height, of being in the centre of the skiing, with reliable snow conditions later in the season; Sölden being larger has the more varied night life, although Hochsölden is by no means lacking in that respect. Some hotels in Sölden have voucher arrangements with others in Hochsölden so that visitors on full pension can obtain hot lunch there.

As a result of the combined lift systems a great variety of runs can be enjoyed. The Innerwald nursery slopes at Sölden are covered by two drag-lifts and a double chair-lift travels from this area to the middle station of the cableway. For the experienced skier the Gaislachkogl 2-stage cableway rises from Sölden to 10,030ft. – the highest in Austria – giving access to some really challenging runs down to Sölden. This was rebuilt for the 1988/89 season and consists of 38 cabins, each holding 24 persons, which has increased the capacity from 450 to 2600 per hour.

The Innerwald chair-lift enables one to return to the middle station without skiing right down to the bottom station of the cableway and also forms a link with the rest of the lift complex, including the Rotkogl area of Hochsölden. Three chair-lifts near the intermediate station give a good selection of medium grade runs back to Innerwald. In addition to the chair-lift rising to Hochsölden from the other side of the village, 2,339ft. to 6,857ft., a 4-seater gondolaway leaves the nearby chair-lift terminal to Giggijoch, 7,444ft. The skiing in this area is wide open and sunny and suitable for medium to advanced intermediate skiers. The runs back to Sölden from the top of the chair-lift are interesting and through wooded terrain, easy and medium. Hochsölden is the entry point for excellent ski touring.

There has been summer skiing on the Rettenbach and Tiefenbach glaciers for some time and this is served by ten lifts, 4 lifts on the former and 6 on the latter. Both areas are connected by a 1,729m. long tunnel and by the Skischaukel lift, thus providing extensive skiing.

In a Few Words: Good skiing for all grades. Hochsölden smaller and situated advantageously for late season skiing, Sölden more scope for night life. Three good ski schools; ski kindergarten (Sölden and Hochsölden); good interlinked lift system; langlauf; ski touring; paragliding; good for parties and young skiers.

Après Ski: Plenty of entertainment in the two resorts, at Hochsölden more intimate and informal, in Sölden more variety. In Hochsölden there is a disco in the Sporthotel Schöne Aussicht. Sölden has a more varied and more exhausting night life. A favourite

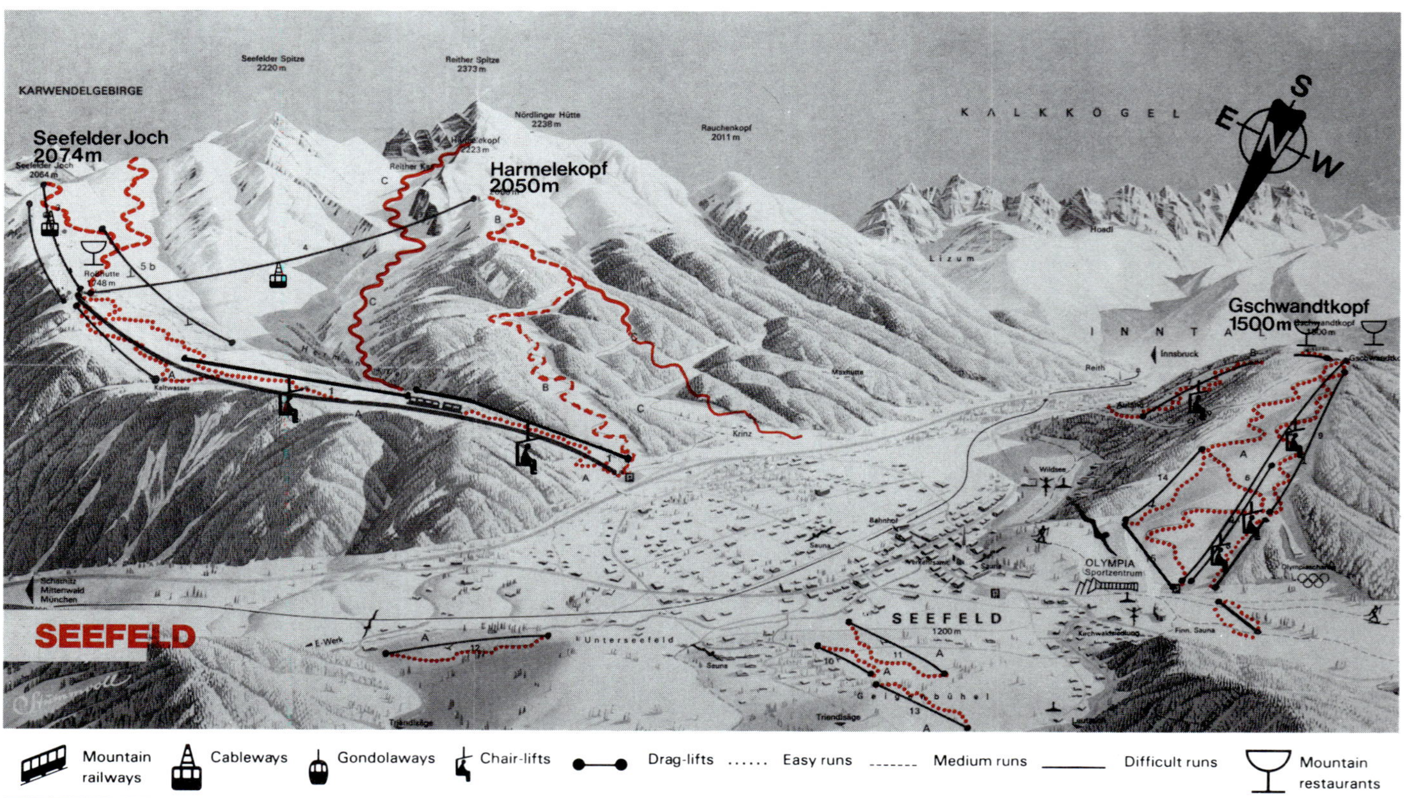

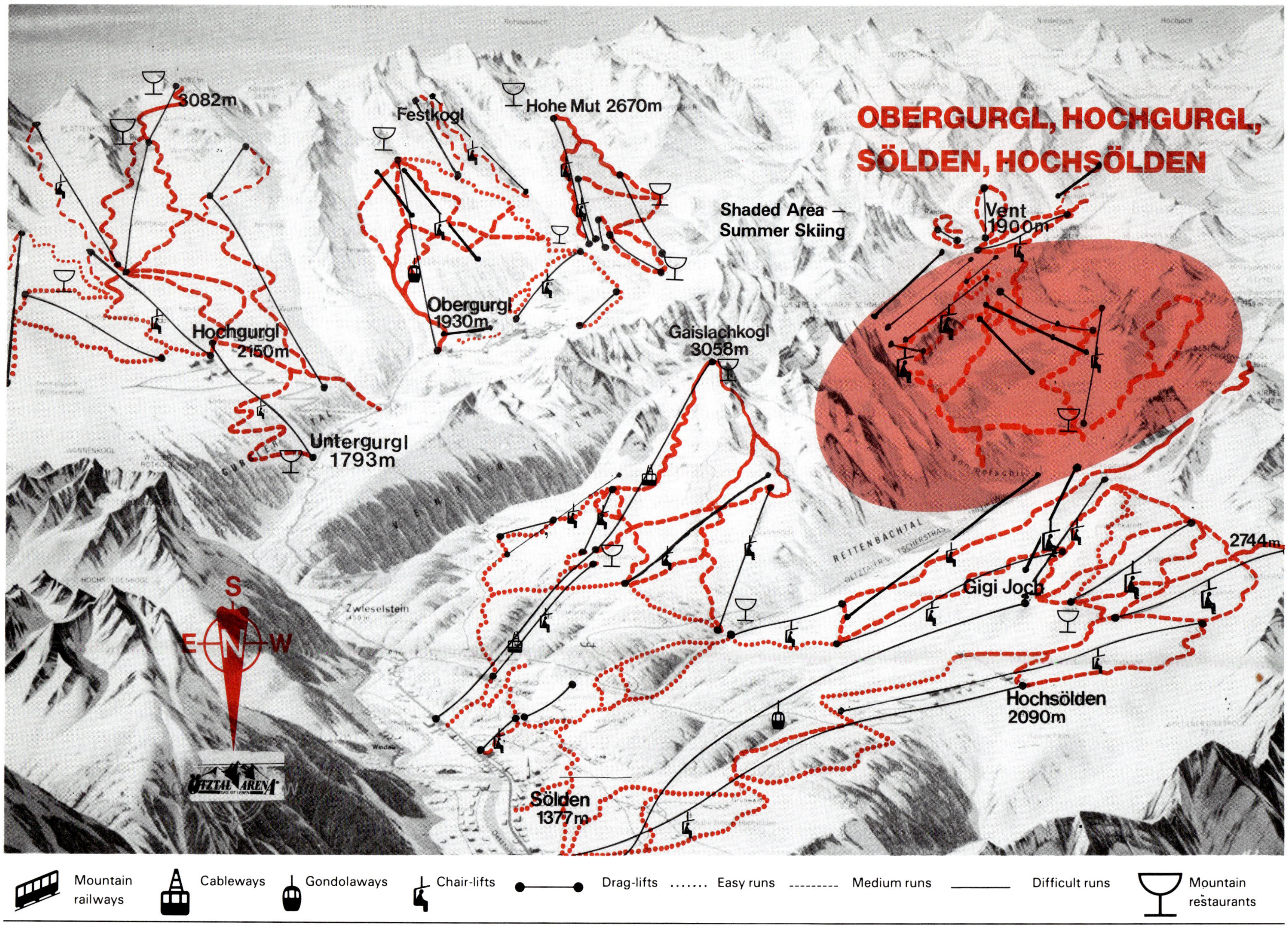
OBERGURGL, HOCHGURGL,
SÖLDEN, HOCHSÖLDEN
3082m
Festkogl
Hohe Mut 2670m
Shaded Area –
Summer Skiing
Vent
1900m
Hochgurgl
2150m
Obergurgl
1930m
Gaislachkogl
3058m
Untergurgl
1793m
Zwieselstein
RETTENBACHTAL
Gigi Joch
2744m
Hochsölden
2090m
Sölden
1377m
S
E
N
W
Mountain railways
Cableways
Gondolaways
Chair-lifts
Drag-lifts
Easy runs
Medium runs
Difficult runs
Mountain restaurants

place with young people is the Après-Ski-Club. More sophisticated is the atmosphere in the Central Hotel. There are six discos in Sölden–Gletscherspalte in the Alpenland, the Après-Ski-Club, Philipp's Kaminstube, Yeti late night disco, Lawine Music Bar in the Hotel Tyrolerhof and the Otzi Bar in the Hotel Bergland. The Bierhimml has live music once weekly. For something different, join one of the Alpenland's evenings to the Gaislachalm, where you can dance to the live Austrian music and sample a few schnaps or glühwein before tobogganing down the 3-mile run to Sölden. There is 9-pin bowling in the Parkhotel and four bowling alleys in the Freizeit Arena. The centrally located Nudeltopf restaurant in Sölden is extremely popular and good value with Italian cuisine offered. For a hearty, no-frills meal, try Armin's Törggelestuben. A regular Landrover service is run to the Gaislachalm during the day, for those taking a day off skiing – there is a very sunny terrace with a beautiful view and good food making it a popular lunchtime haunt.

Sport & Recreation Centre: One of the great attractions of this resort for skiers and non skiers is the Freizeit Arena with its large sports hall where 29 different sports can be played, indoor tennis courts; bowling alley; an indoor swimming pool for adults and one for children; fitness centre, sauna, solarium, steam-bath and massage; an entertainment room, dancing, theatre etc.; congress room, restaurant and cinema.

Recommended Hotels:

Sölden

Hotel Central: A modern luxury hotel in quiet but central position. All bedrooms with private bath, minibar and sitting area. The reception rooms are extremely elegant and beautifully furnished. There are 3 bars and dancing to a lively band and a very nice swimming pool and sauna. Excellent à la carte restaurant, the Ötztaler Stube. Congress rooms and facilities for up to 120 persons. Beauty saloon, underwater massage, sauna, steam bath and solarium.

Parkhotel: A centrally situated family hotel in quiet position near the Sports Centre and about 5 minutes' walk to the Giggihoch lift. A warm atmosphere and good service. Comfortable bedrooms all with bath, wc and telephone. Attractive dining room, bar, stüberl and separate grill for à la carte. The hotel owns a mountain hut where dinner can sometimes be taken and afterwards a toboggan ride down to the village.

Hotel Tyrolerhof: A large modern hotel in a central position, all bedrooms with private bath, spacious dining room, comfortable lounges, one with bar. Dancing in the evenings in the Alm bar. Popular à la carte restaurant 'Kupfer Pfanne'.

Hochsölden

Hotel Edelweiss: An attractive modern hotel with 60 beds, nearly all rooms with private bath, spacious reception rooms with modern decor, large bar, swimming pool with large windows giving a lovely view of the mountains.

Hotel Enzian: This is a lovely comfortable hotel built in traditional Alpine style. All rooms have shower and wc. There is a relaxing reading room/lounge, a TV lounge, sauna and solarium, table-tennis and billiards room; also a very popular café and a large sun terrace. Owners and all the staff most friendly and helpful.

Hotel Hochsölden: A large hotel with a magnificent view from the sun terrace. Two dining rooms, one very attractive, large comfortable lounge and bar. Popular tea-dance at 4 p.m., and dancing in the evenings in the Ski Bar.

VENT

Height of Resort: 6,202 ft.
Height of Top Station: 8,850 ft.
Nearest International Airport: Munich
Map Reference: 3E See page 237
Route by Car: See pages 236-237
Resort Facilities Charts: See page 216
Hotel Reference Charts: See page 229

Vent has always been a well known take-off point for high mountain ski tours both locally and in the nearby peaks and glaciers of the Ötztaler Rundtour region. Many well-known huts such as the Similaun, 9,906ft., Martin-Busch, 8,105ft., Vernagt, 9,040ft., Schöne Aussicht, 9,230ft., Brandenburger, 10,736ft. can be used for week long tours ending in Sölden, Obergurgl or further afield. Today, however, due to the rebuilding of the road from Zwieselstein, Vent has been opened up as a small ski resort, with a good snow record and suitable for beginners to intermediates. On the eastern side of the village there are two drag-lifts for beginners and on the western side a double chair-lift rises to 7,800ft. This is surmounted by a long drag-lift reaching 8,850 ft., the top station. The areas each side of the lift are wide open snowfields above the tree line providing wonderful skiing over north and north-east facing slopes which can be tackled comfortably by the average skier. For those who require greater variety day visits to Sölden and Obergurgl can be made by public transport. The Vent ski school is a good one with most of the instructors speaking English. Guest ski races are held every Friday followed by prize-giving at one of the hotels. There is a 3km. circuit for Nordic skiers.

In a Few Words: A charming 'away from it all' resort and because of its height and the orientation of the runs is good during a long season. Excellent starting point for high mountain touring. Suitable for beginners to intermediates although not a great deal of variety for the latter.

Après Ski: Quite lively for a small resort - there are two disco/keller bars with dancing in the evening. There are several bars and cafés and a reasonable selection of shops, also bowling. An enjoyable evening can be spent joining the torchlight walk up to the Rofenhof, reputed to be the highest farmhouse in Austria, where one is entertained by the family who each play a musical instrument and serve excellent glühwein and jägertee.

Recommended Hotels:

Pension Kellerhof: A charming small hotel recently built and situated at the foot of the chair-lift. All bedrooms pleasantly furnished all with bath, w.c., radio and telephone. Stüberl type restaurant, café/bar, TV room and keller bar for dancing.

Hotel Post: One of the original hotels which was modernised in traditional style in 1980. Comfortably furnished bedrooms many with private bath. Large bar and attractive restaurant with open fire overlooking the swimming pool, where guests can swim free of charge. Sauna. Small lounge. Situated next to the chair-lift.

Haus Wieshof: A pleasant bed and breakfast pension situated opposite the Hotel Post. Bedrooms attractively furnished most with bath or shower, w.c., some with balcony. Comfortable breakfast room which doubles as sitting room.

OBERGURGL/ HOCHGURGL

Height of Resort: 6,322/7,054 ft.
Height of Top Station: 8,648/10,111 ft.
Nearest International Airport: Munich
Map Reference: 3E See page 237
Route by Car: See pages 236-237
Resort Facilities Charts: See page 215
Hotel Reference Charts: See page 228

OBERGURGL:

The highest parish in Austria and the second highest in Europe, Obergurgl is a delightful, small, compact resort with many of its runs ending in the village. Traffic free and with north and north-west facing slopes, the village is acknowledged as having one of the best snow records in Europe. The skiing area, Gaisberg-Hohe Mut, is served by a two-stage double chair-lift starting from the village centre and leading up to Hohe Mut, a rise of 2,382ft., where there is a restaurant from which one has a spectacular view of the mountain peaks and 21 glaciers. The runs down from Hohe Mut are open, steep and enterprising and will test the skill of the most ardent skier. Some 8 km of pistes in this area are now covered by snow cannons. There are very good intermediate runs through the trees off the Steinmann and Sattel lifts, and a popular lunch-time restaurant is situated at the foot of the Steinmann lift, catching the midday sun. Even more so is the Nederhütte at the foot of the Hohe Mut lift, where the quick and efficient waiter service is a joy after a hard morning's skiing. Lunch is good, but even better is the après ski fun with the owner playing live music, dancing and general bonhomie. The ski down used to be alarming but with the snowcat to guide or to carry one down plus floodlighting on the pistes there is no real problem.

Abundant nursery slopes are to be found in the lower Gaisberg area. On the east side of the village lies the gondolaway up to Festkogel, giving a vertical rise of 2,670ft. From this point there are delightful runs back to the village whilst the skiing on the Festkogel plateau itself is suitable for intermediates and beginners and the area is well served by a double chair-lift, 2 drag-lifts and a 4-seater chair-lift. A self-service restaurant is to be found at the middle station.

From the summit this area is surveyed by a revolving camera which relays continuous film, together with weather data, to TV monitors in all the main hotels – a useful guide to planning one's day.

HOCHGURGL:

The Obergurgl lift pass covers the Hochgurgl area and access is by the double chair-lift from Untergurgl, 2km. from Obergurgl, which takes one up to Hochgurgl. This section is covered by snow making guns. The nearby Schermerkar chair-lift connects with the surmounting chair-lifts up to Wurmkogl, 10,111ft. where there is a restaurant with lovely view of the Italian Alps. The runs down, over north and northeast facing slopes, start medium to steep opening up into beautiful wide open pistes. To the left of the Wurmkogl I bubble chair-lift the Schermerspitz double chair-lift rises to the saddle formed by the Schermerspitz and Kirchenkogl peaks. From the top one has delighted open intermediate north facing runs back to base. The Kirchenkar lift in Hochgurgl, with a splendid little restaurant at the top, provides additional intermediate skiing, whilst the Vorderer Wurmkogel drag-lift, on the ridge of the Königstal, serves steeper runs. The final section is a real test as it is too narrow for the piste machines, thence into the gentler Hochgurgl run down to the bottom. Here the ski bus, which runs every 10 minutes and free to Gurgl guests, takes one back to Obergurgl.

In a Few Words: Skiing from your doorstep; high, sunny and a long season; reliable snow conditions; gentle nursery slopes in the village area; skiing for all grades; excellent touring; medium to expensive. Good for families with children. Daily trips to Sölden and Innsbruck.

Après Ski: There is plenty of this in Obergurgl, but not so much in Hochgurgl, which is a smaller and quieter resort. Obergurgl is lively and informal. Popular meeting places after skiing are the Josl country saloon and Krump's Stadl. Slightly more expensive, but equally popular, are the discos at the Hotels Edelweiss and Austria. The evenings of local music, held 3 times weekly in the Hotel Josl are very popular. The Schihaserl Keller Disco (Hotel Fender) in the main square is small but a good atmosphere, playing the golden oldies as well as the latest hits. Occasional musical evenings take place at the cafés, either zither or harmonica. A bowling alley is to be found at the Hotel Alpenland, and the Hotel Austria has a disco and sometimes novelty evenings. The Hotel Riml in Hochgurgl has a squash court.

Recommended Hotels - Obergurgl:

Hotel Alpina: Run by the Platzer family, this four star hotel is situated 5 minutes' walk from centre. It offers first class accommodation in terms of reception rooms, dining rooms and bedrooms. There is a beautiful swimming pool and sauna. A good atmosphere and excellent service. Highly recommended.

Hotel Austria: Situated above the village, 5 minutes' walk from the centre, this is a modern hotel in attractive Tyrolean style, efficiently run by Hans Steiner and his wife. All rooms with private bath and balcony, except singles which have a shower. Long attractive dining room with smaller lounge and bar leading off. Discothèque.

Hotel Crystal: This unusual style hotel of 50 rooms including 17 apartments, situated at the foot of the Festkogel gondolaway was opened in December 1988. It provides a high standard of accommodation, food and service and certainly lives up to its four star category. All bedrooms are with balcony except those on the second floor. The facilities include a large sun terrace, fitness room, solarium, sauna, jacuzzi, steambath, massage, bar/lounge with open fireplace and restaurant.

Hotel Gotthard: A very fine hotel situated above the village about 4 minutes' walk from centre. 88 beds, all rooms with bath, wc and telephone, most with balcony. Large sun terrace, swimming pool, solarium, jacuzzi and sauna. Tastefully furnished throughout and a good atmosphere.

Hotel Hochfirst: Situated near the Festkogel chair-lift, on the left as one enters the village, this is one of Obergurgl's largest (150 beds) hotels. All bedrooms are with bath and balcony, two dining rooms, two lounges, two bars and a very lovely swimming pool, free to guests, sauna, Turkish bath, jacuzzi, massage.

Hotel Jenewein: A popular, luxury style and modern hotel almost at the foot of the Gaisberg chair-lift. Large, attractive bedrooms all with bath, wc., and telephone. Pleasant dining room, attractive lounges. Large sun terrace with ice/bar café overlooking the slopes, Hexenküchl speciality restaurant, sauna, whirlpool and Turkish bath.

Hotel Josl: In a good position, one minute walk from the centre, a very nice pension recently renovated and with a good atmosphere. Comfortable bedrooms, all with bath/shower. Pleasant dining room and also a café-bar which is a very popular meeting place after skiing and in the evenings where locals and visitors come together. Sauna, solarium, large hall with open fire, TV room. Tyrolean duo for dancing.

PITZTAL

Height of Resort: 3,609 ft.
Height of Top Station: 10,761 ft.
Nearest International Airport: Munich
Map Reference: 2D See page 237
Route by Car: See pages 236-237
Hotel Reference Charts: See page 228

The Pitztal, which runs south from Imst was, until 1983, one of Tirol's most inaccessible valleys during the winter. In that year this was all changed by the opening of an underground railway at the head of the valley, thus giving direct access to the Pitztal Glaciers. The approach road is well maintained although there are still dangers of avalanches, but these sections are well known and the road is closed when they are expected.

The small town of Imst lies on the main west-east road between Arlberg and Innsbruck. Most trains stop at Imst with bus connections up the valley The railway to the glacier is 35km. from Imst and 95km. from Innsbruck. The road winds up through Wenns, just by-passes Jerzens (see below) and continues into the Gemeinde of St. Leonhard. Here the valley is known as Innerpitztal. There are numerous delightful hotels and guest houses all the way as one passes the communities of Weisswand, Plangeross, Mandarfen (see the Rifflsee ski area below) and the road finally culminates in a rock wall at Mittelberg, 5,642ft. Here a stupendous engineering feat has pushed an underground railway through rock into the very heart of the glaciers. It does not matter greatly which of the above villages one selects to stay in as the ski bus service connects them all 5 times daily. At the most the journey is 10 minutes.

The Pitztal Glacier Railway (Gletscherbahn & the Glacier Skiing: The railway starts at 5,700ft. and cuts through solid rock for 3.90km. coming out on the Glacier at 8,792ft. difference in height, 3,084ft. The journey takes a mere 7 minutes, there are two trains, one going up as the other is descending and each can take 200 skiers or 1600 per hour.

At the top there is a large self-service restaurant from which the glacier panorama unfolds: it is a stunning sight forming a huge bowl and one has been transported to an area which was previously a ski mountaineers' private preserve. Here one finds a well planned lift system; in the centre is the Pitz Panoramabahn, a fast moving gondolaway, rising to the middle station, 9,908ft., and thence to Hinterer Brunnenkogel, 11,286ft. From this point one has a close up view of the Tirol's highest mountain, the elusive Wildspitze, 12,318 ft. To the right of the central system is the Brunnenkogel drag-lift, 1850 metres long rising to 10,702ft. Further to the right of its base is a shorter drag-lift and these two lifts serve two of the five easy runs in the area. To the left and below the central system is the Mittelergjoch I drag-lift over 2km. in length and rising to 10,439ft., surmounted by Mittelergjoch II drag-lift climbing to 10,761ft and serving two easy runs. Most of the runs from the top stations are red or black with some steep pitches and the majority terminate at the base station of Mittelergjoch I where a chair;lift takes one back to the restaurant.

At this height the snow is always good, the pistes are wide and well kept, the skiing is quite superb and continues throughout the summer. This area would be very cold in early season - our visit was in March and there were no queues. The area also includes 41km. of cross-country runs.

In a Few Words: This has become one of the high skiing areas of which Austria has few. Not to be missed by the keen skier. Quite feasible by bus but obviously better by car. A pity to be in the Imst area with a car and not spend 2-3 days and such a trip could be extended by combining with the Rifflsee and Jerzens ski areas.

Recommended Hotels:

Berghaus Seppl: This hotel owned by the head of the ski school, Sepp Füruter, is situated on the skibus route 9 minutes from the underground railway. Both accommodation and cooking is of high standard. Attractive modern Tirolean wood decor, most rooms with bath/shower, wc and balcony. Indoor swimming pool, sauna and solarium. Large breakfasts and daily choice of menu. Small mobile lift outside the hotel for beginners.

Zirbenhof: Situated close to the Rifflsee ski area and also the local practice slope and tow lift. 48 beds, all rooms with bath/shower, wc and some with balcony. Pleasant reception rooms, choice of menu. The owner helps to create a warm and friendly atmosphere.

Rifflsee Area: Situated at Mandarfen in the Innerpitztal a few minutes short of the underground railway. A single chair-lift rises from 5,380ft. to the Bergstation, 7,446ft. and the attractive Rifflsee Hütte restaurant. One can ski down to the intermediate station of the chair-lift and this combined with the two drag-lifts, Hutten - 800 metres long and Mulden - 400 metres long rising from the restaurant serve 3 red and a blue run over east and south-east facing slopes with splendid views over the Rifflsee to the west. The runs down to the bottom station start with a choice of red or blue over south or south-east facing slopes before combining into a blue in an easterly direction. The height difference from top to bottom is 2,033ft. This is a delightful area providing an alternative to the high glacier skiing and is particularly popular in early season when it is too cold up on the glaciers.

Jerzens: The small village of Jerzens, 3,609ft. is situated above and just off the Pitztal road, 15km. from Imst (6 buses per day). The ski area, on the Hochzeiger mountain, is 3km. above the village approached by a wide, well engineered but steepish road. It is kept open all winter but sometimes chains are needed. A free ski bus service operates regularly throughout the day. Jerzens was the venue for the British Ski Championships, a tribute to its good skiing. The Hochzeiger lifts start in the hamlet of Liss, 4,757 ft., which has a nearby nursery tow and two main lifts up the mountain; one is a single chair-lift and the other an 8-person cabin gondolaway, and both terminate in the middle station area. There are two restaurants in the vicinity. The skiing above the middle station, 6,726ft., is in a large bowl, mostly west facing but with some north-east and south-west aspects. The whole of this area is served by 4 long drag-lifts and a chair-lift. The runs are good and varied over open terrain mostly red and blue but including a black. There is excellent off-piste powder skiing followed by spring snow from March onwards. There are about 40km. of prepared pistes and the runs from the top station to the bottom vary between 5-8km., vertical descent 3,281ft. The whole area is a sun terrace with 6 hours of sunshine even in December. During March one can ski in the sun until 1700 hours or later. The Jerzens/Hochzeiger area has about 2,500 beds in hotels and pensions.

In a Few Words: Surprisingly good skiing for a small resort; well situated for the glacier ski area; langlauf, curling, toboggan run, two discothèques; mostly English speaking instructors; ski kindergarten four year old upwards; ski lifts are automatic, one simply inserts one's ski pass which has a map of the ski area on the back.

Recommended Hotels:

In the quiet village of Jerzens there are three 4 star hotels, the Lamm, Alpenfriede and Jersner Hof. Close to the lift stations one will find four 3 star hotels, the Venetblick, Andy, Panorama and Romantica. All these hotels are family run and provide comfortable accommodation; all bedrooms with bath/shower, wc, TV and telephone. Meals provided are buffet breakfast and 4/5 course evening meals. For something more intimate there is a variety of small pensions and private accommodation.

STEINACH

Height of Resort: 3,432 ft.
Height of Top Station: 6,578 ft.
Nearest International Airport: Munich
Map Reference: 4D See page 237
Route by Car: See pages 236-237
Resort Facilities Charts: See page 216
Hotel Reference Charts: See page 229

One of the most accessible resorts situated just off the autobahn, 26km. from Innsbruck and 12km. from the Brenner Pass. Steinach is a fairly large village with some 5 hotels and a wide range of pensions and apartment accommodation and a good selection of shops, cafés and bars. It is set amidst very beautiful scenery and for the non-skier there are lovely walks, skating, swimming and curling.

The ski area is not a large one; nevertheless a surprising number of varied runs are to be found in the area. In the village itself there are two trainer lifts for beginners whilst the main ski area is situated on the south-western side where a new gondolaway takes one up to the first station. A sunny shelf with trainer lift nearby at a height of 5,414ft. with runs back to the village of 3-5km. over north facing slopes, a vertical drop of 1,970ft., suitable for the inexperienced and more testing runs for the intermediate. From the first station a surmounting chair-lift continues southward to the top station, 6,578ft., with intermediate runs back over north facing slopes. Two further drag-lifts serve the upper slopes whilst from the top station there is an easy run over south facing slopes down to the next village of Gries. For the Nordic skier there is a good variety of langlauf trails through very beautiful countryside, some 100km. in all.

In a Few Words: An interesting village and very accessible. Compact medium sized ski area with a good variety of runs; north facing runs mean the snow is normally reliable. Suitable for beginners to intermediates. Children well catered for.

Après Ski: A good selection of cafés and bars, dancing in many of the hotels, Tyrolean evenings and special events arranged weekly, swimming, skating and excursions to many places of interest.

Recommended Hotels:

Sporthotel Wilder Mann: A well run hotel with comfortable reception hall/lounge, bar, attractive dining room, sun terrace, stüberl. Bedrooms spacious and comfortably furnished, all with bath or shower, radio and colour TV. Large indoor swimming pool, sauna, solarium, underwater massage, playroom, piano bar.

STUBAI VALLEY

Situated 4km. from the Innsbruck-Brenner Autobahn the Stubai Valley is perhaps best known for its Glacier Skiing served by a two stage gondolaway, three chair-lifts and ten drag-lifts, with a top station of 10,499ft. The valley accommodates 5 villages and 4 ski areas all linked by bus services. This report deals with three of the villages and their ski areas:- Fulpmes, which is the largest village and has access to a greater amount of the skiing; Telfes, which shares the ski area with the former; and Mieders on the opposite side of the valley. All three lie at the entrance to the valley. There is a combined lift pass for the whole valley including the link ski buses and individual area passes.

FULPMES

Height of Resort: 2,952 ft.
Height of Top Station: 10,499 ft.
Nearest International Airport: Munich
Map Reference: 2D See page 237
Route by Car: See pages 236-237
Resort Facilities Charts: See page 213
Hotel Reference Charts: See page 227

Fulpmes, set amidst beautiful scenery, lies at the foot of the Schlick skiing area and a free bus service take one to the bottom of the two stage gondolaway. It is a large village and provides a wide range of comfortable accommodation for over 2,800 visitors. There is a good selection of shops, cafés and bars and in addition to skiing a wide range of activities are offered including swimming, skating, curling, cleared walks, bowling, paragliding, snowboarding and tennis.

The Schlick skiing area, suitable for beginners, intermediates and racers, is reached by gondolaway which takes one up to the middle station, Froneben, 4,429ft., where there is a nursery slope with trainer lift, a chair-lift serving an intermediate north-east facing slopes and a gondolaway which rises to Kreuzjoch, 7,007ft. At this top station is a modern restaurant which is sheltered and forms an excellent sun trap. There are no runs down beside this gondolaway and one skis in a north-easterly direction with three possibilities. First, on easy and intermediate runs to the foot of a drag-lift which returns one to the top just above Kreuzjoch. Second, on a blue run to the foot of two parallel drag lifts both of which reach Sennjoch, 7,349ft., which serve easy and intermediate runs back to the base of both lifts. Third, to continue, from this point on a blue run which sweeps round to Schlicker Alm, 5,301ft., to pick up the chair-lift taking one up Sennjoch Hütte where there is a restaurant. The run down is intermediate until half way down and then joins the blue back to Schlicker Alm which is situated in a large sunny bowl with restaurant and trainer lift. It should be mentioned that this area can also be reached by Landrover from Froneben. The run back to the village from Schlicker Alm is blue as far as Froneben and thence intermediate with a few testing bends. For the cross-country skier there are 130km. of trails in the whole of the valley.

TELFES

Height of Resort: 3,281 ft.
Height of Top Station: 10,499 ft.
Hotel Reference Charts: See page 229

This small picturesque village has accommodation for 1,600 visitors and lies about 1km. beyond Fulpmes. It is a quieter village with shops covering the essentials including winter sports equipment. Like Fulpmes it has a station on the mountain line down to Innsbruck main railway station.

Between the two villages there is an excellent sports centre with swimming pools, a very long water chute, saunas, whirlpool, fitness centre, relaxation bath, restaurant, modern concept disco and four indoor tennis courts with professional trainers. Many people ski in the morning and play tennis in the afternoon. The Schlick skiing area is shared with Fulpmes, and both villages have excellent ski schools. A ski bus service links with the chair-lifts up to Froneben.

MIEDERS

Height of Resort: 3,214 ft.
Height of Top Station: 10,449 ft.
Hotel Reference Charts: See page 228

The smallest of the three villages catering for 1,300 visitors, it lies on the opposite side of the valley to Fulpmes and Telfes.

The ski area is served by a single seater chair-lift reaching 5,413ft. At the top there is a trainer lift and a drag-lift stretching about one third of the way down the chair-lift. Although the runs are limited and generally fairly easy there are some 40km of high altitude and well prepared langlauf trails. A number of these are undulated like Norwegian loipe and in places can be really testing. There are also two long distance toboggan runs down to the village. Mieders has its own ski school and bus links to other downhill and cross-country ski areas in the valley.

In a Few Words: A good variety of skiing, most of the year on the glacier; cross-country skiing well catered for with 148km. of prepared trails; charming Tirolean villages with a good friendly atmosphere; après ski fairly lively in Fulpmes; excellent sports centre.

Après Ski: Café Corso in Fulpmes has tea dancing to a lively band from 1700-2000 hours and also dancing until 0300. Often there is a band at the Dorfkrug, a long established inn in the centre and a traditional meeting place for the locals. There are two discos and numerous bars throughout the village and plenty of places to eat with a wide range of menu and prices. The modern but attractive theatre has a variety of performances. One or two evenings a week there is an organised expedition to the Sonnenstein or Vergör mountain restaurants and refreshments are normally followed by a rapid descent to the village by toboggan. There are also sleigh rides, skating, Austrian curling, swimming and tennis.

Telfes and Mieders are much quieter but there are discos in some of the outlying hamlets.

Recommended Hotels:

Fulpmes

Hotel Alte Post: Dating back to 1525, this centrally situated hotel has recently been completely renovated. Attractive bright and beamed ceiling dining room, cosy Tyrolean sitting room, bar, reading and TV rooms, indoor swimming pool, fitness room, sauna and solarium. 42 comfortable bedrooms all with bath or shower.

Hotel Atzinger: From this hotel one has panoramic views of the valley. Run by the family who give it a welcoming atmosphere. ideal for families with young children. Well known for its Tirolean specialities and grills.

Gasthof Stubaierhof: A long established family run pension, all rooms with bath/shower. Quiet central position. Plentiful and good food. Suitable for families it has a children's playroom.

Telfes

Hotel Greier: In a central position this medium size hotel has much wooden decor, particularly attractive dining room with wood panelled ceiling, pleasantly furnished bedrooms all with bath or shower. Stübli, bar, steam bath, sun room, fitness room and massage.

Mieders:

Hotel Alte Post: A traditional Tirolean Hotel, modern style bedrooms nicely furnished, all with bath or shower, telephone, radio, TV connections. Cosy reception rooms; much use made of wood panelling. Central situation.

FINKENBERG

Height of Resort: 2,768 ft.
Height of Top Station: 6,888 ft.
Nearest International Airport: Munich
Map Reference: 4D See page 237
Route by Car: See pages 236-237
Resort Facilities Charts: See page 213

Finkenberg retains its original charm and character. Situated in the Zillertal 3km. from Mayrhofen, it is a quiet village stretching along the Hintertux road, and an excellent choice for families and those who want a peaceful holiday. A gondolaway leads first to a middle station of 5,740ft., thence by a surmounting chair-lift to Penkenjoch, 6,888ft., the entry point to the ski area. There are two restaurants at the top, a rope-tow baby lift and the Hasenmulden I and 10 drag-lifts along with the Nordhang chair-lift. Beginners are well catered for in this area. Medium grade skiers will enjoy the runs to the middle station and the descent to the village 6km. long with a difference in height of 3,936ft. through first open then wooded slopes. Penkenjoch also offers the opportunity of skiing on the Mayrhofen side; the lifts on this side are included in the Finkenberg lift pass. The nursery slopes in the village have their own drag-lift but are sunless, and lunch is best enjoyed at Penkenjoch from where there is a marvellous view of the surrounding slopes and distant mountain peaks.Two excellent ski schools, Klaus Kröll and Franz Stock, cater especially well for children, who may be left in the charge of their instructor all day (in addition to normal kindergarten facilities).

In a Few Words: Quiet but friendly, Finkenberg is good for beginners to intermediate skiers and families; ski schools excellent; within easy reach of Mayrhofen, Lanersbach and Hintertux.

Après Ski: The village is small and quiet with mainly local population. There is little night life – a few bars, a well designed bowling alley and dancing; but for a more lively scene, Mayrhofen is not far away.

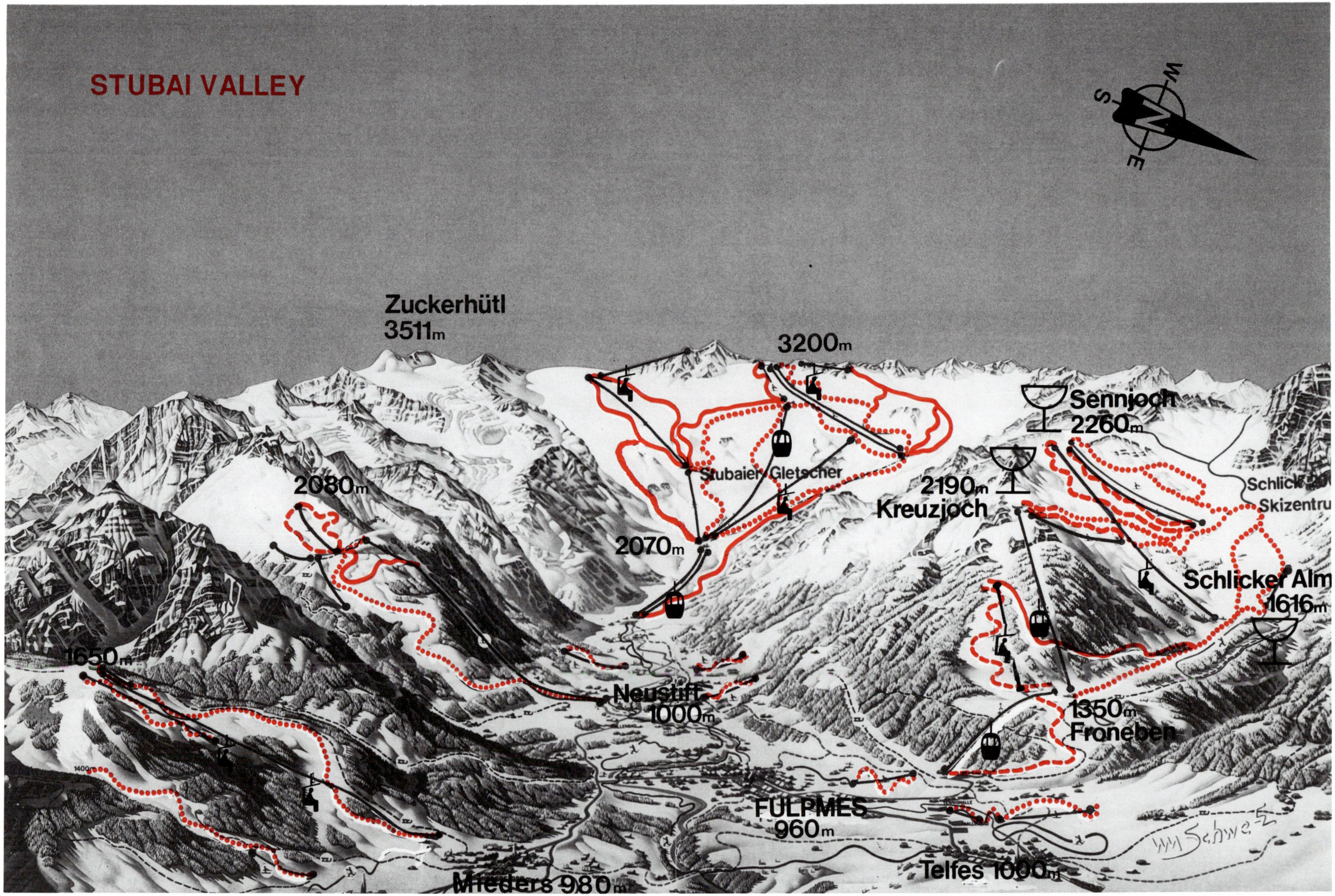

Mountain railways · Cableways · Gondolaways · Chair-lifts · Drag-lifts · Easy runs · Medium runs · Difficult runs · Mountain restaurants

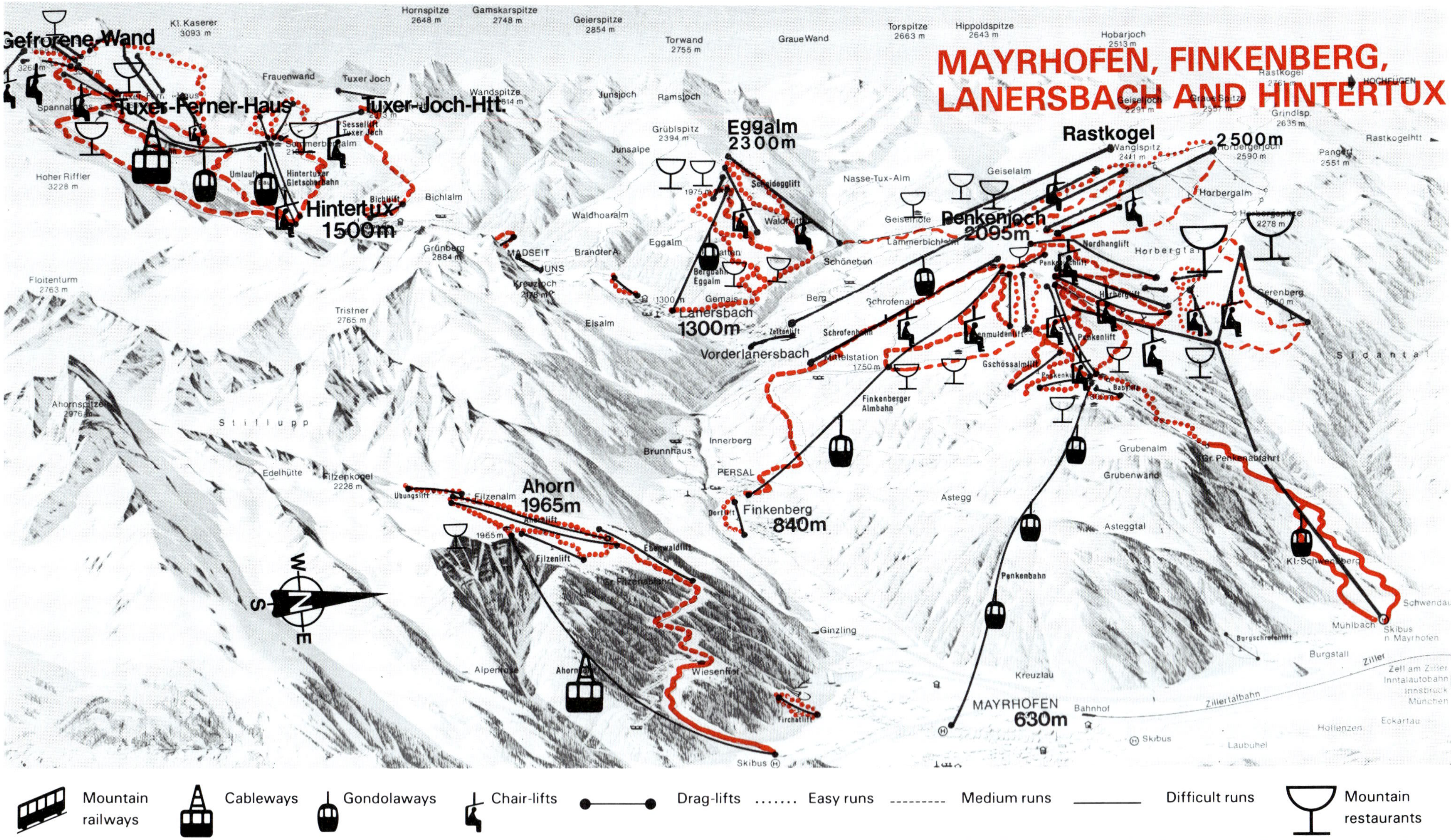

MAYRHOFEN, FINKENBERG, LANERSBACH AND HINTERTUX
Gefrorene Wand
Kl. Kaserer 3093 m
Hornspitze 2648 m
Gamskarspitze 2748 m
Geierspitze 2854 m
Torwand 2755 m
Graue Wand
Torspitze 2663 m
Hippoldspitze 2643 m
Hobarjoch 2513 m
Tuxer-Ferner-Haus
Tuxer-Joch-Htt.
Frauenwand
Tuxer Joch
Wandspitze
Junsjoch
Ramsjoch
Grüblspitz 2394 m
Junsalpe
Eggalm 2300m
Rastkogel
2500m
Horbergjoch 2590 m
Pangert 2551 m
Rastkogelhtt
Grindlsp. 2635 m
Hoher Riffler 3228 m
Hintertux 1500m
Bichlalm
Waldhoaralm
Geiselalm
Nasse-Tux-Alm
Penkenjoch 2095m
Horbergalm
Schneidegglift
Lämmerbichlalm
Schöneben
Nordhanglift
Horbergtal
Grünberg 2884 m
MADSEIT
UNS
Kreuzjoch
BranderA
Eggalm
Lanersbach 1300m
Gemais
Berg
Schrofenalm
Eisalm
Zettenlift
Vorderlanersbach
Mittelstation 1750 m
Gschössalmlift
Penkenlift
Babylift
Finkenberger Almbahn
Floitenturm 2763 m
Tristner 2765 m
Ahornspitze 2976 m
Stillupp
Brunnhaus
Innerberg
PERSAL
Finkenberg 840m
Dorflift
Edelhütte
Filzenkogel 2228 m
Übungslift
Filzenalm
Ahorn 1965m
1965 m
Filzenlift
Ebenwaldlift
Gr. Filzenabfahrt
Grubenalm
Grubenwand
Gr. Penkenabfahrt
Astegg
Asteggtal
Penkenbahn
Kl. Schwendberg
Schwendau
Muhlbach
Skibus n. Mayrhofen
Burgschrofenlift
Burgstall
Ziller
Zell am Ziller
Inntalautobahn
Innsbruck
München
Ginzling
Alpenrose
Wiesenfleck
Firchatlift
Skibus
Kreuzlau
MAYRHOFEN 630m
Bahnhof
Zillertalbahn
Hollenzen
Eckartau
Laubuhel
Sidantal
W N E S
Mountain railways
Cableways
Gondolaways
Chair-lifts
Drag-lifts
.... Easy runs
--------- Medium runs
——— Difficult runs
Mountain restaurants

MAYRHOFEN

Height of Resort: 2,067 ft.
Height of Top Station: 7,283 ft.
Nearest International Airport: Munich
Map Reference: 4D See page 237
Route by Car: See pages 236-237
Resort Facilities Charts: See page 215
Hotel Reference Charts: See page 228

Encircled by steep mountains, the small town of Mayrhofen, with some 3,600 inhabitants, spreads across the floor of the Ziller Valley, a well known area for summer visitors. There is a good selection of hotels, pensions, shops and bars. A great improvement in the transport system for the 1995/96 season is the replacement of the old Penken cableway, which only had a capacity of 650 persons per hour, by a gondolaway with cabins holding 15 persons and moving 2,000 persons per hour (see below). Apart from the skiing in Mayrhofen, visitors can obtain the Zillertal Super Ski Pass covering the use of 165 lifts in the Ziller valley including travel on trains and buses. The skiing around Mayrhofen is divided into three main areas:

Penkenjoch Area: The new gondolaway with 15 person cabins starts from the western side of the village and rises in an arc to the foot of the Penken double and triple chair-lifts, 6,233ft. Here one also finds two restaurants and beginners' lifts. On the top of the Penken one has a good variety of easy to medium skiing, well served by lifts, which include four chair-lifts and the Nordhang chair-lift, along with four smaller drag-lifts. On the north-east side of the mountain there is a good run down from the bottom of the two chair-lifts to Mühlbach, easy to start with but becoming difficult about a third of the way down; whilst on the south-west side of the mountain there is an interesting intermediate run down to Finkenberg, and one can take the gondolaway back to Penkenjoch. The ski area at the top is set amidst very attractive surroundings and is well served by mountain restaurants.

Horberg-Gerent Area: To the north-east of the village lies the lower station of the Horberg gondolaway, reached by skibus, which rises in a north-easterly direction to Horberg, 5,413ft.; there are six restaurants in this area. Here one has the choice of taking the Lärchwald chair-lift to the Penken area or the more recently constructed chair-lift rising northwards to Schafskopf, 7,382ft the highest station in the resort. From this point one can ski eastwards to the foot of the Gerentberg drag-lift and return to the top or continue on a south-west facing run which sweeps round to the foot of the chair-lift, intermediate and some 5km. in length. two further drag-lifts and a double chair-lift have been constructed in the Horberg-Tappenalm area. The Hintertrett 4-seater chair-lift opens in this area for the 1997/98 season. The Gerent area also provides some good powder skiing.

Ahorn Area: This is reached also by cableway, from the southern side of the village, and the skiing at the top, served by a chair-lift and five drag-lifts, is very suitable for beginners and second-year skiers, who are not advised to take the run down from the top to the bottom station of the cableway, which starts off as an intermediate run and becomes difficult towards the end. Next to the top station of the cableway there are two restaurants, at 6,248ft., and although the Ahorn area does not have the same variety as the Penken, it provides a pleasant change of scenery and a fairly challenging run down to the bottom station for the intermediate to good skier Its east facing slopes, normally provide better snow conditions.

In a Few Words: Mayrhofen has a good atmosphere – it's a very friendly resort and although it is widely spread, a free bus service operates to the main cableway terminals. Caters basically for beginners and medium grade; popular with groups and parties; excellent children's ski school; kindergarten 'Wuppy's Kinderland' for children from 3 months to 7 years; Nordic skiing; prices reasonable; lively night scene.

Après Ski: A good variety of activities and entertainment, including indoor swimming pools, saunas, skating, curling, bowling, adventure pool, squash courts, 3 indoor tennis courts, para-gliding, etc. There are several cafés and restaurants where local traditional music is played, along with a number of lively night clubs. The most modern and popular is the Arena underneath the Hotel Strass; the Schlüssel disco and the Papageno, where you can dance well into the night. Another popular spot is the Andreas Keller, attached to the Hotel Kramerwirt. The Post Tenne and the Fuchslöchl are smaller and Tyrolean in style. There are good restaurants at the top of each cableway, lots of cleared walks, and excursions to Innsbruck, Kitzbühel and Salzburg.

Recommended Hotels:

Hotel Elisabeth: A luxurious hotel, tastefully furnished in antique Tyrolean style. The many facilities include a lovely indoor swimming pool, sauna, steam bath, fitness centre and whirlpool free to guests; dancing, Papageno and Mamma Mia Pizzeria.

Hotel Kramerwirt: A charming Tyrolean style hotel of very high standard in all respects, in the centre of the village next to the church. 300-400 years old but completely renovated. Spacious dining room and reception rooms and large, well planned kitchen which ensures good service and food. Good sized bedrooms, all with bath or shower. Complete health centre at top of hotel. Comfortable bar and night club.

Hotel Neue Post: A popular and well run hotel. Comfortable bedrooms, with bath or shower and wc, attractive reception rooms, and the bar 'Tenne' with dancing every evening.

Sporthotel Strass: Adjoins the Hotel Strass, with same owner. All rooms with private bath or shower, balcony, radio and telephone. Swimming pool, sauna, solarium, squash and television room.

Hotel Strass: Conveniently situated next to the Penken cableway terminal; modernised, with good sized bedrooms, all with bath or shower, balcony, radio and telephone; dining room, lounge and two stüberls. A popular hotel.

TUX

(Hintertux, Lanersbach, Madseit, Juns, Vorderlanersbach)
Nearest International Airport: Munich
Map Reference: 4D See page 237
Route by Car: See pages 236-237

HINTERTUX

Height of Resort: 4,920 ft.
Height of Top Station: 10,693 ft.
Resort Facilities Charts: See page 214
Hotel Reference Charts: See page 227

At the head of the valley, about 18km. from Mayrhofen is the small, pretty resort of Hintertux, lying at the foot of the glacier. Its height ensures reliable snow conditions throughout the season, it is a good entry point for high mountain ski touring and there is also summer skiing on the glacier. From the edge of the village, where there is a very large car park, there is a choice of gondolaway or a double chair-lift up to Sommerbergalm, 6,822ft. From this point there are two drag-lifts to the west and a 4 seater chair-lift running north-west to Tuxer-Joch Hütte, 8,318ft. These lifts serve slopes providing easy to medium skiing. The main glacier skiing from the Sommerbergalm is reached by a 4-seater gondolaway or a 'Glacier-Bus' on two cables, 3 metres apart, carrying 24 persons, both of which swing downwards into the valley before rising again to reach the Tuxer-Ferner Haus, 8,725ft., where there is a restaurant and sun terrace. From here twin parallel chair-lifts rise to 10,004ft. and surmounting this is a double chair-lift which travels to the summit, Gefrorene-Wand-Spitze, 10,693ft. Running parallel to the top chair-lift are two drag-lifts allowing one to ski this top section over and over again. The runs down from this high area vary from medium to difficult, depending on the route taken. A superb long variation, starting as an easy traverse, is via the Grosser Kaserer and Olperer, where there are four drag-lifts and parallel to the Lärmstange, a double chair-lift, or one can ski the runs following the line of the lifts back to Sommerbergalm or down to the village. The skiing on the glacier has been further extended by the construction of the 'Schlegeis-Gletscher' triple chair-lift.

In a Few Words: Attractive village with excellent skiing for all standards; 86 km. of prepared runs; wonderful off-piste skiing; excellent ski touring; snow conditions reliable throughout long season; summer glacier skiing.

Après Ski: The Tuxertal as an area provides ski bobbing, toboggan runs, curling, 32km. prepared walks, massage, bowling, swimming, sauna. There is dancing at the Papperla-Pub and the 'Batzenkeller'; fondue evenings, excellent restaurants and café bars.

Recommended Hotels:

Badhotel Kirchler: Constructed in Tyrolean style, 190 beds in hotel and annexe, comfortably furnished rooms all with bath in the modern section. Tiroler stüberl and attractive café-bar with dancing in discothèque in hotel's annexe. Indoor swimming pool, sauna and solarium.

LANERSBACH

Height of Resort: 4,230 ft.
Height of Top Station:8,202 ft.
Resort Facilities Charts: See page 214
Hotel Reference Charts: See page 228

Lanersbach is the largest village of the Tuxertal, sunny and sheltered, on the floor of the steeply rising valley. The Eggalm gondolaway leads from the edge of the village to the Eggalm restaurant, 6,560ft., from which there is a superb view of the Zillertal Alps and here there are open slopes, served by one drag-lift and two double chair-lifts. Medium grade runs through both open and lightly wooded slopes lead to the village, and beginners are catered for by slopes near the top station in addition to the nursery slopes with drag-lifts near the village.

The sunny Rastkogel area is reached from the village by a gondolaway, rising to 6,890ft. The skiing here is mainly above the tree-line and served by a drag-lift and two double chair-lifts, the latter reaching the shoulder of Horbergjoch at a height of 8,202ft. The runs are easy and intermediate. There are two restaurants in the area.

In a Few Words: Agreeable small resort, suitable for beginners to medium grade. The development of the Rastkogel area has extended the skiing considerably, with skiing right back to the village.

Après Ski: Atmosphere informal; various agreeably relaxed cafés, bars, and discothèques. There are weekly guest ski races; swimming; sauna; village festivals; 3 indoor tennis and squash courts.

Recommended Hotels:

Sporthotel Kirchler: Small but well run hotel in the centre of the village. Bedrooms are attractive and comfortable. Pleasant à la carte restaurant and bar, dancing twice weekly in high season.

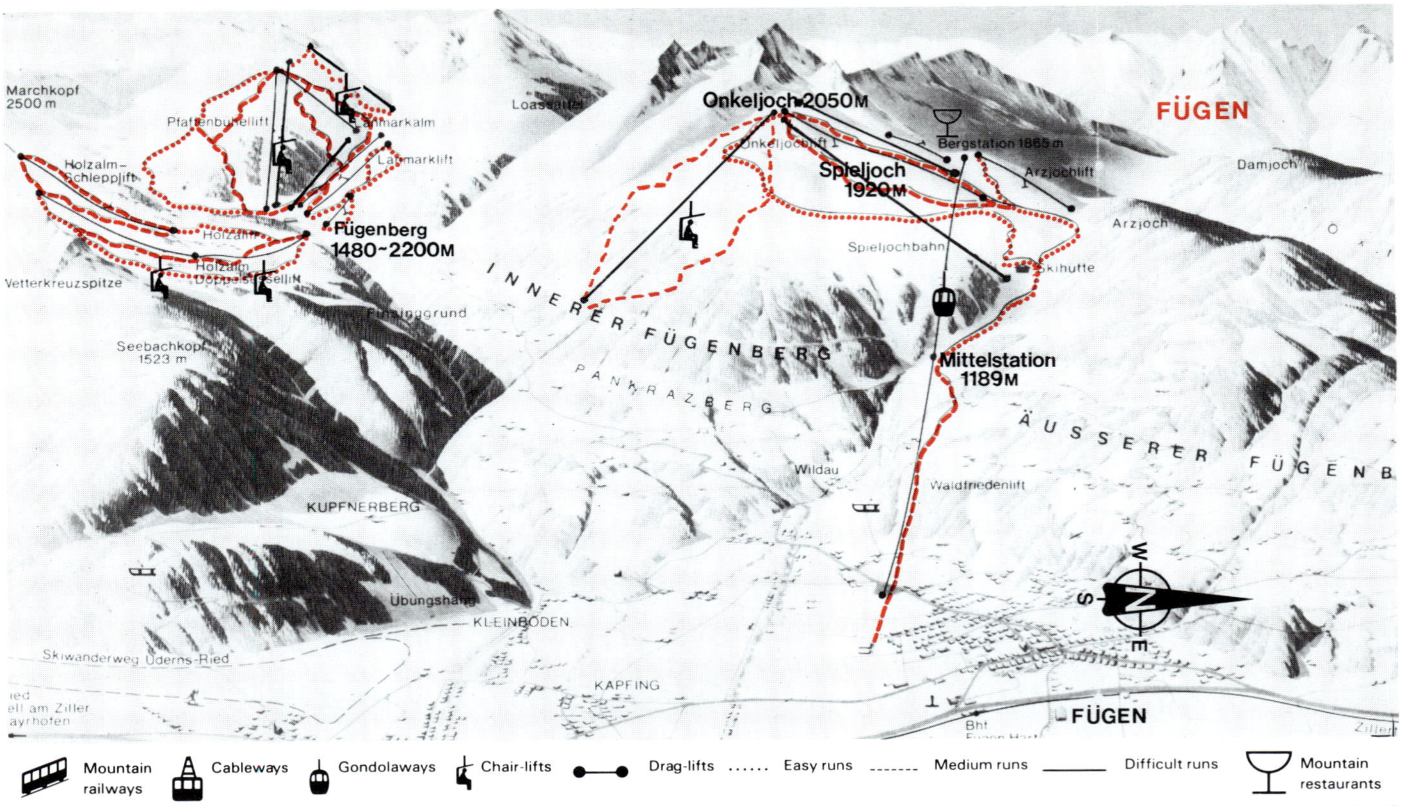

FÜGEN/FÜGENBERG

Height of Resort: 1,853/4,855 ft.
Height of Top Station: 6,888 ft. (Fügen); 7,216 ft. (Fügenberg)
Nearest International Airport: Munich
Map Reference: 4D See page 237
Route by Car: See pages 236-237
Resort Facilities Charts: See page 213
Hotel Reference Charts: See page 227

Fügen is situated at the entrance to the Ziller valley, 7km. from the Zillertal exit from the Munich-Kufstein-Innsbruck autobahn. It is thus easily accessible by road from both Munich, approximately 2 hours, or Innsbruck, approximately 30 minutes. Fügen, a village with 44 hotels and pensions and some 3,700 inhabitants, is a very ancient settlement first mentioned in document in 726 A.D. Like most of the resorts in the Zillertal, Fügen, at only 1,853ft., is relatively low in altitude, which means that the snow coverage on the lower runs can be vulnerable after the end of March. However, as the runs are over smooth grass meadows, only a small amount of snow coverage is required.

Fügen's Local Skiing: Fügen's skiing area is reached by the Spieljochbahn, a gondolaway, the bottom station of which is about 1 mile west of and above the village, and a free bus shuttle service is operated at convenient times for ski pass holders. This 4km. long gondolaway lifts one, via a middle station at 3,834ft., to the Spieljoch Bergstation at 6,117ft. Here there is a restaurant and a choice of drag-lifts, the longest of which reaches up to 6,888ft. From Skihütte a triple chair-lift rises to Onkeljoch, increasing the uphill capacity still further in the area.The runs up at Spieljoch are generally north and north-east facing, and vary from steep to easy. The run all the way down to Fügen, a drop of approximately 5,000,ft. and 7km. in length, is truly magnificent when the snow is good. It is mainly east facing and in parts medium to steep gradient. The run passes the middle station, giving one the alterative of returning again to the top.

A very good and sunny beginner's slope with an easy lift is situated, together with the ski school and ski hire facilities, just below the bottom station. There are three well organised ski schools and the instructors are very friendly.

The Fügenberg Skiing: Although some 13km. distant, the skiing at Fügenberg is considered part of the Fügen area and included in the ski pass. The buses are free for skiers. Fügenberg (little more than a couple of hotels) has three chair-lifts and eight drag-lifts starting at 4,854ft. and reaching 7,216ft. Runs face all points of the compass and vary from steepish to easy. Pleasant skiing for a couple of days or so, even for the proficient.

In addition to the Fügen ski pass there is the Zillertal Super Ski Pass. This allows unlimited use of some 154 lifts in the whole of the Ziller valley, covering the resorts, in addition to Fügen, of Finkenberg, Gerlos, Hintertux (up to 10,693ft.), Lanersbach, Mayrhofen, Ramsberg/Hippach, Kaltenbach and Zell am Ziller. This pass entitles skiers to free travel on buses or on the Zillertal railway.

In a Few Words: A pleasant unspoilt village. The Zillertal has a reputation for its hospitality and Fügen is certainly no exception. Very friendly well organised ski school. Good for beginners and early intermediates. One excellent long run for medium to expert skiers and enjoyable skiing for all standards at Fügenberg, but for them not enough variety for a whole fortnight. However, Fügen makes a good base for area skiing, with the Ziller pass, in all the resorts of the Zillertal. Buses available but one's own car an advantage. Due to low altitude of the village itself the lower runs may be short of snow after March. Cross-country skiing, ski kindergarten, toboggan run. Snowboard Fun Parks in both ski areas.

Après Ski: Après ski in its original form can be found at the Pension Alpina, Pub Aha and in the Hotels Spieljoch, and Kohlerhof, and in Fügenberg the Berghotel and Hotel Lamark. This small village, superimposed with modernity, can produce some evening surprises. The charming Palette, old, small and intimate, alternates between a live band and discothèque. The discos Badwandl, 'Live' and Tenne are also very popular and drink prices are reasonable. Fridays celebrate ski prize giving with a Ski Lehrer's ball, and Saturdays are dance nights. Sleigh rides are available. There is a clinic for a variety of treatments and therapies. All in all a happy time can be had by everyone.

Recommended Hotels:

Pension Elisabeth: Ideally situated beside ski school assembly points and nursery slopes. At the foot of the gondolaway to the main ski slopes. Built in 1975 in attractive modern wooden style with stüberl/ dining room. All rooms with shower/wc. Hub of activity for après ski. Large sun terrace and well balconied.

Gasthof Malerhaus: Situated right by the little Ziller railway and on the bus route to the slopes. Modernised old-style gasthaus run with pride and care by the charming owners, family Haun. Exceptionally good à la carte cooking. Always a little extra something for breakfast. 200m. from skating rink. Two large sun terraces and many private balconies. Good value. Young Mr. Haun speaks English.

Hotel Post: A good hotel in centre of village. Rebuilt in attractive style in 1960. Free swimming pool for guests and twice-weekly saunas. Solarium. Rifle range with automatic targets; and choice of menus.

Luncheon vouchers available. Telephones and showers in all bedrooms.

ZELL im ZILLERTAL

Height of Resort: 1,902 ft.
Height of Top Station: 7,900 ft.
Nearest International Airport: Munich
Map Reference: 4D See page 237
Route by Car: See pages 236-237
Resort Facilities Charts: See page 216
Hotel Reference Charts: See page 229

Zell im Zillertal lies to the heart of the Ziller Valley (Zillertal) where the road divides to continue up the valley or over the Gerlos pass. As it is only 21km. from the Munich-Kufstein-Innsbruck autobahn it is easily accessible by road. Alternatively one can take the little narrow-gauge railway from Jenbach.

Zell im Zillertal has for long been a popular summer resort; its advent as a skiing centre has been more recent. The skiing is divided into two separate areas:

Kreuzjoch Area: The opening of this area in 1978 has transformed Zell am Ziller as a ski resort. It is reached from the centre of the village by a free skibus service, and here a gondolaway takes one up to Wiesenalm, 4,295ft., where there is a very old small mountain restaurant, Grindlalm. From this point there is no skiing back to the village. From Wiesenalm one takes the gondolaway up to Rosenalm, 5,774ft. From the restaurant one looks upon a wide open sunny ski bowl with five drag-lifts and three double chair-lifts, the latter rising to Kreuzjoch, 7,900ft., the resort's top station, serving runs of easy to intermediate standard, over south-west facing slopes. The beginners' and children's ski schools meet at Rosenalm. The run down to Wiesenalm by the side of the gondolaway is of intermediate standard over west facing slopes. Also from Wiesenalm the Sportkarspitz double chair-lift rises south-eastwards and from the top one can cross over to the Kreuzwiesen drag-lift or return to base on a black run.

Gerlosstein Area: The Gerlossteinbahn is situated 3.3 miles from the village and 1,134 vertical feet above it. Buses are fairly frequent, free for skiers, and take 13 minutes to reach the bottom station at 3,048ft. This cableway takes one up to 5,412ft. Here there is a choice of three surmounting lifts, the most important being the Arbiskogel chair-lift to 6,019ft. Runs back to the top station vary from medium to easy. The mainly north facing run all the way down to the bottom station, over 3,000 vertical feet, is a good one (often used as a racecourse) but can be closed for lack of snow on its lower slopes later in the season. The halfway chair-lift Sonnalm, to the south-west of the cableway, converges on the top station, Arbiskogel and gives access to intermediate north-west facing runs back to base or to the lower station on the cableway. The Ramsau chair-lift belongs to the neighbouring resort of Ramsau/Hippach but is included on the Zell ski pass. Apart from the areas mentioned, there are other odd, privately owned, small drag-lifts dotted around, but they play no significant part.

While the snow lasts in the village, beginners and ski school meet just outside the village at the Wimbach-lift (free bus service taking 3 minutes). Later, a beginner's lift is used below the Gerlosstein bottom station, although more usually beginners are taken up to the bowls on the Gerlosstein and Rosenalm. The two ski schools are well organised, friendly and enthusiastic. They hold a guest race every Thursday. There are also 25km. of langlauf trails.

For better skiers Zell im Zillertal makes a most convenient base for skiing all the ten ski resorts in the Zillertal covered by the comprehensive 'Ski Pass Zillertal' which covers 154 lifts (described more fully under Fügen).

In a Few Words: The opening of the Kreuzjoch ski area has greatly improved the facilities of this resort. 47km. of runs of varying grades. Particularly suitable for beginners to intermediate skiers. Advanced skiers have the advantage of the 10 nearby resorts on one pass; free bus service included in the abonnement, but a car a distinct advantage. An unspoilt village which is particularly popular with the less demanding British skiers, and many visitors return year after year.

Après Ski: Unsophisticated but perfectly adequate, many of the hotels having live music, as well as weekly attractions such as schuhplättlers, barbecues and the neverfailing Tiroler abends. Every Thursday evening the ski school prizegiving takes place. The Tourist Office does list skating, curling and tobogganing but because of Zell's low altitude conditions, particularly later in the season, may not be good. The non-skier's pass allows transportation to many pleasant restaurants with large sun terraces. 20km. of cleared walks, and bus excursions to various parts of Austria including Innsbruck, Kitzbühel and the Hintertux glacier, to mention but a few.

A new sports centre open for the 1996/97 season will contain tennis halls, artifical skating and curling rink and play area.

Recommended Hotels:

Hotel Englhof: Beautifully decorated in Tyrolean style. Family owners anxious to please. Overlooks the river Ziller and therefore quieter and nearer the main nursery slopes than most. All rooms have showers, wc and balconies. Large bar-lounge 'Tiroler Stube' with occasional live music for dancing.

Hotel Tirolerhof: A popular hotel, unsophisticated but alive and all-go atmosphere. Situated in the middle of the town on the main street. There are the usual tour specials, e.g. beer evenings, schuhplättler abends and nightly disco, available to all comers. Chinese fondue and greetings glass of wine weekly. Most bedrooms have balconies and 20 have private fridges.

Berghotel Zellerhof: A most attractive hotel and very popular. A variety of small attractions for guests' pleasure, e.g. daily buffet breakfast and evening 'Welcome drinks'; weekly barbecue in keller at small extra charge; meals till 2 a.m. in tiny, ancient grill. All rooms have bathrooms with 2 large basins.

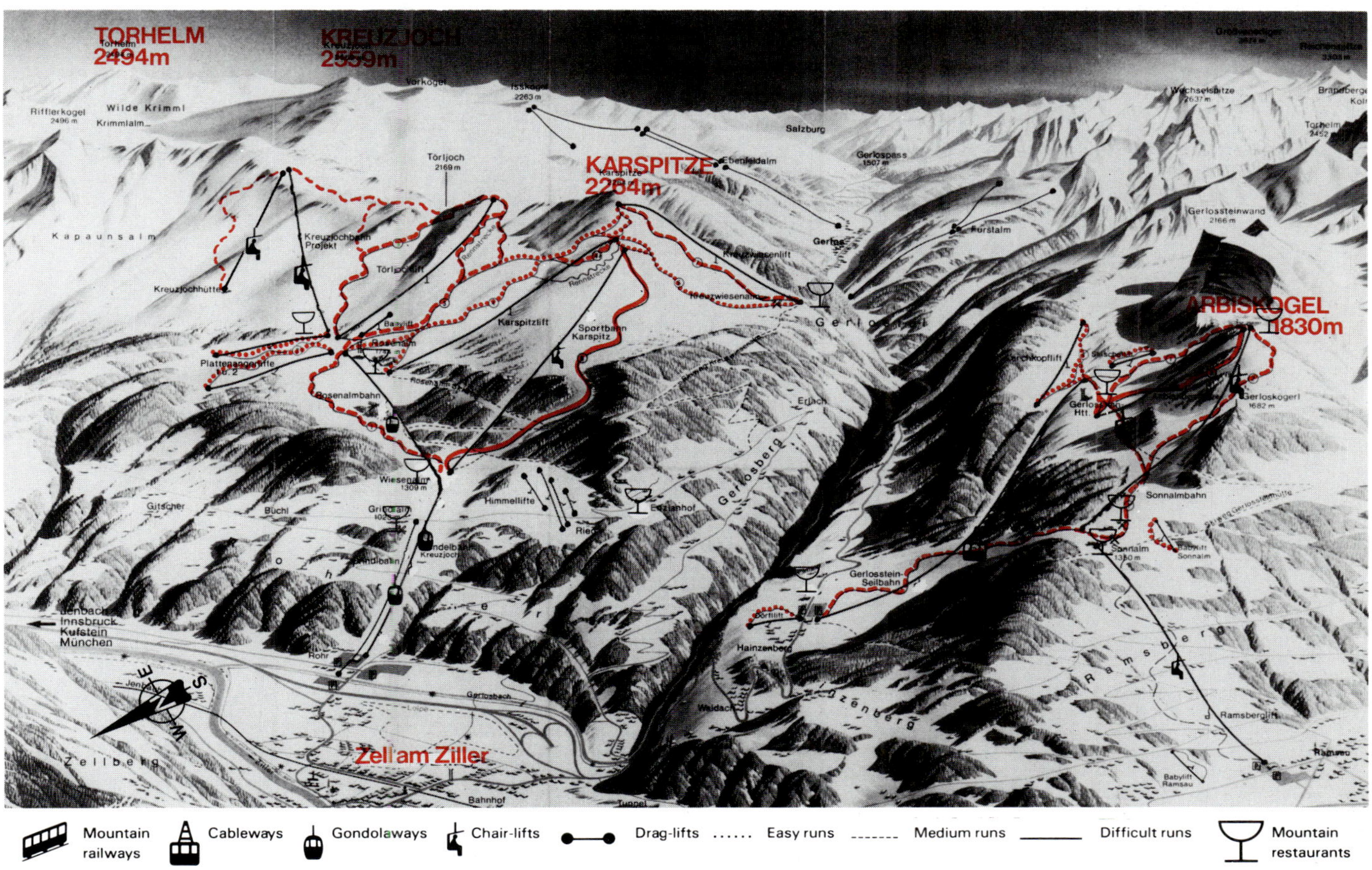

ALPBACH

Height of Resort: 3,281 ft.
Height of Top Station: 6,102 ft.
Nearest International Airport: Munich
Map Reference: 4D See page 237
Route by Car: See pages 236-237
Resort Facilities Charts: See page 212
Hotel Reference Charts: See page 227

Alpbach is a very pretty village with great charm and a happy, friendly atmosphere, small and compact with all its buildings in Tyrolean style. In a nationwide TV contest in 1983 it was voted the prettiest village in Austria. It lies between the Wildschönau and the lower Zillertal and is approached by road from Brixlegg. The skiing is suitable for all standards, but is particularly recommended for beginners to intermediates. The off-piste skiing is excellent. The nursery slopes are very near the village, with their own drag-lifts, and an efficient bus service takes skiers in four minutes to the lower terminal of the Wiedersbergerhorn 2-stage six seater gondolaway and to the Inneralpbach double chair-lift and drag-lift in 6 minutes. The gondolaway rises to the Kriegalm restaurant, 4,429ft., and the second section continues to Hornboden, 6,069ft., with a chair-lift running parallel. Here one finds a restaurant. The skiing in this area has been much improved by the installation of two drag-lifts, both of which converge above the top station of the Gmah 3-seater chair-lift. The two Mulden lifts provide access to easy-medium runs, while the Brandegg lift serves slopes suitable for the medium and advanced skier. The Galtenberg drag-lift from Inneralpbach and the Pögl chair-lift further to the west converge on the lower station of the Pögl double chair-lift which rises towards Wiedersbergerhorn thus providing easy access to the top station for residents of Inneralpbach and more extensive skiing for all concerned. The skiing from the top station includes difficult and medium standard runs, some with 3,000ft. descent and 10,000ft. long, and as the slopes are mostly north facing the snow conditions are generally good and the pistes are well maintained. The runs from the top station to Inneralpbach are covered by snow cannons.

The two ski schools are very well organised, and nordic skiing courses also operate from Inneralpbach, 3km. up the valley.

The lift pass includes the shuttle bus service between the village and the 2-stage gondolaway and also between Inneralpbach. Visitors residing in Alpbach should obtain from their hotel a 'guest card' which allows a reduction on the price of the lift pass. Children under 15 years receive a reduction of about 25-30% on the lift pass. Those under 5 years free if skiing with an adult. Alpbach is the headquarters of a British run club, the Alpbach Visitors Ski Club. Full information can be obtained from the Secretary, Mrs. R. W. (Dinny) Patterson, Bärhaus, 6236 Alpbach, Tirol, Austria.

In a Few Words: Good for groups and families with beginners amongst them, but also catering for the more experienced; ski kindergarten and one for non skiers 3-6 years old; a delightful small village and good value.

Après Ski: Lively and informal.The discothèque Weinstadl at the Alphof Hotel is very popular; so is the Birdy Pub, in Hotel Post and the Hornbeisl in Inneralpbach. Fun too are the sleigh rides to the old inn at Rosmoos followed by quaffing glühwein to the sound of music. At tea-time there is a delicious variety of cakes at the Jakoberwirt, a very popular small bar; or a fantastic selection of ice cream sundaes at the Böglerhof. The large indoor pool has gorgeous views of the Wiedersbergerhorn mountains. Shops include an excellent unisex hairdresser, two good supermarkets plus a good fashion shop and 5 ski equipment shops. Evening babysitting can be arranged through the Tourist Office and there is a good ski kindergarten.

Recommended Hotels:

Hotel Alpbacherhof: A modern chalet-style hotel, with attractive lounge and dining room. Good sized bedrooms, each with balcony, also sun terrace, and indoor swimming pool.

Haus Angelika: This delightful modern chalet-style bed and breakfast pension has beautifully furnished bedrooms, all with bath, attractive breakfast room and sitting room. Main meals taken at Hotel Jakoberwirt.

Hotel Böglerhof: A very fine hotel, spacious and attractively furnished. Large lounge, rebuilt in 1970 with lovely views, elegant dining room and wood panelled stüberl, bar, heated indoor swimming pool, free to guests, sauna, solarium, children's playroom. Bedrooms tastefully furnished; those with bath are particularly attractive.

Hotel Jakoberwirt: Standing on the village square, this old-world inn has much atmosphere. Particularly attractive dining rooms in modern Tyrolean style, comfortable bedrooms and the bar, providing good draught beer, is a popular meeting place. A lively atmosphere and not for quiet people.

WILDSCHÖNAU AREA

Nearest International Airport: Munich
Map Reference: 5C See page 237
Route by Car: See page 236-237

Lying between the Wilder Kaiser Mountains to the north and the Kitzbüheler Alps to the south is the beautiful open valley of the Wildschönau, approached from the Inn valley through the town of Wörgl. The three main resorts are first Niederau; Oberau, a further 3km. away, and last Auffach, another 5km. along the valley. Snow conditions are good here in spite of the relatively low altitude of these resorts, as the valley is protected from the warm southerly Föhn wind by the high Kitzbüheler mountains, and the majority of the runs are on north, north-east or north-west facing slopes. The lift

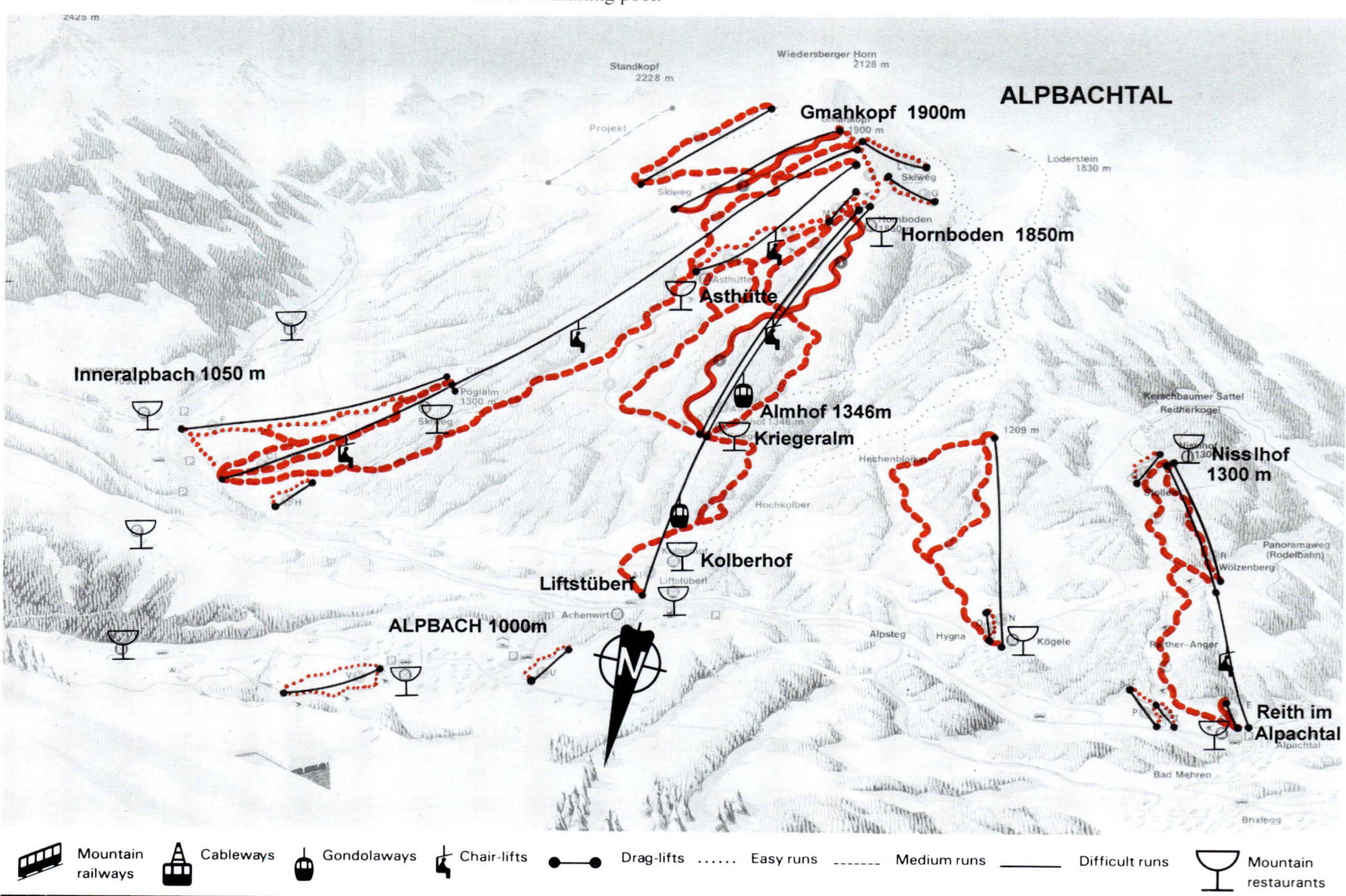

systems of the three resorts are not linked but a bus service runs between them and the lift pass covers all three resorts. All guests in the Wildschönau are entitled to a visitor's pass obtainable from the Tourist Office or hotels. Holders are allowed to use the ski-bus service free of charge. Nordic skiing (langlauf) has become popular in the Wildschönau, and several interesting trails are laid out.

NIEDERAU

Height of Resort: 2,700 ft.
Height of Top Station: 5,333 ft.
Resort Facilities Charts: See page 215
Hotel Reference Charts: See page 228

The largest of the resorts, Niederau, is fairly spread out, with 25 hotels and pensions and around 60 bed and breakfast guest houses and its lift system is the most extensive. An 8 person cabin gondolaway, opened for the 1995/96 season, travels from a terminal to the east of the church to Markbachjoch, 4,750ft. Here there are two gasthofs (from which one has beautiful views over the valley), as well as beginners' slopes served by two drag-lifts, and a restaurant. For the more experienced there are two good red runs back to the village, one being a FIS giant slalom course. The other main lift out of the resort is a single chair-lift to Lanerköpfl reaching 4,750ft and at the top nearby is the attractive Anton Graf Hütte restaurant with sun terrace. A short distance away is a drag-lift which takes one to the highest point in the resort, 5,333ft. From here one can either ski east along the ridge to join the Markbachjoch or all the way down to the village via the excellent FIS approved Downhill course requiring intermediate skills.

In all one has three medium to steep pisted runs back to the village ranging from $2^{1}/_{2}$ to 5km. but there are many good off-piste possibilities in between. All slopes are north or north-east facing through glades and finishing in the village. Immediately south of the village there are excellent nursery slopes served by three drag-lifts. For second week skiers or for those staying at the east end of the resort there is the longer Tennladen drag-lift. Niederau now has two ski schools.

OBERAU

Height of Resort: 3,070 ft.
Height of Top Station: 4,050 ft.
Hotel Reference Charts: See page 228

A delightful village built around its church and an erstwhile 11th century monastery, now the Gasthof Kellerwirt, Oberau is an ideal spot for beginners and intermediate skiers accompanying them. The nursery slopes are served by seven drag-lifts and a baby-lift, the longest rising to Riedlberg, 4,050ft where there is a very attractive restaurant, once an old farmhouse. The Riedlberg lift serves a good steep training slope and is well worth a visit from the neighbouring resorts, especially in the afternoon when the sun reaches the slope. The intermediate skier can easily stay in Oberau, as both Auffach and Niederau are so close at hand, and the lift pass covers all three resorts, including the interconnecting transportation.

AUFFACH

Height of Resort: 3,000 ft.
Height of Top Station: 6,235 ft.
Hotel Reference Charts: See page 227

Auffach is still small but it has grown fairly quickly over the past few years and there are now nine hotels and a selection of pensions and guest houses. There are two sports shops. For a small resort the skiing is good, as the recently extended network of lifts has opened up a variety of runs from a height of 6,235ft. The four-seater gondolaway stops at the middle station, 4,334ft. but one can continue to the top station without alighting. At the middle station there is a delightful modern gasthof, the Berghaus Koglmoos. Supplementing the top section is a drag-lift reaching the same height.

On the summit, the Schatzberg Plateau, 5,800ft., there is a large restaurant with sun terrace and four long drag-lifts interconnecting to the left and a further one to the right. The runs down, over east and north-east facing slopes, vertical descent over 3,000ft., are long and really excellent red and blue gradings with many variations. A special snow-board piste and half-pipe have been installed at this resort.

In a Few Words: Interesting ski terrain amidst beautiful countryside. Plenty of good off-piste skiing and touring; the valley's east-west orientation causes snow conditions normally to be dependable; very popular with the British and ideal for families. Kindergarten (Niederau and Oberau). Prices reasonable, good value. The lift pass covers all three resorts and the ski bus service.

Après Ski: Niederau: Most popular spots are the Cave bar at the Staffler (good discothèque and delicious toasted sandwiches) and the Bichlwirt, where Herbert plays the harp. Discos also operate at the Hotel Vicky, and Dorfstuben Café. There are Tyrolean evenings, sleigh rides, fondue parties, bowling evenings and a weekly prizegiving dance after the ski school races. There is a swimming pool, whirlpools and sauna at the 4 star Vitalhotel Sonnschein and also a sauna/solarium and a small swimming pool at the Hotel Austria. Riding at the indoor school and para-gliding are also available, both with instruction.

Oberau: The Café bars are full, the Hotel Kellerwirt is the favourite spot and the Ski Instructors' Ball takes place every week and is most entertaining, particularly when the instructors do the cabaret. A popular night spot is the Pub Sno-Blau and the Starchenthof with zither music.

Auffach: Here the Keller Bar at the Gasthof Platzl is popular, with an area large enough to seat 150, charming wooden decor and live music once a week. Tyrolean evenings and fondue parties can be arranged. Tobogganing is also available and toboggans can be hired from Weissbacher - Café Martin, where Tyrolean music is played. Above the village, the Bernauerhof is an agreeable place to visit for a drink and sometimes, music. About 1km. down the valley is another popular spot, the Haflingerhof.

Recommended Hotels:

Niederau - Hotel Austria: In a central position. Entrance hall-sitting room attractively furnished and large windows, bar and sun terrace. Modern comfortable bedrooms, all with bath or shower and radio and balcony. Heated indoor swimming pool for guests.

Haus Jochum: Situated 8-10 minutes walk from the village centre and close to the Tennladen lift, these are apartments beautifully furnished and fitted for 2-5 people, four consisting of two bedrooms, bathroom, large living room with balcony or terrace and a fully equipped modern kitchen; three consisting of one bedroom, lounge/living room with kitchen facilities and bathroom. All apartments are equipped with radio, TV, telephone and dishwasher. Free use of laundry and ironing room, as well as fitness and hobby room. Very popular with families and owned by the chief instructor, Franz Jochum and his English wife Janet. Evening meal arranged at nearby hotel if required.

Hotel Staffler: This modern hotel, one minute from the village centre, has an excellent atmosphere. Bright open plan dining room, bar, restaurant, with large sun terrace outside. Comfortable bedrooms many with private bath or shower. Lively keller bar, the 'Cave', for dancing each evening to disco music.

Hotel Vicky: A delightful Tyrolean style hotel 2 minutes' walk from the centre. Run by the owners, Herr & Frau Unger . Attractive dining room with good food, daily choice of menu and generous helpings. Large bar with draft beer, twice weekly 'happy hour' and some popular disco nights with prizes and free drinks. Well furnished bedrooms, fitted carpets, bathroom, wc, telephone and most with balconies.

Oberau - Gasthof Bergland: This excellent 3 star hotel is run by the Erharter family. All 36 bedrooms have bath/shower, wc, balcony, telephone and radio.Spacious dining room with first class service and food, lounge areas, bar, two stubes, fitness centre, solarium, sauna and turkish baths, and sun terrace. 1500 metres from centre but the ski bus stops outside.

Gasthof Kellerwirt: Built as a monastery in the 11th Century and converted to an inn 300 years ago, the Kellerwirt has much historical charm and atmosphere and is the social centre of the village. The long Tyrolean dining room is most attractive with much wooden decor, small sitting room, tap room with draught beer, popular bar in the vaulted wine cellar, large sun terrace. The bedrooms in the old section are comfortable with bath or shower wc, whilst those in the new building are very attractive all with bath and balcony. Sauna, steam bath and solarium in new building.

Chalet Stefanie: Situated next to the ski school meeting place and drag-lift, this is an attractive bed and breakfast pension. Wood panelled stüberl. Most of the pleasantly furnished bedrooms have balcony and a few with private shower. Sauna. It also has a ski hire and equipment shop.

Auffach - Gasthof Platzl: A pleasant hotel with 50 beds, in centre of village, comfortable modern bedrooms, 12 with private bath. Attractive dining room, sitting room, bar and large keller bar, seating 150 persons, with dancing each evening to disco music.

Berghaus Koglmoos: Situated at the middle station of the gondolaway, with skiing to and from the door, the Koglmoos offers delightful flats, with sunny balconies, above its restaurant. Although equipped with a small kitchen and fridge the arrangement includes a set dinner in the restaurant. Car owners can use the road from Auffach which is kept open.

KIRCHBERG

Height of Resort: 2,830 ft.
Height of Top Station: 6,383 ft.
Nearest International Airport: Salzburg
Map Reference: 5C See page 237
Route by Car: See pages 236-237
Resort Facilities Charts: See page 214
Hotel Reference Charts: See page 228

Kirchberg, a large village, situated in the Brixental 6km. from Kitzbühel, is bustling and full of life from early morning to late evening. A good bus and train service connects both resorts. There are many shops of varying size and standard where virtually anything can be purchased. Accommodation ranges from the smart hotels down to a small family gasthof, providing a total of 8,000 beds.

The main skiing is linked with Kitzbühel. The two resorts share many of the same pistes and a single ticket, whether daily or weekly, is good for all the lifts in the area as well as for buses and also the Aquarena in Kitzbühel. The skiing can be divided into five sectors:-

Obergaisberg: At the foot and near the village are the nursery slopes where the ski school meets and this area is serviced by a nursery lift, three drag-lifts and a chair-lift.

Gaisberg: This area with its chair-lift gives access to the giant slalom where World Cup races are held. Guest competitions are also held on this course and medals are awarded. A recently constructed toboggan run is to be found in this area, which is floodlit 4 nights a week.

Maierl: Some 15 minutes' walk up from the valley, but serviced by ski-buses and taxis, one finds three surmounting double chair-lifts passing the Oxalm up to Ehrenbachhöhe, a height of 3,608ft., over a distance of 3,627 metres, this top station is the link with the main ski area. Two surmounting drag-lifts rise from Obwiesen and converge on the top station of the first chair-lift, an alternative means of access.

Klausen: Reached from the village by ski-bus or taxi, the six-seater Fleckalm gondolaway, moving 2,400 skiers per hour, rises to the Ehrenbachhöhe area, where a whole panorama of ski lifts and pistes is at one's disposal. To the left is the Hahnenkamm area (see Kitzbühel). Straight on is the Steinbergkogel, by way of a double chair-lift. This is the highest point of the area, 6,383ft., where one finds a restaurant on a windswept ridge and from here one can ski back to Kirchberg or Kitzbühel and to many other areas.

Pengelstein-Aschau: This long and delightful run from the top of the Pengelstein leads down to the valley and ski-bus returns one to Kirchberg, about half-way down one can take the 4 seater chair-lift back to the top of the Pengelstein.

There are easy and intermediate runs from the top stations of all five areas back to the valley.

Kirchberg has three ski schools and many of the 190 instructors speak English. A special feature is that you can leave the children there from 10 a.m. until 4 p.m., which for those with small children is a great asset.

Another important feature is the ski safari run, which starts at Kirchberg and provides a day's skiing over 37 kilometres ending at Pass Thurn for return by bus or taxi. This route is clearly marked with the sign of the elephant and gives a delightful run for those at intermediate level and passes through all sections of the area.

For those interested in Nordic skiing, this area provides 120 kilometres of runs linked with free use of the ski bus if carrying your equipment, Kirchberg being linked with Brixen and also Westendorf.

In a Few Words: Kirchberg is a resort that offers everything that skiers want and is certainly a place many wish to go back to. Nevertheless it is slightly commercialised: on the whole it is expensive and is influenced by nearby Kitzbühel. The skiing is good and varied with excellent ski-bus services. A very active night life will always guarantee a few hangovers.

Après Ski: Kirchberg offers the widest possible choice of après ski. For coffee and cakes Café Lorenzoni offers an excellent selection. There are 6 night clubs, all with their own particular style and theme. They range from 'Andrea's Tenne', which has its own group and is especially popular amongst the young, to the Kuh Stall, which is more traditional in its decor and music vis-a-vis and La Bamba and the Piccadilly are also popular. The atmosphere quickly builds up and fully justifies the reputation of the Tyrol. Drink prices are expensive and are very similar wherever you go. A great variety of restaurants – try the Boomerang for the excellent kebab – and a wide range of bars and pubs. Special evenings are organised by individual hotels.

Recommended Hotels:

Hotel Landhaus Brauns: Without doubt the most conveniently placed hotel for the skier, standing near the nursery slopes. An elegant hotel with rooms decorated in traditional style. A swimming pool and bar adjoin the reception area. Its capacity of only 48 guests means a personalised service.

Hotel Sonne: A large open-plan reception with adjoining lounge welcomes guests to this pleasant first class hotel. There are a total of 46 bedrooms, all with bath or shower. Most of these are in the new wing, with wide panoramic south-facing windows. There are 18 rooms with balconies. A bar overlooks a superb swimming pool, which also has a sauna and solarium.

KITZBÜHEL

Height of Resort: 2,503 ft.
Height of Top Station: 6,562 ft.
Nearest International Airport: Munich/Salzburg
Map Reference: 5C See page 237
Route by Car: See pages 236-237
Resort Facilities Charts: See page 214
Hotel Reference Charts: See page 228

Kitzbühel is an international resort surrounded by beautiful mountains and lying in a snow pocket, so that in spite of its low altitude good snow conditions usually prevail from mid-December to the end of March, and continue until much later on the higher slopes. It is a fairly large, old and picturesque walled town with colourful painted Tyrolean buildings dating back to the 13th century. It's a place with tremendous appeal for some, though not for others. It caters for everyone, from beginners to experienced skiers, and is ideal for groups of mixed standards. Much of the skiing is above the tree line, but there is an immense variety of runs in the tree line, the latter being particularly suitable when there are stormy conditions and bad visibility. There are four main skiing areas, two on the west facing side of the valley, one on the east, and one on the south.

Hahnenkamm Area: A new high capacity 6-seater gondolaway rises to a height of 5,577ft., giving access to an enormous variety of lifts too numerous to describe individually. This well interlinked system, taking one to a height of 6,562ft., provides a host of runs, mostly of medium standard, ranging from 1.5 to 6.8km. in length. The longer of these lead down to Aurach, Jochberg, Hechenmoos, Aschau, Kirchberg, and Kitzbühel itself. This area alone provides a great selection of enjoyable skiing and is particularly recommended for off piste skiing. Happily the installation of the new gondolaway has almost removed queuing from this bottom station out of the village. The whole of the Streif, Kampen, Ehrenbachgraben/Griesalm and most of the lower slopes of the valley are served by 28 snow cannons, which almost guarantees snow cover for most of the season.

Kitzbüheler Horn Area: A two stage 6-seater gondolaway rises first to Pletzeralm and thence to Alpenhaus, 5,440ft., where there is a large restaurant. From the mid station, Pletzeralm, a cableway reaches the Horn, 6,450ft. On the eastern side of these top stations one can take the intermediate run down to Raintal, returning by chair-lift; or enjoy easy to intermediate skiing to the south served by a network of 5 lifts. Returning to the valley there is a fairly testing run via Pletzeralm and an easy run which winds its way down to Kitzbühel on the left. There is also a 6.5 km. nordic ski trail in this area.

Bichalm Area: From the edge of the neighbouring village of Aurach a chair-lift rises to 5,480ft., and connects with 2 drag-lifts, finally reaching Stuckkogel, a height of 6,100 ft. Here there is good medium grade skiing mostly over south facing slopes and also several fine off-piste runs to Fieberbrunn and Oberaurach or back to the chair-lift bottom station.

Jochberg-Pass Thurn Area: This fourth area is very extensive. It is well sign posted being part of the ski safari and easily accomplished by intermediate skiers. The combined area which has 15 lifts is a good one to ski over when the other areas are crowded. From Jochberg one takes the chair-lift and surmounting drag-lift to Talsenalm and from this point one can easily connect with two further drag-lifts up the Bärenbadkogel where there is excellent skiing in and above the treeline. From the top one can ski back to Jochberg via Talsenalm or across to the foot of the Zweitausender chair-lift at Pass Thurn where a further chair-lift and 5 drag-lifts provide access to runs mostly to medium skiing on north and north-west facing slopes, with the exception of the runs served by the Zweitausender chair-lift, which are very steep and for good skiers only. Snow cannons operate in the Talsen – Wurzhöhe-Süd area.

The Kitzbühel abonnement, which also includes the Aquarena, an outstanding complex of swimming pools, sauna, solarium, massage and sun terrace and bus services, covers the interlinking resorts of Kirchberg, Aurach, Jochberg and Pass Thurn. The whole Kitzbühel area, encompasses over 158km. of downhill runs, served by 63 lifts.

Children: Three year old children and upwards are well looked after in the Ski Kindergarten on the Walt Disney slopes near the foot of the Hahnenkamm. They are taught and entertained from 9.30 am. until 4 pm., thus leaving parents free to ski. Lunch is provided at additional cost. The four ski schools each have their own children's classes.

In a Few Words: An internationally famous town of great character and charm; skiing extensive and varied, for all standards; lift system now first-class; 4 excellent ski schools; plenty of other activities; 120km. of Nordic ski trails; very good value for an international resort.

Après Ski: There is plenty of choice in the way of night clubs and bars. The Tenne has a large dance floor and a good group. Of the various discothèques, the Take Five is the most modern; Praxmair and T5 are very popular. The Café Hölzl is the cheapest and a favourite with the locals. Sigi's Dancing restaurant in the Hotel Zum Jägerwirt is popular – prices reasonable and it has small corners in which to hide away if one wants a little seclusion from the noise. Other activities in Kitzbühel include a casino, indoor swimming pools, cinema, bowling alleys, curling and ice hockey matches, indoor tennis courts and squash courts, bridge, occasionally horseracing, and the wildlife park at Aurach is well worth a visit. The Kurhaus 'Aquarena' has fantastic pools, one normal and one with water massage jets, bars, restaurant, sauna and solarium. Pools are free on the lift pass. The Hahnenkamm museum at the top of the cableway is worth a visit, historically and for memorabilia, and is free. For those who want to know how Franz Klammer felt when he was 'flying on the Hahnenkamm' there is a virtual-reality simulator of the race which one can try out.

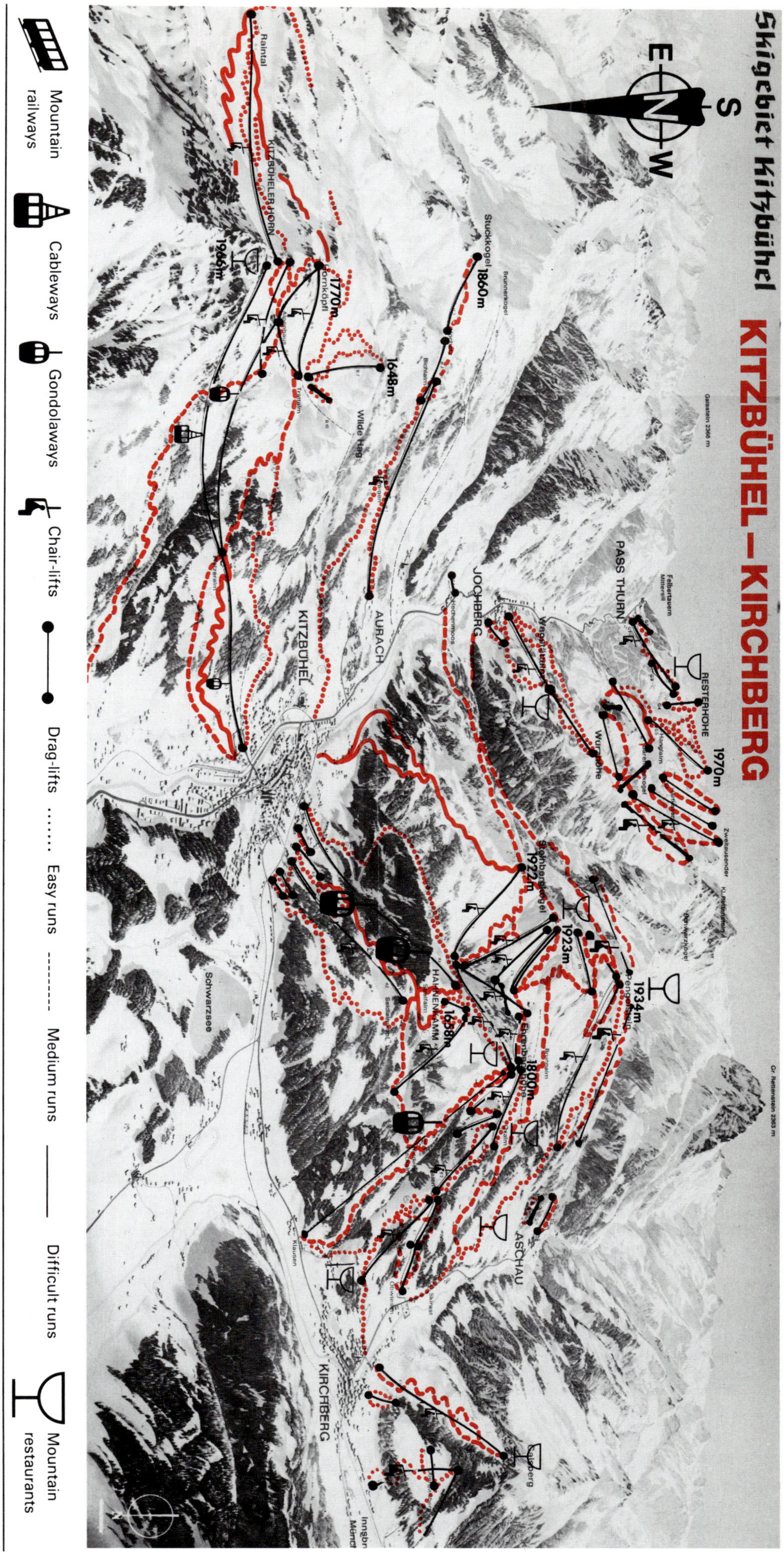

The in-places to meet after skiing are either Praxmair's, Cocktail-bar, Fünferl, Stamperl near the swimming pool or Da Pepe. The museum is well worth a visit, the tea shops are full of tempting delicacies, and as there are a number of cheaper eating places, it's more interesting to make a demi-pension arrangement to be able to take advantage of these. Amongst the most popular are the Gasthof Eggerwirt, Schwarzer Adler, the Zum Zinnkrug (famous for its spare ribs), Chizzo restaurant (Austrian specialities), Sport Stübl for the best fondues, the Goldene Gams for atmosphere and the Hüberstübl. At the cheaper end, but still good value, is La Fonda and the bar oriented Pfiff. If you want to be really in, try the Unterberger, but you have to book well in advance. Something different are the English pubs, 'The Londoner' and 'Big Ben'; S'Lichtl music bar is lively, whilst Highways is a 1950's American bar with a reassembled Buick for its centre piece.If you want a quieter spot and maybe a game of billiards try the Graggauwirt.

Recommended Hotels:

Hotel Erika: Set back in its own grounds in sunny position 5 minutes' walk from the centre. Attractive and bright dining room and bar, with owner's wife serving; buffet breakfast. Cosy reception room, comfortable bedrooms, all with bath/shower, wc., friendly service, swimming pool, sauna and solarium.

Hotel Goldener Greif: One of Kitzbühel's leading hotels, right in the centre. Once an old Tyrolean inn, dating back to 1271, remodernised in 1954, but retains much of its old charm, outside and in. All rooms with bath, high proportion of single rooms. Elegant dining room, à la carte restaurant, lounge with open fire and casino.

Hotel Hofer: Family run hotel, comfortable, friendly, all rooms with bath, cable TV and minibar. Centrally situated, and near Horn and bus stop to Pass Thurn, but very quiet. TV lounge, stüberl, bar. Garage facilities available. Sauna and solarium.

Hotel Zum Jägerwirt: Built in modern Tyrolean style and medium in size, recently renovated to 4-star category, this is a popular hotel, 5 minutes' walk from the centre. Dining room serving excellent food, including a weekly gala evening, comfortable lounge, à la carte restaurant and disco with bar, very well run and friendly service.

Hotel Schweizerhof: Situated close to the Hahnenkamm cableway terminal, this is a very nice family hotel. It has been enlarged in recent years and has lounges, bar, TV room and a nice dining room with first-class food. Pleasant bedrooms, all with private bath. Ideal for children ($3^1/_2$ year-old and over) as hotel overlooks children's ski school.

Hotel Weisses Rössl: This exceptionally fine hotel, centrally situated, is attractively furnished throughout. Dining room, à la carte restaurant, wood panelled stüberl, comfortable lounge area, large bar, panoramic terrace on 4th floor. Spacious and well equipped bedrooms, two room suites also available. The service is efficient and friendly.

FIEBERBRUNN

Height of Resort: 2,625 ft.
Height of Top Station: 6,626 ft.
Nearest International Airport: Salzburg
Map Reference: 6D See page 237
Route by Car: See pages 236-237
Resort Facilities Charts: See page 213
Hotel Reference Charts: See page 227

In the northern 'snowcorner' of the Tyrol, sheltered in a valley of the Kitzbüheler Alps, lies the pretty, old established village of Fieberbrunn. Free ski bus services connect the neighbouring villages of St. Jacob, Hochfilzen, St. Ulrich and Waidring.

The two ski schools are efficient and helpful, with a very good children's ski kindergarten from those 4 years and over. Access to the main skiing area is a little outside the village, within walking distance for the more energetic, otherwise by free bus service. Here a gondolaway rises to Streuboden and thence to Lärchfilzkogel, 5,429ft. A short run down from this top station, leads to the chair-lift rising to Reckmoos, 6,134ft. Also to the recently installed Hochhörndl 4-seater chair-lift which reached 6,626ft. The highest station in the Kitzbühler Alps.

There are six drag-lifts in the area, which serve good skiing over attractive, open and wooded slopes, with a variety of descents back to the village. The surmounting drag-lifts Weissach and Hochkogel, 3,493ft., serve medium runs. In St. Jakob, there is a long chair-lift rising to Buchsteinwand, 5,046ft., with its agreeable restaurant and open fire. Two drag-lifts serve the lower slopes. Fieberbrunn enjoys good snow conditions as it is in an east-west valley with mainly north-facing slopes. It caters well for beginners to medium standard skiers; in addition there is a lift pass available for the surrounding area, served by 71 lifts, and good opportunities for cross-country skiing.

In a Few Words: Very good for beginners, families and intermediates. Snow conditions good, village attractive, prices reasonable.

Après Ski: For a small resort the night life is fairly extensive. The 'Tenne' and River House are two of the main attractions as both have discos; the Londoner Pub is very popular and has live music and various forms of entertainment. The Plauscherl has a good atmosphere and excellent draught beer at the bar. A pleasant evening can be spent in the Pramauer. La Pampa is a very good Mexican restaurant. The new Westernbar in the village centre completes the night life.

Tea dancing is available at the Lindauhof and Enzian Hütte. It is a good family resort, with a relaxed atmosphere and lots of activities for non-skiers including pleasant walks, toboggan runs, skating, a new adventure swimming pool (with separate children's pool) and sauna. Day trips to Kitzbühel, Innsbruck or Salzburg can easily be arranged.

Recommended Hotels:

Hotel Alte Post: A traditional inn with modern annexe behind the main building, situated in the centre of Fieberbrunn. Comfortable and cosy bedrooms with bath or shower, wc, telephone, balcony. Pleasant dining room, à la carte restaurant, bar with draft beer.

Schlosshotel Rosenegg: At one time Napoleon's staff headquarters and Maria Theresa also hunted from here, this is a hotel with history, and much charm and character. Completely renovated in 1991. All bedrooms with bath, radio, TV and telephone and many with balcony. There are also 24 apartments. There is a comfortable lounge; attractive dining room; cocktail bar; 'Kaminstüberl'; candlelight 'Weinstüberl' with open fire and Viennese music; television room; children's playroom and lift. Kindergarten Monday – Friday 09.00-17.00 hours. Swimming pool, sauna, whirlpool, massage etc. An attractive hotel with excellent facilities and a good atmosphere.

ST JOHANN IN TIROL

Height of Resort: 2,180 ft.
Height of Top Station: 5,578 ft.
Nearest International Airport: Salzburg/Munich
Map Reference: 6D See page 237
Route by Car: See pages 236-237
Resort Facilities Charts: See page 214
Hotel Reference Charts: See page 228

The village of St. Johann in Tirol lies at the foot and on the north side of the Kitzbüheler Horn, about l0km. by road from Kitzbühel. It is a traditional Tirolean village with modern sports facilities, easily reached by road or rail. The main by-pass road prevents any through traffic.

On the southern side of the resort, a two section, 6 seater gondolaway rises from the village to Angeralm, 3,937ft, and thence to Harschbichl, 5,578ft., the resort's top station. From here, looking northwards down to the village, runs and lifts fan out from north-east to the west. On the north-eastern side of the gondolaway there are two long surmounting drag-lifts, a drag-lift and surmounting chair-lift and a further chair-lift starting about half-way up rising almost to the top station. To the immediate west of the gondolaway the lower slopes are served by a double and 3 seater chair-lift and a drag-lift, whilst further to the west, from the village of Oberndorf, the first section of the Penzing chair-lift travels to Müllneralm connecting with a 4 seater chair-lift up to Penzing, 4,800ft. This top station provides access to the only black run in the area along with an intermediate run back to Oberndorf, or alteratively one can cross over on an intermediate run linking up with an easy run into St. Johann in Tirol.

Although St. Johann in Tirol is not high, the runs are mainly north-east, north and north-west facing and, being positioned through wide wooded glades, they hold the snow well. The main runs are also covered by snow cannons. The runs on the top section of the mountain are mainly suitable for intermediates whilst those on the lower slopes are most suitable for beginners.

In a Few Words: An attractive alpine village, compact lift system. Northerly oriented slopes through wide wooded glades hold the snow well. Suitable for beginners to intermediates. For those who require greater variety Kitzbühel is only 10km. away. Nordic skiing well catered for with over 75km. of prepared trails. Ski Kindergarten.

Après Ski: Fairly active for a small resort with plenty of cafés and bars. Dancing to live music at the Café Rainer. A popular disco is the Scala. A fine indoor swimming pool, with sauna, solarium and fitness room. Two indoor tennis courts, sleigh rides, rifle range, curling, toboggan run, artificial ice skating rink, bowling alley, fitness centre and ballooning.

Recommended Hotels:

Hotel Fischer: An attractive, family hotel centrally situated in this charming village. The Angerer-Alm Funicular and Hochfeld chair-lifts are about 10 minutes away, giving easy access to the varied skiing covering some 32km. of piste. The hotel is comfortably furnished in traditional Tirolean style with open plan bar and lounge. The dining room is bright and cheerful serving a substantial breakfast buffet and 4 course evening meal. The modern bedrooms all have private facilities, telephone and cable colour TV.

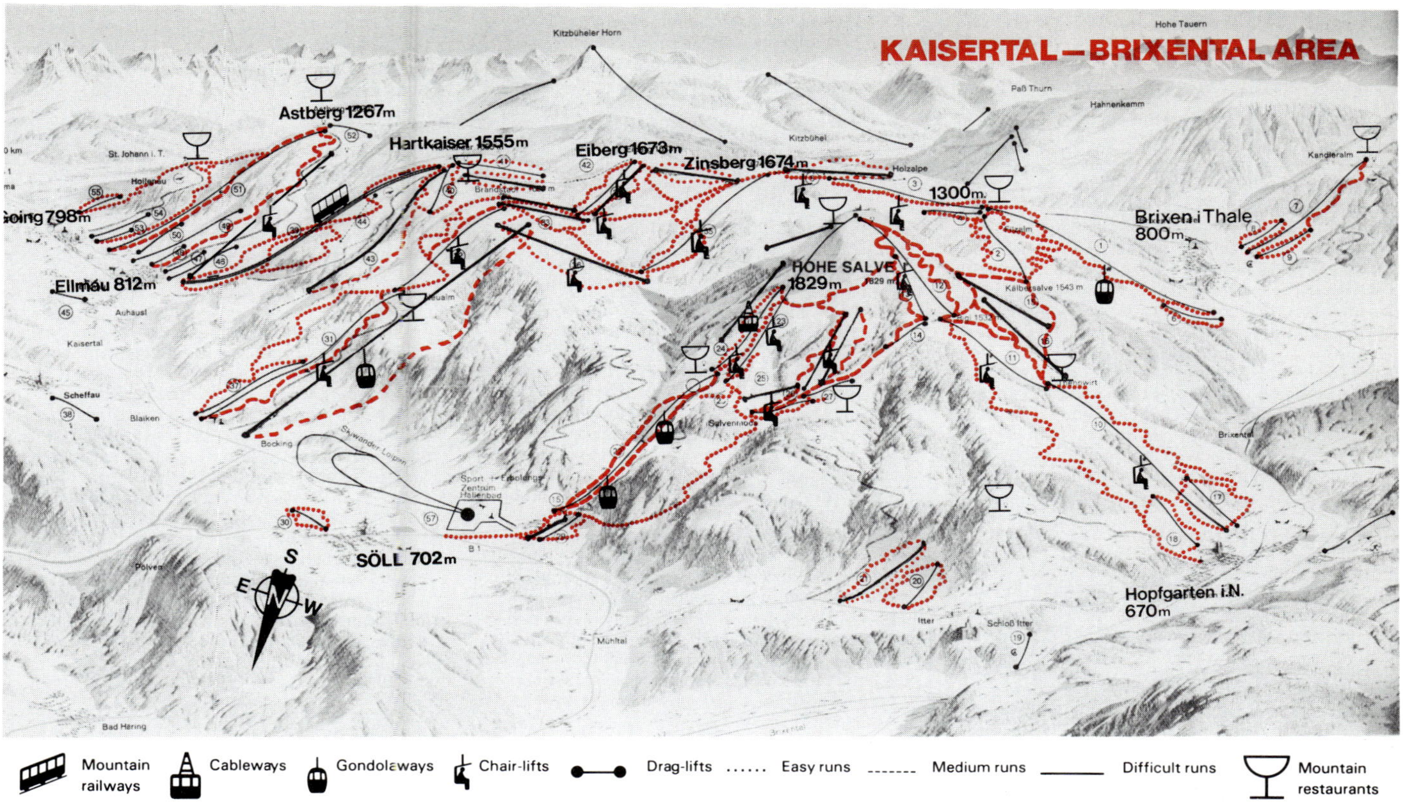

Hotel Europa: This charming hotel is an easy walk from the restaurants, bars and nightlife. The interior is attractively furnished in traditional style with white walls and wooden ceilings. Right next door is the Sports Centre where guests can enjoy the many activities with the added benefit of a 20 % discount on the entrance fee. The free ski bus departs from just 200 metres from the hotel entrance. A special feature of the Europa is the traditional styled dining room where the large open fireplace adds to its already relaxing atmosphere.

SÖLL

Height of Resort: 2,275 ft.
Height of Top Station: 5,998 ft.
Nearest International Airport: Munich/Salzburg
Map Reference: 5C See page 237
Route by Car: See pages 236-237
Resort Facilities Charts: See page 216
Hotel Reference Charts: See page 228

In an open, sunny valley, on the north side of the St. Johann-Innsbruck road, lies the small village of Söll. The old village is centred around a large church and is surrounded by groups of modern hotels, pensions and guest houses. The nursery slopes are extensive, situated about 500m. to the south of the village, with a drag-lift and a baby-lift. A gondolaway with 8 seater cabins 700m. from the village leads to the main skiing area at Hochsöll, 3,595ft., where a drag-lift, a single, a double and 2 quadruple chair-lifts provide a good choice of north-facing runs of intermediate and advanced standard. These include a medium to difficult 2.5km. run and an easy 4.5km. 'Family Run' which includes some narrow parts through wooded terrain, both leading back to Söll. From Hochsöll (via the Hohe Salve chair-lift, 5.990ft. or via cableway or triple chair-lift.), it is possible to reach the connected Hopfgarten circuit, an area which will be enjoyed by medium and advanced skiers. Here four drag-lifts cover the north-facing slopes, giving access to the south-west facing runs to Hopfgarten, from which a three-stage chair-lift returns to the top.

Runs from the top station down to Söll range from 6 to 8km. on mainly north facing slopes. A mountain restaurant with sun terrace provides lunch at the top station and there are more restaurants at Hochsöll. The Skiworld lift pass offers the wider scope of a total of 90 lifts in Söll, Going, Ellmau, Scheffau, Itter, Hopfgarten, Kelchsau, Brixen i. Thale and Westendorf covering some 250km. of runs. Piste supervisors in red and yellow anoraks clearly marked 'Pistenhilfe' now patrol the whole area.

The Söll area provides good and varied opportunities for off-piste skiing and the lift system is well managed.

In a Few Words: A small but popular resort; good ski school; runs well prepared; prices reasonable and good value. The resort can suffer during a mild winter from lack of snow on the lower slopes, but these are now covered by snow cannons and the upper, mainly north facing slopes hold the snow well. Kindergarten at the foot of the gondolaway for 3-5 year olds.

Après Ski: Of Söll's two night clubs, the Whisky Mühle has a disco and special shows in the main season. The Söller Dorfstadl has a good atmosphere for all age groups, whilst Westernsaloon Buffalo's disco is good fun. Bowling is available at the Hotel Tenne, there is an outdoor swimming pool and an indoor pool, sauna and solarium, skating rink, 3 squash courts and a fitness centre. Sleigh rides and tobogganing provide for non-skiers and the toboggan run is tremendous fun in the dark. The toboggan run from Hochsöll to Söll, some 3km. long, is illuminated and the chair-lift operates from 7.30-9 p.m. One high spot of the week is the International Beer Evening at the Hotel Tyrol. Weekly there are guest races with a Snow & Fun party at the Whiskey Mühle. There are also Tyrolean evenings and fondue parties and a number of small bars, but most activities seem to take place in the hotels - recommended for an après ski drink is the Hotel Post;for a cheap evening drink ,'Pub 15' and Pub Austria in Hotel Austria or the 'Vis à vis' bar.

Recommended Hotels:

Gasthof Eggerwirt: One of the original village inns, standing in a central position, recently reconstructed. Attractive dining room and Tyrolean stüberl. Bedrooms very comfortable, all with private bath or shower. Sauna and solarium.

Gasthof Post: This very old hotel was built in the 13th century, attractively decorated outside with frescoes and inside it has vaulted ceilings, thick stone pillars and beautifully carved panels. The restaurant is open to outside guests and the bar is very popular. Bedrooms furnished in old-fashioned style but they are warm and comfortable. Some with bath or shower.

Hotel Tyrol: Renovated in 1991, all rooms with bath or shower, w.c., telephone radio, colour TV and balcony. In quiet position 3 minutes' walk from centre. Large dining rooms with lovely views. House bar and lounge area. Dorfstadl night club in cellar with live band. Sauna, solarium, Turkish bath, spa-pool, heated outdoor swimming pool and fitness room. Lift.

ELLMAU

Height of Resort: 2,689 ft.
Height of Top Station: 5,101 ft.
Nearest International Airport: Munich
Map Reference: 6D See page 237
Route by Car: See pages 236-237
Resort Facilities Charts: See page 213
Hotel Reference Charts: See page 227

Situated between the Kitzbüheler Alps and the Wilder Kaiser mountains, in a wide open sunny valley, is the attractive Tyrolean village of Ellmau. The resort is ideal for beginners as the gentle nursery slopes with drag-lifts are in the village area. For the more experienced the direct route to the main skiing is by mountain railway situated on the south-west side of the village. It is one of the longest and fastest in Austria, rising to the top station, Hartkaiser, 5,101 ft, in 4 minutes. Here there is a restaurant and the link point for the huge Skiworld Wilder Kaiser-Brixental area with 250km. of marked runs served by 90 lifts. The lift pass also covers the lifts at nearby Westendorf.

Ellmau itself has 35 km. of prepared runs, the longest being 5 km with a vertical descent of 1,640 ft. This area is served by the mountain railway, a double chair-lift and 11 drag-lifts. There is a choice of easy and intermediate runs, mainly over north-east facing slopes, back to the village.

The Ellmau ski pass also covers the lifts of the nearby resort of Going, which interlink with the former. The ski-bus service is free with a guest card. Nordic skiers are well catered for with a 10km. trail in the Ellmau area and much longer ones nearby. For more detailed information on the skiing covered by the Skiworld ski pass see separate reports on Söll and Westendorf.

Ellmau Kaiserbad: This leisure complex was opened in 1993 and has an indoor adventure pool with jet stream into an outdoor pool, tennis and squash courts, climbing wall, summer-winter slide and a relaxation centre with sauna, hot whirl pools, Kneipp pools, steam showers, solarium, Vitalcentre, restaurant. There is also a separate adventure pool for children.

In a Few Words: An attractive Tyrolean village; excellent for beginners and good progression slopes for second year skiers. Those of intermediate and advanced intermediate standard will find sufficient variety in the Skiworld area, particularly as Westendorf is covered on the same lift pass. Ski Kindergarten for 4 years old upwards; kindergarten 1-4 year-olds; excellent resort for families. High sunshine record. Due to mainly north- facing slopes snow remains good.

Après Ski: Fairly active with two discothèques and a wide selection of bars and restaurants. Tyrolean evenings are arranged. There is tobogganing, a floodlit run, skating, curling, indoor golf, sleigh rides and 55km. of cleared walks. Excursions are organised to Innsbruck, Salzburg and nearby places of interest.

Recommended Hotels:

Hotel Bär: Situated 5 minutes' walk from the village, this is one of Austria's finest luxurious hotels. Beautifully furnished reception rooms. All bedrooms and apartments attractively designed with bath, wc, balcony or terrace, telephone, radio, TV and minibar. Other facilities include a very fine swimming pool, health centre, turkish bath, sauna, solarium, massage, beauty treatment, gift shop and free kindergarten. Excellent service throughout and highly recommended.

Hotel Hochfilzer: Owned by the Hochfilzer family for 187 years, this centrally situated hotel offers a very high standard of service and cuisine. It is elegantly furnished and its 42 twin bedded rooms and 6 single rooms all have bath or shower, w.c. telephone, radio and balcony. Spacious reception area and dining room, lounge with open fire and bar and several cosy wood panelled stüberls. Swimming and leisure area with large indoor pool, 2 whirlpools, one outside on the sun terrace, Roman thermal bath, sauna, steam bath and Vital-studio.

Pension Claudia: Situated opposite the nursery slopes and also run by the Hochfilzer family. All 16 twin bedded rooms and 3 singles have bath, w.c. and balcony and are attractively furnished. Breakfast room and sitting room; clients taking half board have their evening meal at the Hotel Hochfilzer where they can enjoy its facilities.

WESTENDORF

Height of Resort: 2,624 ft.
Height of Top Station: 6,101 ft.
Nearest International Airport: Salzburg/Munich
Map Reference: 5C See page 237
Route by Car: See pages 236-237
Resort Facilities Charts: See page 216
Hotel Reference Charts: See page 229

This unspoilt village lies in the Kitzbüheler Alps of the Tirol between Wörgl and Kitzbühel, 170km. from Munich's new airport, 100km. from Salzburg and 80km. from Innsbruck. It is easily reached both by train and road from London. It has for many years been a popular resort with British visitors. Certainly English is understood widely and we found friendliness everywhere. All the skiing takes place immediately south of the village, on the Nachtsöllberg, which stands isolated from the other mountains and from the top of which there are breathtaking views in every direction.

Beginners have perfect sunny nursery slopes, now covered by snow cannons, served by three trainer lifts and can soon progress to a fourth rather longer drag-lift.

A great improvement was the installation, in 1987, of the Alpenrosebahn, a two section 6 seater gondolaway. The bottom station is situated 5 minutes' walk from the village centre and the first section. Snow cannons cover both this section and up to the Alpenrosenhütte, above the middle station, 4,310ft. From here there are a number of runs back to the village suitable for beginners up to intermediates, whilst a single chair-lift rises to Choralpe, 6,101 ft. The direct runs back to the middle station from the top of both lifts become very mogulled and graded medium difficult, although in most other resorts one would expect it to be difficult. These runs provide quite excellent and severe technique training for good to expert skiers, with a 1,640 ft. vertical drop. Good novices and medium skiers can avoid the steepest part at the top by taking a long curving path which brings them out halfway down this slope. Even so the remainder of the run is steep for those without adequate technique although the ski schools do manage to bring good second week novices successfully down. There is glorious east and south facing skiing suitable for novices up to medium standard, reached from the top station by a gentle gradient path. Here one arrives at a large area served by 8 drag-lifts, a 4-seater chair-lift and a triple chair-lift, the Fleiding, serving a variety of superb middle gradient south facing runs. Runs from all these lifts interconnect so that one can spend the whole day up here. In the afternoon the faint hearted not up to the steep run back to the middle station can take the chair-lift down to the middle station and ski home from there. Alternatively the recently constructed easy run from the Fleiding chair-lift area ends outside the village and a ski-bus, free to ski pass holders, takes one back to the village. In addition langlauf skiing is well catered for with one circuit of 7km. and a long one, which can be broken into shorter sections, of 18km. to Kirchberg and a further 3km. to Kitzbühel. Snow-boarding, para-gliding and ballooning are also popular. There is now a free ski bus service to the Wilder Kaiser-Brixental ski-circuit. (Westendorf-Brixen). 20 snow cannons now cover the nursery slopes and as far as the top station.

In a Few Words: This deservedly popular resort, although not high, is, because of its predominantly north-west facing slopes, assured of good skiing in a normal year from December till the end of March. Except at weekends, there is absolutely no queueing and one can fit an enormous amount of skiing into one day. An unsophisticated and friendly resort highly recommended for beginners up to good medium standard and for good skiers who do not demand the wide variety of skiing offered by the larger and more expensive resorts. There are three ski schools, Ski School Top, Ski School Westendorf and Ski School Ideal.

Après Ski: A good variety but completely informal. The Mesnerkeller, an attractive part of the Mesnerwirt Gasthof, has a duo with singer for dance music and/ or Tyrolean music and also serves hot foods until 2 a.m. The 'Wunderbar' is modern and lively, providing dance music for all tastes. The 'weekly guests' races prizegiving is held on Fridays for children and on Thursdays for adults in the village hall, called Alpenrosensaal. These are organised by Ski School Westendorf, whilst Ski School Top have their prizegiving on Fridays at the Mesnerkeller and for children at the Kegelbahn Theresianna. If your legs can't take dancing a quiet evening can be spent just drinking in the friendly atmosphere of The Tavern, a comfortable bar, or listening to live music at the Post. Gerry's Inn has a daily Après Ski Party from 4-7 p.m., a livelier replacement of the old-fashioned thé dansant. Other night sponts include Moskito Bar, Kibo Bar and the King's Pub. Finally for a change of menu the Theresiana, Post and Fleidingerhof have a weekly fondue and music evening. Bus trips to Berchtesgaden, Salzburg and Innsbruck make a good day's rest from skiing; as do the 10km. of walks. Lovely sleigh rides, by day or night, are a feature of Westendorf. Most hotels have attractive stüberls where business booms and the helpings are enormous. There is also a variety of entertainment at the recently constructed village hall. Free entrance to skating rink.

Recommended Hotels:

Hotel Post: In a central position and close to the nursery slopes, this old inn has been modernised inside in attractive Tyrolean style. Large light dining room, tap room with draught beer and cosy stüberl; à la carte restaurant. Comfortable bedrooms, all with bath or shower. Zither music in Tyrolean Stube afternoons and evenings.

Sporthotel Jakobwirt: A family run Tyrolean style hotel situated in the centre of the village. Rooms with bath or shower, wc, telephone, radio and balcony. Attractive dining room, two restaurants, comfortable lounge with open fire, bar. Heated indoor swimming pool, sauna and solarium. Lift.

SAALBACH-HINTERGLEMM

Height of Resort: 3,260 ft.
Height of Top Station: 6,845 ft.
Nearest International Airport: Salzburg
Map Reference: 6D See page 237
Route by Car: See pages 236-237
Resort Facilities Charts: See page 215
Hotel Reference Charts: See pages 227-228

A fine skiing area with an interlinking lift system. Both villages have grown from small hamlets and they are now looked upon as one resort. At present there are some 400 hotels and pensions providing some 17,560 beds.

There are altogether 62 lifts in the valley and the system is interlinked. The lift system to the south of the road enables one to reach various north facing runs, ranging from easy to difficult and up to 7km. long. North of the road the lift system gives access to mainly south facing runs, easy to average standard and beyond, of up to 6km. One of the main lifts is the Schattberg cableway, which starts from near the centre of Saalbach. The top station is 6,565ft. with a good restaurant , a large sun terrace and a glorious view. From here, one can take the circuit to Hinterglemm or, in the opposite direction, via Vorderglemm to Saalbach. The south facing slopes near the restaurant are served by the Mulden drag-lift and Limberg 4 seater chair-lift with short runs of 1.5km. and to challenge the more experienced skier there is the FIS 4 km. run, Nord, running parallel with the cableway to Saalbach, a drop of 3,260ft.

An easier run of 7km. for the average skier starts again westwards from the top station and joins the Zell am See-Saalbach road at Vorderglemm, where there is a choice of returning to Saalbach by bus or joining the Schönleiten cableway via Hochwartalm and to the summit of the Wildenkarkogel 6,266ft. The skiing to Saalbach is by way of various easy to medium runs of 6 km. It is also possible to move over to Leogang from the Schönleiten, where there are north facing runs taking in three drag-lifts and a four seater chair-lift. The Saalbach-Hinterglemm abonnement covers the Leogang area. Moving clockwise from the top of the Schattberg cableway one can ski down to the Westgipfel double chair-lift, which rises to the Westgipfel 6,846ft., and from this point has a challenging 5km. run down to Hinterglemm.

Further west in Hinterglemm is an 8 person cableway, mid-point at the Winklerhof, to the top of the Zwölfer, 6,448ft. This point can also be reached from the bottom of the Hochalm double chair by a similar cableway. From here runs of all standards abound, facing east and all about 4km. down to Hinterglemm and include the Men's World Championship Downhill course, the height difference being 3,035ft. Also from this summit the formidable Nord run leads to the north-west of Hinterglemm and back to the bottom of the Hochalm lift. This double chair-lift runs northwards to Hochalm, surmounted by another double chair-lift to the Spieleckkogl with a further drag-lift to the left. A 6-seater chair-lift has replaced the long drag-lift to the top of the Hochalmspitze and from here the skiing is over superb wide, open pistes, improved further by the installation of a 4 seater chair-lift from Sportalm to Hasenauer Köpfl. Down the valley to the east one comes across a further drag-lift which rises north to Reiterkogel, 5,912ft. From this top station particularly recommended is the run to the foot of the Hochalm 6-seater chair-lift; the latter leads to more lovely runs with glorious views. Alternatively it is easy to reach the Bernkogel, 5,809ft. and an easy 4km. run to Saalbach. To the north of Saalbach there is a further series of lifts including a cableway from the village to the FIS start at the Kohlmaiskopf, 5,886ft. leading to a testing run back to the village, and a triple chair-lift and surmounting drag-lift running parallel to this, offer plenty of choice of easy to medium runs back to Saalbach. A ski bus (gratis with ski pass) runs every 20 minutes connecting the two villages, leaving the Schönleiten cableway at Vorderglemm, to the Hochalm lift at Kolling. It is now a fair walk from the middle of Hinterglemm to the bus stops. The area has many good on-piste restaurants/bars; the Pfefferalm was voted the best Stübli in Austria in 1991. Floodlit skiing, which is included in the lift pass, takes place at the Unterschwarzachlift in Hinterglemm every night from 5 pm until 10 pm.

In a Few Words: Well interlinked ski area with loads of variety, suitable for all standards. Nursery slopes extensive with many lifts; suitable for families,

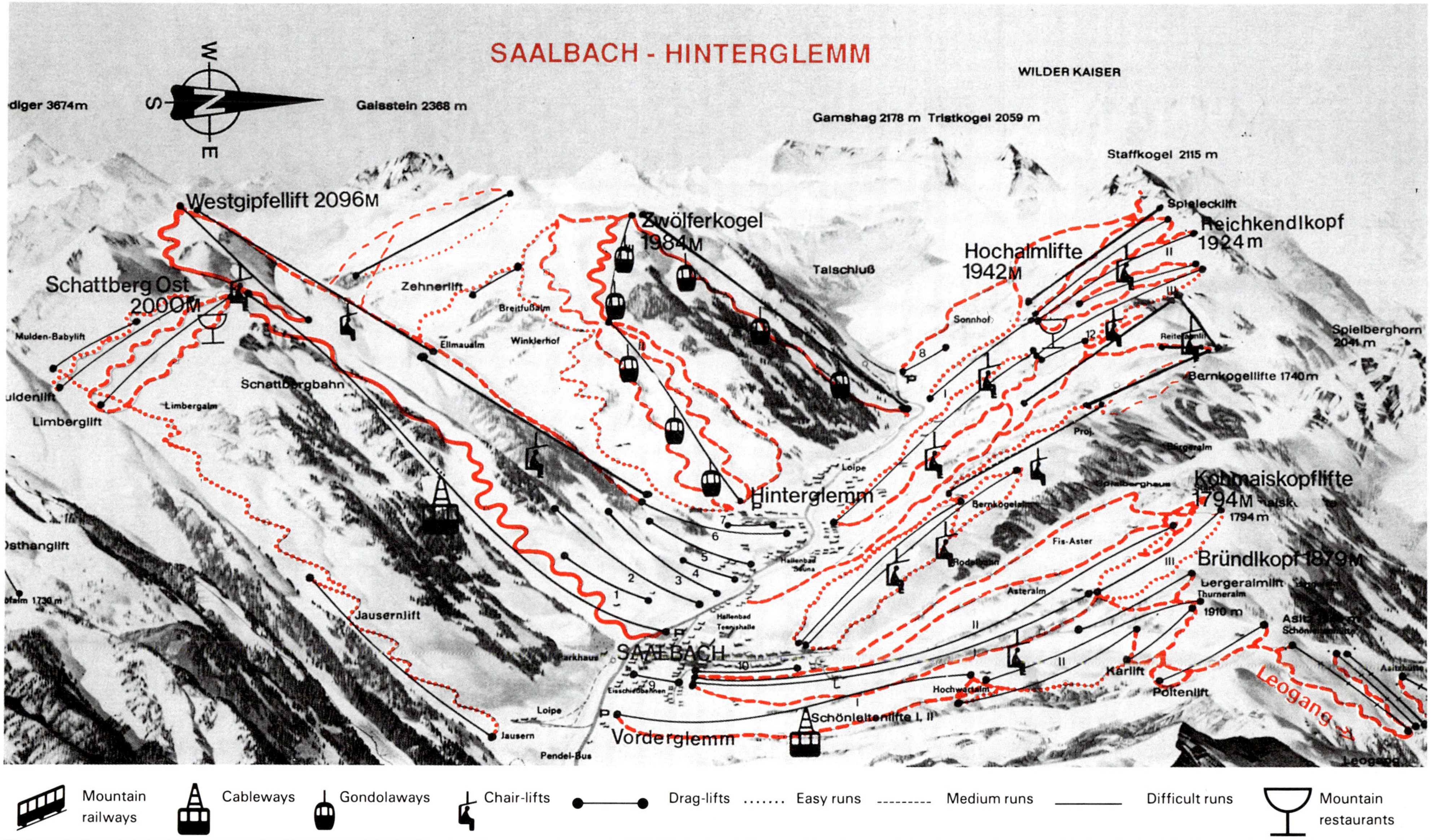
SAALBACH - HINTERGLEMM
WILDER KAISER
Gaisstein 2368 m
Gamshag 2178 m Tristkogel 2059 m
Staffkogel 2115 m
Westgipfellift 2096M
Zwölferkogel 1984M
Hochalmlifte 1942M
Reichkendlkopf 1924m
Spielecklift
Schattberg Ost 2000M
Spielberghorn 2041 m
Bernkogellifte 1740m
Kohlmaiskopflifte 1794M
1794 m
Bründlkopf 1879M
Bergeralmlift
Thurneralm
1910 m
Zehnerlift
Breitfußalm
Ellmaualm
Winklerhof
Talschluß
Sonnhof
Mulden-Babylift
Limberglift
Limbergalm
Schattbergbahn
Osthanglift
Jausernlift
Jausern
Loipe
Pendel-Bus
Parkhaus
SAALBACH
Hinterglemm
Vorderglemm
Hallenbad
Tennishalle
Hallenbad
Sauna
Eisschießbahnen
Proj.
Bergeralm
Fis-Aster
Bernkogelalm
Rodelbahn
Asteralm
Hochwartalm
Karllift
Poltenlift
Schönleitenlifte I, II
Leogang
Mountain railways
Cableways
Gondolaways
Chair-lifts
Drag-lifts
Easy runs
Medium runs
Difficult runs
Mountain restaurants

kindergarten available. With snow making machines on Kohlmais, Jausern, Bernkogel, Zwölfer and Hochalm areas, skiing now possible from 1st December to the end of March. Après ski at Saalbach is better than at many large resorts and Hinterglemm also compares very well; excellent hotels of all grades and good atmosphere in both villages. Saalbach medium to expensive, Hinterglemm medium. Lift pass with good reductions for children and Senior Citizens also covers the Leogang area. Highly recommended.

Après Ski: Saalbach: Lots of night clubs and bars with choice of live music (modern or Austrian) or discos and a number of cafés and restaurants, mostly fairly crowded with a lively atmosphere. It has become much more sophisticated and fairly expensive. Popular with the young is the Visage disco (Hotel Kristall) and Kings (Bergers Sporthotel). The Kuhstall (Alpenhotel) has a two-man Austrian band and its beamed ceilings and panelled walls are decorated with farm implements, cow bells etc. and cow skins covering the bar front. The effect is attractive and the adjoining late night buffet, open till 2 a.m., is excellent. Next door, the Arena Disco has a good group, in another horseshoe-shaped area with cosy alcoves and attractive decor. The restaurant café Sporthotel discothèque appeals to all age groups. It is surrounded by a balcony, the dining room for hotel guests – and above the floor circle hangs a huge illuminated cartwheel. The Taverna in the Hotel Neuhaus, with band, is very popular. The Hinterhagalm is a mountain farmhouse which has been completely rebuilt into a typically Austrian lokal, with rustic style, an Austrian band in the evening and very good atmosphere. For quieter après the Zum Turm Bar under the central church building is fun too. The ski-kindergarten facilities make it an ideal family resort. There's a fine swimming pool, indoor tennis court, 2 lane bowling alley, skating, sleigh rides and toboggan run from Spielberghaus, Hintermaisalm and Maisalm to the village. The standard of the hotels is high and there are several shops, including Berger for fashionable skiwear. A lively atmosphere.

Après Ski: Hinterglemm: Hinterglemm has a lively après ski scene and there is plenty of choice as Saalbach is within easy reach. The cost of evening entertainment is catching up with that of Saalbach. The Knappenkeller which has a discothèque, large, crowded and fun, provides mostly modern music plus some Austrian music, and attached to it is the Londoner Disco which has an open grill cooking hamburgers. An excellent meat fondue, with chips, salad and lots of interesting side dishes, is also available here. The Glemmerkeller at the Hotel Glemmtalerhof, has a 2-man band and disco in the evening. Underneath the Glemmtalerhof is the Alm Bar, with small disco. The Pinzgauer Stüberl (Hotel Wolf) also does a good fondue. It has a discothèque, a part wooden ceiling, heavy beams and stable-style decor, with a large open fire; and has great appeal. Excellent mountain restaurants with considerable variation in price. Nice swimming pool plus sauna and restaurant and 3 indoor tennis courts. Children are admitted to the various kellers and discos, another advantage for families. Try the special Hinterglemmer drink, a large mug of tea, schnapps and rum! The resort has a number of hotels with kindergarten facilities and an indoor swimming pool.

Recommended Hotels: Saalbach

Alpenhotel: This four-star hotel is situated in the centre near the lifts; it is the largest, with 170 beds. Attractive bedrooms all with bath or shower, radio, telephone, colour TV and minibar. There is a wide choice of restaurants and bars:- the Alpenstube for breakfast and dinner, the Vitrine for culinary highlights, the Happy-Saloon where drinks are served in a romantic atmosphere, the Kneipe beerbar, the Kuhstallbar with typical Austrian flair, Thomas-Pub for a quick lunch, the Arena for dancing to live music and the Nightbuffet open until 3 a.m. There is a swimming pool, sauna, whirlpool, vapour-bath, massage, fitness room and conference rooms.

Hotel Bauer: A very impressive medium sized hotel in village centre. Warm and attractive entrance hall, large dining room elegantly designed and beautifully furnished, two sitting rooms with a restful atmosphere. Bedrooms of medium size, nicely furnished, all with bath or shower, wc, balcony, telephone, radio and TV. Popular café with excellent cakes.

Gasthof Neuhaus: The original village inn having much charm and character but almost completely rebuilt. in central position and very popular with visitors and locals. Two bars, one selling draught beer. Large modern dining room and small lounge. The bedrooms in the old building are comfortable, but the rooms in the new wing are very attractive, many with private shower. Keller Bar with band (Heuriger Lokal).

Hotel Saalbacherhof: A large hotel in the centre, efficiently run with friendly and helpful staff. Long and large old-world dining room pleasantly furnished with stüberl leading off. Sitting room on first floor. Large tea room and bar to left of reception area. Bedrooms attractively furnished, all with bath or shower, radio and colour TV.

Recommended Hotels: Hinterglemm

Hotel Glemmtalerhof: A popular hotel in a central position, now completely rebuilt. Very luxurious rooms; large lounge with open fireplace (surrounding reception area). Indoor swimming pool and dancing to band or disco.

Hotel Sonnblick: A comfortable family run hotel situated near to the Reiterkogel chair-lift. Pleasant dining room, exceedingly attractive lounge bar. All bedrooms have bath or shower, wc, TV, some with balcony.

Hotel Wolf: A very nice hotel in central position near the Reiterkogel lift with large sun terrace. Attractive wooden beamed dining room leading off to sitting area with open fire, much antique Salzburgian furniture. A large glass-fronted addition to the bar makes a very pleasant stüberl and sitting room. Comfortable bedrooms, all with private bath or shower and wc, TV, some with balcony. Delightful Pinzgauer Keller Bar, in the form of a stable with open fire and dancing to band. Swimming pool.

LEOGANG

Height of Resort: 2,755 ft.
Height of Top Station: 6,279 ft.
Nearest International Airport: Salzburg
Map Reference: 6D See page 237
Route by Car: See pages 236-237
Resort Facilities Charts: See page 215
Hotel Reference Charts: See page 228

This is a quiet unspoilt resort with hotels and guest houses stretching along the valley. Whilst it is not a compact village it has two important advantages: first, all the slopes are north and north-east facing and therefore hold the snow well; second, it is linked with the larger resorts of Saalbach/Hinterglemm (see separate reports). Adjacent to the village is a 1,200 metre long drag-lift serving two intermediate and one easy run with smaller nursery lifts nearby. The main lift system is 3.5 km by ski bus up the valley where one finds the Asitz gondolaway and a large car park. This two stage system with 8 seater cabins is 3,253 metres long and moves 2,400 persons per hour and rises to the Berghaus Asitz, an excellent mountain restaurant standing at 5,767ft. From this point one can return to the middle station on an interesting intermediate run and continue to the bottom station with the choice of black, red (covered by snow cannons) or blue runs – the latter travels via the Alm drag-lift by which one can return to the middle station.

The link with Saalbach/Hinterglemm is from the top of the gondolaway by skiing down to the foot of the Asitz 4 seater chair-lift which rises 2,578ft. to Kleine Asitz, 6,134ft. To the left three drag-lifts, all rising to the crest, serve excellent intermediate north-east facing runs and the centre lift reaches Grosse Asitz, 6,279ft. where one enters the Saalbach skiing. For the return journey, from this point, one can ski along the crest on an easy run to the top station of the gondolaway. There are also restaurants at the middle and bottom stations of the gondolaway.

In a Few Words: Excellent intermediate skiing, pistes well maintained. Village quieter and less expensive than Saalbach/Hinterglemm and has the advantage of being linked with their ski area under one lift pass. Two ski schools and two ski kindergartens. North and north-east facing slopes hold the snow well. 38 km. of Nordic ski trails.

Après Ski: In the main confined to hotels; several have discos. The swimming pool and sauna at the Hotel Krallerhof is open to Leogang guest card holders. Natural skating rink, riding and 40 km. of cleared walks.

Recommended Hotels:

Hotel Backerwirt: This 3 star modern hotel built on the site of a farmhouse with much of the old wood being used for internal decor. Open fire in the hallway, large dining room, stüberl used for dining and sitting, public stüberl and bar, kellerbar with disco, fitness room and sauna. Large comfortable bedrooms, most with balconies, all with bath/shower, TV and telephone. A family run hotel where guests are made to feel really welcome.

Hotel Krallerhof: Above 4 star rating this luxurious hotel is set well back from the road in its own grounds. Elegant dining room, serving excellent food, sitting area in bars and hall, Alm Bar disco separated from hotel, indoor swimming pool, conference rooms, coffee bar, beauty salon, sauna, steam bath, solarium, massage, fitness room, squash and ski shop. Private drag-lift, ski school and ski kindergarten. Bus to slopes.

Hotel Salzburgerhof: This modern 4 star hotel stands at the foot of the Asitz gondolaway. Well appointed bedrooms with bath/shower, balcony, cable TV, radio and telephone. Attractive dining room, bar and sitting area with open fire, free use of swimming pool 600 metres away, sauna, steam bath, massage and play room.

ZELL AM SEE

Height of Resort: 2,490 ft.
Height of Top Station: 6,500 ft.
Nearest International Airport: Salzburg
Map Reference: 6D See page 237
Route by Car: See pages 236-237
Resort Facilities Charts: See page 216
Hotel Reference Charts: See page 229

Zell am See is a small town, with the suburb of Schüttdorf stretching away to the south. It is in a magnificent position at the water's edge of a large and very beautiful lake with the Schmittenhöhe 'sugarloaf' mountain, 6,500ft., in the background and has the most glorious view across towering, tree covered mountains to the east.

A 4-seater gondolaway leaves from the western side of Zell am See up to Mittelstation. This connects with a series of further lifts up to the top station, Schmittenhöhe, 6,500ft. which, as will be seen from the map, can be reached in four directions. At the top station stands the Berghotel, with a large restaurant and sun terrace with a marvellous view of the ski slopes, town and lake below. From here, on the northern side, short runs lead to the bottom of two drag-lifts and a 3 seater chair-lift, returning one to the top station or just below it. Longer runs lead down to Zell am See via Sonnkogel. On the southern side the Breiteck drag-lift is paired with the slightly longer 3 seater chair-lift, both serving runs on the crest. The Trass 4 km. run from the top via Breiteckalm is a challenge to the experienced skier, descending in a northerly direction to a point halfway down the cableway and from then on parallel to it as far as the terminal, a difference in height of 3,282ft. It is in fact the only difficult run in the area and the longer run of 8 km. from the Berghotel to Breiteckalm and Glockner down to Schüttdorf will be enjoyed by the medium skier. From this point the 6 seater gondolaway takes one back to Bruckberg with its very agreeable restaurant and further 4 seater chair-lift to Glockner. One can then ski down a short distance to the foot of the double chair-lift which goes up to Hirschkogel, 5,641ft. and from here the Breiteck chair-lift connects up with the drag-lift up to Schmittenhöhe. One of the most attractive runs in the above area is the standard run on which world cup races are held. It starts at Schmittenhöhe and travels down via Breiteck, the Mittelstation, ending at the foot of the cableway station, in the valley.

The Sonnalm cableway is close to the Schmittenhöhe terminal and the former travels north-west to Sonnalm, 4,540ft., where there is another very pleasant restaurant. A triple chair-lift then rises to Sonnkogel 6,020ft. and a drag-lift to Hochmais, 5,664ft., with surmounting small drag-lift to Sonnkogel. From this point one can continue to Schmittenhöhe by using the Sonnengrat chair-lift to the west and two further drag-lifts or the triple chair-lift. All the skiing hereabouts is of medium standard,

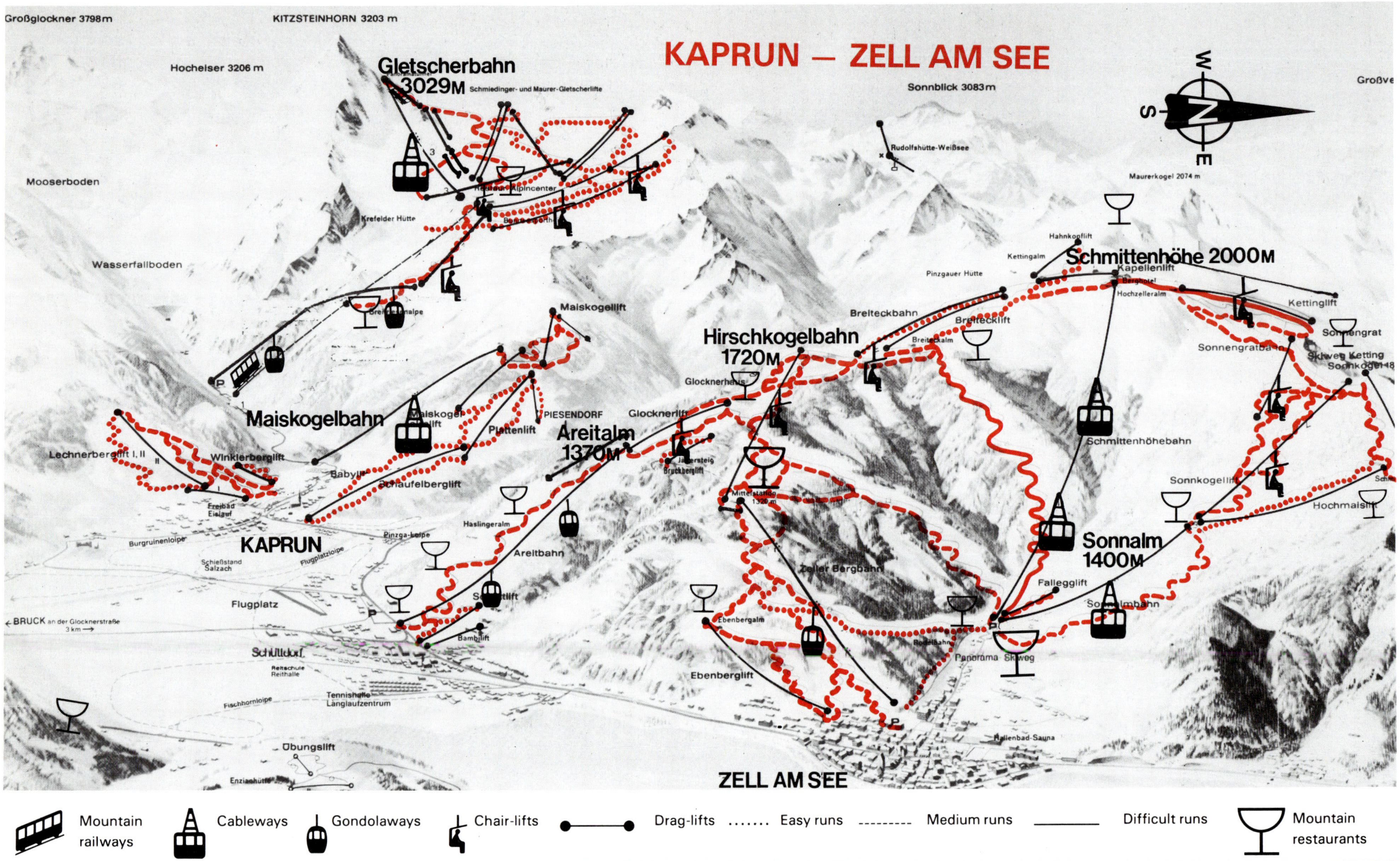
KAPRUN — ZELL AM SEE
Großglockner 3798m
KITZSTEINHORN 3203 m
Hocheiser 3206 m
Sonnblick 3083m
Mooserboden
Wasserfallboden
Gletscherbahn
3029M
Schmiedinger- und Maurer-Gletscherlifte
Krefelder Hütte
Rudolfshütte-Weißsee
Maurerkogel 2074 m
Maiskogellift
Maiskogelbahn
Lechnerberglift I, II
Winklerberglift
Babylift
Schaufelberglift
Plattenlift
PIESENDORF
Areitalm
1370M
Glocknerlift
Bruckberglift
Hirschkogelbahn
1720M
Breiteckbahn
Breiteckllift
Pinzgauer Hütte
Kettingalm
Hahnkopflift
Schmittenhöhe 2000M
Kapellenlift
Berghotel
Hochzelleralm
Kettinglift
Sonnengrat
Sonnengratbahn
Schmittenhöhebahn
Sonnkogellift
Hochmaislift
Sonnalm
1400M
Falegglift
Sonnalmbahn
Zeller Bergbahn
Ebenbergalm
Ebenberglift
Panorama
Haslingeralm
Areitbahn
Bamblift
KAPRUN
Burgruinenloipe
Schießstand Salzach
Flugplatzloipe
Pinzga-Loipe
Flugplatz
← BRUCK an der Glocknerstraße 3 km →
Reitschule Reithalle
Tennishalle Langlaufzentrum
Fischhornloipe
Übungslift
ZELL AM SEE
Mountain railways
Cableways
Gondolaways
Chair-lifts
Drag-lifts
Easy runs
Medium runs
Difficult runs
Mountain restaurants

open and sunny with runs back to Zell am See. It is normally possible to ski right down to the edge of the village until mid-March. The lower slopes are particularly good for beginners.
Across the lake, to the east, the long Ronachkopf chair-lift takes one up to Ronachkopf, 4,875ft. and a medium grade run of about 5.5km., leads down to the lakeside at Thumersbach, with a difference in height of 1,950ft. There are three short drag-lifts on the crest.

In a Few Words: Ideal for beginners and medium skiers: families, groups including non-skiers; plenty of activities; slopes open at the top, broad runs through woods lower down, good choice of accommodation; medium price. Within easy reach of Kaprun (10 mins.) and one pass covers both resorts and the linking bus service.

Après Ski: Informal, unsophisticated and reasonable in price. The Hotel Lebzelter's Lebzelt Keller is a genuine cellar with a vaulted stone ceiling and wooden benches and its restaurant upstairs is good value too, a favourite haunt of younger skiers. They are also regularly to be found at the Pinzgauer Diele, with a discothèque till 2 a.m. and long restaurant bar. Also well frequented are the Crazy Daisy Pub, with live music once weekly; the Disco Viva, the Disco Monte, the Taverne Disco Nr. 1 and the Bierstadl, where one can enjoy 33 different types of beer. Further out, at Schüttdorf, there is a beerhall restaurant and lively band at the popular Café Latini. The Alpenblick stüberl is an agreeable place for a drink and has a guitar player once a week. There is a marvellous selection of walks, a large indoor riding school, a cinema and a variety of good shops. An indoor swimming pool provides simultaneous a view of the skating and ice hockey in the ice stadium. Other activities include tennis, squash, sleigh rides, tobogganning, nordic skiing – 200km. of trails, curling, rifle shooting, ice-surfing on lake, ski touring and alpine flights.

Recommended Hotels:

Gasthof Alpenblick: Situated in Schüttdorf, just off the main road to Kaprun, this is a very charming gasthof. Large dining room decorated in traditional Austrian style, attractive stüberl with zither music each evening, comfortable sitting room and bar. Bedrooms comfortable and some with bath or shower and many with balconies. Nice owner.

Hotel Porschehof: This is an attractive chalet style hotel situated in the Schüttdorf section of Zell am See and conveniently placed for the gondolaway up to the top station. It is pleasantly furnished and has a good atmosphere, the owner worked for many years in the UK and his wife is English. The heated indoor swimming pool, sauna and solarium add to the attractiveness of the hotel.

Grand Hotel Gesmbh & Cokg: Situated on the lakeside, completely rebuilt and re-opened in December 1984. The accommodation now consists of varying size apartments with hotel service. A wide variety of facilities are contained in the hotel complex; Hotel restaurant, lounge, 'Wunder-bar' on the roof; swimming pool, sauna, squash, conference and banqueting rooms. There are also some super-luxe suites available complete with personal sauna, whirl-pool and open fire.

Hotel St. George: This splendid hotel, set in its own grounds, near the centre and 100m. from the gondolaway. Large attractive dining room with pillars and vaulted ceiling and circular open fireplace in the centre. Comfortable and nicely furnished sitting room, bar, heated indoor swimming pool, sauna, gymnasium. The bedrooms are elegantly furnished, all with private bath, wc, radio, TV, telephone, minibar abd balcony. Excellent food.

Hotel Zum Hirschen: Centrally situated, this is a first class modern hotel. Very nice bedrooms, with bath or shower, radio, telephone, minibar, TV and balcony. Pleasant dining room, comfortably and colourfully furnished sitting rooms. Attractive Keller Bar with dancing. Sauna, Turkish bath and whirl-pool.

KAPRUN

Height of Resort: 2,624 ft.
Height of Top Station: 9,938 ft.
Nearest International Airport: Salzburg
Map Reference: 6D See page 237
Route by Car: See pages 236-237
Resort Facilities Charts: See page 214
Hotel Reference Charts: See page 228

Kaprun is a traditional ski village, offering a friendly welcome to visitors and with excellent skiing surrounding it. There are four trainer lifts in the immediate village area and there is good skiing for intermediates and beginners on the shoulder of the Maiskogel mountain. This can be reached in two directions, first by the Schaufelberg drag-lift, which starts near the centre of the village, and from the top one can connect with the Platten drag-lift. From the top of this lift one takes an easy south-westerly short run to connect with the Maiskogel drag-lift, which rises in a north-westerly direction to finish just above the top station of the Maiskogel cableway. The cableway is the second means of reaching this area, and starts about 2km. from the centre of the village, top station 5,021 ft. Four drag-lifts in the top area serve easy and intermediate slopes. The runs down to the village on south to south-east facing slopes are intermediate to start with, through wide wooded glades, leading to easier runs on open sunny slopes.

The main skiing however is on the Kitzsteinhorn, reached by the Gletscher cableway, carrying 1,850 people per hour, surmounted by a 4-seater chair-lift which terminates at the Alpincenter. This is supplemented by a mountain railway, carrying 1,240 persons per hour and terminates at the Alpincenter, 8,060ft. Both these top terminals give access to some marvellous skiing, extending over about 8 square miles of clear, wide open slopes, served by a compact lift system. From the Alpincenter a further cableway ascends in a westerly direction to the top of the magnificent Kitzsteinhorn, 9,938ft. Here one finds a restaurant and a wonderful view looking onto the Grossglockner, the highest mountain in Austria, 12,343ft. Experienced skiers can take the run directly from the top. Beginners take the Gipfelbahn which leads to easy skiing and two short drag-lifts. The runs down to the top station of the mountain railway, where incidentally the restaurant (seating 500 people), is delightful. Running off at right-angles to the top station of the cableway, one has a 4 seater bubble chair-lift travelling in a northerly direction to Schmiedinger-Glacier, and below this and running parallel a drag-lift reaches the Krefelderhütte. At the head of this triangular area formed by the lifts and the ridge one finds two parallel drag-lifts and further to the right two more parallel drag-lifts rising in a north-west facing direction again to the ridge, whilst the Kees drag-lift, the Kitz drag-lift and the longer established Sonnenkar chair-lift have further improved the lift system in this area. This vast triangular glacier provides some marvellous easy to intermediate interconnecting runs. To the right of the top section of the mountain railway the Langwied chair-lift, a 4-seater bubble lift, serves good intermediate runs. Snow conditions are reliable throughout the winter, and this is also an excellent skiing area for summer. It is not possible to ski right down to the bottom station but one can ski down to the Langwied chair-lift. The bottom station of the cableway and the mountain railway are linked with the village by bus services. The TV camera mounted at the top of the Kitzsteinhorn shows a panoramic view of the glacier and is linked to the major hotels and tourist centre, enabling the weather conditions and temperatures to be seen. This is thought to be the first such system in Europe.

In a Few Words: Kaprun is exceptional in Austria for its high glacier skiing and provides comparatively easy and safe skiing and an extensive choice for skiers up to intermediate standard. Also one of the best areas for ski touring. Within easy distance of Zell am See (10 min.) – and one pass covers both resorts and the linking bus service.

Après Ski: There are four discos in the resort. For the pastry lovers, the Morokutti is favourite along with Café Anita and the Café Nindl. There is tea dancing at the Baum-Bar, plus a discothèque and various pensions have a weinkeller. The Kapruner Musikstadl is a very popular nightclub with discothèque. Eating out is fairly inexpensive.

Recommended Hotels:

Gasthof Mühle: Has a large and long dining room seating 150 persons, light and well furnished, with large cartwheels converted into ceiling lights. Bedrooms of good size, all with bath or shower, bathrooms particularly nice. Stüberl. Heated indoor swimming pool 50 metres from hotel.

Sporthotel Kaprun: On the outskirts of the village but the nearest to the cableway stations, this hotel was reconstructed in 1977 and is very attractive. Large reception and dining room area with marble floor. Spacious and light dining room, nicely furnished. Good sized bedrooms, all with bath or shower and most with balconies. Sauna, pleasant stüberl.

HINTHERTHAL

Height of Resort: 3,345 ft.
Height of Top Station: 4,428 ft.
Nearest International Airport: Salzburg
Map Reference: 6D See page 237
Route by Car: See pages 236-237
Resort Facilities Charts: See page 214
Hotel Reference Charts: See page 227

Hintherthal, situated at the head of the Urslay valley, is surrounded by high mountains, dominated by the Hochkönig, 9,662ft., to the north-east. Although not high it has a reputation as a snow-pocket. As the valley is aligned east-west it enjoys long hours of sunshine. It is reached by a good road from Saaffelden (15km. away) via Maria Alm and Hintermoos. Hinterthal is a small, very friendly, unspoilt and picturesque resort with six hotels and nine pensions and a number of private chalets and apartments. It has its own ski school (run by Balthazar Mayer, 27 years a ski instructor, who has taught at Dartmouth, U.S.A. and speaks excellent English). The village comes under the wing of the Tourist Office in Maria Alm (8km. distant).

The Hinterthal Skiing
Two parallel drag-lifts, Faschinglifts I and II, serve an excellent north-facing beginner's slope. As this is not, as is so often the case, the end of a longer run coming from above, the beginner is not molested by fast skiers dashing past. The Sonnleiten drag-lift provides south and south-east facing runs on each side of about 1.5km. with a vertical drop of some 700ft. These are generally intermediate slopes.

The Hochmais lift: A drag-lift takes one up a steep sugar-loaf of a hill giving a variety of descents of up to 3km. with a vertical drop of 1,148ft. This slope, taken down the fall line, provides excellent technique training for good skiers (used occasionally by the Austrian women's team), whilst there are easier routes for the intermediate. Being north-facing, the snow usually remains in good condition and there are a number of excellent deep snow variations down the back side. The Gabühel drag-lift surmounts the Hochmais for some 2km. with a further rise of 1,148ft. In addition to lengthening the return runs to Hinterthal to some 5km. with a height difference of about 2,297ft., it permits skiing down 2km. of south-facing slopes the other side of the ridge to the neighbouring resort of Dienten (see separate report). Returning by chair-lift from Dienten back to the top of the ridge. Eventually, a couple of link lifts along the Gabühel ridge will allow one to ski down to Hintermoos, lower down the valley, and connect with that ski area.

The visitor to Hinterthal is not however confined to the present somewhat limited Hinterthal skiing. One can buy the Saalachtaler 7 day pass which includes 9 lifts on the Aberg (reaching to Langeck, 6,560ft.) and 3 Natrun lifts above Maria Alm, apart from further away skiing at Leogang, Lofer and Maishofen. A bus leaves Hinterthal at 8.50 p.m.daily for the Hintermoos and Maria Alm skiing, returning at midday or 5.00 p.m. One's own car is a considerable asset.

In a Few Words: A pretty and unspoilt little resort. Very suitable for beginners, intermediates and families. Although the Hochmaislift provides steep slopes, not enough variety and length of runs as yet within Hinterthal itself for advanced intermediates and experts. Better skiers can obtain greater variety by skiing also the Hintermoos/Aberg/Maria Alm

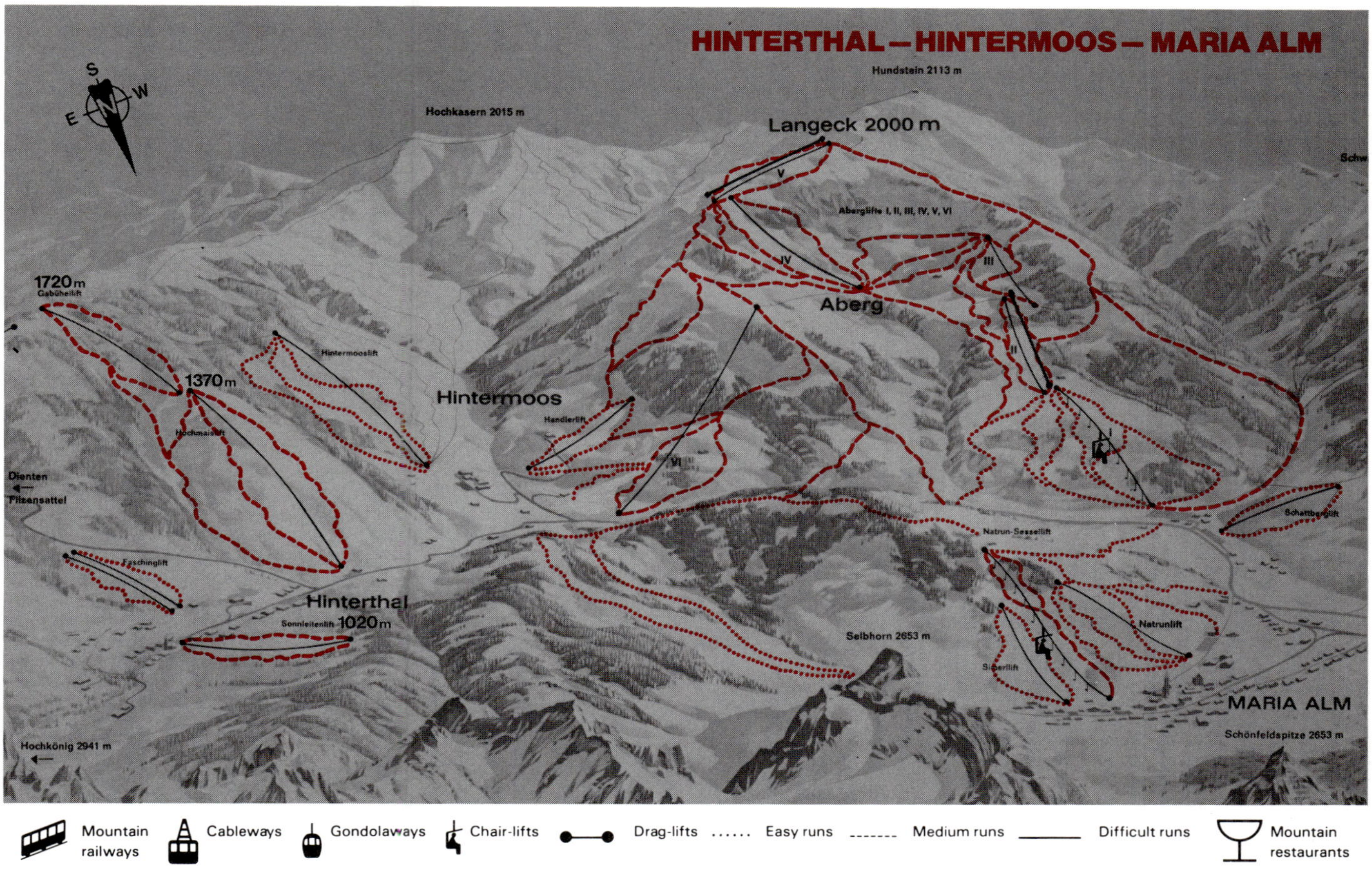

area and beyond with the 7-day Saalachtaler abonnement.

Après Ski: For tea and cakes, the pretty Café Schafhuber is small enough to get warm and crowded, thus becoming the popular gathering place when the lifts stop. The evening après ski is of the do-it-yourself variety but none the less enjoyable for that. The Imschluf (little burrow) under the Wachtelhof is an attractive spot with a four-sided open log fire in the centre of the cellar, round which one can dance to a disco. As from 8 p.m. It's dancing unlimited for those who have the inclination. No entrance fee. Every Thursday there is a popular 'happening' at the Almbar - a dear little wooden hut at the bottom of the baby lift where, drenched in 'atmosphere', you can dance to a live 4-man band from 8.30 p.m. to 1 a.m. The Gasthaus Selbhorn (less atmosphere) advertises nightly dancing in its keller, and the Pension Elisabeth also has a keller/stüberl, surprisingly cosy, where patrons can start up their own disco music if and when the spirit moves them. Pension Ebner's bar can also be turned into disco/dancing, but one must create one's ambience. For drinkers only, there are a number of bars varying in simplicity and economy. The Botenwirt, by the bus stop, is a typical Austrian inn where wine can be drunk alongside the inevitable card-playing locals. For dining out there is the Wachtelhof's restaurant for special treats, the Steinbock, small but pleasant and more modest and with less choice, the old Gasthof Obermussbach. Plenty of natural walks and tobogganning to and from the next village of Dienten. For a day's outing, either sight-seeing or skiing, there are Kitzbühel, Zell am See, Badgastein and rather further, Salzburg, all within worthwhile visiting distance.

Recommended Hotels:

Pension Ebner: The largest of Hinterthal's 9 pensions, detached and situated very close to the highest ski-lift, the Hochmais. The exterior follows the general Land Salzburger style, although the spacious interior is slightly less artistic. Good airy bedrooms, mostly with balconies and all with either private bath or shower and w.c. The pension only does half-pension terms but there is always a reasonably priced menu for those wanting full board. The cooking is done by Mr. Ebner himself.

DIENTEN

Height of Resort: 3,502 ft.
Height of Top Station: 5,747 ft.
Nearest International Airport: Salzburg
Map Reference: 6D See page 237
Route by Car: See pages 236-237
Resort Facilities Charts: See page 213
Hotel Reference Charts: See page 227

Dienten is situated in the lower range of the Hochkönig mountains of Salzburg region with the higher peaks rising to over 9,000ft. and forming a dramatic background to an attractive ski area. The village is compact and well placed; to the north is Hinterthal (see separate report) and to the south Mühlbach. Apart from one small section there are lifts allowing one to traverse the whole area, which although not high has a reputation as a snow pocket. On the north side of Dienten one finds the Gabühel chair-lift rising northwards to Gabühel, 5,360ft., the link with Hinterthal. From here one has easy runs over north facing open slopes towards this resort for the first section developing to intermediate for the run into Hinterthal. The return journey is by chair and drag-lift. The run back to Dienten is over south facing intermediate slopes.

From the southern side of Dienten a 4 seater chair-lift, installed in 1995, rises to Zachhofalm, 5,688ft., with trainer lifts at the bottom and top stations. There are two intermediate tree lined runs back to the valley; one follows the line of the chair-lift and the other following the line of the Bürgl-alm drag-lift which comes up from the north side of the village.

Still on the southern side and next to the bottom station of the chair-lift the Dachegg drag-lift rises to Kollmannsegg, 5,747ft. From here an easy south facing run brings one to the foot of the surmounting Fellersbach drag-lifts and from the top one has a good south facing run down to Mühlbach. The less-than-intermediates should stay at the restaurant because the run down to Mühlbach, closely following the line of the lift, is difficult. Alternatively the less experienced can take the long easy run curving round the foot of the mountain. One then reverses the traverse and arrives back at the foot of the Dachegg drag-lift. Six strategically placed lifts allow the traverse to be made in both directions; the runs are mainly easy on north and south facing slopes, with the exception of the final run following the line of the cableway, into Mühlbach.

For those who require greater variety a further ski area can be reached from Hinterthal – see report under this heading.

For the Nordic skier there are trails of varying length through very beautiful countryside starting from the foot of the Dachegg drag-lift.

In a Few Words: A cosy small resort, a good variety of skiing for beginners to intermediates due to a well placed lift system. A good selection of mountain restaurants so one can stay out all day.

Après Ski: Informal and friendly, the young make for the disco 'Postalm' or Pub 'Dingsda' at the Hotel Post. Twice a week there is dancing to live music in the Hotels Mitterwirt and Salzburgerhof. Several cafés and bars and fondue and glühwein parties are arranged regularly. There are lovely walks into the surrounding countryside.

Recommended Hotels:

Hotel Hochkönig: An old established hotel built in traditional style but renovated in 1981, in a good position two minutes from the Gabühel chair-lift. Bedrooms are comfortably furnished, most with bath/shower. Spacious entrance hall and reception area. pleasantly furnished restaurant where a large buffet breakfast is served, small stüberl with open fire and decorated with hunting relics, the venue for parties when young Willi, the owner, often plays his guitar. There is also a stube much frequented by the locals.

Hotel Salzburgerhof: A family hotel with a good atmosphere, extended in 1981. The reception area leads to an à la carte stüberl on one side and the residents' lounge on the other side. Kellerbar and disco. Sauna. A large buffet breakfast is always served. Bedrooms comfortably furnished, most with bath/shower. Situated about 4 minutes from the Gabühel chair-lift.

THE GASTEIN VALLEY

Nearest International Airport: Salzburg
Map Reference: 6D See page 237
Route by Car: See pages 236-237

This vast panoramic ski area consisting of 3 main villages lies at the head of the Gastein Valley. Dorfgastein is about 45 minutes by coach from Salzburg, Bad Hofgastein 50 minutes and Badgastein approximately 60 minutes, which makes this area one of the most accessible from U.K. airports. All three resorts are linked by a regular and efficient free bus service. Angertal is the skiing link between Badgastein and Bad Hofgastein and it is a good place to start if queues form in the resorts it links. Regular buses also run from Badgastein to two other areas, Graukogel and Sportgastein. The fares for all buses and the train are included in the Super Gastein ski pass. Altogether there are over 250km. of well prepared pistes and each area has suitable skiing for all grades of skier.

DORFGASTEIN

Height of Resort: 2,755 ft.
Height of Top Station: 6,690 ft.
Resort Facilities Charts: See page 213
Hotel Reference Charts: See page 227

A picturesque Alpine village just off the main road, fairly widely spread with a good selection of hotels and pensions. The advantage of this area is that it has excellent protection from south-west winds which sometimes puts the main cableway in Badgastein out of action. For those who do not wish to walk there is a bus service every 30 minutes from the village to the bottom station of the chair-lift, which is supplemented by drag-lifts all rising to Wengeralm. From this point a cableway rises directly to Fulsteck, 6,660ft., supplemented by surmounting lifts. From this top station one can enjoy good open and sheltered slopes. Facing the village on the right (Grossartal side) there are easy and intermediate runs down to the valley returning to the top again by surmounting lifts or by cableway. The run down to Dorfgastein via Fulseck is open at the top and then wide wooded glades to the bottom station, a good selection of blue and red runs. The whole area offers plenty of opportunity for off-piste skiing.

In a Few Words: A good family resort, ski kindergarten where children can be left all day – lunch provided. Most hotels and pensions will make arrangements for babysitting in the evenings. Excellent skiing in its own right plus the extensive ski areas of the neighbouring resorts. 5 Nordic skiing trails. A friendly atmosphere throughout the resort and many people return year after year.

Après Ski: Most hotels have folk dancing and there are informal get-togethers in the lounges and bars. The Kuhbar disco has lots of atmosphere whilst the Disco Ritual at the Hotel Kirchenwirt is popular with the younger set. From the Strohlehenalm the finale of evening entertainment is a torchlit tobog-gan run; this run is open all day. At the bottom of the lift there are two saunas and a solarium. There are horse-drawn sleigh rides into the countryside and also a curling rink.

Recommended Hotels:

Hotel Kirchenwirt: A modern hotel within 300 metres of the lifts and run by the Kostinger family. All bedrooms are large with bath/shower. Some annexe accommodation within 50 metres. Pleasant lounge, dining room, restaurant, bar and sun terrace. K-Keller downstairs with dancing to disco; sauna and solarium. Cosy atmosphere throughout.

BAD HOFGASTEIN

Height of Resort: 2,853 ft.
Height of Top Station: 7,544 ft.
Resort Facilities Charts: See page 212
Hotel Reference Charts: See page 227

Situated just off the main road mid way between Dorfgastein and Badgastein this small town is built around its old centre, a pedestrian zone and consists of some 160 hotels and typical Austrian gasthofs. there and from its panoramic windows one can watch the late afternoon skiers whilst enjoying a drink and keeping an eye out for one's busThere is a free bus service in the village and most of the larger hotels run courtesy buses to and from the car parking area in front of the ski school. This is also the post bus terminal operating buses to all the other ski areas. The indoor tennis centre is also situated there and from its panoramic windows one can watch the late afternoon skiers whilst enjoying a drink and keeping an eye out for one's bus.

The resort enjoys long hours of sunshine from early morning to 1600 hours in February. Its predominantly north-east facing runs ensure good snow and the wide open slopes of the Schlossalm provide excellent skiing and the link with Badgastein via Angertal provides further extensive skiing on the Stubnerkogel.

Its skiing: Schlossalm is reached initially by the mountain railway leaving 100 metres from the parking area, capacity 1,250 per hour and rising to Kitzstein. From this point a surmounting cableway, capacity 600 per hour, reaches 6,724ft.; alternatively one can take the 4 seater chair-lift, Kleine Scharte. Once on the Schlossalm this vast area, served by 8 drag-lifts and 4 chair-lifts, presents no real problems in this respect. The descents to all areas are well defined and one hardly needs to use the same descent during a day's skiing. The 8km. run to Kitzstein via the top of the chair-lift at Hohe Scharte is a must for intermediates upwards; a pleasant rest can be taken at the Aeroplan Hütte just before Kitzstein, where one can decide whether to ski down to the valley, not always an easy run due sometimes to icy conditions and congestion. The alternative is to take the mountain railway down or to ski to Angertal and then get the free bus service to Bad Hofgastein. There are numerous variations for the off-piste skier, particularly to the left of the Hohe Scharte chair-lift and beside the Schloss-Hochalm lift. There are 16 mountain restaurants; of special mention are the Schlossalm, just before the Schlosshochalm lift and the Waldgasthof Café, above the lift office at Angertal, for their cleanliness and good food. To reach Angertal, the link with Badgastein, one takes a predominantly blue run two-thirds of the way down the Schlossalm over wide mogul slopes eventually joining up with the former and the chair-lift up to the Badgastein area. Return is via a double chair-lift and the choice of surmounting drag-lifts.

In a Few Words: Bad Hofgastein's own skiing area on the Schlossalm is excellent for beginners up to advanced intermediates. There are many descents of 8-11 km. and plenty of variations on and off-piste to keep the more advanced skier happy for several days then there are the ski areas of Badgastein and Dorfgastein altogether giving plenty of scope for a 2 weeks' holiday. The town has many attractions for the skier and non-skier. There are numerous shops, restaurants, skating, curling, indoor and outdoor swimming pools, saunas, thermal cures and massage, indoor tennis courts, squash, ski bobbing, riding, sleigh rides and many beautiful walks. The Tourist Office Director and his staff deserve special mention for their enthusiastic aid to tourists. An excellent information centre giving availability of hotel accommodation and all the details one wishes to know about the Valley.

Après Ski: Quite a lively town with a number of discos and dancing to bands.The Glocknerkeller is a club with an ambience of its own. The younger swingers frequent 'Vision', below the Norica Hotel and 'Evergreen', both in the town centre. Belami's disco is situated between Badgastein and Hofgastein, whilst the Gasteiner Tenne, near the centre, is the largest club for dancing in the resort. There are no less than four pubs in the village, Franky's, Tröpferl, 'Tritsch-Tratsch' and Match Box. The Café Weitmoserschlössel, situated in an old castle, is well worth a visit, and so is the Catholic church in the town centre, one of the largest and loveliest Gothic building in the Salzburg region, founded around 894 A.D.

Recommended Hotels:

Hotel Norica: A modern luxury hotel centrally situated in the pedestrian zone. Good sized bedrooms all with bath/shower, TV, and balcony, single rooms with shower, lounge bar on the ground floor with open fire and small dance floor. Two large restaurants with a friendly service, a stüberl leading off. Below the restaurant is a thermal swimming pool with water jet massage facilities, sauna and plunge pool, massage and cure facilities and solarium. High standard of food with three courses of main course or à la carte. A large buffet breakfast is served.

Hotel Palace Gastein: Built in 1967 the Palace Gastein offers every comfort while somehow managing to avoid the somewhat daunting atmosphere its name evokes. The cooking is excellent and each course offers a choice of three dishes, plus a suggested 'cure diet'. Guests can dance nightly to a band in one of the hotel's bars or put their name down for a game of chess, bridge, canasta or backgammon at any time in the card room. Small children can be left for most of the day at the hotel's free kindergarten in the care of a nurse. The heated swimming pool, hairdresser, thermal baths, massage, sauna and sun terrace all contribute to the guests' well-being, candlelight gala once a month adds some extra luxury. A free hotel bus runs a shuttle service to the ski slopes all day. Thermal water can be drunk, free of charge, from a spring tap and 12 thermal baths are included in the all-in rates cure facilities. For the not so young who like comfort without rowdiness or pomp, we can recommend the Palace Gastein.

Pension Paracelsus: A small bed and breakfast pension situated in a quiet street 300 metres from the sports centre and about 7 minutes' walk from the mountain railway. 12 twin bedded rooms and 2 singles all with bath, telephone and balcony. Well furnished. Dining room where a good buffet breakfast is served, on request a simple lunch or dinner will also be provided. Sitting room and television room. Highly recommended.

BAD GASTEIN

Height of Resort: 3,608 ft.
Height of Top Station: 8,809 ft.
Resort Facilities Charts: See page 212
Hotel Reference Charts: See page 227

Situated at the southernmost point of the Gastein Valley Bad Gastein presents an impressive sight. It is the largest of the 3 resorts mentioned, and consists of 135 pensions and hotels, one youth hostel and 47 spa hotels clinging to the mountainside rising from the edge of the river. The centre of the town is mainly old buildings intermingled with a few modern and luxurious hotels along with the swimming pool, one of the largest in Austria which is heated by thermal springs. As one moves away from the centre the typical modern Austrian style hotels become more apparent. The town has been famous for over 600 years for its thermal waters coming from the Graukogel. Parking is limited both in the town and at the lift stations.

The Skiing: This is divided into three main areas: the Graukogel on the east side of the valley, the Stubnerkogel on the west side, which is linked with the ski area of Schlossalm, and the Kreuzkogel at Sportgastein, 5 miles up the valley to the south of the village of Böckstein. The Bad Gastein skiing itself ranges between 3,542ft. and 7,331ft. with a top station of 8,809ft. reached from Sportgastein. There are over 170km. of prepared pistes and 85 km. of Nordic skiing trails along with 50km. on the Graukogel and the Stubnerkogel is from December to mid April and on the Kreuzkogel until early May. The Gastein Super Ski Pass enables one to ski throughout the valley and includes free use of buses and trains between centres. There is also the Golden Skicard. This is a season ticket not only for the Gastein Valley and Grossarl but includes Zell am See, Kaprun, Dachstein Tauern, Dachstein-West, Obertraun and Dolomiti Superski areas. Those travelling by car for a 3 week holiday or more would find this pass a bargain.

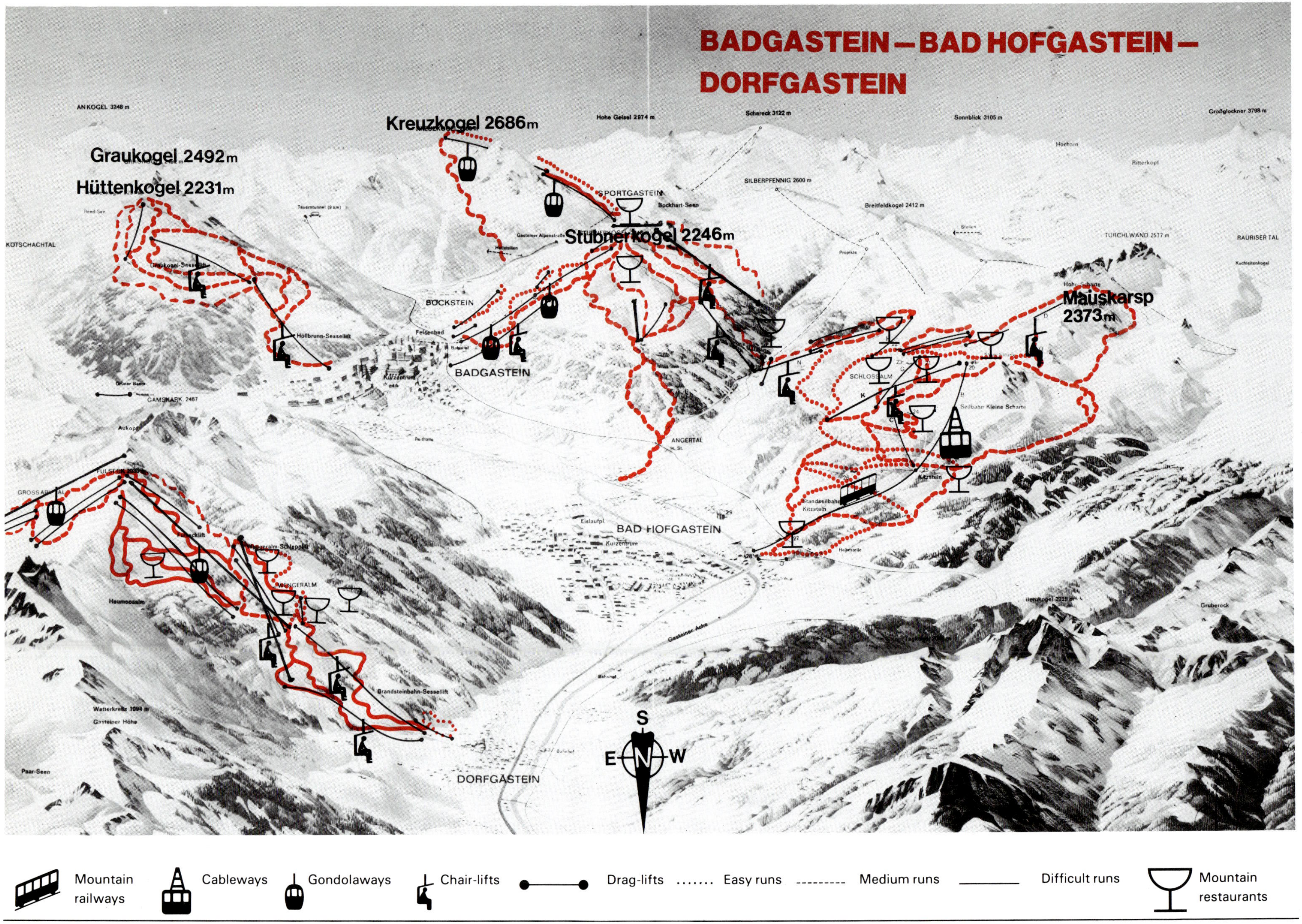
BADGASTEIN—BAD HOFGASTEIN—DORFGASTEIN
Kreuzkogel 2686m
Graukogel 2492m
Hüttenkogel 2231m
Stubnerkogel 2246m
Mauskarsp 2373m
SPORTGASTEIN
BÖCKSTEIN
BADGASTEIN
BAD HOFGASTEIN
DORFGASTEIN
SCHLOSSALM
ANGERTAL
S
E
N
W
Mountain railways
Cableways
Gondolaways
Chair-lifts
Drag-lifts
Easy runs
Medium runs
Difficult runs
Mountain restaurants

Stubnerkogel Area: 3,552ft. - 7,382ft.: From the west side of the town a 6-seater gondolaway, carrying 2,200 persons per hour, first reaches Stubnerkogelbahn and thence continues to Stubnerkogel, with attractive restaurants at the top and middle stations. From the summit there is a variety of easy to medium/difficult east facing runs back to the mid station or on the other side there are more challenging west facing slopes returning to the top by chair-lift and drag-lift. Alternatively one can continue down to Angertal, the link with the Bad Hofgastein area, on a fairly difficult run or take a wooded path of intermediate standard. From Angertal a triple chair-lift quickly takes one up above the tree-line where one takes an intermediate run to the foot of the drag-lift which returns one to the top of Stubnerkogel. Or from the top of the chair-lift one can turn left and by the use of a drag-lift return to the mid station of the gondolaway. A quadruple chair-lift runs from the valley up to the shoulder of the Stubnerkogel is surmounted by the Hirschkar drag-lift which takes one to the eastern flank of this mountain. The most popular run is from the top of Stubnerkogel to Angertal some 7km. in length, two-thirds covered by snow cannons, a route of tremendous variety. From the mid station of the gondolaway to Bad Gastein there are two wooded descents, one easy and one medium, both via the charming Bellevue Alm restaurant which has tea dancing. Both descents can be icy and crowded at times.

Graukogel Area: 3,542ft. - 7,331ft.: A short bus ride from Bad Gastein across a bridge, below a spectacular waterfall, one comes to the bottom station of a single chair-lift which takes one up to the mid station where a surmounting double chair-lift reaches a pleasant restaurant. Nearby a drag-lift rises to 7,331ft. From the top there are two main runs to the mid station, the one on the right is difficult but fun, and the other wide open at the top and thence through wide wooded glades. The descents to the bottom station will present no difficulty for the intermediate. This area is the venue for World Cup races. The slopes are west to north-west facing and keep the snow well. There is a good restaurant within 50 metres of the bottom station. Normally there are no queues in this area.

Sportgastein Area: 5,240ft. - 8,809 ft.: Situated about 20 minutes by bus from Bad Gastein (services hourly during ski periods) is the lower station of the gondolaway and a parking area. Here there are two restaurants: one, Valerie Haus, deserves special mention for its quality of food and reasonable prices. The gondolaway rises to the mid station where there is a self service restaurant; from this point it continues to Kreuzkogel, 8,809ft. After a 20ft. climb one has a spectacular view of the distant mountains. From the top the 11 km. run to Böckstein, over the back of the mountain, is only for the experienced skier as it is very narrow and steep in parts. Looking down from the summit the runs on the right are wide and fairly easy whilst those to the left are intermediate to difficult, over wide and beautiful country with many variations including off-piste skiing. The runs to the valley from the middle station are varied and suitable for all grades of skiers and large areas of off-piste skiing.

In a Few Words: A winter sports and health resort. Excellent skiing facilities for all grades. A wealth of recreational facilities: skating, ski bobbing, Nordic skiing, Austrian curling, sleigh rides, indoor horse riding and competitions, mountain walks in superb scenery, squash, indoor tennis and golf, indoor and outdoor thermal swimming pools, solarium, saunas, bowling etc. An ideal resort for mixed parties of skiers and non-skiers. Plenty of shops and restaurants in the centre and an interesting museum. Increased artificial snow installations.

Après Ski: Well represented at all levels from the Baders Blockhaus and Weismayr discos, which are central and particularly for the younger set, to the Bellevue-Alm, with open fire and more intimate. Pubs include the Schafflinger and the Ski Alm, which is halfway to Böckstein. The hotel Elisabeth Park has a small band and dance area and many other hotels have similar facilities for evening entertainment. For the gambler, as already mentioned, there is the casino.

Recommended Hotels:

Hotel Bellevue: Combines tradition with elegance, centrally situated in its own grounds. All rooms comfortably furnished with bath. Gourmet restaurant with choice of menu for lunch and dinner, buffet breakfast, grill room, cocktail bar and night club. Spacious and beautifully furnished sitting rooms, indoor heated swimming pool, underwater therapy, massage etc. Also owners of the Bellevue-Alm restaurant on the slopes where lunch can be taken by clients on full board arrangements.

Hotel Söntgen: A well run family hotel with a friendly atmosphere, situated on the main street, 250 metres from the gondolaway terminal and 150 metres from the swimming pool. Large informal restaurant with varied menu and buffet breakfast. Most rooms have bath/shower and balconies and there is a large roof garden for sun bathing. The Mühlhäusl disco is downstairs. Guests on full board receive a welcome drink and they can also take lunch at the Waldgasthof or Waldhütte in Angertal as both are owned by the Söntgen.

Haus Nefer: A modern and typically Austrian guest house with a friendly service and bed and buffet breakfast arrangements. All rooms of good size with bath and balcony. Cosy lounge and there is a thermal bath. Good value for those on a limited budget.

WAGRAIN

Height of Resort: 2,952 ft.
Height of Top Station: 6,608 ft. Area: 7,178 ft.
Nearest International Airport: Salzburg
Map Reference: 7D See page 237
Route by Car: See page 236-237
Resort Facilities Chart: See page 216

This friendly resort situated in the Salzburg Region forms part of one of Austria's largest ski areas. Known as the Salzburger Sportwelt, Amadé, or the Three Valleys, it stretches from Filzmoos in the east to Alpendorf in the West, with 320 km. of down hill runs served by 120 lifts, in addition to 220 km. of Nordic ski trails. Nor all the resorts are interlinked by lifts but buses run fairly frequently; a car, however would be an advantage.

Wagrain, set amidst the wooded round top mountains, off the main through road, has much character. It has some 80 hotels and pensions and further accommodation in chalets and apartments for 2,000 guests. Its own ski area covers 40 km. of downhill runs served by 2 gondolaways, 4 chair-lifts and 6 drag-lifts and most of the runs face east and west. The ascent to the skiing is on two sides of the village. On the west a gondolaway rises to Grafenberg, 5,583ft., the link point with the Alpendorf ski area. Two drag-lifts also run parallel with this system with easy runs back to the village, although these become steeper and wooded for the second half of the run in. On the eastern side a two stage gondolaway travels first to Berg and thence to Alpengasthof, the link point for the Flachau ski area. The runs back to the village are intermediate through wide wooded glades. A frequent bus service runs between these two bottom stations of Wagrain.

A short bus ride to the south of Wagrain takes one to Kleinarl, where surmounting chair-lifts travel eastwards to Mooskopf, 6,495ft., the link station for the ski areas of Flachauwinkl and further east Zauchensee. The latter's top station of 7,178 ft. is the highest in the Sportwelt Amadé area.

In a Few Words: Wagrain is a good base to tackle this extensive ski area. The intermediate skier will be happy here and could not ask for a greater variety of runs through picturesque wooded scenery. It requires a good 2 weeks to explore the whose area. The less experienced can select easier routes and these is a choice of 40 mountain restaurants in which to relax for lunch. Good beginners slopes in the village area and a ski kindergarten for children 3-4 years.

Après Ski: One will enjoy the warm and friendly atmosphere in the good selection of bars and cafés and a wide choice of restaurants. For the most active there is an artificial skating rink, indoor tennis court, curling rink, and two discos. Recently opened, a large indoor and outdoor swimming pool with sauna, solarium and restaurant, and horse drawn sleigh rides are available; for the children there are two toboggan runs.

Accommodation: A wide selection of hotels and pensions, an even wider choice of self-catering apartments. The 4 star Sporthotel Wagrain, opened in 1993, is some 450 metres from centre but opposite the Grafenburg gondolaway station. The Hotel Enzian, owned by the Orgonyi family, is centrally situated and the food is excellent. The 3 star Wagrainerhof is central and has dancing once a week.

FILZMOOS

Height of Resort: 3,467 ft.
Height of Top Station: 5,248 ft.
Nearest International Airport: Salzburg
Map Reference: 7D See page 236
Route by Car: See pages 236-237
Resort Facilities Charts: See page 213
Hotel Reference Charts: See page 227

Filzmoos is situated about 50 miles south of Salzburg at the head of a valley at the foot of the impressive looking Bischofsmütze (8,049 ft.), part of the Dachstein group of mountains. It is a most picturesque and sunny small village of 16 hotels, 5 gasthofs, and numerous pensions and chalets with private rooms. It is something of a snow pocket and skiing is generally assured from December till Easter. The main skiing is on the Rossbrand, Rettenstein and Skischaukel Filzmoos-Neuberg.

Rossbrand Area 3,467-5,248ft: This is immediately south of the village and the run down is north-east and north facing, the lower slopes rarely getting the sun and thus the snow is usually in excellent condition. The runs are via wide glades cut through the trees and although comparatively short, the gradient is sufficiently steep, 1,797 vertical feet to be of interest to good skiers as well as novices. This area, served by the Papageno cableway, is best skied early in the morning when it has the eastern sun. There is scope for off-piste skiing through the trees.

Rettenstein Area 3,505-5,380ft: The Rettenstein drag-lift, on the north side of the village, rises to 5,380ft. The slopes face south-west and one can enjoy sunshine for most of the day. The top station is a wide piste cut through the trees offering relatively easy skiing, whilst the run in to the bottom station becomes more difficult.

Filzmoos – Neuberg area 3,467-4,592ft: This area on the north side of the village increases the range of skiing considerably by linking the ski area of Filzmoos to that of Neuberg. The Grossberg chair-lift rises to 4,592ft. and serves intermediate and easy south facing slopes. Further to the north the Mooslehen double chair-lift rises to the crest which divides Neuberg and Filzmoos. Coming up the other side from Neuberg is the Schwaigalm drag-lift, 1,665 metres long; both lifts meet on the crest. The north facing runs to Neuberg and the south facing runs to Filzmoos are partially wooded and suitable for beginners and intermediates. The link back to the Grossberg area is the Verbindungs drag-lift. In the Neuberg valley the Geierberg drag-lift reaches the lower crest on the south side whilst on the north side there are 3 surmounting drag-lifts serving south facing slopes.

East of the village and some 10km. away via Hachau and the Dachstein aerial cableway (5,576-8,856ft.) where glacier skiing is possible in the spring but this can hardly be considered part of Filzmoos, though many summer skiers stay here and drive up every

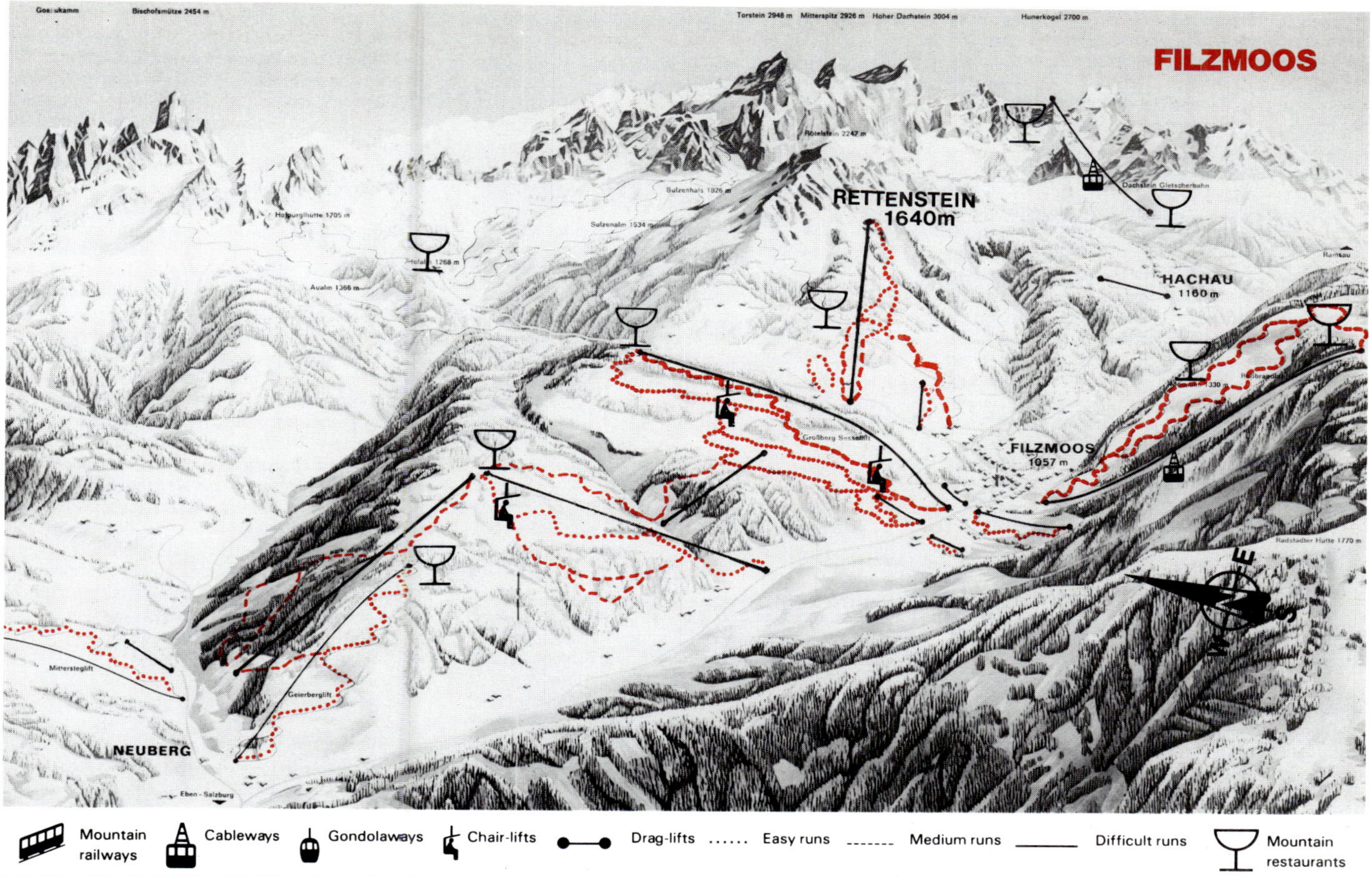

day. Langlauf skiing is also popular with a course of 35km. available.

Salzburger Sportwelt Amadé Ski Pass: For skiers who are looking for variety and the maximum skiing, the above lift pass covers 320 km. of well prepared pistes served by 120 lifts. This can be done from Filzmoos which is one of the 8 resorts covered by the pass. The others are Radstadt, Altenmarkt, Flachau, Zauchensee, Kleinarl, Wagrain and St. Johann/PG.

In a Few Words: An outstanding, pretty, unspoilt and friendly village surrounded by impressive looking mountains. Keeps the sun all day. Most highly recommended for beginners to intermediate, also for families of mixed ability. The skiing is certainly limited for the better skier both in length and variety and cannot be compared with the larger resorts. Nevertheless the runs are steep enough to be of interest to the medium skier and can provide good technique training. We found no queueing for lifts in mid-February, even at the weekend.

Après Ski: Discothèques or live music, you can take your choice – both will be moderate and informal. In the village centre the Mühlradl is another well patronised disco. Its large, wooden mill wheel imitations are extremely attractive. The Alpenkrone organises a weekly fondue evening with dancing to an accordionist. The Alm Bar under the Hubertus Hotel has a discothèque. At the 'Happy Filzmoos' a disco operates daily from 3.30 pm - 6 pm. A good meeting place after ski school is always the Fiakerstüberl, but one has to get there early to be sure of a seat.

Riding stables and toboggan parties. Sleigh rides can be arranged either by day or night. Schnapps provided. The children's ski school, with female instructors, has a novel way of teaching and looking after small learners, plus its own special children's lift and a separate run with a Disney, beginners' slalom.

Recommended Hotels:

Hotel Alpenkrone: The Alpenkrone is beautifully sited, standing alone in full sunshine, above the village and commanding glorious views from its deep balconies running full length on all four sides of the hotel. The impression is one of spaciousness with large bright rooms, open stairways and generous dining room. Decorated with personal tastes, the guests see something pretty and original round every corner. Spacious reception/lounge area; comfortable bar, TV lounge, games room with full sized snooker table. Large sun terrace, swimming pool, whirlpool, sauna, solarium, children's playroom and fitness room. The Alpenkrone is owned and run by John Hampshire and his Austrian wife Rosa. Her efficient calm and his ebullient hospitality make them ideal hoteliers, creating a most happy and welcoming atmosphere where no service is too much trouble. The hotel is, rightly, popular with all nationalities including British parties. A bus, geared to ski school hours, run to and from the hotel.

Sporthotel Filzmooserhof: Ideally situated close to both ski lifts. Breakfasts are of the American buffet style, i.e. help yourself to large varieties of cheeses, breads, hams, sausages, fruit, juices, yoghourts and eggs. A choice of two main courses for dinner. Bedrooms nicely decorated and all with private bath/shower. Sun terrace. Heated outdoor swimming pool, sauna, solarium, massage and gymnasium.

OBERTAUERN

Height of Resort: 5,723 ft.
Height of Top Station: 7,872 ft.
Nearest International Airport: Salzburg
Map Reference: 7D See page 237
Route by Car: See pages 236-237
Resort Facilities Charts: See page 215
Hotel Reference Charts: See page 228

Obertauern is at the top of the old Roman road separating the provinces of Salzburg and Carinthia, and is about 60 miles from the city of Salzburg. It can be reached by plane from Munich and Salzburg airports, thence by train to Radstadt; or by through train Ostende-Radstadt. Transport from Radstadt is by post-bus or minibus. most of its 49 hotels and 21 pensions are modern; they are spread out over about 2km. along the road, both on the summit to the pass and 1km. down the hill to east and west. Obertauern is often likened to Zürs because it is high, being assured of snow from December to the end of April; it lies on top of a pass and has excellent skiing on both sides of the road; in this case the pass runs roughly east-west and the slopes are both north and south facing.

Its uphill transport consists of one cableway, 10 chair-lifts and 15 drag-lifts. Although there are as many as ten entry points from various parts of the village to the ski circus, due to the village stretching over a length of 2km this is not as convenient as one might expect. The mid eastern end is most convenient from a skiing and resort facilities point of view, followed by the western end, but for skiing only. The extreme west end is some distance from facilities. The whole skiing terrain, with its interconnecting lifts, forms one vast skiing circus. Thus one can start out say on the north side of the road, and reach it again from the south. This unique circle covering some 30km. of downhill running can be achieved in either direction although it is best done from east to west on the south facing slopes and from west to east on the north facing. A medium skier can complete the whole circuit in some three hours; although if he does all the runs down from each lift before linking with the next, averaging about 3 hours per lift, the circle can be extended to a couple of days or more, covering 120km. of prepared runs, never skiing down the same run twice. Another feature of this fantastic circus is that the links are designed to be within the capability of very moderate skiers. This is not to say that expert skiers will find Obertauern dull; the circus is generally designed to be done from the middle station, and in many cases there are second stage lifts into higher and steeper terrain providing skiing from difficult to very difficult. The off-piste enthusiast can find many untracked powder runs on the north and south facing slopes and a vast choice of spring snow slopes on the south facing. In vertical drop, the runs are comparatively short, most cases being limited to some 2,000ft., but the feature of this centre is the number of km. that can be covered in a single day rather than the length of any particular run.

The number of beds in the village is 7,100; the uphill capacity of all the transports is 34,190, so that queueing is kept to a minimum. (In this respect there is a choice of 10 lifts that take one out of the village and into the circuit in the morning according to where one's hotel is located; only in the afternoon can one find lengthy queues on the sunnier slopes, particularly at two of the connecting lifts. As stated, one can get into the circuit from any of 9 different points. However the experienced skier will soon discover that the ideal permutation is to ski the north-facing slopes early in the morning starting with the cableway at the west end, working eastwards through this area and crossing to the south facing slopes later when the sun has softened the snow – thus one tends to start in the west on one side of the road and finish in the last of the sun on the west on the other side of the road. One abonnement covers the whole of the Obertauern system. However, there are 9 different companies operating the lifts. This has one great advantage. Each has its own piste making machine and each vies with the other in piste preparation to attract the maximum of skiers to its area. The result is that the runs are perfectly maintained.

Ski Schools: There is a choice of five ski schools asnd two snowboard schools offering ski and/or board tuition, some with excellent children's schools. Starting times and hours are normal but occasionally school meets before breakfast for an early morning visit to the slopes by specially arranging for the early opening of a convenient lift.

In a Few Words: Obertauern is a resort for skiers of all standards but especially favouring beginners up to good medium standard. Everything is exceptionally well organised. The atmosphere is exceedingly friendly. The Tourist Office runs a first class information service under its most helpful director Herr Kindl (excellent English, having spent some years in Canada). The fact that this office is never crowded testifies to the general efficiency and that all visitors are very content. There are also good facilities for cross-country skiing, with 17km. of trails. Obertauern is to be thoroughly recommended for an unsophisticated skiing holiday and is sure of snow.

Après Ski: As Obertauern is for energetic skiers and the ski school starts at 9.00 a.m. the night life can be intense and restricted to a few places, while elsewhere people go to bed early; by 9.30 p.m. the street is deserted . . . everyone is either in bed or in his chosen night spot. There are 4 discos at the Rosshimmel, the Edelweiss, the American Bar and the Römerbar. The Tyroler Keller is usually crowded out with eaters of huge grilled steaks from the open fire. A hot favourite is the Gasthof Taverne, old-established and oozing village atmosphere in its converted cow barn. Here the owner accompanies the vigorous dancing with either Tyrolean music, 'beat' or yodelling. Most places open at 8 p.m. and finish at 2 a.m. Prices are average. There are a few pleasant looking restaurants such as the Lürzeralm and Latschenstub'n where food is served up to midnight, but generally speaking an early en-pension meal (from 6.30 p.m.) is the order of the day. For the skiing fanatic, your après ski can include a run with a difference: one hut owner will switch on floodlights for the last run home . . . if you've stayed drinking till the daylight fades, that is! A splendid sports centre has been recenlty built. This comprises two full size indoor tennis courts which can double as a football pitch or for other organised ball games; three squash courts, bowling, billiards, and restaurant together with a very professional fitness facility with over 20 specialist pieces of equipment. This facility is being increasingly used by national teams and international sportsmen for professional training where the high altitude is of considerable benefit.

Recommended Hotels:

Hotel Kesselspitze: 1$^{1}/_{2}$km. from the village centre of the east side of the pass. A fairly new 'A' category hotel living up to its status in appearance and service. Nursery slopes, one of the 'circus' chair-lifts and one of the ski schools all within a few yards. The Kesselspitze has its own swimming pool, sauna and keller/bar with soft music for dancing. A bus runs 4 times daily to and from the kindergarten and this

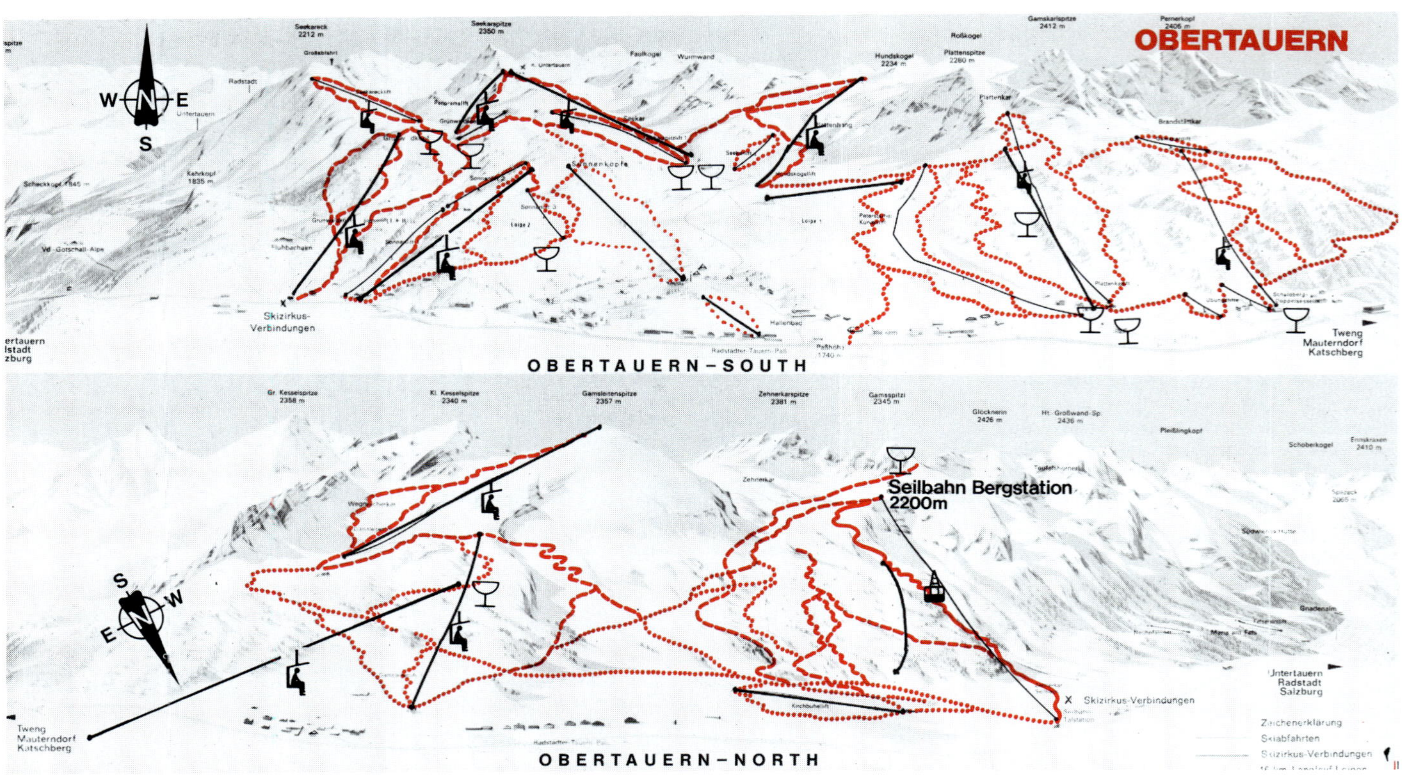

Mountain railways · Cableways · Gondolaways · Chair-lifts · Drag-lifts · ...... Easy runs · ------- Medium runs · ——— Difficult runs · Mountain restaurants

may be used free of charge by guests who want to shop in the village centre without walking the 1½ km. All rooms with bath/shower, wc., balcony and telephone.

Gasthof Taverne: The charming local Oberhumer family have run the Taverne for very many years. (Herr Oberhumer was one of the first ski school lehrers and is now president of the ski club.) It is category 'C', small and full of character, with an attractive stüberl for the en-pension guests instead of the usual bleak dining room. The bedrooms are 'woody' and compact. Part of the Taverne is a very popular night haunt, with nightly shows and song contests, so those looking for spaciousness and peacefulness should not look here. Also a pizzeria.

DACHSTEIN–TAUERN/ SCHLADMING AREA

Height of Resort: 2,443 dt.
Height of Top Station: 6,661 ft.
Nearest International Airport: Salzburg
Map Reference: See page 237
Route by Car: See pages 236-237
Resort Facilities Charts: See page 215

Only one hour from the international airport at Salzburg and linked by a good railway service, the Enns valley offers extensive skiing, served by a number of market towns and small villages. Over 140 km. of pistes with 78 cableways and lifts are provided by several separate companies. A "Ski Paradies" lift pass is available for the whole area and for an extra £9 you can extend your 7 day pass by buying the Top Tauern Skischeck. This is valid for 270 skilifts and 660 km. of piste in the wider region, including Obertauern to the south.

Most of the skiing is on wooded slopes which rise from the valley bottom; in addition there are many areas of prepared tracks for cross country skiers. The skiing is mostly for intermediates, with only a handful of black runs, but what the area lacks in excitement it amply makes up for in terms of charm and a sense of history. Buildings blend into the landscape, the chair-lifts rise above barns and working farms. Every so often a deer will skip off the track into the forest. Just to the south is the huge Hoher Tauern national park, a wilderness area of soaring peaks.

A good road in the valley bottom links the main skiing areas from Pruggern (Galsterbergalm) in the east to Pichl (Reiteralm) 36 km. distant in the west. Schladming, famous in mediaeval times for its silver and copper mining, is the main centre. At the foot of one of the main World Cup downhill ski runs, it has gracefully absorbed skiing into the fabric of the town. Other centres include nearby Rohrmoos together with Haus and Gröbming for the eastern end of the valley.

The area has had a good snow record in recent years and most of the resorts have installed snow cannons. There is a reasonable ski bus system operating, but the distances between the resorts mean that one has to be well organised to visit more than one area in a day. At present only two of the mountains, Planai and Hochwurzen, are linked and then only by a two stage chair-lift at valley floor level.

A neat piste map provides information for each resort, but unfortunately useful route-planning details about lift speeds and lengths, which were included in the past have now been omitted. The whole valley has an uplift capacity of 88,000 people per hour and seldom is it necessary to queue for more than a few minutes.

Planai: This is the oldest established resort with the most extensive skiing. A fast gondolaway, the longest in the valley, reaches the Schladminger Hütte in 15 minutes. From here red and blue runs take one down to the town again with a final black section on the World Cup descent. To get to the pleasant nursery slopes at Weitmoosalm contour round from the top of the gondolaway to Onkel Willi's Hütte and then follow the car/ski road down.

Alternatively there is some good skiing on the top of Planai, 6,213 ft., reached by taking the chair-lift and skiing over to Mitterhausalm. Two long drag-lifts give access to wide pistes excellent for carved turns and mogul skiing. A World Cup event is scheduled for 11-12 January 1998.

Hochwurzen: The bottom slopes are gentle blue runs serving the hotels at Rohrmoos. Avoid these by getting to the bottom of the cableway, four km. from the centre of Schladming. This provides access to the top of Hochwurzen, 6,069ft. Several red runs will take one to other lifts or eventually down to the bottom of the valley beyond Rohrmoos. There is also a 7 km. toboggan run from the top. Floodlit skiing takes place from 1800-2200 at 200 AS per night.

Reiteralm: For the most attractive approach to the mountain, go to the car park closest to the Pichl railway station. Cross the little suspension bridge over the river Enns and one is at the foot of the chair-lift, which provides slow access to the middle station. At the top there is a lovely open bowl with wide pistes and magnificent views across to the Dachstein mountains. Sit on the terrace of the skihütte over a coffee or lunch to watch the action and catch the sun. There is a faster route up the mountain via the gondolaway from Gleiming.

Hauser Kaibling: There is a vertical ascent of 3,609ft. from either the main road or from Haus itself. At the top some striking features attest to the attraction of the Haus World Cup descent and there is a clean and friendly welcome at the Alpine Club's Krummolzhütte. The Gipfellift offers some short black runs and opportunities for skiing off-piste. A blue runs strikes off down to Knapplhof but does not permit descent to the bottom of the valley. Otherwise mostly red runs through the trees give a good descent to the bottom Skistation via the World Cup run. This is popular with the downhill racers.

Galsterbergalm: This area is the least accessible, since to reach the gondolaway requires a five km. drive up the mountain from Pruggern – and tyre chains for the car. It's worth it though, as this is a charming and little-frequented area. From the top of the mountain, Kalteck, 6,481ft., there is a variety of red runs and one black across wide uplands, as well as opportunities for skiing off piste and through the woods. Nestling in a small glade, Galsterbergalm offers the best value gulaschsuppe and kaiserschmarren in the whole valley; and from the top of the gondolaway there is a floodlit toboggan run.

Other Areas: Stoderzinken with three drag-lifts can be reached from Gröbming; and Fageralm, close to Reiteralm, is a small skiing area with 8 lifts. Ramsau on a plateau above the valley is good for cross country skiing and has a few short drag-lifts. The gondolaway to the Dachstein glacier provides access to blue runs only.

Après Ski: The area offers a good range of activities as well as indoor sports facilities, swimming, churches and a museum if the weather is poor. At most of the bottom stations there are open air bistros for that end of the day lager or glühwein. The Hautplatz and nearby streets in Schladming have plenty of bars, cafés and restaurants and for later there is the Sonderbar disco.

In a Few Words: A good value and varied area with charm, little used by the big tour operators. The skiing is mostly red and blue runs on well-wooded broad slopes. A car is helpful but not essential. There is little queueing at lifts and pistes are well managed. Popular with families, recreational skiers and people wanting an area with good alternative activities.

Recommended Hotels:

There are plenty of guesthouses and hotels, spread though the valley. In Schladming the **Alte Poste**, an old coaching inn founded in 1618, has a good reputation and fine restaurant. The modern **Sporthotel Royer** with 130 rooms and many indoor facilities is also to be recommended. To the west in the little village of Pichl can be found the unusual **Pichlmayrgut Hotel**, set on a small bluff with a commanding view of the valley. Based on an old country house and with its own church, it has been sensitively extended. In Gröbming try the reaonably priced **Gasthof Post** (34 beds) in the centre of this attractive small town.

BAD KLEINKIRCHHEIM

Height of Resort: 3,568ft.
Height of Top Station: 6,745ft.
Nearest International Airport: Salzburg
Map Reference:
Route by Car:
Resort Facilities Charts:
Hotel Reference Charts:

Bad Kleinkirchheim, or BKK as it is often called, is in the midst of the Nockberge mountains, about 100 miles south east of Salzburg, in the southern Austrian region of Carinthia. This picturesque ski and spa resort has gained increasing international recognition in recent years from hosting a number of World Ski Championship events, the latest of which were the Ladies Down-hill and Super-G competition held in January 1997.

BKK is linked, by both ski-bus and ski-lifts, with the neighbouring village and pistes of St. Oswald. Also, another by village at Falkert offers some skiing in a separate, slightly higher area, but this is not served by the BKK ski-bus service, nor is it linked with the BKK/St. Oswald ski-lifts. BKK St Oswald and Falkert are all covered by the same lift pass. There is also an arrangement with the skiing area at Turracherhöhe; getting there by bus can be a little tedious, especially in the low season when there is no direct connection, but it is well worth a visit, as the skiing is excellent.

The BKK skiing area has almost 100 km. of well-tended pistes, of varying difficulty well suited to the intermediate skier or snowboarder. Almost all are red runs, the highest or which start above the tree-line and offer outstanding views of the surrounding area, before winding gently through the woods to the valley below. Perhaps the most challenging piste is the K 70 FIS "Franz Klammer" run, named in honour of the famous Austrian skiing champion of the '70s.

BKK and St. Oswald have a combined network of 29 ski-lifts, most of which are drag-lifts, but there are also single, twin and four-seat chair-lifts, and two gondola systems, one of which, the "Kaiserburgbahn", whisks skiers from BKK village to the top station in about 10 minutes. The lift system is well-matched to the pistes it serves and, even in the high season, there is hardly any queueing (except for the peak hour rushes at the start and end of the day). With a little planning, it is possible to link almost every piste without having to resort to the ski-buses, or having to walk more than a short distance to a lift. The pistes are well-served with mountain restaurants, huts and open-air bars, offering all kinds of fare, from local specialities to burgers and chips.

Over 70 instructors provide ski and snowboard instruction at all levels. However, probably because few British visitors have ventured to BKK yet, the quality of the English spoken by the instructors (and hence the value of their instructions) varies greatly from instructor to instructor. Also, as BKK has so few blue runs, the main nursery slope gets rather crowded and quickly worn in the high season.

BKK is a little off the beaten track for the British skier and, in the 1996/97 season only one major British tour operator, Crystal Holidays, offered holidays to the resort. In the low season BKK is probably the "Jewel of the Alps"; with miles of almost empty, well-tended pistes and an enthusiastic local tourist industry doing all it can to encourage more British visitors. In the high season however, from early February onwards (continental schools' half-term holiday time) it is all very different and, literally overnight, the resort changes: the hotels and guest-houses fill to full capacity, the slopes, particularly beginners' slopes, get very busy, as do restaurants, cafés, ski-hire shops, ski school, and so on. The easy-going, helpful nature of the locals becomes more intense and, in some cases, much less helpful. Basically, they don't need us then, and it shows!

In a Few Words: Choose the right time to go and BKK is hard to beat for the intermediate skier. It is all that Austria is renowned for, and more: picturesque, comfortable, welcoming, good variety of pistes, more than adequate lift capacity, excellent hotels, bars and restaurants, thermal pools, après ski activities, in fact just about everything one could wish for on a skiing holiday However, go at the wrong time, i.e., in the busiest part of the high season, and just too many visitors are competing for the resort's resources, both physical and human; result: disappointment and frustration.

Après Ski: Being a spa resort, BKK provides an ideal way to relax tired muscles after a hard day's skiing, by taking a dip in the Romerbad or St. Katherein thermal pools, combined with sessions in the sauna, solarium and jacuzzi (entrance free with the BKK lift pass) For the more energetic there are après ski toboggan runs, ice-skating and curling whilst those looking for a more relaxing way to enjoy the evening air can take a horse-drawn sleigh ride, with a half-way stop at a local tavern. The instructors from "Ski School Krainer" put on a floodlit ski show each Tuesday to entertain visitors and to demonstrate the variety of skiing and snowboarding available in the resort. The show is followed by an open invitation to join the instructors at one of their "locals", usually the Hartlbrau or Brechstube pubs, for a few (or many drinks. There is regular life (traditional) music in the Einkehr restaurant on Tuesday and Thursday evenings and at the Brechlstube during the ski-school presentations on Friday evenings. There are plenty of restaurants in the area to cater for evening meals (although, during the busiest part of the high season, booking is almost essential). BKK also has what must be one of the best calorie-cramming "Café Konditorei" in Austria, and tucking into torte, or a huge ice cream coupe, at the Hunter is an essential experience for anyone with a sweet tooth. For the more savoury palate, an evening meal out at the Groar Küche offers a rustic alternative to hotel restaurant food and the chance to try delicious, pan-fried garlic prawns or special fondue.

Accommodation: The BKK area is well served with a wide selection of accommodation for visitors, ranging from luxury hotels to comfortable guest-houses, bed and breakfast rooms and self-catering apartments. All, even the 4 and 5-star hotels, are run by local families and aim to provide the visitor with the perfect base from which to enjoy the resort's facilities.

UPPER AUSTRIA
HINTERSTODER

Height of Resort: 2,132 ft.
Height of Top Station: 6,232 ft.
Nearest International Airport: Salzburg
Map Reference: 4C See page 238
Route by Car: See pages 236-238
Resort Facilities Charts: See page 214
Hotel Reference Charts: See page 227

The small and attractive village of Hinterstoder lies in a beautiful wooded valley 7km. from the main Linz/Graz road. It is also located 5km. from the end of the valley, thus having the advantage of no through traffic. The valley is open and sunny, and the river Styr winds its way through the village.

The skiing is divided into two main areas, 5km. apart but not interconnected:-

Hinterstoder - Hutterer Höss: From the south-east side of the village, a 6 person gondolaway rises to the middle station. Hutterer Böden, 4,589ft., in 8 minutes. At this point one finds the Berghotel, which overlooks a huge, sunny bowl-shaped skiing area intersected by fingers of woodland. A surmounting double chair-lift rises from this point to Hutterer Höss, 6,232ft., the highest station of the area. Here there are mountain restaurants with magnificent views overlooking the valley below. To the right and left of the top section of the chair-lift there are 8 drag-lifts and 2 double chair-lifts which serve the north-west facing slopes down to the middle station.

Apart from two runs which follow the line of the top chair-lift, the remaining runs served by the drag-lifts are easy to intermediate. The direct run of some 7km. from the top station down to the village through wide wooded glades could be tackled by most second-year skiers with only two difficult sections to manoeuvre. To the right and below the middle station there is a further drag-lift which serves easy and intermediate runs. There is also a cross-country trail of 4km. near the middle station, and one of 25km. in the village area.

Dietlgut – Bärenalm: This second ski area, situated 5km. from Hinterstoder at the end of the valley connected by regular bus service operating daily. A double chair-lift rises from the valley to Bärenalm, 3,946ft., where there are wonderful views. From this point down to the valley again there are intermediate and easy runs. There are also two drag-lifts, one surmounting the chair-lift and one to the right. These serve open and easy runs Hinterstoder has an excellent ski school under the watchful eye of director Helmut Mayr. His good teaching along with his sense of humour is passed to his 40 instructors, and one therefore receives first-class tuition in a happy and enjoyable atmosphere. The ski school operates from the middle station, where there is a trainer lift.

In a Few Words: A charming, small unspoilt ski resort, which will appeal to British skiers. Excellent ski school; beginners to intermediates are well catered for. There are many other resorts in the area so a car is an advantage. An uncommercialised area with a happy and friendly atmosphere.

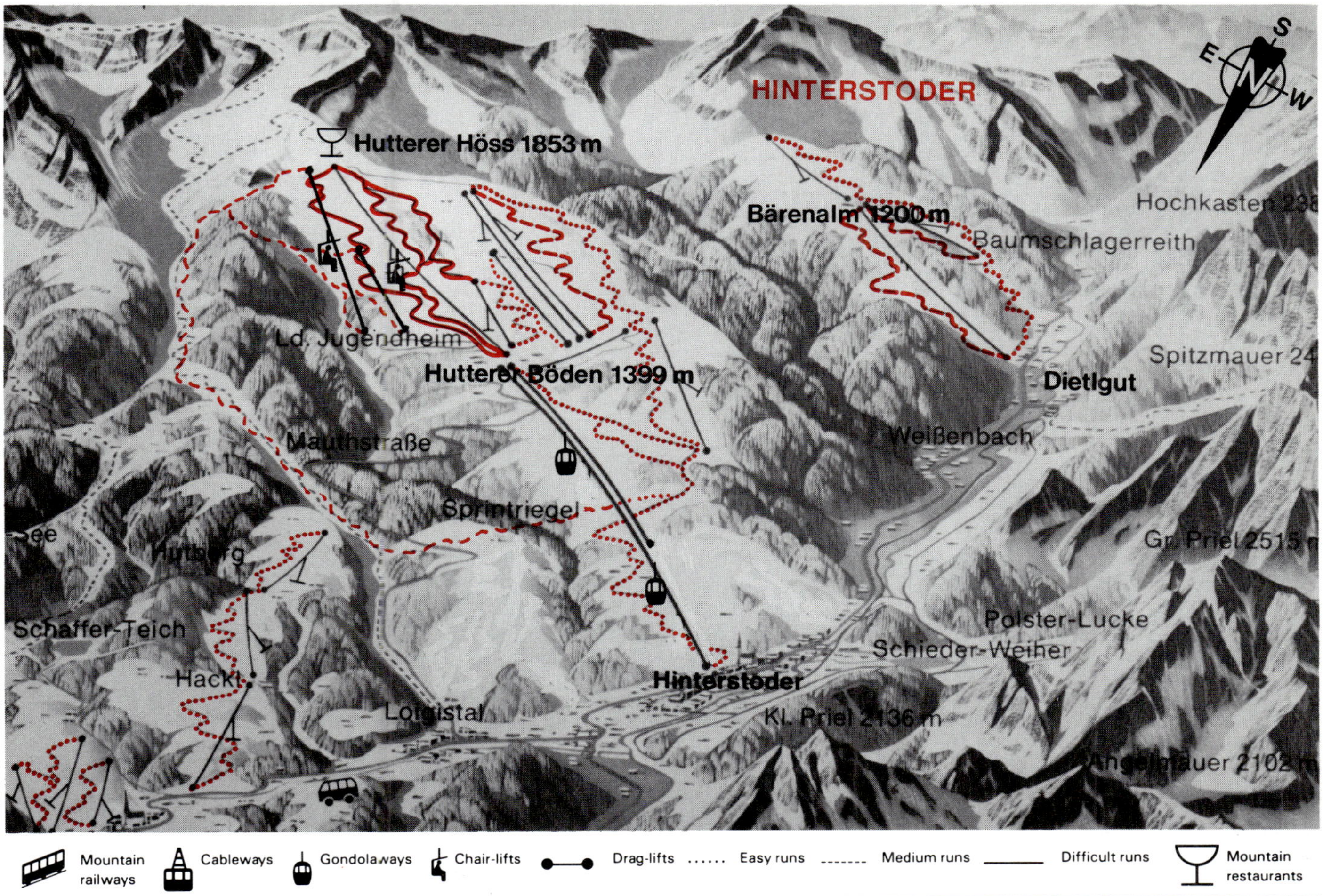

Après Ski: As far as organised entertainment is concerned there is not a lot of choice. Two night clubs: one beneath the Post Hotel has dancing to disco, and there is lots of atmosphere, and its well-stocked bar ensures a happy evening. Many of the hotels and pensions have very pleasant bars, and the ski school organises hilarious farmhouse evenings with tobogganing home afterwards. There is plenty of scope for happy evenings but it is up to the guests to make use of the facilities available.

The village is small and compact, with two general shops with a good selection of sports goods, clothing, food, souvenirs, etc. and the prices are reasonable. Several cafés, hairdresser and a modern youth hostel, which caters for parties of up to 98 persons. This is an impressive and beautiful area, with a background of peaks rising to 8,200ft. For the non-skier there are attractive walks through the countryside, and of course if you have a car this is an advantage, because there are so many small villages and hamlets to be seen.

Recommended Hotels:

Hotel Dietlgut: This beautiful 3 star hotel is situated at the end of the valley, so a car is necessary. Comfortable bedrooms all with bath or shower and five newly constructed apartments with large bedrooms and balcony or terrace. An ideal hotel for the family as there are well organised activities for children and all baby facilities. Attractive reception room and a good traditional Austrian kitchen.

Berghotel Hinterstoder: A large modern hotel situated in an incomparable position above Hinterstoder, at the middle station. The amenities include an indoor swimming pool, massage, gymnastic room, sauna, solarium and a huge sun terrace. The bedrooms are very comfortable, most south facing with balconies. The dining room doubles as a sitting room with large panoramic views overlooking the ski slopes. Special facilites for children and a daily activity programme. A pleasant keller bar with dancing to disco is open from5 p.m. Those making their own way by car must have chains as they will have to negotiate the toll road which is long and fairly steep in places. The only way up is by car or gondolaway, the latter stoppng by about 5 p.m.

Hotel Stoderhof: This is the only hotel in the village area itself. Owned and run by Erich and Ilse Fruhmann, who ensure that guests have a pleasant stay. The tireless Ilse Fruhmann is well known in the district and has been running this hotel now for a number of years. It is ideally situated, only a minute's walk from the gondolaway and the shops. A large airy hall and reception area, with a pleasant dining room leading off at the far end. The kitchen and dining room are the province of Ilse's husband Erich, who is well known in the district for his excellent cooking. The rooms are spacious and comfortable, all with bath or shower and access to a balcony. There is a 'pool' table for guests' entertainment, indoor swimming pool with a large sitting area and a good sauna and solarium. A comfortable reading or writing area on the first floor with a large TV room adjacent to the dining room. Warm and personal attention is one of the important points of this family run hotel.

OBERTRAUN

Height of Resort: 1,968 ft.
Height of Top Station: 6,917 ft.
Nearest International Airport: Salzburg
Map Reference: 3C See page 238
Route by Car: See pages 236-238
Resort Facilities Charts: See page 215

This small village of 10 hotels and pensions overlooks the Halstätter lake and as the high wooded mountains enclose it on three sides, one gets the impression of being rather shut in. If the village does not play its part in attracting visitors, the skiing on the Krippenstein mountain does. From the south-eastern side of the village a 2-stage cableway runs first to Schönberghaus and thence to the Berghotel Krippenstein, 6,917ft. - far better to stay here, where one has magnificent views over the valley and across a panorama of glaciers and peaks stretching out towards Salzburg.

There is skiing on the eastern and western sides of the mountain. On the eastern side there is a 4km. intermediate run, not always pisted, down to the middle station of the cableway over north-east facing slopes. There is no run down to the village from this point, so one takes the cableway down. Still on the eastern side, there are three drag-lifts serving the top area and providing easy runs.

On the western side there is a good intermediate north-west facing 3km. run to the foot of the Gjaidalm cableway, where a drag-lift serves the slopes in this area. Alternatively, from the top one can take the famous Dachstein 'ski autobahn', which includes the above run and then swings north near the foot of the Gjaidalm lower station and thence, north-eastwards to the village, intermediate to start with but a difficult centre section, 12.5 km. long with a vertical descent of 4,963ft.

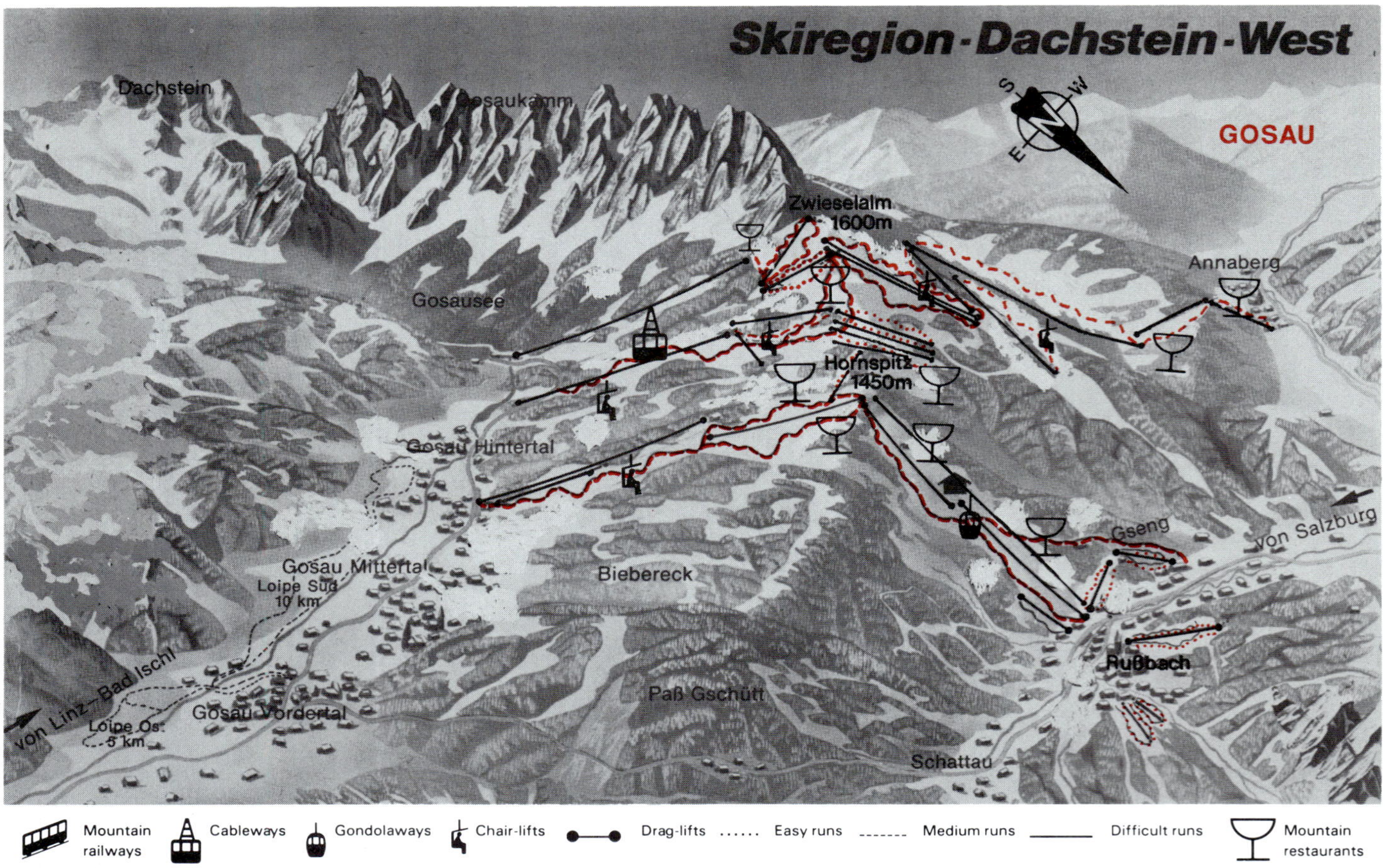

Apart from the downhill skiing, there are some delightful glacier tours of some 21km.

In a Few Words: A resort solely for the experienced skier; disappointing village and little to do for the non-skier. Reliable snow and a late season. If the extensive plans to develop the Hallstätter glacier area materialise, this will be quite something.

Après Ski: Little to do here in the evening apart from a disco and the normal cafés and bars. Hallstatt, on the other side of the lake, is quaint and unusual and well worth a visit.

Recommended Hotel:

Berghotel Krippenstein: At the top station of the cableway, commanding beautiful views of the valley and the surrounding glaciers. A modern hotel of 80 beds, all rooms with bath or shower. Spacious dining room, sitting room and bar. Sun terrace. Sauna.

GOSAU

Height of Resort: 2,460 ft.
Height of Top Station: 5,258 ft.
Nearest International Airport: Salzburg
Map Reference: 2C **See page 238**
Route by Car: **See pages 236-238**
Resort Facilities Charts: **See page 214**
Hotel Reference Charts: **See page 227**

Some 60 minutes by bus from Salzburg one enters Gosau from a rather narrow, shady pass, one comes across a delightful wide, open and sunny valley, dominated by the famous Gosaukamm, a series of peaks at the southern end. The village is split into three main areas, Gosau Vordertal, Mittertal and Hintertal, with the lake of Gosausee marking the end of the valley. The most active section of the village is Gosau Mittertal, which has a magnificent large indoor swimming pool, and a good shopping centre.

There are twelve hotels and pensions providing beds for 1,450 guests, dotted along the valley.

There are a number of small drag-lifts on the lower slopes, but the main skiing is based in two areas, now linked by drag-lifts.

Southern Area: This is the largest area of the two areas and can be reached from the north-western area by link drag-lifts or by taking the bus (free to ski pass or hotel guest card holders) to the edge of the lake of Gosausee, where a cableway and connecting drag-lift takes skiers up to Zwieselalm, a height of 5,258ft., the highest point in the valley. From the top, one has magnificent views across the Gosaukamm and the Dachstein range of mountains. There is a fairly difficult section between the top and the drag-lift, but the latter serves runs suitable for intermediates and beginners. There is a pleasant mountain restaurant here with reasonable prices. The experienced skier will enjoy the piste down to the valley, but there are tricky spots only suitable for intermediates and above. At the bottom one can take two surmounting chair-lifts to the top again and work one's way across to the north-western area. From Zwieselalm there is a pleasant intermediate run across to Annaberg, achieved by using a series of lifts in both directions.

North-Western Area: From a point halfway between Mittertal and Hintertal a fast 4 seater chair-lift rises to the middle station where twin surmounting drag-lifts reach 4,756ft. The pleasant runs down to the middle station or to the valley are not difficult and they more or less follow the line of the lifts. This is a reasonably open area, interspersed with beautiful woods, which is a particular feature of Gosau.

From the top station it is also possible to ski down to the village of Russbach, in the valley on the northern side, returning to the top again by two-stage drag-lifts, and these lifts are included in the ski pass. Gosau is a good Nordic centre, with four prepared runs, two of l0km. and one of 20km.

In a Few Words: A good resort for most recreational skiers, with an interesting variety of skiing on open pistes or through beautiful wooded areas, made possible by 30 strategically placed lifts. Excellent Nordic skiing (langlauf). A long village with bus service to the bottom stations of the lifts. Excellent indoor swimming pool.

Après Ski: There are three discothèques and night clubs but as the village is spread over 5km. and the bus service stops at 1800 hours this creates difficulties. Of the discothèques the one at the Hotel Gosauschmied is well worth a visit. It has lots of atmosphere, and consists of three separate cloister-type rooms. The disco plays from 8 in the evening until 5 in the morning. The Saddle Room at Hotel Koller appears to be the most popular although the Stofferl is worth a visit. Several of the other hotels organise various activities for their guests. Swimmers are well catered for in the very large, pleasant swimming pool. For the non-skier there is riding, skibobbing, sleigh rides and extensive and beautiful walks in the area, particularly the one round the lake Gosausee.

Recommended Hotels:

Hotel Gosauer Hof: Standing in its own grounds in the sunniest part of the valley, this hotel accommodates 50 guests. A number of the bedrooms have private facilities and their own balconies. Pleasant reception room with two sitting rooms leading off. Large sun terrace. A folklore evening is organised at this hotel once a week.

Hotel Sommerhof: Situated near the two-stage Homspitz lift. The largest hotel in the resort, with most impressive accommodation. Attractive hall and reception area. Large bright dining room leads off to the right of the reception, with a smaller dining room to the left. The bedrooms are comfortable, furnished in traditional style, many with private facilities. Ice-bowling and horse sleigh rides.

SPITAL am PYHRN

Height of Resort: 2,624 ft.
Height of Top Station: 6,146 ft.
Nearest International Airport: Salzburg
Map Reference: 4C See page 238
Route by Car: See pages 236-238
Resort Facilities Charts: See page 216
Hotel Reference Charts: See page 229

This very pleasant village, close to Windischgarstener Tal, is spread around its magnificent church, which was once an old monastery. It is near the famous Pyhrn pass, which leads on to Graz. There is no skiing in the immediate vicinity of the village, but the ski bus, takes one 4km. to the foot of the Pyhrn. Here one takes the mountain railway up the Wurzeralm mountain to the Bergstation. The journey of 3km. is covered in 6 minutes, and the capacity is 140, or 1,250 persons an hour. The top station stands at 4,707ft., and here one finds a wide open sunny bowl, with lifts fanning out, the ski school headquarters, the Berghotel Hengl, and other pensions. This is an excellent area for beginners, with 5 drag-lifts in the immediate vicinity. Near the Bergstation and running southward is a double chair-lift rising to 5,363ft. There are intermediate runs back to the foot of the lift and to the top of the mountain railway station, and easy runs back to the lower station of the mountain railway. Rising westward from near the top station is a double chair-lift 2,000m. long and reaching 6,146ft., the highest in the area. Easy runs swing southward, and thence westward to the foot. The ski area is small and compact, but provides much enjoyable skiing for beginners to those up to intermediate standard

In a Few Words: A small, cosy village. Compact and attractive ski area, disadvantage 4km. from the village, but the skibus is free of charge. 25km. of cross-country tracks, 25km. of well kept walks, 4.5km toboggan run, para-gliding school. Ski school, kindergarten.

Après Ski: In Spital itself this is very limited, but Windischgarstener Tal is close at hand. There is however one lively night club attached to the Alpenrose Hotel, which is well known throughout the district and is called the Octopussi. Dancing is normally to disco, but on special occasions they have live music. There is a magnificent public swimming pool, sauna, solarium and also a bowling alley.

Recommended Hotels:

Hotel Alpenrose: A pleasant hotel, situated 600 yards from the village centre on the main road to the skiing area. Comfortable, modern reception rooms and an attractive bar. Total of 44 beds, most rooms having bath or shower.

Berghotel Hengl: This charming hotel is situated in the skiing area itself, near the top of the Bergstation. The bedrooms, 50 in all, are comfortably furnished and all have bath or shower. The dining room is on the first floor, and this has considerable character. In the corner is a huge fireplace and just off is a very pleasant, well stocked bar and sitting room Half pension only is provided here, that is breakfast and lunch, and the evening meal is à la carte. Run by the son of the late Eddy Hengl.

BAD AUSSEE

Height of Resort: 2,296 ft.
Height of Top Station: 6,562 ft.
Nearest International Airport: Salzburg
Map Reference: 3C See page 238
Route by Car: See pages 236-238
Resort Facilities Charts: See page 212

50 miles south-east of Salzburg, Bad Aussee lies in the heart of the Austrian Mountain and Lake District at 2,296ft. above sea level. To the north are the Totes Gebirge whilst immediately to the south is the famous Dachstein Mountain Range. This is principally a langlauf (Nordic skiing) resort.

From mid December until early March there is normally excellent cross-country skiing along a good variety of well prepared trails ranging from low lying and virtually flat routes to those resembling the much more undulating 'loipe' more often associated with Norway. There is a downhill skiing area centred on the nearby Loser Mountain, top station 5,906ft., and a larger area rising to 6,562ft. above Tauplitz. Although there are some testing slopes, the downhill runs are comparatively short and are best suited to beginners and intermediate grade skiers.

Langlauf (Nordic) Skiing: A four-lane 5km. trail passes within fifty metres of Hotel Wasnerin about 2km. south-west of the village centre. These tracks link up with others forming an 12km. circuit. On the other side of the village is a more varied loipe between Altaussee and Grundlsee. There are also a number of interconnecting trails providing a wide choice of routes.

Downhill (Alpine) Skiing: The bottom station of the Loser double chair-lift is about twenty minutes drive from Bad Aussee. From this station, 2,728ft., one can take either the Kurvenlift Sandling rising 1,640ft in 1400m. length to the west, or the first of the two Loser chair-lifts rising a total of some 2,132ft. over a length of approximately 2,700m. to link up with the Loser complex of drag-lifts to the east. Altother there are two chair-lifts and five drag-lifts. These lead to a total of twelve prepared pistes. Incorporated in the complex is a 6km. FIS Downhill run.

There are two routes to the Tauplitz skiing complex. From the village of Tauplitz, 2,919ft., is a long chair-lift rising to 5,330ft. Alternatively one can drive up the Tauplitzalm toll road. This complex comprises 3 chair-lifts and 13 drag-lifts which lead to 25km. of prepared pistes also incorporating a FIS Downhill run. In addition there are 15km. of high level langlauf trails. Both areas have ski schools, facilities for hiring equipment and ample restaurants.

In a Few Words: An ideal centre for nordic ski enthusiasts who wish to travel by car and combine a certain amount of downhill skiing. For those travelling by air, the resort is in easy reach of Salzburg with good train connections. Over 100km. of prepared high and low level nordic ski trails. A reliable snow area.

Après Ski: Being a spa as well as a winter sports resort, there is plenty of entertainment. A wide selection of restaurants, bars, wine taverns and dancing at various hotels and discothèques.
Tobogganing, curling, riding, swimming and hang-gliding are also well catered for.

Recommended Hotels:

Hotel Wasnerin: Situated outside the village and 50 metres from one of the nordic ski trails, this chalet style hotel is extremely good value. Its 30 double rooms and 3 singles are all differently furnished with balconies or bay windows providing panoramic views of the lovely countryside. 25 rooms are with bath or shower and w.c. The reception rooms are pleasant and furnished in traditional style. Good home cooking. Musical evenings and dancing as required.

BRIEF REPORTS ON FURTHER AUSTRIAN RESORTS

AXAMER-LIZUM, 5,150ft.: This small resort was built for the 1964 Olympic Games, 30 minutes by road from Innsbruck. Snow conditions normally reliable until spring; several north-east facing slopes. Attractive area and near to Innsbruck for excursions. Three hotels; height top station 7,670ft.; one mountain railway, five chair-lifts and three drag-lifts; suitable for beginner and all grades of skiers.

BICHLBACH, 3,526ft.: A small resort situated between Berwang and Lermoos and near enough to the latter to make daily visits possible. 12 hotels and pensions; height at top station, 4,150ft.; 1 chair-lift and 4 drag-lifts; suitable for beginners to intermediates now that it is linked with Berwang.

EHRWALD, 3,267ft.: Only 2km. from Lermoos (see separate write-up) artificial skating rink, bowling, sleigh rides; 26 hotels and pensions; height at top station, 9,203ft.; 2 cableways, 1 chair-lift, 6 drag-lifts; suitable for beginners to advanced intermediates.

GERLOS, 4,071ft.: Situated in a sunny position, rounded topped hills, partially wooded, encircle the spacious nursery slopes in the village area. 40 minutes by bus from Zell am Ziller. 96 hotels and pensions; height at top station 6,772ft.; 6 chair-lifts, 20 drag-lifts; suitable for beginners to intermediates, good touring in the area.

IGLS, 2,952ft.: Situated above Innsbruck and 6km. away, this resort with its neighbour Axamer-Lizum was the venue for the 1964 Winter Olympic Games. Ideal for families and parties with non-skiers, being so near a city; skating, ski-bobbing, bobsleigh, swimming, saunas etc.; 43 hotels and pensions; height at top station 7,370ft.; 1 cableway, 1 chair-lift, 6 drag-lifts. Area pass covers 52 lifts. Suitable for beginners to intermediates.

KÜHTAI, 6,500ft.: This small resort at the north end of the Staubaier Alps, reached by road 14km. from Ötz, is one of Austria's highest resorts with safe snow from early to late season, but it can be very cold during early season. A large variety of half and full day ski tours. Three good night spots; 17 hotels and pensions. Height at top station, 8,710ft.; two chair-lifts and 8 drag-lifts. Suitable for beginners to intermediates.

LIENZ, 2,850ft.: A compact town with friendly atmosphere, and capital of the East Tyrol. Ideal for parties of skiers and non-skiers. Two ski areas, Hochstein and Zertersfeld. Skating, curling, riding, kindergarten and good après ski. 38 hotels and pensions. Height of top station 7,520ft.; 1 cableway, 2 chair-lifts, 9 drag-lifts. Suitable for beginners to intermediates.

ST. MICHAEL, 3,609ft.: This charming small resort lies about 25km. south of Obertauern (see separate report) and close to the Katschberg tunnel. It is linked with the nearby resort of Mauterndorf and their combined 11 lifts serve 35km. of prepared runs, suitable for beginners to intermediates. From the top station, Speierect, 7,910ft., one has open skiing, whilst the lower runs to the village are through wide wooded glades which hold the snow well. Comfortable and reasonably priced accommodation can be found in the village where après ski is well catered for in the form of cosy bars, disco, sleigh rides, bowling, swimming and indoor tennis.

FRANCE

ALPE D'HUEZ

Height of Resort: 6,101 ft.
Height of Top Station: 10,988 ft.
Nearest International Airport: Lyon-Satolas
Map Reference: 3D See page 238
Route by Car: See page 236-238
Resort Facilities Charts: See page 217
Hotel Reference Charts: See page 229

Alpe d'Huez faces south and commands a wonderful view of the valley below and the mountains beyond. It is one of the sunniest resorts in the Alps. The spectacular ascent to the resort will be familiar to all television viewers of the Tour de France and gives one a new respect for the competing cyclists.

The main ski area lies north of the village and it is a most impressive and compact lift system and a paradise for beginners and those up to intermediate standard, with a good selection of testing runs for the advanced skier. The lower lift system serves a huge amphitheatre of easy to medium skiing over open south to south-west facing slopes. From the heart of this area a two-stage gondolaway travels northeastwards, first to 6,921ft. where there is a restaurant with sun terrace. This point can also be reached by three parallel drag-lifts running up on the left of the gondolaway, whilst further to the right one finds a series of drag-lifts, which service numerous runs on the slopes below the first station. The area on both sides of the gondolaway is excellent for the novice skier.

The second stage of the gondolaway climbs to Lac Blanc, 8,856ft. Supplementing this section is a chair-lift to the left, whilst to the right a chair-lift runs eastwards to the southern tip of Lac Blanc, where a surmounting chair-lift rises still further to 9,119ft. The testing 5.3km Combe Charbonnière run starts here, descending to the south-east side of the village, a drop of 3,215ft. This area is for the intermediate to good skier.

From the second station of the gondolaway a cableway swings eastwards to Pic Blanc, 10,988ft. Here one has wonderful views of the high mountains in several countries and of the Sarenne Glacier, the venue for summer skiing served by a chair-lift and a drag-lift. The run from the top to the second station of the cableway 'Le Tunnel' is interesting and testing, steepish skiing over the glacier. One gets one's breath back through the tunnel hewn out of the mountainside and one needs it to negotiate the steep drop at the exit, becoming less steep as one nears the second station, a run of 2.7km., with a vertical drop of 2,296ft.

Another testing and difficult run from Pic Blanc is the Sarenne, on a steep , south-facing slope, until one reaches the valley of the same name. It then swings westwards to the foot of the Alp Auris chair-lift, which takes one back to the outskirts of the village – a run of 16km. with a vertical descent of 6,232ft., one of the longest runs in Europe.

The direct runs from Pic Blanc to Lac Blanc are for good skiers only. The direct run from the top to the north side of the village is 7km. and to the southern side 8km. During late season one can make two interesting tours from the south side of the tunnel, the shorter one ending near the airstrip and the other at Huez, whilst on the north side there is a lovely offpiste run to Oz, mainly on north-west facing slopes some 10km. in length, vertical drop 8,265ft. The high mountain skiing with off-piste possibilities is superb in this resort, well organised by the Bureau des Guides. In 1987 a considerable extension was made to the north-east area. From the valley station of Vaujany a cableway (160 persons/cabin) rises in two stages, first to L'Alpette and thence to Dôme des Rousses, 9,212ft. From the valley station of Oz-en-Oisans a gondolaway reaches L'Olmet, whilst a further gondolaway travels south-eastward to the central system. The runs from Dôme des Rousses link with the central system whilst those back to the two valley stations are long easy to intermediate over north-west facing slopes. 30 snow cannons have been installed on the Vaujany runs allowing the return ot this station all season. Total for the whole ski area is now 385 cannons.

Running north from the bottom of the cableway terminal is a further series of three parallel drag-lifts up to Signal, 6,937ft. This point can also be reached by the Grand Sure chair-lift which starts from the western side of the village, runs are easy to medium/difficult over south-facing slopes. Two more interesting runs from Signal are down to the village of Villard-Reculas. Two parallel surmounting drag-lifts bring one back to Signal.

A further ski area is to be found on the southern side of the village. A chair-lift takes one across the gorge to the foot of the Signal de L'Homme double drag-lift which rises to 7,137ft., where there is a south-west facing run of about 3.5km. down to Auris en Oisans, medium/difficult. An extension to this area allows one to take an intermediate westward run to the foot of Le Chatelard drag-lift, where there is a restaurant. The drag-lift connects with the chair-lift back to Signal de I'Homme, where one has a choice of two medium homeward runs of about 4.5km. on north-west facing slopes. The Auris Express, a 4 seater chair-lift, installed for the 1991/92 season, links the village of Auris en Oisans with Alpe d'Huez in under 15 minutes.

This well-equipped resort has 82 lifts moving 90,000 people per hour, serving 100 prepared pistes, totalling 220km. of downhill runs, in addition to eight marked touring pistes. 'Télécentre' lift transports skiers from lower part of resort to main lift base.

There are no immediadiate plans for extending the lift system but faster lifts to the existing ones will be introduced. Improvements will also be made to buildings and sports facilities. Due to the large proportion of English visitors special courses for ski instructors are being held so that they have a good knowledge of the language. There are two special waiting points in the ski school for English speaking skiers near the bottom station of the Grandes Rousses gondolaway.

The Visalp Ski Pass: Available from 2 to 14 days or more and not only covers all lifts in the area and shuttle bus services but allows free entrance to the open-air swimming pool, ice rink, sport and congress hall, local museum and weekly concerts. There is a discount for families of 4 or more persons. A 5-day pass and over allows a day's skiing at Les Deux Alpes and also Serre Chevalier.

In a Few Words: Very impressive; compact lift system with most runs ending in the village area; very sunny; excellent for all grades and for families – kindergarten; good ski school where one can be sure of an English speaking instructor; 385 snow cannons ensuring that the maximum number of runs are kept open during bad seasons. 50km. of prepared trails for nordic skiing; nice hotels and small pensions; good atmosphere. Helicopter link with Les Deux Alpes, 5 minute journey – 295 francs return (minimum 4 persons).

Après Ski: This is definitely to be recommended – swinging, jazzy and great opportunities. There are three night clubs, all discothèques and all small and intimate, but very different in character and 7 'Piano Bars'. Amongst these are the delightful L'Utop at the Hotel Vallée Blanche. The 'Igloo' is one of the most fashionable discos in the resort. There are numerous good restaurants in this resort and the best, if you're a gourmet, is Le Chamois d'Or and Le Lyonnais; La Cordée has excellent food, is small, attractive and open fairly late. The Genepy is also open late and the food is good and also La Crémaillère which remains open all night long. All these restaurants are situated near the skiing area. In the old village, the Étable is cheaper than most and is open for late night snacks. Alpe d'Huez has a cinema showng two different films each evening. It also has a large outdoor heated swimming pool, an indoor pool and an artificial skating rink, Olympic size. A special area for driving a car on ice, instructor and rent-a-car available. An excellent sports centre contains 3 indoor tennis courts, squash courts, golf practice facilities, an indoor climbing wall, archery, shooting, dancing and further facilities for team games and various sports. The sculptured waterfall near the entrance is well worth seeing. Weekly classical music concerts are held at Notre Dame des Neiges, usually featuring their amazingly designed futuristic organ. The acoustics are perfect.

Recommended Hotels:
Hotel Les Gentianes: Situated south-east side of village; bar on the left of the entrance; small sitting room with open fireplace; attractive old-style decor; dining room in wooden decor with oak beams and large windows; all bedrooms with private shower; cosily furnished and wood panelled throughout. Nice small hotel.

Hotel Petit Prince: A modern hotel in a good position, the Grande Sure chair-lift being immediately outside the door. Tastefully furnished bedrooms, mostly south facing, many with bath and balcony; attractive and spacious reception rooms; bar and television room; excellent food and service under the personal supervision of the Amenc family; a good atmosphere.

Hotel Vallée Blanche: In central position near ski school; large sitting room and bar and open fire; card room leading off; large bright L-shaped dining room, most attractive with large white lights and open grill; a long sun terrace running the whole length of the dining room and the sitting room; 15 good sized bedrooms in modern section colourfully decorated with large balconies and all with nice bathrooms, separate wc. and bidet. The old section has 27 rooms which are smaller, all with bath or shower. Soundproofed discothèque, sauna and fitness room. A very nice owner.

LES DEUX ALPES

Height of Resort: 5,412 ft.
Height of Top Station: 11,673 ft.
Nearest International Airport: Lyon-Satolas
Map Reference: 3E See page 238
Route by Car: See page 236-238
Resorts Facilities Charts: See page 217
Hotel Reference Charts: See page 230

This large resort lies in the high sunny valley about $1^1/_2$ hours by road from Grenoble. The village runs from north to south, its wide streets giving a spacious, yet busy, atmosphere. Many of the resort's hotels are at the older, southern end of the village, whilst most shops are on the main street, which runs through the resort. The newer Le Village development is located at the northern approach. The resort is almost entirely at the same level and is less than 20 minutes walk from one end to the other. A free bus service operates to all parts of the village. Skiing is on both sides of the valley.

The more extensive ski areas, including the glacier which is also used in summer, are on the eastern side of the resort. The fastest mode of uphill transport is the Jandri Express which consists of 20 person cable cars on the gondola principle and has a capacity of 1,800 persons per hour. The journey to the middle station, La Toura, 8,530ft., takes 15 minutes. The glacier is a further 10 minutes up the Jandri Express at 10,499ft. At 'La Toura' a variety of chair-lifts

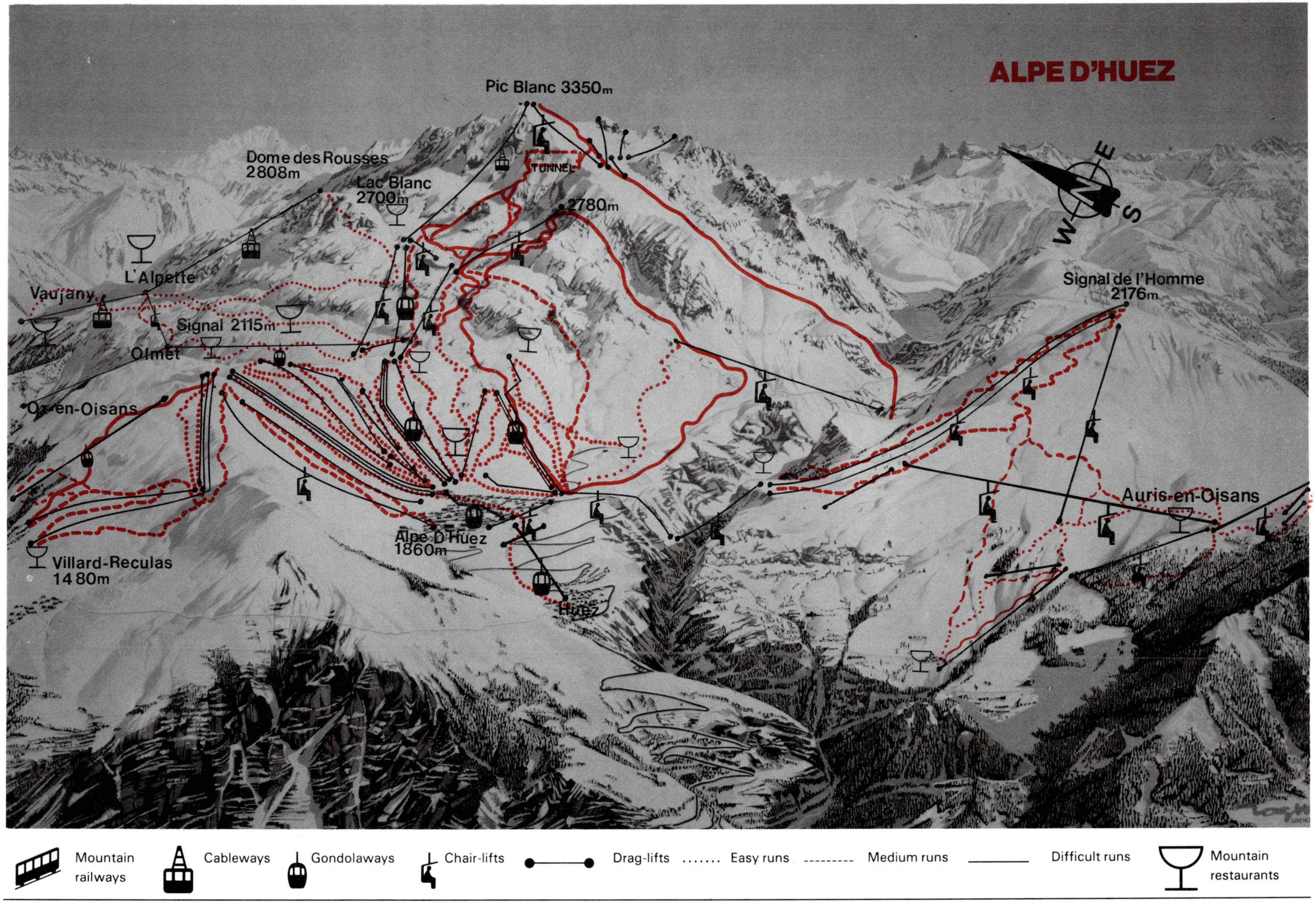

ALPE D'HUEZ
Pic Blanc 3350m
Dome des Rousses
2808m
Lac Blanc
2700m
TUNNEL
2780m
L'Alpette
Vaujany
Signal 2115m
Olmet
Oz-en-Oisans
Villard-Reculas
14 80m
Alpe D'Huez
1860m
Huez
Signal de l'Homme
2176m
Auris-en-Oisans
W
E
S
N
Mountain railways
Cableways
Gondolaways
Chair-lifts
Drag-lifts
Easy runs
Medium runs
Difficult runs
Mountain restaurants

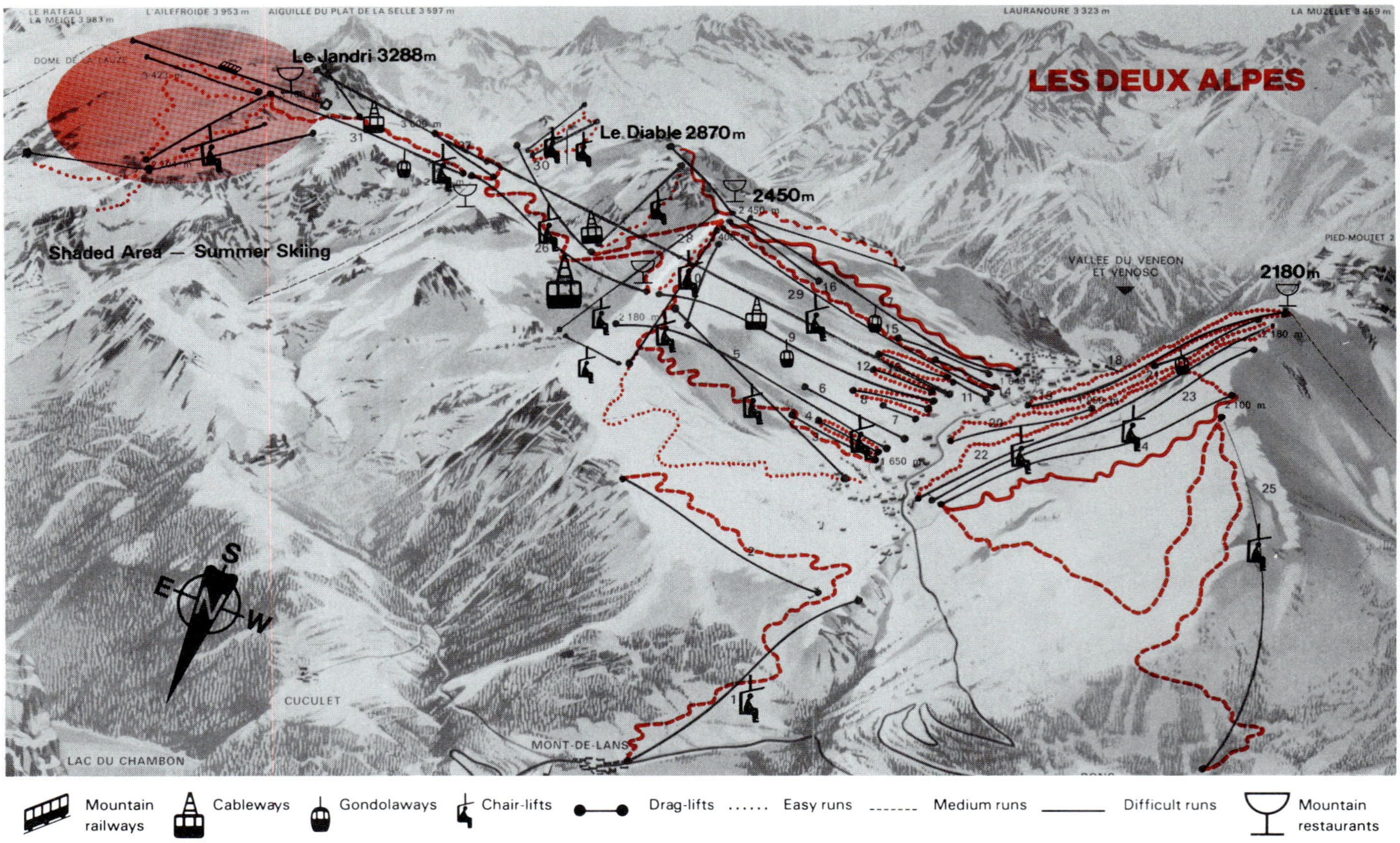

and drag-lifts fan out, and there is the restaurant 'Panoramic'. The top station has one of the highest restaurants in France and is the focal point for the glacier ski area which includes 3 chair-lifts, 7 drag-lifts and a funicular which runs under the glacier. The latter gives access to the viewing platform at 11,483ft., and Mont Blanc can be seen in the distance. There is a link between Les Deux Alpes and La Grave, although a 15 minutes walk is required. Most of the runs on the glacier are blue. Returning to the middle station there is a choice of red and blue runs about 3km in length, which get very crowded late afternoon.

The run from the middle station to the lower end of Les Crêtes, 7,166ft., is not very exciting but variations are possible by breaking off either via the Belle-Combes chair to the Super Diable, 9,227ft., a good black run which provides probably the best and hardest descent to the village, or via the Thuit chair to the higher end of Les Crêtes, 8,038ft., where the Pastorale restaurant is located. From here one can either ski north along Les Crêtes, a wide ridge overlooking the resort or descend directly to the southern end of the village by a variety of red runs or by the notorious Diable which until recently was classed as black! At the northern or lower end of Les Crêtes, one finds the Patache restaurant. Les Crêtes itself is a very popular area for instruction and practice and the wide slope is served by 2 chair-lifts one being a 4 seater. A cableway runs from beside the Patache restaurant up to the middle station, La Toura, 8,530ft. Continuing down the mountain however there is a choice of runs all the way back giving access to any chosen part of the resort, meaning that one can ski virtually to one's own doorstep. All but one of these runs, however, are steep reds and blacks, often icy and bumpy. The one blue run is gentle but narrow, and also crowded in the afternoon. The skiing below Les Crêtes is very varied and access can be gained to these slopes via 2 gondolaways and 3 chair-lifts. A pleasant variation is to go north down to Mont de Lans, by a pleasant red run and return by chair-lift. Lack of snow cover means that this run is rarely open. There is an artificial snow covered black piste, Combe-Valentin, which runs from Les Crêtes to the resort, but this gets very crowded when natural snow cover is limited.

The western side of the resort is excellent for powder skiing after a heavy snowfall, and provides very good piste skiing for the less advanced skier. The Super Venosc 4 seater chair-lift starting from the southern end of the village and the Cimes chair-lift from the northern end meet at the Troika restaurant, 6,890ft., and a number of mainly blue runs give access to both ends of the village and to a number of other chair-lifts and drag-lifts. The Fioc drag-lift at the northern end gives a choice of a blue or black return run or alternatively one can ski north down to Bons village, a 4km. run through trees, and return by chair-lift. The western side of the resort, however, loses its snow cover much faster than the eastern side due to the orientation of the runs.

Venosc, a beautiful old village, lies in the valley at the southern end of the village. It is accessed by an efficient new gondolaway and is well worth a visit. It is a good location for those wishing to combine traditional rustic charm with the extensive piste system of Les Deux Alpes.

Off-piste possibilities are excellent, notably in the Chalance area, around Bellecombes and on the Pied Moutet side of the resort.

A feature of the 6 day lift pass is that it allows for one day's skiing in each of a number of other nearby resorts including Alpe d'Huez, Serre Chevalier, Puy St. Vincent, La Voie Lactée Sud and La Grave, which makes it ideal value for car skiing. The 13 day pass gives up to 2 days skiing in each resort.

In a Few Words: Lift systems excellent, snow reliable with artificial snow making facilities, steep runs down to the resort. Kindergarten, summer skiing. Friendly atmosphere and reasonable value. Ski pass valid for neighbouring resorts.

Après Ski: One thing this resort is definitely not short of is swimming pools; 6 indoor for hotel guests and 2 open to the general public, one of the latter included in the lift pass. The Hotel Bérangère's outdoor pool is built right on the ski slopes. There are four night clubs, between them probably providing something to suit everyone. The L'Avalanche is very small and very loud. The bar front, the chairs, the wall behind the dance floor and the minute dance floor itself are all made of metal and it is popular with the young. It is not the place for a quiet conversation. The Casa has a fairly large dance floor divided in half by a film screen. It also has a piano-bar. The club has thick stone walls, tiny alcoves and is spacious yet cosy. If one wishes to spend a quiet evening in front of open fires there are plenty of crêperies. There are also over forty restaurants and twenty different bars to choose from serving anything from hot chocolate to 'Un Grog', the French version of hot buttered rum! Popular bars include Mikes's Bar and Rodeo; whilst good value restaurants include La Patate. For superior cuisine try the Chalet Mounier. Gégé Pilloud is a regionally renowned patissier and his shop is by the Jandri bottom station. Be sure not to miss sampling some of his 60 flavours of ice cream, cakes and fine chocolate. Les Deux Alpes also has a cinema and a very large skating rink, included on the lift pass, which is open until 11 p.m; bowling alleys, fitness centres and squash courts.

Recommended Hotels:

Hotel Le Bérangère: Situated at entrance to village; this is a large, modern hotel; south-facing balconies; indoor and outdoor swimming pool, Californian bath, sauna; sun terrace; attractive lounge, white decor, open fire, large windows overlooking the sun terrace and swimming pool; large light dining room on the left of entrance; medium sized bedrooms, nicely furnished, wooden decor with white walls, most with balconies, all with bath or private shower; 59 rooms altogether; dining room particularly attractive, large windows, much wooden decor; bar leading off reception area; a very nice hotel.

Hotel Edelweiss: This 3 star hotel is certainly conveniently placed for the lifts. All bedrooms with bath/shower, wc and balcony. Pleasant dining room, lounge with open fire and bar.

Hotel Mounier: One of the first to be built at the far end of the village; large L-shaped dining room, oak beams, windows along the side; attractive small breakfast room, light oak beams, white walls; sitting room, wood decor, open fireplace; bar; small comfortable bedrooms; Jacuzzi, sauna and solarium. Situated at the south end of the village near the Diable gondolaway and the La Rouge chair-lift.

LA CLUSAZ

Height of Resort: 3,608 ft.
Height of Top Station: 7,872 ft.
Nearest International Airport: Geneva
Map Reference: 4B See page 238
Route by Car: See page 236-238
Resorts Facilities Charts: See page 217
Hotel Reference Charts: See page 230

Of the French resorts, La Clusaz until recent years was little known to the majority of British skiers, which is surprising, as it is one of the oldest ski resorts in the French Alps, dating back to 1931. The village itself is quite old and is the centre of various outlying little hamlets each with its own accommodation but coming under the La Clusaz umbrella. The resort has been developed outwardly in chalet style and is picturesque and charming, quite unlike the concrete purpose-built French resorts. The lift system has been carefully sited to connect one area with another and to provide adequate uplift out of the village. The proximity of Mont Blanc, visible from various points, and other high mountains, combined with predominantly north facing runs, ensures an abundance of snow in the average year and skiing until May. La Clusaz is is reached by RN 909, which is always kept open for cars in winter. It is only 30 km. from Anneçy and 50 km. from Geneva.

The resort as a whole has 35 hotels and pensions, mostly small and pleasant which, together with chalets and apartments, provide some 19,500 beds. The lift system, which includes 3 cableways, 2 gondolaway, 14 chair-lifts and 38 drag-lifts, provides a capacity of 48,000 persons per hour. Apart from the downhill skiing described below, which is certainly above average for a resort of this size, the hamlet of Les Confins, 4km. distant, is an important and most popular centre for Nordic skiing (langlauf) with all facilities, including instruction and training for all standards, 9 prepared and marked trails, totalling 42km., and facilities for the hire of all equipment. A further 9 trails (19km.) can be found on Plateau de Beauregard). There is also a well established ski mountaineering and touring school with a variety of interesting and ambitious tours and, unusually, a freestyle school (hot-dogging, aerial and ballet for all standards. La Clusaz held the World Freestyle championships in 1995.

Small buses (Navettes) run at 30-minutes intervals to all outlying ski areas at a small charge.

Downhill Skiing: There are 5 separate areas, taken from west to east:-

Massif de Beauregard 5,412ft.: From the village area, access is by cableway, which is quite prone to queues in peak season. Most of the runs at the summit are suitable for intermediate skiers. From the summit one can ski back to the village by runs through the trees or one can ski on to the Croix-Fry-Merdassier area.

Massif Croix-Fry-Merdassier: There are two ski areas either side of the roadway to Col de Merdassier and include a variety of wide open runs suitable for intermediate skiers. There is a choice of mountain restaurants. By taking either of the Choucas drag-lifts one can ski onwards to the L'Étale area.

Massif de L'Étal 6,429 ft. : The summit of L'Étale is reached either by cableway or by a combination of drag and chair-lifts. The north facing red runs are challenging, with the Tétras particularly recommended.The Transvaal cableway links this with the Massif de L'Aiguille in the event of snow conditions not being suitable.

Massif de L'Aiguille 7,741 ft.: Rising above the village to the south this area provides the most extensive and varied skiing in the resort. It is served by conveniently situated lifts starting from different points in the village. The first stage at Crèt de Merle has nursery slopes and an excellent mountain restaurant. The second stage at Crèt du Loup is reached by either drag or chair-lift and is also the top of the Combe des Juments chair-lift which starts at Les Étages. Runs back to the village are mainly blue with some reds, while one can proceed higher still to the summit by the Aiguille drag-lift. From here one can ski down by a red or blue run, or one can use the Côte 2000 chair-lift to access. The La Balme area via the challenging and newly opened Combe de Fernuy, which is unpisted but marked.

Massif de Balme 7,872 ft.: Probably the best skiing in the resort can be found at La Balme, approximately 4 km. by road from the village. A debrayable gondolaway leads to combe de la Balme from where three chair-lifts continue further upwards. The longest of these chair-lifts leads to the highest point in the resort from which there are excellent view of Mt. Blanc, Dents du Midi and the resort of Flaine. The runs back to the mid station are very challenging but have variants which are suitable for good intermediate skiers, while the hardest runs will satisfy even experts.

Thanks to the well situated and prolific lift system one can start from the village via Beauregard and, proceeding in an anti-clockwise direction, connect on skis with all the above mountain areas, eventually skiing back in the afternoon from La Balme, although this last run entails some langlaufing. In all there are 130km. of marked runs. Alternatively, starting from La Balme, one can cover most of the circuit in a clockwise direction up to and including L'Étale. Skiing in the high season in February we met with no queues. All the runs are interesting and there are gradients suitable for all standards from the expert down to the beginner. There are good opportunities on all these north-facing slopes for off-piste powder skiing.

In a Few Words: Attractive, charming and understandably popular resort, tastefully developed in chalet style around an old village. Skiing for all standards above the average for a resort of this size. Skiing on the five mountains is interlinked. One of the most accessible resorts from Geneva or channel ports. Two kindergartens. Tourist Office staff friendly and helpful. Outstanding facilities for langlauf in beautiful surroundings. In general highly recommended.

Après Ski: Much to do. Artificial skating rink floodlit in evening. Joy rides on snowcats affording marvellous views and photographic opportunities. Cosy rides in tiny horse-drawn carts. There are 20km. of swept paths and 7 different planned walks.

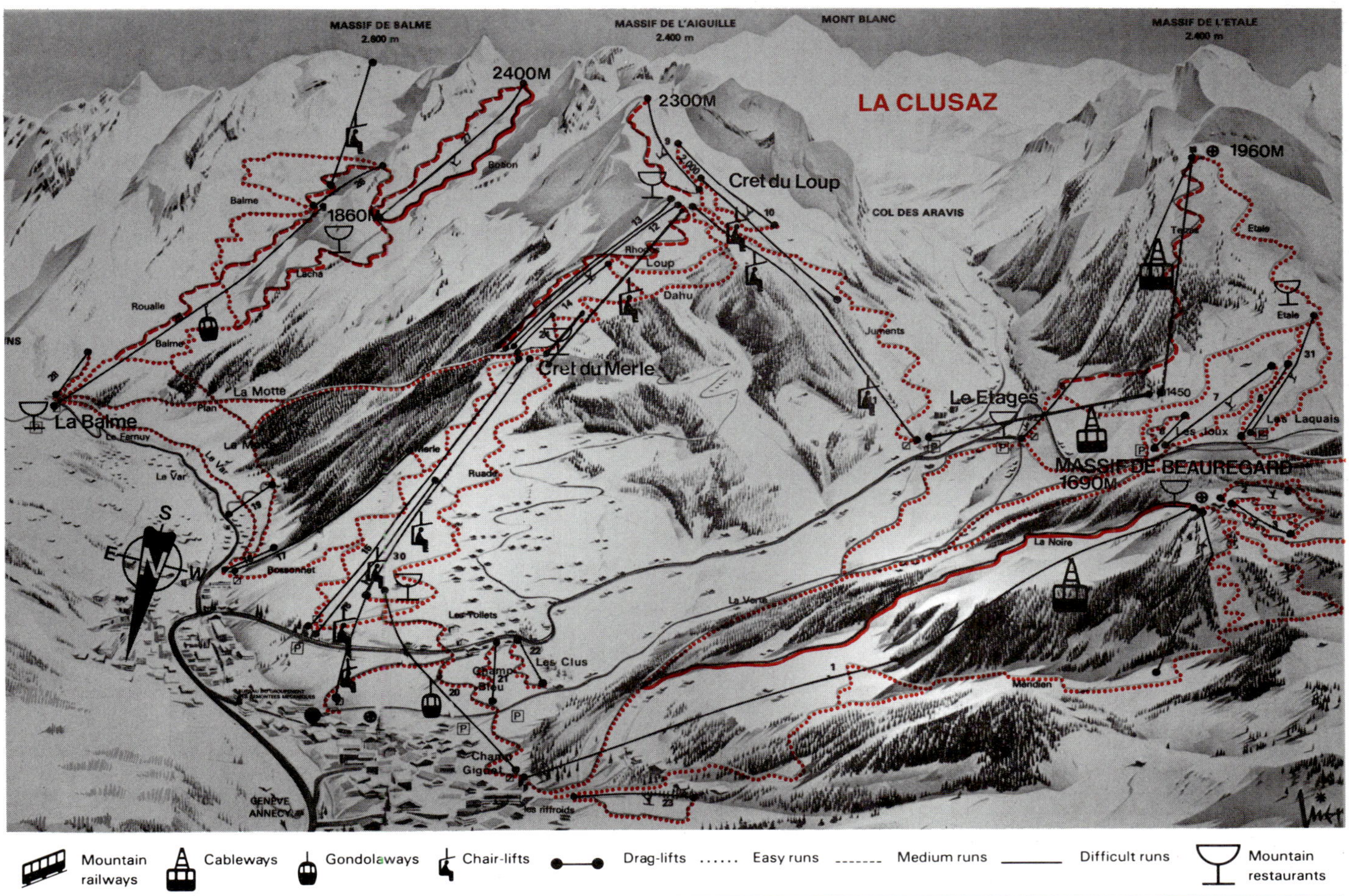

For a change, visit one of the many surrounding farms where the famous Reblochon cheese is made. There is one cinema for the linguist, floodlit cross-country tracks for the energetic, saunas and therapies for the keep-fitters, a wealth of restaurants for the gourmets (total of 30, of which the L'Écuelle, La Ferme and La Chaumière are outstanding) and finally, for the inexhaustible, a choice of 4 discothèques, some for maximum noise and minimum age but all charging identical price per drink, be it water or champagne. L'Écluse, popular with the young, has a surprise setting, being over a little underground torrent, floodlit and running out of harm's way under a glass-encased bridge. Tea shops, crammed with inimitable French patisseries; crêperies and gift shops galore with an interesting emphasis on regional worked minerals and jewellery. Every Monday newcomers are greeted in the square with a free glass of hot wine and some sort of welcoming entertainment such as a film, folk dancing or relevant lecture. Three fitness centres, open air swimming pool, skating rink, hang gliding and paragliding.

Recommended Hotels:
Hotel Beauregard: This 4 star hotel, built in traditional Haut Savoyard chalet style, has been completely renovated and is beautifully furnished throughout. Situated next to the bottom of the Bossomet drag-lift and 20 metres from the ski school. Its 61 bedrooms, all with bath, balacony, telephone, satellite TV and safe, combine a Savoyard setting with comfort. Three restaurants, 3 panoramic lounges with bar and fire place and terrace. Swimming pool, sauna, Turkish bath, solarium, gymnasium and conference rooms.

Pension Bellachat: A modest two-star hotel situated in beautiful surroundings in the very heart of the cross country trails and school. Plentiful food. Sun terrace. 4km. from La Clusaz with a 30-minute bus service till 7.15 p.m. The Balme cableway within half a mile. Good walks. Absolutely no evening entertainment. The Bellachat is ideal for keen lang-laufers who enjoy peace and quiet.

Hotels Carlina and Beaulieu: Sister hotels under one management sharing the same panoramic sunny position overlooking the main ski slopes and 100 yards above the village. The Carlina's indoor heated swimming pool (free) fitness centre, sauna, jacuzzi, solarium, massage and large garage are all shared by Beaulieu guests. both have sun terraces, comfortable bedrooms, card and public rooms. The Carlina's extra star means a head waiter with slightly more sophisticated waiting, larger bedrooms and higher charges! We stayed at the Beaulieu and found the five course dinners excellent, the service quick and the attitude throughout very agreeable.

FLAINE

Height of Resort: 5,250 ft.
Height of Top Station: 8,150 ft.
Nearest International Airport: Geneva
Map Reference: 4B See page 238
Route by Car: See page 236-238
Resorts Facilities Charts: See page 217
Hotel Reference Charts: See page 229

The modern purpose built resort of Flaine lies in a large bowl amidst the impressive Grand Massif in the Haute Savoie. It opened in 1969 but in recent years has extended its skiing, first linking with Samoëns and thence joining up with Morillon and Les Carroz, the latter becoming an important resort in its own right. The Grand Massif area now covers five resorts, those mentioned above plus Sixt, a village with its own skiing and now directly linked into the main system via the piste 'Des Cascades'. Flaine is one of the nearest resorts to the U.K. being 491 miles from Le Havre, 2 hours from Geneva airport and 18 miles from the rail head of Cluses. It is built on three levels, the Forum is the main centre with Flaine Forêt above and Front de Neige below. Flaine has 3 hotels, one hotel Residence and 750 apartments. A new Hamlet has been built beside the road on the Col above the resort. It consists of 65 attractive Norwegian wooden chalets, apartment blocks, a hotel-club and a general store.

The Skiing: The Grand Massif lift pass embraces all 5 resorts with 80 lifts and 263km. of pistes. There is a day pass for the Flaine lifts only. With such a vast network of lifts and runs it is impossible to describe the skiing in detail. It is divided into main areas:-

Flaine's own area:

South of the resort: Here the slopes are predominantly north facing and keep their snow until late season. They are served by the latest uphill transport systems, the main one being a cableway with 30 cars moving continuously, each car holding 25 persons to give a total capacity of 3,000 per hour which can be increased if necessary. Supplementing is a gondolaway along with a number of linking chair and drag-lifts rising to the ridge dominated from east to west by Tête Pelouse, 8,116ft., Les Grandes Platières, 8,136ft., and Tête des Lindars, 8,382ft. Runs criss-cross the whole of this bowl and vary from black, a section of about 3km., through many red to a swinging blue of some 6km. Special mention must be made of the steep black run below Tête Pelouse to Gers although this is not always open. Le Blanchot - highly recommended mountain restaurant on the blue Serpentine run. Excellent food and large sunny balcony, next to the new 4 seater Col de Plate chair-lift.

North of the resort: A triple chair-lift takes one up to Grand Vans, 7,540ft., halfway down the piste to Flaine one can divert up to the excellent Tête de Veret black bowl, particularly good in powder. Alternatively, only with a Guide and the right conditions, one can ski over the back off-piste to the bottom of the Gers lift. Continuing further north from Grand Vans one can ski reasonably gently or steeply down to Lac Vernant: here there are two lifts up to Tête du Pré de Saix, 6,933ft., the limit of the Flaine pass and the start of the Grand Massif pass with runs down to the three neighbouring resorts as described below:-

Runs down to Samoëns 720: A long and interesting descent with many variations. At the start one has the choice between 3 blacks and a red down to what is known as Samoëns 1600, a plateau area previously called Plateau des Saix with scattered restaurants, pensions, lifts and runs for all standards, including beginners. This area can also be reached by road from Samoëns. Continuing down from the plateau the red or black runs channel into wooden glades to the bottom of the gondolaway at Vercland, known as Samoëns 720, where one finds some pensions and restaurants. From here Samoëns village is 4km. and reached by ski bus. It is a beautiful village listed 88th in the French National Office of Historic Monuments and the only ski resort in France to be so listed. The return to the summit from Samoëns 720 is firstly by 4 seater gondolaway to Samoëns 1600 and thence a choice of long chair-lifts in two stages back to Tête du Pré des Saix. The slopes are north facing and the snow is usually good to the bottom of this area which is served by 17 lifts and has the most challenging runs of the outlying resorts.

Runs to Morillon, 2,296ft.: This is the longest and probably the easiest of the runs, some 15km. from Flaine, with the choice of red or blue routes through the trees. These are north facing runs and can provide good powder conditions; the area is picturesque with restaurants dotted about. Morillon is a little farming village now developing as a ski resort, although the main future development is likely to be above at Morillon Grand Massif, 3,546ft., connected with Morillon by a good approach road. The return into the circuit is by a modern 10 seater gondolaway to Morillon Grand Massif and thence by a fast 4 seater chair-lift. This area has 8 lifts.

Runs to Les Carroz, 4,068ft.: This resort can be reached by a number of different routes, most of which provide long and easy runs. Its own skiing is through wooded glades over blue and red runs, mostly west facing and served by 15 lifts. Les Carroz is a large and fast developing resort on traditional lines. Its main lifts out of the resort are situated above the village and unless one is staying at the top end a ski bus serves the lower stations from the village square. These lifts consist of a 6 seater gondolaway and two alternative chair-lift routes. Excellent old chalet style restaurant - Les Molliettes - at bottom of the long, blue Marmotte run. Superb food both at lunch and dinner.

Sixt: This attractive old village lies beyond and above Samoëns at 2,525ft. It has its own skiing, served by two chair-lifts and 5 drag-lifts up to 5,240ft., for which the Grand Massif ski pass is valid. There are two pistes from Flaine area to Sixt but a ski bus operates between Sixt and Samoëns gondolaway for the return journey.

It must be realised that the return to Flaine from all the above areas is a lengthy business and time must be watched if one is to make the vital return link to Flaine from Lac de Vernant before the lifts close.

In a Few Words: A delightfully compact traffic free resort and although purpose built not in any way unattractive. A vast choice of runs and wherever one skis there is a lift to take one further afield or back. Virtually no queueing or walking. Ideal for families as children can be looked after from morning to late evening and for beginners, ski évolutif taught so that long runs can be taken even during the first holiday. Two ski schools, 5 free lifts for beginners. A paradise for intermediates and much also for the advanced skier, particularly with the wealth of off-pistes opportunities. For the advanced skier, Flaine Super Ski runs weekly courses that include powder skiing, ski treks and an introduction to slalom and giant slalom. Deservedly popular with the British. Friendly atmosphere and high standard ski school. Highly recommended. The Flaine Ski Clinic - a flexible English speaking alternative to ski schools, is also recommended.

Après Ski: Everywhere is fairly crowded on the whole as there are only a few venues available. The White Grouse, a traditional half-timbered English owned pub serving draught ale and lager very popular and packed every evening – a good meeting place and chance for everyone to get together. Free vin chaud is offered every Sunday evening outside the Tourist Office. Chez Daniel is an inexpensive crêperie which also has special fondue and raclette soirées each week. Several bars and café provide pastries and hot chocolate at tea time. The Chalet Bissac Terrace is a favourite sunny lunchtime spot. The Chalet Bissac, which is built above the télébenne to Flaine Forêt, has very lively fondue evenings once a week, with plenty of dancing and bonhomie. Cimes Rock Cafe in the resort of Flaine is a lively venue. Varied menu – international to traditional Savoyard fare (ie fondue and raclette). Live (loud) music most nights. Le Chalet Michet provides a meal in an old-style atmosphere and is well known for its raclettes. Disco La Bodega becomes packed up to the early hours of the morning and there is a need for one or two more. Cinema with up-to-date French films and new English ones. Large indoor swimming pool, solarium, gymnasium, skating rink and a very good library with latest English books for which a moderate charge is made. The 'Drive on Ice' school is very popular and also provides entertainment for the spectators.

Recommended Hotels:

Hotel Aujon: Flaine's largest hotel catering mainly for bed and breakfast visitors; breakfast self-service, waitress service for dinner. Pleasant bar and an open plan lounge with log fire. Bedrooms very comfortable, all with bath, wc, telephone and TV. Friendly and helpful staff.

Club Aquarius: All bedrooms are with private bath, wc and TV and there are special four-bedded rooms for families, for which the hotel is particularly suited, having nursery; kindergartem for children up to 7 years old, baby-sitting service and games room. A spacious bar and sitting area with cheminée fireplace in the centre, pleasant dining room, and a separate one for children 2-6 years. Disco once weekly.

Hotel Le Totem: A good three-star hotel and good value. Bedrooms very nicely furnished all with private bath. Pleasant dining room, large lounge bar area attractively designed, terrace and bridge room. Restaurant gastronomic. All south facing rooms with balcony.

Hotel Residence de la Forêt: Excellent apartments; larger than average rooms; reception desk, key and telephone service; take-away meals; lounge, bar, launderette, lock up ski lockers and ski home position.

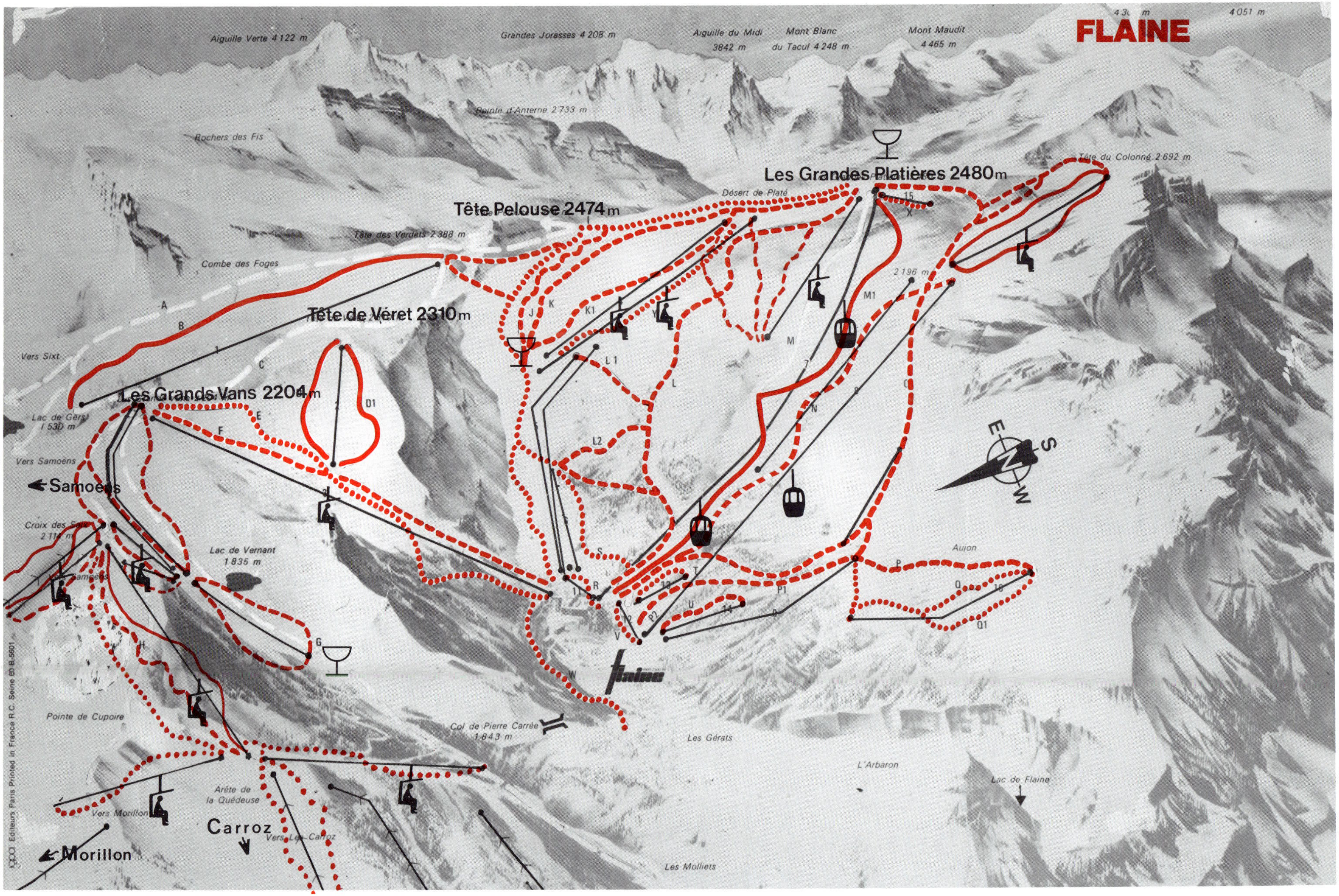

Mountain railways | Cableways | Gondolaways | Chair-lifts | Drag-lifts | .... Easy runs | --------- Medium runs | ——— Difficult runs | Mountain restaurants

LES HOUCHES

Height of Resort: 3,280 ft.
Height of Top Station: 6,455 ft.
Nearest International Airport: Geneva
Map Reference: 5C See page 238
Route by Car: See page 236-238
Resorts Facilities Charts: See page 218
Hotel Reference Charts: See page 230

Les Houches is situated 7km. west of Chamonix at the foot of Mont Blanc, the highest mountain in Europe. It is easily reached by car from Geneva, 90km., via the motorway, the 'Route Blanche', which leads to the Mont Blanc tunnel connecting France with Italy. There are five bus connections with Geneva airport each way per day, taking $1^1/_2$ hours. The village spreads out over some 8km. Les Houches provides a total of 8,000 beds contained in 20 hotels and in numerous chalets and apartments. The lift capacity is 17,300 persons per hour. As Mont Blanc overshadows the village there is little sunshine in the village itself during December and January. All the ski slopes lie to the south, with the result that virtually all the runs are down north facing slopes, allowing skiing until April and beyond.

Skiers have the choice of the Les Houches abonnement covering 17 various lifts and 55km. of pistes, available for 1 to 8 consecutive days, or the 'Ski Pass Mont Blanc', covering 190 lifts and more than 700km. of pistes in 14 resorts (Chamonix, Argentière, Megève, St. Gervais, Les Houches, Vallorcine, Praz-sur-Orly, Combloux, Salanche, Cordon, St. Nicolas de Veroce, Passy, Les Contamines, Montjoies). The pass is available for 3 to 13 consecutive days.

Besides downhill skiing, Nordic skiing (ski de fond) is exceedingly well catered for and very popular.

Les Houches' own skiing: The main uphill transport out of the village to the Bellevue-Col de Voza-Prarion ridge consists of a cableway rising from the west end of the village to Bellevue, 5,904ft. In addition a gondolaway travels from some 700 yards further west, to Prarion, 6,455ft. Between these two systems there is the Maison Neuve chair-lift surmounted by the Kandahar chair-lift, also up to Prarion. There are hotel restaurants at both these top stations, as well as at Col de Voza, midway between the two. Once up there are 9 interconnecting drag-lifts within this general area – and from Prarion there are particularly enjoyable runs westwards towards St. Gervais, with 2 long surmounting drag-lifts and a chair-lift to bring one back. 67 snow cannons can be operated.

To ski back to the village, there are 3 main routes with variations, one medium, one relatively difficult and the third the world-famous 'Piste Verte' international racecourse used for the Men's Downhill in the Arlberg-Kandahar races. These are through wooded glades and provide excellent skiing for all standards up to the expert. From all these runs one can return to either the Bellevue or Prarion bottom stations. In the village itself there are two beginner slopes served by lifts.

In a Few Words: In comparison with other resorts, not the most picturesque or well laid out village, but its scenery could not be more grandiose or magnificent, with the Mont Blanc chain towering above it within illusory touching distance. Excellent skiing of its own for all standards, both downhill and cross-country, with good off-piste powder snow possibilities for the former. For those wanting more variety, a good and generally cheaper base for the 13 other neighbouring resorts covered on the Mont Blanc ski pass.

Après Ski: For a non-skiing day there are many alternatives. A breathtaking trip to the very peak of the Aiguille du Midi by the highest cableway in Europe followed, if you remain vertigo-free, by a swing across the Vallée Blanche in tiny cabins to an Italian peak from where you can descend to Courmayeur. For the less intrepid Italy can be visited via the famous Mont Blanc tunnel, the longest road tunnel in Europe. A natural skating rink is floodlit by night and three different marked walks lead you through pretty wooded scenery. You can watch hockey matches and torchlight slaloms. Bar/restaurants of typical French style are plentiful and two good restaurants, the Pèle and the Peter Pan, as well as their excellent à la carte, feature a Savoyarde fondue where you charcoal-cook strips of meat at the table. The Peter Pan is a 200 year-old chalet/hotel well worth a visit.

Recommended Hotels:

Hotel Beausite: A popular hotel, well run by the owner and where guests return again and again. Very friendly and informal atmosphere. Attractively renovated in wooden style with cheerful bar and open fire in dining room, which is also a good restaurant. All bedrooms with bath or shower, wc, telephone, TV and mini-bar. Sauna. Near skating rink, bus stop and one of the ski school assembly points.

Hotel Bellevarde: Converted farmhouse retaining old-fashioned wooden style. immediately beside Bellevarde chair-lift. Carefully run by young owners. Quiet chalet/annexe adjacent. Sun terrace.

Hotel de la Piste Bleue: Chosen for its good position halfway between the Prarion and Bellevue ski lifts and within 5 minutes' walk from either. (All ski runs back to the village can be made to finish at the door.) Near nursery slopes. Large dining room, sun terrace and two sitting room, bar and billiard room. All bedrooms with bath and most with balconies.

CHAMONIX

Height of Resort: 3,389 ft.
Height of Top Station: 12,604 ft.
Nearest International Airport: Geneva
Map Reference: 5B See page 238
Route by Car: See page 236-238
Resorts Facilities Charts: See page 217
Hotel Reference Charts: See page 229

Built at the foot of Mont Blanc, Chamonix is a large resort steeped in mountaineering tradition, with a lot of charm and many attractive old buildings. Horse drawn carriages,available as taxis, add to the character. In winter people come from all over the world to do the famous Vallée Blanche run, as well as doing the many cross-country runs; in summer it is a great climbing centre, with mountain biking, golf and para-gliding increasing in popularity. Chamonix is easily reached from Geneva in about 1 hour by the'Route Blanche'motorway which runs almost to the resort.

The beautiful Chamonix Valley incorporates Les Houches, at the entrance, Les Praz, Argentière and Le Tour at the end. There are 6 main ski areas, linked by buses from Chamonix Centre and Chamonix Sud. The bus fare is included in ski passes of over 1 day. All the ski areas (see separate report for Les Houches) become very crowded at the weekend and during French school holidays.

Le Brévent Area: Nearest to the centre of Chamonix, on the north-west side of the valley above Chamonix, a six-seater gondolaway runs first to Plan Praz and thence a small cableway goes sharply up to Le Brévent peak, 8,206ft. This top station can now be reached by a series of lifts from La Flégère. The run down to the Plan Praz, with excellent snow throughout the season, is for good skiers, whilst further down to the village it becomes steeper. Depending on the snow, it is possible to ski to the bottom of the main lift. Four lifts to the north of Plan Praz service good runs for intermediates but near the restaurant there is a good selection of slopes for beginners. Brévent also has some interesting off-piste skiing. At the base of the Brévent area are the Savoy nursery slopes.

La Flégère Area: About 1 mile east of the town on the north side of the valley, this is a sunny area with good intermediate skiing. A large cableway reaches Flégère where a chair-lift runs to L'Index, 7,962ft., servicing many varied runs back to the restaurant. Several lifts off to the right give access to good nursery slopes. Only one access lift and therefore very crowded during peak season; when there is not enough snow to ski down, passage on the descending cablecar must be booked.

Les Grands Montets Area: On the south of the valley above Argentière, the extensiveness and quality of the skiing makes this the best area by far for good skiers. However it can take over an hour from Chamonix to the middle station in high season (after buses and queues at the base station). A large cableway to the mid-station at Croix de Lognan, 6,386ft.(recently developed with restaurant), continues up to Les Grands Montets, 10,643ft., with superb views and excellent powder snow for intermediate-advanced skiers. The Grands Montets lift is not included in the lift pass and a supplement of 28F per journey is required. Queues are up to an hour in peak season.To the right of the cableway is the Bochard gondolaway (opened in 1996) to La Pendant, 9,190ft., and several chair-lifts, completing this fabulous area with some challenging runs and vast off-piste potential.

Le Tour Area: Half an hour away by bus, at the head of the valley, this area is rarely crowded. A gondolaway from Le Tour rises to Charamillon, 6,070ft., with its restaurant, and a chair-lift continues to just short of the Swiss frontier. To the east of this system a long chair-lift and connecting drag-lift reach Col de Balme, 7,171ft. where one finds another restaurant. Three further drag-lifts serve these upper slopes, the highest rising to 7,447 ft. – this sunny treeless area is a paradise for novice skiers as most of the runs are easy with a few reds thrown in, including the descent from Charamillon to Le Tour. A new slope to Vallorcine was recently opened in this area. The nursery slopes with 3 button lifts are adjacent to the bottom station of the gondolaway. Excellent off-piste opportunities in this area.

Aiguille du Midi Area: On the south of Chamonix town, the two-stage cableway rises steeply to 12,604ft. in 20 mins. to a large restaurant and the start of the famous Vallée Blanche run which, early in the season, is open only in spells of good weather. One walks through rock tunnels and over a bridge suspended between two peaks, to the tunnel of the Aiguille du Midi itself and the view of the Mont Blanc Massif glacier area below. A walk down a precipitous ridge will be more difficult than the run itself to most; parties are roped together for this descent. This leads onto the glacier before 20km. of unforgettable skiing. Above, the gondolas cross to the Italian frontier on Pointe Helbronner and only operate later in the season.

The traditional Vallée Blanche run itself is not difficult, although the area of the seracs where the glacier breaks up can be tricky. The run should never be done without a guide to show the route avoiding the many crevasses, and apart from expert knowledge of the area making the trip much more interesting, if any accident occurs without a guide the costs involved for rescue are enormous. After the long gentle run down, there is a stiff climb up the side of the valley before descending through woodland to the centre of Chamonix. A clear day makes one fully appreciate the vast beauty of this area. This is one of the finest runs in the world – no skier should miss it. When snow cover is thin on the final run in to Chamonix, mostly along wooded paths, this section can be unpleasant so it is advisable, in such conditions, to take the cog railway to the centre of the resort.

Beneath the Aiguille du Midi are the other main nursery slopes in Chamonix, Les Planards, which has snow-making facilities. There is also off-piste skiing from the middle station of the Aiguille du Midi back to Chamonix Sud. In addition to the regular ESF ski school classes, others are available, touring the pistes in the valley, concentrating on off-piste or Ski Fun Tours which combine instruction with guiding.

In a Few Words: Excellent for cheaper access to high mountain skiing than will be found in purposes built resorts; particularly for the intermediate and good skier; superb off-piste possibilities (guide essential); good lift system although the unlinked areas mean reliance on the bus service without private transport; efficient but very crowded at peak

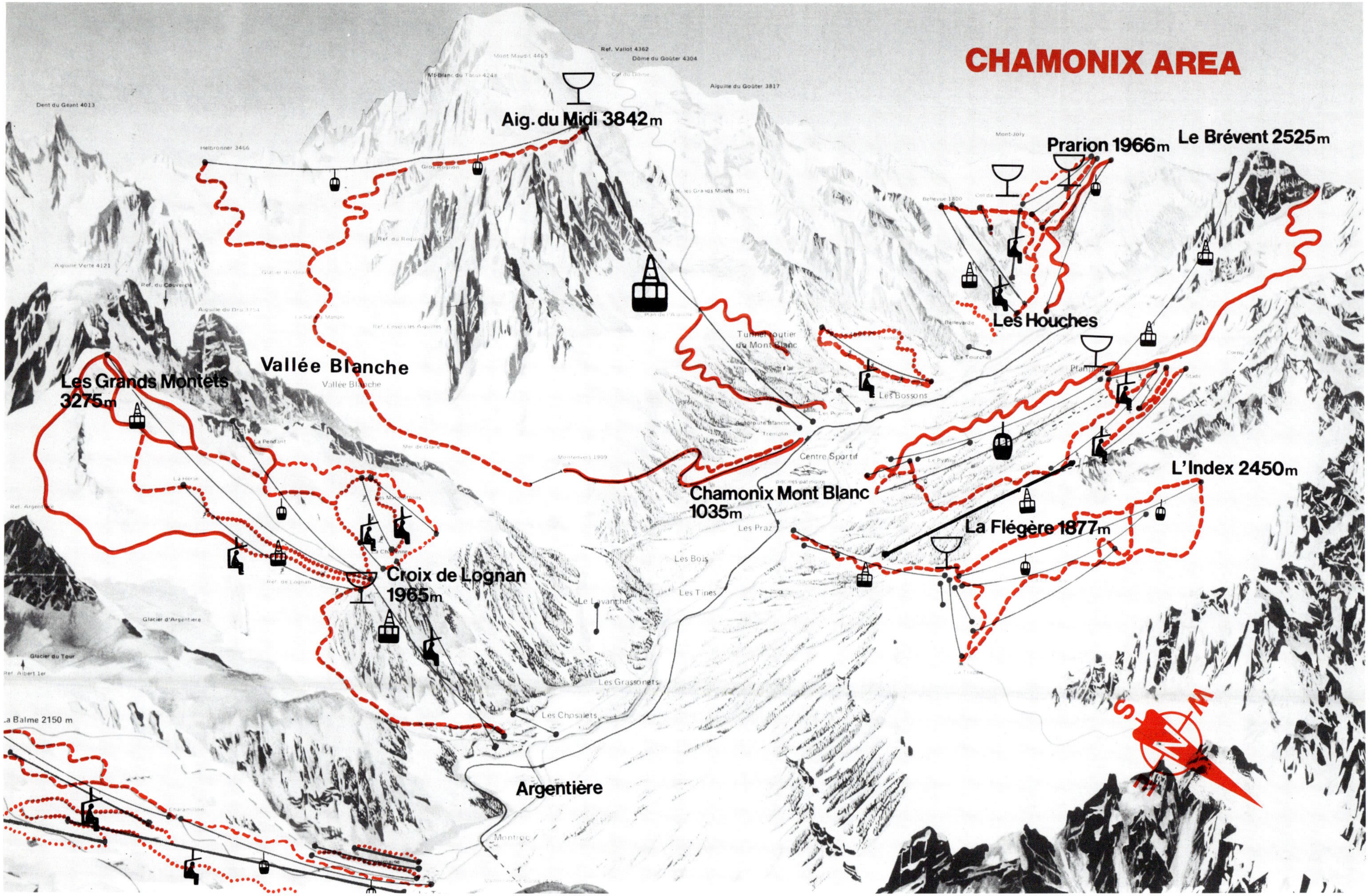

Mountain railways | Cableways | Gondolaways | Chair-lifts | Drag-lifts | ...... Easy runs | --------- Medium runs | ——— Difficult runs | Mountain restaurants

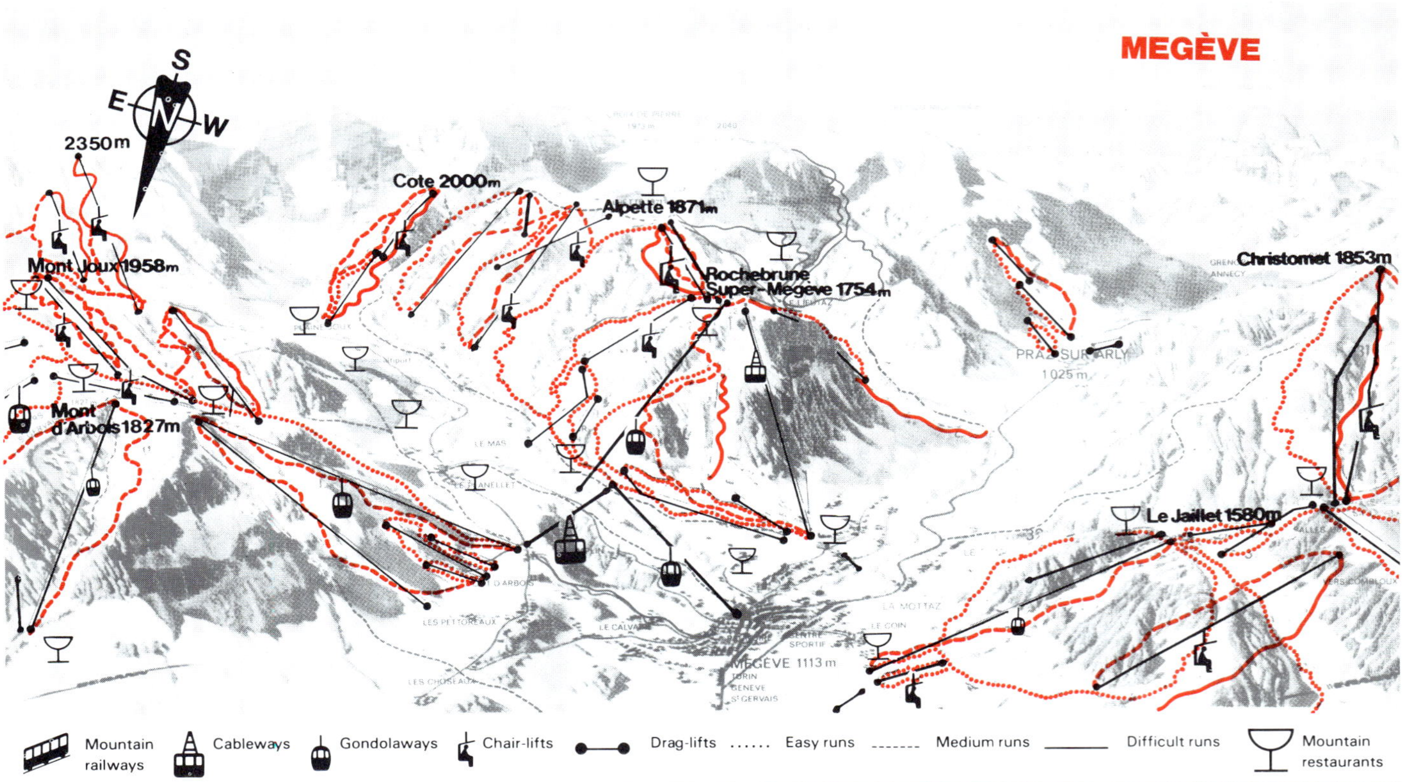

times; excellent snow on all higher slopes throughout season. There are a variety of lift passes covering different areas as well as buses. The resort has a lot of charm and is also interesting for non-skiers.

Après Ski: Chamonix is a large bustling, busy town. There are over 200 restaurants and bars, catering for every taste including Japanese and Oriental. Those wishing to find a lively bar should go to La Choucas Video Bar on Rue du Paccard or Bar Le Brévent, both are noisy and busy. The latter also has a good restaurant. There are also several night clubs: the Blue Night is expensive but worth a visit. Other popular bars are The Driver, Mill Street Pub and Chambre Neuf. Chamonix also has a market on Saturdays, ice skating rinks and a splendid modern sports complex with indoor and outdoor pools, a fitness centre with saunas and steam bath, tennis and squash courts. Nearby Argentière is less expensive and much quieter.

Recommended Hotels:

Hotel Croix Blanche Inn: Under the same ownership as the Mont Blanc, this hotel stands in the central town square; attractive entrance cum small sitting room, elegant breakfast room and bar, comfortable bedrooms. Bed & breakfast only, but has its own excellent restaurant adjoining.

Hotel Hermitage & Paccard: This is a very nice family run hotel, recently completely renovated, standing in its own grounds in a quiet position. All rooms with bath or shower, wc and balcony, long bright dining room, comfortable sitting room and bar.

Hotel Mont Blanc: Could not be more central and adjoining the Tourist Office and ski school, this is one of Chamonix's leading hotels. Large entrance area to reception, elegant dining room on two floors with large, open circular fireplace in the centre, comfortable sitting rooms, bar and large bar area leading to sun terrace and garden, heated open air swimming pool, comfortable and spacious bedrooms, good food and a friendly and efficient service.

Hotel La Sapinière: The original hotel building is old, but with recent extensions. The rooms are large with bath or shower, WC, telephone, TV. There is a luxurious but friendly feel to the hotel which is run by a Franco-American couple. Restaurant, bar, lounge, television room, pool room, fitness room, sauna and massage. Private parking and heated garages. A very quiet location, only five minutes' walk from the village centre, and very close to the Le Brévent lift

MEGÈVE

Height of Resort: 3,651 ft.
Height of Top Station: 7,709 ft.
Nearest International Airport: Geneva
Map Reference: 4C See page 238
Route by Car: See page 236-238
Resorts Facilities Charts: See page 218
Hotel Reference Charts: See page 230

Megève, well established as France's most fashionable ski resort, après ski being pursued just as seriously as skiing, is within an easy distance of Geneva airport. The skiing is divided into three areas, two connected by lifts and the third, Le Jaillet by bus. The Mont Blanc ski pass covers 13 resorts with a total of 190 lifts, serving more than 680km. of marked pistes and includes the local and resort buses.

Rochebrune Area: A great improvement has been made to this area, situated south-west of the town, also known as Super Megève. It can still be reached by cableway from the outskirts but a more convenient gondolaway, Le Chamois, leaves from the centre, behind the church and rises to Le Tour. A further surmounting gondolaway, La Caboche, takes one to Rochebrune summit where one finds a pleasant restaurant, and the start of the Olympique run now covered by 50 snow cannons. Nearby, the Alpette chair-lift and drag-lift rise to 5,754ft., the top station in this area. This transportation combined with several drag-lifts provide a good variety of runs to suit all grades of skiers. The installation of the Petite Fontaine and Jardin chair-lifts and the Rochefort drag-lift now links Rochebrune area with Cote 2000 and both can be reached by cableway from the Mont d'Arbois area.

Mont d'Arbois/La Princesse Areas: A 15 minute bus ride to the south-west of the resort delivers one at the lower terminal of the gondolaway, capacity 2600 persons per hour, which rises to 5,995ft. and connects with 3 drag-lifts covering gentle slopes suitable for beginners. A further 6 drag-lifts and chair-lifts lead to medium and difficult open runs. The area is linked to the St. Gervais area by cableway, and a long gondolaway opens up another area, La Princesse, on the west of Mt. d'Arbois, with a vertical drop of 2,500ft. and providing easy, medium and difficult runs up to 5km. The chair-lift, Mont Joly, which rises to the resort's top station, 7,709ft., provides two challenging runs to base.

Cote 2000: Furthest from the resort, a chair-lift leaves Plaine Joux, surmounted by a 4-seater chair-lift which rises to Cote 2000. From the top one has a choice between difficult and intermediate runs back to base.

Le Jaillet Area: Situated north-west of the resort, Le Jaillet is reached by a modern gondolaway carrying 1,800 persons per hour, and from the top station, 5,183ft. one has the most beautiful view of Megève. A nearby drag-lift rises to a rounded summit, Les Salles, 5,592 ft. with easy runs down to Combloux. From the top of Le Jaillet there is an easy run down to the bottom of the Christomet drag-lift which rises to 6,077ft. with runs back to the bottom station – one medium along the ridge clear of woods; one difficult following the line of the lift, top section open, lower wooded and one difficult with wooded sections. From the bottom, the chair-lift takes one back to Le Jaillet for runs back to the village. There is interesting and varied skiing in this area. A beginner's lift was recently opened at the top station of Jaillet.

In a Few Words: Varied skiing widely spread around the resort; sunny; four kindergartens provide good facilities for families and ski classes for children; easily reached from airport; good, sophisticated and fashionable après ski; expensive but some reasonably priced pensions available. Three underground car parks.

Après Ski: Specialising in après ski, Megève indeed provides all the variety of night life you could wish for. Numerous bars, night clubs and restaurants ranging from the simple and reasonably priced to the chic and expensive, and the gourmet's choice. There is the famous Club des 5 Rues and Caves de Megève where the best French and Swiss Jazz players perform. Sporting activities include 75km. of nordic ski trails, para-gliding, 50 km. of cleared walks, skating, ice hockey, curling, sleigh rides, riding and ski bobbing, and there is a casino, 3 cinemas, bowling alley, 2 indoor swimming pools, indoor tennis court and indoor climbing wall.

Recommended Hotels:

Hotel le Fer à Cheval: A pleasant rustic style hotel near the centre, 27 bedrooms all with bath, and 7

suites all with bath, wc, colour TV and direct dial telephones. À la carte restaurant, bars, sitting rooms, sauna and jacuzzi.

Parc des Loges: This 4 star de luxe hotel standing in its own grounds was completely modernised in 1988. The accommodation consists of 45 rooms and a large selection of apartments and suites with balcony or terrace, fireplace and coloured television. Pleasant sitting rooms, gastronomic restaurant, piano bar, swimming pool, sauna and garage. Central position.

Hotel Mont Blanc: This luxury hotel, near the central square, tourist office, ski school, and gondolaway, was completely rebuilt in 1970. All the bedrooms in the hotel have private bath and there are also 10 suites consisting of bedroom, bath, entrance lobby and sitting room. Apart from the luxurious furnished dining rooms and sitting rooms, there is an art gallery, bank and lecture room. Attractive patio garden. Outdoor swimming pool and restaurant.

VALMOREL

Height of Resort: 4,592 ft.
Height of Top Station: 7,884 ft.
Nearest International Airport: Geneva
Map Reference: 4D See page 238
Route by Car: See page 236-238
Resorts Facilities Charts: See page 218
Hotel Reference Charts: See page 230

Situated south-west of Moutiers, in one of the neighbouring valleys to Courchevel, Valmorel is a French resort with a difference. No skyscraper blocks here – the old buildings have been restored and new ones constructed in traditional chalet style to blend with the old and the surrounding countryside. The ski area continues to develop and there are now 50 lifts and 162km. of pistes with the St. François Longchamp ski area being included as part of the circuit.
The main ski area is on the north-west side of the village, with 2 chair-lifts rising in V-formation, one reaching the crest and the other terminating half-way up. The runs back to the village from these two top stations are easy and intermediate over south-west facing slopes. The crest itself is well served by a long series of 8 interlinking lifts stretching from the hamlet of Combelouvière, 4,101ft., to the highest point on the crest, above the village, 6,621ft., and this system provides a good variety of north-east facing runs, of easy to intermediate standard, down to Combelouvière. From the top station one has the choice of easy and intermediate runs back to the village over south-east facing slopes.

On the south-west side of the resort a two-stage gondolaway rises first to 6,003ft. and the second stage to Col du Mottet, 7,884ft., the highest station in the resort. The runs from the top over east facing slopes are intermediate and difficult whilst those from the first station to the village are easy and north-west facing.

Further to the south-west there is another chair-lift giving access to a selection of easy runs and to the left two surmounting drag-lifts rise to Col Du Gollet, 6,137ft., providing intermediate and difficult north facing runs over the first section and becoming easy nearer the village. There are a number of drag-lifts on the lower slopes in this area which provide, in the main, easy slopes for beginners and second year skiers.

Children from 6 months upwards can be catered for in the Saperlipopette. The 3 year olds and upwards are taught to ski in the Jardin des Neiges and can be booked for morning or afternoon sessions or left there all day with lunch provided. Valmorel is an excellent starting point for the 9 Valleys ski tour. However arrangements must be made well in advance

In a Few Words: Valmorel is very much an unsophisticated family resort, a friendly atmosphere and helpful people. The ski school is well organised, 10 adults to a class. Special initiation stadium for adults and ski évolutif is taught. Beginners to intermediates will be happy here, there are difficult runs but always alternative routes.

Après Ski: It is pleasing to see a new French resort being developed in traditional style, and the farming community remaining part of the scene. The village square is particularly attractive and intersecting traffic free streets are lit at night by imitation oil street lamps. There are 21 restaurants, including six in the mountains, and a night club. There are mountain walks, toboggan runs, cross-country skiing, para-gliding, hang-gliding, horse-drawn sleigh rides, fitness club and fondue and raclette evenings etc. There is a library and games room for children. Specially recommended for eating out is Gril le Creuset where all the food is cooked on an enormous log grill in the restaurant. it is wise to book a table for the evening meal. La Marmite and Chez Albert both provide a warm and friendly service and are recommended. Le Jean's Club is a lively discothèque and very crowded. Each week various forms of entertainment are organised and the 3 hamlets, which make up Valmorel, are connected by télébourg carrying 15 persons and operating from 08.30 a.m. to 11.30 p.m.

Recommended Hotels:
Hotel La Fontaine: A 2 star hotel constructed in chalet style, situated beside the main square. 40 rooms all with bath and with balcony or access to balcony. All rooms have extra bed, very suitable family hotel and baby sitting is available. Bar, Lounge, restaurant 'La Chéminée' – special dishes, charcoal grills, raclettes, savoy and burgundy fondues. Friendly atmosphere.

Hotel Planchamp: A 3 star chalet style hotel with 25 rooms all with bath, TV and direct dial telephones. Nice sitting area with huge log fire and bar adjoining. Most attractive dining room with terrace and excellent menu. Baby sitting available. Good atmosphere.

Hotel du Bourg: A 2 star hotel with 53 rooms all with bath. Buffet Breakfast. Bar with large log fire. TV.

Self-catering: Studios and apartments can be rented in new traditional style buildings. There are studios for 2 and apartments for up to 9 persons. Studios have shower and apartments with bathrooms. Kitchens are equipped with two hot plates, washing up machine and fridge. Linen is supplied but not towels. Baby sitting can be arranged.

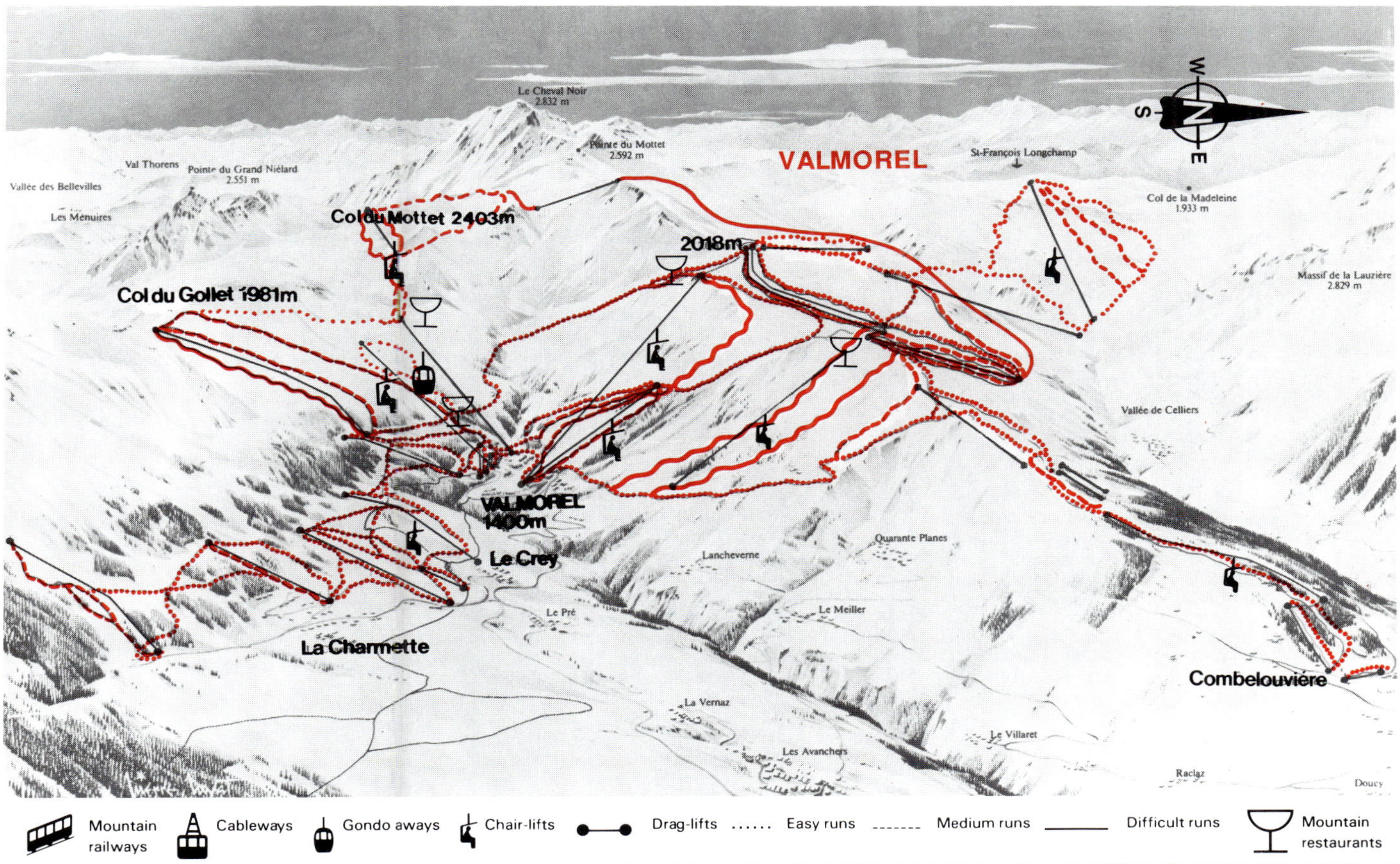

LES TROIS VALLÉES

The Trois Vallées is made up of five well known resorts, Courchevel, Méribel, La Tania, Les Menuires and Val Thorens, reported in the pages that follow. The fifth resort, La Tania, was opened in 1992. Saint Martin de Belleville is now included in the Trois Vallées lift pass and all six resorts are interlinked. The whole area provides some 600 km. of prepared pistes serves by 200 lifts making it one of the largest ski areas in the world.

COURCHEVEL 1850

Height of Resort: 6,013 ft.
Height of Top Station: 8,825 ft.
Nearest International Airports: Geneva/ Chambéry/Lyon
Map Reference: 4B See page 238
Route by Car: See page 236-238
Resorts Facilities Charts: See page 217
Hotel Reference Charts: See page 229

Travelling by air, international flights land either at Geneva, Lyon or Chambéry airports. There are good motorways from Geneva, 90 miles and Lyon, 112 miles, to Chambéry and thence via Albertville to Moutiers, where a well engineered road leads up to Courchevel. Chains are needed at times.

Courchevel 1850 was the first of the resorts built by skiers for skiers in 1946. Unlike many of the modern purpose-built French resorts which followed it is not at all a 'concrete jungle' being most attractively and cleverly laid out, with most hotels and chalets hidden away behind trees which line the pistes. A recent move to add chalet style roofs to many buildings enhances the scene and gives a more alpine appearance.

Courchevel 1850 is the main and highest station. Its immediate satellites are Courchevel 1650, 1550 and 1300, the latter the old village of Le Praz. The most recent extensions to the ski area are at La Tania, sector 1350, where an 8 seater gondolaway and surmounting drag-lift have been installed. Further up, the new 4 seater chair-lift, Dou des Lanches, reaches Col de la Loze and provides an additional link with Altiport 1700 and Méribel. One can ski down to all of these and there are direct links back. Only down the road but skiwise rather out on a limb is Courchevel 1650. This has its own skiing ridge and to reach it on skis one has to go up and across and then ski down. The fact that Courchevel as a whole can accommodate 32,432 visitors and still retain a village-like appearance is because the visitors are dispersed between these five Courchevel resorts. The lifts and pistes are more than capable in handling these large numbers even in high season, in fact the lift capacity is 54,000 per hour. The runs are superbly groomed by 22 snow-cats working mainly at night, supplemented by 474 snow cannons. Courchevel's skiing with its 68 interlinking lifts and some 180 km. of pistes is far too extensive to describe in any detail. Suffice it to say that the main uphill transportation out of the village of 1850 consists of 3 gondolaways starting in one area, Croisette, and taking one up to:-

a) The Col de La Loze, 7,410ft.: Transportation to this area was greatly improved by the refurbishment of the Chenus gondolaway and the replacement of the Coqs chair-lift by a high speed detachable quad. From La Loze one has a large choice of runs back to Courchevel 1850, alternatively many different routes more westwardly through wooded glades to Courchevel 1300 and La Tania. The latter includes two black racecourses, Jean Blanc and Jockeys, in addition to the delightful and easier Bouc Blanc run. From Courchevel 1300 one can return either to Courchevel 1850 or back to Col de la Loze. It should be mentioned that from the latter is one of the runs to Méribel.

b) Verdons, 6,875ft., upward to Vizelle, 8,671ft., and La Saulire, 8,825ft.: A modern 8 seater gondolaway, capacity 2,400 persons per hour, takes one up to Verdons. From here one has the choice of taking a further 8 seater gondolaway to Vizelle or one of the largest cableways in the world, with each cabin holding 160 skiers, up to Saulire. Both of these summits interconnect and are the start of the main runs over to Méribel and beyond. Runs back to Courchevel are numerous and varied but mention must be made of three black descents from Vizelle; also for the courageous and really competent skiers the very steep couloirs from Saulire – Le Grand Couloir and Emile Allais runs. The longest and more usual intermediate run, about 9km., starts south, turns east down wonderfully wide slopes before turning northwards down a valley past Les Creux. From this valley there is a choice of 3 lifts up onto the ridge of Courchevel 1650, with its own 19 lifts and a long easy run down to 1650. Returning up to the ridge there are three routes, blue, red and black, back to the valley and Courchevel 1850.

c) The Jardin Alpin and Biollay Sector: Also starting from Croisette the Jardin Alpin gondolaway rises to the Biollay area which is wonderfully open with numerous linking lifts. Here the beginner and second year skier will enjoy the gently easy runs. It should also be mentioned that many of the hotels and apartments are accessible on skis from this area.

Skiers have the choice of two lift passes:- the Vallée de Courchevel pass covering 1850, 1650, 1550, 1300 and La Tania; or the 3 Valley pass covering all the skiing in Courchevel, La Tania, Méribel, Les Menuires, Val Thorens and St.Martin de Belleville. The round trip from Courchevel through to Val Thorens to the furthest point at Cime de Caron, 10,496ft., can be made in one day by competent skiers but it is a long one. Most competent skiers opt for the full pass but others prefer to choose good weather to go far afield and pay the day supplement on the lesser pass. Courchevel is the most easterly of the Trois Vallées resorts and its slopes face mainly north so under normal conditions it has good snow. Also the slopes above Courchevel 1300 are more wooded thus creating better visibility in bad weather. There are good possibilities for off-piste skiing including the recent extension at Aiguille de Fruit.

A total of 474 snow cannons on many of the runs. Several new, improved lift installations, opening up new ski areas and generally speeding up the flow of traffic. 10 cross-country circuits; 2.5km. Luge run from 1850 to 1550; an Olympic size artificial skating rink was opened in 1990; ice climbing tower, 40 metres high, many kms. of prepared walks; mountain parachute skiing; ski-jumping and floodlit skiing on Ste. Agathe (1,650 metres).

In a Few Words: The dedicated skier's ideal resort; suitable for all standards, pistes wide and well prepared; planning of lift system superb; snow reliable throughout season; good touring possibilities; expensive.

Après Ski: The four Courchevel villages together provide a wide selection of après ski life from the casual to the sophisticated and the food is always the most tempting French cuisine. A popular meeting place is the terrace at the Tremplin, which has a large informal restaurant and cellar with night club, cinema and bowling alley. Good gastronomic restaurants include Les Arches, Le Bateau Ivre, Le Bistrot du Praz, Le Chabichou, Le Paral and Le Yaca. There is an excellent cold buffet at the Soucoupe, on the slopes of La Loze, which is a popular lunchtime eating place; likewise La Bergerie, an old shepherd's hut in existence before Courchevel itself! This is particularly recommended as it has a very good atmosphere, excellent food, dinner and dancing in the evening as well, with free taxi service included. Another very popular lunch spot is the restaurant Altitude 21.

The night clubs include:- Les Caves, De Courchevel, La Bergerie, La Grange, L'Équipe and Le Refuge à Courchevel (1650). For more intimate atmosphere La Mangeoire (1850), a good restaurant with resident pianist. For an evening meal the Yeti at 1650 is much recommended, with various specialities including superb seafood. Le Bel Air (1650) with good food and superb terrace; the Bistrot Du Praz is also known for its excellent food. For specialist cheese dishes La Fromagerie (1850) is to be recommended. So is Le Petit Savoyard (1650) for its pizzeria. The hotels Carlina, Airelles, Caravelle, Bellecôte, Annapurna, Byblos des Neiges, New Solarium, Pralong 2000, Ducs de Savoie, Lana, Grandes-Alpes and Sherpas have indoor swimming pools. There is a large indoor skating rink where very entertaining ice hockey matches are held. There is a good range of shops; chic boutiques, sports shops; comprehensively stocked supermarkets. and the tourist office, 'La Croisette' provides almost everything else – banks, post office, 'salle des fêtes', information desk (English spoken), ski school desk and so on. There are kindergartens at 1650, 1850 and 1550.

Recommended Hotels:
Hotel Le Chamois: Conveniently placed for the Loze lift, completely renovated and providing bed and breakfast only. An excellent hotel with attractively designed reception rooms and bar, also a large sun terrace. Bedrooms have bath or shower and most are with balcony.

Hotel Le Dahu: Facing the Olympic ice Skating Rink, this is another older established hotel, renovated and in a central and sunny position. Attractive dining room with lounge and bar leading off, with sun terrace outside. The bedrooms are comfortably furnished, all with bath or shower and balcony.

Hotel Des Neiges: A 4-star hotel 10 minutes walk from centre. Beautifully furnished and decorated. All bedrooms with bath or shower, many with balcony, reception rooms comfortably equipped, pleasant bar with periodic entertainment, large sun terrace, with charcoal grill at lunchtime on sunny days. Jacuzzi and sauna. Good atmosphere and well run by the charming family Benoist. On the Bellecôte piste.

Hotel Les Ducs de Savoie: Situated in the Jardin Alpin and convenient for the slopes and the village, this 3 star hotel deserves a 4 star rating. Its 72 attractive bedrooms all have bath or shower, telephone, satellite TV, radio and those facing south are with balcony. Lovely restaurant and large sun terrace, lounge bar, indoor swimming pool, jacuzzi, sauna, Turkish bath, solarium, fitness room and games room including billiards. Staff at all levels courteous and helpful and provide a high standard of service.

Hotel La Potinière: A nicely designed hotel. An attractive dining room with beamed ceiling, a well furnished and comfortable sitting room on the first floor opening on to a balcony. All bedrooms pleasantly furnished, all with bath or shower. There is also a large 'brasserie' type bar. Central position.

Hotel Bellecôte: A luxuriously appointed hotel. Savoyarde decor throughout with much use of wood. Swimming pool, treatments; periodic evening entertainments in the bar. Superbly run by Toussaint family. On Bellecôte piste.

Hotel Annapurna: Courchevel has an amazing number of excellent 4 star hotels and this, reputed to be the most modern in the Alps, certainly lives up to its rating. Charming decor, all south-facing rooms for maximum sunshine. 9 suites. 2 restaurants, delightful bar and superb swimming pool, sauna, jacuzzi, with resident health specialists, run by Bernard Jacob; ski lifts and pistes immediately outside. Free bus service runs constantly to and from village centre.

MÉRIBEL

Height of Resort: 4,756 ft.
Height of Top Station: 9,681 ft.
Nearest International Airport: Geneva/ Chambéry, Lyon
Map Reference: 4D See page 238
Route by Car: See page 236-238
Resorts Facilities Charts: See page 218
Hotel Reference Charts: See page 230

The valley of Méribel has one resort with two main centres, Méribel (4,756ft.) and Méribel-Mottaret (5,576ft.) Méribel itself is a village of charm and character exceptional amongst French resorts, its low chalet-style buildings grouped in a woodland setting, on the lower slopes of the mountains rising above it. Its position in the centre of the Trois Vallées gives it access to the ski areas of the Courchevel valley on one side, and Les Menuires/ Val Thorens, which have rapidly developed, in the Vallée des Bellevilles on the other side. The skiing of Méribel itself is divided into two areas and includes 74 marked runs covering 108 km. and served by 57 lifts, 16 gondolaways, 16 chair-lifts, 18 drag-lifts and 7 baby-lifts; the latest being a 4 seater chair-lift alongside the Plattières Gondolaway in Méribel-Mottaret.

From Chaudanne one has the choice of 3 gondolaways and 2 chair-lifts travelling up the eastern and western sides of the valley, making it an ideal plateau for planning one's route for the day. Also a good rendezvous, lift passes can be purchased here and there is direct access to shops and restaurants.

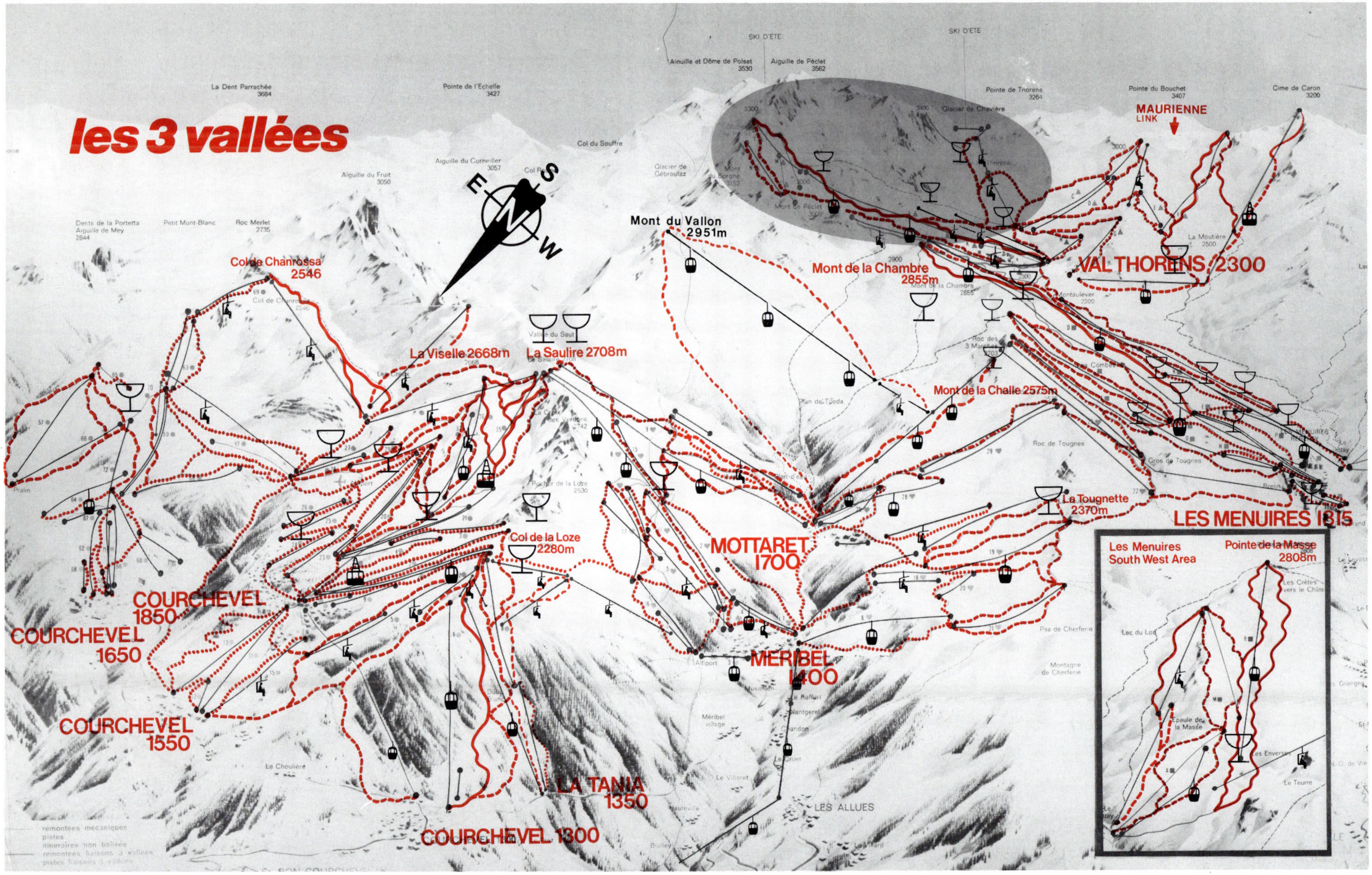

Mountain railways | Cableways | Gondolaways | Chair-lifts | Drag-lifts | ...... Easy runs | --------- Medium runs | ——— Difficult runs | Mountain restaurants

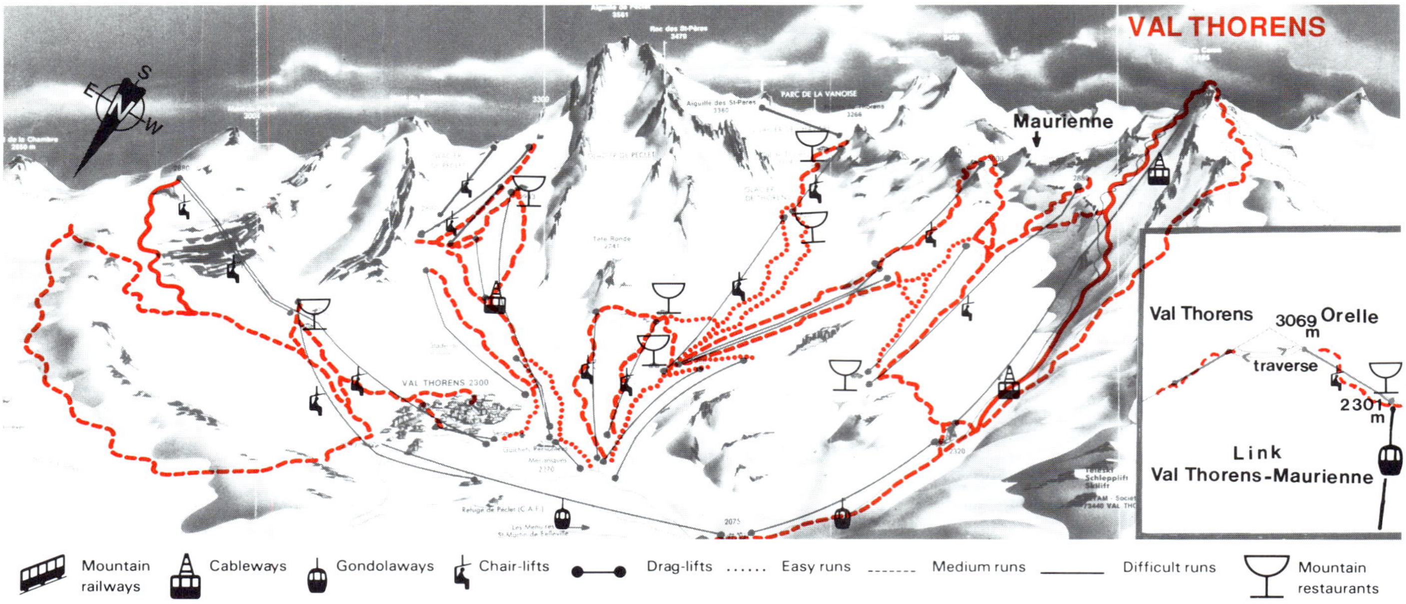

The Burgin-La Saulire lift network extends up the eastern side of the valley and La Saulire, 8,825ft. can be reached by fast gondolas from Méribel and Méribel-Mottaret. La Saulire forms the link with the Courchevel valley. There is one run from Saulire which connects with the Burgin pistes and, the Grande Rosière run is an interesting challenge to the experienced skier. Nearer to the mile long L'Adray chair-lift gives access to more medium grade runs on the north side of Burgin. A gondolaway leads from the north of the village to the airport, connecting with drag-lifts up to La Frasse, about 7,745ft. providing the entry point to easy and medium grade runs on west and north-west facing slopes enabling one to commute down to La Tania and Courchevel via La Loze Pass.

Méribel-Mottaret, best situated from the skiing point of view, is a satellite village built in the same Alpine style as its neighbour and has 22 chalet-apartment buildings, five hotels, commercial centres, restaurants, a club hotel, cinema and one night club, and is linked to Méribel by a series of lifts or by a frequent Navette bus service. Méribel-Mottaret has 10,427 beds, and the chalets in this area are serviced by a gondolaway or by a shuttle bus service. The Plattières three-stage gondolaway rises south-westwards from Méribel-Mottaret to Mont de la Challe, 8,445ft. Whilst the black run from the top to the second station can be tricky, depending on snow conditions, there is a red run which joins with the wide easy pistes leading down from the second station to Méribel-Mottaret.

The gondolaway up to Mont Vallon, 9,684ft., reached by skiing down from the second or top station of Plattières has opened up a new area. It provides access to two red runs either side of the gondolaway, to the south the Campagnol, which returns one to base and Plan Mains chair-lift up to the second station of Plattières. To the north the Combe du Vallon, a fairly taxing run back to Méribel-Mottaret.

A gondolaway rising south-westward from Méribel-Mottaret with surmounting drag lift, Table Verte, opens up more runs to the west. On the western (Les Menuires) side, further lifts connect it to the area below the Tougnètte ridge at Mont de la Challe, 8,445ft. A gondolaway from the outskirts of Méribel itself connects with surmounting lifts rising to the Tougnète, 8,015ft., a further link between Méribel and the Vallée des Belleville and the resorts of Les Menuires and Val Thorens. From the top of Roc de Fer is the start of the black run 'La Face' which will test the skills of the experienced skier. A chair-lift runs west with surmounting drag-lift to a point below Tougnète, 7,475ft., and further drag-lifts serve the runs in this area. There is a good selection of these, 6 to 8km. in length on north and north-east facing slopes. There is also 33km. of cross country skiing and guides are available to give instruction and to organise daily treks of the area. It is also possible to ski back to Les Allues, below Meribel, and surrounding chalets, via marked tracks through the trees known as the 'Itinèraire' route.

Spring skiing is also possible from Tougnète down to St. Martin de Belleville, from where a two stage chair-lift leads back to Méribel, via Cherferie. The Morel and Altiport lifts serve easy runs. The road and tunnel to Méribel-Mottaret bypassing Méribel has made a great improvement. 500 snow guns are in operation, in the Méribel valley.

Children: The E.S.F. have opened 'Les P'Tits Loups' kindergarten at Mottaret for children 3 years upwards; also at Rond Point des Pistes and Olympic Parc (hockey rink). They can ski or play in a protected area with two small drag-lifts and life size cartoon characters. Supervised meals optional.

In a Few Words: A delightful and attractive village with good skiing suitable for all standards, with easy access to the wider range of the Courchevel and Belleville valleys. Méribel-Mottaret smaller and compact; good for families, with kindergarten 'Les Pingouins' for 3-8 year olds. Méribel also has a kindergarten 'Le Club Saturnin' for 18 months – 3 year-olds. Day ski touring; reliable snow; highly recommended but expensive.

Après Ski: Less activity here than in some of the bigger French resorts, but plenty of bars and restaurants with local specialities. Night clubs include the discothèque Dick's Tea Bar, which is slightly out of the village, the Scotts in Méribel and Le Privilegge in Meribel Mottaret. There is an artificial Olympic ice rink and an indoor swimming pool, bowling, hang-gliding, para-gliding, snow shoe tours, fitness rooms with sauna and jacuzzi, squash, 2 cinemas, and some lovely marked mountain walks.

Next to the Olympic skating rink is 'Le Canadien', a 6 lane bowling alley with electronic scoring and below it is the L'Arti-chaud, a live music bar with billiards, open till 0200 hours.

Recommended Hotels:

Hotel Ardray Télébar: A superb chalet style hotel, on the slopes facing the Burgin drag-lift. Beautiful rustic style bedrooms pleasantly furnished, attractive Savoyard dining room, comfortable sitting room with open fire, large sun terrace, friendly atmosphere.

Hotel Grand Coeur: A good four star hotel, near the Tourist Office in the lower part of the village. Attractive dining room and lounge, bar. Bedrooms pleasant and well furnished, all with private bath, telephone and television. Sauna, jacuzzi and fitness room.

Hotel L'Orée du Bois: Situated at the 'Rond Point des Pistes' ski school meeting place. Tastefully furnished bedrooms all with bath or shower, attractively modern style dining room, cosy bar sitting room with open fire.

Hotel Tarentaise: Situated at the top end of Méribel-Mottaret with lovely views. A 3 star hotel with attractively furnished bedrooms all with bath, wc, fitted carpets, telephone, TV and radio alarm. The sitting room and dining room, tastefully decorated, open on to a large sun terrace. An attractive bar with open fireplace.

LES MENUIRES

Height of Resort: 6,068 ft.
Height of Top Station: 9,350 ft.
Nearest International Airport: Geneva
Map Reference 4D See page 238
Route by Car: Se page 236-238
Resorts Facilities Charts: See page 218
Hotel Reference Charts: See page 230

Les Menuires, together with its higher neighbour Val Thorens, was the last but one resort to be constructed to form the famous skiing area of the Trois Vallées. With the other valley resorts of Méribel, Courchevel, and more recently La Tania, all interlinked by lifts, it is claimed to be the largest skiing area in the world. In fact the valley in which Les Menuires lies is the longest in France and constitutes two-thirds of the whole Trois Vallées complex. Les Menuires is reached by road from Moutiers, 27km. distant by CD 515 A. The road rises steeply out of Moutiers and chains may be necessary. There are regular buses each way every day.

Les Menuires is one of the most modern of the purpose-built French skiing stations and its functional architecture of concrete high rise buildings provide good quality accommodation and one soon comes to appreciate the inestimable advantages for the skier of such a layout. In essence the main part of the station, 'La Croisette', is built in the form of a horseshoe, the open side of which faces south and contains the Tourist and ski pass offices, restaurant terraces, ski school and nursery slopes. It does not matter whether one is living within this central area or in one of the complexes on levels above or below, for every building is connected by lifts for both pedestrians and skiers; one can put on one's skis at one's door in the morning and ski back to it in the evening. Indeed in many cases one has the added refinement of taking the hotel lift from one's room, pressing a button marked 'piste' and arriving on the slopes.

The more recently developed 'Les Menuires-Les Bruyères' village, the second main shopping centre, approximately 1km. from 'La Croisette', has some 10,000 beds. Lower type buildings surround the square and here all services are catered for and its lift system connects with the main ski area. Less crowded than 'La Croisette' area.

Les Menuires skiing: The accompanying ski plan gives little idea of the vastness of the skiing area or the seemingly limitless number of inter-connecting lifts. It is impossible to describe the runs in detail, but basically the skiing can be divided into two main areas:

West of the resort: This is the La Masse area, and one skis down into the valley for the ultra-modern 12 seater gondolaway to the Masse shoulder, whence one can go higher either by the Masse II gondolaway, 9,350ft., or the Masse drag-lift, or by one of 6 chair-lifts in the area. All these slopes, varying from medium to difficult, except for one easy run down from the top of Masse I gondolaway, are north, north-east and east facing and can provide superb powder skiing. This area is best skied in the morning. A choice of four lifts returns one to the resort.

East of the resort: This, the larger side, includes 21 lifts, 3 of which start immediately from the 'horseshoe'. The longest are the 2-stage gondolaways Chambre I and II and Les Bruyères I and II to the summit, 9,350ft., from which one can either ski to Val Thorens, Méribel or back to Les Menuires. Another important link on this side is the Les Combes chair-lift connecting with the Les Allamands chair-lift to Roc des Trois Marches, an alternative route to Méribel and Courchevel. On this side of the mountain there is a vast ski area with many blue runs descending to Saint Martin de Belleville (see separate report). The runs back to Les Menuires of all grades are over predominantly west-facing slopes enjoying the full afternoon sun till 5.30 p.m. (February). This side is best skied early in the morning after a snowfall or from mid-day onwards. Later in the season it produces magnificent off-piste spring snow skiing everywhere.

Both sides include treeless runs of approximately 5-6 km. in length and 3,541ft. vertical drop. The ultra-modern Les Bruyères gondolaway I and II, each cabin with 12 seats, has increased the capacity from Reberty to Mont de la Chambre by 3,000 persons per hour. it also allows connections with Val Thorens and Méribel. Les Menuires has 300 snow cannons covering 60 hectares or 120km. of pistes from the sector of Mont de la Chambre over the Olympic Slalom Stadium, the quarters of La Croisette, Preyerand, Reberty to the bottom of La Masses. This equipment, fully automatic, ensures that snow is guaranteed regardless of weather conditions.

Lift Passes: The visitor to Les Menuires has the choice of taking the local ski pass covering 47 lifts and 120km. of pistes or paying for the full Trois Vallées pass covering 200 lifts and 600 km of marked runs. An alternative and probably the most sensible compromise for medium and even expert skiers is to take advantage of the offer of paying a daily supplement on the local pass to cover all the Trois Vallées skiing or a daily supplement for the Val Thorens skiing only. This allows one to choose the fine days for skiing further afield. As a guide to distances and time including travel uphill, the medium skier will take at least one hour to reach Val Thorens, 1 hour for Méribel and 2 hours for Courchevel. Double this to allow for the return journey and it will be seen that a trip over to Courchevel is a full day's excursion, even if only a modicum of the Courchevel runs are to be undertaken. The holder of a 6 day or more Trois Vallées pass is entitled to one day's skiing in each of regions of Val D'Isere/Tignes and La Plagne/Les Arcs, greatly improving opportunities for keen skier.

In a Few Words: A resort tailored entirely for skiers of all abilities. Lacks the atmosphere of the typical old Tyrolean resort but guarantees the maximum skiing per day. Virtually no queues. Fast uphill transport all interlinking. Runs facing all points of the compass, therefore maximum skiing in sunshine with limitless powder and spring snow off-piste possibilities. High enough to be sure of snow from December lst till May. Probably the most highly mechanised ski area in the world. Great scope for 'studio apartments', which are probably the most economical type of accommodation. Highly recommended for those requiring the maximum amount of skiing. But in the resort you will also find 12 hotels, 5 of them 3 and 2 star opened after 1989, of which the newest, 'L'Ours Blanc', 3 star, provides a high standard of food and accommodation.

Après Ski: The skiing is so magnificent that any après ski activities seem almost superfluous. However, the weekly programme of events, available from the Tourist Office, lists a busy schedule, including organised sorties on snow shoes by day and evening cheese-fondue parties in altitude restaurants with night skiing down by torch light and 'snow-cat' excursions. There are two swimming pools, two fitness clubs, skating rink, microlight flights and hang-gliding. There are 2 cinemas, 2 discos and many good restaurants restaurants such as La Ruade (atmosphere), and La Marmite de Géant (specialities), attractive bars and pancake counters, Du Lou Bar is popular and especially worth a visit.

Recommended Hotels:
Hotel Les Christelles: A small 2-star hotel run by young Greeks. Modern bedrooms all with bath/wc. and balconies. Informal dining room and bar. Beautiful sunny position just below the shopping area and right at the foot of a beginner's slope and lift. Connected to the main complex by non-stop cage style lifts running from morning till midnight; anyone can step on free of charge until 6 p.m. . . . fun!

Hotel L'Oisans: A small hotel, neat and compact, with attractive American bar, Le chouka. Central position right in the shopping arcade and opposite one of the resort's most popular restaurants, Auberge de Lanau, under the same ownership.

Hotel Skilt: Privately owned 3-star hotel, one of the first built in Les Menuires. In the centre of the complex and a choice of an Italian or a French restaurant for its residents. Pleasant public rooms and bar, with popular sunny terrace as hub of activity. Most bedrooms have private bath and balcony.

Hotel L'Ours Blanc: A chalet style 3 star hotel opened in December 1990 and standing on the edge of the ski runs. 50 bedrooms and suites all with balcony, bathroom, wc, TV and telephone. Gourmet restaurant with lovely views, lounge with open fire, bar, library, conference room, gym, Turkish Bath and solarium. South facing sun terrace, private parking. Owned and run by M, & Mme. Pascal Casali. Mme. Casali is English.

VAL THORENS

Height of Resort: 7,544 ft.
Height of Top Station: 10,496 ft.
Nearest International Airport: Geneva
Map Reference: 4D **See page 238**
Route by Car: **See page 236-238**
Resorts Facilities Charts: **See page 218**
Hotel Reference Charts: **See page 230**

Situated at 7,544ft. Val Thorens is the highest ski resort in Europe. It is in the same valley, Belleville, as Les Menuires and 8km. further on and 1,476ft. higher up an easy gradient and well engineered roads but snow chains are sometimes necessary. Moutiers is 37km. away at the bottom of the valley and Geneva 159km. Val Thorens, with 3 skiable glaciers above it, caters for skiing during July and August; in winter lifts rise to 10,496ft. allowing 4,506 vertical feet of downhill skiing, whilst in summer lifts reach up to 10,830ft. During the winter season cars must be parked in one of several car parks when not loading and unloading.

Although a modern purpose-built ski station, it was, and continues to be, tastefully developed and at present consists of 15 hotels and 50 apartment buildings providing some 21,500 beds. Its 120km. of marked pistes are served by 1 cableway, 1 funitel, 3 gondolaways, 17 chair-lifts and 9 drag-lifts in winter, giving a capacity of 51,970 persons per hour. In summer a further six lifts come into operation. All lifts are sited to be interconnecting. The uphill transportation has been improved by the installation of the Funitel de Péclet, and enlarged gondola type cabins carrying some 30 persons, specifically designed to operate safely in wind conditions of up to 100km. per hour. This runs from the resort to the summer skiing area. Excellent snow can be relied upon throughout a very long season and the runs are suitable for all standards. Those to the south and west are particularly suitable for beginners. Especially recommended are the runs from Cime de Caron cableway with magnificent views from the top and long, challenging runs back down.

The La Maurienne valley provides further extensive skiing. At present from a height of 9,843ft. one can descend to 7,546ft., known as the Plan Bouchet area, where one finds an Alpine refuge chalet with a large self-service restaurant and overnight dormitory accommodation. One returns to the top by the Rosaël 4 seater detachable chair-lift. Plan Bouchet area can now be reached from the bottom of the Maurienne Valley by a 12 person capacity gondolaway, and a further chair-lift is planned for 1997. The bottom station is situated 6 km from the Fréjus Tunnel (French side) on Highway 6. This beautiful south-west facing valley offers extensive off-piste skiing for intermediates to expert skiers.

The important connecting link with the other 'Three Valley' stations is served by two chair-lifts; Plein Sud and 3 Vallées 1, which connect with two further chair-lifts, 3 Vallées 2 and Bouquetin. From these top stations one can either ski to Méribel via Plan Mains chair-lift, or alterntively ski down to Les Menuires area where there are 5 more access points to Meribel. From this summit the runs back to Val Thorens vary between difficult and medium.

Ski passes are available for just Val Thorens, Vallée des Belleville or the whole of Trois Vallées.There are frequent buses, depending on road conditions, between Val Thorens and Les Menuires. For families with 3 or more children the third and subsequent children receive free passes providing 2 adult and 2 child passes purchased. All the mountain restaurants serve a good selection of food and drink. Lunch at the top of Cime de Caron should be taken early or late to avoid a long queue.

Children: A unique feature of Val Thorens is the Village Marielle Goitschel, a ski school of exceptional quality for children. A team of instructors, most speak English, tailor tuition to the requirements of the children. In addition, the École du Ski Français (E.S.F.) runs two Miniclubs: one is situated at the top end of the resort in the 'Roc de Péclet' block and the other at the bottom end and called Village du Soleil. The E.S.I. 'Ski Cool' also has an excellent teaching programme for adults and children. Évoluski (short skis) for beginners from the age of 14-77 years. There are nurseries for children from 3 months upwards and ski training for the 3 year olds upwards. The existence of these schools must be a major factor to influence the choice of this holiday resort for those with very young children. There are two further ski schools, Prosneige and Ski, Surf, Nature.

In a Few Words: Highest resort in Europe with access to the whole 3 valley region. Compact, efficiently run and friendly. Guaranteed good snow (100 snow cannons just in case). Great scope for deep off-piste powder skiing. Excellent piste maintenance and well run lift system continually being upgraded. New avalanche protection systems installed. Lower slopes particularly good for beginners, others for all standards up to expert. Long hours of sunshine. Excellent 'studio apartment' facilities. Particularly recommended for early or late season holidays and for family holidays where children are keen skiers.

Après Ski: Still rather unsophisticated, but between the 15 hotels you can find a sauna, a solarium, a heated swimming pool, a tea room, and some impromptu and informal dancing. There are also 51 restaurants (plus 10 on the mountain) including a raclette specialist, several bars and three discos. The restaurants are particularly accommodating but if you are a family or group staying in self-catering apartments it is wise to book tables in good time. There are two good take-aways and four crêperies. The restaurant du Lou and Le Scapin are particularly recommended for the best pizzas outside Italy; friendly and efficient service at lunch and in the evenings.

The Centre Sportif caters for indoor tennis (3 courts), swimming, squash, climbing wall, weight lifting, 3 saunas and simulated golf on many of the world's famous courses. La Pause Bar and La Descente are fun and good value; Le Galoubet has a piano bar. Other diversions include snowmobiles, para-gliding and a cinema. Various cocktail parties are given at different centres throughout the season. Ski films are shown and the Novotel organises various dress shows and other forms of entertainment. All visitors should call at the Tourist Office and collect a Val Thorens 'passport' which contains a wealth of information.

Recommended Hotels
Hotel Fitzroy: A centrally situated 4 star modern hotel equipped to the highest international standards. An excellent restaurant, shopping facilities and swimmng pool, sauna and fitness centre are all available at this establishment.

Hotel La Marmotte: A hotel with modern bedrooms and extra 'adjustable' bunk accommodation for children; special cheap rates accordingly. Modern decor throughout with open plan bar, dining room and small sitting area. All bedrooms have private bath, wc., telephone and balcony. Well places in centre of village and directly skiable to and from the slopes.

Hotel Val Clavière: The oldest hotel in Val Thorens, bought by an experienced hotelier who has brought it back to its 3-star rating. All bedrooms have bath, wc., balconies and telephones. Large heated garage and large sun terrace. Open log fire in sitting room. Solarium. Two-level dining room. Dancing twice weekly in bar/lounge. Lift to basement leads straight on to ski slopes and ski lift.

Hotel Val Thorens: A first class modern Mountain-style hotel in a central position alongside the pistes. 81 comfortable, spacious and attractive bedrooms all with bath, direct dial telephone, cable TV, radio and balcony. Impressive 'forum' with lounge area, piano-bar and open fireplace. 3 restaurants, excellent French cuisine, buffet breakfast, large sun terrace. Fitness club, sports shop, boutique and bank.

SAINT MARTIN DE BELLEVILLE: 4,593 ft. For those requiring a more peaceful location than the larger resorts in the Trois Vallée the small resort of St. Martin could be a good alternative. It is the municipal centre of the Belleville Valley in which the resorts of Les Menuires and Val Thorens are situated. It is a typical Savoy village with a 17th century church, town hall, 3 hotels, apartments, shops, bars and restaurants and lies 7 km by road below Les Menuires.

From the skiing point of view there is no disadvantage in staying in St. Martin as it forms part of the huge Trois Vallées network and is included on the lift pass. From the village surmounting chair-lifts St. Martin 1 & 2, the latter being a new 4-seater, rise to Pas de Cherferie, 6,984 ft. and from this point runs lead directly to the Méribel and Mottaret ski area. Alternatively one can ski down, on easy or intermediate runs, to the Les Teppes drag-lift which rises to Mont de la Challe, 8,441 ft., and from this top station there is a long easy run into Les Menuires. Another option is to use a series of lifts on the crest working one's way across to other areas of the Trois Vallées. The runs back into St. Martin are easy and intermediate and 34 snow cannons cover the last 3km into the village.

LA PLAGNE

Height of Resort: 5,904 ft.
Height of Top Station: 10,663 ft.
Nearest International Airport: Geneva
Map Reference: 4D See page 238
Route by Car: See page 236-238
Resort Facilities Charts: See page 217
Hotel Reference Charts: See page 230

La Plagne is made up of six high altitude modern stations and four other villages at lower altitude, combining to produce a large ski circuit with over 210km. of marked runs, many nordic skiing trails and excellent opportunities for off-piste skiing. A big resort with over 45,000 beds, well developed commercial centres and good inter-station transport links. There are 113 lifts carrying 114,000 persons per hour. It is situated 92 miles from Geneva, a journey which normally takes about 3 hours, the last 15 miles being on a winding but wide approach road from Aime. It is also easily reached by train from Chambery, Lyon or Paris.

While the 6 main stations making up the resort are all self-sufficient and separate, they do fall into two main groups based on Plagne Centre and Plagne Bellecôte. Each satellite has its own distinctive atmosphere. Plagne 1800, 5,905ft., is located just below Plagne Centre, 6,560ft., the largest of the stations, which is itself closely linked with Plagne Villages, 6,724ft., by télébus and with Aime La Plagne, 6,789ft., by télémetro. Aime La Plagne, Plagne Bellecôte and Plagne Centre feature very modern architecture whereas the majority of the other high altitude centres have kept to the village/ chalet style.

A navette bus service links Plagne Centre with Plagne Bellecôte, 6,350ft., which is about 2 miles by road. Belle Plagne, 6,693ft., is very close to Plagne Bellecôte and is linked by gondolaway, which like the télémetro and télébus run late into the night, but are only covered by the ski-pass until 5 pm. There is extensive parking in most areas.

The four lower altitude centres are:- Les Coches, 4,757ft., Montchavin, 4,000ft., Plagne Montalbert, 4,429ft., and Champagny en Vanoise, 4,100ft.

The Skiing: The various sectors link very well and can generally be skied in both directions, allowing for much variety. The piste map issued by the Tourist Office breaks down the area into 7 sectors, but these can be reduced to the following main areas for description purposes. The skiing is particularly suitable for families; so too are resort facilities. Some of the red runs would appear to be of lower grade and there are a few testing black runs, but the off-piste possibilities are enormous. La Plagne area is a large open bowl, housing many mini-bowls, flanked by low level skiing through the trees. The runs are particularly well signposted.

Belle Plagne, Plagne Bellecôte and Glacier: Starting from Plagne Bellecôte the gondolaway, one of the longest in Europe, leads past Belle Plagne to Roche de Mio, 8,860ft., where one can take a selection of red or blue runs to the Montchavin sector, Champagny, or return to Plagne Bellecôte or Belle Plagne via the Tunnel des Inversens or Les Bourtes, which requires using a short drag-lift. Alternatively one can continue on the gondolaway from Roche de Mio to the Glacier, 9,840ft., where 4 lifts serve the summer skiing area but is closed in the winter.

It is possible, with a guide, to ski off-piste from the Bellecôte Glacier via Les Bauches to Montchavin. Keeping to the pistes a number of black and red runs lead from the Traversée chair-lift to the Chalet de Bellecôte chair-lift or straight to Col de la Chiaupe, from where one should take the gondolaway up top Roche de Mio to return. The skiing close to Belle Plagne and Plagne Bellecôte is generally easy with the exception of Les Colosses, a red run through the trees close to Bellecôte. There are a number of mountain restaurants in the sector. Skiing to Les Bauches leads one to a popular sun-trap restaurant and on the route for those skiing over to Les Arcs for

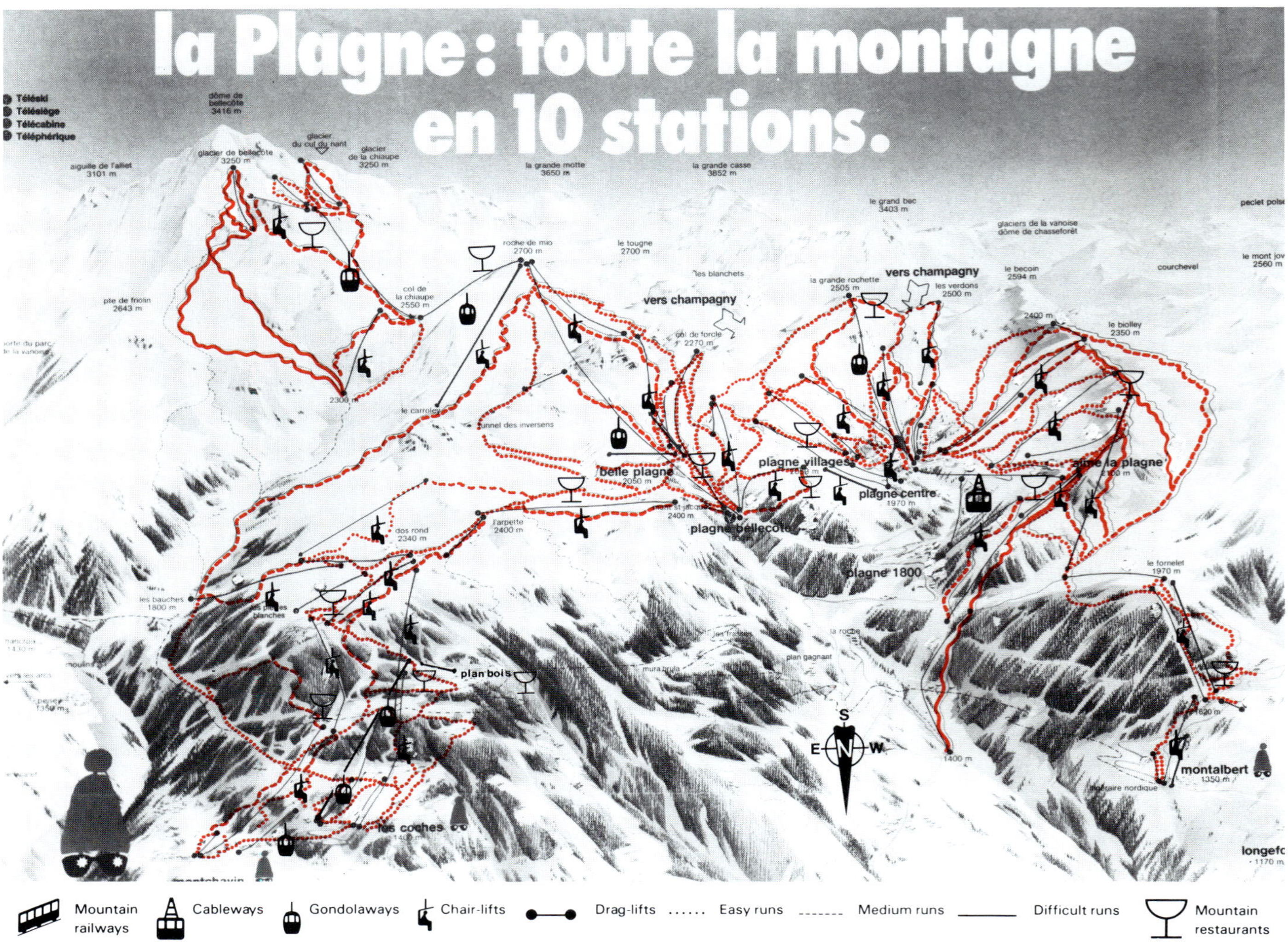

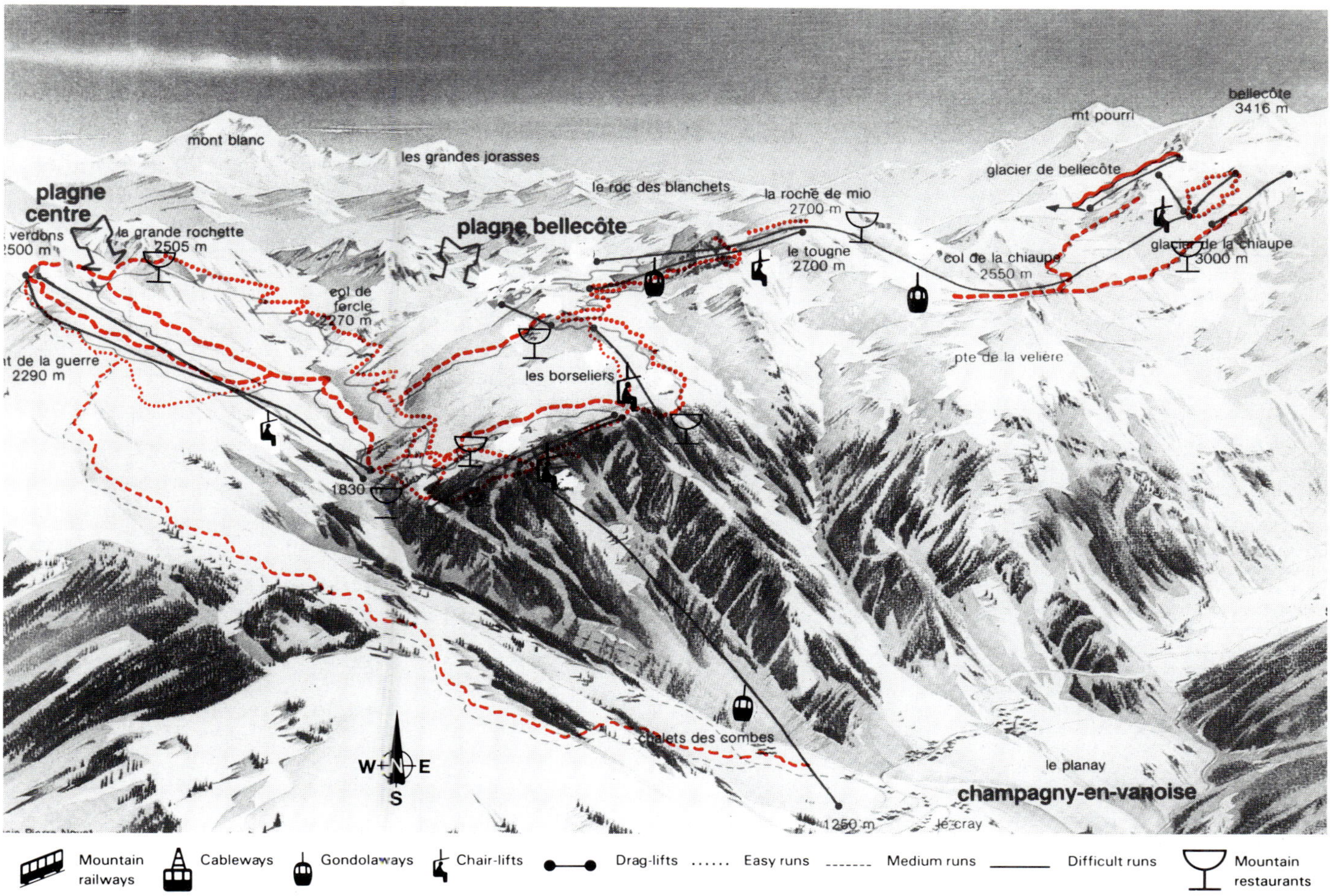

the day. Plagne Bellecôte is also the site for freestyle skiing competitions.

Montchavin & Les Coches: These two stations, with their own well developed lift systems, are linked to Belle Plagne via the Crozats chair-lift or La Salla drag-lifts. They can also be reached from Plagne Bellecôte via the Arpette chair-lift or directly from Roche de Mio. Much of the skiing is wooded with a choice of blue or red runs leading to the same point, which is good for groups of mixed abilities. Particularly attractive is the red run, Pierres Blanches, leading from the popular restaurant of the same name to Le Sauget, another restaurant with a good reputation. Improvements in the Montchavin area include the Lac Noir gondolaway, 12 to a cabin, and moving 2,200 persons per hour; a 6 person chair-lift leading to Pierres Blanches restaurant. A 4 seater Dos Rond chair-lift has replaced the drag-lift.

Plagne Centre, Biolley & Plagne Montalbert: The largest sector, covering also Plagne Villages, Aime La Plagne and Plagne 1800, provides some testing runs as well as a large number of easier, pleasant runs mostly above the treeline. From Plagne Centre, always bustling with activity, uphill transportation fans out in a number of directions. A 4 seater chair-lift leads from near Le France to above Plagne Villages where the skiing is mostly intermediate, and also links directly with Plagne Bellecôte.

The long gondolaway from Plagne Centre (sometimes queues) takes one to La Grande Rochette, 8,220ft., from where a variety of runs lead to Plagne Bellecôte, Champagny en Vanoise or back to base via the Carina or Vega red runs. The Champagny sector is probably easier, reached by using the 'Du'z' drag-lift followed by the Verdons 4 seater chair-lift. The return is via Mercedes, another red run which is quite steep at the top.

Finally, heading south from Plagne Centre, the Bécoin 4 seater chair-lift provides access to another group of runs including Grande Pente and Les Etroits, which have fantastic views across the entire valleys. From Aime La Plagne, there is a variety of red and blue runs to choose from and immediate access to the mainly tree lined runs down to Plagne Montalbert, 4,430ft. Morbleu is a testing black and the long black Emile Allais runs to below Plagne 1800. There is a selection of mountain restaurants.

The Farandole is a tough red running under the chair-lift below 1800 and Les Grenouilles, marked blue but steep at the top. Towards Plagne Montalbert there are a number of blue runs through the trees.

Champagny en Vanoise: This links directly with Belle Plagne and Plagne Centre. From Roche de Mio the Carella run leads to Le Levasset and another long run ends at the foot of the Verdons Sud chair-lift. The Buvette les Borseliers just around the corner is very popular and the resort of Courchevel can be seen across the valley. From here one can return to Belle Plagne by one of two 6-seater chair-lifts or sample a few of the blue and red runs around La Rossa where there is a very popular restaurant, at the top of the Champagny gondolaway and the start of Les Bois run down to the village of Champagny en Vanoise. Skiing this sector in the opposite direction, access from Plagne Centre is from La Grande Rochette gondolaway or the Verdons Nord chair-lift, then a choice of red runs, Kamikaze or Hara-Kiri or blues, Bozelet, down to Les Borseliers. Return to Belle Plagne is by the Quillis drag-lifts. Alternatively, in good conditions, one can take the 10km. Mont De La Guerre red run right down to the village of Champagny en Vanoise.

Children: There are excellent facilities for children with kindergartens/nursery clubs at each of the 10 centres for children from 2 to 6 years. Each 'Club Garderie' as they are known is well run with indoor and outdoor recreation facilities including skiing. Children can be left for a half day, full day or for a series of 6 days, lunch provided. For 8-14 year olds provisions include discovering the mountain in snow shoes, building igloos, and a torchlit descent at Montchavin/Les Coches. Montchavin and Les Coches accept children from 9 months and Belle-Plagne and Plagne Montalbert from 18 months.

Ski Passes: The Plagne weekly ski-pass allows once a week access to the skiing at Tignes, Val d'Isère, Les Arcs and Les Trois Vallées. 25% discounts are given for the over 60's and under 16 years. Children under 7 are free if their accompanying adult purchases a pass. Free lift passes also for persons over 72 years. Passes can be ordered in advance.

In a Few Words: An excellent resort for skiers up to advanced intermediate standard, with guaranteed snow conditions and an excellent lift system; very much a family-orientated resort, much of the accommodation being self-catering; après ski on the quiet side; excellent kindergartens. There are ski schools at each village (ESF) plus two other independent ones in Plagne Centre and Belle Plagne with a total of 550 instructors.

Après Ski: Each station provides various forms of entertainment. To mention a few:

Plagne Centre: A lively atmosphere and extensive shopping facilities. Restaurants abound, of which Le Chaudron must be recommended. Also Le Refuge which has been in the same family for 30 years and provides traditional local dishes at reasonable prices. Domino's and Rolando's Pizzerias are good value. There is no shortage of music and discos with Le Must being very popular, along with King Café.

Plagne Bellecôte: Here a number of bars and restaurants are sited together, with the La Saboia, and Colosses Loisirs all well worth a visit. There is a heated outdoor swimming pool, sauna, natural skating, and dancing at Le Jet night club.

Belle Plagne: A good deal of activity takes place at the Hotel Eldorador and attracts late night revellers. For eating out the Matafan and Chez Moustache are recommended, also Mat's pub and Boderock night club. Sports centre with sauna and bowling.

Plagne Villages: Two good restaurants are the Le Grizzli and L'Oustal.

Plagne 1800: Here La Bartavelle is one of the popular eating spots along with Loup Blanc. The main bar is the Café Couleur.

Aime La Plagne: The highest station has many shops and activities under one roof, and Soupe aux Schuss and L'Arlequin are recommended. Also the Gordon's night club.

Plagne Soleil: A popular eating spot is the small French restaurant Edelweiss whilst the Lincoln Pub is one of the liveliest bars in the area.

Plagne Centre, Bellecôte and Aime all have cinemas. It is also possible to para-glide and hang-glide in the La Plagne area and to hire skidoos (snow motor bicycles). The Bob Raft, the Olympic bobsleigh run, is available in the valley just below 1800, until the run melts in early spring. All main centres have discos, fitness training facitilities, sauna, jacuzzi etc.

Recommended Hotels:

Hotel Christina (Plagne Centre): A pleasant 3 star hotel near the Biollet lifts. 100 beds, most rooms with bath. Soirée dansante with orchestra every Wednesday, sun terrace overlooking ski slopes. American bar, 'Edelweiss Grill' restaurant with cooking over open fires.

Hotel Eldorador (Belle Plagne): A modern chalet style hotel situated at the foot of the slopes. 184 bedrooms, all doubles with bath, telephone, radio and balcony. Large restaurant with terrace, TV room, reading room, games room and piano bar. Free kindergarten for children from 4 years. Friendly atmosphere.

Hotel Eldorador (Belle Plagne): A modern chalet style hotel situated at the foot of the slopes. 184 bedrooms, all doubles with bath, telephone, radio and balcony. Large restaurant with terrace, TV room, reading room, games room and piano bar. Free kindergarten for children from 4 years. Friendly atmosphere.

Hotel Le France (Plagne Centre): Particularly recommended for its very friendly and helpful staff and excellent cooking, this 3 star hotel is close to the centre and can be reached through covered galleries. 160 beds, all rooms with private bath and balcony, of varying sizes. Reliable telephone room, open round the clock. Large sun terrace, spacious restaurant, pleasant lounge, attractive bar, separate TV, reading and lecture rooms. Dancing and cabaret once a week.

Self-catering Accommodation: The majority of accommodation is in self catering apartments varying in size and quality.

LES ARCS

Height of Resort: 5,249 ft. - 6,560 ft.
Height of Top Station: 10,583 ft.
Nearest International Airport: Geneva/Lyon
Map Reference: 4D See page 238
Route by Car: See page 236-238
Resorts Facilities Charts: See page 217
Hotel Reference Charts: See page 230

First launched in 1969/70, Arc Pierre Blanche 1600 is a small village built in the centre of the 37,050 acre Les Arcs skiing area, in the Savoie region of the French Alps and can be reached by a $1^1/_2$ hour journey from Chambéry or a $3^1/_2$ hour drive from Geneva or 2.5 hours from Lyon airports or an 8 mile journey from the main railway at Bourg St. Maurice, which is also connected to Les Arcs by a funiculaire monorail taking 5 minutes. It is the first of a group of villages which now make up the ski centre broadly referred to as Les Arcs. The Golf, Latitudes and Mercure Gran Paradiso Hotels and 15 apartment blocks at Arc Chantel 1800 form the nucleus of the second village and Arc 2000, to the south, is developing rapidly in both size and stature. A direct cableway linking these two latter centres was opened in 1992.

An amazing network of interlinking lifts and runs open up an enormous range of skiing. It is a masterpiece of planning, with many excellent features. Cars are excluded from the village, lifts have sufficient capacity to avoid the necessity of queueing, hotels provide bed and breakfast, demi or full pension, with meal vouchers valid in mountain restaurants. The Les Arcs radio station, on 93.4 FM, gives daily information in French and English on weather, state of runs and other general activities.

Arc Pierre Blanche has been designed to harmonise with its beautiful mountain background. Its unusual buildings are constructed of warm materials, largely wood, set against the rock face, their terraces and balconies forming a giant suntrap. The size of the village and height of the buildings, however, ensure that the atmosphere remains friendly and informal. It is compact and provides all facilities needed. Situated on a plateau on the Massif de la Vanoise, it is surrounded by glacier-topped mountains and good snow conditions are ensured from December to May on the mainly north, north-west or north-east facing slopes. 29 chair-lifts, 45 drag-lifts and two cableways cover the area, with 150km. of marked pistes to choose from, all well interlinked; in addition to deep snow skiing, glacier and 10km. of marked langlauf trails.

Crossing the nursery slopes (which are served by 4 small drag-lifts and the children's ski area) the La Cachette chair-lift rises to a height of 7,052ft., where there is a choice of average or difficult runs to the village. Another easy run from this point veers further west down to Arpette and the delightful round l'Arpette restaurant with its surrounding sun terraces. A long chair-lift goes from here to de Clocheret, 7,774ft. leading to various medium runs to the village or, alternatively take the Clocheret chair-lift to Signal Des Tetes where one connects with the Comborciéres chair-lift in Arc 2000 or the Arpette chair-lift rising to a ridge of 7,905 ft. from which there are a number of varied runs, some fast, using the Piste du Fond-Blanc or de Clair-Blanc.

The run towards Aiguille Grive leads to another restaurant, just above the Arc Chantel (1800) plateau. The double drag-lift de la Vagère serves the intermediate run de Froide Fontaine, or the easy Piste des Grands Mélèzes and the difficult Piste de la Vagère.

The gentle traverse across the ridge from the top of the Arpette chair-lift leads to the other side of the mountain and the Vallée de l'Arc, an area of marvellous skiing country encompassing runs of every standard. A 918ft. ascent on the double drag-lift du Plan Vert to 8,528 ft. offers the choice of long easy runs through deep snow or on the piste through a sheltered valley.

Across the valley, the Grand Col drag-lifts rise to a height of 9,840ft. Whilst a cableway reaches the summit of the Aiguille Rouge, 10,583 ft. and from this point there is a challenging and delightful run down to the village of Villaroger in the Isère Valley, 9,843ft. below. Villaroger can also be reached by the Rhona 2 drag-lift just below Pré St. Esprit.

To take one back to the village, the Bois de l'Ours chair-lift leads up to the ridge again and provides some marvellous views across the valley on the way. The journey can be broken between the two lifts and this offers the option of skiing down to the bottom again, or turning left to join the piste de Malgovert, skiing through the dark pine woods down to Arc Pierre Blanche (1600). From the top of the Deux Têtes drag-lift several runs are possible; left to Arpette via the piste du Clocheret, or right and then directly to the village via the piste de la Cachette.

Further runs particularly attractive for beginners are to be found in the area towards Arc Chantel (1800), which has also been considerably extended during the past few years. Buses run every half an hour between Arc Chantel and Arc Pierre Blanche. Les Arcs ski area is also linked with the valley of Peisey-Nancroix, which has several average to challenging runs. These are cut out amongst the trees making it a particularly attractive area with the advantage of better than average visibility in bad weather.

In Arc 2000 the speed skiing slope is open to visiting skiers, so you can set your own speed record!

In a Few Words: Very well planned lift system and network of runs; almost no queueing. Mainly north facing slopes with good snow conditions; glacier skiing; langlauf; hang-gliding; 2 skating rinks; runs and lifts immediately outside hotels; wide selection of tours; 4 kindergartens; apartments and studios to rent. Ski évolutif method of instruction available, good for beginners who want to learn quickly. Expert skiers can take advantage of the superb variety of runs and accessability of farther reaching skiing throughout the geographical area or try monoskiing and surfing, which is taught by the excellent ski school. The Les Arcs 6 day ski pass also allows one day a week access to the ski areas of Trois Vallées, Tignes, Val D'Isère and La Plagne. The Carte Blanche card allows visitors to participate in various activities.

Après Ski: Lots of activity and a lively atmosphere. At Arc 1800 there are five discos, two at 1600 and one at 2000, five cinemas and a sports club with table tennis, archery, shooting and various indoor games.
The food is excellent at Les Trois Arcs Hotel and theCachette is also recommended. La Pizza is small and crowded but a good bet. Good French specialities are available at L'Arcelle.

The 'First' discothèque in 1600 runs till the early hours of the morning. The Éspace Mont Blanc also holds art exhibitions. Arc 1800 has now become a very active centre. There are four night clubs, the Rock Hill Club, the Fairway, The Carre Blanc and live music every evening in the lounge of the Hotel du Golf, also in Hotel Latitudes. There are several pizzerias and La Galette serves traditional dishes such as fondue and raclette in a friendly atmosphere. Good eating spots too are the Laurus restaurant and the Triangle Noir. Lively bars to end the evening include the 'J.O.' and the Thuria.

At the 'Petit Zinc' (Hotel du Golf) one can enjoy excellent gourmet dishes in sophisticated and calm surroundings as one can in the Gran Paradiso Restaurant. Another pleasant bar/restaurant is L'Equipe. The Santaline, a small friendly restaurant is also to be recommended whilst the Casa Mia serves us delicious Italian specialities

Recommended Hotels:
All are operated by the same company and are very similar throughout. Very bright and sunny rooms with their own radios and telephones, many with individual sun terraces. All have meal vouchers valid for exchange at mountain restaurants. In addition to the hotels there are many apartment blocks with self-contained flats at both Arc Pierre Blanche and Arc Chantel.

Arc Pierre Blanche 1600 Cachette: Half pension, 135 doubles, some twin, some with double beds. Balconies and private bath/wc. Two sitting rooms, two bars. Welcoming, pleasant restaurants.

Charmettes: In same building as Trois Arcs, though only one star. Bed and breakfast. 24 rooms, the smaller ones facing north-west, some with bunk beds but well designed with good use of space. Every two rooms have their own private shower and wc.

Pierre Blanche: Same building as Cachette but all bedrooms with bath. Next to these two hotels is a very large sun terrace with deck chairs and a good view of ski lifts and beginners' slopes. Very nice for sun bathing, meeting friends, having tea. Underneath the same building is the discothèque 'Aquarius'.

Trois Arcs: Full or half pension. About 100 yards from the main square so probably the quietest. 48 doubles all private bath/wc and TV. All south facing rooms have good sun balconies, those with a distant view of Mont Blanc are without. One sitting room and two bars, one with open fireplace. Dining room and a snack restaurant, bright and comfortable, all on first floor. Several bedrooms can have extra beds and there are some 'family' suites.

Arc Chantel 1800 Golf Hotel: A 3-star hotel opened in 1975 with panoramic view of Mont Blanc and the Bellecôte range. All rooms with bath, wc, and balconies. Two restaurants, two bars, one with open fireplace and live music. Night club, The Fairway. Sauna and beauty salon. Full or half pension.

TIGNES

Height of Resort: 6,825 ft.
Height of Top Station: 11,480 ft.
Nearest International Airport: Geneva
Map Reference: 5D See page 238
Route by Car: See page 236-238
Resorts Facilities Charts: See page 218
Hotel Reference Charts: See page 230

For serious skiers, Tignes is hard to beat. Not picturesque, though not ugly, this modern resort offers skiing for 365 days a year. It is set in a vast snow bowl, surrounded by mountains and borders the Vanoises National Park. Tignes has 5 villages in all. The main Tignes Le Lac and Le Lavachet are situated to one side of the lake with Val Claret 2km. beyond. Lac, Lavachet and Val Claret are well connected by free buses producing a single resort atmosphere. Les Boisses and Les Brevières lie further down the valley. Tignes marries extensive first class skiing with convenience. If possible intermediate skiers and below should avoid staying in Lavachet because only challenging runs lead back to this village. For the less experienced Val Claret is a good area. Nowhere is far from the lift system so queueing is minimal except the connection from Val Claret

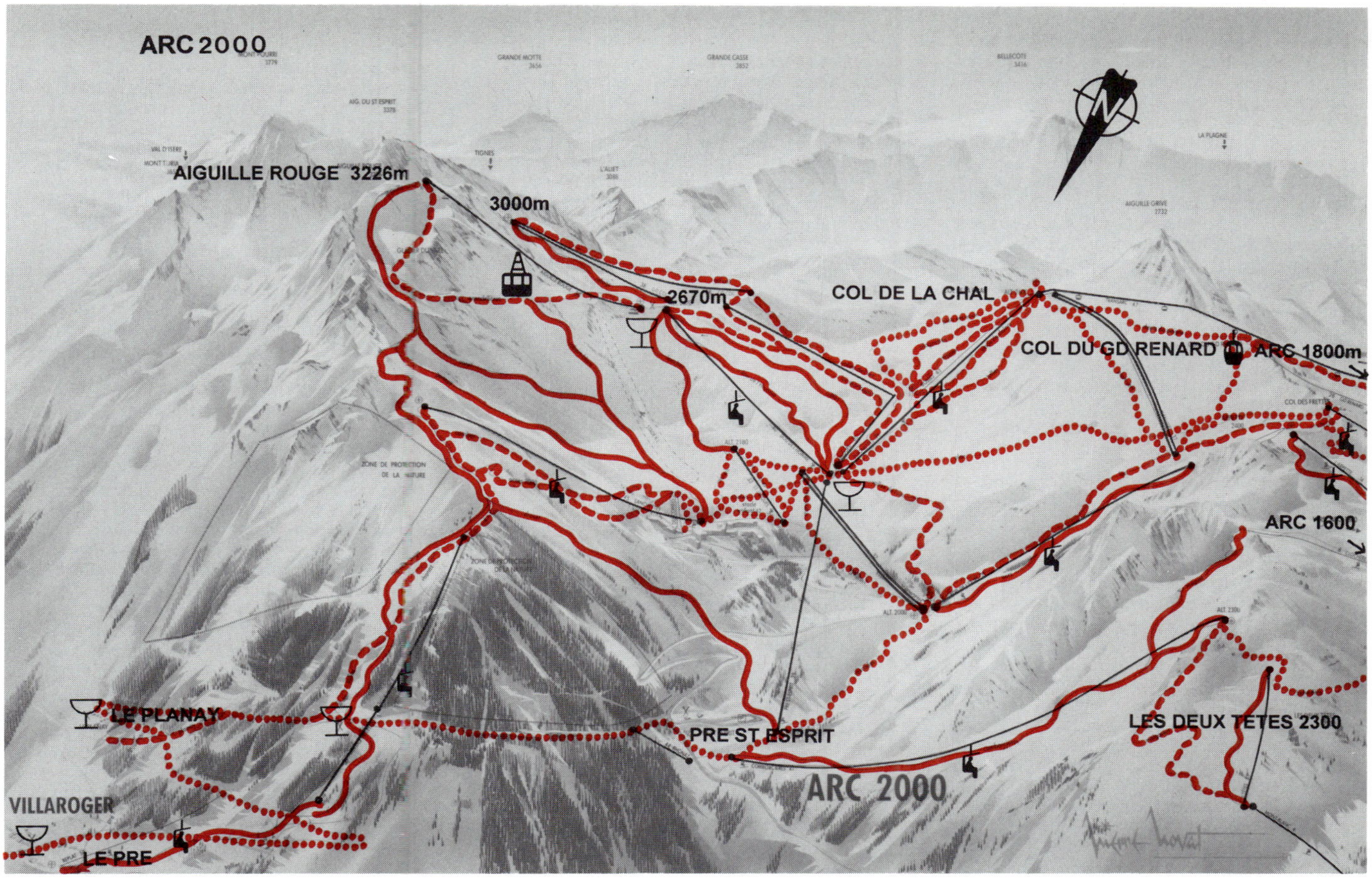

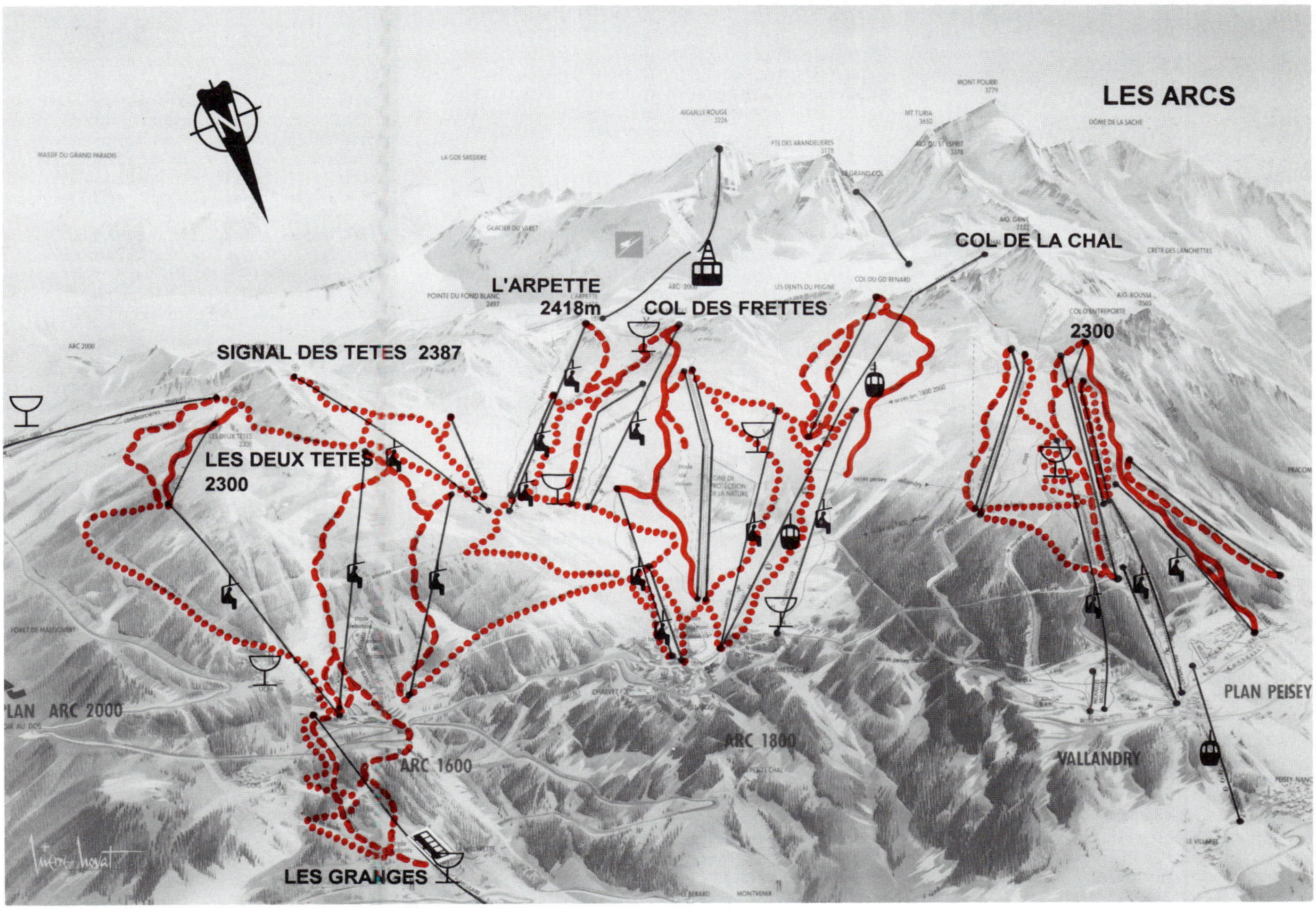

Mountain railways · Cableways · Gondolaways · Chair-lifts · Drag-lifts · ...... Easy runs · ------- Medium runs · ——— Difficult runs · Mountain restaurants

back to Lavachet and Tignes-Les-Brevières. Intermediate and advanced skiers will benefit most from the three good ski schools, ESF, Évolution 2 and Ski School International, which exist in each satellite. They all offer traditional ski classes as well as race training, off-piste, monoskiing, para-gliding and snow-surfing. Tignes shares an efficient lift system with Val d'Isère; the whole Éspace Killy area comprises 100 lifts, 300km. of marked pistes and 10,000 hectares of possible off-piste skiing, including some testing couloirs. Tignes has 21km. of prepared cross-country trails and 50km. of summer skiing served by 14 lifts. The skiing is varied and in addition the area lift pass includes a day skiing at either Les Arcs or La Plagne during the winter season. Skiing is mainly above the treeline on wide open pistes with a wealth of off-piste opportunities. Since the runs almost completely surround the resort it is possible to follow the best of the sun and the snow and not cover the same ground twice in a day.

There are four main skiing areas in addition to the Val d'Isère runs:-

La Grande Motte Area: From Val Claret an underground funicular, carrying 3,000 persons per hour, rises to the restaurant Le Panoramic at Côte, 9,895ft., on the Grande Motte glacier in 6 minutes. From Val Claret a covered 4-seater chair-lift, 'Les Lanches', takes one within a few hundred feet of the top station. The runs back to Val Claret are blue or red. This is an extensive summer skiing area and is being further developed with new lifts. In the winter, conditions permitting, much of the glacier is kept open and a cableway rises to just below the summit of La Grande Motte at 11,480ft. A double chair-lift operates between Col de la Leisse and Cote serving a red run. Additional drag-lifts are in operation during the summer. From the glacier a pleasant sheltered intermediate run descends to Val Claret and a further easier run takes the longer route.

Col du Palet Area: A chair-lift and double drag-lift on the north side of Val Claret lead to a pleasant mountain restaurant from which two further chair-lifts and a drag lift provide access to a variety of easy and intermediate runs, mostly south facing. From the top of the Grattalu lift in this area it is possible to cross over the Aiguille Percée area via the Grand Huit lift, and one can return via the Replat chair-lift and Merle Blanc chair-lift meeting the Grattalu again at the summit.

Aiguille Percée Area: From Lac de Tignes three drag-lifts serve the lower slopes whilst two chair-lifts provide access to the upper. From the top of either chair-lift (and from the top of Grand Huit if coming from Val Claret) one can descend to the chair-lift Aiguille Percée which climbs to the summit of the same name at 9,186ft. It is one of the best landmarks in Tignes and gets its name from a hole in the rock. One can return via a red run following the line of the chair-lift whilst on the northern side there are easy, intermediate and difficult runs down to Tignes and Les Boisses, 6,090ft., situated by a dam and reservoir in the Isère Valley. From here one can continue down through the woods to Tignes Les Brevières, 6,085ft., an old Savoyard village of charm. These are excellent runs with a vertical drop of nearly 3,000ft. with skiing above and below the tree line, best done in the morning when the east facing slopes are in the sun. The return is by La Sache gondolaway and surmounting Marais chair-lift.

Tovière Area: A gondolaway and cableway from Lac de Tignes and the Tufs chair-lift from Val Claret meet at the 8,801ft. summit of Tovière with its popular restaurant. This is the main link with the Val d'Isère skiing with several easy routes down to the middle station of the La Daille gondolaway and from this point one can return to Tovière by the Tommeuses chair-lift. The piste from Tovière to Lac is black with a steep bottom section. The piste, however is wide and one can descend by a series of long traverses. For the less experienced there is an easy blue run with red variants from Tovière to Val Claret.

In a Few Words: Reliable snow, vast and varied skiing, excellent lift system with little queueing. The 5 villages have excellent bus links at resort level and whilst the lift system at altitude is interconnected moving from one ski area to another requires careful planning. Good kindergarten facilities and extensive self-catering apartments and good standard hotels. Extensive summer skiing and some night life.

Après Ski: A good choice of restaurants ranging from economical crêperies and pizzerias to Cordon Bleu cooking. For good value in savoyard cooking L'Osteria at Le Lavachet is recommended and Le Vesuvio - reasonable in price and a good atmosphere. La Côte de Boeuf in Le Lac provides a variety of set menus with a special children's menu, which makes it particularly attractive to family groups. For the immediate post ski drink and get together, L'Arbina at Lac has a lively atmosphere, while across the road at the Neige et Soleil one can recount the day's exploits in the cosy basement bar. La Calèche in Lac is recommended for fondues. There are five night clubs of which Les Chandelles is the most sophisticated, Le Blue Girl the most popular, and Le Stadium attracts the younger set. The others are Jack's Club and Les Caves du Lac, all in Tignes le Lac. Few of these night spots are not well patronised. 'Tignespace', a sports and congress centre at Le Lac has 2 indoor tennis courts, 2 squash courts, gymnasium, turkish bath, saunas, jacuzzis, solarium, massage and a congress hall for concerts, film shows etc. Val Claret also has a fitness centre. There is a small natural skating rink, bowling and a cinema in Tignes Le Lac.

Recommended Hotels:
Hotel Aiguille Percée: Situated in Le Rosset area of Le Lac, a chalet style hotel of 35 bedrooms comfortably furnished, attractive dining room, with large windows, allowing a lovely view, lounge and bar and a large sun terrace.

Hotel Campanules: Situated in Le Rosset, this is a fine modern hotel of medium size, in an elevated position, with a lovely view of the lake and the mountains; most attractive dining room with a large sun terrace outside, lounge with open fire, bar and comfortable bedrooms, all with bath, wc, telephone, radio and TV.

Hotel Neige et Soleil: Overlooking the lake and nursery slope with a pleasant sun terrace and situated by the Tovière gondolaway. Rooms comfortable with private facilities. Excellent food with varied menu, fondue included weekly. The Cellar Bar has atmosphere and is a favourite after skiing meeting place. This is a small and friendly hotel which would not be out of place in a more traditional mountain village.

Hotel Refuge: In a central position opposite the lake and Tovière gondolaway. Reasonably priced for a 3 star hotel. Large rooms with facilities. Bar has open fire and intimate atmosphere. Separate TV lounge. Very good food. All rooms pleasantly furnished in rustic style with bath/shower and wc. 2 lounges and a TV room.

VAL D'ISÈRE

Height of Resort: 5,965 ft.
Height of Top Station: 10,676 ft.
Nearest International Airport: Geneva
Map Reference: 5D **See page 238**
Route by Car: **See page 236-238**
Resorts Facilities Charts: **See page 218**
Hotel Reference Charts: **See page 230**

Once the hunting village of the Dukes of Savoy and developed for skiing as long ago as the 1930's, Val d'Isère is nevertheless essentially a ski resort in the modern French style. A vast ski area is accessible from Val d'Isère and Tignes (see separate heading), with 133 pistes, marvellous slopes for off-piste skiing and an interlinking system of lifts, complex and extensive. The abonnement covers all lifts in the area. Individual tickets have been dispensed with. The bus services are free to all visitors. The Le Fornet cablecar and the Funival are a short bus journey on either side of the village and from the two cableways running from Le Joseray, not far from the village centre, one travels to Solaise and the other converges with the Funival at Bellevarde.

All three systems are supplemented by high speed chair-lifts to cater for peak periods. Additionally, an underground funicular railway runs from La Daille to the top of Bellevarde moving 3,000 persons per hour. An amazing network of drag-lifts and chair-lifts rise in all directions from these top stations, leading to some glorious pistes of all standards and covering such a range that the moderate skier can ski all day without going over the same ground. These runs lead to further lifts disappearing far into the mountains. Most of the drag-lifts are automatic and started off by the skier. There are extensive opportunities for the off-piste skier too, and most of the options are now well documented in a paper back available at good booksellers in the resort.

During high season queueing can get quite bad, especially lifts out of the village and the Le Fornet cableway is often the quickest way out. The situation has been much improved since the opening of the Funival at La Daille and the installation of high speed quad chair-lifts on Solaise and Bellevarde. The easier runs tend to be on the upper slopes, the lower slopes becoming generally steeper. The routes back to the centre of Val d'Isère from the top of Bellevarde and Solaise are fairly testing, particularly below the tree line (whatever their colour coding) and the less experienced skiers tend to descend by cableway. There are reasonably easy routes down to La Daille and Le Fornet. The coding of some of the lower pistes can be misleading and one can expect to find some red runs as challenging as black runs in other resorts and some blues could easily be red.

Bellevarde Area: The cableway from the village and the Funival from La Daille both lead to Bellevarde, 9,100ft., and below a group of apartments are built into the mountain. In addition, two surmounting high speed chair-lifts rise to Bellevarde, running almost parallel with the cableway on the eastern side. Difficult runs return to the village down the steep east-facing slopes such as 'La Face de Bellevarde', a long and challenging Olympic run, and wider easier north facing runs lead down to the La Daille middle station, from which point a variety of medium to difficult wooded runs descend to La Daille. Alternatively two parallel chair-lifts rise up to Tovière with its agreeable restaurant, and over the ridge from here various runs lead to Tignes. Also from Bellevarde 3 chair-lifts, one of which is high-speed, give access to higher, very enjoyable easy runs with the most spectacular view across the snowfields beneath the Point du Grand Pré and Col de Fresse. There are, in addition, a number of off-piste runs from this area down into Tignes and Val Claret.

Solaise Area: A cableway rises to Tête de Solaise, 8,366ft., supplemented by the Solaise Express chair-lift reaching the same area. The top part of the slope back towards the resort is served by a chair-lift. From Tête a large snow bowl with a series of lifts stretches away into the distance to Arcelle, 8,957ft. and L'Ouillette, 10,102ft. Most of the runs here are easy and flattering to the skier, though there are testing red runs from Arcelle to Le Manchet and black from the Tunnel 3000 drag-lift. There is a black and a red route (with a supposedly blue variant) down to the centre of the resort, steep, narrow and often sharply mogulled below the tree line. There is an easier red route and pleasant blue route down to Le Laisinant on the southern outskirts of the resort which connects with the Train Rouge. Now a path has been groomed allowing skiing back to the resort and thus avoiding taking the bus. The nursery slopes are situated in the centre of the village, around the bottom of the main Solaise/Bellevarde cableway stations, where the lifts are free of charge.

Le Fornet Area: There are three ways of reaching this area – by cableway from Le Fornet, by the Leissières chair-lift from Solaise area or by a steep run from the top of the Tunnell 3000 drag-lift, which is rarely open. A long gondolaway rising south-westward from the top of Le Fornet cableway gives access to pleasant open slopes. A further drag-lift and chair-lift lead to the Pisaillas Glacier at over 10,000ft. Most of the lifts on the glacier are open in the winter and summer and there is a longish run from the top to the Cascade chair-lift affording a pleasant variety of undulating skiing compared with most glacier runs. One can return to Solaise via the Leissières lift or descend to Le Fornet by a difficult run under the cableway or by a gentle blue alternative. Given the correct snow conditions tree skiing, off-piste, in this area is the best in the resort and there are several well known off-piste descents which do connect with the lift station, principally Col Pers and Grand Vallon. Always less busy than other slopes.

La Daille: Much has been said about La Daille already, but in addition a well trodden itinerary, the Valley Perdue, leads from the top of the gondolaway right to the bottom of the O.K. run. It can be followed on a series of open snowfields or via a spectacular Gorge. The village is situated at the foot of the world famous World Cup Downhill run and near the entrance to Val d'Isère, La Daille is a functional and self-sufficient complex with supermarket, shops and restaurants. The self-catering accommodation is comfortable and well appointed which is linked by a series of covered walkways to

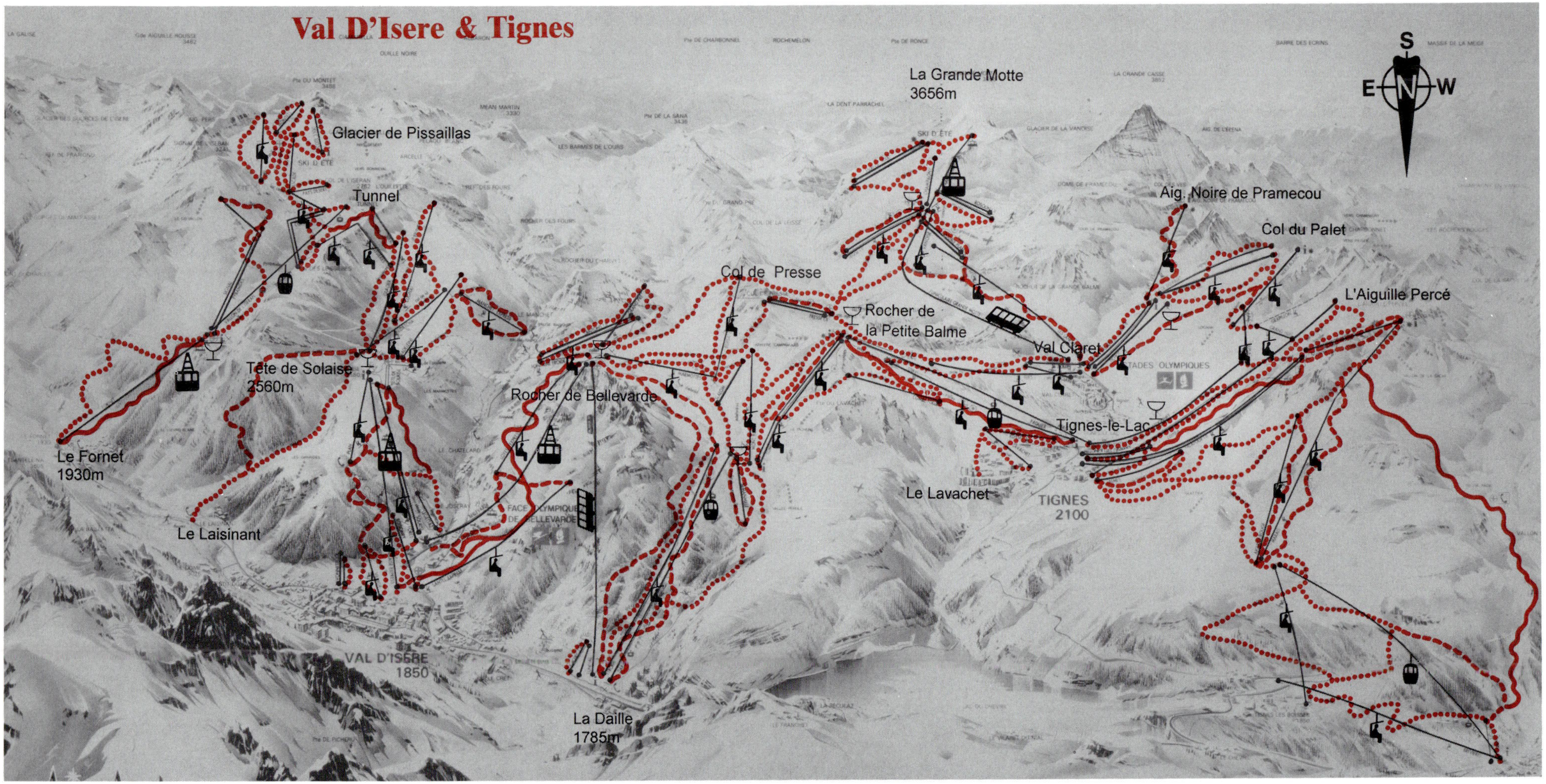

Mountain railways | Cableways | Gondolaways | Chair-lifts | Drag-lifts | .... Easy runs | --------- Medium runs | ——— Difficult runs | Mountain restaurants

the commercial centre. It is marginally cheaper than the main village.

In a Few Words: Val d'Isère and Tignes cover an area of unsurpassed variety and range of skiing, and this is primarily a good skier's resort. There are 5 official ski schools:- E.S.F., Top Ski, Mountain Masters, Évolution 2 and Snow Fun plus many others, smaller but equally official and efficient. Snow conditions reliable for late skiing, good touring area; expensive but good value for the experienced skier. Introduced for the 1992/93 season was the 'faithful client' discount on lift passes. By presenting your pass purchased during one of the three previous seasons, discounts of 5% and up to 20% can be obtained. It is understood that this offer will run from season to season.

Après Ski: Of the various night spots, the Club 21 and Dicks T Bar discothèques are the most popular. Club 21 is crowded mostly with young French people dancing the night away. Dick's T-Bar is for the British, run by an Englishman, its disco opens at 2200 hours and it is also open for afternoon tea and drinks. In addition there are games rooms, swimming pools and a good choice of bars and restaurants. At the Bar Jacques one can eat good Lyonnaise food. La Grande Ourse is an excellent restaurant, but expensive, at the foot of the nursery slopes, with a terrace outside for lunch, but dinner must be booked as tables are limited. The crêpes are too good to be missed for sale on the street. The Crech'Ouna in La Daille is also worth a visit for excellent fondues. Jazz'n Bar is always crowded and plays loud beat music; the Café Face is very popular, with a lively atmosphere. La Perdrix Blanche is always crowded, so booking essential, here one has an extensive menu featuring pizzas, sea food and fresh pasta and is quick and cheap. Popular with the young is the Game Centre. It is advisable for large parties eating out to book tables in good time, for any restaurant.

Recommended Hotels:

Hotel Blizzard: This bright modern hotel in the centre and within easy range of the main lifts has 72 double bedrooms, no singles, all with bath or shower. Best rooms face south away from the main street. Two sitting rooms, dining room and bar. Particularly popular with the young smart French set who appreciate their comfort and good food. 'Knack' discothèque. Late evening meals served in restaurant La Luge.

Hotel La Gelinotte: An attractive chalet style hotel on a tree- covered slope overlooking the village. Antique furniture, cosy bar with classical music, split level dining room. All bedrooms with bath or shower and balconies. Run by the charming Beilins who create welcoming and friendly atmosphere. Free shuttle bus service to the lifts every morning.

Hotel Grand Paradis: This is a large modern hotel, in central sunny position; bedrooms all with private bath, TV and beautifully furnished. Reception rooms are elegant and attractive, bar, lecture room, jacuzzi, Turkish bath, sauna, solarium, games room.

VALFREJUS

Height of Resort: 5,083 ft.
Height of Top Station: 8,979 ft.
Nearest International Airport: Turin
Map Reference: See page 238
Route by Car: See page 236-238
Resorts Facilities Charts: See page 218
Hotel Reference Charts: See page 230

Valfrejus is one of the newest French ski resorts situated on the French-Italian border above the town of Modane. The 8km. approach road from the latter affords good views of the Maurienne Valley and the old fortress which used to guard the road from the other side. There are many hairpin bends and should one be driving in bad visibility there are signs counting down the number of bends before reaching the village. The resort sits above the Frejus road tunnel which links Modane with Bardonecchia, in Italy. The long term plan is a ski link with this resort and also the charming old French resort of Valloire. Valfrejus, set within tree covered slopes, contains chalet style residences, all wood faced and tastefully presented. The ski area is well planned with a compact lift system with runs back to the village on mainly north facing slopes. The uphill transport out of the village to the main ski area is a 6 seater gondolaway and a parallel chair-lift to the middle station where there is a restaurant and 6 drag-lifts serving easy and intermediate runs. The gondolaway continues to the top station, 8,979ft. where there is a further restaurant. From the top, and looking down to the village, there is a black run to the right and passing the middle station and converges to a red before arriving in the village. To the left there are two easy, one wide sweeping, and a red run down to Le Pas du Roc. From this point there are two chair-lifts, one back to the top station and the other to the Col D'Arrondaz Restaurant meeting the chair-lift coming up from Plateau D'Arrondaz. There is a long blue run back to the village from the bottom of the two chair-lifts. The pisted skiing is both above and below the tree line and at present suitable for beginners up to intermediate standard, although there is some very good and challenging off-piste and tree skiing. The resort has two ski schools who provide healthy competition over prices and the quality of teaching.

Children: Well catered for with a nursery for 3 months to 3 year olds and two ski kindergartens for children from 3 to 6 years.

In a Few Words: A pleasant small resort and well worth watching in view of its eventual links with Valloire, thence Bardonecchia (see separate report). Compact village and lift system. Due to its height and mainly north facing runs it holds the snow well. Night life fairly limited at present.

Après Ski: This is a small and fairly new resort, so one must not expect too much. There are three pubs and a restaurant (Le Bardonecchia) offering evening entertainment, a few shops and several other restaurants and bars.

Hotels: There are three 2 star hotels; L'Alpe Hôtel, L'Auberge du Charmaix, and Le Valfrejus.

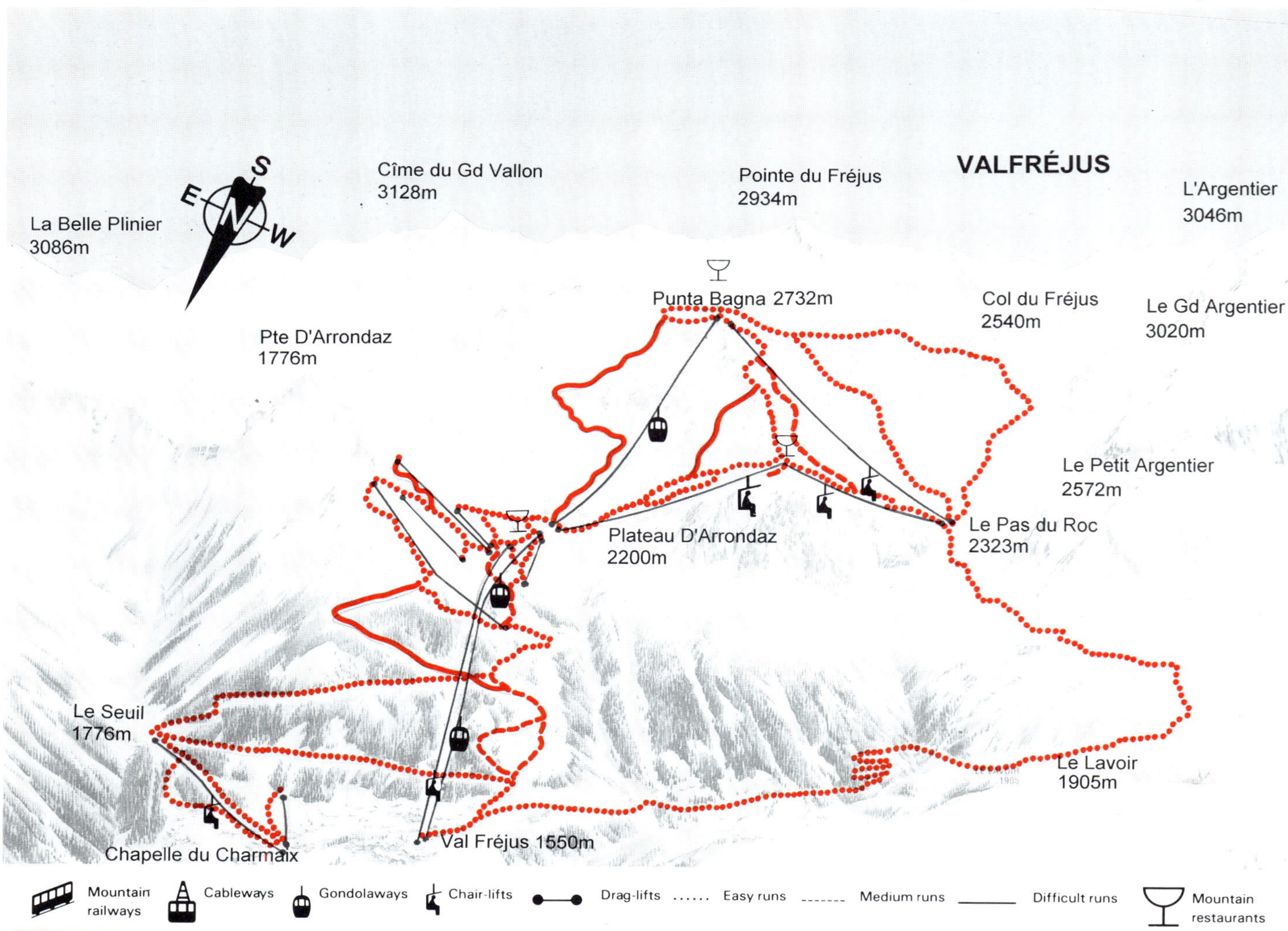

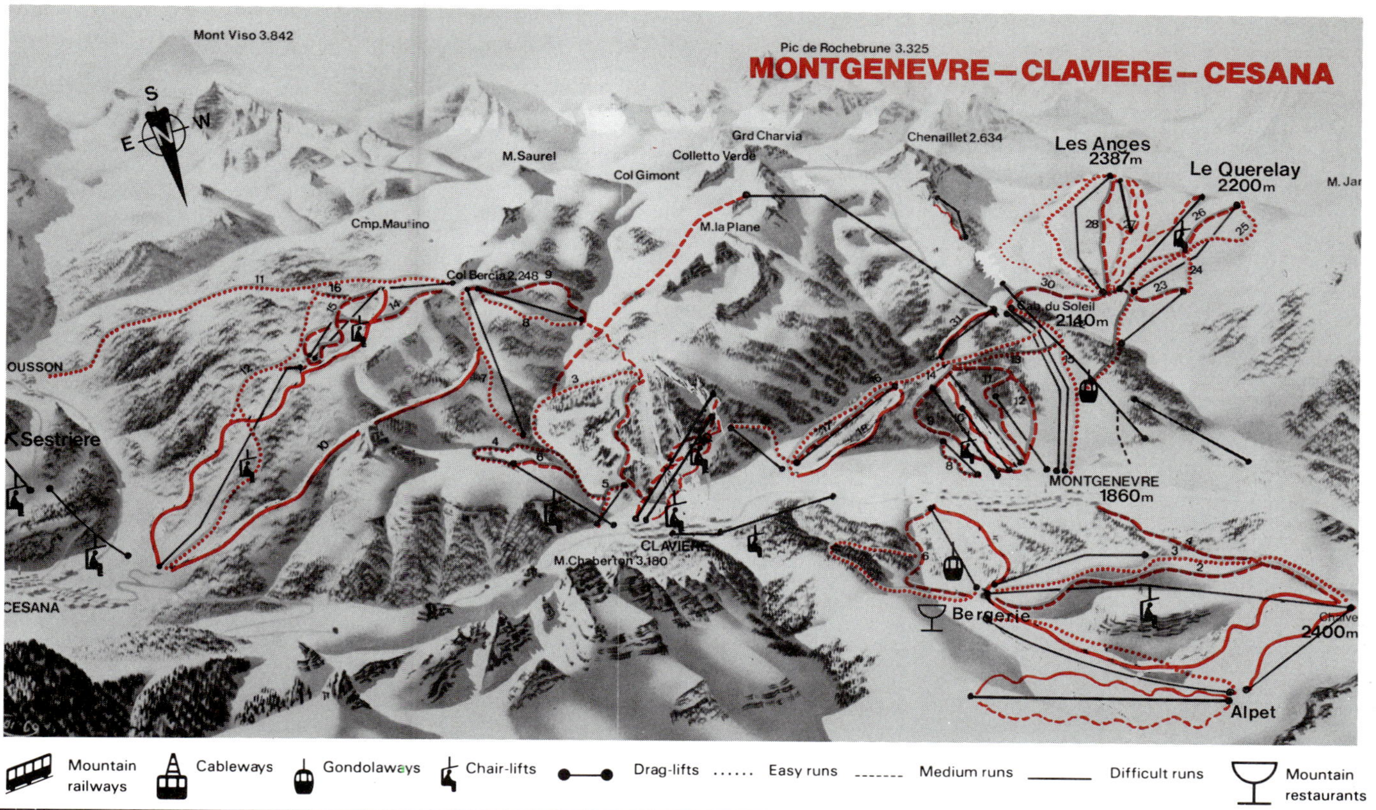

MONTGENÈVRE

Height of Resort: 6,069 ft.
Height of Top Station: 8,326 ft.
Nearest International Airport: Turin
Map Reference: 4E See page 238
Route by Car: See page 236-238
Resorts Facilities Charts: See page 218
Hotel Reference Charts: See page 230

Situated on the French/Italian border this resort can be reached from the Italian side, Oulx – 11km. or from Briançon – 12km. or via the Frejus tunnel from Modane to Bardonnechia. Montgenèvre is an attractive small village, its limited hotel accommodation far outweighed by the large number of privately-owned chalets and apartments. The village is fairly long, running from west to east and the valley is wide and sunny. By road it is very close to Cesana and also within easy reach of other Italian resorts, Sauze d'Oulx, Sestriere and the French resort of Serre Chevalier, Montgenèvre is in fact linked with the Italian resorts of Clavière, Cesana, Sansicario and the Sestriere area. Montgenèvre has two compact lift systems of its own:-

From the eastern edge of the village, a 6 seater gondolaway rises to Bergerie, 7,084 ft. – where one finds the mountain restaurant 2,000 and a sun terrace – thence by chair-lift to Chalvet, 8,560ft. From Chalvet there is a direct south-east facing run, medium/difficult, back to the village of 6km., vertical descent 2,624ft., three runs to Bergerie, easy, medium and difficult up to 2.5km. on south to south-east facing slopes, vertical descent 1,476ft. and the same variety of runs but partially wooded from Bergerie to the village up to 2km. in length, vertical descent 984ft. on south facing slopes.

Running north-westward from Bergerie there is a drag-lift at approximately 45 degrees to the chair-lift, rising to Alpet, this connects with a further drag-lift running up to Chalvet. The run down from the top station towards Alpet is difficult, but the run from Alpet back to Bergerie is easy. From Alpet there are also three runs down to the Baisses Valley, one black and two red each side of the Rocher Rouge chair-lift. From the foot one can continue on a long easy run to the Monquitaine chair-lift, mentioned below or return to Alpet by the Rocher Rouge lift. The chair-lift, Monquitaine, rises in a north-westerly direction from the outskirts of Clavière towards Montgenèvre thus linking the two villages on the eastern side. On the south-western side of the village 2km. run back to the village. Alternatively, one can ski down to two single drag-lifts which rise in U formation to the crest formed by Mount Chenaillet and Mount Janus. The very large ampitheatre of skiing is interesting and enjoyable and due to its north and north-east facing slopes the snow is good and remains so until late season. On the left the Les Anges lift rises to the crest 7,829ft., with three runs, easy, medium and difficult to the lower terminal of up to 3km,. or an easy run back to the village of 7km. vertical descent, 1,791ft. The Querelay lift on the right rises to the same height and provides similar runs down on north-east facing slopes. To relieve the congestion on the Querelay lift a 4 seater chair-lift was installed which runs almost parallel and reaches the same height. The opening of La Crête drag-lift at last provides a link from Les Anges bowl to Rocher de l'Aigle. The lift is quite steep and the run down back to the bowl is black and variable, and no good in late season. A restaurant at the foot of this lift has been opened. Also from the western side of the village the Col du Soleil drag-lift rises to 6,232ft. with short medium runs back to the village. From the western side of the village a gondolaway rises south-eastward to a point above Col du Soleil and from the top, there is a short run north-eastward down to the base of the Rocher de L'Aigle drag-lift which rises to Colletto Verde, 8,326ft., and from here one can ski down to the Italian resort of Clavière and thence across to just above Cesana; from here one can link with the Sansicario and Sestriere skiing, reversing the procedure for the homeward journey to Montgenèvre. The whole area is covered by 62 lifts, 22 of which are in Montgenèvre itself.

In a Few Words: Small resort - two compact ski-lift systems providing good skiing for the beginner up to intermediate plus; sunny; reliable snow due to its mainly north facing runs; not much queueing due to the limited number of hotel beds; the link with the Italian resorts provides a great variety of interesting area skiing. Snow cannons are being increased.

Après Ski: There are several bars and cafés here and three night clubs. Le Boom looks rather like the vaults of a church, only it is not so cold, as it has a large fire burning at one end. There is also a discothèque at The Playboy (English owned) which has an intimate atmosphere. Jamy is a very popular haunt for eating (escargots and steaks particularly good), drinking and socialising. It is very good value and all the ski instructors frequent it. The Refuge bar, specialising in raclettes and crêpes, is one of the most popular daytime haunts, whilst the small Hotel L'Alpet runs a very good family-style restaurant, where excellent French food can be obtained. It is very popular so it's as well to book a day in advance. The Ca Del Sol bar with disco downstairs is much frequented. Lou Pitchounet Restaurant is excellent value; for snacks or fondue try Le Crépouse and for pizzas The Tourmente. The bar at Hotel Rois Mages is popular with English visitors – it has a lively atmosphere and offers live music. The open air ice rink is open until about 10.30 p.m. (but closes early March) and many people make use of this facility.

Recommended Hotels:

Hotel Napoleon: This modern hotel is situated in the centre of Montgenèvre. It is an attractive hotel, with spacious dining room and bar serving good food, set menu and à la carte. Bedrooms are well furnished and many south-facing with small balcony, all with private bath or shower. The bar is a popular meeting place for the locals. The whole hotel has a good atmosphere.

Hotel Valérie: This is a modern style hotel in a central position. Attractive, large dining room with old-style decor, spacious and comfortable. Bedrooms of medium size, nicely furnished, all with private bath or shower. A pleasant hotel with a good atmosphere.

SERRE-CHEVALIER

Height of Resort: 4,500 ft.
Height of Top Station: 9,100 ft.
Nearest International Airport: Turin/Lyon
Map Reference: See page 238
Route by Car: See page 236-238
Resorts Facilities Charts: See page 218
Hotel Reference Charts: See page 230

Serre-Chevalier takes its name from the first peak to be besieged by recreational skiers. The resort now comprises three separate villages and various hamlets that stretch along the main road from Briançon towards Grenoble. The three villages, Chantemerle, Villeneuve and Le Monêtier, are styled SC1350, 1400 and 1500 respectively, but they are normally referred to by their proper names. Briançon now styled SC 1200, has more recently been linked into the same ski network. The resort offers a very extensive and fully integrated skiing area reaching up to 9,100ft and extending to 250 km of marked pistes. It is a traditional French skiing resort with a history stretching back over many decades. In recent years it has sought to re-establish its popularity in the face of competition from newer purpose built stations. In consequence it has developed in an uneasy compromise between traditional French alpine architecture and the extensive modern apartment blocks. Nevertheless it retains that distinctive quality of provincial France that is frequently lacking in the more anglophile and cosmopolitan resorts.

Serre-Chevalier offers the potentially ideal combination of a Southern Alp, Mediterranean climate and north-facing slopes. Located at the top of the Alpe du Sud in the largest larch forest in Europe, good snow conditions allow even the intermediate skier the exhilarating experience of descending off-piste between widely spaced trees to the valley floor. Above the tree line there is a wide range of open piste to suit all abilities. The more experienced will relish the opportunity to enjoy the unlimited, safe and easily accessible off-piste. The range and variety of off-piste skiing attracts large numbers of monoskiers and surfboarders.

Ski Areas: The skiing can be conveniently divided into three areas. The majority of the lifts and the skiers are to be found above the tree line in two adjacent and interlinking snow bowls above the Grande Alpe and the Frejus/Echaillon sections. The piste skiing here is wide and open and for the most part suited to the intermediate skier. There are, however, more than enough pistes suitable to the beginners needs, running from 8,202ft. through the open snowfields and in turn onto roads and tracks that wind gently through the trees to the valley below. For the more competent there is a good choice of steeper runs immediately below the peaks that surround the snow bowls and above Le Monêtier. In addition, there are a very considerable number of beautiful trails and descents through the larch forest of varying severity.

Grand Alpe: Reached from Chantemerle by cableway, gondolaway or chair-lift, or alternatively by connecting lift from Frejus/Echaillon. The Grand Alpe offers a large choice of wide intermediate pistes on the gentle upper slopes of the Serre-Chevalier peak together with an adequate but frequently congested nursery.area. The top of the Prorel drag-lift offers impressive views towards the Vallée de la Durance and the opportunity, after a short climb, to ski to Briançon. The pisted runs from Prorel provide a quiet meandering descent interspersed with boulders, trees and gulleys in marked contrast to more open slopes of Serre-Chevalier. Below the tree line there are numerous tracks suited to all abilities leading through the larch trees to Serre Ratier. The most direct descent is the Route Olympique. Further trails to the village of Chantemerle cut through the trees to the west of Les Eduits where the Aiguillette chair-lift serves two splendid red runs and a lot of tree skiing which is often unused.

For the novice there is a 12km. descent along a very gently sloping road which leads eventually all the way down to Chantemerle. The old chalet hotel and newer piste restaurants at Serre Ratier provide keen competition to the larger and thronging mountain restaurant at Grand Alpe.

Frejus/Echaillon: Two gondolaways will carry you from Villeneuve above the tree line and a new 8 person continuously running gondolaway, the Pontillas, now serves the community at the eastern end of this village and Le Bez. Here a choice of drag-lifts and chairs provide wide, open and flattering piste descents from eastern flanks of Serre Chevalier. The Col du Mea with a good range of steeper and more demanding pistes is set immediately below the ridges of L'Eychauda, Clot Gauthier and the Tête de la Balme. Once again there is a relatively gentle track for the novice leading via Frejus all the way to the valley floor Villeneuve. The Tête de la Balme chair-lift can often prove to be very exposed and cold. However, it offers the link to Monetier or an excellent and predominantly unpisted descent down the east facing valley above Frejus, which remains relatively quiet even when the resort is at its busiest. The Echaillon restaurant is just off the piste and easy to miss. The Pi-Mai restaurant at the small mountain village of Frejus offers higher standards of cuisine than the other modern alternatives.

Le Monêtier: There is ample skiing for the novice close to the valley floor. A combination of chair and drag-lifts will convey the more able skiers through the trees to Bachas, above the tree line, where there is a choice of two chair-lifts. The l'Yret chair gives spectacular views of the Glaciers and mountains in the Park des Écrins and leads to the highest point in the resort's lift system 9,100ft. None of the skiing above Bachas is easy. A descent from the l'Yret chair-lift leads to a connecting lift linking to Frejus/Echaillon section.

In a Few Words: A resort very popular with the French and beginning to be recognised by British skiers as France's best kept skiing secret, which offers superb skiing and well maintained pistes. All abilities are well catered for. There is a choice of long, gentle descents that will complement and encourage the beginner. There is a vast range of safe and easily accessible off-piste skiing for the more able. The resort is not without some alpine charm, and for the determined skier who enjoys a taste of provincial France, the effort of the lengthy journey is well rewarded. The resort has an enviable record for sun and snow, but the lower slopes can become patchy. Crowding and queueing can be severe during the French national holidays and on Sundays when the weekend skiers arrive in droves from Northern Italy and Grenoble, but normally during the week queues are non existant. There are 45km. of prepared trails for Nordic skiing and each village has kindergartens and ski schools for young children.

Après Ski: At night the public telephone box is as busy as anywhere! A great deal of accommodation in the resort is provided by apartments. The occupants tend to be French families hankering after skiing rather than night life. Restaurants are plentiful. Night clubs are rare and expensive. Various discothèques provide entertainment for the younger element, usually at the week-ends. There are ample shopping facilities in each village and the large town of Briançon is only 5 miles distant. There is a swimming pool, skating rinks, cinemas, and ice driving. Some of the recommended restaurants include:- Le Couch'ou at Chantemerle; Le Chazelay and La Marotte at Villeneuve; L'Alpen, Le Barbin and Le Chazal at Monetier; La Bidule at Le Bez.

Recommended Hotels:

Chantemerle (1350):
Hotel de la Balme: A 2 star hotel on the edge of the village. It is a modern hotel built in traditional alpine style with lots of wood and an open fire (bathroom and telephone in all 28 rooms).

Hotel Plein Sud: A luxury 3 star hotel situated at the foot of the main skiing area. 42 rooms all with bathroom, TV, mini-bar, 33 with balcony overlooking the pistes. Large breakfast buffet, indoor swimming pool and fitness room.

Villeneuve (1400):
Le Christiania: A 2 star hotel 100 metres from the Aravet télécabins and full of antiques collected by the owner. Rustic decor.

Cimotel: A 2 star hotel situated close to the Aravet télécabins and very near a modern shopping centre. 44 rooms. Restaurant overlooking the main skiing area.

Hotel Le Lièvre Blanc: A 2 star hotel, informal and friendly, situated in the old part of the village (400 metres from the piste) in traditional alpine building. 27 bedrooms all with bath or shower, good restaurant and lively bar. Run by a Jersey couple, the hotel has its own ski shop and offers a free ski guiding service.

Monetier (1500):
Hotel Alpazur: A 2 star hotel situated 300 metres from the lifts. Large club hotel with 115 bedrooms and continuous activities planned for children and adults.

Hotel Alliey: 2 star, 4th generation owner. Rustic style of decoration. Wood panelling. Excellent wine cellar. 24 rooms. Same family own the 3 star Résidence Le Pré des Ors.

Hotel de L'Europe: 2 star hotel situated in the heart of the village in 15th century buildings. Modernised. 31 rooms.

LE CORBIER

Height of Resort: 5,086 ft.
Height of Top Station: 7,415 ft.
Nearest International Airport: Geneva
Map Reference: 3D See page 238
Route by Car: See page 236–238
Resorts Facilities Charts: See page 217

The resort of Le Corbier is situated in the Savoie amongst the Arvan-Villard mountain range which joins the northern and southern Alps. Due to its open position it often misses the bad weather (or clears up quickly), it lies in a snow-trap area and has a good sunshine record. Reached by a 10 mile mountain road from the Provincial town of St. Jean-de-Maurienne. The latter is 537 miles from Calais (motorway as far as Chambéry thence 45 miles on the Modane road). Both Geneva and Lyon airports are about 100 miles from the resort.

Le Corbier is a typical modern purpose built resort consisting of 6 high-rise apartment blocks joined in the centre by a series of lower buildings. The apartment blocks, somewhat stark, face south onto the slopes, which are floodlit at night and north over the Valley of the Maurienne to the mountains of the Trois Vallées. As is customary with this type of resort there are covered ways at ground level connecting most of the blocks in which are situated supermarkets, shops, restaurants, night clubs and other amenities which make the resort completely self-supporting. Le Corbier is mainly a family resort with visitors from most West European countries.

The Skiing: All the skiing takes place on the mountain topped by Pte. du Corbier, 7,415ft. which has a breadth of some 5km. and is virtually on the 'doorstep' south of the apartments. The slopes are predominately north facing so that snow is assured over a long period under normal conditions. The mountain however is intersected by valleys and gullies so one has the possibility of skiing on east, north-east, north and west facing slopes according to conditions, and it is quite possible to find spring snow on east facing slopes and powder elsewhere on the same day.

There are 29 prepared pistes covering 80km. The runs are excellently graded to suit beginners and intermediates and, if taken down the fall-line, steep and interesting enough for experts. The direct run from the summit is graded black. Over the back of the mountain there are east and south facing runs down to St. Jean-D'Arves with a chair-lift to bring one back. Here there are excellent possibilities for off-piste, spring snow skiing from February onwards as there is from Pte. du Corbier down to the neighbouring resort of St. Sorlin D'Arves which has its own lift network.

The maximum vertical drop on Le Corbier side is 2,350ft. and the runs if taken direct are 3-4km. but extended to 5km. taken by the easier routes. There are 7 chair-lifts and 17 drag-lifts. A further 3 drag-lifts can be brought into operation by the ski school if the snow is short on the lower slopes during late season. Nine lifts start immediately outside the apartments and there are seldom queues. There are three mountain restaurants with sun terraces on Le Corbier side and a popular bar/restaurant in St. Jean d'Arves. Le Corbier ski area is directly linked to that of La Toussuire, Les Bottières and St. Jean d'Arves. These resorts are all on the same lift pass covering 180km. of pistes served by 44 lifts. A shuttle bus operates from the foot of St. Jean d'Arves to St. Sorlin d'Arves and a supplement is payable for skiing at the lattter resort. The 'Chicks Club' is an unusual outdoor 'snow garden' for infants from 3-6 years: an entirely safe fenced–in area, with free mini ski drag where skiing is taught, tests taken and games supervised.

In a Few Words: With predominantly north facing slopes and a base height of over 5,000ft. snow is assured for a long season. Ideal for families, friendly and unsophisticated small resort with a relaxed atmosphere. Above average sun. Minimum queueing allows maximum downhill skiing per day; excellent for beginners to intermediates. For better skiers it could be considered as a cheaper self–catering holiday for one week to get fit before going to a larger resort. Maximum help given by the Interhome staff. Avoid the French school holiday period in February when the resort is very overcrowded. Artificial snow cannons are in operation.

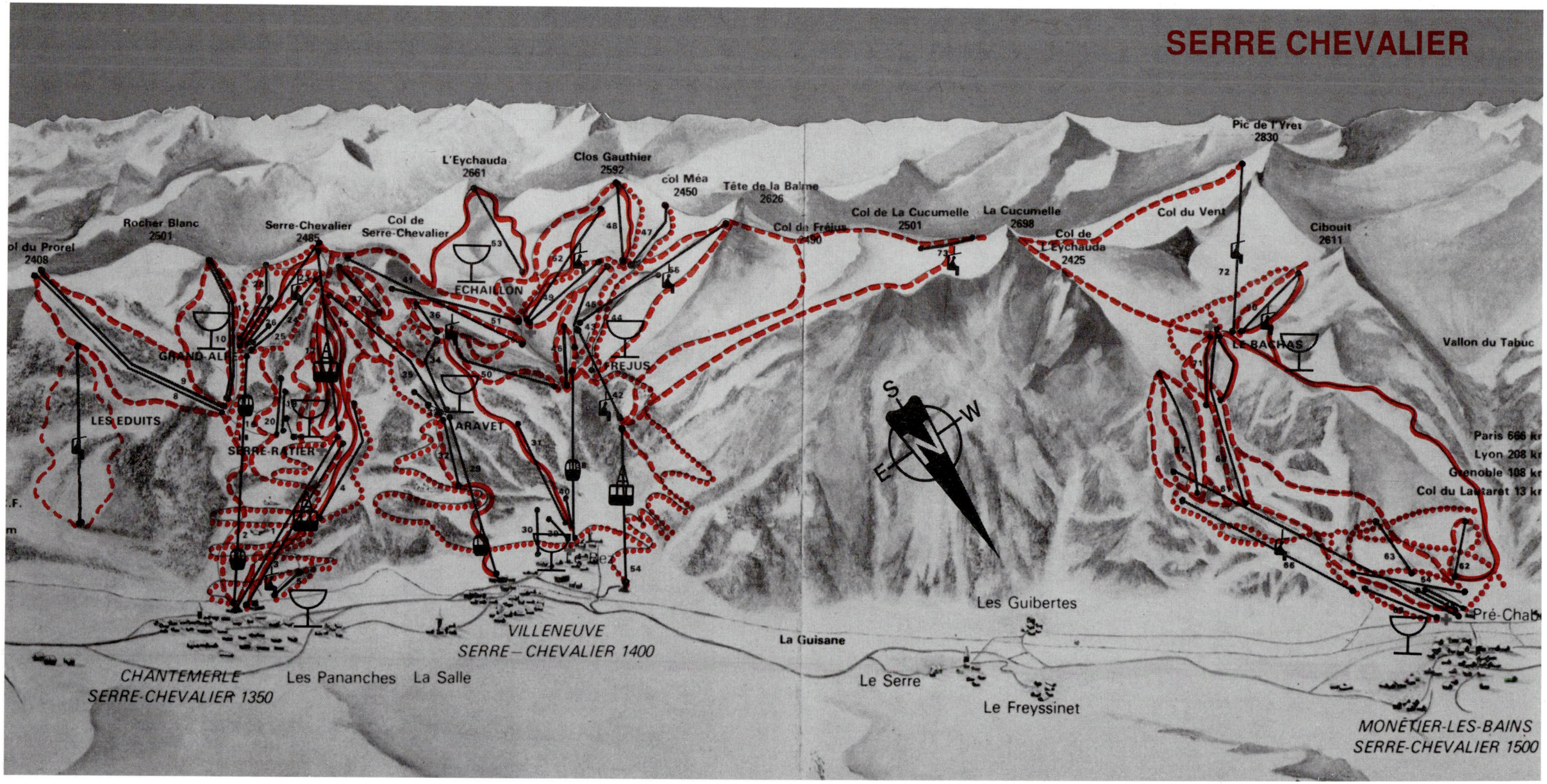

Mountain railways | Cableways | Gondolaways | Chair-lifts | Drag-lifts | .... Easy runs | --------- Medium runs | ——— Difficult runs | Mountain restaurants

Après Ski: Informal and fairly quiet being mainly a family resort. There are two discos – the St. Moritz and The Sweet Club, the latter occasionally has tea dancing. The resort has a good selection of restaurants from the inexpensive but rather basic Le Yeti to the more sophisticated Le Saint Moritz owned by ex-world ski champion, Jean-Noel Augert, providing first class food and service, but priced accordingly. Ice skating rink, para- and hang-gliding, and snow-shoe rambling. There is one amusement arcade, open until midnight and a cinema open nightly.

Accommodation: The Interhome apartments are basically furnished and equipped but like most French accommodation every inch is used, thus the sleeping capacity listed should be taken as somewhat cramped so it is wise to take a slightly larger bedded apartment. Most apartments have balconies and panoramic windows. None of the kitchens have ovens. The central heating and hot water supply is excellent. Blankets are supplied but not linen, the latter can be hired. There are three supermarkets which also have a meal counters for take-away hot food. This saves the bother of cooking. Apartments are cleaned on the day of departure otherwise there is no room service. Each flat has its own ski locker in the basement. There is an excellent crèche for children under 3 years open until 1700 hours daily.

LA TOUSSUIRE

Height of Resort: 5,905 ft.
Height of Top Station: 7,874 ft.
Nearest International Airport: Geneva
Map Reference: 3D See page 238
Route by Car: See page 236-238
Resort Facilities Chart: See page 217

La Toussuire, situated in the Savoie is linked with the resort of Le Corbier, see separate report, to the east and to St. Sorlin D'Arves by shuttle bus which lies further to the south-east. To the north-west of La Toussuire the hamlet of Les Bottières is located. All four resorts are on the same lift pass giving a combined total of 180km. of prepared pistes served by 59 lifts. La Toussuire lies in a spacious sunny bowl and enjoys an average of 6 hours a day sunshine in January. The resort has 12 hotels and pensions and a much larger proportion of apartment accommodation, most of the latter being privately owned. It is older than most French ski resorts and considerable development has taken place over recent years.

La Toussuire Skiing: Those up to intermediate standard will be happy here. Lifts fan out from the village area towards or to the crest running from east to west. All the runs are north, east or west facing so hold the snow well; most are reds but with a good selection of blues. The top station, Tête de Bellard, 7,874ft. with a restaurant is reached by chair or drag-lift with intermediate runs to the village, vertical descent 1,9868 ft. Altogether 6 chair-lifts and 13 drag-lifts serve the area. Good nursery slopes are to be found in the village area and there are 25km. of prepared nordic ski trails. Families are well catered for with a ski kindergarten for children from 3 to 11 years and a crèche/kindergarten for children from 2 months upwards.

Linked Resorts: La Toussuire is connected with Le Corbier by chair-lifts rising each side of the valley separating the two resorts. Using the latter's lifts one can work one's way across down to the foot of the chair-lift at St. Jean D'Arves where a shuttle bus operates to St. Sorlin D'Arves. The return journey to Le Corbier is via the chair-lift at the former station. Les Bottières is connected to La Toussuire by road but can be reached on skis by taking the drag-lift up to Le Grand Truc, 7,247ft., which provides intermediate runs each side of the lift down to base. From the left-hand run one can divert to a fairly steepish red over the crest down to Les Bottières. Two surmounting drag-lifts return one to the crest to re-join the piste to La Toussuire. This whole system with 59 lifts serving 180km. of pistes provides interesting variations for the intermediate, good progressive slopes for the beginner, whilst the advanced skiers will be satisfied for a a time with runs taken down the fall-line along with the variety of off-piste possibilities.

In a Few Words: An excellent resort for families, beginners to intermediates; not many English skiers at present but popular with the French. Well planned lift system, our Correspondent was there during the French school holiday and the maximum wait at the lifts was 7 minutes. Sunny resort and due to the altitude and orientation of the runs snow, under normal conditions, remains good; pistes well groomed.

Après Ski: A wide selection of bars and restaurants along with two discos to liven up the scene.

Accommodation: The largest proportion is in self-catering apartments. There are 12 hotels and pensions.

BARÈGES & LA MONGIE

Height of Resort: 4,265 ft.
Height of Top Station: 8,400 ft.
Nearest International Airport: Tarbes/Toulouse
Map Reference: See Main Map page 238
Resort Facilities Charts: See page 217
Hotel Reference Charts: See page 229

These two resorts in the French Hautes Pyrénées are taken together because they share the same skiing. There are two types of lift passes, one restricting the skiing to the resort area where it is issued, the other covering both resorts which is about 30% more expensive. The boundary line for the former is the Col du Tourmalet. The lifts are all interlinking and it is equally practical to ski from one to the other in both directions. Barèges, a small spa village in the time of Napoleon III, dates back earlier than that. It consists of one main street built on a slope, with old stone buildings on either side. Its hotels are the old traditional type but modernised. Set in a narrow east-west tree line valley with steep mountains on either side. The friendliness of the inhabitants, especially the hotel owners, most of whom have been running their hotels for three generations or more, is very apparent. The British are welcomed and not treated as second class citizens, and the place definitely has character, if quite different from the accepted idea of a winter sports resort. There are 11 hotels and pensions which total 4,200 beds. The Barèges lift capacity overall is 18,210 per hour and there is not much queueing to get out of the village except at weekends and special holiday periods, particularly at Tournaboup station. La Mongie and its satellite Tourmalet, 1km. west, are a complete contrast to Barèges, being modern purpose-built French stations; the former built in somewhat Alpine chalet style, the latter consisting of an enormous self-contained apartment complex. Both are directly on the skiing slopes, facing south and immediately adjacent to a network of lifts. La Mongie has 12 hotels and pensions (totalling 700 beds) but apartments bring the total up to 8,000 beds. The lift capacity overall 20,000 per hour.

The Barèges/La Mongie Skiing: The Barèges-owned lifts and runs reach to the Col du Tourmalet and cover a distance of 12km. The La Mongie area down from the Col is 5km. This does not take into account the many lifts diverging from this main east-west connecting axis. Barèges has 24 lifts, La Mongie 29; 53 in all serving 120km of prepared runs.

From Barèges to La Mongie (on the far left) is about 17km. via runs and lifts so that the return journey alone is 34km. This can be increased enormously by including the north and south diverging runs. As a guide to time, to ski directly from Barèges to La Mongie takes between one and two hours, depending on the standard of skier and the size of the lift queues. The return journey can be done in a shorter time providing the lower slopes to Barèges are open. The direct trip both ways is easily within the capability of a lower intermediate. There are two means of uphill transport out of Barèges; a two stage cableway, infrequent and rather slow, to Ayré (the mountain on the extreme right, providing three steep wood glade runs, one being an international race course); and a gondolaway, La Laquette, a much swifter and more efficient form of mountain access. The last connects to Laquette (second mountain from the right) which is the ski school area with a mass of lifts. There are so many lifts out of La Mongie and Tourmalet that it is impossible to mention them in detail. Suffice it to say that there is a cableway to Taoulet (7,677ft.) and a gondolaway to Pourteilh (7,365ft.) the latter particularly, providing two splendid north facing runs under the gondolaway that are steep and challenging. The chair-lift, 4 Termes, rises from the top of the gondolaway to the highest point in the area, 8,400ft. From here there is an excellent off-piste run down the Cluses valley to Tournaboup in Bargés Valley. This is suitable for ski school groups of modest intermediates. However, the best and longest run in both resorts is the more difficult alternative route back to Barèges via the Coume L'Ayse (the highest point at 7,710ft). The first half is steeply mogulled down to Super Barèges and the whole run back to Barèges is 11km. long. Apart from the extensive pistes with a good selection of bars and restaurants, there are excellent opportunities for off-piste powder skiing on north facing slopes and also for steep, spring snow skiing on virgin south facing slopes. There is a particularly good independent ski school, popular with the British and known for the organisation of off-piste expeditions.

In a Few Words: Two resorts providing really long distance skiing by 53 linked lifts over some 120km. of marked pistes. Excellent for the beginner and intermediate, adequate for the experts, who will find some challenging pistes and considerable off-piste opportunities. After all, Barèges has supplied 15 of the French team over the years, from Henri Cazaux (French champion 1950, manager of the Hotel Igloo) down to, more recently, Annie Famose. Cross-country skiing is also catered for with 12km of trails.

Après Ski: Both have friendly bars for après ski gathering, cinema, a local entertainment organised by the Tourist Office. At Barèges the Igloo, the Richelieu, the Central, L'Europe and Pub L'Oncet with piano bar are especially popular and at La Mongie the bar at the Hotel Pourteilh adds music to its popularity. Both resorts have crêperies for those delicious, made-on-the-spot French crêpes at reasonable prices. Night life is rather low key and unsophisticated everywhere and there are no night clubs with live bands – only discothèques. At Barèges Le Hibou and Le Jonathan are open from 11 p.m to 3 a.m. La Mongie also boasts two discos: La Tutte and the more sophisticated Tito's, up at Tourmalet. Films and slides are shown from time to time in both stations. Simplicity and early nights tend to be the 'norm'. In Barèges the extended thermal baths are open from 4 p.m. to 8 p.m. Swimming, saunas and other recreational activities will be available to visitors.

Recommended Hotels:

BARÈGES

Hotel de l'Europe: Old and unpretentious Napoleonic hotel in village street, completely renovated in 1989, run by three generations of the Lons family. Many bedrooms have 3/4 beds and 50% have balconies; all with bath or shower and wc. Interesting food and generous helpings. Excellent service in large dining room; somewhat inadequate sitting room arrangements but a happy-go-lucky atmosphere compensates. 3 minutes' walk from funicular and 10 from main gondolaway. Sauna and lift in hotel.

Hotel Igloo: The nearest hotel to the gondolaway. Owned and very personally run by Mme. Cazaus andand her husband Henri, former ski champion and present inspector of French ski schools. The hotel has a most friendly atmosphere; attractively decorated with delightful small sitting room, charming dining room and mountain view. Carefully prepared 4-course meals are the owners' pride and any changes of menu are willingly allowed. Visitors would surely be very happy at the Igloo.

Hotel Richelieu: Situated in the village street. Typical old-fashioned French hotel dating back to 1860 and Barèges's heyday as a thermal resort. Run by the Azin family. Pleasant informal atmosphere in bar and sitting room, where guests play their own games. Adequate French menu but good selection of regional specialities à la carte. All rooms with bath or shower and wc. Sauna and lift in hotel. Three minutes from cableway and ten from gondolaway.

LA MONGIE

Hotel Le Pourteilh: A very comfortable and pleasing modern hotel, most efficiently run by the owner, Mme. Ferrand. Right on the nursery slopes and south facing, all bedrooms have bathrooms and separate wc. and 50% have balconies. The Pourteilh has a large and lively bar with good sun terrace. A vast table of hors d'oeuvres is the daily luncheon speciality and dinners include 3 choices for the main course. Guests can lunch up at Tourmalet if they prefer. Heated garage, ski room, games rooms.

Hotel Le Taoulet: Under the same management as the Hotel Pourteilh and enjoying an equally good position immediately overlooking the nursery slopes. A simple little hotel established 20 years ago and having a rustic open-style charm. It shares the same menus with its richer sister-hotel, but offers fewer choices. There is a large sun terrace, open fires and a bar/crêperie with snacks available at all times. Rather unluxurious bedrooms but free use of showers for rooms without private facilities. The Taoulet has no bathrooms.

ST. LARY

Height of Resort: 2,722 ft./5,511 ft.
Height of Top Station: 7,955 ft.
Nearest International Airport: Tarbes/Toulouse
Map Reference: See Main Map page 238
Resorts Facilities Charts: See page 218
Hotel Reference Charts: See page 230

The ski area of St. Lary-Soulan (2,722ft). stretches above the Aure Valley in the region of the French Hautes Pyrénées. St.Lary, a typical Pyrenean village of stone houses and slate roofs, is some 50 miles and 1 hour 20 minutes by bus from Tarbes airport. It is an open and sunny village. Its skiing area starts at Pla D'Adet (5,511ft.) which is reached by cableway (50 capacity) in $4^1/_2$ minutes. It is not practical to ski down to St. Lary (rarely snow and no marked piste) and one returns by cableway. For those with a car there is a road up of 11km. St. Lary has 10 hotels and pensions; Pla d'Adet One, with a further one at Espiaube and environs in addition to 23,000 beds in apartments and holiday centres. Advance reservations can be made on the cableway whcih is useful at weekends when the resort is crowded. It is wise to avoid the French school half-term week when all the lifts are overcrowded.

The Skiing: Surprisingly extensive for a resort of this size. The French are past masters at linking their lifts so that all walking is avoided – the system carries one generally on an axis east to west, and the furthest point reached is about l0km. distant (more if one takes a longer route). The skiing, which starts at Le Pla d'Adet – a sunny bowl, consists of 5 drag-lifts ideally graded to suit complete beginners up to early intermediates.

For better skiers there is a long double chair-lift, surmounted by a drag-lift to approximately 6,560ft. with steepish mogulled runs either back to Pla d'Adet or further afield, directly down the quite challenging north facing La Bassia run and thence through the forest to Espiaube.

For the less experienced skiers a new north facing easy run, 'La Corniche', has been created. This starts at the top of the chair-lift above Pla d'Adet and runs down to the foot of the 4 seater Tortes chair-lift. From this point one can ski down to Espiaube or take the Tortes lift up to La Tourette, 7611 ft. At Espiaube, the centre of the skiing complex, there is a generous choice of 2 long lifts up east facing slopes, a 6-seater gondolaway to Col du Portet (7,267ft.) and a chair-lift surmounted by a drag-lift to La Soumaye (7,775ft.). All these reach the same general area and the runs back to Espiaube are all good, fast, intermediate runs, whilst there is a steeper black run direct from La Tourette. From all these top stations one can continue further afield in a north-west direction down easy runs to Lac de L'Oule, where there are three further lifts up south facing slopes (the longest to the highest point in the resort at 7,955ft.). These give excellent spring snow off-piste possibilities. For the good to expert skier there are extensive unpisted steep north facing powder slopes between Espiaube and Lac de L'Oule.

In a Few Words: It is rare to find such a small inexpensive resort with so many lifts and such extensive skiing (80km. of pistes). Excellent for the beginner up to good intermediate. No waiting except at holiday times. Possible to ski an enormous amount of km. in a day. Good steep north facing powder slopes for good skiers as well as extensive south facing spring snow off-piste possibilities. A most friendly village, unspoilt and unsophisticated. Almost exclusively French skiers except for the British. The keen skier who wants to start early and ski late may prefer to stay up at Le Pla d'Adet; the last cableway down to St.Lary is at 5.30 p.m., the first up is at 8.30 a.m. Cross-country skiing is also catered for along with snowboarding.

Après Ski: There is a selection of cafés, bars and crêperies, both at Pla d'Adet and St. Lary. The latter also boasts two salons de thé but the atmosphere remains subdued rather than boisterous. Fun can be had trying some regional specialities: Rochers des Pyrénées, a sort of cake cooked on a spit over a wood fire and dropped into the shape of a rock; and a fabulous sort of waffle covered with chestnut and whipped cream. A tiny old wooden shop offers an intriguing variety of mountain cheeses with much tasting leading up to each purchase. At the local Sports & Health Centre there is table tennis, volley, basket and medicine ball, and a gymnasium, or *why not* relax after a hard day's skiing in one of St. Lary's spas. There are night clubs; at St. Lary the Luna disco is strictly for teenagers; Les Chandelles has the only live band in quiet surroundings and the popular Le Vinkasou. Le Davidson at Pla d'Adet suits the young.

Recommended Hotels:

Hotel Christinia: Situated at Pla d'Adet, 2,624 ft above St. Lary and right beside the cableway. Very convenient for starting and finishing skiing. Built in 1961, all bedrooms have private baths and wc. Large dining room with panoramic views and big open-sided fireplace, where food is grilled during meals. Salmon from Pyrenean rivers and fondues are served weekly at no extra charge. The owners, M. and Mme. Rieu, look upon their guests as friends and really try to make their stay a happy one. Travel slides of many countries are often shown in the evenings.

Grand Hotel Mir: In the main street, some seven minutes' walk from the cableway. Owned and firmly supervised by Mme. Mir, one of three generations of Mir. Unusually spacious grey stone sitting room with open fireplace; pleasant Austrian-style 'woody' bar; pleasing dining room with good food of great variety. Visitors maintain the same menu is not repeated over a fortnight's stay.

FONT-ROMEU

Height of Resort: 5,895 ft.
Height of Top Station: 7,205 ft.
Nearest International Airport: Toulouse/ Perpignan
Map Reference: See Main Map page 238
Resort Facilities Chart: See page 217

Font Romeu stands on a south facing shelf and the town itself is a pleasant mix of ancient and modern, with a good selection of shops, bars, restaurants,etc., where prices are no higher than in any small town in France. The base station "Les Airelles" is reached by a 6-seater cableway from the main street with a free multi-storey car park immediately opposite, or alternatively by car, a 5-minute drive on good roads. There is ample parking at Les Airelles and also ski school, kindergarten, self-service restaurant, 2 bars and a highly efficient, very reasonable "garderie des skis".

From Les Airelles, a series of chair-lifts and drag-lifts fan out to open up the twin peaks of Calme and Galinera, joined by an easy green run. Calme offers several enjoyable red runs, 4 blues and 1 green, served by 2 chair-lifts and 5 drag-lifts, and 1 black which links with Galinera. Galinera, served by 3 chairs and 5 drags, has 3 interesting black runs, in addition to numerous blues and greens running through wooded countryside, and a liaison via Col del Pam with Pyrénées 2000 skiing area, which has some pleasant but limited skiing. Col del Pam, which has its own parking area, offers a short blue and a short green with 2 drags. All the areas link extremely well, allowing one to move easily from one to another regardless of which lifts or runs are used.

In a Few Words: Well thought out and perfectly groomed ski area, furnished with 460 snow cannons, making it one of the densest areas which can be kept under snow in Europe. Superb for beginners and intermediates, with many off-piste opportunities, although the gradings for some of the runs are perhaps a little high. More for the social skier than the daredevil downhiller! Extremely attentive and helpful lift attendants. But beware weekend visitors from France and Spain who sometimes over-estimate their capabilities and make space hard to find on the more difficult runs. Not crowded and hardly any queues, during the week. A 6-day ski pass in 1996/7 cost only 390FF in low season for those staying in the town itself. A lift pass covering the Neige Catalane ski area, embracing 9 ski stations, all within easy reach, costs just 650FF in low season. There are also 80km of Nordic ski trails of various grades, together with dog sleds, squash and indoor tennis courts, horse-riding, climbing wall, etc.

Après Ski: Eating out is no problem, with a proliferation of restaurants lining the main street, from cheap and cheerful pizzerias to more elaborate but still reasonably priced establishments. There is also a casino, a cinema and 3 discos.

Accommodation: There are more than twenty hotels or apart-hotels ranging from 3-star to non-classified, and a wide selection of self-catering apartments, many of which are also graded by the Tourist Office, but it is worth checking exactly where any of these are, as some will leave you a long uphill walk to the town centre.

LES ANGLES

Height of Resort: 5404 ft.
Height of Top Station: 7614 ft
Nearest International Airport: Toulouse/ Perpignan
Map Reference: See Main Map Page 238
Resort Facilities Charts: See page 217

Picturesquely situated overlooking a large lake completely frozen in winter, the old village with its narrow streets and Gallo-Roman bell tower contrasts with the modern and efficient facilities on the slopes. Skiing is on the humpbacked ridge of Roc d'Aude. There are three access points: via one of the two gondolaways, Les Pelerins and Lou Bac, housed in the same building which also provides locker facilities for ski equipment; via the Jassettes Express 4-seater chair-lift, or via the Pla del Mir drag-lift from the outskirts of the village. The latter can be reached by a free navette, whilst the others all start from the town centre. They all have large parking areas either next to the lifts or within easy walking distance, with town centre overflow parking on a lower level.

The three areas, Les Jassettes, Bigorre and Pla del Mir, offer a network of 6 blues and 13 reds, non-demanding and ideal for intermediates, with links at strategic points allowing easy movement from one run to another for greater variety. For beginners there is a large and gentle plateau just below the summit and a long green run all the way from the peak of Roc d'Aude to the village. For the more advanced, a black run through the trees takes one back to the bottom station of the gondolaways and chair-lift. Plenty of scope for off-piste through the trees.

There are special facilities for snowboarding (Espace Surf) and from time to time freestyle demonstrations of snowboarding take place.

In a Few Words: In total there are 40kms of piste, covering a drop in height of 2624 ft and with its 212 strategically placed snow cannons, good snow cover is maintained on a variety of runs throughout the season so there is something for everyone. Finely groomed pistes, no crowds and no queues, certainly out of school holidays, inexpensive lift passes at 700ff for 6 days in high season. Nordic skiers are catered for with more than 100km of marked pistes and for children the resort boasts a creche, kindergarten and infants' ski school. The mountain restaurants serve simple meals at reasonable prices. Progressive resort which maintains the feel of a real mountain village. The resort is one of the 9 Neige Catalan ski stations and a pass covering all nine can be purchased for little more than the normal six-day pass, giving access to more skiing than anyone could hope to cover in a week.

Après Ski: Strong emphasis on other sporting and/ or outdoor activities, such as ice and snow surfing, and tours of the countryside by Troika or Husky-drawn sled. The Parc Animalier with two trails of 1.5km and 3.5km where one can see various species of animals native to the Pyrénées in their natural habitat. Lessons in scuba diving in the pool (which also offers a free sauna) or for the more advanced scuba diving beneath the ice of Lake Matemale, as well as the more usual ten pin bowling and ice skating. There is a good selection of restaurants of all prices, several bars some of which also serve food. There is also a cinema in the old village.

Accommodation: The capacity of the resort is 18,000 beds. Accommodation is mainly in self-catering apartments or chalets, a great many of which are south-facing with a view of the lake, but some of which can be a reasonable distance from the lifts (up to 3kms). There are also five hotels of various standards and one aparthotel.

ISOLA 2000

Height of Resort: 6,560 ft.
Height of Top Station: 8,563 ft.
Nearest International Airport: Nice
Map Reference: See Main Map page 238
Route by Car: See page 236-238
Resorts Facilities Charts: See page 217
Hotel Reference Charts: See page 229

The sunny resort of Isola lies high in the Chastillon valley easily accessible from Nice Airport, about $1^1/_2$ hours along a good climbing road The road passes the bottom station of the modern Génisserie 4-seater chair-lift, the longest in the Southern Alps and further on, Parking 1900 with its 3 chair-lifts and drag-lift before reaching the main resort, a complex of ultra-modern buildings. This is another purpose-built ski resort surrounded by a huge crescent of sunny slopes, lifts and potential lift sites fanning out from the resort from all sides, and runs from the widely spread top stations converging on the resort. There are 24 lifts, consisting of one gondolaway, 11 chair-lifts and 12 drag-lifts covering the north-east, north and north-west facing slopes (most are north facing). The slopes to the north-western side of the resort are scheduled to have additional lifts, and in this area the chair-lift to La Lombarde is already in operation. At present there are 120km. of prepared pistes. Plans are under way to link up with the Italian village of Santa Anna di Vinado via Col de la Lombarde which will enlarge the ski area considerably.

Central Area: The gondolaway is the central lift from the resort and carries 1,200 persons per hour to a height of 7,609ft., where there is a small restaurant, the Schuss. Supplementing this sytem is the Grands Vallons 4 seater chair-lift, running from Front de Neige to La Cabane. A variety of north facing runs lead back to the resort or Parking 1900. These include one of the most challenging runs, the Super Sapins, running roughly parallel to the gondolaway. An alternative return route is down to the Plateau drag-lift on the east side, rising to a height of 7,806ft. and then skiing down to the resort, or by using either of the two Marmottes drag-lifts to the west, which give access to a good selection of north facing runs to the village or parking area.

The Sistron chair-lift, rising to a height of 8,563 ft., increases the scope of skiing in this area. It gives a drop in height of 2,624ft. and has opened up 20km. of pistes, including a medium and a difficult run. The latter offers the opportunity of first-class off-piste skiing, in the valley parallel to the St. Sauveur valley, previously inaccessible. The top station here provides the most spectacular view – stretching from the Mediterranean as far as Mont Blanc and Mont Rosa. Another improvement is that the previously overcrowded Front de Neige drag-lift has been duplicated, reducing queueing on the journey to the Slalom Stadium, giant slalom course, ski-lift des Parcs and piste des Sapins, which has been adapted to fit in with the Front de Neige lifts. In addition, there have been a number of modifications to existing runs and correction of black spots. The installation of the Merlier chair-lift has opened up some superb skiing in the valley of the same name. A residents' car park for 550 cars has been constructed at the entrance to the resort, making it a pedestrianised area.

Parking 1900 Metres: This area was designed to cope with the heavy weekend influx from Nice, providing space for 1,000 cars, buffet bar, lavatories, ski hire and ticket office. There is an ice Circuit, designed with the help of the late Graham Hill, where one can be taught to drive in one's own car under icy conditions. Day visitors can by-pass the resort by taking either the Combe Grosse lifts, or the Cabane chair-lift rising to a height of 7,691ft. which then leads to the main Pelevos skiing area to the left, or the Col de Valette and Saint-Sauveur area to the right. The Combe Grosse lifts rise to 8,094ft. which provides skiing all day in the sun, on runs of an easy to medium standard, with a drop of 1,968ft. in height. On the north-western side of the resort a chair-lift rises from Parking 1900 up to La Lombarde, 7,741ft. This point is on the Franco-Italian border. The runs back are on south to south-west facing slopes and easy to intermediate standard.

Génisserie 1800 Metres: This base links with the main lift system, as the Génisserie chair-lift, beginning some way from Isola 2000, rises to a point 7,544ft. high. From this top station one can ski across to the base of 3 lifts, first the Saint Sauveur drag-lift with a surmounting chair-lift rising to Sistron, 8,563ft., the resort's top station; second, the Valette drag-lift reaching 7,743ft, and third, the chair-lift rising to La Cabane, 7,844ft. The area consists of north, west and north-west facing runs, and snow conditions remain good until May. Medium to advanced standard runs lead back to Génisserie. Two additional difficult runs have been constructed in this area. They branch off from the main Sistron-Génisserie run, and therefore give the area greater variety.

Children: There are two nurseries. La Pichoun's, staffed by qualified nurses and kindergarten helpers, look after small children and even babies. The children's village, 'Le Caribou', provides indoor and outdoor activities including early skiing tuition. 'Le Club des Juniors' caters for the 6-12 year olds, and here the children learn to ski in a specially equipped area with two small drag-lifts. Indoor activities are also organised. Meals are available and bookings can be made on a half, full or 6 day basis. There are also several reliable babysitters in the resort.

In a Few Words: A well situated resort with an excellent interlinked lift system. Long season with good snow conditions; door to door skiing. Évolutif teaching for beginners; the method of teaching in collective classes is good; good sun; recommended for families; kindergarten; langlauf; sun and snow guarantee; gets better every year. 165 snow cannons are in operation.

Après Ski: Food is available in the restaurants of the 4 hotels and a selection of outside restaurants, serving a variety of specialities. La Tanière and Le Scoop are great fun and very popular, whilst La Spatule and the Hotel Pas du Loup have comfortable piano bars.The Cow Club has an excellent and reasonably priced menu; it is also open at lunchtime when one can eat on the outside terrace. Dress everywhere is very casual. There is a cinema showing French films 6 days a week and English on the seventh. There are excellent sports hire shops, two supermarkets and a bakery. Once a week, weather permitting, there is a torchlight procession by the ski instructors, followed by a firework display. Other activities include: hang-gliding, skating, snowboard park and various competitions, night skiing twice weekly free of charge, heli-skiing and classical music concerts every week.

Aquavallee: This extensive indoor sports and leisure centre is situated in Isola village 25 minutes by bus from Isola 2000. It provides many facilities under one roof, including:- swimming pools, watershutes, gymnasium, squash, sauna, solarium, restaurant, boutique, conference rooms and much more. A pleasant break from skiing!

Recommended Hotels:

Hotel Le Chastillon: The Hotel Chastillon is 4-star with 54 bedrooms all with bathrooms, some with south facing balconies. There are 3 suites for 6 people in each and colour TV,video and mini-bar in all rooms. Its charming open hall with flagstone floor and clumps of evergreen and variegated ivy simulates a courtyard garden. This is overlooked by three tiers of wooden balustrades with the bedrooms leading off them. This is very attractive though limiting in privacy to a certain extent. There is also a television room and bar with sun terrace. The hotel is known for the excellence of its chef and the beautifully designed dining room is superb – large and comfortable, decorated with fresh spring flowers; there is a sun terrace off. Guests can choose their dinner from the à la carte menu, which looks good and is good.

Hotel Diva: This four star hotel was opened in 1988, built in traditional chalet style with 28 rooms and suites all with facilities, including TV and video. Elegantly designed reception rooms, bar with live music, massage and sauna. High standard of cuisine. Magnificent views from the terrace. Easily accessible on skis.

Le Druos: Opened in 1976/77 and under the same management as the other hotels, this is a bed and breakfast hotel with a number of family-sized rooms, situated some way from the shops and ski school, but it is possible to ski to and from the hotel. Bright, flagstoned entrance hall with log fire, lots of flowers and greenery. Bar where sandwiches can be obtained at lunchtime. Good value.

Le Pas du Loup: This 3 star hotel opened at the end of 1973 and has 97 double rooms, all with private bathrooms and TV with video, some with south facing balconies overlooking the ski slopes. Single rooms are also available. Like the other three it has no single rooms – a double room has to be taken with an adjustment in charge. Large modern reception areas, comfortable and always brightened by a beautiful vase of flowers. Two bars, one with terrace, a large dining room with sun terrace, television room, piano-bar and as with the other hotels, one steps straight outside into the ski area. Of the three, this hotel caters best for children.

La Résidence Les Adrets: Situated in the heart of the resort and providing comfortable fully equipped apartments of varying sizes, with direct dial telephone, TV and a laundry service.

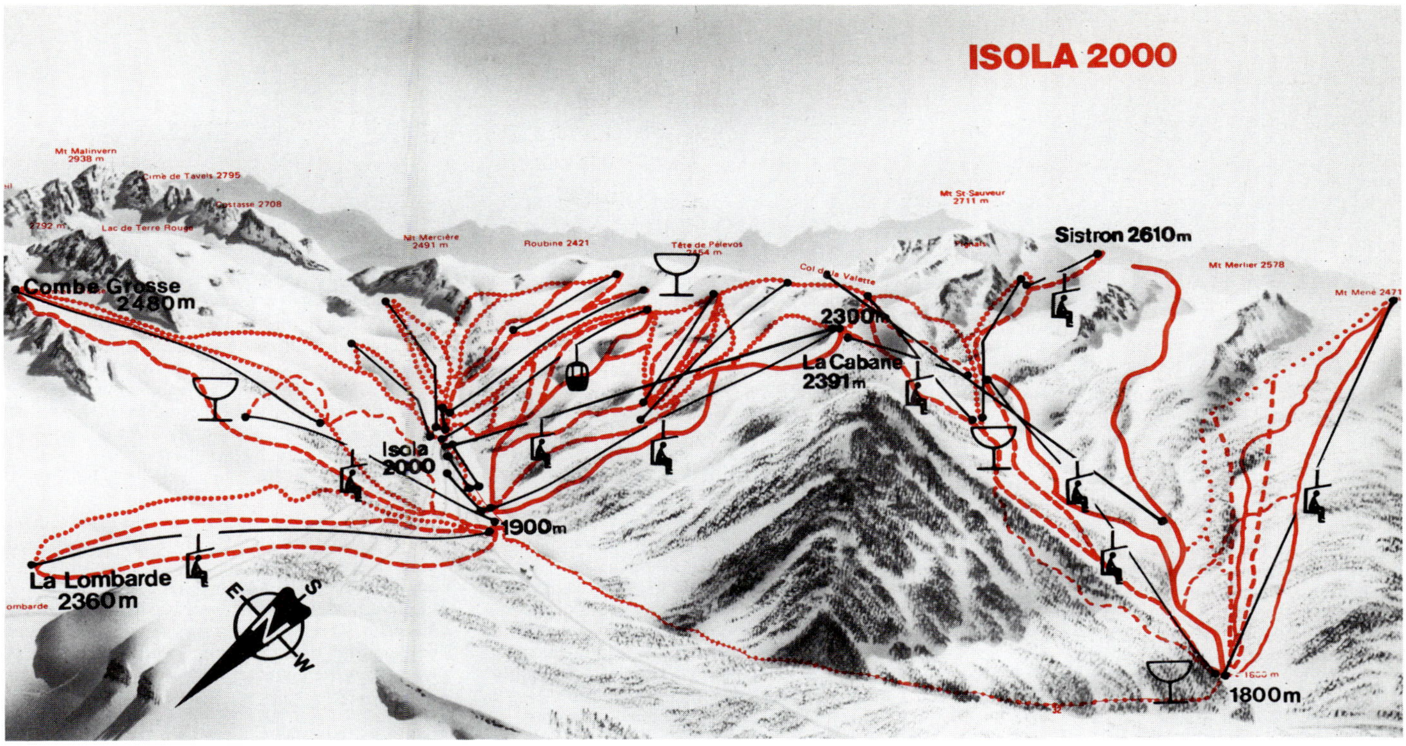

BRIEF REPORTS ON FURTHER FRENCH RESORTS

ARGENTIÈRE, 4,110ft.: Situated at the eastern end of the Chamonix valley, this is a typical small village forming part of the Chamonix lift complex, connection by regular bus service. Direct skiing from Argentière to Les Grands Montets area situated on the southern side of the village. 64 hotels and apartments; height top station 12,486ft.In 1986 a new ski area was introduced, not only increasing the potential but doing much to alleviate the queues at the Argentière-Lognon cablecar. Three lifts were introduced, a gondola from the village to Plan Joran and 2 chair-lifts, plus increased capacity on the Bochard gondola. These serve the La Pendant area, an open bowl and superb off-piste skiing in a succession of large combes stretching over 1,240 acres with a drop of 3,350ft., to the chair-lift. This gives a total of 2 cableways, 1 gondolaway, 5 chair-lifts, 1 drag-lift and 5 additional pistes and trails plus Chamonix complex (see separate report). Suitable for intermediates to advanced skiers.

LA ROSIÈRE 6,069ft.: Situated on a sunny plateau above Bourg St. Maurice and reached by a long twisting road with many hairpin bends. A small sunny village with a few hotels, the main accommodation being in apartments. The skiing over wide open south facing slopes is suitable for beginners to intermediates using the well spread out lifts to criss-cross the area, otherwise the runs are relatively short.. The link with the Italian resort of La Thuile (see page 104) creates a different picture as the combination of the two resorts provides 135km. of prepared pistes served by 33 lifts. The entry point for the La Thuile skiing is via Col de la Traversette, 7,874ft, Night life centres on the various bars, such as Le Relais and the Yeti and also the disco. La Rosière is well placed for visits to the nearby resorts of La Plagne, Les Arcs, Tignes and Val d'Isère.

ST. GERVAIS, 2,685ft.: Lying midway between Chamonix and Megève, to which its ski terrain is connected, St. Gervais is really a small town with a large choice of hotels, casino, cinema and a wide variety of restaurants. The skiing is in two areas, one each side of the valley and the runs are easy to medium. 49 hotels and pensions; height top station, 6,420ft. 1 mountain railway, 3 cableways, 3 gondolaways and 27 drag-lifts, suitable for beginners to advanced intermediates.

VALLOIRE 4,693ft.: Situated between St. Michel de Maurienne and the Col du Galibier, Valloire lies in a sunny valley surrounded by some magnificent ski terrain. Most of the runs face north, north-east and north-west so the snow remains in good condition until late season. Life in the village is cheerful and unsophisticated. 27 hotels and pensions; height top station 8,203ft.; 2 gondolaways, 8 chair-lifts and 21 drag-lifts suitable for beginners but favours the medium to good skier. 130km. of marked runs, (longest 5km.); 2 ski schools, kindergarten, 2 altitude restaurants.

RISOUL 6,013ft.: Another purpose built resort which although small has an amazingly large ski area. This is achieved by sharing on the Risoul/Vars combined skipass the skiing of two neighbouring resorts, Vars-Ste.-Catherine and Vars-les-Claux. Together they make up some 184km. of prepared pistes and very extensive off-piste. The skiing will suit beginners to advanced skiers alike with mile upon mile of long, often challenging runs. Many of the red runs could be graded black and the blacks make even the most adventurous skier pause to consider. One in particular, Les Vautours, is very difficult. 57 lifts soon disperse skiers around the area and onto the upper slopes. The ski school takes great pride in its teaching system, encouraging a high level of ability. Many of the instructors speak English. The well balanced ratio of blue and red runs make this an ideal resort for mixed ability groups or families. Less able skiers will enjoy the length of the runs and the variety. Accommodation is mainly in self-catering apartments with all the necessary shops, bars and restaurants within short walking distance within the main complex. Nightlife is casual, mainly happening in the bars or 'special' evenings in the restaurants. There is one disco.

VAL CENIS 4,593ft.: Situated in the Haute Maurienne, near the National Park of Vanoise and close to the French/Italian border, Val Cenis consists of two old villages, Lanslebourg and Lanslevillarde, about 3km. apart. The well equipped ski area lies on the south-eastern side of the road and stretches up between the two villages to a height of 9,186ft. so one can enter the system from either village. The 60km. of runs are mainly blue and red with a few blacks from the top station, served by a gondolaway, 10 chair-lifts and 12 drag-lifts. The top half of this north-west facing area is above the tree line, and wooded slopes on the lower part hold the snow well. Suitable for beginners to intermediates although some of the direct reds are more testing. The two villages have 14 hotels plus apartment accommodation. Night life is relaxing in the various restaurants and bars and for the more energetic there are two discos.

ITALY

THE ALTA BADIA DISTRICT

The district of Alta Badia, in Bolzano Province, lies at the top of the Val Badia leading up from Brunico. Before the First World War it was Austrian (South Tyrol) and both Italian and German are equally spoken along with the local language, Ladino. Most places still have three names. The Alta Badia, includes the resorts of Pedraces, La Villa, San Cassiano, Corvara and Colfosco is bounded by 3 passes, all kept open in winter. This area is easily reached on the autobahn from Munich into Austria via Kufstein, by-passing Innsbruck and over the Brenner Pass when one continues on the Italian autostrada until the exit at Bressanone.

THE ALTA BADIA SKIING

Once up at Piz La Ila (from La Villa) or Piz Sorega (from San Cassiano) one is within a vast interconnecting ski 'circus' from which one can not only ski to or from either of these two resorts but connect with the resorts of Corvara, Colfosco and Pedraces as well as the Campolongo and Gardena passes – this immediate area may be called the Pralongia area and can perhaps be described as a plateau dotted with hills. Wherever one meets a hill there is a lift up and when one skis down the other side there is a lift taking one further away or alternatively, one to take one back. Everyone skis according to his standard but the less accomplished must be careful not to be lured too far afield lest one has not time to get back by evening. Generally those 'plateau' runs between lifts are relatively short and easy, the emphasis being on the distance one can cover rather than the vertical drop. Overall the runs down to the resorts are steeper and more interesting for the better skier than the interconnections above. Apart from the direct runs down to La Villa and San Cassiano, the Boé and Vallon runs from the gondolaway and chair-lift respectively from Corvara are of special interest. Included in the district abonnement and not to be missed is the cablecar from Passo Falzarego to Lagazuoi 9,111ft., with its 8km. run back to Armentarola. This can easily be achieved by bus even if one does not have a car. There are many other challenging runs outside the immediate Alta Badia area for which one's own car is an asset but not essential. An achievement in distance, some 60km., amidst the most beautiful Dolomite scenery, is the circling of the Sella Massif, the famous 'Sella Ronda'.

The Dolomiti Superski Abonnement System: One cannot appreciate the scope of the skiing in the Alta Badia and beyond without some understanding of the unique abonnement system: this must be the most modern and extensive in the world. It is an astonishing achievement that the Dolomiti Superski Abonnement embraces 464 lifts, covering almost the length and breadth of the Dolomites. This gives tremendous freedom of action for the good skier with a car (although the bus services are extensive) who wants to drive around some 25 resorts picking and choosing the best runs. The Superski Abonnement costs about 10% more than the district pass. The district passes divide the Dolomites into 12 areas, that for the Alta Badia, with which we are concerned, is in itself very generous, allowing the use of 57 lifts over a wide area and covering the resorts of Pedraces, San Cassiano, Armentarola, La Villa, Corvara and Colfosco, up to the passes of Campolongo and Gardena and the Lagazuoi cablecar. This is probably as much territory as most intermediates can cover in a fortnight's holiday.

The issuing of the Dolomiti Superski Abonnement (Superski or District) in each resort is quick and efficient. Once issued, you never have to show it to any lift attendant. You merely pass it through a machine at the bottom of every lift; if there is a bleep it is valid, if not you're out of your particular area or beyond the validity date. Mind-boggling and uniquely efficient; the slopes echo with bleeps everywhere!

In a Few Words: A paradise for the beginner to intermediate skier and a novel experience for the good to expert; the challenging runs are here but rather spread out. A car is an asset. One might say that no-one is a complete skier until he has skied the Dolomites. This a different type of skiing; touring with the aid of lifts with the odd really challenging run thrown in as a bonus - one goes to Zermatt, say, to achieve the maximum amount of vertical downhill feet in a single day; here it is a question of how many miles one can achieve and get back to one's resort by nightfall. All this amongst the most beautiful scenery in the Alps.

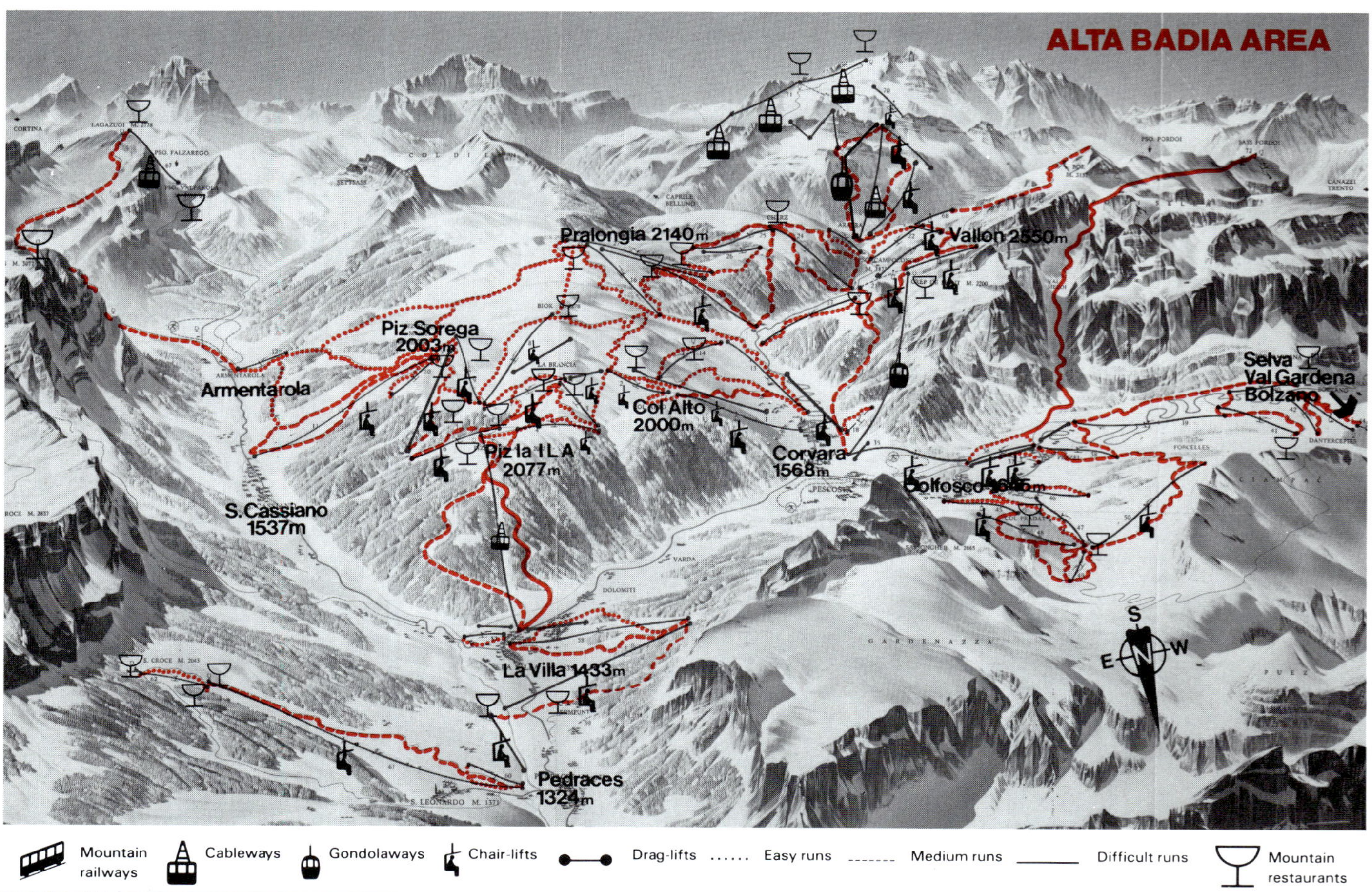

LA VILLA

Height of Resort: 4,870 ft.
Height of Top Station: 6,812 ft.
Nearest International Airport: Venice/Munich
Map Reference: 6B See page 239
Route by Car: See pages 236-239
Resort Facilities Chart: See page 219
Hotel Reference Charts: See page 231

La Villa is situated astride the Brunico-Corvara road where it turns off for San Cassiano and the Falzarego pass. Although widely spread, the bulk of its accommodation is within a few hundred yards of the main lift. The resort was constructed in 1966 (although the original old village stands above it). In all there are 45 hotels, pensions and residences providing 1,767 beds with 672 beds in private houses. It enjoys long hours of sunshine (in February 8 a.m. till 4.30 p.m.). There is an excellent sunny nursery slope. The cableway out of the resort centre rises to Piz La Ila 6,812ft., where one is in the vast Alta Badia ski circuit and here it is quite impossible to apportion the 57 lifts available to any particular resort. The two runs back from Piz La Ila to La Villa, some 2,000ft., descent and 2 or 3km in length, are some of the best in the area. Both are north facing through wooded glades, where the snow is usually excellent. One is a very enjoyable good intermediate run; the other, more direct, is challenging and superb 'Gran Risa', the World Championship downhill course. Good skiers needing to choose between La Villa or San Cassiano as a base (although they are linked by lifts) would probably prefer the former in order to have these very good runs on their doorstep. Two chair-lifts now connect La Villa with Pedraces (see below).

Après Ski: The hotels Ladinia, Aurora and Christiania, being near the end of the ski runs, are popular for coffee and cakes. Dandos music pub is popular with the younger set. Night life is somewhat limited. There are also night spots in San Cassiano, La Villa's 'sister-village' some 3km. away, but here again the taxi problem crops up. Of course much happy drinking can be done in the numerous bars/hotels, starting at the village's popular meeting place, the Hotel Ladina, with heated swimming pool and fitness centre.

Recommended Hotels:

Hotel Christiania: At the top of the village and only 50m. from the ski lift, the Christiania is a modern hotel built in most attractive Tyrolean style, where the key-note is spaciousness with informality. Nice sun terrace, sauna, solarium and whirlpool, large lounge and stüberl/bar popular with residents and non-residents alike. Piano bar. Dress casual. Food and service in dining room both excellent; large choice of menu including a help-yourself salad buffet with 7 varieties at every meal. Owner's wife and French waiter speak good English. Every fortnight there is a very enjoyable cocktail party where guests are made to feel really welcome. We stayed here and would rate the Christiania as 'A' category although it remains 'B' by owner's choice.

Pension Diana: Situated on the main village street and of chalet-style appearance, the Pension Diana offers good value for money. Its lounge/bar and dining room with candles at night are both very pleasant and its menu, although a set one, can be altered if required. Very personally run by the owner Frau Tirel, whose son speaks English and is most helpful. As the rooms are few, early booking is advisable.

PEDRACES – S. LEONARDO

Height of Resort: 4,343 ft.
Height of Top Station: 6,703 ft.
Nearest International Airport: Venice/Munich
Map Reference: 64B See page 239
Route by Car: See page 236-239
Resort Facilities Chart: See page 220

This small village lies just 3km. north of La Villa, it has a good selection of accommodation in its 87 hotels, pensions and residences, providing a total of 940 beds with a further 630 in private houses.

The resort's own ski area is served by a chair-lift rising eastwards from the village to twin restaurants, and here a surmounting drag-lift takes one up to Santa Croce, 6,703ft. with a further restaurant at this top station. The views of the Alta Badia area from this point are breathtaking. The run back to the village, following the line of the chair-lift is about 4km. with a vertical drop of 2,243 ft., will be enjoyed by the intermediate skier. There are nursery slopes at the top and foot of the chair-lift, the latter is also served by a drag-lift. Two interconnecting chair-lifts installed in 1993 link Pedraces with La Villa.

In a Few Words: A charming village and no disadvantage staying here with lift connections to La Villa 3km. away. Pedraces skiing is included in the Alta Badia lift pass.

Après Ski: Limited, with most of the activities centred around the 4 star Sporthotel Teresa with its piano bar, indoor tennis court and covered riding area. Two hotels have heated swimming pools, for guests only. Cosy bars to be found in several of the hotels, in addition to the Badia pub.

SAN CASSIANO

Height of Resort: 5,159 ft.
Height of Top Station: 6,570 ft.
Nearest International Airport: Venice/Munich
Map Reference: 6B See page 239
Route by Car: See page 236-239
Resort Facilities Charts: See page 220
Hotel Reference Charts: See page 231

This old village, in a very sunny position, is situated at the foot of theValparola pass about 3km. up from La Villa and is rather more concentrated. A further $1^1/_2$km. up the pass is Armentarola, which may be considered a satellite as it is connected by lifts. Here there is excellent nordic skiing. San Cassiano has 57hotels and pensions varying from the luxurious to simple totalling 2,014 beds and 1402 beds in private houses. Some 250m. from the centre, a four seater chair-lift rises to Piz Sorega 6,750ft. Here one is within the Alta Badia skiing circuit linking all the neighbouring resorts – see under the 'Alta Badia Skiing'. There are no nursery slopes in the village and the ski school meets at Piz Sorega, where there are excellent beginner slopes. The runs back to the resort consist of a long and beautiful beginner/early intermediate run and steeper good intermediate runs down the line of the lifts. Novices and early intermediates may prefer San Cassiano to La Villa as a resort because of the glorious long and easy run back to the village.

Après Ski: The Hotel Rosa Alpina is the centre of entertainment, offering dancing to a 2-man band. There are 4 hotels with heated indoor swimming pools for guests only and 11 saunas and for the indefatigable, a climb up to the lovely Hotel Diamant can even get you an indoor tennis court and two 9-pin bowling alleys for after ski relaxation.

Recommended Hotels:

Hotel Falzares: A well established, no nonsense hotel chosen for its ideal location in the centre of the village rather than for any frills. All of the rooms have bathrooms, telephone and hairdrier, and many have balconies; simple dining room and bar/lounge, plain Italian cooking and benches outside the front door to sit in the sun and watch the world go by. Suitable for those looking for a modest price and who put convenience before luxuries.

Hotel Rosa Alpina: An extremely attractive, well set out hotel in the very centre of San Cassiano. Dating back well over a hundred years, the Rosa Alpina is beautifully modernised throughout in excellent Tyrolean style; spacious sitting rooms and bars, inviting grill room and dining room with panoramic windows and views. The amenities – many free to guests – include ping-pong, billiards, children's games room, sauna, massage and swimming pool, whirlpool and solarium. All the rooms have telephones, TV on request, private shower/bath/wc, and nearly all have balconies. Also 24 apartments from 2 to 6 persons. Dancing daily. There's a pizzeria and a konditorei. A cocktail party is organised every so often for guests free of charge. An 'English breakfast' is included in the rates. Run by the Pizzinini family for over 50 years.

CORVARA

Height of Resort: 5,143 ft.
Height of Top Station: 7,216 ft.
Nearest International Airport: Venice/Munich
Map Reference: 6C See page 239
Route by Car: See page 236-239
Resort Facilities Charts: See page 219
Hotel Reference Charts: See page 231

Corvara, the largest of the villages in the Alta Badia complex, is situated at the junction of the valleys that lead to Arabba, Grödnertal and La Villa. It is spread over a wide area but the centre is fairly compact and situated on either side of the main road leading to Arabba. There is a good variety of shops and boutiques. 35 hotels and pensions provide beds for 1,759 guests, some 841 beds in private houses and 1,089 beds in apartments.

The ski school meets in the village centre and sessions are from Monday to Friday, 1000-1245 hours. Private lessons are available mornings and afternoons. Children can be left at the ski kindergarten fromn 0930 - 1600 hours to enjoy a full day's skiing.

Just above the ski school is the chair-lift Col Alto, rising to a height of 6,520ft. over a distance of 1,086m. This is one of three lifts that connect Corvara with the magnificent skiing circuit of the Alta Badia, described separately. The runs down from the Col Alto are typical in that they offer a choice of wide and interesting easy to intermediate pistes. To the west of Corvara is the Boé gondolaway, which rises to a height of 7,216ft. From the top station there are magnificent views of the Marmolada and a whole panorama of peaks, snow fields and lifts, including the Alta Badia skiing circuit.

From here a choice of runs down to either Corvara by way of a red piste that takes one across wide snow fields to wooded slopes; or alternatively down to Campolongo, which connects up with the Alta Badia skiing circuit. Also at the top there is a further chair-lift rising an additional 443ft. to Vallon, the highest point in the district at 8,315ft. There are still many lifts and pistes that have not been mentioned but all are interconnected and all offer the same excellent conditions that make this area so popular. One unusual lift is a chair-lift that connects the skiing complex of Colfosco with that of Corvara. This lift is 1,145m. long, but only rises 131ft., and is used purely to transport from one village to the next.

Recommended Hotels (Corvara):

Hotel Sassongher: This first-class hotel is beautifully situated, overlooking the entire village. Being 500m. from the village centre makes it a little inconvenient, but the magnificent views looking south more than compensate. Shuttle buses operate all day to the slopes. It has been tastefully decorated but is perhaps a little 'traditional'. All rooms have a bath or shower, telephone, radio and TV and are very comfortable. A well stocked bar and 2 sitting rooms guarantee guests' comfort. Indoor swimming pool, sauna, fitness club, solarium, massage, Boutique and conference room seating 80 persons.The Sassongher Disco Club is situated in the keller.

Pension Pradat: A pleasant little pension of some 48 beds. Run by the Miribung family, with all the comforts of a typical family pension. All the bedrooms have either bath or shower, with the exception of the 4 single rooms, and are very comfortable, nearly all with balcony. The rooms mostly look south across the whole valley, with fine views of the Boe in the foreground and snow fields to the rear. A small dining room reserved for guests provides excellent and plentiful food. The bar, which doubles as a sitting room, is popular for both visitors and residents. A good family pension in pleasant position.

COLFOSCO

Height of Resort: 5,401 ft.
Height of Top Station: 7,216 ft.
Nearest International Airport: Venice/Munich
Map Reference: 6C See page 239
Route by Car: See page 236-239
Resort Facilities Charts: See page 219
Hotel Reference Charts: See page 231

Colfosco, smaller than Corvara, stands 258ft. higher and 3km. to the west. It has 25 hotels and pensions, catering for 885 guests and some 1,340 beds in private houses and apartments. The village is about $1^{1}/_{2}$km. long with the shops and hotels to either side of the road. The skiing in the village area is more suited to the beginner or intermediate. The 876m. long Col Pradat chair lift rises to a height of 6,560 ft., and from this point a piste leads down into a very wide, sunny bowl. A further choice of 4 lifts to all points of the compass rising from here includes the Forcelles chair-lift to the highest point in Colfosco, 7,216ft.

There are other lifts in the village which are concentrated above and to the west of Colfosco. These serve easy to intermediate runs but, what is more important, they connect skiers up with the huge complex of over 464 lifts covered by the Dolomiti Superski Pass which costs about 10% more than the Alta Badia Pass. For the good intermediate and advanced skier it is well worth the extra expense, but for the less experienced the Alta Badia pass is sufficient for 2 weeks holiday.

Après Ski: Corvara and Colfosco: Popular with the young is the Posta Zirm night club with band and the Disco Greif, and there are the usual hotel bars, restaurants and piano bars. The buildings are very much Tirolean design and decor and the night clubs are no exception and have a cosy atmosphere. A toboggan run has recently been built in Corvara whilst Colfosco has a snowboard half pipe and an indoor climbing wall.

ARABBA

Height of Resort: 5,254 ft.
Height of Top Station: 9,676 ft.
Nearest International Airport: Venice
Map Reference: 6B See page 239
Route by Car: See page 236-239
Resort Facilities Charts: See page 219
Hotel Reference Charts: See page 230

Arabba is one of the ski resorts clustered around the base of the Sella Massif on its south-eastern side and lies at the foot of the Pordoi pass to the west (leading over to Canazei) and the Campolongo pass to the north (leading over to Corvara and the Alta Badia). These passes are kept open in winter. The best route is over the Brenner and via Brunico and the Val Badia.

It is a small resort with excellent skiing. During December and January the sun is limited to 3 and 4 hours per day respectively, but from February onwards it enjoys long hours of sunshine.

The Arabba Skiing: Arabba's immediate local skiing consists of:

(a) The Porta Vescovo cableway and the two section Europa I and II gondolaway; (5,287ft.-8,188ft.), and Carpazza chair-lift (6,426. 8,188ft.), plus the Portados chair-lift which can be used to connect with the former to reach the summit of Porta Vescovo.

(b) The Monte Burz chair-lift (5,281ft.-6,385ft.).

(c) Beginner's tow lift nursery slope south-facing. Two drag-lifts connecting Campolongo Pass and chair-lift from Pass to Crep de Mont, 7,218ft.

(d) Bec De Roces chair-lift from Arabba to Bec De Roces. A drag-lift, Campolongo, is the return lift from Campolongo Pass to Arabba. There are a further 5 drag-lifts to the north of Campolongo Pass.

(e) A cableway, (Sass Pordoi, 7,360,ft.- 9,676ft.), with a lift at the top and two other lifts on the Pordoi pass.

(f) A series of 4 drag-lifts and 2 chair-lifts are in operation to connect Arabba via the Passo Padon with Malga Ciapela (see separate report) the start of the cableway for the Marmolada glacier. The glacier is not on the Superski pass. But holders can obtain a 30% reduction on a day pass.

The Porta Vescovo cableway: This cableway, built in 1972, was supplemented in 1991 by a two stage gondolaway and both provide skiing with a vertical drop of 3,116ft., over entirely north-facing slopes, where the snow remains untouched by the sun. There are some 5 pistes back to the base varying from relatively easy, through medium to difficult. All these are excellent, satisfying descents for all standards of skier (except beginners). The pistes are wide and very well maintained. The steepest runs vary between 3 and 4km., the longest some 6.5km. but three-quarters of the way down one can connect with the Carpazza chair-lift, base 6,426ft., which returns one to the summit and thus extending the skiing in this area until May as it is not necessary to return to the base station of the cableway. There is excellent scope for off-piste powder skiing. There is a restaurant at the summit and directly south are the slopes of the Marmolada 10,977ft., the highest mountain in the Dolomites. The lower station of this mountain, Malga Ciapela, can now be reached from the Arabba area by a series of 6 inter-connecting lifts which are included on the Arabba ski pass.

The Monte Burz chair-lift: This provides two runs of 1,049ft. drop and between $1^{1}/_{2}$ to 2km. back to the village down south-facing slopes, one quite a steep and fast direct route, the other less steep but not without interest for intermediates. From the top of the chair-lift a north-west facing run connects with Le Pale drag-lift which rises to Col De Roces, thus linking Arabba by the Campolongo drag-lift. From the Pass the Costoratta chair-lift connects with the Boe cableway at Crep de Mont, 7,218ft., linking up with the Corvara, La Villa and San Cassiano areas.

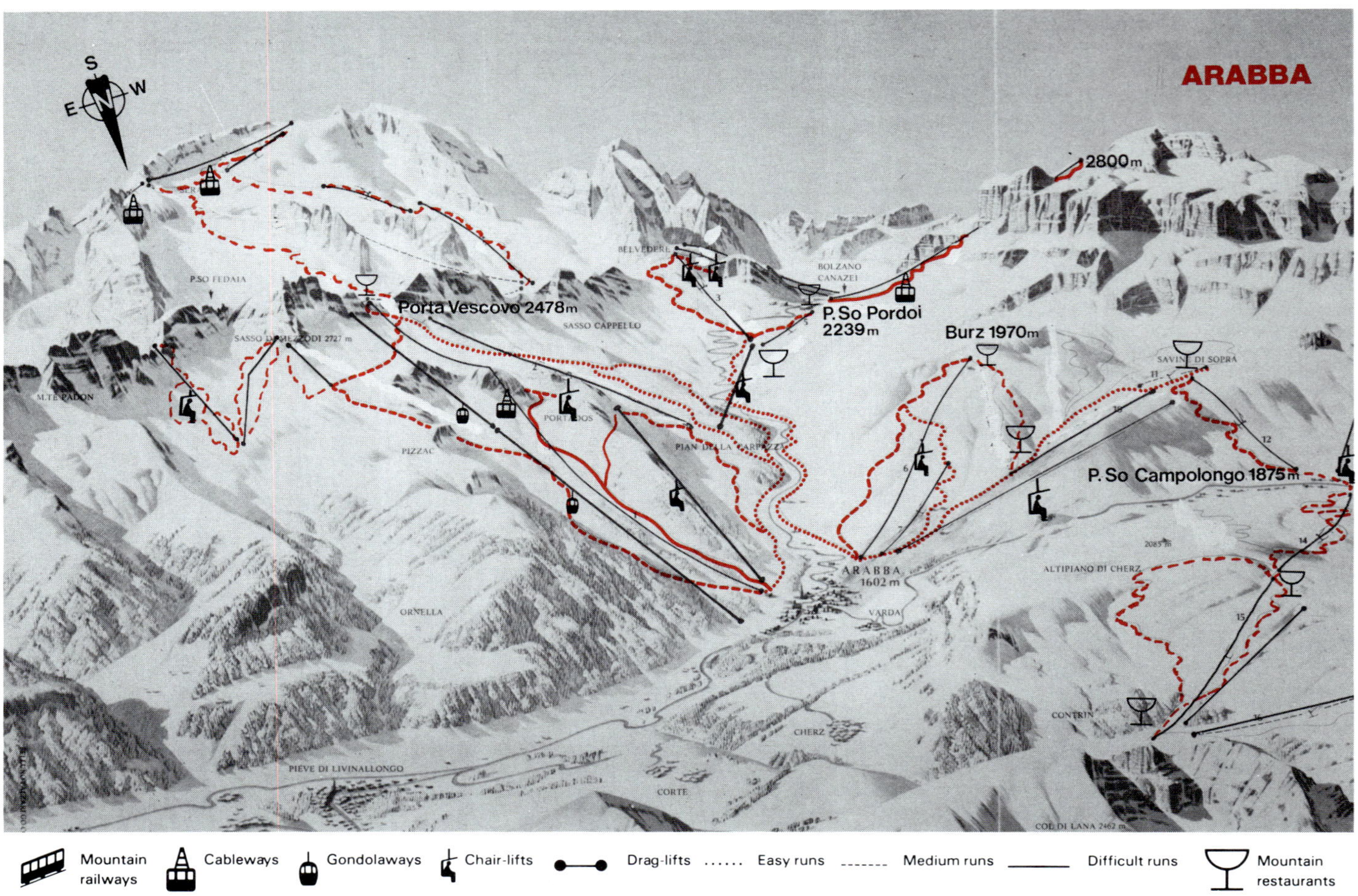

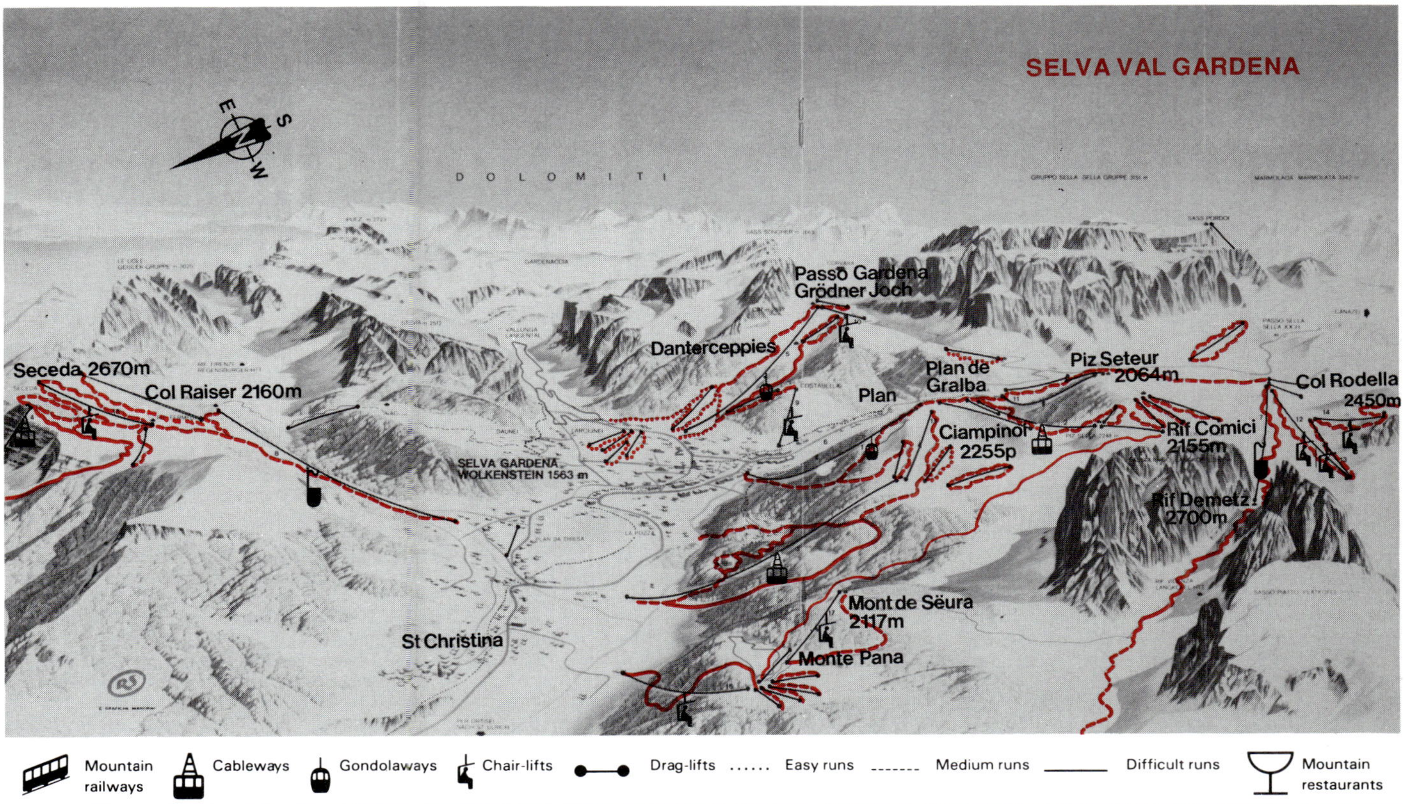

Pordoi Pass: The Fodom chair-lift reaches Pordoi Pass and the connecting lifts are the Saletei or the Lezuo Belvedere chair-lifts. Here the Sass Pordoi cableway rises right into the Sella Massif at 9,676ft., with a drag-lift and chair-lift at the summit. The cableway opens up 3 off-piste black runs – the Val Mezdi, Val Lasties and the run under the Forcella Pordoi cableway itself. From the Pordoi pass, one can ski down and return from the resorts of Canazei and Campitello as well as linking with all the runs of Selva and Val Gardena. Also one can do the whole circuit of the Sella in either direction, some 69km. of skiing.

In Few Words: Arabba provides excellent skiing for all standards. With the Superski pass the skiing available is limitless. Natural skating rink.

Après Ski: The cafés attached to most of the hotels and pensions supply coffee and cakes in a rather uncosy sort of way, there being, as yet, no popular meeting place for skiers to congregate after skiing. Although most pensions advertise their 'Ristorantes' these are pretty basic and would hardly coax one out for a gastronomic evening.

Recommended Hotels:

Pension Evaldo: Lying some 300m. downward from the village centre, the modernised chalet-style Pension Evaldo is sure to please most visitors. Its simple, lightwood 'stüberl', lounge and bar, its pleasing dining room and its neat, clean bedrooms, each with shower/wc., all form an ideal choice of holiday accommodation. Food plentiful and any changes to the set menu may be made each morning before 10 a.m. Whirlpool, sauna, massage and sun room.

Hotel Porta Vescovo: The largest, newest and one of the nicest hotels in Arabba. The whole decor is tastefully modern and woody, with a multitude of super, 'sink-into' chairs in spacious lounges and bar. Nearly all the dining tables are formed into corner banquettes, giving an unusually comfortable and intimate impression. 'Al Fegolé' bar with open fire. Amenities include sauna, solarium, massage pingpong/billiards/card room, sun terrace and sufficiency of deck chairs. All bedrooms have bath or shower and balcony.

SELVA VAL GARDENA

Height of Resort: 5,128 ft.
Height of Top Station: 8,264 ft.
Nearest International Airport: Verona/Munich
Map Reference: 6B See page 239
Route by Car: See page 236-239
Resort Facilities Chart: See page 221
Hotel Reference Charts See page 231

Selva is a small town situated high up in the Val Gardena, in what was until the end of the First World War, the Austrian Sud Tyrol: it is now Italian and its inhabitants speak German, Italian and Ladino, a local language spoken in a few high valleys of the Dolomites. The area is run with a mixture of Austrian efficiency and Italian insouciance. The town is a mixture of old and new chalets and hotels and the main street has a good selection of shops.

Skiing in this part of the Dolomites started when the railway was constructed during the First World War – but the local population had already held races prior to this in 1908 and had even started a ski club! Selva Val Gardena is well known to the British for its pre-Christmas World Cup Men's Downhill race always shown on Ski-Sunday. The town is dominated by magnificent scenery, craggy Dolomite peaks of greyish-pink rock - these peaks come alive at sunset when they seem to glow. There is a network of 81 lifts serving 175km. of prepared pistes and these are connected to the massive Dolomiti-Superski area which contains approximately 1,100km. of pistes and covers over 464 lifts.

Danterceppies area: This area is on the Eastern side of the village and can be entered in a variety of ways – either through the drag-lifts serving the sunny nursery slopes which are right in the village – or by taking the Costabella single chair-lift and skiing down to the gondolaway station. Either way it is the gondolaway which takes one up to the ridge overlooking the Alta Badia region and the route of the Sella Ronda. If one only holds a local Val Gardena pass it is necessary to ski back down to the village on the wide and pretty pistes through the pine woods - most of these runs are intermediate with some steeper parts here and there. There is a restaurant at the top and the small and cosy Panorama which is part of the way down.

At the bottom of these runs below the gondolaway station and alongside the nursery slopes is the restaurant known as 'The Squirrel' or Scoiattolo – here one can eat and drink and on Fridays there is tea-dancing in ski boots, accompanied by some of the ski instructors who sing and play various musical instruments.

Ciampinoi area: On the southerly side of the village lies the Ciampinoi area, reached by a modern gondolaway, constructed in 1989, or chair-lift. From the top station runs fan out in all directions – one can ski down to the village of Selva on steepish, wooded slopes or down to Santa Cristina on wide open pistes and then lower down through woods. One of these runs is the famous F.I.S. Val Gardena Men's Downhill 'Saslonch' which is kept in good condition because it is used for the Italian Team practices and most of the time it is open to the public.

From Ciampinoi one can ski on part of the Sella Ronda down to Plan de Gralba – past the Vallongia mountain restaurant which serves good food and is well known for its excellent apple strudel. From Plan de Gralba one can either ski directly to Selva on an intermediate run or travel back up on the fast Piz Sella cableway - which enables one to ski back to Ciampinoi again.

Overall, medium to good skiers will enjoy the skiing in Selva for its delightful variety of stimulating runs rather than their length; but for those who require even greater variety there is the Dolomiti-Superski Pass, which covers over 464 lifts in the Dolomite area.

Much of the skiing reported elsewhere in this Guide is in itself interlinked, but with one's own transport there are endless possibilities and today the Dolomite area must be unique in the world of skiing.

In a Few Words: Selva itself provides a great variety of medium-length runs, good for all grades whilst the advanced skier can take the Dolomiti-Superski pass, which allows unlimited use of all the lifts in the Dolomite area; village not compact; skiing area dramatic and beautiful. A friendly resort with a good atmosphere; well run ski school; snow-making machines.

Après Ski: Lively and informal, with numerous bars, restaurants and night clubs but fairly scattered as the village is so spread out. The 'Luislkeller' is full of people from about 4.30. p.m. being a popular meeting place for skiers and instructors, the Speckkeller is another good place to meet for a drink after skiing. The Hotels Savoy and Stella both have good discos. One of the most popular night spots is the 'Dali'. The Hotel Laurin has live music most evenings in its keller bar.

There are a number of popular pizzerias (one of the best being 'Ciampinoi' Pizzeria) and cafés. In addition to the resident bands, visiting groups and orchestras appear regularly. Selva also has a covered ice-rink, indoor tennis, bowling and billiards: Ortisei and St. Christina, nearby, have a further selection of night spots if required: Ortisei has ample opportunity for indoor swimming and tenpin bowling; and ice hockey championships take place in Selva on Friday evenings and on Saturdays in Ortisei.

Recommended Hotels:

Hotel Alpino-Plan: Situated at Plan, 10 minutes' walk from the centre of the village, this is a traditional inn, enlarged and providing comfortable accommodation. All rooms with bath or shower, telephone and TV; large sitting room, cosy bar popular with the locals. Good Italian kitchen. Friendly atmosphere, mainly created by owner Luis Demetz, English-speaking ski instructor.

Hotel Antares: A 4-star hotel centrally situated and 3 minutes from the main cableway. Large open-plan lounge with wooden panelling, Alpine style; bar/breakfast area, attractively decorated L-shaped dining room with set menu or à la carte. Swimming pool, sauna, sun terrace. All bedrooms with bath/shower, telephone, radio, and colour TV.

Hotel des Alpes: A modern hotel built in semicircular Alpine style, attractively furnished and decorated. Many rooms with bath or shower and balconies.

Pension Flora: Quite large for a pension with 50 beds, most with bath or shower. Small lounge, café, bar. Centrally situated.

CANAZEI/CAMPITELLO (Val di Passa)

Height of Resort: 4,808 ft
Height of Top Station: 9,684 ft
Nearest International Airport: Venice
Map Reference: 6C See page 239
Route by Car: Pages 236-239
Resort Facilities Chart: Page 219

These attractive twin resorts, 2 km. apart, are situated in the Val di Passa, and offer much of what is best for most skiers – beautiful scenery, a good range of runs for all abilities and access to a vast ski area in the Sella Ronda. Both resorts have very different characters – Campitello has more of a 'village' feel with a quiet nightlife, whilst Canazei is far more cosmopolitan and lively with many shops and boutiques, a swimming pool, sauna, and ice-rink. It is, however a lot noisier, being on the junction of the two major access roads.

Campitello is linked to the Sella Ronda by the Col Rodella cableway, which takes one up to a sunny basin, with spectacular views of the Sella Massif, and served by a small system of chair-lifts. This area is ideal for intermediates and the more intrepid beginner, as it is wide and not overly busy except at the beginning of the day when people are trying to get an early start to ski the Sella Ronda. As this suggests, with the benefit of the Ski Dolomite Pass, this is a good entry point to the 26km tour, which takes in the four passes of Sella, Pordoi, Campolongo and Gardena, and can be completed by intermediates easily in a day.

From Col Rodella there is a beautiful red run down through the trees to Canazei (sadly there is no run back to Campitello), or to Pian Frataces. Following the route of the Sella Ronda (anti-clockwise, a chair-lift takes one out of the valley up to the Belvedere ski area, above Canazei, and the Passo Pordoi with skiing up to 7,874 ft. This is a fair-sized basin. but with a greater variety of skiing for all ability levels (including off-piste). Coupled with its position on the Sella Ronda and the direct cableway served Canazei-Pecol-Col dei Rossi means it gets very busy. Fortunately the area is well served with chair-lifts and queues very rarely form. Nestling under the Massif itself, Belvedere offers dramatic views – also Marmolada and the surrounding mountains – subsequently its restaurant with sun terrace is very popular at lunchtime and not being overpriced is well worth a visit.

The red run down to Canazei via Lupo Bianco is highly attractive, though being quite narrow in places, as it snakes its way through trees and over bridges, is testing even for intermediates, particularly at the end of the day when it is very busy, but is nevertheless great fun.

Cross-country ski trails follow the River Avisio in the Val di Passa from Canazei though Campitello, Mazzin, Pozza, Viga to Moena, all of which are served by the free skibus service.
Canazei ski school has a very well organised system for all grades of skier having a drag-lift and nursery slope in the village. Children too are well catered for, with a kindergarten service under supervised conditions, and a snow adventure playground – the 'Fantaski Spielpark' at nearby Alba for 3 to 6 year-olds. The ski-bus service linking these villages is frequent and so this does not present much of a problem, although it can of course be crowded at peak times.

In a Few ords: These two charming resorts offer the best of both worlds, situated in a beautiful valley providing facilities to meet the needs of the most dedicated skier –snow cannons abound. The easy access to the vast skiing area of the Sella Ronda including the resorts of Selva/Val Gardena and Arabba, and low prices are other attractions of this area. On the other hand a knowledge of Italian or German is a distinct advantage, whilst it is important to know that lunchtimes are strictly observed – almost everything is shut between 12.15 and 2.15 pm, even if you want to buy a lift pass!

Après Ski: Canazei has many bars for those coming straight off the slopes as well as for later on in the evening; Particularly good for a choice of grappa, good music and a lively friendly atmosphere is the Penini Bar, which is very popular between 4.00 and 6.00 pm. There is a reasonable range of restaurants, mainly informal and moderately priced; Try Te Cevena, a cellar eatery in the centre of town. Campitello is very quiet but for a lively atmosphere at the end of the day try da Giulio – a cellar bar. Most of the restaurants here are in hotels as there are not many self-catering apartments, but for a more formal and good value meal, the Kamerloy is worth sampling.

Both villages have discos, but the one with the best reputation although it can be a little overpriced is Il Gatto Negro, which is situated halfway between the two villages.

Recommended Hotels: Canazei has many hotels with not a great deal to divide them; but for a balance of comfort, cost and location, the Bellevue and the Tyrol would be worth considering.

In Campitello the same applies, but the Parkhotel Fedora, though slightly more expensive, has the advantage of being located very close to the cableway station, whereas most are quite a walk away

CORTINA D'AMPEZZO

Height of Resort: 4,078 ft.
Height of Top Station: 10,543 ft.
Nearest International Airport Venice
Map Reference: 4C See page 239
Route by Car: See page 236-239
Resort Facilities Chart: See page 219
Hotel Reference Charts: See page 231

Italy's most fashionable resort, Cortina is an appealing town with a lively international atmosphere but warm and friendly despite its size. It is set in the heart of the Dolomites, surrounded by forests and wide ski slopes, with the craggy red rocks of the mountains towering above it. It has something for everyone and is a resort most keen skiers will want to try. There are five main areas:

Faloria-Tondi Area: A cableway from the town centre rises to Faloria, 6,890ft., where there is a large restaurant and small drag-lift nearby. A series of 5 chair-lifts nearby continue the ascent to Tondi, 7,605ft. Open medium grade runs lead to Faloria and to the foot of the chair-lifts and an interesting 9km. run from Faloria area returns to Cortina. This can be varied by joining the chair-lift at Rio Gere to connect with the Cristallo area.

Cristallo Area: Rio Gere, the bottom station near the Tre Croci Pass, is 6km. from the town centre. The chair-lift rises to Son Forca, 7,280ft.,where there is a restaurant and chair-lift giving access to intermediate skiing. Running northwards a chair-lift climbs to Forcella Staunies, 9,522ft., with a spectacular view. The run down starts steeply, through a long gulley, levelling out as it descends to the first station where less experienced skiers should get off on the way up and continues in a wide arc back to Rio Gere and then a long easy to intermediate run to the town. On the right, going down, is the Mietres-Pierosa area with easy open skiing served by 2 drag-lifts and 2 chair-lifts.

Tofana Area: From the town the cableway rises in three stages to Tofana, 10,543ft. The first station is Col Druscié, 5,725ft. with a black and red run down to the foot of the Colfieré chair-lift running parallel with the cableway and finishing just short of the first station. From Col Druscié the cableway climbs steeply to Ra Valles, 8,027ft. Here one can enjoy open and sheltered intermediate skiing served by two chair-lifts and a drag-lift. The run down from Ra Valles is steep and narrow, graded black to start with, and passes beneath the cableway to the foot of the Rumerlo 4 seater chair-lift. This lift is the centre one of the three surmounting chair-lifts and the top one, a 3 seater, Duca d'Aosta, reaches Pomedes, 7,677ft. This area provides some excellent and sometimes steep intermediate skiing and also links with the easy open skiing of the Socrepes-Pocol area, see below. The cableway from Ra Valles to Tofana only operates in the summer.

Falzarego and Cinque Torri Area: The Falzarego Pass, 7,054ft., is about 15km. by bus from the centre of Cortina, but before reaching this station one passes the Cinque Torre area on the left, which is very attractive and provides intermediate skiing served by two chair-lifts. Further eastwards and near the Pass is a drag-lift and chair-lift providing easy runs to base and one to the Pass. Here the cableway climbs dramatically to Piccolo Lagazuoi, 9,022ft, There are restaurants at the top and bottom stations. From the top one has a choice of an intermediate run back to the Pass or an 11km., not too difficult, run through very beautiful rugged terrain with several restaurants en route. It ends at Armentarola and one returns toFalzarego by taxi and to Cortina by bus.

Socrepes-Pocol Area: Two interlinking drag-lifts and three chair-lifts operate roughly parallel in this area, providing open, gentle runs back with plenty of variations.

In a Few Words: A wide variety of skiing and lots of other activities; Cortina should be enjoyed by skiers of all standards and non-skiers too; lively atmosphere and friendly people; good choice of accommodation, medium to expensive in price. One of the nicest large resorts.

Après Ski: There's no shortage of action here, with tea rooms, bars, restaurants and night clubs; also an excellent riding school, an Olympic ice stadium, ski jump, ice hockey and a public indoor swimming pool. There is a good choice of night clubs, including - Limbo, Bilbo, Belvedere, Metro, Area, VIP Club and Hyppo all offer dancing. Piano bars are to be found at Cristallino d'Ampezzo, Miramonti, Terrazza Viennese and the VIP Club. The Hotel de la Poste is a favourite rendezvous for after-ski drinks, and its sun terrace is usually packed with stylish men and women. Cortina is a resort where the more casual jeans and sweater wearers might feel out of place, whereas the chic and elegantly dressed will be in their element. A resort almost everyone would enjoy.

Recommended Hotels:

Hotel Ancora: This is an attractive and well run hotel, centrally situated and close to the Faloria cableway terminal. Comfortable bedrooms, all with bath; much care has been taken in the design and layout of the reception rooms and the dining room is particularly attractive; sun terrace, American bar and dancing.

Hotel Cortina: Right in the centre, a modern hotel attractively designed, good size comfortable bedrooms, all with bath, the reception rooms elegant and tasfully furnished, bar and small sun terrace. A charming and friendly service.

Hotel de la Poste: Situated in a quiet pedestrian zone, in a central and sunny position, this hotel is one of the most popular meeting places in Cortina. The bedrooms are large and comfortable, all with bath and there are also a number of elegant suites. Beautiful dining room with exceptional food and service. Spacious and attractive reception rooms and a convivial atmosphere in the bar.

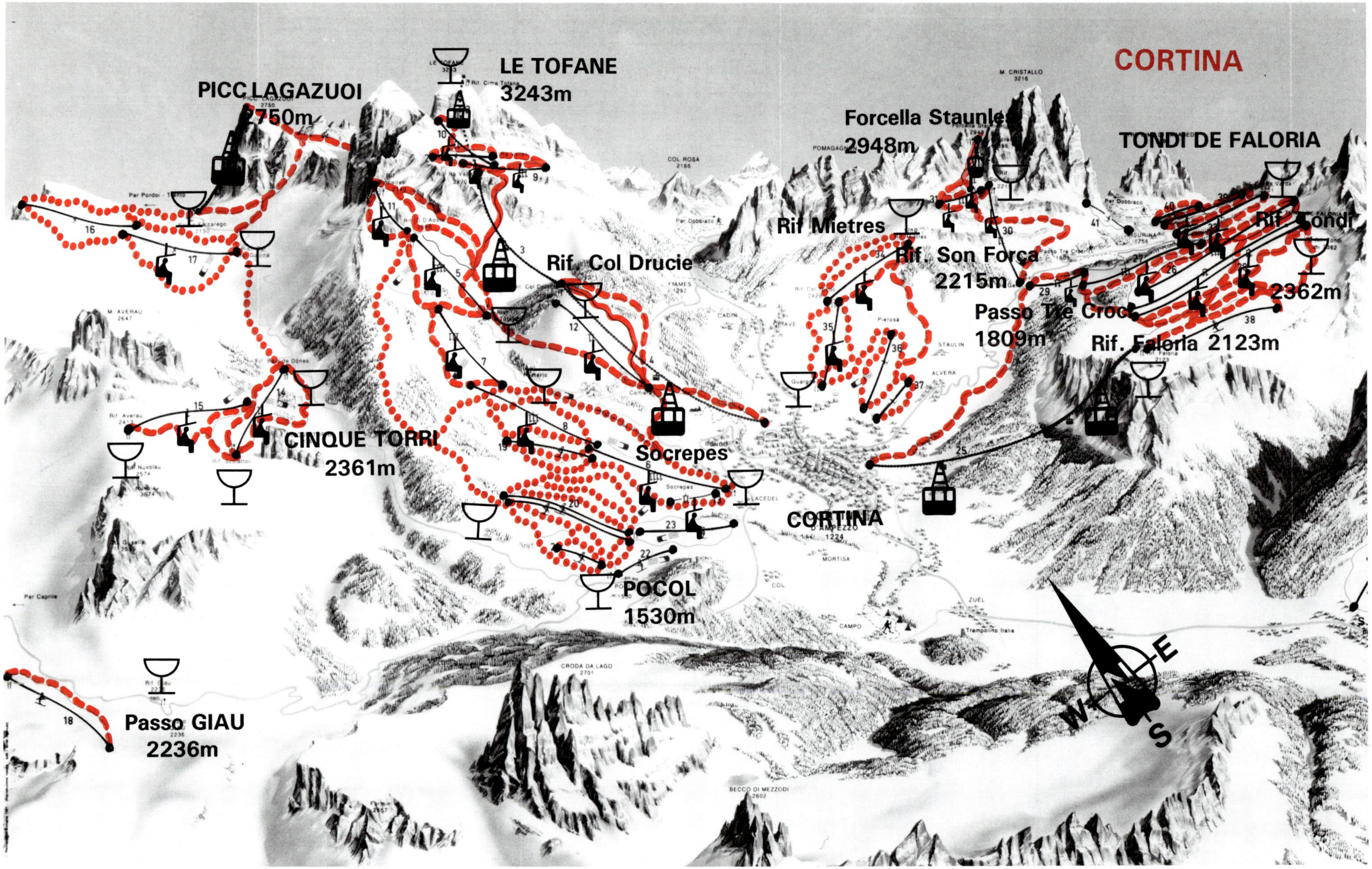

Mountain railways — Cableways — Gondolaways — Chair-lifts — Drag-lifts .... Easy runs --------- Medium runs ——— Difficult runs — Mountain restaurants

Hotel Europe: A modern hotel situated in a central position, near the Olympic stadium. Bedrooms tastefully furnished, although on the small side, all with private bath. Really famous for its food and service. Piano bar; grill room; discothèque VIP Club has become one of the most successful in Cortina. The reception rooms (2 dining rooms, 3 sitting rooms) are beautifully designed and laid out.

Parc Hotel Victoria: This is a very elegant hotel in a central position. The bedrooms are of good size and very cosy, the reception rooms, one large dining room and 5 sitting rooms are most attractive, furnished in local Italian style. The whole hotel has a very good atmosphere.

SAN VIGILIO MAREBBE

Height of Resort 3,939 ft.
Height of Top Station: 7,461 ft.
Nearest International Airport: Venice
Map Reference: 6B See page 239
Route by Car: See page 236-239
Resort Facilities Charts: See page 221
Hotel Reference Charts: See page 231

This delightful small resort situated in the wide open sunny Marebbe valley is some 25 minutes' drive from Brunico, the nearest rail head. There is skiing on each side of the valley.

The main ski area is on Plan de Corones, which is linked to the resorts of Riscone, to the north-east and Valdaora to the east. Lifts from all three resorts converge on the top station at 7,416 ft. Starting from San Vigilio, two surmounting gondolaways rise to Furcia and from this point one can either take the chair-lift rising to Pre de Peres, 6.695 ft. with a fairly steep north facing run back; alternatively run down a little further to pick up the gondolaway to the top station on Plan de Corones. The runs back to the village are easy to intermediate. From the top station one can point one's way north to Riscone or east to Valdaora. To the former one can enjoy the open intermediate run to the half-way stage when it becomes wooded and more difficult to the bottom station. The east facing runs down towards Valdaora are challenging in parts for the intermediate and these are served by 2 chair-lifts and 2 gondolaways. If one continues down to the village surmounting gondolaways return one to the top station. The skiing in this area as a whole is delightful and well served by mountain restaurants, so there is no need to return for lunch.

The skiing on the other side of the valley is limited to a chair-lift rising to Piz de Plaies, 5,425 ft., where there is a bar and restaurant; the runs back are of pleasant intermediate standard. A chair-lift and drag-lift serve the excellent lower nursery slopes. There are excellent facilities for Nordic skiing with 5 trails from 4 to 25km. in length. The longest winds its way to Rifugio Pederü at the end of the Marebbe valley.

In a Few Words: A charming village, excellent compact and attractive ski area. Beginners to advanced intermediates will be happy here. Hardly a queue anywhere. Langlauf and ski-bobbing. A special ski-garden for children, 'Skinopolis', opened in 1993/94 and has proved to be very popular.

Après Ski: Informal and quite active for a small resort. Not expensive. The Hotel Call has a discothèque. There are several bars, pizzerias and restaurants where evenings can be enjoyed in a pleasant and friendly atmosphere. For active types and the non-skier there is a large sports centre with a swimming pool, sauna, solarium, bar, hairdresser, pharmacy and the Igloo Bar. There is skating on a natural rink, ski-bobbing, bowling, pleasant walks, excursions to Cortina, Corvara and Innsbruck, and a tour of the Dolomites.

FORNI DI SOPRA

Height of Resort: 2,975 ft.
Height of Top Station: 6,761 ft.
Nearest International Airport: Venice
Map Reference: 7C See page 239
Route by Car: See page 236-239
Resort Facilities Charts: See page 219
Hotel Reference Charts: See page 231

This delightful village is set deep in the mountains of the Friuli district of Italy. To approach the village from the west it is necessary to negotiate a long pass of about 20 km., which is not difficult as the road is wide and not too steep. A faster approach is from Venice on the motorway. On entering the valley, one is rewarded by magnificent views of the gentle wooded slopes breaking into the dramatic mountains so typical of the Dolomite range.

The village is fairly long and is split into three main areas - Vico, Cella and Andrazza. A large church in Cella and pleasant village square in Vico are the two main focal points. A wide mountain river runs the entire length and to one side of the village. A good selection of shops including sports, food, clothes, hairdressers, etc. provide the needs for most guests.

There are three drag-lifts in the village area ideally suited to first and second year skiers. The longest of the three rises only 550ft. but runs down are interesting and should be managed by most beginners. The other two drag-lifts run parallel and serve their own pistes. These slopes are served by snow making machines. The main skiing area is up the Varmost, reached by a two-stage double chair-lift with a further surmounting chair-lift rising to a height of 6,761ft., (the highest point in the area). The Varmost field, now covered by snow cannons, centres on a

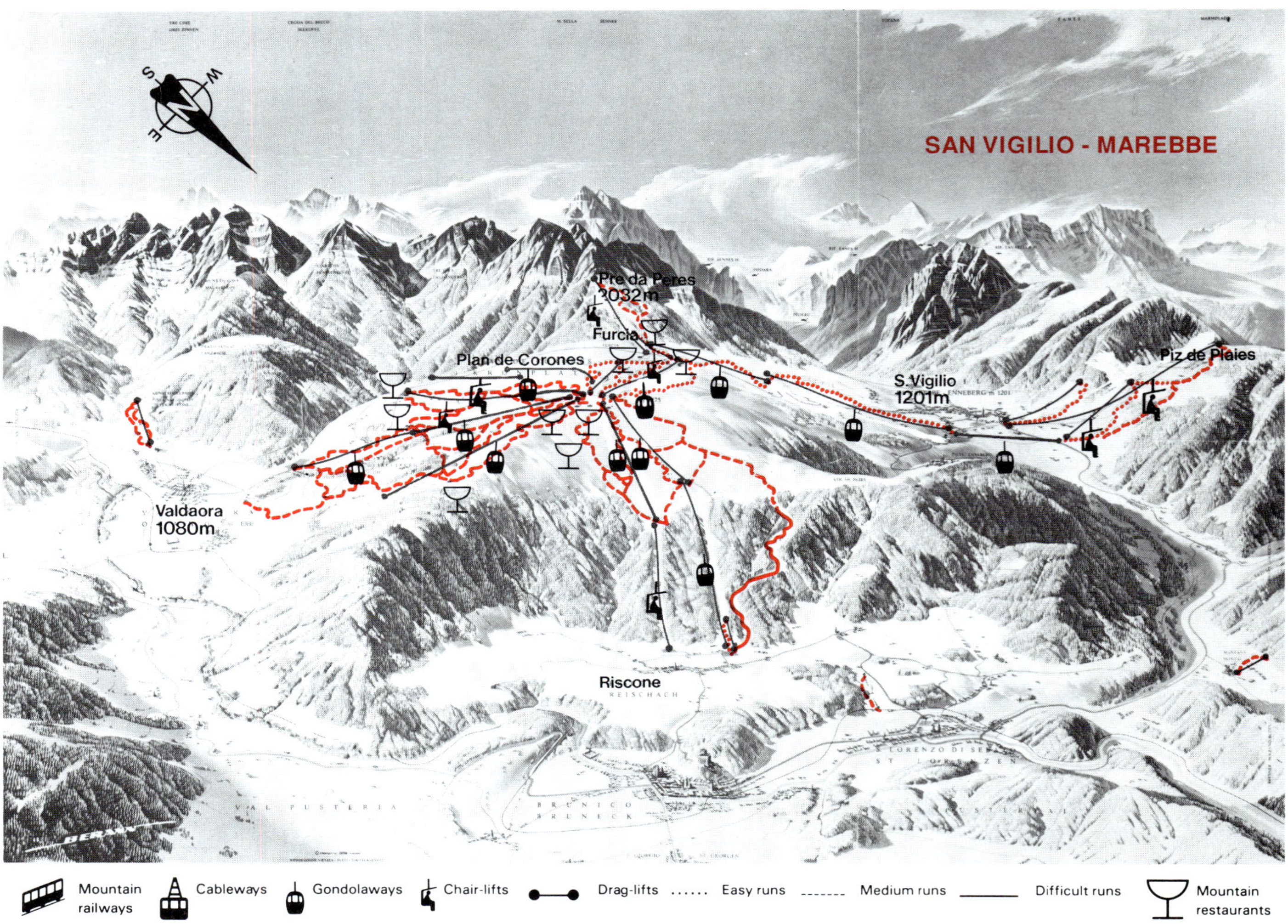

wide south-facing snow bowl, has a vertical drop of 3,800ft., the longest run being 7km. The area has three drag-lifts serving intermediate runs. Two mountain restaurants serve lunch and snacks, so it is not necessary to return to the village. The pistes down to the village can be managed by intermediate skiers but one section will prove rather difficult for some, at the beginning of the final stage. The skiing is over wide open snow fields interspersed with woodland - very picturesque. A 3 seater chair-lift has been opened at Davost, serving a run just short of 1,000 metres with vertical drop of 656ft. It is also covered by snow cannons. There is a 15km. nordic ski trail, a section of which is illuminated at night.

In a Few Words: This is a delightful, small and typically Italian village, with facilities for beginners to intermediates. Happy atmosphere, adequate shopping and après ski and certainly picturesque, with the Dolomites dominating one side. No other well known resorts nearby – Cortina is about 60km. away.

Après Ski: As with many small resorts the après ski is limited. There are however several good restaurants other than hotels and pensions, many of which hold special evenings of entertainment. Other attractions include sports hall with ice rink, gymnasium and indoor tennis court. There are pubs, pizzerias and video bars. A special feature with Forni are some of the spontaneous 'in-hotel' evenings.

Recommended Hotels:

Hotel Davost: A modern hotel ideally situated just beneath the nursery slopes. Comfortable sitting room off hall with good dining room adjacent. Large windows give guests views of the nursery slopes. The food is excellent with pleasant service. Large comfortable bedrooms, all with private facilities. A self-service restaurant is attached for skiers and food is very reasonably priced. A feature is an excellent games room.

Hotel Italia: A modern hotel where the natural stone walls are immediately apparent as one enters. The sitting room is off the main hall and has a 'sunken area' with a large open fireplace, which also doubles as a bar. At the far end a comfortable dining room is open to guests and visitors alike. The bedrooms are very comfortable - many with balconies and all with private facilities. Good English is spoken here so there should be no language problem.

PIANCAVALLO

Height of Resort: 4,265 ft.
Height of Top Station: 6,562 ft.
Nearest International Airport: Venice
Map Reference: See page 239
Route by Car: See page 236-239
Resort Facilities Chart: See page 220
Hotel Reference Chart: See page 231

From a wide, flat valley round Pordenone a steep and tortuous road leads up to Piancavallo, situated on a sunny plateau. The view from here stretches as far as the sea; Venice is about $1^1/_2$ hours' drive away.

Piancavallo is a purpose-built resort, with concrete buildings dotted on the hills amongst the trees and fairly spread out. There are a large number of apartments. The atmosphere is very lively, with a lot of young people. The resort is becoming popular with the English, who are catered for in English-speaking ski school classes. It's a good resort for children and there are a lot of them around. Ski school classes for beginners mix children and adults. The skiing area is served by 15 lifts. The longest is a 3-stage chair-lift rising from near the ski school. From the top one has dramatic views to the coast and the craggy peaks of the Yugoslavian border. There is a small café/bar at the middle station and two medium runs take one to the foot of the lift, where there are nursery slopes served by the Caprioli drag-lift.

Alternatively, a long, easy run links with the slopes served by the Busa Grande, Sauc and Sole lifts. The top station, Tremol, 6,562ft., has a restaurant and a moderately easy run brings one back to the middle station. The Sauc lifts serve east facing slopes and all grades of runs are available. The artificial jump for freestyle skiing is erected here.

In a Few Words: A modern resort with many amenities, but not particularly well laid out – a lot of walking about necessary if one has no car. Skiing at present suitable for beginners to intermediates.

Après Ski: Lively for a small resort – a crowd collects in the bar of the Park Hotel and this is the central meeting place of Piancavallo. There is a covered skating rink. There are various snack bars and pizzerias, including one near the ski school in the Hotel Sport and one in the shopping centre. The excellent shopping centre in the middle of the village is completely under cover, and here the tourist office (A.P.T.), kindergarten, sports shop, boutique, souvenir shop and others can all be visited without going outside. Another block nearby has restaurant, snack bar and games hall with table tennis, small bowling alley and a variety of automatic machines. There is a good choice of night spots: tables are cleared from the centre of the Park Hotel's dining room after dinner for dancing and excellent bands regularly play there. There is a Taverna/discothèque cellar in the Park, and discos at the Sport Hotel and Antares Hotel. It is possible to spend a day in Venice from Piancavallo, but buses do not run conveniently and the best way is for a group to share a taxi. Also worth a visit are Trieste; the Roman town of Aquileia, which has an amphitheatre; and near this the Villa Manin, in Codroipo, which is very beautiful.

Recommended Hotels:

Hotel Edelweiss: Near the chair-lift and ski school. Bar with wooden decor and attractive coloured tile floor. Bedrooms simply furnished, with shower - all 4-bedded. Locked ski racks in corridor. Apartments also available. Bar with restaurant leading off, brightly furnished and wooden panelled. Good disco, 'Gatto Nero'.

Park Hotel Montecavallo: A large, very modern concrete hotel overlooking the village centre. Bedrooms all with shower, comfortably furnished, rather dimly lit. Large, bustling dining room with excellent and friendly service, and views on all three sides; its all round open log fire is very attractive. Above this is a smaller floor on a balcony, where breakfast is taken. Taverna cellar discothèque and bar leading from dining room, which is always full of people. Large and very comfortable sitting area in entrance hall. Basement ski room.

Hotel Regina: Centrally situated. Bedrooms small, carpeted and simply furnished, all with shower, some with balcony, light wooden furniture. Small, light restaurant and larger residents' dining room. Bar with wooden tables and benches and lots of plants. Piano bar.

SELLA NEVEA

Height of Resort: 3,773 ft
Height of Top Station: 5,798 ft.
Nearest International Airport: Trieste
Map Reference: See page 239
Route by Car: See page 236-239
Resort Facilities Charts: See page 221
Hotel Reference Charts: See page 231

From a low plain the mountains forming the Italian/Slovenian border rise dramatically and a remote, twisting road from Chiusaforte leads up to Sella Nevea. The views and sheer rock faces interspersed with waterfalls are exciting and breathtaking. The resort is still being developed and at present only has three hotels, with a small block adjoining the Hotel Canin containing sports shop, souvenir shop, small supermarket and a number of apartments.

The resort normally has snow till May. Sella Nevea is very close to the Slovene border and in the spring a lift from the Slovene side enables skiers from Bovec to ski down the Sella Nevea side. A further lift is projected to complete the all-season interlinking of the two resorts.

A cableway leaves from opposite the Hotel Canin and rises in 5 minutes to the top station, 5,793ft., which is surrounded by sheer-faced craggy peaks. A short walk from this top station is a restaurant, with two drag-lifts serving some easy runs. The glacier in the valley running to Slovenia is clearly visible. The run down to the village passes near a most spectacular cliff and is of moderate difficulty. There are five further drag-lifts near the village centre, most serving easy runs, but one, the Slalom Stadium, providing more difficult alternatives. Pine trees surround the buildings and the thickly wooded lower slopes provide a very beautiful setting.

Guest Card: For clients staying in hotels associated with the Consorzio Servizi Turitici del Tarvisiano e Sella Nevea, a Guest Card allows clients to ski in Tarvisio (see brief report, page 149); also for two days a week at 3 resorts in Austria or 2 in Slovenia. It also allows free use of bus services, entrance to casinos in Kranjska Gora (Slovenia) and Velden (Austria), discounts for ski hire, ice skating, the sports centre in Sella Nevea and at various shops.

In a Few Words: A very small and compact resort with limited facilities, at present suitable for beginners to intermediates but destined for considerable development. Atmosphere very informal, with groups of young people. A resort to watch – when the range of skiing is extended it could be superb – marvellous snow, beautiful scenery.

Après Ski: Each of three hotels have their own discothèques. At the Hotel Canin is the Taverna Canin; and the brightly coloured floor lit from underneath in the Top Sound disco at the Hotel Club Nevea is very striking. The Sporthotel Forte, built in 1981, has a sports centre, indoor swimming pool, sauna, solarium and massage. Night life will no doubt increase in scope with the expansion of the resort.

Recommended Hotels:

Hotel Canin: Part of the main block, this is a modern hotel, with entrance on the lower ground floor, where there is a ski room; and a reception room upstairs, leading into the bar and small residents' dining room. Friendly and helpful family management. Comfortable lounge, TV room, Taverna with disco, covered garage. Excellent regional wine in restaurant. Bedrooms simply and comfortably furnished all with shower and balcony.

Hotel Nevea: Situated just above the central block, some 5 minutes' walk away. Built in 1975, this hotel is wooden panelled throughout. TV and sitting room adjoining attractive dining room, with windows on 3 sides and red wooden chairs. Comfortably furnished sitting area in reception hall. Bedrooms double or 3, 4 and 5-bedded, simply and comfortably furnished; all those on upper floors with balcony and shower, and some with traditional wooden furniture are very pretty. The disco on the lower ground floor is sophisticated in design for such a small resort, and the decor very effective.

SAN MARTINO DI CASTROZZA

Height of Resort: 4,920 ft.
Height of Top Station: 9,053 ft.
Nearest International Airport: Venice
Map Reference: 6C See page 239
Route by Car: See page 236-239
Resort Facilities Charts: See page 220
Hotel Reference Charts: See page 231

Set amidst the dramatic sheer rock faces of the eastern Dolomites, San Martino is $2^{1}/_{2}$ hours' drive from Venice and about 4 hours from Milan or Innsbruck. The village is long and winding and has great charm, with a relaxed and essentially Italian atmosphere. The skiing is fairly widely spread and is divided into four main areas, two now interlinked:

Tognola Area: A free bus service operates from the village centre to the bottom station of the Tognola gondolaway, which rises to Alpe Tognola, 7,095ft., where there is a self-service restaurant and a bar with a sun terrace overlooking a beautiful view. Below this lies a vast bowl served by two drag-lifts and five chair-lifts, providing easy and medium skiing. One run leads to the base of the Cigolera lift rising from 6,422ft., to the other side of Tognola, a height of 7,341ft., overlooking Valcigolera. From the base of the drag-lift a double chair-lift forks off to the left and rises to a higher point; This has become an important junction as two surmounting double chair-lifts coming up from Malga Ces (see below) terminate at this top station, thus linking the two areas. There are fairly steep runs down to both Malga Tognola and Malga Ces. Three medium to difficult runs descend from the top of Alpe Tognola to Fratazza following the line of the gondolaway, within the range of the medium standard skier, and a third branches off to gentler slopes. All of these runs pass through picturesque wooded scenery towards the end.

Malga Ces Area: The Malga Ces chair-lift is also reached by a free bus service two minutes' journey from the village and rises to 5,313ft. Here the Malga Ces and Valboneta drag-lifts serve open, sunny slopes and there is an agreeable restaurant with tables outside. The ascent can be continued by chair-lift to Punta Ces, 7,331ft., where there is another small and simple mountain café, with fantastic views from its sun terrace, worth a visit even if you don't intend skiing down from here. Of the three runs down, two are medium and one is more difficult. Two of these start towards the line of the lift, the more difficult one branching off over narrower, steeper slopes; and the third begins by traversing behind the lift, eventually converging with the others, via the Malga Ces restaurant. As pointed out above two surmounting chair lifts now link this area with Tognola.

Colverde-Rosetta Area: A chair-lift travels from San Martino to Colverde, 6,445ft., on the opposite side to the two previous areas. There is only a gentle $2^{1}/_{2}$km. run through the woods or a shorter one by the della Pale drag-lift. The Colverde-Rosetta cableway rises to 8,823ft., with spectacular views. Skiing here is limited too, on gentle north-east facing slopes. Spring or summer touring is available in this area, but the descent to Colverde should be tackled only by the hardiest and most competent skiers.

Passo Rolle: This is a high pass road some 9km. above San Martino. It is reached by a free bus service and there are a few hotels and pensions. The scenery is quite breathtaking. The Segantini chair-lift rises from 6,373ft. to Capanna Segantini, 7,183ft. A drag-lift and a chair-lift are to be found in this area and on the other side of the road are nursery slopes with beginners' lifts. Above these are some steeper, interesting pistes running down from the Tognazza ridge and reached via the Cavalazza and Paradiso chair-lifts. There is a 7.5 km. Nordic ski trail in this area.

In a Few Words: Widely spread ski areas well served by bus service; an easy-going resort, so far fairly unexploited, with a glorious mountain background; plenty of skiing, very enjoyable for beginners to advanced intermediates; good value.

Après Ski: Night life varies from casual to the more sophisticated. In the Hotel Rosetta, the Tabià is one of the best night spots - dancing to discothèque and with plenty of room and generous seating. The Majestic Hotel Dolomiti provide tea and evening dancing in a more formal atmosphere. A relaxing evening can be spent in the restaurant Drei Tannen, Hotel Savoia, where fondue and other specialist dishes, including Chinese, are provided, with an open fire and gentle music. Other popular places include the Piccolo and Slalom bars, as well as La Stube and Wein Stube bar. A very good pizzeria can be found at Al Lares and at 'La Vecchia Fornace' there is a sauna, bowling alley and a pizzeria.

Recommended Hotels:

Hotel Colfosco: In pleasant position on south side of village towards Fratazza-Tognola cableway and close to a small shopping complex. Owned and run by the Orsingher family for over 70 years; present incumbent Angelo Orsingher very capable and a fund of information; unusual in San Martino in that he speaks excellent English. Hotel atmosphere friendly and relaxed, impressive entrance hall, comfortable sitting room spacious bar; attractive bright dining room, TV room, card room. Cosy breakfast room. All rooms with bath or shower and balcony, many of them have been tastefully re-modernised. Food and service excellent. Piano bar, video games room, snooker and table tennis.

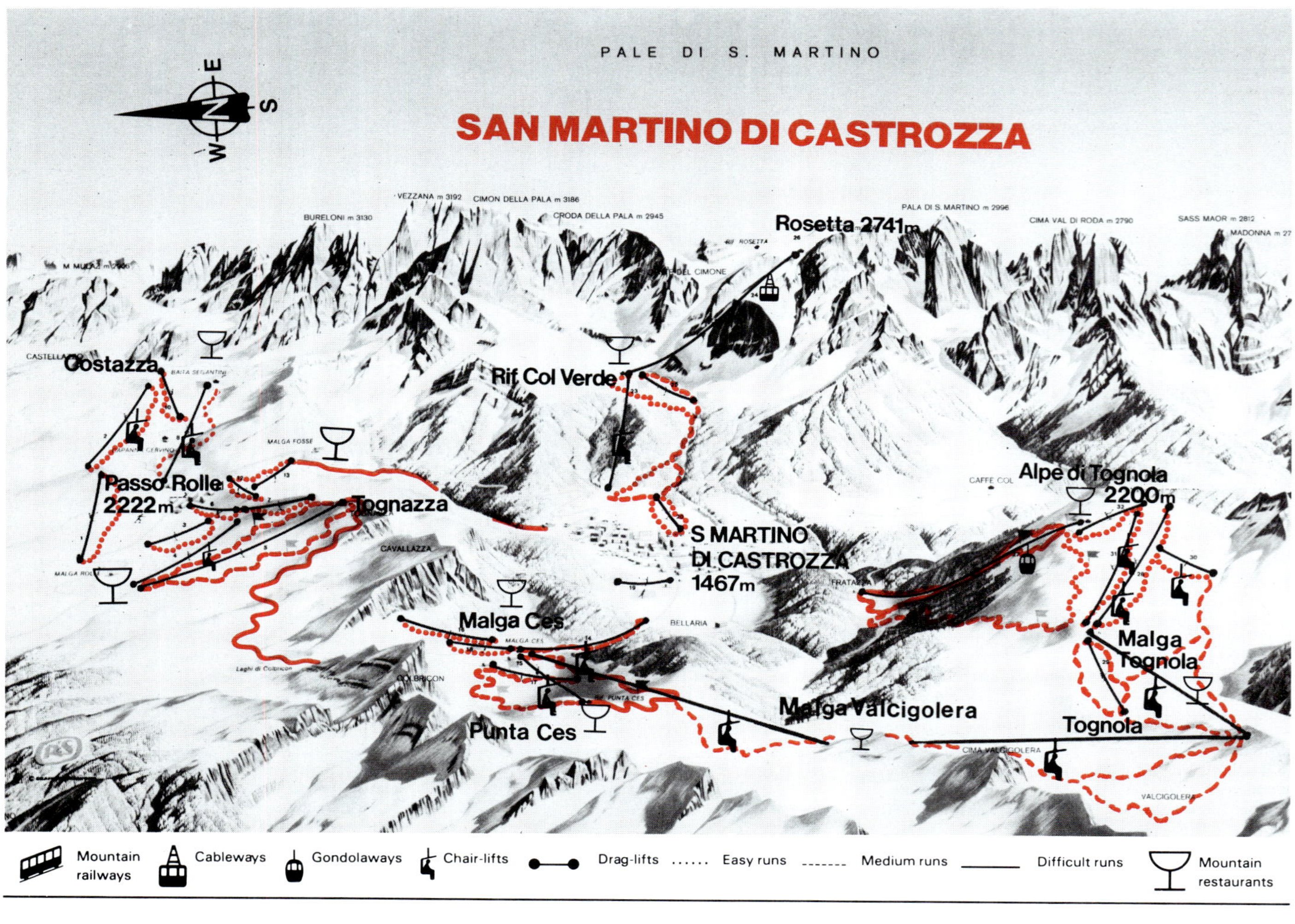

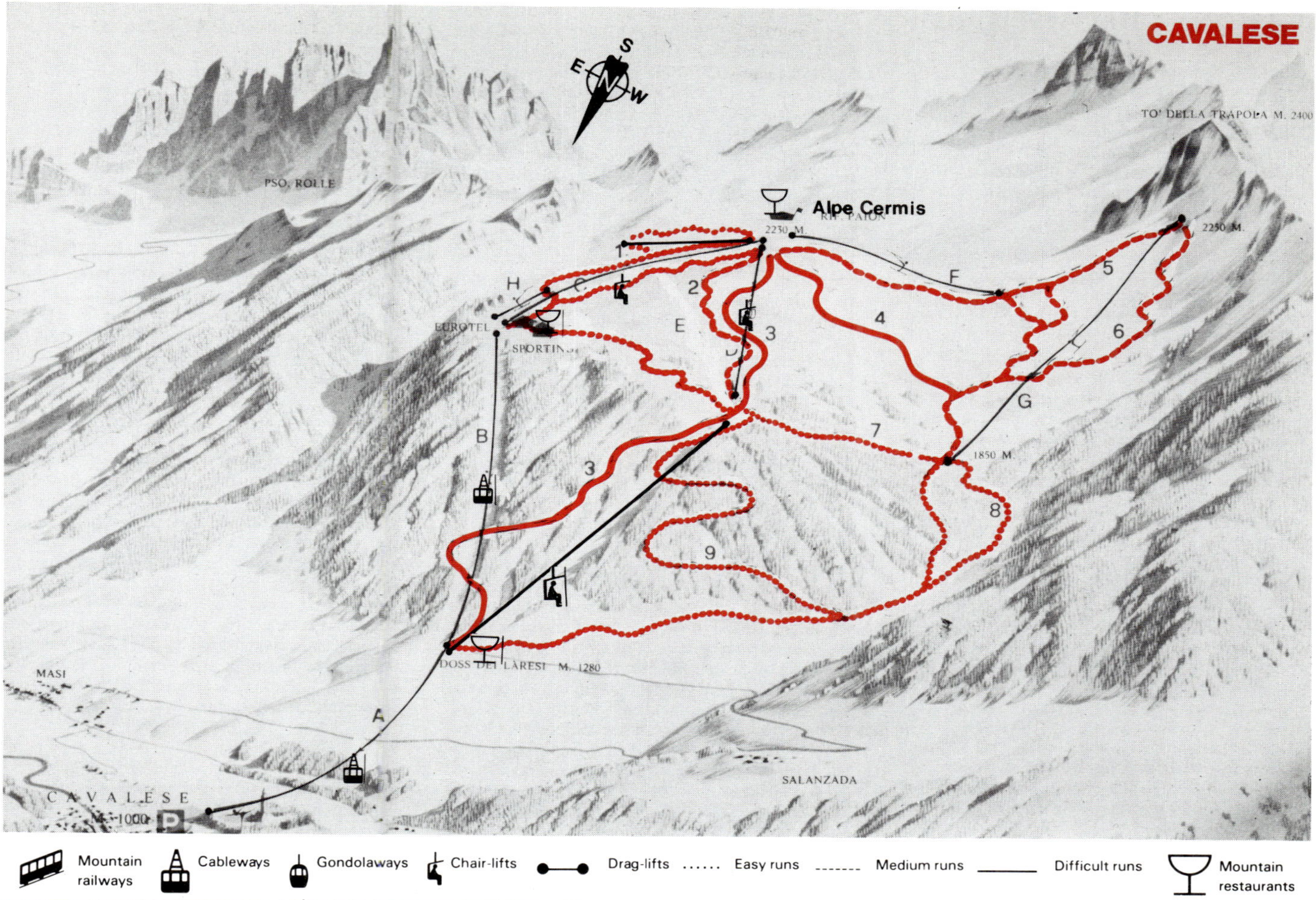

Pension Margherita: In the very centre of the village, this is a small and cosy family-run pension. Cheerful dining room with good cooking in super modern kitchen. Small but comfortable bedrooms. All rooms except singles with bath or shower. Bar/sitting room.

Hotel Savoia: A well appointed hotel two minutes from village centre. Good sized bedrooms elegantly furnished, all with bath or shower and balconies. Spacious reception and lounge area, pleasant dining rooms and separate breakfast room, large comfortable restaurant, Drei Tannen, is adjoining.

CAVALESE

Height of Resort: 3,300 ft.
Height of Top Station: 7,420 ft.
Nearest International Airport: Venice/Milan
Map Reference: 6C See page 239
Route by Car: See page 236-239
Resort Facilities Charts: See page 219
Hotel Reference Charts: See page 231

This delightful resort is of considerable historic interest, dating back to 1300, and consists of some 110 hotels and pensions. It is situated in the north-east Fiemme valley of the Trento Dolomites, 42km. from Bolzano and 60km. from Trento and is accessible by car from the Channel ports via the Brenner Pass. The village lies on the north side of the river Avisio. The skiing is reached by a 2-stage cableway; the first section swings its way southwards across the river to Doss dei Larèsi, 3,900ft. where there is a snack-bar. At the top of the second stage, 6,562 ft., one finds the Eurotel and Sporting Club Hotel, with swimming pool and a range of privately owned, cone-shaped chalets. To the left is the trainer lift for the beginners' ski school. To the right a cleverly laid-out lift system serves a series of interlinking runs. From the top of the cableway a chair-lift rises south-westwards to the summit of Alpe Cermis, 7,335ft., where there is a self service restaurant and a mini club for children from 4 years upwards.

Converging on this point from the north is a further chair-lift, Paion, and from the west a drag-lift, Bombasèl. From this focal point one has a wide choice of runs, easy both sides of the first-mentioned lift, intermediate to the right of and difficult following the line of the second lift, whilst an intermediate run follows the line of the third lift, with a difficult run branching to the north-west. All the skiing is above the tree-line. Further to the west and interlinking with all the runs mentioned, one finds the longest drag-lift, Prafiori, which rises to the highest point in the area, 7,420ft., providing intermediate runs each side to the base.

The most challenging is the difficult Olympic run, which starts from the top of Cermis, following the line of the Paion chair-lift over open north-facing slopes and at the base it swings north-eastward through wooded terrain to the first station of the cableway, 4km. with a vertical descent of 3,135ft. From the first station of the cableway, Doss dei Larèsi, a recently installed 4 seater chair-lift links up with the Paion chair-lift, thus increasing the uphill capacity considerably. Easy wooded runs also wind their way through the lower homeward slopes to this point. The longest run is 6km., from the top of the Prafiori lift, intermediate to the base and easy to Doss dei Larèsi, vertical descent 3,185ft.

For greater variety the resort of Pampeago is only 20 minutes by mini-bus from Cavalese. This resort is linked with Obereggen and 17 lifts provide access to easy and intermediate skiing. Lago di Tesero, 5 km. from Cavalese, has 25 km. of Nordic skiing trails whilst Passo Lavazè, 5,905ft., 10km. from Cavalese, has some 50km. of Nordic ski trails.

In 1991 the World Nordic Ski Championships were held in the Fiemme Valley, and new facilities were constructed including a Press-Congress centre and Ice Hockey Stadium in Cavalese, a Jumping Hill in Predazzo (14km.) and a Ski Stadium in Lago di Tesero (5km.). To explore and enjoy all the resorts in the valley a car is useful, although there are bus services. 80km. of runs in the Fiemme valley are now covered by snow cannons, and also 10km. of the Nordic ski trails.

In a Few Words: Some may be put off by having to take the cableway to the skiing, but this is more than compensated by the fine compact area above the treeline, and interesting wooded variations on the lower slopes. Suitable for parties of mixed skiing abilities; all required to take the lift pass including beginners, orientation of runs ensures good snow conditions.

Après Ski: There's a fair variety, but less organised than some resorts. Dancing in Manarin One Music Hall, two theatres and cinema. Plenty of cafés and wine bars at reasonable prices. For non-skiers there is skating, swimming, tennis and attractive walks, regular bus services to Bolzano and Trento for those who wish further sightseeing.

Recommended Hotels:

Hotel Cavalese: Situated close to the village centre, an unsophisticated small hotel, but efficiently run by the Bonelli family. Comfortable bedrooms, many with private shower and wc. Bright dining room, small lounge and café/bar. Good atmosphere and friendly service.

Hotel San Valier: One of the nicest hotels in the resort 5 minutes walk from the cableway. Built in rustic style, comfortable and attractive reception rooms. All bedrooms tastefully furnished with bath or shower. Swimming pool.

MADONNA DI CAMPIGLIO

Height of Resort: 5,084 ft.
Height of Top Station: 8,640 ft.
Nearest International Airport: Milan
Map Reference: See page 239
Route by Car: See page 236-239
Resort Facilities Charts: See page 220
Hotel Reference Charts: See page 231

Madonna di Campiglio lies in a sheltered, sunny valley in the Brenta Dolomites 210km. from Milan, 3½ hours by road. From the older established centre of the resort Tirolean type buildings stretch out and there is a modern complex at Campo Carlo Magno. The whole village has a superb setting amongst the pine forests and lakes with a beautiful mountain background. The lift network is excellent and there is very little queueing except at Christmas, Carnival week in February, Easter and holiday weekends. The pistes are well maintained and marked, the nursery slopes at Spinale base and Campo Carlo Magno are ideal for beginners and they can progress to the slopes of Groste and Pradalago. Every 30 minutes a bus service links Madonna with the bottom stations of the Groste cableway, Pradalago chair-lift and Campo Carlo Magno. There are also 4 buses a day to the ski area of Pinzolo which gives one the opportunity of visiting the old church of San Vigilio with its Danse Macabre fresco painted in 1539 by Simone Baschenis of Averaria.

Madonna has 4 main ski areas of its own but we are also incorporating in this report the linked resorts of Marilleva and Folgarida.

Cinque Laghi Area: From the west side of the village a cableway rises to Palon, 6,965ft., where there is a restaurant. This area enjoys the sunshine from early morning until early afternoon and provides a good variety of intermediate to advanced runs from the restaurant down to the village entering the pretty wooded slopes towards the end. Alternatively one can take the Patascoss chair-lift to Panculogo rising to 7,470ft. where there is an interesting intermediate east facing run, steep for the first 200 metres, which joins the World Cup run for a short distance then breaking across it to join other runs from Cinque Laghi to the village. Another alternative is to take the 3 Tre chair-lift rising to 7,054ft. where an intermediate run takes one to the Panculogo pistes or the 3 Tre World Cup run. The latter starts off with a sharp descent over north-east facing slopes becoming more torturous and narrow as one reaches the final wooded slopes, an exhilarating run for the good skier. Just up from the World Cup finish a double chair-lift rises 600ft., and this is surmounted by a button lift used by the ski school; here there is a small restaurant.

Pradalago Area: From the village the Pradalago gondolaway, with a capacity of 3,000 persons per hour, rises to 6,890ft. where one finds a restaurant and some 200 metres further down the Rif Viviani, with restaurant, self-service restaurant and kiosk serving snacks. This area enjoys the sun from mid morning to mid-afternoon and the open and gently east and south-facing slopes are fed by two button lifts and two chair-lifts and one of the latter, Fiocco di Neve, provides access to the Genziana pistes, a variety of easy and intermediate north-east facing runs which terminate at the foot of the Genziana chair-lift. From this point one can either ascend to the Pradalago or to Monte Vigo, 7,152ft., where there is a restaurant and the descents to Marilleva and Folgarida begin (see below). From Pradalago itself the pistes leading to the bottom stations are: Nanbino (black) ending at the foot of the Pradalago gondolaway; the Provetti (medium) and Zeledria (easy) both terminating at the foot of the Fortini chair-lift, where one can cross the road and take the gondolaway up to Groste.

Groste Area: The Groste gondolaway (with a capacity of 2240 persons per hour) leaves from a point midway between Madonna and Campo Carlo Magno, first rising to the middle station, Groste, where one finds the Rif Boch restaurant, providing comfort and good food in a delightful setting, and thence to Passo del Groste (8,005ft.). Here one finds a restaurant and a wide open plateau with two parallel chair-lifts rising to 8,497ft. The scenery in this area is beautiful and the runs down by the two chair-lifts are two red and two blue runs as far as Rif Graffer where a red and a blue lead to a path and the base of the Rododendro chair-lift for returning again to the top. Alternatively one can take the adjoining chair-lift up to Monte Spinale. All these predominantly north-west facing slopes keep the snow well and enjoy late morning and afternoon sun. There are good opportunities in the Groste area for off-piste skiing.

Monte Spinale Area: This top station, 6,904ft., can be reached either by the recently installed gondolaway (2,000 persons per hour) leaving from opposite the skating rink or by the Nube d'Argento chair-lift from Campo Carlo Magno with a surmounting chair-lift up to the Monte Spinale restaurant. From here the Groste area can be reached by a pleasant intermediate run to the foot of the Rododendro chair-lift or a direct intermediate run to the bottom station of the gondolaway. The strategically placed lifts allow many variations in this area. There is a good intermediate run from the top to Campo Carlo Magno, or when one reaches the Montagnoli restaurant turn left and a difficult run leads to the centre of Madonna. Again from the top of Monte Spinale, looking down the gondolaway coming up from the village, there are interesting runs down in this area, easy, intermediate and difficult, the latter including the Direttissima. On the west side the top station of this area is served by a 3 seater chair-lift.

Most of these runs are over north-west and west facing slopes which hold the snow well. In addition there is some fine off-piste skiing directly under the cableway and each side of the Direttissima.

MARILLEVA: 4,593 - 7,152ft.: The link point with Marilleva is Monte Vigo, reached by chair-lift from the Pradalago area. At the top there is a pleasant restaurant, Orso Bruno, where the 4½km. piste starts for the run down to Marilleva 1400, starting on gentle open slopes and passing on the way the Doss della Pesa lifts and the latter part through wide wooded glades. Marilleva 1400 is a small purpose built resort with its own ski school and two nursery lifts. There are hotels, shops and restaurants, a swimming pool and a disco. When snow conditions allow, a further descent can be made on fairly steep slopes through the woods to the little village of Marilleva 900, returning by gondolaway. The journey back to Monte Vigo is by a two-stage chair-lift; this can be broken halfway to enjoy the intermediate open pistes of Doss della Pesa, where two chair-lifts serve these slopes. From Monte Vigo one takes the intermediate Malghette piste which finishes at the foot of the Genziana chair-lift for the return to Madonna.

FOLGARIDA: 4,254 - 6,863ft.: As with Marilleva the link point for Folgarida is Monte Vigo where easy and intermediate runs lead to Malghet Aut, 6,082ft. Here there is a restaurant and also the nursery slopes used by the Folgarida ski school. The easy to intermediate runs in this area are served by 4 drag-lifts and the Genzianella chair-lift. From the restaurant there is a choice of runs down to Folgarida; the 7½km. run to the foot of the Belvedere chair-lift is intermediate and tree lined, whilst the Pista Nera is quite a steep and interesting run. The return to the top is by chair-lift or 6-seater gondolaway.

If time allows an hour or so on the Malghet Aut pistes is great fun before taking the chair or drag-lift up to Monte Spolverino, where after a short walk one reaches the drag-lift up to Monte Vigo and the pine woods with most of the 15 hotels constructed in chalet style to blend with the attractive surroundings. Après ski is on the quiet side with discos and bars in the hotels.

In a Few Words: Madonna's link with Marilleva and Folgarida provides a great variety of skiing covering some 150km. of prepared pistes, suitable for all grades. There is nearly always an easy way down for the less experienced and the lift system is well planned and interlinked. The Campo Carlo Magno area is particularly suitable for beginners. A friendly resort should appeal to British visitors.

Après Ski: Skiing is first and foremost but no lack of facilities on this side. Numerous bars frequented during the day and early evening with many serving draught beer. The stylish Bar Suisse is very popular. Apart from hotels there are 31 restaurants plus a further two at Campo Carlo Magno, all serving good Italian food or pizzas after 7.30 p.m. The Belvedere serves good pizzas; the intimate Stork restaurant with a vast selection of wines serves excellent regional and national dishes; it also has an American bar with draught beer and a separate pizzeria open until the early hours. Restaurant Lo Sfizio is particularly recommended.

The Stork discothèque is the largest and most popular in Madonna, with comfortable seating for over 300 arranged around a large dance floor and two bars and its panoramic windows overlooking the beautiful floodlit pine woods. A more intimate disco is Des Alpes, and outside the village, La Zangola.

There is a wide variety of shops in Madonna including reasonably priced supermarkets, an Olympic size indoor swimming pool, a skating rink, Nordic skiing trails and a wide selection of beautiful walks and a few mountain restaurants accessible to non-skiers.

Recommended Hotels:

Pension Cozzio: A superb family run pension situated midway between 3 Tre Pistes and 5 Laghi cableway. Small entrance hall leading to a cosy bar with comfortable seating which overlooks a spacious airy restaurant serving excellent food. Opposite is a lounge/card-TV room. The wood panelled bedrooms are tastefully furnished, with the exception of the 4 single rooms all have bath/shower and wc and plenty of hanging space. Small private disco/bar, table tennis rooms, extra TV room and garage. The owners and staff very friendly and helpful.

Hotel Grifone: A first-class, modern chalet-style hotel situated off the main street a short distance from the Spinale cableway. All rooms with bath, balcony and telephone. Spacious dining room, reading room, lounges and children's playroom. Delightful atmosphere, excellent service and food. L'Orso disco. Very good value.

Hotel Milano: Right in centre, modern family run hotel. 41 good sized bright doubles, 2 singles, all private bath or shower, telephone and balcony. Dining room, sitting room, bar, TV room, children's playroom downstairs. All rooms quite comfortably furnished, a little functional perhaps as regards atmosphere. Owners very helpful.

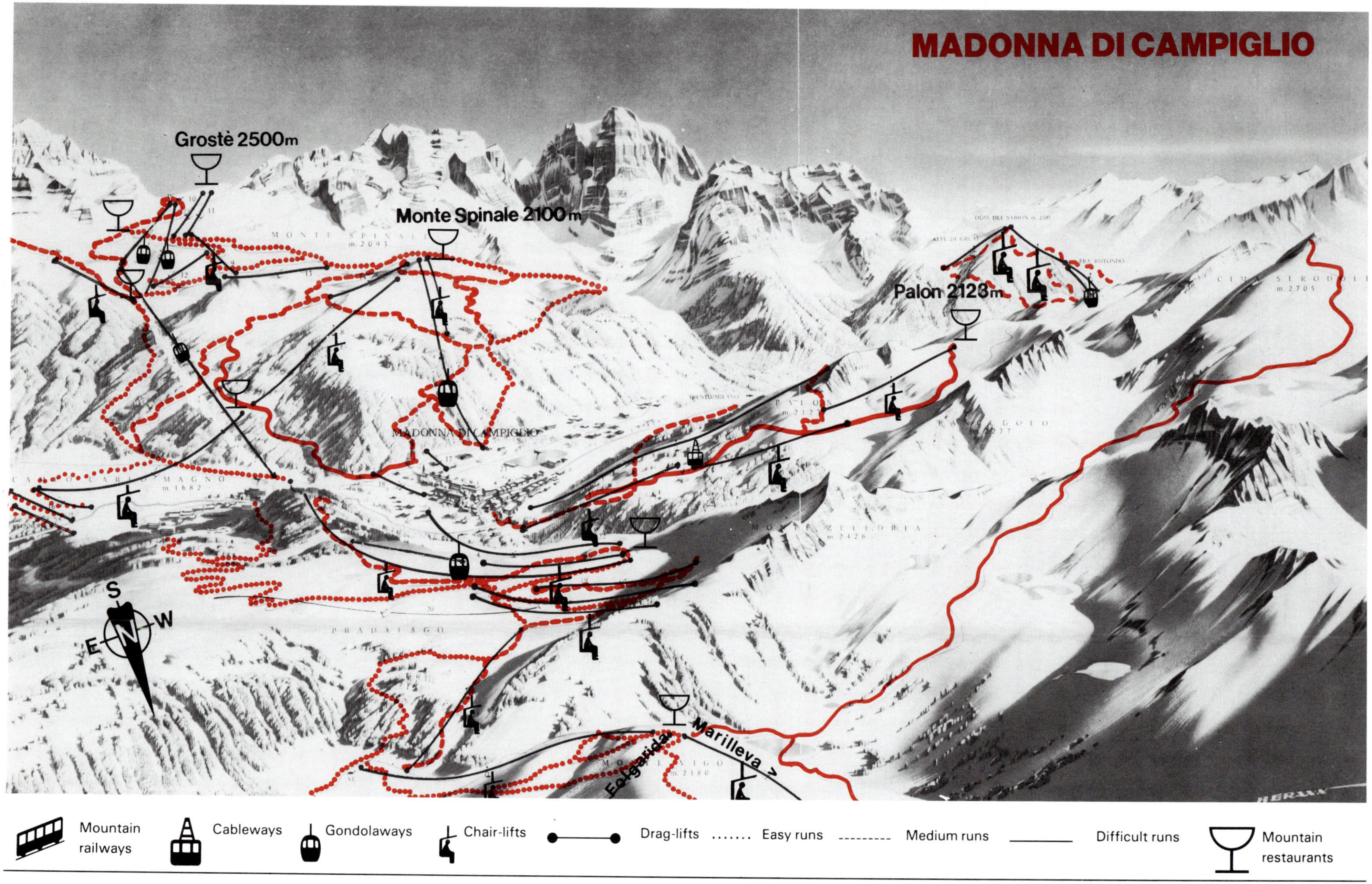
MADONNA DI CAMPIGLIO
Grostè 2500m
Monte Spinale 2100m
Palon 2123m
Folgarida
Marilleva >
S
E
N
W
Mountain railways
Cableways
Gondolaways
Chair-lifts
Drag-lifts
Easy runs
Medium runs
Difficult runs
Mountain restaurants

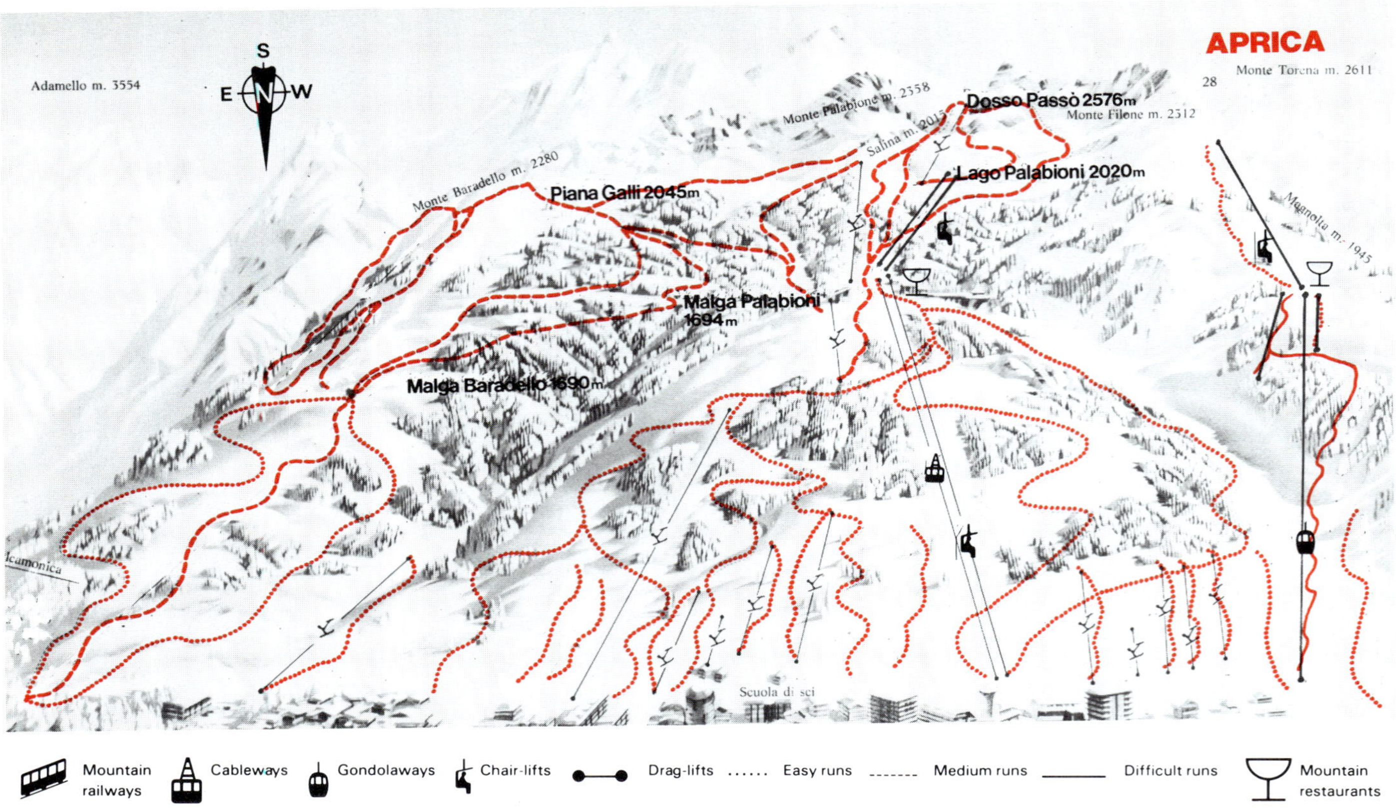

Hotel Miramonti: This attractive recently modernised hotel is situated at the base of the 3 Tre piste and near the 5 Laghi chair-lift. The spacious reception area joins the Piano Bar with a central ornamental fireplace, semi-circular bar and panoramic windows overlooking the village. A breakfast room, doubling as a lounge/card room in the evening, leads to a spacious restaurant with a reputation for good food.

Downstairs a solarium, sauna, children's playroom and garage. The modern apartments with bedroom and sectioned-off lounge with turn down sofa, forming a double bed at night, are all carpeted and the apartments have plenty of hanging space. All have bath/shower, wc, radio and telephone and most with balcony. Some apartments will take 5 persons so particularly suitable for families. A very well managed family hotel.

Savoia Palace Hotel: Centrally situated in the main street, this recently renovated and well appointed first class hotel has 54 good sized doubles and 3 singles, elegantly furnished,all with private bath, telephone, TV, minibar and safe. 12 rooms have balconies. Welcoming entrance hall, attractive sitting rooms with colourful decor, spacious dining room. Characteristic panelled taverna, bar. Nice system of reception rooms leading into each other. Excellently run by director, Signor Mizzaro.

APRICA

Height of Resort: 3,863 ft.
Height of Top Station: 8.448 ft.
Nearest International Airport: Milan
Map Reference: 4C See page 239
Route by Car: See pages 236-239
Resort Facilities Chart: See page 219
Hotel Reference Chart: See page 230

Aprica is situated in the province of Sondrio, on the road between Lake Como and the Brenta Dolomites. A long village, lying in an east-west valley, 164km. from Milan. The ski area is to be found on the south side and the runs face north-east, north and northwest; therefore snow remains good till late season.

The gondolaway and two surmounting drag-lifts on the eastern side of the village have been closed and the skiing is now concentrated on the central and western systems.

From near the centre of the village a gondolaway and a parallel chair-lift climb to Malga Palabione, 5,556ft., where one finds a circular self-service restaurant. To the left there are two drag-lifts serving the immediate area above and below the top station, whilst to the right, surmounting drag-lifts and a chair-lift rise to Dosso Paso, 8,448ft. From this point one has a selection of north and north-west facing runs, open for two-thirds of the way down and wooded towards the top station of the gondolaway, with easy runs back to the village.

The area on the western side of the village is reached by gondolaway rising from Piscina Coperta to Malga Magnolta, 6,150ft. Here there is a modern restaurant situated in a sun trap. Surmounting the gondolaway is a chair-lift rising to 6,759ft, serving an easy run to base. Below the restaurant and running parallel with the gondolaway is a drag-lift with a difficult run to base or one can continue to the village on a run with the same degree of difficulty. On the right of Piscina Coperta one finds a further drag-lift with easy runs. Beginners are well catered for at this resort – no less than 11 drag-lifts, stretching from one end of the village to the other, serve the lower slopes.

In a Few Words: Although the village is long the lift system is compact, providing good facilities for those up to intermediate standard – a few of the runs are classified World Cup standard; beginners well catered for on the lower slopes; northerly orientation of the runs means reliable snow.

Après Ski: One of the most popular night spots is 'Charlie Brown', situated in the centre of the village. There is a discothèque open each evening seating 400 people. There is a good selection of restaurants, cafés and bars. The cocktail lounge is one of the popular meeting places, whilst the Pasticceria Corvi serves delicious pastries and cocktails and so does the Café Tognolini.

Excursions are arranged to nearby Bormio, Sondrio and duty-free Livigno; also to St. Moritz, where skiers can take advantage of the excellent skiing at this famous resort.

Recommended Hotels:

Hotel Cristallo: Close to the ski school and gondola terminal, this is a modern hotel, with open-plan reception incorporating comfortable lounge and bar. Very suitable for families; the TV room sometimes shows children's films; there is a children's playroom with ping-pong; babysitting can sometimes be arranged, and children are made very welcome. All rooms with bath/shower and wc, many can be expanded to take one or two extra beds.

Hotel Larice Bianco: Situated on the nursery slopes near the ski school, this is a charming hotel, run by friendly owners Giovanni and Grazia Polatti. Two small but very comfortably furnished lounges plus TV lounge, bar and large dining room with view over the ski slopes. All rooms with bath/shower and wc. and most with balcony.

Hotel Torrena: Centrally situated but only a very short walk from the lifts and ski school, this is a delightfully furnished hotel with a very agreeable atmosphere. Dining room and wood-panelled bar on ground floor, comfortable lounge on first floor. Modern bedrooms, all with bath/shower and wc. Owners very good company.

SANTA CATERINA

Height of Resort: 5,697 ft.
Height of Top Station: 9,135 ft.
Nearest International Airport: Milan
Map Reference: 4C See page 239
Route by Car: See pages 236-239
Resort Facilities Charts: See page 220
Hotel Reference Charts: See page 231

This charming little resort lies about 12km. south-east of Bormio and a fairly regular bus service links the two. Because of its height and mostly north facing slopes, snow remains good throughout the season. For those keen on high mountain touring Santa Caterina is the nearest entry point to the Ortler and Cevedale regions; some of the finest touring can be found here and also summer skiing. The total lift system consists of one chair-lift and seven drag-lifts.

The main lift system consists of two drag-lifts and one chair-lift. The first drag-lift, which can if necessary be converted to a chair lift, is 1.5 km. in length and rises from above the village to Malga Plaghere, 7,478ft., where there is a small restaurant. One then skis down for about 300m. to the second stage, 1.4km. in length, rising to Cresta-Sobretta, 8,938ft., where a further restaurant is situated and the Vallalpe drag-lift, 770m. in length, rising to 9,135ft. From Cresta-Sobretta there is an easy run of 5 km. sweeping round in a 180° arc to the bottom of the Cresta-Sobretta lift (6km. if taken from the top draglift); or one can divert and go down to the village which gives runs of 8 and 9km. respectively. A chair-lift leaves from the centre of the village and rises to the large Paradiso restaurant, 6,593ft., the ski school area with three beginner's drag-lifts, either of which can be used as link lifts to connect with the Cresta-Sobretta lift.

On the western side there is also a more direct and difficult run of 4km. to the village in addition to two further runs each of 2km., one medium, one difficult, to the bottom of the Cresta-Sobretta drag-lift. All the skiing to this point is wide open, whilst it is wooded down to the village, in most cases fairly wide glades. Off-piste skiing is discouraged until very late in the season and then only with a guide due to avalanche danger.

In a Few Words: A charming resort with friendly people: excellent for beginners to intermediates; good langlauf facilities; reliable snow; good entry point for fabulous high mountain touring. Bormio skiing close at hand. The lift pass covers both resorts and also Livigno.

Après Ski: Quite informal in a relaxed, friendly atmosphere. There are two discos, the Queens in the Hotel Sport and the Zeus Music Palace. A choice of five restaurants-pizzerias and two Crêperies. In the Al Camino Residence one finds a popular Pub where a great variety of music is played. The Taverna of the Hotel Baita Fiorita opens on public demand. For non-skiers there are several pleasant walks and it is possible to take the chair-lift to the Paradiso restaurant and sit in the sun with excellent views of the slopes, returning to the village by chair-lift.

Cars and minibus can be hired to take people to and from Bormio for the swimming pool or evening entertainment, as the last bus leaves at 6 p.m. (Bormio is only 12km. away and has a greater variety of skiing and night life.)

Recommended Hotels:

Hotel Baita Fiorita: A quiet family run hotel in the centre of the village. Nicely furnished rooms all with bath or shower. Large wood panelled dining room and bar. All cooking very 'local', is done by the family. Also a private Taverna for hotel guests with log fire.

Pensione La Pineta: Situated 5 minutes from centre and not far from the chair-lift, this is an excellent pension for families, with a number of bedrooms on two levels which can take up to 5 beds, attractively furnished and most with shower; 2 with bath. Small lounge with open fire; dining room serving food of particularly high quality cooked by the owner.

Hotel Milano: This traditional 2 star hotel is situated 200 metres from the resort centre and 400 metres from the nearest ski lift. All rooms have shower, wc and telephone; two sitting rooms, one with TV, dining room and bar.

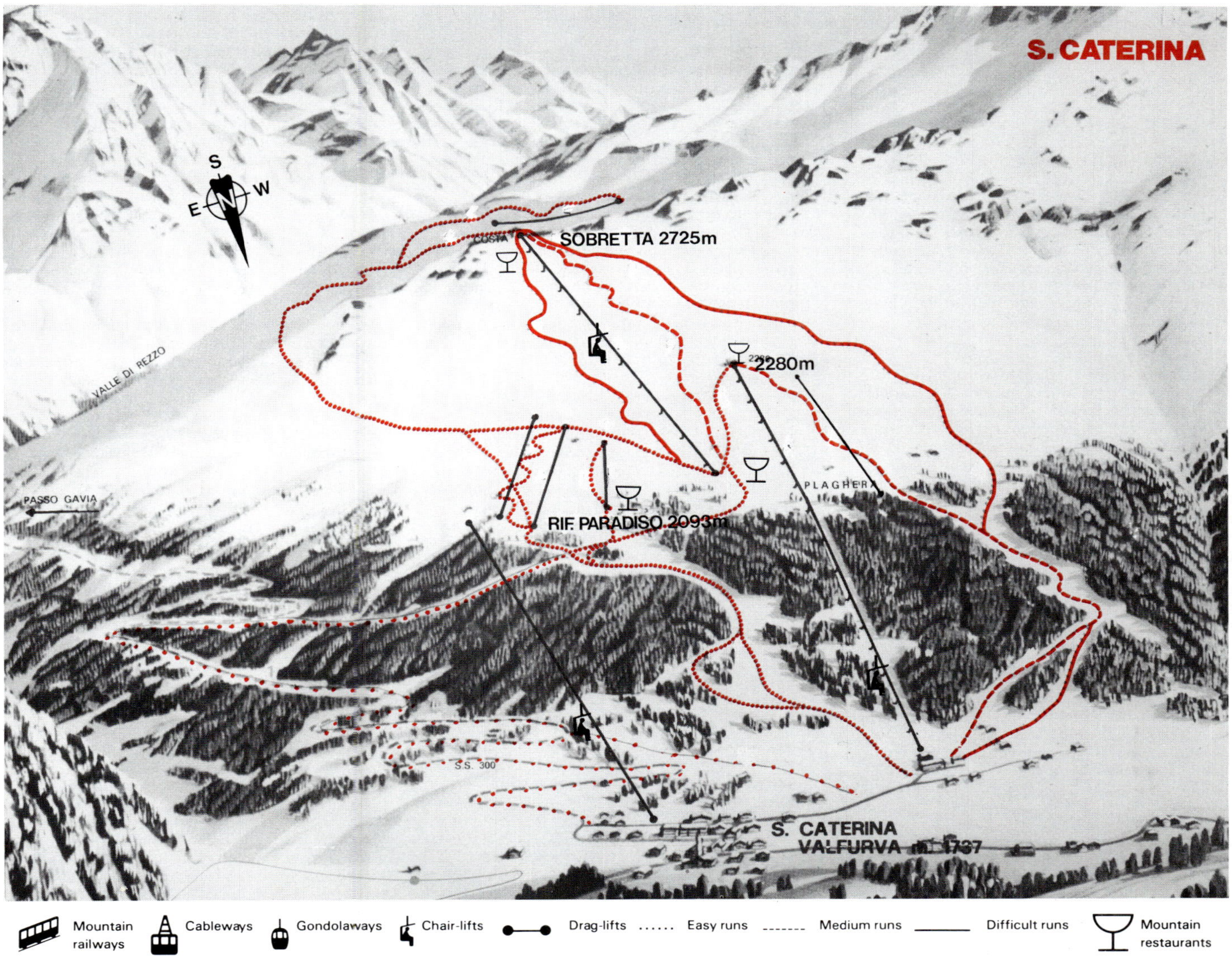

PASSO TONALE

Height of Resort: 6,168 ft.
Height of Top Station: 9,016 ft. (Summer: 9,896 ft.)
Nearest International Airport: Milan
Map Reference: 4C See page 239
Route by Car: See pages 236-239
Resort Facilities Charts: See page 220

One of the highest resorts in Italy situated in the province of Trento. It lies in the open sunny valley between Val di Sole and Val Camonica. This wide valley runs in an east-west direction with the lifts on each side of the road and the pistes, therefore, are predominantly north and south facing. The resort itself is small with some 30 hotels and pensions, shops, supermarkets, cafés and bars lining each side of the village street. The runs are all above the tree line and there is summer skiing on the glacier on the south side with lifts ranging from 9,016 to 9,896ft.

South Side: The runs in this area are not for the faint-hearted but for the advanced intermediate and good skier. From the village a cableway travels southeastwards up to Paradiso, 8,482ft., where one finds a restaurant. From this point a chair-lift rises southwards to Cap Solda, 9,016ft. This is the northern extremity of the glacier where the summer skiing takes place and here there is a restaurant and three parallel drag-lifts rising to 9,896ft. and two ski school trainer lifts. The lifts on the glacier are not normally open in the winter but if snow conditions are poor on the lower slopes then they are operated. The runs back to the village from Cap Solda are intermediate as far as Paradiso, to the right and more or less following the line of the chair-lift. From Paradiso, the difficult Paradiso Direttissima run crisscrosses below the cableway, whilst Paradiso Normale to the left is difficult to start with and thence intermediate for the run in. As the runs are over north and north-west facing slopes the snow conditions are normally excellent.

North Side: The novice to intermediate will be very happy in this area serviced by 16 lifts, 7 of which are trainers for beginners and second year skiers. The main lifts can be divided into two areas: to the west side of the village a 4-seater chair-lift rises northwards to 6,759ft., where one finds a pleasant restaurant. A longer surmounting 4-seater chair-lift reaches the crest at Bleis, 8,268ft. From here intermediates will enjoy the 4.5km. Alpino run back to the village whilst beginners can take the easy Bleis run.

On the east side of the village two parallel drag-lifts rise northwards, the longer one, Cadl I, reaching 7,509ft.; runs back to the village are intermediate. From the top of Cadl I one can cross over eastwards to the Rododendro drag-lift or to the chair-lift, the latter terminating at a very pleasant restaurant, Valbiolo, 7,362ft. From the restaurant the Tonale Occidentale chair-lift swings westwards to 8,3OOft., the east facing run back to the restaurant is intermediate, whilst the south facing run from this point down to the village is easy and about 3½km. in length. From the Valbiolo restaurant a new 4-seater chair-lift runs northward to Passo Contrabandinieri, 8,795ft., serving two excellent runs back to the restaurant. For a change of surroundings it is possible under normal conditions to ski down, with a little langlauf in between, to the larger village of Ponte di Legno which has a much smaller lift system, consisting at present of a chair-lift and surmounting drag-lift providing intermediate, easy and difficult runs back to base. There is a good langlauf trail of 7.5km. here and a further one of 5km. at Passo Tonale.

In a Few Words: A resort with great possibilities; compact lift system; well prepared runs but piste markings not good; height ensures good snow, under normal conditions, for a long season; little or no queueing and not overcrowded at weekends; excellent for beginners to intermediates although there are a limited number of difficult runs.

Après Ski: Informal and not very bright. There is the Embassy disco, five pubs with live music:- Antares, Heaven, Crazy Horse, El Bait and Cantuccio and bars in many of the hotels. There are two swimming pools, an ice rink and toboggan run. For greater entertainment facilities Ponti di Legno is close at hand.

Recommended Hotels:

Pension La Torrette: A pension with 22 beds situated in the centre. All rooms with shower/wc., small dining room, sitting room, bar and pizzeria providing the best pizzas in the village.

Hotel Savoia: A modern hotel well placed for the lifts. 35 rooms all with shower/wc, nicely furnished but some on the small side, spacious bright dining room, comfortable lounge and large bar. Discothèque and garage.

CASPOGGIO

Height of Resort: 3,504 ft.
Height of Top Station: 7,072 ft.
Nearest International Airport: Milan
Map Reference: 4C See page 239
Route by Car: See pages 236-239
Resort Facilities Charts: See page 219
Hotel Reference Charts: See page 231

This small resort of 7 hotels sits on a sunny shelf above a wide, open valley. It is easily reached by road being only 16km. from Sondrio through the attractive Malenco Valley. For a resort of its size Caspoggio has a good, compact lift system and in addition the Chiesa ski area is nearby.

From the edge of the village surmounting chair-lifts rise first to San Antonio, 4,430ft., where there is a chair-lift. The second stage reaches up to Piazzo Cavalli, 5,644ft., here amidst beautiful scenery there is a further restaurant. The ski school operates at Piazzo Cavalli where there is also a trainer lift and a longer lift as classes progress. From this area a longer drag-lift travels eastwards up to Dosso Galli, 7,072ft. the highest station in the resort. From here one has the choice of intermediate runs which sweep round south of Piazzo Cavalli and thence north-westward to San Antonio and the village. For the experienced skier there is the testing FIS run from the top station which more or less follows the line of the lifts. The longest run is 4.5km. with a vertical descent of some 3,500ft.

Chiesa Yalmalenco Area: One can also purchase a day pass for the Chiesa skiing situated on the plateau across the valley from Caspoggio. This is reached by cableway from Costi Battaini which rises to Palu, 6,595ft., here there is a restaurant from which one has wonderful views across the valley. From the restaurant one can ski down on north-west facing runs of intermediate standard to Barchi 5,577ft. and travel back by chair-lift to the restaurant or take another chair-lift from the restaurant which travels south-eastward up to Sasso Alto, 7,654 ft. the highest station, with intermediate north-west facing runs back, Alternatively from the top one can ski down northwards to Casoni, 6,233ft. returning to the top by chair-lift. All the skiing in this area is above the treeline and the runs are easy to intermediate.

In a Few Words: Caspoggio is an attractive small resort with a compact ski area served by a good lift system; suitable for beginners to intermediates; skiers requiring greater variety can also use the Chiesa area; predominately north-west facing slopes in both areas so snow should remain good under normal conditions.

Après Ski: Quiet and informal as with most small resorts. There are several cosy bars and restaurants and disco dancing most evenings in Chiesa Valmalenco and a good deal of organised entertainment. Caspoggio has a natural ice rink. There are plenty of nearby places of interest and excursions are arranged to Bormio, duty free Livigno and St. Moritz.

Recommended Hotels:

Hotel Kennedy: Situated about 8 minutes walk above the village this medium size hotel has comfortable accommodation, most bedrooms with bath or shower and many with balcony. A pleasant dining room and lounge, bar, discothèque with dancing most evenings.

BORMIO

Height of Resort: 4,018 ft.
Height of Top Station: 9,905 ft.
Nearest International Airport: Milan
Map Reference: 4C See page 239
Route by Car: See pages 236-239
Resort Facilities Charts: See page 219
Hotel Reference Charts: See page 231

Bormio, the venue for the 1985 World Alpine Championships, was once an old Roman spa. The old village centre with its cobbled streets surrounded with a variety of modern hotels and villas. Its setting is picturesque, a sunny, sheltered bowl at the foot of the Stelvio pass and its atmosphere is agreeably relaxed.

An extensive network of lifts covers the slopes of Monte Vallecetta, top station Cima Bianca, 9,905ft., otherwise known as Bormio 3000. The distance from the top station to the village is 14km. A 2-stage cableway from the edge of the village rises to its first station, Bormio 2000, where there is a good variety of easy and intermediate runs, thence to the top by cableway or chair-lift running parallel; alternatively the gondolaway from the village to Ciuk and surmounting chair-lift or drag-lift to La Rocca enables one to ski down to Bormio 2000 and join the cableway for the second section. A good variety of runs on open, north and north-west facing slopes, 7 to 10km. in length, lead from the top and the wide selection of lifts on the middle slopes provides numerous variations of runs down through broadly wooded pistes, 2 to 4km. The main lifts on these slopes are the drag-lift from Ciuk to a height of 7,540ft., a chair-lift to La Rocca and a chair-lift to Bormio 2000.

The central area has been much improved by the installation of 4 chair-lifts and all lifts in this area serve runs suitable for all grades of skiers, over north and north-west facing slopes. There are also excellent nursery slopes at both Ciuk and Bormio 2000. From the top station, Bormio 3000, the runs to the village are suitable for all grades of skiers. Snow conditions are normally sufficient to allow skiing to the village area until mid-March, but artificial snow making machines have improved this situation.

San Colombano Area: The recent development of this area has added to the attraction of Bormio's skiing. Unfortunately part of this area was not in operation for the 1996/97 season; as yet it is not known whether it will be for 1997/98. Please check with Bormio Tourist Office. A short time ago there were only two drag-lifts; now there are 3 chair-lifts and 6 drag-lifts serving 35km. of prepared pistes. The two base stations are Oga, 5,019ft. in the Valdisotto, 3km. from Bormio, and Isolaccia, 4,365ft. in Valdidentro, 9km. away, but a bus service links these two stations along with Le Motte in the centre of the area.
From Oga two surmounting chair-lifts rise in a southerly direction to a restaurant at 7,418 ft. which is one of the ski school areas. From Isolaccia the third chair-lift reaches a further restaurant and ski school area with a trainer lift. From this point a short traverse takes one to surmounting drag-lifts rising to Mont Masucco, 7,762ft. The area around both these two top stations provides delightful open skiing for beginners and intermediates served by 3 drag-lifts, one ascending to Dosso le Pone, 8,368ft., the highest point in the area. The intermediate skier will enjoy

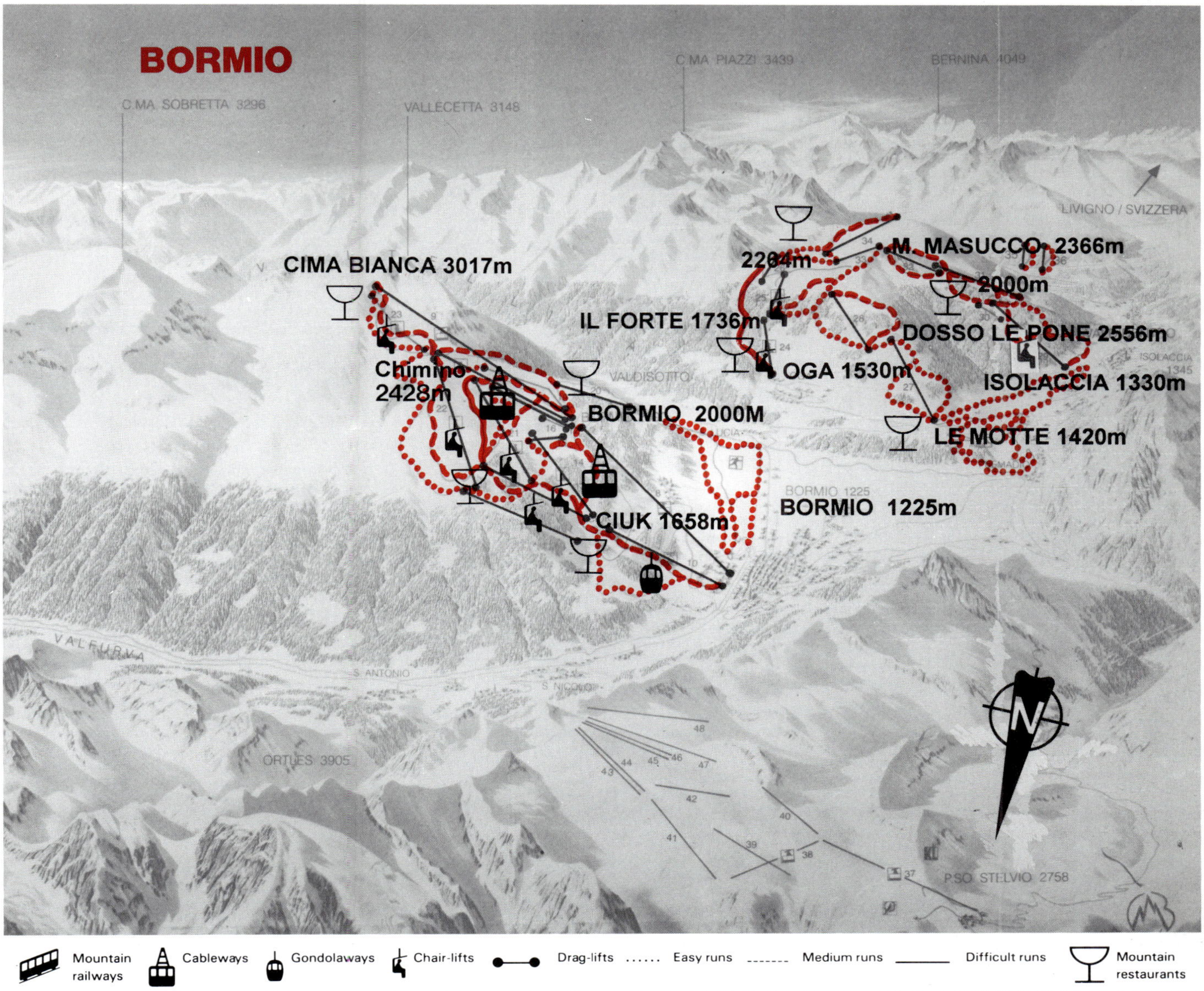

the demanding run through wooded glades from Masucco down to Isolaccia, about 4km. in length with a vertical drop of 3,400ft. The less experienced can take the blue run in the central sector running each side of the linking drag-lifts which come up south-eastwards from Le Motte; a break can be taken at the Il Forte restaurant situated between these two lifts. The run back from the top to Oga is wooded and difficult, about 3km. in length with a vertical descent of 2,450ft. Most of the runs in the area are north, north-east and north-west facing so hold the snow well.

The Bormio lift pass covers this area as it does Livigno and S. Caterina. No photographs are required for lift passes as electronic checking devices are operational at all turnstiles.

There are a number of mountain restaurants offering tempting local dishes. At Bormio 2000 one finds a large self-service restaurant, at Bormio 3000 a smaller bar serving snacks. At Ciuk there are two large restaurants in the hotels and at La Rocca local style mountain restaurants. There are marvellous opportunities for ski touring too from Bormio, in the Ortler and Cevedale regions at 10-12,000ft., with an enormous range of glacier skiing, much helped by well spaced mountain huts. This is also an excellent area for summer skiing for all grades, located on the nearby Stelvio Pass. It is expected that a new ski area will be opened just to the left of La Rocca with the construction of two new drag-lifts, difference in height about 3,280ft., increasing the total length of runs by some 20km. These lifts are the first stage of a new programme to link Bormio to S. Caterina.

In a Few Words: Interesting skiing for all grades, particularly medium to good; fascinating old town, sheltered and sunny and not yet over-commercialised; snow conditions reliable; touring, summer skiing; medium price, good value.

Après Ski: There are not many restaurants outside the hotels themselves. Recommended are the Piccolo Mondo, Taula and Vecchia Combo. Many of the hotels have their own small night spots with juke box, mainly for residents, but outsiders are admitted with drinks at normal bar prices. There are three discothèques, the large Kings Club, where the ski school gathers each Friday for presentations; it has a large dance floor with good lighting and films are also shown here. More intimate and cosy is the Shangri-La. The disco in the Hotel Nazionale is also popular and here reasonably priced drinks are enjoyed around an open fire. The Hotel Aurora's original piano bar is a quiet intimate place to relax in front of a large log fire. The Rezia Piano Bar is also popular. There is in Bormio a superb Olympic-sized swimming pool with water relayed from the radioactive thermal springs beneath Plateau Reit, 3km. from the town centre. Here there is thermal bathing and mud baths. The old Roman bath in a cave outside town is exactly as it was 2,000 years ago. More functions are being put on by some of the hoteliers and restaurant owners: for instance, buses to Bormio 2000 and then snocat to a mountain restaurant for dinner of polenta and sausages and then down on skis; also, night tobogganing at Bormio 2000 organised by the owner of the Hotel Girasole. There are also facilities for riding, squash and skating.

Recommended Hotels:

Hotel Ambassador Chalet: Close to cableway terminal. Attractive restaurant and lounges with wooden decor. English style bar. Bedrooms nicely furnished, nearly all rooms with private shower. À la carte restaurant.

Hotel Funivia: Next to cableway terminal, remodernised half-timbered hotel, with spacious dining room, lounge and bar. Taverna with open log fire and stereo system; television room, games room, sauna and jacuzzi. Bedrooms comfortable, most with private bath or shower and many with balcony. Large sun terrace and garage.

Hotel Genzianella: Immediately opposite the cableway, large bright dining room, sitting room, small TV room and bar. Bedrooms of good size, particularly in the new wing, all with bath or shower. Good for families, children welcome, friendly atmosphere. Taverna discothèque.

Hotel Posta: A very attractive old chalet-style hotel dating back to 18th century, recently upgraded and completely renovated. Situated in Via Roma, intimate style decor, cosy sitting rooms, nice bright dining room, bedrooms tastefully furnished, all with bath or shower. Piano bar, swimming pool, whirlpool, sauna, solarium and fitness room.

LIVIGNO

Height of Resort: 5,958 ft.
Height of Top Station: 9,184 ft.
Nearest International Airport: Milan/Zürich
Map Reference: 4B See page 239
Route by Car: See pages 236-239
Resort Facilities Charts: See page 220
Hotel Reference Charts: See page 231

Livigno is situated in a high, sunny valley near the Swiss border about 40km. from Bormio and one hour by car from St. Moritz. It is 4 hours by road from Milan, Zurich or Munich and is a duty free area. The valley runs in a northerly direction, with ski areas on each side.

Eastern Side: A gondolaway rises from the village centre to the Mottolino restaurant at 7,872 ft., with intermediate runs back to the village of 3 km in length. From Mottolino restaurant one can take the chair-lift up to Monte Della Neve, 9,134 ft., and from this point there is a testing run down to the chair-lift rising to Monte Sponda, 8,269 ft., giving access to various on and off-piste runs. Alternatively from Monte Della Neve one can ski back to the restaurant and down to the village with runs of about 5 km or fork right below Monte Sponda and take an intermediate run to the foot of the Trepalle 4 seater chair-lift which brings one back again to the restaurant. Below Trepalle one finds the Passo d'Eira drag-lift serving easy runs.

Western Side: The main lift system runs from San Rocco, to the south-west of the village and there are further lifts at Santa Maria, to the north-east. A gondolaway from San Rocco rises to Lac Salin, 9,085ft., with a restaurant and a self-service restaurant at the top. Over the crest two parallel drag-lifts serve intermediate west facing runs down to Federia, 8,134 ft. Both lifts rise to 9,184 ft, the highest station in the resort. From this point north-east facing intermediate runs lead back to the village or one can ski down to the Lac Salin chair-lift which returns one to the restaurant again. From the latter one can cross over to the two Blesaccia chair-lifts which serve a variety of intermediate north-east facing runs. From the top station of Blesaccia an easy run follows the crest down to the Costaccia restaurant, 6,767 ft, and thence down to Santa Maria end of the village. From this area a chair-lift rises to the Costaccia restaurant, where the Valandrea-Vetta chair-lift travels southwards to a height of 5,095 ft. These lifts serve easy to intermediate runs.

There are plenty of nursery slopes and limitless offpiste skiing for the expert. Snow remains good throughout a long season because of the valley's high altitude. The 7 day lift pass is also valid for the lifts in Bormio, Santa Caterina, Valdidentro and Valdisotto.

In a Few Words: A fascinating resort, with open sunny slopes and good snow; duty free area (including very cheap petrol) an advantage for motorists; suitable for beginners to intermediates plus; skiing of similar standard in both areas.

Après Ski: Pretty active with plenty of bars, cafés and discos. The erstwhile alpine hut, 'Tea del Vidal', transformed into an old world restaurant, is very popular with young people, and it has the best music. The larger disco 'Cielo' is popular. The Kokodi disco in San Rocco is a more recent addition, so is Marco's Video bar, whilst Foxi's Pub in the centre of the village is one of the most popular drinking places. For eating out there is Mario's Pub where one can get a snack or meal at reasonable prices, the fish restaurant 'Pesce d'Oro' close to the centre provides a wide variety of fish dishes. The Bar Scuola-Sci has long been a popular meeting place with an international atmosphere, here you can enjoy a rest and drink after skiing. There is also a good selection of pizzerias. This is primarily a skier's resort, but there are sleigh rides, an ice rink, para-gliding, tennis, golf range plus excursions to St. Moritz and many other interesting places as alternative activities. There is a good selection of shops taking advantage of the duty free status. Livigno is a very long village and the bus service runs from 8.20 a.m. to 7.30 p.m.– after that taxis are available.

Recommended Hotels:

Hotel Buceneve: Close to the terminal of the Mottolino drag-lift (one can ski to the hotel) in a slightly elevated position with lovely views over Livigno. Furnished in local style, all bedrooms with bath or shower, telephone and TV; spacious lounge, Taverna and dining room. Pleasant and helpful management. Games room with table tennis etc.

Hotel Erica: Opened in 1980 and situated in a central position, this hotel has comfortably furnished rooms, all with bath, shower and wc. Spacious dining room, open plan reception area, lounge and bar.

Hotel Europa: Situated about 11 minutes walk from the village centre and 6 minutes to the Mottolina gondolaway, this comfortable 3 star hotel is attractively furnished. Large lounge and bar, dining room from which one has lovely views, sauna, jacuzzi, solarium and fitness room. Spacious bedrooms all with shower, wc, telephone, TV and minibar; most rooms have balconies.

Hotel Pare: This hotel was opened during the 1971/2 season and has a lovely view overlooking the village. Spacious sitting rooms, cocktail bar, terrace, swimming pool, sauna and solarium. All bedrooms with private bath or shower, many with balconies. Very attractive dining rooms, fitness corner and conference rooms.

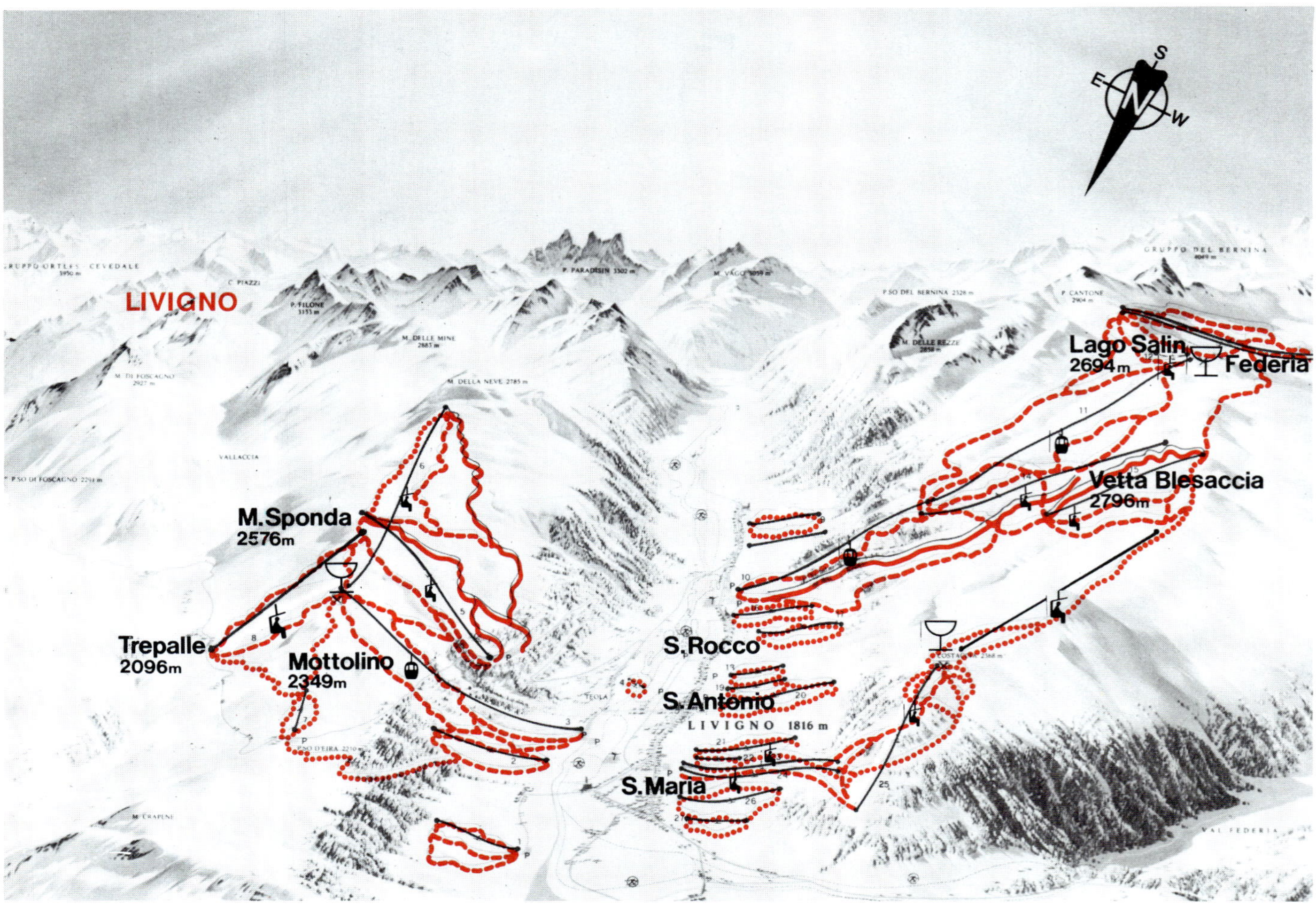

Mountain railways · Cableways · Gondolaways · Chair-lifts · Drag-lifts · Easy runs · Medium runs · Difficult runs · Mountain restaurants

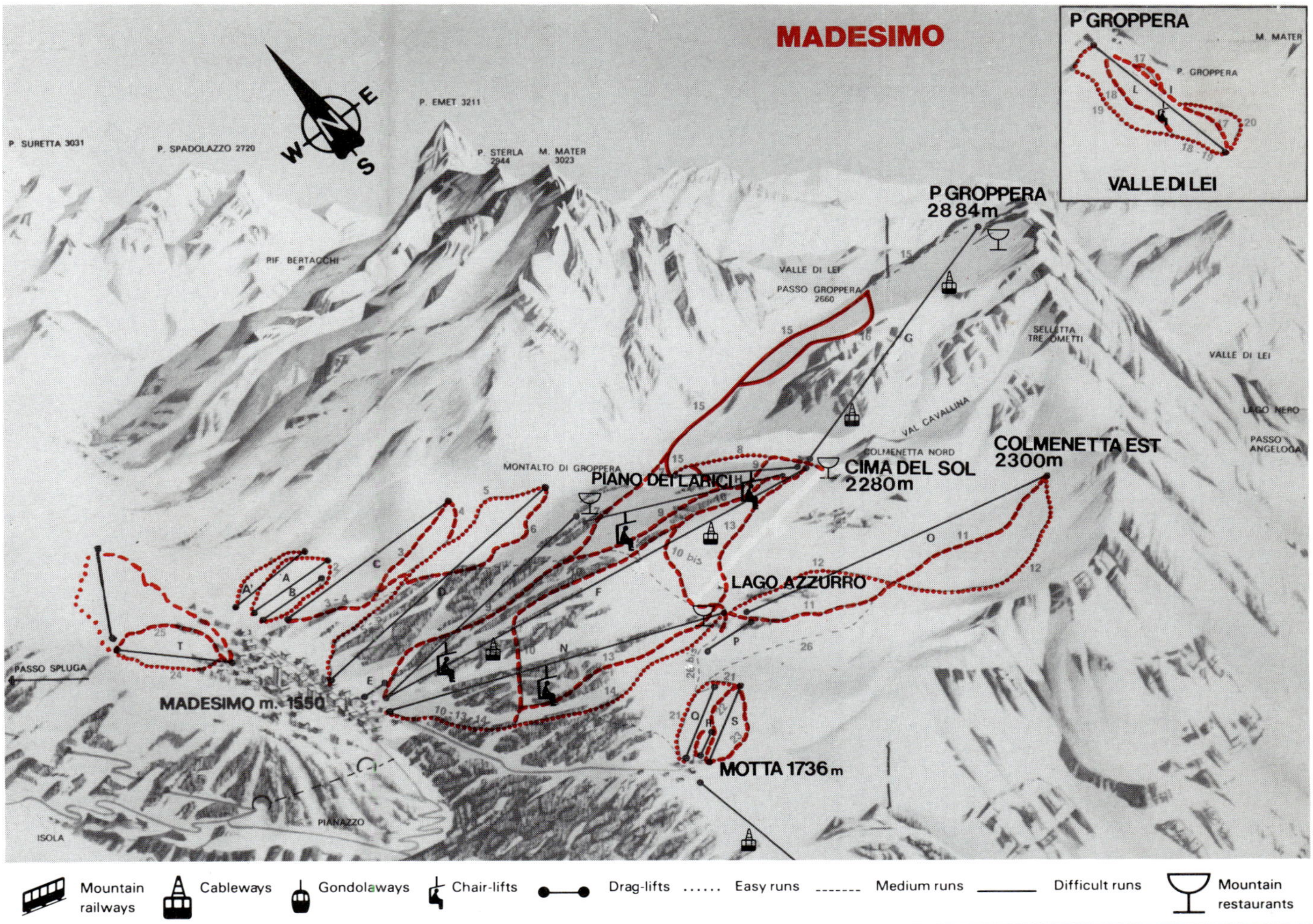

MADESIMO

Height of Resort: 5,085 ft.
Height of Top Station: 9,481 ft.
Nearest International Airport: Milan
Map Reference: 2B See page 239
Route by Car: See pages 236-239
Resort Facilities Charts: See page 220
Hotel Reference Charts: See page 231

Travelling 90 miles north from Milan on the road to the Splugen Pass, which ends in a steep climb through innumerable hairpin bends, one arrives at Madesimo, a modern, middle-sized village in wooded surroundings. Snow conditions are normally good here because of the altitude although the nursery slopes tend to become icy when there is less than average snow.

The ski area is reached by a double-stage cable-way from the village first to Cima del Sole, 7,480ft., with restaurant and sun terrace, then Pizzo Groppera, 9,481ft. From the village a chair-lift runs parallel to the lower section of the cableway up to Lago Azzuro, and from this point a drag-lift rises to Colmenetta Est, 7,545ft. To the left of the cableway two surmounting chair-lifts also connect the resort with the latter station. From the halfway station there are runs of various grades leading to wooded runs lower down, which deteriorate later in the season. There is a small restaurant at the top station, Pizzo Groppera, with a marvellous views and very enjoyable runs over varied terrain lead from here through the Valle di Lei, some 2,000m. in length, with a double chair-lift returning to the top station. Best of all, but fairly difficult is the Canalone run from Pizzo Groppera, starting steeply (the run averages 36° gradient) and leading to a wide and smooth gulley, evening out into a gentler run down to the village, a distance of 5,150m. in total: or one has the choice of returning to the first station of the cableway via the Piano dei Larici chair-lift.

A computerised system for lift passes has greatly improved organisation, the pass covers all lifts, (except one baby lift), including those on the beginner's slopes at Arlecchino and Motta, A snack bar is to be found at the bottom of the Val de Lei run and restaurants at the middle and top stations of the cableway.

In a Few Words: Best suited to medium to good skiers; all runs end in the village, with a compact lift system; snow reliable, village modern with attractive surroundings; medium price, good value.

Après Ski: Night life fairly quiet on the whole. The Cantinone at the Hotel Andossi is very popular with English visitors - it is a log cabin style bar, serving draught beer and wine. The Facsimile Videoteque in the Hotel Torre is probably the most popular in the village and is also open every night. One of the best among the good selection of restaurants is the Tec de L'Urs. Its atmosphere is delightful and it is very good value. At the Edelweiss and Italy Pub, pizzas cooked on open fires are excellent. The tiny bar Osteria Vecchia, near the cableway station, is nearly 200 years old and serves meals whilst a similexcellent.ar establishment 'Dogana Vecchia' provides local specialities. Good fondues are to be found at the Verosa and the Meridiana Hotel's Tavernetta. A very friendly bar, located centrally and only 2 minutes from the cableway, is the 'Sand Iron Pub'.

The mountain restaurant at Cima del Sole is good, providing ample and tasty portions and the Baite del Sole, at the end of one of the runs, has a lovely sun terrace where one can indulge in the delicious plates of smoked beef and cheese. A third mountain restaurant is located at Pian dei Larici. There are some good walks for non-skiers and a snow cat to take them to Baita del Sole to meet skiing companions for lunch! Skating and Nordic skiing are also available.

Recommended Hotels:

Hotel Cascata et Cristallo: Near the cableway terminal, this is a large hotel of 180 beds, all rooms with bath. A large well appointed dining room, large lounge with bar, children's play-room, swimming pool with sauna, large sun terrace. Tavola Calda bar, with friendly atmosphere, the only place in the village to serve pizzas at lunch. A well run hotel with plenty of space.

Hotel La Meridiana: Pleasantly situated in the centre of the village. Characteristic style building with pleasant bar and lounge. Taverna-Piano-Bar has open fire and fondues are frequently arranged. All rooms have bath or shower. Sun terrace, one of the best sun traps in the village.

Hotel Torre: A multi-floor hotel situated centrally only a 4 minute walk from the cableway and most shops. Rooms vary in size but all have bath or shower. Large dining room; TV/sitting room with some indoor games. Very popular Conchiglietta disco.

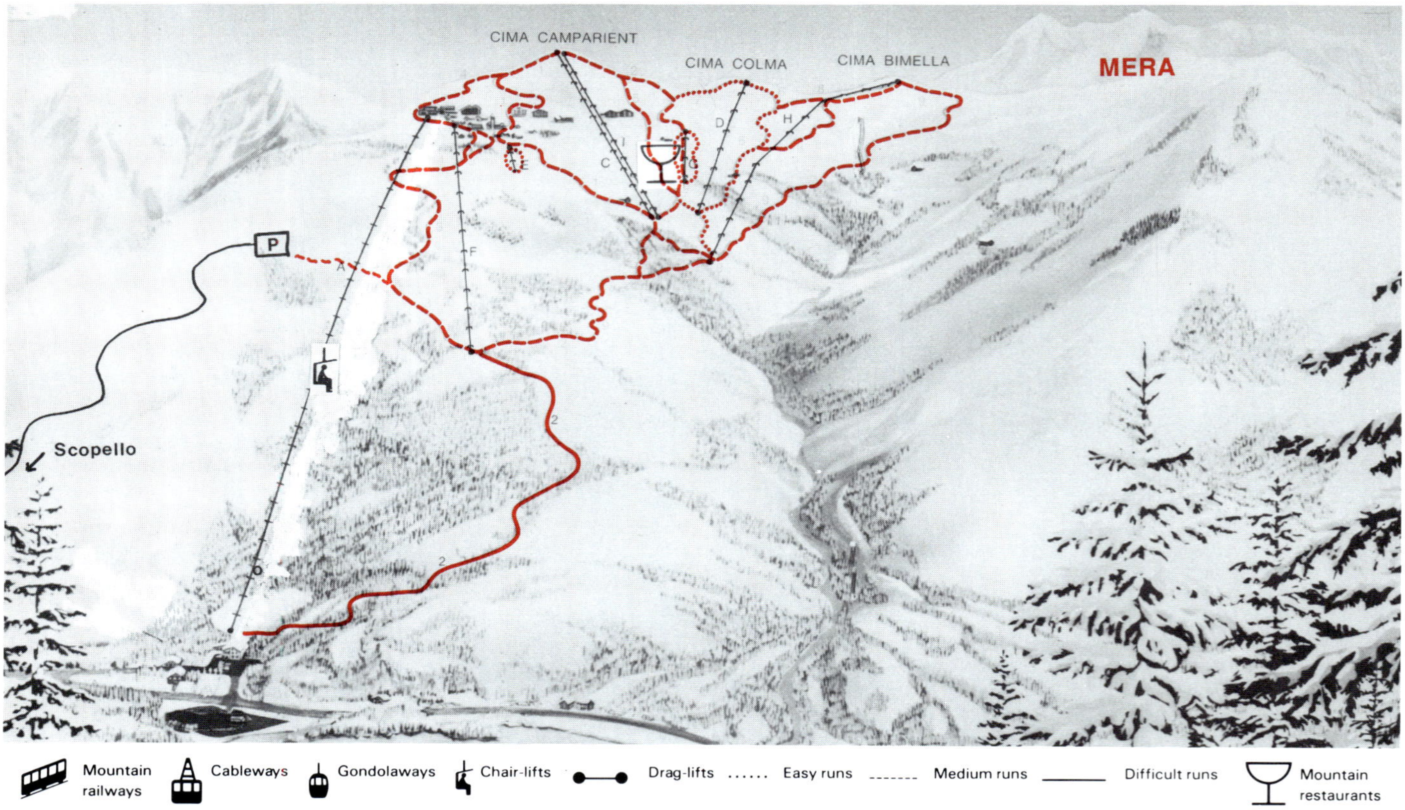

MERA

Height of Resort: 2,200/4,900 ft.
Height of Top Station: 5,900 ft.
Nearest International Airport: Milan/Turin
Map Reference: 7D See page 238
Route by Car: See pages 236-238
Resort Facilities Charts: See page 220
Hotel Reference Charts: See page 231

This delightful small resort lies on a high, open plateau above the Sesia valley, almost equidistant (about 100 km.) from Milan or Turin airports. Mera is reached by a covered chair-lift rising from nearby Scopello, 2,200ft. to 4,900 ft or by road from Scopello to Alpe Trogo, where there is a car park, and one skis down to the foot of Pian Rasto drag-lift which rises to the village. For a small resort Mera has a good and compact interlinking lift system. On the west side of the chair-lift, starting less than half-way down, is a long drag-lift, Pian Rasto, which converges on the top station of the chair-lift and services a medium run which terminates at the foot of the drag-lift; alternatively, one can continue on a fairly difficult wooded run to the bottom of the chair-lift near Scopello.

The main ski area is reached by skiing north-westwards from the top station down to the foot of the double drag-lift (passing a trainer lift on the way) which rises to the top station, Cima Camparient, 5,900ft., providing intermediate runs back both sides of the lift and link runs with the lift previously mentioned. On the right a further drag-lift rises to Cima Colma, which caters for easy runs either side; whilst further to the right a longer drag-lift reaches Cima Bimella and from this point one has good intermediate runs back to the base, or one can continue easterly on an advanced intermediate run to the foot of Pian Rasto drag-lift. Here one can return to the top station of the chair-lift or negotiate the difficult wooded run to the foot of the chair-lift. Although small, the system is cleverly interlinked, providing a good variety of north, north-east and north-westward facing runs over open terrain, except for those to the lower stations.

Mera is a sunny resort, but the northerly orientation of the runs means that snow remains good. There is a small natural skating rink at the Hotel La Baita.

In a Few Words: Essentially a skier's resort, beginners to intermediates; compact lift system, reliable snow; being near Milan and Turin can get crowded at weekends, otherwise no queueing.

Après Ski: This is what you make it and it's mostly centred around the Hotel Capricorno, whilst the Bar Piero is a popular place for a drink. A few shops selling most of the things one requires, along with ski school and sports shop.

Hotel Capricorno: Owned by the lift company. Wood-panelled bedrooms are small but comfortable, floor showers and bathrooms. Dining room with bar adjacent and further room which is the centre of impromptu entertainment and disco.

FOPPOLO

Height of Resort: 4,920 ft.
Height of Top Station: 7,101 ft.
Nearest International Airport: Milan
Map Reference: 3D See page 239
Route by Car: See pages 236-239
Resort Facilities Charts: See page 219
Hotel Reference Charts: See page 231

A fairly modern resort standing at the head of the Brembana valley, 58km. from Bergamo and 110 km. from Milan. The village consists of a cluster of 8 hotels, essential shops, cafés and bars. The ski area is compact, with lifts fanning out from the village and all the main runs, facing west and south-west, ending in the village area. Eleven lifts serve 50km of prepared pistes. Under normal conditions this resort has a good snow record.

Three main lift systems leave the village area. On the southern side, a chair-lift rises to Valgussera, 7,101ft., the top station of the resort. There is no run directly back to the village from this top station so one heads eastward to connect with the Vago and Giretta drag-lifts, the latter's top station 6,845ft., and from here one has easy and intermediate south-west facing runs each side of the lift and back to the village. From the near centre of the village a double chair-lift supplemented by a 4-seater chair-lift rise eastward to Quarta Baita, 5,979ft., with easy runs back to the village.

Surmounting is a further chair-lift and parallel drag-lift to Monte Bello, 6,888ft., where there is a restaurant. From this point one can cross over to the Giretta drag-lift on easy and intermediate south-west facing runs, or ski back to the first station on south-west facing runs; one difficult and one easy.

From the north-east side of the village surmounting drag-lifts rise in a north-easterly direction, first to Tre Stalle, 5,710ft., with easy runs to the village, and thence to Foppane, 7,003ft. From this point there is a difficult run which follows the line of the top lift and an intermediate run which swings out north-westwards and then south to the first station. It is possible to cross over from the north-eastern area to the central area without returning to the village.

In a Few Words: A compact ski area with all the main lifts leading from the village and the main runs finishing in the village. Good snow record. Skating rink. At the head of a valley, so no through traffic. Very reasonable prices.

Après Ski: The night life is much in evidence for a small resort. Lively discothèques are to be found at the hotels Europa, Cristallo and Des Alpes. There are various cafés and bars, and the Pizzeria Serenella is a popular rendezvous. Not much for the non-skier, apart from a natural Olympic size skating rink.

Recommended Hotels:

Hotel Cristallo: Situated next door to the Baita chair-lift and the ski school meeting place, this large, modern hotel has pleasant bedrooms, all with private bath or shower, many with balcony; also interconnecting family rooms. Large bright dining room and spacious lounge. Discothèque.

Hotel Europa: Situated approximately halfway between the Baita chair-lift and the drag-lift going up to Tre Stalle. Bedrooms comfortably furnished. Most have private shower and wc. and some have balcony. Interconnecting family rooms. Attractive reception rooms and thre popular 'Grizzly' discothèque.

Hotel Pineta: Situated a few yards from the Hotel Europa and nearer the Tre Stalle drag-lift, this is a modern hotel under the same management as the Cristallo. All bedrooms with bath or shower and some with balcony. Bright dining room, comfortable lounge/bar.

MACUGNAGA

Height of Resort: 4,352 ft.
Height of Top Station: 9,000 ft.
Nearest International Airport: Milan
Map Reference: 7C See page 238
Route by Car: See pages 236-238
Resort Facilities Charts: See page 220
Hotel Reference Charts: See page 231

Macugnaga is divided into two parts, Staffa and Pecetto, but nevertheless is a village of charm and character. The skiing is two areas.

Staffa-Monte Moro Area: A fast two-section cableway rises from Staffa to Alpe Bill, 5,525 ft., and continues to the summit of Monte Moro, 9,000ft., on the Swiss border, with superb views of the Monte Rosa glaciers and some marvellous skiing, catering for all standards. At the top there are two restaurants and four drag-lifts serving this area, and there are several runs of nearly 5 miles to the first station.

Pecetto-Belvedere Area: A 2-section double chairlift rises to Belvedere, 6,000ft., the resort's most beautiful area, with particularly fine views from the top station. The first section of the chair-lift rises to Burky, where to the right one finds a drag-lift serving a short, easy run. From Burky the chair-lift swings north-westward up to Belvedere, where there is a restaurant with sun terrace. From this top station one has the choice of three runs: to the right of the chair-lift an intermediate run, which can be tricky to start with, depending on snow, conditions, becoming easier towards Burky and joins the easy run down to the village; to the left of the chair-lift an interesting intermediate run sweeps round in an arc clear of Burky down to the bottom station of the chair-lift. The third intermediate run joins the easy run at the foot of the drag-lift.

Beginners are well catered for in the village, with their own drag-lift, and in addition to Macugnaga's skiing a most enjoyable day tour can be made in the spring to Saas Fee in Switzerland for a change of scene. There are two ski schools, a 5km. nordic ski trail in Pecetto and 8km. between Staffa and Isella, as well as surfing and hang-gliding.

In a Few Words: An attractive village, though not compact; friendly, relaxed atmosphere, skiing ideal for beginners to good intermediate standard; night life could be more varied, but throughout prices are good value.

Après Ski: Unsophisticated but lively, with plenty of cheap wine to add to the holiday mood. Casual clothes are all you need, discothèques could be varied by some live music. A favourite haunt for the young is the Flora piano bar; both the Glacier and Roffel Pizzerias are excellent; the Girasole is a favourite sport for fondues; the Jager is a popular rendezvous for tea and delicious cakes, whilst the Taverna del Rosa and Flizzi are to be recommended.

There are many other restaurant/bars where one can enjoy drinks and meals at reasonable prices. The Big-Ben disco on the main road in Staffa is modern with a large bar. Macugnaga is not far from the Italian lakes, which make a delightful day's outing in early spring.

Recommended Hotels:

Hotel Dufour: Situated in Staffa main square, brightly furnished bedrooms all with bathrooms and telephone, small dining room, café bar. Efficiently

Hotel Zumstein: Situated in Staffa, near the main square, this chalet style hotel is one of the best in the resort. Bedrooms of good size, many with shower or bath and balconies, all with TV. Very attractive stüberl type bar, spacious lounges and large dining room with panoramic view. Sauna. Run by the friendly and welcoming Burgener family, this is a popular hotel with lots of atmosphere.

CHAMPOLUC

Height of Resort: 5,478 ft.
Height of Top Station: 8,940 ft.
Nearest International Airport: Turin
Map Reference: 6C See page 238
Route by Car: See pages 236-238
Resort Facilities Charts: See page 219

Champoluc is a small village lying at the head of the lovely Ayas valley, some 27km. by road from Verres on the Turin-Aosta motorway. It has great charm, with only twenty hotels and pensions. To the eastern side of the valley the main lift system is reached by cableway from the village to Crest, 6,560ft., where there are restaurants. A medium to difficult $2^1/_2$km. run leads from here back to the village. For the less experienced skier, there are two chair-lifts at Crest which serve much gentler slopes, returning to the village again by cableway. More competent skiers can travel from Crest by chair-lift and surmounting drag-lift to the top station, 8,940ft., on the southern shoulder of Mt. Betta Forca, to the east of the Sarezza summit. The view from here is glorious, with the Matterhorn, Monte Rosa and a multitude of other peaks spreading out across the horizon. The runs from the top to the middle station are enjoyable, over south, south-east and south-west facing slopes, with a run of 7-8 km., a drop of 3,791ft., the full distance to Champoluc. This becomes wooded but with wide glades, as it approaches the village.

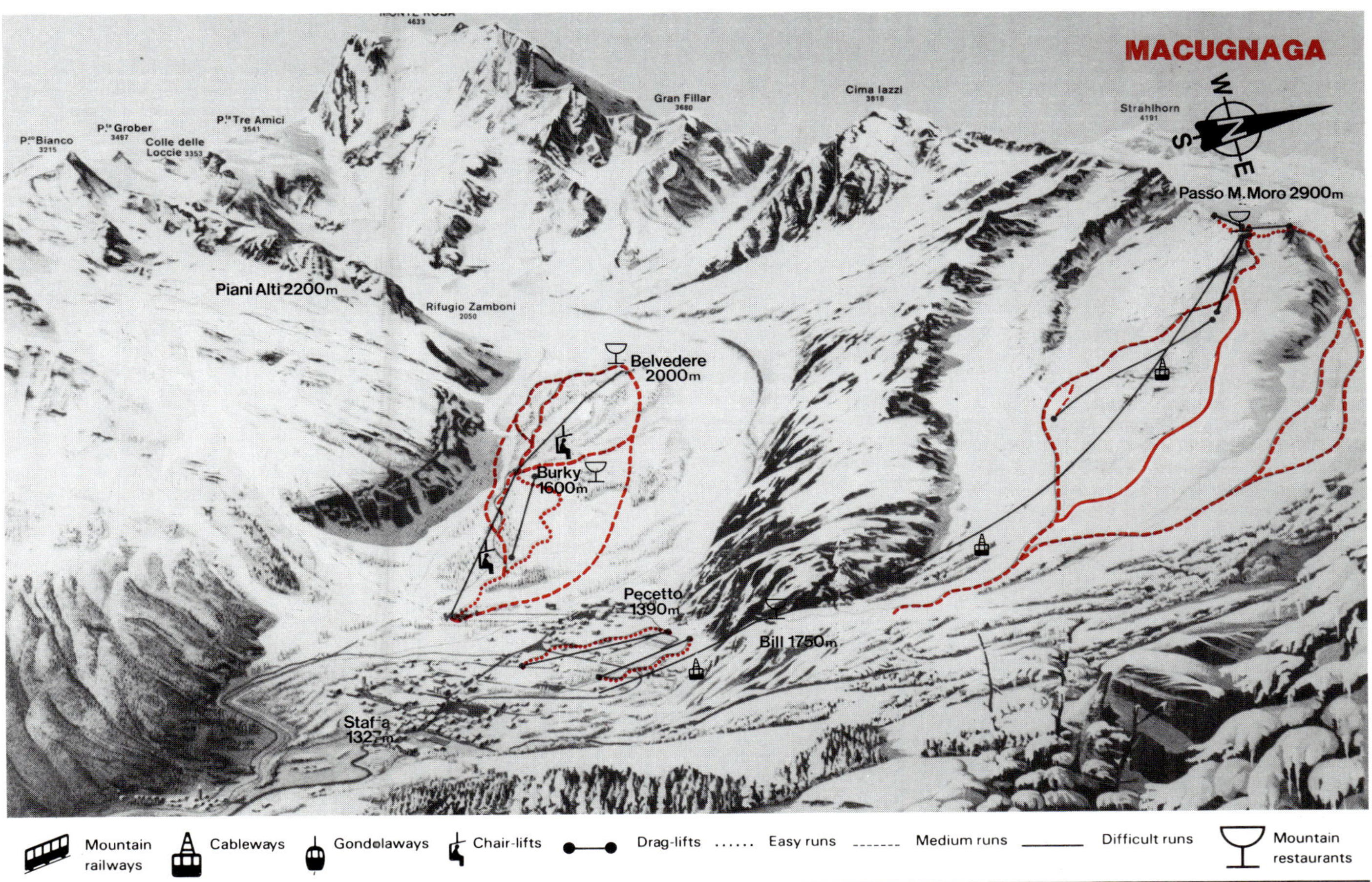

There is also a series of 8 drag-lifts on the western side of the valley above Antagnod, a suitable area for beginners and inexperienced skiers to gain confidence on, as well as a small beginners' drag-lift in the village. For greater variety one can take the Monte Rosa ski pass which embraces the ski areas of Champoluc, Frachey, Stafal, Orsia and Gressoney, providing a combined total of 184km. of runs served by 46 lifts. There are 13 mountain restaurants en route which adds to the enjoyment of a day's skiing amidst very beautiful scenery.

For the expert skier, mountaineering tours are organised accompanied by a qualified guide, with climbs to Colle Sarezza, 8,912ft., Colle Testa Grigia, 9,953ft., Colle del Rothorn, 8,832ft., Corno Vitello, 10,027ft. and many others. For the Nordic skiers there are two attractive circuits, one of 5km. in length and the other 25km., which run through the pine forests and attractive Alpine scenery.

In a Few Words: A small resort of much character with a helpful and friendly atmosphere; queueing rare except for holidays and Sunday; at present relatively unspoilt and inexpensive.

Après Ski: Skiing is the main interest here and night life is fairly small in scale so far, there are various cafés, bars with music and a discothèque, Grand Parson Frachey, where the locals also enter into the spirit of evening entertainment. Turin, Cervinia and Aosta all within easy access. Saint Vincent, 25km. away, is also within easy access with its casino and wider range of night life. Also of interest is the local wood carving; the Antagnod church with its frescoes and the mediaeval castles of Granes, Issogne and Verres.

Recommended Hotels:

Hotel Alpi Rosa: A typical mountain hotel, with old and modern sections, all rooms in the latter have private bath whilst in the former they are smaller and more simply furnished. The pleasant dining room adjoins the lounge/bar and there is a separate television room. A well run family hotel with a good atmosphere.

CERVINIA and Matterhorn Valley

Height of Resort: 6,760 ft.
Height of Top Station: 11,500 ft.
Nearest International Airport: Turin
Map Reference: 6C See page 238
Route by Car: See pages 236-238
Resort Facilities Charts: See page 219
Hotel Reference Charts: See page 231

Cervinia is among the highest resorts in the Alps and one of Italy's top three international ski centres. Easily reached from Turin or Milan airports, with an excellent approach road. It enjoys good snow conditions because of its height for a long season, in spite of the fact that there is plenty of sun and most of its slopes are south-east, south and south-west facing. The Matterhorn dominates the glorious high mountain surroundings and the slopes are wide open with superb, long runs and magnificent spring skiing – it is possible to ski quite comfortably from Plateau Rosa to Valtournenche or Zermatt and back in a day. The village is unexceptional in appearance but has a lively atmosphere.

The ski area is vast and served by an efficient combination of cableways, gondolaways, chair-lifts and drag-lifts.

From the centre of the village a cableway and a parallel gondolaway rise to Plan Maison, 8,382ft and from this point a two stage cableway travels to Plateau Rosa, 11,500.ft on the Swiss border. The drag-lifts beyond on the glacier are Swiss owned and to use these and to take advantage of the novel run to and from Zermatt, a passport and the payment of a daily supplement to the main Cassa in Cervinia is obligatory. The runs from Plateau Rosa to Cervinia are intermediate, some 10km in length and exhilarating. On the way down occasional huts provide expensive but wholesome food and drink giving one the opportunity to admire the breathtaking panorama. From Plan Maison, a series of other lifts are easily reached. The Rocce Nere chair-lift and a three stage drag-lift offer easy runs back to Plan Maison. In the past a more challenging run descended from Furggen, 11,456ft., to Plan Maison; unfortunately the cableway has been closed.

The alternative uphill system from Plan Maison was more recently completed. This consists of a 12 seater gondolaway, carrying 2400 persons per hour, rising to Lago Cime Bianche, 9,225ft., surmounted by a cableway climbing to Plateau Rosa carrying 1,450 persons per hour. It has helped to reduce the queues from Plan Maison to Plateau Rosa but also allows skiers to alight at Lago Cime Bianche to connect with the Lago Goillet 3 seater chair-lift, rising to Col Cime Bianche, 9,728ft., which serves some excellent south-west facing intermediate runs.

On the north-west side of the village, adjacent to the ski school assembly area, the Cretaz drag-lift system runs up almost parallel to the cableway to terminate at 8,192ft, and by a short cross-over the Rocce Nere chair-lift can be reached. From this area a superb variety of intermediate runs are available either to Plan Maison or the village. On the south side of the resort one finds the Carosello system, reached by the Bardoney chair-lift connecting this area from the village with the Cieloalto chair-lift, which rises eastwards to 8,134ft., serving west facing runs back to the village, difficult to start with and becoming intermediate; or one can take the run swinging to the south, difficult at the top and easy for the rest of the way to Lago Bleu, returning by chair-lift of the same name. This area is often sheltered from northerly winds which can affect the Plan Maison pistes.

Cervinia is essentially a skier's resort, catering for all standards. In the spring the off-piste runs, amidst beautiful scenery from Plateau Rosa to Champoluc and Valtournenche should not be missed. The uphill link from Valtournenche to Plateau Rosa consisting of a gondolaway out of the village and thence by surmounting drag-lifts has made this delightful 22km run very popular. Depending on conditions it is not an easy run and should only be tackled by skiers of intermediate standard and above or with a guide. There are generally fewer skiers in this area and the early afternoon snow conditions plus the direction of the slopes, makes it an ideal spot for a picnic lunch followed by some not too strenuous runs. For beginners there are extensive nursery slopes in the village area.

Chamois & Torgnon: A delightful day can be spent at these two smaller resorts down the Valley.

Chamois situated at 5,954ft. is one of the highest communes in Europe and reached by cableway from Buisson. Here one finds 7 lifts serving 6 runs above the village and interesting off-piste runs down to Valtournenche.

Torgnon at 4,884ft. is further down the valley with 6 lifts serving very attractive tree-lined runs in addition to Nordic trails.

Visitors to Cervinia may also be interested to know that apart from the normal resort ski pass there is the Valle d'Aosta ski pass which covers all resorts with a total of over 200 lifts.

In a Few Words: Marvellously long easy medium runs on good snow; spring skiing superb; snow always plentiful throughout long season; skiing for all standards, though only a small number of difficult runs; lots of sun; occasional strong winds at Plateau Rosa; expensive but good value.

Après Ski: Although skiing definitely takes priority, bars, restaurants and night clubs abound and booking in advance is recommended especially at weekends. Ten minutes drive by jeep from Cervinia is Les Clochards where one can enjoy excellent local specialities served in a characteristic atmosphere. The Copa Pan restaurant is attractive but expensive. So is the Café des Guides. The restaurant 'Jour et Nuit' is to be recommended. There is typical d'Aosta cuisine at Maison de Saussures and the Matterhorn specialises in pizza and huge T bone steaks. Most hotel food served in a friendly atmosphere.

Recommended rendezvous after skiing must include Bar Falcone at the Hotel Perruquet, the Dragon Bar and Giuseppe at the Da Compagnoni specialises in cocktails. Amongst the night clubs La Chimera is large and trendy, the Yeti has ski videos, whilst Blow Up Disco and Scotch Club are relatively new.

There is also an ice rink and ample opportunities for tobogganing and the Giomein centre offers table tennis and a swimming pool. Several hotels also have pools, the Hermitage and Cristallo; the latter admits non residents. There is a casino at St. Vincent, 27km away, and every Thursday a coach leaves Cervinia for the Casino at 2045 hours. Residents wishing to take advantage can book seats on the coach, which are free of charge, at the Tourist Office.

Recommended Hotels:

Hotel Breuil: A modern and attractive hotel in the village centre. All bedrooms with bath or shower. The light wood panelling is particularly attractive. Lounge entrance hall, main lounge, American bar and lounge and spacious dining room all tastefully furnished and decorated. Garage.

Hotel Hermitage: This delightful chalet-style 4 star hotel is situated on the outskirts of the village. Beautifully furnished throughout. 18 bedrooms all with private facilities, large sitting room, dining room, American bar, conference room, swimming pool, gym, sauna, turiskh bath, solarium and heated garage.

Hotel Europa: 100 yards from the nursery slopes and 8 minutes from the cableway, this is an unusual shaped hotel in a sunny position. Attractive bar and restaurant and comfortable sitting room, super sun terrace. Nicely furnished bedrooms, all with private bath or shower and many with balconies. Swimming pool, jacuzzi, Turkish bath, sauna, solarium and fitness room. Garage.

Hotel Meuble Gorret: This pleasant small two star hotel is in a central position and 200 metres from the nearest lifts. Family run, all rooms with bath and telephone; bar and TV room.

Meuble Meuble Joli: Simple bed and breakfast house run by Pauline Pession, English wife of a ski instructor. Good English breakfast on request (supplement payable). No private facilities but inexpensive, clean and friendly. Centrally situated opposite nursery slopes above ski school.

Hotel Pellissier: Overlooking the nursery slopes, this is a small modern bed and breakfast house, with comfortable accommodation. Attractive wine bar downstairs, tea room, 'Dragon Bar' with English beer and good pub food (Jackie Pellissier is Welsh).

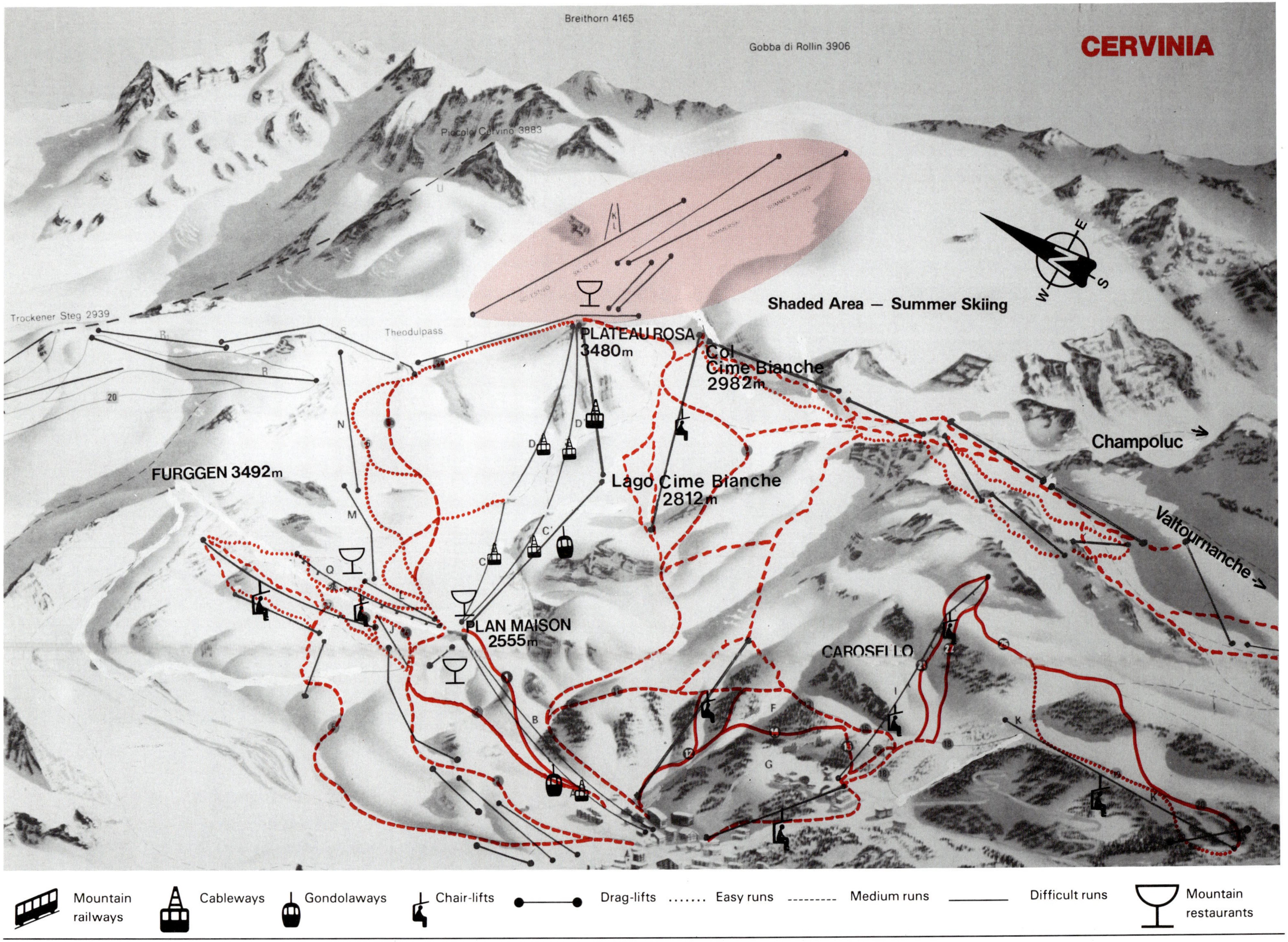
CERVINIA
Breithorn 4165
Gobba di Rollin 3906
Piccolo Cervino 3883
Trockener Steg 2939
Theodulpass
Shaded Area – Summer Skiing
PLATEAU ROSA
3480m
Col
Cime Bianche
2982m
Champoluc
FURGGEN 3492m
Lago Cime Bianche
2812m
Valtournanche
PLAN MAISON
2555m
CAROSELLO
Mountain railways
Cableways
Gondolaways
Chair-lifts
Drag-lifts
Easy runs
Medium runs
Difficult runs
Mountain restaurants

LA THUILE

Height of Resort: 4,757 ft.
Height of Top Station: 8,667 ft.
Nearest International Airport: Geneva
Map Reference: 5C See page 238
Route by Car: See page 236-238
Resort Facilities Chart: See page 220
Hotel Reference charts: See page 231

La Thuile, situated in the Valle d'Aosta, 20 minutes by road from Courmayeur, was once an old mining village which is gradually being restored. Some 500 metres away a well designed complex known as the Planibel has been constructed consisting of a 300 room 4 star hotel, apartment block, 2 swimming pools, indoor football pitch, squash court, gymnasium, sauna, games room, restaurants, shops and disco.

La Thuile is linked with the French resort of La Rosière (see brief report page 31) with a combined total of 33 lifts serving 135km. of prepared pistes. The superior skiing is on the Italian side; the orientation of the runs, east and north facing, ensures good snow conditions over a large area compared to the predominantly south facing shorter runs on La Rosière side. Nevertheless the latter can be more enjoyable when the La Thuile area is very cold, as it can be.

From outside the Planibel complex a 25 person gondolaway and a 4 seater chair-lift rise to Les Suches, 7,218ft.. Here there is a restaurant and some ideal beginner's slopes used by the ski school as well as those at the foot of the gondolaway. Rising from Les Suches over open slopes above the tree line are two chair-lifts and an express chair-lift reaching Chaz Dura, 8,466ft. Runs back to the former station are flattering for the intermediate, whilst those directly to the village through steeply wooded terrain are coded black – these can be avoided, however, by selecting the intermediate runs before reaching Les Suches. These sweep down in wide arcs to each side of the village. On the south-eastern side of Chaz Dura lifts there are 3 further lifts serving easy runs; the third chair-lift travels to the top station, Belvedere, 8,677ft., where one has magnificent views of the Rutor glacier, Mont Blanc and on a clear day the Matterhorn. From Belvedere more challenging north facing runs, red and black, lead down to the Petit St. Bernard road, following the line of the San Bernado chair-lift by which one can return to the top or continue to the village. Running parallel is a further chair-lift travelling up to Chaz Dura with similar runs to base. There are restaurants at the foot of each lift. Good off piste skiing is to be found is this area. There is a snowpark and half-pipe near Gran Testa ski-lift and a baby snowpark next to the baby lift.

La Rosière skiing: See brief report, page 31. This is reached by an easy run from Belvedere down to the Chardonnet chair-lift which rises to Col de Traversette, 7,874ft. where one has fine views of the Isère valley and the layout of La Rosière ski area. The return to La Thuile is a moderately steep run to the foot of Bellecombe drag-lift and from the top of this lift one has a long gentle run back to the village. Alternatively one can connect with Bellecombe 2 drag-lift which travels back again to Belvedere. La Thuile has facilities for nordic skiing with trails ranging from 1 to 10km. Guided Heliskiing tours are also available.

In a Few Words: An unusual resort which has been slow to change its old mining village image to a thriving ski resort. The efficiently run Planibel complex has done much to improve the situation. The lift system is well planned and the orientation of the runs ensures good snow conditions; lack of queues; link with La Rosière is a bonus; runs well posted with numbers as shown on the piste map, not so on the French side. In general good value for money.

Après Ski: Something for most people, cafés and restaurants abound, two very reasonable in price are Lo Creton and La Bricole. The latter is particularly attractive, set in an old oak beamed converted barn; the pasta dishes are highly recommended, and there is also a disco attached. La Bricolette, alongside La Bricole restaurant, is a cosy bar which is very popular in the evenings. Those not staying in the Planibel complex can use the sporting facilities, already mentioned above, for a modest weekly charge. In the complex there is the Fantasia disco and the Rendezvous Pub. On the mountain La Foyer restaurant with sun terrace, situated in the middle of the upper bowl, is a favourite spot for lunch.

Recommended Hotels:

Hotel Planibel: This 4 star hotel with 300 rooms is situated next to the gondolaway some 500 metres from the old village; all bedrooms attractively furnished with bath or shower, wc, telephone, TV, mini bar and balcony; large restaurant, bar with live music, disco and use of all the facilities in the complex. Skiing to the doorstep.

Hotel Edelweiss: A 2 star bed and breakfast hotel with 23 beds, 200 metres from the Planibel complex; basically furnished but all rooms with shower and wc. Breakfast room and bar adjoining. Small ski-lift outside the hotel, ideal for beginners and children.

Hotel Chalet Alpina: Recently re-constructed, this small bed and breakfast hotel chalet is situated 300 metres from lifts. All rooms with shower, wc, breakfast room with bar and lounge area. Good atmosphere mainly created by the owner, Eddie Nico, who speaks English and is efficient and helpful. He is also a ski guide and arranges his own day tours to nearby resorts, such as Courmayeur, Chamonix, Cervinia etc. Good value.

COURMAYEUR

Height of Resort: 4,015 ft.
Height of Top Station: 9,843 ft.
Nearest International Airport: Geneva
Map Reference: 5C See page 238
Route by Car: See pages 236–238
Resort Facilities Charts: See page 219
Hotel Reference Charts: See page 231

Courmayeur lies at the foot of Mont Blanc in the north-west comer of the Aosta valley, within easy reach of Geneva through the Mont Blanc tunnel and served by public buses daily.

The main ski area until spring is the Chécrouit, Cresta d'Arp and Val Veny area. Cresta d'Arp, 9,060ft. is reached by a 4-stage cableway from the village centre (ski lockers available) and from here, generally from March onwards, the testing 12km. off-piste run down to Dolonne begins. Skiers are not allowed to take their skis on the last section of the cableway to Cresta d'Arp unless accompanied by a guide. The uphill journey can be broken at any of the intermediate stations: Plan Chécrouit, 6,000ft., with its good nursery slopes, Lago Chécrouit, 7,330ft., or Cresta Youla, 8,534ft. Leading to the Val Veny area, another cableway rises from the neighbouring village of Entrèves to Mont Chétif, 6,675 ft., from which point there is an amazing close-up view of the immense and beautiful Mont Blanc. On the Courmayeur side there is a choice of medium standard runs from Cresta Youla and Col Chécrouit, these slopes served by 7 drag-lifts and 2 chair-lifts and on the Val Veny side there are 3 chair-lifts and various drag-lifts. Linking both areas is a further chair-lift and 2 drag-lifts. The larger cableway (135 persons) from the village to Plan Chécrouit has made a tremendous difference. Snow making machines now cover 14km. of pistes. There are good langlauf trails in Val Ferret, Entrèves and Dolonne, equipment can be hired in these areas and there are also ski school classes for langlauf. An enormous feat of engineering gives access to the Monte Bianco slopes to the north of Val Veny: a cableway starts near the entrance to the Mont Blanc tunnel swings upward to link Courmayeur with Chamonix, rising to the intermediate stations of Pavillon and Rifugio Torino, to P. Helbronner, 11,254ft. This is the entry point to the glacier and the famous 18 km. Vallée Blanche run to Chamonix (see separate report under Chamonix, page 98). Unfortunately the cableway link with Chamonix skiing only operates in the summer, weather permitting. There are wonderful skiing areas on both the Italian and French sides but these cannot usually be skied until spring and a guide must be taken. Courmayeur is a marvellous ski resort all season for medium to good skiers and for really expert skiers in late season. The 6 day lift pass allows one day's skiing at Pila, Argentière and Chamonix, giving access to the Mont Blanc area.

In a Few Words: This is an attractive village with something for everyone, its charm and tradition centred around the old section. An ideal resort for a family ski holiday. Bed and breakfast arrangements allow one to take advantage of the many inexpensive restaurants. Good medium skiing in Chécrouit/Testa d'Arp area, one disadvantage in that it is not possible to ski back to the village. Not best suited to beginners but some magnificent skiing for the medium to experienced skier with 111 acres controlled by 316 snow guns. Good langlauf facilities.

Après Ski: Will suit all ages, plenty of bars, Bar Roma, Steve's and Ziggy's very popular; tea rooms – note Cafe Della Posta. There are many excellent yet reasonably priced restaurants: particularly good are the Terrazza, Al Camin and the Pierre Alexis. Pizza bars, such as the Bar du Tunnel, are also excellent value. For the young and energetic there are three discothèques to choose from. A number of the hotels also provide their own entertainment. Three hotels have swimming pools, one normally open to the public and there is a pool at Pré St. Didier about 6km. from Courmayeur. One cinema. An Olympic size skating rink which is also open in the evenings. Shopping is good, but as expensive as in the larger Italian towns, except at the market held on Wednesdays where some bargains are to be found. There are 25 mountain restaurants in all, well placed, efficiently run and with excellent local dishes particularly at La Grolla and Maison Vielle. In addition, the popular Maison de Filippo at Entrèves will complete a day's skiing with the most delicious meal.

Recommended Hotels:

Hotel Excelsior Parigi: A 3 star hotel situated two minutes walk from the cableway. Modern and spacious dining room, comfortable lounge and bar, TV room, games room, sauna and solarium. Nicely furnished bedrooms all with bath or shower, TV and telephone, most with balconies.

Hotel Meuble Laurent: A cosy well run bed and breakfast hotel situated 200 metres from the main square. Friendly owners always ready to welcome their guests. Bedrooms simply furnished, some with shower and wc. Comfortable breakfast and TV room. Sun terrace.

Hotel Royal: Another first class hotel in a central position, 155 beds, all rooms with bath. Modern, attractive decor throughout, large lounges and dining room, bars. Efficient and friendly service. Sauna and outdoor swimming pool.

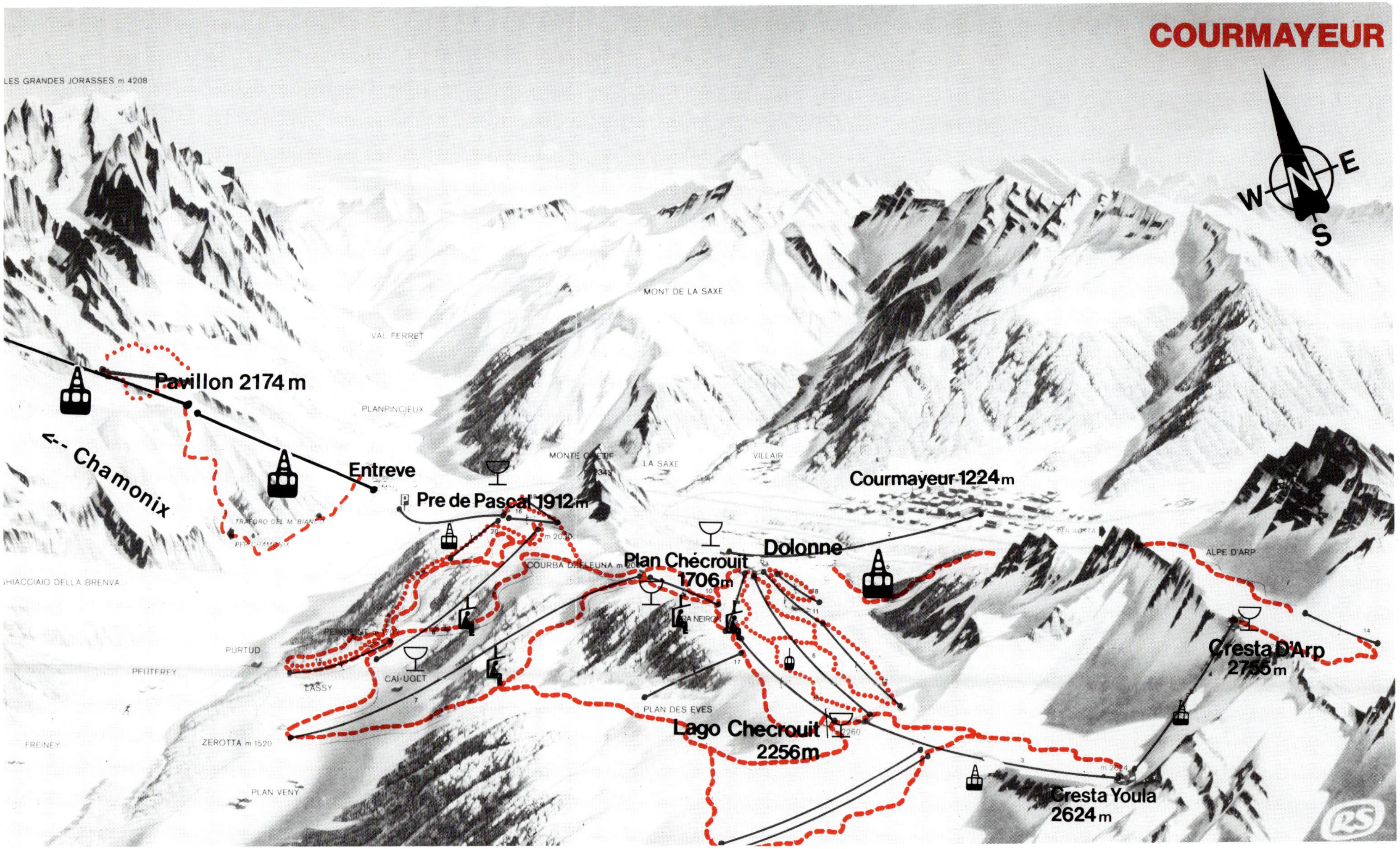

Mountain railways | Cableways | Gondolaways | Chair-lifts | Drag-lifts | ...... Easy runs | --------- Medium runs | ——— Difficult runs | Mountain restaurants

PILA

Height of Resort: 4,500/5,800 ft.
Height of Top Station: 8,660 ft.
Nearest International Airport: Turin
Map Reference: 5C See page 238
Route by Car: See pages 236-238
Resort Facilities Charts: See page 220
Hotel Reference Charts: See page 231

Considerable development has taken place at this resort situated above the historical town of Aosta. Reached by road or six seater gondolaway from the outskirts of Aosta, first to Les Fleurs, 4,500ft., and thence to the heart of the resort. At one time the main accommodation and entertainment had to be found in Aosta, but now with five extensive Residences and seven hotels one has a wide choice of accommodation in Pila itself. The uphill transportation moves 16,300 skiers per hour. Situated near a large town such as Aosta one must expect crowds at weekends.

The ski area is almost an amphitheatre of lifts and runs. On the eastern side, a 4 seater chair-lift rises to Chamolé, 7,573ft., whilst running parallel slightly further south, a 3 seater chair-lift rises to a similar height. Both lifts serve north-west facing intermediate and easy runs through wide wooded glades to their bases. From the southern side there are two main lift systems out of the village. To the left the 4 seater chair-lift rises to Lago Leissé, 7,811ft., whilst to the right an 80-capacity cableway swings south-westwards to Grand Grimod, 7,379ft., with its restaurant and sun terrace. From both top stations there are easy and intermediate north facing runs to the village.

Skiing down from the top of the cableway on the western side one finds another restaurant and a good selection of intermediate runs served by four lifts. A long drag-lift, Couis II, rises to 8,660ft., the highest station in the resort. From this point one has wonderful skiing in an open sunny bowl and one can ski back to base or continue down to the foot of the Grimondet 2 seater chair-lift which rises southwestwards to 7,703ft., and serves fairly open skiing fringed by woods.

In a Few Words: A progressive resort; compact and well planned lift system serving 70km. of prepared pistes; excellent for intermediates but lesser grades well catered for; open skiing combined with wide wooded glades; majority of runs facing north, north-east and north-west, therefore hold the snow well; five mountain restaurants.

Après Ski: For a developing resort a good selection of restaurants, pizzerias, bars and cafés. For dancing there are three discothèques and a piano-bar. A good range of shops; supermarkets; skating rink; saunas, solarium and massage. Easy access to Aosta, parts of which date back over 2,000 years, where there is a wide range of entertainment.

Recommended Hotels.

Hotel Chalet des Alpes: A comfortably furnished hotel, all bedrooms with bath or shower, pleasant sitting room and TV area. Heated indoor garage.

Further Accommodation:

Reservation Centre: Tel: 0165 521148

BARDONECCHIA

Height of Resort: 4,304 ft.
Height of Top Station: 9,022 ft.
Nearest International Airport: Turin
Map Reference: 4E See page 238
Route by Car: See pages 236–238
Resort Facilities Charts: See page 219
Hotel Reference Charts: See page 231

Bardonecchia lies at the end of the Frejus road tunnel which links France with Italy. It is, therefore, very accessible by road via Modane and also by air, Turin being about 2 hours away. The town lies in a wide valley with three ski areas on the western side all interlinking and one on the north-eastern side reached by ski-bus.

Campo Smith Area: A double and single chair-lift rise from the valley station to the sunny middle station, Pian Del Sole, 5,085ft., where there are two restaurants. There are two drag-lifts in this area, which serve easy open runs for the inexperienced, and a chair-lift rising towards Colomion. To the left of the restaurants a long drag-lift reaches Colomion, 6,890ft., where there are a number of options on predominantly red runs, the run on the right of the drag-lift ran be tricky as it is fairly closely wooded. From Colomion, where there is a further restaurant, one can cross over the Les Arnauds area (see below). The nursery slopes are at Campo Smith valley station served by a small drag-lift.

Les Arnauds Area: From the valley station a double chair-lift reaches a small restaurant and a long surmounting drag-lift takes one up to Pra Magnan, 7,152ft. This system provides interlinking runs to the Campo Smith and Melezet areas on either side. From the top there are two variations, to the left a

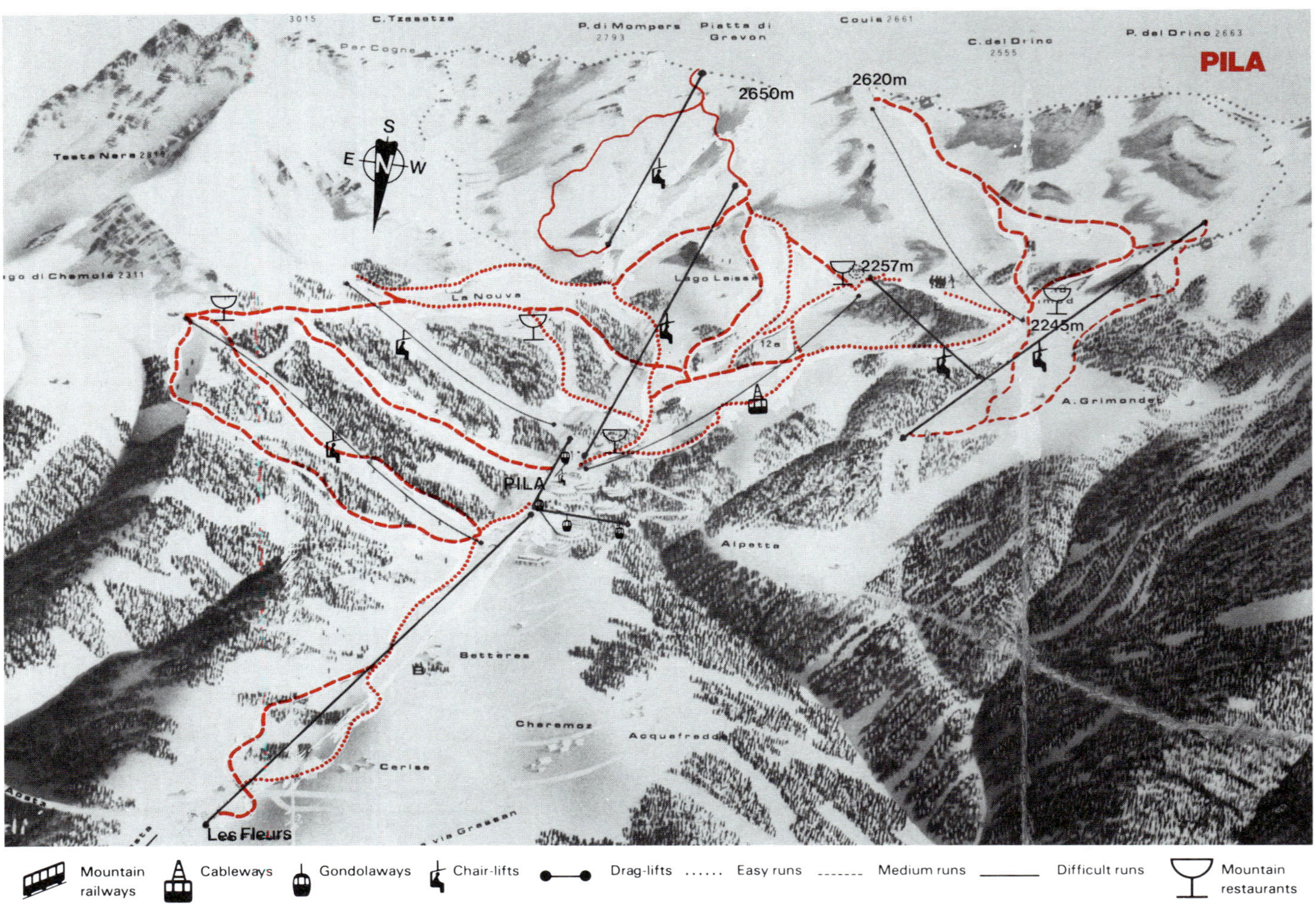

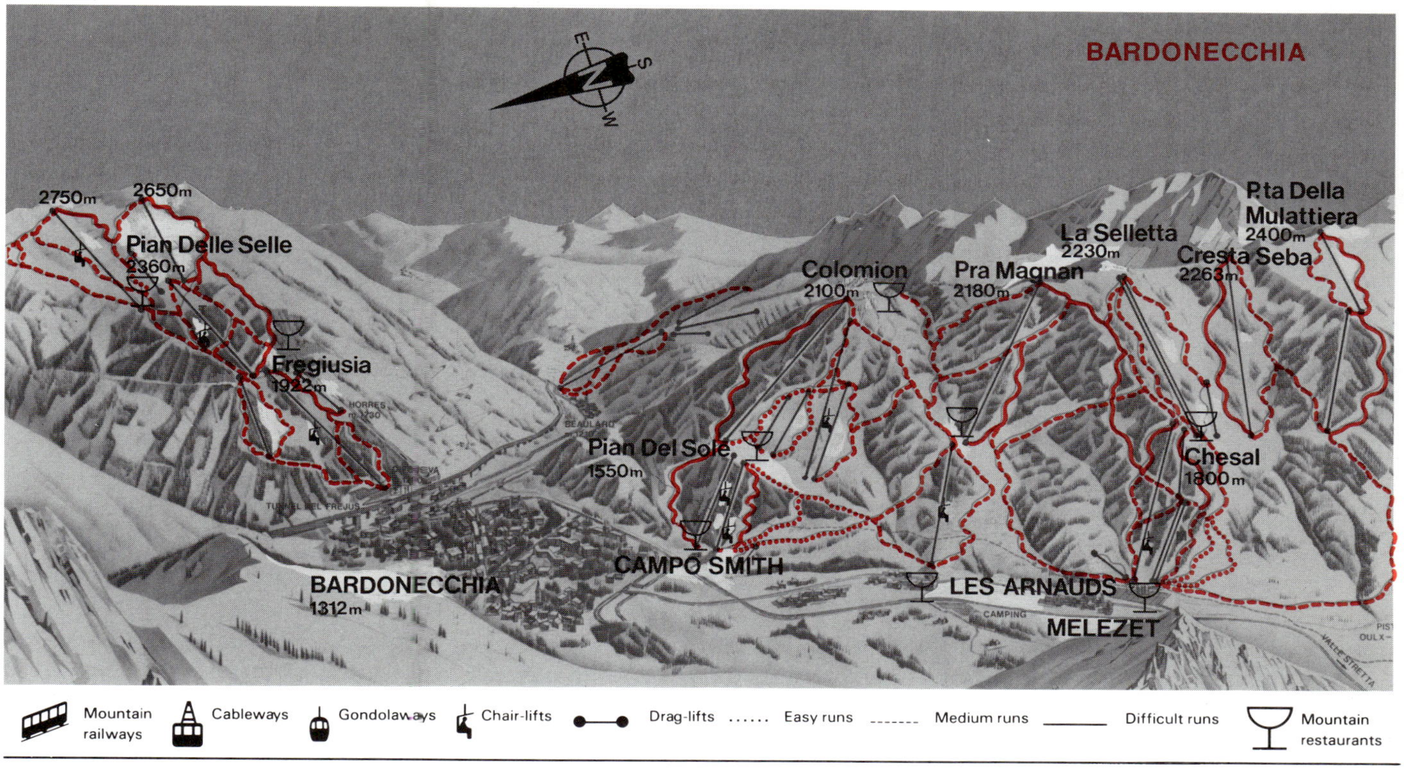

heavily mogulled run whilst to the right a wide fast piste. All runs back to the valley station are intermediate.

Melezet Area: An abundance of skiing in this area, the runs well prepared and better marked, also the lower slopes appear to hold the snow well. At the valley station one finds a nursery area with drag-lift and a double chair-lift rising to Chesal, 5,905ft. Here there is a restaurant and beginner's slopes served by a drag-lift. The system up to Chesal is also supplemented by two parallel drag-lifts surmounted by a single drag-lift. The runs back to base are ideal for beginners. From Chesal two parallel drag lifts climb to La Selletta, 7,316ft., providing delightful intermediate runs back to the middle station. Further to the right of Chesal a long drag-lift and two surmounting drag-lifts reach Cresta Seba, 7,425ft., and Della Mulattiera, 7,874ft., respectively. The runs from both top stations are for intermediates and above.

Jefferau Area: The base station is reached by bus and here a long double chair-lift ascends to Fregiusia, 6,304ft., with its restaurant. Two drag-lifts each side serve the upper part of the slopes. From Fregiusia a further double chair-lift leads one into the Jefferau–Pian Della Selle area where the delightful open slopes never appear to be crowded. This area has a short drag-lift and on the right a longer one rising to 8,694 ft. To the left a new chair-lift, Testa del Ban, reaches the resort's top station, 9,022ft.; both serve intermediate runs whilst the shorter lift to the centre provides access to easy skiing. The runs down to the valley station each side of both chair-lifts, are in the main, intermediate.

In a Few Words: A fairly extensive ski area most suited for intermediate skiers although beginners are well catered for in three nursery areas; well planned lift system moving 22,000 skiers an hour and serving 140km. of prepared pistes, 13 km. covered by snow cannons. Good selection of small mountain restaurants giving a friendly service; efficient ski-bus service included in lift pass; no lift queues during the week but very crowded at weekends and during holiday periods.

Après Ski: Considering the size of the town it lacks amenities. Food and drink are very reasonable and the atmosphere is typically Italian, a selection of bars and cafés and a few good restaurants. Two discos, Popeyes and Charie Brown, the former appeared to be the most popular and livelier of the two. A number of shops selling Italian merchandise but not particularly cheap although there is a very reasonably priced sports shop. There is an indoor tennis court and one cinema.

Recommended Hotels:

Hotel Tabor: This two star hotel situated in the centre, provides comfortable accommodation, all rooms with private shower, wc. Dining room and an à la carte restaurant, sitting room and bar.

Hotel Des Geneys: A three star hotel standing in its own grounds near the centre. A long established family hotel which was recently refurbished. All bedrooms have wall to wall carpeting, private bath, wc, telephone and TV. Breakfast rooms, restaurant, bar, bridge room, TV room and fitness room.

LIMONE

Height of Resort: 3,300 ft.
Height of Top Station: 7,054 ft.
Nearest International Airport: Turin
Map Reference: See main map page 236
Route by Car: See page 236
Resort Facilities Charts: See page 220
Hotel Reference Charts: See page 231

Dating from Roman times, the town of Limone is a happy mixture of ancient and modern, where the traditional sights of an old Italian town, blend happily with modern shopping facilities. Easily reached from Turin, Genoa, Nice and Milan, and only 60km. from the Mediterranean Coast, the town has been a favourite centre for walkers for many years, with superb views down to the Piemonte Plain. The skiing area, known as the 'Riserva Bianca' is north and north-west facing and is formed by the linking of the three valleys of Limone, Colle de Tenda and Limonetto. This creates one expanse of runs giving 80 kilometres of pistes, served by 25 lifts, of which 5 are chair-lifts. There is an excellent selection of mountain restaurants which, as well as those in the town, serve many traditional Piedmontese dishes. These combining with the sunny temperament of the inhabitants must make Limone one of the friendliest Alpine resorts. The 'Ski School di Riserva Bianca' has an office at all three villages. 'Riserva Bianca' is divided into four areas all interlinked with the exception of Val di Cros mentioned below.

Val di Cros Area: On the south-east edge of the town a chair-lift rises to restaurant Capanna Chiara, 5,690ft., a surmounting drag-lift continues south-eastwards and thence swings south to 7,100ft. Above and to the left of the restaurant one finds two further drag-lifts serving west and north-west facing slopes. All lifts provide a variety of runs on the upper slopes and down to base for intermediate skiers. It should be mentioned that the restaurant Capanna Chiara serves excellent food under the direction of the genial Luciano. The nursery slopes are located to the right at the foot of the chair-lift, these are extensive and have their own lifts.

Sole Area: On the south-western side of Limone a further chair-lift swings in the same direction to Sole, 4,900ft. where there is another good restaurant (try the cannelloni). The 'Olympica' run used during the Italian Championships and the Ladies World Cup Championships follows the line of this lift back to the village. This lift is the Gateway to the 'Riserva Bianca' proper and the first of a series by which one can traverse across the 3 valleys to the French frontier. From the restaurant at Sole, three surmounting draglifts take one up to Alpetta, 6,850ft. On the way up one passes a long drag-lift, Belvedere, to the right and a 4 seater chair-lift on the left, which together serve a good variety of runs in the area and back to Limone. To continue the traverse, from Alpetta one skis down westward to the foot of the Pian del Leone drag-lift which rises southward to the Capanna Nicolin restaurant, where excellent food can be obtained. A surmounting drag-lift rises from the restaurant to the highest point, 7,054ft., where one has magnificent views of the Piemonte Valley amid the Monte Viso. From this point descend via a short but interesting ridge route to Cima Cabanaira, 6,560ft., where another fine restaurant, 'Baita 2000', is situated.

Colle di Tenda: The link lift for this valley is the long Cabanaira chair-lift which rises westward from the Colle di Tenda complex to the 'Baita 2000' restaurant. One can descend to Colle di Tenda by a fairly testing run which more or less follows the line of the lift or by an easier route. At the base, 4,600ft., one finds a modern complex consisting of the hotel 3 Amis, with swimming pool, shops and restaurants. Three small drag-lifts serve the immediate slopes in the area but the link lift with the next valley is the Colle di Tenda which rises to 6,010ft. From this point one skis into the third valley and down to Limonetto.

Limonetto: From the outskirts of this small village a chair-lift rises to the Testa de Runc restaurant and to the south, four drag-lifts serve the open slopes in this area. The top lift, Del Colle, reaches the ridge on the French frontier at 6,230ft. where one has wonderful views of the mountains and wooded slopes of Les Alpes Maritimes. Having enjoyed a good lunch at the excellent restaurant Porta della Neve just above Limonetto, the reverse traverse can be made to Limone. If you have eaten too much or cannot gather enough strength for the return journey on skis, do not worry, there is a bus service from Limonetto or Colle di Tenda to Limone.

In a Few Words: A small town full of character and friendly people; excellent ski area, pistes well maintained by 17 snowcats; a manager for each area in touch with each other by VHF Radio; suitable for beginners to advanced intermediates; north and northwest facing slopes ensures reliable snow.

Après Ski: This is fairly active with 4 major discothèques, of these the Lanterna and 'Boccaccio' are particularly comfortable and well appointed. Several of the hotels also have their own discos or tavernas. There is an abundant choice of good cafés, bars and restaurants, also a swimming pool in the 3 Amis hotel, one cinema and an ice rink.

Recommended Hotels:

Principe Grand Hotel: 42 bedrooms all with bath or shower, wc., telephone and TV. Opposite the Sole chairlift. It was here that King Umberto II used to stay. A very well appointed first class hotel with comfortable lounge, most attractive dining room, TV. room and a Disco. The hotel is most ably run by Livio Bottero.

Hotel Tripoli: This modern hotel situated midway between the Sole chairlift and the town (4 minutes from each) run by the Donolato family, very well appointed and has a comfortable lounge and bar and pleasant restaurant. There is a small Taverna downstairs with disco music. All the bedrooms have a bath or shower and wc. and are very well furnished.

Hotel Touring: Situated by the main street in the village, this hotel, run by the friendly Victor Chiesa and his family, has a comfortable lounge and dining room. There are 34 bedrooms of which 25 have private bath or shower with wc.

Hotel 3 Amis: This modern large hotel is situated in the Colle di Tenda and is therefore centrally placed for access to the whole ski area. Besides the usual appointment of lounges, bars and dining room, this hotel has a large indoor swimming pool. There are 70 bedrooms all with private bath or shower and wc.

SANSICARIO

Height of Resort: 5,576 ft.
Height of Top Station: 8,826 ft.
Nearest International Airport: Turin
Map Reference: 4E See page 238
Route by Car: See pages 236-238
Resort Facilities Charts: See page 221

Situated high in the Susa valley, only 12km. from Oulx, on the Paris-Rome main line, little more from Bardonecchia, exit for cars via the tunnel from Modane and 2½ hours from Turin airport, Sansicario is therefore very accessible. As a winter sports resort it is strategically placed, insofar that it does not have a vast area of skiing in its own right, but this is unimportant as it has direct access to the facilities of the linked resorts on each side. From near the hotels, uphill transportation moving east will take skiers to Fraiteve, the entry point to the well-organised lift system of Sestriere (see separate report); or from Sansicario ski south-westward and one reaches the lower station of the Rafuyel chair-lift, the link lift for the skiing in the strangely beautiful 'Mountains of the Moon', thence to Clavière and on to Montgenèvre the operation can be carried out in reverse. The combined lifts of the resorts involved number some 65, and the total kilometres covered depends on the route taken, but with careful planning and timing there is sufficient skiing to stimulate the most ardent skier.

Sansicario's skiing: Strictly speaking, the Sansicario skiing stretches from Mount Fraiteve's summit, 8,826ft., down to just south-east of Cesana Torinese, 4,461ft. The slopes are mainly west-facing, and are served by strategically placed lifts, 3 chair-lifts and 8 drag-lifts, where there is little waiting except at weekends, when it is packed. The runs are well laid out. From the summit there are two intermediate runs spreading out lower down to 18 major pistes. The top section is open, but lower down wooded, some of it fairly closely. One can stop at the intermediate stations and travel back to the top, or travel directly down to Sansicario, or onwards still further to the valley below. Wherever one is in this area, the cleverly placed lifts allow one to arrive back on skis in the centre of the village.

In a Few Words: An excellent resort for the real enthusiast, intermediate to advanced, who wants to ski all day and go to bed early, as there is little else to do! At present not an ideal resort for the beginner or even the second-year skier. Neither is it highly satisfactory for young children. Very crowded at weekends.

Après Ski: This is a small, fairly basic resort, very Italian in atmosphere, where amenities at present do not live up to its extensive skiing possibilities. Food and drink are reasonably cheap. There is a disco in the Hotel Sansicario complex, a recreation centre with swimming pool, Turkish bath and sauna. The old village of Sansicario, which is about 10 minutes' walk down the mountain has an attractive bar/restaurant with good food and atmosphere.

Recommended Hotels:

Hotel Sansicario: At present the only second class hotel in the resort. Built in a complex consisting of the hotel itself in two sections, plus a large self-service cafeteria, restaurant and adjoining bar. Bedrooms for individual guests brightly decorated, all with bath; for groups intercommunicating rooms, one with bath and the other with shower. Sitting area, lounge/bar, breakfast room. There is a supplementary charge for guests wishing to eat in the hotel restaurant.

SAUZE D'OULX

Height of Resort: 4,950 ft.
Height of Top Station: 8,145 ft.
Nearest International Airport: Turin
Map Reference: 4E See page 238
Route by Car: See pages 236-238
Resort Facilities Charts: See page 221
Hotel Reference Charts: See page 231

The village of Sauze d'Oulx is very easily accessible by rail, road or air - 80km. from Turin. It is divided into an interesting old section and a much less attractive modern part. The atmosphere is always one of informal gaiety and it is a particularly favourite resort with British skiers.

The landscape is very beautiful, many of the ski runs leading through woods of larch trees. The network of lifts is compact and well planned. Some distance from the village centre, a chair-lift rises to Sportinia, 7,052ft., and here there is a small group of hotels and restaurants. Various easy, wooded runs lead back to the village. From Pian Della Rocca a 4 seater chair-lift rises to Triplex, 8,145ft., where there is excellent off-piste powder skiing and adjacent to this is a chair-lift, rising southwards to Rocce Nere, 7,980ft. Upon reaching the top one can ski down the other side into the bowl where the Rio Nero drag-lift and the 4 seater Nouvo Basset chair-lift are located. Both give access to good, open skiing in this area. To the west of the Rio Nero lift is the Col Basset drag-lift which is the link lift with the neighbouring resort of Sestriere and the other linked resorts of Sansicario, Clavière and Montgenèvre (see separate reports). To the north-west is the Rio Nero lift which is the direct link with Sansicario, Clavière and Montgenèvre. There is a choice of runs to the village via Sportinia or to the foot of either the Bourget or Clotes/Lago Nero draglifts; the latter can also be reached via a chair-lift from the village, or to Jouvenceaux, below Sauze d'Oulx. The very top of these runs is open but the slopes become widely wooded for two-thirds of the way down.

To the left of the village the twin Gran Comba 3 seater chair-lift rises to 6,175ft., the Chardonet twin drag-lifta continuing from here to a height of 7,280ft., giving access to fairly open runs to the village, or across to the small Costa-piana ski lift, taking one to a further height of 7,572 ft. From here one can ski down to the foot of the Tausieres drag-lift, rising to 7,962ft. and have the choice of three runs, either right down to the village; to the terminal of the Moncrons drag-lift; or to Pian della Rocca chair-lift, then on to Sportinia via Primo Sole/Le Bourget/Lago Pilone. The lift system is compact and well interlinked and provides a good variety of skiing of medium standard with runs up to 8km. in length. The nursery slopes are served by the Clotes chair-lift, starting just above one of the ski school offices. The lift pass covers Sestriere, Sansicario and Clavière with the possibility of purchasing a daily extension for Montgenèvre (France).

Moncrons: The trip from Sauze d'Oulx to Montgenèvre and back is a full day's hard skiing for the good intermediate skier. Many of the lifts are being improved and a new link is planned from Moncrons to Pragelato.

In a Few Words: Skiing suitable for medium to good standard; compact system; well maintained pistes; its link with the 'Milky Way' makes Sauze d'Oulx an attractive proposition for the really good skier; informal and lively and good for parties and young people; piste marking should be improved; lift passes reasonable with children under 8 skiing free; medium prices, good value.

Après Ski: For its size Sauze d'Oulx has a fairly active night life and the atmosphere is one of gaiety. There are several discos, the most popular being the Cotton Club and Andy Capp. For drinks and eating out there is a good selection; the Hotel Derby has a large attractive bar with a huge open fire at one end. Moncro cocktail bar with music and popular with the young, is adjacent to the Derby. La Griglia, provides the best pizzas and spaghetti. Don Vicenzo's and L' Canton are reputed to be the best restaurants but very expensive. Other good restaurants include La Grangia, Villa Daniela, Del Falco, Del Borgo, El Fujot, Old Inn and Le Pecore Nere. Lampione's, in the old village serves good draft beer, as does the Scotch bar. Andy Capp bar and also the Schuss are very popular. The ski area is served by excellent mountain restaurants – to mention five, Capanna Kind in Sportinia, Ciao Pais in Clotes, Bar Clotes, Ristorante Belvedere (Genevris) and Bar Chamonier in the Bowl near the Nuovo Basset chair-lift..

Recommended Hotels:

Hotel Derby: A small modern hotel in central position with plenty of atmosphere, a pleasant dining room. Its large attractive rustic lounge bar with open fire is a popular meeting place; the bedrooms are tastefully furnished and comfortable. Delfo Baccon and his wife run a very good hotel and the service is personal and friendly.

Hotel Holiday Debili: An attractive modern hotel in the village centre, possibly the best in Sauze d'Oulx. Bedrooms nicely furnished, all with bath or shower and most with balcony, telephone and radio, spacious and comfortable reception rooms furnished in traditional Italian style. Real Italian food and plenty of it. Owned and efficiently run by English speaking Debili family.

Hotel Monte Genevris: The original inn of the village enlarged and modernised, providing simple accommodation, bright dining room and lively café bar. A friendly run family hotel with helpful staff, particularly suitable for young people.

Hotel Savoia Debili: A large old established hotel in the centre of the village. Bright and comfortable bedrooms, large reading and television rooms and pleasant bar in the lounge hall.

CLAVIÈRE

Height of Resort: 5,774 ft.
Height of Top Station: 6,676 ft.
Nearest International Airport: Turin
Map Reference: 4E See page 238
Route by Car: See page 236-238
Resort Facilities Chart: See page 229

A small village situated in the Susa Valley on the French border with 9 hotels and pensions accommodating some 600 guests and a further 400 in apartments. The shopping facilities, including a supermarket, are good and prices reasonable. Clavière is a quiet resort set amidst woodland scenery and a very good atmosphere prevails.

Although Clavière's own ski area is limited to 50 km. of prepared pistes served by 4 chair and 8 drag-lifts, it forms part of the huge Milky Way embracing 400 km. of marked runs served by 100 lifts. Clavière's main slopes face north with runs through fairly wooded terrain and therefore under normal conditions hold the snow well. The immediate neighbouring resorts of Montgenèvre (see separate report) to the west and Cesana to the east link well with Clavière lift-wise, with easy and intermediate runs back to the resort.

The nursery slopes on the outskirts of the village are served by a drag-lift and a chair-lift.

In a Few Words: A pleasant small village with a good atmosphere; reasonable prices; suitable for all grades of skiers with the direct entry to the Milky Way's 400 km. of marked runs served by 100 lifts. Free lift pass for children under 8 years when accompanied by an adult.

Après Ski: Not for the active après skier, but there are a fair number of restaurants, bars and crêperies, natural ice skating rink and 15 km Nordic ski trail. For those requiring a great variety, Montgenèvre is only one km. away.

Recommended Hotels:

Hotel Passero Pellegrino: This 3 star hotel is situated in the centre of the village, 100 metres from the ski school and some 200 metres from the lifts. Pleasant dining room, comfortable lounge with TV area, bar and coffee shop. All bedrooms with shower, wc and telephone. The hotel also has a separate chalet-style apartment building with its own open plan lounge connected to the hotel by the restaurant.

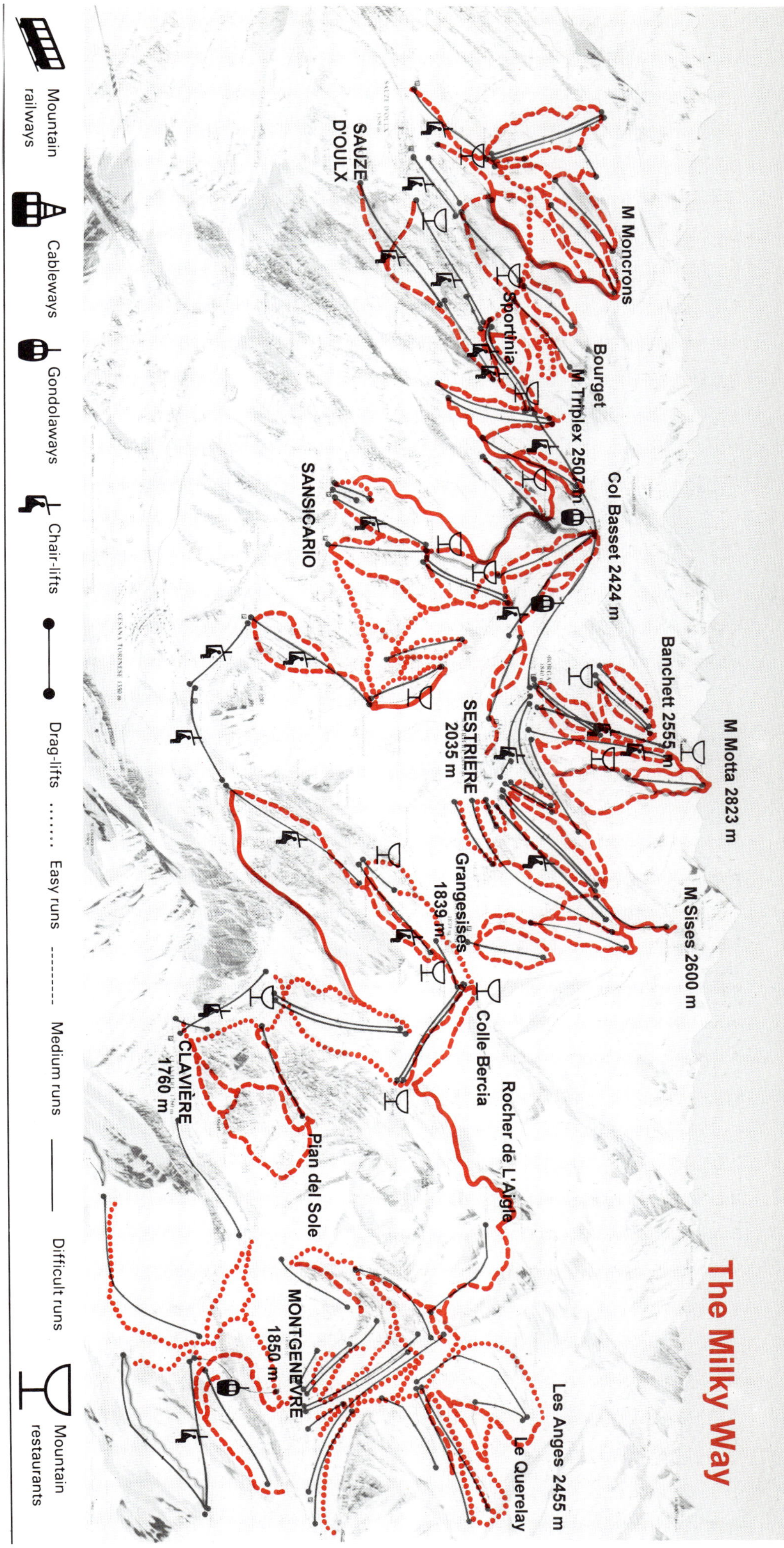

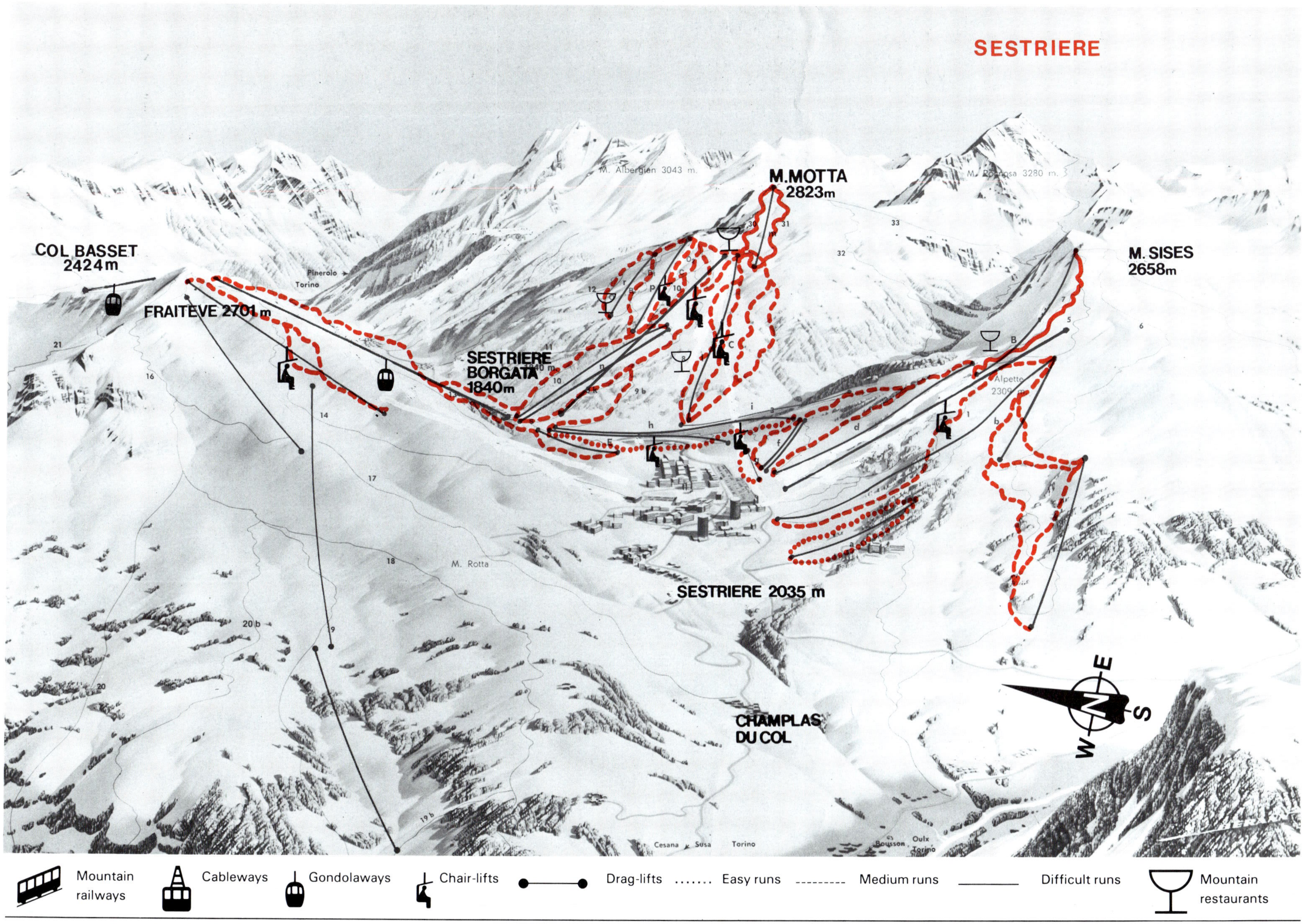
SESTRIERE
M. Albergian 3043 m.
M. Rognosa 3280 m.
M.MOTTA 2823m
M. SISES 2658m
COL BASSET 2424m
FRAITEVE 2701 m
Pinerolo
Torino
SESTRIERE BORGATA 1840m
Alpette 2300 m
M. Rotta
SESTRIERE 2035 m
CHAMPLAS DU COL
Cesana
Susa
Torino
Bousson
Oulx
Torino
N
S
E
W
Mountain railways
Cableways
Gondolaways
Chair-lifts
Drag-lifts
...... Easy runs
--------- Medium runs
Difficult runs
Mountain restaurants

SESTRIERE

Height of Resort: 6,666 ft.
Height of Top Station: 9,175 ft.
Nearest International Airport: Turin
Map Reference: 4E See page 238
Route by Car: See pages 236-238
Resort Facilities Charts: See page 221
Hotel Reference Charts: See page 232

Sestriere is part of an interconnected skiing area known as La Via Lattea - The Milky Way - and the lift pass covers over 350km of pistes. It has one of the best high mountain lift systems in the Alps, and provides excellent skiing for the widest possible range of skier, from complete novices to the advanced. It is 2 hours from Turin airport and is situated 22 km from the Frejus motorway and the Rome-Paris railway line at Oulx. It is a modern ski resort but with a long tradition, which hosts World Cup skiing. It is set amidst impressive mountain scenery. The skiing is conveniently to hand, with a large area of nursery slopes next to the resort, and all main ski runs finish there also. The main skiing areas are:

Monte Sises/Alpette Areas: Two drag-lifts leave from the south-east side of the resort which end just above Alpette, 7,504 ft., where a surmounting drag-lift rises to Monte Sises, 8,638 ft., serving a difficult run to base. From the resort there is also a 4 seater chair-lift, Cit Roc, which terminates short of Monte Sises. From these top stations one has a choice of intermediate runs back to Sestriere or Grangesises of about 5 km. At the latter station there is a residence of the same name providing self catering accommodation and also a restaurant. The lifts from here connect one with the main system. Alternatively from Monte Sises or Alpette one can ski over to Sestriere Borgata 2 km north-east of Sestriere which is the base station for Banchetta/Mont Motta and Col Basset/Mont Fraiteve ski areas.

Banchetta/Mont Motta Areas: Well served by lifts the main two being 4 seater chair-lifts, Nuova Nube and Chisonneto Banchetta. A surmounting drag-lift takes one up to Monte Motta, 9,175 ft , the resorts highest station. The runs down each side of the drag-lift are demanding but those on the lower slopes are delightful, both on and off-piste, through wooded terrain. Two chair-lifts connect Borgata with Sestriere.

Col Basset/Monte Fraiteve Areas: From Sestriere Borgata a fast gondolaway rises to Col Basset, 7,952ft., which is the link point with the Sauze D'Oulx ski area (see separate report). From the top one can ski back to Borgata on an enjoyable intermediate piste or take the long winding easy run of about 8 km which ends on the approach road to Sestriere. Monte Fraiteve, 8,778 ft., is reached from Col Basset by drag-lift and this is the link point for Sansicario, Clavière and Montgenèvre (see separate reports). Once on the Sansicario side of the mountain it is possible to ski down to Cesana and transfer by chair-lifts to the other side of the valley and thence to Clavière.

Apart from its connection with the Milky Way and other neighbouring resorts, Sestriere appears to be leading the way with artificial snow installations. Some 700,000 square metres can be given snow cover which means that virtually all the resort runs can be protected against bad snow seasons.

In a Few Words: A purpose-built ski resort with all its advantages: lift system well planned, with little queueing; open and sunny with good snow from early to late season; well maintained pistes; direct links with 4 neighbouring resorts and the Milky Way. Good value for money for a high resort and highly recommended for all grades of skiers. Extensive snow making installations. Some of the red runs do not seem to justify their grading; they are easier than one might expect, but no less fun for that. If there is any criticism it is that some of the lifts and pistes are not clearly marked, with name boards missing or illegible, and some of the mountain restaurants were disappointing. Free lift pass for children under 8 years if accompanied by an adult.

Après Ski: A wide choice, varying from inexpensive pizzerias to more expensive well appointed restaurants. The best pizzas were to be found at 'Pinkies' where a champion pizza maker threw the pastry around with great skill - an entertainment in itself. A good selection of shops. A favourite of the younger set is Bar Sestriere discothèque. The Tabata disco is the most popular whilst the Black Sun discothèque is large, seating 200. Club Colombière has an open air heated swimming pool, with sauna and gymnasium and there is a further pool at Borgata Sestriere. The Sports Palace has tennis and basket ball courts, a fitness centre, skating rink, a driving on ice school, cinema and tourist flights.

Recommended Hotels:

Hotel Cristallo: A large modern hotel opposite the main cableway terminal, comfortable bedrooms, most with private bath, a large long bright dining room, two spacious sitting rooms and two bars. Dancing in the Cristallino sometimes with band, otherwise discothèque. Good service.

Hotel Miramonti: A medium-sized hotel at the entrance to the village. Accommodation for 60 guests in attractively decorated bedrooms, pleasant dining room and lively bar much patronised by the locals.

Hotel Olympic: A medium-sized hotel in quiet position, all bedrooms with private bath and balcony. A well-designed sitting room with bar and sitting room leading off. Under the personal management of the owner Eric Guiot.

BRIEF REPORTS ON FURTHER ITALIAN RESORTS

ABETONE, 6,105ft.: A long-established resort, situated on the southern side of the Tuscan-Emilian Alps, between Florence and Lucca. A largish village with a good variety of restaurants and bars, discothèques and cinemas. 25 hotels, height of top station 7,085 ft.; 4 cableways, 6 chair-lifts, 9 drag-lifts. Suitable for beginners to intermediates.

ANTERMOIA, 4,920ft.: A small sunny resort in the province of Bolzano, only two hotels and three pensions. Several cosy bars and two good discos. Three surmounting drag-lifts, to station 7,216ft. Good intermediate runs up to 6km. in length and plenty of opportunity for off-piste skiing. Suitable for beginners to intermediates. A very friendly village atmosphere.

GRESSONEY, 4,455ft.: The Gressoney valley is approached from Ponte St. Martin, the exit from the Aosta motorway. There are three separate ski areas linked by bus, Gressoney St. Jean, the largest of the three, 8km. further on Gressoney La Trinité and at the head of the valley, another 3km. away, is Staval, standing at the foot of the Monte Rosa. The combined ski areas provide a good variety of skiing with reliable snow conditions. Night life on the quiet side. Height of top station (Staval) 8,946ft.; combined lift: 2 gondolaways, 4 chair-lifts, 10 drag-lifts; suitable for beginners to advanced intermediates.

LURISIA TERME, 2,624ft.: This resort is a famous spa situated in a wooded valley 104 km. due south of Turin and 128km. from Genoa. Little skiing in village but good compact area reached by gondolaway or bucket lift terminating at the Gran Baita restaurant, here mostly open skiing served by 6 lifts. When snow allows the run back to the village is about 7km. 15 hotels and pensions, shops, restaurants, bars and discos. The resorts of Frabosa, Prato Nevoso and Artesina are all within 20km. Suitable for beginners to intermediates.

MALGA CIAPELA (Marmolada), 4,743 ft.: Malga Ciapela as yet is hardly a resort, it is a cluster of six hotels with further accommodation in nearby villages. Marmolada is the mountain towering above; its summit is 11,022ft., the highest in the area. The top section is glacier so here there is summer skiing as well. If you have not skied the Marmolada then you have something to look forward to, wonderful wide open skiing above the tree line and mainly on north facing slopes, and the intermediate will enjoy the run from the top station to the village of some 12km. From the village and on the left facing the mountain a three stage cableway rises first to Antermoia (no skiing back from this point), thence to Serauta where there is a large self-service restaurant and finally to the top station which terminates below the summit at 10,712 ft. From here intermediate and good skiers will take the run which follows the line of the cableway as far as the second station, Serauta and then swings north-westwards down Passo Fedaia where one can return to Serauta by a chair-lift and surmounting drag-lift. From Passo Fedaia, continuing on an easy run towards the village following the line of the Tabià Palazza chair-lift, one comes to the Capanna Bill restaurant which is a good place to meet your less experienced friends for lunch, as this point can be reached from Malga Ciapela by surmounting drag-lifts which serve easy slopes.

From Capanna Bill a chair-lift rises westwards to Passo Padon, 8,218ft. and it is here there are link lifts with Arabba. This links the Marmolada area with the rest of the Dolomite circuit. On the Marmolada side the runs back from Passo Padon to Capanna Bill are intermediate with one section fairly difficult; from here, as pointed out before, there are easy runs back to the village. At present essentially a skier's resort; excellent open high mountain skiing; a good interlinking lift system of its own and with the whole of the Dolomiti area. 15 km. cross-country circuit.

NEVEGAL, 3,382ft.: Situated 12km. south-east of the provincial capital of Belluno. A long village with 20 hotels and pensions. Not a high resort but mainly northerly orientated runs served by 2 chair-lifts and 12 drag-lifts. Height of top station 5,471ft. Night life on the quiet side, a selection of bars and restaurants and two popular discos. Belluno nearby whilst Cortina and Venice are not far away. Suitable for beginners to intermediates.

SOLDA, 6,068ft.: Situated in the Ortles-Cevedale range, 19 miles from the Stelvio Pass, this very pleasant high Alpine village has a good snow record. 38 hotels and pensions; height at top station 8,2O0ft.; one cableway, 2 chair-lifts, 11 drag-lifts; suitable for beginners to advanced intermediates; a very good touring area.

TARVISIO, 2,460ft.: This thriving town is situated in the north-east corner of Italy close to the Slovenian and Austrian borders. The town is old and full of interest with 40 hotels and pensions. The skiing is in two areas and covers Tarvisio and Valbruna, 6km. away, served by one cableway, 4 chair-lifts and 7 drag-lifts. Height of top station 5,872ft. Nordic skiing is well catered for with over l00km. of marked trails. Night life is active with a good selection of bars and restaurants and a number of lively discos. Suitable for beginners to intermediates and Nordic skiers. Guest card from certain hotels allows skiing in three Austrian resorts and two in Slovenia. Also the use of ski bus, free entrances in Casinò Kranjska Gora (Slovenia) and Velden (Austria), and discounts for ski rental, skating, disco entrance, Sports Centre in Sella Nevea and various shops.

TERMINILLO, 6,920ft.: Rome's nearest ski resort, about 1 hour from the capital, so ideal for visiting this city. A selection of restaurants and bars, night clubs and a swimming pool. 16 hotels; height of top station 7,259ft., 1 cableway, 1 chair-lift, 13 drag-lifts. Suitable for beginners to advanced intermediates.

SWITZERLAND

ADELBODEN

Height of Resort: 4,436 ft.
Height of Top Station: 7,644 ft.
Nearest International Airport: Zurich/Berne/Geneva
Map Reference: 3D See page 240
Route by Car: See pages 236-240
Resort Facilities Charts: See page 221
Hotel Reference Charts: See page 232

A medium-sized, pretty village reached after a climb up 16km. of winding road from Frutigen. There is one main street with shops and hotels to either side and the village has a delightful Alpine atmosphere, with a background of glorious scenery. There is accommodation in hotels and pensions for around 1,400 and a further 7,000 beds provided by chalets and apartments. In addition to its own four separate ski areas Adelboden is linked to its neighbour Lenk in the next valley, giving considerably increased scope.

Silleren-Geils-Hahnenmoos Area: Silleren is the most recently developed area and is reached by gondolaway leaving from the centre of Adelboden, rising to Sillerenbühl and from the restaurant, where a three-piece band plays at lunchtime, one has beautiful views of the surrounding terrain. A drag-lift coming up from the Aebi restaurant converges on this top station which combines with the nearby Sta[illegible]l drag-lift, serving several red and one black north-west facing runs.

From Sillerenbühl one can ski to Geils, which lies in a wide sunny bowl, where there is a further restaurant. Here there is a choice of two chair-lifts and one gondolaway, all serving runs over wide open slopes. One of the chair-lifts rises in a southerly direction to Luegli, 6,822ft., from which point there are two runs, one black and one blue, of about 2km. on north facing slopes back to Geils; the post bus returning from here to Bergläger. A gondolaway, travelling in a north-westerly direction from Geils, leads to Hahnenmoos, 6,404ft., and there is an easy run of 2km. from here down to Geils. The longer chair-lift from Geils travels to Laveygrat, 7,216ft., giving the choice of a difficult and a medium run to Geils, both about 2km. in length on north-east facing slopes. There is also a very interesting 5km. medium run to Gilbach, through wooded slopes towards the end.

The Lenk area can be reached by skiing down the far side from Hahnenmoos. There is a restaurant at the top of the cableway. A series of lifts in the Lenk area lead back to its top station of Metschstand, 6,882ft., and from here it is possible to ski down a 3km. run to Geils or a 5km. run to Bergläger.

Tschentenalp Area: This lies to the north west side of the village and Tschentenegg itself, 6,357ft., is reached via the Schwandfeldspitz gondolaway. At the top there is a very agreeable restaurant and a variety of runs descending north and north-west facing slopes. The Möser chair-lift and Tschentenalp drag-lift return one to the top station, the runs – medium and difficult either side of the drag-lift and to the base of the drag-lift – are most enjoyable, as well as the medium run to the foot of the chair-lift. The run back to Adelboden is about $2^1/_2$km., with a difference in height of nearly 2,000 ft.

Boden Area: A drag-lift from the west side of Boden rises to Kuonisbergli restaurant, 5,690 ft. From this point a drag-lift rises to Höchsthorn, 6,242ft. This provides a very pleasing, medium to difficult run on the left side of the lift down to Boden on north-east facing slopes of approximately 3km. in length. To the right a run links up with the four medium grade runs from Kuonisbergli down to Boden, which are approximately 2.5km. in length. These are over north and north-east facing slopes. Further to the north a drag-lift leads up to Fleckli, 6,188ft., which gives access to medium and difficult runs to the base and to the village on east and south-east facing slopes of some 3km. in length, with vertical descent of 1,722ft. An excellent bus system serves the whole area.

Engstligenalp Area: The cableway from Birg (south of Adelboden) rises to Engstligenalp, 6,442ft., where there are pensions and restaurants. There are no runs back to the village from here and the return journey made by cableway. Two surmounting drag-lifts rise to Tschingelochtighorn, 7,644ft., and one medium/difficult and one medium run of about, $2^1/_2$km., vertical descent 1,246ft., over north-west, facing slopes, lead back to the restaurant. There is a trainer lift nearby. From this point the ski touring areas can be reached, providing long and short tours in the Wildstrubel region and long tours to Kandersteg and Crans/Montana. Good nordic ski trails in this area as well as in Boden.

Children: The hotels Beau-site, Adler, Crystal and Steinmattli all have good facilities for small children.

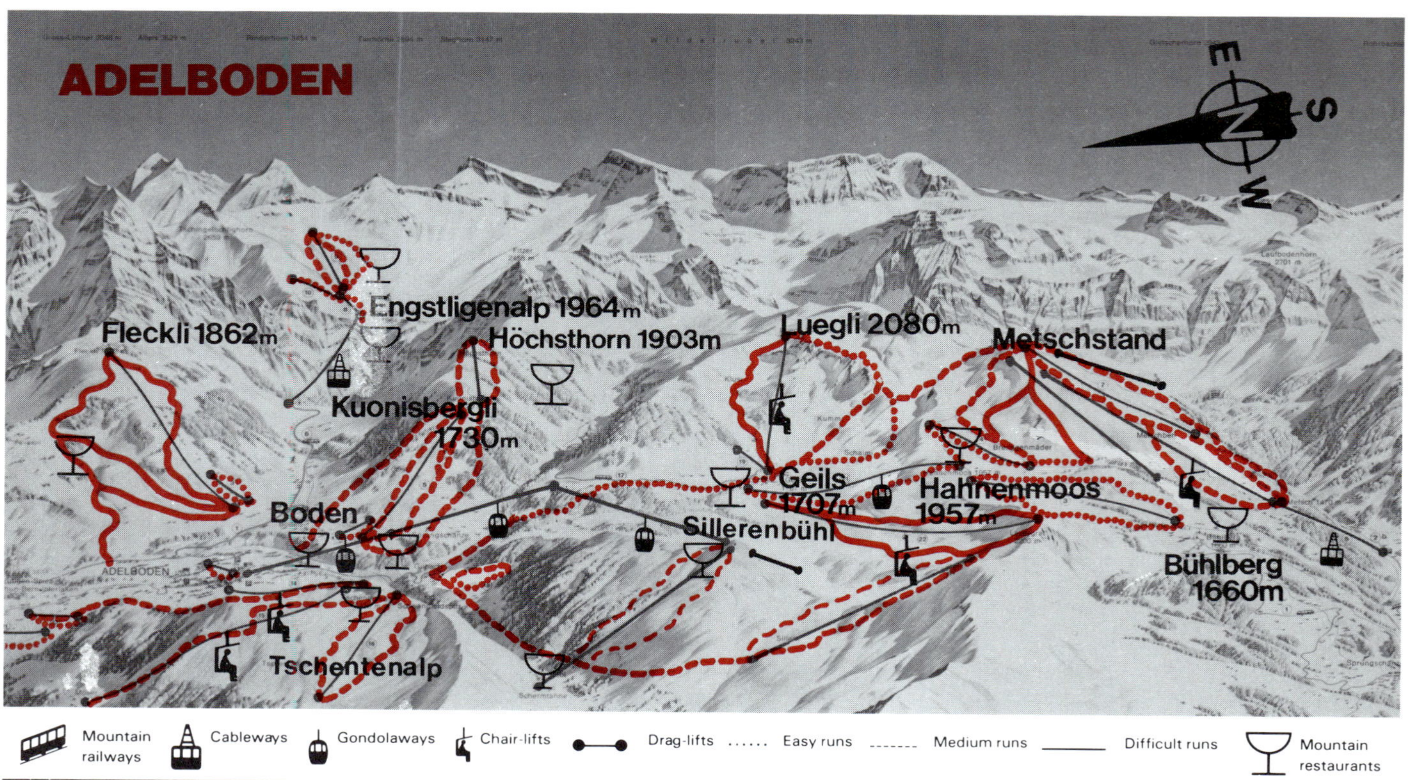

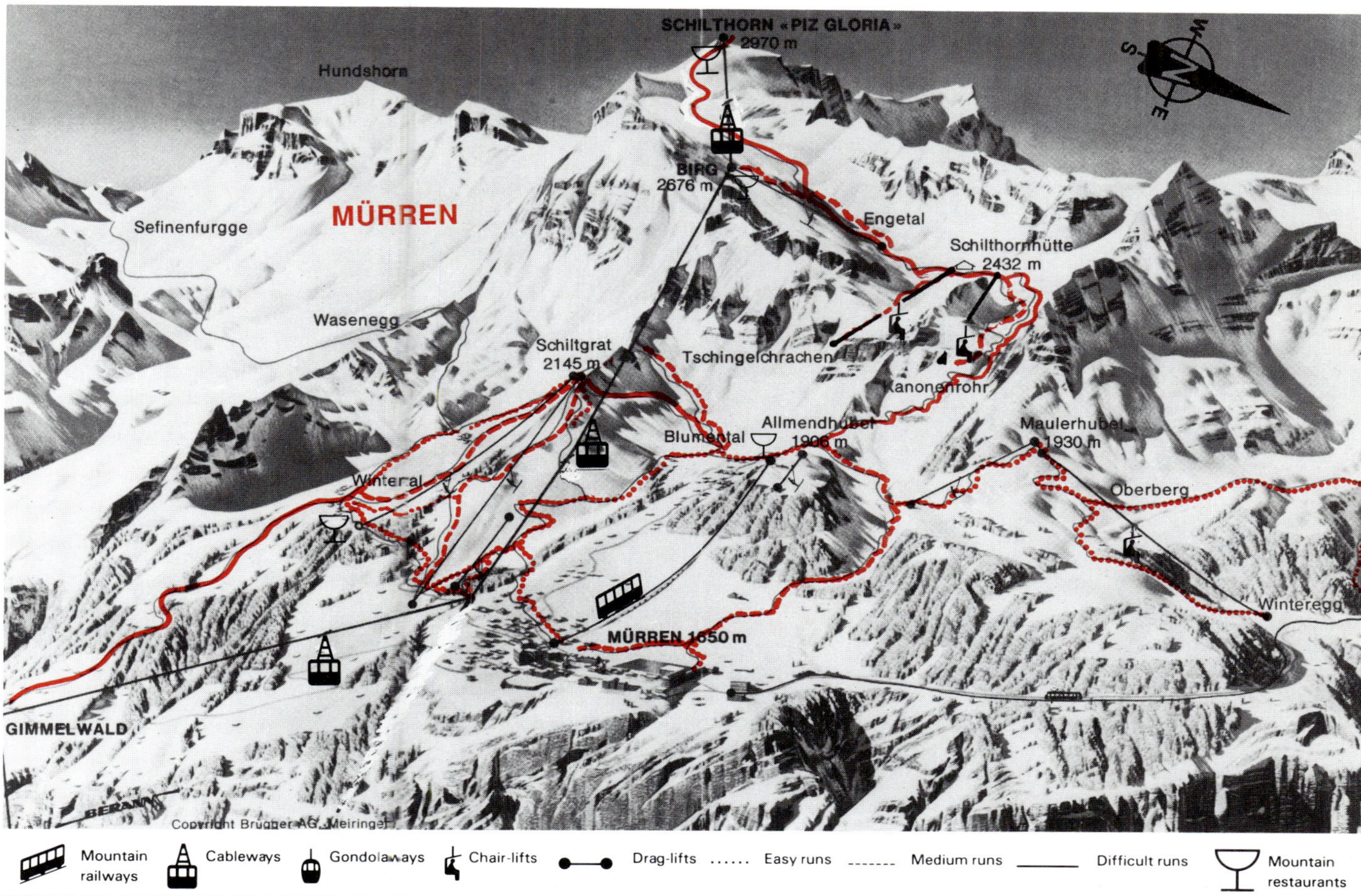

MÜRREN

Height of Resort: 5,362 ft.
Height of Top Station: 9,748 ft
Nearest International Airport: Zurich
Map Reference: 3D See page 240
Route by Car: See pages 236-240
Resort Facilities Charts: See page 223
Hotel Reference Charts: See page 233

A small village on a high and sunny shelf overlooking the Lauterbrunnen valley and reached by mountain railway or by cableway from Stechelberg, Mürren is one of the most delightful ski resorts in the Alps, remaining almost unchanged over the last 36 years, and car-free. The buildings blend harmoniously with the lovely surroundings. There are only 14 hotels and pensions with accommodation for 850, a further 1,200 beds being provided by the chalets and apartments. The skiing facilities have been much developed in recent years and the four-stage cableway with capacity of 100 from Stechelberg to Schilthorn is a magnificent feat of engineering, culminating in the revolving restaurant at the summit. There are three main ski areas:

Schilthorn Area: The Schilthorn, or Piz Gloria, was the setting for the James Bond film, 'On Her Majesty's Secret Service', and what a dramatic setting it is. From Mürren the cableway rises to Birg, 8,780ft., where there is a restaurant and sun terrace perched above a precipitous rock face. The cableway continues to the summit, 9,748ft., where one finds the magnificent revolving restaurant from which there are wonderful views of the surrounding peaks.

From the top there is a steep and challenging black run, which includes the 'Kanonenrohr', right back to Mürren, narrow and exposed in places and definitely not for the faint hearted. From Birg there are comparatively easy routes which meet the run from the top station at Engetal. Two new chair-lifts in this bowl give more scope on snowsure slopes for intermediate skiers. A drag-lift returns one to Birg for those who prefer to take the cableway down to Mürren. The descent from the Schilthorn forms the top section of the famous Inferno race down to Lauterbrunnen, 16km. in length with a vertical descent of some 7,000ft., one of the longest downhill races in the world.

Schiltgrat Area: The Schiltgrat drag-lift, runs almost parallel to the cableway and terminates at 7,038ft., where it is met by the Gimmelen drag-lift rising from the restaurant at its base. From the top of both lifts there are runs of varying difficulty, including the famous Kandahar course. There is a pleasant run from the top, above and below the tree line, to Gimmelwald returning to the resort by cableway.

Allmendhubel-Maulerhubel Area: Allmendhubel, 6,273ft., is reached by mountain railway from the village centre and easy runs return to the village. A steep run leads down to the foot of a drag-lift which takes one to Maulerhubel, from which point there is an interesting run to the village, or enjoyable easy and intermediate runs of about 4km. to Winteregg. A train returns one to Mürren or a chair-lift to the top of Maulerhubel.

Sports Centre: A superb sports centre includes indoor swimming pool, sauna, steam bath, jacuzzi, massage, solarium, fitness room, squash courts, games room, TV room and library. The sports hall provides facilities for basket ball, tennis and football. In addition there are outdoor ice rinks with skating, curling and ice hockey. Most of these facilities are free to those staying in the resort's hotels or chalets.

In a Few Words: A typical Alpine resort; friendly and good for families, with kindergarten; langlauf; good nursery slopes in village area; efficient tourist office; within easy reach of Wengen and Grindelwald; snow reliable; compact lift system; skiing suitable for all grades.

Après Ski: Informal, with dancing in various hotels every night with lively atmosphere. The attractive Tächi bar/night club in the Hotel Eiger, has an inviting open fire; its restaurant looks over the Jungfrau range and there is a cosy stübli serving

In a Few Words: Skiing for all grades, though only a small number of difficult runs; village compact and charming, with beautiful scenery; good for families; kindergarten; many slopes north-west to north-east facing; good atmosphere.

Après Ski: Lots of night life, with good choice of night clubs and bars and an informal and lively atmosphere. Favourite with younger people is the Berna discothèque. Of universal appeal is the Alte Taverne (Hotel Nevada Palace), converted from 6 very old wooden houses into a barn-style room with a gallery overlooking the dance floor and enough seats for 200. The Muusfalle Disco at the Hotel Victoria Eden is open every night.There is also a good restaurant. Raclettes and fondues are available in nearly all restaurants, and pizzas and Italian food in the restaurants Kreuz and Alfredo. Another excellent restaurant is the Tartare in the Hotel Huldi and the Wildstrubel in Boden. The Alte Taverne in the Adler Hotel has a band and the Domino has an attractive apéritif bar. Some of the restaurants have Swiss music.

Recommended Hotels:

Hotel Steinmattli: This 4 star hotel is 3 minutes' walk from the village centre and from the Sillerenbuhl; gondolaway. Large lounge, dining room, à la carte restaurant, bar, whirlpool and sauna. Attractive bedrooms, all with bath, wc, balcony, TV, radio and telephone. Kindergarten in hotel.

Parkhotel Bellevue: Two minutes' walk from centre, situated above the village. Large reception sitting area, bright dining room in two sections with large windows, sun terrace. Bedrooms of good size, most with bath. Night club 'Scotch Club 69', very nice swimming pool and sauna.

Swiss specialities. Popular also is the disco in the 'Inferno' bar at the Hotel Mürren. The Hotel Jungfrau has a large room with an excellent restaurant. There is a disco at Bliemli Keller. The Stäger Stübli is the bar frequented by ski instructors and locals and has a very good atmosphere. Its restaurant is also highly recommended, particularly for cheese fondues. The various mountain restaurants also provide evening fondue and raclette parties, to be followed if desired by an exhilarating return to the village by toboggan.

Recommended Hotels:

Hotel Eiger: One of the nicest hotels in Mürren, near the station, with wonderful views over the valley; bedrooms very comfortable, all with bath and nearly all with balcony. The top floor is very attractive. Spacious dining room, comfortable lounge and popular Tächi bar, large sun terrace. Swimming pool, sauna, solarium and fitness facilities. Conference room. Very well run by family Stähli-von Allmen.

Hotel Jungfrau: An old established chalet-style hotel, modernised inside and standing next to the nursery slopes in a sunny position. Good sized bedrooms, all with bath, attractive dining room, popular 'Im Gruebi' bar. Jungfrau Lodge adjacent, all rooms with bath. Free access to sports centre.

Hotel Palace: This hotel was recently completely reconstructed and modernised. Its 50 bedrooms are attractively furnished all with private bath, wc. Well planned and comfortable reception rooms. Baby sitting service during day and evening. Popular Inferno Bar, completely renovated in 1991,with dancing to disco. Free access to sports centre.

GRINDELWALD & WENGEN

Height of Resort: 3,393/4,187ft.
Height of Top Station: 8,157ft. (11,333ft.)
Nearest International Airport: Zurich
Map Reference: 4C See page 240
Route by Car: See pages 236-240
Resort Facilities Charts: See page 222
Hotel Reference Charts: See page 232

These two quite separate resorts share the same extensive ski area and are linked by a highly efficient mountain railway. Both have great charm and character. Wengen vies with Mürren for the title of the 'birthplace of Alpine skiing'. Certainly the railway from Wengen to Kleine Scheidegg (built in 1910/11) and the Lauberhorn drag-lift (now a 4-seater chair-lift) provided early skiers with the first uphill transport and gave Britain one of its most famous clubs, The Downhill Only (DHO). The Club has its headquarters in Wengen and runs training schemes for promising young British racers during Christmas and Easter. Wengen is situated on a wide sunny shelf overlooking the precipitous Lauterbrunnen valley, with access only by mountain railway, the resort being traffic free. It has superb views of the Jungfrau range and is one of the most scenic resorts. It is very popular with the British, particularly families, who are made to feel very welcome.

Grindelwald is also a long established ski resort and a famous climbing centre, set in a gentle valley below the dramatic peaks of the Jungfrau, Mönch, Eiger and Wetterhorn. Between them Grindelwald and Wengen have a wide variety of skiing on and off-piste to suit all grades of skiers with the famous north wall of the Eiger forming the background.

Kleine Scheidegg Area: Trains from both Grindelwald and Wengen meet at Kleine Scheidegg, 6,762ft., and on both sides there are intermediate stations to which one can descend and from which skiers can return to their respective resorts. Another mountain railway climbs from Kleine Scheidegg to Eigergletscher, 7,612ft., and continues through a tunnel inside the Eiger to **Jungfraujoch, 11,333ft.**, and from the panoramic restaurant one has dramatic views but **no ski runs apart from an off-piste route down the Aletsch Glacier (guide essential).** From Eigergletscher there are runs below the Eiger to the foot of the Salzegg drag-lift and the un-pisted routes of Black Rock and Oh God leading to the high speed Wixi chair-lift. This is a superb area for powder skiing. The Wixi chair-lift and a high speed 4 seater chair-lift from Kleine Scheidegg rise to the top of the Lauberhorn with runs both to Kleine Scheidegg and back to Wengen, the latter including the famous World Cup course. This area has been further improved by the triple chair-lift from Wixi to Fallboden thus linking with the Salzegg drag-lift and the Arvengarten high speed chair-lift. En route to Wengen the Bumps drag-lift and Innerwengen chair-lift serve popular practice slopes. On the Grindelwald side the Arvengarten chair-lift gives access to Kleine Scheidegg and together with the Honegg and Tschuggen drag-lifts and the Gummi chair-lift provides the link with Männlichen. There are runs of 7 to 8½km. down to Grindelwald, open at the top and wooded to just above the resort.

Männlichen Area: A two stage gondolaway from Grindelwald and an improved cableway from Wengen meet at Männlichen, 7,333ft. Here there is an enormous snow bowl, and in addition to the gondolaway the upper section is served by two chair-lifts. There is a most pleasant descent of 4,237ft., over 8½km. in length to Grindelwald Grund. To ski back to Wengen the only route is via Kleine Scheidegg and if heading in this direction it is worth exploring the pistes and off-piste routes served by the linking lifts extending above and below the tree line. The Gummi chair-lift gives access to some particularly fine powder skiing and the snow is usually good in this predominantly north facing area.

'First'-Oberjoch Area: This area on the north-eastern side of Grindelwald is reached by gondolaway, the lower terminal being about 8 minutes' walk from the station. It travels via Bort to Grindel, where the Schreckfeld restaurant is situated, thence up to 'First' and its restaurant with superb views down to the village and across to the Jungfrau - Eiger range. The slopes are mainly south facing and are renowned for their spring snow, with powder retaining well on the upper slopes. There are 6 drag-lifts in the area and a 4 seater chair-lift, which rises to Oberjoch, 8,157ft. The upper runs are fairly gentle, but the 8km. descent to Grindelwald is more challenging, particularly if the direct black route under the gondolaway is taken. The red Grindel run is a pleasant alternative and the gondolaway can also be used to descend from any of the stages. Alternatively one can descend from the top of the Schilt drag-lift on a blue and red making a pleasant scenic route back to the village church.

Mürren: The Jungfrau Region pass is a good buy for the keen skier and gives those staying in Grindelwald and Wengen the opportunity of visiting Mürren as well (see separate report). This pass does not cover the moutain railway journey Eigergletscher-Junfraujoch. Supplement 1994/95 was 45.50 S. Frs.

In a Few Words: Two villages with great history, though differing in character, Wengen is smaller and more compact, Grindelwald a little livelier and accessible by car. Both share a vast ski area. The two resorts have excellent facilities, including kindergartens and efficient helpful Tourist Offices. Both good for families, all standards of skiers and a warm reception for British visitors.

Après Ski Grindelwald: The one long main street houses some excellent shops and boutiques and the well-stocked and reasonably priced Migros and Coop shop for those on self-catering arrangements. Non-skiers can take advantage of Grindelwald's proximity to Wengen and Mürren as well as Interlaken for a day's outing, and there are plenty of other activities: tobogganing, beautifully kept walks. The sports centre houses a large indoor skating rink used for major international competition, 4 curling rinks, an indoor swimming pool, games room, sauna and solarium. Non skiers can also spend a pleasant day at Bussalp, 5,905ft., situated on the sunny side of Grindelwald. It is reached by bus and at the top there is a restaurant with wonderful views of the high mountains. Here there are lovely walks, tobogganing and cross-country skiing trails. As Grindelwald is easily accessible by car, a lot of Swiss tend to come up for the weekends and the village has a lively and happy atmosphere. Dress tends towards the comfortably elegant, away from jeans and can be quite formal in the Hotel Regina. There are excellent and varied evening entertainments offered all over the village; amongst these, a disco and very pleasant ambience can be found in the Challi-Bar (Hotel Kreuz). Other night spots are the Spider night club at the Hotel Spinne and the Cava-Bar (Hotel Derby) and the Plaza Club (Hotel Sunstar). The Expresso Bar is very popular with the locals and has considerable atmosphere; so is the Gebsi-Bar at the Hotel Eiger.

Recommended Hotels Grindelwald:

Hotel Belvedere: This superior 4 star hotel, one of the best known in the area, was completely renovated in 1994. It is family run and owned, providing very comfortable accommodation. All rooms and suites with bath, radio, satellite TV, minibar, safe, hairdryer, bath robes and balconies. Dining room, à la carte restaurant with piano music, elegant lounges with panoramic views, piano-bar. Indoor swimming pool, jacuzzi, sauna, Turkish bath, massage, solarium and children's games room. Free parking.

Hotel Derby-Bahnhof: Situated right by the station, this is a popular hotel with very good accommodation; all rooms with bath, wc. and balcony. Large and pleasant dining room, very popular Gaststube, always filled with skiers. The Cava Bar has dancing in the evenings.

Hotel Eiger: This is a family and cosy 4 star hotel, all bedrooms with private bath or shower, radio, minibar and television, south facing rooms with balcony. There are also 12 apartments with 2-6 beds and kitchen. In the same building, the popular restaurant Swiss Chalet and Gepsi-Bar in rustic style. Sauna and hot whirlpool.

Grand Hotel Regina: Standing in the centre of the village, this is a luxury hotel in every way, but still retains a warm and friendly atmosphere. All its rooms and suites have private bath or shower and they are attractively and comfortably furnished. The two dining rooms and sitting rooms are spacious and beautifully appointed. There are two bars. The hotel also has a very fine swimming pool with sauna and solarium, which are free to guests. Beauty salon. A chalet-style annexe with luxury apartments is connected with the main hotel by a covered passage-way.

Après Ski Wengen: Skiing takes priority here – the night life is fairly subdued and often skiing takes over here too, with night ski jumping and torchlight descents after the Wengernalp fondue evenings, the merry makers guided by local experts! There are various somewhat expensive restaurants and discothèques and hotel dancing. Sina's Pizzeria offers excellent Italian dishes. Alternatively, there are much cheaper eating spots serving snacks, or menu of the day. One finds a lively disco 'Tiffany' in the Hotel Silberhorn complex. Popular bars with British visitors are the Pickel, the Tanne and Sina's Pub. Good swimming pools and saunas can be found at the Sunstar and Park Hotels, and there are excellent shops, and hairdressers of a very high standard. The tone is casual by night, fashion being in the main confined to ski wear. Mountain restaurants are widely spread. There are plenty of activities for non-skiers too – excursions to neighbouring areas, artificial and natural ice rinks, ice hockey and curling and floodlit ski jumping amongst them. For greater excitement there is the possibility of helicopter or small plane trips, which vary enormously in length and price, flying close to the north face of the Eiger is an experience.

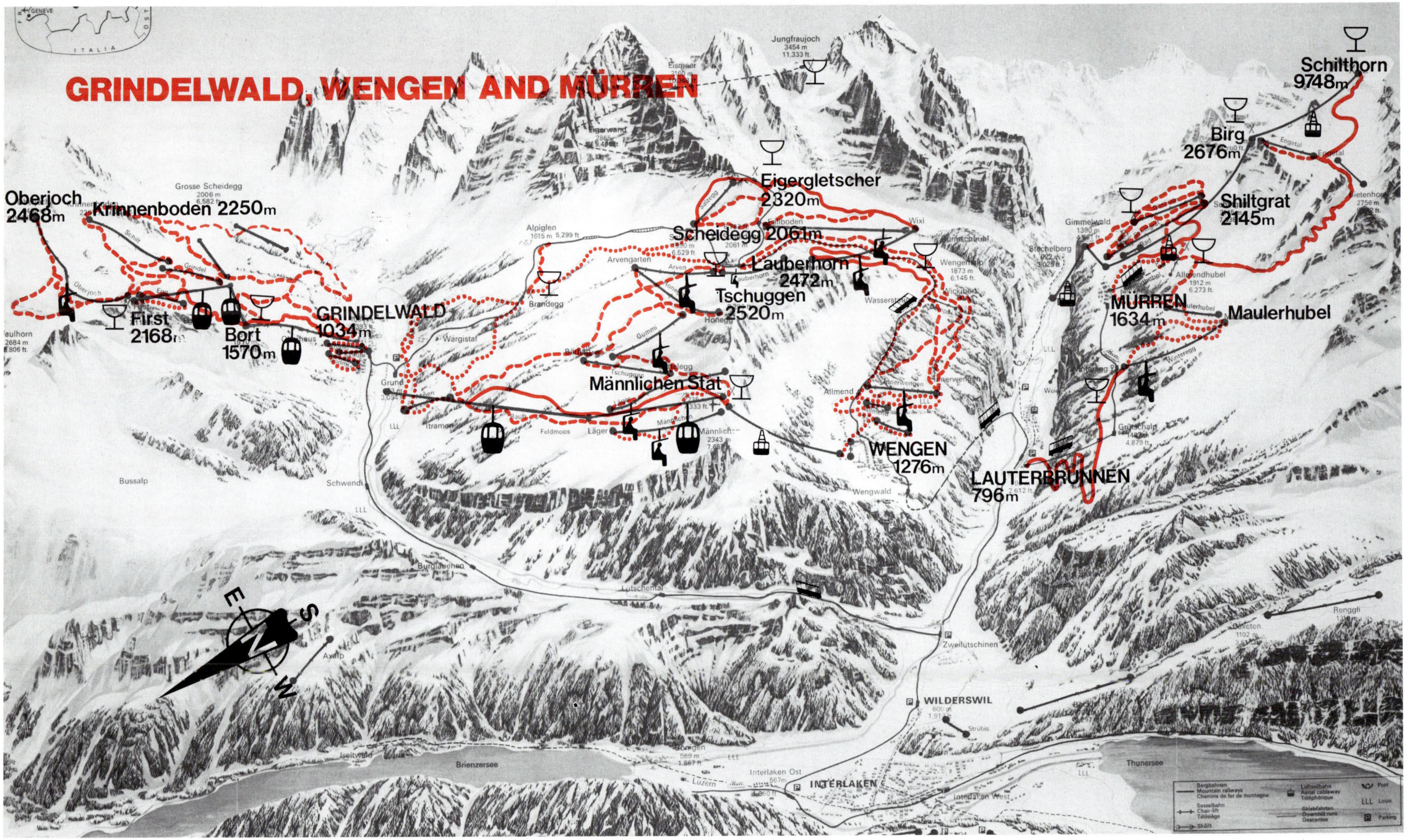

Mountain railways | Cableways | Gondolaways | Chair-lifts | Drag-lifts | ...... Easy runs | -------- Medium runs | ——— Difficult runs | Mountain restaurants

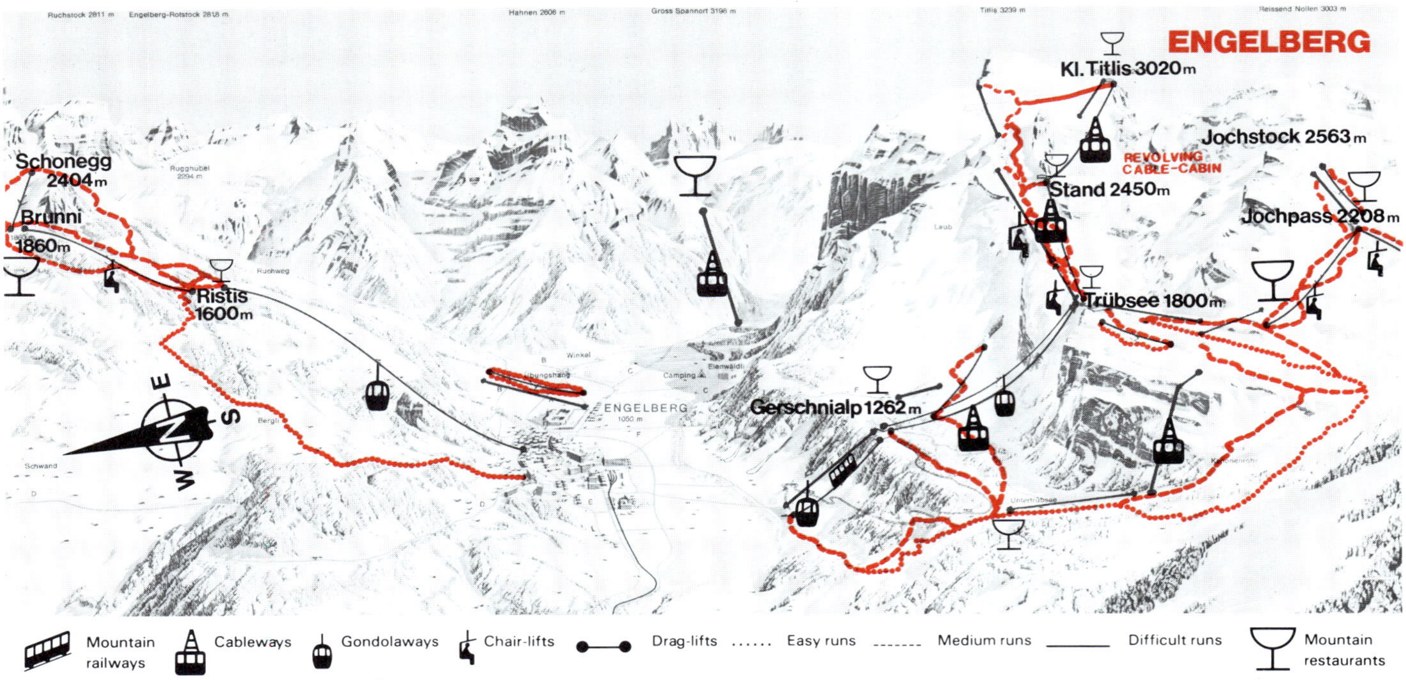

Recommended Hotels Wengen:

Hotel Bellevue: A well appointed hotel with a warm and welcoming atmosphere. Pleasant rooms with private facilities, most with balconies, all with telephone and radio. Family and connecting rooms available. Good lounge, TV room and bar. Food recommended as are the excellent pots of tea. Has one of the best views in Wengen of the Jungfrau and Lauterbrunnen valley. 10 minutes walk from the station.

Hotel Falken: A traditional Swiss family-run hotel with a welcoming atmosphere from both management and staff. Near the centre, convenient to the cableway, shops and railway. Most of the bedrooms have private bath and many have balconies. Comfortable sitting room, small bar, pianist, large bright dining room and sun terrace. TV room.

Hotel Regina: A large hotel of 160 beds in a sunny position near the centre. Comfortable bedrooms, a large proportion with private bath. Well appointed reception rooms, one dining room, choice of 4 menus at no extra charge, including one vegetarian and one fish; speciality restaurant "Chez Meyer's", one club room, large lounge, sun terrace and 2 bars.

Hotel Schweizerheim: A small friendly family run hotel set in quiet position below the station overlooking the Lauterbrunnen valley, 10 minutes walk from centre. Good value for money with clean, comfortable and sizeable rooms, all with bath. Pleasant restaurant, two lounges, Swiss mountain style bar, sun terrace. Excellent food and ample portions. The family provides musical entertainment. Good atmosphere.

Hotel Silberhorn: One of the most popular family hotels in Wengen situated in the centre and efficiently run. There is a complex of restaurants, bars, the Tiffany disco and a hairdressing salon. Double and single rooms. Whirlpool.

Hotel Victoria-Lauberhorn: Standing in the main street, 2 minutes from the station, this is an excellent large hotel much recommended by guests. It has been completely renovated and most tastefully redecorated, skilfully combining local and modern styles. 50 double and 12 single bedrooms, all with bath/shower, radio, TV and safe. Elegant dining room, sitting room, 2 bars including the à la carte restaurant which serves meals and delicious snacks.

Hotel Wengener Hof: Set in its own grounds about 7 minutes walk from the station, this delightful 4 star hotel has 24 double rooms and 12 singles all with bath. Free shuttle bus service.

bath or shower and some with balconies. Elegantly furnished dining room, lounge, and bar from which one has wonderful views of the surrounding mountains.

Hotel Sunstar: A modern 4 star hotel situated in the centre of the resort and offering a high standard of accommodation. All bedrooms are tastefully furnished, twins with bath and singles with shower. Much wood decor and tapestries. A superb swimming pool with panoramic windows and lovely views of the mountain ranges. Sauna and solarium. Restaurant, bar, cosy lounge with open fire.

ENGELBERG

Height of Resort: 3,444 ft.
Height of Top Station: 9,906 ft.
Nearest International Airport: Zurich
Map Reference: 4C See page 240
Route by Car: See pages 236-240
Resort Facilities Charts: See page 222
Hotel Reference Charts: See page 232

Engelberg is one of the oldest resorts in Switzerland, winter sports were introduced there in 1887 and the first rail connection with Lucerne made in 1898. Its famous Benedictine monastery founded in 1120, lies in a beautiful valley, with high mountains on three sides but nevertheless is open and sunny. There is a good rail service from Zurich airport, changing at Lucerne and from this point the journey takes one hour, alternatively by car 35 minutes. The old part of the village has great charm. The skiing is divided into three main areas, one on the north side of the village and two on the south side.

Gerschnialp-Titlis: Two minutes by bus from the centre of the village one finds the fast and efficient gondolaway which rises to Trübsee, 5,904ft. This has replaced the old funicular railway to Gerschnialp and the surmounting cableway to Trübsee, although both are retained to carry excess loads during peak periods. The journey can be broken at Gerschnialp, 4,140ft., where the nursery slopes are served by two drag-lifts, alternatively there is a cross-country skiing circuit, and also an easy 3.5km. toboggan run back to the village. Stand, 8,036ft., can be reached from Trübsee either by two surmounting chair-lifts or by cableway and here one finds a restaurant with sun terrace overlooking the Titlis Glacier. From Stand, the Rotair revolving cable-cabin carrying 80 persons (see Comment) rises to Titlis, 9,906ft., the top station. From the sun terrace of the restaurant one has magnificent views of the glacier below and the high distant mountains the Matterhorn, Jungfrau, the Eiger and others and one can see as far as Zurich and Basle on a clear day. The run back to Stand starts deceptively easily but it turns into a steep narrow piste full of moguls later on and is certainly for the experienced skier. From Stand to Trübsee there is a good variety of intermediate to easy skiing. Particularly interesting and somewhat challenging are the Erika variations by the Laubergrat chair-lift. The run from Titlis to the village is some 12km. in length with a vertical descent of 6,462ft.

Trübsee-Jochstock: At Trübsee one finds the Sporthotel and restaurant and drag-lifts serving easy slopes, it is also the start of a long cross-country trail through beautiful scenery. Across the lake from Trübsee and on the southern tip, stands the restaurant Alpstübli with a vast sun terrace. From here a 4 seater chair-lift reaches Jochpass, 7,249ft., and converging on this point is a chair-lift coming up from Engstlenalp, which provides pleasant south-west facing runs to its base. It should be mentioned that Engstlenalp is a favourite area for snowboarders. From Jochpass and rising eastwards are double drag-lifts terminating at Jochstock, 8,413ft., which serve intermediate runs over south-west facing slopes. This is a delightful skiing area with something for everyone. From the Alpstübli restaurant there are long easy and intermediate runs back to the village. On the descent most runs converge at the Unter-Trübsee mountain restaurant, where huge, cream-filled meringues are a must, perhaps washed down with haus-kaffee and schnapps.

Brunni-Schonegg Area: The Brunni cableway from the north of the village arrives at Ristis, 5,248ft., where there is a restaurant, from here a chair-lift rises to Brunni, 6,101ft., to connect with a further drag-lift to Schonegg, 6,692ft. A medium to difficult run leads from Schonegg to Brunni over west facing slopes and a medium run from Brunni to Ristis on south-west facing slopes. There is quite an interesting run from Ristis of about 7km. over west and south-west facing slopes to the village, vertical descent 3,248ft., but the snow disappears from the lower section fairly early on.A new, winter and summer, 600 metre bob run has been opened in this area.

Cross-country skiing is well catered for with 5 trails, 3-5 to 15km. The Tourist Centre organises courses and good package arrangements are available. Extensive facilities are to be found in the sports centre:- ice rink with spectators gallery, curling hall with 3 rinks, changing rooms and waxing room for cross-country skiers; 2 indoor tennis courts and a fitness room.

In a Few Words: Skiing for all grades, particularly medium to good skiers, with reliable snow on higher slopes; fine selection of glacier tours; plenty of activities for non-skiers; marvellous scenery; interesting village; good organisation.

Après Ski: Informal and fun. Tea dancing takes place at weekends in several hotels. Favourite with teenagers is the Spindle bar, a large disco with rustic decor and a lively atmosphere. Also popular are the Coffee restaurant and dance club 'Matter'; the Bierlialp with disco and Casino Carmena with bar and dancing to live music – the prices are reasonable. The Caribbean Dream Life bar at the Central and the Pub at the Hotel Engel are favourite drinking holes for many visitors whilst the Alpenclub holds its own against most of the night spots. As well as the night life, there are curling and ice hockey matches, international ski jumping, skating, tobogganing (a 2 mile run) and night-time torchlight skiing for guests every week. A school for para-gliding, 25 miles of cleared walks, an indoor swimming pools and covered sports centre for various entertainment .

Recommended Hotels:

Hotel Bellevue Terminus: Centrally located, next to the skibus stop. Large lounge, spacious dining room with high panelled ceiling, comfortable bedrooms, particularly those with bath.

Hotel Central: This very comfortable, modern hotel is pleasantly furnished and carpeted throughout. All rooms with bath/shower, telephone, radio, colour TV and mini bar. Free entry to indoor swimming pool, sauna and solarium. Attractive dining room and restaurant, grill room and Caribbean dream-life bar. Good atmosphere.

Hotel Crystal: A centrally situated modern hotel, all rooms with bath/shower, telephone, colour TV and minibar, carpeted throughout. Attractive small dining room leading to rustic style restaurant. Reduced entry to swimming pool in the Hotel Central opposite.

Hotel Hess: A well established hotel in central position. Large comfortable lounge, attractive Stübli speciality restaurant with bar and dancing to pianist. Large screen TV room with video; conference rooms,. solarium, sauna. All bedrooms with bath/shower, telephone, radio, TV and minibar.

Hotel Eden: Delightful and friendly, recently modernised family run hotel next to the station. Excellent cuisine, cooked by the owner and served by his wife, makes dining a very special occasion, further enhanced by a carefully chosen and excellent wine cellar. Bedrooms and guest rooms simply but comfortably furnished. 10 bedrooms, all with bath/shower, telephone, radio TV, safe and minibar; TV room, buffet breakfast, children's playroom; sauna, solarium, terrace.

ANDERMATT

Height of Resort: 4,738 ft.
Height of Top Station: 9,842 ft.
Nearest International Airport: Zurich
Map Reference: 5C See page 240
Route by Car: See pages 236-240
Resort Facilities Charts: See page 221
Hotel Reference Charts: See page 232

Andermatt is a medium sized village of great character., and with a warm atmosphere, situated in a high, sunny valley to the north of the St. Gotthard Pass. The skiing is excellent, catering very much for the experienced skier.

The main skiing is in the Gemsstock area, reached via a fast 2-stage cableway from the west end of the village, rising first to Gurschen, 7,018ft., where there is a restaurant and serving these lower, easier slopes is a chair-lift and drag-lift. The second stage of the cableway terminates at Gemsstock, 9,842ft., and from here there is a fantastic view over the mountains. The Sonnenpiste run back to Gurschen, to the left, is medium to difficult standard and it can become more exacting under the very often changeable weather conditions. The runs to the right of the cableway are testing and the centre one should not be attempted by any but the most competent. The run descends evenly between deep crevasses but when it reaches the glacier wall it becomes extremely steep, with danger of a drop of 200ft. over the edge. Beyond the wall the run becomes less steep but is still very narrow, requiring restricted and frequent turns until it ends, at the base of the Gurschen chair-lift. The run either side are not so testing but nevertheless they are for good skiers. This is fine skiing for those of sufficiently advanced standard, with its north facing slopes and excellent snow – amongst the best in the Alps. The run to the village from Gurschen again is not easy and provides varied terrain. The total descent, from Gemsstock to Andermatt is 5,000ft.

To the east of the village is the Nätschen-Stockli area, reached by mountain railway and chair-lift. Here one long and two shorter drag-lifts serve open, south-facing slopes, a very good alternative when there has been a heavy snowfall on the Gemsstock slopes. The train continues to the Oberalp Pass, where there is another drag-lift. Oberalp gives access to some easy touring to Dieni, with extensive open slopes served by 2 chair-lifts and 4 drag-lifts. Another train journey, in a westerly direction, leads to Hospental, where a chair-lift and drag-lift serve the Winterhorn slopes. Further west is Realp where there is a very good beginners' slope served by a drag-lift. All these areas provide easy to medium standard skiing and there is very good touring in the surrounding areas, with mountain huts placed at strategic intervals. There are also enjoyable off-piste runs over the far side of Gemsstock, with spectacular views, down to the St. Gotthard Pass. Langlauf facilities are very good at this resort and one of the best trails is from Andermatt to Realp and back, about 20km.

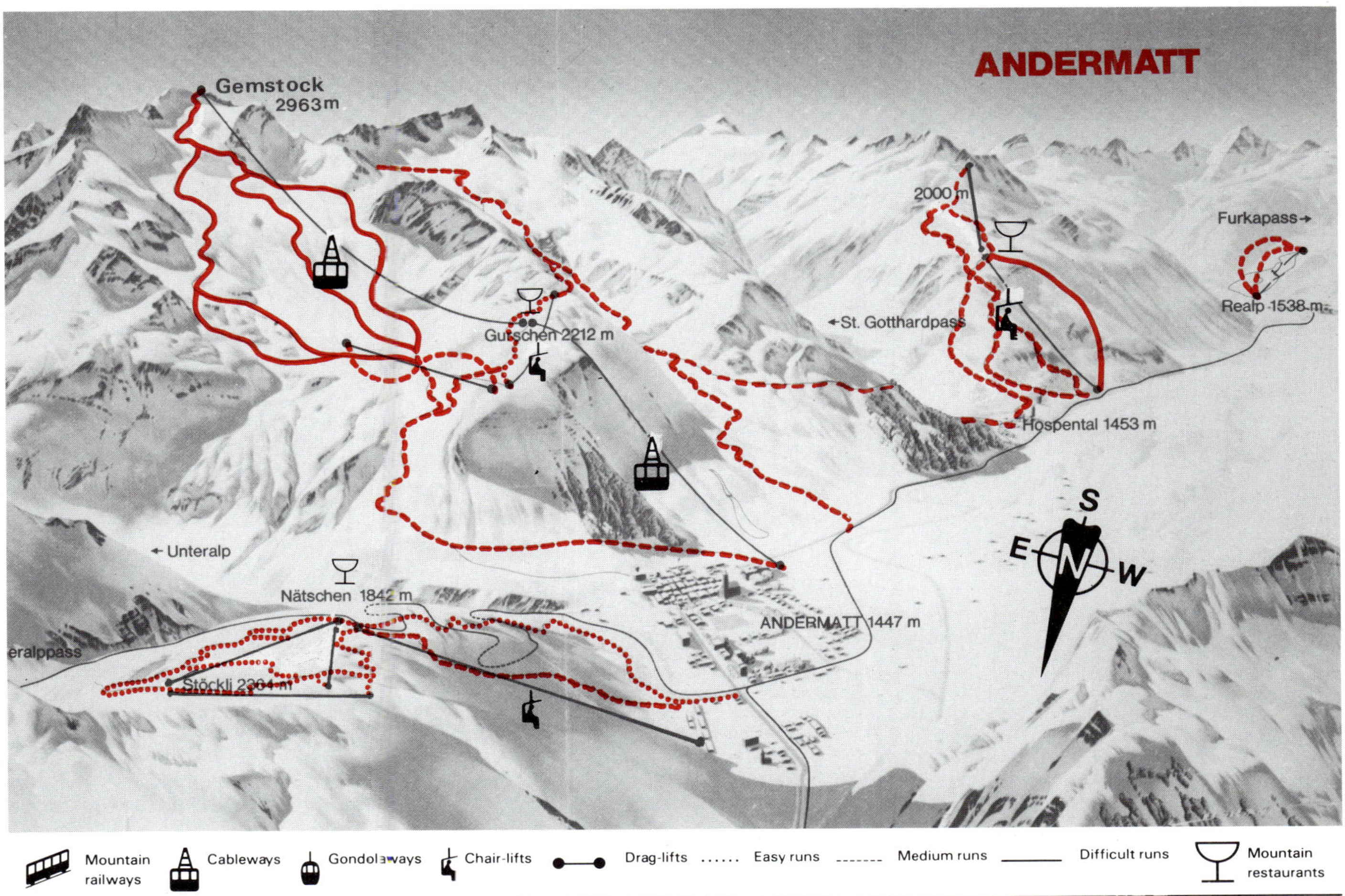

In a Few Words: A delightful and picturesque village; good for families; reliable snow throughout a long season; excellent ski touring; skiing available for all standards but medium to very experienced skiers will benefit most; little queueing except at holidays and weekends. Medium in price and good value.

Après Ski: Night life is informal and lively. The most popular spot is the Downhill which belongs to gold medal winner, Bernard Russi, and is run by Toni Aeschbacher. It has either live music or disco and is therefore very popular and crowded. Several hotels organise special evenings; there are sleigh rides, tobogganing, curling, a natural ice rink, a sauna and fitness centre.

Recommended Hotels:

Hotel Bergidyll: One of the most popular hotels in Andermatt, old established but modernised, pleasant and comfortable bedrooms, large restaurant and bar. Cosy lounge with open fire. A very good atmosphere and much recommended.

Hotel Drei Könige: A centrally situated 3-star hotel. Comfortable rooms, all with bath or shower, mostly with small sitting area and very nicely furnished. Elegant dining room. Excellent food, sun terrace, a popular meeting place. Fitness/health studio with sauna, solarium, whirlpool, massage and steam bath.

Hotel Krone: This hotel was completely rebuilt in 1970 but still retains its Swiss character. Reception area, bar café, spacious dining room, à la carte restaurant, Kronen-Stübli upstairs sitting room and television, comfortable modern bedrooms all with bath or shower/wc. and all with telephone. A fitness and physiotherapy centre with sauna/solarium free, is attached to the hotel. A well run hotel with excellent service.

Hotel Sonne: Rebuilt in 1986 in Swiss chalet style, all rooms with bath/shower, wc, radio and telephone. Attractive rustic style restaurant. Sauna & fitness room. Conveniently placed for cableway station and cross-country trails.

BRAUNWALD

Height of Resort: 4,264 ft.
Height of Top Station: 6,233 ft.
Nearest International Airport: Zurich
Map Reference: 5C See page 240
Route by Car: See pages 236-240
Resort Facilities Charts: See page 221
Hotel Reference Charts: See page 232

Braunwald, in north-east Switzerland, is a delightful car-free village set amidst pine and sycamore woods and is reached by a drive of some two hours from Zurich along the southern shore of Lake Zurich. Turning off through Glarus, the provincial capital, one reaches Linthal, where a mountain railway climbs up to Braunwald, situated on a sunny shelf. The lack of cars in the village makes it an ideal resort for children. The first section of the gondolaway is 3 minutes walk from the village centre, which takes one to the ski school assembly spot, where the Café Uhu is also located. From this point the second section, with triple cabins, each cabin holding 15 persons, rises through wooded slopes to Grotzenbühl, 5,240ft., where there is a restaurant. From here, a chair-lift continues the ascent across an impressive ravine and past craggy, icicle-hung cliffs to the top of the ridge at Seblengrat, 5,904ft., where it meets the top of the Bächital chair-lift coming up from the north facing slopes over the ridge. The descent on the south facing side of the ridge is medium to steep to begin with and evens out into a gentle run of about 3km. down to the base of the gondolaway.

Alternatively, still on the southern side, one can take the shorter run down to the Mattwald drag-lift up to Grotzenbühl and thence to the top station again. From the south-western side of the village a long double chair-lift travels northwards to Berghaus Gumen, 6,232ft. It rises steeply over the last section, which is above the treeline and an area that can be rather exposed. A drag-lift also serves the upper slopes. From this top station restaurant there are intermediate runs over open slopes down each side of the lifts, all directed towards Grotzenbühl, and thence easy runs back to the village through pretty, wooded scenery.

There is a magnificent view from Seblengrat over the next valley, where you can see the village of Schwanden. The run in this valley is reputedly the longest and most interesting in Braunwald, leading into a wide, open bowl. After a heavy snowfall, however, this area is normally closed for a short time, but when open it can be skied by all grades. There is also a very steep run for expert skiers from Braunwald down to the valley, open only during the earlier part of the season. These runs are not shown on the map as they are frequently closed. There is in addition a 8km. langlauf circuit on the slopes below Grotzenbühl.

In a Few Words: A very friendly and lively village, with no cars, ideal for children; skiing mainly suitable for beginners to intermediates; slopes mostly south facing and very sunny; excellent ski school.

Après Ski: The immediate place to meet after ski school is the Café Uhu Cristal, at the foot of the slopes, which has delicious ice cream specialities. The Tourist Office, next to the top of the mountain railway, gives all information on the day's activities, e.g. which hotels have music for dancing that evening. There is a lively atmosphere for such a small resort. One very popular haunt after skiing and in the evening is the Gade keller bar in the Alpenblick Hotel, with rustic decor and full of locals as well as visitors; it has a juke box and serves reasonably priced draught beer. Films are also shown regularly in the Alpenblick with English soundtrack.

Recommended Hotels:

Hotel Alpenblick: This attractive hotel is surrounded by trees and situated next to the terminal of the mountain railway. Traditional and efficiently run with a friendly, relaxed atmosphere, catering well for families. In addition to a comfortable lounge/reception room with adjoining bar there is a separate café/restaurant and the Gade keller bar, a popular meeting place for the young after skiing and in the evening. Bedrooms, most with private bath, are comfortable, tastefully decorated and generously furnished, and have minibar, telephone and radio. The residents' dining room is light and spacious, with windows on two sides, and a superb view overlooking the valley.

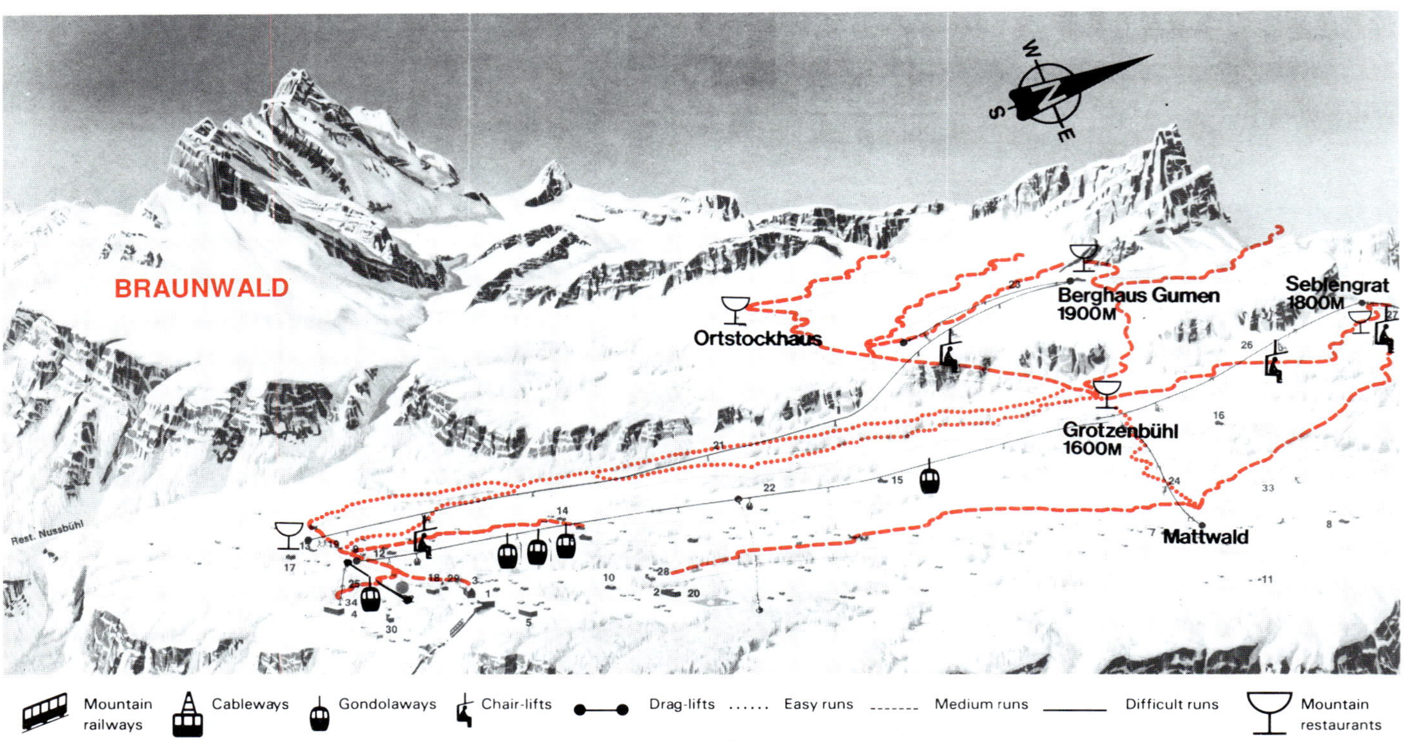

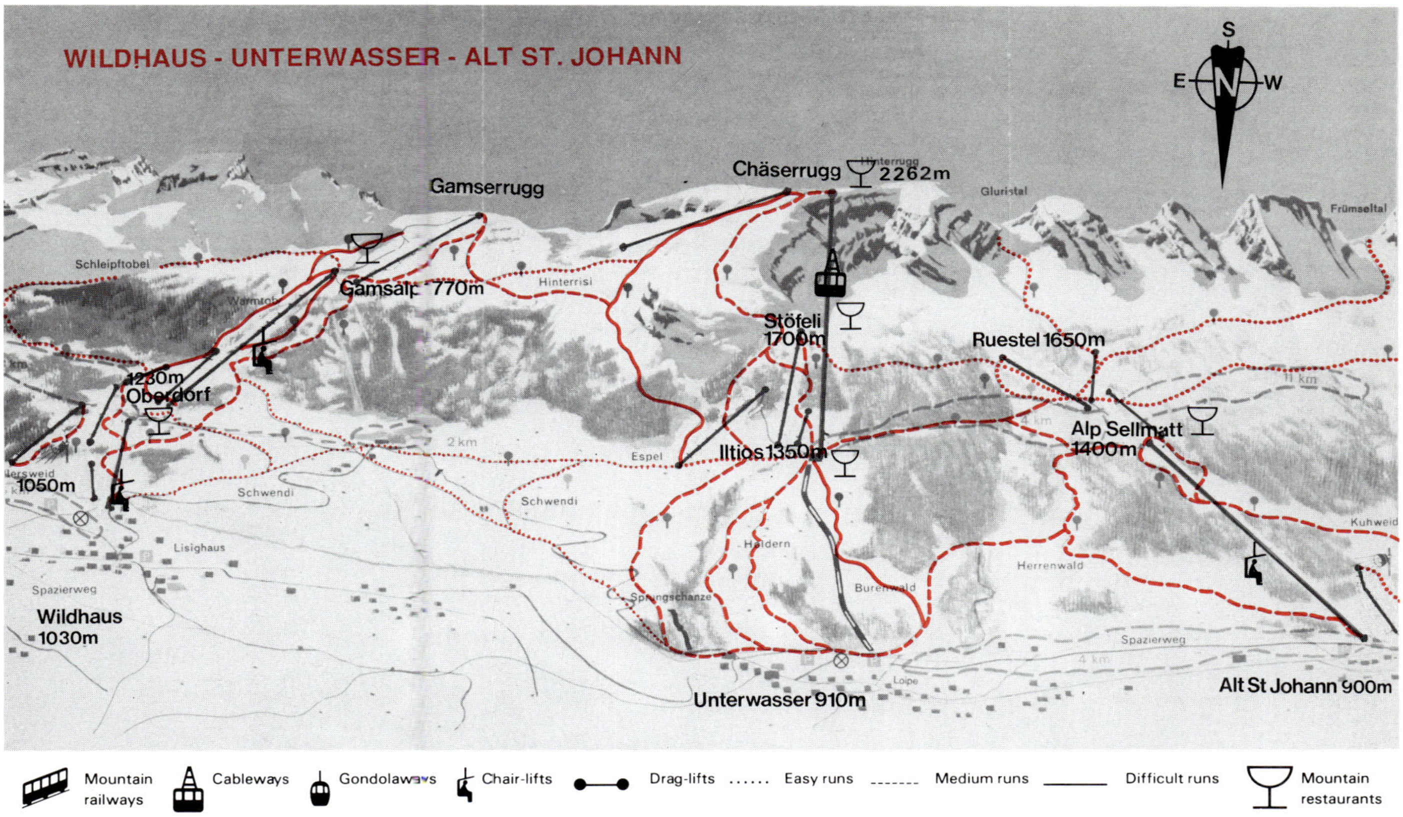

Hotel Alpina: Situated in the village centre, a popular medium-grade hotel with pleasant atmosphere. Many rooms with bath/shower, those south facing with balcony, all with radio and telephone. Attractive restaurant with view over valley, which guests can use at other times; also dining room. Annexe with 4 rooms. Small but light and comfortable bedrooms. Lounge with TV.

Hotel Bellevue: A very large hotel which has been modernised, and a member of the Klub Kinderfreundlicher Schweizer Hotels, which cater specifically for families. Indoor swimming pool, whirlpool, sauna and open air ice-rink (open to the public). Games room as well as room with amusements for small children. Vast amount of space. Large bedrooms which can take extra beds, bright and modernised, most with bath or shower and balcony. Large main dining room with superb view over valley; à la carte restaurant; modern style bar with arched windows.

WILDHAUS

Height of Resort: 3,395 ft.
Height of Top Station: 7,423 ft.
Nearest International Airport: Zurich
Map Reference: 6B See page 240
Route by Car: See pages 236-240
Resort Facilities Charts: See page 223
Hotel Reference Charts: See page 233

Cross the Rhine from Vaduz, the capital of Liechtenstein, through the old town of Buchs and continue westwards along a spectacular mountain road for about 17 miles to enter Wildhaus, 3,395ft., followed after 2 miles by Unterwasser, 2,985ft., and Alt St. Johann, a further 2 miles. The road continues for about 40 miles via Wattwil to Zurich.

Each village has a network of lifts on the north-facing slopes and the runs interconnect so one has access to 20 lifts (the Obertoggenberg lift pass includes the whole area) and runs to suit all standards of skiing, including floodlit runs at Wildhaus. There are extensive facilities for cross-country skiing, including 35km. of prepared trails.

Wildhaus: Near the ski school a four seater chair-lift takes one to Oberdorf, 4,051ft., with two drag-lifts for beginners. A 3-seater chair-lift to Gamsalp, 3,641ft., and from there a drag-lift to Gamserugg, 6,888ft., where there are difficult or medium runs, or a medium run across to the Unterwasser lifts. Easy runs from either the Wildhaus or Unterwasser area lead down to Schwendi, where the Gaden mountain restaurant should not be missed.

Unterwasser, 2,985-7,413ft.: A mountain railway reaches to Iltios, 4,428ft., where there is a large restaurant with sun terrace. From here a cableway climbs to Chäserugg, 7,413ft., with a fine view over the Walensee to the Swiss Alps. There is a restaurant and drag-lift here also. A variety of medium runs are available back to Iltios (via the restaurant at Stöfeli) or across to Gamsalp. Three drag-lifts are near Iltios, including one to Stöfeli, 4,346ft. to 5,576ft., from Espel, 4,133ft. to 4,821ft., and a trainer lift. An 11km. cross-country trail with short cuts, via Alp Sellamatt, begins at Iltios.

Alt St. Johann, 2,952-5,412ft.: A chair-lift takes one to Alp Sellamatt, 4,592ft., with its restaurant and from here two drag-lifts to Ruestel, 5,412ft., provide easy runs back to Sellamatt and across to Iltios.

Advanced skiers who need more of a challenge can take a difficult 2-hour tour from the top of the Schwägalp-Säntis cableway, which is reached by road from Wildhas. The tour ends in Unterwasser.

In a Few Words: Skiing for all grades, with interesting traverses between the lift systems. Good resort for families; kindergarten and good children's ski school. Long village, but a lively atmosphere and plenty of extra activities, including curling, skating and swimming.

Après Ski: There is a swimming pool with sauna open to the public attached to the Hirschen Hotel, and this hotel is one of the main centres of night life. Its James' Club has a band in the evening, and its Pferdestall discothèque, with stable decor, is very popular. The Sonne Hotel has an excellent, attractively decorated restaurant and raclette-stübli; also a pub with dancing. There is dancing to band at Hotel Alpenblick and the Hotel Alpenrose has a modern fitness centre. Excursions are available to St. Gallen and Vaduz, and there is a good selection of shops in Wildhaus and Unterwasser, including a craft shop and sports shops. There is a weekly sleigh ride to the delightful Gade restaurant at Schwendi, which can also be reached by road – this is an old farmhouse which completely retains its original character. A variety of suggested activities are available from the Tourist Offices, and Wildhaus and Unterwasser are resorts that a non-skier would not feel stranded in.

Recommended Hotels:

Hotel Alpenblick: Near the ski school and lifts, this newly renovated family hotel has 18 double and 3 single rooms comfortably furnished, all with shower. A lovely restaurant at the 'Gräppelen-Bar' with live music each evening.

Hotel Hirschen: One of the largest hotels. In the same family for 110 years. There are two annexes adjacent. The rooms are luxurious and facilities include a swimming pool with bar, sauna, games room and two bowling alleys. It is one of the social centres for the village, with dancing to a disco every evening.

Hotel Selun: A small hotel opposite the Alpenblick run by the local butcher. The rooms are modern and comfortable and there is a sitting room, but one looks elsewhere for other entertainment.

Hotel Sonne: A modern chalet-style hotel at the top at the village with a very friendly atmosphere. Rooms are luxurious in the traditional style and there are 3 self-contained flats. Swimming pool, sauna, solarium, 2 restaurants in addition to residents' dining room, which is attractively candlelit in the evening, and bar with dancing, all wood-panelled, providing a choice of entertainment.

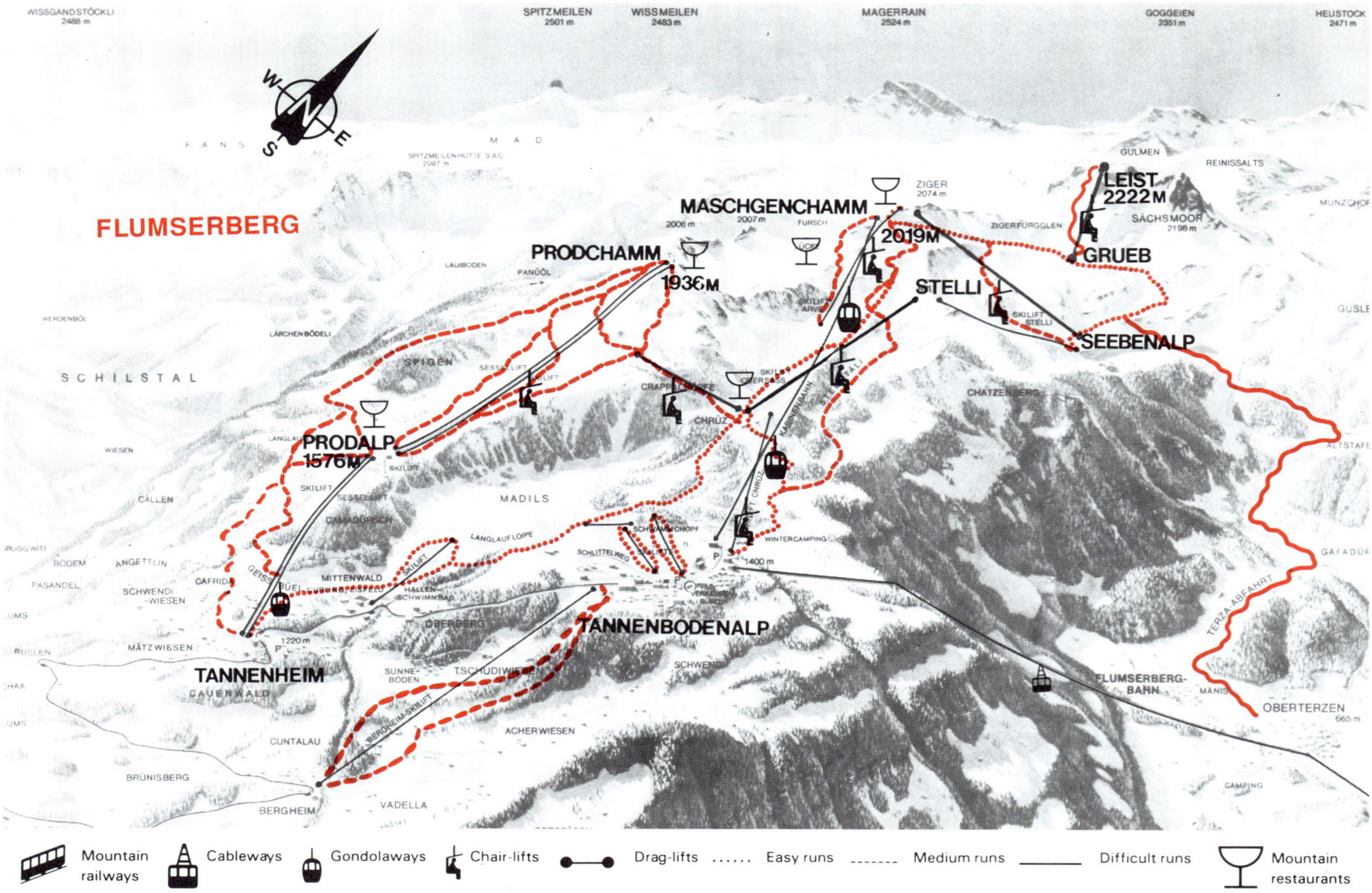

FLUMSERBERG

Height of Resort: 3,280 ft./4,592 ft.
Height of Top Station: 7,287 ft.
Nearest International Airport: Zurich
Map Reference: 6B See page 240
Route by Car: See pages 236-240
Resort Facilities Charts: See page 222
Hotel Reference Charts: See page 232

Only about hour's journey from Zurich, Flumserberg can be reached by cableway from Unterterzen, or by a winding mountain road. The Flumserberg area includes the villages of Bergheim, 3,187ft., Tannenheim, 4,001ft., and Tannenbodenalp, 4,592ft., 800 metres apart, which are linked by road and through their ski areas. They form a resort which is very much on the move, with new lifts being built and projected and accommodation increased. The Twärchamm chair-lift enables one to ski both areas without returning to base. The upper terminal of the cableway is at Tannenbodenalp where the nursery slopes and the larger part of the accommodation are situated. Flumserberg lies in a snow pocket, and in spite of its relative lack of altitude the lifts normally remain open till the end of April. Situated on a sunny terrace overlooking a valley, the area provides a variety of accommodation, with particular emphasis on apartments and chalets. There are various hotels and 'club' hotels, apartments which can be hired by groups for self-catering, and there are good facilities for children.

The skiing is divided into two main areas:-

Tannenheim Area: A 12-person gondolaway rises from Tannenheim, 4,001ft., to Prodalp Hotel restaurant, 5,168ft., and a 4-seater chair-lift continues the ascent to Prodkamm, 6,366ft. Here there is a restaurant and one has a beautiful view over the valley, vast areas of ski-touring snowfields extending into the distance. Open south facing intermediate runs of about 4km. lead down to Tannenheim, and one can also ski across to join the Maschgenkamm area by forking off to the left from Prodkamm on an east facing intermediate run to the foot of the Obersäss drag-lift.

Tannenbodenalp Area: From the north-west edge of the village a gondolaway rises to Maschgenchamm restaurant, 6,622ft., from which one has glorious views of the surrounding countryside. Supplementing the lower section is a 4 seater chair-lift reaching Chrüz, about a third of the way up, with easy runs back to the village. The upper section of the gondolaway is also supplemented by a 4 seater chair-lift serving intermediate runs from the top to the base. In the centre and crossing below the gondolaway, is the Obersäss 4 seater chair-lift. The two upper lifts allow interesting variations on easy and intermediate runs on south east facing slopes without returning to the village. All 4 seater chair-lifts can be used to get from Tannenbodenalp to Maschgenchamm, thus fully supplementing the gondolaway.

On the north-eastern side of the top station one can ski down to the frozen lake of Seebenalp by taking the longer easy run or the more direct intermediate approach. From Seebenalp, a drag-lift takes one up to Stelli on the ridge and from here one has a wooded run back to the village, which can be taken off-piste in spring snow. Alternatively one can take the chair-lift from Seebenalp back to the top station. From the top, and also on the north-east side, there is a 7km. run down to Oberterzen, which is easy until Seebenalp, and becoming difficult as it winds its way through the valley, a vertical descent of 4,474ft. One returns to Tannenbodenalp in 10 minutes by the gondolaway. On the north-eastern side of the top station a chair-lift, running from Grueb (halfway down the easy Seebenalp run) to Leist, 7,287ft., extends the range of skiing for the advanced skier. On the southern side of Tannenbodenalp there are intermediate runs down to the small village of Bergheim, with a drag-lift back to Tannenbodenalp. From Tannenbodenalp one can see the lower langlauf circuit, which lies between the two areas; a higher, more demanding one lies above Prodalp. In addition, there is a vast, magnificent ski touring field extending into the depths of the Flumserberg mountains.

In a Few Words: A lively and friendly resort, very popular with the Swiss and excellent for families. The slopes are in the main wide, gentle and open, sometimes wooded, with plenty of opportunity for off-piste skiing and a good choice of descents; most marked pistes are of easy and intermediate standard. Efficient lift system with little queueing. On a sunny terrace but with good snow till late season. Skiing area extended by present and projected lift construction. Good base for ski touring. Less expensive than many Swiss resorts.

Après Ski: The Slalom bar, next to the Tannenboden Hotel, is the centre of night life in Tannenbodenalp, with live music; and in the afternoon, the large café/bar in the old Tannenbodenalp Hotel is full of atmosphere, wooden panelled and festooned with antlers; the Alpina Hotel also has live music daily at tea-time and in the evening and an informal atmosphere; whilst the Chuestall bar has live music from 1700 hours and a wide variety of fondues. In Tannenheim, the Hotel Edy Bruggmann has an attractive large octagonal restaurant with dance floor and music; below is the Edy-bar, a dimly lit keller bar with disco, popular with young people. Nearby is the pleasant Bergroch café. There is a natural ice rink, sleigh rides, prepared nordic ski trails and 20km. of cleared walks. All the hotels have restaurants open to the public.

Recommended Hotels:

Hotel Alpina: Situated just across the road from the Tannenbodenalp ski-lift and gondolaway, this hotel has been reconstructed and is now a modern hotel, informal in atmosphere. One enters on ground floor level and the light and comfortable reception area and dining room are on the next floor. Agreeable dining a room with view over the valley, and black birds painted on the windows to prevent real birds from crashing into them. Friendly and quick service, appetising and satisfying meals. Bedrooms with shower/wc. On the ground floor, lively bar with band in afternoon and evening.

Sporthotel Baselbieterhaus: Near the lifts, this is a hotel which provides especially economical accommodation for groups; often large groups of children, or families. Rooms with up to 6 bunk beds for children, with wash-basin and floor showers, basic and simply furnished. 16 rooms with bath or shower. Dining room and sitting rooms. Games room for children.

Hotel Tannenboden: Over 80 years old, this is a completely wooden hotel, with the fish-scale effect of the wooden tiled exterior characteristic of old buildings in this part of Switzerland. Simply but comfortably furnished bedrooms, carpeted, all with wash-basins. Shower on each floor. Those under the roof have sloping ceilings. The panelled dining room has windows on three sides; the café/bar is popular with locals and has a hunting atmosphere with deer's heads on the walls and chandeliers made of antlers. A building of great character. The rustic Slalom bar has live music. The Garnihotel next door has 20 modern bedrooms all with bath, wc., radio. Also solarium and sauna.

PIZOL

Height of Resort: 1,686 ft. (Bad Ragaz)
1,755ft. (Wangs)
Height of Top Station: 7,283 ft. (Bad Ragaz)
7,306 ft. (Wangs)
Nearest International Airport: Zurich
Map Reference: 3D See page 240
Route by Car: See pages 236-240
Resort Facilities Charts: See page 223
Hotel Reference Charts: See page 232

The Pizol mountain overlooks the town of Bad Ragaz and the village of Wangs, the former primarily a spa situated in the valley of the early Rhine, offering skiing as an additional activity. It is only an hour away from Zurich and can easily be reached by road or rail at any time of year. A 2-stage 4-seater gondolaway rises in 25 minutes to Pardiel where there are three houses with youth hostel type accommodation. From Pardiel, 5,373ft., a drag-lift rises to Laufboden, 7,283ft., and from here there is a choice of runs of easy to medium standard over wide open slopes. There are two other drag-lifts which serve the slopes below Pardiel, a small one covering an excellent beginners' slope, and a longer one, Schwamm, which caters for the most difficult run in the area, vertical descent 921ft.

A similar area can be reached from the small village of Wangs, some 10 minutes' drive from Bad Ragaz. The skiing is very much like that on the Bad Ragaz side, but the slopes narrower. From the edge of Wangs village a gondolaway rises to Furt, 4,992ft., with its restaurant and from here two surmounting drag-lifts reach the top station, 7,306ft., where one finds another restaurant and a drag-lift serving the top slopes. From the restaurant one can cross over and ski down to Bad Ragaz, via Laufböden and Pardiel, mainly on intermediate or difficult runs over northerly orientated slopes or return to Wangs with a choice of an easy run or a difficult run, the latter closely following the line of the lifts, giving a vertical descent of some 5,500ft. It seems a pity that the two top stations are not yet linked by lifts. Although both base stations are low the upper areas served by drag-lifts have a much longer season. Nordic skiing is also available.

In a Few Words: Bad Ragaz, being a spa resort, has a good variety of recreational facilities; the skiing could be improved considerably by link lifts at the top. A good base for those with a car wishing to visit nearby ski resorts.

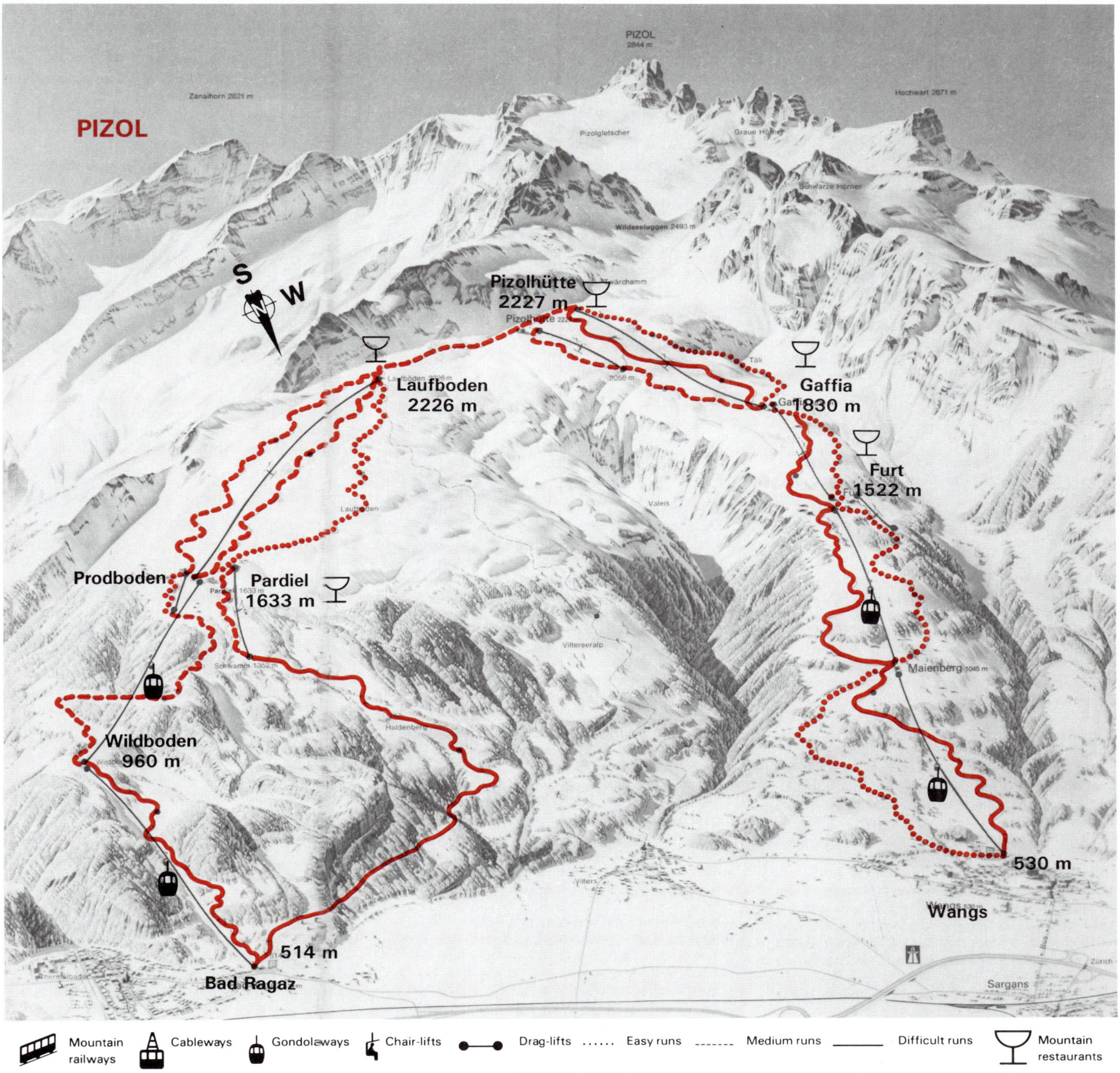

Après Ski: Swimming is well catered for with two indoor and one outdoor heated pools, the thermal water being pumped from the mountains 4km. away. There is an indoor tennis centre, and other forms of sport and entertainment as well as excursions to nearly places of interest.

Recommended Hotels:

Hotel Derby: Situated on the edge of Bad Ragaz, by the foot of the gondolaway, a small, informal hotel, with modern bedrooms, all with bath or shower. Bar popular with locals. Cinema, bowling, and sometimes live band for entertainment.

Hotel Sandi: Situated near the station , this is a very comfortable, modern and efficiently run hotel. Dining room beautifully decorated with flowers, excellent cuisine formally presented. Carpeted bedrooms with a vast amount of storage space, balcony, spacious bathroom with temperature-controlled taps; radio, telephone.

Hotel Garni Rössli: A bed and breakfast house centrally but quietly situated. Bedrooms have balcony, radio, TV, telephone, bath/shower and wc. Comfortable sitting room, restaurant.

FLIMS – LAAX
FALERA

Height of Resort: Flims: 3,615 ft.
Laax: 3,346 ft.
Height of Top Station: 9,902 ft.
Nearest International Airport: Zurich
Map Reference: 5C & 6C See page 240
Route by Car: See pages 236-240
Resort Facilities Charts: See page 222
Hotel Reference Charts: See page 232-233

After travelling on the motorway south-west from Chur for 10km. one takes the approach road to the right, which is steep in places, and one arrives in Flims 11km. later, whilst Laax is 5km. further on. The mountain road runs through picturesque scenery with magnificent views across the Vorder Rhein valley. Much development of the ski area has taken place over recent years which is known as the 'White Arena' and its interlinking lift system consists of 32 lifts serving 220km. of marked pistes.

FLIMS
This resort is made up of two villages 1km. apart, Flims Waldhaus and Flims Dorf. Although the latter is more convenient for the skiing the former is more attractive with a larger number of hotels and shops camouflaged by beautiful trees which line the streets. The skiing is divided into three areas:

Foppa - Naraus - Cassons Grat: From the south west side of Flims Dorf a triple chair-lift rises to Foppa, 4,658ft., where one finds a pleasant restaurant. The easy run back to the village follows the toboggan run which is about 3km. in length. The second stage of the chair-lift reaches Naraus, 6,036ft., where there is another restaurant. Runs back each side of the chair-lift are intermediate whilst the two drag-lifts in the area which cross the chair-lift provide access to easy and medium runs. Near the foot of the lower drag-lift is the restaurant Spalegna. This is small, interesting and not too crowded since it is a little off the beaten track. Next door is a little gem 'Raclette-Treff', where mainly raclette is served. This is a must for a different lunch, but seating only about 10, some planning is required. The final ascent to Cassons Grat is by a small cableway, and here at a height of 8,858ft. is a further restaurant from which, after a climb of about 100 metres, there are magnificent views of the whole area and the surrounding peaks. The run back to Naraus is difficult but for the less experienced an enjoyable intermediate run swings westwards to Segneshütte and thence south-east to Foppa. From Nauraus there is an easy and enjoyable run across to Startgels, the top of the gondola lift from Flims.

Startgels - Grauberg: From the south-west of Dorf a 2-section gondolaway swings its way up to Startgels, 5,216ft., where there is a deservedly popular Italian restaurant, Trattoria Startgels. There are easy runs back to both Dorf and Waldhaus. A triple chair-lift reaches Nagens from Startgels, giving access to a difficult slope, Platt'Alva, leading back to Startgels. From Startgels also, a cableway reaches Grauberg, 7,309ft., and the Segnes-Hütte restaurant is situated below this top station. To the left of the cableway intermediate runs are to be found down to Startgels and Foppa whilst to the right, an easy run to start with links up with the difficult run from Nagens to Startgels. There is a straight forward run from here down to Flims with flattering schusses. About halfway down watch out on the right for the sign for the Runcahöhe restaurant. This requires poling down a long path, but it is worth it. The variety, quality and price of the food, plus the ambience of this restaurant make a visit there one of the priority items of the holiday. A short bumpy path gets one quickly back to the piste.

Nagens Area: Crossing over on an easy run from top station Grauberg and passing an excellent restaurant on the way, one reaches the Nagens area served by 4 drag-lifts and a triple chair-lift. This is delightful open south facing skiing with runs to suit the inexperienced and intermediate skiers. From here one can move across and up eventually to La Siala and thence across to Vorab, all by relatively easy skiing. Alternatively via the foot of Nagens one can take either of the two difficult runs down to Plaun, 5,282ft., the link with Laax. A chair-lift takes one back to the foot of Nagens's lowest drag-lift. From this vast snowfield there are wonderful views across the valley to the Laax area (see below).

LAAX
Laax is 5km. from Flims and the ski area embraces the villages of Murschetg and Falera. The largest is Laax, an attractive resort with a lake, numerous guest houses and hotels. Murschetg is situated near the foot of the lifts. Falera, 3km. to the west of Laax, is an attractive small village with limited shopping facilities and only two hotels. A ski bus, free of charge for skiers, connects all three villages. The skiing is divided into three areas:

Murschetg - Crap Sogn Gion: A cableway rises from the complex to Crap Sogn Gion, 7,283ft., where there is a hotel with restaurant facilities for non-residents. The cableway runs late to service dances at Hotel etc. This point can also be reached from Murschetg by taking the 12 person gondolaway to Curnius and the 4 seater chair-lift to Crap Sogn Gion. From the top one has a good selection of runs: a difficult south-east facing piste follows the line of the cableway and to the right, intermediate runs follow the line of the drag-lifts to the bottom station and easy runs to Falera near the bottom of the run to Murschetg, where there is a restaurant, Larnags. Although in a busy area an excellent and good value lunch can be obtained. To the left of the top station one finds excellent intermediate and difficult runs down to Plaun and the link chair-lift with La Siala. This lift closes early and one should always check.

Crap Sogn Gion - Crap Masegn: The cableway from Crap Sogn Gion rises to Crap Masegn, 8,126ft. which is the link with the Vorab Glacier area (see below). To the right of this top station, which has an Italian restaurant, 'Das Elefant', there are easy and intermediate south-west facing runs down to Midada Sut, following the line of the long chair-lift which returns one to the top. Runs of the same grade descend over south-east facing slopes to the foot of Treis Palas drag-lift, which rises to the crest beneath the cableway. To the left of the top station a short intermediate run over north-east facing slopes leads to the second stage of the gondolaway to Vorab, whilst a long east facing run of the same grade crosses to Plaun for Nagens area.

Crap Masegn - Vorab Glacier: From Crap Masegn inexperienced skiers can take the two-stage gondolaway to the Glacier restaurant, whilst others can ski down to the first station and pick up the second stage. From the restaurant a double drag-lift rises north-west to the highest point of the whole area, 9,902ft., and to the left a chair-lift forks out westwards to 9,307ft. From both top stations the runs to the restaurant and to the middle station of the gondolaway are easy. For the experienced skier an exhilarating, difficult south facing run leads down to the foot of Midada Sut chair-lift, whilst from the Glacier restaurant an interesting intermediate run over east facing slopes terminates at Plaun to connect with the chair-lift to Nagens area.

Lift pass: One lift pass covers the White Area of Laax, Flims and Falera with a total of 225km. of well prepared runs. Single tickets are for non-skiers only. Included in the lift pass is the ski-bus, which covers the whole area.

In a Few Words: An extensive ski area with a well laid out lift system providing runs for all grades. Well placed mountain restaurants amidst beautiful scenery. Extensive langlauf trails and plenty of cleared walks for the non-skiers. One of the most attractive resorts in the Alps, sophisticated and one of the most popular resorts with the Swiss, Germans and Italians.

Après Ski: Flims has a number of night clubs, a popular one being the 'Caverna' in the Bellevue Hotel with a cellar more than 400 years old. There are many excellent restaurants with local, Swiss and international cuisine (fondue, raclettes, Italian etc.) There is a large choice of swimming pools all in the hotels but open to outside visitors as well as a public pool in Laax; bowling, skating, curling, and the Park Hotel Waldhaus Flims and Hotel Signina, Laax each have two indoor tennis courts. The Sports centre Prau la Selva, between Flims and Laax, has ice skating, ice hockey, curling, shooting gallery and a fitness club. Other activities include ballooning, hang-gliding, para-gliding and riding. Laax has a good choice of restaurants and two night clubs, the established Casa Veglia and the Camona. Both have live music and disco. Two of the most convenient spots for an après ski drink are the 'Iglu Bar' in Flims and the 'Crap Bar' in Laax-Murschetg, both at the foot of the lower lift stations.

Recommended Hotels – Flims:

Albana Sporthotel: A medium-sized hotel ideally situated next to the ski lifts. A very pleasant reception area decorated with rustic furniture. A staircase with a huge window running the full height of the hotel leads outside guests to a comfortable restaurant situated on the first floor. Excellent food is served to guests in their own rustic style restaurant. The bedrooms are large, comfortable and well furnished, all with bath or shower. Indoor car park. An 'English Pub' is open to visitors.

Hotel Adula: A truly superb hotel situated in Flims Waldhaus. As one enters the reception, the comfortable sitting rooms lead off to the right. The dining room leads off to the left. A gourmet restaurant, the Barga, well known in Flims, is off the reception area. A pianist plays here every day and guests can eat specialities of the house in front of an open fire. In addition, the restaurant La Clav serves Italian food with a selection of exquisite Italian wines. A large swimming pool, sauna, steambath and massage are a particular feature of the hotel.

Park Hotel Waldhaus: This is the largest and most luxurious hotel in Flims. Situated in Waldhaus this pleasant elegant hotel boasts the best facilities which include indoor tennis, a magnificent swimming pool, 2 bars, 2 restaurants (including an Italian restaurant). The numerous reception rooms are comfortable. The whole complex which includes 5 separate buildings are all connected by heated underground walkways. A pleasant bar provides the focal point of many good evenings.

Recommended Hotels – Laax:

Sporthotel Happy Rancho: A very large hotel situated about 600m. from the main lift complex. Unusual in design insofar as the hotel is split into about nine separate units all under the same roof. The whole is connected by a concourse in the basement with 9 lifts connecting each section. Accommodation consists of 60 double rooms and 40 beautifully equipped apartments – some with their own separate fireplace. Some of the facilities include: fitness/gymnastics room, swimming pool,

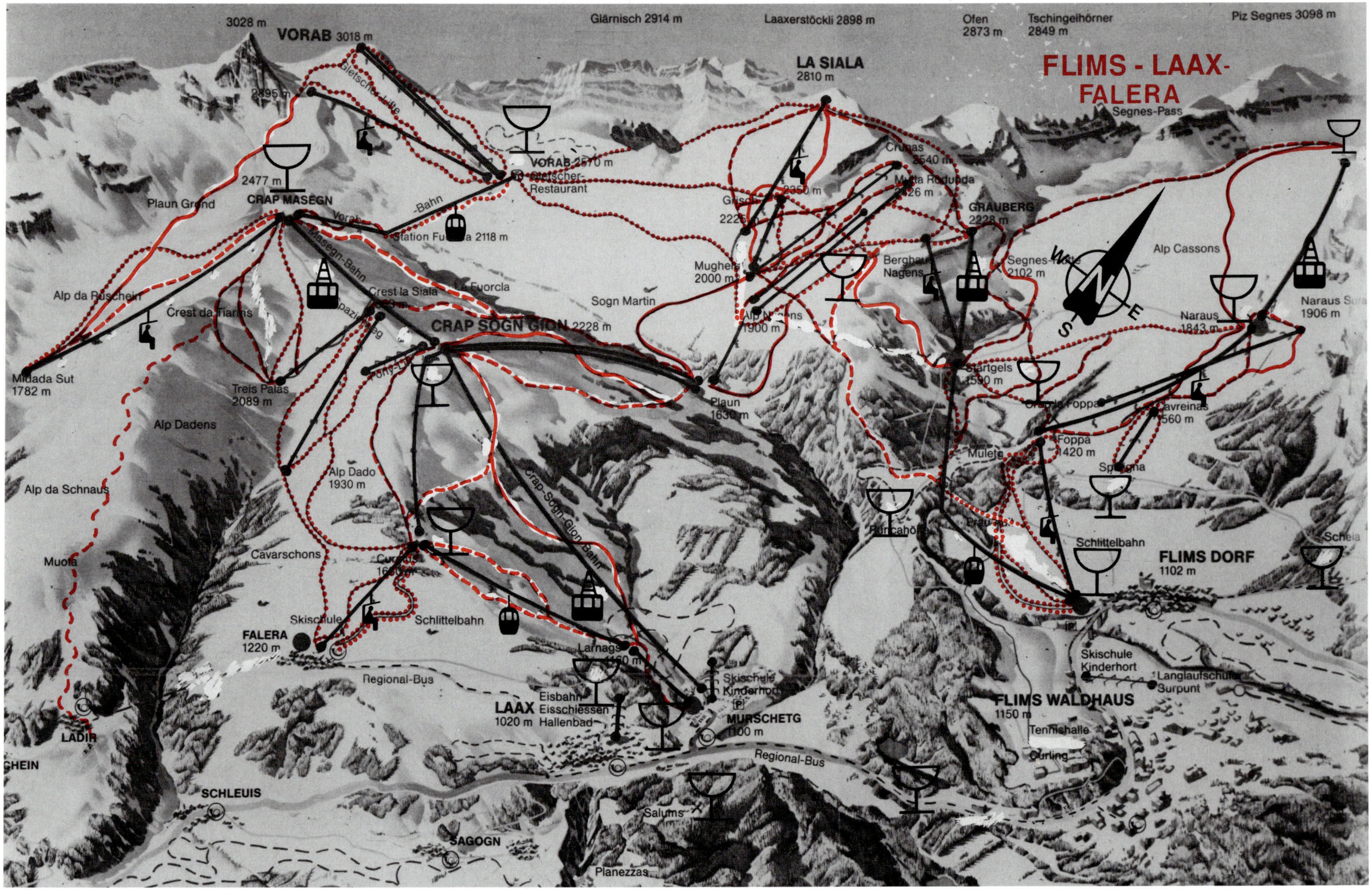

Mountain railways — Cableways — Gondolaways — Chair-lifts — Drag-lifts — ...... Easy runs — --------- Medium runs — ______ Difficult runs — Mountain restaurants

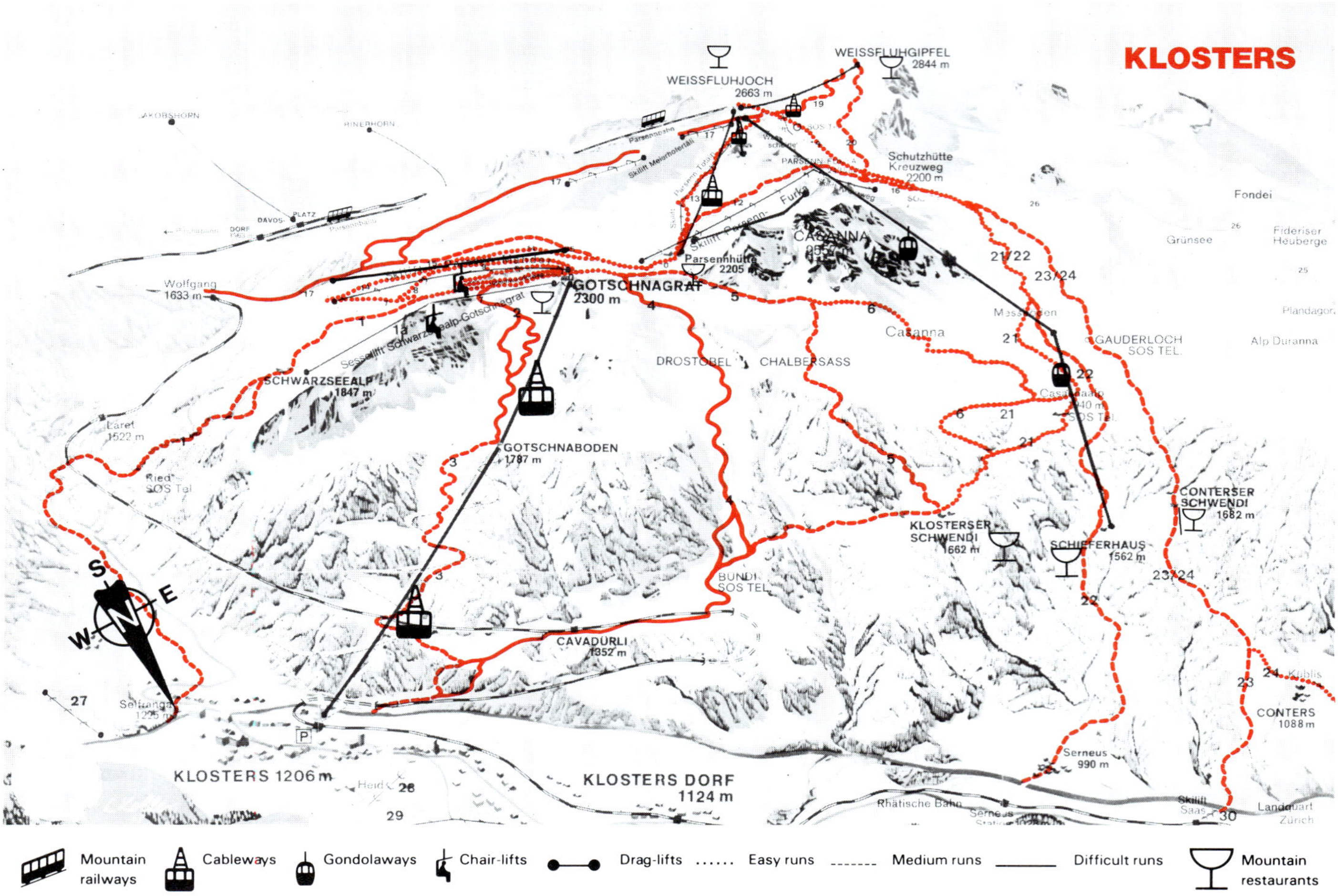

sauna, massage, hotel ski instructors and guides, ski kindergarten, solarium, ski acrobatics instructions (in the summer). This latter is on an artificial ski slope outside with a jump into a specially constructed swimming pool. The reception is large and luxurious with the main dining room leading off. This is light and airy. All guests are made welcome by a party on their first night. Other events are arranged throughout the week. This first class hotel is ideal for families, the single or the elderly. All facilities laid on.

Hotel Larisch: A very pleasant small hotel situated away from the village centre. As well as the 20 double bedrooms there are 5 apartments ideal for family use. A pleasant light and airy dining room provides a beautiful view up the mountain. A sauna is provided for guests. Pleasant sitting rooms. A swimming pool in the hotel next door is available free to guests of the Hotel Larisch.

Hotel Riva: Beautifully situated on the banks of the lake in Laax. Medium sized hotel with large pleasant reception. Leading off is the main dining room decorated in rustic style with a separate room for wild 'Fondue Parties' which are a speciality of the hotel. The main bedrooms all consist within 'apartment blocks' of 3 or 4 rooms per apartment. Each room has its own lock. These rooms all share the bathroom of the apartment. Bedrooms are comfortable and well equipped. Skating on the lake is immediately adjacent to the hotel. Swirmming pool. A pleasant bar.

SAN BERNARDINO

Height of Resort: 5,249 ft.
Height of Top Station: 8,283 ft.
Nearest International Airport: Zurich
Map Reference: 2B See page 240
Route by Car: See pages 236-240
Resort Facilities Charts: See page 223
Hotel Reference Charts: See page 233

This attractive small resort lies at the southern end of the famous tunnel of the same name, some 2 hours' drive from Zurich. It is situated in a sunny position near the Italian border surrounded by scattered pine woods.

From the western side of the village a gondolaway rises westwards to a pleasant mountain restaurant, 6,397ft., and nearby a trainer lift. From the restaurant a drag-lift, Tre Uomini, continues westwards to the top station, 8,283ft. Here, well above the tree-line, one can take an easy run southwards to the foot of the Rotond drag-lift which rises to 8,218ft. There are easy runs down both sides of this lift and from the base one can continue down to the restaurant, all runs over open, east facing slopes. From the top station of the Tre Uomini drag-lift and on the northeast side there are good intermediate runs down to the restaurant swinging out north-eastwards and thence curving round south-eastwards all over wide open slopes. From the restaurant to the village there are intermediate runs each side of the gondolaway through wide wooded glades to start with but becoming narrower towards the village. On the south east side of the resort there is a 600 metres long drag-lift serving easy runs for beginners. Nordic skiing is also well catered for with 25km. of trails through beautiful wooded countryside.

In a Few Words: A small attractive resort with a compact lift system serving 50km. of well prepared runs. Because of its height and the orientation of the runs the resort, under normal conditions, has a long season. Suitable for beginners to intermediates. Excellent facilities for Nordic skiing with 25km. of marked trails.

Après Ski: Normal facilities for a small resort, cosy bars and restaurants. Disco dancing at the Hotel Albarella which also has a very fine swimming pool. A natural skating rink, curling and pleasant walks through the beautiful surrounding area. Excursions are also arranged to Locarno, $1^1/_2$ hours away.

Recommended Hotels:

Hotel Albarella: Situated on the edge of the village 5 minutes' walk to the nursery slopes and about 6 minutes to the foot of the gondolaway, the attractive modern Hotel Albarella has 130 beds. It is made up of apartments for 2, 3 and 4 persons all with bath, wc, balconies, radio and telephone, all comfortably furnished. The hotel's extensive facilities include: restaurant, grill room, lounge with open fire, disco/bar, indoor swimming pool, skittle alley, games room, conference rooms and sun terrace.

KLOSTERS

Height of Resort: 3,908 ft.
Height of Top Station: 9,262 ft.
Nearest International Airport: Zurich
Map Reference: 6C See page 240
Route by Car: See pages 236-240
Resort Facilities Charts: See page 222
Hotel Reference Charts: See page 232

Klosters, situated in the Grisons, is reached by the Rhaetian railway from Landquart. It still retains its village atmosphere and is considerably smaller and thus more attractive than Davos, a further 10km. up the line. It is a fashionable and sophisticated resort, ranging from large first class hotels to the smallest pensions and is divided between Klosters Platz, the main part, and Dorf, about 2km. apart. There are three ski and snowboard schools with good nursery slopes and drag-lifts, free for pupils, adjacent to the village. Before describing its enormous scope for downhill skiing, one should mention that Klosters is popular for nordic skiing, with several prepared tracks into the Vereina Valley and to Serneus ranging up to 50km. (including one on which owners can exercise their dogs!). There is a toboggan run from Gotschnaboden and the usual other winter sports facilities, i.e. skating rink, curling, sleigh rides, swimming, para-gliding. It is, however, for downhill skiing that Klosters is justly famous and there are two main areas: the Gotschna-Parsenn area, which is linked with Davos and the Madrisa area. A free bus service operates every 20 minutes between Klosters Platz and Klosters-Dorf and every hour to Serneus, Monbiel and Selfranga.

Madrisa Area: Constructed in the 1960's, this area is reached from Dorf by the Klosters-Madrisa gondolaway rising to 6,322ft. At the top station one finds the Saaser Alp mountain restaurant, a very long drag-lift, the Schaffürggli, rising to 7,852ft. and for novices, the double Saaser Alp drag-lifts. Further over to the north-west is another long lift, the Glattegen, to 7,249ft. All these are interconnecting and as the slopes are generally south-east, south and south-west they get the sun throughout the day and there are excellent possibilities for spring skiing. The slopes here are well maintained and ideal for beginners to intermediates. In addition there is a network of walks, dotted with benches, so that the Madrisa is an area where the whole family can keep in touch, whether skiers or not. Also an ideal area for small children with its own kindergarten. The longer runs are 3km. back to the restaurant, whilst the rather more challenging run from here to the bottom station is 6km. Perhaps the best runs, however, and certainly the longest, are those over the saddle on the other side of the Schaffürggli lift down the Schafcalanda from the Madrisa lift, rising to 8,338ft. to the Zügenhüttli drag-lift, from where one can return to Saaser Alp, or continuing down either via the village of Schlappin (deserted in winter), or by the remote and charming restaurant Erika and thence down the long valley back to Klosters Dorf. This beautiful run, over 9km., is a memorable experience and should not be missed. Although graded as 'difficult', this is only in relation to the other runs in the area and in fact there are no sections that a moderate skier could not manage in suitable conditions.

Gotschna-Parsenn Area: The Gotschnagrat cableway is situated in Klosters Platz, just behind the railway station. The first section rises from 3,936ft. to Gotschnaboden, 5,861ft., the second to Gotschnagrat, 7,544ft., total height difference 3,608ft. Capacity on the first section is 1,200 persons per hour and 1,400 on the second section. The Gotschna-Parsenn abonnement includes five cableways, two gondolaway, three chair-lifts and 12 drag-lifts including 3 in the village. This permits one to connect with all the Davos Parsenn skiing including the highest point, the Weissfluhgipfel, 9,260ft. and includes the Parsenn funicular up from Davos and a reduction on other Davos ski areas of Pischa, Jakobshorn/Bramabüel, Schatzalp/Strela and Rinerhorn (for details see under Davos). An abonnement for the two areas Klosters/Davos includes 55 ski lifts in one abonnement, the REGA pass. It is available for 2-22 days and not expensive.

This superb Parsenn area is too large to describe in detail. Suffice it to say that it contains some of the longest runs in the world and caters for every standard of skier from beginner to expert. Runs back to Klosters from Gotschnagrat average about 5km., whilst those to Serneus, Saas and Küblis, from where one returns by Rhaetian bahn, can be anything up to 14km. The Casanna run to Klosters and the famous Küblis run, to quote but two, can be tackled by relative beginners. At the other end of the scale, the steepness of the Wang under the cableway to Gotschnaboden is breathtaking. There is a large choice of off-piste runs through wooded terrain, down to Klosters/Serneus and stations lower down the valley. As these slopes are generally north-east facing, the powder snow can be excellent. Dotted around the whole area are attractive and unspoilt mountain restaurants. As mentioned under Davos the 6 seater gondolaway, operating from Schifer Haus restaurant to Weissfluhjoch carrying 1,700 persons per hour and called the Parsenn Schiferbahn, has improved the skiing tremendously in this area.

In a Few Words: Klosters is a charming resort and a good alternative to Davos for people who prefer the smaller more attractive village. Skiing for all grades in some of the best skiing terrain in the world. Good ski schools; extensive langlauf; kindergarten; variety of night life; sophisticated; expensive but excellent value abonnement. New lift ticket system 'top card' (see Davos report).

Après Ski: A good selection of night life, with Davos only 10km. away for further variety if required. There are bars, restaurants and night clubs in all price ranges. The Hotel Vereina has piano music in its Scotch Bar. The rendezvous in Klosters is the Chesa Grischuna – tables must be booked for the evening; the food is good and prices are not outlandish. The attractive, dimly lit Casa Antica is a popular and lively discothèque with good music and atmosphere. The Kir Royal in the Silvretta Parkhotel alternates between live and disco music. In Klosters-Dorf the Madrisa Bar and Rufinis both provide lively discos.

Recommended Hotels:

Hotel Chesa Grischuna: An attractive chalet style hotel, exquisitely furnished in typical Grisons style. The bedrooms are pretty and cosy, most of them with private bath. The Chesa restaurant is one of the most popular meeting places in Klosters for lunch (large terrace) and dinner. A pianist entertains for tea and during the evening during high season. Bar, bowling.

Grand Hotel Vereina: An excellent hotel in the centre of the village. It lays special emphasis on its very good facilities for children; and is a hotel of first-class amenities and comfort without ostentation. 160 beds, most rooms with bath, spacious reception rooms, Scotch bar, brasserie bar, children's playroom, kindergarten, indoor swimming pool, solarium, free sauna from 4 to 7 pm, sun terrace.

Silvretta Parkhotel: Opened in December 1990, this 4-star chalet hotel has 110 rooms, all with bath or shower, telephone, TV, minibar and safe. Facilities include an à la carte restaurant, an Asian restaurant, a cosy stüberl, a piano bar, the Kir Royal night club with dancing to band or disco. The fitness centre has a bowling alley, swimming pool, sauna, Turkish bath, solarium and massage. There is also a beauty salon, kindergarten and an extensive covered car park.

Hotel Steinbock: This pleasant hotel, 3 minutes' walk from the Gotschnagrat cableway, is decorated in traditional wooden style and is centrally situated, near the beginners' lifts and on the bus route to Madrisa. All rooms with bath/shower, telephone, radio, TV and minibar. Gourmet restaurant. Sauna, Turkish bath and whirlpool. Very popular, particularly with the locals.

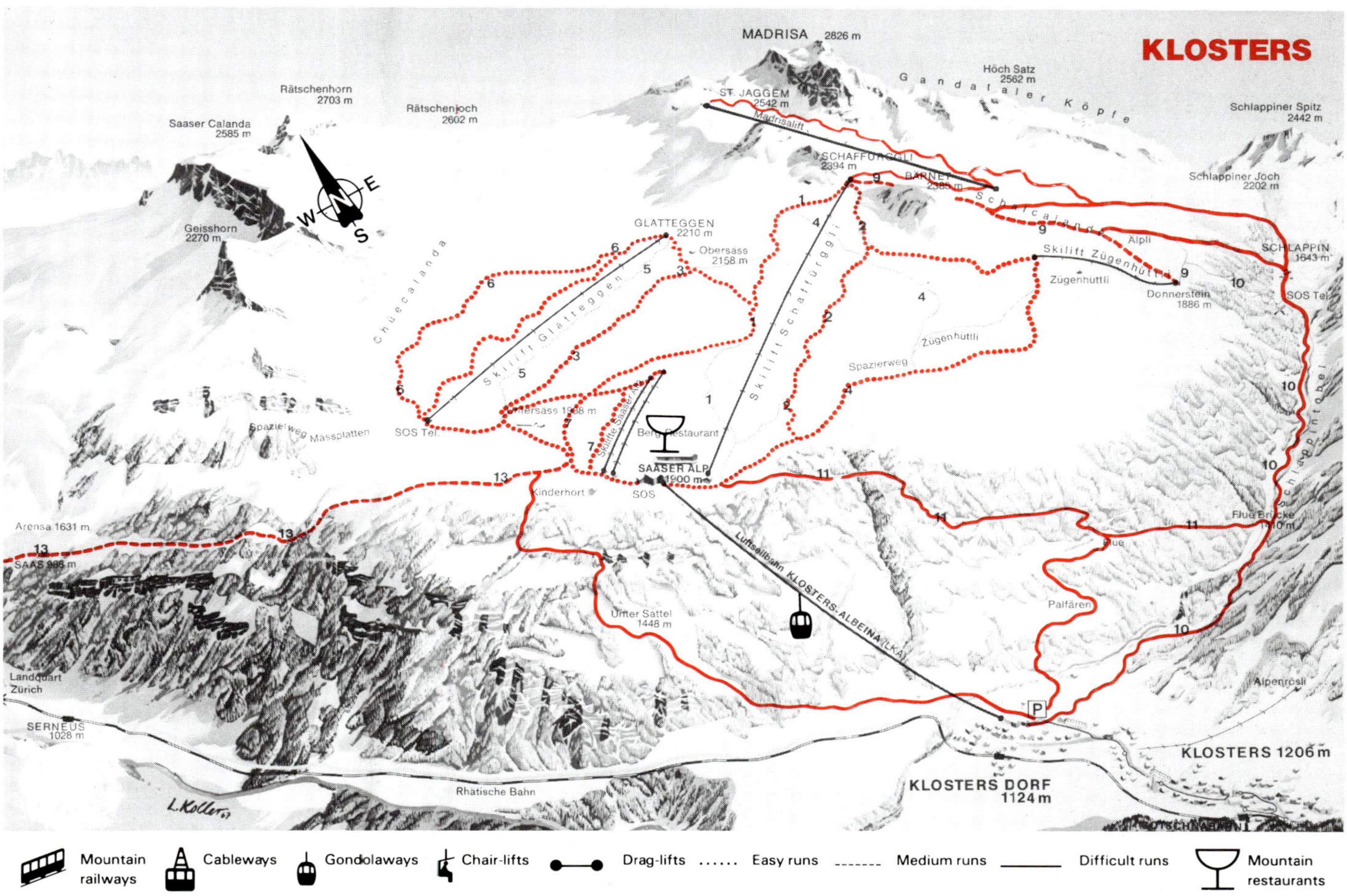

DAVOS

Height of Resort: 5,118 ft.
Height of Top Station: 9,262 ft.
Nearest International Airport: Zurich
Map Reference: 6C See page 240
Route by Car: See pages 236-240
Resort Facilities Charts: See page 222
Hotel Reference Charts: See page 232

Davos is the highest town in Europe and Switzerland's largest ski resort. The town straddles a through route for some 2 miles, the buildings themselves do not add to Alpine splendour but for skiers this is compensated by some of the world's longest, varied and beautiful ski runs. The resort is divided into Dorf and Platz accessible by train from Zurich. Trains leave Zurich for Landquart every 60 minutes, where there is a connection to Davos. By car much of the road from Zurich to Landquart is motorway and the remaining 30 miles from Landquart is over a well maintained road.

Accommodation of all types is available from 90 hotels and 3,900 chalets and holiday apartments. Facilities in the resort include:- ski touring, Nordic skiing, snowboarding, hang gliding, 84km. of cleared walks, 6 indoor and outdoor curling rinks, 14 indoor swimming pools, 1 cinema, a tennis, squash and badminton centre, toboggan run with curved banks, riding school and hall, an ice sports stadium and a 22,000 square metres skating rink in Platz. Convention centre with theatre performances, concerts, lectures, exhibitions and sports events, a gaming room. In the mountains there are some 25 restaurants to choose from. The Davos Kirchner Museum opened in 1992 and is devoted to the work of the German expressionist painter and also of considerable architecural merit. In the same year a winter sports museum was opened.

The five main ski areas have 88 runs totalling some 270km. in length. The areas are linked by buses running at 5 minute intervals during the day along the valley road. The Parsenn, Schatzalp-Strelapass and Gotschna areas are linked above the valley. Klosters which has access to the Parsenn also has 13 runs on the Madrisa mountain totalling some 60km. and can be regarded as part of the area; indeed the REGA ski pass covers all the skiing in Davos and Klosters, together with all buses and interconnecting trains.

Rinerhorn Area: Reached by car on the Platz to Glaris road, or every 60 minutes by a 10 minute train journey from Platz or every 20 minutes by bus (free service). A 6 seater gondolaway rises to Jatzmeder in under 10 minutes (1200 persons per hour). The journey through the trees is very beautiful. At Jatzmeder there is a rustic type restaurant with open fire, where the grills are good, so is the apfelstrudel with vanilla sauce. In this area there is skiing for all standards. To the left of Jatzmeder and a short run down, one finds two parallel drag-lifts rising to Juonli, 7,832ft., from which there are easy, intermediate and difficult runs, in addition to a special run for children. Further to the left one finds the Hubel rustic type restaurant and drag-lift more suitable for beginners. To the right of Jatzmeder further parallel drag-lifts rise to Nüllisch Grat, 8,197ft., serving runs for all standards. The runs in the area are usually quiet and there can be very good powder snow. Below Jatzmeder three runs continue through the woods and fields to the Glaris end of the Rinerhorn chair-lift bottom station. Pistes in the area are from 1-5km. in length.

Jakobshorn Area: The main cableway to Ischalp, 6,350ft., starts near Platz railway station, capacity about 770 persons per hour. At Ischalp there is a restaurant and a second cableway rises to Jakobshorn, 8,417ft., with its restaurant and sun terrace. The most difficult and well-known run down is the Jakobshorn Nord, with moguls to start with, thence intermediate and an easy run in as one approaches Ischalp. To the right is the Usser Isch drag-lift serving two 2km. long intermediate runs. From half-way down one can pick up easy runs to Ischalp and to the base of the Clavadeler Alp drag-lift which rises to short of Jakobshorn; these two top stations are connected by a short cableway. To the right of Clavadeler Alp and running parallel, is the Jatz drag-lift, which has a restaurant at the top, the runs down are intermediate. Also converging on this top station is a shorter lift serving easy runs. There are two interesting runs to the valley each side of Jakobshorn which are not controlled and therefore are not always open. To the right looking down is the 4km. Teufi run where one passes a pleasant rustic restaurant. To the left is the Mühle run down to the cosy Landhaus Frauenkirch restaurant.

From Ischalp a drag-lift rises to Bramabüel, 8,130ft. The two 3km. runs each side are difficult to start with, this area is well-known for its large moguls and thence intermediate after about one km. for the run into Ischalp. There are paths down to Platz from Ischalp and the base of Clavadeler Alp drag-lift, both are about 4km and are easy to ski except one small section. In December 1995 a new chair-lift was opened from the valley to Usser Isch, 6,804ft., with the Panorama restaurant at the top station.

Schatzalp-Strelpass Area: The Schatzalpbahn funicular railway rises from Platz to Schatzalp, 6,068ft., where there is an attractive old 4-star hotel, a prepared walk and toboggan run down to Platz. From Schatzalp a recently installed chair-lift links with a drag-lift up to Strelapass, 7,636ft. There are only two drag-lifts at this level, one mainly serving beginners slopes, and the other the difficult and intermediate runs from the top of Strelagrat, 8,125ft., back to Schatzalp. There are also off-piste runs from this summit to Arosa and Glaris. From Strelapass the Hauptertäli cableway crosses eastwards to connect with the Haupter Tälli drag-lift which rises to Weissfluhjoch, 8,740ft., thereby linking this area with that of the Parsenn.

The Parsenn Area: The funicular railways rise 3,622ft., in two stages from Dorf to Weissfluhjoch, 8,740ft., (1,080 and 1,160 persons per hour respectively). From the first stage Höhenweg, 7,210ft., there are three difficult runs back to Dorf. From Weissfluhjoch, where the avalanche centre is sited, there are easy runs down to Höhenweg also to the foot of the Haupter Tälli drag-lift to the south-west and to the Parsennhütte to the north-east. The run down the west side of the Meierhofer Täli drag-lift is more difficult. The highest station in the whole area, Weissfluhgipfel, 9,262ft., is reached by cableway in under 3 minutes from Weissfluhjoch, it takes up to 100 persons. There is a restaurant at this top station and wonderful views of the surrounding area. Both runs down are difficult until they join some of the most interesting runs in the area leading from Weissfluhjoch to Küblis, 14km., Saas, Serneus

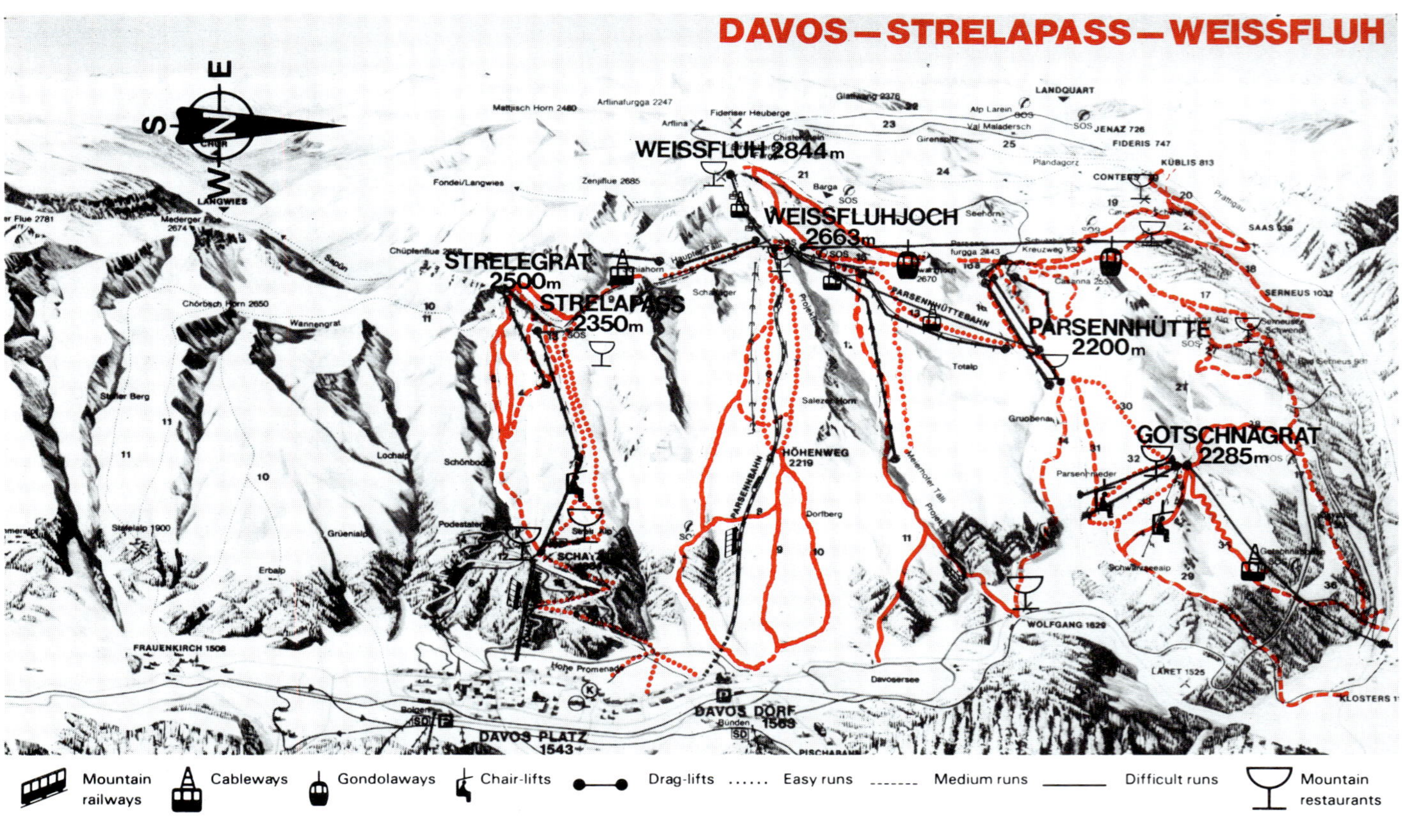

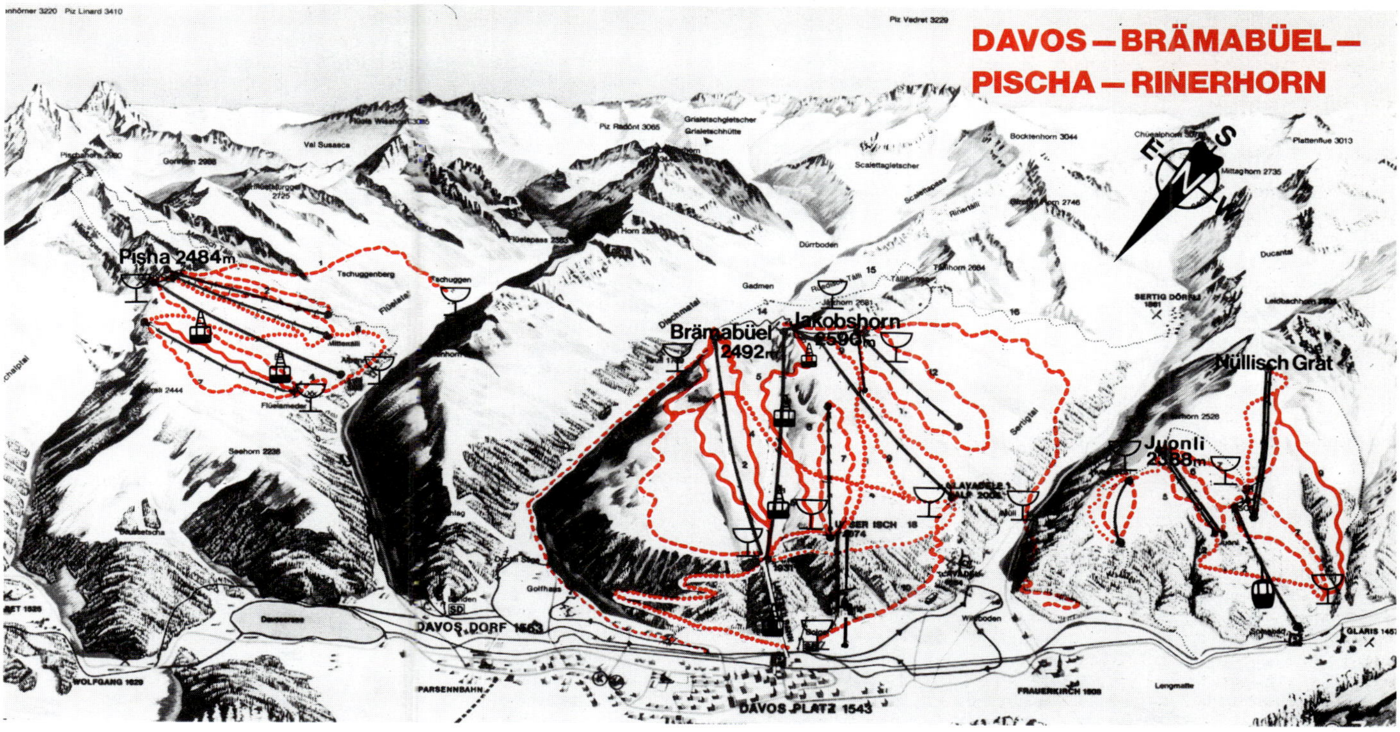

Mountain railways | Cableways | Gondolaways | Chair-lifts | Drag-lifts | ...... Easy runs | ------- Medium runs | ______ Difficult runs | Mountain restaurants

and Klosters. At the end of all these long runs one can return to Davos by rail, except from Serneus where one has to take the bus to Klosters. A 6 seater gondolaway from Schifer to Weissfluhjoch has changed the face of skiing on the north side with a direct return to Weissfluhjoch. All four runs have restaurants en route. From Klosters it is also possible to return to the Parsennhütte by the Gotschnagrat cableway. At the latter's top station there is a restaurant and two lifts in the area serving intermediate and easy runs. From the Parsennhütte one can take the cableway, up to Weissfluhjoch or ski down to Wolfgang and take the train or the bus back to Davos.

Pischa Area: Reached by bus, free service, leaving from near the Parsennbahn every 15 minutes between 0800-1600 hours. The journey to Dorfji, 780ft., above Davos takes about 10 minutes. It is not possible to ski back to Davos. This area is above the tree line and is entirely on its own. From Dorfji the Pischabahn cableway rises 2,210ft., to Pischa, 8,076ft., in about 8 minutes. Generally the skiing is not exciting but it is a useful area for intermediate skiers who require less crowded and sunny slopes. There are ten variations of descent served by three drag-lifts in addition to the cableway. Most of the runs are about $2^{1}/_{2}$km. in length, the standard run which is wide and fast is longer. There is also an interesting unmarked run to the north-east of the Pischabahn, on the ridge before the descent one has a wonderful view of the surrounding peaks and Davos. There are four restaurants in the area.

Ski Pass with Integrated Microchip: Since winter 1994/95 it is even easier to ski in the Davos/Klosters region – the entire area was the first region in Switzerland to have the new type of **Hands Free System** installed. The new credit card size ski pass – a top card with individual programming – can be read and checked at the turnstiles without any physical contact, i.e. there will no longer be any need to insert the ski pass into a scanner; it can simply stay in your pocket or wallet. This will mean less queueing at the ski resorts, particularly at peak times.

Beginners & Children: Beginner's slopes and lifts in Platz are located at Bolgen, near the Jakobshorn cableway lower station. Those in Dorf are at Bünda, about 400 metres from the start of the Parsenn railway. There are beginner's and children's classes and ski kindergartens for 3-10 year olds at Bünda and Pischa.

In a Few Words: Superb skiing catering for all standards, about 30% of the runs are for beginners, 40% for intermediates and 30% for experts. Noted for its long runs; off-piste skiing can be excellent with day tours being a special feature when conditions are right. Pistes are well maintained and the vast lift system transports 39,000 persons per hour (55,000 per hour in Davos/Klosters area combined). Whilst the runs are well marked, improvements could be made by showing the destination and distances on the posts. Increased lift capacity from valley stations still required along with 4 seater chair-lifts instead of the long drag-lifts. Bus and train connections between areas are good, and there is a wide selection of mountain restaurants and plenty of activities for the non skier.

Après Ski: Masses of bars and restaurants and 16 night clubs with live music and discothèques. These night spots vary considerably in standard. In Dorf a popular stop after skiing is the Parsenn hotel for beer and Käsekuchlein (cheese tart), for cakes try Café Weber. The Hotel Derby's Palüda Bar is delightfully decorated in Grisons style and you can sit in a cosy bar on the balcony, or near the dance floor and enjoy a meal cooked on a large open grill, with music in relaxed style. There is a good grill room at the Hotel Flüela (Dorf), a small stübli, dancing and good food, effective decor and wayout music at the La Bohème, one of the best spots.

A rustic atmosphere can be found in the small Chämi bar where there is taped pop/rock music for the young clientele; the Central has a piano bar which is very popular, and the food is good there. Also good value is the Montana, with open fireplace and rustic decor. The Hotel Europe (Platz) is impressive, with two night clubs, four restaurants and piano bar. The Post Hotel has a very good restaurant. The Pöstli Corner for après ski drinks and snacks, whilst the Pöstli night club is sophisticated with live music, it is not cheap, neither is the Cabanna club with disco and live music. More reasonable is the Jakobshorn club with its small disco bar.

For those staying in apartments there are many places for eating out, to mention but a few:- Restaurants Central and National are two good basic places to eat; excellent pasta/pizza will be found at Pizzeria Padrino; also in the Hotel Davos Face. The Golden Dragon Chinese restaurant in the Hotel Terminus in Platz is upmarket. The cinema shows English films and there are indoor swimming pools, riding, skating, ice hockey, squash, tennis and romantic sleigh rides to the beautiful surrounding valleys.

Out of Town: Hubli's Landhaus restaurant at Laret serves very good nouvelle cuisine, whilst the restaurants at Teufi & Islen and the Frauenkirch Landhaus all have good basic menus.

Recommended Hotels:

Hotel Bellavista: Situated in Platz near the Horlauben bus stop, and Congress Hall. Completely rebuilt in 1987/88, a family run hotel with restaurant, lounge with cheminée, bar, sauna, conference room. All bedrooms with bath, wc, direct telephone, radio-clock, colour TV and safe. Parking and garage.

Club Hotel: This large 300 bed hotel is situated in Davos Platz. Most of the accommodation is in studios or apartments all with private bath and wc. and equipped with minibar and foldaway beds. The large bar and dining room is open plan with large tables, very suitable for parties and families. Indoor swimming pool, 2 saunas, fitness room and massage, table tennis and two squash courts.

Hotel Derby: One of the best hotels in Switzerland, most efficiently run under the personal supervision of the manager, Hans Rudolf Schmid. Situated in Dorf, 180 metres from the Parsennbahn, in a sunny position, set back from the main street in its own grounds. Comfortable, well furnished rooms, completely renovated in 1994. Spacious reception room and bar, an attractive two-tiered dining room with excellent food and service. New conference centre for 200 persons.

Delightful Palüda Grill. Indoor swimming pool, sauna, health and fitness centre, massage, curling and kindergarten.

Hotel Flüela: A de luxe hotel situated in Dorf and a short walk from the Parsennbahn. Many of the bedrooms have been remodernised. Spacious and attractively designed reception rooms, elegant cocktail bar, piano entertainment and attractive stübli in Grisons style. Indoor swimming pool, solarium, sauna, Turkish bath, massage, hairdresser and Credit Swiss Bank. The Hotel Flüela has been in the Gredig family for over 130 years. Special 'Ski Packages' at beginning and end of season.

Hotel Meierhof: An excellent modern hotel in Dorf, centrally situated and furnished in delightful traditional style. All rooms with bath and many with balcony, attractive dining room, cosy grill room with adjoining piano bar, first class cuisine and cellar. Particularly friendly, helpful manager.

Post Hotel: Attractively refurnished and with a modern wing, this hotel is in Platz. Nice bedrooms, spacious and well appointed public rooms. Indoor heated swimming pool, night club, boutique, sauna.

Hotel Schweizerhof: A first class hotel in Platz with a choice of several reception rooms, elegant dining room. Spanish bar, resident band, heated indoor swimming pool, sauna, solarium, masseur and roof garden sun terrace.

Hotel Sonnenberg: A quiet family hotel in Dorf, providing comfortable accommodation, friendly atmosphere, good food and efficient service. Swimming pool, sauna and solarium. Ten minutes' walk from Parsennbahn.

Hotel Terminus: In Platz and conveniently situated for the Jakobshorn lifts. Attractive wood panelled à la carte restaurant, large dining room, bar, stübli which is popular with the locals, and a Chinese restaurant.

LENZERHEIDE-VALBELLA

Height of Resort: 4,822/5,062 ft.
Height of Top Station: 9,397 ft.
Nearest International Airport: Zurich
Map Reference: 6C See page 240
Route by Car: See pages 236-240
Resort Facilities Charts: See page 222
Hotel Reference Charts: See page 233

Lenzerheide-Valbella lies in a beautiful area and is made up of two attractive villages, about 2km. apart and separated by the Heidsee lake. The scope of its skiing is wide and contrasted, and it is served by an excellent lift system. The wide, sunny valley runs north to south and the hotels and chalets are surrounded by pine trees on the lower slopes. 28 hotels and pensions provide only 2,400 beds, and the numerous chalets and apartments a further 12,000. The efficient lift systems, with 37 lifts and capacity for 33,000 persons per hour give access to 156km. of marked pistes. A free shuttle bus service enables one to reach all main terminals in either of the two ski areas without difficulty.

Eastern Area: A two stage cableway rises to Rothorn, 9,397ft., departing from a terminal between the two villages and easily reached via a small drag-lift on the north of Lenzerheide 100m. from the Hotel Danis. The journey to the first station, Scharmoin, 6,232ft., takes 6 minutes, where there is a very nice panoramic restaurant; there is another at Rothorn with wonderful views, and the second stage journey takes 8 minutes. Supplementing the first section up to Scharmoin there is a 4-seater gondolaway with 99 cabins in all. A steep and fairly difficult run leads from the top over north-east facing slopes, the piste straight at first, then twisting until it reaches a 600m. tunnel broken by a bridge midway. This is not for the faint hearted as there is a climb round a ridge at the exit with a sheer drop first to one side, then the other, before one reaches the lovely open piste, which will be much enjoyed by medium skiers. It starts steeply and descends over north-west facing slopes for about 5km. to Scharmoin, vertical descent 3,165ft. Four drag-lifts in this area give a wide variety of skiing on treeless slopes. At the top of the Schwarzhorn, reached by chair-lift, one has a view over the valley to Hörnli, Arosa. Runs from Scharmoin to the foot of the cableway are about 2km. in length through wide glades, and from top to bottom the run is about 13km., vertical drop 4,428ft.

Western Area: Quite different from that on the opposite side of the valley, this area is covered by an intricate and superbly contrived lift system, and one can begin or end at either side of either village. From the southern side of Lenzerheide, the Tgantieni triple chair-lift rises to 5,674ft., where there are two good restaurants. A surmounting triple chair-lift goes to Piz Scalottas, 7,636ft., with another restaurant. A run of 3km. leads from here to the village, vertical descent 2,690ft., or by skiing across to the foot of two further surmounting drag-lifts, Pedra Grossa, with its Alp Nova restaurant, and Piz Gertrud, one can weave one's way towards the Valbella side. The Piz Gertrud almost reaches Piz Danis, 8,191ft., and from here there is a run to Lavoz, with another restaurant and drag-lift to just below the Stätzerhorn, 8,446ft. One can ski straight down to Valbella from here, or take advantage of a

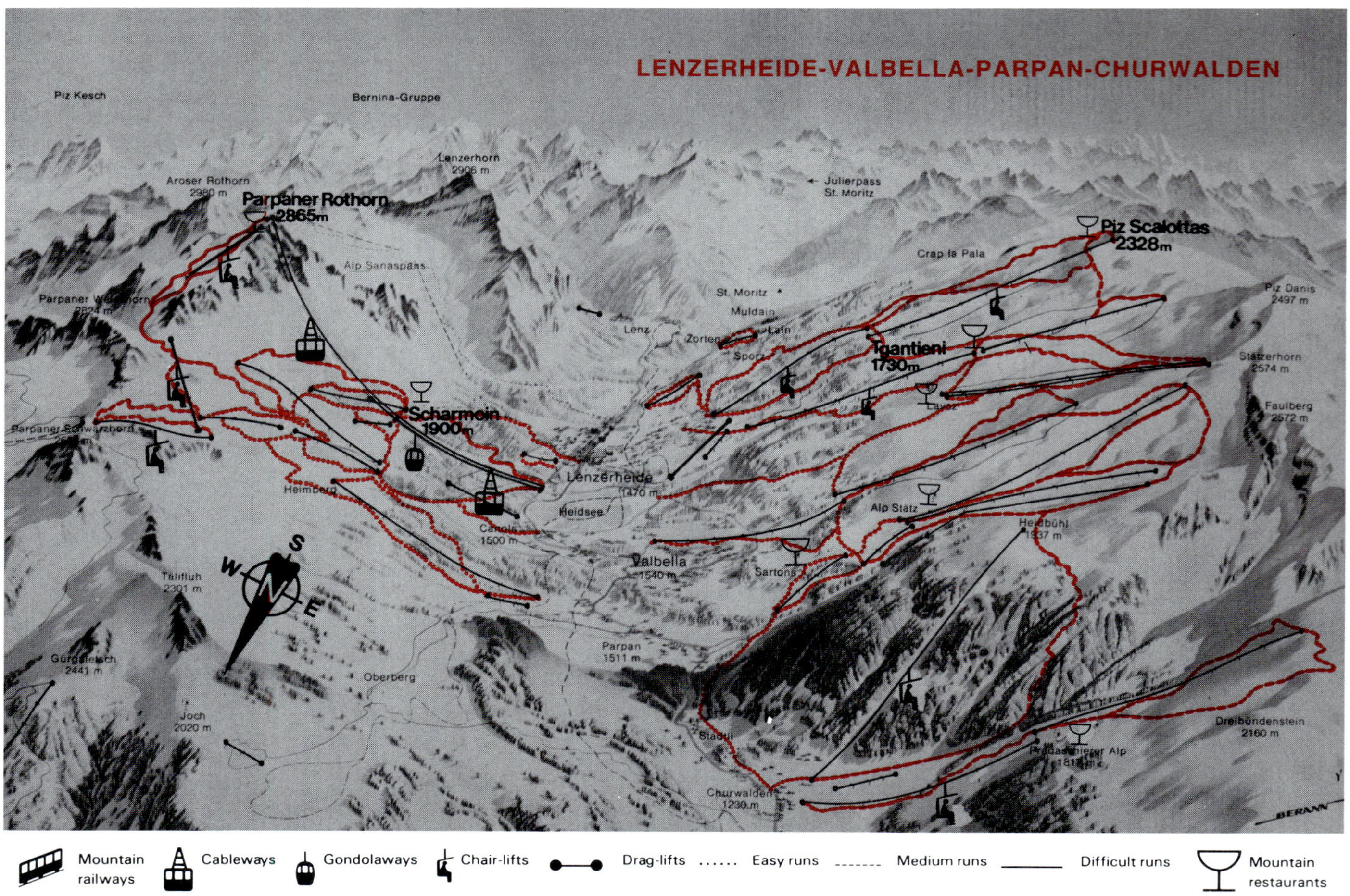

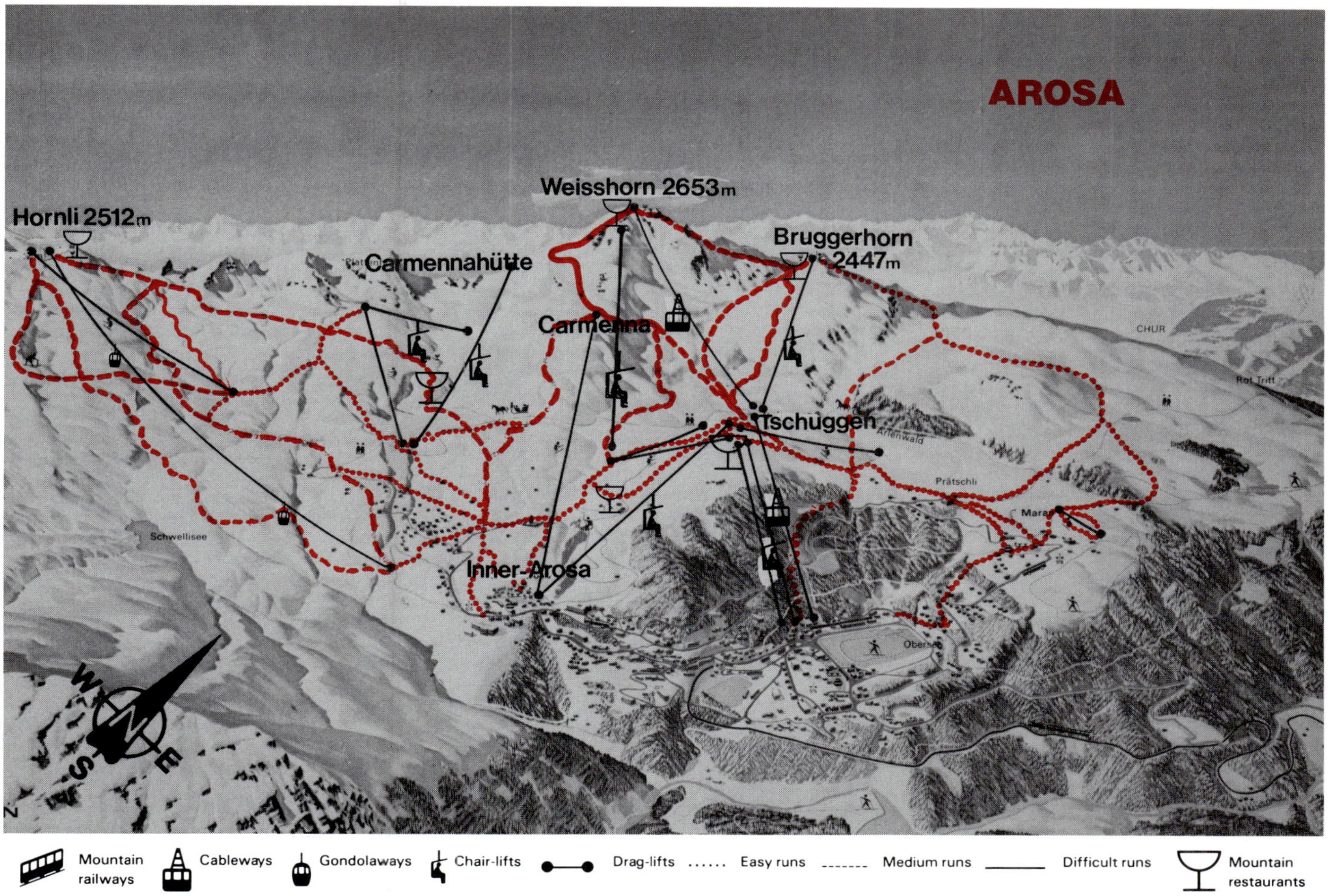

further six drag-lifts on these slopes, providing some enjoyable medium skiing. Alternatively one can ski down to Churwalden, taking in a further three lifts. At the end of a day's skiing one can return to Lenzerheide by bus or make one's way through the same series of lifts in the other direction to Tgantieni. It is an interesting area and provides some excellent skiing. The upper slopes are above the tree line and the wooded slopes are open enough to give ample space to turn, mainly east and north-east facing. By zig-zagging down to the lower terminal each time, crossing this network once, produces total downhill running of 18-20km. in length and vertical descent of 15,000ft.

In a Few Words: Excellent and varied skiing, suitable for all standards, particularly medium to good intermediate, catered for by two compact lift systems; 13 well placed mountain restaurants; attractive scenery; reliable snow. Friendly atmosphere. A very good family orientated resort, with special ski classes and kindergartens for children aged 2 upwards; langlauf.

Après Ski: Many hotels have night clubs, and amongst the most popular is the night spot in the Hotel Waldhaus and Posthotel (Valbella) and the Tic Tac Club and Joy-Club in Lenzerheide. There is a night club, the Heini Hemmi-Bar in Hotel Valbella Inn. Lenzerheide also has a large natural ice rink, 50 km. of nordic ski trails, cleared walks, curling, tobogganing, indoor tennis, squash and bowling, and there is a road from Scharmoin to the valley with sledge rental. Ski-bobbing, ice hockey, sleigh rides and swimming are also available.

Recommended Hotels:
Grand Hotel Kurhaus: A large modern style hotel with long bright dining room and attractive grill room; two elegant sitting rooms; stübli type bar; dancing to band or disco; tastefully furnished bedrooms, all with bath or shower and many with large south-west facing balconies. Indoor swimming pool, sauna and massage.

Hotel Lenzerhorn: In the centre of Lenzerheide village and near the skating rink and ski school meeting area. Large bright dining room; rustic style à la carte restaurant with dancing to pianist; small stüberl; cosy and nicely furnished sitting room; modern style bedrooms with radio, most with bath or shower.

AROSA

Height of Resort: 6,000 ft.
Height of Top Station: 8,658 ft.
Nearest International Airport: Zurich
Map Reference: 6C See page 240
Route by Car: See pages 236-240
Resort Facilities Charts: See page 221
Hotel Reference Charts: See page 232

Arosa is a village built on a fairly steep incline at the head of the Schanfigg valley and is reached by a road climbing for 31km., rising 3,645ft., with a further 600ft., to climb to reach the western side of the village from the entrance (10 minutes by bus or half an hour's brisk walk). Its mountain background is glorious; the winding main street stretches from one end to the other with most of the hotels lining either side, and a view to the south over a horizon of snowy peaks. There is accommodation for around 8,000 visitors. The lift system is excellently linked so that whichever end of the town one's hotel is, it is easy to interchange from one ski area to the other, and there is a free bus service for everybody.

Oversee Area: On the eastern side, the main lift is the Weisshorn cableway, newly built for the 1992/93 season, with a capacity of 1,200 persons per hour. First it climbs to the middle station, 6,603ft., with a restaurant, 'Brügger Stuba', with a large sun terrace. The second stage travels to Weisshorn, 8,658ft., where there is a restaurant with two large sun terraces and a moving staircase to the top of the mountain. Alternatively, turning off to the right from the first station, a double chair-lift rises to Brüggerhorn, 8,004ft., with another restaurant. In the area of the first station of the cableway one finds the Tschuggen east drag-lift supplemented by a triple chair-lift and the west drag-lift along with the Ried drag-lift which all serve the slopes east and west of the first station. From the bottom station the Ried drag-lift, a 4-seater chair-lift rises to just below the Weisshorn summit.

Inner-Arosa Area: To the west, the Hörnli 6-seater gondolaway travels to Hörnligrat, 8,179ft., where there is a restaurant and sun terrace. It has a capacity of 2,000 passengers per hour. The Hörnli chair-lift starts about halfway up this slope and converges with the top station. Two ingeniously arranged drag-lifts, the Plattenhorn and Carmenna, form the link which enables skiers to move freely across these extensive, open and sunny slopes from one area to the other, finishing wherever they choose. This area was further improved by the installation of the Bänkli double chair-lift, rising northward from the base of the Plattenhorn drag-lift past the Carmennahütte to the ridge below the Weisshorn. A second chair-lift, Obersäss, starts from the Carmennahütte running northwestward to the top station of the Plattenhorn drag-lift. A triple chair-lift also links Inner-Arosa to Arlenwald Road and thence by second stage of the cableway to Weisshorn and from here a marvellous panorama spreads out before one.

The open, upper slopes provide medium to difficult skiing, whereas beginners will find the lower slopes suitably gentle. The slopes towards the eastern side are south facing but snow normally remains good because of the high altitude. The Hörnli area consists mainly of east and south-east facing runs and conditions are best here in the afternoon. Runs are up to 5 or 6km. in length, difference in height 3,000ft. Extensive ski touring is possible as far as Lenzerheide, Davos and Klosters. Ice hockey, skating, curling and Bavarian curling are available on a choice of ten rinks:- a covered artificial one 33

× 66 metres, an open-air artificial rink, 55 × 99 metres, and natural rinks at Maran and Inner-Arosa, making a total area of about 15,000 square metres. Instruction is available for all sports. A high standard of food will be found in the mountain restaurants. The Alpenblick is near the foot of the gondolaway, its excellent rosti not to be missed, and the Café-Fertig is well worth a visit. For non skiers there are over 40 km. of cleared walks from which one can reach all the mountain restaurants and ski areas. For non-skiers lift passes are half the normal price.

In a Few Words: A very enjoyable resort for most standards of skiing, perhaps somewhat limited for the most advanced. Excellent for family groups with children, who are well catered for, with babysitters and kindergarten available; good ski touring; snow-shoe walking, sledging, horse-drawn sleighs, in-golf, para-gliding; plenty of cleared walks; good range of hotels; après ski varied. Excellent snow record.

Après Ski: Available at all hours! There is a good choice of night spots, most of them fairly casual in style. There are plenty of outdoor activities for non-skiers, more than 40km. of beautiful walks up through the woods to the snow-covered pastures, a passenger flight with the hot air balloon 'Arosa', skating rinks, curling, and sleigh rides along the famous Arlenwald Road. The Arosa-Kulm Hotel was completely rebuilt some years ago but its old much-loved bar has been preserved and transplanted into the new entertainment area and their bands are some of the best in the resort. The Post Hotel has an excellent restaurant and pizzeria; the Post Bar is still a lively dancing spot. There are good restaurants as well as dancing at the Carmenna Gada, or the discos 'Nuts' and the 'Kitchen Club' at the Hotel Eden. The Tschuggen Hotel has a ballroom and orchestra for traditionalists. Various hotels provide a relaxing atmosphere with a pianist in the bar.

Recommended Hotels:

Arosa Kulm Hotel: Close to the slopes and cableways, this renovated hotel boasts rooms decorated with personal taste. Superb food served in different restaurants. Extensive wine cellar. Theme nights. English speaking staff. Located within is the fitness and beauty college, (sauna, massage, gymnasium, solarium, hairdressing). Swimming pool and children's playground.

Hotel Bellevue: A very nice first class hotel with every modern comfort. Spacious and pleasant entrance hall adjoining extensive lounge, Bündnerkeller restaurant open until the small hours, renowned for excellent service and cuisine. Bedrooms very comfortable, all with bath or shower, fitness centre with sauna, whirlpool and Kneipp bath. Under personal supervision of the owner, Mrs. D. Hold.

Hotel des Alpes: A very good first class hotel, centrally situated and conveniently placed for the Carmenna lift. Good size and attractively designed bedrooms nearly all with private bath. Spacious reception rooms with elegant decor, cosy bar with pianist, sunny roof terrace.

Hotel Hold: A small but extremely popular hotel opposite the Arosa Kulm and well placed for the Hörnli gondolaway. Cosy bedrooms nicely decorated, homely reception rooms and the long bar room is a popular meeting place. Efficient and friendly service.

Hotel Tschuggen: An impressive modern building, completed in 1971, well situated for the Carmenna lift. Very smart entrance hall with attractive bar sitting room adjoining. Large dining room with wooden ceiling and windows along two sides, twice weekly gala evenings, three à la carte restaurants, long sitting room with wooden beams and pillars, grill room. Tschuggen night club with dancing to orchestra in dance bar. Roof garden restaurant and swimming pool, sauna, massage, beauty parlour, bridge room, stübli with bowling alley, Italian restaurant 'La Vetta', ski shop and nursery. Ski-bus shuttle service. Dress formal in dining room and ballroom.

ST. MORITZ

Height of Resort: 6,088 ft.
Height of Top Station: 10,837 ft.
Nearest International Airport: Zurich
Map Reference: 6D See page 240
Route by Car: See pages 236-240
Resort Facilities Charts: See page 223
Hotel Reference Charts: See page 233

St. Moritz forms the centre of a vast ski area, linked by lift systems, rail and road, the surrounding resorts in some cases nearer the major lifts than St. Moritz itself - Pontresina- Diavolezza/Lagalb, Muottas Muragl, Corvatsch-Silvaplana and Sils-Furtschellas. St. Moritz is a large resort with a wide range of accommodation, with hotels of every type providing 5,750 beds and apartments a further 6,800. The skiing is divided into 5 areas:-

Corviglia Area: A mountain railway rises from the town centre of St. Moritz Dorf via Chantarella to Corviglia, 8,156ft., where there is a large restaurant with sun terraces. Runs from Corviglia fan out in all directions. To the south-west is the Salastrains chair-lift, with two restaurants (Zuberhütte and Salastrains), the Suvretta chair-lift and Signal chair-lift with restaurant Chasellas at the base and the Trutz restaurant at the top of the chair-lift and the Paradiso chair-lift with the Paradisohütte nearby. Runs down to Marguns, south of Corviglia, lead off in a north-easterly direction and to the south-west, a drag-lift and chair-lift rise to Plateau Nair and provide runs to Marguns and over the easy, open slopes to Corviglia. All runs in this area, apart from the tricky 'Flying Kilometre' are easy to medium-difficult. For those staying in St. Moritz Bad wishing to reach the Corviglia area one takes the cableway which connects with the Signal chair-lift and this runs parallel with the Salastrains chair-lift. Two miles of runs covered by snow machines.

Piz Nair Area: A cableway from Corviglia travels to Piz Nair, 10,029ft. Here there is a restaurant with fantastic views of distant surrounding mountains. Challenging and exciting runs down to Marguns are to be found in this area, served by the Fuorcla-Grischa chair-lift, ranging from medium-easy to medium-difficult in standard.

Corvatsch Area: 6km. by road from St. Moritz and above Silvaplana. From Surlej, where there is a restaurant, a 2-stage cableway rises to Murtél, 8,865ft., with further restaurant this section is covered by snow machines. Here two drag-lifts converge, one from Mandras, the other from Margun-Vegl, and a chair-lift leaves the base of this second lift, at right angles to it, and ascends to Giand'Alva, from this point one can enjoy the long Hahnensee black run down to St. Moritz Bad with its very pleasant restaurant about half way down. Murtél can now be reached from Alp Surlej by a quad chair-lift opened in 1993, making it unnecessary to ski all the way down to Surlej to get the cableway up again. It has also done much to reduce the waiting time for the latter, particularly during the morning rush. The second stage of the cableway reaches Corvatsch, 10,837ft., where there is a restaurant and an amazing view. A run from Corvatsch over the glacier divides into two and merges again at the foot of the Mandras lift: both within the capability of a good-medium skier. On the whole the runs are suitable for medium good standard and provide interesting and delightful skiing over both north and south facing slopes.

Celerina-Marguns Area: As well as the gondolaway travelling from Celerina to Marguns, 7,470ft., a drag-lift and chair-lift from Plateau Nair and Corviglia give access to runs down to this station, where there are two good restaurants. The skiing here is open and sunny, in a vast snow-bowl. The Trais Fluors chair-lift, to the north, reach a height of 9,060ft., and from the top is a run to Celerina of about 4km. via Marguns, vertical descent 3,384ft., or another to the base of the Glüna chair-lift. To the west a further chair-lift on Piz Grisch has extended the skiing in this area. All runs finish at either Marguns or Celerina. The Marguns-Celerina run is partly covered by snow machines.

Sils-Furtschellas Area: This is a relatively new ski area beyond Corvatsch and above Sils Maria. It is included in the Sport Bus itinerary. The cableway with its related chair-lift has transformed Sils Maria from a predominantly summer resort into an excellent winter one.

Already from the Furtschellas top chair-lift, 9,184ft., one can ski to Surlej-Corvatsch bottom station. The Curtinella drag-lift connects the two areas in both directions.

In short, the network provides yet another complete skiing area in the Upper Engadine.

The large cablecar takes one from Sils to Furtschellas, 7,583ft., where there is a restaurant and above this five interlinking drag-lifts spread out over a very wide area. The skiing, including the runs back to Sils, is mainly north facing, excellent and varied, suited to all grades of skiers. It was noteworthy in late March that, whilst there were enormous queues at the Corvatsch, there was no waiting on any lift in this area.

The following ski areas are easily accessible from St. Moritz by bus or car; Diavolezza; Piz Lagalb; Bernina-Paradiso Bianco; Languard; and are given under Pontresina: see separate report.

In a Few Words: The scale of St. Moritz is immense – its skiing, its hotels, its international set; the skiing provides plenty of variety for the advanced and intermediate skier, with excellent lifts, road and rail transport; good in March/April when it is less crowded; extensive areas covered by snow machines thus ensuring a long season a resort the good skier must visit once.

Après Ski: St. Moritz is world-famous for its night life, and this is certainly in the grand style, mainly sophisticated and expensive, with both sexes dressed to kill in glamorous evening attire - however, there's scope for jeans and sweaters too. In the Badrutt's Palace Bar you can dance to a lively band or in their King's Club discothèque. The Chesa Veglia has two typically Swiss-style restaurants, and serves excellent food cooked on spits. There is a wealth of non-skiing activities, fitness centres, the famous Cresta Run and the bob run, skating, swimming, curling, riding, large indoor tennis and squash centre, winter golf and polo tournaments, thrilling horse and greyhound races as well as cricket on the frozen lake, cinema and two interesting museums apart from the fun of being an onlooker of the exciting scene. The children's clubs are mainly open all day and several hotels also have arrangements for looking after children. If you're not feeling on top of the world as you should do in St. Moritz, there is a Health-Spa Centre, which includes mineral baths, drinking cure, peat packs, the Kneipp cure, and physiotherapy. There is not time in one visit to see and do everything, there's so much going on. The atmosphere is stimulating, the variety limitless.

Recommended Hotels:

Hotel Bären: A pleasant well-run family hotel in quiet position, 5 minutes from the centre. Decorated in traditional Swiss style, spacious bright dining room, comfortable sitting room, bar and very attractive swimming pool free to hotel guests.

Hotel Crystal: This superior 4 star hotel is centrally situated. All bedrooms are in Swiss pine or nut, with bath and shower, hairdryer, minibar, TV, radio and safe. Lounge with open fire, à la carte restaurant serving Italian specialities, fitness centre. Completely renovated in 1997, and a very well run hotel.

Hotel Kulm: A world famous hotel situated in a central and sunny position, overlooking the lake and the mountains of the Upper Engadine. 300 beds in 200 rooms with private bath, spacious in size and warmly furnished. Elegant and tastefully furnished public rooms: dining room, 10 sitting rooms, two bars, heated indoor swimming pool with sauna, massage, gym. Ice-skating and curling rinks with resident pros, sun terrace and rustic restaurant, child care facilities, "Sunny-Bar" dancing/nightclub with live music.

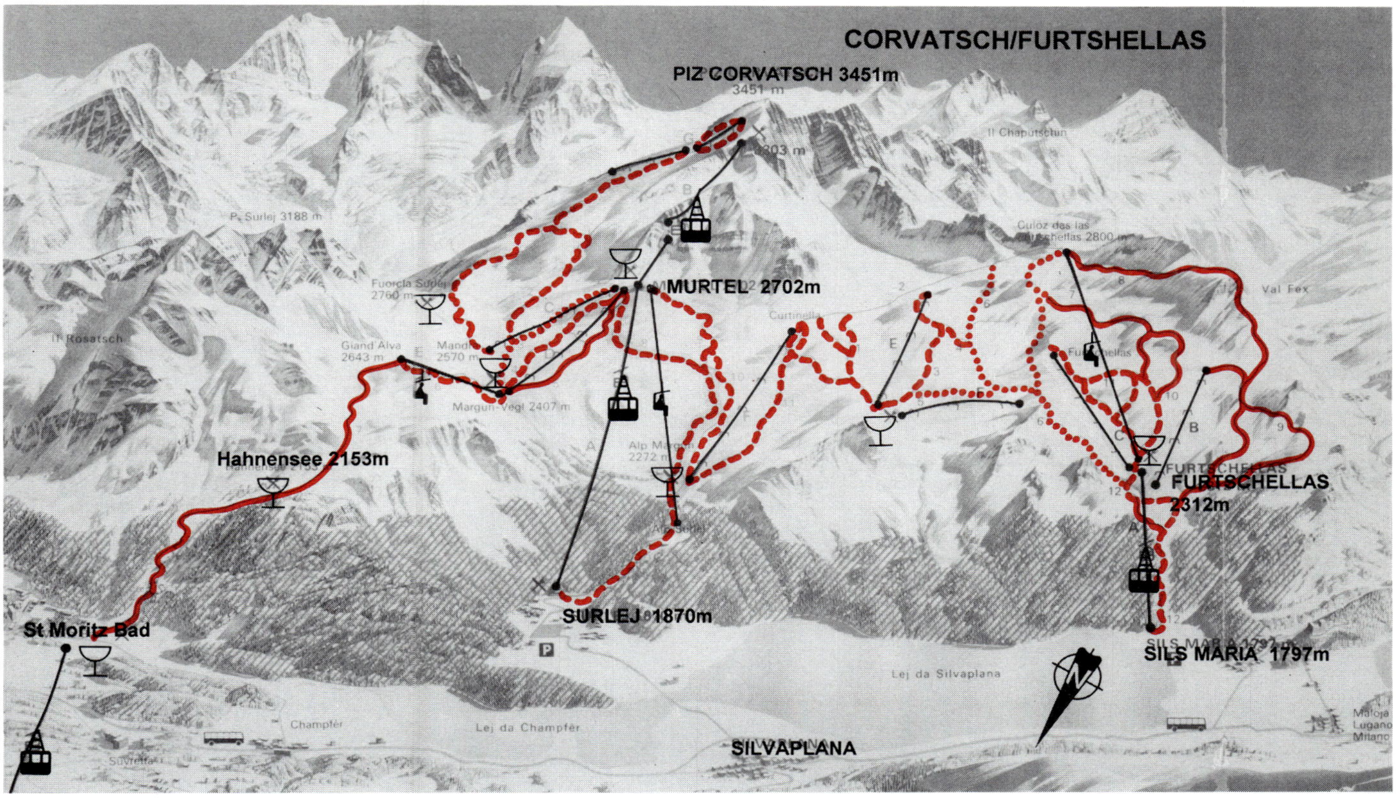

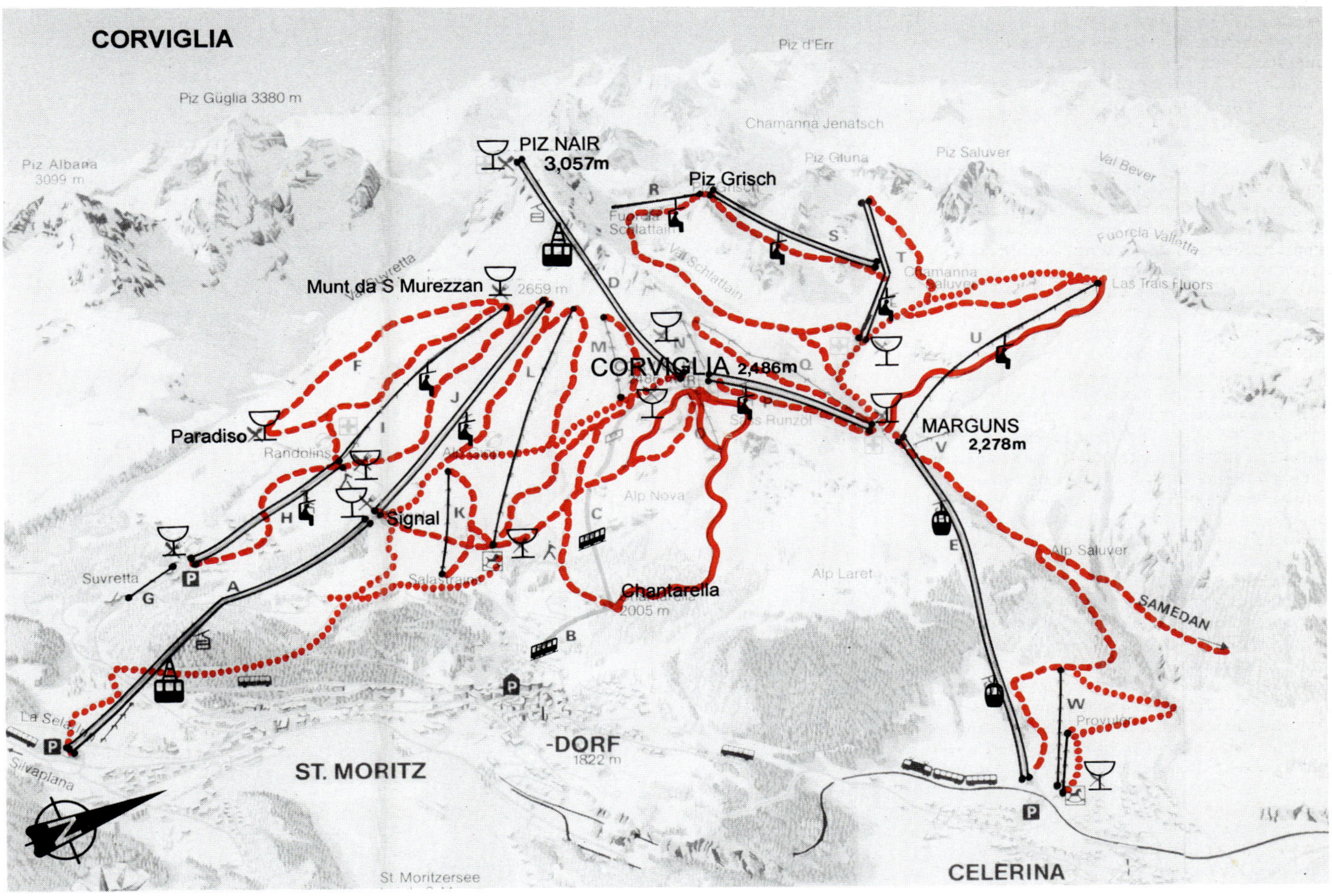

Mountain railways	Cableways	Gondolaways	Chair-lifts	Drag-lifts	...... Easy runs	------- Medium runs	——— Difficult runs	Mountain restaurants

Badrutt's Palace Hotel: This famous multispired, extravagantly designed hotel was opened in 1896 and is one of the largest in St. Moritz. Everything about this hotel is magnificent, its spacious reception rooms, superlative restaurants and beautifully comfortable bedrooms, with everything maintained in tip-top conditions. Service is impeccable, as of days gone by. Extensive facilities include swimming pool, whirlpools with massage centre, 3 saunas, a gymnasium and a nearby bar, ice rink, squash court, indoor golf, bridge room with hostess, exclusive boutiques and hairdresser. Own officially recognised Ski School and Palace Ski Shop.

Hotel Chesa Guardelej: Situated in St. Moritz-Champfer in a quiet position. Consisting of 10 Engadin-style houses connected by underground walkways. Attractive decor throughout, particularly the restaurant. Extensive facilities include swimming pool, sauna, solarium, massage room, gymnasium, squash court, billiards room, large garage and shuttle bus service.

Hotel Schweizerhof: A large hotel in the centre. All bedrooms with private bath, reception rooms is attractively decorated, particularly the Piano Bar which has dancing. Children's playroom and 'Stübli' après ski bar. Restaurant Alca for traditional dishes.

PONTRESINA

Height of Resort: 5,972 ft.
Height of Top Station: 9,827 ft.
Nearest International Airport: Zurich
Map Reference: 7D See page 240
Route by Car: See pages 236-240
Resort Facilities Charts: See page 223
Hotel Reference Charts: See page 233

Pontresina is situated amongst some of the most glorious scenery in the Alps and enjoys exceptionally long hours of sunshine. Although full of hotels and pensions of all categories it has managed to preserve its character as a traditional Engadine village with its narrow main street hemmed in by ancient houses. As will be seen in this report, Pontresina, like many other Engadine resorts, has widely spread skiing areas and it is not a resort where one steps out of the hotel onto the lifts. A good deal of time is spent travelling to the various areas, but the runs in each area are so varied that one is well rewarded; in fact one can almost ski a different run each day during a fortnight's holiday. The large skiing areas of Diavolezza and Piz Lagalb provide superb nearby skiing; these, linked with a half hourly inter-area sport-bus service, make Pontresina a first class resort. The bus service, the railway and entrance fee to the swimming pools of Pontresina and St. Moritz are included in the Engadiner abonnement. The ski areas of Lagalb, Bernina, Diavolezza, Languard and Muottas Muragl are regarded as within Pontresina's sphere of influence, whilst the skiing above St. Moritz and Celerina (Corviglia, Piz Nair, Marguns, etc.) together with Corvatsch and the area above Sils Maria may be said to be within the St. Moritz sphere. In fact, thanks to the sport bus, it is now just as easy to reach all the vast skiing available in the Engadine from Pontresina as it is from St. Moritz. The ski areas adjacent to Pontresina are:

Diavolezza Area, 6,906ft.-9,827ft.: 9km., and 13 minutes by bus from Pontresina, the Diavolezza cableway goes up to 9,827ft. At the top there is a drag-lift and a chair-lift. The direct run back to the bottom station is a glorious one for moderate skiers and even beginners. For the more experienced there is the famous Morteratsch 10km. glacier run.

Piz Lagalb Area, 6,979ft.-9,563ft.: This area is but a further km., and 3 minutes on from Diavolezza. A cableway rises to 9,563ft. Formerly the runs were only for competent skiers but a by-pass, just below the top station, makes it possible to avoid the somewhat alarming top slope so that moderate skiers can now manage to ski this area.

Languard Area, 5,937ft.-8,068ft.: This is Pontresina's immediate skiing area, just above the village. It consists of a drag-lift serving a good south facing, sunny nursery slope and above it, a longish chair-lift taking 9 minutes to reach the charming restaurant at the top, 8,068ft., from which one has a beautiful view; vertical difference 1,265ft. The run down is mostly through a west facing gulley and fairly steep; for intermediates and above.

Muottas Muragl Area, 5,729ft.-8,429ft.: Muottas Muragl is 5 minutes from Pontresina by bus. A mountain railway, originally intended as a scenic point with the best views in the upper Engadine, rises to 8,055ft., where there are two drag-lifts and a trainer lift. There is an excellent restaurant with a sun terrace. The skiing is suitable for the family and the area is certainly worth a visit.

The following skiing areas are also easily accessible from Pontresina by bus or car. Figures in brackets indicate bus travelling time. See under St. Moritz:-

Celerina: For the Marguns area (15 minutes)
St. Moritz: For Corviglia and Piz Nair (20 minutes)
Surlej: For the Corvatsch area (30 minutes)
Sils: For Furtschellas area (40 minutes)

It is noteworthy that although Sils is over half an hour away, any competent skier, by using the interlinking lifts, can ski back all the way to St. Moritz, thereby saving 30 minutes of the return bus journey. This glorious series of runs should certainly

PONTRESINA

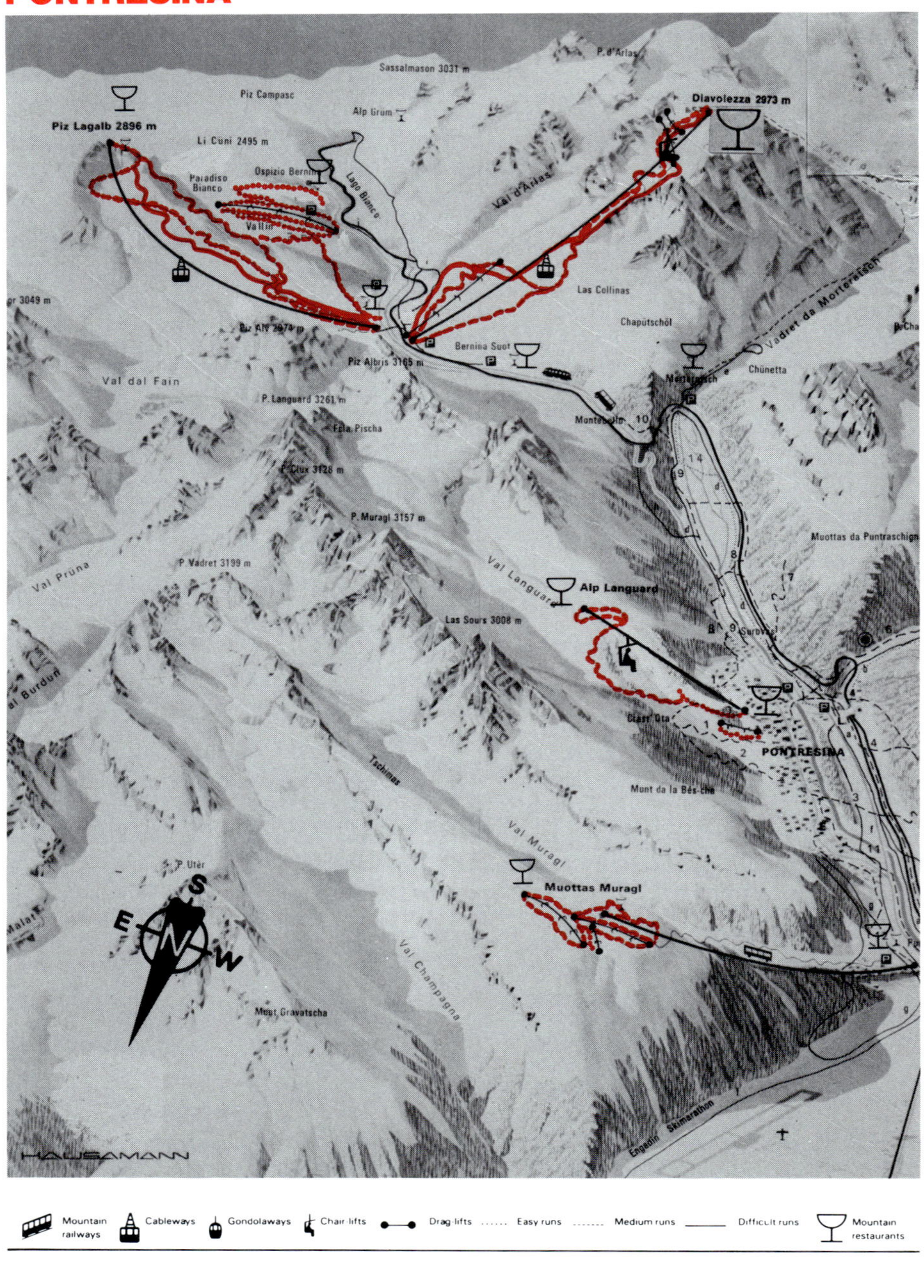

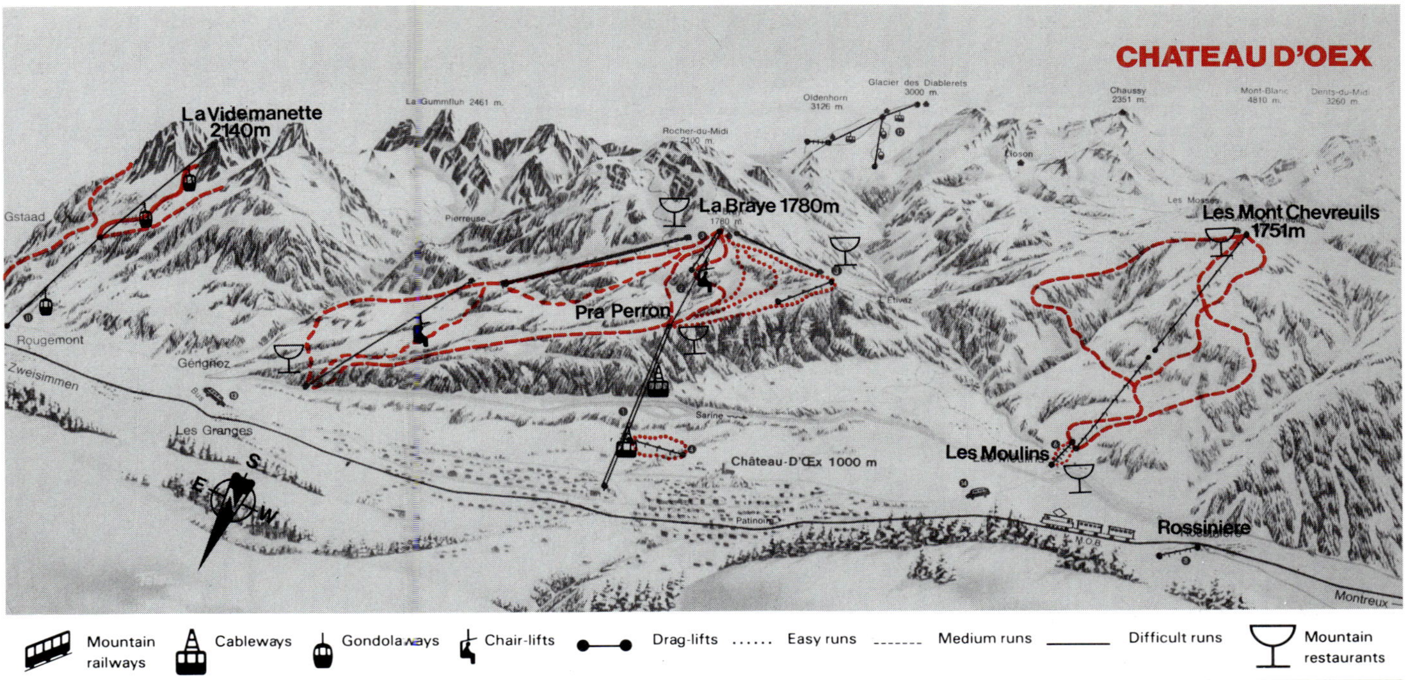

not be missed. Such then is the enormous scope of runs available for the downhill skier. In addition there is unlimited scope for ski mountaineering and touring from February till April. Pontresina is a winter sports centre in the broadest sense of the term. The terrain particularly lends itself to cross-country skiing (langlauf), through beautiful and varied scenery over no less than 60km. of prepared trails, and a further 90 are available outside the Pontresina area, Indeed the cross-country skiing possibilities in the Engadine are probably unsurpassed in the Alps. Each year more and more visitors are taking to this form of skiing. In addition there are two free skating rinks, 11 curling rinks, ice hockey, swimming pool, sleigh rides and 120 miles of walks.

In a Few Words: Pontresina caters for almost every type of winter sport, whilst its overall opportunities for skiing, both langlauf and downhill, would be hard to beat anywhere in the Alps. The vast skiing resources of its immediate areas and the Engadine as a whole are now accessible; one has to acquire the habit of hopping on and off the sport buses! Many skiers will prefer the relatively cheaper prices and peaceful atmosphere of Pontresina to the sophistication St. Moritz.

Après Ski: There is no need for Pontresina visitors to feel beckoned by the gaieties of St. Moritz. Apart from the mostly small dance floors in the hotels, there are four lively and amusing night spots as well as one discothèque, where one can enjoy informal surroundings. Long skirts and dark suits are only necessary in the luxurious hotels. For those not tied to full or half pension, there is a wealth of restaurants to discover, ranging from the small local haunts with hardly a tourist in sight to the smart enticing restaurants with first class menus. The price range is correspondingly varied. The Sarazena restaurant, a very old private house, charmingly converted, with an adjoining wooden minstrel's gallery for guests to sit and overlook the dancers of the night club, is particularly attractive. The Kronen Stübli has a pleasant atmosphere and good food. At the other end of the scale the Hotel Muller's Arven Stübli and the Bernina's Locanda are enjoyable. To sum up: there's plenty of après ski in Pontresina; to own a car is a bonus but far from essential.

For those who want a change from skiing, Pontresina has a lot to offer: miles of scenic, prepared wooded walks and tracks, exciting sleigh ride excursions, trips by horse-drawn bus to the Roseg valley, large skating rink (free to visitors), and an impressive indoor swimming pool. Sun terraces and comfortable chairs everywhere are the rule rather than the exception.

Recommended Hotels:

Hotel Engadinerhof: The exterior belies the interior. Once this is appreciated the Engadinerhof is the sort of hotel one returns to. The hotel has been owned by the same family and run for families for many years. Mrs. Heinrich takes a personal interest in the management and her guests obviously feel that the Engadinerhof is their personal home. There is no ostentation yet one's every comfort has been studied Spacious, light pine-panelled dining room with excellent and plentiful food. Instead of the usual rather dull formation of chairs, the lounge is arranged with a quantity of individual tables and banquettes for 4, which produces a relaxed and secluded atmosphere. There is also a good sized floor for dancing. Across the street there is an excellent sun terrace with chaise-longues reserved for guests.

Sport Hotel: Excellently situated in the centre of the village and opposite a sport-bus stop, the Sport Hotel belongs to the Pontresina Commune and is efficiently run by its alert young manager and wife, who both speak excellent English. The bedrooms have lovely views over the mountains and forests, all have radio and telephone. A popular feature of the hotel is the breakfast buffet, a liberal and varied help-yourself affair, which eliminates the necessity of a large lunch. Television room, table tennis room, various games kept at reception for family entertainment. The Nordeska bar is small, cosy with an open fire and a relaxed atmosphere. Here you can dance in a tiny space if you feel like it. For a change you may eat in the hotel's stübli with a deduction from your normal bill.

Hotel Steinbock: Under the same ownership as the Hotel Walther and next door to it. An inn since 1651 and has now become a most attractive small hotel, modernised with a charming stübli as well as the normal dining room. The 30 bedrooms are all with bathrooms. An easy-going atmosphere and good value for money.

CHATEAU D'OEX and ROSSINIÈRE

Height of Resort: 3,380 ft.
Height of Top Station: 5,741 ft.
Nearest International Airport: Geneva
Map Reference: 2D See page 240
Route by Car: See pages 236-240
Resort Facilities Charts: See page 221
Hotel Reference Charts: See page 232-233

Chateau d'Oex lies on the side of an open valley of the Pays d'Enhaut in the Gstaad Super Ski Region, which stretches past Gstaad to Zweisimmen at the eastern end, including the resorts of Rougemont, Saanen, Schönried and Saanemöser, to the tiny village of Rossinière to the west. Most of these have their own ski areas and although they are not to any extent interlinked, a ski pass is available for the whole area, including the train, providing a tremendous variety of skiing on mainly north-facing slopes. Good snow conditions therefore normally prevail in spite of the relatively low altitude. Chateau d'Oex itself is a village of great charm and character, with a friendly and relaxed atmosphere.

There are two lift systems. A cableway (renewed in 1993) from the village centre rises to Pra Perron, 4,018ft., surmounted by a chair-lift reaching La Braye, 5,346ft. There are restaurants at both top stations. The La Montagnette drag-lift runs parallel and ends above La Braye at 5,576ft. On the west side of this system are 2 drag-lifts, the top one, Tête du Grin, rising to 5,741ft.; both lifts serve easy linking runs. On these higher slopes the skiing is easy to medium. Runs of easy, medium and difficult standards, of about $3^1/_2$km., lead down to Pra Perron on open and wooded slopes. There is a medium 8km. run from La Braye when snow conditions allow, and a 4km. run from the middle station, wooded in parts to the neighbouring village of Gérignoz from which a chair-lift and a surmounting drag-lift allow skiers to reach the top of La Braye again. A free bus travels between Gérignoz and Chateau d'Oex.

The second area, Les Moulins, is closer to the neighbouring village of Rossinière, about 2km. away. Three drag-lifts culminate at Monts Chevreuils, 5,445ft., with restaurant. Various intermediate runs lead back to the lower terminal. Rossinière itself is a delightful and very small village, almost entirely built of wooden chalets, grouped around a central square and rising up the hillside. It is very quiet but

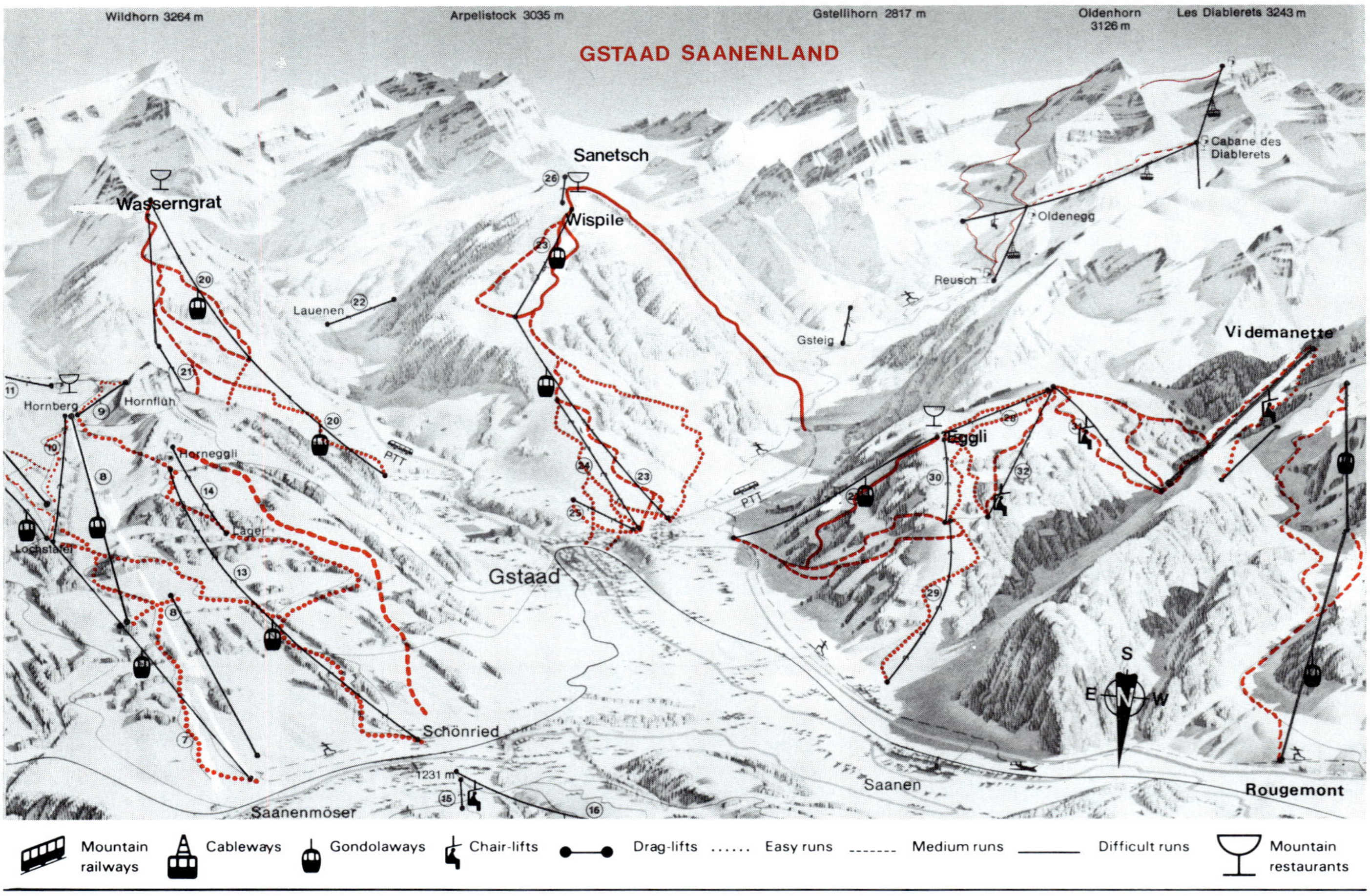

the valley's skiing can be reached from here.

In a Few Words: A very warm and attractive resort with a varied amount of activity of its own and a good range of skiing available in the neighbouring resorts. High standard of hotels, small and friendly atmosphere. Good for beginners to advanced intermediate skiers. Extensive facilities for langlauf. Hot air ballooning centre with international competitions in January each year.

Après Ski: This isn't sophisticated but it's fun – there is a discothèque at the Richemont which gets going rather late and becomes crowded with young people energetic enough to keep it going. The Bon Accueil's cellar bar has a tremendous ambience - open fire, dim lighting and music if you feel like dancing. There is a discothèque Le Ranch at the Hotel Les Bouquetins and another, My Love, at the Hotel La Rocaille. There are a number of good restaurants in Chateau d'Oex - the Hotel de Ville, the Ermitage, the Hotel La Rocaille and the Bon Accueil are all recommended. Other activities include good walks, a riding school (for indoor and outdoor riding); and there is an ice rink with curling, ice hockey, ski-bobbing, a cinema, an interesting museum, and a cheese-making centre. For more sophisticated night life Gstaad is only 20 minutes' drive away.

Recommended Hotels:

Chateau d'Oex

Hotel Beau-Séjour: Situated next to the cableway terminal to La Braye, one minute walk from centre. An old established hotel, comfortable bedrooms, many modernised with private bath or shower and balcony. Large bright dining room and sitting room lounge with large south facing windows with view over valley. Attractive à la carte restaurant, bar and café. Friendly and helpful owners.

Hotel La Rocaille: Situated on the north-east side of the village, 6 minutes walk from the centre, this hotel can accommodate 52 guests. All rooms elegantly furnished, all with private facilities, direct dial telephones, colour TV, radio and safes. The apartments are fully serviced. Dining in 'Au Train Bleu' restaurant-grill or in the 'Café des Boissons' which has a delightful atmosphere with wooden panelling and beamed ceiling. Piano Bar disco and café-terrasse.

Hotel Victoria: Not as the name implies, but a small cosy hotel, 33 beds. Bedrooms colourfully furnished, all with bath or shower and many with balconies and lovely views. Small, warm sitting room and attractive dining room; an extremely nice family hotel and owner.

Rossinière

Rossinière is a very small and quiet village and is about 2km. from Chateau d'Oex. It is on the main railway line, but own transport is an advantage.

Chalet-Hotel La Colline: High up the south facing hillside, reached by crossing a bridge over the stream with a marvellous view over the valley, this is more of a family home than a hotel, with a warm and intimate atmosphere. Under the ownership of M. Claude Martin, who offers full pension arrangements, as well as bed and breakfast or half board. Meals are taken round a large table together. Baby-sitting can be arranged.

Hotel de Ville: Chalet-style hotel in the village centre, it basically provides dormitory accommodation for 20, with or without breakfast, plus 3 single rooms. Good for parties, friendly atmosphere.

GSTAAD SAANENLAND

Height of Resort: 3,308 ft.
Height of Top Station: 6,461 ft.
Nearest International Airport: Geneva
Map Reference: 3D See page 240
Route by Car: See pages 236-240
Resort Facilities Charts: See page 222
Hotel Reference Charts: See page 232

In 1994 it was decided that Gstaad and its 6 neighbouring villages, Saanen, Schönried, Sannenmöser, Lauenen, Gsteig and Turbach should join forces and operate under one tourist office, Gstaad Saanenland. The combination of the resorts provides 2,300 beds in hotels and some further 10,00 in chalets and apartments.

Gstaad Saanenland lies in a wide sunny valley and its villages, set amidst beautiful wooded scenery, have much charm and character. With few exceptions the skiing in the area is mainly for beginners to intermediates. With the Gstaad Super Ski Pass, however, the variety of skiing is considerably extended to 250km. of runs served by 69 lifts which includes Les Diablerets with its Spring glacier skiing. Furthermore it also allows one to ski in Adelboden-Lenk and the Alpes Vaudoises resorts.

The Gstaad Saanenland skiing can be divided into 5 main areas:-

Eggli Area: A gondolaway travels in 12 minutes from the west side of the village to Eggli, 5,117ft., where there is a pleasing restaurant with a large sun terrace. This is the link with Saanen, with two surmounting drag lifts converging on this station. This point is also the link with Rougemont. Easy runs lead down the line of the top lift, and one can ski across to the Fäng chair-lift and travel to Eggli Stand, 5,478ft. This can also be reached by chair-lift to Eggli and another chair-lift from Chalberhöni, in the next valley. Skiing in this area is interesting, through wide wooded glades on mainly north and north-east facing slopes, steep in parts. Runs to Gstaad are 3-4km. in length, vertical descent 2,100,ft., and to Saanen 5km., a drop of 2,116ft.

Wispile Area: From the south-west of the village a 2-stage gondolaway rises first to 5,183ft. From this point easy and medium runs lead to the village over north facing slopes, a drag-lift runs parallel to the lower half, with a trainer lift at the bottom. The second station is Wispile, 6,265ft., where there is a restaurant. There are medium to difficult runs over north-east facing slopes from the top to the first station, and the total distance of the runs from top to bottom is 4-5km., vertical descent 2,950ft.

Wasserngrat Area: Reached from the southeast side of the village by a 2-stage gondolaway, rising in 16 minutes to Wasserngrat, 6,461ft., where there is a restaurant. The steep upper slopes, particularly the Tigerrun, even out halfway down and from here gentle runs lead to the village over mainly north facing slopes, distance 5km., a drop of 2,804ft. There are several variations back to the village.

Schönried + Horneggli + Rellerli Area: The village of Schönried lies north-east of Gstaad, connected by bus or train, with its ski area on both sides of the road. On the south-east side a gondolaway rises to Horneggli, 5,806 ft., where one finds a restaurant and the Läger drag-lift with a top station of 5,938ft. Both lifts serve blue and red runs and one black to base through attractive wide wooded glades. On the north-west side of the village another gondolaway with surmounting drag-lift reach the Rellerli restaurant, 6,013 ft. A testing run follows the line of the lifts back to Schönried whilst a long easy run of about 4 km. sweeps round in a wide arc to the village.

Saanenmöser – Saanerslochgrat Area: The main lift system from the village is a two section gondolaway travelling south-eastwards to the restaurant at Saanenwald, another gondolaway with surmounting drag-lift reaches Hornfluh, 6,203 ft. Five drag-lifts on the upper slopes serve easy runs (with the occasional red) and link with the Schönried area.

In a Few Words: Skiing fun, with wider range available in surrounding areas. Mainly north, north-east and north-west facing slopes, making up for the lack of altitude. Good for families and non-skiers, Junior-Club Playgroup run by the ski school, kindergarten; sophisticated and lively.

Après Ski: Gstaad is renowned for its night life, which includes several good restaurants and night clubs. The Café Olden on the ground floor has a bar and restaurant with dancing in a slightly nostalgic atmosphere; the Cave below is more rustic in style with dancing, and food available from open grills. The Palace Hotel is another old-world luxury hotel and has a good night club, the Green Go, with an international band, modern decor, frequented by guests dressed in anything from jeans to dinner jackets. There's a swimming pool to plunge into just outside, if you need to cool off! Another very popular spot is the Chesery, a pretty chalet, with hotel, restaurant offering a varied menu and an excellent piano bar. Ristorante Rialto with bar serves Italian specialities in a cosy atmosphere. About 2 miles outside Gstaad is the Chösterli, a rustic 17th century inn with countless little rooms and alcoves and an intimate atmosphere, yet with room for 500 people. It has a large dance floor with live and recorded music, and does very good meals and late night specialities. They also do lunch and you can ski down to it from Wispile - it's well worth a visit. Club 95 disco at the Hotel Victoria is very popular. Gstaad also has a cinema with films in various languages, a large indoor swimming pool, tennis hall with 3 courts, and a curling rink hall.

Recommended Hotels: Gstaad

Garni Hotel Alphorn: Small hotel next to the Hotel Rütti; very nicely furnished; modern bedrooms with bath or shower, fridge and balcony; small sitting room; two cosy beamed-ceiling restaurants; small swimming pool.

Hotel Bellevue: Situated in a large private park, 5 minutes from the centre. All rooms with bath/shower, wc, radio, TV, self-dialling telephone, minibar. For entertainment, piano bar recommended. Bellevue kitchen is honoured with 15/20 points by the Guide Gault Milau for its excellent food.

Sporthotel Rütti: Close to the Wispile and Eggli gondolaways, 16 minutes from the centre. A modern hotel, sitting room to right of reception, white walls and natural wooden decor; large bright dining room, rustic pizzeria with sun terrace outside; good medium-sized bedrooms all with private shower, wc, family rooms with beds for children on a half floor in same room.

Sporthotel Victoria: A very comfortable family hotel in the traffic-free centre. Sitting room on left of reception leading to modern breakfast room; large, bright dining room and beyond a very large wood panelled bar Club 95, where there is dancing to disco; popular stübli-type restaurant and a new brasserie with wintergarden where speciality dishes are served; bedrooms comfortably furnished, all with bath and shower.

ROUGEMONT

Height of Resort: 3,175 ft.
Height of Top Station: 7,399 ft.
Nearest International Airport: Geneva
Map Reference: 2D See page 240
Route by Car: See pages 236-240
Resort Facilities Charts: See page 223
Hotel Reference Charts: See page 233

In the Pays d'Enhaut valley, midway between Chateau d'Oex and Gstaad - about four or five miles from each - lies Rougemont, a medium-sized, very attractive and completely unspoilt village built almost entirely of wooden chalets with many carved and painted facades. Most of the village is on the south facing side of the valley and a 5 minute walk northwards, crossing the stream which runs through the village, leads to the terminal of a gondolaway. This rises via one intermediate station the Videmanette, 7,399ft., a spectacular journey through towering vertical rock faces. At the top there is an excellent restaurant with tables in the sun.

The more intrepid skier can begin the run down from here; alternatively there is a 2-car gondolaway – 8 persons per car, by-passing the initial steep slopes and from its lower terminal, there are various short runs of easy, medium and difficult standard in a wide open, sunny bowl, leading to the foot of a chair-lift, with a glorious view of the surrounding peaks. The long run down to the village, of about $7^1/_2$km., can be taken over medium or difficult pistes and is quite beautiful - one of the best in the whole valley passing through wooded slopes as it descends. A variation of the descent, taking the Eggli lifts, links it with Gstaad.

In a Few Words: Excellent skiing, on mainly north facing slopes of medium standard, with abonnement available extending the range over the Pays d'Enhaut valley; good nordic skiing facilities. Very local atmosphere in village, good value and within easy reach of other resorts for more varied skiing and night life if required.

Après Ski: No night clubs but Chateau d'Oex and Gstaad are nearby for those wanting this form of entertainment. The bars in the hotels are full of atmosphere and mostly cheerful and lively, particularly the Grizzli Bar in the Hotel Viva. The Café du Cerf is a very old chalet, and there's a fascinating antique shop in a stable. Basically however, Rougemont will be best enjoyed by keen skiers rather than by those who want a lively night life.

Recommended Hotels:

Hotel Valrose: A hotel with 27 beds, light and agreeable with view over the mountains. Many bedrooms with balcony. Large attractive dining room; special fondue and raclette room. The bar in typical Rougemont style in the centre of life, lots of card games. Very good atmosphere; M. Cottier, the owner, provides all general information on Rougemont and is extremely helpful.

LES MOSSES

Height of Resort: 4,756 ft.
Height of Top Station: 7,708 ft.
Nearest International Airport: Geneva
Map Reference: 2D See page 240
Route by Car: See pages 236-240
Resort Facilities Charts: See page 222
Hotel Reference Charts: See page 233

A winding road leaves Chateau d'Oex and about 9 miles away, at the top of the Col des Mosses mountain pass lies the small village of Les Mosses. A road divides the two main skiing areas. All facilities - ski-lifts, car park, hotels, restaurants and shops are compactly arranged in the centre. The buildings are mostly modern, with some chalets scattered on the surrounding slopes. Snow conditions here are excellent despite plenty of sun . Les Mosses seems to get a snowfall when many other resorts do not; it is high and many of the slopes are north facing. Skiers of all standards are catered for, from the beginner to the advanced. On the western side of the road the slopes are covered by a network of 8 interlinking drag-lifts (the highest point reached is Les Parchets, 6,260ft.). These slopes are where the ski school mainly operates and, when snow conditions in neighbouring resorts are inadequate, do become crowded with day visitors.

Since the closure of the gondolaway up to Pic de Chaussy the area on the eastern side of the road is limited to three drag-lifts, one of which, the Praz-Corret, rises to 5,648ft. All three serve easy to intermediate interconnecting runs.

Nordic skiing is well catered for with two trails of 6 and 8km. Floodlit skiing from 20-2200 hours served by the Bébert draf-lift. Les Mosses has a very young atmosphere and aims to provide excellent skiing at the most reasonable prices possible.

In a Few Words: Fairly modern resort with excellent snow and sun; good for families and groups of young people; special package with accommodation and abonnement for six Alpes Vaudoises resorts provides good range of skiing; very good value.

Après Ski: Les Mosses is essentially a resort for keen skiers, and the only real night spot is the Bar Les Fontaines with discothèque operating till 2 or 3 in the morning. The short drive to Leysin, Les Diablerets or Chateau d'Oex offers more variety if required. All these resorts are about 15-20 minutes by car. There are good restaurants at the Relais Alpin-Hotel and Hotel Les Fontaines, both modern in style, and the Chaussy restaurant with more traditional decor. A lot of competitive skiing events take place here in conjunction with Les Diablerets and there are ice hockey matches and torchlight skiing followed by a festive meal.

Recommended Hotels:

Hotel La Sapinière: Small hotel just off main road, near ski school. 30 beds, all double rooms, many with balcony. Restaurant/bar/sitting room all open plan. Rooms bright and comfortable, good for families.

Restotel Keller: The largest and most central hotel, modern with bright decor and comfortably furnished. 40 beds, all rooms with shower. Large restaurant serving excellent food and gigantic portions! (at lunchtime you can eat outside in the sun). The owners M. and Mme. Stucki are very welcoming and like to have English guests.

VILLARS

Height of Resort: 4,264 ft.
Height of Top Station: 7,216 ft.
Nearest International Airport: Geneva
Map Reference: 2D See page 240
Route by Car: See pages 236-240
Resort Facilities Charts: See page 223
Hotel Reference Charts: See page 233

The central street of Villars curves gently uphill, with a background of pine-covered slopes, overlooking the Rhône valley and its vineyards around Aigle. It is a sunny village, consisting mostly of chalet-style buildings and attractive shops, and there are two smaller villages on its outskirts, Chesières and Arveyes. A large number of chalets provide accommodation, far outnumbering the beds provided by the hotels. Its link with Les Diablerets (see separate report) has vastly extended the ski area.

Villars - Bretaye Area: The main ski area, Bretaye, 6,068ft., is reached by taking the mountain railway, with two stops en route, rather slow and crowded at rush hours. Once there, however, this is the nerve centre of the Villars skiing, with runs and lifts spreading out from it in all directions. The three main ones in the area, rising to the summit of Chamossaire, 7,216ft., Petit Chamossaire, 6,989ft. and Chaux Ronde, 6,657ft. From Chamossaire one has a marvellous 360° view of the area for miles around. The runs down from this point to Bretaye are varied, easy to medium, on south-east facing slopes, about 2km. in length, vertical descent 1,148ft. Just below Bretaye a drag-lift rises north-west to Roc d'Orsay where there is a restaurant; it should be mentioned that this station can be reached by gondolaway from the north of Villars village. From Roc d'Orsay one can ski down to Bretaye or take the testing run 'Bouquetins' which turns off the right hand ridge into a steep narrow gulley before one reaches the 'Aiguille' hump. It is about 3km. in length, 4km. from the top of Chamossaire, clear of woods over south and southeast facing slopes, vertical descent 2,780ft. One can end the run at the foot of the Roc d'Orsay gondolaway or in the village centre. The runs down from Petit Chamossaire are more suitable for the good performer, one medium/difficult and the other difficult, some glade running on south-east facing slopes. The latter run ends by the terminal of the Lac Noir chair-lift which takes one up to the summit of Chaux Ronde, 6,657ft., on which two parallel drag-lifts also converge from Bretaye. From the top of the chair-lift there is an exciting and testing north facing run down to the bottom and a drag-lift takes one up to Bretaye. There is a choice of easy and testing runs from the top of both drag-lifts to Bretaye, about 1km. in length over west facing slopes. There is also a direct run from Chaux Ronde down to Villars, turning left at the bottom of the two drag-lifts, following the line of the railway and swinging away from it after the Col de Soud and thence to the village, about 5km. with a vertical drop of 2,450ft., skiing all the way. Alternatively one can keep left before Col de Soud and run down to La Gryonne Valley and take the chair-lift and drag-lift back to Bretaye, or the two chair-lifts up to Chaux-de-Conche. From this point one can ski to Les Diablerets. The Villars ski pass covers the Diablerets lifts. There are four restaurants in the Bretaye area and one of the best is at Lac des Chavonnes, whilst the restaurant at Bretaye itself has a large seated picnic area, an ideal resting point for families.

Barboleusaz-Les Chaux Area: This area is linked to Bretaye and can also be reached very easily from Barboleusaz, 10 minutes away from Villars by road or mountain railway. On the Villars side there are easy runs down to La Rasse and here surmounting drag-lifts take one up to Les Chaux, 5,904ft., and its restaurant. The gondolaway from Barboleusaz reaches this point (see separate report adjoining). The intermediate runs back to La Rasse are open and interesting and one can return to Bretaye by chair and surmounting drag-lift. Beginners are well catered for with nursery slopes and trainer lifts in the Villars village area and further slopes at Bretaye.

In a Few Words: A charming resort with a good atmosphere in lovely wooded countryside; good interlinking lift system, which has recently been improved by the introduction of high speed quad chair-lifts, and the interlink with Diablerets has vastly extended the skiing. Some modernisation required to avoid queues at lifts leading to the top stations. Plenty of non-skiing activities; kindergarten run by the Swiss Ski School.

Après Ski: There is plenty of variety here in the way of bars, restaurants and night clubs, but the night life in Villars is at its best in high season – once the snow disappears from the lower slopes the resort becomes much quieter. The Vieux Villars is recommended for raclettes. The Bridge Pub and the Mini Pub are certainly worth a visit, whilst the discos Na Zdrove and El Gringo's are fun. The latter's complex also has an excellent restaurant, Chez Chi Chi. There is a very good Italian restaurant with Italian-style decor, Peppino's, at the Eurotel, with a different group playing every month. The Sporting has a good restaurant, bar and mini-pub. Another restaurant worth a visit for its delicious Italian specialities is 'Mon Repos'. Other bars worth a visit are Chez Jo,The Bridge Pub and Frowling. There is also a large artificial skating rink (not open to the public all the time) with restaurant and bowling alley. There are three indoor swimming pools and a very well equipped fitness club with instructor, massage and solarium. Indoor tennis centre with 6 courts, squash and sauna.

Recommended Hotels:

Hotel L'Écureuil: A charming small chalet-style hotel set back from the road to Gryon, 300m. from the village centre. 54 beds, all rooms with private bath, telephone, radio, TV, sunny terrace and most with a kitchen. Excellent restaurant, and delightful owners.

Eurotel: This first class hotel, opened in 1975/6 and completely renovated in 1993, is 300m. from the town centre. 270 beds, 124 double rooms, 29 singles all with bath. Large dining room and attractive Peppino Italian restaurant. Very comfortably furnished rooms, some with kitchen section and fridge, beds which fold up into the wall to make a large sitting room. Swimming pool, sauna, solarium and fitness centre, games room.

Grand Hotel du Parc: Set back in its own beautiful grounds, this large first class hotel is 5 minutes' walk from, the centre. Good sized bedrooms attractively furnished, all with bath and shower and most with balconies; large bay window sitting room; long, bright, elegant dining room with fairly formal, old-world atmosphere and excellent food; pre-lunch cocktails served on an ice bar outside; lovely swimming pool where babies are taught to swim every morning, and sauna; conference room; play room, Tavern; bar piano bar; fitness centre and two private ski-lifts.

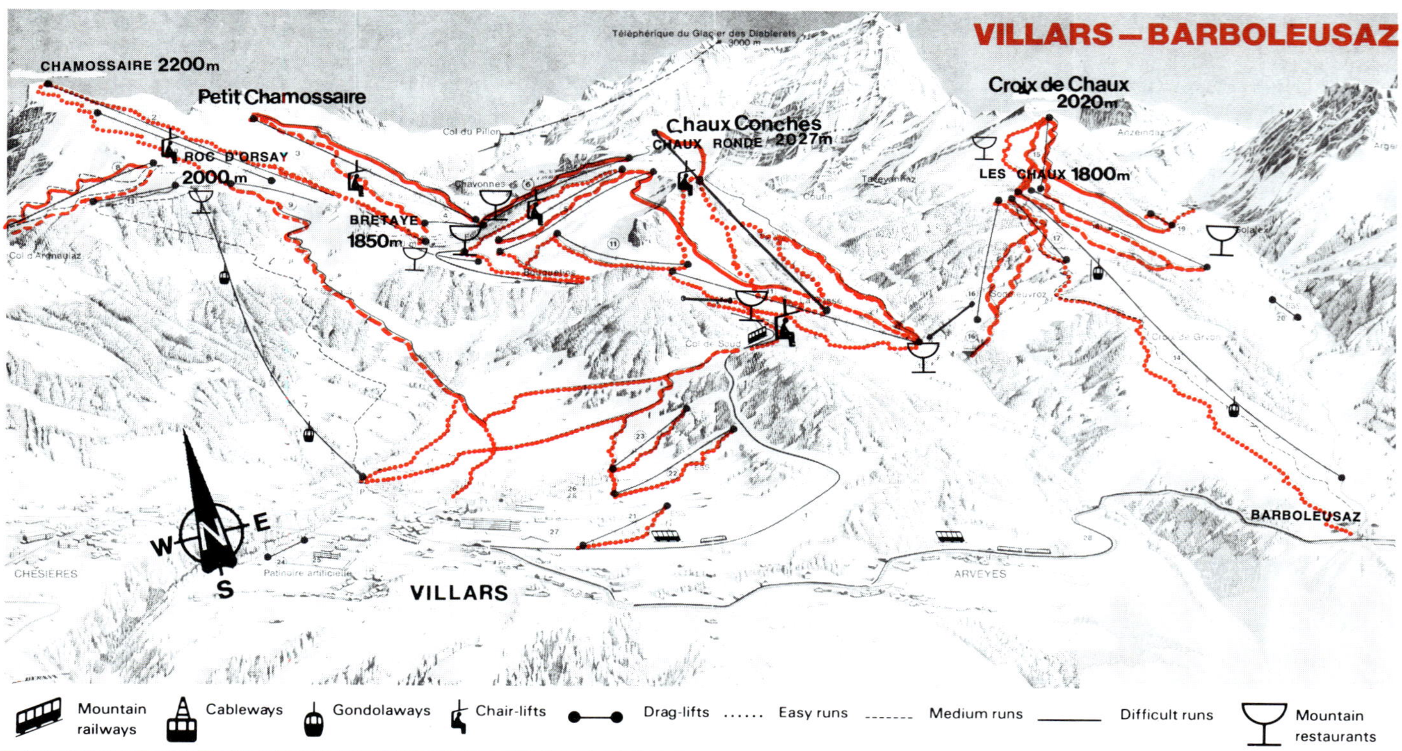

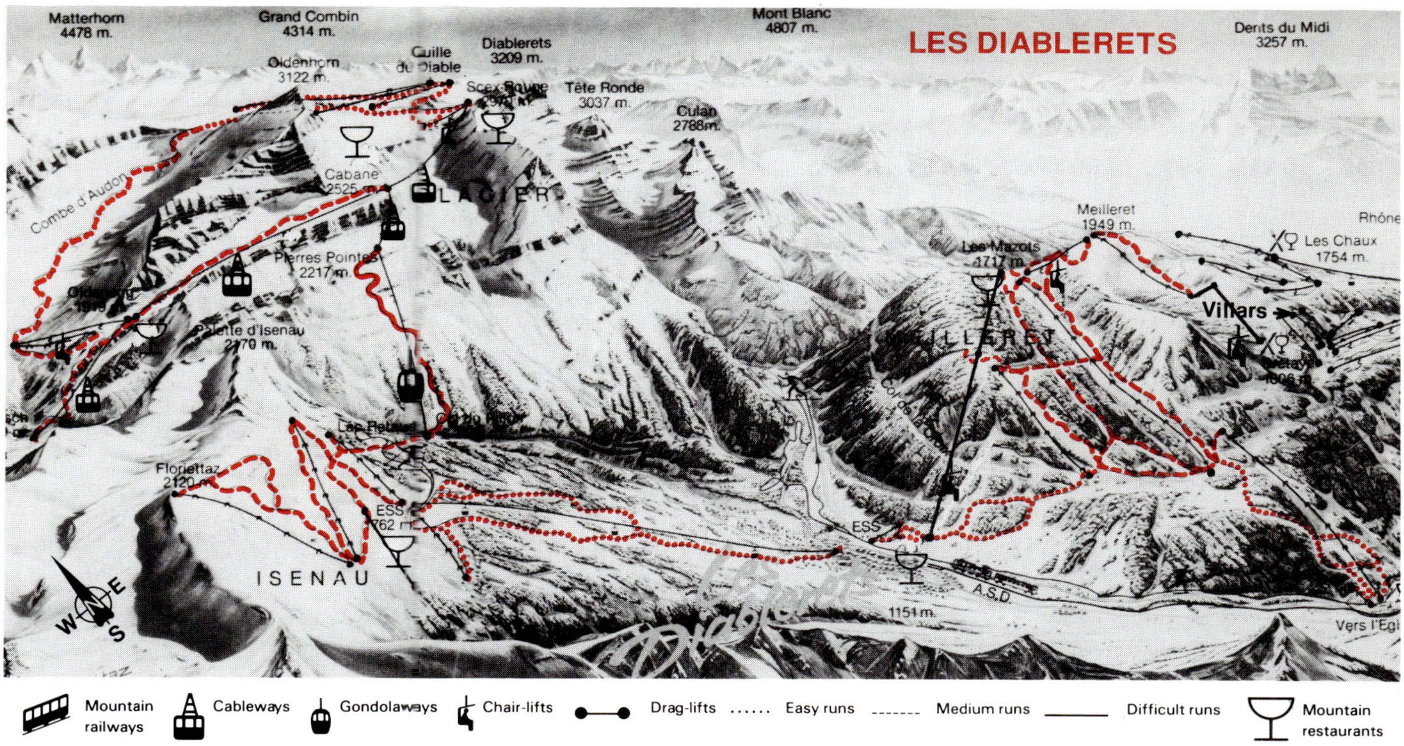

Hotel Renardière: A very attractive chalet-style hotel with three similar style annexes within 15-40m. of the main building, set in their own grounds 5 minutes' walk from the centre. All bedrooms with bath or shower, tastefully furnished; in main building wood panelled dining room most attractively decorated with windows along two sides; large sitting room with open fire; grill room; bar; quiet and cosy atmosphere.

BARBOLEUSAZ and GRYON

Height of Resort: 3,970 ft.
Height of Top Station: 6,626 ft.
Nearest International Airport: Geneva
Map Reference: 2D See page 240
Route by Car: See pages 236-240
Resort Facilities Charts: See page 221
Hotel Facilities Charts: See page 232

Barboleusaz is hardly a village, more of an outpost formed by a group of buildings near the Les Chaux gondolaway terminal. Ten minutes from Villars by road or mountain railway, it has its own tourist office, a few hotels, many café-restaurants and a good teashop. Further along the road from Villars is the lovely old country village of Gryon, with picturesque wooden chalets lining its narrow sloping streets.

Barboleusaz is well placed for the Les Chaux ski area, which interlinks with the whole Villars system when there is sufficient snow on the lower slopes, giving an extensive range of skiing. The gondolaway rises to Les Chaux, 5,904ft., where there is a restaurant. From or to Les Chaux, four drag-lifts are available, one rising to Croix des Chaux, 6,626ft. An easy 5km. run over west and south-west facing slopes leads down to Barboleusaz, difference in height 2,656ft. The four drag-lifts serve the more difficult higher slopes over varied terrain, wooded in parts. By following the line of the right hand drag-lift, the descent leads to the La Rasse series of drag lifts which take one to Bretaye, the hub of Villars' ski area (see Villars report).

In a Few Words: Small and secluded with friendly atmosphere and not far from Villars for more activity if required. Good skiing linking with Villars, mostly easy to medium standard. Extensive langlauf facilities. One can avoid taking the rather crowded mountain railway to start the day's skiing by taking the speedy gondolaway.

Après Ski: An absolutely delightful log cabin refuge which can be reached on skis or by road, is Frience, run by Leo Crameri, with a warm and friendly atmosphere and good food and drink. If you want a lively night life Villars is nearby, whilst Montreux is only 40 minutes drive.

Recommended Hotels:
Hotel Cremaillère (Barboleusaz): Small and attractive chalet with very nice owners. Close to lift terminal and one can ski to hotel. Sun terrace with lovely view. Bright restaurant/bar, breakfast room. 12 bedrooms all with wooden walls and balcony.

LES DIABLERETS

Height of Resort: 3,936 ft.
Height of Top Station: 9,840 ft.
Nearest International Airport: Geneva
Map Reference: 2D See page 240
Route by Car: See pages 236-240
Resort Facilities Charts: See page 222
Hotel Reference Charts: See page 233

After leaving the Geneva-Brig motorway at Aigle, 23km. later one arrives at Les Diablerets, which is a small village with chalet-style buildings, surrounded by impressive mountains. The area is very beautiful and its lift system is vast for so small a resort, with glacier skiing all year round. The link-up with Villars has increased the ski area considerably, with 230km. of prepared pistes including the Alpes Vaudoises (Leysin-Les Mosses-Villars-Diablerets). Les Diablerets itself is under one lift pass. There are two separate ski areas in addition to the glacier area.

Glacier des Diablerets: The largest and highest ski area, reached by gondolaway from the Col du Pillon, 4 miles from the village. This rises to Pierres Pointes and provides runs suitable for good skiers only. A surmounting cableway continues up to Cabane des Diablerets, 8,276ft. (Tête aux Chamois). It can also be reached from Reusch, 2km. from Col du Pillon, and this cableway rises to Oldenegg, connecting with another to Cabane des Diablerets. The 3½km. run to Oldenegg from here is of good medium grade over open north-east facing slopes, 1,971ft. descent. The 4km. medium grade run and 3km. difficult Chamois run both lead to Reusch from Oldenegg, becoming wooded as they descend, with vertical drop of 1,902ft. The top station on the Glacier des Diablerets, 9,840ft., is reached by cableway from Cabane des Diablerets. The view here is vast and indescribably beautiful. A long chair-lift, 3 drag-lifts and a snow-bus serve the glacier which is open for summer skiing too. Here there is also a Nordic ski-trail of 6km. for use during summer. There is a very pleasant restaurant at the top station of the cableway, as well as at all other stations excepting Pierres Pointes. The run from the top goes to the south of the Oldenhorn peak and is straight and gentle to start with, becoming steeper and trickier and providing some exciting skiing in the Combe d'Audon. A chair-lift takes one back up to Oldenegg. From Glacier des Diablerets to Oldenegg the run is 11km. in length with vertical descent of 4,000ft., and if one continues down to Reusch this provides a magnificent 14-15km. run with 6,000ft. descent. Good skiers will love it.

Isenau Area: A gondolaway rises from the north of the village to 5,904ft., where there is a restaurant and large sun terrace with a glorious view of the valley below and the Diablerets massif beyond. There is a drag-lift to the south-west of the restaurant. A short drag-lift rises to the north-east to provide easy to medium runs in a wide, sunny bowl, leading down to the foot of the Floriettaz drag-lift which rises to Col des Andérets, 8,822ft. A 2km. run over south facing slopes take one to the base of the Isenau drag-lift, and from the top of this an interesting 6km. run leads down to the village, when snow conditions allow, vertical descent about 2,000,ft. This area on the whole caters for beginners to medium grade, and a new drag-lift La Crua, for beginners, was opened in 1993. One can also ski from Isenau to Col du Pillon gondolaway bottom station, which is also the departure point for the bus back to the village. There is a snowboard park in this area.

Meillerets-Les Mazots Area: To the right of the approach road, 1km. from the village is Vers l'Église, from which point two surmounting drag lifts reach Les Mazots, where one finds a restaurant. A 6km. toboggan run starts from this point. Two further well-spaced drag lifts produce excellently interlinked runs through mainly wooded slopes; the skiing is interesting of medium to good-medium standard. Les Mazots can also be reached from Les Vioz by a 4 seater chair-lift with an intermediate station at La Jorasse. The upper slopes are open, and from Les Mazots a chair-lift rises to Meillerets, 6,494ft. The Laouissalet drag-lift to the south-east of Meillerets has opened up a wide sunny bowl with good off piste possibilities. This is also the link lift with Villars (see separate report).
Children: There is a kindergarten, 'Le Coin des

Petits Diables' for children from 3-6 years and a ski kindergarten, 'Le Diablodocus' Parc for 3-8 year olds.

In a Few Words: Small and quiet in spite of its vast lift system; friendly atmosphere. Langlauf; para gliding, ski school, superb high mountain skiing – helicopter available; within close reach of many other resorts. The interlink with Villars has extended the skiing considerably.

Après Ski: This is fairly quiet but there are a few appealing night spots. At the Parc des Sports is Saloon La Pote discothèque as well as an ice-rink with a restaurant 'La Potinière'. La Couronne is a very picturesque old chalet restaurant specialising in cheese dishes. The restaurants take it in turn to hold special evenings. The Auberge de la Poste, the old village inn, has a typical restaurant. There is an artificial ice rink with skating free to all guests, curling and outdoor curling. The Grand-Hotel has a special club, Residence Meurice, which is free for hotel guests. It has sauna, massage and a large, heated indoor swimming pool.

Recommended Hotels:

Hotel Mon Abri: Situated at the entrance to the village, ten minutes' walk from the centre. Bar room and old-world grill room for outside guests; large bright dining room, wooden decor; extremely nice modern bedrooms in the modern section of the hotel, all with private bath or shower, whilst those in the old section are comfortable, wood panelled in typical Swiss style. Large sun terrace.

Ermitage Hotel and Residence Meurice: Situated in the centre of the village; large reception area/ sitting room and further raised level sitting room leading into long, bright, nicely decorated dining room with wonderful view of mountains. Good medium-size bedrooms all with bath or shower, most with balconies. Apartment-type bedrooms in Residence Meurice converting into sitting rooms, all with bath. kitchen and fridge, most with balcony; conference room, night club, swimming pool; very nice and efficient staff.

Hotel Les Lilas: An extremely attractive small chalet-style hotel; most attractive dining room with fireplace. Heavy beamed ceilings with rustic style decor, beautifully furnished and providing a cosy atmosphere; bedrooms very attractive with slanting beamed ceilings and exquisitely furnished, all with shower and wc. Well known for its 'Traditional Cuisine'.

LEYSIN

Height of Resort: 4,134/4,760 ft.
Height of Top Station: 6,658 ft.
Nearest International Airport: Geneva
Map Reference: 2D See page 240
Route by Car: See pages 236-240
Resort Facilities Charts: See page 222
Hotel Reference Charts: See page 233

Leysin, in the centre of the Alpes Vaudoises and an hour's drive from Lausanne, rates as the eleventh largest winter sports resort in Switzerland. It is steeply built, facing south and overlooking the Rhône valley, and made up of two village centres on different levels. A car is therefore a great advantage, although various taxi services operate. Because of its height and high sun record the snow is at its best during the earlier part of the season, when the social life also flourishes. The main skiing is to the north-east of the village, and a gondolaway travels in 8 minutes to La Berneuse, 6,658ft. Here there is a revolving restaurant with sun terrace allowing wonderful views of the Rhône valley and surrounding mountains. From this point a wide bowl opens up before one and after skiing down these slopes to Lac d'Ai one can take the Chaux de Mont chair-lift to a height of 7,100ft., under the Tour d'Ai peak. A run of medium standard down wide open south-facing slopes leads to the foot of the Ai chair-lift which returns one to La Berneuse. From here there are two medium to easy runs to the village over south-facing slopes, open at the top and becoming wooded as they descend, but with wide pistes, about 4km. in length with a vertical descent of 2,395ft. Another closely wooded run ends on the eastern side of the village. A second gondolaway runs from near the lower terminal of the Berneuse lift to just below the Lac de Mayen, 6,301ft., and a chair-lift continues the ascent to the crest surrounding the Lac d'Ai. A widely wooded run, open to start with, leads down from Lac de Mayen to the village over south and south-east facing slopes, about 4km. in length. Four chair-lifts, Mayen - Bryon, Bryon - Le Fer, Le Fer - Choulet, and Solepraz - Les Ars, constructed in 1982, opened extensive terrain with over 60km. of well prepared pistes.

There are also nursery slopes surrounding the village on three sides, all served by drag-lifts, and three further drag-lifts on the western side serving short wooded runs.

In a Few Words: The keen skier will not find sufficient scope in Leysin alone, although there is some good off-piste skiing, but its wide variety of other activities make it suitable for parties or families including beginners and non-skiers; a snow nursery for children aged 4-6 years, open daily from 9.30 a.m. until 12 noon; within easy reach of other Vaudoise resorts, including Les Mosses and Les Diablerets; snow best in early season; two langlauf courses; lots of sun! and prices reasonable.

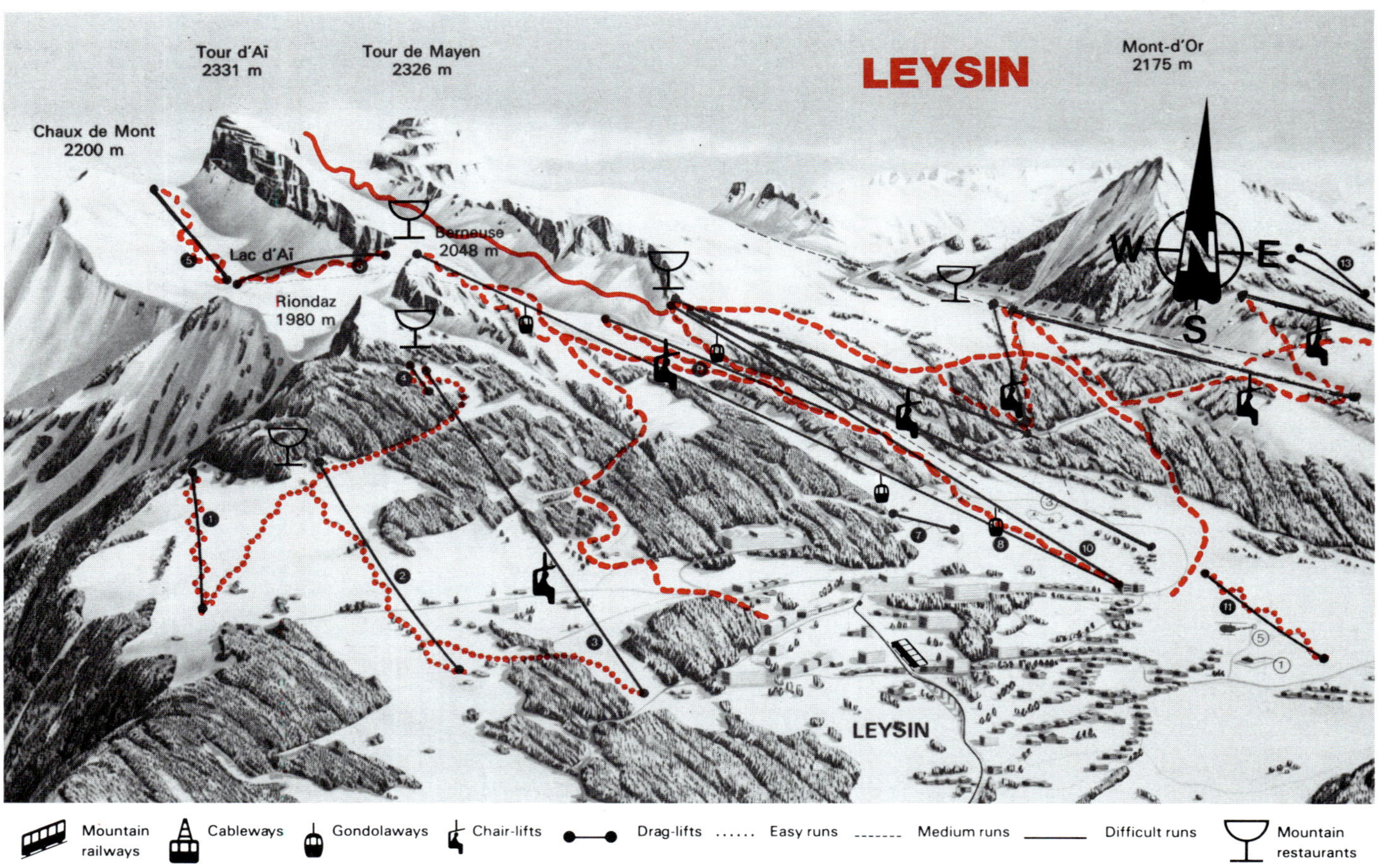

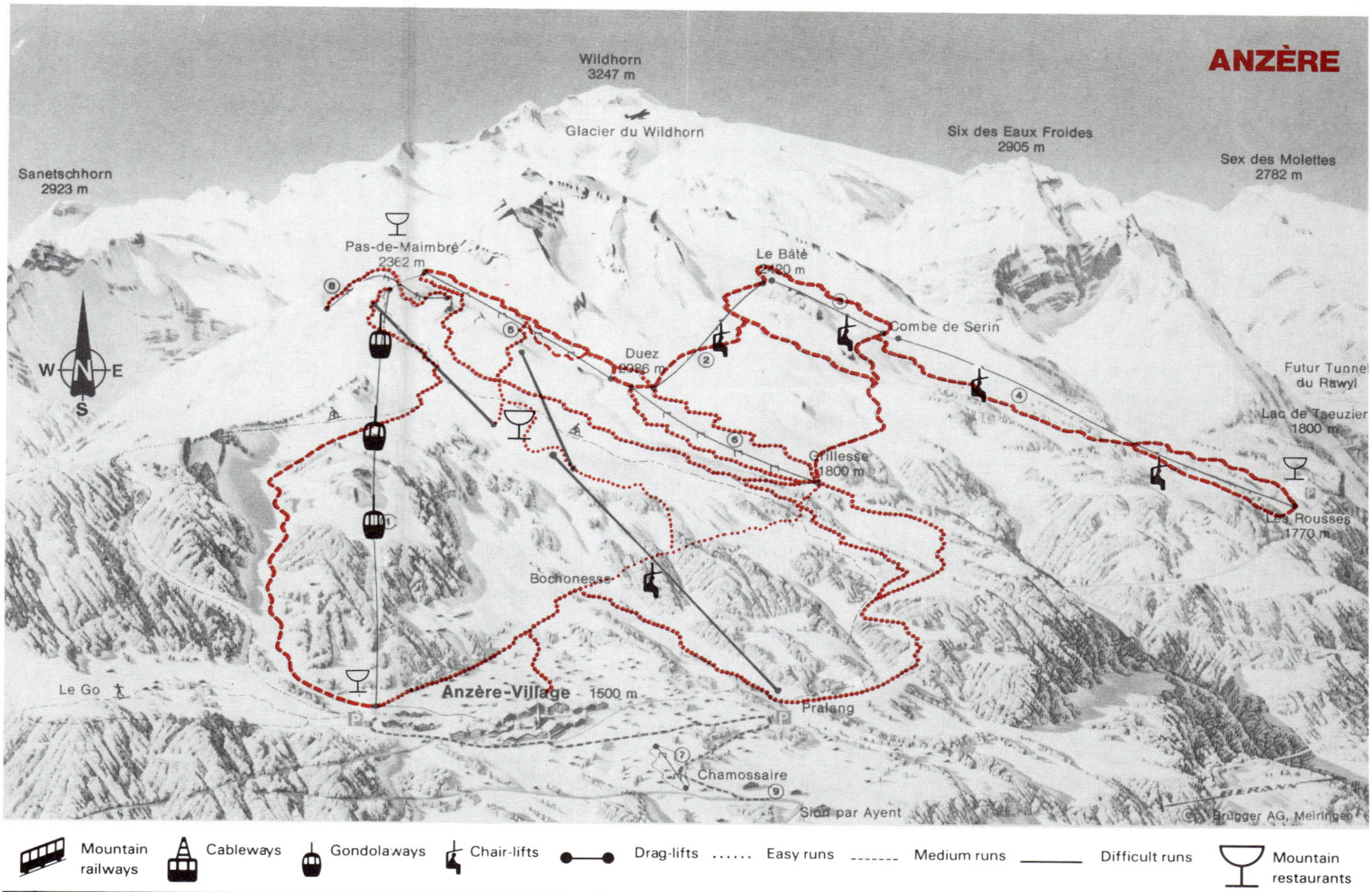

Après Ski: There is quite an international community based in Leysin with a lot of young people and there are several discothèques. 'The Club 94' is very popular. The Cesar discothèque at the Central-Résidence is very stylish. The Vagabond Club's bar is always full of life, however quiet things are elsewhere. The Café de Leysin, more expensive, has excellent cuisine; Le Chasseur is good value with a friendly atmosphere. The fondue and raclette evenings at the Prafandaz restaurant at the top of the lift, are a special attraction in rustic surroundings. The tax de séjour included in hotel prices gives a reduction to the skating rink, tennis and squash courts in the Sports Centre and for ski-passes and indoor swimming pool. In addition there is curling and ice hockey matches. There are torchlight downhill and ski races weekly.

Recommended Hotels:

Hotel Central-Résidence: This hotel really deserves the description of a first class international hotel. Superb use of colour and natural materials (wood, stone, leather) in decor; very comfortably furnished. Attractive alcoved dining room with fire open all round; cocktail piano-bar with open fire; excellent food and an agreeably relaxed atmosphere. Cesar discothèque with dark blue lights and dark wood decor very effective. 200 beds, all rooms with bathrooms, kitchenette and south-facing balconies, radio, telephone and security drawer. Swimming pool, sauna, fitness room, massage. Highly recommended.

Club Vagabond: A unique, self-contained hotel at the top of the hill, run by very agreeable and helpful Canadians, providing accommodation; meals (at one sitting); catering mainly for young people. Young and lively atmosphere. log cabin style bar and discothèque with draught beer. 50 beds, 2, 3, 4 or 5 to a room, most rooms south facing with balcony and with plenty of space. Sun terrace off dining room, sitting room with open fire leading from bar.

ANZÈRE

Height of Resort: 4,920 ft.
Height of Top Station: 7,937 ft.
Nearest International Airport: Geneva
Map Reference: 2D See page 240
Route by Car: See pages 236-240
Resort Facilities Charts: See page 221
Hotel Reference Charts: See page 232

Anzère is a modern well planned ski resort in the Valais region of Switzerland built in the mid sixties, easily accessible, sunny and compact, providing everything required by most holiday skiers. It is good for those of medium skiing ability and for the absolute beginner too, and particularly for families with teenagers or small children, who should probably rent one of the well equipped, easily run and most comfortable apartments or chalets. If however, your leanings are towards big, bare, bleak and really challenging skiing and an old alpine village then Anzère is not your style.

Anzère lies at 4,920ft., on a sunny plateau with woods of pine and larch, on the southern slopes of the Bernese Alps, looking across the Rhone Valley toward a panoramic view of the Valaisian Alps (13 mountains over 4,000 metres high). Anzère is only about 2 hours from Geneva by good rail and road connection, the road up from the valley is an easy and good one in winter and Sion, the capital of the Valais, is only about 10 miles distant.

The ski area is reached either by a 4 seater gondolaway from the upper west side of the village to Pas de Maimbré, 7,747ft., or a 2 seater chair-lift from Pralan, below and east of the village, which connects with the Les Luys and Tsalan drag-lifts. This chair-lift, which has a restaurant at its top station, is more convenient for those staying in the Pralan area and its capacity of 1,200 persons per hour has greatly reduced the queues at the gondolaway during busy periods. At Pas de Maimbré there is a restaurant and sun terrace from which one has unsurpassed views of some of the highest peaks in the Alps. One also finds the nursery slopes served by a trainer lift; this is an alternative area to the nursery slopes in the village with two baby lifts. From the top station the main skiing is mostly open over south and south-east facing slopes served by 3 drag-lifts with an east facing gully down the Combe de Duez and a drag-lift to pull one back. Skiing to the resort is either by the Piste des Masques, which is covered by snow cannons, graded black but not difficult, or an easier run to Pralan. From Duez one can ski further east by taking the Duez-le-Bâté 2 seater chair-lift to 7,937ft., the highest station in the resort and one can enjoy a long east facing run to Les Rousses, the latter half through trees. This very popular and pretty run can be tackled even by beginners as there are alternative routes with many off-piste varieties, some rather more challenging. At Les Rousses there is a charming wooden restaurant set amidst the pines. On the large sun terrace one can grill one's own sausages, steaks etc. It is difficult to tear oneself away from this lovely venue to return to Combe de Serin 3-seater chair-lift. At this point one can either take a surmounting chair-lift up to Le Bâté or ski down south-west to Grillesse.

In general the skiing is most suitable for intermediates and beginners but the more expert can have fun by taking the steeper line. There are good opportunities over the whole area for off-piste skiing although several slopes are avalanche-prone and care must be taken at certain times.

Cross-country skiers are well catered for in lovely surroundings; so are snowboarders, with two schools, and there is a 3.1 km toboggan run.

In a Few Words: A pretty and compact village, long sunshine hours and some of the best views in Alps. Many chalets and apartments owned by British and therefore an English atmosphere. Excellent for families. Good English speaking ski school. Exceptionally friendly and relaxed atmosphere everywhere. Somewhat limited variety of skiing and greatly lacking north facing slopes particularly for late season skiing. Paragliding school.

Après Ski: The main village square is blissfully out of bounds to motor traffic and gives Anzère much of its charm. Around it are a few nice little restaurants, unpretentious and serving well cooked dishes in welcoming interiors, also a pizzeria, a salon de thé and a crêperie.

In the centre of the village there are two night clubs, Les Masques de Bois and the King Kong. There is skating and curling up until the end of February, a beautiful swimming pool with special rates for visitors, and Salon 'Rio' with 6 billiard tables. Spaghetti, flambée and excellent steaks are to be found at Chez Juio. Every Monday an enormous cauldron of hot spiced wine is heated up and distributed free to all visitors. There are also 6 good sports equipment and sportswear, shops and boutiques. There is really everything one needs in the way of cosmetics, pharmacy, 2 supermarkets catering for the majority of Anzère visitors who are staying in a beautiful chalet or apartment.

Besides the restaurants mentioned in Anzère itself, it is fun to venture further perhaps to Ayent or Arbaz a few kilometres away and at the latter you can find the Restaurant du Lac à Arbaz which serves fresh trout cooked over an open fire, as well as fondues, raclette and other local specialities, well worth the 3 kilometres by taxi or bus if you are without a car. Nearer at hand in Anzère for dancing is La Diligence at Hotel de la Poste which has music until 3 a.m.

Recommended Hotels:

Hotel Eden: Built in 1983 this is a pleasant apartment hotel with nicely furnished studios and apartments each with kitchenette and fridge and bathroom. A pleasant restaurant, comfortable lounge, bar and for the more active a gymnasium and games room.

The Hotel des Masques: Beautifully situated on one side of the main square and with a sunny outlook, 42 bedrooms all have bath, wc. radio, telephone and balcony, and are decorated and furnished with a pleasing use of colour and material, pretty lampshades, warm carpets etc. The sitting room has a circle of deep cushioned seating around an open central log-fire with copper chimney above, and is set open plan between a bright dining room and a small bar. Beneath the hotel and with separate entrance is the popular discothèque 'Masque de Bois' open from 9 p.m-2 a.m through the season. During high season it usually has a band.

The Hotel Zodiaque: Set on the other side of the square and much bigger, having 140 beds. All bedrooms with bath/wc., radio, telephone and balcony and having fantastic views. A proportion of the accommodation consists of apartments with kitchenettes. Extremely modern in furnishing and decoration, very comfortable, with a leaning towards spot lights and some piped music. 2 bars, snack and grill room, sauna and largish discothèque underneath the hotel, called King Kong which is always lively and in high season sometimes has musicians such as 'Los Paraguayos' or a group or a singer as well. Card room, bridge and backgammon are played. TV and cinema.

LES 4 VALLÉES SKI AREA

The Four Valleys complex, of which Verbier forms a part, has developed considerably over recent years. In the process smaller resorts in the area are expanding and four of these resorts are reported under the above heading.

VERBIER

Height of Resort: 4,921 ft.
Height of Top Station: 10,916 ft.
Nearest International Airport: Geneva
Map Reference: 2E See page 240
Route by Car: See pages 236-240
Resort Facilities Charts: See page 223
Hotel Reference Charts: See page 233

Verbier has expanded tremendously over recent years to become one of the best organised resorts in the Alps. It lies in the Valais region on an extensive, open plateau. The lifts and cableways are well placed and within easy access of the village. The abonnement covers a total of 100 lifts in 4 valleys serving 400km. of pistes. Accommodation is amply provided and there is an abundance of chalets, many available to visitors either staffed or for self-catering. The traditional character of the village has been carefully retained and new developments blend well with the old. A free bus service operates around the village from 0830-1900 hours.

The main lift system runs from the east of the village and consists of two gondolaways and one double chair-lift rising to Les Ruinettes, 7,215ft., where many lifts and varying degrees of skiing can be found. The 1994/95 season saw the opening of the 'Funitel', a large type of gondola moving 2,000 persons per hour and running from Les Ruinettes to Attelas I which connects with the cableway to Mont Gelé, 9,918ft. To relieve the pressure on the Attelas region a heavy-duty cableway was opened in 1987 season from La Chaux to Col des Gentianes, with connections to the Mont Fort area. One of the largest in Switzerland, each of two 150 place cars makes the journey in just over 6 minutes. Three chair-lifts to the east of Les Attelas provide good skiing for beginners to medium skiers and one chair-lift rises to the Col de Chassoure to connect with a gondolaway from Tortin. A cableway from Tortin opens up the glacier skiing below Mont Fort and an even higher lift reaches near the summit of Mont Fort, 10,916ft. This is also for summer skiing. From Tortin one can ski, on fairly easy runs, to Siviez, Veysonnaz, Thyon 2000 and Haute Nendaz, altogether an enormous skiing area covered on the same abonnement.

Mont Fort Area: Unless you are going to ski the Mont Fort area every day it is better to pay the supplement for this area when skiing there.

The second ski area is Savoleyres. A gondolaway rises from the village and some excellent south facing runs are found either back to the village or on a drag or chair-lift. Spring snow is excellent on this south facing side. The north facing slopes of Savoleyres provide excellent piste skiing and interesting runs through the woods to La Tzoumaz (also known as Mayens-de-Riddes), where a gondolaway returns to Savoleyres. Three drag-lifts and two long chair-lifts are found on this north side. The off-piste skiing is limitless and with runs cut between trees, skiing is enjoyable even with poor visibility.

Good mountain restaurants are found at the top and bottom of the mountain lifts . The small restaurant Au Mayen just below the chair-lift up to Les Ruinettes is particularly good with a very friendly service. Also good is the restaurant Les Marmottes, below the drag-lift on south Savoleyres and Café Central at La Tzoumaz. The Carrefour restaurant at the top of Off piste, 'Chez Danny' under the Medran chair-lift and the Mont-Fort Cabane on the Mont-Fort - Chaux route. A more recent restaurant, L'Olympique, was opened at the top of Attelas I.

Those who prefer small village surroundings can stay at Le Châble, which has direct access by gondolaway to Verbier and a direct connection to the lifts travelling to Les Ruinettes and Attelas. Or one can stay in Veysonnaz, Haute-Nendaz, Siviez or Mayens-de-Riddes which all have direct access to the slopes (see separate reports).

Ski Tours: Several tours can be undertaken; two suggestions:-

Half-day – Verbier, Mont Fort, La Chaux, Verbier, about 22km. Suitable for advanced skiers.

One day – Verbier, Attelas, Tortin, Siviez, Greppon Blanc, Thyon 2000, Mayens-de-l'Ours, Siviez, Haute-Nendaz, Verbier, about 35km. Suitable for intermediate and advanced skiers.

The Verbier abonnement also covers the ski area at Brusons, a small resort opposite Verbier which has expanded extensively and there are further plans for development. A free bus runs from Le Châble to Bruson and there is an interesting run back to Le Châble through very small villages.

Overall, Verbier ranks as one of the top skiing resorts. There is an excellent sports centre with facilities for swimming, tennis, squash etc.

20 snow making machines enable skiers to ski down to the resort and beginners to practice on the nursery slopes. All runs have been marked and colour coded to match up with the map of the area.

There are good family rates on the Verbier abonnement which makes it more reasonable for families. For example, a family consisting of 2 adults and 2 children (4-16 years) have the opportunity of getting a complete family abonnement for the price of two normal adult tickets. The two ski schools arrange excursions to the four valleys daily – this is a superb day's skiing with views over the Rhône valley.

In a Few Words: Skiing excellent for all standards. Limitless off-piste for those with knowledge of the mountains; efficiently arranged lift system, although some bottle-necks, this is being improved all the time by the extensive construction of new lifts and replacement of older lifts. Very sunny; extensive nursery slopes; good for young children in early season; excellent kindergarten for 3 to 10 year-olds. Summer skiing.

Après Ski: Verbier has a good selection of restaurants, clubs, bars and even a burger bar to appeal to most tastes and pockets. Starting with restaurants, Verbier boasts one of the best restaurants in Switzerland, being the 'Rosalp', rated 3 'toques' in the Gault et Millout guide. The several Swiss-style restaurants include 'Montpelier', 'La Grange' (recommended for raclette and fondue), 'La Luge' – an excellent grill and bar. The 'Écurie', 'Caveau' and 'Braconnier' are also recommended. On the slightly less opulent style, Verbier has a selection of pizzerias including 'Fer à Cheval', 'Borsalino', 'Al Capone' and 'Chez Martin'; all are warm and friendly. There are a couple of speciality restaurants – 'Phoenix' (Chinese) and 'Le Mignon' (Creole, amongst a Swiss selection) – this is highly recommended. Verbier has several night clubs with dancing to band or disco. 'The Farm' is probably the most exclusive and expensive and is reputed to pull regulars from as far away as Geneva. Marshall's is very popular and slightly less expensive than The Farm. The Tara is popular and The Scotch Club, a perennial favourite for the younger set. The bars in Verbier including Pub Mont Fort, Nelson, Jacky's Bar and New Club are always buzzing. The Milk Bar, Harold's Hamburgers', Jesse's Grill and Juice Bar, Tart'in and Le Monde des Crêpes are also popular after skiing, for sweet and savoury snacks respectively.

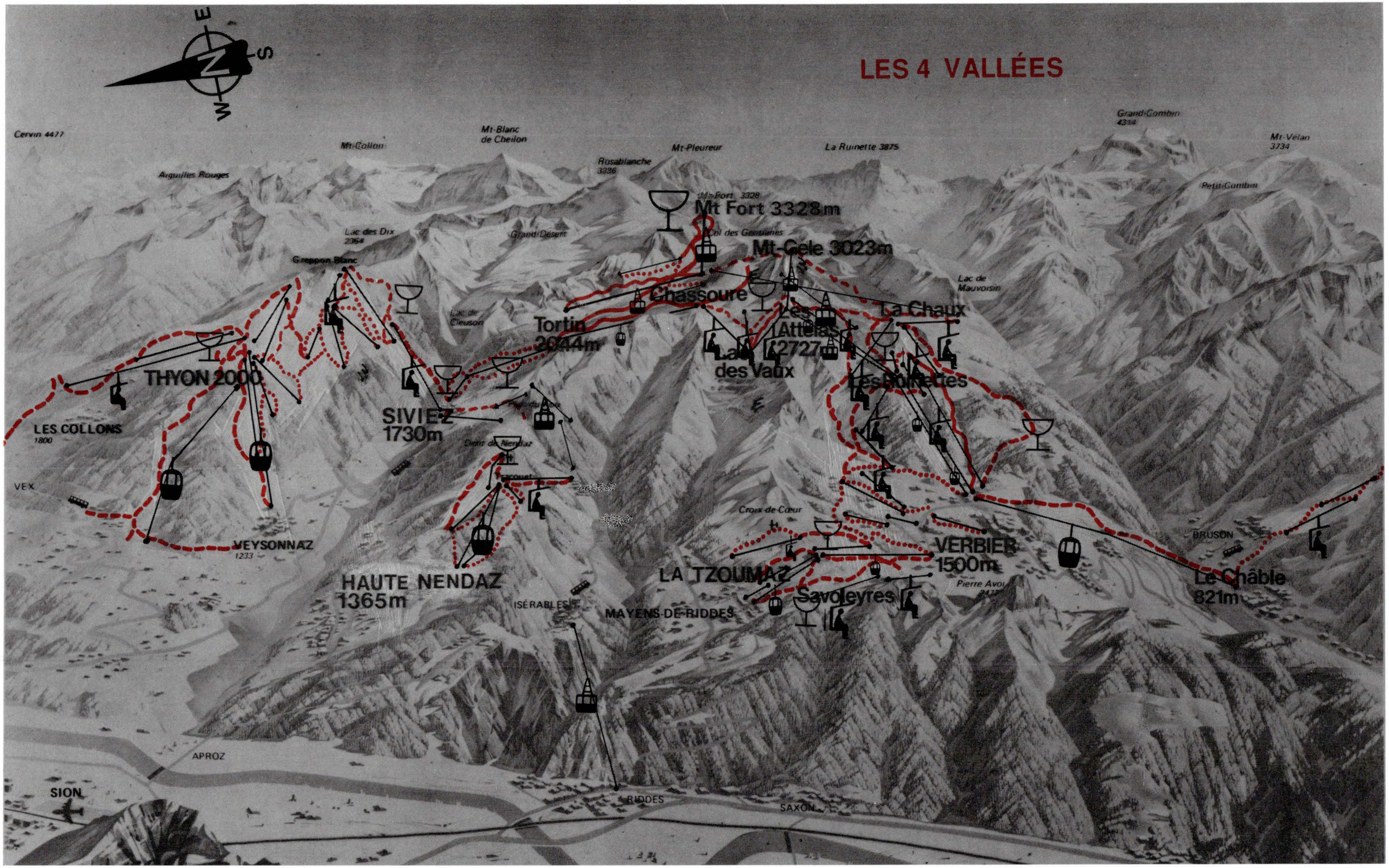

Mountain railways — Cableways — Gondolaways — Chair-lifts — Drag-lifts .... Easy runs --------- Medium runs ——— Difficult runs — Mountain restaurants

Recommended Hotels:

Hotel de Verbier: A long established family run hotel situated on the edge of the main square and about 450 metres from the Medran gondolaway. Pleasant dining room and spacious wooden beamed lounge with bar which is a popular meeting place. Private fitness centre 100 metres away. Relaxed and friendly atmosphere. Discounts on ski passes, ski hire, shopping and private sports centre.

Hotel Alba: This large and attractive 170 bed hotel is centrally situated in one of the streets leading to the main square. The cosily furnished bedrooms all have bath and wc. The dining room, lounge areas and well designed bar are all beautifully furnished. A buffet style breakfast is always served. Fitness room, solarium and sauna. Heated car park. Also conference facilities for up to 80 persons.

Hotel Bristol: This modern chalet-style hotel is situated near the main square. All bedrooms are with bath, wc, colour TV and mini-bar. The restaurant is on the ground floor, along with shops and ski locker room. The reception area is on the third floor and reached by lift. A good hotel for the keen skier requiring simple accommodation at reasonable prices.

Hotel de la Poste: A pleasant, family type hotel, situated near the village square. Comfortable rooms, some with bath or shower. Large sunny dining room, restful lounge-bar and TV room. Swimming pool.

Hotel Eden: This comfortable family run hotel stands in the main square. All bedrooms have shower, wc., balcony, radio & telephone. Lounge & residents dining room where buffet breakfast is served. 'The Nelson Pub' serving 30 types of beer.

Hotel L'Auberge: Situated in a sunny position, under the same management as the Hotel de la Poste. Simple but pleasant rooms, with bath or shower. Games room including bar opening onto large sunny terrace. Meals taken at the Hotel de la Poste.

Hotel Rhodania: Situated in main street, all rooms with private bath or shower, very modern and smart reception area. The Spaghetteria restaurant specialises in spaghetti and Italian dishes. Popular disco – 'Le Farm Club'.

VEYSONNAZ

Height of Resort: 4,045 ft.
Height of Top Station: 10,916 ft.
Nearest International Airport: Geneva
Map Reference: 2E See page 240
Route by Car: See pages 236-240
Resort Facilities Charts: See page 223

Situated on the northern side of the Four Valleys furthest away from Verbier, Veysonnaz is a small mountain village 13km. from Sion. Many chalets in Valaisian style have been constructed in recent years and the total bed capacity is 4,000, with some 150 beds in hotels.

From the eastern side of the village a gondolaway rises just above Thyon 2000: to the left and right of this main lift are the drag-lifts, Combyre I and II, which serve the intermediate runs on the upper slopes. Further to the left the Piste de l'Ours gondolaway serves the famous piste of the same name, where some of the best skiers in the world have competed. A demanding run of 3.5km. with a vertical drop of 2,592 ft. is kept in good condition by 28 snow making machines covering 15 km. of runs. To the south of Thyon 2000 a series of drag-lifts on Greppon Blanc, provide access to a good variety of easy and intermediate runs above the treeline and these lifts also allow one to traverse across to the run down to Siviez Nendaz. Here one picks up 3 surmounting drag-lifts connecting with the Tortin gondolaway up to Col de Chassoure, or the cable-way via Col des Gentianes to Mont-Fort, the entry points for the ski area above Verbier. From either Col de Chassoure or Mont Fort one can work one's way back to Veysonnaz.

In a Few Words: Veysonnaz has a compact lift system of its own and the skiing, mainly over west and north-west facing slopes, is best suited for second year to intermediate skiers, whilst the advanced skier has access to this huge area served by 100 lifts.

Après Ski: As with most small resorts it is limited: there is disco dancing, a selection of restaurants and bars and a heated indoor swimming pool.

Accommodation: A wide selection of chalets and self-catering apartments on which we can send you details.

MAYENS-de-RIDDES (LA TZOUMAZ)

Height of Resort: 4,921 ft.
Height of Top Station: 10,916 ft.
Nearest International Airport: Geneva
Map Reference: 3E See page 240
Route by Car: See pages 236-240
Resort Facilities Charts: See page 222

This village, known by the above two names, is reached from Riddes, halfway between Martigny and Sion, on a good approach road of 13km. It is a small, but growing, village consisting mainly of chalets and apartments, most of them recently constructed, providing over 7,000 beds with a further 125 in hotels, the best being the The Hotel Beau-Site. There is a well stocked supermarket, ski hire shops, restaurants and bars. The village is well situated at the foot of the gondolaway which takes one up to the top station at Savoleyres, 7,723 ft. From this point there are south facing runs on the Verbier side, well known for its spring snow, and excellent north facing runs down to Mayens-de-Riddes which also provides first class off-piste opportunities. On the way the café Chez Simon, at the foot of the Savoleyres Nord drag-lift, is well worth a visit. The runs in both areas are well groomed and most suitable for the intermediate skier.

Rising from the village and running parallel with the gondolaway a chair-lift and surmounting drag-lift serve the slopes immediately above the resort.

In a Few Words: Strategically placed for the 4 Vallées ski area and the north facing slopes of Savoleyres on the doorstep. Accommodation is considerably less expensive than the neighbouring resorts in the 4 valleys.

Après Ski: Quiet and definitely for the ski enthusiast. Many happy hours can be spent in the restaurants, disco and bars where one will enjoy a warm and friendly atmosphere. Swimming pool, sauna, skating, para-gliding and toboggan run.

NENDAZ

Nendaz embraces the resorts of Haute-Nendaz and Siviez, the latter being 1,200ft. higher. They are linked by lifts and by a shuttle bus service and in an ideal position for the '4 Vallées' skiing.

HAUTE-NENDAZ

Height of Resort: 4,478 ft.
Height of Top Station: 10,916 ft.
Nearest International Airport: Geneva
Map Reference: 2E See page 240
Route by Car: See pages 236-240
Resort Facilities Charts: See page 222

Situated on a sunny shelf overlooking the Rhône Valley, Haute-Nendaz spreads from the older part to Nendaz-Station where most of the hotels, apartments and shops are located. Like its neighbour Verbier, the greater part of the accommodation is in chalets and apartments, providing over 16,500 beds, and still increasing, in addition to 3 hotels and 5 pensions.

Looking at the map it will be seen that the Verbier skiing is to the right and the Veysonnaz-Thyon area to the left. The link-point for both being Siviez (see report below) which can be reached in 20 minutes by a frequent ski bus service or on skis as follows: Take the cableway, installed in 1992, next to the car park, up to Tracouet, 7,218ft., where there is a large self-service restaurant with sun terrace. This is also the area for the ski school with 4 drag-lifts, one serving the nursery slope; also a free amusement park for children. To continue to Siviez one takes the Les Fontaines drag-lift which connects with the cableway to Plan-du-Fou, 7,972ft., where there is a pleasant restaurant. From this point one has some delightful easy skiing all the way to Siviez.

To ski to the Veysonnaz-Thyon area one takes the Novelly chair-lift from next to the Siviez car park. There is a very pleasant mountain restaurant there. A surmounting drag-lift leads to the crest of the Greppon Blanc, 8,858ft., where one finds lovely, easy to intermediate skiing on west facing slopes above the tree line. Here one comes across Thyon 2000, a small, purpose built resort where both gondolaways coming up from Veysonnaz and Mayens-de-L'Ours meet. On the north-east slopes there are many lifts serving these wide open, easy pistes. There are plenty of places to have lunch at Thyon or at the top of the Novelly chair-lift. This circuit alone provides a splendid days skiing with plenty of variety.

To reach the Verbier skiing from Siviez one takes the 4 seater chair-lift to Tortin, 6,706ft., with its own self-service restaurant which tends to get crowded at noon. Here one has the choice of taking the gondolaway to Chassoure, 8,989ft; or the cableway to Col des Gentianes, 9,514ft., with connecting cableway to the top station Mont Fort, 10,916ft. This area is on the glacier where summer skiing takes place, served by drag-lifts. There is a self-service restaurant at Col des Gentianes (see separate report on Verbier). On the return journey to Tortin the run is black and often heavily mogulled, therefore more suitable for experienced skiers. One can however, take the gondolaway down to Tortin. It is suggested that when taking day trip to the Verbier skiing, it is wiser to take the shuttle bus from Haute-Nendaz to Siviez only taking 20 minutes, thus giving one more time.

In a Few Words: A well placed resort for the '4 Vallées' ski area; much more reasonably priced than its larger neighbour; interlinked with the main circuit with a back-up shuttle bus service; suitable for all grades of skiers; nordic skiing well catered for; sports centre, high standard apartments.

Après Ski: A good selection of bars and restaurants, 4 disco night clubs which include Les Flambeaux, which is perhaps the most popular; it has a pizzeria next door. Le Mazot is a pleasant café bar opposite the Tourist Office where one can recover with draft beer from the day's skiing. To mention a few of the restaurants, Le Robinson is intimate and exclusive; Mont-Rouge, large with good food and service; Sporting, small and rustic; Le Grenier and Les Etagnes near the gondolaway are well worth a visit; whilst the Edelweiss is unpretentious and favoured by the locals – always a good sign, and is next door to the bus station. Le Pub Phénix and Piano Bar Tchin-Tchin are good value. Le Vieux-Chalet is specially recommended, 10 minutes from centre, whilst down in the old village, La Place has character. There is an artificial skating rink; sports centre with squash, fitness room, massage, sauna and solarium.

Accommodation: Mainly in a wide range of chalets and self-catering apartments, and we would be pleased to let you have detailed information.

SIVIEZ

Height of Resort: 5,675 ft.
Height of Top Station: 10,916 ft.
Nearest International Airport: Geneva
Map Reference: 3E See page 240
Route by Car: See pages 236-240
Resort Facilities Charts: See page 222

A small purpose built resort situated to the east and nearly 1,200ft. higher than Haute-Nendaz, linked lifts and also reached by frequent bus services from

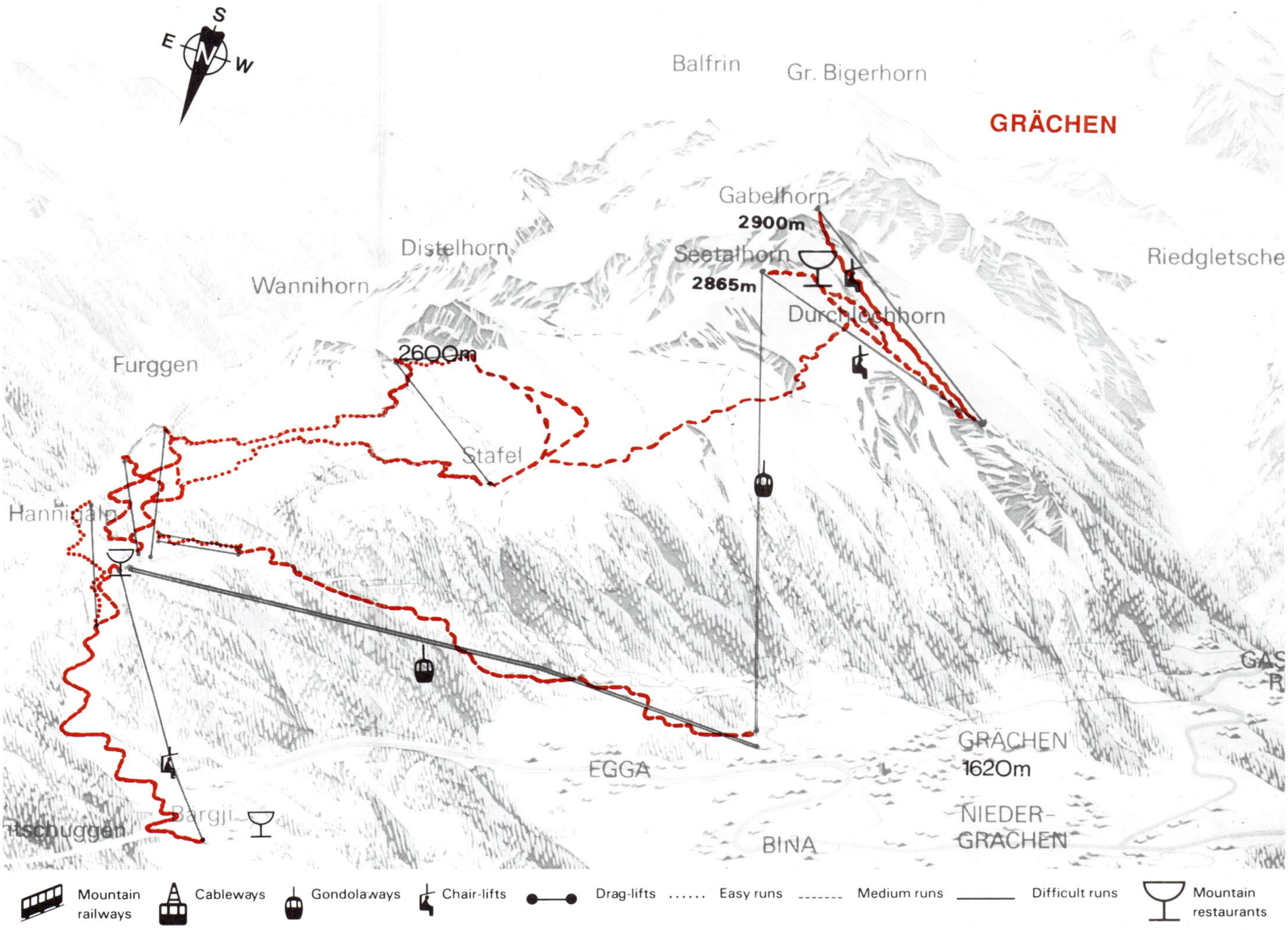

the latter. One hotel and a half a dozen apartment buildings, the essential shops and a surprising choice of restaurants make this an ideal centre for skiing almost all of 'Les 4 Vallées' region. From Siviez a 4 seater chair-lift takes one to Tortin where there is the choice of the Mont Fort cable car or Tortin Gondola which connects with the vast area of skiing above Verbier. On the north-east side a chair lift and surmounting drag-lift to Greppon Blanc giving access to the Thyon 2000 and Veysonnaz areas while on the west side, the Siviez chair-lift and surmounting drag-lift offer easy skiing as well as entry to all the runs above Haute Nendaz. At the top of the drag-lift there is another attractive and pleasant mountain restaurant.

In a Few Words: A small modern resort ideally placed for the dedicated skier.

Après Ski: This is really what you make of it in a small friendly resort. Haute Nendaz is quite close for those with their own transport.

GRÄCHEN

Height of Resort: 5,313 ft.
Height of Top Station: 9,528 ft.
Nearest International Airport: Geneva
Map Reference: 3E See page 240
Route by Car: See pages 236-240
Resort Facilities Charts: See page 222
Hotel Reference Charts: See page 232

Grächen has quickly expanded with the recent development of its ski slopes. It is perched high on a sunny shelf on the eastern side of the valley which leads on to Zermatt, and looks across towards an imposing group of towering mountains. There is an old, pretty village centre, surrounded by numerous chalet-style hotels and new chalets, and most of these appear to be available for renting. The resort is very suitable for families, the skiing being easy to medium on north-west and west facing slopes. Snow conditions are good in late season. The lift system has been extended and there is absolutely no queueing and no hassle, Grächen is one of the most restful resorts one could choose.

The skiing is divided into two areas:

Hannigalp-Wannihorn area: The main skiing area is just above the treeline on north-west facing slopes, reached by a gondolaway from the eastern side of the village, only 5 minutes from the centre, to Hannigalp, where there is a restaurant seating 500 people, in addition to a smaller cosy Swiss style restaurant seating 50. Alternatively, one can travel to Hannigalp on the long chair-lift which runs from Bargji – there is a delightful log-cabin restaurant here. From Hannigalp there is a choice of 4 drag-lifts, but to avoid any walking one can ski down to the base of the lowest, the Paradiesli, and connect with the other two. This is an easy run. The two higher drag-lifts run almost parallel up to Furggen and from here there are variations of easy and intermediate descents back to Hannigalp. From Furggen one can also make a long traverse across to Stafel and ascend to Wannihorn, 7,528ft., via a further drag-lift. This provides a difficult run from Wannihorn to Stafel, but intermediate skiers who don't wish to attempt it can traverse back across the same slope and return to Hannigalp. There is a trainer lift at the base of the higher Furggen drag-lift. To return to the village there is a long and varied easy to medium west facing run from Hannigalp, very icy in the morning and slushy in the late afternoon, a wide piste with trees either side; or one can take the medium to difficult run down to Bargji.

Seetalhorn-Gabelhorn area: This area is reached by gondolaway starting from the southern side of the village and rising to Seetalhorn, 9,415ft., where one finds a restaurant. From this top station there are easy and intermediate runs, northwest facing, by the chair-lift down to Plattja, 8,087ft. From the base one can cross over on a difficult run to pick up a second chair-lift which reaches Gabelhorn, 9,528ft., the highest station in the resort. The north-west facing runs down each side of this lift are all difficult. From these upper slopes it is not possible to ski directly down to the village. One can however, cross over on intermediate and difficult north-east facing runs leading to the Hannigalp area.

Children: Excellent facilities for children between 3-6 years are available in the Schnöö's Super Children's Ski Paradise' situated on Hannigalp and reached by gondolaway from the village. Equipped with its own miniature ski lifts and runs, toboggan runs and igloos – this is completely free of charge. There is also an indoor heated play area where parents can leave their children all day to be looked after and fed by a trained staff for a reasonable charge. Full information from the Tourist Office, tel: 028 56 27 27.

In a Few Words: A small village, greatly improved ski area giving the resort a longer season; popular with families; indoor sports centre with curling and tennis, sunny and fairly quiet. Excellent facilities for children, 3-6 year-olds, in their own 'Ski Paradise'.

Après Ski: There are numerous tea rooms, restaurants and bars but the atmosphere is restful and uncrowded. Many of the visitors to Grächen stay in self-catering chalets. There is dancing at the Grächerhof and the Walliserhof hotels. The charming log cabin restaurant at Bargji is reached by following the main road through Egga, the upper part of the village, from which you can just see the tip of the Matterhorn, and you can drive to within 5 minutes walk of the restaurant. There are wood fires and raclettes and fondues are served. There is a beautiful view across the valley. Special weeks are held during the season at all-in prices. There are two swimming pools in hotels and a skating rink, but Grächen is definitely not a resort for night swingers.

Recommended Hotels:

Hotel des Alpes: On the western side of the village, about 2 minutes from the centre, this is a chalet-style hotel with red furnishings giving it a warm atmosphere. Separate restaurant and bar, with special feature a heated sun terrace. All bedrooms have shower/wc. telephone and balcony. Rooms can take extra beds for children. Frau Ruff is very helpful and speaks good English.

Hotel Élite: Built in 1970 in traditional style, this small well-run hotel is situated fairly near the Hannigalp gondolaway, towards the upper end of the village, about 5 minutes from the centre. Bedrooms, most with bath, are very comfortable, with south-facing balcony overlooking the village, the Weisshorn in the background. Small, light and attractive dining room with wooden beams also facing south, with terrace outside. Very good food cooked by the owner. Separate lounge, bar/reception area, whirlpool, sauna and solarium. M. Reynard, the owner, offers a personal service to guests.

Hotel Hannigalp: This centrally situated hotel has been run by the same family for nearly ninety years. Large dining room with windows on three sides, à la carte restaurant, a particularly attractive bar with a good atmosphere, comfortable sitting rooms. All bedrooms with bath or shower, wc, balcony, direct telephone, radio and TV. Indoor swimming pool, sauna, solarium, whirlpool, table tennis and tennis court.

CRANS-MONTANA

Height of Resort: 4,920 ft.
Height of Top Station: 9,840 ft.
Nearest International Airport: Geneva
Map Reference: 3D See page 240
Route by Car: See pages 236-240
Resort Facilities Charts: See page 222
Hotel Reference Charts: See page 232-233

Crans-Montana is really made up of two separate but adjoining centres, sharing the same beautiful surroundings and ski terrain, and the same facilities are available to visitors of either resort. Set in the heart of the Valais region, it is reached by a $2^1/_2$ hour drive from Geneva, a half hour bus journey from the railhead of Sierre, or a slightly longer journey by cableway; there is also an air link from Geneva to Sion.

The resort is built on a wide plateau overlooking the Rhône valley, with a magnificent view in every direction. The ski terrain is varied and interesting, much of it above the treeline, with gullies and paths threading through massive rocks and beautiful pine woods on the lower slopes. The main area is towards the Wildhorn and Wildstrubel mountains which lie behind Crans-Montana, and provides some 160 km. of pistes, the well-planned and extensive lift system removing any possible feeling of crowding.

Les Violettes-Plaine Morte Area: The Violettes Express, with 6-seater gondolas, rises from the east of Montana to Les Violettes, 7,355ft., where there is a restaurant. Here one of the major changes to the lift system for the 1995/96 season was the 'Funitel' rising to Plaine Morte, 9,840ft., with its excellent restaurant built round three sides of the terminal, giving fantastic views. The 'Funitel', a continuously moving gondola type system, consists of 20 cabins, each holding 30 persons,- which increases the capacity on this sector from 480 to 1,600 persons per hour.Three drag-lifts serve these fairly easy slopes and one can also cross to the glacier drag-lift (also used for summer skiing and snowboarding) and ski on the glacier. From Les Violettes there is a superb run down to the foot of the cableway which medium skiers can enjoy; best conditions for this are in the morning. On the way down are the La Toula drag-lift and chair-lift which lead to the slopes of Mt. Bonvin, offering the choice of two fast descents, or access to the Aminona-Mt. Bonvin ski area. Better skiers usually prefer to ski to the foot of the La Barmaz 4 seater chair-lift or Cabane de Bois drag or chair-lift and return to Les Violettes, as the steeper and more interesting part of the piste is on these upper slopes, the last stretch through the woods being very gentle. In addition, there is a most spectacular off-piste run, the Faverge, for good skiers only; it leads from Plaine Morte through an entirely different valley to Aminona, vertical descent 4,920ft. Another particularly enjoyable run, with fascinating scenery, starts off at Les Violettes and ends at the foot of the Bella Lui area.

Cry d'Err-Bella Lui Area: There is a choice of 3 lifts to Cry d'Err, 7,436ft., and Bella Lui, 8,725ft. From Montana a 6-seater gondolaway goes to Cry d'Err via Grand Signal, where there is a restaurant. Cry d'Err can also be reached by gondolaway from Crans, and one passes La Menbé restaurant about halfway up. The Crans-Chetzeron gondolaway leads to Chetzeron with yet another restaurant, a drag-lift completes the journey from here to Cry d'Err. From Cry d'Err, Bella Lui is reached by either cableway or drag-lift. These slopes are open and mainly south facing with a network of lifts making the area a vast playground for beginners to medium skiers, with limitless variety of runs and glorious views. There are five well-spaced mountain restaurants, and the slopes are open at the top, becoming wooded lower down. The descent from Bella Lui can be taken fast by good skiers by keeping up high on the ridge, crossing it to the left and joining the Piste Nationale, a lovely run for competent skiers. It can also be joined at Cry d'Err by crossing the ridge beyond the gondolaway station. One can return to the top of the Piste Nationale, using the drag or chair-lift, and from here there are also fast runs, finishing in the fairly close woods by the Les Barzettes-Les Violettes gondolaway station. Another run which is fun starts behind and above the Bella Lui cableway terminal, turning off to the right and eastwards over a ridge, descending through various gullies and finishing with a steep traverse to Les Violettes. At Bella Lui there is a small bowl which can be skied by using a drag-lift, and which also permits one to cross over to Cabane de Bois.

Aminona-Petit Bonvin Area: A short bus journey from Montana leads to a gondolaway, its top station Petit Bonvin, 7,872ft. This area can also be reached by skiing from Plaine Morte through the Faverges. There is a beginner's drag-lift near the little cabin café and gentle slopes which lead down to a pleasant medium run crossing through the woods to Aminona. On the western side of the gondolaway, starting at Plumachit, a new 4 seater chair-lift, 'La Tza', with a capacity of 2,400 persons per hour, rises to Petit Bonvin. The descent starts with an easy run becoming steeper on the way down. This lift replaces the two previous chair-lifts.

It is not possible to detail the immense variety of runs in Crans-Montana. In addition to snowboarding, which is also extremely popular here, nordic skiing is particularly well catered for, with 50km. of prepared trails including some interesting tracks through the woods. Marvellous ski touring is accessible from Crans-Montana as well, to Mont Bonvin, Wildstrubel and the Wildhorn. Also hot air ballooning, para-gliding and ski-surfing. Free shuttle bus service every 20 minutes to all parts of the resort. Free covered car parks at all cableway stations.

In a Few Words: One of the most beautiful settings anywhere, with varied skiing for all grades; good interlinked lift system, well provided with mountain restaurants; sunny; well organised resort.

Après Ski: Lively in both, with plenty of choice. In Crans the Sporting, with casino, bars, large restaurants and dancing to a group is popular but expensive. A favourite spot for teenagers is the Pacha Club with bar dancing to disco; Absolut also has a disco and English style decor. Le Madison (Hotel Central) has a group and occasional floor show. The night club 'Aux Noctambules', near the Supercrans tower, always has a lot going on but gets noisy and somewhat out of hand. The Number One discothèque lives up to its name and is very good. After 2200 hours the Memphis piano bar has a lively atmosphere and good music. Amongst the various restaurants, the Cisalpine in Montana, near the gondolaway terminal, has timbered rooms with open fire, a good atmosphere and excellent foods – raclettes, fondues, grills, etc. In Montana, Auberge de la Diligence has ambience and serves Lebanese specialities, whilst La Poste offers good French dishes. In Crans the Rôtisserie de la Reine is expensive but with superb cuisine; Le Vieux Moulin is much cheaper and you can get a set menu there; the Primavera, is also very good value. Le Raccard specialises in international cuisine, is elegant and provides excellent service. Reasonably priced snack meals can be obtained at the Vieux Moulin; and the Miedzor Hotel has a delightful small bar and restaurant. Worth trying also are the Petit Paradis in Bluche for Valais specialities, La Cave restaurant in Crans. Among popular meeting places are the Grange Bar and Café du Centre in Montana, the latter offering folk music, and the Pub in Crans. There are comfortable bars with friendly atmosphere in most hotels.

Recommended Hotels:

MONTANA

Hotel Crans Ambassador: In a beautiful setting overlooking Montana, about ten minutes from the centre and 100m. from the Cry d'Err lifts, and one can ski back to the hotel. Provides apartments as well as 56 double and 8 single rooms, all with bath, balcony; and 6 beautifully furnished luxury suites. Large attractive sitting room, long panelled dining room and carnotzet for regional dishes, all serving excellent food. Card room, swimming pool with bar, solarium, jacuzzi, sauna, health and beauty centre, fitness and conference rooms. Expensive. Regular mini-bus service.

Hotel St. Georges: Quiet hotel in its own pine garden 100m. from the main square. 40 rooms all recently renewed with bath, colour TV, radio, direct dial phone, minibar and safe-box; most of them are south facing with balcony. Different restaurants - international, French, Italian and Swiss atmosphere - comfortable and cosy sitting rooms, piano bar with live music every evening. Friendly management and lots of personal attention. Conference room up to 15 seats with modern technical material. For your health, sauna and solarium.

Hotel Vermala: In a sunny situation with fine views to the south and with wooded land behind. At the Vermala end of Montana, but the free and frequent local bus stops right outside and takes only 5 minutes to the very centre of Montana, skating rink, etc. It takes even less time to the bottom stations of the Cry d'Err and Grand Signal cableways, which are only a few minutes' walk either on or off skis. There are 70 beds in comfortably furnished rooms all with bath or shower and wc. and almost all have south facing balconies and wonderful views. Bright and cheerful sitting room, dining room and bar. The food is good and specialities such as fondue and raclette can be enjoyed.

CRANS

Hotel Miedzor: Modern, neat and comfortable, this charming small hotel is in a quiet but central position in Crans. 14 double and 3 single rooms, all with bath or shower, balconies, radio, telephone and some with tiny kitchen and fridge; attractive furnishings. Pretty, colourful restaurant with good cooking. Small sitting room with open fire and nice bar with pianist from Christmas to March (no dancing).

Hotel Royal: This charming 5 star hotel was completely renovated in 1994. It has 42 south facing rooms with balcony, 12 north facing, all with bath, wc, radio, TV, minibar and direct dial telephone. The reception rooms offer comfort and a warm atmosphere. Special bridge room with hostess, and a pianist plays each evening in the restaurant and bar. The hotel is set amidst the pine trees with lovely views, and only 2 minutes' walk from centre.

CRANS – MONTANA

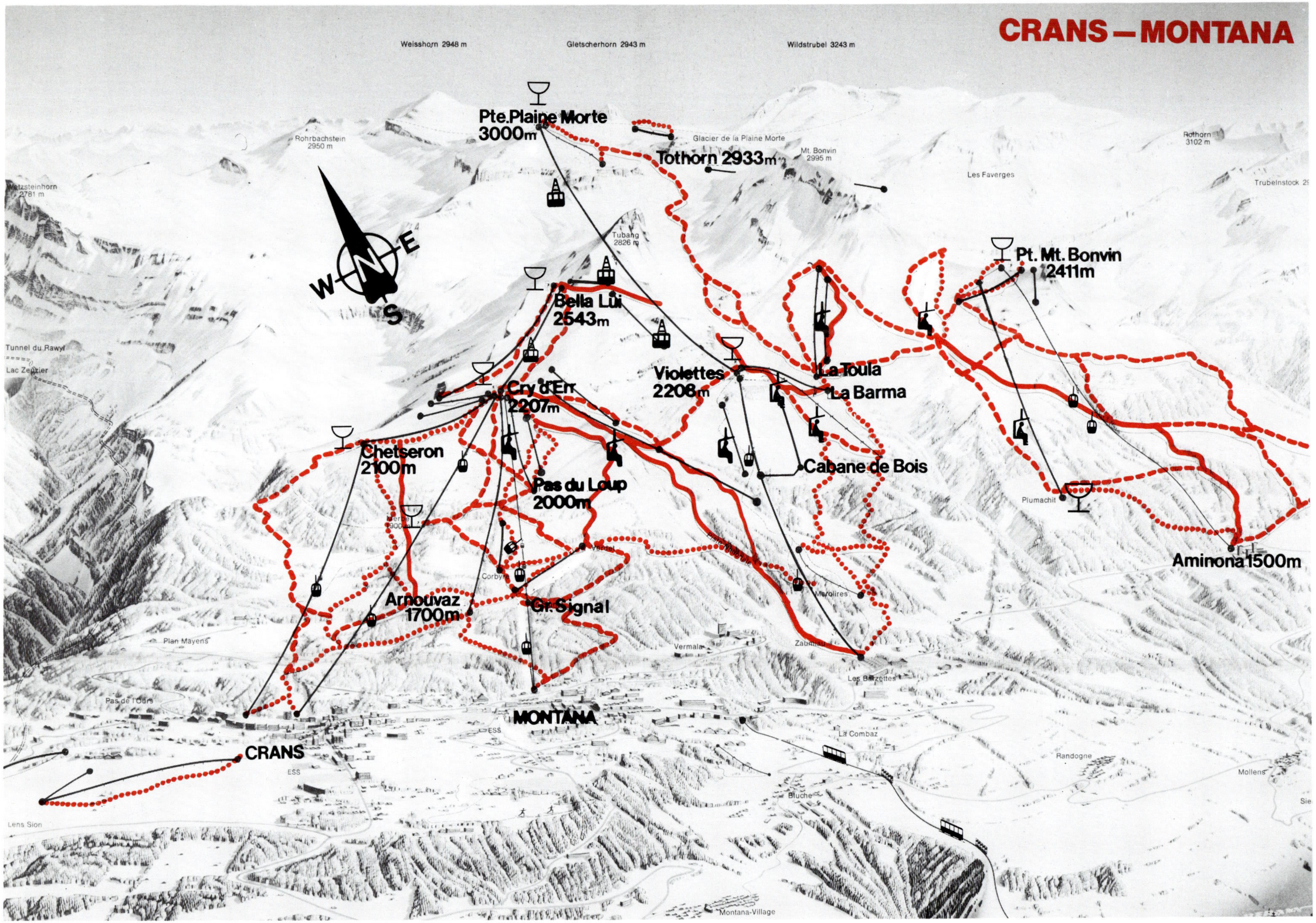

Mountain railways · Cableways · Gondolaways · Chair-lifts · Drag-lifts · ...... Easy runs · --------- Medium runs · ——— Difficult runs · Mountain restaurants

ZERMATT

Height of Resort: 5,315 ft.
Height of Top Station: 12,788 ft.
Nearest International Airport: Geneva
Map Reference: 3E See page 240
Route by Car: See pages 236-240
Resort Facilities Charts: See page 223
Hotel Reference Charts: See page 233

Dominated almost everywhere by the magnificent Matterhorn, Zermatt, with Europe's highest tree line, is an all year round ski resort. It combines a busy and thriving mountain resort in a most beautiful area of the Alps, with an excellent range of high mountain skiing in Switzerland's most southern mountain resort.

Zermatt is accessible by the Zermatt railway or by road via Visp to Tasch – it takes about 12 minutes from Tasch to reach Zermatt by train or taxi. There are 60 return journeys each day during peak season from 06.00-23.30. Cars are not allowed in the resort. The narrow streets are served by horse-drawn sleighs, electric taxis, four solar powered ski buses, and electric delivery vehicles. In the picturesque village there are still groups of old farmhouses and barns. There is an Alpine Museum with skiing and climbing relics and reconstructions of old Zermatt dwellings and a concert hall.

Accommodation of all types is available from 5-star hotels to simple rooms. An availability board and telephone is at the station.Facilities in the resort include para-gliding school, ski touring, heli-skiing, mountain climbing, skating, curling, tobogganing and ice-hockey; indoor swimming pools, cinemas, saunas, indoor tennis, squash and bowling. For langlauf enthusiasts, advanced classes are run on high altitude trails. There are many shops offering the latest ski fashions and several supermarkets and some 40 or so mountain restaurants. Several distinguish themselves by the charm of their interiors and the quality of their food. Those currently serving very good food and specialities as well as giving pleasant service are mentioned in the text below. In spite of having so many facilities, Zermatt's prices are not among the most expensive in middle-sized Swiss resorts.

Zermatt's three main ski areas have some 45 runs totalling over 150km in length. The areas are partially interlinked – plans for complete interlinking have met with commercial and environmental opposition. In addition, Cervinia and Valtournenche, with which Zermatt is interlinked, have over 150km. of marked runs served by 36 lifts. A supplement is required for Cervinia lifts.

Gornergrat-Stockhorn Area: Reputed to be the highest, above ground, rack railway in Europe rising 4,855ft. from the village to Gornergrat, 10,170ft., and moving 2,800 people per hour. After passing Riffelalp station, there is a magnificent view of the Matterhorn. From Gornergrat a two-stage cableway continues to Hohtälligrat, 10,789ft., with its cableway to Rote Nase 10,650,ft. and then to Stockhorn, 11,180ft., giving access to the Platte and Triftji areas where skiing is particularly good in spring. These areas are very steep and are often heavily mogulled. With fresh snow the powder skiing can be marvellous. Below these areas is Gant, which gives access to Blauherd or up the Platte drag-lift and from there to the Triftji drag-lift. Below Gornergrat is a wide expanse of often sunny slopes served by drag-lifts. The runs are wide and easy to Riffelberg with the exception of a tricky start. Trains run back to Gornergrat every 10 minutes. To avoid this start take the slower train (48 minutes) which stops at all stations, including the Landtunnel station, a little before the Ritty turn-off, and get out at Rotenboden just below Gornergrat or at Riffelberg and take the drag-lifts upwards. The comfortable Riffelberg Hotel restaurant's best feature is the panoramic view. It was a setting for the film 'Women in Love'. Below Riffelberg, the widened gallery section leads to skiing more challenging than the blue grading indicates. Lower down is the picturesque Ritty's for Zermatt's most consistently fine mountain-hut cooking (by Bruno, previously pastry chef at the Zermatterhof Hotel): try the quiche, the rosti, the käsesschnitte and the famous apfelstrudel – in fact everything is good. Half a mile below, turning left past Simi's (try the Nudeln Carbonara and grilled Bratwurst) is the passenger lift to Furri, connecting with cableways up to Furgg, Schwarzsee, Trockener Steg and the Klein Matterhorn. The road past Alm (which serves sensational fresh trout) can usually be skied to Zermatt. Also below Gornergrat there is an exciting red run through Kelly's Gully down to Grünsee and then either to Riffelalp or to Gant. Before Gant is the Findeln-Gletscher, now rebuilt and open.

Sunnegga/Blauherd-Rothorn Area: The Sunnegga high speed underground funicular railway rises to Sunnegga, 7,509 ft. (2,600 per hour). From Blauherd a new cableway rises to Rothorn, 10,170ft., with its restaurant. From Rothorn there are three choices of skiing. There is a medium grade run over south facing slopes which divides near Fluhalp with one branch towards Blauherd and the other (sometimes closed), to Gant (via Fluhalp restaurant which serves excellent goulasch soup) with its link to the Triftji area. There is the Kumme Valley below the Rothorn, with three runs and a triple chair-lift back to Rothorn. Also is the option of continuing down the valley or taking one of two steep runs near Tuftern leading into Zermatt.

From Blauherd, 8,470ft., the easier runs descend to Findeln via Sunnegga where it can be perilously icy inspite of the fully automatic 'snow guns' operating from just below Rothorn down to the National 4-seater chair-lift. There are also several pistes from Blauherd through meadows and then along mountain paths leading down to Zermatt. One is the challenging National downhill race run to the foot of the chair-lift of the same name which returns skiers to Blauherd. From Sunnegga, popular lunchtime stops are the chalet restaurants in Findeln, among which are: Adler – try the pot au feu; Chez Vrony – try the rosti and the apple tart and 'Chez Franz and Heidy' for ossa buco with polenta and also the chocolate mousse.The recently opened Enzian Restaurant run by Anni and Toni Strametz, is small with a friendly atmosphere and delicious food. Intermediate skiers can then take the moderate slope to Findeln chair-lift returning to Sunnegga.

Good skiers can take the often icy path to Findelenbach station. Skiers may stop at Othmar's Hütte – try the muesli, the hot apple cake, the delicious carrot cake and their café fertig or at Ried – sample their strudel with vanilla sauce.

Furri-Trockener Steg - Schwarzsee - Klein Matterhorn - Cervinia and Valtournenche Areas: A gondolaway and a cableway both rise to Furri, 6,115ft., (2,700 per hour) and from there one cableway rises to Schwarzsee, 8,480ft., a second to Trockener Steg, 9,642ft., a third leads to these stations via Furgg, 7,900ft., whilst a two section 4 seater chair-lift rises from Furgg to above Trockener Steg, terminating at 9,947ft. Schwarzee can also be reached from Furgg by the 5 cabin gondolaway, each cabin holding 15 persons. From Trockener Steg is Europe's highest cableway to the Klein Matterhorn, 12,533ft. It is advisable to enquire about the weather before making the ascent as it can be bitterly cold. The Gandegg Hütte below Klein Matterhorn is full of atmosphere, providing good food and a very cheerful service.

Klein Matterhorn: The station ends on the north side of the peak and a tunnel about 200 yards long leads to the pistes down to Plateau Rosa, and to Cervinia. From the centre of the tunnel is a passenger lift to the foot of a hundred or so steps. At the top is a safety viewing platform with a 360° panorama with breathtaking views of Mont Blanc and Gran Paradiso. (both about 40 miles away). From Klein Matterhorn, the run into Zermatt is about 17km. direct via Furgg-Furri and about 20km. if via the Furgg-Schwarzsee cableway, making it one if Europe's longest marked ski runs. Access to Trockener Steg and Cervinia and the glacier area which stretches about 6km. from Gobba di Rollin, 12,793ft., past Plateau Rosa to Trockener Steg with 9 drag-lifts, is initially by a single piste which can be testing if the ridge is icy followed by slopes varying from moderate to quite steep. Trockener Steg station is well equipped with boot and ski lockers where skiers can leave their equipment.

Cervinia, Valtournenche and Trockener Steg: After the ridge there are two branches to the Cervinia runs, one near the Plateau Rosa which also leads to Valtournenche and the other beside the Theodulpass. It is quicker to get the day ticket back by buying it at a cableway station on the Swiss side although it is cheaper in Italy, particularly for those under 16. The Swiss day ticket allows unlimited use of the Cervinia lifts though a very early start is needed to take advantage of this as the main cableway back to Testa Grigia, (Plateau Rosa) in Switzerland may take up to two hours. It is wiser to plan the day in order to leave Cervinia by 2 p.m. and never select a Sunday for your skiing visit. Remember that the shops in Cervinia close between noon and 4 p.m. and that lunchtime service can be leisurely. (Try Ristorante Pavia with its sun terrace and delicious food). The first part of the return journey from Valtournenche is via Cervinia by bus or taxi (about 20 minutes). The descents to Trockener Steg after the ridge merge with the run from Plateau Rosa, 11,416ft., just beyond the Theodulpass below Furgghorn. These runs on the Theodul glacier are gently inclined for beginners. It has excellent deep snow skiing after snowfalls. Two long parallel drag-lifts lead towards the ridge which marks the Italian border, one rises to Furggsattel, 11,040ft. and the other connects with the shorter drag-lifts to the Theodulpass, 10,705ft. and Plateau Rosa.

Trockener Steg to Furgg, Schwarzsee and Furri: From Trockener Steg, where the automatic snow guns now operate down to Furri via Furgg, the runs are on open slopes, at first moderate as far as the bottom of the Theodul drag-lift and later of increasing gradient to the bottom of the Garten Poma lift at Furgg. The Garten run is often mogulled on the west side as is the lower part on the east where it meets the Theodul-Furgg run. From Furgg downwards you can avoid the steep and often icy run direct to Furri (sometimes closed), by taking the lift from Furgg to Schwarzsee, for an interesting range of runs immediately below the Matterhorn. Three difficult runs descend through narrow gulleys towards Furri There is a testing run via the Hörnli drag-lift which is never prepared by snow-cats. It is also the run closest to the Matterhorn. A fourth easier run, the White Pearl, via Stafelalp to Zermatt, is very picturesque.

Furri to Zermatt: The Gornergrat, Trockener Steg and Schwarzsee runs into the village all converge near Furri where the lift can be taken to the village. Many skiers make their way to the mountain restaurants such as the Furri (excellent pot au feu, lasagne al forno). The run from Furri into Zermatt, which generally has snow from December to the end of April, now that it has snow cannon cover, can be skied by moderately good skiers. A incentive not to take the gondola down at the end of the day is the 16th century restaurant Zum See (try the spinach tortellini and the sacher torte) and the Restaurant Blatten for the best cakes in the mountains and for dinner on Wednesday evenings.

Powder Snow Skiing: The principle areas for untracked snow are around the Triftji and Gornergrat-Upper Kelle areas. Other areas on the main slopes are around Rothorn, at the bottom of the Ried meadows; between the Garten lift and the Matterhorn; between Hörnli lift and the Matterhorn. For those able to pay the price, there are helicopter tours with guides to Monte Rosa, Alphubel and Aeschihorn. In all these areas avalanche warnings should be heeded.

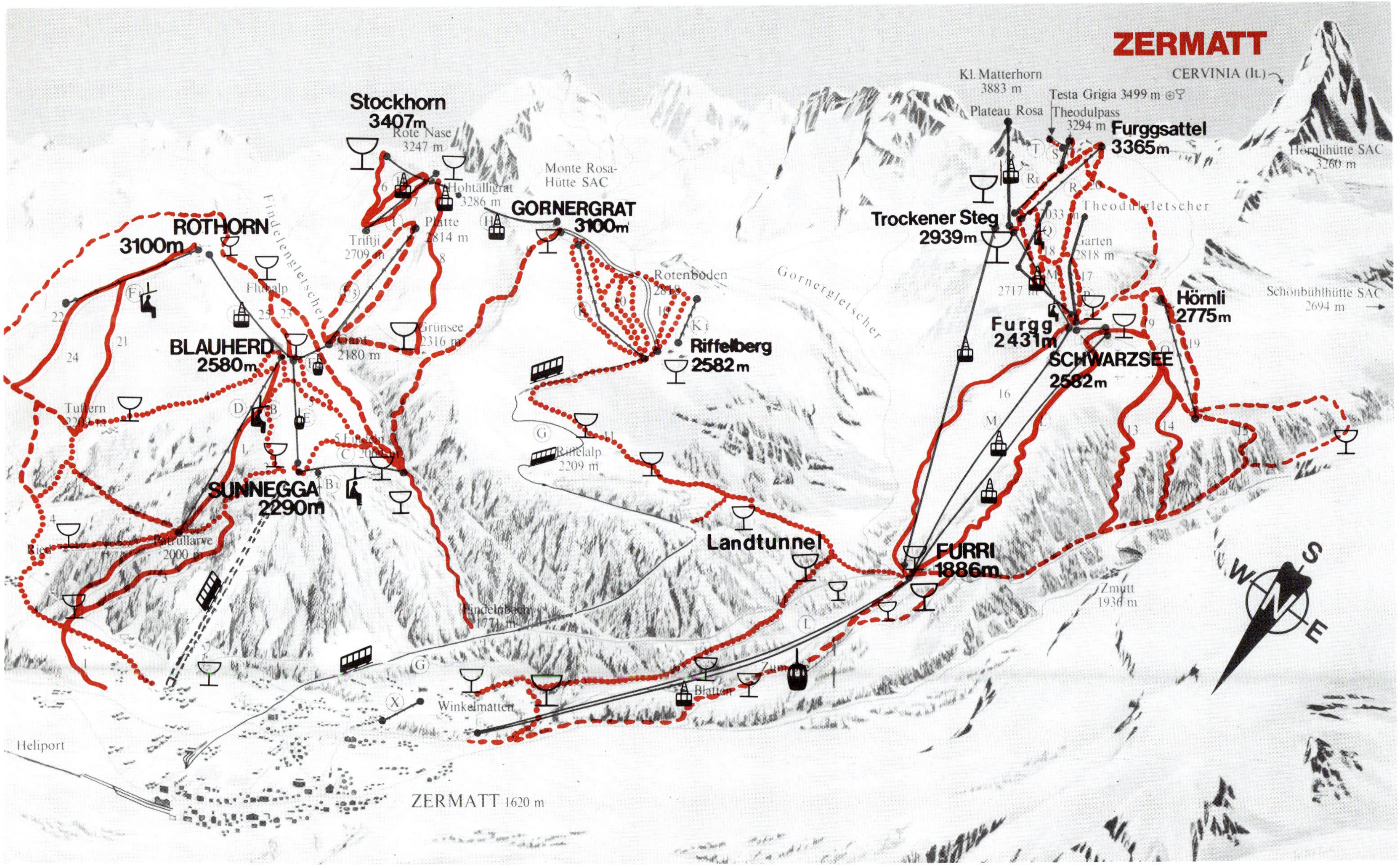

Mountain railways | Cableways | Gondolaways | Chair-lifts | Drag-lifts | ...... Easy runs | --------- Medium runs | ——— Difficult runs | Mountain restaurants

Ski Classes: Ski classes are all day only, from Monday to Saturday as well as from Sunday to Friday, and are available from the age of six. The school is the biggest, though perhaps not the best in Switzerland, due mainly to some of the classes being over-large. It is run by the dual management team of Roman Perren and Beny Graven. The standard of instruction is usually good and recognises the demand for classes solely in English.

Beginners and children: For class 1 skiers there is a small slope in the village. Class 2 generally skis below Sunnegga where there are easy runs served by the Eisfluh T-bar and a small hand tow. The traditional run for beginners is from Rotenboden to Riffelberg. Children's ski classes start at 6 years old. There is a nursery at the Hotel Nicoletta and Hotel La Ginabelle. There is good sledging along the paths from Furri into Zermatt.

Spring & Summer Skiing: Zermatt has one of the longest skiing seasons – 365 days a year. There are high altitude tours (Haute Route) until late spring. In summer there is skiing from about 0700-1300 hours daily, between Klein Matterhorn and Trockener Steg, where 9 ski-lifts move about 8,600 persons per hour, serving some 25km. of prepared pistes; the longest being 7km. with a vertical 3,290ft. One can enjoy lunch at Trockener Steg and equipment can be left there before returning to the village.

In a Few Words: Superb, exciting skiing, catering for all standards. There are more runs for medium and good skiers than for beginners. Snow conditions remain good for a long season with skiing possible throughout the year above Trockener Steg. Ski reports are given each morning on Radio Zermatt (Channel 7) at 8.10 a.m. and 9.10 a.m. Weather conditions on the slopes are also shown on video in most hotels. There is a vast lift system but only three entry points from the resort and only partial linking between areas, so a fair amount of walking is necessary. There are 5 electro-solar ski-buses. The village is delightful with a lively nightlife and renowned for outstanding eating places on and off the slopes.

Après Ski: For many it starts earlier in Zermatt than most resorts with lunch in one of the mountain restaurants. Most of these restaurants also serve teas. In Zermatt itself, there are about ten teatime rooms, among which are Conditorei Hörnli, Café Fuchs, Café Zellner and Biners and about 40 bars among which are Elsie's (known for its snails and oysters), the Monte Rosa bar, the Papperla Pub, and the busy crêperie near the ski school offices. If you still have the stomach for it, there are about 80 restaurants to choose from which include the Corbeau d'Or at the Mirabeau Hotel; the Avenstube at the Hotel Pollux, Le Mazot (for good grills) and Le Gitan (excellent grilled lamb and gratin dauphinoise). There is the Spaghetti Factory at the Hotel Post for pasta, the China Garden for Chinese cooking and the Vieux Valais for pasta and excellent pizza.

Well advertised on billboards in the main streets are special events, galas, theme dinners, live bands and cinema programmes. The most popular places for dancing are Le Village disco especially with the young and the Hotel Alex and the Zermatt Yacht, Golf and Country Club for the sophisticated. The Lady Pollux has a disco often with a live band as do the Hotels Mont Cervin, Zermatterhof, Bristol and Simi's Hotel – the two latter have folkloristic music Doors open around 9.30 p.m. For a group it is best to reserve in advance and arrive by 10.00 p.m.

Recommended Hotels:

Hotel Alex: In a quiet, sunny position with a view of the Matterhorn and close to the Gornergrat station. Luxury hotel, built and decorated in the best traditional Valais style, with the addition of superb apartments with open fire and TV on the fourth floor. Large south facing terrace, luxurious indoor pool, sauna and excellent masseur! Restaurant one of the best in Zermatt. Dancing in night club. The owner, Alex Perren, was a well known mountain guide and instructor. Indoor tennis court and a squash court.

Hotel Garni Derby: A delightful chalet-style hotel in main street, near Gornergrat station. Most rooms with private bath and balcony; attractive tea-rooms and restaurant where guests can take lunch or dinner. Sun terrace, with service, on main street.

Hotel Mont Cervin: One of the Seiler group of hotels. Situated in the centre of the village, this is a large hotel with reception rooms matching its size. Attractively decorated sitting rooms and three dining room areas, providing superb food and excellent service. The bedrooms are large and tastefully furnished, many with balcony. The indoor swimming pool is one of the finest to be found at any hotel, well planned, with massage, sauna, solarium and fitness room; conference rooms. Residence Mont Cervin with 15 luxury suites.

Hotel Nicoletta: Situated off the main street, opposite the ice rink. Reopened in July 1986 after extensive rebuilding. 122 rooms all renovated in 1997, several suites with 2-4 rooms; all with private bath/shower and wc, telephone, radio, TV and fridge, those south facing with balcony and Matterhorn view. Hotel restaurant, à la carte restaurant, piano bar, lounge. Swimming pool, sauna, sun terrace, solarium. Children's playroom, and private kindergarten (winter only), carnotzet, pharmacy and kiosk in same building.

Parkhotel Beau-Site: This hotel enjoys lovely panoramic views, it is a 4 star and situated 4 minutes walk from the centre. The 73 bedrooms are nicely furnished, all with bath, telephone and radio, most have balconies. The extensive facilities include a large comfortable sitting room, attractive dining room, grill for à la carte meals, cosy bar with candlelit alcoves, swimming pool, sauna, whirlpool, turkish bath and solarium. Large sun terrace. A well organised hotel and much recommended.

Hotel Walliserhof: An old Valaisian hotel, with sun terrace in front, has been completely renovated inside and the decor is most attractive. All bedrooms are with private bath and tastefully furnished, two dining rooms, sitting room and bar. Owned and supervised by Ruth Inderbinen, who is very friendly and helpful.

Hotel Zermatterhof: A large hotel of 148 beds standing in its own grounds in the centre of the village. Bedrooms of good size and tastefully furnished. All with private bath or shower, TV, minibar, some with jacuzzi. Elegant and spacious reception and dining rooms including de luxe French restaurant.Two bars and pianist. Large swimming pool, sauna, steambath, solarium and fitness room. Very, efficient and friendly service.

SAAS FEE

Height of Resort: 5,905 ft.
Height of Top Station: 11,811 ft.
Nearest International Airport: Geneva
Map Reference: 4E See page 240
Route by Car: See pages 236-240
Resort Facilities Charts: See page 223
Hotel Reference Charts: See page 233

Saas Fee, situated amidst beautiful scenery, at the end of the Saastal Valley just over an hour by post bus from the main rail station of Brig, can be easily reached by train from Zurich or Geneva. By car, few difficulties should be experienced, but chains are essential. One takes the Zermatt road from Visp branching off left at Stalden.

Completely carless, there are large covered and open air car parks at the entrance to the village, all transport in the village is by small 'electro' trucks, this gives a very quiet and relaxed atmosphere to the whole village. Quite large and some distance from one end to the other, with the centre divided from the main lift area by a river, Saas Fee has grown from a small Valais farming village to one catering well for skiers seeking an authentic village, with modern facilities, yet without the expense or sophistication of larger and better known international resorts.

The skiing, which is divided into three main areas, is either good for beginners, or excellent for advanced intermediate upwards. Although there is some excellent easy skiing suitable for second week to third year skiers on the Fee glacier and in the Felskinn area, reaching it from the top stations and returning to the village can be daunting for the less experienced.

For absolute beginners the nursery slopes are ideal, although early in the season can be in the shade for much of the day. Both nursery slopes and main lift stations are at one end of the village and can be a few minutes' walk from the village centre, longer from the main area for Chalets. The Alpin Express cableway, first section installed in 1991, and the second section was opened for the 1994/95 season. The cableway has improved the situation considerably, as will be seen below. There is, however, a good selection of hotels of all grades adjacent to the main lifts. For those staying in the centre or beyond there are facilities to leave boots and skis near to the ski school and lifts which are secure and plentiful.

Being high, with glacier skiing up to 11,811ft., snow is almost guaranteed, but early season can be cold, heavy snowfalls can lead to piste closure until avalanche clearance has been done. For those aspiring to improve their skiing and tackle all types of terrain few places can be better suited. On the main runs back to the village, the longest being 9km., almost everything is encountered from easy 'motorway' on the glacier, to steep mogul fields. Due to restricted usable areas on the glacier and steep mountain sides lower down, 'off piste' possibilities are limited.

Spielboden-Längfluh Area: A gondolaway from the west side of the village rises to Spielboden, 7,962ft., where there is a restaurant. A cableway, holding 60 persons, runs from here to Längfluh, 9,416ft., with a further restaurant and a chair-lift, and a wonderful view of the high mountain peaks and seracs of the Fee glacier. A 5km. run leads back to the village, testing for the medium skier and exhilarating for the good skier. As an alternative to this run, take the new lift, installed for the 1994/95 season, from Längfluh which travels up the glacier and from the top one can ski over to Felskinn.

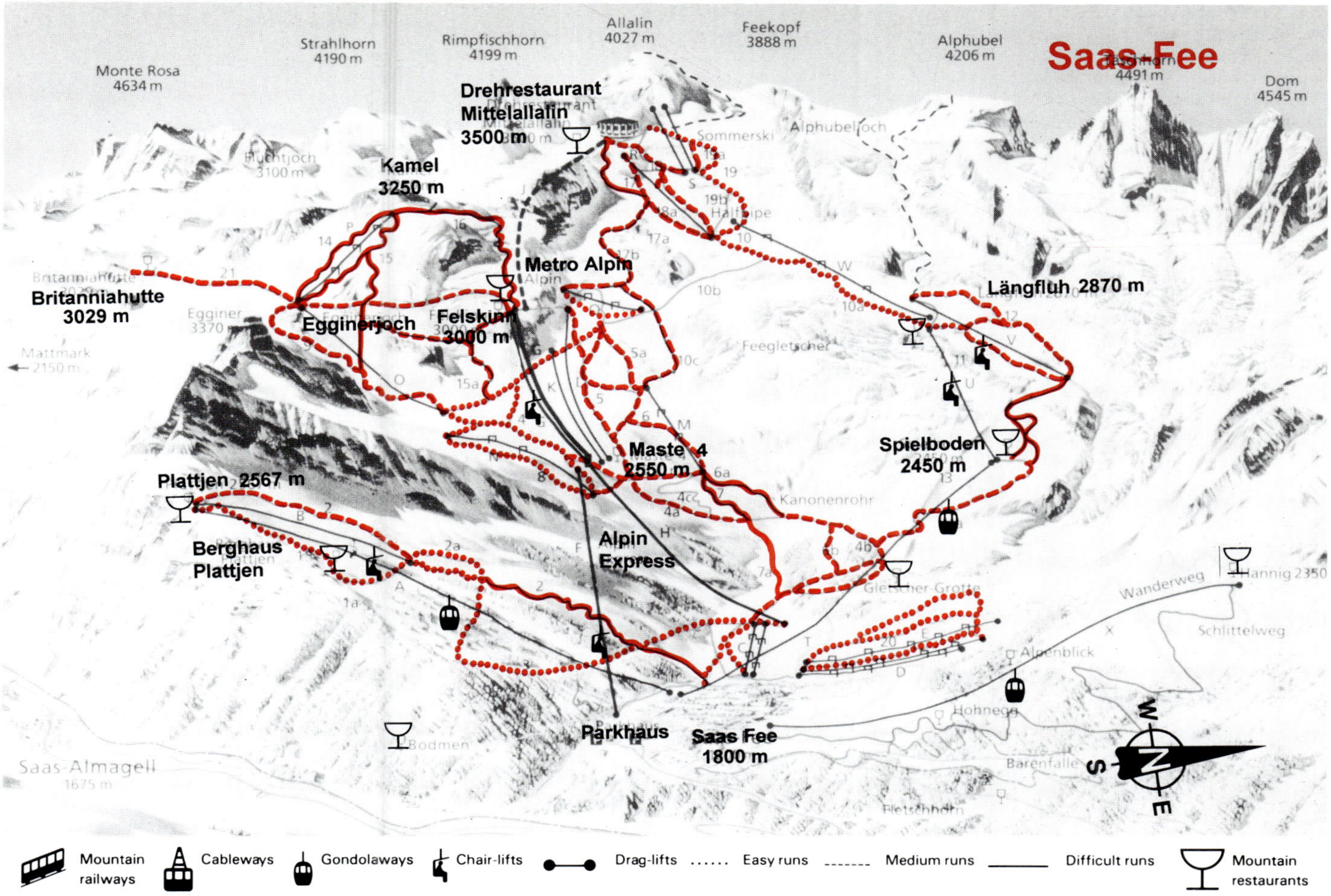

Felskinn-Mittelallalin Area: A great improvement has been made to the approach of this area by the Alpine Express cableway. It leaves from the edge of the car park, situated at the entrance to the village, and climbs to Maste 4 and its restaurant, 8,366ft. On the northern side there are three drag-lifts and the longest, Egginer 2, terminates near Felskinn, 9,750ft. where one finds the entrance to Metro Alpin. The second stage of the Alpin Express cableway rises from Maste 4 up to Felskinn. 9,834ft., thus providing a direct link from the village with the Metro Alpin.

From the western side of the village a cableway holding 60 persons rises to Felskinn in 7 minutes, a vertical rise of 3,600ft.

The runs between Maste 4 and Felskinn served by the three drag-lifts mentioned above and one on the south side provide superb easy to intermediate skiing, whilst the runs below Maste 4 to the village become more difficult with the longest run being about 7km. Above Maste 4 on the southern side there are two further drag-lifts, one rising to Egginerjoch, 10,171ft., with a red run to base and from the top, and with a little climbing, poling and finally schussing one arrives at Felskinn. The second lift reaches Kamel, 10,660ft., with two black runs to base and a third black to Felskinn.

At Felskinn is the entrance to Metro Alpin, opened in 1984 and one of the world's highest underground railways. It rises to Mittelallalin, 11,500ft., with its revolving restaurant from which one has marvellous views of the surrounding area. On the north side there are three drag-lifts and 22km. of prepared runs which is the summer ski area. The top lift reaches 11,811ft. and from this point there are glorious runs to the village via Längfluh or Maste 4 of some 9km. with a vertical descent of 5,600ft.

To summarise, now the second stage of the Alpin Express up to Felskinn is completed it has off-loaded the pressure on the Felskinn cableway on the west side of the village and provided a more even distribution of access for the visitors living in the village; whilst weekend skiers will have immediate access from the car park to the Felskinn skiing and the area above it, without having to make the long walk through the village to the west side.

Plattjen Area: A gondolaway travels from the west side of the village to Plattjen, 8,343ft., where there is a restaurant. A chair-lift serves the top section so that it is unnecessary to ski right to the village. Runs are steep to medium. There is however an easy run through the trees to the village.

Hannig Area: The gondolaway up to Hannig has been closed but this area remains open for tobogganning and it has 20km. of marked footpaths with lovely walks down the mountain.

In addition to these immediate ski areas, some of the best touring territory in the Alps is accessible from Saas Fee, and the famous Haute Route to Chamonix and Verbier starts here.

In a Few Words: Delightful and unspoilt; friendly atmosphere; no cars; good for families with young children after mid-February; kindergarten; first-class lift system; efficient ski school; reliable snow throughout a long season; November until April; well placed, but limited, mountain restaurants; excellent for beginners and more advanced skiers, but limited in between; summer skiing; superb touring accessible.

Après Ski: Starting at lunch time, or after skiing the Rendez-vous near to the ski school is popular. For lunch or evening meal, unsophisticated, but full of atmosphere the small restaurant Zur Schaferstube is a must, situated at the edge of the village near to the Staffelwald lift, food is excellent – reservations advised. Although many guides recommend the Café Domino for après ski teas, the Sporting Café and Restaurant in the village centre is highly recommended for both teas and meals, being friendly and much used by locals. For evening entertainment most of the action is subdued and takes place in the various hotels. Discos and dancing at the Popcorn at the Dom Hotel, 'Nightlife' at Metropol Grand Hotel and Le Club at the Ferienart Walliserhof. The bars 'Why Not', 'Go-inn', 'Happy Bar' and 'Nesti' are all popular evening gathering places. There are several good restaurants including Restaurant Hohnegg, Cheminée, La Ferme. Good pizzerias are Boccalino, or Steakhouse Phillipe below the excellent romantic Hotel Beau Site. For a special evening out dinner at the Waldhotel Restaurant Fletschhorn (marked on piste maps near langlauf track), reached by a delightful 20 minute walk through woods along a lighted path, is well worthwhile.

There are a number of good clothing and sports shops, together with banks, bookshops and chemists etc. A visit to the Saas Museum should not be missed; much of the heart of Saas Fee can be better understood from the well displayed history.

Indoor Sports Centre: Saas Fee has one of the finest indoor sports centres in the Alps, with 2 tennis courts; fitness room; swimming pool; whirlpool; steam bath; sauna; solarium and massage.

Recommended Hotels:

Hotel Allalin: A re-built aparthotel with the attractive use of 300 year old timber. All rooms with private bath, TV, telephone and balcony. Two restaurants, one on the 'Walliser-Kanne' serving specialities such as fondue, raclette, etc. Comfortable lounge, sitting room, sauna and whirlpool. Close to Hannig cableway.

Pension Bergfreude: Situated in a central but quiet position off the main street, a charming chalet-style pension completely renovated, many rooms with bath/shower as well as with balcony. The dining room is brightly furnished, with connecting bar and lounge, with comfortable, agreeable atmosphere. Large sun terrace. Very well run by friendly and helpful Burgener family.

Hotel Christiania: Well placed for the major cableways, a modern chalet-style family run hotel with a large sun terrace in front. Comfortable bedrooms, modern decor, all with bath or shower, telephone, TV, minifridge, safe, and balconies. Spacious light dining room, restaurant. Sauna, Turkish bath and solarium.

Hotel Dom: A comfortable traditional style hotel in a central position. 77 beds, all rooms with bath/shower, wc, spacious dining room, lounge, Internet corner and the best snowboard bar in town. Restaurant serving Swiss specialities. Personal and friendly atmosphere.

Hotel Marmotte: A small 3 star family hotel with 39 beds, all rooms with bath/shower. Situated some 500 metres from centre and efficiently run by the owners Karl and Eva Dreier. Pleasant reception rooms, sauna, spa-pool and solarium. Food exceptional, prepared and cooked by Karl.

Ferienart Walliserhof: A centrally situated 4 star chalet style hotel, elegantly designed interior with much use of wooden decor creating a cosy atmosphere. 50 twin or double bedrooms and 4 singles with bath or shower, wc, telephone, radio, TV, minibar and balcony. Spacious lounge areas with open fires, attractive dining room, 2 bars, swimming pool with jet streams, sauna, massage, fitness room, solarium, games room and sun terrace. Dancing each evening to band.

BRIEF REPORTS ON FURTHER SWISS RESORTS

BIVIO, 5,825ft.: Situated on the west side of the Julier pass, 22km. from St. Moritz, this small village with hotels and pensions providing 1,000 beds has a quiet and friendly atmosphere. Only 4 drag-lifts, but 30km. of prepared pistes and an excellent centre for touring. Top station 8,399.ft. Cosy restaurants, bars and a discothèque. Suitable for intermediate skiers.

LENK, 3,608ft.: Situated in the Bernese Oberland at the head of the Simmen valley and linked with Adelboden (see separate write-up), this attractive village provides a wide range of facilities, skating, curling, cross-country skiing, swimming, kindergarten; 30 hotels and pensions; height at top station, 6,880ft.; 1 cableway, 2 gondolaways, 3 chair-lifts; 10 drag-lifts, plus Adelboden lifts; suitable for beginners to advanced intermediates.

SAMNAUN, 6,036ft.: Lying at the head of the valley by the same name in the north east corner of Switzerland, this resort is linked with the Austrian resort of Ischgl (see separate report), thus providing a wide range of skiing. It also has the advantage of being in the duty-free zone. There is skating, curling, nordic skiing, swimming, dancing and a good selection of restaurants and bars. 13 hotels and pensions plus Ski Haus Alp Trida (44 beds); the latter is situated in the heart of the ski area. It has the world's first double-decker cableway holding 180 persons, in addition to 4 chair-lifts, 8 drag-lifts plus the lifts in Ischgl. Suitable for beginners to advanced intermediates.

ST CERGUE, 3,600ft.: One of the nearest resorts to Geneva airport, direct transfers under 1 hour. A popular resort for families and the Children's Club for 2-8 year olds is part of the attraction. 9 hotels and pensions; height at top station 5,600ft.; 1 mountain railway, 1 chair-lift, 7 drag-lifts; particularly suitable for families and skiers up to intermediate standard.

ST. LUC, 4,500ft.: Situated 34 minutes by road from Sierre, this is an ideal small resort with 55km. of pistes, the longest being 6.5km. Because of its height and mainly north-east facing slopes the snow holds well throughout the season. There are four restaurants and four café/bars, a disco, natural skating rink and a kindergarten. Four hotels and apartments provide a total of some 3,800 beds. Height of top station, 9,924ft; one chair-lift, 6 drag-lifts. Easy to reach from the channel ports or from Geneva and particularly suitable for families and skiers up to intermediate standard.

SILS MARIA, 5,894ft.: Although well provided for in its own right, Sils Maria is in a good situation for other resorts in the Engadine, particularly the Corvatsch area, 5km. by road, or one can ski across from Sils Maria top station. It is obviously cheaper to stay at a small resort and use the very good sports bus service to the larger nearby resorts. There is also skating, curling, sleigh rides, lovely walks, mountain restaurants and Nordic skiing. 16 hotels and pensions, height at top station 9,184ft.; one cableway, one chair-lift, 4 drag-lifts. Suitable for all grades of skiers.

LIECHTENSTEIN

MALBUN

Height of Resort: 5,248 ft.
Height of Top Station: 6,560 ft.
Nearest International Airport: Zurich
Map Reference: 6B See page 240
Route by Car: See pages 236-240
Resort Facilities Charts: See page 223
Hotel Reference Charts: See page 233

This delightful country between Austria and Switzerland will have an appeal for everyone, especially the romantic. The old world charm of Ruritania, that imaginary state of so many stories, is all here in the Principality of Liechtenstein. Malbun lies in the upper end of a side spur of the Samina valley. An excellent approach road from the capital, Vaduz, connects to the resort via a tunnel, making easy access.

Set in a bowl-shaped landscape, the mountains rise around the village like a large amphitheatre, thus ensuring long hours of sunshine. To the north east of the village is the main ski area, rising to a ridge of 6,560ft. A chair-lift takes one to this ridge in the direction of Sareiserjoch from the edge of the village. The skiing here is open. An interesting medium run of 2km. begins on the south-west facing slopes, curving round to the north-west facing slopes and reaching the village after a vertical descent of 1,312ft. A drag-lift leaves the south-west side of the village, rising to Hocheck, 6,055ft., and easy runs of 1½km. over north-east facing slopes lead back to the village. There is an excellent beginners' slope served by a drag-lift. Altogether the resort has 4 drag-lifts and one double and one 4 seater chair-lift, and all have good access from the centre of the vi llage. In the ski school most of the instructors speak English so there should be no language problem here.

In a Few Words: A small and fairly quiet resort; skiing good for beginners and families but otherwise limited; runs and lifts to and from the village; reliable snow; reasonable in price.

Après Ski: There is not a great variety, and night life centres on the Turna Hotel with attractive Taverna discothèque and good value draught beer. The Hotel Galina has a snow-board bar open from 1100-1700 hours. Vaduz, the capital of Liechtenstein, is only 17km. away, where there are many shops. There are a number of cleared walks. Prices reasonable compared to most ski resorts.

Recommended Hotels:

Hotel Gorfion: Run by Klaudi Zechner-Schwärzler, the former being daughter of Ruth and Helmut Schwärzler, well known to visitors to Brand, as the Scesaplana hotel in that resort is run by them also. The Gorfion is of modern design, large bedrooms all with bath and most with balconies, carpeted throughout. Spacious dining room, sitting room and bar. Sun terrace, indoor swimming pool and children's playroom.

Malbuner Hof: Run by Florian Mitterhuber. A luxury hotel affording all comforts with good size bedrooms tastefully decorated and furnished. All have bath, wc., radio, telephone and a balcony. Good indoor swimming pool, sauna, steambath, massage and solarium, and adjoining this there is a changing room and storage facilities for ski equipment.

PORTES DU SOLEIL

FRANCE/SWITZERLAND

PORTES DU SOLEIL SKIING AREA

This huge area known as the Portes du Soleil lies between the Lake of Geneva and Mont Blanc covering the Savoy Chablais, part of the French Haute Savoie, and the Swiss Bas Valais. It encompasses some 14 valleys (400 square miles) and to the south-east it is bounded by the Dents du Midi which loom over most runs. It claims to be the largest international ski area with over 650km. of prepared pistes, served by 219 lifts (access to which are now all automatic) and connecting no less than 13 ski resorts, 8 in France and 5 in Switzerland as follows:-

France: Abondance, Avoriaz, Chatel, La Chapelle d'Abondance, Les Gets, Montriond, Morzine and St. Jean D'Aulps.
Switzerland: Champéry-Planachaux, Morgins, Torgon, Val d'Illiez-Champoussin and Les Crosets.

All of the above resorts are on the main Portes du Soleil ski pass and passports are required to ski over the frontiers. To keep the pistes in good order there are 80 snow cats and 900 maintenance staff. It is impossible to describe such a vast ski area in any detail but the area plan shown will be easier to read if the ski area is divided into three:

(a) The main circuit
(b) The two 'off-shoot' circuits – Torgon to the northand Morzine/Les Gets to the south.
(c) The resorts not yet linked to the main area by lifts.

The Main Circuit: This circuit covers, anti-clockwise, the resorts of Chatel, Avoriaz, Planachaux-Champéry, Les Crosets, Champoussin, Morgins, Super Chatel and back to Chatel. The final lift links were completed in 1981/82. The whole can easily be tackled by an intermediate except for the very steep 'wall' on the Swiss side between Avoriaz and Planachaux. This can be avoided by taking the chair-lift down or by skiing the circuit in an equally interesting clock-wise direction. In fact the circuit should be done in both directions as completely different runs and views are involved. Taking only the most direct lift connections, leaving the many tempting variations to be tackled piecemeal on other days, the complete circuit will take the average skier between 5-6 hours in either direction. A full day if lunch is to be fitted in at one of the many mountain restaurants.

The 'Off-Shoot' Circuits:

The Torgon Area: This is a linked extension to the north of the Main Circuit and is reached either from Morgins or Chatel via Super Chatel. It has its own circuit, travelling out by one route and back by another, it is an extensive area in itself, the return trip from Morgins requiring some 5 hours or from Chatel $3\frac{1}{2}$ hours. This area should not be missed as the views across the Rhône valley are superb. On a clear day one can see right through to the Bernese Oberland, with the Eiger, Mönch and Jungfrau clearly visible and at one point there are views down to the eastern end of Lake Geneva. There is a steepish mogulled red section on the outward journey, but within the capabilities of intermediates. For experts the black 'Torgon Wall' is an optional extra. All in all a very satisfying area.

Morzine - Les Gets Area: There is an extension to the south-west of the Main Circuit and to allow the maximum time this is best tackled from Avoriaz. One skis down to Les Prodains, the bottom station of the Avoriaz cableway, where there is a navette (ski bus) shuttle service to either the Pleney or Nyon lifts (allow 30 minutes each way from Avoriaz). Alternatively one can ski over to Super Morzine and take the gondolaway directly down to Morzine. The most direct round trip from Morzine to Les Gets will take about $1\frac{1}{2}$ hours, but this is but a tiny bite of a large cherry as these two resorts cover an extensive area. Many days can be profitably spent here. The skiing is mainly blue and red runs with some black runs above Nyon and the backside of Mont Chéry.

The Unlinked Resorts: La Chapelle d'Abondance is linked to Torgon and Super-Chatel with the La

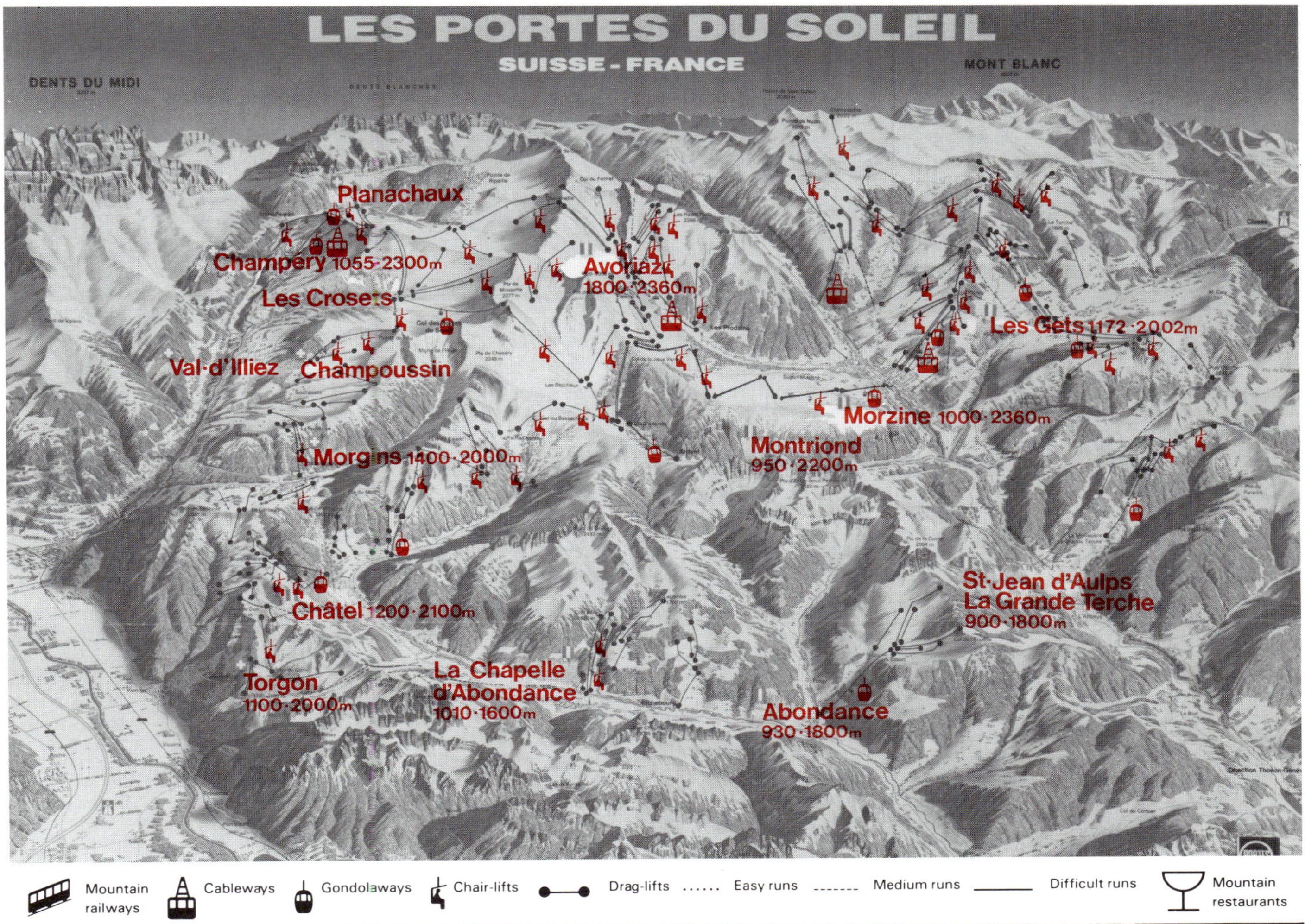

Pantiaz cablecar. St. Jean d'Aulps, with over 3,000 vertical feet of downhill, will eventually to be linked to Les Gets, whilst Montriond which has limited skiing at present is linked to the main circuit by Navette bus. These resorts are worth a visit if one has a car, perhaps at weekends when they are far less crowded than the main area. An excellent free brochure is available in all Portes du Soleil resorts which shows in detail and very clearly all the sections in the Portes du Soleil with their most direct links and estimated skiing times between each. As stated all circuits are within the capabilities of an ntermediate but experts will find some 20 steep black runs distributed around the area. Although this is not a high altitude ski area, the highest point being some 7,700ft., one should expect to ski the circuit into April because the lift system has been very well planned with south facing slopes usually having chair-lifts as opposed to the drag-lifts prevailing on the north facing slopes.

To Sum Up: The Portes du Soleil is highly recommended and a 'must' for any enthusiastic skier. By the end of 2 weeks there will be many pistes still unskied let alone the off-piste possibilities. Our Assistant Editor, Peter Forbes, has now spent 5 weeks exploring the area during March and found no serious queues.

The Resorts: In the following pages it will be seen that seven resorts are written up on a full report basis, Avoriaz, Chatel, Les Gets, Morzine, St. Jean d'Aulps, Champéry and Morgins and the remainder briefly reported.

AVORIAZ

Height of Resort: 5,904 ft.
Height of Top Station: 7,743 ft.
Nearest International Airport: Geneva
Map Reference: 5B See page 238
Route by Car: See pages 236-238
Resort Facilities Charts: See page 217
Hotel Reference Charts: See page 229

One of France's purpose built ski resorts, the first building was constructed in 1966/67. It is one of the nearest resorts to Geneva airport, and a bus takes one from the airport to the edge of Avoriaz in two hours. Cars are banned in the village, and they are really unnecessary as it is so well-planned, and horse drawn sleighs are used during the winter. The lifts are very near by, and you can ski right back to your doorstep. This is a particular advantage for family ski parties. There are many Résidences and two main shopping areas, one in the Place du Snow and the other in Place Centrale which provide almost everything that one requires, whilst other parts of the village are also equipped with shopping facilities. The Children's Village, run by Annie Famose, contributes greatly to Avoriaz as a family resort; it is very well run - it has its own two drag-lifts and a building containing reception, nursery, creative room, playroom and restaurant. It accepts children from the ages of 3 to 16.

Les Hauts Forts: This area is served by two drag-lifts and a chair-lift on the lower slopes, and a further two drag-lifts and chair-lift on the upper slopes. The summit of Les Hauts Forts, 7,413ft., can be reached by using the system, or by taking the 4 seater chair-lift from the village. The lower north-facing slopes provide easy to medium runs. From the top station there is a choice of easy and medium north-west facing runs back to the village, whilst a selection of difficult runs, including the superb black run 'Crozats', swing westward down to Les Prodains, and from this point one takes the cableway back to the village. Alternatively, before reaching Les Prodains one can take the chair-lift back to the top of the Hauts Forts runs.

Plateau Les Lindarets: The nursery slopes are situated on this plateau, reached by a choice of two lifts. Especially interesting medium and easy runs lead down through the beautiful tree-line over the far side. One finds a good selection of restaurants with large sun terraces in this area, which also provides a link with Chatel.

Cubore: The triple Cubore chair-lift opens up the valley north-west of Avoriaz. It is reached by taking the Chavanette drag-lift, and from the top one takes the easy run down to the chair-lift, which climbs over the top of the ridge up to Pointe de Vorlaz. Here one has the choice of skiing back down the same side on a medium to difficult run or by taking the short, fairly steep medium run on the far side to the foot of the chair-lift, taking the lift back to the top station; alternatively, one can continue down the valley, joining up with the Mossette run, or the parallel run travelling down to the foot of the Lindarets drag-lift. This is an easy but very long run, a lot of it being a straight schuss, but very pleasant as it travels through beautiful valley scenery. In 1993 a 4 seater chair-lift was installed linking Les Brocheaux with Pointe De Mossette, extending the skiing in this area
.

Pas de Chavanette: The Chavanette drag-lift is reached via the first Les Hauts Forts lift crossing the ridge, and it ends at the Swiss border. Three medium easy runs go down to Avoriaz, or you can cross towards Champéry, either down a black run which is very steep and normally heavily mogulled, or by taking a chair-lift and an easy run to Les Crosets. An attractive return route is to take the gondolaway from Les Crosets to Pointe de Mossette and restaurant, from which it is possible to ski back to the bottom of the Lindarets drag-lift.

Avoriaz provides the real ski enthusiast with a good variety of runs and there is plenty of scope for offpiste skiing both open and wooded. It is an excelient resort for the family. One has a choice of 3 ski-lift passes:- (1) Beginners' pass, covering the plateau lifts and the cableway only; (2) lifts in Avoriaz area only; and (3) the Portes du Soleil pass – particularly good for those who enjoy area skiing as it covers 13 resorts, 8 in France and 5 in Switzerland, served by over 224 lifts and covering 650km. of prepared and marked runs in addition to a wide variety of off-piste skiing.

In a Few Words: There is a good variety of skiing for the real enthusiast, particularly with the Portes du Soleil lift pass, although a good ski lift map of the area is seriously missing. An excellent resort for families, with well-run Children's Village; two central baby-sitting services.

Après Ski: A variety of restaurants. The Flo runs a good, inexpensive self-service restaurant, whilst a more expensive but good restaurant is situated above it, both with sun terraces overlooking the pistes. The Hauts Forts restaurant serves a delicious meal; equally so the restaurant of the de luxe hotel Les Dromonts, whilst La Taverne and La Mamma provide very good food. The Petit Vatel is to be recommended for good value as well as good food. The Brin de Folie (Snow complex) pizzas, spaghetti and grills. The small mountain restaurant Le Petit Pin is popular. The Refuge Vérard, half way down to the Les Prodains cableway, serves good food and is occasionally open at night – one finishes the evening by skiing or otherwise to the bottom of the cableway. There are two cinemas, showing French and English films, and an ice rink, bowling alley, a fitness centre and two squash courts.

Accommodation: The only privately owned hotel-residence in Avoriaz is Les Hauts Forts and the other hotel, the de luxe Les Dromonts. There are various residences, including the Ruches, which has a restaurant and Le Quarter de la Falaise, situated near the car park at the entrance to the resort. The latter has a fast food restaurant. The above residences have studio-type accommodation with kitchenette. There is a great variety of self-catering studios and apartments to be found in Avoriaz, and the organisation Avoriaz Location can provide the smaller studio-type accommodation with kitchenette to apartments accommodating up to 7 persons with full-sized kitchens properly equipped. Radio Avoriaz (92.1Mhz) broadcasts throughout the day giving details of skiing conditions and local news.

MORZINE

Height of Resort: 3,281 ft.
Height of Top Station: 7,874 ft.
Nearest International Airport: Geneva
Map Reference: 5B See page 238
Route by Car: See pages 236-238
Resort Facilities Charts: See page 218
Hotel Reference Charts: See page 230

Taken as a whole, Morzine seems like a village being in two parts joined by a causeway; the original old Savoyard village clustered round the church at the foot of the hill, with the more recent traditional ski resort, one of the oldest in France, above and nearer the slopes. The upper area has been growing steadily since its inception in 1934 and this is where the Tourist Office and most hotels and pensions are situated.

Morzine is on route des Grandes Alpes (RN 202) 63km. from Geneva airport and 30km. from the rail heads of Thonon and Cluses, with a regular bus service from Geneva, Thonon and Cluses. The quickest route by car is from Cluses motorway exit. It lies in the south-west of the vast skiing area of the Portes du Soleil with its 650km. of pistes and 228 lifts. It forms a link between Avoriaz and Les Gets to the south-west. 1988 saw the opening of a direct link on skis between Morzine, via Super-Morzine, with Avoriaz. As a result Morzine considers itself as the heart of the Portes du Soleil and now likes to be known as Morzine/Avoriaz. This is understandable as it in fact created Avoriaz which opened in 1966. Morzine has always been connected by an efficient Navette service running every 15 minutes to the bottom of the Avoriaz cableway at Les Prodains and this alternative route continues.

There are now four ways into the mountains from the resort:- via the Pleney gondolaway, 200 metres from the main square and Tourist Office; the Super-Morzine gondolaway 200 metres north west and by Navette services to both the Nyon and Avoriaz cableway bottom stations every 15 minutes, free on the ski pass. The skiing can be briefly described as follows:-

The Morzine/Les Gets Skiing: The Pleney skiing lies immediately south of the resort where there are a number of reasonably priced hotels right on the slopes. This was Morzine's original ski area. Access to Pleney, 5,131ft., is by modern 6-seater gondolaway with a parallel back up to the older cableway. Pleney can also be approached by the usae of 4 seater chair-lift with links to a 3 seater chair-lift, thus minimising queueing. From the top there is a very wide choice of runs either directly back to the resort down north facing slopes or eastward to link with the Nyon skiing. All this area is heavily wooded with runs through glades, a great boon in bad light. The area has 27 lifts to choose from criss-crossing all the slopes, in addition to the Les Gets skiing, see separate report, available on the other side of the ridge. There are two routes over to Les Gets, one from above Pleney, an easy run through woods, and the other via the long Charniaz chair-lift to Col du Ranfolly, 5,459ft. Of the many varying grade routes from Pleney to Morzine special mention must be made of the blue runs, which are outstanding, and the last 2km. including the nursery slopes are covered by 100 snow making guns, which ensures the lower slopes being kept open until late season. The ski routes from Pleney to Nyon and back are excellently planned with many alternatives to suit all standards. Most of the Nyon skiing is west facing afternoon skiing, as well as Super-Morzine, see below, when Pleney north slopes are in the shade. Nyon has two well known runs, red and black respectively, both served by chair-lifts to Pointe de Nyon, 6,666ft., and Chamossière, 6,606ft. The latter also has a red alternative and this run back to Morzine is about 11km. One can also reach or return from the new high speed Nyon cableway by Navette. For those prepared to confine themselves to this beautiful and varied area there is the Morzine/Les Gets ski pass.

The Super-Morzine Skiing: Opened in 1988 this was a large hitherto unused sunny plateau. Apart providing Morzine with skiing on its south side it gives a direct ski link with Avoriaz. The connection has necessitated constructing six new lifts. From Morzine one mounts the 6-seater gondolaway to Super-Morzine, with two restaurants, and further height is gained on a 4-seater chair-lift. From this top station the runs are wide, open and undulating. The whole trip takes about 30 minutes, the same as the alternative route by Navette and cableway. The return run includes two lifts as far Super-Morzine where one must take the gondolaway down, there being no ski run. The whole area is easy blue skiing, marvellous for beginners and intermediates but rather boring for the expert who would use it merely as a means of getting from A to B. Best in the afternoon sun. An exposed area so it can be very cold in bad weather.

In a Few Words: The largest of the Portes du Soleil resorts. Very well situated for easy access from the U.K. Excellent varied and limitless skiing for all standards. Heavily wooded on the south slopes for visibility in bad weather. Greatly enhanced by the new ski access to Avoriaz. A traditional ski resort with charm and a relaxed atmosphere, unlike the modern purpose-built resorts such as Avoriaz. Although low in altitude the north slopes hold the snow well assisted by snow guns. 97km. of Nordic ski trails divided into five circuits through superb countryside. Kindergarten. Excellent resort for families and non-skiers but rather spoilt by the amount of traffic passing through.

Après Ski: A vast variety of leisure activities for non-skiers and après skiers. For the energetic there is swimming in 30 hotels, curling, an Olympic size skating rink, para-gliding, sightseeing flights, heli-skiing, aerobics, conducted snow-shoe walks tracing flora and fauna, cameras and binoculars at the ready, bowling, billiards etc. Highly popular are the inter-hotel races and video descents available to participants at the price of a blank tape. For the less active one can watch ice hockey, international ice dancing, concerts, dress shows as well as two cinemas. If you are not worried about your figure there are a wide variety of crêperies and patisseries. Three night clubs provide lively entertainment until the small hours. Restaurants abound all sizes and prices. The pride of Morzine is La Chamade with its expensive and cheaper sections, both offering excellent cuisine, whilst at the 'Grand Restaurant' prices and cuisine live up to the title. Auberge De La Combe à Zorre in a lower bracket is immensely popular but be prepared to enjoy the Savoyard specialities in close proximity to fellow diners. For atmosphere, candle light, log fire etc. Le Café Chaud is unbeatable, but if fondues are not your favourite food then keep to the darkened little bar for a cocktail. Traditionalists should try Le Brulot, a brasserie with changing set menus at reasonable prices and more space to accommodate the usual crowds. Shopping excellent with some 130 shops and boutiques.

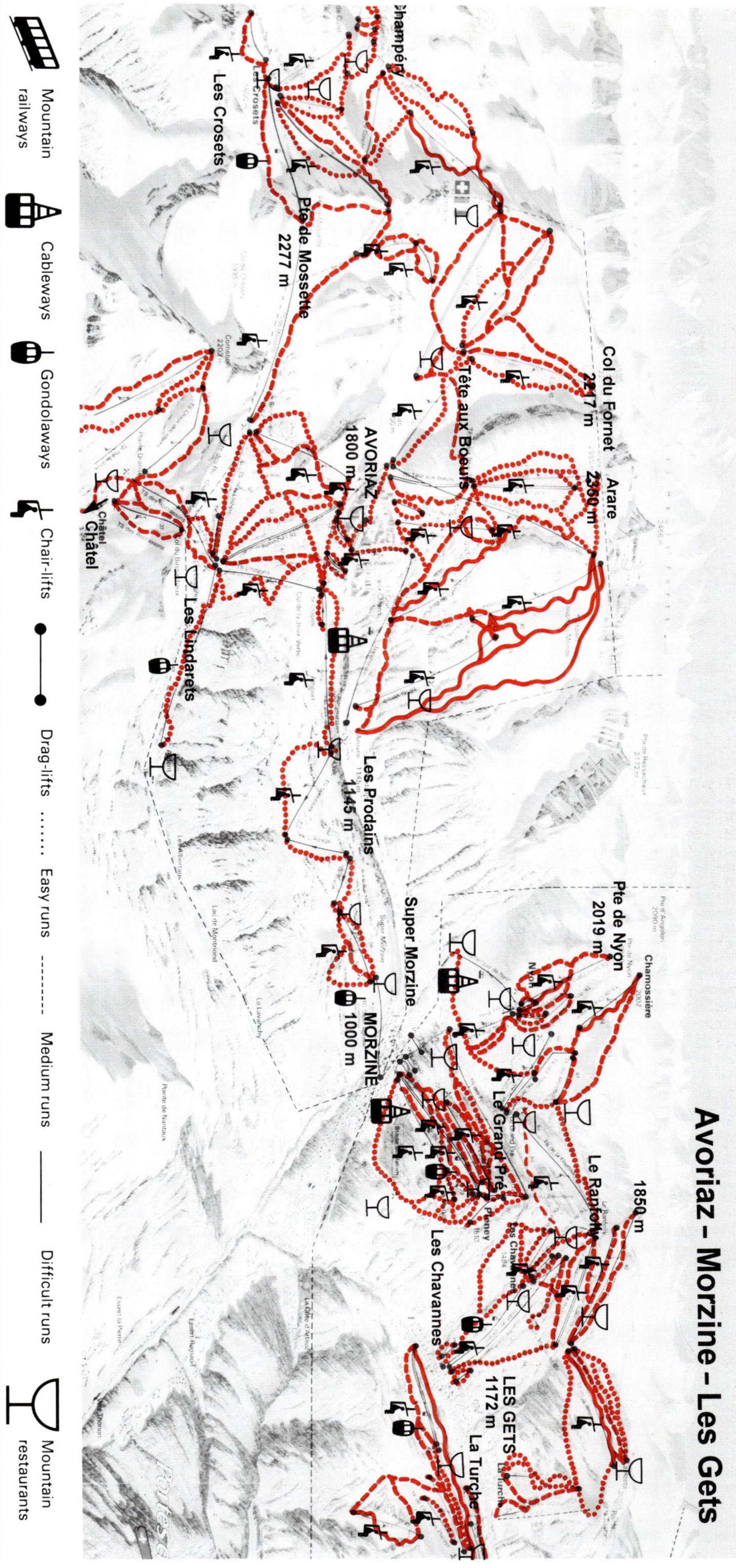

Recommended Hotels:

Hotel Le Tramplin: This 3-star hotel is in a prime position adjoining the gondolaway Pleney and the ski school assembly point. Built in 1936 by the Taberlet family and still run by them. All rooms with bath or shower and balcony. Guests can have lunch on the south facing balcony overlooking the slopes. Weekly 'festive evenings'. Covered garage included in rates. Lift.

Hotel L'Equipe: A 2-star hotel built in 1956 by the Béard family who continue to run it, excellent situation close to the Pleney gondolaway and skiable back to the door. All rooms have balconies, bath or shower. Indoor swimming pool with bar and a very popular bar attached to the hotel which gets very rowdy immediately after skiing.

Hotel Igloo: We spent a very comfortable week here. A unique 2-star bed and breakfast hotel without restaurant. There is a small attractive dining room and adjoining kitchen for use of the guests, this is fully equipped and kept immaculately clean by the staff. An oven-ready dish from the supermarket or takeaway provides the ideal solution for ravenous but economical skiers. Breakfast and bar drinks are served in bedrooms upon request. Small gymnasium and sauna. Rates are very reasonable, garage parking is free, near shops and lifts. The general atmosphere is delightfully easy going. Highly recommended.

LES GETS

Height of Resort: 3,844 ft.
Height of Top Station: 6,069 ft.
Nearest International Airport: Geneva
Map Reference: 4B See page 238
Route by Car: See pages 236-238
Resort Facilities Charts: See page 217
Hotel Reference Charts: See page 230

Les Gets is situated on the summit of a Col some 55km. from Geneva. It can be reached by car via the Mont Blanc motorway to Cluses exit or via Thonon in about 1$^1/_2$ hours, or by train with bus connections. Les Gets is one of the older French resorts, opened in 1937 and has spread southwards from the old village down both sides of the main road. It has 27 hotels and some 12,000 beds in chalets and apartments. It enjoys the Mont Blanc climate which ensures plenty of snow and one of the characteristics of its situation is that after a snowfall the airflow is from the north thus keeping the powder in excellent condition. As there are no high mountains in the immediate vicinity it enjoys well above the average hours of sunshine. Les Gets is the most southerly of the resorts forming part of the vast Portes du Soleil skiing region and itself has over 130km. of pistes served by 59 lifts. It is directly linked, over its northern ridge, with Morzine and Nyon, an area of equal size with mainly north facing slopes, and thence with Avoriaz. One has the choice of the local pass, which covers Les Gets–Morzine, or the Portes du Soleil pass. Les Gets skiing and also that of Morzine is heavily wooded, a great boon for skiing in bad weather. The slopes are over rockless grassy meadows, thus skiing is possible with very sparse snow coverage.

The local skiing is divided between two areas, the lower stations of each being approximately 400 metres walk apart but linked by free transport:-

Mont Chéry: On the west side of the village a modern 6 seater gondolaway rises to the half-way stage where there is a good restaurant and sun terrace. From here a number of interlinking chair and drag-lifts reach the summit, 5,979ft. These east and south-east facing slopes are best skied in the morning sun. There is also excellent skiing for the afternoon on the other side of Mont Chéry over north and north-west slopes. Here there are three challenging black runs with red alternatives. From the end of each run a chair-lift returns one to the summit. The runs back to Les Gets are red or black.

Les Chavannes: On the east side of the village one finds the nursery slopes with three trainer lifts and access to Les Chavannes by a 4 seater gondolaway or a modern 4 seater chair-lift which continues beyond Chavannes to provide a link down to Morzine. At Chavannes there are six restaurants with another above and a number of lifts upwards giving access southwards to a very large bowl shaped area with runs, red and blue, facing all points of the compass. This area is served by six long lifts including a very fast modern chair-lift to Ranfolly, 6,069ft., Les Gets top station, and a 4 seater to La Rosta. Above Chavannes one can ski down northwards to Nyon above which includes two black runs each of some 2km. or to Morzine. One has the choice of two routes back to Les Gets. The most direct route Les Gets-Morzine return takes between 1$^1/_2$-2 hours, but there is masses of skiing on the Morzine side. Skiing down from Chavannes to Les Gets is within everyone's capability over long easy slopes.

Nordic skiing is well catered for with over 18km. of prepared trails graded into three stages of difficulty. There are also 30km. of cleared walks.

In a Few Words: Excellent and extensive skiing for all standards, limitless with the Portes du Soleil pass. Good off-piste opportunities through the trees over rockless slopes. Challenging black runs for experts. Excellent family centre including non-skiers. Very crowded during school holidays and much traffic in the streets. High recommended for January skiing with long hours of sunshine. In bad weather the extensive runs through wooded glades provide good visibility. Three ski schools; 3 categories of kindergartens and well placed mountain restaurants, most of which set aside areas for picnic lunches.

Après Ski: As befits a French resort, Les Gets is rich in restaurants and the choice is exciting. Undoubtedly one of the most popular is Le Schuss where reservations are essential, middle of the village and middle prices perhaps explains its popularity as apart from the Savoyarde specialities the cuisine is hardly soignée. A short pull uphill reaches Le Labrador; here one dines in quiet spaciousness. For a thoroughly gastronomic evening Le Mont-Chéry is not to be missed, with sophisticated decor, quiet atmosphere and not an unreasonable bill.

The Restaurant La R'mize is excellent, whilst Le Tyrol with its open wood fire has a good reputation and serves food until 1 a.m. Another gastronomic 'must' is dinner at Les Alpages restaurant, where the rich smells of haute cuisine alone are worth a visit, book and fill your wallet. There are of course a wide variety of crêperies; stand-up stalls for the not too tired and not too rich or indoor crêperies for one's choice. Pâtisseries and tea shops are numerous and crowded. There are two cinemas with a frequent change of programmes but they rarely carry sub-titles. The only heated indoor swimming pool is at the hotel La Marmotte which is open to the public. After dark Les Gets calls itself the 'youthful resort', the L'Igloo disco being one of the most popular haunts, no live bands but frequent cabarets. Ice rink and fitness centre.

Recommended Hotels:

Hotel La Marmotte: An attractive 3 star hotel privately owned by Mme. Mirigay who runs it with efficiency and the personal touch is immediately apparent on arrival. An ideal situation opposite the gondolaway up to Les Chavannes and at the foot of the pistes. The cooking is traditional and regional but the restaurant is not open to non-residents. Breakfast and lunches are mostly buffets. There is a weekly fondue evening and an organised outing on skis, plus guide, every 10 days. Heated indoor swimming pool, sauna, solarium, massage, children's playroom, billiards, ping-pong, sun terrace and large heated indoor garage.

Hotel Stella: A 2 star bed and breakfast hotel on the main road and near the nursery slopes and the Chavannes lifts. Unpretentious and easy going but extremely comfortable. Run by the three Baud brothers who speak English and are out to please. Snacks available almost any time from the café-bar. Lift, large sun terrace and covered garage and easy parking. Sauna.

Hotel Les Alpages: A very comfortable 3 star hotel some 100 metres uphill from the end of the village but accessible on skis from adjacent slopes. All bedrooms with bath, separate wc and telephone. Sauna, solarium, games room, billiards, baby sitting service and garage. A large south facing terrace adjoining the excellent gourmet restaurant.

CHATEL

Height of Resort: 3,9378 ft.
Height of Top Station: 6,890 ft.
Nearest International Airport: Geneva
Map Reference: 5A See page 238
Route by Car: See pages 236-238
Resort Facilities Charts: See page 217
Hotel Reference Charts: See page 229

Chatel is an old Savoyarde village and since 1953 has gradually increased in size to become an international ski resort. There are 27 hotels providing over 1,500 beds and some 2,400 chalets and apartments with 15,000 beds. Most of the newer buildings have been built on the outskirts of the old village and the resort as a whole has become large and widespread and situated on different levels. Chatel is situated just below the Pas de Morgins in the Savoy Chablais of the Haute Savoie. The pass is kept open throughout the winter and the resort is easily accessible by motorway from the Swiss side via Lausanne (68km.) Aigle, Monthey and Morgins. There are through trains from Paris to Thonon with connecting buses to Chatel. On the Swiss side bus services from Geneva are limited as are the services from the railhead Monthey.

Chatel is probably the largest of the resorts with direct access to vast Portes du Soleil area.

Chatel Ski Lifts and Skiing: To be properly understood this section should be read in conjunction with the description given in the previous pages on the whole of the Portes du Soleil area. The main lifts, which are entirely adequate for the number of beds in the resort area, are:- 2 cableways, 12 chair-lifts and 24 drag-lifts.

For the Super Chatel Area: From the centre of the village one reaches Super Chatel by a direct gondolaway or a two stage chair-lift and at the top one finds a large west facing bowl served by a number of interconnecting lifts. The skiing in this area is suitable for beginners and intermediates with the exception of two black runs. It is the starting point for the long runs northward to Torgon and southward to Morgins and beyond. There is a restaurant and hotel at the top of the gondolaway, and a self-service restaurant for 700 persons. The runs back down to Chatel can be tackled by most skiers.

For the Le Linga Area and Beyond: The important Le Linga gondolaway is at L'Essert situated below and 1$^1/_2$km. from Chatel. It is really a satellite resort to Chatel with its own hotels, apartments and shops. Visitors may prefer to make this their base as there is a free night shuttle bus service from 1800-2400 hours. During the day it is possible to ski from the upper part of Chatel to L'Essert with the help of the village lifts, but in practice it is quicker to take the Navette service operating from the church square every 20 minutes. The Le Linga recently renewed 12 person cableway is surmounted by a modern 3 seater chair-lift to 6,890ft. There are really satisfying wood glade runs back to the bottom station with a choice of blue, red or black runs. There is a restaurant half way down, below which it is possible to cut off to the right to end in Chatel or to continue to the bottom and take the Navette back. From the top station of the chair-lift to reach Avoriaz one travels westward then southwards and on the way one finds five restaurants in a sunny position at Plaine Dranse. A further sunny restaurant will be found at Pré le Joux, which is another starting point for skiing also for skiing to Avoriaz. All the skiing in this area is of excellent intermediate standard, whilst the Chaux Des Rosées 3 seater chair-lift provides access to a challenging black run as well as red variations.

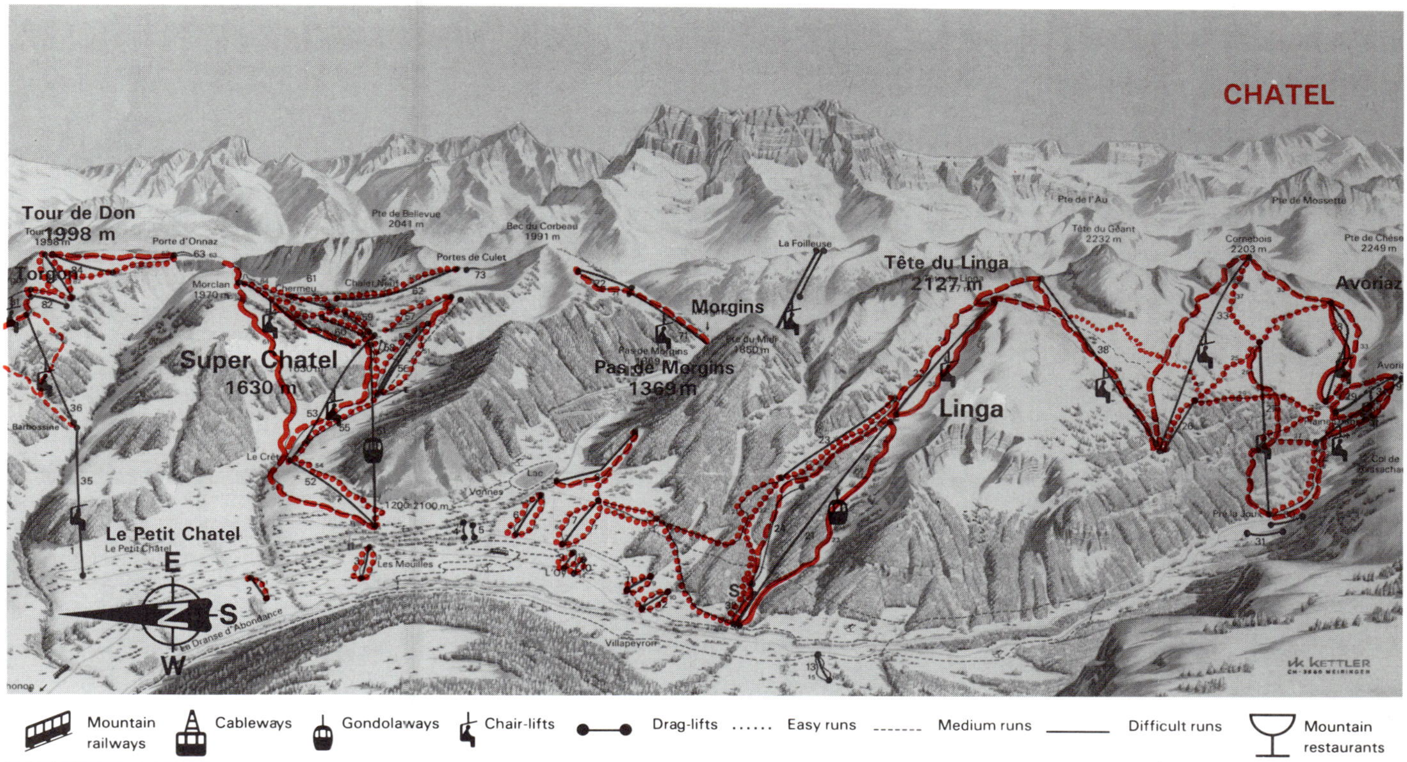

The Village Lifts: The village is well equipped with beginner and trainer lifts – altogether there are 16. These also serve a very useful purpose in getting one to the various levels of the resort.

The Ski Abonnements: Visitors have the choice of 2 lift passes. A Chatel 5 non-consecutive days pass plus one day Portes du Soleil is good value and convenient if the weather is bad. The 'Portes du Soleil' pass covers the full area and represents better value for money for the intermediate skier over a period of 6 days. Other passes can be purchased varying from a half day to the whole season.

In a Few Words: Chatel is situated at the junction of two valleys and enjoys above average hours of sunshine. It provides an excellent central access to the wonderful Portes du Soleil skiing region. It is particularly suitable for those with cars who may wish, at times, to short-circuit some of the runs, thus getting further afield by driving direct to Morgins, or if going towards Avoriaz, to Pré la Joux. Also by car some of the non-connected resorts are easily accessible from Chatel. The resort is spread out but there are Navette connections to all parts – no fares. Covered parking for 500 cars. Many visitors will prefer self-catering apartments, please refer to the Club section. The skiing is suitable for all standards.

Mainly French visitors but a marked increase of British, Belgian and Dutch.

Ski Schools: Several options are available. A special beginner package comprises five days of group lessons including a six day Chatel pass. L'École de Ski Français (ESF) and the Ski École International 'Portes du Soleil' are tailored for beginner and intermediate grades respectively. Two other ski schools are Snowride and Henri Gonon. Snow board, telemark and ski carving lessons given by both these schools.

Children: Children are well catered for in the Marmottons Village created by instructress and infant teacher Catherine Thoule. It is open every day 0830-1730 hours for infants and children from 14 months upwards, and is open from Christmas onwards. The 'Village' has its own ski-lifts and qualified staff who organise ski and snow activities, toboggan rides, indoor games etc. Approximate prices for 6 days are as follows:- Crêche only with meal – 670FF; full activities with meal 1050FF. Daily rates are also available. Space, however, is limited so it is advisable to book in advance.

Après Ski: There are 27 hotels and all have restaurants but if one is eating out one should choose a restaurant, and there are some 20 of them, as the hotels tend to close their dining rooms early. Eating out in Chatel is a big business and at weekends it is essential to book a table. For the largest and surely the best nouvelle cuisine menu, visit the Fleur de Neige whose chef holds the Regional first prize cookery award. A most impressive, but not cheap, menu which includes many rare dishes which few people have sampled before.

A fascinating antique barn, Le Vieux Four, is worth a visit, not perhaps for the quality of the food but the sheer age of the building. One eats in cowsheds on milking stools, the whole place has a tremendous atmosphere, reasonably priced but slow service. La Cordée has a reputation for good food and is not too expensive. La Bonne Menagère has good food and atmosphere and La Ripaille au Linga is excellent value. So is Le Renard a short distance away, and the Contrebandiers has a band every evening. The Pierrier is also a good restaurant serving local dishes. There are plenty of crêperies, from comfortable cafés, to mobile vans which keep up the Haute Savoie traditions of serving crêpes and sharp schnapps to revive the skier after a hard day. Le Choucas, a bed and breakfast hotel, serves specialities, mainly cheese, in its bar. There is bowling and a night bar in the Blue Lagoon.

Popular bars include Les Armaillis, La Godille, La Taverne, Le Tunnel and L'Isba. The Séquoia disco on The Morgins Road is very popular. There are two cinemas showing up-to-date films daily, one showing English films once a week. There are guided tracks on snow shoes, a skating rink, visits to a cheese making farm, and a weekly market.

Recommended Hotels:

Hotel Perdrix Blanche: This 2 star hotel is situated at Pré de la Joux at the end of the valley; the 9 bedrooms are all with bath and satellite TV, cosy lounge and bar; a friendly atmosphere prevails and the food is good.

Hotel Fleur de Neige: This hotel has a long standing reputation for its high standards, particularly the restaurant where diners from outside are turned away nightly. The reception rooms are elegantly furnished and all rooms are with private facilities and there are some suites. A very helpful and hard working manager. Guests have a large choice of menu. It is possible to put on skis at the hotel and ski to the main Linga lift and also to return on skis so being situated some 600 metres from the centre of Chatel is in no way an inconvenience.

Hotel Lion D'Or: This hotel has recently been modernised with 35 new rooms all with private facilities. M. Maxit has been the proprietor for 21 years and helps to create a pleasant atmosphere in this old established and centrally situated hotel. The bar is very popular with locals.

Hotel Macchi: Run by the same family for 19 years and situated 300 metres from the centre and 500 metres from the ski school assembly point. A modern hotel, all rooms with private facilities and balconies. South facing terrace, à la carte restaurant and highly recommended for its food. Mainly French clientèle and they return again and again. Covered garage.

ST. JEAN D'AULPS/ LA GRANDE TERCHE

Height of Resort: 2,624 - 2,952 ft.
Height of Top Station: 5,905 ft.
Nearest International Airport: Geneva
Map Reference: 5B See page 238
Route by Car: See pages 236-238
Resort Facilities Charts: See page 218
Hotel Reference Charts: See page 230

St. Jean d'Aulps with its 10th century abbey is a sleepy little Savoyard village which has not yet woken up to the opportunities afforded by a small modern ski resort, La Grande Terche, on it doorstep. The village could be considered somewhat backward with only one modernised hotel out of four, 3 restaurants and no night life. When one speaks loosely of St. Jean d'Aulps as a ski resort one really means La Grande Terche village, 3km. to the west up a wide well engineered road. This has a hotel residence, a number of attractively designed apartments and two excellent restaurants. St. Jean d'Aulps lies on the Grandes Routes des Alps (RN 202) only 57km. from Geneva airport and 6km. from Morzine and Montriond with access into the main Portes du Soleil circuits. La Grande Terche will eventually be linked with Les Gets. Meanwhile it has formed its own circuit with the Bellevaux valley and within the next 2 years it should be linked with the resort of Praz de Lys.

The Skiing: Grande Terche/Val d'Enfer combining as the skiing domaine of Roc d'Enfer.

The Grande Terche: Compared with the main Portes du Soleil resorts the skiing is limited but the Grande Terche is a skier's mountain and what it lacks in variety it makes up for in quality. The area as a whole has 34km. of pistes served by 16 lifts and it was the venue of the French National Championships in 1983. From Grande Terche village a 6-seater gondolaway, due to be replaced by a cableway, rises, seemingly almost sheer at times, in 8 minutes to a plateau at Terche 1500. Here are the nursery slopes with 3 lifts, a restaurant and Nordic ski circuit. Two parallel drag-lifts take one up to Grande Terche 1800. From here the north facing runs back to the bottom station through glades give a vertical drop of some 3,000 feet of consistent gradient. Although graded blue and red it is one of those excellent 'race course' that can be turned into black by taking the steepest line. A very satisfying run where one has to 'work' all the way. About halfway down a long drag-lift can be used to return to a height of 5,577ft., so that one can repeat the steeper part of the run without going all the way down.

Returning to the top of Grande Terche 1800 one can ski southward down a glade to the bottom of the Combe de Graydon chair-lift and from the top of this lift at Col de Graydon, 5,905ft., there are a variety of red and blue runs down open east facing slopes back to base.

Val d'Enfer/Bellevaux Valley: Opened in 1988, one can now ski from Col de Graydon on generally west and north-west facing intermediate slopes to a little resort, La Cheverie, situated above Bellevaux. (it is at this point the link will be made with Praz de Lys). From here one takes two lifts up to Col de Follys and thence down east facing slopes to Grandes Terche village. This circuit has almost doubled the skiing and provides a very enjoyable and picturesque run of about 7km. The full Portes du Soleil pass is valid in the area whilst there is also a choice of the Grande Terche pass or one for the full Roc d'Enfer area.

In a Few Words: Limited but good skiing greatly enhanced by opening up the Bellevaux valley. Although a low resort north facing runs keep their snow well. Grand Terche village is relaxed and friendly with none of the rush and crowds to be found in the main Portes du Soleil ski areas and yet within easy reach for those with their own car. A good choice of reasonably priced apartments, many being British owned.

Après Ski: Energetic night revellers must go to nearby Morzine. The locals of Jean d'Aulps are no night birds nor do they cater for any. Emphasis is on quietness, calmness and sound sleep. Lights stay on later up at Grandes Terche where at the excellent L'Enfanle restaurant one is encouraged to overeat and linger on. There is dancing at the Auberge de la Terche twice weekly to band or disco.

Recommended Hotels:

Hotel Le Perroudy: A most attractive 2 star hotel situated in St. Jean d'Aulps. Built in 1980 and personally run by the young Desroches family. 15 double rooms each with bath, w.c., direct line telephone and balcony, Restaurant, free covered garage and lift. 4 Navettes per day up and down from Grande Terche.

Auberge de la Terche: A 3-star hotel right at the foot of the gondolaway at Grande Terche. Half the hotel is 'residence' and en pension or self catering terms are optional. Dancing twice weekly.

CHAMPÉRY

Height of Resort: 3,450 ft.
Height of Top Station: 7,400 ft.
Nearest International Airport: Geneva
Map Reference: 2D See page 240
Route by Car: See pages 236-240
Resort Facilities Charts: See page 221
Hotel Reference Charts: See page 232

Champéry is in the Canton de Valais near the French border, within easy reach of Geneva and in the heart of the 'Portes de Soleil'. It is a picturesque village, with wooden chalets lining the main street, and lies at the foot of towering mountains known as the Dents du Midi.

The nursery slopes, apart from one in the village, are on Planachaux, which is reached by cableway, leaving from the railway station, two 125 person cabins, or chair-lift from Grand Paradis. Rising to 5,875ft., these slopes are south facing, very sunny, and provide very easy to medium runs being served by 18 lifts. There are many restaurants offering a wide choice, their south facing terraces commanding majestic mountain views. There is also a small shop, useful for running repairs and leaving skis and boots.

To ski across to France (passport needed) one takes the chair-lift up the famous Chavanette; at the top is the border and a medium run leads down from here to Avoriaz. The 4 seater chair-lift from Les Crosets to the Pointe de Mossettes, 7,400ft., gives access to a 6km. run down to the Lindarets chair-lift (which also connects with Avoriaz) and the attractively situated restaurant Les Marmottes nearby. Champéry can be reached again via the Pas de Chavanette, a very steep descent, but less intrepid skiers can take the chair-lift. Day tours can be made to the surrounding resorts, including Morzine and Chatel. From Planachaux the runs down to the valley are easy and intermediate, some 4-6km., ending at the foot of the Grand Paradis chair-lift where one can return to the top or take the minibus back to the village.

In a Few Words: A charming small resort with access to extensive skiing and linked with Avoriaz and other Portes du Soleil resorts - see Introduction; open, sunny slopes above tree-line; excellent for beginners and all grades.

Après Ski: Varied and reasonable in price for a Swiss resort. The liveliest spot is the Levant with disco, popular with the locals, and specialising in fondues and raclettes. There's a cheap snack bar at Le Pub; the bar in the Hotel de Champéry is a favourite after skiing spot, and has a pianist in the evenings. The Vieux Chalet serves Swiss specialities, and Le Farinet is an excellent restaurant; their pizzas and fondues are highly recommended and prices are reasonable. There are several more good restaurants, bars and pubs with music and dancing. The sports centre has artificial skating and curling rinks, a swimming pool, sauna, solarium, fitness room, massage and restaurant.

Recommended Hotels:

Hotel Suisse: A first class hotel in the centre of the village. Entirely renovated in 1986. Five minutes from the main cableway. All rooms with private bathroom/shower. Lounge, piano bar, Victor Huge à la carte restaurant. Efficient service and friendly atmosphere.

Hotel Beau-Séjour: Standing in its own grounds a short distance from the Planachaux cableway terminal, this is an attractive old chalet-style family hotel efficiently run. The lounge is comfortable. All rooms have private bath or shower, wc, radio, TV, telephone and mini-bar. Its Vieux Chalet is open each evening and excellent fondue bourguignonne is served.

Hotel de Champéry: One of the longest established hotels in the resort. Attractive bar with resident pianist and cosy lounge. The bedrooms are tastefully furnished and most have bath and balcony. A gay atmosphere prevails. Sauna open to outside guests, massage and large games room.

Hotel des Alpes: Ten minutes' walk from the cableway, this chalet-style hotel is owned by François Rieme and he and his wife run a very efficient and friendly house. The modern and nicely furnished bedrooms all have private bath. The reception rooms are attractive and retain a Swiss atmosphere.

MORGINS

Height of Resort: 4,593 ft.
Height of Top Station: 6,890 ft.
Nearest International Airport: Geneva
Map Reference: 2D See page 240
Route by Car: See pages 236-240
Resort Facilities Charts: See page 223
Hotel Reference Charts: See page 233

Morgins is situated in the Bas Valais and has been an Alpine resort since 1820. Before World War II it was a skiing resort much favoured by the British and indeed still has British associations. In 1970, finding itself situated in the developing Portes du Soleil ski region the resort underwent considerable modernisation with some old hotels being pulled down and replaced. Morgins with only 390 inhabitants, however, still retains much of its charm with many old chalets and farms remaining. It will retain its existing charm as the only planned expansion over the next 10 years is an additional 1,200 beds. The railway station at Aigle, on the Simplon line with fast trains from most points including Geneva, is only 27km. distance with good connections. The fastest road route is from Geneva on the motorway via Lausanne, Aigle, Monthey and Troistorrents. Alternatively one can take the shorter route via Thonon, Chatel and over the Morgins Pass which is always kept open in the winter.

Morgins is a small and open village with only 3 hotels, including one bed and breakfast, providing 265 beds and 880 chalets and apartments with a total of some 5,500 beds and 10 restaurants. It is an important resort being in the heart of the Portes du Soleil region with its 650km. of prepared pistes. The resort enjoys above average hours of sunshine.

Morgins Lifts & Skiing: To be properly understood this section should be read in conjunction with the description of the Portes du Soleil area reported in the Introduction. There are two main ski routes out of Morgins being part of the main circuit of the Portes du Soleil:-

On the North Side: A triple chair-lift takes one up a north facing mountain to La Foilleuse where there is a large (550 seats) restaurant and from which there are splendid views of the impressive Dents du Midi with Mont Blanc in the background. The installation of a chair-lift for the 1990 season now facilitates the return to La Foilleuse for the run back to Morgins. Wider intermediate slopes then stretch out towards the west and Champoussin. The longest run in this immediate area being Les Bochasses, which steepens towards the bottom. There are plans to piste the slopes west of La Foilleuse. The Sepaya run at Champoussin is wide and relaxing and good for

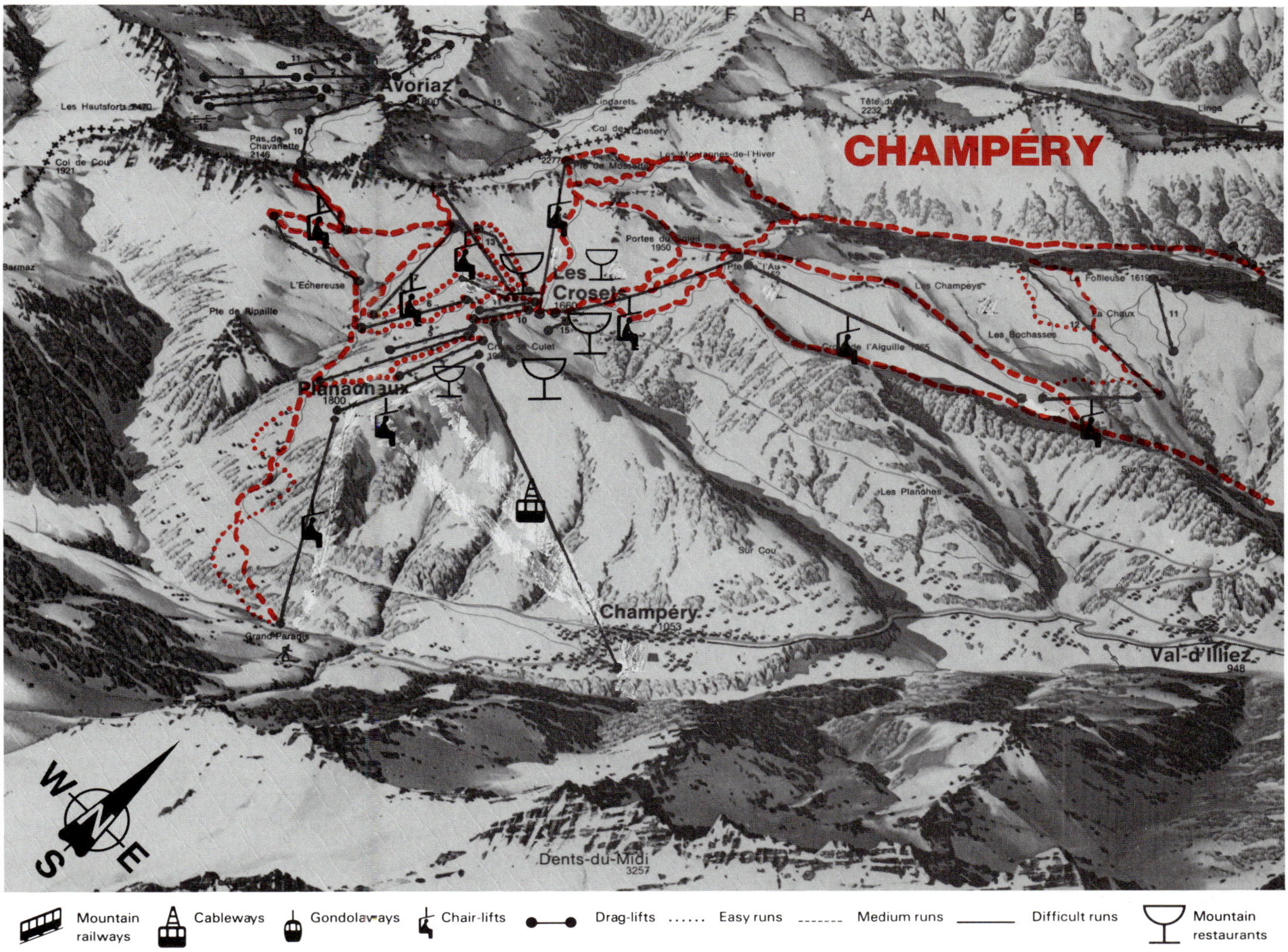

building intermediate confidence. The recently installed triple chair-lift, Les Champeys, to the peak above Champoussin opens up a wider skiing area within the immediate vicinity of Champoussin. This area leads deeper into the Portes du Soleil circuit through Les Crosets and across the frontier into Avoriaz. The furthest point of the Morgins area is the Pointe de L'Au, 7,060ft., which peaks between the Les Crosets and Champoussin valleys. It affords a fast return on the east or a steep mogully adventure to the south and eventually a gentle return to Champoussin. The run back to Morgins is good, through wooded glades with a 4-seater chair-lift half way down to pull one back to the top. Always fun and this run is particularly useful in bad visibility.

On the South Side: Three lifts, the first a 4-seater chair-lift, surmounted by a charming restaurant, followed by three drag-lifts takes one up to Porte de Culet. Here the south facing slopes, close to the 4 seater chair-lift, provide excellent nursery skiing. From this point the runs back to Morgins are fairly long reds and blues over south facing slopes. Continuing northwards over the top one skis down to Super Chatel over a variety of very pleasant, fast, blue runs. From Super Chatel one has the choice of the long run to Torgon and La Chapelle D'Abondance or continuing the circuit down to Chatel and through Le Linga to Avoriaz.

To get from the south side to the north side entails a walk of only 5 minutes if one uses a village lift to gain height. There are several beginners' lifts in the village area serving excellent nursery slopes whilst Nordic skiing is well catered for with prepared trails running through the woods, 3, 8 and 9km. in length.

In a Few Words: An attractive old world village lying in the very heart of the vast Porte du Soleil ski area. Parts are modernised, open and uncluttered. Skiing suitable for all standards and recommended as a base. Easy road access over the Morgins pass to Chatel. English generally understood. Above average sunshine.

Après Ski: Being a small village this is obviously limited. There is skating, a tennis hall with two courts and prepared marked walks. A good choice of 'fun' restaurants and small cafés:- Savolaire, Café Le Bazot, cakes and ices, Café du Valais, grills on a wood fire, Café La Buvette with a very pleasant woody atmosphere. Café Les Fontaines-Blanches serves a wide selection of cheese specialities and the Restaurant-Bar La Bergerie includes frogs legs on the menu! There is one disco Le SAF. Morgins in the heart of the Portes du Soleil is most appealing, it has a certain openness often sadly missing in the more congested resorts. Peace and quiet prevails and their motto is 'Morgins, mon oxygène'.

Recommended Hotels:

Hotel Beau-Site: A small and very old established hotel owned and run by the family Diserens. No rooms with private facilities, but public bathroom and 2 showers and now run on a bed and breakfast basis. What is lacking in modern facilities is more than compensated by the warmth, care and attention to guests given by the owners.

Hotel Bellevue: A 3 star hotel with a total of 80 beds all with facilities and including 22 suites, each with electric ring and bar arrangement. There is a swimming pool, Carnotzet for all cheese specialities, créperie-pizzeria, hairdressing and beauty parlour, boutique and a large sun terrace.

BRIEF REPORTS ON THE REMAINING RESORTS:

It should be noted that the height of the top stations given is the top station of that particular resort. If, however, it is one of the linked resorts, the highest point that can be reached by lifts is 7,874ft.

France:

Abondance: 3,050-5,905ft.: Situated below Mount Cauffé, an attractive small village. The skiing is served by 13 lifts. Not a linked resort but easy access by car to Chatel.

La Chapelle D'Abondance: 3,314-5,249ft.: Now linked with Torgon and situated between Abondance and Chatel so easy access by car to the latter. A typical small Savoyarde village. The skiing is served by 12 lifts.

Montriond: 3,116-7,218ft.: At present this resort has limited skiing served by a cableway and 2 lifts. By car easy access to Morzine and Les Gets.

Switzerland:

Champoussin: 5,511-7,546ft.: On the main circuit and situated close to Val d'Illiez, this small village has limited accommodation so the 8 lifts in the immediate vicinity are adequate and for good skiers there is the whole of the Portes du Soleil. There are a few restaurants and bars and a disco.

Les Crosets: 4,378-7,564ft.: A good place to stay but there are only two hotels, the immediate area is served by 12 lifts, one of them, the gondolaway, travels to Pointe de Mossetts, 7,400ft., where there is a 6km. run down to the Lindarets drag-lift which gives access to Avoriaz.

Torgon: 3,609-562ft.: A linked resort via Super Chatel or Chapelle d'Abondance, the immediate ski area is served by 8 lifts and the famous 'Torgon Wall' is for experts only. The village is of medium size, with hotels, chalets and apartment accommodation. Several restaurants and discos. From the village one has a lovely view of Lake Geneva.

ANDORRA

ANDORRA

This tiny Principality of some 470 square km. is situated high in the Pyrenees between France and Spain. The official language is Catalan but Spanish and French are widely spoken and English is being taught in schools. The capital is Andorra la Vella situated in the south-west, disappointing at first sight with the narrow streets full of cars and crowds of people buying duty free goods in the masses of shops. Access from the UK by air is via Toulouse or Barcelona being 180km. and 226km. away from the capital respectively.

Being a cheap and duty free state has attracted British and other tour operators, whose clients were the only skiers to be seen on the slopes mid-week. This situation is changing as will be seen under Soldeu/El Tarter. Weekends can be crowded with Spanish skiers from Barcelona and Valencia and French from Toulouse. There are five ski resorts, Soldeu/El Tarter, Pas de la Casa/Grau Roig, Arinsal, Pal and Arcalis. The first two are each counted as one resort. Arinsal and Pal share a single lift pass.

Andorra is a delightful area and being duty free the prices are very reasonable. For the 1997/98 season a lift pass covering all 5 Andorran resorts will cost about 3,500 Pts per day. So the experienced skier can have a very enjoyable two weeks holiday staying the first week at La Massana and covering Pal, Arinsal and Arcalis, the second week at Canillo or Soldeu for the two remaining resorts.

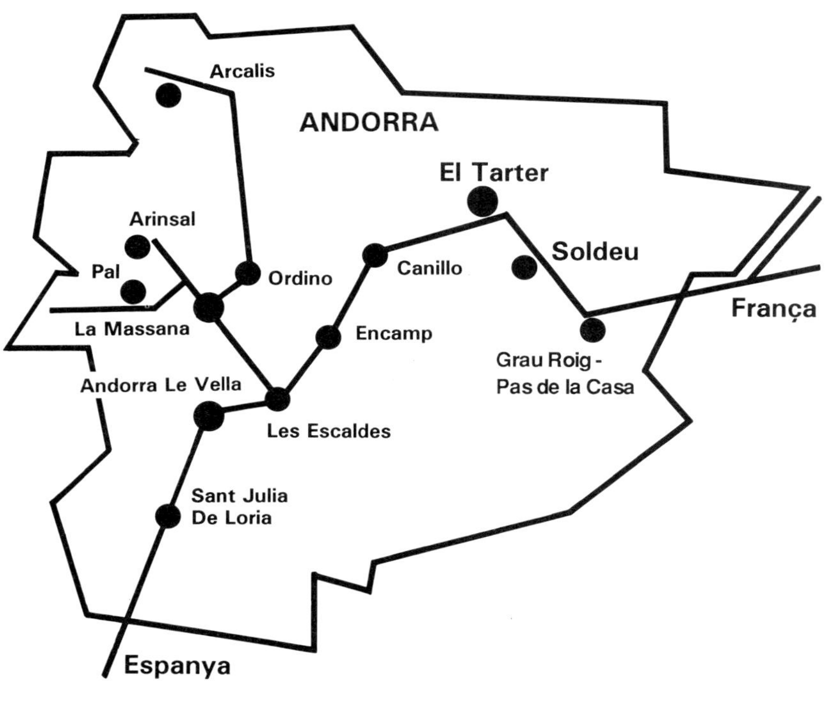

SOLDEU/EL TARTER

Height of Resort: 5,900 ft.
Height of Top Station: 8,400 ft.
Nearest International Airport: Barcelona
Map Reference: See Main Map page 236
Resort Facilities Charts: See page 225
Hotel Reference Charts: See page 234

Soldeu/El Tarter, one of five resorts in the Principality of Andorra, is an area deserving of far more attention than it receives. The two, linked villages provide a large and varied ski area, noted for sunshine as well as plenty of snow. The skiable terrain has been laid out to suit most grades of skiers. The 1996/97 season saw the opening of an 8 person gondolaway, moving 1,500 passengers per hour. The bottom station is on the Soldeu side of the valley and it rises to the Espiolets Plateau, 7,710 ft. in less than 5 minutes. Running parallel, but starting the other side of the valley and reached from the village by crossing a high foot-bridge, is the bottom station of the Espiolets chair-lift which rises first to middle station, where skiers can join and continue to the Espiolets Plateau.

The chair-lift rises to a middle station where skiers can join to continue to the top, the Espiolets Plateau at 7,710ft. This is the centre of the 'Soldeu' side of the mountain, being the arrival of all but two of the drag-lifts, and the departure point for most of the runs. It is the site of the excellent nursery slopes and their six beginner drag-lifts, overlooked by a large mountain restaurant, the ski school, heated children's crêche, etc. A long drag-lift, now the greatest bottle-neck on the mountain, links the lower end of the nursery slopes with a the top of the Belvedere (now called La Solana) from where the average skier can enjoy a variety of runs, either back to the Espiolets plateau, the village of Soldeu, or the El Tarter side of the mountain. Access to this side can also be gained direct from the plateau following a gentle green path, and further down, on an extension of the 'green' run which finishes at the bottom of the El Tarter chair-lift.

The El Tarter side of the mountain is accessed by two chair-lifts, one double and a detachable 4 seater (at 5,431ft.), rising from the large 1,000 place car park, and the hotels and attractive modern urbanisation of El Tarter, to the open Riba Escorchada valley. Here there are six lifts including the one already mentioned, which links to the Espiolets plateau, and a 4 seater chair-lift, rising southwards, surmounted by two parallel drag-lifts converging on Tossel de la Llosada, 8,400 ft. From this point one has astounding views over the capital, Andorra La Vella, and half the Pyrenees range. The Soldeu side of the mountain can also be rejoined from here, or from the top of the El Tarter chair-lift along what has aptly become known as the 'winter wonderland' path through the forest. This sunny and delightful area will witness all future expansion, with the entire western side scheduled for development. The skiing, covering some 65km,. provides something for every grade.

Challenging runs, which have been widened for the advanced skier, include steep ones following the line of both chair-lifts down to Soldeu and El Tarter. Runs are mainly through wide wooded glades on north and north-east facing slopes. Off-piste skiing is superb, and there are several connecting tracks through the woods. Also in the area near the top of the chair-lift three beginners lifts and a restaurant have recently been constructed. A ski school also operates from here. There are still many more possibilities for expansion which it is hoped to exploit in future years. Some 244 snow cannons now cover 14km of the runs.

The ski school, under Director Miquel Casal and subdirectors Alex Santiago and Mike Archer, is of an exceptionally high standard. At peak season there are over 100 English speaking BASI qualified instructors, plus around 50 Spanish, Argentinian and Andorran, together teaching 800 to 1000 persons per week. Soldeu boasts a 90% ski school attendance

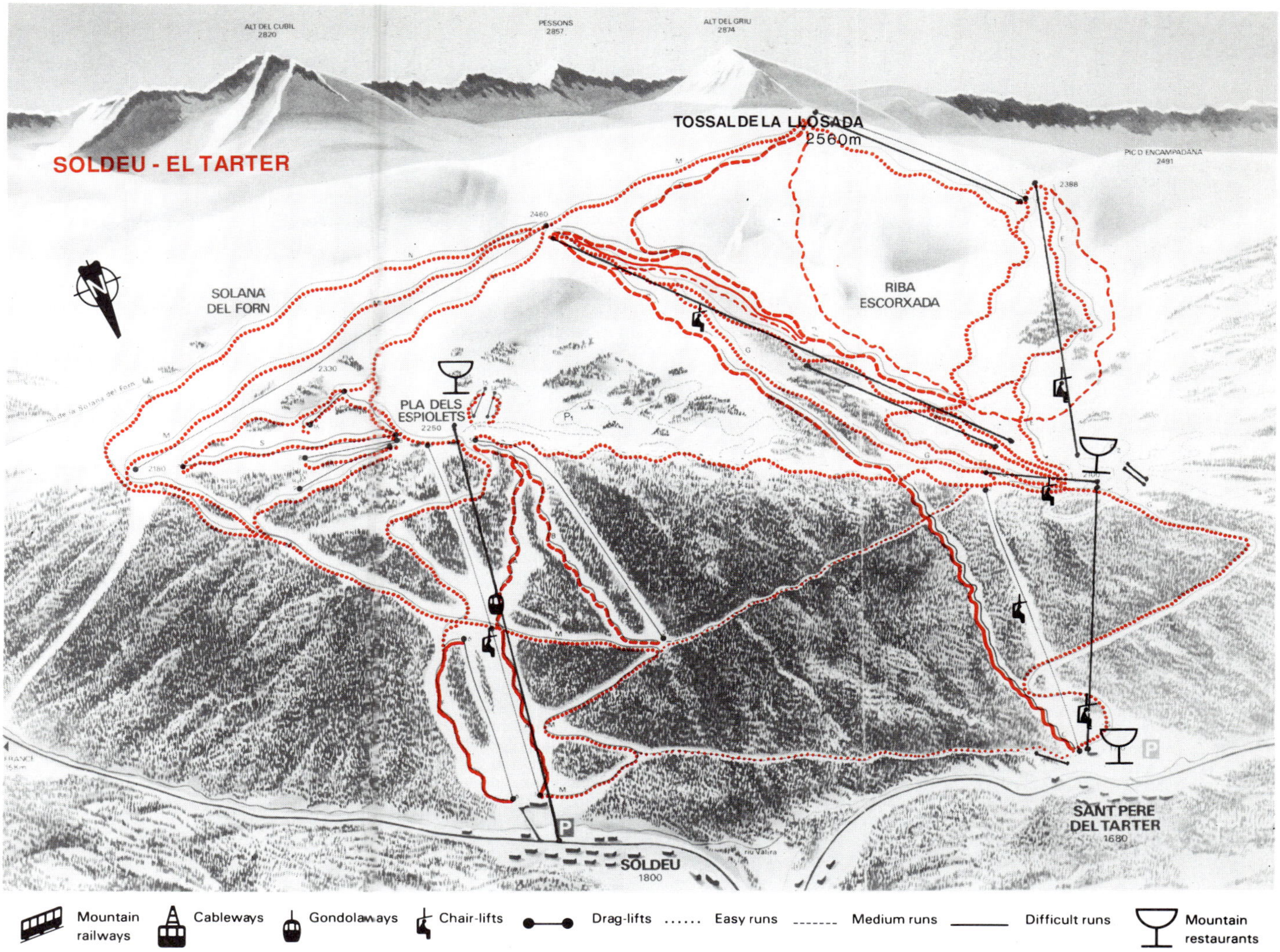

and a very low accident rate as the majority of skiers are in controlled conditions. Being taught to ski in English is never a problem, although you may have to tune into a New Zealand or Canadian accent. The grading system, to ensure classes of the same level of progress is most efficient. Weekly end of course tests are well structured and administered with the same degree of enthusiasm, friendliness and encouragement for which this ski school has become renowned. There is also a crêche facility at the ski school for skiing mums and enquiries can be made to Mike Archer at the ski school.

The ski school also provides snowboard and telemark classes and every Thursday downhill by torchlight. Also every week they organise a helitransfer from Soldeu to Grau Roig.

The lift pass includes bus transport to the nearby village of Canillo which has a sports centre, ice rink, swimming pool, squash and various restaurants and discos.

For those who prefer Nordic skiing, there are 2 tracks, one of 7km. which starts near the top of the Soldeu chair-lift, and one of 5km., from the top of the Tarter chair-lift.

The installation of new lifts has relieved the queue problems and the new management has changed the resort for the better, with many development plans for the future. Recently, however, they have encouraged bus loads of Spanish school children to the resort by giving special mid-week prices, and as a result it is now the most crowded resort in Andorra.

In a Few Words: Of the five, the most established resort for British skiers; varied ski terrain with 60km. of prepared pistes; suitable for beginners to intermediates but with some challenging runs for the more advanced; excellent ski school with high standard instruction; good off-piste possibilities; crêche and kindergarten.

Après Ski: There is a good choice of restaurants in Soldeu/El Tarter, some informal and some smart. Solineu and Bonnell's are best for lunch and Pussycat reasonably smart for dinner. The Canadian and English run Hotel Roc San Miquel has a pleasant bar and a restaurant. Fat Al's Bar and the Aspen Bar, situated in the resort centre, with restaurant and discothèques are the most popular après ski venues.

Recommended Hotels:

Hotel Del Tarter: Completely refurbished in 1991, accommodating 80 guests in 37 comfortable rooms all with private bath, wc and TV. Popular with English skiers, relaxed friendly atmosphere, excellent food in pleasant surroundings, bar, separate TV room, sauna. Ski locker per room provided in basement and also children's room with TV. Light evening meals available earlier for small children. Situated at the bottom of the chair-lift to the Riba Escorxada. Excellent family hotel run by Mr & Mrs Daniel Mateu, who mix well with their guests. Spacious family suite.

Hotel Parador Canaro: Situated half way between Soldeu and El Tarter this spacious hotel is built of traditional local stone & timber. 18 double rooms all with bath and wc. Pleasant traditional dining room and bar with large sun terrace a small gentle slope beside the hotel, with its own 3 small ski lifts for beginners.

Hotel Naudi: Situated only 200 yards from the lifts in Soldeu, another traditional hotel with bar and downstairs spacious dining room looking out onto the mountain. Very comfortable lounge with large sun terrace. Sleeps 120 in 60 tastefully furnished rooms, all with bath (this includes annexe across the road).

Hotel Roc St. Miquel: A small English-owned hotel, recently refurbished, run as a chalet with accommodation for 24 guests. All rooms with private bath and wc. Bright dining room with Cordon Bleu cooking. Popular bar with open house buffet.

Sporthotel: This 4 star hotel with 400 beds has recently been completed. Attractive and well furnished throughout, and its 'Picadilly' Pub is very popular.

GRAU ROIG/PAS DE LA CASA

Height of Resort: 6,725 ft.
Height of Top Station: 9,350 ft.
Nearest International Airport: Toulouse/Barcelona
Map Reference: See Main Map page 236
Resort Facilities Charts: See page 225

Pas de La Casa is on the northern side of this twin resort, with pistes skirting along the French-Andorran border that affords one's first view of Andorra on approaching it from France. The sprawling chaotic town, with some 10,000 beds in hotels and apartments, dispenses duty-free goods to coach loads of French day trippers as well as catering for skiers. Grau Roig (pronounced Roich) on the southern side of the divide separating it from Pas, is only 10 minutes bus ride from Soldeu, but plans to link the two will have to overcome local opposition. It has a well designed base station with a large car park, several restaurants and bars, kindergarten, shops, picnic area and a small hotel. There are no plans to increase the accommodation.

The slopes on both sides are wide open and hold some interesting descents and in most years offer excellent off-piste possibilities. The principle runs on both sides are covered by snow making machines guaranteeing a 5 months season. The central system consists of 4-seater chair-lifts coming up to the crest from both base stations, with a series of drag-lifts on either side of the chair-lifts. The skiing is, therefore based on the yo-yo principle of a lift up and runs following the line of the lifts down. Both stations are well served by trainer lifts.

Two lifts have been installed on the right of the Grau Roig and one on the opposite slope, taking the development in the direction of Soldeu.

Four mountain restaurants are to be recommended:- 'Col Blanc' at the top of the chair-lift; 'Costa Rodana' on the right of the Pas ski area which can be reached on skis or by road; 'Piolet' in Grau Roig by the Montmalus area and the excellent 'Refugi dels Bessons' by the lake.

In a Few Words: Now looked upon as one of Andorra's top resorts and one of the top five in the Pyrenees; 29 lifts serving 85km of prepared pistes and still extending; north-west and north-east facing slopes tend to hold the snow well; ideal for beginners to advanced intermediates. After Arcalis, this resort has the most reliable snow in Andorra; sometimes the season covers a period of 6 months.

Après Ski: Plenty going on in Pas with masses of bars, restaurants and shops. For evening entertainment there is a choice of six discothèques.

Accommodation: A wide selection of pensions, hotels and self-catering apartments in Pas de La Casa.

ARCALIS

Height of Resort: 6,364 ft.
Height of Top Station: 8,530 ft.
Nearest International Airport: Toulouse/Barcelona
Map Reference: See Main Map page 236
Resort Facilities Charts: See page 225

This purpose built resort in the north-west corner of the Principality was opened in 1983/84 and is located at the head of a large valley 24km. from Andorra la Vella. At present there is no accommodation in the area the nearest being in El Serrat, 6km., or Ordino some 9km. away. After passing through a short tunnel one comes across the base station with its two large restaurants, snack bar and two bars. There is also a kindergarten and crêche facilities and a free 150 metre baby drag-lift for up to 10 year olds. The organisation of ski hire, ski school and lift passes is also done at the base station and similar facilities at the middle station which is reached by a shuttle bus service or by the two lifts mentioned below.

From the base station two parallel drag-lifts, L'Hortel I & II rise south-eastwards, the longer of the two reaching 7,380 ft, serving an easy run to the middle station and intermediate runs back to the base station. Also from the base station a high speed detachable 4 seater chair-lift, the longest vertical lift in the Pyrenées, was opened for the 1995/96 season. This rises south-eastwards to some 8,000 ft. serving a variety of excellent runs to both the base and middle stations.

From the middle station three further drag-lifts, two short ones serving easy runs and a long one, l'Abarsetar, travelling south-eastwards to 7,710 ft, from the top a long red run winds its way through wooded glades to the base station.

The longest lift is Les Portelles 3 seater chair-lift, starting just above the middle station and travels southwards to the crest below Arcalis summit, 8,366 ft. Here one can view this very beautiful ski scene, open at the top and fairly wooded lower slopes. Following the line of the lift down there is a red run on the right and a black on the left joining the red halfway down.

In the valley to the west of the base station a 4 seater chair-lift, with a beginner's drag-lift at the foot, rises to 8,530 ft. terminating just above Les Portelles top station. This has relieved the pressure on the latter and opened up excellent blue and red north facing runs and also some brilliant off-piste skiing. A red run leads to the base station and a winding path takes one back to the middle station.

All lift passes for Arcalis, Arinsal and Pal are valid for the bus travelling between all 3 resorts.

In a Few Words: A beautiful ski area; delightful and challenging piste skiing and very enjoyable off-piste through wide wooded glades; predominately north facing slopes holding the snow well; good for beginners to intermediates; scope for considerable development, part of which already implemented; only snag no accommodation near the lift system.

Après Ski: At present, there is little going on so one has to visit La Massana or Andorra la Vella where there is a fair amount of activity.

Hotel Accommodation: The nearest is at El Serrat, some 6km. from the base station, or Ordino, 9km.

ARINSAL

Height of Resort: 5,085 ft.
Height of Top Station: 8,530 ft.
Nearest International Airport: Toulouse/Barcelona
Map Reference: See Main Map page 236
Resort Facilities Charts: See page 225

Situated on the western side, Arinsal, which a few years ago used to be a small village, has grown into a large and thriving resort with many hotels, apartment blocks, restaurants, bars/pubs and discos. It has the largest growth in Andorra but in comparison its skiing is at present limited. The base station, situated on the northern outskirts of the resort, has restaurants, bars, ski shops, apartments and parking for 700 cars. From here a chair-lift rises to the middle station, Comallemple, 6,427ft., which is the real centre of Arinsal skiing. This station can also be reached by road which is always kept open, and this is parking space along with extensive restaurant facilities, 3 ski shops, ski school with 40 English speaking instructors a children's nursery, 4 trainer lifts and lockers for equipment and clothes.

The skiing is situated in a huge bowl shaped area above the treeline with a compact lift system travelling mainly westward. On the right the 4 seater, Les Fonts, chair-lift carries 2,000 skiers per hour up to 7,677 ft, where one finds the 'Igloo' snack bar, to the left the Bambi chair-lift rises to 6,890 ft, where there is the Obelics snack bar and above surmounting drag-lifts reach Port Negre, 8,530 ft, the top station. From here one has wonderful views of the beautiful countryside and a selection of easy and intermediate runs over east and north-east facing slopes to the middle station. The series of lifts allows one to break one's journey at various stages to return to the top. One of the three black runs can be reached from Port Negre by skiing down to La Capa drag-lift rising to the peak of the same name, the second is from the middle to the base station and the third down into the adjoining Cubil Valley from the top of the La Tossa drag-lift.

In a Few Words: Well planned and compact lift system; good facilities at middle station; most of the skiing above the treeline; under normal conditions reliable snow; suitable for beginners to intermediates. Fully automatic computer controlled York Snow making equipment.

Après Ski: This has expanded considerably.There is Ciscos Bar and restaurant situated in a converted barn providing reasonable priced drinks against background music for impromptu dancing. The Skydance disco, in the Gothard Hotel, is enjoyable; so is that in the Hotel Solana. The small restaurant La Neu provides excellent ribs and steaks but does not stay open late. Other bars and restaurants include 'La Granja' and 'La Riba' which have live music most nights and a night bus connects them all. In the restaurant 'Jan', next to Ciscos, one can enjoy good, but pricey, local dishes. At several village restaurants, however, a 3 course meal with wine can be obtainedat a reasonable price. Further entertainment to be found in La Massana and Andorra la Vella.

Recommended Hotel:

Hotel Solana: Situated in the centre of the village this family run hotel offers comfortable accommodation, all roms with bath/shower, wc and most with balcony. Dining room with buffet breakfast and choice of menu for dinner. Large bar/lounge, cosy bar with open fire, games room, disco, swimming pool, sauna and jacuzzi, pub and garage.

PAL

Height of Resort: 6,069 ft.
Height of Top Station: 7,769 ft.
Nearest International Airport: Toulouse/Barcelona
Map Reference: See Main Map page 236
Resort Facilities Charts: See page 225

Situated on the western side of the Principality is the village of Pal and continuing eastwards along a winding approach road one comes to the ski area, opened in 1982/83, which is rather an unusual one. Its top extremity follows the line of the crest from peak Del Cubil, 7,769 ft, the highest point, down to the base station, 6,069 ft, about 3½km. in length. The interlinking lifts and runs are spaced on the right-hand side stretching down to the road below. Along the road parking spaces have been created near the bottom stations of four widely dispersed lifts, which could be termed the lower base stations. This means at peak periods skiers are quickly dispersed over the whole system and not having to approach it from one point. At the base station there is a loop road for further parking and a very attractive wooden constructed lodge, "La Chubella' with bar and restaurant, which becomes very crowded at lunchtime, a kindergarten and four trainer lifts. The layout of the ski area is very American with most of the runs through wooded glades and becoming fairly open near the top station. From near the base station a chair-lift rises to Pla de la Cot, 6,829 ft, where there is a further restaurant and two trainer lifts. From here one has a selection of intermediate runs following the line of the lifts and one can return up again or connect with lifts rising to the top station, peak Del Cubil. Interesting intermediate runs are served by these three lifts, (a chair and two drag-lifts) whilst to the right of the top station fairly closely wooded red runs reach Col de la Botella with a chair-lift back to join the main system. From the top there is a run along the crest of about 3km. down to the La Caubella restaurant at the base station, red to start with and thence blue.

In a Few Words: Not everyone's type of skiing but a well thought out lift system for an unusual ski area leading to little or no queues even during peak periods; good for beginners to intermediates but favours the latter; good off-piste. Although Pal and Arinsal are separate resorts they are managed by the same company and joint passes for both resorts are available.

Après Ski: In La Massana or Andorra la Vella.

Accommodation: Limited in Pal village but hotel and apartment accommodation in La Massana or Andorra la Vella.

BULGARIA

BOROVETS

Height of Resort: 4,265 ft.
Height of Top Station: 8,300 ft.
Nearest International Airport: Sofia
Resort Facilities Charts: See page 225
Hotel Reference Charts: See page 235

Borovets is situated amidst the pine forests in the Rila mountains 70km. south of Sofia, about $1^1/_2$ hours by coach. It is the starting point for climbing the Musala, 9,597ft., the highest peak of the Balkan peninsula. About 150 days a year with thick snow cover excellent for winter sports. Abundance of ultra-violet rays. Lack of pollution. It is the second largest skiing resort in Bulgaria with 11 hotels and 2 villa zones. A free bus service operates morning, lunchtime and evenings. There are lock-up facilities for ski equipment in the ski area, for which a small charge is made.

The Skiing: Borovets hosted the World Cup, both slalom and giant slalom, in March 1981 and for this event built an entirely new lift system and constructed new runs through the trees. It has some of the best skiing in Bulgaria for intermediates up to expert. The slopes are mainly north facing and have challenging steep sections as one would expect for a World Cup venue. The lifts cover two distinct areas:

The World Cup Area: Access is by the latest French 6-seater gondolaway which rises to Yastrebets in 22 minutes. It is 4,827 metres long and has a capacity of 1,200 persons per hour. From here one can ski down southwards to join four drag-lifts which serve a large area of open and sunny east facing slopes. The first lift serves easy slopes whilst the remaining four provide access to a selection of longer intermediate runs. If one wishes to take the gondolaway down there is a 5 minute climb to the top station.

Alternatively by traversing under the top station one can join the run to the village further down. There is a two section drag-lift, the top ending just below the upper section of the gondolaway and the bottom starting from the village some way from the lower gondolaway terminal. From the top of the gondolaway it is possible to ski down following the line of the drag-lifts, which in fact is the World Cup run – a very pleasant red well within the capabilities of intermediates. To regain the gondolaway one has two alternatives, trek through the woods to the lower station or take the drag-lifts to the top and ski down the red or black run to the middle station of the gondolaway.

The Original Area: This is situated to the left of the World Cup area and consists of a chair-lift 1 900 metres long and rising to Sitnyakovska in 15 minutes, and a second chair-lift, 1310 metres long, rising to Martinovi Baraki and 3 small button ski tows for beginners. One ski school meets here and the ski terrain is varied with interesting steep sections as well as good easy runs for beginners. The other ski school meets at the Olymp Hotel.

In a Few Words: Although not yet comparable with the larger Alpine resorts, the skiing is good for all standards with some steep and fast runs through glades for the expert. Although runs are not always well linked, the wide pine glades allow skiing in bad weather. The best Bulgarian resort for the more experienced skier. Two good ski schools with mostly English-speaking instructors and small classes; good equipment hire facilities. 15km. of trails for Nordic skiing.

Après Ski: Entertainment is in the hotels with games rooms and dancing to bands in the dining rooms and discos. With free enterprise on the increase many small bars have appeared; these have plenty of atmosphere and prices are considerably cheaper than those in hotels. Particularly recommended is Peters Bar opposite the gondolaway. Balkantourist arrange a varied programme of entertainment, such as visits to a typical farm house, folk evenings, films and video, wine tasting and ski presentations etc. Sofia is well worth a visit by local transport or tour bus, both of which are extremely cheap. There are lovely walks in the area.

Recommended Hotels:

Hotel Bor: A pleasant hotel. 37 twin-bedded rooms and 8 singles all with bath, only single rooms have balconies. Buffet breakfast provided and the restaurant is open from 0800 to 2300 hours with a non-stop service. Panoramic sun terrace for guests.Taverna for local dishes. Dancing in the dining room. Duty free shop.

Hotel Edelweiss: A nice family chalet-style hotel with a good atmosphere, under the same management as the Bor. 64 twin-bedded rooms and 14 singles all with shower. Some rooms with balconies. Restaurant service from 0800 - 2300 hours. Dancing in restaurant. Sun terrace.

Hotel Olymp: A good modern 3 star hotel situated 50 metres from one of the ski runs and 9 minutes' walk from the gondolaway. 360 beds in twins/ triple rooms all with showers, wc, lounge area, large restaurant, bar/disco, sports centre with swimming pool, sports hall, gym, saunas and solarium.

Hotel Rila: 3 stars, is an original hotel-complex for mountain tourism designed by the French firm Les Arcs. The complex is made up of 200 twin bedded rooms all with bath, wc, TV and balcony and 350 studios, each sleeping 2-4 persons, with bath, wc, kitchenette and balcony. Restaurant service: Rila restaurant - 380 seats. Iskar restaurant 200 seats, a folk stye restaurant 170 seats, coffee shop 30 seats; a night club 140 seats; a day bar 100 seats; snack bar 100 seats.
There is a shopping centre and a currency Coracom shop, fitness centre with saunas and medical centre, a barber and hairdresser.

PAMPOROVO

Height of Resort:. 5,345 ft.
Height of Top Station: 6,335 ft.
Nearest International Airport:. Plovdiv
Resort Facilities Charts: See page 226
Hotel Reference Charts: See page 235

Pamporovo is situated in the Rhodope mountains in the southern part of Bulgaria close to the Greek border. The mountains are more like rounded-top hills, thickly pine-clad and very beautiful. Pamporovo has a reputation for fine windless weather and about 186 winter days are fine.

The Skiing: The runs are predominantly north and north-west facing and skiing is possible from December to the second half of April. The nearest chair-lift is about 650 metres from the hotels, this has a capacity of 600 persons per hour and reaches the Stoudenets hut at the middle station. Some 2km. from the village in the Malina-Ardashla area one finds a further two chair-lifts; the first, with a capacity of 375 per hour, rises to the middle station; the second a 3 seater with a capacity of 1,800 persons per hour reaches Snezhanka (Snow White) peak, 6,317ft. Here there is a television tower and coffee bar from which one has lovely views into Greece. This point can also be reached from the Studenets hut by chair-lift. To the left (east) one can take a drag-lift up a steep slalom slope, 'The Wall'. The run down is black and is the site for Europe Cup slalom events. On the eastern side of this area there is also another drag-lift serving a good blue practice run. In all there are 25km. of well prepared runs, the longest being blue of 3.8km. from the peak down to Ardasla. Most runs are easy for beginners to early intermediates, the exceptions are the steep slalom slope and the interesting giant slalom course of some 2km., splitting into two halfway down and ending at Ardasla chair-lift, or Two Bridges drag-lift. Both are graded black and have been used for the Europa Cup races. All runs are through glades cut through the pine forests. The main nursery slopes are below the bottom station and south facing served by a drag-lift. There are alternative nursery slopes behind the Snezhanka Peak. The bottom stations are served by bus from the village and both have ski storage rooms. The ski school appears excellent with most instructors speaking English. The equipment for hire is modern and of good quality.

In a Few Words: A pretty, sunny and unsophisticated resort generally windless and safe from avalanche dangers. Skiing suitable for beginners to early intermediates, the black runs are sufficiently challenging but would not be enough to satisfy the better skier for more than a day or two.

Après Ski: Local fiery drink, Mustika, is cheap and very effective. Almost every hotel has dancing to a live band in the dining room, plus night clubs and bars and discos in the basement. Average opening hours are between 2200-0400 hours, but the latter often depends on the 'spirit' of the moment. Shops are fairly scarce: there are local currency shops selling mainly souvenirs. Pamporovo has two particularly delightful restaurants: a typical Rhodope style Tavern, presided over by a seemingly ferocious brigand, who cooks and serves the famous whole lamb, spit roasted, which is eaten with one's fingers – do not ask for a knife and fork! This fantastic dinner is followed by boisterous folk music and singing. In 1991 an English pub, 'The White Hart', opened and is to be found near the Mourgavets Hotel.There is also an enchanting old water mill converted into a restaurant and this visit is best planned by day so as to enjoy the scenic drive. Excursions include trips to Plovdiv, the second largest city in Bulgaria, Istanbul and other places of interest.

Recommended Hotels:

Hotel Perelik: A large hotel of grand style. 199 twin–bedded rooms, 10 single rooms and several apartments all with bath/shower. Two dining rooms, 2 sitting rooms, 4 bars and swimming pool. Sauna, water/electric treatment room, children's room, games room, bowling alley, Taverna for local cooking, dancing nightly.

Hotel Mourgavets: 75 twin-bedded rooms and 8 single rooms, all with private bath, balconies, telephone and television. Spacious dining room, 8 sitting rooms and 2 bars. Buffet style breakfast and large choice of menu for other meals. Disco, games room and day bar on top floor with inspiring panorama; resident dentistry. Free bus service to lifts.

SPAIN

LA MOLINA

Height of Resort: 4,726 ft.
Height of Top Station: 8,315 ft.
Nearest International Airport: Barcelona
Map Reference: See Main Map page 236
Route by Car: See pages 236-240
Resort Facilities Charts: See page 225
Hotel Reference Charts: See page 234

La Molina is a long established ski resort set high in the Eastern Pyrenees, 160km. or 3½ hours by train from Barcelona and 20km. from Bourg Madame on the French border; it is a resort built specifically for skiing. The central hotel area is on the Puig Llançada mountain and reached by chair-lift from the railway station or by road, and is close to the main lift system (parking is possible at several of the lower lift terminals).

The extensive La Molina area, the central and eastern side, on the Puig Llançada mountain is connected to the western area (the Supermolina area, rising to Tossa d'Alp) by a small gulley which runs from the bottom of Torrente Negro almost to the foot of the lower Tossa d'Alp chair-lift. Tossa d'Alp is the link station with Masella.

La Molina Area: Two surmounting chair-lifts run from the hotel area up to the Costa Rasa restaurant, 6,757ft. To the right of the chair-lift is the ski school with two parallel drag-lifts. The Pista Trampolina to the right of the nursery slopes is a very suitable run for beginners, and so is the Pista Larga. Above the restaurant Costa Rasa there are a further three parallel drag-lifts. The longest, Torret Negre 1, rises to 7,376ft., some 500ft. below the summit, and from this point runs of about 4km. lead down to the valley over north and north-west facing slopes, following approximately the lines of all these lifts, with vertical descent of 2,650ft. A further series of three lifts on the eastern side serve mainly intermediate runs.

Supermolina Area: This area is situated on the western side of the Puig Llançada mountain and extends to the Tossa d'Alp area. The start of the Supermolina area is a quarter of an hour's walk from the main hotel area of La Molina and is connected by road, in the Supermolina hotel area there are three short practice drag-lifts and the ski school meeting place. From this point a 2-stage chair-lift, the Montana Sagrada, rises to the Costa Rasa restaurant and running parallel with the top section is a drag-lift. Above the restaurant is the Soley de Comella drag-lift, which terminates less than halfway down the Torret Negre drag-lift and therefore it is possible to link up at this point with the La Molina runs or to return to the Supermolina hotel area. There is a run from the bottom of the Sole de Comells drag-lift through a narrow valley, terminating 300m. from the bottom of the chair-lift. These are all easy runs over north-facing slopes. To reach Tossa d'Alp one crosses over to the bottom of the Puig d'Alp chair-lift which travels westwards to 7,506ft., and from this point connects with a further chair-lift up to Tossa d'Alp, 8,315ft. Here is a very pleasant restaurant, the Nido de Aguila (Eagle's Nest), which also has sleeping accommodation and which serves reasonably priced meals and drinks. From this point one has wonderful views of the surrounding area. As pointed out before, this is the link station with Masella. There are a variety of runs back to the foot of the chair-lift, varying from easy to medium over north-east facing slopes. There is no direct run to the Supermolina hotel area and therefore one has to take transportation or be prepared for a longish walk.

In a Few Words: Essentially a skier's resort, with most of the lifts covered by one pass. Strategic links still required to make the La Molina-Supermolina-Masella circuit a good one.

Après Ski: The Hotel Adserá, where excellent fondues are served and the Hotel Solineu-Palace has a swimming pool and a lively discothèque and sometimes groups. There is a disco at the Roc Blanc Hotel. But La Molina is very much a skier's resort. Shopping is limited - there is a very good supermarket at Supermolina with a gift and sports shop attached, selling attractive items at reasonable prices. In Super molina there are three good restaurants worth visiting:- Roc Blan, Bodegon and El Bosc. The Sport Hotel runs a good cheap restaurant, but avoid weekends. Masella is about an hour's walk, with very spectacular views in the Cerdanya valley, and the picturesque village of Puigcerdi is worth a visit - it dates back to the 13th century and has a good range of shops. The main advantages are that in Spain the drinks are cheap, the atmosphere is friendly and carefree and the hotel staff love children and make them very welcome.

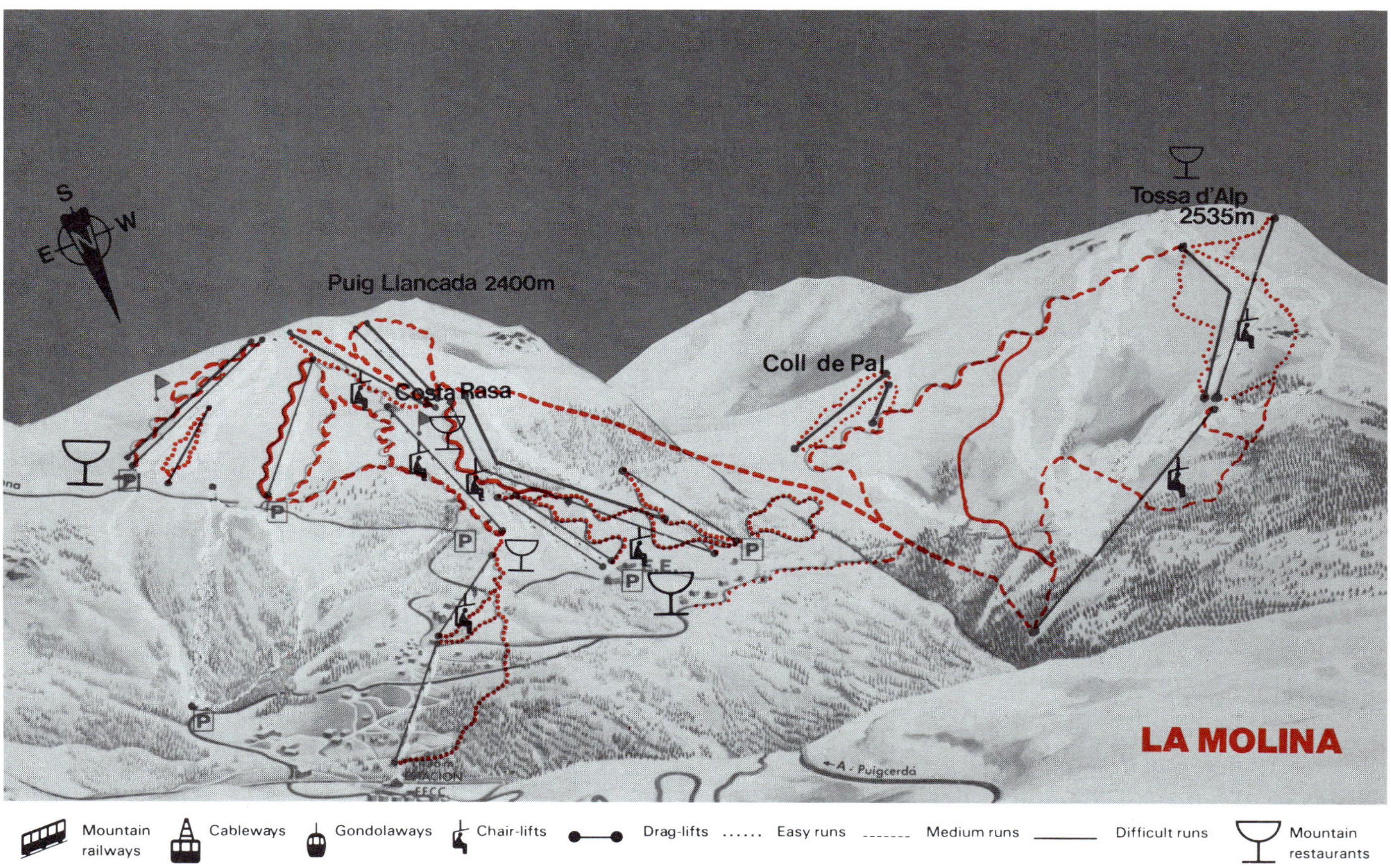

Recommended Hotels:

Hotel Adserá: 400m. from the central chair-lift, this is an oldish hotel in local mountain style, largely rebuilt, 38 double rooms, 2 singles, all with bath, some with balcony, comfortably furnished. Dining room, large wood panelled lounge with open fire and bar; TV, table tennis, ski hire; El Tirrol snack bar/restaurant adjoining; ski films shown weekly. Soundproofed disco in basement. Very friendly and informal atmosphere.

Hotel Solineu-Palace: Originally the Palace hotel but recently combined with the Solineu to form one building. Situated in Supermolina, this first class hotel provides excellent accommodation. 95 double rooms all with bath or shower with attractive views over the valley. Two nicely furnished dining rooms, large comfortable and well furnished lounge with open fire along with two bars. Swimming pool and solarium, lively discothéque.

MASELLA

Height of Resort: 5,258 ft.
Height of Top Station: 8,331 ft.
Nearest International Airport: Barcelona
Map Reference: See Main Map page 236
Route by Car: See pages 236-240
Resort Facilities Charts: See page 225
Hotel Reference Charts: See page 234

Situated in the Eastern Pyrenees 175km. from Barcelona airport, Masella cannot as yet really be termed a resort. It has one hotel and a few apartments; nevertheless, in a good snow season, the skiing geared to this limited accommodation is excellent. Apart from its own ski area there is a link via Tossa d'Alp with the Super Molina skiing - see separate report.

From Pla de Masella, where there is a nursery slope with drag-lift, a 2-section double chair-lift rises to Pleta de Castanys, 6,390ft., where there is a further beginners' area with drag-lifts. Supplementing the chair-lift is a drag-lift which runs almost parallel and terminates nearby the top station of the chair-lift. The runs from this area back to the bottom station are easy to medium, through wide wooded glades over north and north-east facing slopes. Those who require greater height should ski down to Pla de Tornadors, a third of the way down, or debus on the way up to connect with a further chair-lift which rises west of south to Cap del Bosc, 7,053ft. This is a favourite meeting place, being a sun trap with a small bar at hand. From this point one has a choice of easy runs back to the base or to the village, open to start with and wooded further down. Experienced skiers can take the challenging run down to the village, which is fairly closely wooded. Other alternatives from Cap del Bosc: First, ski down on an open, north-west facing medium run to the foot of the Fondo Coma Oriola chair-lift and return by this lift; or, second, take the drag-lift which rises south-eastwards to Tossa d'Alp, 8,331ft., where one finds the Eagle's Nest refuge-restaurant and the runs down to Super Molina (reported under La Molina).

Looking towards Masella, however, to the left there is the difficult Fondo Coma Oriola run and also an intermediate run, both west facing, down to the foot of the Fondo Coma Oriola chair-lift; to the right an intermediate run 4km. in length via Puig d'Alp leads to the resort; whilst in the centre easy runs lead their way back to the lower station. Good skiers, however, will take the testing Coma Parahona, open on the top section and wooded lower down to Pla de Masella, about 3.5km. In length, vertical descent 3,085ft.

In a Few Words: For a small resort it has an extensive ski area set amidst beautiful wood and scenery and served by a compact lift system. Being 87 km from Barcelona it is very busy at weekends and during holiday periods, but during the week visitors have the slopes to themselves.

Après Ski: Very little après ski, mainly centred on the discothèque in the Hotel Alp. More extensive entertainment will be found in Puigcerda 15 minutes journey down the valley, whilst duty free Andorra is only 45 minutes away by car.

Recommended Hotels:

Hotel Alp: A large modern L-shaped hotel. Bedrooms simply decorated, with modern Swedish style furniture, all with bath. Large lounge with open fire, long bar and area for television, cards, billiards. Spacious dining room serving typical Spanish food with a choice of menu. Indoor swimming pool, overlooked by night club/disco. Sauna. Separate games and play room. Mini-club for children 6 to 12 years old.

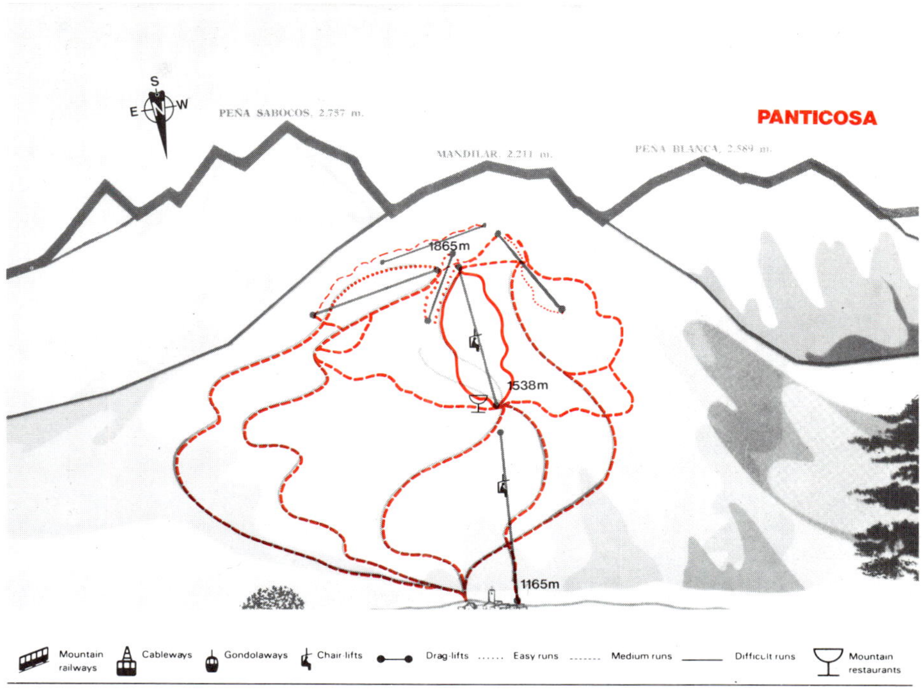

PANTICOSA

Height of Resort: 3,821 ft.
Height of Top Station: 6,209 ft.
Nearest International Airport: Zaragoza
Map Reference: See Main Map page 236
Route by Car: See pages 236-240
Resort Facilities Charts: See page 225
Hotel Reference Charts: See page 234

At the head of the Tena valley, 168km. from Zaragoza airport, 19km. from the French border and only a few km. from Formigal, Panticosa, contrary to most Spanish winter sports resorts, is refreshingly, not purpose built. It is an unspoilt mountain village with narrow cobbled stone streets and main square, surrounded by traditional style houses. Panticosa lies in a sheltered position, being protected by two mountain ranges, Argualas and Picos del Infierno, both rising to over 10,000ft. The skiing is on the Mandilar mountain and about 500m. from the village centre. The Santa Cruz double chair-lift rises southwards in ten minutes to 5,061ft., where there is a restaurant and beginner's slopes. Surmounting, is a further double, Petrosos, chair-lift, which reaches in seven minutes the top station, 6,209ft., where there is another nursery ski area with a beginner's drag-lift, about 50 yards long. Facing the village one finds to the right a drag-lift coming up from the north-east and converging on the top station, whilst to the left a further drag-lift comes up from the north-west towards the top station. There is also a beginners lift and a long drag-lift serving the area above the top station. To the right there is an easy run down and to the left there is a choice of intermediate runs to the base of the drag-lift and down to the restaurant. Two advanced intermediate runs follow the line each side of the upper chair-lift to the restaurant. The run down from the restaurant to the village is intermediate, but inexperienced skiers can of course take the chair-lift down again. As the slopes face north, north-east and north-west snow remains good over open terrain, which becomes slightly wooded towards the village. For Nordic skiers (langlauf) there is a 5km. FIS trail in the area.

In a Few Words: Small ski area but well laid out; orientation of the runs means reliable snow under normal circumstances; limited to beginners and those up to intermediate standard; charming old village; langlauf.

Après Ski: This is more active than in some Spanish resorts. The Los Diablos discothèque is very popular and so is Morlans Bar (Hotel Morlans) with charcoal grill specialities. The restaurant is in the main square and attracts many guests; so does the Fonda Sanpietro restaurant. The historical town of Jaca is only 40km. away and is well worth a visit. In Panticosa itself there is a supermarket and a good range of small shops.

Recommended Hotels:

Hotel Escalar: Situated about 150m. from the main square in an elevated position. Bedrooms comfortably furnished, all with shower/bath, telephone and TV. Attractive dining room, a small lounge with TV and a large lounge with bar and pinewood walls.

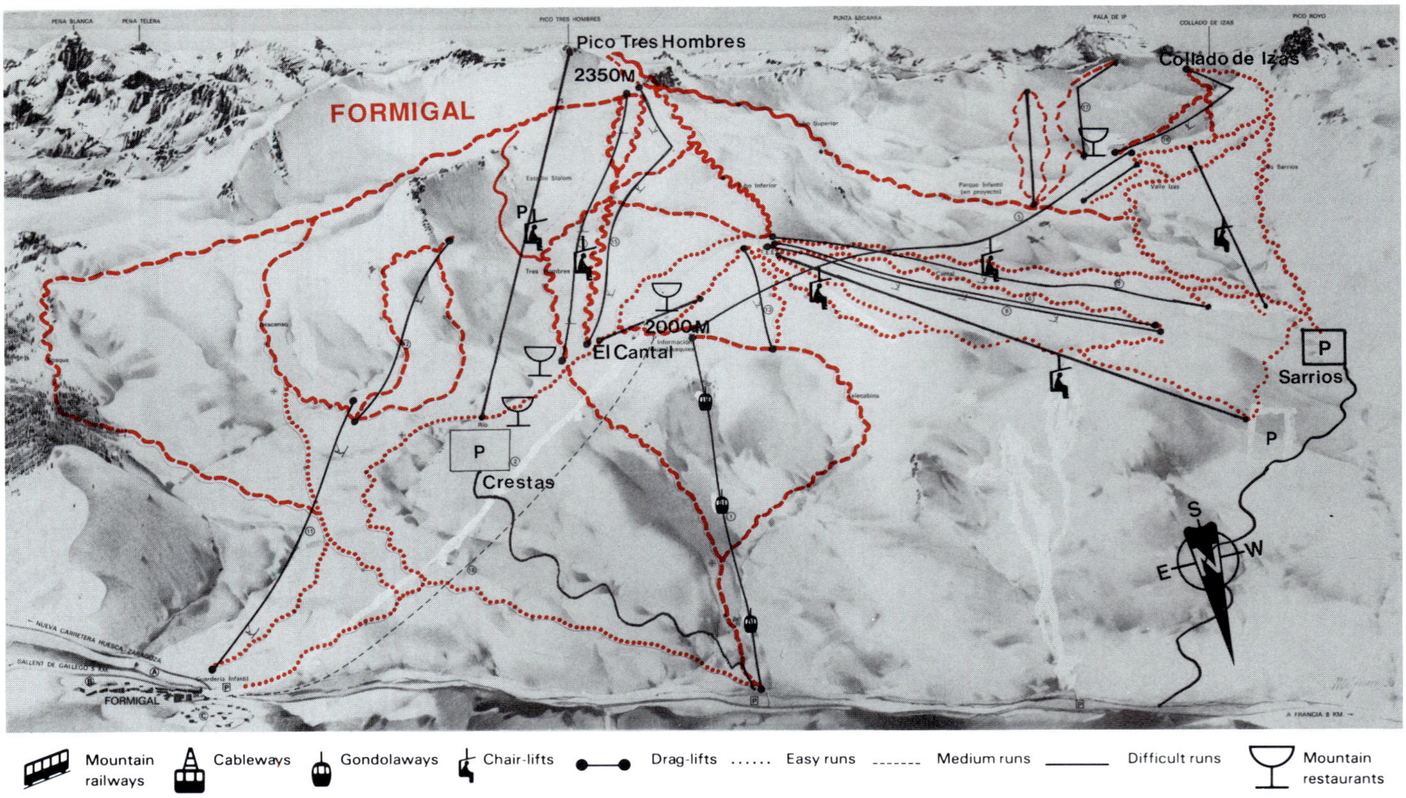

FORMIGAL

Height of Resort: 4,920 ft.
Height of Top Station: 7,920 ft.
Nearest International Airport: Zaragoza
Map Reference: See Main Map page 236
Route by Car: See pages 236-240
Resort Facilities Charts: See page 225
Hotel Reference Charts: See page 234

This is the Spanish equivalent of the French purpose-built ski resort. It is set high in the Pyrenees 166km. from Zarogoza, a journey of $2^1/_2$ hours by bus. The village has none of the traditional atmosphere of the old-style ski resort, but has the advantage of uncrowded, wide, open, sunny slopes, with good snow as these are mainly north-facing and a well planned, compact lift system with no queueing. The slopes are snow-covered pasture land with no obstructions and skiing is superb both on and off piste.

The ski area has three main entry points: first, from parking area Crestas situated above and south-west of the village and the bottom station of the new 4 seater chair-lift; second, from the parking area west of the village where the Sextas gondolaway rises to El Cantal, the hub of the ski area; and third, still further west, is Sarrios parking with two chairs and 3 drag-lifts.

In the central area El Cantal at the top of the gondolaway there is a self-service restaurant and coffee shop with large sun terraces. The views from here of the Central Pyrenees, stretching across the Midi d'Ossau and the Picos del Infierno, are glorious, and it is on these gentle slopes that the ski school operates. From El Cantal a triple chair-lift runs south-westwards and a surmounting drag-lift rises to just below Collado de Izas. The runs which follow close to the latter are intermediate but there are long easy runs to the foot of the two chair-lifts at Sarrios parking. One of these returns to the Collado de Izas area and the other to El Cantal. Beginners' slopes, served by 3 drag-lifts, lie between these.

From Crestas parking area a new 4 seater chair-lift rises to Pico Tres Hombres, 7,920ft., and to the right another chair-lift and a drag-lift travel in the same direction terminating at 7,009ft. Beautiful 5-7km. north facing runs lead down to the village from these top stations which are mainly intermediate, with vertical descents up to 3,000ft.

On the eastern side and above the village two surmounting drag-lifts serve intermediate runs from the top and easy runs lower down. Skiing throughout is suitable for all grades but favours the intermediate and novice skiers. The only disadvantage of this wonderful open terrain is that on a windy day it can be cold.

In a Few Words: A skier's resort, with excellent lift system; sunny; no queueing or crowding except during holiday periods; kindergarten; good value. Snow cannons cover the runs down to the village on the eastern side of the gondolaway and the central area.

Après Ski: Lively bars, with the added attraction of cheap drinks, especially wine. The Hotel Formigal has two bars which are always full and have a good atmosphere. The Hotel Nievesol has a noisy and very casual discothèque which is very popular with teenagers. Try Pub Collins or Tres Hombres Pub as an alternative. Shops are adequate without being especially interesting, and include two good sports shops, boutique and a patisserie selling delicious cakes. There is little activity for the non skier but a very attractive walk to the village of Sallent, some 4km. away. Sallent has its own selection of shops.

Recommended Hotels:

Hotel Formigal: A first class hotel, well furnished bedrooms, 96 doubles, 16 singles, and apartments for 6-8 persons, all with bath,telephone and TV, many with balcony. Attractive dining room serving excellent food, and guests can lunch at the mountain restaurant if preferred; tastefully designed lounge; playroom, TV and video room; large sun terrace; two bars; saunas, hydro massage, sun bed and gymnasium.

Hotel Eguzki-Lore: Built in 1971 in Tyrolean style, recently renovated and beautifully furnished throughout. All bedrooms have bath and shower, telephone and TV. Attractive timbered dining room, comfortable sitting room, charming bar, solarium. Good atmosphere and friendly service.

Hotel Nievesol: In the centre of Formigal ski station. 120 double rooms, 13 singles, all with bath telephone and TV. Dining room, large lounge and bars; playroom, discothèque.

SIERRA NEVADA

Height of Resort: 6,888 ft.
Height of Top Station: 10,308 ft.
Nearest International Airport: Malaga/Granada
Resort Facilities Charts: See page 225
Hotel Reference Charts: See page 234

Sierra Nevada is the southernmost ski resort in Europe, 20 miles from the beautiful city of Granada, 62 miles by road from the coast at Motril and 100 miles from Malaga. The world alpine ski championships were held here in 1996. It is the central massif of the Cordillera Penebetica, stretching 70 miles from the valley of the Almeria to the Lecrin and here stand two of the highest mountains in Spain, the Mulhacen, 11,421ft., and the Veleta, 11,381 ft. The scenery is dramatic, the highest peaks perpetually snow covered, the lower slopes marked with huge boulders and tumbling streams. Amid this background lies village of Sierra Nevada, 6,888ft., with its top station at 10,308ft., near the summit of the Veleta.

The slopes are vast and open, above the treeline and mainly north, north-west and north-east facing, providing excellent snow conditions from November to May. The sun's rays are exceptionally strong and great care must be taken to avoid burning, even if one is not spending long hours on a glacier or the higher slopes. Sierra Nevada is very beautiful and provides a complete contrast to other ski resorts with its southern Spanish atmosphere, lack of crowding and queueing for lifts except at weekend and carnival weeks. As well as magnificent snow there is often marvellous powder snow and spring snow later in the season. Extensive artificial snow making machines, strategically placed on the main runs, ensure that prolonged dry weather need not be a serious problem. The resort has a good medical centre with resident doctor and X-ray equipment.

The Skiing and Uphill Transport: To prepare for staging of the 1996 World Championships an intensive development programme was commenced in 1990. This involved constructing 11 new lifts, some of which will open up new areas and some which will replace lower capacity existing lifts.

Borreguiles: This constitutes the main skiing area. Two gondolaways take one up to Borreguiles area, in which is the meeting place for everyone including the ski school classes. For the beginner initially there is a 4-seater chair-lift and several drag-lifts. When one has graduated from that slope, there are two further longer drag-lifts serving ideally graduated slopes. A new detachable 4 seater chair-lift provides a good variety of intermediate runs above Borreguiles. All this is open fast skiing with some medium gradient mogul slopes. From the Borreguiles area the Veleta II drag-lift rises towards the summit, but slightly higher; the Antonio Zayas drag-lift reaches the top station at a height of 10,308ft, where one has marvellous panoramic views and on a clear day one can look across the Mediterranean to Africa.

From the top of both lifts there are three main descents. Facing downhill, these are:

(a) Keeping to the right, the longest run in the resort of 5½ km., a drop of 3,428ft. back to the village via the Parador slopes. These are beautiful open slopes, within the capabilities of the advanced novice.

(b) Directly back to Borreguiles down a wide steepish slope where continuous turning is necessary. This is graded difficult but can be tackled by an intermediate without qualms.

(c) By bearing left, there is a choice of two beautiful runs to the Laguna las Yeguas whence there is a chair-lift to pull one back over the ridge to return to Borreguiles. A short challenging run from below the radio telescope is definitely worth including in this itinerary. Alternatively one can take the long Laguna chair-lift which terminates at about the same height as the Antonio Zayas lift. There are delightful red runs to base each side of the lift, or from the top one can join the runs mentioned in (a) and (b) above. Also within the large Borreguiles bowl are two further lifts which provide a link with the long swinging runs of Monachil (see below).

From the village and running parallel on the eastern side of the gondolaways is the 3 seater Genil chair-lift rising to its restaurant at 8,233ft. This connects with the 3 seater Stadium chair-lift reaching 9,807ft. From the top one can join the run to the village mentioned under (a) above or return to the restaurant on a steepish red and thence to the village with a choice of two blue runs.

Borreguiles is a sun trap and here there are three mountain restaurants. The runs down to the resort vary between fairly easy to medium steep.

Monachil: This east-facing area is reached by the new 4 seater Jara chair-lift from the resort rising 1,066 ft., and connecting with the Monachil chair-lift which links with Borreguiles and provides an alternative route to Borreguiles. The Monachil area provides a great variety of superb skiing from easy, through medium to steep slopes. In this area are the two runs graded black which in Spain denotes very difficult although they would not be considered so by the experienced skier. This area is hardly ever crowded even at weekends.

From the village one can also take the Parador chair lift (6,888 - 8,036 ft) eastwards which also serves as access to the higher hotels and apartments in the resort. From the top there are a number of red and blue runs back to the resort.

The whole of the Sierra Nevada skiing offers tremendous potential to the off-piste enthusiast either with its high level powder or after prolonged sunshine, even in January, on spring snow, where one can ski virtually everywhere. There are no hazards or precipices and the slopes are virtually avalanche-free. January is usually a period of prolonged fine weather. Even at this time of year one can continue skiing till very late in the afternoon. The sun does not leave the village till 6 p.m. Snowfalls mostly come in February and March but even then it is said that one can expect 8 out of 10 days to be fine. The resort does not close until the second half of May.

In a Few Words: A resort with a difference. One literally feels on top of the world. No higher mountains to cast early shadows. Extended skiing hours in the sun even in January, as hot as March in the Alps. Informal and friendly atmosphere, especially the ski school who teach the Austrian method. Whilst the miles of pistes are ideal for everyone up to good intermediate, blasé good to expert skiers, used to the top Alpine resorts, will find the runs insufficiently challenging; but for them the limitless expanse of off-piste skiing could provide compensation. Having made these points it should be mentioned that being so far south and open terrain it can be affected by weather and winds, more so than resorts further north. This is a chance one takes. Ski kindergarten for children up to 6 years old.

Après Ski: Skiing is the main attraction in Sierra Nevada and night life is informal and limited to a discothèque in the Metro Hotel and the Piano-Bar at the Hotel Rumaykiyya which has a cosy atmosphere and live music is played every evening. There is a good selection of bars and pubs: Sierra Nevada 2000 is recommended for pasties, hot chocolates and drinks; Big Foot Bar in the Mont Blanc building is

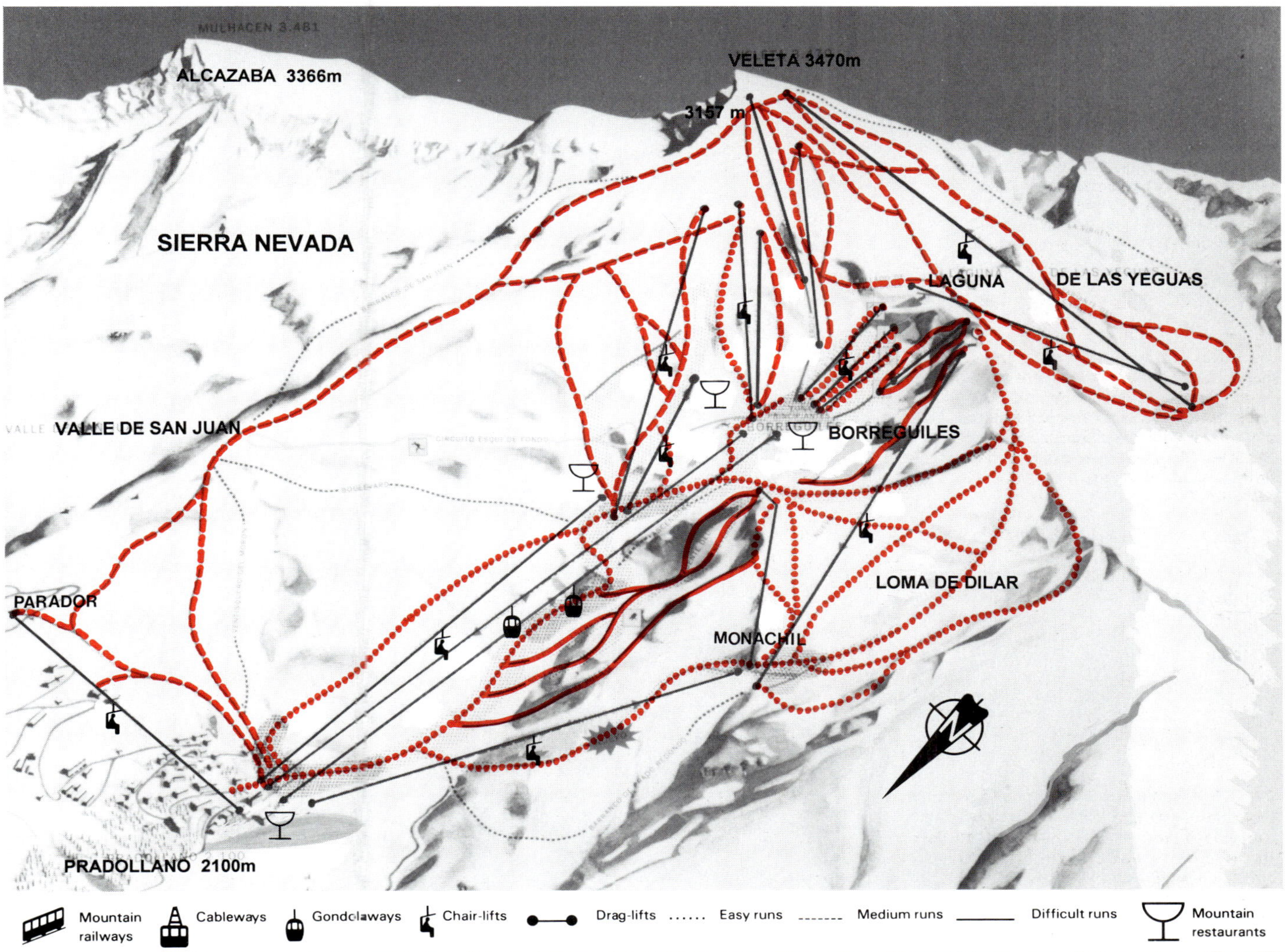

very popular and El Bistro in the main square has a good atmosphere. A wide choice of restaurants include Ruta del Veleta – serving meat to shell fish; Midas for atmosphere and good food; and Tito Luigis for good value. La Chiminea disco bar in the Primavera building is a popular night spot. Granada is quite close and provides a wider choice of clubs and restaurants if required.

Recommended Hotels:

Hotel Melia Sierra Nevada: A first-class 4-star hotel adjacent to the main square and only 5 minutes from the ski-lift systems. 500 beds, all rooms with bath, telephone, satellite TV and radio. Sauna and massage, indoor swimming pool. Dining room and large bar on first floor. Spacious lounges. Popular café and snacks on the ground floor. Large disco from 11 p.m. informal dress for dinner; suit and tie not required.

Hotel Melia Solynieve: This is the reconstructed Solynieve taken over by the Melia group. It is a 3-star hotel adjacent to the main square. 183 bedrooms all with bath, wc., telephone and radio. Pleasant dining room, large lounge and bar area; discothèque.

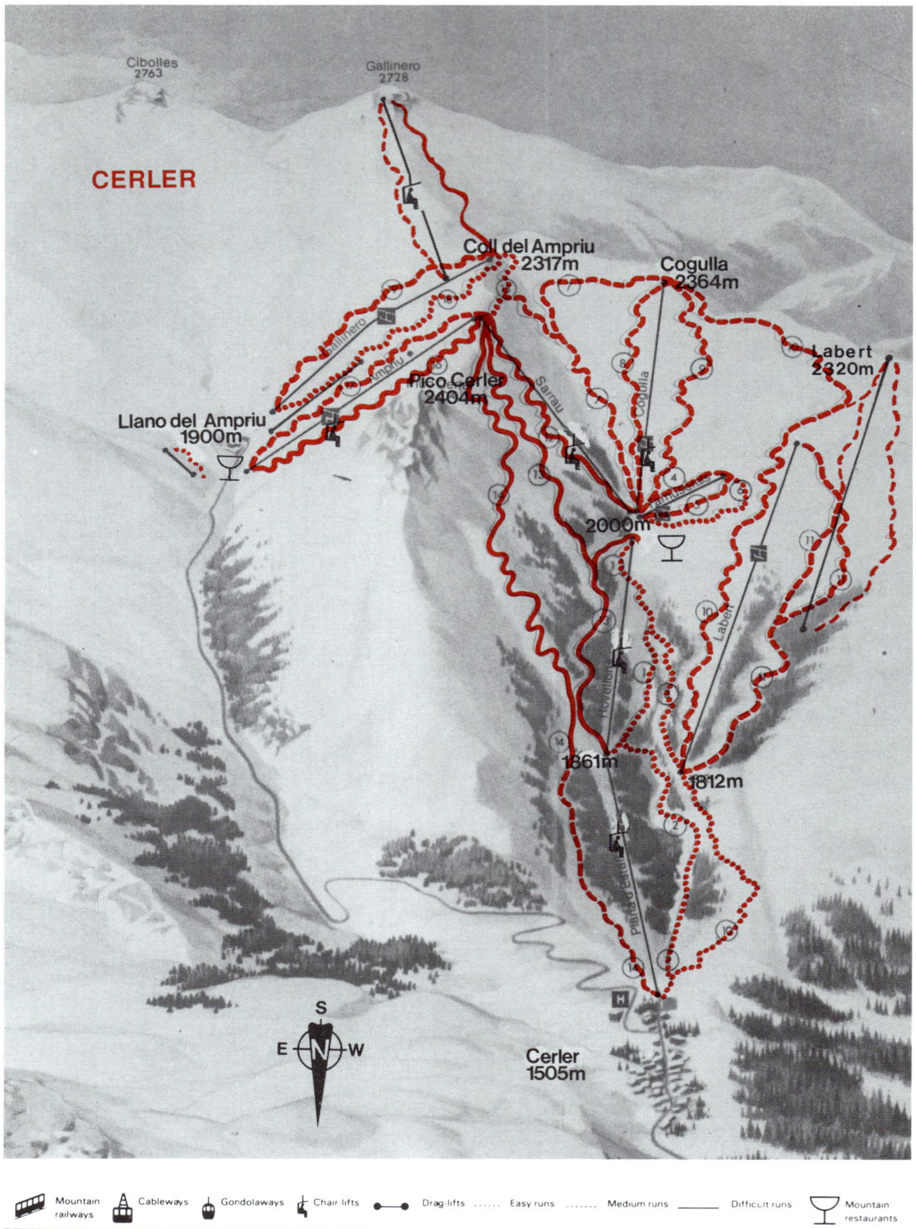

CERLER

Height of Resort: 4,936 ft.
Height of Top Station: 8,628 ft.
Nearest International Airport: Zaragoza
Map Reference: See Main Map page 236
Route by Car: See pages 236-240
Resort Facilities Charts: See page 225
Hotel Reference Charts: See page 234

Situated in the upper Aragonese Pyrenees, 228km. from Zaragoza airport and 289km. from Barcelona. If one is travelling by car from the Channel ports, one leaves the main motorway at Barbastro and shortly before arriving at Cerler one passes through the delightful old village of Benasque. The purpose-built resort of Cerler, consisting at present of only two hotels and several apartment blocks, sits just above the old village. Benasque with 12 hotels is only a few kms. away.

The ski area to the south is an amphitheatre in shape, open at the top and wide wooded glades halfway down, with the runs funnelling towards the bottom station, where the restaurant 'El Molino' is situated. The runs are predominantly north, northwest and north-east facing, but the ski area is protected from the north and north-east winds by the Maladeta range, rising to 11,165 ft. The 'hub' of the ski area is reached by surmounting chair-lifts; the first rises to 6,104ft., and the second to Cota 2000, which has recently been developed, where there is a restaurant and the ski school area with beginner's drag-lifts. To the right of the second stage of the chair-lift a long drag-lift rises almost parallel to a point 548ft. higher. From the restaurant itself a chair-lift reaches Cogulla, 7,754ft., whilst to the left of the restaurant a chair-lift rises south-eastwards to the ridge at 7,600ft., where it meets a further chair-lift coming up on the eastern side from Llano del Ampriu. A drag-lift also climbs the eastern side from the latter station to Coll del Ampriu, 7,600ft.

The 1993 season saw the development of the new ski area 'El Gallinero', which is reached by skiing down a short distance from the top of the Coll del Ampriu drag-lift to pick up the Gallinero 4 seater chair-lift. This rises towards the summit of the same name, terminating at 8,628ft., which makes it the highest top station in the Pyrenees. The run down on the right to base is intermediate whilst the one on the left is a 2.6km. black with a vertical descent of 2,066ft. Both runs are north facing over wide open slopes.

The runs down to Llano del Ampriu vary from easy to difficult, about 2km. in length over east to northeast facing slopes. Here there is a new service area with restaurant, bar and sun terrace; a children's play garden, ski rental and lift pass shop. On the western side of the ridge one has a wide choice of runs down to the restaurant and to the village – the most challenging for the advanced intermediate follows the line to the right of the main lift system, whilst to the left the intermediate will be happy with the runs from the top to the bases of the upper lifts and to the village itself. Runs to the bottom station are about 7km. in length, with vertical descent of 3,700ft., open for the first half and leading to wide wooded glades over the lower section.

In a Few Words: Essentially a skier's resort; compact lift system; reliable snow; not particularly suitable for beginners; favours second year to advanced intermediates. 80 snow cannons in operation.

Après Ski: There is a livey disco in the Hotel Cerler, whilst in Benasque there are a further three, along with quite interesting bars. The swimming pool at the Hotel Monte Alba is attractive. A popular meeting place is the Sky Bar in the old village, owned by one of the ski instructors. For non-skiers the restaurant at the top of the second chair-lift has a very large sun terrace, and there are many lovely walks amongst the beautiful scenery surrounding Cerler. This area has much wild life, such as the ibex, wild boar, etc. The old village of Cerler is delightful, with a beautiful church. Shopping is limited but Benasque provides quite a good variety.

Recommended Hotels:

Hotel Monte Alba: Modern and attractive, well furnished and a good atmosphere. All bedrooms with bath. Comfortable bar/lounge; television room; indoor swimming pool; sauna and solarium; billiards and table tennis. Large sun terrace with lovely views.

BAQUEIRA BERET

Height of Resort: 4,920 ft.
Height of Top Station: 8,267 ft.
Nearest International Airport: Tarbes
Map Reference: See Main Map page 236
Route by Car: See pages 236-240
Resort Facilities Charts: See page 225
Hotel Reference Charts: See page 234

Baqueira Beret, a purpose-built resort, is situated in the Aran valley high in the Pyrenees, 330km. from Barcelona, 140 km. from Lourdes and 160km. from Toulouse in France. It is reached in the winter by highway N230 travelling via the Viella tunnel.

Created by Luis Arias, the famous Spanish skier, 24 times champion of Spain, it has a well laid-out lift system serving a large variety of runs favouring the medium to good skier.

From the south-east side of the village a 4-seater chair-lift rises to 5,904 ft. and at the top there is a restaurant. Directly above is the ski school area served by twin parallel drag-lifts and a shorter drag-lift to the left. Flanking this area are two main systems. On the right the Pla de Baqueira chair-lift rises southward to 7,216 ft. where one finds another restaurant and running parallel with the chair-lift is the Pla de Baqueira drag-lift, which towards the top swings away south-eastward. A 4-seater detachable chair-lift 'Mirador Express' (2,880 skiers per hour) rises from 5,904ft. to the top station in 8 minutes. The 2.4km run which follows the line of this lift has been extended to some 100 metres in width. From all top stations mentioned so far, the runs over north and north-west facing slopes, are for medium to good skiers and there is only one easy run and that is from the ski school area to the village.

The Bonaigua - Argulls area to the south-west of the resort was extended for the 1994/95 season. It is now served by four chair-lifts and a drag-lift reaching Tuc de la Llanca, 8,267 ft., the resorts highest station. At Port de la Bonaigua a small service area has been constructed consisting of a self-service restaurant, toilettes, ski rental, ticket sales and parking. This can be reached by road through the Bonaigua Pass. The area is linked to the main system mentioned above.

Further up the valley to the east, just above Orri, one finds a series of three lifts (one chair and two drags). One of the latter, the Luis Arias, rises to 8,200ft. From this point one can ski over the whole area mentioned so far, back to the village, the longest run being the 'North Face-Waterfall', 5.5km. with a vertical descent of 3,281ft. Alternatively one can tackle the difficult north-east facing runs down to Orri, 6,068ft. Orri with its parking space has become an important link point between Baqueira and the recently developed areas of Beret 1800. Just above Orri the Vista Beret chair-lift rises eastwards to 6,888ft., with intermediate runs back to base, or from the top, one can cross over on a north-east facing intermediate run, to Beret 1800 where one finds a self-service restaurant, equipment hire facilities and a ski school. To the right of Beret 1800 the De la Reina chair-lift rises south-eastwards to 7,251 ft., and to the left the Clot de L'Us chair-lift climbs in the same direction to 7,218ft. The runs from both top stations to base are intermediate mainly over north and north-west facing slopes, whilst from the top of the latter lift one can cross over to the base of the Dossau chair-lift which reaches Tuc du Dossau, 8,235ft. This lift provides access to enjoyable wide open skiing over west facing slopes for good skiers back to Beret 1800. At this base there is also a 745 metres long chair-lift which serves the only easy slope in the area. The present complex allows one to cross over in both directions from Beret 1900 to Baqueira thus providing extensive skiing for intermediate to good skiers. The distance by road from Baqueira to Beret 1800 is 8km.

Snow-making System: In addition to the 171 snow guns covering 9 km. of runs along the Mirador piste, Argulls access and North-Face Waterfall, there is now a new system of 71 snow guns, covering 5km of runs. They are: Pins, Stadium, Clot der Os and Pla Beret,

In a Few Words: One of Spain's foremost resorts. Well planned and compact lift system. A good variety of runs, favouring the medium to good skier;well maintained slopes, with lifts open all the time, and well organised. Extensive helicopter skiing. Due to its height and orientation of the slopes, good snow is assured under normal conditions and most of the skiing is above the treeline. Nursery school for 3-8 year olds. Primarily a skier's resort and one to watch in the future, as it is still extending.

Après Ski: As the resort grows, so do the après ski facilities. Tiffany's disco at the Hotel Montarto is always well attended, the Tuc disco is also very popular, and the most recent one to open is the Disco-Bar Lobo. The Residential Centre Baqueira 1500 complex contains hotels, apartments, restaurant, supermarket, sports shop and other services. Below the Hotel Ruda is another supermarket, bank, clothes shop, restaurant and bar. Most apartment blocks have their own small café/ restaurant and shop below. There are 3 hotels and a good selection of bars and restaurants, La Borda being the best of the latter, but don't miss the 'tapas' restaurant El Tamarro.

The small town of Viella, 8 miles away, has many shops, discos, restaurants, bars and a bowling alley, and there are a number of small Aranese villages between Baqueira and Viella, which are interesting and many of which have delightful restaurants and bars. In Viella a new sports complex was recently opened, this has two swimming pools, ice skating rink, gymnasium, sauna, jacuzzi and other sports facilities. Unfortunately there is no connecting bus service, taxis are about £8.00 each way.

Recommended Hotels:

Hotel Montarto: A large modern hotel with 304 beds, forming part of the Residential Centre. All rooms with bath or shower. Spacious reception rooms, furnished in modern style with much wooden decor. The centre of entertainment is Tiffany's discothèque.

Hotel Ruda: The latest hotel to be built, with 40 rooms all with bath. A pleasant bar and lounge area. Of modern design and a high standard throughout.

Other Hotels: La Creu, Garons and La Cuma all situated at nearby Salardu.

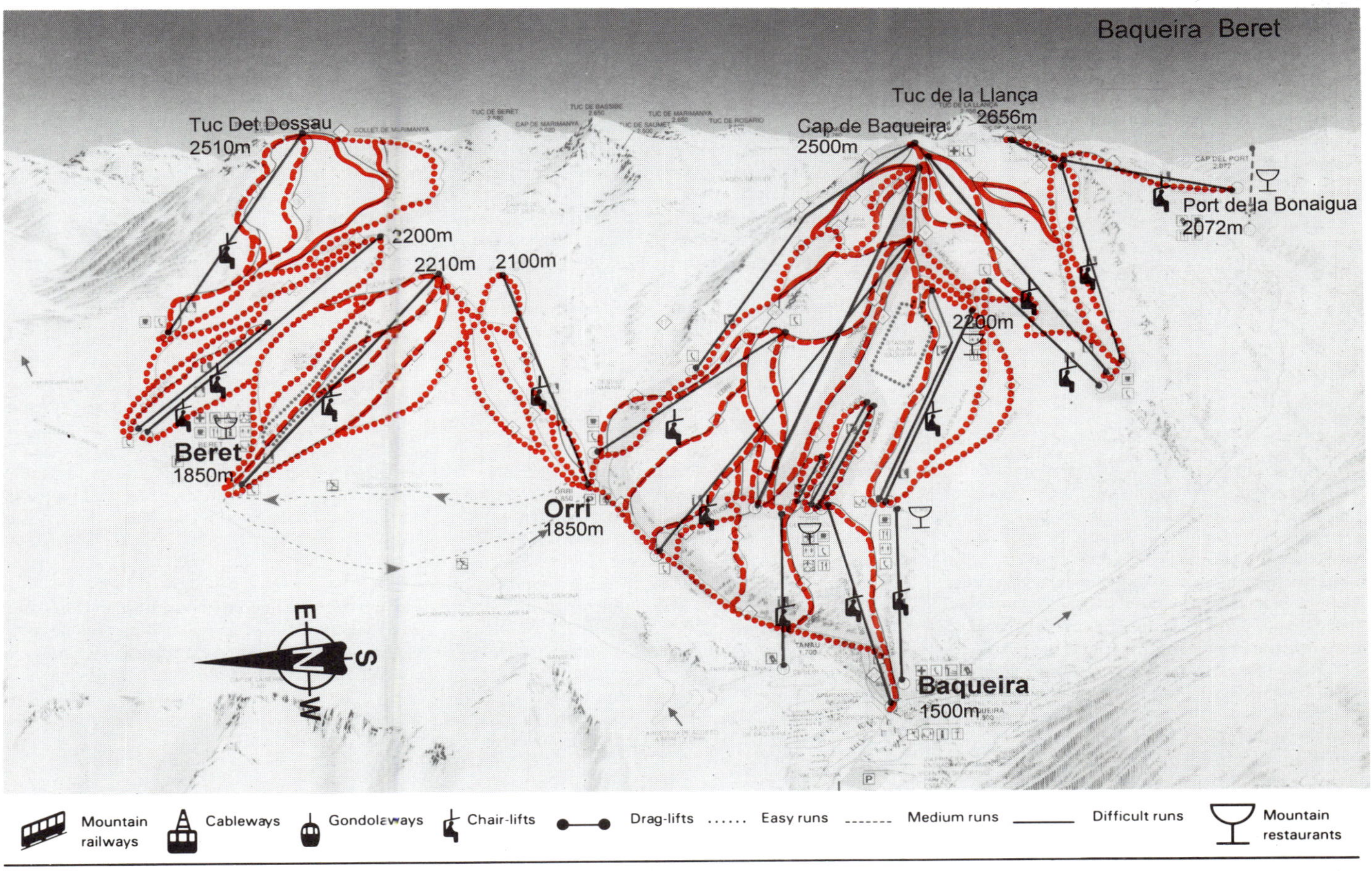

GERMANY

To those of us familiar with skiing in Germany, it is a matter of considerable astonishment that so few Britons seem to be aware that it is a country that offers excellent Alpine areas, as well as cross country skiing. Furthermore, it is certainly worth noting that there are five skiing regions - and henceforth we are referring to Alpine or downhill skiing - that are, paradoxically and geographically speaking not Alpine! These are in the Bavarian Forest (south east of Nürnberg) the Black Forest (between Strasbourg and Stuttgart), the Eifel (on the Belgian border south of Aachen), the Sauerland (between Köln and Kassel) and the Harz (on the inner German border south of Braunschweig). It is therefore very often feasible to sneak some skiing in Germany even if one is on a short visit to, for example, the industrial or commercial centres.

There are over 300 places registered with the German Tourist Board as having ski lifts and prepared and policed pistes - and probably half as many again that are not registered.

At present this guide can only report on 8 leading resorts that all lie close to the border with Austria, along the foothills of the Alps. Much of the skiing is first class, but it is true - and it has its advantages - that all these places became more or less prosperous before the advent of the skiing boom, and skiing has become only a part of their way of life, albeit an important part. Summer tourism, mountain climbing, walking, cross country skiing, the 'cure' all claim equal priority - so you will not find anywhere the purpose built ski resorts such as in France.

One of the side effects of this is that often the ski runs are some distance from the village centre and from each other, and in many areas it is almost essential to have a car. (There usually are buses, but it is tiresome to be dependent upon them).

German skiing should be taken on an opportunity basis, as it is by the Germans; and because most of the resorts are easily accessible on the excellent German road system, they tend to be very full at weekends, if conditions are good. Conversely, on weekdays queues are virtually non-existent, even in the high season. The skiing itself can be very good indeed - and, since one is in Germany, the lifts work, they open and close on time, and the pistes are beautifully prepared whilst there is still plenty of room for 'birds nesting', which seems to be very much in vogue with the locals, who spread over new powder snow like locusts on the harvest. The mountain restaurants tend to be numerous, large, efficient and not expensive. It is also possible to find board and lodging in the valleys at extremely reasonable prices. Ski-lift passes cost much the same as elsewhere. Any skier who finds himself in Germany in the season with a spare day or two, or more, would be foolish not to sample the local product.

BAYRISCHZELL

Height of Resort: 2,630 ft.
Resort Facilities Charts: See page 224

Bayrischzell is a beautiful uncrowded village lying at a height of 2,630ft. on the German Alpine road south east of Munich, 5 miles from the Austrian border. It is easily approached by a motorway from Munich, and is therefore a place to be avoided at weekends! In common with other German resorts, it caters for the Nordic skier (Langlauf) as much as for a downhiller, for the summer holidaymaker as much as for the skier. It is therefore well equipped with numerous hotels and restaurants, pensions, ski schools - and the ubiquitous discothèque. The Hotel Alpenhof is strongly recommended. There are two skiing areas in addition to the kindergarten slopes in the village.

The Wendelstein: A cable car rises from the outskirts of the village to the top of the Wendelstein (6,029ft.), where it meets the Cog railway which climbs up from the eastern side. The run down the eastern side is frequently unpisted, never easy, always steep, and sometimes unfrequented. Having finished the run you return to the summit on the Cog railway. The west side has two drag-lifts at the top, each giving a rise of 853ft. The run all the way down into the valley back to Bayrischzell is, after a faintly daunting first hundred feet, suitable for an enjoyable family outing.

The Sudelfeld: The ski area here may be reached by chair-lift from Bayrischzell in the west or from Rosengasser in the east by drag-lift, or direct from the Alpenstrasse - or the run down from the Wendelstein - in the north. It consists for the most part of wide open snowfields of medium gradient, with the odd gentle or steep slope thrown in for good measure. It is criss-crossed by some 22 ski lifts, always enabling one to return eventually to one's start point whatever piste numbers are followed. The longest single lift carries one over a height difference of 1,248ft., the shortest 164ft., and the vertical drop from the topmost lift to the lowest car park is 2,067ft.

It provides another ideal family circus for skiers of all standards, with the emphasis on the intermediate or beginner. It is well sprinkled with restaurants and glühwein pumps for those in need of re-fuelling.

BERCHTESGADENER LAND

Height of Resort: 1,837 ft.
Resort Facilities Charts: See page 224

Berchtesgaden lies at the extreme south eastern tip of Germany, at a height of 1,837ft., an old town that became prosperous on account of its salt mines and abundant high quality wood. (Today its salt mines are worked for both salt and tourism). The Kurdirection is most helpful and go-ahead, and is obviously trying to boost the winter reputation of the area. The town planning has been very strictly controlled, so all new buildings fit in well with the character of Berchtesgaden - huge hotels are not allowed. There are some 10 or 12 with between 40 and 70 rooms with numerous smaller hotels around. There is little après ski as such, but excellent food can be found, especially in the restaurant at the Kur and Kongress Haus, the Prinz Regent Luitpold, and an orchestra plays daily at tea time, also in the Kur Haus, in the grand traditional manner. More rowdy traditions are carried on at Oberau and Königssee nearby, where 'Bavarian Evenings' are held twice a week. A swimming hall, with indoor and outdoor pools, water shutes and whirlpool, was opened in March 1997.

Berchtesgaden itself is already more a centre than a ski resort in its own right, which is why the ski area is often referred to as the Berchtesgadener Land, ie the district of Berchtesgaden. The town itself boasts virtually no skiing, but there are 5 different ski areas nearby – 4 within 6km. and 1 within 15km. with good bus connections. Pride of place must go to the Jenner area.

Jenner: 5km. to the south of Berchtesgaden lies the village of Königssee where you will find a bob/luge run, and also the start of the Jenner-bahn lift, which lifts the skier in 2 stages (but you do not have to leave your enclosed 2 seater gondolaway at the half way stage, 3,641ft.) to over 5,400ft. The top ski area is served by 2 chair-lifts and 2 drag-lifts all of about 592 vertical ft.; the pistes are wide, well prepared and suitable for the intermediate skier, whilst being steep enough to keep the interest of the advanced.

The run from the middle station down to Königssee winds through the woods along a piste some forty metres wide. It must make a superb downhill race course (it has a FIS A homologation certificate), and is a joy to ski. It does, however, get crowded at weekends as it is virtually the only way down to the car park at Königssee.

Rossfeld/Oberau: With a ticket called 'Ski Ohne Grenze' (ski without border – so-called because the border between Austria and Germany runs through the ski circus), one can play the combinations of lifts in the Rossfeld/Oberau complex. The vital thing to realise is that one should leave one's car at Oberau and then take the bus (included in one's ticket) up to Rossfeld. From there is a newly developed and somewhat complicated circus offering superb skiing for all standards. There are some 7 inter-connecting lifts serving different hills. The longest run is 6km, easy enough for anyone, yet fast and long enough for the expert to find exciting if taken straight and nonstop.

Hochschwarzeck: 8km. due west of Berchtesgaden, and 1,640ft. higher, can be found a ski area consisting of one 2 seater chair-lift, which rises a further 984ft., and four drag-lifts. The run from the chair-lift is appropriate for intermediate skiers, whilst the others qualify as nursery slopes.

Götschen: The Götschenkopf lift rises 1,148ft. and provides some excellent if limited skiing. The main slope is much used in these parts for Giant Slalom racing, whilst the 'back way round' provides 'motorway' skiing - there is nothing daunting for the tyro or the timid, whilst the more skilled or adventurous can put their skis together and schuss all the way down the middle of the road, so to speak. There is a third, often unpisted, route that goes down to Bischofswiesen on the valley floor - fun but not to be taken in error when your car is parked a mile and 984 vertical ft. up the road at the bottom of the Götschen lift, for there is as yet no lift up from Bischofswiesen!

GARMISCH-PARTENKIRCHEN

Height of Resort: 2,632 ft.
Resort Facilities Charts: See page 224

Garmisch-Partenkirchen is without question the most famous skiing resort in Germany - indeed it is the only one that many a skier has heard of. Not only did it host the Winter Olympics in 1936, but it has more recently been the site of the World Championships (1978), and every year World Cup Races like the Kandahar combination of downhill and 'Super G'. By any standards it is a resort on the grand scale and it is a source of amazement that it should ever be omitted from ski guides.

The twin towns of Garmisch and Partenkirchen are separated only by the Loisach river, and now form one large town. The Loisach valley in which it sits is very broad at this point, and through it ran the main, ancient trading route for the Romans from Augsburg into Italy. The valley floor is at a height of 2,632ft. here, and is dominated to the north-west by the Kramer 6,499ft., the north-east by the Wank, 5,840ft., to the south-east by the towering rock wall of the Wetterstein, 7,871ft., and to the south-west by the Grosser Waxenstein, 7,321ft.; and, rearing even higher behind that mountain, Germany's highest, the Zugspitze, 9,731ft. It is most impressive scenery.

Garmisch-Partenkirchen is within 90km. of Munich. Its skiing, given the right snow conditions is of the highest order. Unfortunately these two facts, when combined, make Garmisch-Partenkirchen a crowded place on sunny weekends, when traffic jams and lift queues are not uncommon at peak periods. However, if you can get to Garmisch-Partenkirchen on weekdays, you will have uninterrupted use of some 40 marked and manicured pistes of varying standards, and at heights from 2,788ft. to 8,692ft.; and there are 52 ski lifts, including 4 with a height difference of over 3,280ft. For convenience the territory is divided into four areas, mostly interconnected apart from Zugspitze.

Eckbauergebiet: The Eckbauer is a comparatively small and gentle hill. It rises to a height of 4,061ft., the top can be reached in a semi-enclosed 2 seater gondolaway of some antiquity. This Eckbauerbahn is nearly 3 kilometres in length, and provides one with a pleasant, gentle descent of 1,640ft. vertical drop to the former Olympic Ski Stadium, into which 4 ski jumps – one a 70 metre hill – deposit their competitors, and from beside which the lift starts. At the top of the Eckbauer there is one small drag-lift giving a 132 foot rise, which serves a good second or third day slope – smooth and wide but with a definite gradient. There is also a restaurant. Visitors should certainly visit this little area at least once, and they may indeed find it an excellent place to go when there are crowds elsewhere - one might describe it as good for a family Sunday outing.

Hausberg/Kreuzeckgebiet: The Hausberg/ Kreuzeck area caters for the majority of skiers who come to Garmisch Partenkirchen, and it has a justifiably high reputation. Two parallel cableways rise from the valley floor at the south of the town, separated by some 2½km. The eastern one is the Hausbergbahn, which rises to 4,363ft. It is the most popular lift to the upper skiing areas, with shelters at its foot, ski and snowboard schools and equipment hire shop, and boasts the worst queues at peak hours. The western lift is the Kreuzeckbahn which takes you up from 2,517 to 4,419ft. Between the 2 lifts at the top of the ridge lies a skiing area including the Kreuzjoch, served by some 10 interconnecting lifts, most of whose runs are in the middle or easy category. The majority of skiers, once up in this area, seem to stay there for the day, rather than ski down again to the valley bottom. But it is in skiing down that the advanced skier will find runs of real interest – and fame – names to be conjured with (or heard on television) like the Kandahar, the Olympia, the Hornabfahrt. Both the Kandahar and the Horn are officially designated as difficult, but there are normally by-passes open for the inexpert or faint hearted. The expert or the bold may well find a fast wide race track before him, recently prepared for a world cup or similar race, in immaculate condition, with virtually no-one else in sight. Such places are rare indeed in the Alps today, and the opportunity for fast skiing should be grabbed by those who want it. However, it should perhaps be said that although these runs were in perfect condition when your correspondent was lucky enough to ski them after a metre of new snow had fallen, they do have a reputation for becoming extremely icy in parts. In good conditions you will find no better runs anywhere.

It should be added that there are, of course, easy runs down back to the car parks, so no-one need ever come down by the cableway so long as there is snow to ski on.

Osterfeldergebiet: This area is reached by the Alpspitzbahn, which starts at the bottom of the Olympia and Kandahar runs referred to above, and which can carry 500 people per hour up to the Osterfelderkopf at 6,724ft. Once there one realises that one has arrived in the high Alps: the views are breathtaking, and the weather can be very cold. (But the knowledge that the Zugspitze area lies even higher over the ridge prevents one getting too carried away). Below the arrival point is a circus of 5 lifts. These include the Bernadein lift which provides a run somewhat narrower than the norm here, and thus more challenging. Near the top of the Bernadein is the Hochalm, where a good restaurant is to be found, and from where one can take another short cable way back to the Osterfelderkopf. Alternatively, access is by means of 2 button lifts - the Längenfelderlifts - to some wide snow fields. To and from these fields goes the one link with the Kreuzjoch area.

The Osterfelder area provides extremely good skiing, although there are no really long lifts. It also provides, as described, access to the Kreuzeck/Hausberg areas, and often quicker access at peak times than waiting for the Hausberg or Kreuzecklifts themselves.

The Wankgebiet: The Wankbahn 4 seater enclosed gondolaway lifts up to 800 people per hour from 2,329ft. to a height of 5,756ft. The top station is excellently planned with sun terraces, two large restaurants etc., and it even includes a special room for those who have brought their own food and drink.

The self service restaurant, is large, warm, efficiently run and remarkably inexpensive. However, the reader may be more interested on what is available outside! There he will find a ski circus of six inter-connecting lifts, with runs varying from the extremely easy to the steep. The Esterberglift is 950 metres long, and lifts its passengers 1,248ft. This is the one for the advanced skier, whilst all the others serve comparatively easy, and short, runs.

A word of warning: The map of ski runs shows two descending from the Wank back to the bottom station. One of them from the bottom of the Sonnenlift is not pisted, is steep, and can be shut sometimes on account of avalanche danger. The other run is called the Esterbergabfahrt, and continues 'down' from the bottom of the Esterberglift referred to above. However, the next 500 metres involve some amount of poling and skating, which may waste some 15 minutes and a lot of breath, although this problem has been partially solved by the installation of a 60 metre long drag-lift. The end of this 8km. run is, admittedly, downhill, but of the wood-path variety, and not especially exciting. Many people return to Garmisch by the way they came up – on the Wankbahn. On this occasion, there is no loss of face!

The skiing on the Wank is good, without being outstanding, in a resort where there is plenty of outstanding skiing. However, you get 'owt for nowt', and when there are massive queues elsewhere, you will often find little or no waiting here.

Zugspitze: This area might possibly be the most famous in Germany, as it has had a long time to establish its reputation. The Zugspitzbahn, which runs from Garmisch-Partenkirchen to an underground station just below the summit of the Zugspitze, was built over 60 years ago. It is a cog railway, which takes about an hour from the town centre, or half an hour from the Eibsee station. The statistics are: Garmisch-Partenkirchen to summit 18.7km., rise 2,296-8,692ft., capacity 350 people per hour. This capacity proved totally inadequate to meet the demand when skiing increased in popularity, and a cableway was built which runs from Eibsee to the very summit of the Zugspitze, at 9,676ft., giving a rise of 6,724 vertical feet in ten minutes. One cannot ski from the summit, but a 100 persons capacity cableway completed in 1992 takes one down to the glacier station, 'Sonn Alpin', where there is a very good self-service restaurant with sun terrace. Since January 1988 the new tunnel and station of the cogwheel train has been inaugurated, and skiers get off the train right in the skiing area called 'Platt'. In 1993 a 3 floor self-service restaurant was opened on the Zugspitze summit and through its panoramic windows one can see – given good visibility - into Austria (ten feet away – one is on the border!), Italy, Liechtenstein and Switzerland. Unfortunately Mont Blanc is said to be out of range! But the countries may be irrelevant – suffice it to say that one gets one of the most magnificent views of the Alps to be found anywhere – and, therefore, as any true Alpine skier will agree, one of the finest views in the world.

The skiing on the Zugspitze is all contained in the bowl below the summit, where there are 9 drag-lifts and a double chair-lift. The snow conditions are usually perfect - there is never any ice, and there is good snow from the start of October (when the ski schools hold their first refresher courses there) until mid-May. There is snow, as such, all the year, as the top part of the ski bowl is actually on a glacier, and the bottom of it by a glacial lake. The other conditions are, as in all high Alpine areas, less predictable, and subject to sudden change. The runs are what you make them, as you can ski anywhere unless there are avalanche warnings. Certainly they appear on the whole not very steep, but if you stay in the fall line for long, it will be fast enough for anyone. And, of course, there is plentiful off-piste skiing, and ski tours abound in spring.

If you go by rail, you should get out at the Tunnelfenster or Riffelriss stops, which are just after the train emerges from the tunnel and from these runs a piste for skiers of intermediate standard over some 6km. down to Eibsee. Like so many runs at Garmisch-Partenkirchen – indeed in Germany – this is cut like an eight lane motorway through the forest, especially for skiing, and so good visibility is ensured, there is no problem over finding one's way, and the gradient is such that the fast skier can indeed go fast whilst the less experienced have room to traverse and brake.

Garmisch-Partenkirchen is a holiday and convention resort 365 days a year. Any skier of intermediate standard or better should seize the opportunity to ski there, given two provisos. First, avoid the weekend, particulary between 0900-1100 hours; second check the runs are open all the way to the valley floor. Under those conditions it is a place not to be missed. A well organised tourist office offers extremely competitive packages.

MITTENWALD

Height of Resort: 3,018 ft.
Resort Facilities Charts: See page 224

Mittenwald is to be found in the Isar valley, which partly carries the road from Garmisch Partenkirchen in the direction of Innsbruck. It is on the Austrian border between the massive Wettersteingebirge, of which the Zugspitze is one, and the similarly imposing Karwendelgebirge. Some 300 years before skiing came to Mittenwald it was famed for its violin makers – and it is still so today. It is also a health resort, and one realises from the average age the hotel guests that skiing is of secondary importance to the town. Nevertheless, if one were in a position to spend a couple of days here, it is an opportunity to be grabbed on account of the Karwendelbahn.

Karwendel/Dammkar: The naming of this particular skiing area is somewhat complicated by the fact that the lift is called the Karwendelbahn, but the ski run is known as the Dammkar, which is reputed to be the longest downhill run in Germany. The cableway rises from 3,018-7,261ft. in a single span. Underneath the lift the virtually vertical face of the mountain gives every indication of being the home of many a potential avalanche – and so it is. (Sometimes even the main Garmisch-Innsbruck trunk road has to be closed because of the threat). However, in normal conditions when the runs are open – and they skirt round the steep face to the north – they are safe enough, but steep and difficult. Also a 4,264ft. drop can feel a very long way, so the Dammkarhütte halfway down often provides a welcome place of refreshment. One of the features of this area is the tunnel which runs through 400 metres of the mountain top to bring the skier to the start of the run and away from the extremely daunting features of the peak itself. Previously one had to wend one's way with one's ski over one's shoulder up and down paths and steps which were not unknown to turn the imaginative into immobile wrecks! But the run has always been a wonderful challenge, and still enables the adventurous to find the soft snow nowadays so quickly destroyed by piste preparation.

Kranzberg/Luttensee/Wildensee: Immediately to the North West of Mittenwald lies the Hoher Kranzberg, a mere hill in comparison with its large neighbours, at 4,160 ft. It hosts a very ancient chair-lift and 7 drag-lifts varying in length from 150 metres to 650 metres, which cater for the beginner to intermediate skier.

The Rieger Hotel is most comfortable with swimming pool, sauna etc., and its food is excellent, ranging from a magnificent self-service breakfast where you can take your pick of fruit juice, cereals, eggs, meats, cheeses, yoghurts, etc., to a dinner menu which includes a fondue bourguignonne that is very good indeed. In the cellar it has a bar with (gentle) live music and a dance floor, known as Rischon: a most agreeable place.

OBERAMMERGAU

Height of Resort: 2,624 ft.
Resort Facilities Charts: See page 224

Oberammergau is, of course, the world famous home of the unique Passion Play staged every ten years in the fulfilment of the oath so to do, taken in 1633, by the villagers, provided the Almighty lifted the black death from them. The actors all come from the town.

Kolbensattel: The four lifts collectively known as the Kolbenlifte and 4 beginners lifts are to be found on the west side of the valley. The chair-lift rises slowly - from 2,921 to 4,100ft. and from it there is a choice of several very easy runs down to the bottom again. The pistes run through the trees, so are particularly advantageous in bad light, and are wide and well maintained.

Laberjoch: On the opposite side of the valley is to be found the Laberkabinenbahn - a small cable car system which lifts one from 2,624 to 5,522ft. in ten minutes. It is an old system, catering mainly for summer tourists and expert skiers. The runs back to the bottom station are not wide, nor are they prepared: indeed, in many places they are narrow and precipitous, and, in your correspondent's short experience, covered in waist high, heavy new snow! This run should not be attempted by anyone short of either skill or courage.

A well known resort for Nordic skiing with 90km. of prepared trails.

The Hotel Böld, run by the Hans family, has established a long and friendly relationship with Britons, especially with members of the forces who have been staying there regularly for many years. It is an excellent hotel with a very high standard of cuisine, and with the friendly atmosphere that seems to pervade all in Oberammergau. There is a wide choice of hotels where a typical Bavarian atmosphere prevails.

OBERSTAUFEN/STEIBIS/ THALKIRCHDORF

Height of Resort: 2,808 ft.
Resort Facilities Charts: See page 224

Oberstaufen is one of the leading summer and winter resorts of the Oberallgäu. It is the home of the 'Schrothkur' and abounds in picturesque houses and expensive shops which cater for the wealthy 'curetakers'. It has many excellent small hotels, guesthouses, apartments and more recently hotels of international standard.

It is in the immediate areas of Thalkirchdorf and Steibis (which is some 5km. east of Oberstaufen, on the Alpine Str.), that the majority of the downhill skiing is to be found. There are, of course, cross country trails scattered all over the area, and the skiing, which earns for this area a rightful place in a list of visits with the best ski runs in Germany, is to be found on the Hochgrat.

Hochgrat: The modern Hochgrat gondolaway lifts one from 2,808-5,602ft. onto the Hochgrat shoulder. Pause there if you like to see the chamois searching for food on the 6,083ft. summit above, and then launch yourself onto the 'FIS Abfahrt' – and down the gun barrel if you dare. This fires you from a short but rapid chute onto a very steep, wide slope, and the top area is often unbeaten snow. There is a less hair-raising way round but in any case only competent skiers should attempt this mountain. The intermediate skier will find less testing ways down, and the expert can grapple with large, steep mogul fields, and some near vertical sections to be found directly under the lift. There is now a drag-lift on the Hochgrat. This mountain is well worth a visit, and is as challenging as any in Germany. The bottom station of the lift is to be found by going on through Steibis for 4km. on the 'main' road, which is, in winter, a cul de sac. It ends at the lift – but go slowly, because not only is the road narrow, hilly and full of bends, but much frequented by large military vehicles from the British Army Adventure Training Centre which has been in this area since about 1967 – long before the lift was built.

The Steibis Ski Area: Above Steibis itself there is a ski area served by eight modern ski lifts and one very ancient single seater chair-lift, designed primarily for summer use, which it is not necessary to take, other than to reach the beginners slopes so sensibly sited at the top of the mountain. These are, of course, able to be used for a longer season than the nursery slope beside the village. The twin Bärenloch lifts serve a good intermediate run, whilst above it the Fluh provides runs on some very steep slopes.

The Thalkirchdorf Area: The north facing slopes over the Konstauzer Ach above Thalkirchdorf provide superb, custom built skiing,with new snow making machines, primarily for the beginner and intermediate skier, but the expert may appreciate the fact that they are seldom crowded, so one can ski without danger.

There are some 7 major lifts, of which the double chair Hündlealpbahn is the largest.

It is possible to buy a 'Skipass Oberstaufen' which covers all these areas in addition to a 2 hour visit to the adventure swimming hall 'Aquaria'. But you really need a car also to get the best out of them.

OBERSTDORF

Height of Resort: 2,756 ft..
Resort Facilities Charts See page 224

Oberstdorf, where the World Nordic Skiing Championships were held in 1987, is the leading winter sports resort of the Allgäu region of Germany, where it lies at a height of 2,756ft. at the head of the Iller valley. In fact this region probes into neighbouring Austria, enabling Oberstdorf to proclaim itself Germany's southern most spa and holiday resort. In common with other German towns of the type, it is beautifully equipped with modern sporting, recreational and business conference facilities, and it is famous for its ski flying hill (where a jump of 193 metres has been recorded) and its magnificent ice stadium The resident population numbers about 11,000, who probably give equal importance in their commercial and private lives to summer tourism, Alpine skiing, Nordic skiing, other winter sports, and 'cure' activities.

There are three main skiing areas – the Nebelhorn, the more recently developed Fellhorn and the Söllereck area. A ski-bus service links all areas.

The Nebelhorn: This mountain peak is 4,592 ft. higher than Oberstdorf, and, as the crow flies, some 5km to the east. (As the skier schusses, it is 7km. away). One can be lifted right to the summit, where the view is comparable to the finest in the Alps.

The cableway from Oberstdorf rises in 2 stages to the Bergrestaurant Hoefatsblick at 6,337ft. A further new cableway rises from this station to the peak of the Nebelhorn, 7,296ft. Supplementing this top system are two surmounting chair-lifts. One can disembark at either stage and ski back down – more of that later. Alternatively, from the second stage, one can stay in the small bowl one has reached, where 2 chair-lifts operate, one of which ascends to the very peak.

From the Bergrestaurant Hoefatsblick the run down to the Seealpe middle station is designated 'black' in the brochures, and we believe this is justified. It is a marvellous run of over 3km., with a drop of 2,138ft., most of which are achieved in the first $1^1/_2$km., leaving just enough to enable one to keep free-wheeling as far as the cableway without having to walk over the last part. A chair-lift also serves the top section (5,446 – 6,314ft.).

The final stage from Seealpe to the town runs through the woods, but is superior to the typical wood-path run. There are several open snow fields, and one short but precipitous mogul slope – again with an easier way around. (incidentally along a separate route but over the same terrain there is a toboggan run of immense popularity). In short, the Nebelhorn offers some excellent challenging skiing, providing there is snow to bring one down to the bottom, and tolerable weather to allow one to enjoy the top.

Söllereck/Schrattenwang/Höllwies: This area provides easier skiing than the Nebelhorn and Fellhorn areas, but there is good variation provided by five separate but interconnecting lifts. There are two approaches to the area: One is by the Söllereckbahn chair-lift which rises from 3,280 to 4,412ft. in eleven minutes from its start point some 3km. distance from Oberstdorf, on the Kleinwalsertal road. The other main lift goes up the mountain from the other side. This is the Höllwieslift, 2,657-4,330 ft., and 1,970m. in length, making it the longest drag-lift in Germany.

The Fellhorn: The Fellhorn Cableway is to be found some 6km. from Oberstdorf, up the Stillachtal past the famous ski-flying hill. Its cabin holds 100 people and whisks 720 people per hour three quarters of the way up the Fellhorn in 6 minutes, rising from 2,966 to 5,840ft. From that station one gains access to part of the ski circus in the Fellhorn bowl, including 3 long drag-lifts and three chair-lifts, and the magnificent, sometimes challenging, 'red' run back down to the bottom station.

However, most people prefer to press on to the Fellhorn summit, which is reached in a second cableway which lifts you a further 615ft. in 3 minutes. You are now at the top of probably the best skiing bowl in Germany which could hold its own – provided always conditions were good – with any in the Alps. There are steep slopes, middling slopes, gentle slopes: There are open slopes and wooded slopes, pisted slopes and soft snow slopes. There are some 5 drag-lifts, several restaurants, and, on a week day in the high season, no queues. Added to this already exceptionally attractive proposition, is the ability to take one of the lifts – the double Bierenwang lift – up to the Kanzelwand ridge. Along this ridge runs the border with Austria, and as a result of excellent mutual cooperation between the authorities and lift companies of the 2 countries, one can ski down into the Austrian ski complex of the Kleinwalsertal. From the top of the Kanzelwand there is a superb wide run with a vertical drop of 984ft. to a 3 seater chair-lift which takes one to the top again, or you can drive on all the way down to the Austrian village of Riezlern, a further 2,296 vertical feet below, returning by gondolaway. The run is not as good as those on the German side, but adds yet further variety, and is easier. The less experienced skier could use this for a long run, and take the Felhorn lift back down at the end of the day. The Fellhorn ticket is valid at the Kanzelwand Gondola too. In addition, one can purchase a special ski pass encompassing all skiing areas in the Austrian Kleinwalsertal and the three resorts of Oberstdorf.

Recommended Restaurant/Après Ski: The Almenhof in the hamlet of Rubi some 3 km. north-east of Oberstdorf itself, served your correspondent with one of the best steaks he has ever eaten. Cooked on a charcoal grill, it tasted superb and it could be cut with a fork – and it was, for demonstration purposes! Live Bavarian music is played by a live Bavarian band – on the whole a place of genuine 'untouristy' excellence. There are many good restaurants which can also be recommended.

REIT IM WINKL

Height of Resort: 2,296 ft.
Resort Facilities Charts: See page 224

The village of Reit im Winkl ('Clearing in the Corner') lies at a height of 2,296ft. on the German Austrian border 60km. west of Salzburg and 30km. north of Kitzbühel. It has some 3000 inhabitants. The village itself is in the middle of a wide valley ideally situated for langlauf skiing, for which it is justly famous. Apart from good and abundant nursery slopes near the village, the Alpine skiing – or the start of it is to be found 5km. up the German Alpine Road at Seegatterl. Here there is a huge, efficiently run car park, whence one takes a bus up to Winklmoosalm, 3,860ft. The next stages consist of 2 gentle drag-lifts which take you a further $2^1/_2$ kilometres, into Austria, and a huge ski bowl. This is the 'Steinplatte Ski Paradies'.

Steinplatte: There is access to the Steinplatte ski area both from the German and the Austrian side, and it caters for an enormous number of skiers. The pistes are legion, well manicured by several squadrons of piste machines, and for the most part, never narrower than 50 metres. The main artery is the Kammerköhr 4 seater chair-lift and the new Kapellen 6-seater chair, which run up the centre of the circus and is capable of delivering about 4000 skiers an hour onto the slopes where they can meet those arriving by chair-lift from Austria, or those taking yet another drag-lift from the German side. The final journey to the very top can either be by chair-lift or drag-lift, and finishes at 6,135ft. There are a further three serving the 'Ski Paradies', and whilst the majority of the pistes are suitable for all levels of skiers – mainly due to the fact that one really can traverse afar if turning is not one's speciality – there are some extremely taxing options for the expert. The place has many mountain restaurants, where German Marks and Austrian Schillings are equally readily accepted. Most skiers stay in the Steinplatte area until it is time to go home, which can mean a very busy run down to the car park. But that is not all that is unusual about it, for the run is 9 kilometres long. It drops 3,280 vertical feet, so the gradient is gentle, yet constant. Even the slowest skier has only to walk about 30 yards, and some parts are quite fast enough to practice linked turns.

This resort is unhesitatingly recommended as an ideal resort for a family which includes beginners as well as seasoned skiers.

RESORT FACILITIES CHARTS

INDEX

NORTH AMERICA

Name of Resort	Aspen Mountain	Aspen Highlands	Buttermilk	Alpine Meadows	Beaver Creek	Big Sky	Breckenridge	Copper Mountain	Crested Butte
State or Province	Colorado	Colorado	Colorado	California	Colorado	Montana	Colorado	Colorado	Colorado
Telephone/Fax Area Code	970	970	970	916	970	406	970	970	970
Telephone Number	925.1220	925.1220	925.1220	583.4232	845.5712	995.5000	453.1643	968.2882	349.2222
Fax Number	925.9024	925.9024	925.9024	583.0963	845.5728	995.5001	453.5000		349.2397
Height of Resort	7,945ft	8,040 ft.*	7,870ft.*	6,835ft	8,100ft	7,500ft	9,610ft	9,600ft	9,375ft
Height of Top Station	11,800ft	11,800 ft.	9,840ft.	8,440ft	11,440ft	11,150ft	12,213ft	12,360ft	12,162ft
Cableways	Nil	Nil	Nil	Nil	Nil	1	Nil	Nil	Nil
Gondolaways	1	Nil	Nil	Nil	Nil	1	Nil	Nil	Nil
Chair-lifts	7	8	6	11	11	10	13	15	9
Drag-lifts	Nil	2	1	1	Nil	3	3	4	4
Total Lift Capacity per Hour	10,755	9,145	7,500	16,000	22,000	21,000	26,450	29,250	18,000
Ski School Instructors	175	175	175	100	275	20	290	200	
Natural Skating Rinks	Nil	Nil	Nil	Nearby	1	Nil	Yes	Yes	Nil
Artificial Skating Rinks	1	1	1	Nearby	1	Nil	Nil		2
Curling Rinks	Nil	Nil	Nil	Nil	Yes	Nil	Nil		Nil
Ice Hockey	Yes	Yes	Yes	Nearby	Yes	Nil	Nil		Nil
Sleigh Rides	Yes	Yes	Yes	Nearby	Yes	Yes	Yes	Yes	Yes
Riding	Yes	Yes	Yes	Nearby	Yes	Nil	Yes	Nil	Yes
Sports Centre	3	Yes	Yes	Nearby	Yes	Nil	Yes	Yes	Yes
Indoor Tennis	3	Yes	Yes	Nil	Yes	Nil	Yes	Yes	Nil
Hang-Gliding	Nil	Nil	Yes	Nil	Nil	Nil	Nil	Nil	Yes
Para-Gliding	Yes	Yes	Yes	Yes	Nil	Nil	Nil	Yes	Yes
Heated Swimming Pools (public)	1	Yes	Yes	Nearby	Nil	Nil	Yes	Yes	Nil
Heated Swimming pools (hotels)	Yes	Yes	Yes	Nearby	Yes	Yes	Yes		Yes
Sauna Baths	Yes	Yes	Yes	Nearby	Yes	Yes	Yes	Yes	Yes
Bowling	Nil	Nil	Nil	Nearby	Nil	Nil	Yes	Nil	Nil
Cinema	4	Yes	Yes	Nearby	Yes	Yes	Yes		Nil
Kindergartens	Yes	Nearby	Nearby	Yes	Yes	Yes	Yes	Yes	Yes
Mountain Restaurants	4	2	3	1	5	Yes	2	Yes	13
Night Clubs with Bands	Yes	Yes	Yes	Nearby	2	Yes	Yes		3
Discothèques	Yes	Yes	Yes	Nearby	1	Nil	Yes	Yes	Nil

* Height of lowest station

RESORT FACILITIES CHARTS

NORTH AMERICA

Name of Resort	Deer Valley	Heavenly Ski Resort	Hunter Mountain	Jackson Hole	Keystone	Killington	Lake Louise	Lake Placid
State or Province	Utah	California	New York	Wyoming	Colorado	Vermont	Alberta	New York
Telephone/Fax Area Code	801	702	518	307	970	802	403	518
Telephone Number	649.1000	586.7000	263.4223	733.2292	468.2316	422.3333	522.3555	523.1655
Fax Number	649.1910	588.5517	263.3704	733.2660	468.4105	422.4391	522.3774	523.9275
Height of Resort	7,200ft	6,200ft	1,601ft	6,311ft	9,300ft	1,047ft	5,400ft	1,200ft
Height of Top Station	9,400ft	10,167ft	3,202ft	10,450ft	11,980ft	4,241ft	8,650ft	4,415ft
Cableways	Nil	1	Nil	1	Nil	Nil	Nil	Nil
Gondolaways	Nil	Nil	Nil	Nil	2	2	Nil	Nil
Chair-lifts	11	18	11	7	18	23	8	9
Drag-lifts	Nil	6	5	1	3	8	3	Nil
Total Lift Capacity per Hour	22,800	33,000	18,200	9,000	32,700	53,039	19,667	10,135
Ski School Instructors	170	165	150		200	300	45	100
Natural Skating Rinks	Nil	Nil	Nearby	Nearby	Yes	1	Nearby	5
Artificial Skating Rinks	Yes	Nil		In Jackson	Nil	1	Nil	4
Curling Rinks	Nil	Nil	Nil	Nil	Nil	Nil	Nearby	1
Ice Hockey	Nil	Yes	Nil	Nil	Yes	Nil	Nearby	3
Sleigh Rides	Yes	Yes	Nearby	Nearby	Yes	Yes	Yes	Yes
Riding	Yes	Nil		Nearby	Yes	Yes	Nil	Yes
Sports Centre	Yes	Yes	Nearby	Nearby	Yes	5	Nearby	Yes
Indoor Tennis	Yes	Nil	Nearby		Yes	3	Nearby	Nil
Hang-Gliding	Yes	Yes		Nil	Nil	Nil	Nearby	Nil
Para-Gliding	Nil	Yes		Nil	Nil	Nil	Nearby	Nil
Heated Swimming Pools (public)	Yes	Yes	Nearby	Nil	Nil	Yes	Nil	Nearby
Heated Swimming pools (hotels)	Yes	Yes		Nil	Yes	Yes	Nearby	10
Sauna Baths	Yes	Yes	Yes		Yes	Yes	Nearby	20
Bowling	Yes	Yes		Nil	Yes	Yes	Nearby	Yes
Cinema	Yes	Yes	Nearby	Nearby	Yes	7	Nearby	3
Kindergartens	Yes	Yes	Yes	Yes	Yes	Yes	Yes	Yes
Mountain Restaurants	Yes	6	1	2	2	1	2	2
Night Clubs with Bands	Yes	Yes			Yes	22	Nearby	Yes
Discothèques	Yes	Yes	Yes	Yes	Yes	2	Nearby	

NORTH AMERICA

Name of Resort	Mammoth Mountain	Mont Ste.-Anne	Park City	Purgatory	Snowbird	Snowmass	Squaw Valley	Steamboat
State or Province	California	Quebec	Utah	Colorado	Utah	Colorado	California	Colorado
Telephone/Fax Area Code	619	418	801	970	801	970	916	970
Telephone Number	934.2571	827.4661	649.8111	247.9000	742.2222	925.1220	583.698587	879.6111
Fax Number	934.0600	827.3121	649.5964	385.2131	742.3300	925.9024	583.5970	879.7844
Height of Resort	7,940ft.	580	6,900ft	8,795ft	8,100ft	8,208ft	6,200ft	6,900ft
Height of Top Station	11,053ft.	2,625	10,000ft	10,991ft	11,000ft	11,835ft	9,050ft	10,500ft
Cableways		Nil	Nil	Nil	1	Nil	1	Nil
Gondolaways	2	1	1	Nil	Nil	Nil	1	1
Chair-lifts	26	6	7	9	8	17	32	20
Drag-lifts	2	5	Nil	Nil	Nil	2	4	3
Total Lift Capacity per Hour	53,000	17,760	23,000	14,000	10,200	24,000	47,370	31,500
Ski School Instructors	350	160	200	100	120		120	200
Natural Skating Rinks	Yes	Yes	Nil	Nil	Nil	Nil	Nil	Nil
Artificial Skating Rinks	Nil	Yes	Yes	Nearby	Nil	Yes	2	1
Curling Rinks	Nil	Yes	Nil	Nil	Nil	Nil	Nil	Nil
Ice Hockey	Yes	Yes	Nil	Nil	Nil	Nil	Nil	1
Sleigh Rides	Nearby	Yes	Yes	Yes	Nil	Yes	Nil	Yes
Riding	Nil	Yes	Yes	Nil	Nil	Yes	Yes	Yes
Sports Centre	Nearby	Yes	Yes	Nearby	Nil	Yes	Nil	Yes
Indoor Tennis	Nil	Yes	Yes	Nil	Nil	Nil	Yes	Nearby
Hang-Gliding	Yes	Yes	Nil	Nil	Nil	Nil	Nil	Nil
Para-Gliding	Yes	Yes	Nil	Nil	Nil	Nil	Nil	Nil
Heated Swimming Pools (public)	Yes	Yes	Yes	Nearby	Nil	Yes	1	Nil
Heated Swimming pools (hotels)	Yes	Yes	Yes	5	5	Yes	4	Yes
Sauna Baths	Yes	Yes	Yes	Yes	7	Yes	2	Yes
Bowling	Nil	Yes	Yes	Nearby	Nil	Nil	Nil	Yes
Cinema	Nearby	Yes	Yes	Nearby	Yes	Nil	Yes	
Kindergartens	Yes	Yes	Yes	Yes	Yes	2	Yes	Yes
Mountain Restaurants	Yes	6	4	3	2	5	10	5
Night Clubs with Bands	Yes	Yes	Yes	Yes	3	Yes	4	10
Discothèques	Yes	Yes	Yes	Yes	Nil	Nil		

RESORT FACILITIES CHARTS

NORTH AMERICA

Name of Resort	Stowe	Sugarloaf	Sun Valley	Taos	Telluride	Vail	Whistler/ Blackcombe	Winter Park
State or Province	Vermont	Maine	Idaho	New Mexico	Colorado	Colorado	B. Columbia	Colorado
Telephone/Fax Area Code	802	207	208	505	970	970	604	970
Telephone Number	253.3000	237.2000	662.4111	776.2291	728.3856	845.5712	932.3928	726.5514
Fax Number	253.3406	237.2718	622.2051		728.6364	845.5728	932.9623	726.1572
Height of Resort	1,559ft	1,400ft	5,760ft	9,209ft	8,745ft	8,200ft	2,214ft	9,010ft
Height of Top Station	4,393ft	4,237ft	9,150ft	11,817ft	11,890ft	11,250ft	7,160/7,494ft	12,060ft
Cableways	Nil	Nil	Nil	Nil	Nil	Nil	Nil	Nil
Gondolaways	1	1	Nil	Nil	Nil	1	1	Nil
Chair-lifts	8	17	15	8	9	19	29	20
Drag-lifts	2	2	Nil	2	1	5	4	2
Total Lift Capacity per Hour	12,550	17,035	23,380	10,700	10,100	45,370	46,000	33,710
Ski School Instructors	200	155	160	100	80	700	500	250
Natural Skating Rinks	Nil	1	Nil	Nil	1	1	5	1
Artificial Skating Rinks	Nearby	1	2	Nil	1	1	1	3
Curling Rinks	Nil	Nil	Nil	Nil	Nil	1	Nil	Nil
Ice Hockey	Nearby	Yes	Yes	Nil	Yes	Yes	Nil	Yes
Sleigh Rides	Nearby	Nil	Yes	Nil	Yes	Yes	Yes	Yes
Riding	Nearby	Nil	Nil	Nil	Yes	Yes	Yes	Yes
Sports Centre	Nearby	Yes	Yes	Nil	Yes	Yes	Yes	Yes
Indoor Tennis	Nearby	Nil	Nearby	Nil	Nil	Yes	Yes	Nil
Hang-Gliding	Nil	Nil	Yes		Yes	Nil	Nil	Nil
Para-Gliding	Nil	Nil	Yes		Yes	Yes	Yes	Nil
Heated Swimming Pools (public)	Nearby	Yes	Nil		Nil	Nil	Nil	Yes
Heated Swimming pools (hotels)	Yes	Yes	2	Yes	Yes	Yes	Yes	Yes
Sauna Baths	Nearby	Yes	Yes	Yes	Yes	Yes	Yes	Yes
Bowling	Nearby	Nil	Yes	Nil	Nil	Nil	Nil	Nil
Cinema	Yes	Nil	Yes	Nearby	Yes	Yes	Yes	Yes
Kindergartens	Yes	Yes	Yes	Yes	Yes	Yes	Yes	Yes
Mountain Restaurants	9	Yes	5	2	Yes	9	10	7
Night Clubs with Bands	Yes	Yes	Yes	Yes	Yes	5	Yes	4
Discothèques	Yes	Nil	Nil	Nil	3	Yes	4	

AUSTRIA

Name of Resort	Alpbach	Bad Aussee	Badgastein	Bad Goisern	Bad Hofgastein	Berwang	Brand
Province	Tyrol	Steiemark	Salzburg	U. Austria	Salzburg	Tyrol	Vorarlberg
Tourist Office Director	R. Danler	A. Schupfer	E. Schett	S. Mittendorfer	Karl Nobis	H. Werner	L. Reinhard
Telephone/Fax Area Code	(05336)	(03622)	(06434)	((06135)	(06432)	(05674)	(05559)
Telephone Number	5211	54040-0	25310	8329	7110	8268	555
Fax Number	5012	54040-7	253140	8329-74	711031	8436	555-20
Total Visitor Beds	2,500	3,680	7,300	2,300	8,000	2,310	1,550
Height of Resort	3,281 ft	2,296 ft	3,608 ft	1,640 ft	2,853 ft	4,398 ft	3,412 ft
Height of Top Station	6,102 ft	6,562 ft	8,890 ft	3,280 ft	7,544 ft	5,395 ft	6,297 ft
Mountain Railway	Nil	Nil	1*	Nil	1*	Nil	Nil
Cableways	Nil	Nil	1	Nil	1	Nil	Nil
Gondolaways	1	Nil	8	Nil	8	Nil	Nil
Chair-lifts	5	2	15	1	15	4	5
Drag-lifts	15	8	29	2	29	6	8
Total Lift Capacity per Hour	19,000	8,000	69,000	850	69,000	20,000	11,278
Ski School Instructors	60	15	110	7	70	38	50-60
Average sunshine hours - village area							
December	4	$5\frac{1}{2}$	4	6	5	4	3
January	5	6	5	7	5	5	$3\frac{1}{2}$
February	$5-6\frac{1}{2}$	7	6	8	6	7	$5\frac{1}{2}$
March	8	8	7	9	8	8	$7\frac{1}{2}$
April	8-9	9	8	11	9	9	9
Natural Skating Rinks	2	Yes	1	1	Nil	Nil	Nil
Artificial Skating Rinks	Nil	Yes	Nil	Nil	1	Nil	Yes
Curling Rinks	Yes	Yes	Yes	Yes	Yes	Nil	Yes
Ice Hockey	Yes	Nil	Nil	Nil	Yes	Nil	Yes
Tobogganing	Yes	Yes	Yes	Yes	Yes	Nil	Yes
Sleigh Rides	Yes	Yes	Yes	Yes	Yes	Yes	Nil
Riding	Nil	Yes	Yes	Nil	Yes	Nil	Yes
Sports Centre	Nil	Yes	Yes	Nil	Yes	Nil	Yes
Indoor Tennis	Nil	Yes	Yes	Nil	Yes	Nil	Yes
Hang-Gliding	Nil	Yes	Nil	Nil	Yes	Yes	Nil
Para-Gliding	Yes	Tes	Nil	Nil	Yes	Yes	Yes
Heated Swimming Pools (public)	Yes	Yes	Yes	Nil	1	Yes	Nil
Heated Swimming pools (hotels)	Yes	Yes	Yes	2	Yes	Yes	Yes
Sauna Baths	Yes	Yes	Yes	3	Yes	2	10
Bowling	Nil	Yes	Nil	3	Nil	Nil	Yes
Cinema	Nil	Nil	Yes	Nil	Nil	Nil	Nil
Kindergartens	2	Nil	Yes	2	2	1	Yes
Mountain Restaurants	4	Yes	21*	3	21*	4	4
Night Clubs with Bands	Nil	Nil	2	Nil	1	1	Yes
Discothèques	2	Yes	4	Nil	4	Nil	Yes

*Gastein Valley

RESORT FACILITIES CHARTS

AUSTRIA

Name of Resort	Leogang	Lermoos	Mayrhofen	Nauders	Niederau (Oberau & Auffach)	Obergurgl/ Hochgurgl	Obertauern	Obertraun
Province	Salzburg	Tyrol	Tyrol	Tyrol	Tyrol	Tyrol	Salzburg	U. Austria
Tourist Office Director	G. Madreiter	Maria Peer	Thekla Erler	G. Riedl	Hilde Thaler	Mag. Kienpointner	D. Kindl	J. Puchinger
Telephone/Fax Area Code	(06583)	(05673)	(05285)	(05473)	(05339)	(05256)	(06456)	(06131)
Telephone Number	234	2401	6760	220	8255	466	7252	351
Fax Number	7302	2694	6760-33	627	2433	353	7515	34222
Total Visitor Beds	3,820	1,642	7,900	3,800	6,080	3,900	6,500	1,310
Height of Resort	2,755ft.	3,623 ft	2,067 ft	4,590 ft	2,700 ft	6,322/7,054 ft	5,723 ft	1,968 ft
Height of Top Station	6,279ft.	7,215 ft	7,283 ft	9,022 ft	5,333 ft	10,111 ft	7,872 ft	6,917 ft
Mountain Railway	Nil	Nil	Nil	Nil	Nil	Nil	Nil	Nil
Cableways	1***	Nil	1**	Nil	Nil	Nil	1	2
Gondolaways	5	1	3	1	2*	1	Nil	Nil
Chair-lifts	19	5	10	3	1	10	11	Nil
Drag-lifts	39	4	16	12	26	11	14	5
Total Lift Capacity per Hour	73,800***	12,500	34,930**	16,700	32,000*	22,000	35,000	3,000
Ski School Instructors	80	75	160	70	80	80	100	20
Average sunshine hours - village area								
December	6	6	4	4	4	5	5	1
January	7	6	5	5	5	5-6	5	2
February	8	7	6	6	6	6	8	5
March	9	8	7	6-7	8-9	6-7	8	7
April	10	9	8	7	9	8	9	9
Natural Skating Rinks	Yes	1	Yes	Yes	Yes	1	Nil	1
Artificial Skating Rinks	Nil	Nil	Nil	Nil	Nil	Nil	Nil	Nil
Curling Rinks	Yes	Yes	Yes	Nil	Yes	2	Nil	Nil
Ice Hockey	Nil	Nil	Nil	Nil	Yes	Nil	Nil	Nil
Tobogganing	Yes	1	Yes	Yes	Yes	Nil	Yes	1
Sleigh Rides	Nil	Yes	Yes	Yes	Yes	Nil	Yes	Yes
Riding	Yes	Nil	Yes	Yes	Yes	Nil	Nil	Yes
Sports Centre	Nil	Nil	Yes	Nil	Nil	Nil	Yes	Nil
Indoor Tennis	Nil	Nil	Yes	Yes	Nil	Nil	Yes	Nil
Hang-Gliding	Yes	Yes	Yes	Yes	Nil	Nil	Nil	Nil
Para-Gliding	Yes	Yes	Yes	Yes	Yes	Nil	Nil	Yes
Heated Swimming Pools (public)	Yes	2	Yes	Nil	Nil	Nil	Nil	Nil
Heated Swimming pools (hotels)	3	4	7	Yes	Yes	15	11	Nil
Sauna Baths	1	Yes	Yes	Yes	Yes	Yes	Yes	Yes
Bowling	Nil	Nil	Yes	1	Yes	Yes	Yes	Yes
Cinema	Nil	Nil	Yes	Nil	Nil	Nil	Nil	Nil
Kindergartens	Yes	Ski	Yes	Ski	Ski	Ski	Yes	Yes
Mountain Restaurants	6	4	14	6	12	8	12	4
Night Clubs with Bands	Nil	1	Yes	2	Nil	2	2	Nil
Discothèques	Yes	1	7	Yes	Yes	4	2	1

*including Oberau and Auffach **including Finkenberg ***including Saalbaach/Hinterglemm

AUSTRIA

Name of Resort	Raggal	Saalbach/ Hinterglemm	St. Anton	St. Johann In Tirol	Schruns	Seefeld	Serfaus
Province	Vorarberg	Salzburg	Arlberg	Tyrol	Vorarlberg	Tyrol	Tyrol
Tourist Office Director	Barbara Bickel	W. Rinner	H. Wagner	P. Wallner	C. Fiel	M. Tschoner	S. Tschuggmall
Telephone/Fax Area Code	(05553)	(06541)	(05446)	(05352)	(05556)	(05212)	(05476)
Telephone Number	345	7272	22690	62218	72166	2313	6239
Fax Number	380	7900	2532	65200	72554	3355	6813
Total Visitor Beds	560	17,130	7,987	2,562	2,491	8,600	4,200
Height of Resort	3,332 ft	3,260 ft	4,210 ft	2,296 ft	2,275 ft	3,872 ft	4,682 ft
Height of Top Station	4,264 ft	6,845 ft	9,222 ft	6,233 ft	7,544 ft	6,890 ft	8,858 ft
Mountain Railway	Nil	Nil	1**	Nil	Nil	1	Nil
Cableways	Nil	1***	9	Nil	1	2	1
Gondolaways	Nil	5	2	2	1	Nil	2
Chair-lifts	1	19	36	6	6	6	5
Drag-lifts	5	39	40	10	4	17	10
Total Lift Capacity per Hour	4,340	73,800***	110,000**	20,100	14,620	16,000	24,871
Ski School Instructors	15	200	300	80	35	100	180
Average sunshine hours - village area							
December	2	6	2	5	5	$6^1/_2$	6
January	4	7	3	6	$5^1/_2$	7	7
February	6	8	4-5	7	6	$7^1/_2$	7
March	8	9	7	8	6-7	8	8
April	10	10	8	9	7		8
Natural Skating Rinks	Nil	Nil	1	Nil	Nil	1	1
Artificial Skating Rinks	Nil	Yes	Nil	1	Nil	1	Yes
Curling Rinks	Nil	Yes	5	Yes	Nil	40	Yes
Ice Hockey	Nil	Yes	Nil	Yes	Nil	Nil	Nil
Tobogganing	Nil	Yes	Yes	Yes	Yes	Yes	Yes
Sleigh Rides	Nil	Yes	Yes	Yes	Yes	Yes	Yes
Riding	Nil	Yes	Nil	Nil	Nil	Yes	Nil
Sports Centre	Nil	Yes	Nil	Yes	Nil	Yes	Nil
Indoor Tennis	Yes	Yes	Yes	Yes	Nil	Yes	Yes
Hang-Gliding	Nil	Nil	Nil	Nil	Nil	Yes	Nil
Para-Gliding	Nil	Yes	Yes	Nil	Yes	Yes	Yes
Heated Swimming Pools (public)	Nil	2	Nil	1	1	1	Yes
Heated Swimming pools (hotels)	Nil	18	Yes	Yes	5	40	3
Sauna Baths	Yes	Yes	Yes	Yes	Yes	52	Yes
Bowling	Nil	Yes	Yes	2	Nil	Yes	Yes
Cinema	Nil	Nil	Yes	Nil	1	Yes	Nil
Kindergartens	Yes	Yes	Yes	Yes	1	Yes	Yes
Mountain Restaurants	2	40	11	12	3	10	3
Night Clubs with Bands	1	5	3	2	Yes	8	2
Discothèques	1	15	13	1	Yes	6	Yes

**including Lech and Zürs ***including Leogang

RESORT FACILITIES CHARTS

AUSTRIA

Name of Resort	Sölden/ Hochsölden	Söll		Spital am Pyhrn	Steinach	Stuben	Tschagguns
Province	Tyrol	Tyrol		U. Austria	Tyrol	Arlberg	Vorarlberg
Tourist Office Director	C. Niederstetter	C. Berger		H. Fachberger	K. Hasenbacher	R. Pichler	T. Leach
Telephone/Fax Area Code	(05254)	05333)		(07563)	(05272)	(05582)	(05556)
Telephone Number	22120	5216		249	6270	399	72457
Fax Number	3131	6180		70076	2110	399-4	73940
Total Visitor Beds	9,662	4,100		1,900	2,300	620	3400
Height of Resort	4,436/6,857 ft	2,275 ft		2,624 ft	3,432 ft	4,592 ft	2,275 ft
Height of Top Station	10,030 ft	5,997 ft	*Area*	6,146 ft	6,578 ft	7,872 ft	6,903 ft
Mountain Railway	Nil	Nil	1	1	Nil	1**	Nil
Cableways	2	1	1	Nil	Nil	9	Nil
Gondolaways	1	2	6	Nil	1	2	3
Chair-lifts	18	13	27	2	3	36	2
Drag-lifts	11	16	55	7	7	40	4
Total Lift Capacity per Hour	47,255	36,330	113,758	9,320	5,000	110,000**	12,000
Ski School Instructors	190	100		10-30	50	30	25
Average sunshine hours - village area							
December	5	7			3	2	4
January	5½/7	8			4	4	4
February	6-8	9			5	5	5
March	6½	8-9			7	6-7	6
April	7/9-10	11			8	7	6½
Natural Skating Rinks	1	Yes		Yes	Yes	Nil	Nil
Artificial Skating Rinks	Nil	Yes		1	Nil	Nil	1
Curling Rinks	3	1		5	Yes	Nil	1
Ice Hockey	Yes	Nil		Nil	Yes	Nil	1
Tobogganing	Yes	Yes		Yes	Yes	Nil	Yes
Sleigh Rides	Yes	Yes		Yes	Yes	Nil	Yes
Riding	Nil	Yes		Yes	Yes	Nil	Yes
Sports Centre	Yes	Nil		Yes	Nil	Nil	Nil
Indoor Tennis	Yes	Nil		Nil	Nil	Nil	Yes
Hang-Gliding	Nil	Yes		Yes	Yes	Nil	Yes
Para-Gliding	Yes	Yes		Yes	Yes	Nil	Yes
Heated Swimming Pools (public)	Yes	1		Yes	Nil	1	Nil
Heated Swimming pools (hotels)	6	Yes		Nil	Yes	2	3
Sauna Baths	Yes	Yes		Yes	Yes	15	5
Bowling	Yes	Yes		Yes	Nil	Nil	Yes
Cinema	1	Nil		Nil	Nil	Nil	Nil
Kindergartens	Ski	Yes		Ski	Yes	Ski	1
Mountain Restaurants	17	8		6	3	3	4
Night Clubs with Bands	Yes	Yes		Nil	1	Nil	Yes
Discothèques	Yes	Yes		1	1	1	Yes

** including St. Anton, Lech & Zürs

AUSTRIA

Name of Resort	Vent	Wagrain		Westendorf	Zell am See	Zell am Ziller	Zürs
Province	Tyrol	Salzburg		Tyrol	Salzburg	Tyrol	Arlberg
Tourist Office Director	C. Niederstetter	N. Krenn		T. Wurzrainer	H. Brugger	W. Strasser	U. Jochum
Telephone/Fax Area Code	(05254)	(06413)		(05334)	(06542)	(05282)	(05583)
Telephone Number	8193	8448		6230	770	2281	2245
Fax Number	8174	8449		2390	2032	228180	2982
Total Visitor Beds	1,220	5,000		4,380	6,000	5,103	1,508
Height of Resort	6,202 ft	2,952ft		2,624 ft	2,490 ft	1,902 ft	5,590 ft
Height of Top Station	8,850 ft	7,178ft	*Area*	6,101 ft	6,500 ft	7,900 ft	8,036 ft
Mountain Railway	Nil	Nil	Nil	Nil	2**	Nil	1*
Cableways	Nil	Nil	Nil	Nil	4	1	9
Gondolaways	Nil	3	8	1	4	1	2
Chair-lifts	1	3	30	4	11	6	36
Drag-lifts	3	8	82	8	38	13	40
Total Lift Capacity per Hour	3,450		130,000	17,640	71,930**	23,800	110,000*
Ski School Instructors	15-20	80		100	200	100-130	140
Average sunshine hours - village area							
December		4		4	4½	5	4-5
January		5		5	5	5	5-6
February		6-7		7	6	5	5-7
March		8		8	7	7	6-8
April		9		9	8½	7	7-8
Natural Skating Rinks	Nil	Nil		1	Yes	Yes	Nil
Artificial Skating Rinks	Nil	Yes		Nil	Yes	Yes	Nil
Curling Rinks	Nil	Yes		Nil	Yes	Yes	Nil
Ice Hockey	Nil	Nil		Nil	Yes	Nil	Nil
Tobogganing	Yes	Yes		Nil	Yes	Yes	Nil
Sleigh Rides	Yes	Yes		Yes	Yes	Yes	Yes
Riding	Nil	Nil		Nil	Yes	Nil	Nil
Sports Centre	Nil	Nil		Nil	Yes	Yes	Nil
Indoor Tennis	Nil	Yes		Nil	Yes	Yes	Nil
Hang-Gliding	Nil	Nil		Nil	Yes	Yes	Yes
Para-Gliding	Nil	Yes		Yes	Yes	Yes	Yes
Heated Swimming Pools (public)	Nil	Nil		Nil	Yes	Yes	Nil
Heated Swimming pools (hotels)	Yes	3		Yes	Yes	Yes	Yes
Sauna Baths	Yes	Yes		2	Yes	3	Yes
Bowling	Yes	Nil		2	Yes	Yes	Nil
Cinema	Nil	Nil		Nil	Yes	Nil	Nil
Kindergartens	Yes	Yes		Ski	Yes	Ski	Ski
Mountain Restaurants	Nil	Yes		12	25	4	
Night Clubs with Bands	Nil	Nil		Yes	Yes	Yes	Nil
Discothèques	Yes	2		2	Yes	Nil	Yes

*including Lech and St. Anton

**including Kaprun

RESORT FACILITIES CHARTS

FRANCE

Name of Resort	Alpe d'Huez	Avoriaz*	Barèges/ La Mongie	Chamonix	Chatel*	Courchevel	Flaine	Font-Romeu
Province	Isère	H. Savoie	H. Pyrénées	H. Savoie	H. Savoie	Savoie	H. Savoie	H. Pyrénées
Tourist Office Director	Aimé Heldt	P. Perinet	A. Sabathie	B. Prud'homme	P. Bernard	J. L. Leger	Mlle. C. Sals	C. Portello
Telephone/Fax Area Code	(476)	(450)	(562)	(450)	(450)	(479)	(450)	(468)
Telephone Number	11.44.44	74.24.24	92.68.19	53.00.24	73.22.44	08.00.29	90.80.01	30.68.30
Fax Number	80.69.54	74.18.25	92.69.13	535890	73.22.87	08.15.63	90.86.26	30.29.70
Total Visitor Beds	32,200	16,080	4,200	11,494	16,524	33,000	5,300	20,000
Height of Resort	6,101 ft	5,904 ft	4,265/5,905 ft	3,389 ft	3,937 ft	6,013 ft	5,250 ft	5,895 ft
Height of Top Station	10,988 ft	7,710 ft	8,400 ft	12,604 ft	6,890 ft	8,825 ft	8,150 ft	7,205 ft.
Mountain Railway	Nil	Nil	1	1	Nil	Nil	Nil	Nil
Cableways	5	1	1	5	Nil	1	Nil	1
Gondolaways	9	2	2	7	2	9	2	Nil
Chair-lifts	24	20	7	14	12	15	6	7
Drag-lifts	46	18	42	20	34	43	19	26
Total Lift Capacity per Hour	90,000	47,185	38,216	60,000	41,630	64,533	27,240	18,000
Ski School Instructors	164	120	80	300	60	400	100	20
Average sunshine hours - village area								
December	5	6	4	3	5	6	5	4
January	5½	6	5	4	6	6½	5½	5
February	6½	6	6	5	7	7½	6	6
March	7	9	6	6	8	9	7	7
April	8	10	8	7	9	10	8	8
Natural Skating Rinks	Nil	Nil	Nil	Yes	Yes	Nil	1	Nil
Artificial Skating Rinks	1	1	Nil	Yes	Yes	1	Nil	Yes
Curling Rinks	1	Nil	Nil	Yes	Nil	Nil	Nil	Nil
Ice Hockey	Yes	Yes	Nil	Yes	Nil	Yes	Yes	Yes
Tobogganing	Nil	Nil	Nil	Nil	Nil	Yes	Nil	Nil
Sleigh Rides	Nil	Yes	Nil	Nil	Yes	Yes	Nil	Nil
Riding	Nil	Nil	Nil	Yes	Nil	Nil	Nil	Yes
Sports Centre	Yes	Yes	Nil	Yes	Nil	Yes	Yes	Yes
Indoor Tennis	Yes	Nil	Nil	Yes	Nil	Nil	Nil	Yes
Hang-Gliding	Yes	Yes	Nil	Yes	Nil	Yes	Yes	Yes
Para-Gliding	Yes	Yes	Yes	Yes	Yes	Yes	Yes	Yes
Heated Swimming Pools (public)	Yes	Nil	Nil	Yes	Nil	Nil	Yes	Yes
Heated Swimming pools (hotels)	Yes	Nil	Nil	Yes	Yes	6	Nil	Yes
Sauna Baths	Yes	Yes	Yes	Yes	Yes	Yes	Yes	Yes
Bowling	Nil	Yes	Nil	Yes	Yes	Yes	Nil	Nil
Cinema	2	Yes	1	Yes	2	3	1	Yes
Kindergartens	Yes	Yes	Ski	Yes	Yes	Yes	Yes	Yes
Mountain Restaurants	14	13	5	9	9	13	8	Yes
Night Clubs with Bands	Nil	2	Nil	Nil	Yes	Yes	Yes	Yes
Discothèques	Yes	3	2	4	2	Yes	Yes	Yes

*See Portes du Soleil for Linked Resorts

FRANCE

Name of Resort	Isola 2000	La Clusaz	La Plagne	La Toussuire	Le Corbier	Les Angles	Les Arcs	Les Deux Alpes	Les Gets*
Province	Alpes Maritimes	H. Savoie	Savoie	Savoie	Savoie	Hautes Pyrenées	Savoie	Isère	H. Savoie
Tourist Office Director	M. Deuelay	L. Godde		J-L. Laÿs	André Dann	G. Cousin	J.M. Silva	P. Brand	Mme. F. Richard
Telephone/Fax Area Code	(493)	(450)	(479)	(479)	(479)	(468)	(479)	(476)	(450)
Telephone Number	23.15.15	32.65.00	09.79.79	56.70.15	83.04.04	04.32.76	07.12.57	79.22.00	75.80.80
Fax Number	23.14.25	32.65.01	09.70.10	83.02.99	83.02.90	30.93.09	07.45.96	79.01.38	79.76.90
Total Visitor Beds	8,075	9,200	39,500	5,500	6,050	18,000	28,999	30,000	11,400
Height of Resort	6,560 ft	3,608 ft	5,904 ft	6,095 ft	5,085 ft	5,249 ft	5,249 ft/6,562 ft	5,412 ft	3,834 ft
Height of Top Station	8,563 ft	7,872 ft	10,663 ft	7,874	7,415 ft	7,874 ft	10,583 ft	11,673 ft	6,069 ft
Mountain Railway	Nil	Nil	Nil	Nil	Nil	Nil	1	1	Nil
Cableways	Nil	3	1	Nil	Nil	2	1	4	2**
Gondolaways	1	2	8	Nil	Nil	Nil	3	3	3
Chair-lifts	10	13	30	6	12	2	29	24	22
Drag-lifts	12	38	74	13	32	19	45	30	28
Total Lift Capacity per Hour	26,000	49,500	114,000	15,000	27,859	15,900	82,000	63,113	55,147**
Ski School Instructors	60	180	550	55	45	40	230	310	110
Average sunshine hours - village area									
December	4	4	5	5	6½		5	7	7
January	5	6	6	6	7		6	8	8
February	5	6	7	7	8		7	8	8
March	6	7	8	7½	9		9	10	10
April	7	7½	9	8½	10		10	11	10½
Natural Skating Rinks	1	Nil	2	1	Nil	Nil	2	Nil	Nil
Artificial Skating Rinks	Nil	1	Nil	Nil	Yes	Nil	Nil	1	Yes
Curling Rinks	Nil	Nil	Nil	Nil	Nil	Nil	Nil	Nil	Nil
Ice Hockey	Nil	Yes	Nil	Yes	Nil	Yes	Yes	Nil	Nil
Tobogganing	Nil	Nil	Yes	Nil	Nil	Yes	Nil	Yes	Nil
Sleigh Rides	Nil	Yes	Nil	Yes	Nil	Nil	Nil	Nil	Yes
Riding	Nil	Nil	Nil	Nil	Yes	Yes	Yes	Nil	Nil
Sports Centre	Nil	Nil	Nil	Nil	Nil	Yes	Yes	Yes	Nil
Indoor Tennis	Nil	Nil	Nil	Nil	Nil	Nil	Nil	Nil	Nil
Hang-Gliding	Nil	Yes	Yes	Yes	Nil	Nil	Yes	Nil	Yes
Para-Gliding	Nil	Yes	Yes	Yes	Yes	Nil	Yes	Yes	Yes
Heated Swimming Pools (public)	Nil	1	Yes	Nil	Yes	Yes	Yes	2	1
Heated Swimming pools (hotels)	1	Yes	Nil	1	Yes	Nil	Nil	7	3
Sauna Baths	Yes	Yes	Yes	Yes	Yes	Yes	2	Yes	4
Bowling	Nil	Nil	Yes	Nil	Nil	Yes	Yes	2	Yes
Cinema	1	1	Yes	1	Yes	Yes	5	1	2
Kindergartens	Yes	Yes	10	1	Yes	Yes	3	2	Yes
Mountain Restaurants	10	10	22	3	2	2	4	6	9
Night Clubs with Bands	Nil	Nil	Yes	Nil	Yes	Nil	Yes	Nil	Nil
Discothèques	2	3	Yes	2	2	1	Yes	3	1

*See Portes du Soleil for Linked Resorts **Including Morzine

RESORT FACILITIES CHARTS

FRANCE

Name of Resort	Les Houches	Les Menuires	Megève	Méribel	Montgenèvre	Morzine*	St. Lary
Province	H. Savoie	Savoie	H. Savoie	Savoie	H. Alpes	Haute Savoie	H. Pyrénées
Tourist Office Director	J. Didier	Régine Jay-Grillot	A. Seigneur	J. M. Choffel	M. Perretta	M. Monné	Martine Gibert
Telephone/Fax Area Code	(450)	(479)	(450)	(479)	(492)	(450)	(562)
Telephone Number	55.50.62	00.73.00	21.27.28	08.60.01	21.52.52	74.72.72	39.50.81
Fax Number	55.51.71	00.75.06	93.03.09	00.59.61	21.92.45	79.03.48	39.50.06
Total Visitor Beds	9,300	23,000	12,746	34,668	8,000	18,000	18,800
Height of Resort	3,280 ft	6,086 ft	3,617 ft	4,756/5,576 ft	6,069 ft	3,281 ft	2,722/5,511 ft
Height of Top Station	6,455 ft	9,350 ft	6,630 ft	9,681 ft	8,326 ft	7,874 ft	7,955 ft
Mountain Railway	1	Nil	Nil	Nil	Nil	Nil	Nil
Cableways	1	Nil	2	Nil	Nil	2**	1
Gondolaways	1	8	5	16	2	3	1
Chair-lifts	3	19	13	16	7	22	9
Drag-lifts	12	18	22	18	16	28	22
Total Lift Capacity per Hour	16,000	50,886	50,625	62,000	22,500	55,147**	25,205
Ski School Instructors	52	160	180	250	80	110	60
Average sunshine hours - village area							
December	1	5	5½	5	7	5	4
January	2	6	6½	6	7	6	5
February	5	8	7½	8	7	7	5
March	8	9	8	8	10	8	8
April	8	10	9	9	10½	9	9½
Natural Skating Rinks	1	Nil	Nil	Nil	1	Nil	Nil
Artificial Skating Rinks	Nil	1	2	Yes	Nil	Yes	1
Curling Rinks	Nil	Nil	1	Nil	Nil	Yes	Nil
Ice Hockey	Yes	Nil	Yes	Yes	Yes	Yes	Nil
Tobogganing	Nil	Nil	Nil	Nil	Yes	Nil	Nil
Sleigh Rides	Nil	Nil	Yes	Nil	Nil	Nil	Nil
Riding	Nil	Nil	Nil	Nil	Yes	Nil	Nil
Sports Centre	Nil	Yes	Yes	Yes	Nil	Yes	Yes
Indoor Tennis	Nil	Nil	Yes	Nil	Nil	Nil	Yes
Hang-Gliding	Nil	Yes	Nil	Yes	Nil	Yes	Nil
Para-Gliding	Yes	Yes	Yes	Yes	Yes	Yes	Nil
Heated Swimming Pools (public)	Nil	2	Yes	1	Nil	Nil	Nil
Heated Swimming pools (hotels)	Yes	Nil	Yes	Yes	Nil	30	Nil
Sauna Baths	Yes	5	Yes	Yes	Yes	22	2
Bowling	Nil		Yes	Yes	Nil	1	Nil
Cinema	Nil	Yes	2	2	1	2	2
Kindergartens	Yes	3	3	2	1	Yes	1
Mountain Restaurants	3	17	30	10	Yes	16	3
Night Clubs with Bands	Nil	Nil	1	Yes	Nil	Nil	2
Discothèques	Nil	2	8	2	2	3	3

*See Portes du Soleil for linked resorts **Including Les Gets

FRANCE

Name of Resort	*St.Jean d'Aulps	Serre Chevalier	Tignes	Val d'Isère	Valfrejus	Valmorel	Valmorel Area	Val Thorens
Province	H. Savoie	H. Alpes	Savoie	Savoie	Savoie	Savoie		Savoie
Tourist Office Director	L. Lavanchy	R. Sanchis	J. P. Garnier	M. Giraudy	J-L. Ratel	Mme. M. Martin		F. Gros
Telephone/Fax Area Code	(450)	(492)	(479)	(479)	(479)	(479)		(479)
Telephone Number	79.65.09	24.98.98	06.15.55	06.06.60	05.33.83	09.85.55		00.08.08
Fax Number		24.98.84	06.45.44	06.04.56	05.13.67	09.85.29		00.00.04
Total Visitor Beds	2,160	30,000	28,000	26,408	3,500	8,513		21,000
Height of Resort	2,962 ft.	4,500 ft	6,825 ft	5,965 ft	5,083 ft	4,592 ft		7,544 ft
Height of Top Station	5,905 ft	9,100 ft	11,480 ft	10,676 ft	8,979 ft	7,884 ft		10,496 ft
Mountain Railway	Nil	Nil	2**	2**	Nil	Nil	Nil	Nil
Cableways	Nil	3	4	4	Nil	Nil	1	2
Gondolaways	1	6	6	6	2	1	2	3
Chair-lifts	3	16	49	49	4	9	12	17
Drag-lifts	12	47	41	41	6	22	36	9
Total Lift Capacity per Hour		70,500	135,000**	135,000**	15,140	29,170	41,725	51,970
Ski School Instructors	20	250	450	400	65	80		170
Average sunshine hours - village area								
December	4	4	3	4	4	3½		7
January	5	5	4	5	5½	5½		8
February	7	5	6	6	6	7		9
March	8	6	8	8	6½	7		9
April	9	7	9	9	7	8		10
Natural Skating Rinks	Nil	2	1	1	Nil	Nil		Nil
Artificial Skating Rinks	Nil	1	Yes	Nil	Nil	Nil		Nil
Curling Rinks	Nil	Nil	Nil	Nil	Nil	Nil		Nil
Ice Hockey	Nil	Nil	Nil	Yes	Nil	Nil		Nil
Tobogganing	Yes	Nil	Nil	Nil	Nil	Nil		Nil
Sleigh Rides	Nil	Yes	Yes	Nil	Nil	Nil		Nil
Riding	Nil	Yes	Yes	Nil	Nil	Nil		Nil
Sports Centre		Yes	Yes	Yes	Nil	Nil		Yes
Indoor Tennis		Nil	Yes	Nil	Nil	Nil		Yes
Hang-Gliding		Yes	Yes	Nil	Yes	Nil		Nil
Para-Gliding		Yes	Yes	Yes	Yes	Yes		Yes
Heated Swimming Pools (public)	Nil	1	Nil	1	Nil	Nil		Yes
Heated Swimming pools (hotels)	1	Yes	Yes	Yes	Nil	Nil		Yes
Sauna Baths	Nil	Yes	Yes	Yes	Nil	Yes		Yes
Bowling	Nil	Nil	Yes	Nil	Nil	Nil		Nil
Cinema	Nil	2	1	1	Nil	Yes		1
Kindergartens	Nil	3	1	Yes	Yes	Yes		Yes
Mountain Restaurants	2	11	6	13	3	6		11
Night Clubs with Bands	Nil	Yes	Nil	3	3	Nil		Yes
Discothèques	2	Yes	Yes	7	Nil	1		Yes

*See Portes du Soleil for linked resorts **Combined Tignes/Val d'Isère

RESORT FACILITIES CHARTS

ITALY

Name of Resort	Aprica	Arabba*	Bardonecchia	Bormio	Canazei/Campitello (Val di Fassa)	Caspoggio/ Chiesa	Cavalese Val di Fiemme	Cervinia
Province	Sondrio	Belluno	Torino	Sondrio	Bolzano	Sondrio	Trento	Aosta
Tourist Office Director	A. Negri	D. Lucia	R. Pelle		A. Weiss	B. Pedrolini	Dr. G. Travaglia	F. Maquignaz
Telephone/Fax Area Code	(0342)	(0436)	(0122)	(0342)	(0462)	(0342)	(0462)	(0166)
Telephone Number	746113	79130	99032	903300	602466	451150	241111	949086
Fax Number	747732	79300	980612	904696	602278	452505	230649	949731
Total Visitor Beds	6,500	2,010	1,808	6,443	50,000	2,500	29,000	5,700
Height of Resort	3,863 ft	5,254 ft	4,304 ft	4,018 ft	3,937ft	3,504 ft	3,300 ft	6,760 ft
Height of Top Station	8,448 ft	9,676 ft	9,022 ft	9,905 ft	8,878ft	7,072 ft	7,874 ft	11,500 ft
							Area	*Area*
Mountain Railway	Nil	Nil	Nil	Nil	Nil	Nil	Nil	2
Cableways	1	2	Nil	2	7	1	3	15
Gondolaways	1	2	Nil	1	5	Nil	2	7
Chair-lifts	4	10	9	7	27	4	25	15
Drag-lifts	18	13	15	6	19	4	22	34
Total Lift Capacity per Hour	15,000	30,000	22,000	14,400	98,531	10,450	63,000	75,400
Ski School Instructors	80	25	100	150	250	41	12	120
Average sunshine hours - village area								
December	3	3	7	4	3	5	6½	5
January	6	4	17	4-5	4	6	7	6
February	8	9½	7½	6-7	8	7	7½	7
March	9	10	8	8	9	8	8½	8
April		10	10	9	10	10	9	9½
Natural Skating Rinks	2	Yes	Yes	Nil	3	Yes	Yes	1
Artificial Skating Rinks	Nil	Nil	Nil	1	1	Nil	1	Nil
Curling Rinks	Nil	Nil	Nil	Nil	1	Nil	Nil	Nil
Ice Hockey	Nil	Yes	Nil	Yes	1	Nil	1	Yes
Tobogganing	Nil	Yes	Nil	Nil	Nil	Yes	Yes	Yes
Sleigh Rides	Nil	Nil	Nil	Yes	Yes	Yes	Nil	Nil
Riding	Yes	Nil	Nil	Yes	Nil	Nil	Nil	Yes
Sports Centre	Yes	Nil	Yes	Yes	Nil	Yes	Yes	Yes
Indoor Tennis	Nil	Nil	Yes	Yes	Nil	Nil	Yes	Nil
Hang-Gliding	Nil	Nil	Nil	Nil	Yes	Yes	Yes	Nil
Para-Gliding	Yes	Yes	Nil	Nil	Yes	Yes	Yes	Yes
Heated Swimming Pools (public)	1	Yes	Yes	Yes	Yes	1	Yes	2
Heated Swimming pools (hotels)	Nil	Yes	Nil	Yes	Yes	1	Yes	3
Sauna Baths	Yes	Yes	Yes	Yes	Yes	Yes	Yes	2
Bowling	Nil	Nil	Yes	Nil	Yes	Nil	Nil	Nil
Cinema	1	Nil	Yes	Yes	Yes	Nil	Yes	1
Kindergartens	Nil	Nil	Nil	Nil	Yes	Nil	Yes	Nil
Mountain Restaurants	3	11	10	7	50	Yes	14	15
Night Clubs with Bands	Nil	Nil	Nil	Yes	Yes	Nil	Nil	Nil
Discothèques	2	Nil	Yes	3	Yes	Yes	Yes	4

*Dolomiti Superski Pass available at supplementary charge covering 464 lifts in the area

ITALY

Name of Resort	Clavière	Champoluc/ Antagnod	Cortina*	Corvara/ Colfosco*	Courmayeur	Foppolo	Forni di Sopra	La Villa*
Province	Torino	Aosta	Belluno	Bolzano	Aosta	Bergamo	Udine	Bolzano
Tourist Office Director		O. Frachey	Dr. D. Gentile	Dr. D. Dapunt	Dr. C. Canepa	M. Marchesi		M. Canins
Telephone/Fax Area Code	(0122)	(0125)	(0436)	(0471)	(0165)	(0345)	(0433)	(0471)
Telephone Number	878856	307113	3231	836176	842060	74101	886767	847037
Fax Number	878888	307785	3235	836540	842072	74101	886686	847277
Total Visitor Beds	1,617	11,000	22,700	5,914	17,614	1,650	2,528	2,407
Height of Resort	5,774 ft	5,478 ft	4,018 ft	5,143/5,401 ft	4,015 ft	4,920 ft	2,975 ft	4,870 ft
Height of Top Station	6,676 ft	8,940 ft	10,543 ft	7,212 ft	9,843 ft	7,101 ft	6,761 ft	6,812 ft
Mountain Railway	Nil	Nil	Nil	Nil†	Nil	Nil	Nil	Nil
Cableways	Nil	Nil	6	2	7	Nil	Nil	2†
Gondolaways	Nil	1	Nil	1	2	Nil	Nil	1
Chair-lifts	4	11	23	22	8	3	4	22
Drag-lifts	8	5	10	32	9	10	3	32
Total Lift Capacity per Hour	12,000	21,200	45,057	65,800†	23,560	15,000	7,700	65,500†
Ski School Instructors	40	30	150	80	100	20	10	58
Average sunshine hours - village area								
December	6	5	6	4½	3	6	6	6
January	7	6	6½	5	4	7	7	7½
February	8	7	7½	6	6	6	8	8
March	9	8	8	7	8½	8	9½	8½
April	10	8	8½	8	10	9	10	9
Natural Skating Rinks	Yes	Nil	Yes	1	Nil	Yes	Nil	Yes
Artificial Skating Rinks	Nil	Yes	Yes	Yes	1	Nil	1	Nil
Curling Rinks	Nil	Nil	Yes	2	Yes	Nil	Nil	Yes
Ice Hockey	Nil	Nil	Yes	Yes	Yes	Yes	Yes	Yes
Tobogganing	Nil	Nil	Yes	Yes	Nil	Nil	Nil	Yes
Sleigh Rides	Nil	Nil	Nil	Yes	Nil	Nil	Nil	Yes
Riding	Nil	Nil	Yes	Yes	Yes	Nil	Yes	Yes
Sports Centre	Nil	Nil	Yes	Nil	Yes	Yes	Yes	Nil
Indoor Tennis	Nil	Nil	Yes	Yes	Yes	Nil	Yes	Yes
Hang-Gliding	Nil	Nil	Yes	Yes	Yes	Nil	Yes	Yes
Para-Gliding	Nil	Nil	Yes	Yes	Yes	Nil	Yes	Yes
Heated Swimming Pools (public)	Nil	Nil	Yes	Yes	Yes	Nil	1	Yes
Heated Swimming pools (hotels)	Nil	Nil	Yes	Yes	3	Nil	Nil	Yes
Sauna Baths	Nil	Yes	Yes	Yes	Yes	Nil	2	Yes
Bowling	Nil	Nil	Nil	2	Yes	Nil	Nil	Yes
Cinema	Nil	Nil	1	1	1	Yes	Nil	Nil
Kindergartens	Nil	Nil	Yes	Ski	Ski	Yes	Nil	Nil
Mountain Restaurants	4	6	20	11	21	10	3	3
Night Clubs with Bands	Nil	Nil	2	2	Nil	Nil	Nil	Yes
Discothèques	1	2	9	4	3	3	1	Nil

*Dolomiti Superski Pass available at supplementary charge covering over 464 lifts in the area

†Alta Badia area lifts

RESORT FACILITIES CHARTS

ITALY

Name of Resort	La Thuile	Limone	Livigno	Macugnaga	Madesimo	Madonna di Campiglio	Malga Ciapella* (Marmolada)	Mera
Province	Aosta	Cueno	Sondrio	Novara	Sondrio	Trento	Belluno	Vercelli
Tourist Office Director	Dr. C. Canepa	P. Grosso	P. Bormorini	R. Pirazzi	F. Fontana	Gastone Rossi	D.Gentile	
Telephone/Fax Area Code	(0165)	(0171)	(0342)	(0324)	(0343)	(0465)	(0437)	(0163)
Telephone Number	884179	92101	996379	65119	53015	442000	721319	78024
Fax Number	885196	927064	996881	65119	53782	440404	721319	
Total Visitor Beds	3,080	16,821	8,334	3,080	7,250	26,700	2,046	700
Height of Resort	4,757ft.	3,300ft	5,958ft	4,352ft	5,085ft	5,084ft	4,743ft	2,200/4,900ft
Height of Top Station	8,667ft.	7,054ft	9,184ft	9,000ft	9,461ft	8,640ft	10,712ft	5,900ft
Mountain Railway	Nil	Nil	Nil	Nil	Nil	Nil	Nil	Nil
Cableways	Nil	Nil	Nil	2	2	1	2	
Gondolaways	1	Nil	3	Nil	Nil	4	Nil	Nil
Chair-lifts	14	6	11	2	7	15	2	1
Drag-lifts	18	25	16	9	7	10	5	7
Total Lift Capacity per Hour	36,570**	22,000	42,000	7,924	17,486	28,500	6,741	5,500
Ski School Instructors	28	80	50	30	55	160	13	15
Average sunshine hours - village area								
December	4	5	7½	4	4½	6½	6	8
January	6	6	8	5	5½	7	6½	8
February	7	7	8	8	7	7½	7	9
March	8	8	9	9	9	8¼	8	10
April	9	9	10	9	10	9	9	11
Natural Skating Rinks	Nil	Nil	Yes	2	1	Yes	Nil	Yes
Artificial Skating Rinks	1	1	Nil	Nil	Nil	Nil	Nil	
Curling Rinks	Nil	Nil	Nil	Nil	Yes	Nil	Nil	Nil
Ice Hockey	Nil	Nil	Yes	1	Yes	Nil	Nil	Nil
Tobogganing	Nil	Nil	Nil	Nil	Yes	Nil	Nil	Yes
Sleigh Rides	Nil	Nil	Yes	Nil	Nil	Nil	Nil	Nil
Riding	Nil	Nil	Yes	Nil	Nil	Nil	Yes	Nil
Sports Centre	Yes	Nil	Nil	Nil	Yes	Yes	Nil	Nil
Indoor Tennis	Nil	Nil	Nil	Nil	Nil	Nil	Nil	Nil
Hang-Gliding	Nil	Nil	Nil	Yes	Nil	Nil	Nil	Nil
Para-Gliding	Nil	Yes	Yes	Yes	Nil	Yes	Yes	Nil
Heated Swimming Pools (public)	Yes	Nil	Nil	Nil	Nil	1	Yes	Nil
Heated Swimming pools (hotels)	Nil	2	Yes	Nil	2	4	Yes	Nil
Sauna Baths	Yes	Yes	Yes	Nil	2	Yes	Yes	Yes
Bowling	Nil	Nil	Nil	Nil	Nil	Nil	Nil	Nil
Cinema	Nil	1	Yes	Nil	Yes	Yes	Nil	Nil
Kindergartens	Nil	Nil	Nil	Nil	Nil	Nil	Nil	
Mountain Restaurants	5	5	5	5	3	13	Yes	3
Night Clubs with Bands	Nil	Nil	Nil	Nil	Nil	Nil	Nil	Nil
Discothèques	1	4	Yes	2	Yes	5	Nil	3

*Dolomiti Superski Pass available at supplementary charge covering over 464 lifts in the area **including La Toussuire

ITALY

Name of Resort	Passo Tonale	Pedraces	Piancavallo	Pila	S. Cassiano*	S. Caterina	S. Martino di Castrozza
Province	Trento	Bolzano	Pordenone	Aosta	Bolzano	Sondrio	Trento
Tourist Office Director	A. Gregori	M. Canins	Sr. Predieri		M. Canins	G. Confortola	
Telephone/Fax Area Code	(0364)	(0471)	(0434)	((0615)	(0471)	(0342)	(0439)
Telephone Number	903838	839695	655191	521148	847037	935598	768867
Fax Number	903895	847277	655354	521437	847277	935598	768814
Total Visitor Beds	6,100	1,570	7,800	2,810	3,502	1,900	9,170
Height of Resort	6,168ft	4,264ft	4,500/5,800ft	4,343ft	5,159ft	5,967ft	4,920ft
Height of Top Station	9,895ft	6,703ft	6,562ft	8,660ft	6,570ft	9,135ft	9,053ft
Mountain Railway	Nil	Nil	Nil	Nil	Nil	Nil	Nil
Cableways	1	2†	Nil	1	2†	Nil	1
Gondolaways	Nil	1	Nil	1	1	Nil	1
Chair-lifts	14	22	3	9	22	1	13
Drag-lifts	14	32	13	2	32	7	9
Total Lift Capacity per Hour	30,000	65,800†	11,000	16,300	65,800†	7,065	24,000
Ski School Instructors	70	10	20	70	65	80	100
Average sunshine hours - village area							
December	5	6	7	6	5	3½	5
January	6	6½	7	7	7	4-5	6
February	7	7	8	8	8	6	7
March	8	8	8½	9	9	7	8
April	9	8	8½	11½		8	9
Natural Skating Rinks	1	1	Nil	Yes	Yes	Yes	1
Artificial Skating Rinks	Nil	Nil	1	Aosta	Yes	Nil	Nil
Curling Rinks	Nil	Yes	Yes	Nil	Yes	Nil	Nil
Ice Hockey	Nil	Yes	Yes	Nil	Yes	Nil	Nil
Tobogganing	Yes	Yes	Nil	Yes	Yes	Nil	Nil
Sleigh Rides	Yes	Yes	Nil	Nil	Yes	Nil	Yes
Riding	Nil	Yes	Nil	Aosta	Yes	Yes	Yes
Sports Centre	Nil	Nil	Nil		Yes	Yes	Nil
Indoor Tennis	Nil	Yes	Nil		Yes	Nil	Nil
Hang-Gliding	Nil	Yes	Nil		Yes	Nil	Yes
Para-Gliding	Nil	Yes	Nil	Nil	Yes	Nil	Yes
Heated Swimming Pools (public)	Nil	Nil	Nil	Aosta	Yes	Nil	1
Heated Swimming pools (hotels)	2	Yes	Nil	1	1	1	Yes
Sauna Baths	2	Yes	Nil	2	3	Yes	5
Bowling	Nil	Nil	Nil	Nil	2	Nil	1
Cinema	Nil	Nil	Nil	Aosta	Nil	Nil	1
Kindergartens	Nil	Nil	Ski	Yes	Yes	1	Nil
Mountain Restaurants	4	Yes	4	5	Yes	3	11
Night Clubs with Bands	Nil	Yes	Nil	Aosta	1	Yes	Nil
Discothèques	1	Nil	2	4 + Aosta	Yes	Yes	1

*Dolomiti Superski Pass available at supplementary charge covering over 464 lifts in the area †Alta Badia area lifts

RESORT FACILITIES CHARTS

ITALY

Name of Resort	Sansicario	S. Vigilio di Marebbe	Sauze d'Oulx	Sella Nevea	Selva* Val Gardena	Sestriere
Province	Torino	Bolzano	Torino	Udine	Bolzano	Torino
Tourist Office Director		Franz	R. Pelle	L. Lazzaro	Dr. R. Mussner	R. Pelle
Telephone/Fax Area Code	(0122)	(0474)	(0122)	(0433)	(0471)	(0122)
Telephone Number	811175	501037	858009	54026	792277	755444
Fax Number	811315	501566	850497	54005	792235	755171
Total Visitor Beds	690	3,184	4,333	2,650	5,400	16,839
Height of Resort	5,576ft	3,939ft	4,950ft	3,773ft	5,128ft	6,666ft
Height of Top Station	8,826ft	7,461ft	8,145ft	5,793ft	8,264ft	9,175ft
Mountain Railway	Nil	Nil	Nil	Nil	Nil	Nil
Cableways	Nil	Nil	Nil	1	4	Nil
Gondolaways	Nil	12	Nil	Nil	4	1
Chair-lifts	1	8	9	Nil	27	4
Drag-lifts	9	11	16	7	42	24
Total Lift Capacity per Hour		49,000	18,197	5,040	79,523	23,000
Ski School Instructors		50	130	30	100	100
Average sunshine hours - village area						
December	6	6	6½	3	4	8
January	7	6½	7	3½	5	8½
February	8	7	8	4-5	7	9½
March	9	8	9	6-7	8	10½
April	10	8½	10	7-10	8-10	12
Natural Skating Rinks	Nil	1	Nil	1	Yes	Yes
Artificial Skating Rinks	Nil	Nil	Yes	Nil	1	Nil
Curling Rinks	Nil	Nil	Nil	Nil	Yes	Nil
Ice Hockey	Nil	Nil	Nil	Nil	Yes	Nil
Tobogganing	Nil	Nil	Nil	Yes	Yes	Nil
Sleigh Rides	Nil	Nil	Nil	Nil	Yes	Nil
Riding	Nil	Nil	Nil	Nil	Yes	Nil
Sports Centre	Yes	Nil	Nil	Yes	Yes	Yes
Indoor Tennis	Yes	Nil	Nil	Nil	Yes	Yes
Hang-Gliding	Nil	Nil	Nil	Nil	Yes	Nil
Para-Gliding	Nil	Nil	Nil	Nil	Yes	Yes
Heated Swimming Pools (public)	1	1	Nil	Nil	Nil	Nil
Heated Swimming pools (hotels)	Nil	4	2	Yes	3	1
Sauna Baths	1	3	1	1	Yes	2
Bowling	Nil	1	1	Nil	3	Nil
Cinema	1	Nil	1	Nil	Nil	1
Kindergartens	1	1	Yes	Nil	Yes	Nil
Mountain Restaurants	4	12	11	3	Yes	6
Night Clubs with Bands	Nil	Nil	Yes	Nil	Yes	2
Discothèques	Yes	1	4	2	4	1

*Dolomiti Superski Pass available at supplementary charge covering over 464 lifts in the area

SWITZERLAND

Name of Resort	Adelboden	Andermatt	Anzère	Arosa	Barboleusaz/ Gryon	Braunwald	Champéry*	Chateaud'Oex
Province	B. Oberland	Uri	Valais	Grison	Vaud	Glarus	Valais	Vaud
Tourist Office Director	R. Lymann	Estner Imnasty	A. Gollut	M. Vincenz	M-P. Praz	B. A. Brunner	E. Caballero	P. Sublet
Telephone/Fax Area Code	(033)	(041)	(027)	(081)	(024)	(055)	(024)	(026)
Telephone Number	6738080	8720450	3992800	3775151	4981422	6431108	4792020	9242525
Fax Number	6738092	8720451	3992805	3773135	4982622	6432574	4792021	9242526
Total Visitor Beds	8,900	1,300	7,312	7,550	2,123	1,360	6,761	4,100
Height of Resort	4,438ft	4,738ft	4,920ft	6,000ft	3,970ft	4,264ft	3,450ft	3,280ft
Height of Top Station	7,644ft	9,842ft	7,937ft	8,658ft	6,626ft	6,232ft	7,400ft	5,741ft
Mountain Railway	Nil	1	Nil	Nil	1**	1	1	1
Cableways	1	2	Nil	2	Nil	Nil	1	1
Gondolaways	3	Nil	1	1	2	4	1	Nil
Chair-lifts	4	4	3	7	5	3	6	2
Drag-lifts	20	6	8	6	15	Nil	11	13
Total Lift Capacity per Hour	27,350	11,250	9,220	21,700	25,000**	5,650	15,000	9,870
Ski School Instructors	50	40	40	150	20	40	30	40
Average sunshine hours - village area								
December	6	4	7	6	6	6	4	4
January	6½	4½	7	6½	8	7	5	6
February	7½	5	8	8	9	8	6	6
March	8½	6	9	10	10	9	7½	7½
April	9	7	11	11½	12	9-10	9	9
Natural Skating Rinks	Nil	1	Nil	2	Nil	Yes	Nil	Nil
Artificial Skating Rinks	1	Nil	1	2	Nil	Nil	1	Yes
Curling Rinks	Yes	Yes	1	3	Nil	Nil	1	Yes
Ice Hockey	Yes	Nil	Yes	Yes	Nil	Nil	Yes	Yes
Tobogganing	Yes	Nil	Nil	Yes	Nil	Nil	Yes	Nil
Sleigh Rides	Yes	Yes	Yes	Yes	Nil	Yes	Nil	Yes
Riding	Yes	Nil	Nil	Nil	Nil	Nil	Yes	Yes
Sports Centre	Yes	Nil	Nil	Yes	Nil	Nil	Yes	Yes
Indoor Tennis	Nil	Nil	Nil	Yes	Nil	Nil	Yes	Nil
Hang-Gliding	Yes	Yes	Yes	Yes	Nil	Yes	Nil	Yes
Para-Gliding	Yes	Yes	Yes	Yes	Yes	Nil	Yes	Yes
Heated Swimming Pools (public)	Nil	Nil	1	Yes	Nil	1	Yes	Nil
Heated Swimming pools (hotels)	2	Yes	Nil	7	Nil	2	Nil	Yes
Sauna Baths	6	4	4	Yes	Nil	3	Yes	Yes
Bowling	Nil	Nil	Nil	2	Nil	1	Nil	Nil
Cinema	1	Nil	Nil	1	Nil	1	Nil	Yes
Kindergartens	1	Ski	Yes	3	Yes	Nil	Yes	Yes
Mountain Restaurants	9	4	3	6	Yes	5	5	3
Night Clubs with Bands	2	Nil	Nil	Yes	Nil	Nil	2	Yes
Discothèques	3	2	3	Yes	Nil	Nil	2	Yes

*See Portes du Soleil for linked resorts **including Villars

RESORT FACILITIES CHARTS

SWITZERLAND

Name of Resort	Davos	Engelberg	Flims/Laax	Flumserberg	Grächen	Grindelwald	Gstaad-Saanenland	Haute-Nendaz Siviez
Province	Grison	Obwalden	Grison	St. Gallen	Valais	B. Oberland	B. Oberland	Valais
Tourist Office Director	Bruno Gerber	F. Miller	U. Barandun	M. Manhart	F. Miller	J. Luggen	D. von Weissenfluh	P. O. Bourban
Telephone/Fax Area Code	(081)	(041)	(081)	(081)	(027)	(033)	(033)	(027)
Telephone Number	4152121	6373737	9209200	7201818	9562727	8541212	7488181	2895589
Fax Number	4152100	6374156	9209201	7201819	9561110	8541210	7488183	2895583
Total Visitor Beds	19,598	5,900	9,813	7,200	6,800	8,900	12,300	16,763
Height of Resort	5,118ft	3,444ft	3,615ft	3,287ft	5,313ft	3,393ft	3,308ft	4,478ft
Height of Top Station	9,262ft	9,906ft	9,902ft	7,287ft	9,528ft	8,157ft	6,461ft	10,916ft
Mountain Railway	3**	1	Nil	Nil	Nil	8***	Nil	Nil
Cableways	10	4	4	2	Nil	5	5	7*
Gondolaways	5	3	3	2	2	2	12	12
Chair-lifts	4	5	11	10	3	12	16	34
Drag-lifts	34	10	14	4	9	23	41	47
Total Lift Capacity per Hour	55,000**	25,000	41,200	21,125	11,400	39,350***	50,000	72,448*
Ski School Instructors	200	100	150	70	40	100	250	180
Average sunshine hours - village area								
December	5½	2	7	6	3	4	5	5
January	6	3	8	6	4	4	6	5
February	7	4	9	8	6	9	6-7	7
March	9	5	10	9	7½	10	7	8
April	11	6-7	11	10	8	10	8	8
Natural Skating Rinks	1	1	Yes	2	1	1	3	Nil
Artificial Skating Rinks	1	1	Yes	Nil	Yes	1	1	1
Curling Rinks	12	3	Yes	Yes	Yes	4	4	1
Ice Hockey	Yes	1	1	Yes	Yes	Yes	Nil	Yes
Tobogganing	Yes	Yes	Yes	Yes	Nil	Yes	Yes	Yes
Sleigh Rides	Yes	Yes	Yes	Nil	Yes	Nil	Yes	Nil
Riding	Yes	Nil	Yes	Nil	Yes	Nil	Yes	Nil
Sports Centre	Yes	Yes	Yes	Nil	Yes	Yes	Yes	Yes
Indoor Tennis	Yes	Yes	Yes	Nil	Yes	Nil	Yes	Nil
Hang-Gliding	Yes	Yes	Yes	Yes	Yes	Yes	Yes	Nil
Para-Gliding	Yes	Yes	Yes	Yes	Yes	Yes	Nil	Yes
Heated Swimming Pools (public)	Yes	2	Yes	Nil	Nil	1	1	Nil
Heated Swimming pools (hotels)	16	4	Yes	Nil	2	4	7	Nil
Sauna Baths	10	7	Yes	2	3	8	Yes	Yes
Bowling	Nil	Nil	Nil	Yes	Nil	Yes	Yes	Nil
Cinema	1	1	Nil	Nil	Nil	1	1	Nil
Kindergartens	1	2	Yes	Nil	Yes	Yes	Ski	Yes
Mountain Restaurants	25	11	13	6	3	20***	24	25*
Night Clubs with Bands	Yes	Nil	Yes	Yes	Nil	Yes	Yes	Yes
Discothèques	Yes	2	Yes	Yes	1	Yes	Yes	4

*Total lifts in 4 valleys **including Klosters ***including Wengen and Mürren

SWITZERLAND

Name of Resort	Klosters	Lenzerheide/ Valbella	Les Diablerets	Les Mosses	Leysin	Mayens-de-Riddes	Montana/ Crans
Province	Grisons	Grison	Vaud	Vaud	Vaud	Valais	Valais
Tourist Office Director	M. Accola	W. Ziltener	J. F. Morerod	J. J. Derron	A. Fricker	P. Gaillard	W. Loser
Telephone/Fax Area Code	(081)	(081)	(024)	(024)	(024)	(027)	(027)
Telephone Number	4102020	3843434	4923358	4911466	4942244	3061851	4850404
Fax Number	4102010	3845383	4922348	4911024	494616	3066493	4850460
Total Visitor Beds	8,400	6,760	5,000	3,050	6,934	5,625	39,500
Height of Resort	3,980ft	5,052ft	3,936ft	4,756ft	4,134ft	4,921ft	4,920ft
Height of Top Station	9,262ft	9,397ft	9,840ft	7,708ft	7,218ft	10,916ft	9,840ft
Mountain Railway	3†	Nil	Nil	Nil	Nil	Nil	1
Cableways	10	2	4	Nil	Nil	7*	2
Gondolaways	5	1	2	Nil	2	12	5
Chair-lifts	4	9	4	Nil	7	34	8
Drag-lifts	34	27	15	12	10	47	28
Total Lift Capacity per Hour	55,000†	32,350	16,200	10,500	13,420	72,448*	41,000
Ski School Instructors	100-200	100	24	15	60	25	150
Average sunshine hours - village area							
December	5	6	3	6	5	6	7
January	6	6½	4	6	6	7	8
February	8	7	6	7	8	8	9
March	10	8	8	8	8	9	11
April	11	8½	10	9	8	10	11
Natural Skating Rinks	Yes	1	Yes	1	Nil	1	2
Artificial Skating Rinks	Yes	1	1	Nil	1	Nil	1
Curling Rinks	4	12	4	Nil	2	Nil	5
Ice Hockey	1	Yes	Yes	Nil	Yes	Nil	Yes
Tobogganing	Yes	Yes	Yes	Nil	Nil	Yes	Yes
Sleigh Rides	Yes	Nil	Yes	Nil	Yes	Yes	Yes
Riding	Nil	Nil	Nil	Nil	Yes	Nil	Yes
Sports Centre	Nil	Yes	Nil	Nil	Yes	Nil	Yes
Indoor Tennis	Nil	Yes	Nil	Nil	Yes	Nil	Yes
Hang-Gliding	Yes	Yes	Yes	Nil	Yes	Nil	Yes
Para-Gliding	Yes	Yes	Yes	Nil	Yes	Yes	Yes
Heated Swimming Pools (public)	Nil	1	Nil	Nil	Yes	1	Yes
Heated Swimming pools (hotels)	7	7	Yes	Nil	Yes	Nil	6
Sauna Baths	6	6	Yes	Nil	3	1	Yes
Bowling	3	Yes	Nil	Nil	Nil	Nil	1
Cinema	Nil	1	Nil	Nil	1	Nil	1
Kindergartens	2	3	Yes	Nil	Nil	Yes	4
Mountain Restaurants	11	17	6	5	4	25*	10
Night Clubs with Bands	Nil	3	Nil	Nil	1	Nil	Nil
Discothèques	4	3	Yes	1	2	Nil	10

*Total lifts in 4 valleys †including Davos

RESORT FACILITIES CHARTS

SWITZERLAND

Name of Resort	Morgins*	Mürren	Pizol (Bad Ragaz & Wangs)	Pontresina	Rougemont	Saas Fee	St. Moritz	San Bernardino
Province	Valais	B. Oberland	St. Gallen	Grisons	Vaud	Valais	Grisons	Grison
Tourist Office Director	S. Monay	P. Lehner	D. Simmen	M. Lergier	P. Bovay	Frank Bumann	H. Danuser	G. Trippolini
Telephone/Fax Area Code	(024)	(033)	(081)	(081)	(026)	(027)	(081)	(092)
Telephone Number	4772361	8568686	3021061	8388300	9258333	9571457	8373333	941214
Fax Number	4773708	8568696	3026290	8388310	9258967	9571860	8373366	941155
Total Visitor Beds	6,695	2,000	2,364	5,200	2,170	7,200	12,575	1,800
Height of Resort	4,593ft	5,362ft	1,686/1,755ft	5,972ft	3,175ft	5,905ft	6,088ft	5,249ft
Height of Top Station	6,896ft	9,652ft	7,306ft	9,827ft	7,399ft	11,811ft	10,837ft	8,283ft
Mountain Railway	Nil	8††	Nil	3†	1	1	3†	Nil
Cableways	Nil	5	Nil	7	Nil	4	7	Nil
Gondolaways	Nil	2	4	1	1	3	1	1
Chair-lifts	3	12	Nil	13	2	2	13	1
Drag-lifts	15	23	7	34	1	18	34	4
Total Lift Capacity per Hour	17,790	39,350††	3,200	65,000†	800	26,410	65,000†	5,600
Ski School Instructors	40	30	12	65	10	80	180	50
Average sunshine hours - village area								
December	4	4	7	$6\frac{1}{4}$	6	4	6	5
January	5	4	$7\frac{1}{2}$	$7\frac{3}{4}$	7	5	6-7	5
February	$6\frac{1}{2}$	5	$7\frac{1}{2}$	7	$7\frac{1}{2}$	7	7-8	6
March	8-9	6	8	$9\frac{3}{4}$	8	8	9	6
April	9	6	$8\frac{1}{2}$	11	9	9	10	7
Natural Skating Rinks	Yes	Nil	Yes	Yes	Nil	Yes	5	1
Artificial Skating Rinks	Nil	Yes	Nil	Nil	Nil	Nil	1	Nil
Curling Rinks	Yes	Yes	Nil	Yes	Nil	Yes	Yes	1
Ice Hockey	Yes	Yes	Nil	Yes	Nil	Yes	Yes	Yes
Tobogganing	Nil	Yes	Yes	Nil	Nil	Yes	Yes	Nil
Sleigh Rides	Yes	Nil	Yes	Yes	Nil	Nil	Yes	Nil
Riding	Yes	Nil	Yes	Nil	Nil	Nil	Yes	Nil
Sports Centre	Yes	Yes	Nil	Yes	Nil	Yes	Yes	Nil
Indoor Tennis	Yes	Yes	Yes	Nil	Nil	Yes	Yes	Nil
Hang-Gliding	Nil	Yes	Yes	Yes	Yes	Yes	Yes	Yes
Para-Gliding	Yes	Yes	Yes	Yes	Yes	Yes	Yes	Yes
Heated Swimming Pools (public)	Nil	1	Yes	1	Nil	Yes	1	1
Heated Swimming pools (hotels)	Yes	1	Yes	4	1	7	10	Yes
Sauna Baths	1	3	7	Yes	1	3	18	Yes
Bowling	Nil	Nil	Nil	1	Nil	Nil	Nil	Yes
Cinema	Nil	Nil	Nil	1	Nil	Yes	1	Nil
Kindergartens	Yes	1	Yes	1	Nil	Yes	3	Nil
Mountain Restaurants	4	7	Yes	11	Yes	10	12	Yes
Night Clubs with Bands	Yes	Nil	Nil	Yes	Nil	Yes	Yes	1
Discothèques	1	3	Nil	Yes	1	Yes	5	1

*See Portes du Soleil †combined Pontresina-St. Moritz ††including Grindelwald and Wengen

SWITZERLAND

Name of Resort	Verbier	Veysonnaz	Villars	Wengen	Wildhaus	Zermatt	Malbun (Liechtenstein)
Province	Valais	Valais	Vaud	B. Oberland	St. Gallen	Valais	
Tourist Office Director	P. Messeiller	H.B. Fragnière	E. Fassbind	J. Brunner	C. Sutter	Amadé Perrig	Ursula Schlegel
Telephone/Fax Area Code	(027)	(027)	(024)	(033)	(071)	(027)	(075)
Telephone Number	7753888	2071053	4953232	8551414	9999911	9670181	2636577
Fax Number	7753898	2071409	4952794	8553060	9992929	9670185	2637344
Total Visitor Beds	25,000	3,650	10,000	7,400	2,500	13,500	1,150
Height of Resort	4,921ft	4,045ft	4,264ft	4,187ft	3,395ft	5,315ft	5,248ft
Height of Top Station	10,916ft	10,916ft	7,216ft	8,157ft	7,413ft	12,778ft *Area*	6,560ft
Mountain Railway	Nil	Nil	1**	8†	1	2	Nil
Cableways	7*	7*	Nil	5	1	15	Nil
Gondolaways	12	12	2	2	Nil	7	Nil
Chair-lifts	34	34	5	12	3	15	2
Drag-lifts	47	47	15	23	14	34	5
Total Lift Capacity per Hour	72,448*	72,448*	25,000**	39,350†	18,000	75,400	6,620
Ski School Instructors	170	20	75	40-60	60	175	15
Average sunshine hours - village area							
December	$6\frac{1}{2}$	6	7	4	5	$3\frac{1}{2}$	5
January	$7\frac{1}{2}$	7	8	$5\frac{1}{2}$	$6\frac{1}{2}$	4	$5\frac{1}{2}$
February	$8\frac{1}{2}$	8	9	7	$7\frac{1}{2}$	$6\frac{1}{2}$	6
March	$9\frac{1}{2}$	9	$9\frac{1}{2}$	8	8	8	$6\frac{1}{2}$
April	11	10	10	9	9	9	7
Natural Skating Rinks	Nil	Nil	Nil	1	Yes	2	1
Artificial Skating Rinks	1	Nil	Yes	1	Yes	1	Nil
Curling Rinks	Yes	Nil	Nil	10	4	12	Nil
Ice Hockey	1	Yes	Yes	Yes	Nil	Yes	Nil
Tobogganing	Yes	Nil	Nil	Yes	Yes	Nil	Yes
Sleigh Rides	Nil	Nil	Nil	Nil	Yes	Nil	Nil
Riding	Yes	Nil	Yes	Nil	Yes	Yes	Nil
Sports Centre	Yes	Yes	Yes	Nil	Yes	Nil	Nil
Indoor Tennis	Nil	Nil	Yes	Nil	Yes	Yes	Nil
Hang-Gliding	Yes	Nil	Nil	Yes	Yes	Nil	Yes
Para-Gliding	Yes	Nil	Yes	Yes	Yes	Yes	Yes
Heated Swimming Pools (public)	2	1	Yes	Yes	2	Yes	Nil
Heated Swimming pools (hotels)	Yes	Nil	Yes	Yes	2	16	4
Sauna Baths	Yes	1	Yes	2	8	20	3
Bowling	Nil	Nil	1	Yes	Yes	1	Nil
Cinema	1	Nil	1	1	Nil	1	Nil
Kindergartens	Yes	Ski	Yes	Yes	Yes	Yes	Yes
Mountain Restaurants	25*	25*	8	20†	6	35	1
Night Clubs with Bands	Yes	Nil	Nil	Nil	2	7	Nil
Discothèques	4	2	2	3	2	4	1

*Total lifts in 4 valleys **including Barboleusaz †including Grindelwald and Mürren

RESORT FACILITIES CHARTS

GERMANY

Name of Resort	Bayerischzell	Berchtes-gadener Land	Garmisch-Partenkirchen	Mittenwald	Oberammergau	Oberstaufen	Oberstdorf	Reit im Winkl
Province	Oberbayern	Bayern	Bavaria	Oberbayern	Bavaria	Oberallgäm	Bayern	Oberbayern
Tourist Office Director	K. Sterr	E. Wittmann	P. Maninger	E. Eichhorn	Angela Karl	F. Haüg	M. Schmidl	H. Schuster
Telephone/Fax Area Code	(08023)	(08652)	(08821)	(08823)	(08822)	(08386)	(08322)	(08640)
Telephone Number	648	9670	180-6	33981	1021	93000	700-0	80020
Fax Number	1034	63300	180-755	3355	7325	930020	700236	80029
Total Visitor Beds	2,250	3,050	8,957	6,700	1,601	5,573	6,325	5,000
Height of Resort	2,630ft	1,837ft	2,362ft	3,018ft	2,624ft	2,808ft	2,756ft	2,296ft
Height of Top Station	6,562ft	5,905ft	9,730ft	7,362ft	5,524ft	5,577ft	7,362ft	6,069ft
Mountain Railway	1	Nil	1	Nil	Nil	Nil	Nil	Nil
Cableways	Nil	2	4	Nil	1	Nil	5	Nil
Gondolaways	1	2	8	1	Nil	1	1	Nil
Chair-lifts	2	2	4	1	1	2	5	6
Drag-lifts	22	27	27	7	7	30	17	16
Total Lift Capacity per Hour	23,000	19,600	52,000	6,600	8,120	18,000	22,750	25,000
Ski School Instructors	60	60	200	120	30	100	200	40
Average sunshine hours - village area								
December		4	6	5	3	6	5½	5
January		5	6	5	4½	7	6	5
February		6½	9	6	5½	8	7½	7
March		9	11	7	6½	9	9	9
April		10	11½	9	9½	10	10	10
Natural Skating Rinks	1	4	Yes	Nil	1	Nil	Yes	Nil
Artificial Skating Rinks	Nil	Nil	Yes	Yes	Nil	Yes	Yes	Nil
Curling Rinks	Nil	1	Yes	Yes	Nil	Yes	Yes	Yes
Ice Hockey	Nil	1	Yes	Yes	Nil	Yes	Yes	Nil
Tobogganing	Nil	5	Nil	Yes	Nil	Yes	Yes	Yes
Sleigh Rides	Yes	Yes	Nil	Yes	Nil	Yes	Yes	Yes
Riding	Yes	Yes	Yes	Yes	Nil	Yes	Yes	Nil
Sports Centre	Nil	Yes	Yes	Yes	Yes	Yes	Yes	Nil
Indoor Tennis	Nil	Yes	Yes	Yes	Yes	Yes	Yes	Yes
Hang-Gliding	Yes	Yes	Yes	Yes	Yes	Yes	Yes	Nil
Para-Gliding	Yes	Yes	Yes	Yes	Yes	Yes	Yes	Nil
Heated Swimming Pools (public)	Nil	Yes	2	Nil	1	Yes	Yes	3
Heated Swimming pools (hotels)	Yes	Yes	16	8	1	Yes	36	11
Sauna Baths	Yes	2	19	5	2	12	5	2
Bowling	2	3	Yes	Yes	Yes	1	Yes	2
Cinema	Yes	2	Yes	2	Nil	Yes	1	Nil
Kindergartens	Yes	Yes	Yes	1	1	Nil	Nil	Nil
Mountain Restaurants	12	20	11	11	5	5	6	14
Night Clubs with Bands	Nil	Nil	Yes	4	Nil	Yes	Yes	2
Discothèques	Yes	3	5	3	1	5	4	1

NORWAY / ROMANIA

Name of Resort	Geilo	Hemsedal	Lillehammer	Voss	Poiana Brasov	Predeal	Sinaia
Province				Brasov	Brasov	Prahova	
Tourist Office Director	E.T. Bere	E. Eliassen	Hafjell Alpine Centre	B. Christensen	Silviu Coman		
Telephone/Fax Area Code	(320)	(320)	(061)	(56)	(0040)		
Telephone Number	91300	60156	277078	510051	68 262 389		
Fax Number	91850	60537	277008	511715	68 150 504		
Total Visitor Beds	2,694	2,065	3,580	1,380	2,423	2,359	3,130
Height of Resort	2,610ft	2,132ft	656ft	285ft	3,345ft	3,427ft	2,624t
Height of Top Station	3,500ft	4,921ft	3,412ft	2,952	5,844ft	4,821ft	6,560ft
Mountain Railway	Nil	Nil	Nil	Nil	Nil	Nil	Nil
Cableways	Nil	Nil	Nil	1	2	Nil	4
Gondolaways	Nil	Nil	Nil	Nil	1	Nil	Nil
Chair-lifts	4	5	3	4	Nil	Nil	1
Drag-lifts	14	11	6	4	7	7	1
Total Lift Capacity per Hour	21,000	24,200	11,500	8,500	6,600	2,000	-
Ski School Instructors	25	15	8	15	150	32	24
Average sunshine hours - village area							
December	5	4½	5	4	5	5	5
January	6	5	7	4½	5	6	6
February	9	8	9	7	6	7	6½
March	10	9	11	8	7	7	7
April	11	11	12	10	7	9	1
Natural Skating Rinks	Yes	Nil	Yes	Nil	Nil	1	2
Artificial Skating Rinks	Yes	Nil	Yes	Nil	1	Nil	Nil
Curling Rinks	Nil	Nil	Yes	Nil	Yes	Nil	Nil
Ice Hockey	Nil	Nil	Yes	Nil	1	Nil	Nil
Tobogganing	Nil	Nil	Nil	Yes	Yes	Nil	
Sleigh Rides	Yes	Yes	Yes	Yes	Yes	Yes	Yes
Riding	Yes	Yes	Yes	Nil	Yes	Nil	Nil
Sports Centre	Yes	Yes	Yes	Yes	Yes		Yes
Indoor Tennis	Nil	Nil	Yes	Nil	Nil		Nil
Hang-Gliding	Nil	Nil	Nil	Yes	Nil		Nil
Para-Gliding	Nil	Yes	Yes	Yes	Nil		Nil
Heated Swimming Pools (public)	1	Nil	Yes	Yes	2	Nil	Nil
Heated Swimming pools (hotels)	7	1	Yes	Yes	1	1	2
Sauna Baths	10	4	Yes	7	3	1	3
Bowling	Nil	Nil	Nil	Yes	Yes	1	Nil
Cinema	1	Nil	1	1	1	Yes	1
Kindergartens	3	Yes	Yes	Nil	1	1	Nil
Mountain Restaurants	8	1	Yes	Yes	3	3	3
Night Clubs with Bands	Yes	1	Nil	Yes	4	Yes	Yes
Discothèques	Yes	Yes	Yes	Yes	6	Yes	Yes

RESORT FACILITIES CHARTS

SPAIN

Name of Resort	Baqueira Beret	Cerler	Formigal	La Molina	Masella	Panticosa	Sierra Nevada
Province	Lerida	Huesca	Huesca	Gerona	Gerona	Huesca	Granada
Tourist Office Director	R. Buil			J.T.I. Alsina		J. Bazan	M. Mendoza
Telephone/Fax Area Code	(973)	(974)	(974)	(972)	(972)	(974)	(958)
Telephone Number	644455	551012	488126	892031	890106	487248	249100
Fax Number	644488	551617	488313	145048	890078	487455	249122
Total Visitor Beds	4,100	1,100	2,020	1,588	1,000		6,200
Height of Resort	4,920ft	4,936ft	4,920ft	4,726ft	5,258ft	3,821ft	6,888ft
Height of Top Station	8,235ft	8,628ft	7,920ft	8,315ft	8,331ft	6,209ft	10,308ft
Mountain Railway	Nil	Nil	Nil	Nil	Nil	Nil	Nil
Cableways	Nil	Nil	Nil	Nil	Nil	Nil	Nil
Gondolaways	Nil	Nil	1	Nil	Nil	Nil	2
Chair-lifts	14	4	6	9	3	2	12
Drag-lifts	7	8	13	6	6	4	5
Total Lift Capacity per Hour	25,500	6,280	15,200	13,630	7,000		31,965
Ski School Instructors	80	40	70	60	31		350
Average sunshine hours - village area							
December		4	7	4	6		7
January		5	7½	4	6		7
February		5	8	5	7		8
March		6	8½	6	7½		8½
April		7	9	7	7½		9
Natural Skating Rinks	Nil	Yes	Nil	Nil	Nil	Nil	Nil
Artificial Skating Rinks	Nil	Nil	Nil	Nil	Nil	Nil	Nil
Curling Rinks	Nil	Nil	Nil	Nil	Nil	Nil	Nil
Ice Hockey	Nil	Nil	Nil	Nil	Nil	Nil	Nil
Tobogganing	Nil	Nil	Nil	Nil	Nil	Nil	Nil
Sleigh Rides	Nil	Nil	Nil	Nil	Nil	Nil	Nil
Riding	Nil	Nil	Yes	Nil	Nil	Nil	Yes
Sports Centre	Nil	Yes	Nil	Yes			Yes
Indoor Tennis	Yes	Yes	Nil	Nil			Yes
Hang-Gliding	Nil	Nil	Nil	Nil			Yes
Para-Gliding	Yes	Nil	Nil	Nil			Yes
Heated Swimming Pools (public)	Nil	1	Nil	Nil	Nil	Nil	Yes
Heated Swimming pools (hotels)	Nil	2	Nil	Yes	1	Nil	2
Sauna Baths	Yes	2	1	2	1	Nil	6
Bowling	Yes	Nil	Nil	Nil	Nil	Nil	Nil
Cinema	Nil	Nil	Nil	Nil	Nil	Nil	Nil
Kindergartens	3	2	Yes	1	1	Nil	Yes
Mountain Restaurants	4	2	4	5	2	Yes	4
Night Clubs with Bands	Nil	1	Nil	Nil	Nil	Nil	Nil
Discothèques	2	5	Yes	Yes	1	Yes	10

ANDORRA

BULGARIA

Name of Resort	Arcalis	Arinsal	Grau Roig/ Pas de la Casa	Pal	Soldeu/ El Tarter	Borovets	Pamporovo
Province	Ordino	La Massana	Encamp	Encamp	Canillo	Sofia	Smolia
Tourist Office Director		H. Garner	Joan Viladomat	H. Garner	M. Canauggia		
Telephone/Fax Area Code	(376)	(376)	(376)	(376)	(376)		(359)
Telephone Number	836963	838438	820391	838438	851151		3021 417
Fax Number	839225	838738	823036	838738	851337		3021 711
Total Visitor Beds	762	4,100	7,500	4,100	6,000	4,740	2,620
Height of Resort	6,364ft	5,085ft	6,726ft	6,069ft	5,900ft	4,300ft	5,345ft
Height of Top Station	8,530ft	8,530ft	9,350ft	7,769ft	8,400ft	8,300ft	6,335ft
Mountain Railway	Nil	Nil	Nil	Nil	Nil	Nil	Nil
Cableways	Nil	Nil	Nil	Nil	Nil	Nil	Nil
Gondolaways	Nil	Nil	Nil	Nil	1	1	Nil
Chair-lifts	4	3	8	3	7	2	5
Drag-lifts	8	10	21	11	14	12	13
Total Lift Capacity per Hour	13,500	12,000	30,715	11,400	22,000	9,500	15,200
Ski School Instructors	40	60	150	80	140	100	60
Average sunshine hours - village area							
December	5	6	7	6	7		2½
January	6	7	8	7	8		4
February	7	8	9	8	9		4½
March	8	9	10	9	10		5
April	9	10	11	10	11		6
Natural Skating Rinks	Nil	Nil	Nil	Nil	Nil	Nil	Nil
Artificial Skating Rinks	Nil	Nil	Nil	Nil	Yes	Nil	Nil
Curling Rinks	Nil	Nil	Nil	Nil	Yes	Yes	Nil
Ice Hockey	Nil	Nil	Nil	Nil	Yes	Nil	Nil
Tobogganing	Nil	Yes	Nil	Nil	Nil	Yes	Nil
Sleigh Rides	Nil	Nil	Nil	Nil	Nil	Nil	Nil
Riding	Yes	Yes (5km.)	Nil	Yes	Nil	Nil	Nil
Sports Centre	Yes	Yes (5km.)	Nil	Yes	Yes		Nil
Indoor Tennis	Nil	Yes (5km.)	Nil	Yes	Nil		Nil
Hang-Gliding	Nil	Nil	Nil	Nil	Nil		Nil
Para-Gliding	Nil	Nil	Nil	Nil	Nil		Nil
Heated Swimming Pools (public)	Yes	Nil	Nil	Nil	Yes	Nil	Nil
Heated Swimming pools (hotels)	Yes	Yes	2	Yes	Yes	Yes	Yes
Sauna Baths	Yes	Yes	Yes	Yes	6	Yes	Yes
Bowling	Yes	Yes (5km.)	Nil	Nil	Nil	Yes	Yes
Cinema	Nil	Nil	1	Nil	Nil	Yes	Nil
Kindergartens	Yes	Yes	Yes	Yes	Yes	Yes	Yes
Mountain Restaurants	3	7	4	Yes	2	Yes	9
Night Clubs with Bands	Nil	5	Yes	Nil	2	5	Nil
Discothèques	Nil	4	Yes	Nil	2	2	Yes

'BEFORE YOU GO'

A skiing holiday is fun but much of the pleasure comes from achievement, by the mastery of physical skill which means physical effort which requires physical fitness. Happiness must be earned. The fitter you are when you arrive for your holiday, the better chance you have of enjoying it.

How fit are you? Let's see. Take an ordinary kitchen chair, step up onto it and step down again immediately. Keep on doing this steadily for one minute, changing the leading leg each time. Then breathe in! breath out! in! out! in! out! in! and hold that breath. If you can hold it for sixteen seconds you are about average. Eighteen seconds is good. Twenty seconds or more is excellent. If you have rated high on this test you know your work and/or your play is keeping you fit and in good physical condition, then you can, if you wish, cut out the conditioning training below and go straight to the pre-ski exercises.

But if your score is low then you must think about what we call conditioning training. Before we go on to this, what about your weight? If you are overweight then you must try and shed those excess pounds. The extra load they put on your heart, lungs and muscles makes the job of getting fit much more difficult. Cut out starchy food – bread, potatoes, sweets. Don't eat between meals. Cut out sugar, reduce the alcohol intake. You can eat plenty of lean meat, fish without batter, eggs and green salad. No peas or beans. We are hoping that you have a few weeks in hand before your holiday starts so that there should be no need for a crash course and the dieting can be done steadily with a gradual reduction in weight.

CONDITIONING TRAINING

Now for your conditioning training.
Conditioning training is based on a daily period of continuous exertion which causes you to breathe more quickly and your heart to beat faster. The fitter you get the more effort you can sustain without distress. The simplest way of providing continuous exercise is by a daily period of walking, running or cycling, but the amount done should be accurately measured in terms of time and distance and over a six week period. The target you set yourself in respect of both time and distance should steadily rise.

Walking is probably the easiest to arrange. Settle on a walk from your home or your office that you know is definitely 1 mile. A person of average fitness should cover this in 12 minutes. Set yourself a target for walking every day, increasing the stint until after six weeks you can cover 3 miles in 40 minutes.

If you prefer cycling you should be able to cover 2 miles in just over 6 minutes and you should improve daily on this until at the end of six weeks you can cover six miles in just over a quarter of an hour.

Running is in some ways the best conditioning training of all. You may find it difficult to run a mile in your present state of fitness but start with a mixture of running and walking and doing this you should be able to cover one mile in 12 minutes. Gradually increasing the proportion of running each day. At the end of six weeks you should be able to run, without walking, a mile in under 9 minutes.

Ladies can reduce the target times by 25%

FALLING EXERCISE

It is surprising how afraid people are of falling and for the beginner particularly at skiing, it is impossible to learn without falling quite a large number of times and it is worthwhile practising the art of falling with the minimum risk of injury. Practise this simple daily exercise. Stand in what you might call the skiing position – feet together, knees bent forwad, lean forward from the hips and look forward. (One of the important points about falling is always to try and fall sideways or backwards if you can. The most serious injuries invariably come from a toss forward. If you realise you are getting out of control then this exercise will help you to fall to the side or backwards.) Crouch low by giving at the knees. To fall to the right, as the knees give they should both move to the right allowing yourself to fall sideways on the outside of your right thigh, but don't put your right hand down to break the fall. Push it across in front of your body – that is to your left – you will then strike the ground or floor with your right thigh and find yourself rolling over immediately onto your back. Try and be as limp and relaxed as you can as you fall.

PRE-SKI EXERCISES

Try and find time to do 15 to 20 minutes each day following the schedule of exercises given below:

Leg Strengthening

1. Stepping up exercise. This follows the same procedure as for the step up test given earlier. Start with one minute stepping and gradually increase the dose daily until you can step up and down for two to three minutes without distress.

2. Squatting. Stand in an upright position, feet slightly apart. Squat down on your heels. At first, if necessary, hold on lightly to the back of your chair to help to keep your balance. Start with four or five squats and increase these daily until twenty squats come easily to you.

3. Squat jumps. This is a strenuous exercise to be introduced as you get fitter. From the squatting position spring upwards by stretching and pushing off with your legs. On landing go back into the squat position and repeat. Two or three squat jumps at first and then repeat them to six to ten times as you get stronger.

4. Ankle rolling. Sit on a table with your legs dangling. Rotate the feet with as big a circular movement as possible, moving them first in one direction and then in the other. 10 to 20 circles.

5. Feet rocking. Stand upright. Get up on your toes then lower your heels and raise your toes off the ground using your feet like rockers. Make each rocking movement as full as possible. Rock forwards and backwards 10 to 20 times and perform the exercise as slowly as possible.

Shoulder Strengthening

6. Press-ups. Sergeant majors' favourite! Lie on the floor face down, place hands – palms down – on the floor beside your shoulders, press away from the floor until your arms are straight and your body is supported by your hands and toes. Bend the arms and return slowly to the starting position. You should start with at least four press-ups and increase daily until at least ten can be performed.

7. Weight swinging. Get an easily held object – medicine ball, stone, bag of sand, weighing about 4-6 lbs. Holding it in one hand swing the arms forward and backward six times, change hands and repeat. Make each movement as full as possible, well back and then forward and upward with a straight arm until the weight is almost perpendicular overhead. Increase repetitions until twenty can be performed with each hand.

8. Getting up exercise. Sit on the floor with the kitchen chair seat towards you, level with your hips. Draw your knees up, keeping the soles of your feet on the floor. Turn and place both hands on the seat of the chair. Without moving your feet, press down with your arms until you have gained the standing position. Repeat this three or four times with the chair on your right side and then again with the chair on your left side.

Back and Abdomen Strengthening

9. Feet circling. Lie on your back, press your hands, palms down, against the floor, keeping the knees straight describe as big a circle as you can with your feet. In a full circle your feet will pass over your head. Repeat, changing the direction of the circle, four repetitions in each direction to begin with, increased to ten but remember to keep those knees straight!

10. Sitting up. The same starting position but place hands on your knees, palms down, sit up and bend forward allowing your hands to slide down towards your feet and try to get your head to touch your knees. Four times at first increasing to ten.

11. Rocking. Lie face down, bend your knees and grasp your ankles behind you. Raise your head and shoulders clear of the floor, now rock forwards and backwards on your stomach with as big a movement as possible. Six times at first increasing to twelve.

12. Stretch and relax. Lie on your back, stretch your arms above your head, that is along the floor, the backs of the hands resting on the floor. Try consciously to push your feet and hands away from your body. That is, stretch out on the floor as far as you possibly can. Try hard to get a big stretch of the whole body from the tips of your fingers to your toes. Then completely relax your muscles and repeat four to six times.

If you follow the programme set out above you will be fit for anything skiing has to offer.

HOTEL REFERENCE CHART — AUSTRIA

Resort/Hotel	Owner/Manager	Area Code	Telephone No	Total No. Beds	Double Rooms	Single Rooms	With Bath/ Shower	Dining Rooms	Sitting Rooms	Bars	Dancing with Band	Discothèques	Swimming Pool	Village Centre (metres)
Alpbach		05336												
Alpbacherhof	A.Bischofer		5237	110	55	—	All	2	2	1	No	No	Yes	100
Angelika	J.Steinlecher		5339	30	13	4	All	1	1	No	No	No	No	50
Böglerhof*	Fam.Moser-Duftner		5227	110	43	6	All	3	2	1	Yes	No	Yes	Central
Jakoberwirt	Fam. Radinger		5223	45	20	5	No	4	1	1	No	No	No	Central
*Plus apartments														
Auffach		05339												
Platzl	S.Fill		8928	60	31	3	22	2	1	1	Yes	No	No	Central
Koglmoos	Fam.Metzler		8889	Apartments				1	1	No	No	No	No	5000
Bad Aussee		06152												
Wasnerin	H.Steinbichler		2108	70	30	3	25	1	2	1				
Badgastein		06432												
Bellevue	Fam.Wührer		25710	200	80	60	All	3	3	2	Yes	Yes	Yes	200
Parkhotel Söntgen	G.Windischbauer		2235	138	43	52	60	1	1	1	No	Yes	No	150
Bad Goisern		06137												
Agathawirt	H.Schenner		8341	90	42	6	All	2	1	1	No	Yes	Yes	2500
Bad Hofgastein		06432												
Norica	B. Sandl		8391	155	67	21	All	2	1	1	No	Yes	Yes	Central
PalaceGastein	F. Dold		67150	317	118	92	All	4	4	2	Yes	Yes	Yes	200
Paracelsus	E.Stadelmann		6667	26	12	2	All	1	1	1	No	No	No	
Berwang		05674												
Edelweiss	J.Sprenger		84230	40	18	4	All	1	1	1	No	No	No	
Brand		05559												
Beck	W.Beck		306	66	33	—	All	1	1	1	Yes	No	Yes	Central
Colrosa	O.Beck		225	75	36	3	36	1	1	1	No	No	Yes	Central
Garni-Gulma	F.Bertel		246	35	14	3	All	1	1	No	No	No	No	Central
Hämmerle	E.Hämmerle		213	90	36	19	27	2	1	1	No	No	No	Central
Lagant & Zaluanda	H.Schwärzler		285	75	35	2	All	Yes	Yes	Yes	No	No	Yes	200
Scesaplana	H.Schwärzler		221	128	59	5	All	2	1	3	No	Yes	Yes	100
Walliserhof	R.Meyer		241	85	38	8	All	1	1	1	No	No	Yes	200
Bürserberg		05552												
Burtschahof	H.Maurer		65307	36	18	1	18	1	1	1	No	Yes	Yes	3000
Taleu	R.Moschler		63257	60	30	—	All	3	1	2	No	Yes	Yes	Central
Damüls		05510												
Damülserhof	W&J.Klauser		210	100	50	6	All	2	3	2	No	Yes	Yes	Central
Madlener	G.Madlener		221	65	29	6	13	Yes	Yes	Yes	No	Yes	No	300
Dienten		06461												
Hochkönig	W.Scherbinek		216	51	24	2	All	Yes	Yes	Yes	No	No	No	300
Salzburgerhof	O.Bacher		217	75	31	2	All	Yes	Yes	Yes	No	Yes	Yes	100
Dorfgastein		05433												
Kirchenwirt	Fam.Köstinger		251	58	28	2	All	Yes	Yes	Yes	No	Yes	No	300
Ellmau		05358												
Claudia	H.Hochfilzer		2501	35	16	3	All	1	1	1	No	No	No	100
Hochfilzer	H.Hochfilzer		2501	140	66	8	All	3	2	1	No	Yes	Yes	Central
Der Bär	C.H. Windisch		2395	100	31	4	All	2	4	2	Yes	Yes	Yes	400
Faschina		05515												
Rössle	E.Schäfer		252	30	15	—	9	1	No	No	No	No	No	Central
Fieberbrunn		05354												
Alte Post	J.Eder		6257	160	60	3	All	1	1	1	No	No	No	Central
Schloss Rosenegg	O.Eberhardt		6201	*300	116	10	All	3	1	1	No	No	Yes	Central
*Plus apartments														
Filzmoos		06453												
Alpenkrone	J.Hampshire		280	104	49	6	All	1	3	1	No	No	Yes	1100
Filzmooserhof	R.Webinger		232	80	38	4	All	1	1	1	No	No	Yes	200
Fügen		05288												
Elisabeth	J.Haun		2972	50	All	4	20	1	1	1	No	No	No	300
Malerhaus	E.Haun		2278	45	22	1	All	2	1	1	No	Yes	No	100
Post	Fam.Ritzl		3212	118	54	10	All	3	1	1	No	No	Yes	Central
Fulpmes		05225												
Alte Post	H.Krösbacher		2358	70	33	7	All	1	1	1	No	No	Yes	Central
Atzinger	K.Atzinger		3135	64	27	5	—	2	2	1	No	No	No	1000
Stubaierhof	Fam.Deutschmann		2266	46	19	1	All	1	1	1	No	No	No	Central
Furx		05522												
Peterhof	H.Schmind		42882	50	20	—	All	2	1	—	No	No	No	7km
Galtür		05443												
Alpina	H.Walter		8264	33	16	1	5	1	—	1	No	No	No	200
Alpen Hotel	F.Lorenz		8206	80	36	7	All	1	1	1	No	Yes	No	100
Post	A.Türtscher		8422	110	52	6	All	3	2	1	Yes	Yes	No	Central
Gargellen		05557												
Bachmann	F. Helmut		6316	70	33	3	All	2	1	1	No	No	Yes	50
Gargellenhof	I.Kessler		6274	60	28	4	23	1	1	1	No	No	No	500
Madrisa	H.Rhomberg		6331	130	55	12	55	3	2	1	No	Yes	Yes	200
Silvretta	H.Schaper		6308	65	26	9	All	1	1	1	No	No	Yes	200
Gaschurn		05558												
Rössle	A.Kessler		8331	106	49	7	All	3	2	2	No	No	Yes	50
Verwall	W.Durig		8206	206	69	33	11	1	1	1	Yes	No	Yes	1000
Sonnblick	L Tschanun		8212	101	42	5	47	2	4	1	Yes	Yes	Yes	200
Gosau		06136												
Gosauerhof	A.Loserer			50	24	2	15	2	1	1	No	No	No	400
Sommerhof	T.Wallner		8258	70	26	2	All	2	1	1	No	Yes	Yes	
Gurtis		05525												
Leni	E.Grass		82617	20	9	2	—	1	1	1	No	No	No	350
Hinterglemm		06541												
Sonnblick			648	28	13	2	11	1		No	No	No	No	Central
Glemmtalerhof	C.Breitfuss		7135	120	53	9	All	2	2	2	Yes	Yes	Yes	Central
Wolf	T.Wolf		7346	80	37	6	All	2	2	1	Yes	No	Yes	100
Hinterstoder		07564												
Dietlgut	K Wendl		52480	47	22	3	All	1	1	1	No	No	No	5 Km
Hinterstoder	I. Sedlak		5421	128	23	—	All	2	1	1	No	Yes	Yes	10 Km
Stoderhof	E.Frühmann		5266	75	37	7	All	3	2	2	No	Yes	Yes	Central
Hinterthal		06584												
Ebner	W.Ebner		8164	60	20	—	All	1	1	1	No	Yes	No	Central
Hintertux		05287												
Kirchler	J.Kirchler		312	183	85	10	70	2	2	1	—	Yes	Yes	Central
Hochsölden		05254												
Edelweiss	H.Fender		2298	60	25	10	All	Yes	Yes	Yes	No	No	Yes	Central
Enzian	U. Riml		2252	94	42	10	All	4	3	1	No	Yes	Yes	Central
Hochsölden	G. Gurschler		2229	94	42	10	All	2	3	2	Yes	No	No	Central
Ischgl		05444												
Post	R.Wolf		5233	130	46	15	40	1	1	1	Yes	No	Yes	100
Sonne	E.Zangerl		5302	60				1	1	1	No	Yes	No	100
Tirol	A.Elmar		5216	46				1	1	1	No	No	No	100
Madlein	G.Aloys		5220	140	65	10	All	3	1	1	Yes	No	Yes	200
Kaprun		06547												
Kaprun	S.Grainer		8625	150	65	20	All	3	1	1	No	Yes	No	1850
Mühle	J.Nindl		8254	100	40	2	All	2	3	3	No	No	No	400

HOTEL REFERENCE CHART — AUSTRIA

Resort/Hotel	Owner/Manager	Area Code	Telephone No	Total No. Beds	Double Rooms	Single Rooms	With Bath/ Shower	Dining Rooms	Sitting Rooms	Bars	Dancing with Band	Discothèques	Swimming Pool	Village Centre (metres)
Kirchberg		**05357**												
Brauns	G. Schmolz		2545	48	22	4	All	1	1	1	No	No	Yes	200
Sonne	E.Nemetz		2402/3	90	37	9	44	2	2	1	No	No	Yes	300
Kitzbühel		**05356**												
Erika	B.Schorer		4885	84	42	—	All	2	3	1	No	No	Yes	20
Goldener Greif	J.Harisch		4311	80	40	6	All	2	1	1	No	No	No	Central
Hofer	H.Hofer		3013	50	21	7	All	2	1	1	No	No	No	300
Jägerwirt	S.Bartenstein		4281/3	140	67	6	All	3	2	2	No	Yes	Yes	200
Schweizerhof	H. Affenzeller		2735	80	38	4	All	1	1	1	No	No	No	200
Weisses Rössl	W.Hirnsberger		2541	70	31	7	All	2	1	1	No	No	No	100
Klösterle		**05582**												
Albona	K.Kessler		224	30	12	3	5	1	1	1	No	Yes	No	Central
Lanersbach		**05287**												
Kirchler	E.Kirchler		201	65				1	1	1	No	No	No	Central
Laterns		**05526**												
Bergfrieden	J.Nesensohn		230	58	27	4	All	1	1	1	No	No	No	
Kühboden (Innerlaterns)	Fam. Vith		234	75	29	10	All	2	2	3	Yes	Yes	No	200
Gapfohl	G. Mangold		233	150	20	—	All	3	4	1	No	Yes	No	3000
Lech am Arlberg		**05583**												
Berghof	Fam.Burger		2635	84	37	10	All	3	2	1	No	No	No	100
Rudboden	Fam.Schuler		2508	15	6	3	5	1	No	No	No	No	No	500
Tannbergerhof	H.Jochum		2202	51	21	9	All	2	3	1	No	Yes	Yes	Central
Leogang		**06583**												
Bäckerwirt	Fam. Frick		204	60	25	10	All	2	-	2	No	Yes	No	Central
Krallerhof	Fam. Altenburger		2460	150	71	8	All	1	2	1	No	Yes	Yes	2.5km.
Salzhurgerhof	Fam. Hörl		7310	90	45	-	All	2	1	1	No	No	No	3.5km.
Lermoos		**05673**												
Alpenrose	F.Petz		2282	39	18	3	All	1	1	1	No	No	No	200
Edelweiss	M.Gerber		2214	220	100	20	All	3	1	1	No	No	Yes	100
Mayrhofen		**05285**												
Elizabeth	Fam.Thaler		2929	70	24	10	All	4	2	2	Yes	Yes	Yes	150
Kramerwirt	H.Kröll		2615	150	72	8	All	Yes	Yes	Yes	Yes	No	No	Central
Neue Post	F.Pfister		2131	195	80	20	All	4	1	1	Yes	No	No	Central
Strass Sporthotel	Frau Roscher		2205	117	51	15	All	2	1	3	No	Yes	Yes	50
Strass	Fam. Roscher		2205	130	50	19	All	3	1	3	Yes	Yes	Yes	50
Mieders		**05225**												
Alte Post	H.Debern		2513	50	24	2	All	Yes	Yes	—	—	—	—	Central
Nauders		**05473**												
Almhof	Fam.Kröll		313	85	40	4	All	2	3	2	Yes	Yes	Yes	100
Alpina	S.Jennewein		349	32	15	2	All	1	1	1	No	No	No	100
Maultasch	E. Zemm		235	120	50	7	All	1	1	1	Yes	No	Yes	Central
Niederau		**05339**												
Austria	E. Blachfelder		8188	85	36	7	All	2	1	2	No	No	Yes	Central
Staffler	Herr Thaler		8222	64	30	4	28	1		1	No	Yes	Yes	150
Vicky	M.Unger		8282/3	54	25	4	All	1	1	1	No	Yes	No	200
Oberau		**05339**												
Kellerwirt	H.Keller		8116	65	29	6	All	3	2	2	No	No	No	Central
Stefanie	S.Margreiter		8383	17	5	4	All	1	1	No	No	No	No	Central
Bergland	Fam. Erharter		8250	72	36		All	Yes	Yes	Yes	No	No	No	
Obergurgl		**05256**												
Austria	H.Steiner		282	60	25	10	32	1	1	2	No	No	No	
Gotthard	G.Scheiber		335	88	39	10	All	1	2	1	No	No	Yes	100
Hochfirst	Fam. Fender		231/2	180	67	4	All	2	2	2	No	No	Yes	300
Jenewein	D.Schöpf		203	74	35	4	All	2	1	1	No	Yes	No	Central
Josl	H.Gstrein		205	40	17	—	All	2	1	2	Yes	Yes	No	Central
Crystal			454	100	50		All	Yes	Yes	Yes	No	No	No	
Alpina	K. Platzer		295	150	72	6	All	2	2	1	No	No	Yes	500
Obertauern		**06456**												
Kesselspitze	Fam.Lürzer		7264	110	50	10	25	1	2	1	No	Yes	Yes	1500
Taverne	H.Oberhumer		7229	40	17	3	All	1	1	3	Yes	Yes	No	Central
Wisenegg	G.Sager		7272	60	26	4	15	2	2	1	No	No	No	2,000
Ohertraun		**06131**												
Krippenstein	H. Moser		7527	80	32	9	19	1	1	1	No	Yes	No	1500
Pitztal (Mandarfen)		**05413**												
Zerbenhos	J.Pechtl		8284	48	23	2	All	2	1	1	No	No	No	
Raggal		**05553**												
Nova	V.Burtscher		222	60	28	2	1	1	1	Yes	Yes	Yes	No	200
Saalbach		**06541**												
Alpenhotel	Fam.Thomas		6660	*170	39	11	All	3	1	3	Yes	Yes	Yes	Central
Bauer	J.Bauer		2130	70	30	6	All	2	2	2	No	Yes	Yes	Central
Neuhaus	F.Breitfuss		7151	120	50	18	All	3	1	1	Yes	No	Yes	Central
Saalbacherhof	J.Dschulnigg		7111	155	65	15	All	2	3	2	No	Yes	No	Central
St. Anton am Arlberg		**05446**												
Arlberg	P.Ennemoser		2210	98	42	14	35	2	1	2	Yes	Yes	No	300
Post	R. Alber		2213	120	56	9	All	1	1	1	Yes	Yes	No	Central
Rosanna Stüberl	Fam.Flühler		2400	78	39	—	All	2	1	2	No	No	No	50
Schwarzer Adler	K.Tschol		2244	112	48	17	All	4	3	2	No	Yes	No	Central
Valluga	F.Kertess		3263	50	22	6	16	2	1	1	No	Yes	No	400
Berghelm	W. Tschol		2255	50	21	8	All	1	1	1	No	No	No	200
St. Johann in Tirol		**05352**												
Europa	E. Mechs		62285	50	Apartments		All	3	1	1	No	No	No	150
Fischer	G. Fischer		623320	65	31	4	All	1	1	1	No	No	No	Central
Schruns		**05556**												
Alpenrose	K.Mäser		72655	80	34	3	All	2	1	2	No	No	Yes	500
Chesa Platina	A.Trunsperger		72323	40	17	4	All	2	1	1	No	No	No	500
Irma	J.Walsch		72452	15	7	1	All	1	1	—	No	No	No	125
Seefeld		**05212**												
Hiltpolt	Herr Hiltpolt		2253	70	30	8	All	1	1	1	No	No	No	Central
Karwendelhof	F.Wilberger		2655	85	39	7	All	2	1	2	Yes	No	No	100
Philipp	H.Kögl		2301	120	55	10	All	2	2	1	No	No	No	300
Post	A. Albrecht		2201	180	72	26	70	1	2	3	No	Yes	No	Central
Serfaus		**05476**												
Alpenhof	K. Schuler		6228	70	30	8	All	2	1	1	No	No	No	200
Cervosa	H.Westreicher		6211	130	56	11	All	3	4	2	Yes	No	Yes	400
Edelweiss	A.Geiger		6223	45	21	3	All	1	1	—	No	No	No	150
Schwarzer Adler	K.Luggen		6221	50	41	9	37	1	1	1	No	No	No	200
Sölden		**05254**												
Central	Fam.Waschl		2260	160	71	20	All	2	2	2	Yes	No	Yes	200
Tyrolerhof	S.Falkner		2288	85	35	15	All	1	1	2	Yes	No	No	Central
Park	Fam. Gürschler		2250	85	33	11	All	2	2	Yes	No	No	No	100
Söll		**05333**												
Eggerwirt	B.Weiss		5236	52	22	2	All	1	2	1	No	No	No	200
Post	J Bliem		5221	38	17	4	5	2	1	1	Yes	No	No	Central
Tyrol	J Schernthanner		5273	134	61	8	All	1	3	2	Yes	Yes	Yes	300

HOTEL REFERENCE CHART — AUSTRIA

Resort/Hotel	Owner/Manager	Area Code	Telephone No	Total No. Beds	Double Rooms	Single Rooms	With Bath/ Shower	Dining Rooms	Sitting Rooms	Bars	Dancing with Band	Discothèques	Swimming Pool	Village Centre (metres)
Steinach		**05272**												
Wilder Mann	G. Hörtnagl		6270	85	25	8	All	3	3	1	Yes	No	Yes	Central
Stuben		**05582**												
Albona	H.Brandle		712	40	18	4	22	1	1	2	No	Yes	No	Central
Telfes		**05225**												
Greier	F.Wehinger		2226	50	20	2	All	1	2	1	No	No	No	Central
Tschagguns		**05556**												
Alpila	E.Bahl		72250	27	13	1	All	1	1	1	No	No	No	400
Cresta	H.Ammann		72395	60	26	8	All	2	1	1	No	No	Yes	Central
Vent		**05254**												
Post	Fam.Pirpamer		8119	60	25	10	All	3	1	1	No	No	Yes	Central
Kellerhof	V. Scheiber		8109	23	10	—	10	1	1	1	No	Yes	No	Central
Wieshof	M.Scheiber		8128	12	5	2	All	1	1	—	No	No	No	Central
Westendorf		**05334**												
Jakobwirt	Fam.Ziepl		6245	100	45	6	All	3	2	2	No	Yes	Yes	Central
Post	G. Ager		6202	80	40	—	All	2	1	2	No	No	No	Central
Windischgarsten		**07562**												
Schwarzes Rössl	G.Baumschlager		311	39	17	5	17	2	2	No	No	No	No	Central
Zell am See		**06542**												
Alpenblick	Herr Siegl		2431	150	57	13	37	3	1	1	No	No	Yes	
Grand	G. Flacké		2388	*320	35	8	70	2	2	2	No	Yes	Yes	50
Zum Hirschen	E.Pacalt		2447	85	41	3	All	4	2	2	No	Yes	Yes	200
St. George	Fam. Holleis		3533	75	32	5	All	2	1	1	No	No	Yes	400
Porschehof	G. Weissenbacher		7248	80	36	7	All	2	1	1	No	No	Yes	2000
Zell am Ziller		**05282**												
Tirolerhof	Fam. Egger		2227	80	39	2	41	1	1	2	No	Yes	Yes	Central
Zellerhof	A. Müller		2612	70	29	11	All	2	1	1	No	No	No	Central
Englhof	Fam. Hans Hotter		3134	65	31	3	All	3	3	1	No	No	No	100
Zürs am Arlberg		**05583**												
Alpenrose-Post	H.Hauptman		22710	170	65	40	All	5	1	2	Yes	No	Yes	Central
Edelweiss	J.Strolz		26620	123	45	25	All	2	1	2	No	Yes	No	Central
Lorünser	H.Jochum		22540	125	47	31	All	2	2	1	No	No	No	Central
Mathies	F.Antonino		22790	40	16	7	All	2	3	2	No	No	No	Central
Zürserhof	F.Skardarasy		25130	181	72	37	All	3	2	1	Yes	Yes	No	500

*Plus apartments

HOTEL REFERENCE CHART — FRANCE

Resort/Hotel	Owner/Manager	Area Code	Telephone No	Total No. Beds	Double Rooms	Single Rooms	With Bath/ Shower	Dining Rooms	Sitting Rooms	Bars	Dancing with Band	Discothèques	Swimming Pool	Village Centre (metres)
Alpe d'Huez		**476**												
Les Gentianes	M.Serrat		80.35.76	27	9	7	All	1	1	1	Yes	No	No	
Petit Prince	M.Amenc		80.33.51	80	40	—	All	1	1	1	No	No	No	300
Vallée Blanche	C.Thomas		80.30.51	90	40	2	36	Yes	Yes	Yes	No	Yes	No	500
Avoriaz		**450**												
Les Dromonts	SICA-Residence		74.08.11	84			40	1	1	1	No	No	No	Central
Le Snow	SICA-Residence		74.06.11	250	Studios		All	2		1	No	No	No	Central
Barèges		**462**												
L'Europe	M.Lons		92.68.04	89	—	—	34		1	1	No	No	No	Central
Igloo	H. Cazaux		92.68.10	46	22	2	All	2	2	1	No	No	No	Central
Richelieu	M. Azin		92.68.11	69	34	4	All	1	2	1	No	No	No	Central
Chamonix		**450**												
Croix Blanc Inn	J. Morand		53 00.11	62	33	3	All	—	1	—	No	No	No	Central
Hermitage & Paccard	L. Paccard		53 13.87	70	30	5	30	Yes	Yes	Yes	No	No	No	300
Mont Blanc	J. Morand		53.05.64	95	33	4	All	Yes	1	1	No	No	Yes	Central
Chatel		**450**												
Fleur De Neige	C. Neuvecelle		73.20.10	95	45	4	All	2	2	1	No	No	No	600
Lion D'Or	N. Maxit		73.22.27	80	25	Nil	All	1	1	1	No	No	No	
Macchi	M. Macchi		73.24.12	64	32		All	1	1	1	No	No	No	300
Perdrix Blanche	G. Vuarand		73.22.76	19	9	–	All	1	1	1	No	No	No	6km
Courchevel		**479**												
Ducs De Savoie	Rene Guth		08.03.00	144	72	—	All	1	2	1	No	No	Yes	400
Le Chamois	Mm. Feron		08.01.56	85	30	—	30	—	1	1	No	No	No	50
Le Dahu	R. Puglièse		08.01.18	60	30	—	Yes	1	1	1	No	No	No	Central
Des Neiges	H. Benoist		08.03.77	90	42	6	All	1	2	1	No	No	No	500
La Potinière	H. Michel		08.00.16	80	30	4	All	1	1	2	No	No	No	Central
Bellecote	R. Toussaint		08 10.19	105	48	10	All	Yes	Yes	Yes	No	No	Yes	500
Annapurna	C. Pinturault		08 04.60	154	61	—	All	1	3	1	No	No	Yes	1500
Flaine		**450**												
Aujon	M. Blazy		90.80.10	410°	150	25	All	1	1	1	No	Yes	No	Central
Club Aquarius			90.81.66	372*	126	—	All	1	1	1	No	Yes	No	Central
Le Totem	G. Cremieux		90.80.64	108	54		All	1	1	1	No	No	No	Central
Isola 2000		**493**												
Le Chastillon	N. Jabre		23.10.60	108	54	—	54	1	1	1	No.	No	No	Central
Le Druos	G. Marguet		23.12.20	84	39		39		1	1	No	No	No	600
Le Pas du Loup	N. Jabre		23.11.71	194	97	—	97	1	1	2	No	No	No	50
Diva			23.17.71		28	—	All	Yes	Yes	Yes	No	No	No	600
La Clusaz		**450**												
Beauregard	R. Duffes		32.68.00	130	46	15	61	3	3	1	No	No	Yes	100
Bellachat	Mme. Gallay		02.40.50	65	30	—	All	1	1	1	No	No	No	3000
Carlina	M. Ruphy		02.43.48	144	72	—	All	2	3	2	No	No	Yes	300
La Mongie		**562**												
Le Pourteilh	Mme. Ferrand		55.40.04	80	38	2	All	1	2	1	No	No	No	Central
La Taoulet	Mme Ferrand		95.40.26	50	22	1	10	1	1	1	No	No	No	Central
La Plagne		**479**												
Eldorado			09.12.09	358	174	10	All	Yes	Yes	Yes	No	No	No	
Christina	M. Theanor		09.28.20	100	50	—	46	1	3	1	No	No	No	Central
Le France	P. Burnet		09.28.15	160	80	—	All	1	3	1	No	No	No	Central
Les Arcs		**479**												
Golf			41.43.43	600	300	—	All	4	2	2	No	Yes	No	Central
Pierre Blanche/Cachette	M. Assier		07.70.50	350	175	—	All	2	2	1	No	Yes	No	Central
Trois Arcs	Mlle. Touraille		07.78.78	96	48	—	All	3	1	2	No	No	No	Central
Les Deux Alpes		**476**												
La Bérangère	R. Lherm		79.24.11	120	50	9	All	1	1	1	No	No	Yes	150

HOTEL REFERENCE CHART — FRANCE

Resort/Hotel	Owner/Manager	Area Code	Telephone No	Total No. Beds	Double Rooms	Single Rooms	With Bath/ Shower	Dining Rooms	Sitting Rooms	Bars	Dancing with Band	Discothèques	Swimming Pool	Village Centre (metres)
Mounier	R. Mounier		80.56.90	74	37	—	All	1	3	1	No	No	No	Central
Edelweiss	J.C.Ponsard		79.21.22	90	34	1	All	1	1	1	No	No	Yes	Central
Les Gets		450												
La Marmotte	Fam.Mirigay		75.80.33	120	45	3	All	1	2	1	No	No	Yes	100
Les Alpages	Mme. Thibon			40	20	—	All	1	2	1	No	No	No	200
Stella	Fam.Baud		75.80.40	80	31	—	All	1	1	1	No	No	No	150
Les Houches		450												
Beausite	Mme. Perrin		55.51.16	36	18	—	All	1	1	1	No	No	No	Central
Bellevarde	Mme. Paillou		54.41.85	23	10	1	2	1	—	1	No	No	No	300
De la Piste Bleue	D. Gonin		54.40.66	50	25	—	16	1	2	1	No	No	No	500
Les Menuires		479												
Les Christelles	A. Fsaossis		00.66.05	62	30	—	All	2	1	1	No	No	Yes	200
L'Oisans	B. Di Benedetto		00.62.96	38	18	—	All	1	—	1	No	No	No	Central
Skilt	M. Olias		00.63.52		50	—	40	2	2	1	No	Yes	No	Central
L'Ours Blanc	P. Casali		00.61.66	100	50	—	All	1	1	1	No	No	No	500
Megève		450												
Le Fer à Cheval	M. Sibuet		21.30.39	65	30	—	All	1	1	1	No	No	No	250
Mont Blanc	G. Boisson		21.20.02	117	38	26	All	2	10	1	Yes	Yes	Yes	Central
Parc Des Loges	D. Aubrun		93.05.03	'00	47	6	All	1	1	1	No	No	No	50
Méribel		479												
Grand Coeur	J. Zedde		08.60.03	98	49	—	All	1	1	1	No	No	No	50
L'Orée du Bois	R. Chardonnet		00.50.30	60	30	—	All	1	1	1	No	No	No	1000
L'Ardray Télébar	A. Bonnet		08.60.26	52	26	—	All	1	3	1	No	No	No	2000
Méribel Mottaret		479												
Tarentaise	R. Stephenson		00.42.43	90	45	—	All	1	1	1	No	No	No	300
Montgenèvre		492												
Napoléon	M. Matarasso		21.92.04	100	45	3	45	1	3	1	No	No	No	Central
Valérie	R. Baume		21.90.02	67	32	3	All	1	1	1	No	No	No	Central
Morzine		450												
L'Équipe	M.Beard		79.11.43	110	35	—	All	1	1	2	Yes	Yes	Yes	100
Igloo	M.Baud		79.15.05	58	29	—	All	—	1	—	No	No	No	200
L.Tramplin	G.Taberlet		79.12.31	90	36	All	1	3	1	No	No	No		100
St.Jean D'Aulps		450												
Perroudy	Mme.Desrouchy		79.63.64	30	15	—	All	1	1	1	No	No	No	100
Terche	M.Bruno		79.62.09	250	121	4	All	3	—	1	Yes	Yes	Yes	3 km
St. Lary		562												
Christiania (Pla d'Adet)	M. Rigu		98.44.42	54	24	—	All	1	1	1	No	No	No	Central
Grand Hotel Mir	Fam. Mir		39.40.03	50	22	5	All	1	1	1	No	No	No	150
Serre Chevalier		492												
Plein Sud (1350)	B. Chabrand		24.17.01	84	38	4	All	1	1	1	No	No	Yes	160
Le Christiania (1400)	M. Paul		24.76.33	54	26	2	All	1	1	1	No	No	No	50
Le Lievre Blanc (1400)	T. & J. Hickey		24.74.05	75	20	1	26	1	1	1	No	No	No	Central
Alliey (1500)	E. Buisson		24.40.02	49	23	3	19	2	1	1	No	No	No	Central
Alpazur (1500)	J. Aelion		24.40.41	290	115	—	75	1	1	2	No	No	No	
Tignes		479												
Aiguille Percée	M. Baudin		06.52.22	65	25	—	All	1	1	1	No	No	No	
Les Campanules	D. Reymond		06.34.36	80	36	—	All	1	1	1	No	No	No	30
Neige et Soleil	J.Davat		06.32.94	65	28	4	All	1	1	1	No	No	No	Central
Val D'Isère		479												
Blizzard	M. Cerboneschi		06.02.07	144	72	—	All	1	2	1	No	Yes	No	Central
Gelinotte	C. Beilin		06.06.73	44	22	2	All	1	3	1	No	No	No	800
Grand Paradis	B. Boulais		06.11.73	100	40	—	All	1	1	1	No	No	No	100
Valmorel		479												
La Fontaine	0. Hoffer		24.28.44		40	—	All	1	1	1	No	No	No	
Planchamp	M. Chevalier		09.83.91	100	50	—	All	2	1	1	No	No	No	100
Du Bourg	A. Mason		09.86.66	120	54	—	All	1	-	1	No	No	No	Central
Val Thorens		479												
Fitzroy	M.Loubet		00.04.78		36		All	Yes	Yes	Yes	No	No	Yes	Central
La Marmotte	M. Montero		00.00.07	56	22	—	All	1	1	1	No	No	No	Central
Val Clavière	B. Garcin		00.00.33	100	49	—	All	2	2	1	No	No	No	Central
Val Thorens	B.Branko Perkov		00.04.33	160	80	—	All	3	2	1	No	No	No	Central

HOTEL REFERENCE CHART — ITALY

Resort/Hotel	Owner/Manager	Area Code	Telephone No	Total No. Beds	Double Rooms	Single Rooms	With Bath/ Shower	Dining Rooms	Sitting Rooms	Bars	Dancing with Band	Discothèques	Swimming Pool	Village Centre (metres)
Aprica		0342												
Cristallo			746159	60	20	4	All	1	1	1	No	No	No	Central
Larice Bianco	G. Polatti		746275	60	20	3	All	1		1	No	No	No	400
Torena	A. Corvi		746112	30	15	—	All	1	1	1	No	No	No	Central
Arabba		0436												
Evaldo	Herr Evaldo		79109	48	22	4	All	1	—	1	No	No	No	300
Porta Vescovo	S. Cattameo-Guerra		79139	121	56	—	All	1	1	2	No	Yes	No	Central
Bardonecchia		0122												
Des Geneys	R.Bosticco		99001	110	50	7	All	1	3	1	No	No	No	300
Tabor	G.Rossi		9857	42	16	2	21	2	1	1	No	No	No	Central

HOTEL REFERENCE CHART — ITALY

Resort/Hotel	Owner/Manager	Area Code	Telephone No	Total No. Beds	Double Rooms	Single Rooms	With Bath/ Shower	Dining Rooms	Sitting Rooms	Bars	Dancing with Band	Discothèques	Swimming Pool	Village Centre (metres)
Bormio		**0342**												
Ambassador Chalet	M. Dei Cas		904625	50	20	2	All	1	3	1	No	No	No	300
Funivia	G. Bonacorsi		903242	65	35	4	All	1	1	1	No	No	No	800
Genzianella	G. Andreola		904746	77	37	3	All	1		1	No	No	No	800
Posta	G. Pelosi		904753	102	47	8	55	1	1	1	No	Yes	No	Central
Caspoggio		**0342**												
Kennedy			558055	105	50	5	All	2	1	1	No	Yes	No	500
Cavalese		**0462**												
Cavalese	R. Bonelli		30306	55	25	—	Yes	1	1	1	No	No	No	100
San Valier	M.G.Zorzi		31285	84	42	—	All	1	1	1	No	No	No	100
Cervinia		**0166**												
Breuil	L. Herin		949537	76	37	6	All	1	1	1	No	No	No	Central
Cristallo	C. Paga		943411	220	100	20	All	3	3	1	No	Yes	Yes	600
Europa	Sig. Odisio		948660	118	57	4	All	1	3	2	No	No	No	200
Meuble Joli	M. Pession		949394	24			—	1	—	1	No	No	No	Central
Pellissier	M. Pellissier		949088	18	6	6	All	1	—	2	No	No	No	Central
Champoluc		**0125**												
Alpi Rosa			307135	60		Yes	Yes	1	1	1	No	No	No	
Cortina		**0436**												
Ancora	F. Bertozzi		3261	131	60	11	All	1	4	1	No	Yes	No	Central
Europa	E. Cardazzi		3221	94	42	10	All	2	3	1	No	Yes	No	
Parc Victoria	M. de Dominis		3246	80	36	8	All	2	3	1	No	No	No	Central
De la Poste	R. Manaigo		4271	133	51	31	All	2	4	1	No	No	No	Central
Cortina	F. Apollonio		4221/2	80	35	10	All	2	2	1	No	No	No	Central
Corvara		**0471**												
Pradat	Fam. Miribung		836159	40	18	4	18	1	1	1	No	No	No	800
Sassongher	R. Pescosta		836085	90	40	10	All	2	2	2	No	Yes	Yes	500
Courmayeur		**0165**												
Royal	G. Marzi		846787	186	90	6	All	2	1	1	No	No	Yes	Central
Foppolo		**0345**												
Cristallo	S.E.F. Lift Co		74026	125	60		All	1	3	2	No	No	No	2500
Europa	M. Bellini		74103	43	21	1	All	1	1	1	No	Yes	No	
Pineta	M. Marchesi		74035	50	19	2	All	1	2	1	No	No	No	
Forni Di Sopra		**0432**												
Davost	E. Cambio		88103	70	27		All	1		1	No	No	No	250
Italia			88040	64	29	6	All	1	1	1	No	No	Yes	1800
La Thuile		**0165**												
Planibel			884541	598	300		All	Yes	Yes	Yes	No	Yes	Yes	500
Edelweiss			884144	23			All	1	—	1	No	No	No	300
Chalet Alpina	E. Nico		884187	28	11	3	All	1	1	1	No	No	No	500
La Villa		**0471**												
Christiania	L. Prossliner		847016	55	25	4	All	3	3	1	No	No	Yes	100
Diana	Frau Tirel		85035	36	18	—	All	1	1	1	No	No	No	300
Limone		**0171**												
3 Amis	G. Mormone		928175	140	70	—	All	1	1	1	No	Yes	Yes	6km
Principe	L. Bottero		92389	80	38	4	All	1	1	1	No	No	No	500
Touring	Sig. Cungo		92393	61	32	2	25	2	2	1	No	No	No	Central
Tripoli	D. Giordano		92397	60	26	9	All	1	2	1	No	Yes	No	300
Livigno		**0342**												
Bucaneve	B. Talacci		996201	63	26	12	All	2	1	1	No	No	Yes	300
Europa	S. Strobl		996278	110	50	—	All	1	2	2	No	No	No	500
Pare	G. Hadinger		970623	78	38	2	All	1	4	1	No	No	Yes	1500
Erika	S. Peiti		996034	68	35	3	All	1	1	1	No	No	No	Central
Macugnaga		**0324**												
Dufour	D. Rabboglatti		65529	32	14	2	All	1	1	1	No	No	No	Staffa
Zumstein	Fam. Burgener		65118	76	32	12	All	1	1	1	No	No	No	Staffa
Madesimo		**0343**												
Cascata & Cristallo	T. Ciocca		53108	170	70	10	All	1	2	2	No	Yes	Yes	Central
Meridiana	A. Maranesi		53160	52	26	3	All	1	1	2	No	Yes	No	Central
Torre	S.U.A		53234	107	51	5	All	1	2	1	No	No	No	Central
Madonna Di Campiglio		**0465**												
Cozzio	R. Cozzio		441083	50	22	6	24	1	2	1	No	Yes	No	Central
Grifone	L. Chemini		442002	68	34	—	All	1	2	1	No	Yes	No	800
Milano	Sig. Sommadossi		441210	84	41	2	All	1	2	1	No	No	No	Central
Miramonti	G. Pellegrimi		441021	78	36	6	All	1	1	1	No	No	No	100
Savoia Palace	F. Mizzaro		441004	111	54	3	All	1	3	1	No	No	No	Central
Malga Ciapela		**0437**												
Marmolada	H.O.M.A.N.		722041	160	76	1	All	2	2	2	No	Yes	Yes	Central
Mera		**0163**												
Capricorno	B. Maurizio		78003	50	24	2	—	2	1	2	No	Yes	No	Central
Piancavallo		**0434**												
Montecavallo	C. Mirco		655251	228	7	All	Yes	Yes	No	Yes	No			
Regina	F. Mazzega		655166	120	50	—	All	2	1	1	No	No	No	Central
Pila		**0165**												
Chalet des Alpes	G. Chabod		521017	50	19	2	All	1	2	1	No	No	No	800
San Cassiano		**0471**												
Falzares	A. Crazzolara		849496	40	18	2	All	1	1	1	No	No	No	Central
Rosa Alpina	P. Pizzinini		849500	90	48	8	All	2	2	2	Yes	No	Yes	Central
Santa Caterina		**0342**												
Baita Fiorita	A. Enrichette		903214	42	17	1	All	1	2	1	No	Yes	No	Central
La Pineta			935509	24	11	2	All	1	1	1	No	No	No	950
Milano			925117	135	61	7	All	1	2	1	No	No	No	300
San Martino		**0439**												
Colfosco	A. Orsingher		68319	86	35	9	All	1	2	1	No	No	No	150
Margherita	M. Marini		68140	35	14	3	12	1	1	1	No	No	No	Central
Savoia	F. Lott Liebener		68094	130	61	10	All	2	2	2	No	No	No	200
San Vigilio		**0474**												
Condor	Fam. Leimegger		501017	51	21	7	All	2	1	1	No	No	No	250
Excelsior	P. Heinrich		501036	35			All	1	1	1	No	No	No	100
Sauze D'Oulx		**0122**												
Derby	D. Baccon		850176	34	7	5		1	1	1	No	No	No	Central
Holiday Debili	G. Debili		850260	80	37	6	All	1	1	1	No	No	No	Central
Monte Genevris	G. Eydallin		850086	54	23	8	4	1	1	1	No	No	No	Central
Savoia Debili	S.& G. Debili		850184	80	39	2	16	1	1	1	No	No	No	Central

HOTEL REFERENCE CHART — ITALY

Resort/Hotel	Owner/Manager	Area Code	Telephone No	Total No. Beds	Double Rooms	Single Rooms	With Bath/ Shower	Dining Rooms	Sitting Rooms	Bars	Dancing with Band	Discothèques	Swimming Pool	Village Centre (metres)
Sella Nevea		0433												
Canin	Fam. Gimona		54019	64	30	—	All	2	1	1	No	Yes	No	Central
Nevea	F. Gironi		54043	140	60	—	All	1	2	1	No	Yes	No	Central
Selva		0471												
Alpino-Plan	L. Demetz		795134	63	30	3	All	1	1	1	No	No	No	1000
Antares	C. Bianchi		795400	100	40	5	All	1	1	2	No	No	Yes	Central
Des Alpes	P. Pitscheider		795184	49	19	13	All	2	1	1	No	No	No	Central
Flora	H. Schenk		79531	37	18	1	10	1	1	1	No	No	No	Central
Sestriere		0122												
Cristallo	P. Rubinich		7234	136	60	16	All	Yes	Yes	2	No	Yes	No	Central
Miramonti	R. Jaime		7048	66	30	6	30	Yes	Yes	1	No	No	No	300
Olympic	E. Guiot		77344	50	22	6	All	1	1	1	No	No	No	100

HOTEL REFERENCE CHART — SWITZERLAND

Resort/Hotel	Owner/Manager	Area Code	Telephone No	Total No. Beds	Double Rooms	Single Rooms	With Bath/ Shower	Dining Rooms	Sitting Rooms	Bars	Dancing with Band	Discothèques	Swimming Pool	Village Centre (metres)
Adelboden		033												
Bellevue	H. Richard		673 41 73	101	41	19	60	2	2	1	Yes	Yes	Yes	200
Stein Mattli	Fam. Romer		673 39 39	118	59	-	All	1	1	1	Yes	No	No	300
Andermatt		041												
Bergidyll	R. Fryberg		887 14 55	40	20	3	9	1	1	1	Yes	No	No	Central
Drei Könige	A. Renner		887 00 01	40	18	3	All	2	1	—	No	No	No	Central
Krone	A. Alpenalp		887 00 88	83	31	15	40	4	1	1	No	No	No	Central
Sonne	Fraur Nager		887 12 26	60	25	5	All	2	1	1	No	No	No	Central
Anzère		027												
Zodiaque	M. Christen		399 16 16	140	40	30	All	2	1	2	No	Yes	No	Central
Eden Roc	R. Moos		399 31 00	136	70	—	All	2	1	2	No	No	No	100
Arosa		081												
Des Alpes	L. Hüppi		378 73 73	80	30	20	All	1	1	1	No	No	No	100
Arosa Kulm	C. Ziegler		377 01 31	231	93	44	All	5	2	2	Yes	Yes	Yes	1500
Bellevue	D. Hold		377 12 51	110	46	18	All	2	1	1	No	No	No	300
Hold	G. Hold			40	16	8	12	1	1	1	No	No	No	500
Tschuggen	H.-R. Rütti		377 02 21	235	93	47	All	4	2	2	Yes	No	Yes	1000
Bad Ragaz (Pizol)		081												
Derby	D. Maron			35	15	5	All	1	1	1	Yes	No	No	500
Sandi	Fam. Sandi		302 17 56	80	22	36	All	1	1	1	No	No	No	600
Garni Rössli	Z. Madera		302 32 32	36	14	6	All	1	1	No	No	No	No	200
Barboleusaz		024												
Cremaillere	P. Graf		498 21 55	29	13	2	—	1	1	1	No	Yes	No	Central
Braunwald		055												
Alpenblick	Fam.Gredinger		643 15 44	100	40	20	30	2	2	2	No	No	No	Central
Alpina	R. Schweitzer		643 32 84	55	18	12	All	1	1	–	No	No	No	300
Bellevue	M. Vogel		643 30 30	100	46	8	40	2	3	1	Yes	Yes	Yes	300
Champéry		024												
Des Alpes	F.Rieme		479 12 22	45	18	4	20	1	2	1	No	No	No	400
Beau-Séjour	G.Avanthey		479 17 01	39	17	5	All	1	1	1	No	No	No	100
De Champéry	O. de Reynier		479 10 71	133	63	9	All	1	1	1	No	No	No	Central
Suisse	E. & C. Berra		479 07 07	80	40	–	All	2	2	2	No	Yes	No	Central
Chateau D'Oex		026												
Beau-Séjour	C. Haas		924 74 23	72	30	12	All	1	1	1	No	No	No	Central
La Rocail	I. Nicolin		924 62 15	24	12	—	All	2	—	1	No	No	No	500
Crans		027												
Miezdor	J Mudry		481 44 33	32	15	2	All	1	1	1	Yes	No	No	100
Royal	C. Fattore		481 39 31	104	50	4	All	1	2	1	No	Yes	No	Central
Davos		081												
Derby	H.R. Schmid		417 95 00	180	82	16	All	2	2	2	No	No	Yes	Central
Flüela	E. Marlés		410 17 17	130	60	20	All	3	3	1	No	PB	Yes	Central
Meierhof	R. Frey		416 82 85	130	60	10	70	2	1	1	No	PB	Yes	Central
Morosani Post Hotel	M. Grubser		413 74 74	200	90	20	All	3	3	3	Yes	Yes	Yes	Central
Schweizerhof	M. Demisch		413 26 26	150	57	36	All	2	3	1	No	PB	Yes	Central
Sonnenberg	R. Weber		416 10 22	65	27	10	All	2	1	2	No	No	Yes	500
Terminus	S. Ritter			106	45	16	47	1	1	1	No	No	No	300
Bellavista	Fam. Moser		417 56 00	48	24	—	All	1	1	1	No	No	No	500
Engelberg		041												
Bellevue			637 12 13	130	48	34	All	2	2	1	No	No	No	Central
Central	Fam. Ruckstuhl		639 32 32	80	37	6	All	3	2	2	No	No	Yes	100
Crystal	D. Fioretti		637 21 22	45	18	9	All	2	1	—	No	No	No	300
Hess	E. Hess		637 13 66	52	24	4	16	1	1	1	No	PB	No	
Eden	Fam. Reinhardt		639 56 39	25	7	2	All	2	1	1	No	No	No	100
Flims		081												
Albana	R. Alder		911 23 33	60	28	3	All	2	1	1	No	No	No	Central
Adula	P. Hotz		911 01 61	180	79	22	All	3	2	1	No	No	Yes	300
Park Waldhaus	J. Müller		911 01 81	265	106	54	All	4	2	3	Yes	No	Yes	500
Flumserberg		081												
Alpina	A. Güller		733 12 32	51	21	9	18	2	1	1	Yes	No	No	200
Baselbieterhaus	Mr. Kuhn		733 16 43	120			16	1	3	1	No	No	No	100
Tannenboden	H. Kurath		733 24 08	65	20	12	20	2	2	1	Yes	No	No	100
Grächen		027												
Des Alpes	F. Ruff		956 22 44	50	18	6	All	1	1	1	No	No	No	150
Elite	G. Reynard		956 16 12	48	21	3	All	1	1	1	No	No	No	250
Hannigalp	R. Andenmatten		956 25 55	40	20	2	All	3	4	1	No	No	Yes	100
Grindelwald		033												
Belvedere	Fam. Hauser		854 54 54	100	45	10	All	2	2	1	No	No	Yes	250
Derby-Bahnhof	C. Märkle		854 54 61	125	50	25	All	1	1	1	Yes	Yes	No	50
Eiger	B. Heller		853 21 21	90	41	8	All	2	1	2	No	No	No	Central
Regina	H. Krebs		854 54 55	180	80	20	All	2	2	2	No	PB	Yes	20

PB = Piano Bar

HOTEL REFERENCE CHART — SWITZERLAND

Resort/Hotel	Owner/Manager	Area Code	Telephone No	Total No. Beds	Double Rooms	Single Rooms	With Bath/ Shower	Dining Rooms	Sitting Rooms	Bars	Dancing with Band	Discothèques	Swimming Pool	Village Centre (metres)
Gstaad		**033**												
Alphorn	Fam. Reichenbach		744 45 45	32	11	10	16	1	1	1	No	No	Yes	1500
Bellevue	F. Salverda		748 31 71	88	33	22	All	2	1	1	No	No	No	200
Victoria	H. Oehrli		744 14 31	54	25	4	All	1	1	1	Yes	No	No	Central
Rütti	H. Rytz		744 29 21	16	4	All	1	1	1	No	No	No	1500	
Klosters		**081**												
Chesa Grischuna	H. Guler		422 22 22	42	16	10	17	1	1	1	No	No	No	Central
Grand Vereina	A. Dietlhelm		422 61 91	160	65	25	90	2	3	2	No	No	Yes	Central
Steinbock	S. Barblan		422 45 45	80	37	4	All	2	—	1	No	No	No	200
Silvretta Park Hotel	U. Erpenbeck		422 61 21	216	75	4	All	3	2	2	No	Yes	Yes	Central
Laax		**086**												
Happy Rancho	S. Demola			300	60	12	All	2	1	1	Yes	Yes	Yes	300
Larisch	H. Kern		921 47 47	• 70	20	5	27	2	2	—	No	No	Yes	Central
Riva				54	27			1	No	1	No	No	Yes	Central
Lenzerheide-Valbella		**081**												
Grand Kurhaus	R. Poltera			130	58	14	All	2	2	2	Yes	Yes	Yes	Central
Lenzerhorn	R. Bossi		384 11 05	52	18	17	8	3	1	1	No	No	No	Central
Les Diablerets		**024**												
Mon Abri	G. Nussbaumer		492 34 81	40	17	6	All	2	1	1	No	Yes	No	800
Ermitage & Res Meurice	A. Givel			150	70	10	All	2	1	2	No	Yes	Yes	Central
Les Lilas	J. Matti		492 31 34	20	8	2	5	2	1	1	No	No	No	500
Les Mosses		**025**												
Sapiniere	J. Durgnat			30	5	—	—	Open Plan		1		No	No	Central
Restol Keller	F. Stucki			40	21	—	All	1	—	1	No	No	No	Central
Leysin		**024**												
Central-Résidence	P. Moret		494 12 11	200	69	17	All	2	2	1	No	Yes	Yes	500
Club Vagabond	D. Gross		494 13 21	50	–	—	—	1	1	2	No	Yes	No	300
Montana		**027**												
Crans Ambassador	J. Rey		481 48 11	130	61	8	All	1	2	1	No	No	No	250
St. Georges	R. Grunder		481 24 14	85	35	15	All	3	1	1	No	PB	No	100
Vermala	G. Plozza		481 28 73	60	21	15	All	1	1	No	No			
Morgins		**024**												
Beau-Site Garmi	G. Diserens		477 11 38	30	12	6	—	1	1	1	Yes	No	No	200
Bellevue	G. Torrione			80	22	8	All	2	1	1	No	Yes	Yes	100
Mürren		**033**												
Eiger	Von Allmen/Stähli		855 1331	90	36	8	All	1	1	1	No	Yes	Yes	500
Jungfrau	S. & O.Emmenegger-Jordan		855 4545	100	52	11	All	1	2	1	Yes	No	No	200
Palace	A. Dietler		855 2424	100	48	2	All	3	1	2	No	Yes	Yes	300
Pontresina		**081**												
Engadinerhof	E. Heinrich		842 62 12	140	58	24	60	1	1	1	No	No	No	Central
Sport	H.& R. Pampel		842 63 31	145	53	33	75	1	1	1	No	No	No	Central
Steinbock	C. Walther		842 63 71	52	23	6	All	2	1	—	No	No	Yes	100
Rossinière		**026**												
La Colline	C. Martin			15	6	3	—	1	1	No	No	No		800
De Ville	B. Pinotit			20	Dorm	3		1	—	—	No	No	No	Central
Rougemont		**026**												
Valrose	A. Cottier		925 81 46	27	12	3	All	2	1	1	No	No	No	Central
Saas Fee		**027**												
Allalin	T. Zurbriggen		957 18 15	80	39	-	All	2	1	1	No	No	No	200
Bergfreude	0. Burgener		957 21 37	40	16	8	All	2	1	1	Yes	No	No	200
Christiania	K. Burgener		957 31 66	50	20	10	All	1	1	1	Yes	No	No	Central
Dom	R. Anthamatten		957 26 31	77	26	10	All	1	1	2	No	No	No	Central
Marmotte	K. Dreier		957 28 57	43	19	5	All	1	2	1	No	No	No	300
Walliserhof	B. Anthamatten		958 19 00	110	50	4	All	1	2	2	Yes	Yes	Yes	Central
St. Moritz		**081**												
Bären	Fam. Degiacomi		833 56 56	115	47	18	All	2	2	1	No	No	Yes	300
Crystal	F. & B.Daxer		832 11 65	144	62	20	All	1	1	1	No	No	No	Central
Kulm	Dir Hunkeler		832 11 51	300	125	50	All	3	10	2	Yes	No	Yes	200
Palace	D.R. Bachofen		837 10 00	370	170	30	All	5	18	2	Yes	Yes	Yes	Central
Schweizerhof	U. Höhener		837 07 07	150	71	14	All	1	1	4	Yes	Yes	No	Central
Chesa Guardalej	P. Kampher		832 23 73	220	110	—	All	3	1	1	Yes	Yes	Yes	2000
San Bernardino		**092**												
Albarella	H. Ellmauer			130	65	—	All	2	1	1	No	Yes	Yes	800
Verbier		**027**												
Alba	P. Zuber		775 29 00	150	70	10	All	1	1	2	No	No	No	500
Bristol	M. Contat		771 65 77	48	14	6	All	—	—	—	No	Yes	No	Central
L'Auberge	A. Oreiller		771 62 72	40	15	10	All	Yes	Yes	Yes	No	No		120
Eden	B. Douchet			38	18	2	All	1	1	1	No	No	No	Central
De la Poste	A. Oreiller		771 66 81	60		13	23	1	1	1	No	No	Yes	Central
Rhodania	0. Guignard		771 61 21	80	33	11	All	1	1	1	No	Yes	No	200
De Verbier	P. Bruchez		771 66 88	64	31	2	All	1	1	1	No	No	No	Central
Villars		**024**												
Écureuil	C. Seeholzer		495 27 95	54	27	—	All	1	1	1	No	No	No	500
Eurotel	S. Muller		495 31 31	350	145	25	All	2	1	2	No	No	Yes	300
Parc	P. Chevrier		495 21 21	110	50	10	All	3	3	2	No	No	Yes	500
Renardière	M. Plattner		495 24 92	24	—	All	1	1	1	No	No	No	300	
Wengen		**033**												
Falken	Fam.Cova		856 51 21	85	36	13	39	1	3	2	No	No	No	300
Regina	G. Meyer		855 15 12	175	79	17	All	2	1	1	No	No	No	200
Schweizerheim	E. Lauener		855 11 12	40	15	9	All	1	2	1	No	No	No	500
Silberhorn	H.Zinnert		856 51 31	140	54	7	All	1	2	3	Yes	Yes	No	Central
Victoria-Lauberhorn	S. Castelein		856 51 51	120	57	12	All	1	2	2	No	No	No	100
Wengener Hof	H. Zinnert		855 28 55	64	24	12	All	1	2	1	No	No	No	500
Bellevue	E. Graf		855 11 21	70	33	6	All	2	3	1	No	No	No	100
Sunstar	M. & E. Leemann		856 51 11	154	77	15	All	2	1	1	No	No	Yes	Central
Wildhaus		**071**												
Alpenblick	M. Weibel			39	18	3	All	2	—	1	Yes	No	No	Central
Hirschen	S. Walt		999 22 52	130	60	20	All	2	1	3	No	Yes	Yes	Central
Selun	O. Thoma			24	8	5	All	1	1		No	No	No	Central
Sonne	P. Beutler		999 23 23	50	24	1	All	2	1	1	No	Yes	Yes	Central
Zermatt		**027**												
Alex	A Perren		967 17 26	140	63	8	All	2	1	3	No	Yes	Yes	100
Derby	P. Borriello			45	17	6	20	1	1	1	No	No	No	Central
Mont Cervin	W. Pinkwart		966 88 88	267	122	22	All	3	2	2	No	No	Yes	Central
Nicoletta	H. J. Walther		967 01 51	115	59	—	All	2	1	1	No	PB	Yes	Central
Parkhotel Beau-Site	F. Schwegler		967 41 41	140	63	10	All	4	1	1	No	No	Yes	200
Walliserhof	R. Inderbinen		966 65 55	54	24	6	All	2	1	1	No	No	No	Central
Zermatterhof	J.P. Lanz		966 66 00	148	60	25	All	2	2	2	No	PB	Yes	Central

PB = Piano bar

LIECHTENSTEIN

Resort/Hotel	Owner/Manager	Area Code	Telephone No	Total No. Beds	Double Rooms	Single Rooms	With Bath/ Shower	Dining Rooms	Sitting Rooms	Bars	Dancing with Band	Discothèques	Swimming Pool	Village Centre (metres)
Malbun		**075**												
Gorfion	Fam. Schwärzler		264.18.83	70	35	—	All	1	1	1	No	No	Yes	100
Malbunerhof	P. Sparber		263.29.44	70	22	3	All	2	2	1	No	No	Yes	Central

HOTEL REFERENCE CHART — SPAIN

Resort/Hotel	Owner/Manager	Area Code	Telephone No	Total No. Beds	Double Rooms	Single Rooms	With Bath/ Shower	Dining Rooms	Sitting Rooms	Bars	Dancing with Band	Discothèques	Swimming Pool	Village Centre (metres)
Baqueira Beret		973												
Montarto	D.M. Espanol		64.44.44	304	134	32	125	2	1	1	No	Yes	No	Central
Cerler		974												
Monte Alba	T. Sanchez		55.11.36	250	119	12	All	2	2	2	No	No	Yes	200
Formigal		974												
Eguzki-Lore	J. Zabalza		48.80.75				All	1	1	1	No	No	No	
Formigal	I. Ramos d'Angelo		48.80.34	210	96	12	All	1	1	2	No	Yes	No	
Nievesol	A. Salvador			278	133	12	All	2	2	2	Yes	No	Yes	
La Molina		972												
Adserá	J. Adserá		89.20.01	90	38	2	All	2	2	2	No	Yes	No	1500
Solineu-Palace	J. Riera		14.51.19	95	—	—	All	2	1	2	No	Yes	Yes	
La Solana	J. Poos		89.20.00	60	27	3	All	1	1	1	No	No	No	1500
Masella		972												
Alp	Mr. Masip		89.01.51	300	146	2	All	1	1	1	No	Yes	Yes	Central
Panticosa		974												
Escalar	L. Guillen		48.70.08	80	40	—	All	2	3	1	No	Yes	No	Central
Sierra Nevada		958												
Melia Sierra Nevadas	F. Sarabia		24.91.11	525	140	25	All	1	1	2	No	Yes	No	Central
Melia Solynieve	F. Sarabia		24.91.11	427			All	1	1	1	No	Yes	No	Central

HOTEL REFERENCE CHART — ANDORRA

Resort/Hotel	Owner/Manager	Area Code	Telephone No	Total No. Beds	Double Rooms	Single Rooms	With Bath/ Shower	Dining Rooms	Sitting Rooms	Bars	Dancing with Band	Discothèques	Swimming Pool	Village Centre (metres)
Arinsal		376												
Solana	A. Solana		835127	180	80	5	All	1	1	1	No	Yes	Yes	100
Soldeu/El Tarter		376												
Del Tarter	Mr & Mrs Mateu		851165	80	40	—	All	1	1	1	No	No	No	—
Roc St. Miquel	C & M Leonard		851079	24	12	—	All	1	1	1	No	No	No	300
Bruxelles	M. & Mme.Tricoire		851010	54	16	2	—	1	1	1	No	No	No	Central
Parador Canaro	J.Farre		851046	54	18	—	All	1	—	1	No	No	No	1500

HOTEL REFERENCE CHART — ROMANIA

Resort/Hotel	Owner/Manager	Area Code	Telephone No	Total No. Beds	Double Rooms	Single Rooms	With Bath/ Shower	Dining Rooms	Sitting Rooms	Bars	Dancing with Band	Discothèques	Swimming Pool	Village Centre (metres)
Poiana Brasov														
Alpin	I. Cherghescu			272	129	—	All	Yes	Yes	Yes	No	No	Yes	1000
Bradul	G. Ilescu			136	55	26	All	Yes	Yes	Yes	No	Yes	No	
Predeal														
Cioplea				288	136	14	All	Yes	Yes	Yes	Yes	Yes	No	
Rozmarin	S. Bodeanu			300	145	5	All	2	1	1	No	Yes	No	
Sinaia														
Alpin	G. Ianta			122	66	4	All	2	—	1	Yes	Yes	No	10km
Montana	M. Chitic			350	153	12	All	3	2	2	Yes	Yes	Yes	Central

HOTEL REFERENCE CHART — SCOTLAND

Resort/Hotel	Owner/Manager	Area Code	Telephone No	Total No. Beds	Double Rooms	Single Rooms	With Bath/ Shower	Dining Rooms	Sitting Rooms	Bars	Dancing with Band	Discothèques	Swimming Pool	Village Centre (metres)
Aviemore		01479												
Stakis Badenoch	Miss J.Keyes		810261	54	8	—	All	1	2	2	Yes	No	No	500
Alt Na Craig	M. & J. Clifton		810378	20	8	1	1	1	2	2	No	No	No	700
Cairngorm	Barratt		810233	47	16	7	18	1	1	3	Yes	No	No	Central
Coylumbridge	Stakis		810661	400	168	4	All	2	3	4	Yes	Yes	Yes	2000
Craiglea Guest House	H. & A. Nunn		810210	24	10	2	1	1	1	—	No	No	No	Central
High Range	F. Vastano		810636	20	6	—	All	1	No	Yes	No	No	No	500
Aviemore Highland Hotel	J. Gatenby		810771	250	99	4	All	1	1	2	No	No	No	1000
Boat of Garten		0147983												
Craigard	M. Robinson		206	43	17	5	8	1	2	1	No	No	No	350
Boat	D.B. Wilson		258	70	29	7	All	2	1	2	No	Yes	No	Central
Carrbridge		0147984												
Carrbridge	J. MacGregor-Smith		202	99	43	11	13	1	1	2	No	No	No	
Glenshee		01250												
Altamount Chalets	A. Steeple		3324	118			All	—	—	No	No	No	No	
Angus	A. Scott		2455	—	68	18	All	1	2	2	Yes	Yes	Yes	Central
Dalmunzie	S. Winton	0125085	224	34	15	1	15	1	3	1	No	No	No	Central
Fife Arms	G. Bowman	013383	644	—	65	20	80	1	1	2	Yes	Yes	No	
Glenshieling	S. Jones	01250	4605	12	4	2	1	1	2	—	No	No	No	
Log Cabin Hotel	A. Finch	0125081	288	26	13	—	13	1	1	1	No	No	No	800
Spittal	M. Stewart	0125085	215	100	36	8	44	1	—	1	Yes	Yes	No	
Kingussie		015402												
Duke of Gordon	Mr & Mrs Welsh		302	96	34	8	8	1	1	1	No	Yes	No	
Royal	B. Justice		898	80	32	4	26	1	1	2	Yes	No	No	Central
NethyBridge		0147982												
Nethy Bridge *Inc.Dormitories	A.Pru		203	170*	12	12	All	1	6	4	Yes	Yes	No	Central
Newtonmore		015403												
Mains	J. Hilton		206	58	22	10	2	1	2	2	No	No	No	

HOTEL REFERENCE CHART — BULGARIA

Resort/Hotel	Owner/Manager	Area Code	Telephone No	Total No. Beds	Double Rooms	Single Rooms	With Bath/ Shower	Dining Rooms	Sitting Rooms	Bars	Dancing with Band	Discothèques	Swimming Pool	Village Centre (metres)
Borovets														
Bor	Balkan Tourist			88	37	8	All	1	1	No	Yes	No	No	Central
Edelweiss	Balkan Tourist			146	64	14	All	1	2	1	No	No	No	Central
Rila	Balkan Tourist			1250	550	—	All	2	4	4	Yes	Yes	No	Central
Pamporovo														
Murgavec	Balkan Tourist			164	75	8	All	1	8	2	No	Yes	No	Central
Perelik	Balkan Tourist			465	199	10	All	2	2	4	No	Yes	Yes	Central

HOTEL REFERENCE CHART — NORWAY

Resort/Hotel	Owner/Manager	Area Code	Telephone No	Total No. Beds	Double Rooms	Single Rooms	With Bath/ Shower	Dining Rooms	Sitting Rooms	Bars	Dancing with Band	Discothèques	Swimming Pool	Village Centre (metres)
Austlid		**61**												
Holiday Centre *Inc.Cabins	P. & G. Stephensen		228513	375*	24	6	30	2	2	1	No	Yes	No	
Dalseter		**61**												
Dalseter	E. Gillebo		299910	150	64	26	81	1	4	1	Yes	No	Yes	
Fefor		**61**												
Fefor	R. Jacobsen		290099	256	100	15	All	2	3	1	Yes	No	Yes	
Geilo		**67**												
Bardola	F.A. Walhovd		85400	250	102	—	All	1	2	3	Yes	No	Yes	
Geilo	F. Mietle		85511	144	72		All	1	4	2	Yes	Yes	No	
Holms	P. Olsen		85622	130	65	—	All	1	1	2	Yes	Yes	Yes	
Hemesdal		**320**												
Viking-Hemesdal	P. Christoffersen		79102	140	55	—	All	2	1	2	Yes	Yes	No	
Lillehammer		**61**												
Lillehammer Touristhotel	L. Koppervik		286000	330	155	—	All	1	2	2	Yes	No	Yes	
Oppland	P. Halsa		258500	140	60	10	All	1	3	2	Yes	Yes	Yes	
Victoria Rica	0. Gudim		250049	220			All	1	2	3	Yes	No	Yes	
Nordseter		**61**												
Lillehammer	Fam. Vestol		264004	83	37	9	All	1	3	2	Yes	No	Yes	
Nevra	Fam. Khaliq		269067	120	50	20	55	1	3	2	Yes	No	No	
Norefjell		**321**												
Fjellhvil	Fam. Ertzeid		49174	100	45	2	All	2	4	1	Yes	Yes	No	
Sjusjøen		**62**												
Fjellstu	E. Halla		363408	120			25	Yes	Yes	Yes	Yes	No	No	
Sjusjøen	K.Lein		363401	140	69	—	All	1	3	2	Yes	No	Yes	
Panorama	H. Nilsson		363451	110	48	4	All	1	1	1	Yes	No	No	
Skeikampen/Gausdal		**61**												
Skeikampen	L.B. Anderson		228505	285	68	17	All	2	2	1	Yes	No	Yes	
Gausdal	Fam. Smith-Erichsen		228500	260	120	10	All	2	7	2	Yes	Yes	Yes	
Spåtind		**61**												
Spåtind	S. Johansen		9056	84			All	1	5	1	Yes	Yes	Yes	
Ustaoset		**32**												
Ustaoset	E. Svelland		87161	145	54	36	89	1	4	2	Yes	Yes	Yes	
Voss		**56**												
Fleischers	O. Fleischer-Tonjum		511155	120	51	20	All	1	4	2	Yes	No	Yes	
Kringsjå	K. Klemetzen		511627	40	16	2	15	1	2	1	No	No	No	
Park Voss	J.B. Anderson		511322	76	24	22	48	1	2	3	Yes	No	No	
Vang	T. Tillung		512145	35	13	4		2	1	1	No	No	No	
Youth Hostel	Y.H.A.		512017	200			All	1	1	No	No	No	No	
Wadahl		**61**												
Wadahl	T. Wadahl		298300	180	80	20	All	1	3	2	Yes	No	Yes	

TO YOUR RESORT BY CAR & AIR

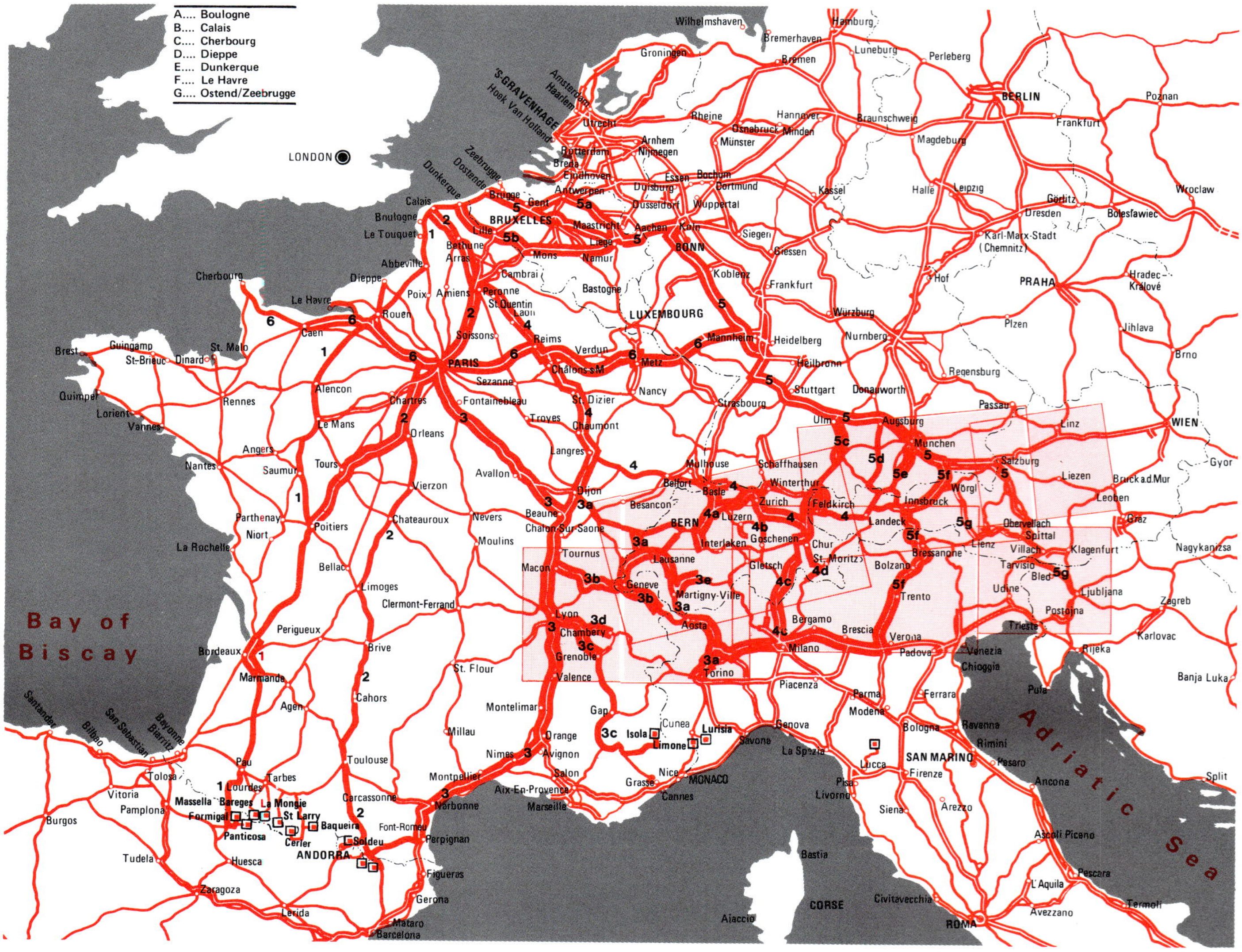

TO YOUR RESORT BY CAR & AIR

Country/Resort	Map Reference	Airport* (Charters)	Travel by Air Onwards time Hours	Main Map Route No. Calais (B) Le Havre (F)	Country Map Route No.	Total distance Channel Ports Miles	Km.
AUSTRIA							
Alpbach	4D	Salzburg	2.45	F6/5	5f	767½	1235
Auffach	5D	Munich	3.15	B5	5f	709½	1142
Axamer-Lizum	3D	Innsbruck	0.45	F6/5	5e	774	1246
Bad Aussee	3C	Salzburg	2.15	B5	5h	807	1299
Badgastein	6D	Salzburg	2.00	B5	5	781	1257
Bad Goisern	3C	Salzburg	2.00	B5	5h	760	1223
Bad Hofgastein	6D	Munich	1.45	F6/5	5	830	1336
Berwang	3C	Munich	2.50	B5	5e	704½	1134
Bichlbach	3C	Munich	2.40	F6/5	5e	756	1217
Brand	1D	Zurich	2.55	F6/4	4	580	933
Bürserberg	1D	Zurich	2.40	F6/4	4	622	1001
Damüls	1D	Zurich	3.15	B2/4	4	601	96
Dienten	6C	Salzburg	2.30	B5	5	832	1224
Ehrwald	3D	Munich	3.00	F6/5	5e	750	1207
Ellmau	5C	Innsbruck	1.45	B5	5f	709	1141
Faschina	1D	Zurich	3.00	F6/4	4	626	1007
Fieberbrunn	5C	Munich	3.55	B5	5f	718	1156
Finkenberg	4D	Munich	3.30	F6/5	5f	768½	1237
Filzmoos	7D	Salzburg	1.45	B5	5	766	1233
Fontanella	1D	Zurich	3.00	B2/4	4	580	934
Fügen	4D	Innsbruck	2.30	B5	5e	720	1159
Fulpes	4D	Innsbruck	1.00	B5	5e/f	734	1181
Galtür	2E	Innsbruck	2.15	F6/5	5e	806½	1298
Gargellen	1E	Zurich	3.10	F6/4	4	636	1024
Gaschurn	1E	Zurich	4.00	B2/4	4	591	951
Gerlos	5D	Munich	3.30	B5	5f	739½	1190
Gosau	2C	Salzburg	2.10	B5	5h	812	1307
Gurtis	1D	Zurich	2.30	F6/4	4	611½	984
Hinterglemm	6D	Salzburg	1.45	F6/5	5	849	1366
Hinterstoder	4C	Salzburg	2.30	B5	5h	770	1239
Hinterthal	6D	Salzburg	2.30	B5	5	757	1218
Hintertux	4D	Munich	4.00	B5	5f	745½	1200
Hochgurgl	3E	Innsbruck	2.15	F6/5	5e	808½	1301
Hochsölden	3E	Innsbruck	2.00	B5	5e	747½	1203
Igls	4D	Innsbruck	0.30	F6/5	5e	773	1244

Country/Resort AUSTRIA	Map Reference	Airport* (Charters)	Travel by Air Onwards time Hours	Main Map Route No. Calais (B) Le Havre (F)	Country Map Route No.	Total distance Channel Ports Miles	Km.
Ischgl	2D	Innsbruck	2.30	B5	5e	746	1201
Jerzens	3D	Munich	3.30	B5	5e	743	1196
Kaprun	6D	Salzburg	2.30	F6/5	5	837½	1348
Kirchberg	5C	Salzburg	2.15	B5	5f/5g	715	1151
Kitzbühel	5C	Salzburg	2.00	B5	5f/5g	716½	1153
Klösterle	1D	Zurich	3.55	B2/4	4	589	948
Kuhtai	3D	Innsbruck	1.00	F6/5	5e	790½	1272
Lanersbach	4D	Munich	3.55	B5	5f	742	1194
Laterns	1D	Zurich	2.30	F6/4	4	611½	984
Lech	2D	Innsbruck	2.30	B2/4	4	599½	965
Leogang	6D	Salzburg	1.45	B5	5	792	1275
Lermoos	3D	Munich	3.00	F6/5	5e	750½	1208
Lienz	6E	Salzburg	3.30	B5	5g	749	1205
Mayrhofen	4D	Munich	3.25	B5	5f	734	1181
Mieders	4D	Innsbruck	1.00	B5	5e/f	734	1181
Nauders	2E	Innsbruck	3.20	F6/5	5e	809	1302
Niederau	5C	Munich	3.00	B5	5f	704	1133
Oberau	5D	Munich	3.05	F6/5	5f	757	1218
Obergurgl	3E	Innsbruck	2.15	B5	5e	755	1215
Obertauern	7D	Salzburg	2.30	F6/5	5	832½	1340
Obertraun	3C	Salzburg	2.15	B5	5h	807	1299
Pertisau	4C	Munich	2.45	B5	5e	720	1159
Raggal	1D	Zurich	2.45	F6/4	4	620	998
Saalbach	6D	Salzburg	1.30	B5	5	792	1275
St.Anton	2D	Innsbruck	2.15	B2/4	4	601½	968
St.Leonhard im Pitztal	3D	Munich	3.40	B5	5e	750	1207
Schruns	1D	Zurich	3.30	F6/4	4	627	1009
Seefeld	3D	Innsbruck	0.45	F6/5	5e	755½	1216
Serfaus	2D	Innsbruck	2.30	B5	5e	740½	1192
Sölden	3E	Innsbruck	1.45	F6/5	5e	800	1288
Söll	5C	Salzburg	2.15	B5	5f	701	1128
Sonntag	1D	Zurich	2.45	B2/4	4	579	932
Spital a. P.	4C	Salzburg	2.40	B5	5h	803	1292
Steinach	4D	Munich	3.00	B5	5f	743	1196
Stuben	2D	Innsbruck	2.15	F6/4	4	635	1022
Telfes	4D	Innsbruck	1.00	B5	5e/f	734	1181
Tschagguns	1D	Zurich	4.00	F6/4	4	626	1107
Vent	3E	Innsbruck	2.00	B5	5e	755	1215
Wagrain	7D	Salzburg	2.00	F6/5	5	816½	1314
Westendorf	5D	Munich	3.00	B5	5f/5g	709½	1142
Windischgarsten	4C	Salzburg	2.30	B5	5h	803	1292
Zell am See	6D	Salzburg	2.00	F6/5	5	835	1344
Zell am Ziller	4D	Munich	3.30	B5	5e	728	1173
Zürs	2D	Innsbruck	2.30	B2/4	4	590½	950

Not necessarily the nearest airport but the ones used by the majority of the Tour Operators for charters. Nearest international airport is shown at the head of each resort write-up.

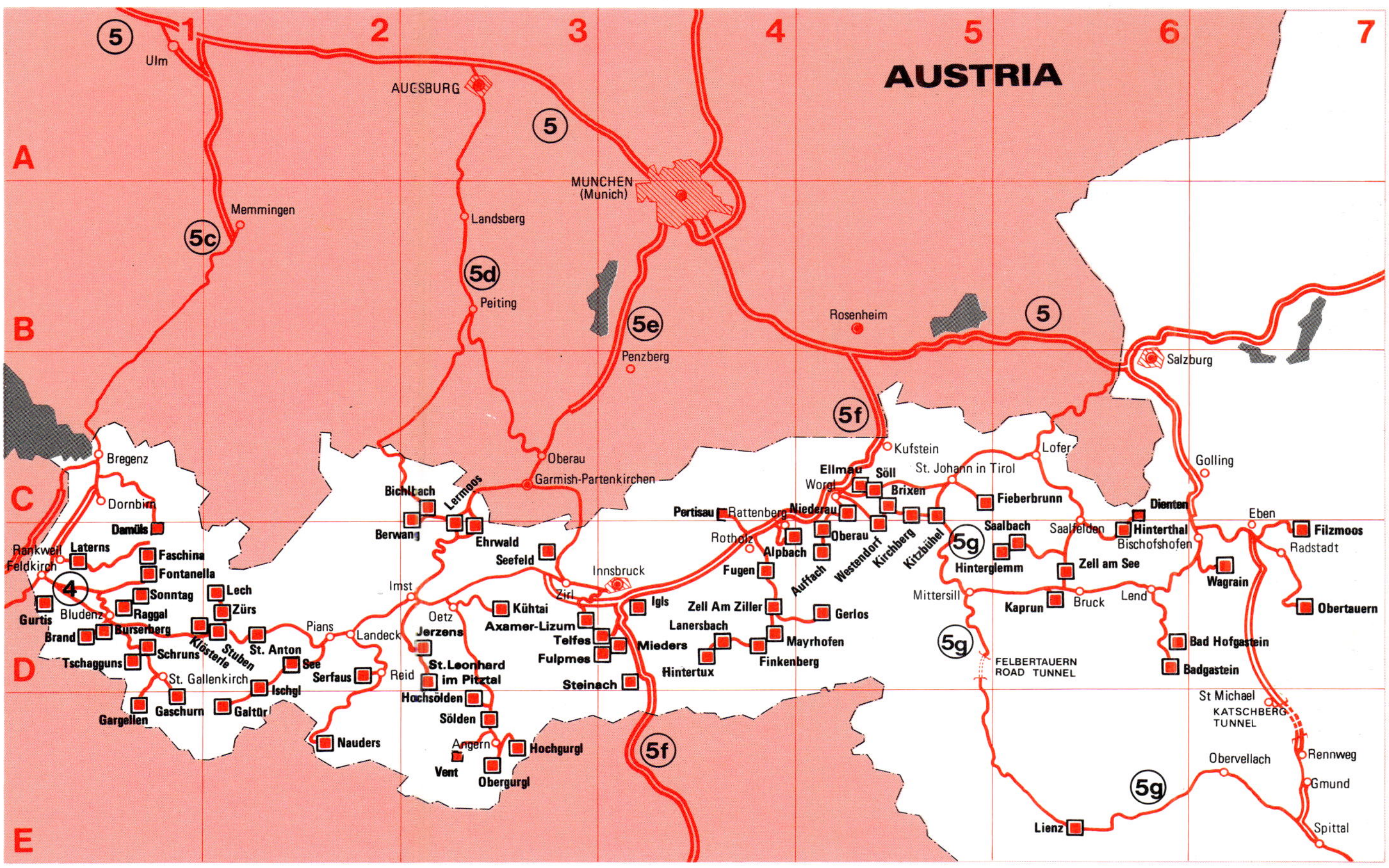

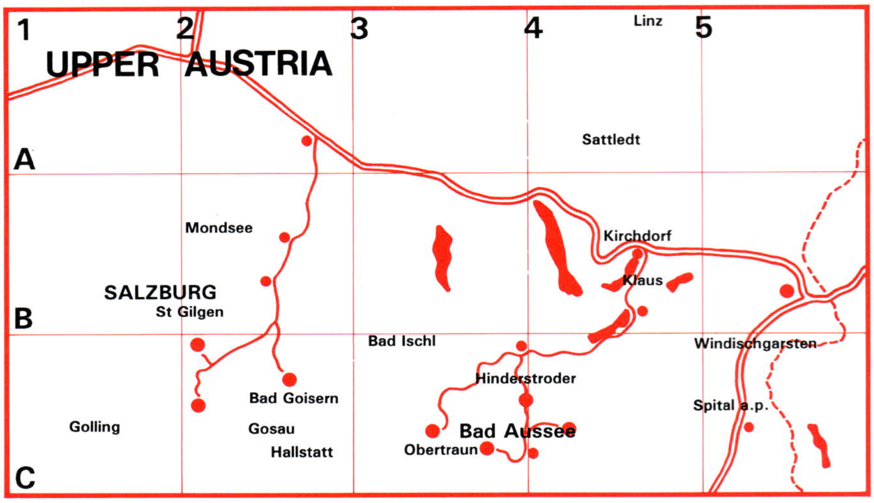

Country/Resort	Map Reference	Airport* (Charters)	Travel by Air Onwards time Hours	Main Map Route No. Calais (B) Le Havre (F)	Country Map Route No.	Total distance Channel Ports Miles	Km.
FRANCE							
Alpe d'Huez	3D	Lyon	2.45	F6/3	3c	516	830
Argentière	5B	Geneva	2.35	F6/3	3b	510	820
Avoriaz	5B	Geneva	2.00	B2/3	3b	555½	894
Chamonix	5B	Geneva	2.30	F6/3	3b	505	813
Chatel	5A	Geneva	1.45	B2/3	3b/f	522	840
Courchevel	4D	Geneva	3.00	B2/3/3c	3d	547½	881
Flaine	4B	Geneva	2.30	F6/3	3b	491	790
Font-Romeu	Main Map	Toulouse	4.00	F3	Pyrenees	710	1142
Isola 2000	Main Map	Nice	1.30	B2/3/3c	Main Map	738½	1189
La Clusaz	4B	Geneva	1.15	F6/3	3b	491	790
La Plagne	4D	Geneva	3.00	B2/3/3c	3d	612	985
La Toussuire	3D	Geneva	4.10	B/2/3/3c	3D	543	874
Le Corbier	3D	Geneva	4.15	B2/3/3c	3d	547	880
Les Arcs	4D	Geneva	4.00	F6/3/3c	3d	563	906
Les Deux Alpes	3E	Lyon	3.00	B2/3	3c	580	933
Les Gets	4B	Geneva	2.30	F6/3	3b	491	790
Les Houches	5C	Geneva	2.30	F6/3/3c	3b	498	801
Les Menuires	4D	Geneva	3.15	F6/3/3c	3d	533	858
Megève	4C	Geneva	2.30	F6/3	3b	502	808
Méribel	4D	Geneva	3.00	B2/3/3c	3d	601	968
Montgenèvre	4E	Turin	2.00	F6/3	3c	556	895
St.Gervais	4C	Geneva	2.45	B2/3	3b	549	884
Serre Chevalier	4E	Turin	3.00	F6/3	3c	543	874
Tignes	5D	Geneva	4.30	B2/3/3c	3d	633	1019
Val d'Isère	5D	Geneva	4.35	F6/3/3c	3d	573½	923

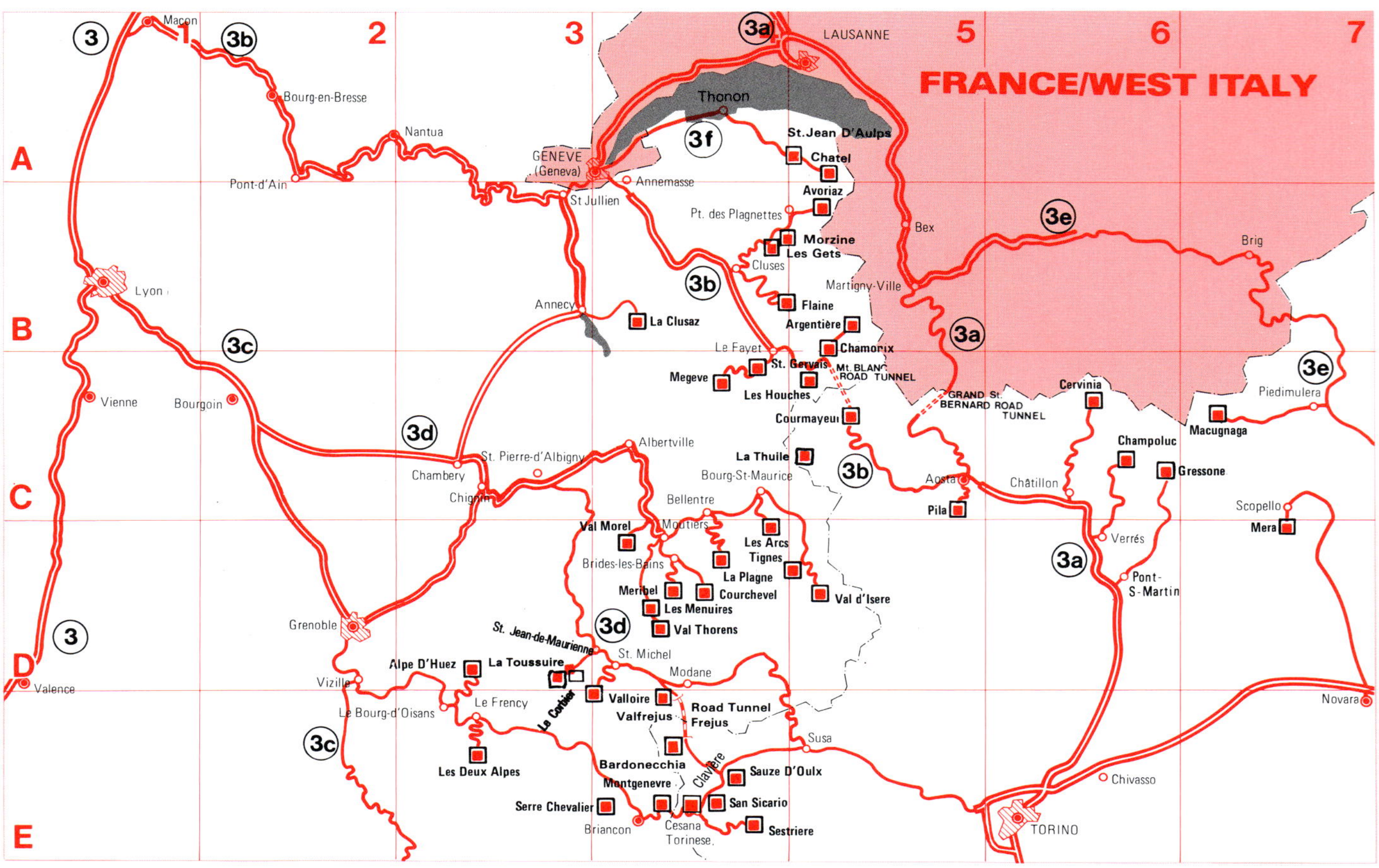

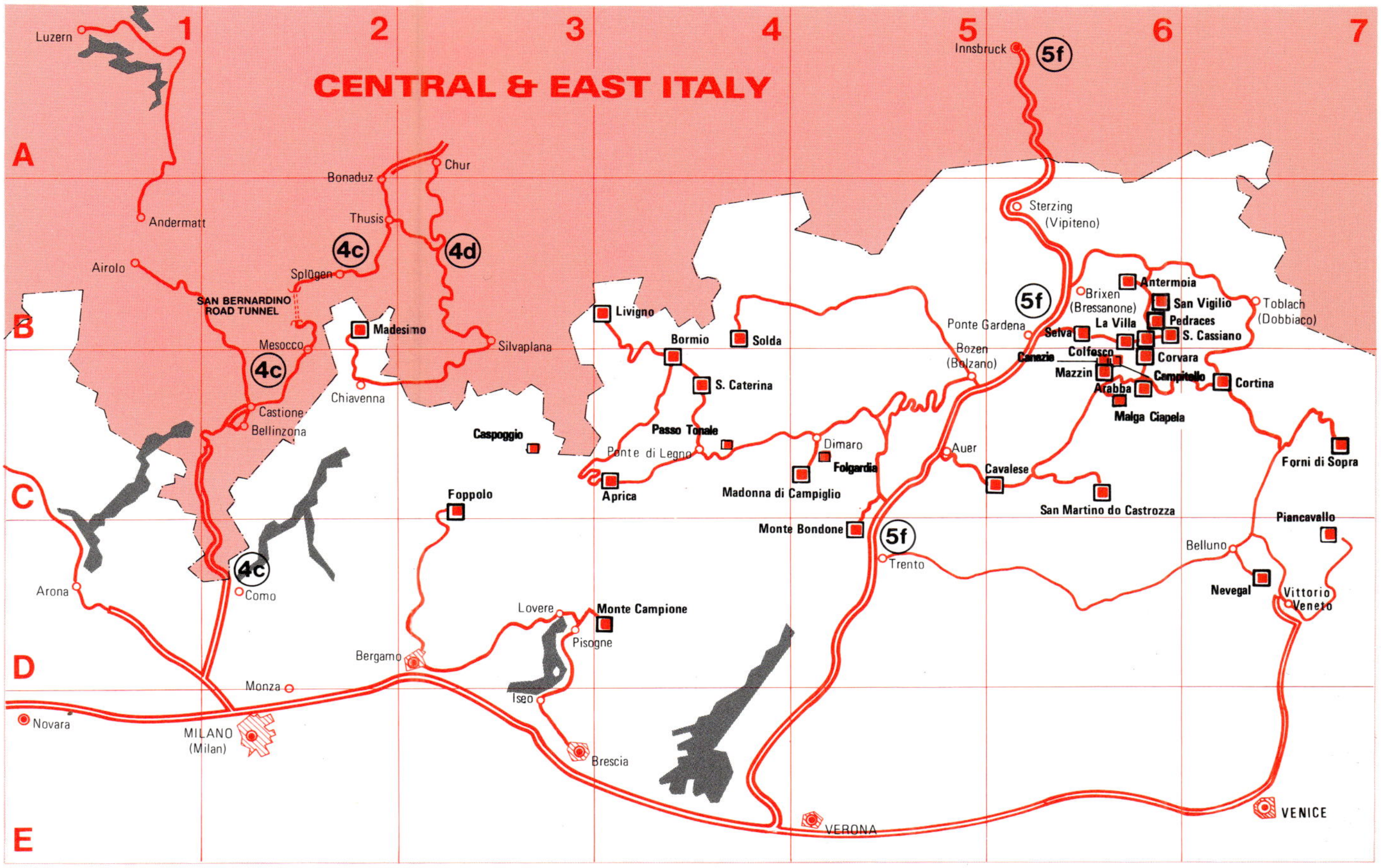

Country/Resort	Map Reference	Airport* (Charters)	Travel by Air Onwards time Hours	Main Map Route No. Calais (B) Le Havre (F)	Country Map Route No.	Total distance Channel Ports Miles	Km.
FRANCE							
Valloire	4E	Geneva	4.30	B2/3/3c	3d	556	895
Valmorel	4D	Geneva	3.00	F6/3/3c	3d	522	840
Val Thorens	4D	Geneva	3.25	F6/3/3c	3d	604	973
Valfrejus	4E	Geneva	4.30	B2/3/3c	3d	568	915
WEST ITALY							
Bardonecchia	4E	Turin	2.30	B2/3/3c	3d	578	930
Cervinia	6C	Turin	2.25	B2/3	3a	620	998
Champoluc	6C	Turin	2.20	F6/3	3a	570½	918
Clavière	4E	Turin	2.00	B2/3/3C	3D	556	895
Courmayeur	5C	Turin	2.40	B2/3	3b	573	922
La Thuile	5C	Turin	3.00	B2/3	3b	589	982
Macugnaga	7C	Milan	2.15	F6/3/3a	3e	601½	968
Mera	7D	Milan	2.30	B2/3	3a	710	1142
Pila	5C	Milan	3.15	B2/3	3a	596½	960
Sansicario	4E	Turin	2.40	F6/3/3c	3d	578	930
Sauze D'Oulx	4E	Turin	2.25	F6/3/3c	3d	568	914
Sestriere	4E	Turin	2.55	B2/3/3c	3d	635	1022
CENTRAL & EAST ITALY							
Abetone	Main Map	Pisa		B5	5f	817	1316
Antermoia	6B	Innsbruck	1.50	F6	5f	907	1459
Aprica	4C	Bergamo	3.30	B5	5f	913½	1470
Arabba	6C	Verona	3.30	B5	5f	823	1324
Bormio	4C	Bergamo	4.00	F6	5f	995½	1602
Campitello	6C	Venice	3.30	B5	5f	852	1420
Canazei	6C	Venice	3.20	B5	5f	849	1415
Cavalese	6C	Verona	2.00	B5	5f	834	1342
Caspoggio	3C	Milan	3.30	B5	5f	928	1546
Colfosco	6C	Verona	3.20	B5	5f	812	1306
Cortina	7C	Venice	3.00	B5	5f	831½	1338
Corvara	6C	Verona	3.15	B5	5f	817	1316
Folgarida	5C	Verona	2.00	B5	5f	857	1430
Foppolo	3D	Bergamo	2.00	F6/3	3a	703	1131
Forni di Sopra	7C	Venice	2.50	B5	5f	870½	1401
La Villa	6B	Verona	3.30	B5	5f	816	1313
Limone	Main Map	Turin	2.00	F6/3	3a	680	1133
Livigno	4B	Bergamo	5.00	B5	5f	901½	1451
Lurisia	Main Map	Turin	2.00	F6/3	3a	682	1098
Madesimo	2B	Milan	3.00	F6/4	4d	685½	1103
Madonna di C.	5C	Bergamo	3.00	B5	5f	861	1385
Malga Ciapela	5C	Innsbruck	2.00	B5	5f	834	1342
Monte Bondone	5D	Verona	1.50	B5	5f	848	1415
Monte Campione	4D	Verona	1.30	F6/3	3a	739½	1190
Nevegal	7D	Venice	2.30	B5	5f	903	1453
Passo Tonale	4C	Bergamo	3.30	B5	5f	975	1630
San Cassiano	6B	Verona	3.45	B5	5f	823	1325
San Martino di C.	6C	Verona	3.00	F6/5	5f	907	1460
S.Caterina	4C	Bergamo	3.45	B5	5f	949½	1528
San Vigilio	6B	Innsbruck	2.00	B5	5f	808	1300
Selva	6B	Verona	3.00	F6/5	5f	908½	
Solda	4B	Verona	3.15	B5	5f	859½	1383

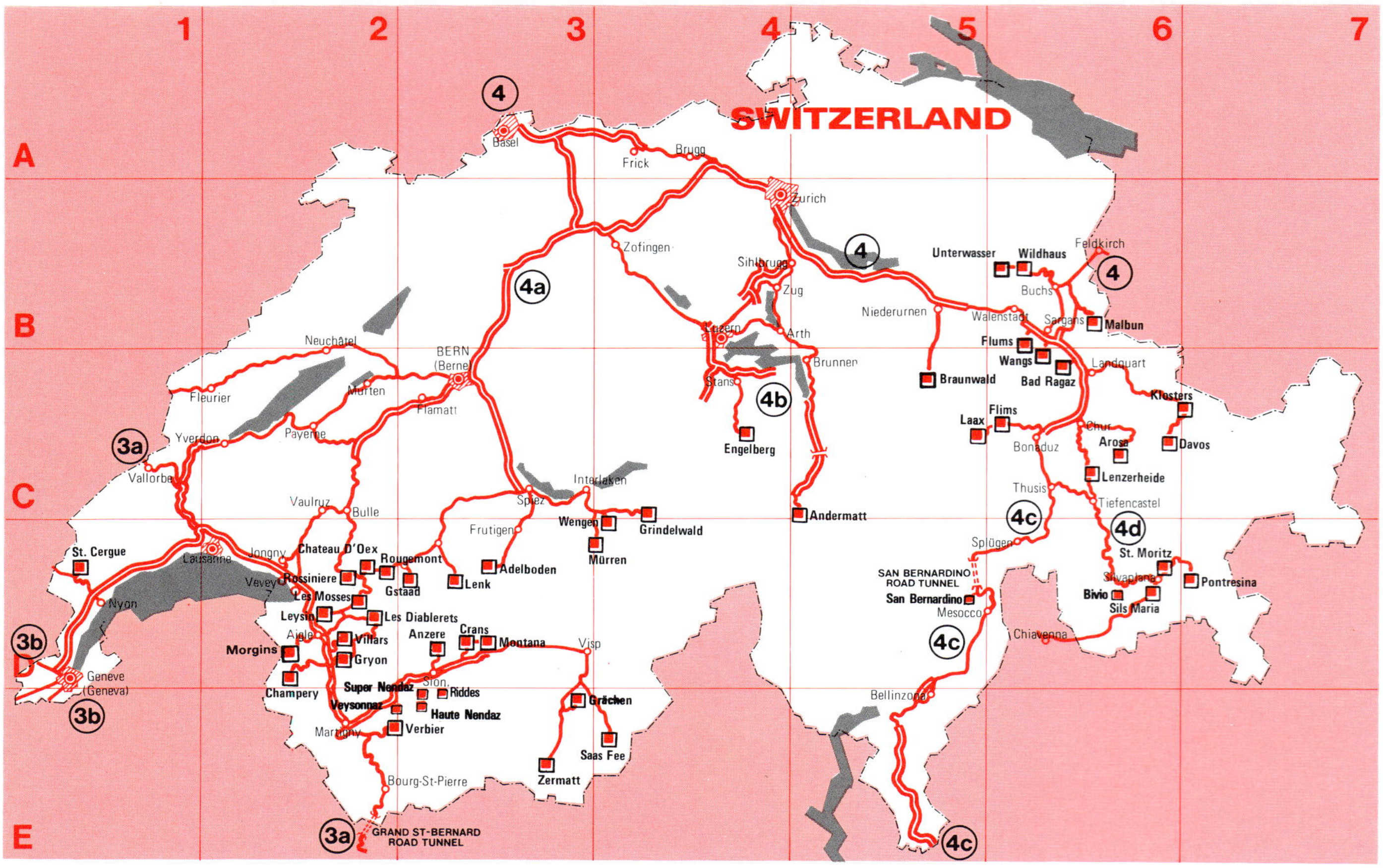

Country/Resort	Map Reference	Airport* (Charters)	Travel by Air Onwards time Hours	Main Map Route No. Calais (B) Le Havre (F)	Country Map Route No.	Total distance Channel Ports Miles	Km.
SPAIN							
Baqueira Beret	Main Map	Zaragoza	4.20	F1	Pyrenees	624½	1005
Cerler	Main Map	Zaragoza	4.30	F2	Pyrenees	713	1148
Formigal	Main Map	Zaragoza	4.00	F1	Pyrenees	626	1007
La Molina	Main Map	Gerona	4.00	F3	Pyrenees	683½	1100
Masella	Main Map	Gerona	3.30	B2	Pyrenees	742	1194
Panticosa	Main Map	Zaragoza	4.45	B1	Pyrenees	757½	1219
ANDORRA							
Soldeu	Main Map	Toulouse	4.00	F3	Pyrenees	671	1172

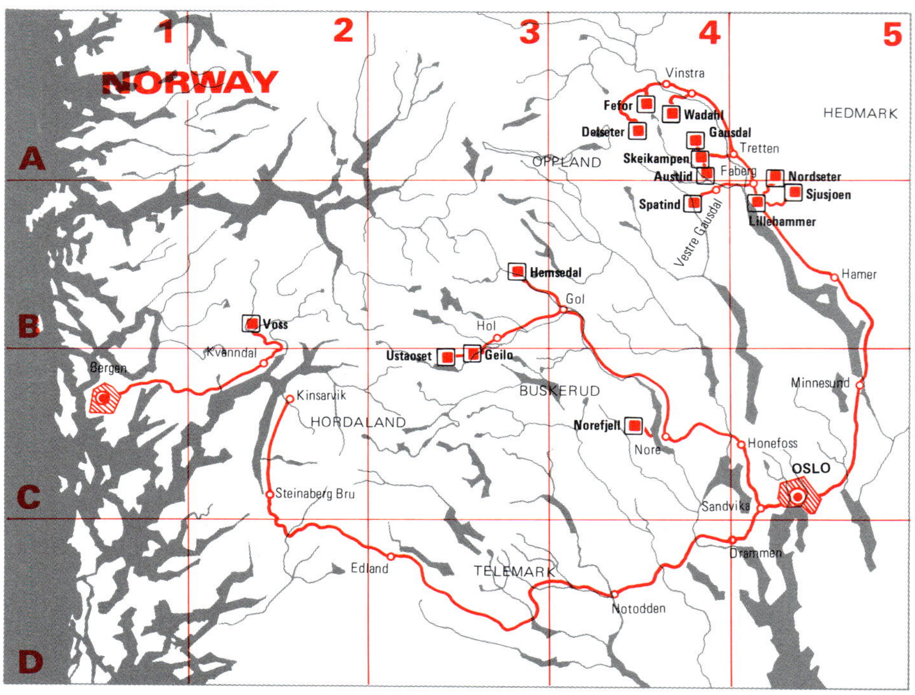

Country/Resort	Map Reference	Airport* (Charters)	Travel by Air Onwards time Hours	Main Map Route No. Calais (B) Le Havre (F)	Country Map Route No.	Total distance Channel Ports Miles	Km.
SWITZERLAND							
Adelboden	3D	Zurich	4.00	B2/4	4a	424½	844
Andermatt	5C	Zurich	3.00	B2/4	4a	539	868
Anzère	3D	Geneva	2.30	B2/3	3a	565½	910
Arosa	6C	Zurich	3.45	B2/4	4	576½	928
Bad Ragaz	6C	Zurich	1.20	B2/4	4c	596½	960
Bivio	6D	Zurich	4.00	B2/4	4a	594	990
Champéry	2D	Geneva	2.15	B2/3	3a	535	861
Chateau d'Oex	2D	Geneva	2.15	B2/4	4a	539	867
Crans/Montana	3D	Geneva	3.00	B2/3	3a	578	930
Davos	6C	Zurich	4.00	B2/4	4	594	956
Engelberg	4C	Zurich	3.30	B2/4	4b	485	782
Flims	6C	Zurich	4.00	B2/4	4	571	919
Flums (Flumserberg)	6B	Zurich	1.40	B2/4	4	548½	883
Grächen	3E	Geneva	4.00	B2/3	3a	601	967
Grindelwald	4C	Zurich	3.30	B2/4	4A	522	840
Gryon	2D	Geneva	2.15	B2/3	3a	477	768
Gstaad	3D	Geneva	2.30	B2/4	4a	548	882
Haute-Nendaz	3E	Geneva	3.10	B2/3	3a	589	982
Klosters	7C	Zurich	3.45	B2/4	4	569	916
Lenk	3D	Zurich	4.15	B2/4	4a	537½	865
Lenzerheide	6C	Zurich	3.00	B2/4	4d	568½	915
Les Diablerets	2D	Geneva	2.15	F6/3	3a	480	773
Les Mosses	2D	Geneva	2.30	F6/3	3a	479	771
Leysin	2D	Geneva	2.30	F6/3	3a	479	771
Malbun	6B	Zurich	2.15	B2/4	564	567	912
Mayens-de-Riddes	3E	Geneva	3.15	B2/3	3a	582	970
Morgins	2D	Geneva	2.00	F6/3	3a	476	767
Mürren	4D	Zurich	4.05	B2/4	4a	533	858
Pontresina	7D	Zurich	4.00	B2/4	4	611½	984
Rossinière	2D	Geneva	2.15	B2/4	4a	536	863
Rougemont	2D	Geneva	2.20	B2/4	4a	543	874
Saas Fee	4E	Geneva	3.45	B2/3	3a	602	968
St.Cergue	1D	Geneva	1.00	F6/3	3b	475	764
St.Moritz	6D	Zurich	4.15	B2/4	4d	606	975
San Bernardino	5D	Zurich	4.00	B2/4	4c	611	983
Sils Maria	6D	Zurich	4.05	B2/4	4d	604½	973
Super-Nendaz	3E	Geneva	3.20	B2/3	3a	596	993
Unterwasser	6B	Zurich	2.30	B2/4	4	563½	907
Verbier	2E	Geneva	3.00	B2/3	3a	577	897
Veysonnaz	3E	Geneva	3.10	B2/3	3a	589	982
Villars	2D	Geneva	2.00	F6/3	3a	476½	767
Wangs	6C	Zurich	1.15	B2/4	4	591	951
Wengen	4D	Zurich	4.00	B2/4	4a	530	853
Wildhaus	6B	Zurich	2.00	B2/4	4	562	904
Zermatt	3E	Geneva	4.30	B2/3	3a	611½	984

* Not necessarily the nearest airport but the ones used by the majority of the Tour Operators for charters. Nearest airport is shown at the head of each resort write-up.

powder

There's more than
one-way
of falling down a mountain

TAKING A CAR TO THE SNOW

Driving rather than flying to your skiing holiday makes mountains of sense. Apart from avoiding the nightmare of having to manhandle skis and all the other awkward clobber through crowded airports, there are many advantages in driving to the snow. Once the car has been loaded up at home there are no further luggage problems until arrival at the resort. One has complete freedom to plan one's own itinerary and to enjoy driving through the countryside with breaks at interesting places en route, instead of the long distance view from a cramped aircraft seat. At the resort a car can be useful for visiting nearby resorts (see page 273) or if the snow conditions are not good at your chosen resort.

But, of course, there are preparations to be made before loading up your car and heading for the resort. Inform your insurance company you are going away and ensure they supply you with a Green Card for the car before you leave. This gives you cover whilst abroad and proves to any member of foreign officialdom that your car is insured.

It may seem like an obvious point, but ensure your car is up to the job of transporting you and your luggage the 1,000 or so miles to the slopes and back. It's advisable to have the car fully serviced. For added peace of mind, take out continental car breakdown cover, too. 'All Car-Skiing' holidays listed in pages 7-8 include AA 5 Star insurance for cars under 10 years old.

Depending on the size of your car and the amount of kit you want to take. You may wish to consider a roof rack, which is one of the most practical and cost efficient ways of carrying the skis, but a more more elegant and fuel efficient method is a roof-mounted ski pod. These lockable wedge-shaped containers are streamlined and can keep several pairs of skis, boots and poles both safe and dry.

Snow chains are also a must for any trip to a ski resort. In fact in most countries it is illegal to drive on certain Alpine roads without carrying a set of snowchains to ensure effective road grip in icy conditions. For the purchase of car roof boxes and snow chains from Snow Chains Euro Products, members can obtain a discount of 10% by presenting the vouchers in page 296.

Other essential cold weather equipment for the car includes a large can of de-icer, a scraper and a small folding show shovel.

Driving on ice- or snow-covered roads doesn't require any special skills, just a healthy respect for the car's abilities and limitations. When pulling away on an icy road, select the highest gear the car will comfortably accept and ease the power on gently. Accelerate and steer smoothly, avoiding any snap changes of direction or speed that may break the wheels' grip on the road. Try and predict what manoeuvres you are going to have to make, and avoid touching the brakes as much as possible. On down gradients select a low gear, say second, and let the engine braking slow you down.

If you are driving on fresh snow the technique is the same, but try not to drive in the wheel tracks of the car in front, as there is more grip on the virgin surface. And once you have fitted the snow chains – usually a five-minute operation – be prepared to slow down dramatically. They offer an outstanding purchase on many zero-grip surfaces but must be looked after if they are to survive for any length of time.

Once at your hotel, chalet or apartment you want to ensure that the car is safe and protected from the elements during your stay. If you do not have access to an underground car park, there is little to worry about short of an avalanche – most cars have been tested to withstand conditions many times worse than the average ski resort can muster. A frost blanket for the windscreen would help get the car moving faster in the mornings, but the scraper and de-icer are usually more than enough. If there is a massive snowfall, well, you've got the shovel to dig yourself out. Securitywise, all the usual safety measures such as deadlocks, alarms and immobilisers should be used at all times wherever you park. Thieves go on holiday too.

CAR CHECK

(1) **Condition of car:**
Complete service before departure.

(2) **Battery:**
Must be in tip top condition; if in doubt, have it checked.

(3) **Anti-freeze:**
Correct proportion for Alpine temperatures.

(4) **De-icer:**
Large can, plus scraper and shovel.

(5) **Rear view mirrors:**
On both sides of car.

(6) **Spares kit:**
Also spare ignition key.

(7) **First aid kit.**

(8) **Warning triangle**:
Compulsory in most European countries.

(9) **Headlights:**
Adjust or adapt for driving abroad.

(10) **Approved GB sign:**
Place on rear of car.

(11) **Official documents:**
A valid driving licence for all persons driving;
Car registration document (if you are not the owner of the car you will need a letter of authorisation from the owner);

Insurance certificate and green card;

Car breakdown insurance.

ROMANIA

POIANA BRASOV

Height of Resort: 3,345 ft.
Height of Top Station: 5,844 ft.
Nearest International Airport: Bucharest
Resort Facilities Charts: See page 224
Hotel Reference Chart: See page 234

This resort is 190km. from Bucharest, reached by a good approach road. It is situated on the Poiana plateau overlooking the town of Brasov, 20 minutes away by bus. Poiana Brasov is a modern purpose-built resort with a compact ski area. From the Hotel Teleferic a cableway rises south-westward towards Kanzel peak, terminating at 5,821ft. To the right and running parallel is an open gondolaway rising to 5,592ft., whilst on the eastern side of the village a further cableway reaches the peak of Postavarul at a height of 5,844ft. Drag-lifts at both top stations serve the easy open slopes whilst the runs down to the village from both upper stations are varied, open at the top, leading to wide wooded glades. To the left the difficult Valea Lupului run of 3km. and the easy Tourist run of 4km. To the right and from the top station of the Kanzel cableway a good medium run with variations ends in the village whilst an easy 4km. run arcs round to the north-east side. Shorter runs of varying standards follow the line of the two main lifts. In the village area a drag-lift serves the trainer slope and a longer lift provides access to a 400m. medium run. Both of these slopes are floodlit at night. Most of the runs are north-west facing.

In a Few Words: A delightful purpose-built resort situated in some of the finest scenery in the Carpathians. A compact lift system and north west facing slopes ensure good snow. For a small resort a good variety of runs but the advanced skier would find it limiting.

Après Ski: Being only 20 minutes from the large town of Brasov there is plenty to see and do. The resort itself has facilities for swimming, skating, ski bobbing, sleigh rides and riding. Night life is active with four night clubs with bands and discothèques.

Recommended Hotels:

Hotel Alpin: A first class hotel opened in 1976. Next to the Hotel Soimul and accommodates 282 guests, all rooms with private bath, wc, sun terrace and satellite TV. Indoor swimming pool, massage and sauna.

Hotel Bradul: Situated alongside the trainer slope and also next door to the Hotel Sport, which houses a ski hire shop. The reception rooms are of good size and comfortably furnished in traditional style. All bedrooms have bath/shower and wc. and there are also apartments consisting of a twin-bedded room, sitting/dining room with radio and folding bed and a large bathroom. Connected to the Hotel Sport by covered passage leading to a cellar bar and discothèque.

Hotel Ciucas: Situated between the Alpin and Soimul hotels, this is the resort's largest hotel, built in 1976. It has 480 beds in single and twin-bedded rooms and also apartments, all with private bath TV and telephone. Extensive reception rooms, large sun terrace, ski hire shop, sauna and massage.

PREDEAL

Height of Resort: 3,427 ft.
Height of Top Station: 4,821 ft.
Nearest International Airport: Bucharest
Resort Facilities Charts: See page 224
Hotel Reference Charts: See page 234

Predeal is 146km. from Bucharest and lies almost halfway between Sinaia and Poiana Brasov. The hotels in the centre of the village are of older design but new hotels have been constructed on the perimeter overlooking the village. The ski area is about 1km. from the village (a mini-bus service operates between) and is small and compact. Access to the top station is by chair-lift rising to the Clabucet Plecare Hotel, 4,821ft. To the right there is a drag-lift which travels halfway up the slope at 45° to the chair-lift. On the western side of the top station there is a trainer lift serving the open slopes in this area. The runs down under the chair-lift are difficult, fairly closely wooded most of the way. To the left of the chair-lift, facing the village, there are easy runs down through wide wooded glades of about 2km., whilst in the centre one finds easy to medium runs to the bottom station, again through wooded glades of 1.7km. The last half of this slope is floodlit at night, useful for skiers taking early holidays when the days are not so long. All runs face north and north-west so snow remains good throughout the season.

In a Few Words: A sunny resort set amidst very beautiful pinewood scenery; excellent for beginners and intermediates, whilst experienced skiers would find it limiting, but Sinaia and Poiana Brasov are only 20km. away on either side.

Après Ski: The resort has facilities for skating and swimming. There are also sleigh rides, bowling and two cinemas. There are many walks through very beautiful scenery. Several of the hotels have dancing to band or discothèque. Evening trips to Brasov, Poiana Brasov and Sinaia.

Recommended Hotels:

Hotel Cioplea: A first class hotel standing on high ground overlooking the resort with magnificent views. 290 beds in 10 suites, 2 single rooms, 129 double and 4, 3-bedded rooms. Bedrooms on the small side but well planned with compact furnishing, all with bath and most with balcony. Large marble floor entrance hall leading to comfortable sitting room. Bright and gaily decorated dining room. Mini-bus service from hotel to ski slopes. Discothèque.

Hotel Orizont: An elegant 3 star modern hotel 400m. from the centre with panoramic views of the surrounding mountains. 146 twin bedded rooms, 6 singles and 4 suites.. All rooms with bath. Extensive reception rooms, swimming pool, sauna, restaurant with band seating 300.

Hotel Rozmarin: First class hotel, situated 250 m. from centre. 126 beds in 4 suites, 29 double and 20, 3-bedded rooms. Restaurant, brasserie and bar.

SINAIA

Height of Resort: 2,624/3,280 ft.
Height of Top Station: 6,560 ft.
Nearest International Airport: Bucharest
Resort Facilities Charts: See page 224
Hotel Reference Charts: See page 234

This resort is a mixture of old and new without any dramatic clash. King Carol built a hunting lodge here in 1883. It was not until 1920, however, that Romanians began to ski here in large numbers, and the first skiers from Western countries started to arrive about 1964. It is the nearest of the three resorts to Bucharest, being only 127km. away.

Like the other two resorts it has a compact ski area, but is more highly mechanised. A two-stage cableway travels west from the village to the Hotel Alpin, which is the first station, and then continues to Furnica Peak, a height of 6,560ft. This top area is open and served by two chair-lifts and four drag-lifts. The skiing is easy to medium with the exception of two east facing runs from the top station to the Hotel Alpin, $2^1/_2$km. in length with a vertical descent of 2,296ft. From the Hotel Alpin there are two easy runs back to the village mostly through wide wooded glades. Runs from the top station to the village are about 5km. in length with a vertical descent of some 3,900ft. There are five restaurants on the upper slopes so it is not necessary to return to the village for lunch.

In a Few Words: A compact ski area and lift system and the intermediate skier will be happy here. No skating in the resort but there is a ski-bob run.

Après Ski: The two hotels mentioned below have dancing to bands and several bars provide good food and music. The Hotel Montana's cellar bar specialises in grills and gypsy type music for dancing and has a very good atmosphere. There is also swimming, saunas, bowling, sleigh rides and two cinemas.

Recommended Hotels:

Hotel Alpin: As mentioned above, this hotel is next to the first station of the cableway, some 9km. by road from the village. Lovely views overlooking the Prahaova valley. An old style hotel but with good sized bedrooms, all with bath and wc. Two dining rooms and dancing to a band. A good hotel to be in if skiing is first and foremost.

Hotel Montana: Completed in 1975 and situated in the centre of the resort and next to the cableway terminal. Bedrooms on the small side but well planned, all with bath and wc. A number of family suites. A main restaurant offering good and varied menu, second restaurant for small groups or parties and a self-service restaurant. Dancing each evening to a band in main restaurant. Bar cellar furnished in traditional style with specialist grills, dancing and Romanian folk music. Sports shop, beauty parlour and other small shops make up the complex below the hotel. Large indoor swimming pool and undercover car park. Sauna.

NORWAY

Apart from usually good and reliable snow conditions, Norway has one of the greatest blessings a country can have in these days - a small population! These advantages, added to its natural beauty of mountains, hills, forests, fjords and lakes and a generally slower pace of life, makes it a good land in which to take a skiing holiday.

Classification of Resorts: The resorts and ski centres in Norway have three classifications:

Alpine: Geilo, Voss, Hemsedal, Norefjell (Oslo is not classified under any one heading in this book as it could come under all). Alpine in Norway means long and varied machine-prepared pistes, with one up to minimum standard for Giant Slalom, a few ski-lifts, qualified ski instruction, hire of Alpine ski equipment, and a mountain restaurant, café or hut serving refreshment.

Touring and Downhill Slalom: Fefor, Gausdal, Skeikampen, Wadahl, Dalseter, Lillehammer, Spåtind. A slalom hill of minimum international standard, qualified ski instruction, hire of both Alpine and touring ski equipment and marked touring trails. Some of these also have machine-prepared pistes.

Touring only: Ustaoset and Austlid. Necessitates good varied touring terrain, touring trails marked and specially prepared.

Grades of Hotels & Accommodation: Skiing hotels are usually in 3 or 4 grades. A Høyfjellshotell, Mountain Hotel, offering a high degree of comfort and facilities and a high position above sea level. A Turisthotell, Tourist Hotel, can offer the same standards but not be on the mountain. A Fjellstue, here translated as a Mountain Lodge, has mountain surroundings but a more informal atmosphere and usually lesser degree of comfort and fewer facilities; it is often just as nice to stay in. Fjellkro provides pub-like accommodation and is cheaper.

OSLO

See Map: Page 240

Although most of Oslo's well spread out population of about 400,000 seem to take to their skis each weekend and evening after an early finish to the day's work, they can be soundlessly swallowed up in the vast and beautiful area of Oslomarka in the wooded hills surrounding Oslo on three sides; the fourth side is bounded by the Oslo fjord, and one can, if one wants, quickly be quite alone in a noiseless and apparently people-less scene of snow and trees lovely enough to stir the most unromantic heart
Oslomarka is divided into districts called Nordmarka, Vestmarka, Ostmarka (north, west, east) and Krokskogen amongst others. It has about 2,600km. of marked and extremely well maintained trails, over fifty of which are floodlit at night as are the slalom hills and ski-lifts. The terrain is varied so that beginners on cross-country skis can happily start off plodding across the frozen lakes and gently up and down short and easy trails until becoming good enough to go for miles over widely differing trails.

Tryvann Ski Centre: Tryvann Ski Centre consists of three separate hills; Tommkleiva, Tryvannskleiva and Wyllerløypa. They are all situated in Nordmarka. All slopes are floodlit. Cross-country lovers are also catered for with a fantastic network of ski tracks.

Tommkleiva is an excellent area for training with children and beginners. The hill has three tracks and two lifts.
Tryvannskleiva with its three slopes and two lifts is probably the best of the Tryvann Ski Centre pistes for free-style and Telemark. At the foot of the slopes there is a cosy wooden lodge with self-service restaurant and pleasant surroundings. At the top of the slopes is a kiosk selling food and hot drinks.

Wyllerløypa provides skiing for the more experienced skier. There are two lifts, one 1,260 metres long with a vertical descent of 1,509 ft.

Opening times: Mon-Fri 10.00-22.00.
Sat-Sun 10.00-17.00

Transport to Tryvann Ski Centre: By tram no. 1 (Frognerseteren) from the centre of Oslo to Voksenkollen station, next to the Ski Service Tomm Murstad. Here skis, boots, snow boards etc. can be hired, waxed and repaired. A bus can transport you from Voksenkollen station to the slopes, and this bus can also pick you up from the most central Oslo hotels.

Tel: + 22 14 54 82

Grefsenåsen Alpine Centre: An alpine centre consisting of two separate hills; Trollvannskleiva and Grefsenkleiva. These small ski centres with altogether four slopesand two lifts, are situated fifteen minutes by car from the centre of Oslo, still far from the hustle and bustle of the city centre. You can buy food and hot drinks adjacent to the slopes.

Opening times: Mon-Fri 15.00-21.00.
Sat-Sun 10.00-17.00

Transport to Grefsenåsen Alpine Centre: To get to Trollvannskleiva take a bus no. 56 (Solemskogen). This bus goes all the way up to the alpine centre on Sundays, all other days it stops five minutes walk away from the slopes. In order to get to Grefsenkleiva take either bus no. 31 or 32 (Grorud/Tonsenhagen). They both stop close to the alpine centre. There are also good parking facilities close to the hills.

Tel: + 22 08 23 70

Ingierkollen Slalom Centre: Situated south-seat of the centre of Oslo, this hill has three slopes and two lifts. The slopes are aimed both at beginners and more advanced skiers.

Opening times: Mon-Fri 17.00-22.00. Sat 10.00-18.00. Sun 10.00-20.00

Transport to Ingierkollen Slalom Centre: From the centre of Oslo take either bus no. 83B, which stops just by the slopes, or train south-bound (end station Ski) to Kolbotn station.

Tel: + 66 80 19 45

Kirkerudbakken Alpine Centre: This alpine centre is idyllically situated west of Oslo. Kirkerudbakken can offer free facilities for very young children in a separate children's slope. There is also a half-pipe for snow-boarders. In addition there are five ordinary slopes and three lifts.

Opening times: Mon-Fri 16.00-22.00.
Sat-Sun 10.00-18.00

Transport to Kirkerudbakken: Train from the centre of Oslo (end station Asker) to Sandvika station, then bus no. 161 which goes all the way to the slope.

Tel: + 67 13 33 68

Kolsåsheiser Slalom Centre: This small slalom centre has one slope for children with a separate lift, and one ordinary slope with two lifts, in addition to a half-pipe and big jump for snow-boarders. The centre is situated west of Oslo, approx. 20 minutes by car. There is a kiosk and café for visitors.

Opening times: Mon-Fri 10.00-22.00.
Sat-Sun 10.00-18.00

Transport to Kolsåsheiser Slalom Centre: Take bus no. 143 from the centre of Oslo. The bus stops just by the slope.

Tel: + 67 53 13 26

Vardåsen Ski Centre: This alpine centre is situated west of Oslo, about $^1/_2$ hour drive direct from the city centre, and has one slope and one lift.

Opening times: Mon-Thurs.15.00-21.30.
Fri. 15.00-21.00. Sat-Sun 11.00-18.00

Transport to Vardåsen Ski Centre: Take a train from the city centre of Oslo west-bound (end station Asker) to Asker station. Then take bus no. 704 (Borgenåsen) directly to the ski centre.

Tel: + 66 78 43 09

Non-skiing activities in Oslo: Visit the **Holmenkollen Ski Jump** (close to Tryvann Ski centre) where a lift takes one up to the top of the ski jump tower, with a beautiful view over Oslo and the Oslo Fjord. International World Cup ski jumping competitions are held there once each year, usually the second week in March. The Norwegian Royal Family has been present every year since 1906, and the late King Olav V jumped there himself as a young man. There is a Ski Museum, cafeteria and souvenir shops under the ski jump. To get to Holmenkollen Ski Jump take tram no. 1 (Frognersteren) to Holmenkollen station.

At the top of Tryvannskleiva slalom track is situated the Tryvannstårnet television tower with a view covering 30,000 sq. km. There is a kiosk in the tower. To get to Tryvannstårnet take tram no. 1 (Frognerseteren) to Frognerseteren station, and walk for approx. ten minutes.

Experience the museums at Bygdøy, i.e. the **Viking Ship Museum**, **Kontiki Museum**, **Fram Museum**, **Norwegian Maritime Museum** and the **Norwegian Folk Museum**. All these museums can be reached by bus no. 30 from Oslo city centre, or by ferry (only between 15th April to 15th September) from the Town Hall harbour (the Bygdøy ferry).

Other interesting museums and sights in the city centre are the **Resistance Museum** at Akerhus Fortress, the **Munch Museum** containing paintings by the Norwegian painter Edvard Munch, the Vigeland sculptures in the **Vigeland Park** and the **National Gallery**. There are also plenty of theatres and cinemas, the latter showing English, French, Italian and Russian films.

Hotel Accommodation: Closest to the slopes are: Holmenkollen Park Hotel Rica (tel: 22 92 20 00), Soria Moria (tel: 22 14 60 80), Voksenåsen Hotell (tel: 22 14 30 90), Lysebu (tel: 22 14 23 90). To the west of Oslo you have among others the following hotels: Vettre Hotel og Konferansenter (tel: 66 90 22 11), Holmen Fjordhotell (tel: 66 84 72 80) and Rica Hotel Oslofjord (tel: 67 54 57 00). In downtown Oslo the largest hotels are: Radisson SAS hotels (tel: 22 11 30 00 and 22 17 10 00), Hotel Continental (tel: 22 82 40 00), and Grand Hotel (tel: 22 42 93 90). There are many small and less costly ones too.

AUSTLID MOUNTAIN LODGE

Ski Touring
See Map: page 240

A journey of $3^1/_2$ hours by train or 230km. by road from Oslo leads to Austlid Mountain Lodge, 5km. south of Gausdal/Skeikampen, set in a gentle wooded background beside a small lake. The surrounding area is for ski touring only and contains many beautiful trails through the woods and above them to the mountain plateau. All facilities for ski touring are available.

Austlid Feriesenter: The old wooden mountain lodge was rebuilt in 1971 and renovated in 1993 and provides accommodation for 65 guests, with both modern comfort and a traditional Norwegian rustic atmosphere. All the rooms in the main building have shower/wc., telephones and TV. Sauna. Warm and colourful sitting room with open fire, bright dining room, good food. Downstairs bar and dancing to disco 5 nights a week. 50 chalets surrounding the hotel taking up to 6 people each. All have TV and telephone.

DALSETER

Ski Touring and some Downhill
See Charts: page 235
See Map: page 240

Dalseter lies between the Jotunheim mountain range to the west and Mt. Ruten, 4,920ft., to the east, from the top of which is a view across most of the mountains of southern Norway, and there is a most enjoyable run down from here to the mountain hotel. More than 120km. of marked trails spread out amongst the magnificent countryside, over frozen lakes and through forests and mountains. The ski school meets near a 750m. drag-lift rising 560ft in 5 minutes.

Dalseter Mountain Hotel: Guests are escorted by car from Lillehammer station to the hotel, lying at 2,800ft. Built in 1964 and fully licensed, this hotel provides excellent comfort and service and has a convivial atmosphere. All bedrooms with telephone, TV, radio, private bath or shower and wc. One of the four sitting rooms has a circular open fireplace with copper chimney. French windows open onto sun terrace with a marvellous panorama of characteristic Norwegian mountain scenery. indoor swimming pool, mechanical gymnasium, table tennis, 3 saunas. Dancing every night except Sundays. Ski and boot hire (Nordic and Alpine), instruction for Nordic and Alpine skiing.

FEFOR

Ski Touring and some Downhill
See Chart: page 235
See Map: page 240

This resort consists of a mountain hotel and 24 chalets each sleeping from 6 to 24 persons, situated at a height of 2,800ft. in the Gudbrandsdal region, and surrounded by the Jotunheim mountains to the west, Dovre to the north and Rondane to the east. It is 13km. from Vinstra, and from Oslo 4 hours by train or 290km. by road. Guests are met at the station by car. The surrounding countryside is formed of frozen lakes and gentle mountain slopes, with vast forests and open plateaus above them. 250km of marked and well prepared ski touring trails penetrate this vast landscape. A 700m. drag-lift is situated 500m. away from the hotel, rising nearly to the summit of Mt. Feforkampen, height rise 700ft. Gentle descents lead down from here, suitable for the beginner to intermediate skier, and an excellent ski school is run by instructors who speak fluent English. Primarily, however, it is an excellent area for ski touring.

Fefor Hotel: In a beautiful setting, this hotel is a rambling complex of old and new sections. Many guests are regulars, from Holland, Germany, Scandinavia and England, and English seems to be the lingua franca. There are floodlit skating rinks near the hotel, and table tennis, and billiards. An indoor swimming pool, saunas, solarium and a squash hall. A band plays every evening in the dance room adjoining the bar. Two spacious dining rooms serving good food; two sitting rooms, one very large, the other smaller and quieter with open hearth furnished 19 traditional style. All of the 100 double rooms, 13 suites and 15 single rooms have private bath, wc. and satelite TV. Skis and boot hire; ski instructor. Dog and horse sledging and fishing through the ice for trout.

GEILO

Alpine
See Charts: pages 224-235
See Map: page 240

Scandinavia's best-known and largest ski resort, Geilo, is reached by train from Bergen in 3 hours or from Oslo in $3^1/_2$. The journey from Oslo by road, which is open all the year round, is 240km. There are 18 hotels and pensions plus a number of chalets and apartments. Geilo lies on the edge of the Hardanger plateau at a height of 2,610ft. In an undulating landscape, and has an agreeable village atmosphere. With the exception of Voss and Hemsedal, it caters much more for the downhill skier than other Norwegian resorts. There is also plenty of après ski with dancing in 7 hotels, 5 discothèques, cinema, shops and cafés, sleigh rides, 8 heated swimming pools and saunas. All information on activities is available at Geilo Tourfist Office. There are 4 chair-lifts, including two 4 seaters, and 14 drag-lifts.

The Geilo chair-lifts: Three chair-lifts rise to Geilohogda, 3,460ft., and these are the main means of access to many of the well prepared pistes. At the top is a restaurant with a panoramic view. The good skier will enjoy the 900m. Ola run, tricky in parts; and for the medium skier the 1,000m. Geilo piste or the 1,100m. Sonja piste will be less intimidating. All these runs lead to the foot of the chair-lifts, ending through narrow wooded paths. There are a number of other runs in the area. The Geilo drag-lift is near these chair-lifts, and also the ski school office and the sunny nursery slopes.

Korkertrekkeren drag-lift: (2,225-3,000 ft.) This is this area to ski if the wind blows hard from the west! Several steep and challenging 500m. runs descend from here, as well as two medium descents, the Mini Korken and Anne pistes. Runs through the woods lead to the base of the two longer drag-lifts, where there is a small café.

Havsdalstrekkene IV and V: (2,990-3,500 ft.) Twin drag-lifts reach the top of Havsdalshovda, a rounded mountain with open sunny slopes sweeping down in a curve which flattens out towards the end. Beginners and medium skiers will enjoy these runs.

Havsdalstrekkene I and II: (2,990-3,465 ft.) Twin drag-lifts terminate near the Geilohogda restaurant. Three different pistes lead down, suitable for beginners to good skiers, through wooded slopes. There is a small café for drinks and snacks at the bottom. There is also a children's drag-lift, with play area set well away from the main lifts.

The Vestlia chair-lift: (2,550-3,465 ft.) This chair-lift and four drag-lifts, two are children's lifts, rise from the south side of Geilo, and there is a cafeteria at the top abd bottom. The runs down from here are longer and interesting, over north facing slopes, and therefore hold the snow well until the end of the season. The experienced will enjoy the Asle piste, 1,300m. long; and the medium skier will prefer the Randi, 1,500m. These runs converge at the foot of the chair-lift. The Bear run is longer and gentler. All these pistes are well maintained and the surroundings are superb.

Halstensgard drag-lift: On the south-west side of the village a drag-lift rises north westwards from the ski centre to about 3,600ft. From the top to base there is a difficult run to the right and two intermediate runs to the left. A small cafeteria is situated at the foot of the lift.

Geilo is a well organised resort, with 9 piste-preparing machines, snow cannons, 18 lifts serving 32 pistes with a total of 25km. of prepared runs, five of which are F.I.S. World Cup standard. There are 7 café/restaurants on the pistes, 2 floodlit runs, 4 ski schools, 7 ski rental shops, ski patrols and a ski taxi service.

Touring is also available in the surrounding mountains, especially to the north, in the Hallingskarvet area, above the treeline. There are more than 200km. of marked and prepared touring trails. The ski schools are first class.

Children: Excellent facilities for children with the Children's House, The Hugo Club and The Troll Club, providing specially protected areas, some with small ski lifts, along with organised activities such as fancy dress skiing, snow sculpturing etc. In addition all children under 7 years are entitled to free ski lift passes.

Every year at the end of April the famous Skarverennet race is held with some 10,000 participants, rather like Norway's national day on skis!

Recommended Hotels:

Bardola Hotel: This hotel has been completely transformed in recent years into a first class modern hotel. It is situated to the east of the village in lovely surroundings near the ski school, and the Havsdalshovda and Arne ski-lifts. The largest hotel in Geilo, it has 57 double rooms, 45 singles and suites, all of which have bath or shower and a refrigerator; all modern and comfortable. Spacious sitting rooms on two floors are linked by an open circular stairway, and are colourful and comfortably furnished. Bright dining room, good food. Three bars, each in a different style and with many places to sit; TV lounge; 2 saunas; hairdresser, basement games room with different amusement machines; also down here is the discothèque and lively and popular night club, fairly well separated from the rest of the hotel. Indoor and outdoor swimming pool, curling hall.

Geilo Hotel: This hotel was completely renovated in 1990, and is situated in the west part of the village, a short walk from the Geilo chair-lift and the ski school. Most bedrooms spacious, 72 doubles, all with private bath/wc, minibar and TV. Pleasant sitting rooms, large bright dining room with piano bar. Dancing on Fridays and Saturdays from 20.00 to 01.00, games room, fitness room sauna and jacuzzi. Owner/manager is very helpful, and a happy atmosphere prevails.

Dr. Holms Hotel: In a central and convenient position, but off the main road. Geilo chair-lift is on one side, and ski school and a drag-lift on the other, and one can ski back to the hotel. Totally rebuilt in 1989 it now has 124 bedrooms and suites accommodating 250 guests, all rooms with bath, telephone, TV and minibar. Attractive and comfortably furnished reception rooms; ski-bar with pleasant sun terrace; 'Vinstuene' – a cosy restaurant where one can drink good wine and enjoy a small dish of tapas. The 'swim and trim' facilities include a swimming pool, children's pool, jacuzzi, sauna, solarium and gymnasium. Beauty salon, bar with open fire, dancing to orchestra 6 nights a week on spacious dance floor. Convention facilities all in one wing with 10 conference rooms and flexible assembly rooms accommodating up to 250 persons.

NOREFJELL

Alpine
See Charts: page 235
See Map: page 240

Norefjell lies l0km. off the main Oslo-Bergen road, 115km. or $1^1/_2$ hours' drive from Oslo. It is one of Norway's best known resorts, set amidst the most lovely scenery, above the beautiful Lake Kroderen and surrounded by mountains and forests. Its snow conditions remain good from December to April, and it was the venue for the 1952 Winter Olympics for the downhill events. In addition to the vast area of marked trails for ski touring, there is a ridge running above the tree-line for 14km. southward from Gråfjell to Ravnåsen, which provides superb varied slopes on either side suitable for downhill skiing.

Eight drag-lifts, one 4 seater and two 2 seater chair-lifts provide access to these ski slopes. Two are 2,000m. long, rising 2,000,ft. to Fjellhvil. The experienced skier will find the Olympic giant slalom course here, long and fairly steep, with vertical drop of 2,000ft. Another lift surmounts this one, travelling a further 2,600m. with height rise of 1,050m., and from here there are a variety of runs of different standard. Near to Norefjellstua is a small tow-lift providing easy skiing for beginners and children. There is an excellent and enthusiastic ski school here and equipment can be hired at the hotels (there are two pensions in addition to the large hotel).

Fjellhvil Hotel: This hotel is in a beautiful setting overlooking the lake and has been rebuilt and extended. It reflects the good qualities of modern Scandinavian design, whilst retaining many traditional features. It is run by Mr. and Mrs. Ertzeid, and is conveniently situated 50m. from the ski lifts. 50 bedrooms, including a few singles, most with private shower/wc., some with bath. Two spacious and colourful lounges, one with open fire, large dining room, cafeteria and bar fully licensed. Sauna; and table tennis; informal dancing 6 nights a week to a band. Usually a keen skiing clientèle.

NORDSETER

Ski Touring and some Downhill
See Charts: page 235
See Map: page 240

Nordseter is 14km. from Lillehammer (a regular bus operates between the two) and lies at a height of 2,780,ft. There are two drag-lifts providing short, gentle runs suitable for beginners and children. The Nevra lift is close to the hotel, 500m. long with height rise of 295ft.; the Nordseter lift is 600m. long rising 400ft., and in addition there is a small rope tow for children. The touring country is extensive, with gentle slopes and is sheltered and mainly wooded. There are half-day tours which allow one to return to the hotel for the superb cold table lunch; alternatively the whole day tours enable one to take lunch in a distant mountain hut or to ski down to Lillehammer itself, an interesting excursion. One tour, mainly over open country above the treeline, leads to the prettily situated Pellestova mountain pension with its café. Nordseter has a morning kindergarten and ski school for all ages. There are also weekly ski competitions for guests and a ski film is shown once a week. There is a mountain chapel 5 minutes from the Nordseter Høyfjellshotell.

Nevra Høyfjellshotell: In a pleasant situation at the edge of the tree line. Of 50 double rooms, 42 have private bath/wc.; 20 singles, 16 with bath or shower/ wc. Several spacious sitting rooms, attractively furnished and overlooking the wooded hills beyond, as does the pleasant dining room. Good food and service. Visitors from many countries. Dancing every evening with band from 21.00 to 00.30. Attractive bar; hire of skis and boots for Alpine and touring. Resident ski instructor. Own lift next to hotel.

Lillehammer Høyfjellshotell: This is a solid, red painted building, set in fairly flat, prettily wooded countryside. 37 double rooms all with bath or shower/ wc., 9 single rooms. Large pleasant dining room, several comfortably furnished roomy sitting rooms. Big dance room with bar. Indoor swimming pool, sauna, solarium and playroom; hire of touring and slalom skis and boots; resident ski instructor.

SKEIKAMPEN/GAUSDAL

Ski Touring and Downhill
See Charts: page 235
See Map: page 240

The undermentioned two mountain hotels are neighbours and share the same magnificent touring terrain and ski-lifts. They are set at 2,500ft. in the mid-Gudbrandsdal region, beautiful and wild, and are dominated by Mount Skeikampen, 3,500ft., on whose lower slopes the two hotels stand, overlooking the woods from a point just above the treeline. They are reached by a 220km. drive from Oslo or a 3 hour train journey to Tretten station, and guests of either hotel are met by car at the station. There are over 200km. of marked and signposted ski tours through the superb scenery of this area, penetrating deep into the rolling mountains and crossing dense forests, frozen lakes and vast open plateaus.

A two-stage drag-lift on Mt. Skeikampen caters for the downhill skiing, starting from the Gausdal Hotel and travelling 600m., its second section continuing a further 1,400m. with height rise of over 1,000,ft. These lifts can also give a good start to the ski tourer planning to cross the mountains further afield. A seventh drag-lift was opened on the west side of Mt.Skeikampen in January 1988, 1200 metres long with a height rise of 900ft., and a ninth drag-lift in 1995. The downhill runs are of medium standard, over marvellous snow both on and off-piste. The views from Mt. Skeikampen are glorious, with the ranges of the Jotunheim and Rondane mountains stretching far into the distance. At the foot of the lifts are 'ski in' bars so that groups, including children or beginners, can rendezvous during the day's skiing. The ski school is run by the Austrian instructor, Franz Hartweger; the short ski method is also taught. Classes cater for downhill and cross-country skiing.

Skeikampen Mountain Hotel: This is one of the best hotels in Norway, with the atmosphere of a beautiful country house, furnished with care and taste,completely modernised and 24 new rooms added in 1988. In the 6 sitting rooms there are oriental carpets on the floors, tapestries, antique grandfather clocks, chests and chairs. Paintings and prints on the walls are original and by well known Norwegian artists. 85 comfortable and prettily furnished bedrooms, 53 doubles, 10 junior suites, 2 suites, 14 singles, all with private bath/wc. 28 apartments close to the hotel all with 2 bedrooms, sitting room with open fire, shower, wc, sauna, telephone and TV. An atmosphere of relaxation and well-being with food and service to the same standard. One bar and for the wine connoisseur a bodega downstairs with brick walls and arches, entered through a wrought-iron gateway. Furnished with a few small wooden tables and chairs, it forms an intimate and attractive setting for a special evening, with a wide choice of wines. In a spacious dancing room a duo or trio band plays every evening. Two saunas, one for men, one for women. Gymnasium with mechanical apparatus and sunlamps. Heated indoor swimming pool and solarium is a great attraction, in an attractive setting with garden type cushioned cane chairs and tables around it. At one end of the pool large French windows look out on to the snow. Skis and boot hire; ski instruction.

Gausdal Høifjellshotell: Owned and run by the same family for more than 50 years. The Gausdal Hotel is a large, comfortable established family type hotel, particularly good for children and teenagers. Games room and playroom. Plenty of entertainment such as competitions and outdoor activities. Swimming pool, disco and ski shop. All bedrooms have private bath or shower/wc TV and radio. Several comfortably furnished spacious lounges and smaller, quieter sitting rooms. The dining room is large and particularly bright, having windows on either side, and serving plenty of enjoyable food. Swimming pool, solarium and two saunas. Small ice hockey rink. Friendly bar and a dancing room which seats 250, where a band plays every night except Sundays. Comfortable well run family hotel with plenty going on and lots of fun for the whole family. Skis and boot hire; ski instruction.

SJUSJØEN

Ski Touring and some Downhill
See Charts: page 235
See Map: page 240

Sjusjøen is 22km. from Lillehammer and can be reached from there by bus. At 2,780ft. it is the same height as Nordseter, which is not far away to the north-west. It is within easy touring distance of both Nordseter and Hornsjo, but lying deeper into the mountain area. The ski terrain is similar to that surrounding Nordseter, gentle and mainly protected by woods. Downhill skiing is catered for by a drag-lift 900m. long rising 492ft. Sleigh rides are arranged, for 2 to 8 persons in one sleigh. This is one of Norway's major ski touring areas embracing Lillehammer, Nordseter, Hornsjø and Pellestova with approximately 300km. of marked and machine prepared double trails. Dog sleigh ski tours.

jusjøen Fjellstue (Mountain Lodge): A two-storey E-shaped building, its original section once a farmhouse, 250 years ago. In a sunny situation with pretty wooded surroundings, enlarged in recent years and modernised. 110 beds; all rooms have private shower/wc, some balconies. Cosy sitting rooms with open hearth and homely atmosphere. Spacious dining room serving typically Norwegian dishes. 300 year old fireside room with beautiful antique furniture. Dancing room with dancing six times a week. Sauna; fully licensed.

Sjusjøen Høyfjellshotell (Mountain Hotel): A large modern three-storey building; 69 rooms all with shower/wc, radio and TV. Large dining room, 5 sitting rooms, 2 bars. Dancing nightly to live music except Sundays. Heated indoor swimming pool; sauna; hire of skis and boots; frequent bus service to Lillehammer.

Sjusjøen Panorama Hotel: In a pleasant situation with open views. All 50 rooms with shower/wc. Attractive dining room serving good Norwegian fare; friendly service. Cosy sitting rooms, one with open fireplace. Dancing nightly; bar; sauna; ski instruction; skis and boots for hire.

HEMSEDAL

Alpine
See Charts: page 235
See Map: page 240

A journey from Oslo of 230km. by road or 4 hours by train (including a 30 minute bus ride) leads to Hemsedal, which is surrounded by magnificent mountain ranges. The resort is considered to be one of the best Alpine ski areas in Norway due to the well prepared pistes, efficiently run lifts and good skiing conditions of the 40km. of slalom pistes which are suitable for beginners and advanced skiers. There is also ski touring in the high and open mountain ranges.

The downhill skiing area lies to the south-west, on the slopes of Totten, 4,560ft. The runs down are quite steep and uneven in places and will be enjoyed by intermediate to good skiers. There are drag-lifts and five chair-lifts here, in addition to the trainer lift. 7 of the Totten lifts run parallel up the steep lower slopes, the longer rising to 3,610ft., difference in height 1,400ft.; and the 4 on the upper slopes are spaced well apart, the highest rising to 4,851ft., difference in height 1,310ft. The surrounding mountains, Mt. Saata, 4,950ft., to the south, and Skogshorn, 5,270ft., to the west, provide wide touring areas. Good facilities are available for hire, ski school and weekly lift tickets. Lift tickets have three price periods, high and low season and mid-week tickets which are 30% reduced in low season.

Viking Hemsedal Hotel: The hotel is 3km. from the ski-lifts, which can be reached by bus, and in the centre of the very small village, height 1,980ft. Completely rebuilt, with 55 double rooms, comfortably furnished, most with private bath or shower and wc. One modern and comfortable sitting room. Two bright dining rooms with generous provision of typical Norwegian food. Popular bar; bar downstairs with dancing most evenings till 03.00. A well run and friendly hotel.

Other Hotels and Pensions: Viking Skogstad Hotel, Fossheim Gjestehus, Breistolen Fjellstue, Hemsedal Gjestehus.

Chalets: There is a good choice of chalets and apartments for renting and full information can be obtained from:- Tourist Office, N-3560 Hemsedal, Tel. 320 60156.

In addition to the above accommodation the resort has a further hotel and pension, 6 apartment centres, 2 chalet centres and 6 camping sites all with winter insulated cabins.

Seven restaurants and four discos.Free kindergarten and ski bus service.

LILLEHAMMER

Alpine and Touring
See Charts: pages 224-235
See Map: page 240

Lillehammer, venue for the 1994 winter Olympic Games, is a small and pretty town nestling in a valley next to the beautiful Lake Mjøsa. It is a 2½ hour journey by road or rail from Oslo, and to the north of it lies the vast, high Gudbrandsdal mountain region, wild and remote, with its marvellous touring possibilities over miles of gently rounded mountain tops. There are also lovely walks through the snowladen pine woods nearer the town. In the town itself there are shops, restaurants and cafés. Other facilities include skating and curling rinks, sleigh rides, dog sleigh skiing, bobsleigh and luge run, several museums and three cinemas.

In addition, there is an enormous expanse of touring terrain, with some 400km. of marked trails and a ski bus service to Nordseter or Sjusjøen, both half an hour away.

Whilst there are masses of Nordic ski trails near at hand, Alpine ski runs are not in the immediate vicinity of Lillehammer. The main Alpine centre is at Hafjell, 15km. north of Lillehammer, with regular bus connections. This compact area, with 23km. of prepared runs through wide wooded glades, is served by 3 chair-lifts and 6 drag-lifts moving 11,500 persons per hour. The skiing is suitable for all grades, consisting of blue, red and black runs: the longest being about 4-5km. with a vertical descent of 2,695ft. 8km. of the runs are covered by snow cannons. At the base there is a children's lift and a beginners' lift serving easy runs. There are three restaurant/cafeterias in the ski area, hotels, guest houses, apartments and cabins to rent in the immediate vicinity. This area staged the women's and men's giant slalom and slalom events during the 1994 Winter Olympic Games.

In Olympic Park, just outside the centre of Lillehammer, one finds the Hakon Hall, a large indoor arena, ski jumps, a small alpine run, free style arena, etc. This is where six Olympic events were held in 1994.

Lillehammer Hotel: In a pleasant position a little above the town centre, in its own wooded grounds about 10 minutes' walk from the ski centre. Long low buildings with 330 beds, large dining room, 2 sitting rooms and reception hall with open fireplace. Indoor and outdoor swimming pools, sauna and solarium. Dancing nightly to band.

Oppland Hotel Lillehammer: Situated a few minutes walk from the town centre with a most beautiful view of Lake Mjøsa, this hotel accommodates 140 guests in 60 double and 10 single rooms all with shower, wc, telephone, radio, satellite TV, mini-bar and hairdryer. À la carte restaurant, Piano-bar with international entertainers, bar and restaurant with dancing, swimming pool with saunas and solarium, comfortable lounges and conference and banquet facilities for 250 persons.

Victoriarica Hotel: Centrally situated 500m. from railway station. Renovated in 1982, with a total of 180 beds, all rooms with private bath/w.c. and colour TV. Dining room, three modern bars, restaurant, comfortable sitting room, TV lounge, bar. Dancing every evening.

SPÅTIND MOUNTAIN HOTEL

Ski Touring and some Downhill
See Charts: page 235
See Map: page 240

This hotel stands alone at the side of Lake Synn, at a height of 2,700ft. Its nearest station is Dokka, a 3 hour train journey from Oslo, and it is 188km. distance by road. It is surrounded by beautiful mountain scenery, with Olavskampen rising to 4,200ft. and Mt. Spåtind to 4,600ft. Downhill skiing is catered for by two drag-lifts 300m. and 900m. long and there is also a short rope tow for children. The runs down are fairly gentle on the whole, suitable for medium skiers with some easier runs for beginners. The surrounding countryside provides some superb ski touring, with many miles of marked trails crossing vast tracts of undulating open land and acres of woodland interspersed with beautiful lakes.

Spåtind Høyfjellshotell: This is a modern 3-storey hotel, having 84 bedrooms all with bath or shower/wc., and 9 cabins for 4 to 8 persons, also with bath and wc. Several sitting rooms and bars are large and lofty, with striking modern architecture and furnishings. Dancing every night, band and discothèque and small 'night club' open till 3 a.m. A lively hotel which tries hard to please its guests and provides good food well served. Sauna; ski and boot hire; child-parking; ski instruction. Indoor and outdoor swimming pool.

USTAOSET

Touring
See Chart: page 235
See Map: page 240

Ustaoset is 11km. to the west of Geilo and midway between Oslo and Bergen on the main railway, it can also be reached by a 260km. road journey from Oslo though not from Bergen in winter. Its magnificent surrounding countryside stretches across Europe's largest mountain plateau, the Hardangervidda and to the foothills of the Hallingskarv massif, 6,550ft., and provides many miles of glorious touring. One of these tours leads to Geilo, which makes an interesting diversion. There are many small privately owned chalets scattered on the slopes as well as the hotel.

Ustaoset Høyfjellshotell: A large, modern brightly lit, luxurious oasis in all that snow. Deep pile carpeting, and comfortable, roomy sofas and chairsfurnish the four spacious sitting rooms where log fires burn cheerfully. Good food is well served in the attractive dining room. 145 beds with private bath/wc and 8 new apartments. Two busy bars; dancing every night, discothèque or 'night club' downstairs; sauna;table tennis; playroom and conference facilities for up to 100 persons. Swimming pool.

VOSS

Alpine
See Charts: pages 224-235
See Map: page 240

One of Norway's top resorts. Voss is only one hour by train from Bergen, on the Bergen-Oslo main railway line, which crosses the mountains of the fjord country. It is 5½ hours from Oslo. Voss was the site of the Alpine World Cup finals in 1971 and men's slalom and grand slalom in 1974, 1977, and 1984, with an exceptionally good grand slalom course. It has four piste-preparing machines and a number of varied runs, and is an appealing village near the beautiful Lake Vangs amid lovely scenery. There are various good value ski packs available, but these have to be arranged and prepaid abroad. Skis and boots can be hired from Voss Ski & Surf and Gausel Skiutleige.

Hangur Area: The 3,500,ft. long cableway rises 2,200ft. and gives access to the whole of the skiing terrain, travelling from Voss to Hangur, where the ski school office and the Hangur restaurant are situated. A chair-lift and a drag-lift rise another 500ft., and from here there are various easy runs on mainly open but some wooded slopes, suitable for beginners and children. All these end by the restaurant near the terminals of the cableway and chair-lift.

Traastoel Area: An 800m. run from the top of the Hangur chair-lift leads to the foot of Traastoel chair-lift and this rises 850ft. back to Hangur; or one can ski down to join the last stretch of the 1,200m. giant slalom run. The beginning of the giant slalom run, with a ski jump to the right of it, can be reached by crossing to the Bavallen chair-lifts, one 2 seater and one 4 seater, rising 950ft.

Slettafjell: By descending from the top of the Hangur chair-lift over wide open slopes, down to two 3,600ft. long drag-lifts which rise 900,ft., one reaches various easy to intermediate runs about 1,600m. long to the bottom of the drag-lifts, where there is a cafeteria, serving meals and drinks, with a sun terrace. Behind the cafeteria there is a children's ski play area with a short lift.

Raugstad: A long 1 to 1½ hour run for average skiers leads right down to Voss, first over open slopes then through spruce and silver birch woods.

Ski Touring: There is a marvellous run from Lonahorgi, 4,236ft., 6km. above the top of the cableway. The slopes are open and become steep in places. A further 8 illuminated trails in the district. Total prepared trails 45km.

Voss Ski & Surf/Ski School: This has 10-12 instructors and no language problems, teaching whenever required. Normal lessons 2 hours. Minimum age for children is 7 years.

Hangur Cafeteria: A large and busy self-service restaurant. All hotels will give demi-pension so that it is not necessary to return to Voss for lunch.

Après Ski: Only the hotels remain open after 4.30, except on Thursdays, when the shops stay open till 7.00. There is a good cinema open four evenings a week, which shows a variety of films in English. Fleischers Hotel provides glogg for après ski afternoons, as also do Rondo Sportell and Park Hotel Vossevangen. The discothèque at the Hotel Jarl is open every evening except Mondays and the 'Mons Nye Sound and Lighting' disco at the Rondo Sportell is open every evening. The 'Top Spot' dancing bar at Fleischers is open from Monday to Saturday. Café Stationen at Park Hotel Vossevangen open until 0100 hours. They also have the 'Pentagon' disco open every evening. Bergen is close enough for a day's outing for a change of scene.

Recommended Hotels:

Fleischers Hotel: Near the Hangur cableway and lake, this is an old building with a welcoming atmosphere. Bedrooms in the old building are well furnished and those in the modern wing are very agreeable, all with private bath/wc. Several comfortable sitting rooms, with open hearth. Pleasant dining room with lake view, and good food well served. Band with après ski dancing 20.30-01.00. Indoor swimming pool and two saunas. This hotel has a long established reputation with British visitors, and is fully licensed.

Park Hotel Vossevangen: Next to the lake and completely redecorated in 1982, not far from the cableway and in the middle of the village. Bedrooms fully carpeted, modern furniture, comfortable; telephone, private bath or shower/wc. Spacious sitting rooms. Log fires. Dancing every night except Tuesdays in the 'Leonardo Dancing'. Bright dining room and sun terrace overlooking lake and mountains. A long-established hotel with friendly service and fully licensed.

Kringsjå Pension: Quietly situated in a small garden, and well run by family owners. Three cosy sitting rooms and bar (wine and beer). Small bedrooms simple but clean and neat, 15 doubles, 2 singles, one 5-bedded, all with shower and wc. Excellent food; sauna. A friendly and informal pension, very comfortable and homely atmosphere, and good value.

Vang Pension: In the main street, two floors above electrical appliance shop. 17 bedrooms, small, basic, clean and neat, some 3-bedded. 5 public showers, 6 wcs, laundry room. Small modern dining room, sitting room and bar. Sauna. Beer and wine only. Popular and reasonable.

Youth Hostel: 10 minutes' walk from the station, in a position overlooking the lake. 2 and 4-bedded rooms, all with private shower/wc. Sauna, exercise room, sports room, dining room, lounges, cafeteria. Prices very reasonable and pre-bookable.

WADAHL

Ski Touring and some Downhill
See Charts: page 235
See Map: page 240

Wadahl lies at 3,000ft. in the Gudbransdal area, 17km. from Vinstra station, from which guests are met by car, one hour's drive from Lillehammer and 4 hours by rail, or 270km. by road from Oslo. The surrounding landscape is very beautiful and the hotel looks across to the Jotunheim peaks and glaciers, the Rondane range and Mt. Snöhetta. Pistes are well prepared and cater for beginners to average skiers and are directly reached from the hotel entrance by slope about 1,000 metres down to the Gålå Skiarena, where one finds 5 drag-lifts, 200-1,150m. long and a chair-lift, 1,300m., rising 950ft. in 5 minutes with pistes of varying lengths and levels of performance.

There is a small practice slope just outside the hotel, floodlit at night, with a ski-lift for children and beginners. There are 200km. of marked ski touring trails.

Wadahl Høyfellshotell: An attractively built, long, low modern hotel looking over lakes and wooded lower slopes to Mt. Snohetta and beyond. All of the 95 comfortable double rooms have private bath/wc. Several interconnecting cheerful sitting rooms brightly coloured rugs and curtains of typical Norwegian style, open log fireplaces. Dining room and other reception rooms have views across the snowfields and woods. Excellent food quickly served. Two bars, one running almost whole length of dining room, overlooking it through wide arches in white painted walls hung with brightly coloured Norwegian tapestries. Dancing every evening, except Sundays, as there is a band in the hotel and the mountain lodge, 150m. away, has a discothèque. Occasional fancy dress evenings. Ski and boot hire; ski instructors; indoor swimming pool with saunas and solarium.

SWEDEN

Few British skiers have had experience of skiing in Sweden. This large country with a vast amount of open space has a great variety of ski resorts catering for alpine and Nordic skiing. The resorts have much character and are set amidst beautiful scenery. Accommodation ranges from first class hotels down to well equipped log cabins, for those who prefer self-catering. A great effort is made to provide facilities for children and most hotels have their own kindergartens. The ski slopes are well maintained and the larger resorts have a good range of lifts. At many resorts the runs and trails are floodlit to allow longer skiing hours during early season. The ski schools are of high standard whilst sports shops have a good selection of equipment for hire.

From the U.K. by air there are regular flights to Stockholm and Gothenburg with connecting internal flights to airports nearer the resorts, and thence by rail or car. Like Norway, many of the resorts only have one main hotel which provides all the facilities required for an enjoyable holiday. Chalets and log cabins normally provide supplementary accommodation.

ÅRE - DUVED

Two of Sweden's best resorts are situated within a few kilometres from each other, not interlinked by lifts but connected by bus, a 5 minute journey. Located in a wide sunny valley running east to west with the Areskutan mountain rising to 4,658 feet to the north and facing the lake of Åre on the southern side and only 85km. from Östersund airport.

ÅRE - 1,300 ft.

The larger of the two villages and fairly extensive with traditional and modern buildings in attractive surroundings. Most of the ski area is south, south-east and south-west facing and about half of it is above the tree-line. It is well equipped mechanically with 30 lifts. From the centre the cableway, the only one in Sweden, rises to below the summit of the Åreskutan mountain, 4,180ft., where there is a restaurant. On the way up one has wonderful views of the ski area and its lift system. On the eastern side (right) a chair-lift runs almost parallel to the cableway to just below the halfway point serving the difficult Slalombacken run and the World Cup run, from the top of the chair-lift one can also cross over on an easy wooded run to the western side. Further to the east there are two trainer lifts and a mountain railway which leaves from near the Tourist Office and connects with a chair-lift surmounted by a drag-lift up to Mörvikshummeln with four further lifts to the right. All these lifts serve mainly intermediate runs back to the village. On the outskirts of the eastern sector the long Tott drag-lift leaves Hotel Sunwing rising to Totthummeln and from here one has an easy run back to base or one can cross over on an intermediate run to the top of the mountain railway. Serving the intermediate runs on the eastern side at the top of the cableway is a further chair-lift. On the western side (left) of the cableway a 4-seater chair-lift rises to Café Olympia and a surmounting gondolaway reaches just short of the top station. The runs back to the middle station are intermediate and easy whilst those to the village are fairly closely wooded medium to difficult. Further to the west the easier runs are to be found. Four surmounting drag-lifts reach the top station of the cableway and individually provide access to easy skiing. Two further lifts serve the lower slopes. There is a good variety of runs for all grades and plenty of off-piste skiing and many miles of langlauf trails. Children are well catered for in their own ski school. One ski pass covers both resorts,

Après Ski: Après ski life is fun. The most popular bars are in the Hotel Diplomat and Hotel Sunwing, where for 2 hours cheaper drinks are available. After dinner there are a number of places to dance: the 'Country Club' at the Hotel Åregården is very popular with disco and often live groups. The Sunwing Hotel has dancing 6 nights a week to disco or live music. Åre Fjällby is one of the main centres of attraction with two restaurants, bar and disco.There is a good selection of restaurants such as the 'Marmite', 'Bakfickan', 'Bistro' and 'Villa Tottebo' all serving good food in rustic surroundings.

Recommended Hotels:

Hotel Åregården: Situated in the market place, a charming old wooden hotel renovated in 1986. The 40 rooms are simply furnished but comfortable; bed and breakfast arrangements. Pleasant restaurant, 3 sitting rooms, discothèque.

Hotel Åregardarna: An apartment hotel opened in 1981 consisting of small two-storey houses equipped to a high standard. Night club.

Hotel Diplomat: A popular hotel with 100 beds, all rooms with shower or bath and TV. Spacious dining room with excellent menu, wine and cheese restaurant in the cellar, 4 sitting rooms, Skier's Bar with 'Lucky Hour' half price drinks between 3-6 p.m., cocktail bar, conference rooms, sauna and dancing at least twice weekly.

Hotel Sunwing Åre: A large hotel/aparthotel situated next to ski-lift and slopes. 80 rooms, 104 apartments. Pleasant restaurant serving delicious food, live entertainment and dancing normally 4 nights a week during the winter season, 2 bars. Alternatively for younger guests is the discothèque - open 4 nights a week. Comfortable sitting rooms, several conference rooms for all kinds of groups. Large pool, whirlpools, saunas. Mini Club and the Club 13 in winter for younger guests.

DUVED

A small village lying 5 minutes by bus to the west of Åre made up of small hotels, chalets and the necessary shops including two large supermarkets. Duved has a compact lift system of 13 lifts, all running due north to the near summit of the Mullfjället rounded top mountain giving a height difference of some 1,600ft. From the northern outskirts of the village the 'Dall' drag-lift rises towards the summit and terminates about three-quarters of the way up. Further to the right there are two surmounting drag-lifts on the upper slopes and from the top, if one skis down southwestwards, one picks up the remaining lift, 'Västra Paradis', which travels up to the highest point and provides easy runs each side. The skiing down to the village can be varied considerably by using the above lifts with easy and intermediate runs over south facing slopes. In the village area there are two rope tows and a drag-lift. On the eastern side the Englands drag-lift, constructed in 1988, links the Tegefjälls area with Duved. The skiing here makes a pleasant change from the Åre area, a 5-minute bus journey away. Both resorts normally have excellent snow conditions with a long season from November to May.

Après Ski: Après ski life is not as lively as in Åre. The Hamrestugan café with its large sun terrace is very popular. There are a number of restaurants and bars where one can spend many happy hours and for further entertainment Åre is close at hand.

Recommended Hotels:

Hotel Viking Renen: Situated in the centre, this hotel provides a high standard of service. 45 hotel rooms and 43 apartments with a total of 370 beds. Restaurant and cosy bar, comfortable sitting room, children's playroom, sauna.

Forsa: Almost a separate village with over 70 cabins giving a total of 400 beds. All cabins centrally heated with well equipped kitchens, shower/wc., colour TV, clock radio. Access to restaurant, sitting rooms, conference rooms, bar and sauna. One can opt for self-catering or full board.

RIKSGRÄNSEN (1,550 ft.)

Riksgränsen is the most northern resort in Scandinavia, situated in Lapland on the Norwegian border, and in line with Narvik, 40km. away. The resort can be reached by train or car. a 2 hour journey from Kiruna airport. Due to its northern extremity the ski season does not start until the last week in February and carries on into the summer. Two double chair-lifts and four drag-lifts serve the skiing which is to be found on the north, east and western sides of the mountain. There is little queueing as the Riksgränsen Hotel is the only one in the area. The first chair-lift leaves from close to the hotel and rises to Bergstation and from this point an easy run 'Tassen' to the right takes one to the lower terminal of the second chair-lift, which rises to 3,000ft. There are intermediate and difficult runs each side of the lifts; good skiers will choose the 'Branten' run with slopes of 40 degrees. One trail is called the 'Beer Run', as at the end, skiers are awarded a cold beer before making the 5 minute train journey back to the hotel. Nordic skiing and touring is much in evidence here, with trails up to 20km., and the hotel provides guides for such tours.This centre is for all grades of skiers for late season and summer skiing. During the midnight sun period, 18th May to 18th July, many people camp in the area and ski most of the night or there is fishing and canoeing on the lake and lovely walks into the mountains. if the weather is not good one can take the train or car to Kiruna or Narvik. Après ski entertainment is organised in the hotel.

Hotel Riksgränsen: Extended many times since the hotel was built in 1920 and now provides a good selection of accommodation from 4-bedded rooms to modern twin-bedded rooms with bath/shower. Spacious dining room, large sitting rooms, TV rooms, 5 saunas with showers, a large discothèque and bar.

SCOTLAND

Many years of developed skiing in Scotland have contributed to a firm foundation for a successful tourist operation, winter and summer, in the Highlands. The five developed areas are at Cairngorm, Glenshee, Glencoe, The Lecht and Nevis Range.

It should not be imagined that a winter holiday in a Scottish Ski Centre is one totally dedicated to the sport of skiing. While the skier's every reasonable wish is catered for, the Highlands have set out to provide an interest for everyone. Of these the most obvious is the countryside itself. All the ski areas are in glorious country and are approached from villages in the valleys. The Countryside Commission for Scotland has used its influence from the beginning to see that the beauty and serenity of the valleys and hills remains as unimpaired as is possible for the enjoyment of everyone. Be it rock, heather, burn, scree, loch or forest, it's all there within a stone's throw of your centre.

How to Get There: Access to the Highlands is possible by road, rail and air. Improved roads now enable motorists to take motorways and major trunk roads all the way to Inverness. At present the western route via M1, M6, A74, M74,to Glasgow provides the least mentally energetic route. From Glasgow one branches off on A82 to Glencoe and Nevis Range, or via M73, A80, M80 and an improved A9 to Perth and Aviemore. From Perth the A93 takes one to Glenshee. The Lecht is located near the summit of the famous Cockbridge to Tomintoul road (A939). The area can be reached from Aviemore by continuing north on the A9 and reaching the A938 via Boat of Garten (The Osprey Village) and Nethybridge.

Alternatively, it can be reached from 'Royal Deeside' by continuing north on the A93 past Glenshee and cutting off to the A939 4 miles after passing through Braemar. Allowing for a 500 mile journey from London, British Rail also have motor rail from points south to Aberdeen, Inverness and Stirling.

There are sleeper services from Euston to Aviemore, Glencoe via Bridge of Orchy or Fort William, Nevis Range via Fort William and Glenshee via Perth. Scheduled air services fly from the South to Inverness and Aberdeen.

Snow Conditions: Snow normally lies above 2,000 feet in Scotland and the treeline is a little below this level. Due to the maritime weather influence most snow accumulates in the gullies and coires where it can reach depths of twenty feet or more. The wind quickly scours any loose snow off the ridges and exposed places. Pistes are therefore largely self-constructed with the assistance of snow fencing. There are periods, however, when snow blankets of powder in Alpine proportions can penetrate as low as the 1,000ft. level giving a new dimension to the terrain. Be prepared for the unusual since two feet of powder is not unknown in May, as is spring snow in January. The seasons seem to be getting later - from December to May, but November skiing is often possible.

Snow forecasts are published in newspapers from 1st December to 30th April and a ski report can be obtained by telephoning Ski Call 01891 500 440 or Ski Hotline 01891 654 654. Information is also available on the Scottish skiing pages on Ceefax and Oracle.

Car Preparations: One of the recurring problems of snow falling below 2,000ft. is the blockage of access roads. These are the A9 at Drumochter (1,500ft.) when approaching Aviemore from Blair Atholl, and the Cairngorm mountain road to the Car Park (2,000ft.), the Black Mount of Rannoch, just south of Glencoe on the A82 (1,140ft.) and the Devil's Elbow summit (2,180,ft.), on theA93 just south of the Glenshee Company's development. The A939 Cockbridge to Tomintoul road is famous for its closure in winter but road realignment and improved snow clearance have made this a much less frequent occurrence.When coming by road in unsettled weather it is as well to telephone the motoring organisations in Scotland and to listen to radio reports of road conditions. As an added precaution against being caught in blizzard conditions make sure that you have in your car: a shovel, a snow mat (a doormat will do), food and hot drink, and your protective clothing. It is wise to have winterised tyres or chains.

Touring: This can be arranged professionally in the Cairngorm and Glenshee areas. Generally, it is not advised to leave the developed areas where ski patrols keep a watchful eye on the pistes, unless you are in the company of experienced ski mountaineers who can advise on the survival precautions needed. Over 2,000 feet, Scotland's climate is Arctic for considerable periods during the winter and spring.

Ski Gear: Nowadays ski gear is carefully thought out and well designed. Nevertheless, an anorak and waterproof trousers to go over the lot helps in Scottish mist conditions to keep you dry. Have spare woollies to put on and remember that the extremities, head, hands and feet need special protection. Double knit woolly hat, gloves with warm inners (mitts are best for children), and well insulated ski boots. Well fitting goggles against wind and blown snow are essential.

Sports shops and ski hire are available at or close to all the ski areas, so that skiers' every need can be met.

Après Ski: The only ethnic addition to the normal local night life in Britain is the 'ceilidh' at which variations of folk music with a Scottish flavour are introduced. Scottish country dancing is not over indulged nor is the kilted image - rather the reverse with more emphasis on the international folk/rock cult. Discos and dances take place in each area every weekend in season with the usual bar entertainment thrown in.

Accommodation: Modern accommodation can be booked either by package arrangement, as on the Continent, through travel agents, with the advice of local travel associations or direct. One has the usual choice of hotels from one star upwards with surprisingly good value at two star level, bed and breakfast establishments and camping sites in every village with an increasing number of apartments for small groups, chalets and cottages. There is also farmhouse accommodation available.

An interesting development is the rise of independent or denominationally sponsored hostels. The SYHA Hostels have been joined by others in key positions. Compass Centre, Glenshee; Lagganlia (Lothian Region) Centre, Insh Hall Centre and Christian Centre at Kincraig; Abernethy Centre, Nethy Bridge; Garnock Outdoor Centre, Glencoe. All of these provide comprehensive ski package arrangements on a communal basis and there are others in outlying areas which provide ski services to the snow by minibus. Courses for skiers, mountaineers and instructors are organised at Glenmore Lodge, the Scottish Sports Council mountain training centre.

Instruction: This is conducted by ski schools, the majority of which are members of the Association of Ski Schools of Great Britain. Training of instructors is conducted by the British Association of Ski Instructors with popular courses in April and May each year on Cairngorm. The Scottish National Ski Council also runs courses for Ski Leaders. The standard is high as evidenced by the shortage of Grade 1 instructors because of their popularity abroad! All skiing hotels have an arrangement with the local ski school and private or children's instruction can easily be obtained.

GLENCOE SKI CENTRE

(1,150ft. - 3,636ft.)

One of the most scenic of the ski developments is the series of lifts which rise on Meall A' Bhuridh (pronounced Meal a Voorie) above Rannoch Moor. It has the reputation of providing some of the best skiing in Scotland and was taken over by Glenshee Ski Centre in 1995. (Tel. 01855 811226). The car park is half a mile from the Kingshouse junction on the A82 and is clearly signposted. A restaurant, ski hire, ski school, a double access chair-lift and extended car park complete the base installation. The Museum of Scottish Skiing and Climbing is to be released in the redeveloped of the base station.

The Plateau tow gives access to the upper reaches of the mountains as well as the superb beginners' area. The Plateau Café is to be rebuilt with the seating capacity to be doubled. The *'Chateau Plateau'* is the main building at Plateau level, which also has the Glencoe Ski Club Hut and a steep T-bar tow which connects with the summit T-bar and button tow.

There are six runs off the summit ridge between the rock formations. The Etive Glades, the Spring Run and the Fly paper are outstanding. Most skiing takes place above the access chair-lift, but for a few weeks each year – generally in January and early February – the longest descent in Scotland (2,500 ft.) from the summit to the car park is possible. You will have achieved something if you can do it without stopping.

The nearest railways station is Bridge of Orchy (10 miles) on the scenic West Highland line adjacent to Bridge of Orchy Hotel (23 beds) where, given some initiative by the visitor, a lift can be arranged to the slopes. The Kingshouse Hotel (40 beds) is reputedly the oldest hostelry in Scotland and is popular with skiers, being the closest to the ski centre. Further down the glen the Clachaig Inn (?? beds), a former Scottish Pub of the Year with its annual beer festival in February and March each year is a must, and the Glencoe Hotel (25 beds) on the shores of Loch Leven, 12 miles from the chair-lift. There is plenty of choice in terms of price and facilities in the locality (Fort TIC Tel: 01397 703781).

GLENSHEE SKI CENTRE

(2,000ft. - 3,504ft.)

The Glenshee ski area lies on either side of the A 93, with lift complex beginning right by the road at a height of 2,159ft.

Stretching over three valleys and including four Munros, Glenshee Ski Centre offers skiers some of the most extensive skiing in Scotland. Flanking the highest pass in Scotland, the A93 Braemar to Blairgowrie road, access to the slopes couldn't be simpler. Seven lifts operate from car park level, linking up with 19 others, to form Scotland's largest lift system, servicing an impressive 40km. of marked piste.

On the 'sunnyside', initial uplift consists of three pomas and one chair-lift, leading over to Meall Odhar (3,019ft.) and a Snowboard fun park. Over the back of this valley, skiers and boarders can delight in the wide open pistes of Coire Fionn and the ever popular Glas Maol bowl. A tow runs almost the full length of the coire to the summit of Glas Maol (3,504ft.) offering breathtaking views and the opportunity to ski Glenshee's longest runs – 2km.

On the opposite side of the road to sunnyside, a chair-lift and button tow ascent the Cairnwell Mountain (3,059ft.). From the summit skiers can pick their way down the infamous Black Tiger run or opt for the slightly more forgiving Thunderbowl. Alternatively a traverse along the ridge leads on to the gentle bunny run and Butcharts Coire. Three other tows service this north-east ridge, and these can be reached via the Thunderbowl or by a short lift from roadside level ascending the former artificial slope. This route also leads you on to the two tows on Carn Aosda (3,003ft.). Two of the lower slopes on this side have the advantage of snow-making facilities with a capacity to produce 14,500 square meters of snow when required.

Glenshee not only offers challenging skiing for advanced and intermediate skiers; beginners are also well catered for with excellent nursery slopes right beside the car park. In addition, cross country skiing has ben practised for many years in this area with many unmarked trails around Loch Vrotachan.

The centre operates its own Ski and Snowboading School with a team of 40 qualified instructors catering for all standards, with race training and timing facilities available on request. On-site ski, snowboard and clothing hire are also available for your convenience. Moreover, excellent value midweek and weekend packages combine lift tickets, ski hire and instruction at unbeatable prices. Other facilities include a newly refurbished shop selling a wide range of outdoor gear and souvenirs, 3 large cafés and restaurants (2 licensed and all with toilets servicing the hill and base station), disabled toilet facilities, a first aid post manned by a qualified team of ski patrollers and free parking for 1,400 cars and 50 coaches.

Glenshee is to join forces with four top European resorts, Val d'Isère, Meribel, Verbier and Courmayeur, as it hosts one leg of the 1998 European Mogul Challenge. It is hoped the event will run on the Tiger, providing spectators the chance to watch the mogul bashing skills of both professionals and amateurs being tested to the limit on this the steepest venue on the circuit!

There is a thriving Tourist Association, whose members offer all types of accommodation. The Dalmunzie Hotel (34 beds), the highest in Glenshee, offers elegant luxury in magnificent surroundings. The Spittal of Glenshee Hotel (48 beds) was specially designed for skiers in Scandinavian open-plan. The Log Cabin Hotel at Kirchmichael (25 beds) was built as a ski lodge from whole Norwegian pine logs. Braemar (9 miles), well known for its 'Gathering', offers the Fife Arms Hotel (120 beds), comfortable in its baronial style, which has package arrangements for skiers, as does the fully refurbished Invercauld Arms Hotel (68 rooms), and there is a host of friendly guest houses. Blairgowrie, though away from the slopes, provides accommodation of every type for skiers, from the Angus Hotel with sauna, swimming pool and nearby squash court, to the large self-catering Altamount Chalet Park, and the Glenshieling at Rattray, a licensed guest house which welcomes skiers.

Fuller details are obtainable from the Glenshee Lift Company (Tel: 013397 41320), Glenshee Tourist Association (Tel: 01250 5509), and the Braemar Tourist Information Centre (Tel: 013397 41600).

CAIRNGORM

(1,800 - 3,620 ft.)

The Cairngorm mountains lie to the east of the Spey Valley, which runs northwards from Dalwhinnie to Grantown-on-Spey, a distance of some 40 miles. Roughly midway at Aviemore there is a ten mile road into the hills to the car parks and access lifts just above the treeline at about 1,800 and 2,000ft. The valley is highly developed as a near all-the-year-round playground. Winter and summer tourism can merge with some startling effects. One can in May, within the hour, ski the White Lady and sail on Loch Morlich. The amenities for non-skiers can make the family or sporting holiday a reality. Some of the activities offered are golf (7 courses), pony trekking, fishing, dinghy sailing and wind-surfing, canoeing, gliding, cycling, as well as artificial ski slopes should the mountain be stormbound. There are diversions with visits to distilleries, wild life parks, nature trails, clan museums, alpine plant nursery, private steam railway, the osprey observation point and the reindeer house. A focal point for 'fun' is the Aviemore Mountain Resort with its ice rink, film theatre as well as a go-cart track.

The main Highland railway line, (excellent overnight express service direct from London), runs the length of the valley on its way to Inverness which is also served by Dalcross airport, 35 miles from Aviemore. Other road distances to Aviemore are from London 511 miles, Glasgow 140 miles and Edinburgh 127 miles.

The Spey Valley is divided into two districts, Badenoch and Strathspey. Badenoch begins at the Drumochter Pass (1,484ft.) which when crossed gives some idea of conditions to be expected at the Cairngorm car parks. The A9 road bypasses Dalwhinnie (34 miles) with its prominent distillery and rapidly descends to Newtonmore (25 miles). Both villages have had a tradition of skiing tourism since the turn of the century. Four miles further up the A9 is Kingussie (20 miles), capital of Badenoch, where the redcoats were besieged over 230 years ago in Ruthven Castle. Hotels include the Victorian-styled Royal Hotel (65 beds) and the granite-built Star Hotel (75 beds). The lochside village of Kincraig (15 miles) stands above the river Spey, the hamlet of Insh and its scenic loch. Sailing, canoeing and fishing can be enjoyed here. Kincraig is a small haven of good value with two sought-after hotels, the Ossian Hotel (20 beds) and the Lynwilg Hotel (20 beds), which is further up the A9 towards Aviemore. Beyond Aviemore one enters Strathspey which is a more open part of the valley with rolling forest-clad hills and turbulent rivers. Boat of Garten (15 miles) provides two hotels, the Boat Hotel (52 beds) and the Craigard Hotel (35 beds) in a secluded setting near the heath-fringed golf course. A few miles after crossing the River Spey Nethybridge (17 miles) provides plenty of beds for the winter visitor, including the baronial Nethybridge Hotel (75 beds).

Back on the old A9 – the new one sweeps north towards Inverness over the Slochd pass (1,200ft.) – the next village is Carrbridge (17 miles), the home of a number of ex-British team members and a strong skiing tradition. It has the most northerly railway station in the valley and is the railhead for Dulnain Bridge and Grantown-on-Spey. Skiing hotels are the Carrbridge Hotel (96 beds) and the Struan House Hotel (34 beds). The Lochanhully Lodge a little way down the A939 is a development of fifty 4-bedded chalets amongst the birch trees. This road leads onto Grantown-on-Spey (20 miles), a county town tourist resort long before the ski boom started. The Craiglynne Hotel (101 beds) and Ben Mhor Hotel (42 beds) have been popular with skiers for many years.

Aviemore Mountain Resort (10 miles, 700ft. a.s.l.) is the acknowledged focus of activity in the valley, with four very modern hotels in the resort: the de-luxe Four Seasons Hotel with the finest plate glass views in town, the Badenoch Hotel, the Mercury Hotel and the Aviemore Highlands Hotel. Between them they account for over 600 beds, mostly with private bathroom. The other end of the scale is provided by the Aviemore Chalets Motel; 80 apartments in 4-bed units with shower. For those looking for very high quality self-catering holidays, there is the Scandinavian Village, again situated in the Aviemore Main Resort complex. They offer a very high level of comfort and convenience in apartments or houses with full central heating, attractive decor, fully equipped kitchen, complete with dishwasher; colour TV and a host of other comforts.

Thriving establishments include the Cairngorm Hotel (40 beds) opposite the station, the High Range Motel complex comprising chalet accommodation, La Taverna bistro bar and a touring caravan park and the Coylumbridge Hotel (266 beds), which is a self-contained conference hotel, rooms mostly with private bath, with three bars, tennis courts, and a swimming pool and fitness centre.

Glenmore (4 miles) is the hamlet at the eastern end of Loch Morlich, where two burns converge in the natural amphitheatre below Cairngorm itself. The large caravan and camping site lies between the mountain road and the water-borne amenities by the loch. In summer the scene is more like the Riviera with the pines, fine sand and basking humanity.

The ski area is served by a total of 17 ski lifts. When approaching up the mountain road a spur road leads off left into the Coire na Ciste car park (1,800ft.), snack bar and access chair-lift. Here a system of six lifts over a distance of 3,500 yards provide skiing for every level of skier. The main beginners area lies at the top in the Ptarmigan bowl. The centre ground is steep with the East and West Walls as well as the centre gully providing challenging skiing, while intermediates can enjoy the Aonach poma lower down.

Continuing up the mountain road by 'windy ridge' the main car park is reached at about 2,000ft. in Coire Cas. The Day Lodge provides a self-service restaurant, café-bar, ski and snowboard hire, shop, ticket office and a snack bar.

From here there is a choice of four access lifts. On the right is the Fiacaill Ridge Poma. In the centre the Car Park tow and on the left the double chair to the Shieling (2,600ft.), serve the Coire Cas and White Lady system of five lifts including a chair to the Ptarmigan snack bar (3,600ft.) where both Ciste and Cas systems meet. The Day Lodge Poma provides a lower level link from the Coire Cas car park to Coire na Ciste.

The whole absorbs about 6,000 skiers and on holidays and weekends it is advisable to take to the road really early to get the benefit of skiing before the lift queues form. Lifts close in winter at 4.15 p.m. but this is extended to as late as 5.30 p.m. in springtime when daylight hours are longer. The Spring Snow Festival will be held from 20 - 22 March 1998.

A regular bus service operates daily from Aviemore to Cairngorm and a free shuttle bus is provided between Coire na Ciste and Coire Cas car parks as conditions dictate. Information can be obtained from the Cairngorm Chair-lift Company, Tel: 01479 861261; the Aviemore Mountain Resort, Tel: 01479 810 624; and the local Tourist Board, Tel: 01479 810 363.

THE LECHT

(2,000ft to 2,700ft)

The Lecht ski area opened in 1977 and has seen a steady expansion since then. It now has 6 main Poma lifts and 6 beginners lifts. Two slopes on opposite sides of the access road are suitable for national slalom races. The remaining area is ideally suited for beginner and intermediate level and its main market is the family group coping with all levels of skiing ability. The area is safe and compact with all facilities (restaurant, ski hire, ski school, toilets, shop and créche) close to the access road and car parks. It prides itself on having a friendly family atmosphere.

The area is sheltered from the prevailing winds and often operates when both Cairngorm and Glenshee (45 mins by car) are stormbound.

The Lecht also has a 200m floodlight plastic slope, with bumps and natural contours, guaranteeing skiing regardless of snow conditions.

Accommodation is available at Corgarff (2 miles) and Strathdon to the South and at Tomintoul (7 miles) to the North. All information and bookings from Lecht Ski Company Tel No. 019756 51440, Fax No. 019756 51426). Gordon District Tourist Board (01224 632727) and Moray District (01343 542666).

NEVIS RANGE

(2,000 ft. - 4,000 ft.)

Scotland's highest ski area, Nevis Range (Tel: 01397 705825) is situated on the northern slopes of Aonach Mor, which looks over at the rocky face of Ben Nevis, Britain's highest mountain. Opened for the 1989-90 season, Nevis Range boasts Scotland's only gondola lift, a six-seater which provides access from the car park just above sea level to the Snowgoose Restaurant and the ski area itself.

From the Snowgoose restaurant, which shares the gondola top station building with a bar, shop and first aid facilities, a quad chair continues up to link with four ski tows serving the wide open slopes of Aonach Mor, including the main runs in the Snowgoose Bowl. A further three beginner lifts are situated adjacent to the restaurant.

Beginners' facilities have been further improved by the installation of a double chair-lift and drag-lift due east of the top gondola station.

At the top the gentle summit runs have a stunning backdrop of Ben Nevis, whilst in the north-east facing corries a new lift has been constructed, which will provide skiers and snowboarders with some of he most exhilarating "wilderness" skiing Scotland has to offer. This area, Coire Dubh, is a wide, open and sheltered coire usually filling with early season snow. There are lots of entry points into the coire providing many variations for competent skiers. The new lift "Braveheart" is a ski on, ski off 2-seater with a capacity of 800 skiers per hour. Skiers will be able to return to the Snowgoose Restaurant using the Rob Roy T-bar and Great Glen chair-lift.

All this lies only 7 miles north of Fort William by the A82 road, which leads on to Spean Bridge 4 miles further east, providing the nearest accommodation for the area. At Fort William there is a full range of accommodation from simple bunk houses to the sumptuous Inverlochy Castle.

Lochaber, now with two ski areas, is rising to the challenge of offering visitors to the area an all-year-round destination.

Information from: Nevis Range Development Company (Tel: 01397 705825); Fort William and Lochaber Tourist Board - Tel: 01397 703781

AUSTRALIA

by Sasha St. Clair

Australia is a continent of 8.5 million square kilometres/3.3 million square miles: a land of extreme contrasts; desert that equals the Sahara, tropical rain forests to match those of Brazil, glorious parrots, snakes and other reptiles, animals that carry their young in a pouch and hop, the aboriginals who have occupied this land for more than 40,000 years, oppressive heat and our joy – beautiful snow.

The Aussie snow sport resorts are scattered over an area of about 1,400 square km./370 square miles. Starting in Tasmania, the most southern state where snow falls are minimal, the only commercial operation is Ben Lomond. This has a summit of 1,572 meters or 5,157 feet, and offers good intermediate facilities. The Victorian and New South Wales resorts are situated in the Great Divide Mountain Range, which runs from Melbourne up the east coast to just south of Brisbane. Here higher mountains around the 2,100 m./7,000 ft. mark are to be found. These mountains are older than the Grand Canyon and have a rounded shape from millions of years of weathering, not the sheer ruggedness of the European Alps, but still maintain a rugged beauty of their own.

All major commercial resorts have extensive snowmaking systems, thus ensuring a snow guarantee with most accommodation packages. Few drag-lifts are found, Aussies like the comfort of chairs. Most skiing is done below the tree-line, so conditions are generally pleasant due to the lack of wind, plus a lot of fun. All areas are within a few hours drive of either Sydney or Melbourne international airports. Most resorts have ample village accommodation, with a good variety of restaurants, retail outlets and service facilities. Towns that provide service facilities are below the snowline, and can be considerably cheaper than on-slope accommodations.

Cross-country skiing is a very popular sport and all ski resorts have marked trails. This can be a magnificent way of discovering the snow-clad Aussie Bush. If driving, chains are must be carried by law and must be fitted in designated areas. Most access roads are sealed, and conditions should be checked prior to driving as roads can be closed without notice. All operations are situated in National Parks, so a small entrance fee per vehicle should be expected. In my opinion, skiing is now more economical in Australia than in New Zealand, although the snow is damper, and there is not the vertical rise available that is offered over the Tasman Sea in New Zealand. The Kiwi snow is of far a drier quality, due primarily to the altitude and southern latitudes – hence the reputation.

We include include brief information on six popular Australian resorts.

PERISHER BLUE SKI RESORT

Height of Base Station: 5,511 ft.
Height of Top Station: 6,837 ft.

Made up of ski four areas, Perisher Valley, Smiggins Hole, Blue Cow and Guthega ski area, thus forming largest ski resort, covering 3751 acres with a choice of 50 lifts and four resorts serving over 150km of trails. The combined area is now known as Perisher Blue. With more than 24 commercial lodges, plus various club lodges scattered over the resort, it is no wonder that just about every Aussie skier has at one time skied Perisher Blue. Offering wide, groomed slopes, extensive snow making and gentle learning areas, it is the ideal beginner and intermediate resort. Advanced skiers have the Olympic Bowl and Steppes areas which provide challenging runs, but this resort comes into its own for the intermediate skier, or the skier who manages to grab a few days each season. There is always a trail that will give enjoyment and flatter your skiing style.

For those wishing to improve the command of their skis, ski school is the place to go. There are over 250 instructors who cater to all tastes, from first timers to experts, for those wishing to brush up or maybe wishing to try a different style: eg telemark or cross country, as this area has some very enjoyable trails that should not be missed. The Ski Tube gives convenient central access to this resort, without the disadvantages of driving.

Blue Cow, and Guthega, which started as a winter recreation area for staff of the Snowy Mountains Authority, has grown through the 80s to become a popular family area. Blue Cow itself opened in 89, so all facilities are new. It is a purpose-built ski area with modern facilities, and an excellent access system.

The Ski Tube, specifically built for this resort is a rack, rail train and travels through 6.5 km of tunnels from Bullocks Flat to Perisher, then on to Blue Cow, a trip that only takes 19 minutes including stops, arriving within the resort centre at Australia's highest ski area. This part of the resort offers runs like "Escape" and "Pony Ride" for the beginner, through to the famous "Kamikaze" at advanced expert level. The intermediate has some challenging runs to choose from: "Stampede", which is an F.I.S. slalom course, to name but one.

Number of Lifts: 50
Total Lift Capacity per hour: 45,980
Grade of Runs: 30% beginners;
60% intermediates; 10% advanced
Season: From early June to mid October
Resort/Area Telephone: 61 64 59 4495
Fax: 61 64 57 5485

MT. BULLER

Height of Base Station: 5,249 ft
Height of Top Station: 5,872 ft.

This resort has the second largest lift capacity in Australasia, 38,500 skiers per hour, offering a magnitude of options for everyone from the absolute beginner to the G.S. racer, with a wide variety of trails, including some to Mt. Stirling. The Après ski scene is abundant, with some 24 restaurants and bars to choose from, all within easy walking distance of ski accommodation that will suit any taste. For those who wish to try something different in the way of alpine activities there is Australia's only mile high undercover ice skating rink, in the centre of the village. An extensive snowmaking system ensures a good coverage when mother nature is misguided. Mt. Buller has over 80 km. of trails with the longest being 2.5 km. Most skiers' introduction to Buller, will be on Bourke St. & Baldy runs which are for beginners, from where access is gained to the lift system. The intermediate and advanced skier may wish to ski straight to Bull Run Quad or Tyrol T-Bar from their lodges; or try great runs such as Slalom Gully and Powder Keg for the advanced; or the Chute for the intermediate.

Number of Lifts: 24
Total Lift Capacity per hour: 38,500
Grade of Runs: 25% beginners;
45% intermediate; 30% advanced
Season: From mid June to mid October
Resort/Area Telephone: 61.57.77.6077

FALLS CREEK

Height of Base Station: 4,921 ft
Height of Top Station: 6,043 ft.

A pleasure to ski at, friendly staff, efficient management, great skiing and one of the best laid-out of the Victorian ski resorts. Falls offers European-style village atmosphere, with facilities to match. It is a pleasant change to ski from your lodge in the morning, and be able to ski back home in the evening, after an exhilarating day's skiing. Falls caters for all, from the absolute beginner to the die-hard bump skier. It consists of two major areas, in the form of bowls on either side of Frying Pan Spur. These bowls give good sheltered skiing in most conditions and offer over 60 runs serviced by 22 lifts. Try the Village Bowl for some exhilarating bumps or blow out on the steeps; Sun Valley gives good all-round skiing for everyone, or try the Maze area if skiing the trees is your passion. On the main ridge, overlooking the Village Bowl, is located the Cloud Nine Restaurant, combining fantastic views with great food. An excellent base for the cross-country or touring enthusiast, with access to many trails and day shelters within the Bogong National Park – a resort appealing to all tastes.

Number of Lifts: 22
Total Lift Capacity per hour: 25,414
Grade of Runs: 17% beginners; 53% intermediate; 30% advanced
Season: From early June to mid October
Resort/Area Telephone: 61.57.57.2718
Fax: 61.57.57.2287

MT. HOTHAM

Height of Base Station: 4,756 ft
Height of Top Station: 6,053 ft.

The highest Alpine Resort in Victoria, Hotham offers a drive-through access to most lodges in the village. This area brings back some great skiing memories, and offers challenging runs for all, the strange thing being that the beginners' areas are situated on the summit, a true Down Under Resort. A road separates these areas from the intermediate and advanced runs, and 1995 saw the opening of a bridge for skiers over the road. Hotham offers some of the most challenging skiing in Australia. Heavenly Valley is an appropriate name for this bowl, which can give most advanced skiers a wide and varied day's skiing: on the bumps or, if you have a taste for it, off-piste powder. Most intermediate skiers will progress rapidly to black runs, as Hotham has a happy knack of bringing out the best in a skier's ability.

Long fabled Australia Drift will be served for the first time this year by the new T-bar Drift Lift. Mt. Hotham also has a vast selection of trails; they are accessed from Hotham & Davenport Village and are within walking distance, or a convenient shuttle ride.

Number of Lifts: 9
Total Lift Capacity per hour: 16,285
Grade of Runs: 21% beginners;
38% intermediate; 41% advanced
Season: From early June to early October
Resort/Area Telephone: 61.57.59.3508
Fax: 61.57.59.3692

THREDBO ALPINE VILLAGE

Height of Base Station: 4,478 ft
Height of Top Station: 6,683 ft.

Located in a valley with the village situated opposite the ski area, giving magnificent views of the slopes and their excellent facilities, the village consists of modern apartment blocks and lodges, set amongst native bush. Skiing is set on groomed slopes and well-planned runs scattered amongst the trees, and cater for all types and levels of skier. Beginners have a secluded area served by 5 lifts, accessed by the Merits chair. Intermediates have an excellent choice, and the advanced skier has a wide variety with such runs as Funnel Web, High Noon and the Face to name a few.

Thredbo has the reputation of being Australia's version of Aspen: this is an up market resort featuring condo's, boutique shops, silver service restaurants and penthouse suites. Touring and cross-country skiers have not however been forgotten, with challenging trails at their disposal.

One trip well worth taking is to Mt. Kosciusko, but first check with ski patrol on snow and weather conditions.

Number of Lifts: 13
Total Lift Capacity per hour: 16,000
Grade of Runs: 11% beginners;
42% intermediate; 47% advanced
Season: From early June to early October
Resort/Area Telephone: 61.64.57.6275
Fax: 61.64.57.6063

MT. BUFFALO

Height of Base Station: 4,767 ft
Height of Top Station: 5,282 ft.

Situated amongst some of Victoria's most beautiful scenery. Buffalo has two ski areas: Cresta & Dingo Dell. Dingo Dell is best suited to the Beginner and Intermediate, areas with gentle slopes, are ideal for those wishing to try skiing in an uncrowded relaxed atmosphere. Cresta (sometimes known as Tatra) has a greater variety of runs that suit all levels of skiing, although, best for the Beginner or Intermediate, with one short Advanced run. Several Cross Country trails are marked on the Mt. Buffalo Plateau and a trip that is guided by a National Park Ranger can be very rewarding and interesting. The Chalet at Mt. Buffalo is worth a mention as it provides Old World Style accommodation. This establishment was first opened in 1909 and is a favourite all year round with those who appreciate Alpine Country.

Number of Lifts: 7
Total Lift Capacity per hour: 4,600
Types Of Runs: 45% beginners; 35% intermediate; 20% advanced
Season: From June to September
Resort/Area Telephone: 61 57 55 1466
Fax: 61 57 55 1802

MT. BAW BAW SKI AREA

Height of Base Station: 4,829 ft
Height of Top Station: 5,127 ft.

Mt. Baw Baw ski area is a convenient field, being the closest to Melbourne and often underrated, due largely to the facilities when compared to the better known areas. This has a beneficial side, being the lack of queues, giving more skiing and uncrowded slopes. Offering both Nordic skiing and Downhill, X-C is provided via sheltered and well marked trails across the Baw Baw plateau. Grooming of these trails ensures enjoyable skiing. The Downhill side is not to be forgotten either with groomed snow gun sheltered runs catering for the beginner through to the advanced skier. An excellent learning environment will have you progressing to enjoy the intermediate trails within a short time.

Intermediates have a wide selection with trails, Champagne and Slam Dunk or the sweeping Shirley's Slide, and for the advanced, a couple of pleasant runs. Baw Baw is an excellent choice of resort for the person or group thinking of trying skiing, be it Cross Country or Downhill.

Number of Lifts: 8
Total Lift Capacity per hour: 6400
Types Of Runs: 25% beginners;
64% intermediate; 11% advanced
Season: From June to October
Resort/Area Telephone:61 51 65 1122
Fax: 61 51 65 1122

BEN LOMOND

Height of Base Station: 4,790 ft
Height of Top Station: 5,144 ft.

It is only fair to include Australia's most southerly ski area in Tasmania. Located in the Ben Lomond National Park, and one of only two Downhill ski areas in Tasmania. Being run in the true Apple Isle style, the atmosphere is more in keeping with that found in a small club field, not on a ski area of this size. Ample private club lodges give this field a friendly, relaxed approach to skiing in general. Ben Lomond caters mainly to beginners and intermediates. The village, located in a bowl, from where ski lifts radiate out to the surrounding gentle slopes, past these are the intermediate slopes. This resort offers a good family or group environment, where fun is the key word. Jacob's Ladder on the road just prior to the area, is spectacular with its 6 hair pin bends, vertical drops and no safety railing, adding to the aura of this ski field.

Number of Lifts: 8
Total Lift Capacity per hour: 4,815
Types Of Runs: 30% beginners; 60% intermediate; 10% advanced
Season: From July to September
Resort/Area Telephone: 64 03 72 2444
Fax: 64 03 44 9533

NEW ZEALAND

by Sasha St. Clair

The Maori have an expression; "When God created heaven and earth he put a little bit of something in each country: everything that was left over he put in New Zealand". One does not have to go far to experience this, as within a short drive you will encounter sub-tropical forests, beaches of white sand, fjords, trout-laden crystal clear streams and lakes, geologically young mountains that, if you use your imagination, you can see growing. Amongst this beauty the occasional glacier can be seen, groaning and creaking as its massive forces carve out yet another valley. The Fox Glacier is currently growing at the phenomenal rate of 1 metre per day.

The Kiwi has a fanatical reputation as a recreational pursuits enthusiast. This is only too apparent when one takes a jet boat ride or a bungy jump. Extremes seem to be the norm, and this love of sport has extended to the snow sport arena. The abundance of ski resorts available down under has always astonished me in relation to the population of Australia and New Zealand. The alpine terrain in the Southern Alps of New Zealand alone is greater in area than that of the European Alps. Heli and glacial skiing operations can be enormous – one particular operator covers more terrain than that found in the Italian Alps.

New Zealand consists of two major islands, both approximately 1,000 km. by 200 km. The North Island, ranging in climate from sub-tropical to temperate and supporting 75% of the population, has 5 snow sport operations, 2 commercial, 1 Heli-ski and 2 club fields. Two major mountains rise from a plain and on the larger one, Mt. Ruapehu, an active volcano, is situated. In the recent past it was common practice to climb to the rim of the volcano, descend and swim in the heated snow-edged pools, which has since ceased after the last major eruption, but it is still worth the climb. The strength of these eruptions is only too apparent, as at the foot of Mt. Ruapehu is Lake Taupo (238 square miles), the crater from a volcanic explosion some 1,800 years ago.

The South Island contains the bulk of the snow sports operations. Scattered throughout is a myriad of Glacial, Heli-skiing, Commercial and Club areas, all of which are worth a visit. The South Island is totally different in physical appearance to the North, having been sculptured by the forces of ice and water and blessed with an alpine mountain range running the length of the island. Clubs' ski fields are spartan with a base and accommodation building. Generally serviced by a rope tow, these can offer inexpensive challenging skiing, and queues that consists of more than 6 or 7 people are busy days. Heli-skiing in the Southern Alps, south of Christchurch, is world famous for the magic of skiing in a bowl that has not been skied for weeks. Just you, a guide and half a dozen other skiers, is a treat that everyone at least once in their lifetime should experience. Commercial areas are scattered throughout, from Invincible at Glenorchy south of Queenstown, (a small new field for 95), to Mt. Lyford or Rainbow Valley just north of Christchurch. Waiorau Nordic is the only commercial vehicle testing and cross-country ski area, with overnight huts, hire, base building and storage buildings in New Zealand. Snow conditions are generally light and dry.

All areas are within convenient driving distance from major airports. Christchurch contains the South Island's only international airport, although another should open in Queenstown in late 1996. The north Island is accessed through Wellington or Auckland international airports.

New Zealand's ski areas are not resorts, but consist of base buildings supplying day requirements. Accommodation is not generally available on the ski areas, although two areas, Whakapapa and Cardrona, do have condo's available. All operations are serviced through local towns, and are below the snowline. Driving to a ski area is on average about 30-40 minutes. Chains must be carried and fitted in designated areas; most access roads are private and unsealed, and a road toll is charged. Good warm clothing should be kept available as weather conditions can change without warning, due to the proximity to the South Pole and the turbulence created when air flow northwards hits the narrow high mountain ranges of the South Island.

Fishing Enthusiasts: Nothing to do with skiing, but if you are travelling to New Zealand and are keen on fishing the expert to contact is Brian Cox, Tel: 64 3 443 7512. Mention this Guide and you will receive a good service!

We are including brief information on twelve ski areas along with Heli-skiing.

CARDRONA SKI RESORT

Height of Base Station: 5,474 ft
Height of Top Station: 5,610 ft.

Nestling in the heart of the Southern Lakes District, Cardrona offers a convenient location between Wanaka and Queenstown, with ample choice of accommodation and entertainment. Reliable snow falls, gentle undulating slopes for the beginner, challenging terrain for the intermediate and advanced, together with modern facilities, kiddies corral, good commercial transport and ample parking make this a very popular family field. Two major bowls are serviced by quad chairs. McDougals, predominantly the beginner intermediate area, has wide gentle groomed runs with small diversions can make for fun intermediate skiing. Captain's quad is the bowl of choice, providing a selection for the most discerning skier, be it wide open groomed runs, off-piste chutes, bumps, or a coffee to watch the air-heads. Cardrona also offers supreme views of Lake Wakatipu, Lake Hawea, the Remarkables and Coronet Peak and because of this is favoured by film crews. Cardrona has acquired an excellent reputation for the services offered to all, including the disabled skier. Constant renovations and improvements to facilities, featuring on-mountain accommodation and new licensed restaurant make for pleasant and enjoyable skiing.

Number of Lifts: 5
Total Lift Capacity per hour: 6,070
Grade of Runs: 20% beginners; 55% intermediate; 25% advanced
Season: From late June to mid October
Resort/Area Telephone: 64.3.443.7341
Fax: 64.3.443.8818

CORONET PEAK

Height of Base Station: 3,937ft
Height of Top Station: 5,315 ft.

At this resort one will find a variety of wide groomed runs, covered from summit to base by a multi-million dollar snowmaking system which was installed in summer 1991. This system proved itself when Coronet Peak opened earlier than it ever has before for a full season. 1994 saw the opening of a new detachable quad chair which was desperately needed to replace the old double Shirt Front chair-lift. Coronet caters for all, with facilities for the beginner, served by either the Happy Valley or Blue Gum pomas, with a pleasant learning environment. Intermediates and advanced skiers may choose from groomed runs to mogul fields, served by the new quad. For the expert, Coronet has off-piste chutes in the Back Bowls area. Night skiing is offered until 8 pm, or for those who wish to "ski extreme", try Heli-Guides New Zealand (see separate report). Queenstown is the town with the international reputation for fine food, shops and bars, situated on Lake Wakatipu; Shotover and the Kawarau river are famous for their jet boat rides, rafting and the bungy jumping, hence Coronet Peak's reputation as the "extreme sport" holiday destination.

Number of Lifts: 6
Total Lift Capacity per hour: 6,900
Grade of Runs: 10% beginners; 55% intermediate; 35% advanced
Season: From mid June to October
Resort/Area Telephone: 64.3442.4620·
Fax: 64.3.442.4624

MT. HUTT SKI AREA

Height of Base Station: 5,200ft
Height of Top Station: 6,807 ft.

The overall shape of this ski area is that of a bowl, with the major black runs on the surrounding ridges. Being the most well known within Australasia, Hutt's reputation increased after hosting the 1990 World Cup, and in 1989 & '91, F.I.S. races. Northern hemisphere race teams use Hutt as a summer training area. This resort has a multi-million dollar snowmaking system which produces consistent snow to ensure early opening every ski season. Mt.Hutt offers a wide variety of terrain from beginner to expert Try the south face if steep runs are your passion. This area was recently purchased by the Mt. Cook Group, owners of Mt. Cook Line, the Remarkables and Coronet Peak, so packages are offered. Whilst in Methven try the Hot Air Balloon, the Jet Boat ride on the Rakaia River, or for great skiing, Mt. Hutt Heli-Ski (see below).

Number of Lifts: 10
Total Lift Capacity per hour: 9,200
Grade of Runs: 25% beginners; 50% intermediate; 25% advanced
Season: From early May to mid October
Resort/Area Telephone: 643.308.5074
Fax: 64.3.302.8697

Mount Hutt Helicopter is a heli-taxi, operating a Hughes 500 for scenic flights and general heli-skiing, departing from the car park at Mt. Hutt ski area within the Mount Hutt range. It provides, in combining the North Peak with Mt. Hutt Ski Area, a magnificent bowl for the intermediate skier and an unforgettable introduction to heli-skiing. The Hutt Range has runs such as Diamond Face, Triple Treat or Snowboarder Alley for the more advanced skier. The Taylor Range and Black Hills provides the advanced intermediate to expert skier with long challenging runs, and the area offers over 40 different runs. Give a thought to using the Heli-Taxi service from Methven or Mt. Hutt for the best views of the Southern Alps and Canterbury Plains, but be warned once you have flown in a chopper it is an experience that will whet the appetite and can be habit forming.

OHAU SKI FIELD AND LAKE OHAU LODGE

Height of Base Station: 4,921 ft
Height of Top Station: 6,315 ft.

This no hype ski area is owned and operated by Mike and Louise Nielson, a family atmosphere being the key difference compared to the larger commercial areas. Ideally situated between the Southern Lakes and the Canterbury ski fields, Ohau can boast the longest T-Bar in the Southern Hemisphere. This serves great vertical and advanced skiing to the right of the T-bar, and to the left excellent intermediate runs. In 1991 Ohau had over 6m./19.5ft. of snow, the best fall since '68. Beginners are not forgotten here, with several good runs at their disposal. Snowmaking on the lower slopes, main trails and beginner's area ensure ample coverage whenever needed. Superlative powder skiing and unparalleled views of the Southern Alps and Mount Cook are here for those who don't mind a short climb to the summit. If you like basic skiing for realistic prices, a friendly atmosphere and to get away from it all, this is the area for you.

Number of Lifts: 3
Total Lift Capacity per hour: 1,300
Grade of Runs: 20% beginners; 40% intermediate; 40% advanced
Season: From July to October
Resort/Area Telephone: 643.438.9885
Fax: 64.3.438.9885

THE REMARKABLES SKI AREA

Height of Base Station: 5,314 ft
Height of Top Station: 6,420 ft.

This area, opened for the 1985 season, has proved to be very popular: well constructed with modern chair-lifts, it is a delight. A word of caution though – this area does need a good cover of snow to be enjoyable, unlike Coronet Peak which has major summer groomed slopes and only needs 20 cm. of snow to be fun. Ski passes are interchangeable between both areas. The main lifts consist of 3 chairs and a tow for beginners, the Alta double chair serves runs mainly for the advanced beginner and intermediate. Sugar Bowl quad runs up on the left and serves predominantly the intermediate, but also a few advanced runs. Shadow Basin off to the right is primarily intermediate and advanced. The Remarkables also has some cross-country trails with spectacular views of Lake Wakatipu and Queenstown.

Number of Lifts: 7
Total Lift Capacity per hour: 6,620
Grade of Runs: 30% beginners; 40% intermediate; 30% advanced
Season: From late June to late October
Resort/Area Telephone: 643.442.4615
Fax: 64.3.442.4624

TREBLE CONE

Height of Base Station: 4,101 ft
Height of Top Station: 6,102 ft.

This is the ski area postcard photos are taken from, let alone post card runs. Treble Cone can claim some of the best runs in New Zealand for the advanced skier, and for adventurous skiers a 20 minute climb to the summit is most rewarding. The installation for the 1996 season of a high speed 6 saeater chair-lift, the first in the Southern Hemisohere, has made Treble Cone a more realisticly priced area. Intermediate and advanced skiers are in their element here, with bumps, off-piste, and steep and deep powder all to be found. For the beginner, the Platter lift has a wide gentle slope with good coverage from the snowmaking system. Snowboarders have a natural half-pipe with an appropriate name, the Gun Barrel. Extensive snowmaking has improved the scope of this area, ensuring early opening and coverage on beginners' areas. Parapenting is another favoured sport from this field, due to the ideal air flow through the picturesque Matukituki Valley.

Number of Lifts: 5
Total Lift Capacity per hour: 5,000
Grade of Runs: 10% beginners; 50% intermediate;

35% advanced
Season: From 1 July to 21 September
Resort/Area Telephone: 643.443.7443
Fax: 64.3.443.8401

TUROA SKI RESORT

Height of Base Station: 5,249 ft
Height of Top Station: 7,618 ft.

One of only two commercial ski areas in the North Island, and the second largest in New Zealand, Turoa is situated on the south western face of Mt. Ruapehu. It offers modern facilities, a large car park and sealed road access. There are a few runs of up to 4 km. Turoa has an excellent intermediate area, plus a separate beginner's area. The intermediate skier has plenty of runs with ample scope to progress to the more difficult advanced level. For the advanced Turoa offers some superb groomed runs, and for the adventurous there is some great off-piste skiing in the posted area or in the fringe areas to the field.

Try climbing to the summit for breath-taking views of the Tasman Sea, Mt. Egmont, or just to ski back down; but please check with Ski Patrol as they must know where you are going and your time of return as this mountain can be very dangerous.

Number of Lifts: 12
Total Lift Capacity per hour: 12,600
Grade of Runs: 20% beginners; 55% intermediate; 25% advanced
Season: From June to late October
Resort/Area Telephone: 646.385.8456
Fax: 64.6.385.8992

WHAKAPAPA

Height of Base Station: 5,331 ft
Height of Top Station: 7,545ft.

This is undoubtedly New Zealand's largest and most popular ski area, situated on Mt. Ruapehu, and only a 4 hour drive from either Auckland or Wellington. Expenditure of 22 million dollars over the last 7 years has resulted in a remarkable ski resort, boasting New Zealand's highest restaurant, Knoll Ridge Chalet. Whakapapa is a varied and challenging ski field. One thing you must try is the three hour climb to Crater Lake, which offers magnificent views and excellent skiing to either Turoa or Tukino ski fields, but start early and inform ski patrol of your plans. Whakapapa offers excellent learners' areas, situated to the left of "Lorenz's" restaurant.

Most North Island skiers learnt to ski on this skifield. Happy Valley has an extensive snowmaking system that assures ample coverage of the lower slopes and a consistent learning environment. Intermediates have ample scope, with some high long runs which are very challenging. Advanced skiers will enjoy the top half of the mountain, with steep runs like Back Stage, Yankee Slalom or Far West for uncrowded skiing. This area has runs for everyone, and can give anyone a run for their money. Ruapehu weather can be very changeable, so dress accordingly.

Number of Lifts: 25
Total Lift Capacity per hour: 23,000
30% beginners; 45% intermediates;
25% advanced
Season: From early June to mid November
Resort/Area Telephone: 64.7.892.3738
Fax: 64.7.892.3732

MOUNT DOBSON

Height of Base Station: 5,500 ft.
Height of Top Station: 6,600 ft.

Mt. Dobson has New Zealand's largest learner's area, renowned for sunny slopes, taking advantage of a 3km wide basin. Dobson is the ideal learner's field with vertical drop of 1,361 ft., also giving the intermediate a good choice. From the summit it is possible to see Mt.Cook, with views through to the Pacific Ocean and then back to the Southern Alps. Good parking and the advantage of being able to ski from your car to the lifts and back to your car at the day's end may appeal. This fields ability, to give the confidence needed to ski some of the more demanding ski areas. Mt. Dobson has a reputation for a long and consistent season. Ample scopes for the off piste skier, seldom taken advantage of, so try this mountain for some good skiing, you will be pleasantly surprised.

Number of Lifts: 4
Total Lift Capacity per hour:2,300
Grade of Runs: 20% beginners;
50% intermediates; 30% advanced
Season: From late June to mid October
Resort/Area Telephone: 03 685 8039
Fax: 03 685 8039

MOUNT LYFORD

Height of Base Station: 4,100 ft.
Height of Top Station: 5,101 ft.

Mt. Lyford owned and operated by Jenny & Doug Simpson, is New Zealands first true alpine development to include a land subdivision known as Mt. Lyford Wilderness Retreat. Offering, ice skating, fishing, golf and hot pools, all within a few minutes drive. The field itself has great potential and is being developed at a realistic pace, offering good intermediate and advanced runs with modern facilities. The base has a natural ice skating area for those wishing to try it. Excellent groomed cross country trails, plus a good reputation for reliable snow falls, give this field an all round appeal. The development and opening of the Mt.Terako Ski Area in the '92 season with 4 new poma lifts provided separate access to the easterly facing Lyford field. Mt. Lyford is a ski development not to be missed, as you travel south to the better known areas. It is very convenient distance from the ferry for the skier from the North Island, who wishes a day or two of skiing on uncrowded slopes at this twin field resort.

Number of Lifts: 6
Total Lift Capacity per hour:2,200
Grade of Runs:20% beginners; 40% intermediates; 40% advanced
Season: From early June to mid October
Resort/Area Telephone: 03 315 6178
Fax: 03 315 6178

PORTER HEIGHTS

Height of Base Station: 4,200 ft.
Height of Top Station: 6,495 ft.

Porter Heights, being the closest commercial ski field to Christchurch, has a relaxed atmosphere, excellent facilities with a good short access road, and ample parking. Good skiing for the intermediate, near the lifts, great skiing for the advanced, off the ridges and back bowls make the Heights live up to its name. "Big Mama" is the most famous run at Porter Heights, being the longest and steepest run known in New Zealand, with a vertical drop of 2,631 ft. An alternative is to try the awesome Bluff Face to get the adrenalin flowing. Beginners are not forgotten either, with two separate areas at their disposal. Snowboarders have a half pipe that was constructed in '91. For the ski tourer, try the ridge that is a favourite haunt of the locals.

Number of Lifts: 5
Total Lift Capacity per hour:
Grade of Runs: 20% beginners;
50% intermediates; 30% advanced
Season: From mid June to mid October
Resort/Area Telephone: 03 318 4731
Fax: 03 366 6061

RAINBOW VALLEY

Height of Base Station: 5,052 ft.
Height of Top Station: 5,774 ft.

Rainbow Valley Ski Area offers pleasant bowl skiing, having a very wide groomed area on either side of the double chair, giving the adventurous beginner or intermediate skier ample scope. The advanced skier has the East Face lift which services steep but short runs. Heli-skiing is available by prior arrangement or when weather permits. A good learner's area to the side of double chair is a reserved, slow area, ensuring safe and comfortable skiing – this is a reasonably priced ski area. The St Arnaud Range offers some of the best cross country and ski touring areas.

Number of Lifts: 4
Total Lift Capacity per hour: 2,200
Grade of Runs: 30% beginners;
60% intermediates; 10% advanced
Season: From mid June to mid October
Resort/Area Telephone: 03 521 1861
Fax: 03 521 1861

HELI-SKIING

Harris Mountains Heli-Ski with offices in Queenstown and Wanaka have over 18 years experience, and have developed into the largest Heli-ski operation outside Canada, with a choice of over 380 runs off 190 peaks in a 2,600 sq. km. area and have Fat boards for hire. HMH host the New Zealand Powder 8's annually, so if you think you and a friend are up to standard send a fax. There is incredible terrain to select from, offering all standards from the intermediate through to the extreme skier, with options for all – a three run day through to the full Max Vertical 75,000 ft. odyssey.

Being New Zealand's most extensive heli-ski operation, Harris Mountains caters for the tastes of all skiers as well as providing some excellent Snowboard areas. There are a variety of runs with no trees to dodge, in magnificent bowls, sheltered basins, and unique mountain ranges. Cruises on lake Wanaka at the day's end are an optional extra. For the more scenic hearted try skiing the Tyndall Glacier, an experience not to be missed. The main areas of operation are The Doolans, Harris Mountains, Buchanans, Branches, Tyndal Glacier and McKerrow ranges.

Harris Mountains launched a Snowcat Skiing Operation in 1996, the first of its kind in the .Southern Hemisphere.

Tel: 64.3.443.7930 Fax: 64.3.443.8876

New Zealand Heli-Guides operate a private charter and guided heli-skiing venture, specialising in small intimate groups and filling a market gap that has been overlooked, with a guide to client ratio of 1:3 preferred; 1:4 maximum or larger groups by prior arrangement. The company also operates a heli-taxi service to the ski areas. An additional service is offered for those adventurous souls who wish to ski the back bowls of these areas, with pre-arranged pick-up points. For the serious skier who desires those uncrowded long runs of deep virgin powder, including a gourmet picnic lunch to share with a couple of friends in a chosen area, wherever possible arrangements can be made. For those wishing to ski several South Island ski areas or maybe a North Island area, fixed wing aircraft and helicopters are at their disposal. Single day charter is available but 2 to 14 day bookings will be given priority. Each person is assigned a personal Instructor/Guide to ensure that, beginner or expert, they will enjoy the day's heli-skiing, in some of the most beautiful snow covered Alpine country in the world. Whether your taste is for Alpine, Nordic, Telemark, snowboarding or ski touring, heli-skiing is the only way to go for that ultimate thrill.

Tel: 64.3.442.8151 Fax: 64.3.442.8151

Southern Lakes Heliski: Operating from the heart of the Southern Lakes District, in Queenstown, Southern Lakes covers a wide variety of terrain with extensive options. Choose from glacial skiing, conventional skiing in the Hector Mountains, The Remarkables, Thomson Mountains, Richardson Mountains and the Harris Mountains – a total area of over 2,200 sq. km. to choose from, each with its own particular benefits; snowboards are a speciality of the house. Competent beginners are catered for, through to the expert off-piste skier. Try the Thomson Mountains where Mt. Nicholas station is located, have a day's skiing and then a leisurely sunset cruise back to Queenstown on board the vintage Steamship Earnslaw, or just party in the licensed Honky-Tonk piano bar as you reminisce on the skiing highlights the day has offered. Southern Lakes logo sums it up perfectly: "Simply Superb".

Tel: 64.3.442.6222 Fax: 64.3.442.7867

Alpine Guides Westland: Fox Glacier Wilderness Skiing. Licensed to operate anywhere in the Westland National Park, Fox Glacier Wilderness Skiing offers exceptionally high drop off points, 8000ft/2438m on the head of the neves. The main pickup points, Chancellor Hut and Almer Hut on the Fox & Franz Josef Glaciers, are the highest Neves within New Zealand. Try their "door to door" a 1 hour Cessna flight from Queenstown, over the Forests of Westland's World Heritage Park to the Franz Josef airstrip, a twenty minute Helicopter flight over huge icefalls to the Fox Glacier snowfields. Throw in a couple of 7 to 12 km runs down the glacier, with marvellous views of the Tasman Sea and Mt. Cook, a great lunch on the snow, and top it off with a sunset return flight to Queenstown. Six hours in a single run with a 3000 ft 914 m vertical drop through fantastic ice flows and a guide who knows the glacier like no-one else, are just too good to be true.

Skiers need to be fit intermediates, but a choice of runs is available for advanced and expert. With over 20,000 acres to choose from, there is surely a perfect run to enjoy. Normal downhill equipment is fine for day trips, but for multi days touring bindings required. These are available for hire at Fox Township, and some good warm ski clothing will make this a very pleasant escape.

Tel: 64 3 751 0825
Fax: 64 3 751 0857

Methven Heliskiing: Part of Alpine Guides Mt. Cook Ltd., this operation is renowned for its thoroughness and safety that caters to all levels of alpine sport. Flying into the Arrowsmith and Ragged Ranges, over ski runs with names like Masterblaster and Holy Moses, you are grateful that your guides are fully trained. Even so, your heart still pumps, but for the intermediate there is no need for concern with excellent runs such as Reischek Glacier. 6 km of joy, complete with ice falls and awesome views of the Southern Alps. There is always a run to choose from with over 100 named and many more to be found within the 800 square kilometres of mountain range at your disposal. With 3000 vertical meters being completed in three to four runs, not a bad day's skiing, and no lift queues. For the skier from overseas, Methven Heliskiing offers a new and challenging experience not to be missed.

Tel: 03 302 8108

Snowrange Heliskiing: The North Islands only licence & promoted heli-ski operator, with ski guided trips to the majestic Ruahine Ranges south east of Mt. Ruapehu. This mountain range has a good snow fall, offering challenging runs, to those of all skiing abilities. Snowrange guarantee a vertical of 3,048 m 10,000 ft in a day or a half day offering 1,828 m 6,000 ft from over 70 runs at their disposal, including the better known ridges like Te-Hekegna, Hikurangi and Whanahuia. These saddles offer magnificent runs and the experience of a life time, with beautiful scenery as an additional bonus.

Tel: 64 6 328 2869
Fax: 64 6 388 1011

Alpine Guides Ski The Tasman: This is the second and better known ski experience, and has been in operation since the late 1960s, under the banner of Alpine Guides. Ski the Tasman could be misleading in as much as this is only one of several Glaciers used in their operation. The Tasman being the largest of all the Glaciers (27km or 16.75ml) in New Zealand, offers the grandeur of ice caves, gigantic ice pinnacles, and crevasses. With up to 30 meters or 98 feet of snow falling per year on the main divide this ensures incredible skiing, which starts with a flight in a fixed wing aircraft up to the Tasman Saddle, which is an immense snowfield that marks the start of the glacier's flow. Your run starts with gentle bowls, then down to huge open slopes, with a total of 10 kilometres. At the end of which is waiting a delicious lunch before your next descent in the afternoon sun. The standard is intermediate or above. Alpine Guides also operate High Guiding, Ski Touring and a Climbing school.

Tel: 64 3 435 1834 Fax: 64 3 435 1898

CHILE

by Sasha St. Clair

A warm and friendly country, sadly tarnished by recent history in the eyes of most Europeans. This is not justifed – Chile and Argentina are the safest of all South American countries to visit, safer than most European cities. Chileans are warm and friendly, making the experience of travelling much more enjoyable. Try the magnificent seafoods or Curanto, a feast that requires a day to prepare, well worth the trip on its own.

Chile is a long coastal nation 4329km long averaging 180km wide, containing climatic extremes: the highest hottest desert and some of the coldest temperatures, overshadowed by the awe inspiring Andes Mountain Range, with Cerro Aconcagua towering 22,840ft. Throw in a few hundred volcanoes, with the main ridge less than 200 miles from the Pacific Coast, and you get one hell of a range to ski. It's the home of approximately 14 ski areas, two for the cross country skier, and five of which are major international ski resorts; Portillo, Valle Nevado, La Parva, Termas de Chillan and El Colorado. These are the resorts that few Europeans visit, with the exception of race teams and ski instructors.

Today adventure sport enthusiasts are also taking advantage of uncrowded slopes, modern facilities and the relaxed life style. Castellano (Chilean & Argentine, Spanish) is the major language, but most Chileans speak English, with the exception of the indigenous people. One has the opportunity to ski Antarctica through local operators in southern Chile, or Andes Powder Guides, but who needs a helicopter when pristine off piste is available at every area? This is a country which makes snow sports thoroughly enjoyable.

Santiago, a perfect base for your holiday, has five ski areas within a short commute. Lan Chile offer packages and regular flights from Madrid, Miami & Frankfurt. Background information supplied by Chris I. Lizza and South American Ski Guide.

EL COLORADO/ FARELLONES

Height of Base Station: 7,972 ft.
Height of Top Station: 10,935 ft.

This is one of the most popular ski resorts in Chile due mainly to size and lifting capacity, high altitude ensuring good snow conditions and proximity to Santiago. Colorado has a large beginner's area based at the village of Farellones. The ski area proper is Villa Colorado, the modern facilities at the base lodge of El Parador is where most will start their skiing adventure. Summit skiing is accessed via Silla Colorado: the ride on this lift is enough to start the adrenalin going, sharpen your wits for the run down – enjoy this one. Advanced skiers will be in their element here, if you can imagine it: this is the resort that will fulfil your fantasies, from steep and deep to down right scary. Views of Valle Nevado, La Parva and Santiago are best from the higher slopes and are a photographer's delight.

Number of Lifts: 16
Total lift capacity per hour: 13,800
Grade of Runs: 40% beginners;
20% intermediates; 40% advanced
Season: From June to mid October
Telephone: 56 2 201 3704 or 698 2164 or 2463344

LA PARVA

Height of Base Station: 8,760 ft.
Height of Top Station: 11,909 ft.

A small resort area known throughout the world, famous as the summer training area for northern ski teams, or the downhill speed skiing on the mountains north face. But don't let this reputation put you off – slopes are here for everyone. Bumps and powder skiers will love the runs served by the Las Tortolas chair-lift, adventure skiers have La Chiminea chute that dreams are made of. A charming little village on the mountain ridge is mainly the home of Chile's wealthy families, the accommodation for us poor skiers being off the area, just down the valley or in Santiago. La Parva has access to Valle Nevado & El Colorado via lifts, well worth the effort.

Number of Lifts: 14
Total lift capacity per hour: 13,800
Grade of Runs: 15% beginners;
55% intermediates; 30% advanced
Season: From late June to mid November
Telephone: 56 2 231 3411
Fax: 56 2 217 3250

PORTILLO

Height of Base Station: 8,241 ft.
Height of Top Station:10,984 ft.

Another of Chile's famous international resorts, laid back skiing and friendly atmosphere, the majestic Hotel Portillo is situated on a lake, high in the Andes. Peaks of 14,000ft. tower around Portillo; this is another site for speed skiing, 124mph is the entry level here. Two lifts are specially designed, the Va et Vient lifts, Condor and Roca Jack are unique to the area, pulling 4 & 5 skiers respectively. Conventional lifts could not operate where these do – thanks to the designer Jean Pomagalski access to great powder skiing is a short ride. This area has great skiing for all, smokers be warned, highest lift is nearly 11,000; I sounded like a Labrador, must quit. Portillo's owners were instrumental in the establishment of the current World Cup circuit, racing here is second nature. Best beginner's run is Canarios; intermediates should enjoy Juncalillo and Los Tuneles, advanced Roca Jacks, Garganta and Condor, and there is a FIS downhill and GS course here for the not too faint at heart. Simply superb!

Number of Lifts: 12
Total lift capacity per hour: 9,200
Grade of Runs: 20% beginners;
30% intermediates; 50% advanced
Season: From June to mid October
Telephone: 56 2 231 3411
Fax: 56 2 231 7164

TERMAS DE CHILEAN

Height of Base Station: 5,900 ft.
Height of Top Station: 8,200 ft.

Access here is by a 45min flight from Santiago, thence 80 km. by car. On arrival one finds an attractive Tyrolean style village, set on the side of a volcano with views of a beautiful valley, an all year round resort favoured by families, crowds are never a problem here, queues are unheard of. The lower ski area is through the trees – this will improve your turns! the upper is open and well maintained, and a short climb to the summit is rewarded with spectacular views of the crater.The bonus is some great off piste skiing back to the base area. Like most Latin American resort areas all forms of snow/adventure sports are available, even a snowmobile area. All skiing abilities are suited to this resort, and the longest slope here a mere 11 km. The Hotel Pirigallo, in the centre of the resort area, has a spa centre, restaurant and bar. If you think you deserve a little pampering, try a mud bath.

Number of Lifts: 8
Grade of Runs: 20% beginners;
30% intermediates; 50% advanced
Season: From late June to early October
Telephone: 56 2 233 1313
Fax: 56 2 231 5963

ANDES POWDER GUIDES

Andes Powder Guides is small and personal, run by Chileans and ex Vail, Deer Valley ski instructor Rob Petrinovic and his wife Alexandra, both very knowledgable in local customs, filming locations, spectacular scenery, resorts, rivers for rafting and some great fishing spots. Their services are all year round, catering to those who wish to get off the beaten track. If you wish to ski pristine virgin snow that Warren Miller dreams about, this is the adventure operator for you. Andes Powder Guides are the only guiding service catering to small groups, who wish to ski areas few foreigners see. Areas of operation are from Chile's northern border to Cape Horn, specializing in downhill, snowboarding, tele, cross country and ski mountaineering in the winter. For a personal holiday with a difference or to visit and ski many resorts, give them a go.

Management Company Name: Andes Powder Guides/Altue Expeditions
Postal Address: Casilla 52757, Cerreo Central, Santiago, Chile
Telephone: 56 2 232 1103
Fax:56 2 233 6799

VALLE NEVADO

Height of Base Station: 9,450 ft.
Height of Top Station: 12,040 ft.

High in the Andes, 60 kilometres distant from downtown Santiago stands the spectacular Hotel and Condos complex, and perched on top of a cliff, the Valle Nevado Hotel at 3025m., modern and the lifts only a minute or so from your door. No matter what your passion, here it can be fulfilled, restaurants, good service, snow boarding, hang or para gliding, snowmobiling or the plain old downhill, this area can push you to the limits if desired. Valle Nevado Resort is suitable to all levels of snow sports ability, beginners have El Prado chair, intermediates try the undulating El Mirador quad, advanced lets dance try the Bosa Nova Bowl. An additional feature is the interconnecting lifts providing an incredible 26,500 acres or 10,700 hectares of mountain range and 41 lifts in total, more than 100 kilometres of piste skiing encompassing all three resorts of: La Parva, 8,760ft. El Colorado, 7,972 ft and Valle Nevado, 9,925 ft. – yes, these are base elevations, with literally thousands of acres of snow for your enjoyment. Try a day heli-skiing, if for no other reason than to take a friend, watch an Andean Condor soaring or just be alone to enjoy this magic area with a fine bottle of Chilean

Number of Lifts: 9
Total lift capacity per hour:7,500
Grade of Runs: 15% beginners;
40% intermediates; 45% advanced
Season: From late June to mid October
Resort/Area Telephone: 56 2 206 0027
Fax: 56 2 208 0695

ANTUCO

Height of Base Station: 4,293 ft.
Height of Top Station: 5,413 ft.

Set aside a volcano of 3585 m. bearing the same name and at its base is an emerald green lake created by a lava flow, sounds scary, but you have more chance of winning the lottery than being caught by mother nature. Two small ski areas operate on this mountain, all lifts are ground pullers. Expect primative facilities but good uncrowded skiing, although not offering the challenge of the more famous northern areas, some acceptable runs can be found. Hell forget the skiing and enjoy the beautiful surroundings, or the unpretentious hospitality I constantly find in Chile, these alone are worth a day's diversion.

Number of Lifts: 2
Total lift capacity per hour:
Grade of Runs: 35% beginners;
50% intermediates; 15% advanced
Season: From July to mid September
Resort/Area Telephone: 56 2 32 2651

VILLARRICA-PUCON

Height of Base Station:4,593 ft.
Height of Top Station: 7,054 ft.

I have spoken before of the lakes and volcanos that give the southern Chilean ski areas so much splendour. Long runs through the lava flows, provide excitement-laden boarding and skiable half pipes. After ascending and absorbing the vista, appreciate the expanse of uncrowded slopes. Here there is ample room for all preferences of snow sports. The lifts are logically located to take advantage of the volcanos extensive topography. Although a few hours from Santiago (793 km.) this area is well worth the inconvenience.

Number of Lifts: 7
Total lift capacity per hour: 7,500
Grade of Runs: 60% beginners;
25% intermediates; 15% advanced
Season: From late June to November
Resort/Area Telephone: 56 4 544 1901

ANTILLANCA

Height of Base Station: 3,445ft.
Height of Top Station: 4,757ft.

Tucked away in a national park way down south, 1046 km. from Santiago. This area is unfortunately overlooked by many visitors, unless exploring the regions of San Carlos de Bariloche, Argentina. A visit to the valcanoes summit puts all in perspective, looking down its white slopes to the plain, further the surrounding forrests and in the distances a few more volcanoes. Skiing one has a choice of well groomed trails or some great off piste, a great area for cruising. The upper mountain is treeless, whilst the village and lower slopes are set amongst the trees. This area has a club background and was originally founded back in 1935; skiing came in the fifties. The atmosphere I found to be friendly and relaxed, with quite a few families.

Number of Lifts: 4
Grade of Runs: 25% beginners;
50% intermediates; 25% advanced
Season: From June to October
Resort/Area Telephone: 56 6 423 2297

ARGENTINA

by Sasha St. Clair

Argentina has many vistas for the traveller, sub-tropical to antarctic, vibrant cities: Buenos Aries one of the worlds melting pots of culture is home to the Tango. The Latin women are beautiful and well dressed – if I was into modelling would be the place to discover new faces. Here a basic knowledge of Spanish is beneficial, although a few Argentines do speak English.

Argentina is a large country over 3,000 by 1,200 miles; travelling can be long and arduous, but the Latino temperament does make the journey pleasurable. You're on holiday, sit back and enjoy, throw away the time table, don't be impatient. If red meat is your passion, this is the home of great steaks, bar-b-que's, The Pampas, miles of rich flat ranch land, Patagonia, extremes in wildlife and climates and sparsely populated, the Lakes Region with its magnificent alpine lakes, crystal clear waters surrounded by what we snow sports nutters crave, the Andes, rugged and primal in nature, where our inhibitions can be thrown to the wind.

Five major ski areas are close to two major resort cities: one of which is Mendoza, Argentina's third largest city and famous for its wines. San Carlos de Baraloche is a lake paradise; the ski areas nearby are Las Lenas, Los Penitentes, Gran Catedral, Valecitos. Chapelco, farther south, is serviced by another magical little town on a lake, San Martin de Los Adnes, population about 10,000. There are another 12 ski operations scattered down the Andes in Argentina; these are generally basic but very good skiing, two are specifically for the cross country enthusiast in the southern most regions of Patagonia and Terra del Fuego. If you have an adventurous passion try the wild side Antarctica – make inquires locally at Ushuaia.

CHAPELCO

Height of Base Station: 4,100ft.
Height of Top Station: 6,496ft.

This is my favourite Latin ski area, not just for the skiing but mainly for the service town of San Martin de Los Andes and its beautiful fish laden lake. Skiing Chapelco is relaxing and uncrowded. The treeless upper mountain is the exclusive domain of the intermediate and advanced skier. The lower slopes do offer some good intermediate skiing in the moss-covered Lenga trees, but most intermediates will find the first step off Cerro Teta a little intimidating; once over this it is good fun skiing. What this area lacks in the vertical of its northern brothers is compensated for by the speed of the lifts and lack of queues. The beginners' area is wide and well located just outside the Base complex and above the gondola's top station. Nordic skiers have more than ten km. of set trails. San Martin, permanent population 14,000, is a great little place, excellent restaurants, shops and après life, there is even a small casino, for more information go and see for yourself. While here spend a couple of days exploring the lakes and skiing the Chilean areas.

Number of Lifts: 10
Total lift capacity per hour:12,800
Grade of Runs: 25% beginners;
35% intermediates; 40% advanced
Season: From June to October
Resort/Area Telephone: 54 9 722 7460

CERRO BAYO SKI RESORT

Height of Base Station: 3,314 ft.
Height of Top Station: 5,510 ft.

Nestled in the heart of Argentina's magnificent Lakes District, Cerrois 80 km north of Bariloche so offers the international traveller a convenient location, simple choices in accommodation and entertainment. Chapelco and Antillanca are a short distance further north. The base town of Villa Angostura is a small village like all small lake hamlets in this region famous for the fishing. This is a small operation with six lifts the trails are through the trees so provide good shelter in adverse conditions. The intermediate and advanced skier will enjoy this area, there is some good steep sections and a few bumps. I suggest that it should be part of a compulsory stop enroute to other northern Argentine and Chilean ski resorts, a great way to see and ski both countries and well worth the diversions from the one stop tourist resorts.

Number of Lifts: 6

GRAN CATEDRAL

Height of Base Station: 3,400 ft.
Height of Top Station: 6,725 ft.

This is the mountain that started the Latin reputation for awesome downhill skiing. Gran Catedral boasts the greatest number of lifts in South America, 32 at the last count. The main feature is a 25 seat cable car that traverses 3 km and climbs 800 meters in under ten minutes. This is a large mountain and needs to be, as during peak season queues are a common sight, the ski school has in excess of 500 instructors. The long trails back to base are challenging, starting from a cornice down through chutes and eventually trees on the lower mountain. This variety has a charming tendency to make the same run feel and look different.

The top has intermediate and advanced with a choice of good groomed trails or some great bumps and the upper gullies make natura; half-pipes. Try the FIS course descending over metres in three kilometres. Have a meal at Piedre del Condor at the top of the mountain where the food and views are as spectacular as the women. Nineteen kilometres from the base town of Bariloche, which has a population of about 120,000 and is constantly growing along with its international reputation. Situated on the shores of lake Nahuelhuapi, one of the famous seven lakes.

There is everything here for either the jet-setters or the more average visitor: over 100 eateries, cinemas, discos and plenty of watering holes, so stay in the city if you enjoy the après life. There is also an excellent beginners' area, and 20 km. of good and well marked Nordic trails. Bariloche has several smaller ski areas all within a 100 km range; Cerro Otto is just a few minutes commute and has a small novice area. Chall-Huaco is another Pilquitron is about an two hour drive and finally Cerro Bayo (see separate report). If visiting these latter areas, take the extra time and travel the Seven Lakes route to Chapelco and a few Chilean areas. You will transit some of the most beautiful country in the world. So have fun here; that is what Bariloche region is all about – *fun!*

Number of Lifts: 32
Total lift capacity per hour:22,400
Grade of Runs: 30% beginners; 45% intermediates; 25% advanced
Season: June to October
Resort/Area Telephone: 51 94 460053

VALLECITOS

Height of Base Station: 9,510 ft.
Height of Top Station: 10,825 ft.

The Mendoza ski club operate this area which offers good intermediate and advanced skiing in a treeless environment, a couple of days and you will want to try the other less commercial areas within Argentina. Beginners have a good clean area with its own single chair, intermediates try the T-Bar, Advanced take the high roads and blow yourselves out on the chutes and bowls at Filo de Loma Blanca, if off piste is your taste this is one area Argentina is famous for, you will have to traverse a bit but its worth it. These smaller areas are well worth the diversion from the popular and sometimes pretentious destinations. Don't make the mistake of comparing them to other areas, just enjoy the uncrowded and friendly attitudes, this will make for a much more memorable skiing holiday.

Number of Lifts: 5
Total lift capacity per hour:1,450
Grade of Runs: 20% beginners;
60% intermediates; 20% advanced
Season: June to October
Resort/Area Telephone: 5461 250972

LA HOYA

Height of Base Station: 4,462ft.
Height of Top Station: 6,955 ft.

Another of the smaller Areas and the most southern of the Lakes Region ski operations, 265 km south of Bariloche and in the middle of the fruit belt. There is good fishing here too. Now to skiing. Here the season can run into November. The skiable terrain is worth the diversion well off the beaten track, an adequate novice area with a few challenging runs for the intermediate and advanced skier. This is the type of area that makes skiing fun and pleasurable.

Number of Lifts: 4
Total lift capacity per hour:2,600

LAS LENAS

Height of Base Station: 7,300 ft.
Height of Top Station: 10,597 ft.

Las Lenas is a purpose built ski resort and can claim the greatest vertical drop in the Southern Hemisphere, 1,230 metres/4,035 ft., the third greatest in the new world. This is a busy resort with a futuristic design and where the Brazilian jet-set rule, so brush up on your Portuguese. Here 4,000 vertical feet off piste run is like heli-skiing, but if you want to flash your cash you can use a real chopper also, pretentious fool. Everyone promises light and dry – well, here in the Andes you will find that elusive powder. The expansive resort offers a wide variety of trails for all, from the first timer to the World Cup Racer, all have ample scope and more importantly heaps of room. There are off piste trails here where you can ski without seeing another person, or where a seven kilometre run can be tackled by the blue and green skier. The steep 1 in 2 quad chair Marte is just that; if you think you are good, try skiing the chair line; this run will put your carjones in your throat. For the Pajareos there are plenty of cornices and chutes to plumate down. Three lifts are necessary to get you to the top and will ensure that you do not ski the same run twice in a day, there is also a 1.2 km. long quad close to the village that has a few respectable trails if you want to show off. If après life is a big part of your holiday, casino, discos and 10 restaurants. At night this place can be as exhausting as any double diamond run.

Number of Lifts: 12
Total lift capacity per hour: 8,700
Grade of Runs: 20% beginners;
40% intermediates; 40% advanced
Season: June to mid October
Resort/Area Telephone: 541 313 2121
Fax: 541 313 2121

LOS PENITENTES

Height of Base Station: 8,465 ft.
Height of Top Station: 10,479 ft.

Located on the road between Santiago and Mendoza just 25 km. east of Portillo, one of the few easily accessed resorts from Chile. A good lifting plan has opened this resort to runs exceeding six km. Situated in a valley with the Andes towering towards 4,000 m on three sides creates a grandeur to the ruggedness of this mountainscape. The trails are treeless and well groomed, the novice area is adequate, but this mountain is ideal grounding for all skiers to progress to a higher level. The intermediate will not tire looking for new challenging runs. Advanced skiers will discover some very challenging off piste skiing in the most unexpected places, try a few chutes here if you dare. Good tele skiing is found in the gullies that proliferate this area. Cross country skiers will appreciate the ten km. of cut trails. Los Penitentes is named after the Pinnacle rock formations giving a cathedral like appearance; and with a little imagination one can even see the monks.

Number of Lifts: 7

Resort/Area Telephone: 54 6 123 4049
Fax: 54 6 123 3239

BOLIVIA

CHACALTAYA

Height of Base Station:17,130 ft.
Height of Top Station: 17,785 ft.

Outside La Paz is the world's highest ski area: 5,220 m. or 17,130 ft., yes – this is the base elevation and a mere vertical drop of 200 m. or 655 ft. More of a novelty to ski, rather than a skiing holiday destination. It has several claims to fame, the closest to the equator, the fastest lift and the only southern ski area with a season that is in the same months as those in the northern hemisphere. So leave at the end of your season and spend a couple of months discovering the Latin world before hitting the southern areas. Situated because of the altitude on a permanent glacial snowfield.

Below the lift shed is the restaurant – this is incidentally the world's highest. Behind the lift shed is a sheer cliff, so be warned: don't over shoot the lift unless you are into base jumping and have on a parachute or fantastic for para-gliding. This is snow sport at its bare essentials – true no frills skiing at the elevation of a Mt.Everest base camp. This is for those of you who want somewhere different to brag about to your friends about, and believe me Chacaltaya is just that. Don't expect a resort, facilities are Spartan but the lack of oxygen creates a simpatico relationship with the areas affectionados. La Paz is an exotic city for a stop-over and a great place to experience the delights of Bolivian hospitality.

Number of Lifts: 1
Season: November toMarch
Resort/Area Telephone: 591 232 4682

JAPAN

by Sacha St. Clair

Japan's population resides in 20% of the country: the remaining 80% comprises uninhabitable mountains, so outdoor activities and snow sports are an important part of life to this nation. The Japanese are fastidious in all things they do. Their lifestyle is one of the most formal, orderly and precise I have encountered in all my travels. As a whole they are an honest and polite race who value the individual, as well as society. One is immediately aware of these attitudes oon arrival in this fascinating country. Their approach towards skiing is just as enthusiastic as anything they do – no laid back skiing styles here. The average skier practises the skiing stances and is very proud of the appearance projected on the ski slopes. The après lifestyle is a non event with the exception of other foreign visitors. Most nationals retire early (10-11 pm) and concentrate only on the skiing. The exception and best part about skiing Japan are the proliferation of hot springs to relax in after a hard day or night's skiing.

The skiers are courteous and to watch they appear like the US ski instructor demonstration team. The piste skiing is excellent if on weekends a little crowded, so ski weekdays. Few nationals will venture off piste so we foreigners usually take advantage of this situation. There are in excess of three hundred ski operations catering to all persuasions of snow sport activities in Japan, on the islands of Honshu and Hokkaido. They even have indoor ski slopes with man-made snow with different runs from bumps to beginner. Cross country skiing has a very large following here also and set trails can be found at most ski resorts. Many guides are written on Japan alone, including a good comprehensive English guide, 'Ski Japan' by T.R. Reid – this is not the fledgling industry that most Europeans wrongfully assume it is.

The 98 Winter Olympics will be hosted in Nagano City and its environs from the 7th-22nd Feb. 1998. The theme is simple; from around the world – to flower as one, I want to make winter my friend, and meet people from all over the world. My dream will come true in Nagano. 'One Heart – One World'. The host venues where the games events are: Nagano City, Yamanouchi (Shiga Kogen), Hakuba, Karuizawa and Nozawa Onsen. 68 events in seven sports will be held in these categories; Skiing, Skating, Ice Hockey, Biathlon, Bobsleigh, Luge and Curling. Aerials will feature for the first time, Snowboarding as an exhibition sport.

A few warnings: go mid-week avoid holidays and weekends, book accommodation well in advance, and most important if your boot size is larger than 27 cm, book them also or take your own boots and clothing. Speaking of equipment the fashions on the slopes will astound, no el cheapo ski suites here, or old skis, it's all new and well maintained. I'm convinced they dry-clean their clothes each night.

If you hate music from loud speakers, take a good walkman and set of headphones; most resorts provide this invasive and annoying service.

The ski areas covered are a random sampling.

FURANO

Furano is two and a half hours from Sapporo and another 10 minutes to this famous Prince resort chain ski area. Two ski resort owned by Prince offers some great skiing; the big drawback is that one lift each way connects both areas, so pick the time of day that provides the best weather and least crowds and ski that half. This is an intermediate or lower ski area and has the normal set-up, the better you ski the higher up you ski. Despite hosting World cup events, there is not much for the advanced skier – this is a good sit back and cruise mountain.

Management
Area Phone: 81 167 22 1111
Area Info Phone: 81 167 23 1042
Accommodation Service: 81 167 22 5777

Mountain Information
Mountain: Mt. Furano
Highest Lifted: 3,966ft.
Base Alt.: 787 ft.
Season Open: December
Season Close: April
No. Lifts: 19
Types Of Runs:41% Beginners, 38% Intermediates, 21% advanced

HAKUBA

Hakuba township is situated in the centre of a magnificent 20 mile valley and is the service town for a dozen or so ski areas, making a great base for resorts like Happo-one, Sun Alpina, Iwatake, Goryu Toomi and Tsugaike. There are other smaller towns where accommodation can be found, all resorts and towns are accessed by the local alpine mini train that traverses the valley. Many of these ski areas are sister resorts so good package deals can be organised. Hakuba will host the Cross-Country, Ski Jumping, Nordic Combined, Men's and Women's Downhill and Super Giant Slalom events for the 98 Winter Olympics.

HAPPO ONE

Happo One [pronounced Hap-poe-oh-nay] (Hokujo, Hakuba-mura, Nagano Pref.) Rated Japan's number one resort and a main venue for the 98 Olympics Downhill and Cross-Country events. Just 15 minutes' ride outside Hakuba. This is the area that Yankee hot shots come to for the chutes and awesome, extreme faces on the north side of the mountain off the ridge to Mt. Karamatsu. Here you can try the downhill course: use the Alpen Quad for access, or try Skyline. But don't let me scare you off – this is predominately an intermediate area. Snowboarders here are few and far between, due to an extra charge for their passes and much of the area (two-thirds) is restricted from their use; they must also take a competency test first. Here also most will encounter a language problem, but this is diminished due to all the workers from downunder.

Management
Happo One Kanko Kyokai: 81 216 72 3066
Tokoyo Office: 81 3 3409 2355
Accommodation: 81 219 72 3232

Mountain Information
Mountain: Mt. Karamatsu
Summit Alt.: 9,620 ft
Highest Lifted: 5,905 ft
Base Alt: 2,493 ft.
Season Open: December
Season Close: May
No. Lifts: 33 lifts
Grade of Runs: 20% beginners, 50% intermediates, 30% advanced

KUSATSU SHIRANCE

Kusatsu Shirane (Kusatsu-machi, Gumma Pref.) This area is for the intermediate and lower and has a tendency to be crowded. Some challenging bumps can be found and the hot springs here are a great diversion from the lack of challenging runs, so sit back relax and ski this mountain in the same style, you're on holiday. While here give Manza Ski-jo a try for some more fun intermediate and a couple of

expert days' skiing.
Management
Area Phone: 81 279 88 6111
Accommodation Service: 81 279 88 3277

Mountain Information
Season Open: December
Season Close: April
No. Lifts: 15

MYOKO AREA

Myoko Suginohara/Kokusai (Myoko, Kogen-cho, Niigata Pref.) This area is a must if you are visiting the Nagano games and only 30 min. by train. It is three separate areas: Akakura, Shin-Akakura and Ikenotaira, but don't worry – a combined lift pass makes life easy. The first thing I was aware of was the pristine beauty of this area, m that supplies some of the most spectacular views one could imagine. This is mainly an intermediate and lower standard area but with a little perseverance a couple of short expert runs can be located up high with the exception of Maruyama lifts right. This is one of the few ski resorts where you get to ski amongst the trees, making it all the more enjoyable.

Management
Resort Phone: 81 255 87 2165
Koykai: 81 255 86 3911
Accommodation: 81 255 86 2871

Mountain Information
Mountain: Mt. Myoko
Summit Alt.: 8,050 ft
Base Alt.: 2,296 ft.
Season Open: December
Season Close: April
No. Lifts: 13
Grade of Runs: 45% beginners; 43% intermediates; 12% advanced

NAEBA

Naeba (Mikuni, Yuzawa-machi, Niigata Pref.) This is a large and busy resort, which has become famous for hosting countless international ski events and its proximity to Tokyo. Hence here you are first astounded by the accommodation complexes – 4,000 rooms at the Naeba Prince Hotel, one of a resort chain that when visiting Japan you can not help but notice. The annual number of skier visiting is around 3,000,000, three times the average of other national resorts. Lifting capacity insures that queues are few and far between, but this does mean that slopes are always crowded. There is an excellent beginners' area and intermediates will find trail with easy bumps to wide groomed trails. For more challenging runs go up high where the skinny trails are and the more challenging bumps are. The steep stuff is at the top and with only a couple of runs these do get crowded from skiers experiencing the Gondola.

Management
Area Phone: 81 257 89 2211
Area Info Phone: 81 257 89 2121

Mountain Information
Mountain: Mt. Takenoko
Highest Lifted: 5,872 ft.
Base Alt.: 2,952 ft.
Season Open: December
Season Close: April
No. Lifts: 39
Grade of Runs: 30% beginners; 40% intermediates; 30% advanced

NISEKO

Niseko (Kuttchan-cho & Niseko-cho, Hokkaido). Six different ski operation come under the Niseko umbrella, the principal areas being Niseko Higashiyama, Niseko Annupuri Kokusai, Niseko Kokusai Hirafu, but lift tickets are not transferable. Niseko Weiss and Niseko Kokusai Miowa are much smaller and mainly frequented by locals – now that should tell you something. This is one of the most photographed areas in Japan, so watch out for camera bug obstacle in the most inconsiderate places. This is a massive resort which can give all skiers good value for the price of a ticket, so ski one day at each area, then party in the hot springs in the villages.

Management
Postal Address:
Ski Area Phones: Niseko Miowa 81 136 58 2016
Kokusai Hirafu 81 136 22 5151/ 0109
Higashiyama 81 136 44 1111
Annupuri Kokusai 81 136 58 2080
Tourist Info: 81 136 44 2468

Mountain Information
Mountain: Mt. Niseko Annupuri
Highest Lifted: 3,937 ft.
Base Alt.: 984 ft.
Season Open: November
Season Close: April
No. Lifts:
Niseko Kokusai Hirafu: 22
Niseko Higashiyama: 8
Niseko Annupuri Kokusai: 8
Grade of Runs: 21% beginners; 38% intermediate; 41% advanced

NOZAWA ONSEN

Nozawa Onsen (Nozawa Onsen-mura, Nagano Pref.) Onsen means hot springs. This area is famous for its on slope free hot spring baths, some mixed and naked, so don't be bashful – this is an honest way of making new friends. Now to the skiing, lifting is great and so are the runs off piste and on. Not a small resort by any standard. If you want to get steep and deep try the back side down through the trees. Intermediates will love this area with it good wide trails, afternoons I preferred – that's when the good bumps start appearing. If you want to show off there are some good bumps below the lifts also, but to gather a crowd, try some ballet. You will find many good advanced run and a few good cliffs if that's your passion. Intermediates will love this area so to will the beginner or the cruising skier where wide trails are plentiful. Many of the bars and restaurants here have their own hot springs to relax in after a good meal and the day's skiing. Here you can check out the history of skiing in Japan, because this is where it all started, a great museum houses many surprises, also look for the single chair-lift under Hikage lift.

Management
Kyokai: 81 269 85 3166
Accommodation Service: 81 269 85 2068

Mountain Information
Mountain: Mt. Kenashi
Highest Lifted: 5,413ft
Base Alt.: 1,837ft
Season Open: December
Season Close: April
No. Lifts: 27
Grade of Runs: 40% beginners; 30% intermediates; 30% advanced

SHIGA KOGEN

Shiga Kogen (Yamanouchi-machi, Nagano Pref.) is about 28 miles from Nagano City. This is the largest ski area in Japan and about twice the size of Vail. It comprises of 22 independent ski operations although one pass covers all. Shiga Kogen will host the 98 winter Olympic events of Men's and Women's Super Slalom and Slalom events. This area with around 72 lifts all up, includes some from the distant past with wooden chairs; an aerial tram to the latest gondolas so getting up the hill is never usually a problem. Mt. Yokote and Mt. Shiga have some great advanced runs, and most skiers will need quite a few days to discover all the lifts, let alone trails. Here your standard of skiing doesn't matter, there is plenty of mountain for everyone and so much terrain to choose from. You will also find a food establishment or accommodation house to match any time period from pre-war to ultra modern western.

Management
Area Phone: 81 269 34 2404
Accommodation Service: 81 269 34 2404

Mountain Information
Summit Alt.: 7,462 ft.
Base Alt.: 4,346 ft.
Season Open: December
Season Close: April
No. Lifts: 72
Grade of Runs: 25% beginners; 55% intermediate; 20% advanced

TAZAWA-KO KOHGEN

Tazawa-ko Kohgen (Obonai, Tazawako-machi, Akita Pref.) A quiet and uncrowded resort, one of the few to be found in Japan. Set in one of the prettiest rural prefectures with a lake crowning this magic place. The skiing is good value – ten lifts provide great advanced skiing up high, and a couple of runs at the lower. Intermediates will find mid mountain to their taste although once past the drop off at the top of Champion lift, most will enjoy this long run, let alone the views of the crater lake. Beginners have the lower areas, which do get a little crowded but not like the more easily accessed resorts. Within easy travel, there are another two ski areas located on this mountain, but access to these is by ski touring only or public transport: they are Akita-ken Tazawa-ko and Tazawa-ko Minami. It's worth spending a few days exploring this great region.

Management
Area Phone: 81 187 46 2011
Accommodation Service: 81 167 43 0307

Mountain Information
Mountain:
Highest Lifted: 3,937 ft.
Season Open: December
Season Close: April
No. Lifts: 10
Grade of Runs: 21% beginners; 38% intermediates; 41% advanced

ZAO ONSEN

Zao (Zao Onsen, Yamagata-shi, Yamagata Pref.) This is a traditional Japanese ski resort that dates back to the twenties and is encased in old style charm. Beginners have a magnificent areas: one in particular offers some of the best views and is a must for the camera buff. Intermediates have several good areas from which to choose, from wide cruising runs to a few bumps runs that will make for some good exercise. Advanced skiers will enjoy the Oh-mori quad lift that has a 38° slope The Wall, and about a 450m. run of fun. For the photographers, go up to the summit and capture the hoar frost on the trees locally known as the monsters – Zao is famous for this extremely regular and unusual spectacle.

Management
Area Phone: 81 236 94 9328
Tourist Information Service: 81 236 41 1212

Mountain Information
Mountain: Mt. Jizo
Summit Alt.: 5,594 ft.
Base Alt.:2,558 ft.
Season Open: December
Season Close: April
No. Lifts: 46
Grade of Runs: 35% beginners; 50 % intermediates; 15% advanced.

KOREA

Korea is not just a manufacturing country, with a few student that we are constantly aware of protesting on the news. Here one can and will find an enchanting Oriental nation that has magnificent Palaces and Shrines, markets that will tax your credit cards limits. Great restaurants, bustling cities and most important to us snow freaks, great skiing. Yes, skiing – the resorts here are new and engulfing technological changes as they happen.

There are nine major destinations all within a 25 to 270 kilometer range from Seoul most are true Asian style resorts catering to year round activities and include a large hotel complex with additional sporting choices all under the same roof. Night skiing is very popular at the closer downtown areas.

Seoul Resort is just thirty minutes from downtown on Baekbong mountain with three lifts. Chonmasan Ski Resort is 32 km. and has seven lifts plus an artificial slope for year round training. Bears Town Resort 36 km. with another 7 seven lifts, Yangji Resort is 60 km. with six lifts, Daemyung Ski Resort has six quads and is 88 km., Suanbo Aurora Valley is 2 hrs or 140 km. south east, with three lifts, Alps Resort has five lifts and 205 km. north east a short 40 minute flight, Yong Pyeong Resort 213 km. or 40 min. flying and 5 min. taxi ride then a choice of 16 lifts, finally Muju south 270 km. 50 min. flying has seven lifts and the longest slope in Korea 3.2 km. plus a 48 k cross country course. Most of the ski areas are challenging, some excellent off piste skiing is available. It is wise to ski at the more distant resorts from Seoul, crowding does decrease with distance. So for somewhere a little different give Korea a go take a few days as a stopover en route to Japan or one of the Southern Hemisphere destinations.

SOUTHERN AFRICA

Southern Africa is not the destination one would expect to find in a ski guide. I myself have visions of wildlife parks, the Savannah and diamonds. Not of high mountain ranges and an annual covering of skiable snow. Several famous mountain names, one on the equator are snow capped and do suffer from the ravages of the occasional adventurous snow sport fanatic. Their names synonymous with Africa and you should recognize Mt. Ruwenzori, Mt. Kilimanjaro in Tanzania and Mt.Kenya in Kenya. At these mountains there are no ski operators as such, but many tourist guides who are only to happy to helicopter lift the diehard pilgrim in for the a day's snow sports.

Southern Africa boasts several skiing operations further south, all of which are small club style ones. Generally the snow falls are very unreliable, so when the snow comes all head to the hills in South Africa a total of five; Cathedral Peak, Matroosberg, Mont Aux Sources, Underberg and Witsies Hoek. For those who have a passion for cross country skiing, try the Drakenberg mountain range where most of the clubs are located. Do not expect exotic resorts with chairs, lifts are ground pullers, nor great vertical drops. Facilities are primitive by European standards, but do provide some very good skiing. The snow is usually wet and heavy and the snowfalls can be irregular and sparse, so if the powder is scarce do a little sightseeing. The service towns are built in the famous South African style, gracious hotels that will pamper your fetishes. So you can relax and rest in the lap of luxury if club accommodations are to spartan for you. If you desire the exotic try Lesotho and Thabana Ntlenyama, just a short distance form the infamous Sun City. Further information can be requested by writing to: the Secretary, South African Ski Association, P.O. Box 418003, Craighall, Johannesburg 2024, South Africa, Fax 27-11-789-1181 or check with South African Airways.

POLAND

ZAKOPANE

Height of Resort: 2,460/3,280 ft
Height of Top Station: 6,517 ft
Nearest International Airport: Cracow

Situated in a niche between the foot of the Tatras and gentle slopes of Pogorze Gubalowskie, Zakopane is a tourist village of a universal character. It is Poland's largest centre for winter sports, as well as the country's most famous tourist resort, offering activities and facilities for holiday-makers of all ages throughout a year. Owing to its most beautiful location, easy accessibility of the mountains and rich exotic highland folklore Zakopane has been attracting and inspiring distinguished artists and has earned itself an important place in the Polish and European cultural heritage. It has hosted many international conferences festivals and sports events including International Federation of Ski World Championships in 1929,1939 and 1963 and the Universiad in 1993. The town has a well developed network of hotels, holiday houses and rooms to rent in private pensions or villas most of them preserving the features of traditional Zakopane Style characteristic to the region. Central to Zakopane is its main Kropowki promenade with shops, restaurants, bars, cafeterias bustling with life, tourists, musicians and occasionally a flock of sheep, grazing around the town. Zakopane has rapidly developed in the latter part of this century, it is however relatively unspoilt and has preserved its small-time highland character.

The Skiing: Zakopane has four main skiing areas: Kasprowy Wierch, Gubalowka, Butorowy Wierch and Nosal:

The cableway to **Kasprowy Wierch** (1,987m) starts from Kuznice and has a capacity of 210 persons per hour. It is advisable to book your tickets in advance through your hotel or at 'Orbis' tourist office. There is a mountain shelter and a restaurant at the top of the station. From Kasprowy Wierch the main run leads north to Hala Gasiennicowa through Kociol Gosiennicowy and then from Karczmisko it twists and turns all the way down back to Kuznice. The route is 7 km long over 990m difference in altitude. The other route from Kasprowy leads via Hala Goryczkowa down to Kuznice. The ski run is wider and more comfortable, however, it can become icy at its lowest part. Kasprowy is also served by two chair-lifts from Hala Gasiennicowa (1600m) and Hala Goryczkowa (1334m) offering two shorter (1,190 and 1,730m) spectacular runs down the steep upper part of the mountain.Both routes are used in ski competitions and are licenced by international ski organisations. The runs from Kasprowy are suitable only for advanced skiers.

The region of Gubalowka (1,120m) is one of the best developed centres for skiers of intermediate ability. The funicular of a capacity of 860 persons per hour will carry you to the top of the mountain ridge. Bars, restaurants, wooden villas spread over the gentle slopes of the mountain are facing the most beautiful panorama of the Tatras and attract many visitors. The two main runs face south (1,160m) and south-east (740m). The top of Gubalowka is used by many beginner's ski schools and a number of drag-lifts are in operation. Popular with families an with virtually no queueing for the funicular involved, Gobalovka skiing can be a very relaxing and enjoyable experience.

Butorowy Wierch (1,160m) is also suitable for intermediate skiers. It is served by a double chair-lift of a capacity of 720 persons per hour. The run is rather steep and narrow to start with and it gradually widens and becomes more comfortable at its lowest part.

Nosal (1,206) has a slalom run which is mainly used during official competitions, it is however accessible to individuals at other times. The comfortable (1,500m) ski run leads eastwards through the other side of the mountain to Kuznice. The nursery slopes in and around the edge of the town are ideal for beginners with drag lifts, ski-hire shops, ski-schools all ready and available.It is all still quite informal; however continuously developing and well responding to the growing demand.

In a Few Words: A unique resort with great atmosphere, life and culture within easy reach of most immaculate environment of Tatra National Park where its most welcoming magnificent scenery draws hundreds every year to hike and climb in the summer and ski in winter. The ski facilities and runs are not yet comparable with the standard of larger alpine resorts, however the cost of staying and skiing in Zakopane is still cheap for all what it has to offer. Well worth visiting and having a memorable holiday, will be appreciated by all mountain lovers.

Après Ski: Cheap wining and dining all around the town in stylish restaurants, tavernas or if you prefer in tiny welcoming mountain shelters. The average meal will cost from 1.50-5.00. A few night clubs, night shops and a casino as well as art galleries, museums to visit and explore. Also if you fancy a trip out of town a historic city of Cracow or a trip to old Wieliczka Salt Mine are highly recommended.

Recommended Hotels: To make the most of your stay in Zakopane you should book your stay through TRIP Travel Agency. Their pensions: Bialy Potok, Telimena, Pan Tadeusz and other offer at present the highest standard of accommodation. All rooms with private facilities, telephone satellite TV, radio. All situated most conveniently within easy access to mountain trails.

IMPRESSIONS ON AUSTRALIAN AND NEW ZEALAND SKIING

by Judy Skeats

Skiing and snowboarding in the Antipodes offer very different experiences from the European areas. There are also some stark differences between Australian skiing and that found in New Zealand and between the North and the South Island in New Zealand. Australia offers shorter runs in general and less vertical descent but the opportunity to ski through blue gum trees, see wombats crossing the pistes or foraging amongst tree stumps below the lifts and hear exotic bird calls should not be missed. Australia's resorts are reasonably well developed with chair-lifts being the norm, but accommodation on site can be very expensive. Many people stay in nearby towns and 'commute' to the skiing. Most of Australia's resorts are situated in New South Wales (near Canberra) and Victoria and are resorts generally much more extensive than their New Zealand counterparts, though Tasmanian skiing is a notable exception to this.

The two largest resorts in Australia compete fiercely for business. Thredbo has Australia's highest restaurant and marginally higher skiing whereas the recently expanded Perisher Blue area (which has now linked up Perisher, Blue Cow Mountain, Smiggins and Guthega) extends across a wider ski area. both have great character and are well developed in terms of the services offered. These include snow cannons, locker facilities, ski patrollers and a ski hosting/guiding service which is available free on certain days. Intermediate skiers and above just arrive at the advertised rendezvous at the appointed time and a volunteer ski guide will take them around the area. There are also arrangements for children and ski school similar to those found in Europe. In Australia a number of the ski schools have reciprocal arrangements with Austrian and Swiss ski schools so it isn't unusual to be taught by Europeans.

The word 'resort' isn't used in New Zealand – many of the skifields are tiny (some have only three very basic rope-tow lifts) and are run by clubs. It is therefore unusual to be able to stay at the field and travelling times of 30-40 minutes to the ski area are not unusual. Whatever the size, most of the ski areas have some form of ski school and ski/boot hire facilities.

South Island New Zealanders are enthusiastic sportspeople and good cheap skiing is a priority. The fashion-conscious tourists may find themselves at the larger skifields around Queenstown and Wanaka or at Mount Hutt or Whakapapa, but most of the smaller privately owned clubs (which are nevertheless open to the public) offer unpisted slopes and just a lunch hut with basic sandwiches and canned drinks but often challenging skiing. Even in larger places there is rarely a choice of eating places, few toilets and only a basic ski clothing shop on the mountain. However, casual tourists are encouraged to try skiing, and the ski shops in the main ski towns offer the option of hiring ski clothing by the day as well as skis and boots etc (the Australians do this too). Most of the tourists to New Zealand are from Japan and Korea, easily spotted in their bright multicolour ski suits. Native New Zealanders tend to be less fashion conscious, spending their money on the many extreme sports offered (heliskiing, climbing, white water rafting, bungee jumping etc.) rather than on expensive new equipment or hotels. In 1995 the old Salomon SC81 boots were still much in evidence and many skiers stayed in local budget accommodation which may include backpackers' hostels.

The published piste maps of New Zealand skifields do not necessarily give a good guide to the range of skiing – one lift may appear to serve three different runs of different grades whereas the casual observe may only see a wide unmarked expanse with little difference in gradient. For better skiers the off-piste areas and back bowls are challenging (though not always open due to weather conditions) and can be much more extensive than the so-called pisted areas. One small slope, Craigieburn near Christchurch, boasts that it is extreme skier Glen Plake's favourite skifield because of the enormous extreme skiing possibilities. There are a number of heliskiing operations in New Zealand took on both islands. Those most well known are at the Fox and Tasman Glaciers, Harris mountains and from the Southern Lakes.

In New Zealand's North Island the ski areas are large and well developed, offering most of the facilities found at European resorts and a ski guiding service similar to that found at the premier resorts of Thredbo and Perisher Blue in Australia. However both Turoa and Whakapapa are situated on Mt. Ruapehu, an active volcano which erupted in June and July 1996 causing considerable damage and sadly disrupting the skiing season which runs from June to November. Both resorts are very popular as they are only about four hours' drive from Auckland – which appeals to overseas tourists offered day trips and the Auckland population who travel down for weekends.

In New Zealand even some of the larger commercial ski areas are reached by unmade roads so snow chains are often mandatory and 4-wheel drive vehicles preferred. Mount Hutt, a well developed commercial area near Christchurch (and under the same management as the more famous Remarkables and Coronet Peak areas near Queenstown) can only be reached by a drive up a long untarred and exposed road, unsealed apparently because the mountains are still young in global terms and still moving. This and other ski areas have a number of 'closed days' due to bad weather conditions; the slender width of a country surrounded by great expanses of sea means that the whole country is susceptible to frequent and very sudden weather changes. New Zealand skiers are used to listening for radio bulletins to find out which skifields are open or closed each day depending on wind, bad snow, collapsed roads etc but conditions can also change dramatically within one day. For this reason ski passes are offered on a daily basis as the norm, with one-week passes being very unusual.

Larger ski areas in Australia and New Zealand offer Frequent Skier programmes allowing discount on their ski passes once the individual has clocked up a certain number of ski days. However at around $35-50 per day, passes in both Australia and New Zealand look expensive in comparison with the pro-rata rates available across Europe. An additional cost is that of getting up and down to the skifields; coaches are available from larger towns. There may also be road tolls (mainly New Zealand) or National Park entry fees (mainly Australia). Hitchhiking from the bottom of the main connecting roads is quite popular amongst young tourists and travellers trying to keep costs down. Accommodation in all the main ski areas can be expensive and in short supply.

In order to make full use of the available snow and to offset the effect of the closed days in New Zealand and the shorter ski season in Australia, most of the ski areas offer night skiing under floodlights. As so few people stay at the ski area itself nightlife is generally basic and undeveloped, although Thredbo and Perisher Blue in Australia boast a few nightspots.

A final word of warning, about – of all things – Keas, the New Zealand mountain parrots. These large intelligent birds are notorious for pecking at anything that interest them, which can include car windscreen wipers and tyres, any dark bags and equipment etc. Personal belongings and ski equipment are usually safe from thieves in the smaller ski fields, but the inquisitive Keas will peck at anything! their razor sharp beaks can shred video camera cases etc.!

Skiing in both Australia and New Zealand can offer many new and exciting challenges for the 'off' season in the northern hemisphere.

For reports on Australian and New Zealand resorts/ski areas see pages 255-259.

SNOWBOARDERS' CHART

Resorts marked •allow members a reduction on hire rates and in many cases for the purchase of clothing and equipment. The rates quoted are, in the main, for standard equipment. The member must produce his/her membership card. Please refer to the Club section.

Country/Resort	Snowboard/ Fun Park	Half pipes	Collective Instruction			Equipment Hire	
			Days	hours daily	cost *Pts*	Days	Boots & boards *Pts*
ANDORRA							
Arcalis	Yes	Yes	5	3			
Pas Dela Casa	Yes	Yes	5	3	9,050/11,125	5	3,000
Soldeu El Tarter	Project	Yes	5	4			
AUSTRIA					*AS*		*AS*
Alpbach	Yes	Yes	5	2	1000	5	1200
Auffach	Yes	Yes	3	2	1040	3	900
Badgastein	No	Yes:3	3	4	1400	3	1100
Bad Aussee	No	No	3	2	1000	3	645
Bad Hofgastein	No	Yes	3	4	1400	3	1100
Berwang	No	No	3	2	900*	3	960
Brand	Yes	Yes	5	3	1200	5	1500
Damüls	No	Yes	5	4	2000	3	1700
Dienten	No	Yes	3	2.5	1050	3	900
Dorfgastein	No	Yes	3	4	1400*	3	1100*
Ellmau	No	No	3	2	1200	3	750
Fieberbrunn•	Yes	Yes	3	2	900	3	750
Filzmoos	No	No	4	2	1150*	4	1000*
Finkenberg	No	Yes	3	4	1500*	3	750*
Fontanella/Faschina	No	No	5	4	1400*	5	1310*
Fügen	Yes	Yes	3	2	1400	3	600
Fulpmes	Yes	Yes	5	2	2390	5	770
Galtür	Yes	No	3	2	990	3	960
Gargellen•	Yes	Yes	3	2	900	6	1095 (boards only)
Gaschurn	Yes	Yes	3	3	1900	3	750
Gosau	No	No	3	2	800*	3	600*
Hinterstoder	No	Yes	3	2	800	3	600
Hintertaal	No	Yes	3	2	950	3	885
Hintertux/Lanersbach	Yes	Yes: 2	3	2	1100	3	900
Ischgl	Yes	Yes	3	2	1700*	3	750*
Jerzens	No	No	3	2	1200*	3	1155*
Kaprun	Yes	Yes	3	2	1350*	6	1780*
Kitzbühel/Kirchberg	Yes	Yes	3	4	1150	3	1020
Lech	Yes	Yes	4	4	2000	4	1460
Lermoos•	No	Yes	4	2	1050*	6	1730*
Mayrhofen	Yes	Yes	3	2	1200	3	750
Nauders	Yes	No	3	2	930	3	600
Niederau	Yes	at Auffach	3	2	1040	3	900
Oberau	Yes	at Auffach	3	2	1040	3	900
Obergurgl/Hochgurgl•	Yes	Yes	6	2	1850*	6	1800
Obertauern	Yes	Planning	3	2	1350	6	1450*
Obertraun	Yes	No	3	2	900	3	510
Saalbach/Hinterglemm	Yes	Yes: 2	3	3	1500*	3	1140*
St. Anton	Yes	Yes	3	2	1280	6	1490
St. Johann in Tirol	Yes	Yes	6	4	2000	6	1920
Schruns	No	Yes	3	4	3000	3	Included
Schladming	Yes	Yes	3	4	1200*	3	1310*
Seefeld•	No	Yes	3	2	1200	6	1560
Serfaus	Yes	No	3	2	1030*	3	1100*
Sölden/Hochsölden	Yes	Yes	3	4	1110	3	900*
Söll•	Yes	Yes	3	2	1140	3	1340
Sonntag-Stein	No	Yes	3	2	1100*	3	1610
Stuben	No	Yes	3	4	1440	3	840 (boards only)
Tschagguns	Yes	Yes	6	4	1400	6	1800
Vent	No	No	3	2	900	3	1050
Wagrain	Yes	Yes	3	2	990	3	900
Westendorf•	No	Yes	3	4	1180*	6	1160
Zell am Zee	Yes	Yes	3	2	1350*	6	1310*
Zell and Ziller•	No	Yes	3	2	810	6	1310
Zürs	No	No	6	4	1980	4	1460*
FRANCE					*Francs*		*Francs*
Alpe d'Huez•	Yes	No	6	2.30	670	6	725*
Avoriaz•	Yes	Yes	5	2.5	800	6	750
Chamonix	Yes	Yes	3	3	660*	3	450*
Chatel•	No	Yes	5	3	600	6	660
Courchevel•	Yes	Yes	5	3	930*	6	795
Flaine•	Yes	Yes	6	3	695	6	589
Font-Romeu	Yes	Yes	5	4	650*	5	400*
Isola 2000•	Yes	Yes	6	2	540	6	600
La Clusaz	Yes	Yes	5	4	760	6	728
Le Corbier	Yes	Yes	6	2.5		6	900
Les Angles	Yes	Yes	6	3	660	6	600
Les Arcs•	Yes	Yes	5	2	550*	6	790
Les Deux Alpes•	Yes	Yes	6	4	900*	6	676
Les Gets	Yes	No	6	2.5	600	6	550*
Les Houches	No	No	3	2.5	320		
Les Menuires•	Yes	No	6	2.5	750	6	725
Megève•	Yes	No	6	4	910	6	725

*
1996/97 rates

SNOWBOARDERS' CHART

Country/Resort	Snowboard/ Fun Park	Half pipes	Collective Instruction Days	Collective Instruction hours	Collective Instruction cost	Equipment Hire Days	Equipment Hire Boots & boards
FRANCE					***Francs***		***Francs***
Méribel•	Yes	Yes	5	2.5	750	6	759
Montgenèvre	Yes	No	6	2.5	600*	6	690
Morzine	Yes	Yes	6	2	540	6	550
St. Lary•	Yes	No				6	724
Serre Chevalier•	Yes	No	6	5	900*	6	725
Tignes•	No	No	6	3	725*	6	725
Val d'Isère•	Yes	Yes	6	3	708*	6	725
Valfrejus•	No	No	3	2	350	6	630
Valmorel•	Yes	No	6	2.3	585	6	630
Val Thorens•	Yes	No	5	3	600*	6	725
GERMANY					***DM***		***DM***
Berchtesgadenerland	Yes	Yes	5	3	184*	5	160*
Garmisch-Partenkirschen	No	Yes	5	3	188	5	250
Oberammergau	No	No	3	2		3	99
Oberstaufen	No	No	5	3	150*		
Oberstdorf	Yes	Yes	5	4	279*	5	110
Reit im Winkl	No	Yes	3	3	170	3	75
ITALY					***Lire***		***Lire***
Arabba	No	Yes	5	3	180,000*	6	130,000
Bardonecchia	No	No	5	2	160,000*	5	90,000*
Bormio	No	No	6	2.5		6	190,000
Canazei/Campitello	No	Yes	5	3	165,000	6	120,000
Cavalese	No	No	5	2	130,000	5	108,000
Cervinia	No	No	6	2.45	190,000	6	150,000
Champoluc	No	No	6	3	190,000	6	210,000
Cortina	No	No	6	2.5	400,000		
Courmayeur	No	No	6	3	180,000*	6	100,000*
La Thuile	No	No	6	2	135,000	6	120,000
Limone	No	No	6	2	200,000		130,000
Livigno	No	Yes	6	2	190,000	6	150,000
Madonna	Yes	Yes	5	2	230,000	5	200,000
Macugnaga	No	Yes	6	2	190,000		240,000
Pila	No	No	1	4	70,000	1	25,000
PassoTonale	No	Yes	6	2	160,000	6	Included
San Vigilio	No	Yes	5	3	200,000	5	200,000
Sauze d'Oulx	No	No	6	3	180,000*	6	100,000*
Selva	Yes	Yes	3	2	165,000	3	105,000
Sestriere	No	No	Private lessons only				
LIECHTENSTEIN					***S.Fr.***		***S.Fr.***
Malbun	Yes	Yes	5	4	300	5	235
NORWAY					***N.Kr.***		***N.Kr.***
Geilo	Yes	Yes	6	2	840		1,000
Hemsedal	Yes	Yes	5	1	410*	5	1,300
Lillehammer	Yes	Yes	3	1.50	370*	3	750*
Voss	No	No	3	2	300*	3	450*
SPAIN					***Pts.***		
La Molina	No	No					
Masella	No	Yes	5	4	8,250	5	7,500
SWITZERLAND					***S.Fr.***		***S.Fr.***
Adelboden	Yes	Yes	5	4	170*	6	207*
Andermatt	No	No	3	2	150*	6	182*
Anzère•	Yes	Yes	5	3	140	6	182
Arosa•	Yes	Yes	5	2	200	6	207
Braunwald	Yes	Yes	5	4	230	5	190*
Champéry•	Yes	Yes	5	2	150*	6	130
Chateau d'Oex	Yes	No	3	2	66	3	45
Crans/Montana•	Yes	Yes	5	2	200	6	157
Davos•	Yes	Yes	5	4	215	6	207
Engelberg•	Yes	Yes	5	4	358	6	164
Flims/Laax•	Yes	Yes	3	5	230*	6	207
Flumserberg•	Yes	Yes	3	2	79	6	207
Grächen	No	Yes	5	2	170*	6	207
Grindelwald•	Yes	Yes	5	4	275*	6	192
Gstaad-Saanenland•	Yes	Yes	5	2	165	6	207
Haute-Nendaz	Yes	Yes	5	5	234	6	182
Klosters•	Yes	No	3	4.5	175	6	207
Lenzerheide•	Yes	Yes	5	4		6	207
Les Diablerets•	Yes	Yes	6	2	156	6	207
Leysin•	Yes	Yes	6	2	130	6	207
Morgins•	Yes	Yes	5	2	120	6	207
Mürren	No	Yes	3	2	147	3	129
Pontresina•	Yes	Yes	5	4	285	6	207
Saas Fee•	Yes	Yes	5	3	156*	6	207
St Moritz•	Yes	Yes	5	2	280	6	207
Verbier•	Yes	Yes	5	2	170	6	160
Veysonnaz	No	No	4	2	110	4	156
Villars•	Yes	Yes	6	2	110	6	207
Wengen•	Yes	Yes	6	3	204	6	207
Wildhaus•	Yes	Yes	4	2	200	6	182
Zermatt•	Yes	Yes	3	2	135	6	207

*1996/97 rates

SAFETY ON THE SLOPES

by Barney Harford

Skiing can be a very dangerous sport. In this respect it is pretty much like other things in life like crossing the road and driving a car. However if you observe the following rules your exposure to danger on the slopes will be greatly reduced.

- Obey all notices posted on the piste, beside lifts and at cable car stations. Never ski on pistes that are marked as closed.
- Ski at a speed consistent with your ability such that you are in control at all times. Adjust your speed according to the gradient of the slope and visibility.
- The skier below has priority. It is therefore your responsibility to avoid slower skiers when overtaking on the piste.
- Never stop before terrain bumps or blind rises. Someone may be coming and be unable to see you. If you fall in such a position scramble quickly to the side.
- Always ski with consideration for others. If you are an advanced skier that means not cutting up slower skiers. If you are a beginner or intermediate that means not getting in the way of better skiers by attempting to ski slopes that are too hard for you.
- Skiing with companions is safer than skiing alone. Never ski alone off-piste.
- Never stop in the middle of the piste. Always stop at the edge.
- Collisions are one of the most common causes of injury in skiing. Be aware of everything that is going on around you on the piste. Never start without looking behind you. Plan your course up to 50m ahead of you.
- Ensure that your bindings are correctly adjusted for your weight and standard. Check with an instructor if you are unsure. Check the safety release of your bindings every morning to make sure that they have not frozen up.
- Do some warming up and stretch exercises before you start skiing every morning and afternoon. Cold muscles tear much more easily than warm ones.
- Never ski down a piste after it has been closed for the night as there will be no more safety checks until the next morning.
- Make sure that you are always adequately dressed at all times, and particularly when you are at glacier level, when the temperature can be as low as -20 degrees and it is often windy. Be very aware of the possibility of hypothermia setting in if it is is cold or you are slightly unwell. Watch out to see whether companions are shivering, being lethargic. Victims of hypothermia lose the ability to help themselves.
- Watch out for symptoms of frostbite in yourself and your companions. Exposed flesh turns white and becomes numb.

Remember that most skiing injuries result from poorly adjusted bindings and collisions. Be safe on the piste and make sure that you enjoy your time in the mountains.

SELECTING YOUR RESORT

BEGINNERS: It will be seen that we have excluded some resorts from the point of view of beginners. This is not because these resorts, with the exception of a few, do not have good beginners' slopes, but because they are large international centres, where one pays for the name and the extensive facilities offered. Beginners, unless they have money to throw away, do not require this and they would be much wiser to select the small or medium sized centre, of which there are many.

FAMILIES: Parents taking young children between the ages of 3 to 8 years for the first time should select a resort with kindergarten or ski kindergarten facilities, mentioned elsewhere.

HEIGHTS OF RESORTS: If you are taking your holiday between mid-December and early March, all the resorts in this Guide, *given normal weather conditions*, will have skiable snow. If you are taking your holiday before or after this period, the general principle with the exception of Norway and Sweden, is to select a reasonably high resort; this does not always apply, however, as many resorts are situated in 'snow pockets' whilst other low altitude resorts have extensive north facing slopes, where the snow remains good (see below). For instance, when snow conditions were bad in several areas, we have experienced better skiing conditions at some low altitude resorts with extensive north facing slopes than at much higher resorts with a preponderance of south facing slopes.

DIRECTION OF THE MAIN SLOPES: We show in the charts the direction in which the *main* slopes face; the importance of this is briefly explained below.

North Facing Slopes: These only receive the slanting rays of the sun, thus ensuring the lowest ground temperature, consequently the snow remains good and powdery for much longer periods. Such areas become increasingly important during the latter part of the season.

South Facing Slopes: Unless the weather is overcast, south facing slopes are fully exposed to the direct rays of the sun for most of the day and powder snow conditions only prevail immediately after a snow fall. Furthermore, in late season the snow begins to wear thin, particularly if there have not been good pre-season falls to form the hard base. In late season the snow also tends to become soggy and heavy after midday. Against this, south facing slopes have one big advantage: after the hot sun on them during the day the low temperature at night hardens the surface to form a 'spring snow' so that in the morning and up until about 1100 hours one can ski almost anywhere. This is not only a great feeling but, to our mind, the finest skiing of all.

East and West Facing Slopes: These slopes, to a lesser degree, share the advantages and disadvantages of the north and south facing slopes. East facing receive the sun in the morning and west facing in the afternoon. As for the slopes facing the intermediate points of the compass, the north-east and north-west facing slopes would normally have better snow conditions, particularly in late season, than those facing south-east or south-west.

SKI TOURING: High mountain touring is a delightful form of skiing and the experienced skier should devote some time to it. All the resorts marked in the charts with 'T' are good entry points for the touring areas. Half day, full day or longer tours can always be arranged, but it is essential to have a qualified guide with you. This type of skiing is best enjoyed during late season.

			Most Suitable for					Main Slopes Face								
Country/Resort	**Height Resort (feet)**	**Height Top Station (feet)**	**Beginners**	**Second Year**	**Intermediate**	**Advanced Intermediate**	**Advanced**	**North**	**North East**	**North West**	**South**	**South East**	**South West**	**East**	**West**	**Touring**
AUSTRIA																
Alpbach	3,281	6,102	*	*	*			N								
Auffach	3,000	6,235	*	*	*				NE					E		
Axamer-Lizum	5,550	7,670	*	*	*	*		N	NE							
Badgastein	3,608	8,809	*	*	*	*	*	N	NE	NW	S	SE	SW	E	W	
Bad Goisern	1,640	3,280	*	*					NE	NW						
Bad Hofgastein	2,853	7,544	*	*	*	*	*		NE							
Berwang	4,398	5,395	*	*	*			N	NE			SE		E		
Bichlbach	3,526	4,150	*	*					NE					E		
Brand	3,412	6,297	*	*	*								S	E		
Bürserberg	2,919	5,904	*	*	*							SE		E		
Damüls	4,680	6,585	*	*	*							SE	SW			
Dienten	3,502	5,747	*	*	*			N			S					
Dorfgastein	2,755	6,690	*	*	*	*	*	N		NW						
Ehrwald	3,267	9,203	*	*	*	*				NW			SW			
Ellmau	2,689	5,101	*	*	*			N	NE							
Fieberbrunn	2,625	6,626	*	*	*			N								
Filzmoos	3,467	5,248	*	*	*			N	NE		S					
Finkenberg	2,768	6,888	*	*	*	*						SE		E		
Fontanella/Faschina	3,772/4,920	6,560	*	*	*			N	NE			SE	SW	E		
Fügen	1,853	6,888	*	*	*			N	NE		S			E		
Fügenberg	4,855	7,216	*	*	*				NE					E		
Fulpmes	2,952	10,499	*	*	*	*		N	NE					E		
Galtür	5,796	7,544	*	*	*				NE							T
Gargellen	4,628	7,600	*	*	*				NE					E		
Gaschurn	3,280	7,546	*	*	*	*		N	NE							T
Gerlos	4,071	6,772	*	*	*					NW		SE				
Gosau	2,460	5,248	*	*	*			N						E		
Gurtis	2,952	4,522	*	*											W	
Hinterglemm	3,260	6,845	*	*	*	*		N	NE	NW	S	SE		E		
Hinterstoder	2,132	6,232	*	*	*			N		NW						
Hinterthal	3,345	4,428	*	*	*			N								
Hintertux	4,920	10,693	*	*	*	*			NE							T
Hochgurgl	7,052	10,111	*	*	*	*			NE					E		
Hochsölden	6,857	10,030	*	*	*	*	*		NE			SE		E		T
Igls	2,952	7,370	*	*	*			N		NW						
Ischgl	4,600	9,394	*	*	*	*				NW						
Jerzens	3,609	10,761	*	*	*	*			NE				SW		W	
Kaprun	2,624	9,938	*	*	*	*		N	NE					E		T
Kirchberg	2,830	6,383	*	*	*	*	*	N	NE	NW						
Kitzbühel	2,053	6,562	*	*	*	*	*	N	NE	NW	S	SE	SW	E	W	
Klösterle	3,608	7,166	*	*	*			N	NE	NW					W	
Kühtai	6,500	7,950	*	*	*			N		NW				E		T
Lanersbach	4,230	8,202	*	*	*	*						SE		E		T
Laterns/Furx	2,952	5,854	*	*	*						S		SW			
Lech	4,712	8,099	*	*	*	*	*	N			S	SE		E	W	
Leogang	2,775	6,279	*	*	*	*		N	NE							
Lermoos	3,623	7,215	*	*	*				NE					E		
Lienz	2,850	7.520	*	*	*						S		SW			
Mayrhofen	2,067	7,283	*	*	*	*		N	NE			SE		E		
Mieders	3,214	10,499	*	*	*	*		N	NE					E		
Nauders	4,590	9,002	*	*	*			N								
Niederau	2,700	5,333	*	*	*			N								
Oberau	3,070	4,050	*	*				N								
Obergurgl	6,322	8,648	*	*	*	*		N		NW						T
Obertauern	5,723	7,872	*	*	*	*		N	NE	NW	S	SE	SW			T
Obertraun	1,968	6,917		*	*	*			NE	NW						T
Pertisau	3,083	4,865	*	*					NE							
Raggal	3,332	4,264	*	*	*			N		NW						
Saalbach	3,260	6,845	*	*	*	*		N	NE		S		SW			
St.Anton	4,210	9,222		*	*	*	*	N			S	SE	SW	E	W	
St.Johann in Tirol	2,180	5,578	*	*	*			N	NE	NW						
Schladming	2,443	6,611	*	*	*			N		NW						
Schruns	2,275	7,544	*	*	*	*		N	NE	NW			SW		W	T
Seefeld	3,872	6,890	*	*	*			N						E	W	
Serfaus	4,682	8,858	*	*	*				NE		S	SE		E		

Country/Resort	Height Resort (feet)	Height Top Station (feet)	Most Suitable for: Beginners	Second Year	Intermediate	Advanced Intermediate	Advanced	Main Slopes Face: North	North East	North West	South	South East	South West	East	West	Touring
AUSTRIA																
Sölden	4,518	10,030	*	*	*	*	*		NE					E		T
Söll	2,275	5,998	*	*	*			N						E		
Sonntag/Stein	3,700/4,264	5,741	*	*						NW						
Spital am Pyrhn	2,624	6,146	*	*	*					NW					W	
Steinach	3,432	6,578	*	*	*			N	NE							
Stüben	4,592	7,872		*	*	*		N		NW						
Telfes	3,281	10,499	*	*	*	*		N	NE					E		
Tschagguns	2,275	6,903	*	*	*	*		N	NE	NW						T
Vent	6,202	8,850	*	*	*				NE							T
Wagrain	2,748	6,605	*	*	*				NE	NW						
Westendorf	2,624	6,101	*	*	*			N		NW	S			E		
Windischgarsten	1,968	2,821	*	*							S		SW			
Zell am See	2,490	6,500	*	*	*					NW			SW	E		
Zell am Ziller	1,902	7,900	*	*	*			N					SW		W	
Zürs	5,590	8,038	*	*	*	*	*		NE					E	W	
BULGARIA																
Borovets	4,265	8,300	*	*	*	*		N						E		
Pamporovo	5,345	6,335	*	*	*			N								
FRANCE																
Alpe d'Huez	6,101	10,988	*	*	*	*	*			NW	S	SE	SW			
Argentière	4,110	12,486			*	*	*	N	NE		S		SW			
Avoriaz	5,904	7,710	*	*	*	*	*	N	NE	NW					W	T
Barèges/La Mongie	4,265/5,905	8,400	*	*	*	*		N	NE	NW				E		
Chamonix	3,389	12,604			*	*	*	N	NE		S		SW			T
Chatel	3,937	6,890	*	*	*	*	*	N	NE	NW						
Courchevel	6,013	8,825		*	*	*	*	N	NE	NW					W	T
Flaine	5,250	8,150	*	*	*	*	*	N	NE	NW					W	
Font-Romeu	5,895	7,205	*	*	*			N	NE			SE		E		
Isola 2000	6,560	8,563	*	*	*	*		N	NE	NW					W	
La Clusaz	3,608	7,872	*	*	*	*	*	N		NW				E		
La Plagne	5,904	10,663	*	*	*	*	*	N	NE	NW					W	
La Corbier	5,085	7,415	*	*	*			N	NE							
La Toussuire	5,904	7,874	*	*	*									E	W	
Les Angles	5,404	7,614	*	*	*						S	SE		E		
Les Arcs	5,249/6,560	10,583	*	*	*	*	*	N	NE	NW						
Les Deux Alpes	5,412	11,673	*	*	*	*	*	N	NE	NW		SE		E	W	
Les Gets	3,834	6,069	*	*	*	*	*	N	NE	NW			SW	E		
Les Houches	3,280	6,455	*	*	*	*	*	N						E		T
Les Menuires	6,068	9,350	*	*	*	*	*	N	NE					E		
Megève	3,651	7,709		*	*	*		N	NE	NW	S				W	
Méribel	4,756/5,756	9,681	*	*	*	*	*	N		NW					W	T
Montgenèvre	6,069	8,326	*	*	*	*	*	N	NE							
Val Cenis	4,593	9,186	*	*	*			N		NW						
Val d'Isère	5,965	10,676		*	*	*	*	N	NE	NW	S				W	T
Valfrejus	5,083	8,979	*	*	*			N	NE	NW						
Valloire	4,692	7,720	*	*	*	*		N	NE	NW						
Valmorel	4,592	7,884	*	*	*			N				SE				
Val Thorens	7,544	10,496	*	*	*	*	*	N		NW					W	
St.Lary	2,722/5,511	7,955	*	*	*	*		N	NE							
Serre Chevalier	4,500	9,100	*	*	*	*		N	NE							
Tignes	6,825	11,480		*	*	*	*	N	NE	NW	S			E	W	T
GERMANY																
Bayrischzell	2,630	6,562	*	*	*	*				NW						
Berchtesgaden	1,837	5,905	*	*	*				NE	NW	S				W	T
Garmisch-Partenkirchen	2,362	9,730	*	*	*	*	*	N						E	W	T
Mittenwald	3,018	7,362	*	*	*			N	NE							
Oberammergau	2,624	5,524	*	*	*											
Oberstaufen	2,808	5,577	*	*	*	*		N	NE	NW						T
Oberstdorf	2,756	7,362	*	*	*						S	SE		E	W	T
Reit im Winkl	2,296	6,069	*	*	*	*		N			S					
ITALY																
Abetone	6,105	7,085	*	*	*						S		SW			
Antermoia	4,920	7,216	*	*	*				NW		S					
Aprica	3,863	8,448	*	*	*			N	NE	NW						
Arabba	5,254	9,676	*	*	*	*		N	NE	NW	S					
Bardonecchia	4,304	9,002	*	*	*	*		N		NW					W	
Bormio	4,018	9,905	*	*	*	*		N	NE	NW						T
Campitello	4,752	9,684	*	*	*	*	*	N		NW	S			E	W	
Canazei	4,808	9,684	*	*	*	*	*	N		N W	S			E	W	
Caspoggio	3,504	7,072	*	*	*					NW						
Cavalese	3,300	7,874	*	*	*			N		NW						
Cervinia	6,760	11,500	*	*	*	*					S	SE	SW			T
Champoluc	5,478	8,940	*	*	*						S	SE	SW			T
Clavière	5,774	6,676	*	*	*	*	*	N	NE							
Colfosco	5,401	7,216	*	*	*	*.		N	NE	NW			SW	E	W	
Cortina	4,018	10,543		*	*	*	*	N	NE	NW	S		SW	E		
Corvara	5,143	7,216	*	*	*	*		N	NE	NW			SW	E	W	
Courmayeur	4,015	9,843		*	*	*		N	NE		S	SE				T
Folgarida	4,260	8,213	*	*	*	*	*	N		NW	S	SE	SW	E	W	
Foppolo	4,920	7,101	*	*	*						S		SW		W	
Forni di Sopra	2,975	6,761	*	*	*						S		SW			
Gressoney	4,450	9,000	*	*	*							SE	SW	E	W	
La Thuile	4,757	8,667	*	*	*	*		N						E		
La Villa	4,870	6,812	*	*	*	*		N	NE	NW			SW	E	W	
Limone	3,300	7,054	*	*	*	*			NE			SE		E	W	
Lurisia	2,624	6,560	*	*	*			N								
Macugnaga	4,352	9,000	*	*	*				NE		S					T
Madesimo	5,085	9,461	*	*	*	*		N	NE	NW						
Madonna	5,084	8,640	*	*	*	*	*	N		NW	S	SE	SW	E	W	
Malga Ciapella	4,743	10,712	*	*	*	*	*	N						E		
Marilleva	4,593	7,152	*	*	*	*	*	N		NW	S	SE	SW	E	W	
Mera	2,200/4,900	5,900	*	*	*			N	NE	NW						
Monte Bondone	3,280	6,888	*	*	*			N		NW						
Monte Campione	3,937	6,412	*	*	*						S	SE	SW			
Nevegal	3,382	5,471	*	*	*			N						E	W	
Passo Tonale	6,168	9,016	*	*	*	*		N			S					

Country/Resort	Height Resort (feet)	Height Top Station (feet)	Most Suitable for					Main Slopes Face								
			Beginners	Second Year	Intermediate	Advanced Intermediate	Advanced	North	North East	North West	South	South East	South West	East	West	Touring
ITALY																
Piancavallo	4,265	6,562	*	*	*						S	SE				
Pila	4,500/5,800	8,660	*	*	*	*		N	NE	NW						
San Cassiano	5,159	6,570	*	*	*	*		N	NE	NW			SE	E	W	
Santa Caterina	5,697	9,135	*	*	*			N								
San Martino	4,920	9,053	*	*	*	*	*		NE		S			E	W	
Sansicario	5,576	8,826	*	*	*	*	*							E	W	
San Vigilio	3,939	7.461	*	*	*	*	*	N			S			E		
Sauze d'Oulx	4,950	8,145	*	*	*	*	*	N	NE	NW						
Sella Nevea	3,773	5,782	*	*	*										W	
Selva	5,128	8,264	*	*	*	*	*	N		NW			SW		W	
Sestriere	6,666	9,175	*	*	*	*	*			NW	S					
Solda	6,068	8,200	*	*	*	*		N								
Tarvisio	2,460	5,783	*	*	*								SW			
Terminillo	6,920	7,259	*	*	*	*		N			S					
ROMANIA																
Poiana Brasov	3,345	5,844	*	*	*					NW						
Predeal	3,427	4,821	*	*	*			N		NW				E		
Sinaia	2,624	6,560	*	*	*			N	NE							
SPAIN																
Baqueira Beret	4,920	8,267	*	*	*					NW				E		
Cerler	4,936	7,754		*	*	*		N	NE	NW			SW		W	
Formigal	4,920	7,920	*	*	*	*		N							W	
La Molina	4,726	8,315	*	*	*	*		N	NE	NW					W	
Masella	5,258	8,331	*	*	*			N	NE	NW					W	
Panticosa	3,821	6,209	*	*	*			N	NE	NW				E	W	T
Sierra Nevada (Solynieve)	6,888	10,308	*	*	*	*	*	N	NE	NW						
ANDORRA																
Arcalis	6,364	8,366	*	*	*				NE	NW						
Arinsal	5,085	8,530	*	*	*				NE					E		
Grau Roig/Pas de la Casa	6,726	9,350	*	*	*			NE	NW							
Pal	6,069	7,769	*	*	*			N	NE	NW						
Soldeu/El Tarter	5,900	8,071	*	*	*	*		N	NE							
SWITZERLAND																
Adelboden	4,438	7,644	*	*	*	*		N	NE	NW						
Alt St.Johann	2,952	5,412	*	*	*			N					SW		W	T
Andermatt	4,738	9,842	*	*	*	*	*	N		NW	S		SW			
Anzère	4,920	7,937	*	*	*						S	SE				T
Arosa	6,000	8,658	*	*	*	*					S	SE				
Barboleusaz/Gryon	3,970	6,626	*	*	*			N			S					
Bivio	5,825	8,399	*	*	*			N	NE							
Braunwald	4,264	6,232	*	*	*			N			S					
Champéry	3,450	7,400	*	*	*	*	*	N			S					
Chateau d'Oex/Rossinière	3,280	5,741	*	*	*			N		NW			SW			T
Crans/Montana	4,920	9,840	*	*	*	*	*				S	SE	SW	E	W	T
Davos	5,118	9,262		*	*	*	*	N	NE	NW	S	SE	SW		W	T
Engelberg	3,444	9,096	*	*	*	*		N		NW			SW		W	T
Flims	3,615	9,902	*	*	*	*	*				S	SE		E		
Flumserberg	3,287/4,592	7,287	*	*	*	*					S	SE			W	
Grächen	5,313	9,528	*	*	*	*				NW						
Grindelwald	3,393	8,157	*	*	*	*	*	N		NW	S					
Gstaad	3,308	6,461	*	*	*	*		N	NE	NW						
Haute Nendaz	4,478	10,916	*	*	*	*	*	N		NW	S	SE	SW	E	W	T
Klosters	3,980	9,262		*	*	*	*		NE		S	SE	SW	E	W	T
Laax	3,346	9,902	*	*	*	*	*				S	SE		E		
Lenk	3,608	6,880	*	*	*	*			NE	NW				E	W	
Lenzerheide/Valbella	4,822/5,052	9.397	*	*	*	*			NE	NW				E	W	
Les Diablerets	3,936	9,840	*	*	*	*	*	N	NE		S					T
Les Mosses	4,756	7,708	*	*	*			N	NE	NW				E	W	
Leysin	4,134	7,218	*	*	*	*					S	SE				
Mayens-de-Riddes	4,921	10,916	*	*	*	*	*	N		NW	S	SE	SW	E	W	T
Morgins	4,593	6,890	*	*	*	*	*			NW			SW			
Mürren	5,362	9,748	*	*	*	*	*				S	SE	SW			T
Pizol (Bad Ragaz/Wangs)	1,686/1,755	7,283	*	*	*			N								
Pontresina	5,972	9,827	*	*	*	*	*	N	NE	NW	S			E	W	T
Rougemont	3,175	7,399	*	*	*			N	NE	NW						
Saas Fee	5,905	11,500	*	*	*	*	*	N	NE	NW		SE			W	T
St.Cergue	3,600	5,600	*	*	*											
St.Moritz	6,088	10,837		*	*	*	*	N	NE		S	SE	SW	E	W	T
Samnaun	6,036	8,962	*	*	*	*					S	SE	SW			T
San Bernardino	5,249	8,283	*	*	*											
Siviez	5,675	10,916	*	*	*	*	*	N		NW	S	SE	SW		W	T
Unterwasser	2,985	7,413	*	*	*			N	NE	NW						
Verbier	4,921	10,916	*	*	*	*	*	N		NW	S	SE	SW	E	W	T
Veysonnaz	4,045	9,918	*	*	*	*	*	N		NW	S	SE	SW		W	T
Villars	4,264	7,216	*	*	*	*	*	N		NW	S	SE	SW		W	
Wengen	4,187	8,157	*	*	*	*	*	N	NE	NW	S		SW		W	T
Wildhaus	3,395	7,413	*	*	*	*		N			S					
Zermatt	5,315	12,778		*	*	*	*	N	NE	NW	S				W	T
LIECHTENSTEIN																
Malbun	5,248	6,560	*	*					NE				SW			

TOTAL MARKED RUNS, THE LONGEST RUN AND THE LARGEST VERTICAL DESCENT IN FEET

Country/Resort	Total Marked Runs km	Longest Run Km	Vertical Descent in feet
AUSTRIA			
Alpbach	45	8	2,821
Auffach	10	4	3,280
Badgastein*	270	11	4,921
Bad Goisern	10	5	1,640
Bad Hofgastein*	270	11	4,921
Berwang	40	3.5	997
Brand	30	8	3,004
Bürserberg	15	4	3,280
Damüls	30	6	1,905
Dienten	40	4.5	2,560
Dorfgastein*	270	11	4,921
Ellmau	35	5	2,412
Fieberbrunn	60	5	2,624
Filzmoos	32	2.5	1,968
Fontanella/Faschina	18	3	1,640
Fügen/Fügenberg	45	10	4,593
Fulpmes	48	13	5,018
Galtür	40	3.5	1,377
Gargellen	25	7	2,952
Gaschurn	100	10	3,937
Gosau	65	4.5	2,798
Hinterstoder	35	6	1,312
Hinterthal	80	8	1,640
Hintertux/Lanersbach	122	12	5,673
Ischgl	200	14	3,280
Jerzens (Pitztal)	30	5	3,280
Kaprun	130	8	3,713
Kirchberg	157	8	4,101
Kitzbühel	158	8	4,101
Klösterle	50	11	3,558
Laterns/Furx	27	4.8	1,312
Lech	260	5	3,387
Lermoos	30	5	3,937
Mayrhofen	90	6	4,248
Nauders	55	8	4,265
Niederau	40	7	2,624
Oberau	10	1	1,476
Obergurgl/Hochgurgl	110	8.5	4,265
Obertauern	100	7.5	3,280
Obertraun	20	11	4,921
Raggal	25	5	2,624
Saalbach/Hinterglemm	200	8	3,563
St.Anton	260	8.5	4,928
St.Johann in Tirol	60	7	3,800
Schruns	40	11	5,200
Seefeld	25	6	2,952
Serfaus	80	7	3,118
Sölden/Hochsölden	180	12	5,494
Söll	30	6	3,725
Spital am Pyhrn	15	5	2,591
Steinach	12	6	2,952
Stuben	260	4	3,280
Tschagguns	45	10	4,952
Vent	15	5	2,591
Westendorf	45	8	3,477
Windischgarten	17	1.5	
Zell am See	130	8	4,002
Zell am Ziller	45	7	5,363
Zürs	180	5	3,281
*Gastein Valley			
BULGARIA			
Borovets	50	6	3,609
Pamporovo	20	3.8	1,574
FRANCE			
Alpe d'Huez	220	16	6,591
Avoriaz	150	5	3,641
Barèges/La Mongie	91	11	3,609
Chamonix	171	24	9,097
Chatel	82	5	3,214
Courchevel	180	10	4,600
Flaine	150	12	4,743
Font-Romeu	80	10	4,330
Isola 2000	120	6	2,657
La Clusaz	130	6	4,921
La Plagne	208	15	6,562
La Toussuire	180 (area)	5	2,335
Le Corbier	120	5	2,335
Les Arcs	170	15	7,874
Les Deux Alpes	196	13	6,560
Les Houches	50	6.5	3,075
Les Menuires	120	6	3,608
Megève	150	3.4	2,952
Méribel	120	8	3,937
Montgenèvre	60	6.5	2,460
St. Lary	100	4	2,768
Serre Chevalier	250	4.5	4,757
Tignes/Val d'Isère	300	6	3,936
Valmorel	55	5	3,910
Val Thorens	120	3	2,952
GERMANY			
Bayrischzell	40	5	3,056
Berchtesgaden	50	6	3,937
Garmisch Partenkirchen	120	8	3,281
Mittenwald	16	6.5	4,265
Oberammergau	20	4	2,700
Oberstaufen	35	6	2,794
Oberstdorf	42	7	3,622
Reit im Winkl	50	9	3,280
ITALY			
Antermoia	17	6.7	2,296
Aprica	60	7	3,937
Arabba	60	6.5	3,116
Bardonecchia	140	11	4,921
Bormio	80	10	5,533
Cavalese	70	7	3,216
Cervinia	200	22	6,562
Champoluc	43	6	3,281
Clavière	50	4	4,921
Cortina	160	11	5,669
Corvara/Colfosco	150	8	3,937
Courmayeur	100	6	3,281
Foppolo	50	3	1,900
Forni di Sopra	16.9	2.80	3,937
La Thuile	135	11	4,101
La Villa	150	8	3,937
Limone	100	6	3,200
Livigno	100	4	3,280
Macugnaga	40	7.5	4,264
Madesimo	50	5.5	4,215
Madonna di Campiglio	150	7	2,952
Malga Ciapela	26	12	5,969
Passo Tonale	80	4.5	5,872
Piancavallo	30	4.5	1,968
Pila	70	4.5	1,804
San Cassiano	150	6	3,165
Santa Caterina	40	5	3,227
San Martino di Castrozza	80	3.5	2,296
SanVigilio	85	5.5	3,526
Sauze d'Oulx	100	6	3,195
Sella Nevea	20	3.8	2,132
Selva	175	10	3,700
Sestriere	120	7	5,084
ROMANIA			
Poiana Brasov	15	4	2,296
Predeal	6	1.7	1,246
Sinaia	30	5	1,312
SPAIN			
Baqueira Beret	75	3.6	3,300
Cerler	30	7	3,000
Formigal	49	7	3,000
La Molina	40	6	3,590
Masella	53	6.5	3,050
Panticosa		3.5	2,378
Sierra Nevada	60	7.4	4,493
ANDORRA			
Arinsal	28	6	3,314
Grau Roig/Pas de la Casa	73	2.5	2,131
Soldeu	65	8	2,800
SWITZERLAND			
Adelboden	80	8	2,624
Andermatt	65	7.5	5,019
Anzère	40	6	2,827
Arosa	70	6	2,952
Barboleusaz/Gryon	50	5	2,624
Braunwald	25	6	1,968
Champéry	120	4	2,296
Chateau d'Oex/Rossinière	50	6	2,952
Crans/Montana	160	7.5	4,920
Davos/Klosters	315	12	6,675
Engelberg	50	12	6,462
Flims/Laax	220	14	6,562
Flumserberg	50	12	5,577
Grächen	35	5.5	3,280
Grindelwald/Wengen	195	15	4,592
Gstaad (area)	250	14	5,249
Lenzerheide/Valbella	150	9	4,920
Les Diablerets	120	12	5,436
Leysin	60	5	2,952
Mürren	150	15	7,216
Pizol	50	8.5	5,577
St. Moritz/Pontresina	350	10	3,609
Rougemont	50	7.5	3,896
Saas Fee	100	14	5,832
St. Moritz	240	12	5,022
Verbier (4 Vallées)	400	18	8,200
Villars	120	6	2,952
Wildhaus	60	5	4,264
Zermatt	230	15	7,228
LIECHTENSTEIN			
Malbun	20	2.5	1,312

HOW THEY RISE

We give a list of resorts, contained in this Guide, shown in order of height and we also show their top stations in height order. Where resorts are linked e.g. Sölden/Hochsölden we have given the highest station to both resorts.

AUSTRIA

Height of Resort	feet	Height of Top Station	feet
Hochgurgl	7,054	Jerzens (Pitztal)	10,761
Hochsölden	6,857	Hintertux	10,693
Kuhtai	6,500	Fulpmes	10,499
Obergurgl	6,322	Telfes	10,499
Vent	6,202	Mieders	10,499
Obertauern	5,723	Hochgurgl	10,111
Serfaus	5,682	Hochsölden	10,030
Zürs	5,590	Solden	10,030
Galtür	5,796	Kaprun	9,938
Axamer-Lizum	5,150	Ischgl	9,394
Hintertux	4,920	St.Anton	9,222
Fashina	4,920	Ehrwald	9,203
Fügenberg	4,855	Badgastein	8,890
Lech	4,712	Bad Hofgastein	8,890
Damüls	4,680	Serfaus	8,858
Gargellen	4,628	Vent	8,850
Ischgl	4,600	Obergurgl	8,648
Stuben	4,592	Lanersbach	8,202
Nauders	4,590	Lech	8,099
Sölden	4,518	Zürs	8,038
Berwang	4,398	Kühtai	7,950
Lanersbach	4,230	Zell am Ziller	7,428
St. Anton	4,210	Stuben	7,872
Gerlos	4,071	Obertauern	7,872
Seefeld	3,872	Axamer-Lizum	7,670
Fontanella	3,772	Gargellen	7,600
Sonntag	3,700	Galtür	7,544
Jerzens	3,609	Schruns	7,544
Badgastein	3,608	Gaschurn	7,526
Klösterle	3,608	Lienz	7,520
Bichlbach	3,526	Igls	7,370
Dienten	3,502	Mayrhofen	7,283
Filzmoos	3,467	Finkenberg	7,283
Steinach	3,432	Fügenberg	7,216
Hinterthal	3,345	Lermoos	7,215
Brand	3,412	Klösterle	7,166
Raggal	3,332	Obertraun	6,917
Alpbach	3,281	Tschagguns	6,903
Telfes	3,281	Seefeld	6,890
Gaschurn	3,280	Fügen	6,888
Ehrwald	3,267	Saalbach	6,845
Lermoos	3,263	Hinterglemm	6,845
Saalbach	3,260	Gerlos	6,772
Hinterglemm	3,260	Dorfgastein	6,690
Mieders	3,214	Wagrain	6,660
Pertisau	3,083	Fieberbrunn	6,626
Oberau	3,070	Damüls	6,586
Auffach	3,000	Steinach	6,578
Gurtis	2,952	Zell am See	6,578
Igls	2,952	Fontanella	6,562
Laterns	2,952	Kitzbühel	6,562
Furx	2,952	Faschina	6,560
Fulpmes	2,952	Zell am See	6,500
Bürserberg	2,919	Kirchberg	6,440
Bad Hofgastein	2,853	Brand	6,297
Lienz	2,850	Leogang	6,279
Kirchberg	2,830	Auffach	6,235
Finkenberg	2,768	Hinterstoder	6,232
Dorfgastein	2,755	Spital am Pyhrn	6,146
Leogang	2,755	Alpbach	6,102
Wagrain	2,748	Westendorf	6,101
Niederau	2,700	Söll	5,997
Ellmau	2,689	Ellmau	5,997
Fieberbrunn	2,625	Bürserberg	5,994
Kaprun	2,624	Laterns	5,854
Spital am Pyhrn	2,624	Furx	5,854
Westendorf	2,624	St. Johann in Tirol	5,578
Kitzbühel	2,503	Dienten	5,747
Zell am See	2,490	Berwang	5,395
Gosau	2,460	Niederau	5,333
Söll	2,275	Filzmoos	5,248
Schruns	2,275	Gosau	5,248
Tschagguns	2,275	Sonntag	5,149
St. Johann in Tirol	2,180	Pertisau	4,865
Hinterstoder	2,132	Gurtis	4,592
Mayrhofen	2,067	Hinterthal	4,428
Obertraun	1,968	Raggal	4,264
Windischgarsten	1,968	Bichlbach	4,150
Zell am Ziller	1,902	Oberau	4,050
Fügen	1,853	Bad Goisern	3,280
Bad Goisern	1,640	Windischgarsten	2,821

BULGARIA

Height of Resort	feet	Height of Top Station	feet
Pamporovo	5,345	Borovets	8,830
Borovets	4,300	Pamporovo	6,335

FRANCE

Height of Resort	feet	Height of Top Station	feet
Val Thorens	7,544	Argentière	12,486
Tignes	6,825	Chamonix	12,604
Isola	6,560	Les Deux Alpes	11,673
Alpe d'Huez	6,101	Tignes	11,480
Les Menuires	6,086	Val d'Isère	11,480
Montgenèvre	6,069	Alpe d'Huez	10,988
Courchevel	6,013	La Plagne	10,663
Val d'Isère	5,965	Les Arcs	10,583

HOW THEY RISE

FRANCE

Height of Resort	feet	Height of Top Station	feet
La Mongie	5,905	Val Thorens	10,496
La Toussuire	5,905	Méribel	10,496
Avoriaz	5,904	Les Menuires	10,496
La Plagne	5,904	Courchevel	10,496
Font-Romeu	5,895	Serre Chevalier	9,100
Les Deux Alpes	5,412	Valfrejus	8,979
Flaine	5,250	Isola 2000	8,563
Les Arcs	5,249/6,560	Barèges	8,400
Le Corbier	5,085	La Mongie	8,400
Valfrejus	5,083	Montgenèvre	8,326
Meribel	4,756	Flaine	8,150
Valloire	4,692	St.Lary	7,955
Valmorel	4,592	Valmorel	7 884
Serre Chevalier	4,500	La Toussuire	7 874
Barèges	4,265	La Clusaz	7 872
Argentière	4,110	Valloire	7 720
Chatel	3,937	Avoriaz	7 710
Les Gets	3,834	Le Corbier	7 415
Megève	3,617	Font-Romeu	7 205
La Clusaz	3,608	Chatel	6 890
Chamonix	3,389	Megève	6 630
Les Houches	3,280	Les Houches	6 455
St. Jean d'Aulps	2,962	St. Gervais	6 420
St. Lary	2,722	Les Gets	6 069
St. Gervais	2,685	St. Jean d'Aulps	5 905

GERMANY

Height of Resort	feet	Height of Top Station	feet
Mittenwald	3,018	Garmisch-Partenk.	9,730
Oberstauten	2,808	Oberstdorf	7,362
Oberstdorf	2,756	Mittenwald	7,362
Bayrischzell	2,630	Bayrischzell	6,562
Oberammergau	2,624	Reit im Winkl	6,069
Garmisch-Partenk.	2,362	Berchtesgaden	5,903
Reit im Winkl	2,296	Oberstaufen	5,577
Berchtesgaden	1,837	Oberammergau	5,524

ITALY

Height of Resort	feet	Height of Top Station	feet
Cervinia	6,760	Cervinia	11,500
Sestriere	6,666	Malga Ciapela	10,712
Passo Tonale	6,168	Cortina	10,543
Abetone	6,105	Bormio	9,905
Solda	6,068	Campitello	9,684
Livigno	5,958	Canazei	9,684
Pila	5,800	Courmayeur	9,843
Clavière	5,774	Arabba	9,676
Santa Caterina	5,697	Madesimo	9,461
Sansicario	5,576	Livigno	9,184
Champoluc	5,478	Sauze d'Oulx	9,175
Colfosco	5,401	Sestriere	9,175
Arabba	5,254	Sansicario	9,175
San Cassiano	5,159	Santa Caterina	9,135
Corvara	5,143	San Martino	9,053
Selva	5,128	Bardonecchia	9,022
Madesimo	5,085	Passo Tonale	9,016
Madonna	5,084	Gressoney	9,000
Sauze d'Oulx	4,950	Macugnaga	9,000
Antermoia	4,920	Champoluc	8,940
Foppolo	4,920	La Thuile	8,667
San Martino	4,920	Pila	8,660
Mera	4,900	Madonna	8,640
La Villa	4,870	Aprica	8,448
Canazei	4,808	Selva	8,264
La Thuile	4,757	Folgarida	8,213
Campitello	4,752	Solda	8,200
Malga Ciapela	4,743	Cavalese	7,874
Marilleva	4,593	San Vigilio	7,461
Gressoney	4,450	Antermoia	7,216
Macugnaga	4,352	Colfosco	7,212
Bardonecchia	4,304	Corvara	7,212
Piancavallo	4,265	Marilleva	7,152
Folgarida	4,260	Foppolo	7,101
Bormio	4,018	Abetone	7,085
Cortina	4,018	Caspoggio	7,072
Courmayeur	4,015	Limone	7,054
San Vigilio	3,939	Monte Bondone	6,888
Monte Campione	3,937	La Villa	6,812
Aprica	3,863	Forni di Sopra	6,761
Sella Nevea	3,773	Clavière	6,676
Caspoggio	3,504	San Cassiano	6,570
Nevegal	3,382	Piancavallo	6,562
Cavalese	3,300	Lurisia	6,560
Limone	3,300	Monte Campione	6,412
Monte Bondone	3,280	Forni di Sopra	2,975
Mera	5,900	Tarvisio	5,798
Lurisia	2,624	Sella Nevea	5,793
Tarvisio	2,460	Nevegal	5,471

SPAIN

Height of Resort	feet	Height of Top Station	feet
Sierra Nevada	6,888	Sierra Nevada	0,308
Masella	5,258	Cerler	8,628
Cerler	4,936	Masella	8,331
Baqueira Beret	4,920	La Molina	8,315
Fornigal	4,920	Baqueira Beret	8,267
La Molina	4,726	Formigal	7,920
Panticosa	3,821	Panticosa	6,209

ANDORRA

Height of Resort	feet	Height of Top Station	feet
Grau Roig/Pas de C.	6,725	Grau Roig/Pas de C.	9,350
Arcalis	6,364	Arinsal	8,530
Pal	6,069	Arcalis	8,530
Soldeu/El Tarter	5,900	Soldeu/El Tarter	8,400
Arinsal	5,085	Pal	7,769

SWITZERLAND

Height of Resort	feet	Height of Top Station	feet
St. Moritz	6,088	Zermatt	12,778
Arosa	6,000	Saas Fee	11,500
Pontresina	5,972	Verbier	10,916
Saas Fee	5,905	Haute Nendaz	10,916
Bivio	5,825	Mayens-De-Riddes	10,916
Siviez	5,675	Veysonnaz	10,916
Mürren	5,362	St.Moritz	10,837
Zermatt	5,315	Engelberg	9,906
Grächen	5,313	Flims	9,902
San Bernardino	5,249	Laax	9,902
Malbun	5,248	Pontresina	9,827
Davos	5,118	Andermatt	9,714
Valbella	5,052	Crans/Montana	9,840
Verbier	4,921	Les Diablerets	9,840
Mayens-De-Riddes	4,921	Villars	8,840
Crans/Montana	4,920	Mürren	9,748
Anzère	4,920	Grächen	9,528
Lenzerheide	4,822	Lenzerheide	9,397
Les Mosses	4,756	Valbella	9,397
Andermatt	4,738	Davos	9,262
Morgins	4,593	Klosters	9,262
Flumserberg	4,592	Samnaun	8,962
Haute Nendaz	4,478	Arosa	8,658
Adelboden	4,438	Bivio	8,399
Braunwald	4,264	San Bernardino	8,283
Villars	4,264	Grindelwald	8,157
Wengen	4,187	Wengen	8,157
Leysin	4,134	Anzère	7,937
Veysonnaz	4,045	Les Mosses	7,708
Klosters	3,980	Adelboden	7,644
Barboleusaz	3,970	Lenk	7,644
Les Diablerets	3,936	Unterwasser	7,413
Flims	3,615	Wildhaus	7,413
Lenk	3,608	Champéry	7,400
St. Cergue	3,600	Rougemount	7,399
Champèry	3,450	Flumserberg	7,287
Engelberg	3,444	Pizol/Wangs	7,283
Wildhaus	3,395	Leysin	7,218
Grindelwald	3,393	Morgins	6,890
Laax	3,346	Barboleusaz	6,626
Gstaad	3,308	Malbun	6,560
Chateau d'Oex	3,280	Gstaad	6,461
Rossinière	3,280	Braunwald	6,232
Rougemount	3,175	Chateau d'Oex	5,905
Unterwasser	2,985	Rossinière	5,905
Alt St. Johann	2,952	St. Cergue	5,600
Pizol/Wangs	1,755	Alt St. Johann	5,412

LINKED & NEARBY RESORTS

On the left we show resorts directly linked by lifts and on the right nearby resorts which, in most cases, are covered by the area lift pass.

AUSTRIA

Resort	Linked with	Nearby Resorts
Badgastein	Bad Hofgastein	Dorfgastein
Bad Goisern	–	Obertraun
Brand	–	Bürserberg
Damüls	–	Fontanella/Faschina
Dienten	Hinterthal	–
Fulpmes	–	Mieders, Telfes
Gargellen	–	Gaschcurn, Schruns, Tschagguns
Gosau	Rusbach	–
Ischgl	Samnaun (Switz.)	Galtür
Kaprun	–	Zell am See
Kitzbühel	Kirchberg, Jochberg, Pass Thurn	
Lech	Zürs	St. Anton, St.Christoph, Stuben
Lermoos	–	Biberwier, Ehrwald
Mayrhofen	Finkenberg	Lanersbach, Hintertux
Niederau	–	Oberau, Auffach
Obergurgl	–	Hoghgurgl, Sölden/ Hochsölden
Saalbach	Hinterglemm, Leogang	Zell am See, Kaprun
St. Anton	St. Christoph, Stuben	Lech, Zürs
Serfaus	–	Fiss
Sölden	Hochsölden	Vent. Obergurgl, Hochgurgl,
Söll	Going, Ellmau, Hopgarten,Brixen i Thale	Westendorf
Zell am See	–	Kaprun, Saalbach, Hinterglemm

FRANCE

Resort	Linked with	Nearby Resorts
Abondance	10 resorts, Portes du Soleil, see page 195	–
Alpe d'Huez	Vaujany, Oz en Oisans, Villard-Reculas, Huez en Oisans, Auris en Oisans	–
Avoriaz	10 resorts, Portes du Soleil, see page 190	–
Chamonix	Courmayeur (Italy)	Argentière, Le Tour, Les Houches
Chatel	10 resorts, Portes du Soleil, see page 192	–
Courchevel	Méribel, Les Menuires, Val Thorens, St. Martin de Belleville, La Tania	
Flaine	Samoëns, Morillon, Les Carroz Sixt	
Le Corbier	La Toussuire, St. Jean D'Arves	St. Sorlin
La Plagne	Les Coches, Montchavin, Montalbert, Champagny	–
Les Gets	10 resorts, Portes du Soleil, see page 192	–
Megève	St. Gervais, Combloux, St. Nicolas de Veroce	–
Montgenèvre	Italy: Clavière, Cesana, Sansicario, Sestriere, Sauze d'Oulx	–
Morzine	10 resorts, Portes du Soleil, see page 190	–
Val d'Isère	Tignes	
Valmorel	St. François, Longchamp	–

ITALY

Resort	Linked with	Nearby Resorts
Bormio	–	Santa Caterina, Livigno
Cavalese	–	Pampeago, Obereggen
Cervinia	Valtournanche, Zermatt (Switz.)	
Courmayeur	Chamonix (France)	–
Madonna di C.	Folgarida, Marilleva	–
Selva	Corvara, Colfosco, La Villa, San Cassiano, Ortisei, Santa Christina, Canazei, Arabba, Campitello	
Sestriere	Sauze d'Oulx, Sansicario, Cesana, Clavière, Montgenèvre (France)	

SWITZERLAND

Resort	Linked with	Nearby Resorts
Adelboden	Lenk	–
Andermatt	–	Hospental, Realp
Champéry	10 resorts, Portes du Soleil, see page 194	–
Champoussin	10 resorts, Portes du Soleil, see page 194	–
Chateau d'Oex	–	Rossinière, Rougemont, Saanen, Gstaad, Schönried Saanemöser, Zweisimmen, St. Stephan
Davos	Klosters	–
Flims	Laax, Falera	–
Grindelwald	Wengen	Mürren
Gstaad	Schönried,Saanenmöser, Zweisimmen, St Stephan, Saanen,Rougemont	Rossinière, Chateau d'Oex,
Les Crosets	10 resorts, Portes du Soleil, see page 195	–
Les Diablerets	Villars, Barboleusaz, Les Chaux	–
Morgins	10 resorts, Portes du Soleil, see page 194	–
Mürren	–	Grindelwald, Wengen
Pontresina	–	Celerina, Samedan, St. Moritz, Sils, Silvaplana
Saas Fee	–	Saas Grund
St. Moritz	Celerina	Pontresina, Samedan, Silvaplana, Sils
Torgon	10 resorts, Portes du Soleil, see page 195	–
Verbier	Le Châble, Bruson, Mayens-de-Riddes, Haute Nendaz, Siviez, Veysonnaz,Thyon 2000	
Wildhaus	Unterwasser, Alt St. Johann	–
Zermatt	Cervinia (Italy)	

ARTIFICIAL SNOW INSTALLATIONS

Of the resorts published in this Guide we show those that have snow cannons in operation. Unless stated otherwise they operate from the village area to the height shown along with the total length of the runs covered.

Country/Resort	Village Height Feet	To a Height of Feet	Total Length of Runs covered Km
AUSTRIA			
Alpbach	3,281	6,233	20
Badgastein (whole valley)	3,608	6,233	38
Berwang	4,398	5,262	2
Brand	2,919	5,577	8
Bürserberg	2,919	4,101	3
Finkenberg	2,768	6,873	2.5
Ellmau	2,689	5,085	4.5
Fieberbrunn	2,625	4,265	6
Filzmoos	3,467	5,577	2.5
Finkenberg	2,268	6,873	20
Gaschurn	3,280	7,546	15
Gosau	2,460	3,937	4
Hinterstoder	2,132	3,937	10
Ischgl	4,600	7,546	(100 cannons)
Lech	4,712	8,005	10
Mayrhofen	2,067	7,382	12
Nauders	4,590	8,858	30
Obergurgl	6,322	7,054	8.4
Obertauern	5,723	7,168	10
St. Anton	4,210	7,168	18
St. Johann in Tirol	2,180	5,577	7
Seefeld	3,872	6,890	14
Serfaus	4,682	7,710	60
Sölden/Hochsölden	4,518	7,447	10
Söll	2,275	4,593	12
Steinach	3,432	5,905	9
Westendorf	2,624	5,806	12
Zell am See	2,490	5,249	34
FRANCE			
Alpe d'Huez	6,101	8,858	22
Chamonix	3,389	4,626	(45 cannons)
Courchevel	6,013	8,858	66
Flaine	5,250	7,218	(20 cannons)
Font-Romeu	5,895	7,218	54
La Plagne	5,904		(65 cannons)
Les Arcs	5,905	6,562	7
Les Deux Alpes	5,412	6,890	4.5
Les Menuires	6,068	9,350	16
Méribel	4,756	8,858	17.1
Montgenèvre	6,069	5,249	6
St. Lary	2,722/5511	6,069	7.5
Serre Chevalier	4,500	7,218	13
Tignes	6,825	9,843	(201 cannons)
Val d'Isère	5,965	8,202	(125 cannons)
Valmorel	4,592	6,003	6
Val Thorens	7,544	9,843	(72 cannons)
ITALY			
Bardonecchia	4,304	7,218	13
Bormio	4,018	9,843	6
Cavalese	3,300	7,874	45
Cervinia	6,760	7,913	7
Cortina	4,018	6,890	51
Corvara/Colfosco	5,143	7,216	40
Courmayeur	4,015	6,562	(316 cannons)
Foppolo	4,920	6,890	3
Forni di Sopra	2,975	4,921	8
La Thuile	4,757	8,202	10
Limone	3,300	4,921	8
Livigno	5,958	8,878	12
Macugnaga	4,352	6,562	(30 cannons)
Madesimo	5,085	9,180	9.5
Madonna di Campiglio	5,084	8,202	25
Piancavallo	4,265	5,413	10
Pila	4,265	7,540	10
S. Cassiano	5,159	6,570	40
S. Martino di C.	4,920	7,218	25
Santa Caterina	5,697	8,878	20
San Vigilio	3,939	7,461	60
Sauze d'Oulx	4,950	6,562	5
Selva Val Gardena	5,128	7,218	80
Sestriere	6,666	9.175	85
SWITZERLAND			
Crans/Montana	4,920	7,218	3
Engelberg	3,444	5905/7,874	3
Grächen	5,313	7,453	15
Grindelwald	3,393	7,218	15
Haute Nendaz	4,478	4,921	3
Klosters	3,908	5,249	4.3
Leysin	4,134	6,719	(16 cannons)
Pontresina	5,972	8,202	4.5
Saas Fee	5,905	6,069	3
St. Moritz	6,088	9,772	15
Verbier	4,921	7,218	3
Wengen	4,187	7,546	10
Zermatt	5,315	10,181	17

NORDIC SKIING (LANGLAUF)

A sport Scandinavians enjoy in their thousands has spread in a remarkable fashion during the last few years. Nordic skiing should not be confused with ski mountaineering as the trails are gentler and near the resort. The equipment is different, skis being narrower and lighter, boots more flexible and bindings allow the heel to be raised. Whilst Norway is by far the best country for this type of skiing, for example, within 20 minutes of Oslo there are some 2,000km of marked trails, 150km floodlit, many resorts in the Alps have realised the appeal and enjoyment of Nordic Skiing. In the following charts we outline the resorts which cater to this type of skiing.

Instruction: One requires little instruction for this type of skiing. We understand that all the resorts listed provide instruction either in class or privately.

Hire of Equipment: We understand that all the resorts mentioned hire special skis, sticks and boots. Whilst at some resorts the hire rate are cheaper than those for Alpine skiing, others are higher.

MARKED & PREPARED NORDIC SKIING (LANGLAUF) TRAILS IN THE ALPS

Country/Resort	Total Marked Trails in km.
AUSTRIA	
Alpbach	17
Bad Aussee	180
Badgastein	35
Bad Goisern	50
Bad Hofgastein	37
Berwang	15
Brand	30
Bürserberg	14
Dorfgastein	18
Ellmau	10
Fieberbrunn	40
Filzmoos	35
Fügen/Fügenberg	40
Fulpmes	130
Galtür	45
Gargellen	10
Gaschurn	45
Gosau	45
Gurtis	5.8
Hinterglemm	18
Hinterstoder	23
Hinterthal	38
Hintertux	18
Ischgl	48
Jerzens (Pitztal)	2.8
Kaprun	200
Kirchberg	77
Kitzbühel	120
Klösterle	14
Lanersbach	18
Laterns/Furx	27
Lech	18
Lermoos	45
Mayrhofen	20
Nauders	40
Obergurgl	13
Obertauern	17
Obertraun	15
Raggal	10
Saalbach	18
St. Anton	40
St. Johann in Tirol	74
Schruns	18
Seefeld	200
Serfaus	60
Sölden/Hochsölden	16
Söll	35
Spital am Pyhrn	35
Tschagguns	21
Vent	4
Westendorf	35
Wildschönau	38
Windischgarsten	60
Zell am See	200
Zell am Ziller	21
Zürs	19
BULGARIA	
Borovets	63
Pamporovo	25
FRANCE	
Alpe d'Huez	50
Avoriaz	45
Barèges/La Mongie	45
Chamonix	40
Chatel	25
Courchevel	50
Flaine	15
Font-Romeu	80
Isola 2000	5
La Clusaz	70
La Plagne	89
Le Corbier	35
Les Arcs	15
Les Deux Alpes	20
Les Houches	35
Les Menuires	30
Megève	70
Méribel	33
Montgenèvre	20
St. Lary	15
Serre Chevalier	45
Tignes	30
Val d'Isère	20
Valmorel	22
GERMANY	
Bayrischzell	50
Berchtesgaden	50
Garmisch-P.	200
Mittenwald	17
Oberammergau	90
Oberstaufen	120
Oberstdorf	60
Reit im Winkl	80

Country/Resort	Total Marked Trails in km.
ITALY	
Bardonecchia	15
Bormio	15
Caspoggio	40
Cavalese	70
Cervinia	5
Champoluc	30
Cortina	58
Corvara/Colfosco	40
Courmayeur	30
Forni di Sopra	15
La Villa	40
Limone	8
Livigno	40
Lurisia	12
Macugnaga	16
Madesimo	4
Madonna di C.	28
Mera	22
Passo Tonale	12
Piancavallo	20
Pila	29
San Cassiano	40
Santa Caterina	15
San Martino di C.	29
San Vigilio	25
Sauze d'Oulx	3
Sella Nevea	6
Selva	91
Sestriere	35
ROMANIA	
Poiana Brasov	3-4
Predeal	6
Sinaia	30
SPAIN	
Baqueira Beret	7
Cerler	5
La Molina	5
SWITZERLAND	
Adelboden	40
Andermatt	20
Anzère	22
Arosa	27
Crans/Montana	50
Barboleusaz/Gryon	31
Braunwald	22
Champéry	7
Chateau d'Oex	61
Davos	75
Engelberg	47
Flims	60
Flumserberg	20
Grächen	16
Grindelwald	33
Gstaad	118
Haute-Nendaz	28
Klosters	50
Laax	100
Lenzerheide/Valbella	50
Les Diablerets	30
Les Mosses	44
Leysin	49
Morgins	15
Mürren	2
Les Arcs	15
Pizol	20
Pontresina	150
Les Houches	35
Rougemont	40
Saas Fee	8
St. Moritz	150
San Bernardino	14
Montgenèvre	20
Verbier	30
Veysonnaz	10
Serre Chevalier	45
Villars	46
Wildhaus	23
Zermatt (Tasch)	42
LIECHTENSTEIN	
Malbun	19

SKI SCHOOL RATES

For Children see Ski Kindergarten Rates - Page 279

Country/Resort	Class Instruction Consecutive Days 6 Days 4 Hours Daily unless stated otherwise
AUSTRIA	**A.S.**
Alpbach	1250 (5 days)
Badgastein	1690
Bad Goisern	1100 (5 days)
Bad Hofgastein	1340
Berwang	1370 (5 days)
Brand	1100 (3 hours - 5 days)
Bürserberg	1050* (3 hours - 5 days)
Damüls	1280 (5 days)
Dienten	1440 (5 days)
Dorfgastein	1450
Ellmau	1280
Fieberbrunn	1450
Filzmoos	1460
Finkenberg	1300/1370
Fontanella/Faschina	1300 (5 days)
Fügen/Hochfügen	1260
Fulpmes	1280*
Galtür	1450
Gargellen	1400 (5 days)
Gaschurn	1490*
Gosau	1200*(5 days)
Hinterstoder	1200 (5 days)
Hintertux	1760
Ischgl	1380/1450*
Kaprun	1150
Kirchberg	1400
Kitzbühel	1400
Lanersbach	1760
Lech am Arlberg	1570
Leogang	1450*
Lermoos	1270*
Mayrhofen	1490
Nauders	1340
Obergurgl	1590
Obertauern	1450
Saalbach/Hinterglemm	1550*
St. Anton	1580
St. Johann in Tirol	1390
Schruns	1950
Seefeld	1400*
Serfaus	1550*
Sölden/Hochsölden	1600/2300
Söll	1900
Spital am Pyhrn	1200 (5 days)
Steinach	1200
Tschagguns	1400
Wagrain	1450
Westendorf	1350/1380
Wildschönau	1300
Zell am See	1550
Zell am Ziller	1640*
Zürs	1980
FRANCE	**Francs**
Alpe d'Huez	920* (5.5 hours)
Avoriaz	800 (5 hours)
Barèges	480 (3 hours)
Chamonix	770*
Courchevel	1350
Flaine	700
Font-Romeu	400 (2 hours)
Isola 2000	520* (2 hours)
Le Corbier	440* (2.5 hours)
La Clusaz	750*
La Plagne	560* (2 hours)
La Toussuire	475 (2.5 hours)
Les Angles	900
Les Arcs	890* (5 hours)
Les Deux Alpes	595
Les Gets	390 (3 hours)
Les Houches	810*

* 1996/97 rate; where two rates are shown the first is low season rate

Country/Resort	Class Instruction Consecutive Days 6 Days 4 Hours Daily unless stated otherwise
FRANCE	**Francs**
Les Menuires	750 (3 hours)
Megève	780/980
Meribel	958* (5 hours)
Montgenèvre	515
Morzine	800*
St. Lary	446/617 (2 hours)
Serre Chevalier	800
Tignes	585* (3 hours - 5 days)
Val d'Isère	680 (3 hours)
Valfrejus	760/800 (5 hours)
Valmorel	585 (2.5 hours)
Val Thorens	690 (3 hours)
ITALY	**Lire**
Bardonecchia	170,000 (2 hours)
Bormio	150,000 (2.5 hours)
Canazei/Campitello	165,000 (3 hours)
Cavalese	130,000 (2 hours)
Cervinia	190,000 (2.45 hours)
Champoluc	190,000 (3 hours)
Clavière	140,000 (2 hours)
Cortina	270,000 (2.5 hours)
Corvara/Colfosco	195,000* (3 hours)
Courmayeur	190,000* (3 hours)
La Thuile	163,000 (2.5 hours)
La Villa	195,000* (3 hours)
Limone	130,000/200,000* (2 hours)
Livigno	105,000/120,000 (2 hours)
Madesimo	110,000/130,000 (2 hours)
Madonna	216,000 (3 hours)
Passo Tonale	115,000 (2 hours)
S. Caterina	130,000 (2 hours)
S. Martino	190,000* (3 hours)
San Vigilio	180,000/200,000*
Sauze d'Oulx	180,000* (3 hours)
Sella Nevea	250,000
Sestriere	220,000 (3 hours)
San Cassiano	195,000* (3 hours)
Selva	230,000
SWITZERLAND	**S. Francs**
Adelboden	170 (5 days)
Andermatt	150* (5 days)
Arosa	185* (5 days)
Anzère	125 (3 hours - 5 days)
Braunwald	170 (5 days)
Champéry	250 (6 hours - 5 days)
Chateau d'Oex	196
Crans/Montana	155 (3 hours - 6 days)
Davos	210
Engelberg	358 (5 days)
Flims	156
Flumserberg	175
Grächen	157 (2 hours - 5 days)
Grindelwald	192* (5 days)
Gstaad - Saanenland	200
Haute Nendaz	234 (5 hours - 5 days)
Klosters	250 (4.5 hours)
Lenzerheide	195/298 (5 days)
Les Diablerets	189*
Leysin	130 (2 hours)
Mayens-de-Riddes	130 (3 hours - 5 days)
Mürren	123 (2 hours)
Pontresina	190 (5 days)
Saas Fee	163* (3 hours - 5 days)
St. Moritz	185
Verbier	238
Veysonnaz	127 (3 hours - 5 days)
Villars	110* (2 hours)
Wengen	204 (3 hours)
Wildhaus	140
Zermatt	215
Malbun (Liechtenstein)	150 (5 days)

LIFT PASSES ALLOWING UNLIMITED USE OF RESORT LIFTS

The rates in this table allow unlimited use of the resort lifts for a period of 6 or 13 days (unless stated otherwise) during high or low season. Where resorts are linked the price of the area ski pass is given. The low season period at most resorts is normally the last 3 weeks in January and the first week in February. Some of the lower resorts may allow the reduced rate after mid March. Nearly all resorts allow substantial reductions for children. One of the best arrangements for family groups is the 4 Valley ski pass (Verbier/Haute Nendaz etc), a family of 4 with 2 children under 16 years only require 2 lift passes. These must be purchased at the resorts concerned.

Country/Resort	**Low Season**		**High Season**	
	6 Days	**13 Days**	**6 Days**	**13 Days**
AUSTRIA	**A.S.**	**A.S.**	**A.S.**	**A.S.**
Alpbach	1,200	1,970	1,380	2,160
Badgastein	1,690+	3,030+	1,990+	3,580+
Bad Goisern	890*	1,610 (10 days)*	890*	1,610 (10 days)*
Bad Hofgastein	1,690+	3,030+	1,990+	3,580+
Berwang	1,650+++++	2,720+++++	1,795+++++	3,020+++++
Brand	1,350	2,195	1,690	2,740
Bürserberg	1,350	2,195	1,690	2,740
Damüls	1,390	2,405	1,545	2,670
Dienten	1,420	2,495	1,580	2,715
Dorfgastein	1,690+	3,030+	1,990+	3,580+
Ellmau	1,455	2,450	1,455	2,450
Fieberbrunn	1,430	2,415	1,590	2,680
Finkenberg	1,965++	3,650++	1,965++	3,650++
Filzmoos	1,695++++++	2,860++++++	1,785++++++	3,010++++++
Fügen/Fügenberg	1,965++	3,650++	1,965++	3,650++
Fulpmes	1,790	3,170	2,010	3,170
Galtür	1,360	2,480	1,585	2,850
Gargellen	1,710+++	3,020+++	1,940+++	3,430+++
Gaschurn	1,710+++	3,020+++	1,940+++	3,430+++
Gosau	1,105*	1,865*	1,390*	2,340*
Hinterstoder	1,250*	2,320*	1,390*	2,575*
Hintertux	1,965++	3,650++	1,965++	3,650++
Ischgl	1,685*	2,945*	1,800*	3,230*
Kaprun/Zell am See	1,820	3,090	1,970	3,320
Kirchberg/Kitzbühel	1,700	3,060	1,890	3,400
Lanersbach	1,965++	3,650++	1,965++	3,650++
Lech am Arlberg	1,920++++	3,360++++	2,130++++	3,730++++
Lermoos	1,615+++++	2,720+++++	1,795+++++	3,020+++++
Mayrhofen	1,965++	3,650++	1,965++	3,650++
Nauders	1,490	2,695	1,745	3,090
Obertauern	1,610	2,750	1,745	3,270
Obergurgl	1,840	3,030	2,090	3,370
Saalbach/Hinterglemm/Leogang	1,650*	2,715*	1,940*	3,160*
St.Anton am Arlberg	1,920++++	3,330++++	2,130++++	3,730++++
St. Johann in Tirol	1,420	2,515	1,620	2,775
Schruns/Tschagguns	1,710+++	3,020	1,940+++	3,430+++
Seefeld	1,615+++++	2,720+++++	1,795+++++	3,020+++++
Serfaus	1,910	3,325	2,140	3,820
Sölden/Hochsölden	1,820	3,030	2,100	3,430
Söll	1,455	2,450	1,455	2,450
Spital am Pyhrn	1,250	2,320	1,390	2,575
Stuben	1,920++++	3,330++++	2,130++++	3,730++++
Wagrain	1,695++++++	2,860++++++	1,785++++++	3,010++++++
Westendorf	1,480	2,520	1,480	2,520
Wildschönau	1,540	2,615	1,540	2,615
Zell am Ziller	1,965++	3,650++	1,965++	3,650++
Zürs am Arlberg	1,920++++	3,360++++	2,130++++	3,730++++

*1996/97 Rates; + Gastein Valley Pass; ++ Ziller Valley Pass including glacier; +++ Montafon Pass; ++++ Arlberg Pass; +++++ 'Happy Ski' Card covering 10 Resorts; ++++++ Sportwelt Amadé Pass covering 8 resorts

FRANCE	**Francs**	**Francs**	**Francs**	**Francs**
Alpe d'Huez	1,000	1,697	1,000	1,697
Avoriaz	928+	1,614+	928+	1,614+
Chamonix	930	1,640	930	1,640
Chatel	928+	1,614+	928+	1,614+
Courchevel	1,080+++	1,903+++	1,080+++	1,903+++
Flaine	860++++	1,630++++	860++++	1,630++++
Font-Romeu	590*	1,240*	760*	1,600*
Isola 2000	525*	987*	656*	1,234*
La Clusaz				
La Plagne	985*		985*	
La Toussuire/Le Corbier	550	1,031	700	1,290
Les Arcs	960*	1,710*	960*	1,710*
Les Deux Alpes	601	1,339	890	1,785
Les Gets	928+	1,614+	928+	1,614+
Les Houches	930	1,640	930	1,640
Les Menuires	1,080+++	1,930+++	1,080+++	1,930+++
Megève	731*	1,279*	840*	1,470*
Méribel	1,080+++	1,903+++	1,080+++	1,903+++
Montgenèvre	650	1,070	650	1,070
Morzine	928+	1,614+	928+	1,614+
St. Lary	650		700	
Serre Chevalier	875*	1,475*	875*	1,475*

LIFT PASSES ALLOWING UNLIMITED USE OF RESORT LIFTS

Country/Resort	Low Season 6 Days	High Season 13 Days	6 Days	13 Days
FRANCE	**Francs**	**Francs**	**Francs**	**Francs**
Tignes/Val d'Isère	1,005	1,820	1,005	1,820
Valfrejus	502	942	590	1,108
Valmorel	682		857	
Val Thorens	1,080+++	1,903+++	1,080+++	1,903+++

*1996/97 Rates; + Portes du Soleil Pass; +++ Trois Vallées Pass; ++++ Grand Massif

Country/Resort	Low Season 6 Days	High Season 13 Days	6 Days	13 Days
GERMANY	**D.M.**	**D.M.**	**D.M.**	**D.M.**
Garmisch-Partenkirchen	260	438	260	438
Oberstaufen	145	245 (12 days)	145	245 (12 days)
Oberstdorf	239+	388+	251+	408+
Reit im Winkl	223	378	248	420

+ Area Pass

Country/Resort	Low Season 6 Days	High Season 13 Days	6 Days	13 Days
ITALY	**Lire**	**Lire**	**Lire**	**Lire**
Arabba	243,000+*	421,000+*	279,000+*	484,000+*
Bardonecchia	162,000	400,000(12 days)	192,000	400,000(12 days)
Bormio	220,000++	335,000++	245,000++	375,000++
Canazei/Campitello	243,000++++	421,000++++	279,000++++	484.000++++
Cavalese	210,000	360,000	248,000	431,000
Cervinia	260,000	405,000	260,000	405,000
Clavière	210,000+++*	364,000+++*	230,000+++*	428,000+++*
Cortina	243,000+*	421,000+*	279,000+	484,000+
Corvara/Colfosco	243,000+*	421,000+*	279,000+	484,000+
Courmayeur	212,000*	367,000*	245,000*	453,000*
Forni di Sopra	155,000	337,000	180,000	393,000
La Thuile/La Rosiere (France)	200,000*	320,000*	225,000*	384,000*
La Villa	243,000+*	421,000+*	279,000+	484,000+
Limone	170,000*	280,900*	190,000*	305,000*
Livigno	220,000		245,000	
Madonna di Campiglio	230,000*	376,000*	250,000*	417,000*
Madesimo	220,000		230,000	
Piancavallo	156,000*	338,500*	180,000*	390,000*
Sauze d'Oulx	210,000+++*	364,000+++*	230,000+++*	428,000+++*
S. Caterina	220,000++	335,000++	245,000++	375,000++
San Cassiano	243,000+*	421,500+*	279,000+	484,000+
Sansicario	210,000+++*	364,000+++*	230,000+++*	428,000+++*
San Martino				
San Vigilio	219,000*	380,000*	252,000*	436,000*
Selva Val Gardena	243,000+*	421,000+*	279,000+	484,000+
Sestriere	210,000+++*	364,000+++*	230,000+++*	428,000+++*

*1996/97 Rates; + Dolomiti Superski Pass; ++ Area Pass; +++ 'Milky Way' Pass (6 Resorts)++++Val Di Fassa Pass

Country/Resort	Low Season 6 Days	High Season 13 Days	6 Days	13 Days
SWITZERLAND	**S.Francs**	**S.Francs**	**S.Francs**	**S.Francs**
Adelboden/Lenk	204	340	204	340
Andermatt	187*	291*	187*	291*
Anzère	173*	284*	173*	284*
Arosa	187	295	219	347
Braunwald	168*	295*	168*	295*
Champéry	210+++++*	372+++++*	210+++++*	372+++++*
Chateau d'Oex	233+	389+	233+	389+
Crans/Montana	255	413	255	413
Davos/Klosters	207++	444++	259++	444++
Engelberg	193	263	193	263
Flumserberg	188	309	188	309
Flims/Laax	270	450	270	450
Grächen	201	343	201	343
Grindelwald	232+++	380+++	232+++	380+++
Gstaad-Saanenland	233+	389+	233+	389+
Haute-Nendaz	282++++++	487++++++	282++++++	487++++++
Lenzerheide	219	358	219	358
Les Diablerets	233++++	389++++	233++++	389+++++
Leysin	233++++	389++++	233++++	389++++
Mayens-de-Riddes	282++++++	487++++++	282++++++	487++++++
Morgins	210+++++*	372+++++*	210+++++*	372+++++*
Mürren	232+++	380+++	232+++	380+++
Pontresina/St.Moritz	258	430	258	430
Rougemont	233+	389+	233+	389+
Saas Fee	260*	465*	260*	465*
Verbier	282++++++	487++++++	282++++++	487++++++
Veysonnaz	282++++++	487++++++	282++++++	487++++++
Villars	233++++	389++++	233++++	389++++
Wengen	232+++	380+++	232+++	380+++
Wildhaus	184	291	184	291
Zermatt	296	526	296	526
LIECHTENSTEIN				
Malbun	110	125(10 days)	136	170(10 days)

*1996/97 Rates; + Gstaad Super Ski Region Fass; ++ Rega Pass Davos/Klosters; +++ Jungfrau Region Pass;
++++ Alpes Vaudoises Pass (Leysin-La Léckerette-Villars-Les Diablerets inc. glacier); +++++ Portes du Soleil Pass; ++++++ 4 Valley Pass covering 100 lifts including Mont Fort

EQUIPMENT HIRE RATES

-It is regretted that all resort sports shops are not shown in this table as those that are missing failed to return the rate sheets. Resorts marked • allow members a reduction on hire rates and in many cases for the purchase of clothing and equipment. The rates quoted are, in the main, for standard equipment. The member must produce his/her membership card. Please refer to the Club section.

	Skis and Bindings				Boots				Snowboards & Boots	
	Adults		Children		Adults		Children			
Country/Resort	**6 Days**	**13 Days**	**6 Days**	**13 Days**	**6 Days**	**13 Days**	**6 Days**	**13 Days**	**6 Days**	**13 Days**
ANDORRA	*Francs*	*Francs*	*Francs*	*Francs*	*Francs*	*Francs*	*Francs*	*Francs*	*Francs*	*Francs*
Arinsal•	276	554	207	426	161	330	109	223	410	810
La Massana•	276	554	207	426	161	330	109	223	410	810
Pal•	276	554	207	426	161	330	109	223	410	810
Pas de la Casa•	276	554	207	426	161	330	109	223	410	810
Soldeu•	276	554	207	426	161	330	109	223	410	810
AUSTRIA	*A.S.*	*A.S.*	*A.S.*	*A.S.*	*A.S.*	*A.S.*	*A.S.*	*A.S.*	*A.S.*	*A.S.*
Bad Goisern	550	800	400	600	300	420	200	320	-	-
Brand	600	1100	360	700	480	700	280	520	1680	2700
Fieberbrunn•	600	1055	330	624	330	588	210	364	1500	-
Gargellen•	565	1040	295	540	295	540	180	350	1095++	1935++
Hinterstoder	770	1400	450	840	310	560	175	280	-	-
Hochgurgl•	750	1500	420	770	420	770	240	450	1800	4305
Ischgl	720	1300	180	390	300	520	180	390	1920	4160
Kaprun	900	1465	450	730	520	865	260	430	1956	3018
Laterns	675	1288	350	730	380	755	250	500	1520	3015
Lermoos•	600	1300	425	690	400	820	195	410	1730	3060
Nauders	450	910	330	676	270	559	200	364	-	-
Niederau	450	975	270	585	180	390	120	260	-	-
Obergurgl•	750	1500	420	770	420	770	240	450	1800	4305
Obertauern•	900	1620	380	730	350	630	200	590	1150	1990
Seefeld•	685	1175	250	530	355	640	225	330	1120	1910
Söll•	495	855	305	515	265	405	175	340	1343	2340
St. Anton•	660	1100	450	850	390	680	220	410	1490	2480
Steinach•	600	1200	300	600	240	480	120	240	1320	2480
Westendorf•	410	810	310	570	270	510	180	310	1160	2155
Zell am Ziller•	540	1080	360	720	360	720	240	480	1310	2640
FRANCE	*Francs*	*Francs*	*Francs*	*Francs*	*Francs*	*Francs*	*Francs*	*Francs*	*Francs*	*Francs*
Alpe d'Huez•	338	675	150	299	182	364	81	161	725	1449
Argentière•	450	823	182	331	250	477	140	257	800	1487
Avoriaz•	384	766	150	299	206	413	80	161	725	1449
Chamonix•	398	799	171	343	398	799	171	343	819	1642
Chatel•	329	657	140	279	219	438	95	190	660	1319
Courchevel 1650•	387	775	166	332	208	418	89	179	725	1449
Courchevel 1850•	398	799	171	343	215	430	92	185	819	1642
Flaine•	338	675	150	299	182	364	80	161	589	1055
Isola 2000•	387	775	224	439	208	418	131	263	795	1594
La Clusaz•	383	719	122	227	234	444	156	296	728	1372
La Plagne										
Plagne 1800•	419	784	198	330	254	438	182	316	800	1457
Belle Plagne•	350	652	140	274	240	415	110	220	739	1340
Plagne Bellecôte•	384	766	150	299	206	413	80	161	725	1449
Plagne Centre•	335	678	146	291	190	386	84	167	725	1464
Aime 2000•	384	766	150	299	206	413	80	161	725	1449
Champagny en Vanoise•	286	538	142	267	192	358	96	110	626	1170
Montalbert•	291	599	141	294	164	351	76	158	600	1244
Les Coches•	325	614	123	216	155	253	98	164	628	1146
La Tania•	395	792	141	283	197	396	85	170	761	1527
Le Corbier•	299	577	140	263	299	577	115	215	585	1105
Les Arcs•	395	792	152	306	200	396	96	192	750	1504
Les Carroz•	400	880	100	220	175	385	100	220	626	1375
Les Deux Alpes•	338	769	150	299	182	407	80	161	676	1351
Les Menuires•	338	675	150	299	182	364	80	161	725	1449
Megève•	338	675	150	299	182	364	80	161	725	1449
Méribel•	387	775	166	332	208	418	89	179	795	1594
Meribel Mottaret•	338	675	150	299	182	364	80	161	725	1449
Morzine•	323	559	153	268	165	286	100	165	610	1058
Risoul•	280	545	140	245	158	300	105	190	615	1140
St. Lary•	371	759	188	384	171	351	120	243	724	1482
Serre Chevalier•	384	766	150	299	206	413	80	161	725	1449
Tignes•	338	675	150	299	182	364	80	161	725	1449
Val d'Isère•	384	766	150	299	206	413	80	161	725	1449
Val Frejus•	324	650	170	338	175	352	118	232	600	1206
Valloire•	255	455	133	237	127	227	96	172	551	983
Valmorel•	299	597	133	267	161	322	72	143	630	1259
Val Thorens•	338	675	150	299	182	364	80	161	725	1449
Vaujany•	255	455	133	237	127	227	96	172	510	920
Villards de Lans•	293	698	143	368	157	376	77	198	595	1470
ITALY	*Lire*	*Lire*	*Lire*	*Lire*	*Lire*	*Lire*	*Lire*	*Lire*	*Lire*	*Lire*
Foppolo•	40,000	60,000	30,000	45,000	20,000	30,000	15,000	25,000	-	-
Limone•	45,000	58,000	31,000	38,000	31,000	38,000	28,000	35,000	148,500	193,000
Macugnaga•	48,000	71,000	40,000	58,000	41,000	52,000	24,000	36,000	-	-
NORWAY	*Kr*	*Kr*	*Kr*	*Kr*	*Kr*	*Kr*	*Kr*	*Kr*	*Kr*	*Kr*
Sjusjøen•	255+	395+	175+	245	-	-	-	-	-	-
Wadahl•	350	500	280	430	290	500	290	500	840	1400
Nordseter•	285	495	260+	375+	195	335	-	-	480	828
		+Including boots								
SWITZERLAND										
Adelboden	105	165	36	53	52	89	28	44	207	331
Andermatt•	103	165	36	53	52	89	28	44	182	299

EQUIPMENT HIRE RATES

It is regretted that all resort sports shops are not shown in this table as those that are missing failed to return the rate sheets. Resorts marked allow members a reduction on hire rates and in many cases for the purchase of clothing and equipment. The rates quoted are, in the main, for standard equipment. The member must produce his/her membership card. Please refer to the Club section.

Country/Resort	Skis and Bindings Adults 6 Days	Skis and Bindings Adults 13 Days	Skis and Bindings Children 6 Days	Skis and Bindings Children 13 Days	Boots Adults 6 Days	Boots Adults 13 Days	Boots Children 6 Days	Boots Children 13 Days	Snowboards & Boots 6 Days	Snowboards & Boots 13 Days
SWITZERLAND	*S.Francs*	*S.Francs*	*S.Francs*	*S.Francs*	*S.Francs*	*S.Francs*	*S.Francs*	*S.Francs*	*S.Francs*	*S.Francs*
Anzère•	105	165	36	53	52	89	28	44	157	254
Arosa•	105	165	36	53	52	89	28	44	157	254
Braunwald•	105	165	36	53	52	89	28	44	157	254
Celerina•	105	165	36	53	77	121	28	44	207	331
Champéry•	105	165	58	94	52	89	28	44	157	254
Chateau-d'Oex	105	165	58	94	52	89	28	44	157	254
Crans/Montana•	105	165	36	53	52	89	28	44	157	254
Davos•	105	165	36	53	52	89	28	44	157	254
Engelberg•	105	165	58	94	52	89	28	44	157	254
Flims•	105	165	36	53	52	89	28	44	157	254
Flumserberg•	105	165	36	53	52	89	28	44	157	254
Grächen	105	165	58	94	52	89	28	44	157	254
Grindelwald•	105	165	36	53	52	89	28	44	157	254
Haute-Nendaz	105	210	36	53	52	89	28	44	182	299
Klosters•	105	165	36	53	52	89	28	44	157	254
Laax•	105	165	36	53	52	89	28	44	157	254
Lenzerheide•	105	165	36	53	52	89	28	44	157	254
Les Diablerets•	105	165	36	53	52	89	28	44	157	254
Leysin•	105	165	36	53	52	89	28	44	157	254
Morgins•	105	165	36	53	52	89	28	44	157	254
Mürren	105	165	36	53	52	89	28	44	207	331
Pontresina	105	165	36	53	52	89	28	44	207	331
Reideralp•	105	165	36	53	52	89	28	44	207	331
Rougemont•	105	165	36	53	52	89	28	44	157	254
Saas Fee•	105	165	36	53	52	89	28	44	157	254
St. Moritz•	105	165	36	53	77	89	28	44	157	254
Samnaun•	105	165	36	53	52	89	28	44	157	254
Silvaplana•	105	165	36	53	52	89	28	41	157	254
Verbier•	110	180	50	85	55	90	35	45	210	315
Villars•	105	165	36	53	52	89	28	44	157	254
Wengen	105	165	58	94	52	89	28	44	207	331
Wildhaus•	105	165	36	53	52	89	28	44	207	331
Zermatt•	105	165	36	53	52	89	28	44	157	254
SWEDEN	*S.Kr.*	*S.Kr.*	*S.Kr.*	*S.Kr.*	*S.Kr.*	*S.Kr.*	*S.Kr.*	*S.Kr.*	*S.Kr.*	*S.Kr.*
Duved	515	1030 +Including Boots	310	620	310	620	210	420	845	1690
SPAIN	*Pts.*	*Pts.*	*Pts.*	*Pts.*	*Pts.*	*Pts.*	*Pts.*	*Pts.*	*Pts.*	*Pts.*
Sierra Nevada•	4900	9800	3500	7000	2800	5600	1750	3500	-	-

SKI KINDERGARTENS

Whilst every care has been taken in compiling this information we advise parents to re-check with the Tourist Office before booking their holiday. Prices in the table below, in most cases, provide for 2 hours ski school in the morning and 2 hours in the afternoon but this varies at some resorts. Where lunch is included in the price or shown as a separate charge, children are normally cared for during the mid-day break. Where lunch is not included children should be collected after the morning ski school. **In all cases parents should check these facts when booking their children into the Ski Kindergarten.**

Country/Resort	Age Groups From	Age Groups To	Times From	Times To	Prices 6 Full Days Low or High Season	Cost of Lunch Daily
AUSTRIA					A.S.	A.S.
Alpbach	3	5	0915	1600	1580+	Inc.
Badgastein	3	15	1000	1600	2750*	Inc.
Bad Hofgastein	3	4	0900	1500	1985	Inc.
Brand	3	14	1000	1415	1050+	100
Damüls	2	6	1000	1600	1280+	Inc.
Dienten	4		1000	1500	1440+	130
Dorfgastein	3	15	0930	1600	1750*	Inc.
Ellmau	3	12	1000	1600	1250	100
Fieberbrunn	4	12	1000	1530	1300*	120*
Filzmoos	3	14	1000	1530	2020*	Inc.
Finkenberg	4		1000	1530	2090*	Inc.
Fontanella/Faschina	4		1000	1600	1300+	100
Fulpmes	4	15	1000	1500	1290*	Inc.
Galtür	4	14	1000	1530	1930	Inc.
Gargellen	4	6	1000	1500	1700+	Inc.
Gaschurn	3	12	1000	1500	1490*	110*
Hinterstoder	4	7	0930	1600	1600+	Inc.
Hintertux/Lanersbach	4	8	0900	1630	1950	Inc.
Kirchberg	4	12	0930	1500	1940	Inc.

Country/Resort	Age Groups From	Age Groups To	Times From	Times To	Prices 6 Full Days Low or High Season	Cost of Lunch Daily
AUSTRIA					AS.	AS.
Kitzbühel	3	14	1000	1600	1750	Inc.
Lech am Arlberg	3	4	0900	1600	1440	80
Mayrhofen	4	14	1000	1500	2270	Inc.
Nauders	3	10	1000	1500	2030*	Inc.
Niederau	2	6	0930	1630	800	110
Obergurgl	3	5	1000	1600	1490	180
Obertauern	4	13	1000	1600	1450	130
Saalbach/Hinterglemm	4		1000	1600	2270*	Inc.
St. Anton am Arlberg	5	14	0900	1630	2445	Inc.
St. Johann in Tirol	4	12	0930	1600	1200	50
Schruns	3	6	0900	1600		
Seefeld	4	12	1000	1600	1740+	Inc.
Sölden	3	8	0930	1530	2100	100
Söll	5	14	0945	1600	1850	100
Wagrain	2	4	1000	1600	1900	Inc.
Westendorf	3	15	1000	1530	1350	100
Zell am See/Kaprun	4	12	1000	1600	1700	–

+ 5 days   *1996/97 rates

SKI KINDERGARTENS

Whilst every care has been taken in compiling this information we advise parents to re-check with the Tourist Office before booking their holiday. Prices in the table below, in most cases, provide for 2 hours ski school in the morning and 2 hours in the afternoon but this varies at some resorts. Where lunch is included in the price or shown as a separate charge, children are normally cared for during the mid-day break. Where lunch is not included children should be collected after the morning ski school. **In all cases parents should check these facts when booking their children into the Ski Kindergarten.**

Country/Resort	Age Groups From	Age Groups To	Times From	Times To	Prices 6 Full Days Low or High Season	Cost of Lunch Daily
FRANCE					**Francs**	**Francs**
Avoriaz	3	12	0900	1730	975	45
Chamonix	4	12	0900	1700	1300*	Inc.
Courchevel	2	12	0930	1630	960*	60
Flaine	3	12	0900	1700	1220	Inc.
Isola 2000	4	8	0900	1700	1300*	Inc.
La Clusaz	3½	6	0830	1800	1205*	57*
Les Angles	3	10	0930	1630	1000	40
Les Arcs	3	8	0845	1745		
Les Deux Alpes	4	6	0915	1700	1325	Inc.
Les Menuires	4	12	0900	1515	820	78
Megève	3	10	0900	1800	2340*	Inc.
Montgenèvre	3	5	0900	1700	750	–
Morzine	4	12	0930	1700	740	–
Tignes	4	12	0930	1700	1540*	Inc.
Val d'Isère	3	5	0930	1700	1540*	–
Valfrejus	3	6	0900	1700	750	–

+ 5 days *1996/97 rates

Country/Resort	Age Groups From	Age Groups To	Times From	Times To	Prices 6 Full Days Low or High Season	Cost of Lunch Daily
ITALY					**Lire**	**Lire**
Canazei/Campitello	4	10	0830	1730	305,000	Inc.
Cortina	4	15	0930	1530	850,000	Inc.
Corvara/Colfosco	3	6	0930	1600	310,000+*	Inc.
Courmayeur	2	12	0900	1600	420,000*	Inc.
San Cassiano	3	6	0930	1600	310,000+*	Inc.
S. Vigilio/Marebbe	3	10	0900	1600	250,000+	Inc.
Selva Gardena	4	12	0930	1600	390,000	Inc.

+ 5 days *1996/97 rates

Country/Resort	Age Groups From	Age Groups To	Times From	Times To	Prices 6 Full Days Low or High Season	Cost of Lunch Daily
SWITZERLAND					**S.Francs**	**S.Francs**
Adelboden	4	6	0900	1600	170+	16+
Andermatt	4	12	1000	1500	150+*	7
Arosa	4	14	0945	1615	165+	15+
Champéry	3	7	0930	1630	260+	Inc.
Chateau d'Oex	3		0900	1600	210	Inc.
Crans/Montana	3	6	0930	1600	300+	Inc.+
Davos	3	10	0830	1630	200+	10+
Engelberg	3	6	0930	1420	218+	Inc.+
Flims/Laax	4	7	0930	1500	280	Inc.
Flumserberg	3	8	1000	1600	145	20
Grächen	3	8	1000	1600	240*	–
Grindelwald	6	16	1000	1600	192+*	16+*
Klosters	4	16	0945	1600	195+	16+
Lenzerheide	3	6	0930	1600	195	20
Les Diablerets	3	7	0945	1530	245	Inc.
Mürren	4		1000	1200	123	–
Pontresina	3	16	0930	1530	190+	18
Rougemont	5	16	0900	1500	190	10
Verbier	3	10	0830	1700	239*	11*
Veysonnaz	3	6	0930	1600	220+	Inc.
Villars	3	10	0900	1600	300*	Inc.*
Wildhaus	2	10	0930	1630	140*	15+
Zermatt	6	12	1000	1600	255	Inc.

+ 5 days *1996/97 rates

KINDERGARTENS

Whilst every care has been taken in compiling this information, parents should check with the Tourist Office, Ski School or Kindergarten before making their holiday arrangements. Most Kindergartens provide lunch, a few do not and this should be checked. If a Kindergarten is not shown against the resort of your choice, please ring the Tourist Office (see Resort Facilities Charts) and they will advise if there is one or suggest alternatives. **In all cases parents should check these facts when booking their children into the Kindergarten.**

Country/Resort	Name	Tel. No.	Age Group From	Age Group To	Days Open From	Days Open To	Times From	Times To	Price including Lunch Daily A.S.
AUSTRIA									
Alpbach	Alpbach Aktiv	5351	3	8	Mon.	Fri.	0915	1600	1300
Badgastein	Grüner Baum	25160	3	15	Mon.	Sat.	0930	1600	2400*
Berwang	Gästekindergarten	8268	2	12	Mon.	Fri.	1330	1630	–
Brand	Hotel Lagant	285	2	5	Mon.	Fri.	0800	1800	1500
Dorfgastein	Ski School	538	3	15	Mon.	Fri.	0930	1630	2300*
Filzmoos	Ski School	370	3	12	Mon.	Fri.	0930	1530	–
Galtür	Gästekindergarten	8565	3	12	Mon.	Sat.	1000	1530	1930
Gargellen	Ski School	6401	2	5	Mon.	Fri.	0915	1530	1700
Gaschurn	Hotel Mardusa	8211	4	11	Sun.	Fri.	1000	1500	1995*
Kaprun	Skischule Pregenzer	8238	2	12	Sun.	Fri.	0900	1700	1650*
Kirchberg	Mini Club Total	3720	3		Mon.	Fri.	0900	1700	1500
Kitzbühel	Tourist Office	2155	For list of Baby Sitters				–	–	–
Lanersbach	Gästekindergarten	87420	2	12	Mon.	Sun.	0930	1530	1560
Lech am Arlberg	Tourist Office	2161	For list of Baby Sitters				–	–	–
Mayrhofen	Wuppy's Kinderland	63612	3 m.	7	Mon.	Fri.	0800	1800	1850
Niederau	Ski School	2200	2	8	Mon.	Fri.	0930	1630	1460*
Obertauern	CSA Ski School	7336	2	4	Sun.	Fri.	0900	1600	2280
Obertraun	Ski School	596	4	6	Mon.	Fri.	0900	1600	1900*
Saalbach/Hinterglemm	Hotel Theresia	74140	2	7	Mon.	Fri.	1000	1600	2000*
St. Anton am Arlberg	Jugendcenter	2526	2½	5	Sun.	Fri.	0900	1630	1580
Serfaus	Gästekindergarten	6628	1	10	Mon.	Sat.	0900	1630	1000
Zell am See	Feriendorf Hagleitner	56343	3	6	Mon.	Sat.	0930	1530	1200
Zürs am Arlberg	Kindergarten Zürs	2245	3	5	Sun.	Fri.	–	–	–

*1996/97 rates

KINDERGARTENS

Whilst every care has been taken in compiling this information, parents should check with the Tourist Office, Ski School or Kindergarten before making their holiday arrangements. Most Kindergartens provide lunch, a few do not and this should be checked. If a Kindergarten is not shown against the resort of your choice, please ring the Tourist Office (see Resort Facilities Charts) and they will advise if there is one or suggest alternatives. **In all cases parents should check these facts when booking their children into the Kindergarten.**

Country/Resort	Name	Tel. No.	Age Group From	Age Group To	Days Open From	Days Open To	Times		Price including Lunch Daily
FRANCE									**F.F.**
Alpe d'Huez	Les Eterlous	804327	6 m.	14	Mon.	Sun.	0900	1745	–
Avoriaz	Les Petits Loups	740038	3 m.	5	Sun.	Fri.	0900	1800	1200
Chamonix	Halte-Garderie	533668	3	12	Mon.	Fri.	0745	1830	1195*
Chatel	Village des Marmottons	733379	1	3	Mon.	Sun.	0930	1600	670*
Courchevel 1850	Le Village des Enfants	083584	2	12	Mon.	Sun.	0900	1900	–
Courchevel 1650	Vacances des Petits	083584	2	7	Mon.	Sun.	0900	1700	–
Flaine	Garderie des Petits Loups	908782	6 m.	4	Sun.	Fri.	0900	1700	760 No lunch
Isola 2000	Les Pitchauns	231178	2	10	Mon.	Sat.	0900	1700	1135*
La Clusaz	Club des Mouflets	326957	8 m.	4	Sun.	Fri.	0830	1800	
La Plagne:									
Plagne Centre	Marie Christine	091181	2	6	Sun.	Fri.	0900	1700	1050*
Plagnes Villages	Foret des Enfants	090440	2	6	Sun.	Fri.	0900	1700	1050*
Aime la Plagne	Maison des Lutins	090475	2	6	Sun.	Fri.	0900	1700	1050*
Plagne Bellecote	Maison de Dorothée	090133	2	6	Sun.	Fri.	0900	1700	1090*
Belle Plagne	Jardins des Neige	090668	1.5	6	Sun.	Fri.	0900	1700	1070*
Plagne Lauze 1800	Garderie Plagne 1800	092250	3	6	Sun.	Fri.	0900	1700	1050*
Plagne Montalbert	Les Bambins	097733	2	6	Sun.	Fri.	0900	1700	1050*
Les Arcs 1800	Pommes de Pin	415542	1	6	Mon.	Sat.	0830	1800	–
Les Deux Alpes	Bonhomme de Neige	790677	2	6	Sun.	Fri.	0730	1800	900
Les Menuires	Le Village des Schroumps	006379	3 m.	7	Mon.	Sat.	0900	1715	1400
Megève	Meg Loisirs	587784	3	6	Sun.	Fri.	0800	1800	–
Méribel	Club Saturnin	086690	2	8	Sun.	Fri.	–	–	–
Méribel Mottaret	Club les Pingouins	004646	3	8	Sun.	Fri.	–	–	–
Morzine	Garderie L'Outa	792600	2 m.	4	Mon.	Sun.	0830	1800	–
Serre Chevalier	Les Poussins	240343	6 m.	6	Mon.	Sun.	0900	1700	1365*
Tignes	Les Marmottons	065167	3 m.	10	Mon.	Sun.	0845	1700	–
Val d'Isère	Le Petit Poucet	061397	3	8	Mon.	Sun.	0900	1700	1185
	Isabelle Nursery	411282	3	8	Mon.	Sun.	0900	1700	1185
Valfrejus	Les Diablotins	053616	3 m.	3	Sun.	Fri.	0900	1700	740 No lunch
Valmorel	Saperlipopette	098445	6 m.	8	Sun.	Fri.	0830	1700	–
Val Thorens	Mini Club E.S.F.	000286	3 m.	3	Sun.	Fri.	0900	1700	1350
		*1996/97 rates							
ITALY									**Lire**
Aprica	Kinderheim Biancaneve	746521	4	12	Mon.	Sat.	–	–	240,000
Courmayeur	Kinderheim Checrouit	842477	6 m.	3	Mon.	Sat.	0900	1600	–
Livigno	Biancaneve	996279	3	10	Mon.	Sat.	–	–	–
Madonna di Campiglio	Ski School	41140	3	10	Mon.	Sat.	–	–	–
San Vigilio	Skinopolis	501049	3	10	Mon.	Sat.	0900	1600	–
Selva	Ski School	792045	3	10	Mon.	Sat.	0900	1600	300,000
		*1996/97 rates							
SWITZERLAND									**S. Francs**
Adelboden	Kindergarten	733489	2	6	Mon.	Fri.	0900	1700	145
Anzère	Garderie d'Anzere	3992800	2	8	Mon.	Fri.	0830	1700	–
Arosa	Parkhotel	3770165					–	–	–
Champery	Garderiere Snoopy	4792020	2		Mon.	Fri.	0900	1700	225*
Chateau d'Oex	Ski School	9246848	2	8	Mon.	Sat.	0900	1600	–
Crans/Montana	Bibiland	418142	3	6	Mon.	Sat.	0900	1830	–
Davos	Pinocchio	462454	2.5	10	Mon.	Fri.	0830	1630	200*
Engelberg	Swiss Ski School	6373040	3	6	Mon.	Fri.	0900	1630	275*
Flims/Laax	Ski School	9111438	4	10	Mon.	Fri.	0930	1500	300
Flumserberg	Ski School	7333939	3	8	Mon.	Fri.	0930	1615	265
Grindelwald	Kinderclub	8535200	3	10	Mon.	Fri.	0930	1600	210*
Gstaad	Tourist Office	7488181	Babysitting service		–	–	–	–	–
Lenzerheide	Hotel Valbella Inn	3843636	3		Mon.	Fri.	0900	1630	210
Les Diablerets	Ski School	4922002	3	6	Sun.	Fri.	0900	1700	245
Mayens-de-Riddes	Garderie La Toumaz	3061851	2	12	Mon.	Sun.	–	–	–
Mürren	Tourist Office	8568686	3		Mon.	Fri.	–	–	–
Pontresina	Hotel Saratz	8394000	3	10	Mon.	Fri.	0930	1815	235
Saas Fee	Bären Klub	572484	3		Mon.	Fri.	0900	1700	300*
St. Moritz	Parkhotel Kurhaus	8322111	3	8	Mon.	Sat.	0900	1630	–
Verbier	Les Stroumpfs	7716585	6 m.	5	Mon.	Sun.	0830	1700	288*
Veysonnaz	Garderie Ski School	2072141	3	10	Mon.	Fri.	0900	1630	220
Villars	La Trotinette	372237	6 m.	6	Mon.	Fri.	0830	1845	–
Wengen	Tourist Office	8551414	3	7	Sun.	Fri.	0845	1630	150
Zermatt	Hotel Nicoletta	9670151	2 1/2		Mon.	Fri.	0900	1700	250
		*1996/97 rates							

Telephone Numbers: For area codes please refer to Resort Facilities Charts

FOOD PRICES

Prices given in the undermentioned table are approximate. There is a great variation in price between the small and larger international resorts but the greatest difference is in the quality of the products. Nearly all resorts have supermarkets.

Prices in local currency

Items	Austria *A.S.*	France *Francs*	Italy *Lire*	Switzerland *S. Francs*
Butter 1kg	60-78	32-50	7,000-15,000	12.60-16.00
Cheese 1kg	69-169	35-68	11,500-20,000	17.50-23.00
Bacon 1kg	90-220	70-95	12,000-20,000	22.00-23.00
Ham 1kg	130-279	52-80	20,000-35,000	25.00-29.00
Beef 1kg	139-300	70-100	22,500-33,000	20.00-45.00
Lamb 1kg	119-149	69-80	15,000-20,000	24.00-35.00
Veal 1kg	129-280	80-120	18,000-28,000	36.00-45.00
Sausages 1kg	80-150	45-60	14,000-16,000	15.00-18.00
Poultry 1kg	40-100	25-59	5,000-7,000	20.00-25.00
Potatoes 1kg	9-15	4-10	800-1,200	1.60-2.70
Tomatoes 1kg	20-40	13-19	4,000-4,600	3.90-4.20
Onions 1kg	12-15	6-13	1,300-2,000	2.00-2.15
Apples 1kg	16-35	8-14	2,100-3,400	2.10-3.80
Tea 1/2kg	25-80	67-75	14,000-20,000	8.00-15.00
Coffee 1/2kg	39-60	30-60	8,000-14,000	7.20-13.90
Sugar 1kg	15-17	8-9	1,000-2,500	1.50-1.90
Bread, large loaf	25-30	5-12	3,300-4,000	3.90-4.80
Eggs, 12	20-36	11-13	2,900-3,500	4.10-5.40
Soup, large tin	14-30	12-18	3,200-3,500	1.80-6.00
Marmalade, large jar	20-30	15-16	3,500-6,400	3.70-4.20
Jam, large jar	20-30	15-18	3,500-5,000	3.90-4.50
Peas, frozen large pkt	20-37	9-12	3,000-3,500	4.80-5.80
Beans, frozen large pkt	25-40	12-18	3,100-3,500	4.30-5.80
Spinach, frozen large pkt	21-35	8-12	2,600-3,700	3.90-4.90
Milk, 1 litre	9-12	4-6	1,900-2,150	1.75-1.90
Wine, 1 litre	34-60	10-15	2,700-3,300	8.00-10.50
Beer, 1 large bottle	12-15	6-7	1,800-2,200	1.50-2.10
Gin, 1 bottle	129-190	67-82	14,100-18,000	23.90-40.90
Whisky, 1 bottle	169-300	89-109	13,000-25,000	23.00-42.90
Cigarettes, local 20	30-40	13-15	2,700-3,500	3.50-3.90
Cigarettes, British 20	35-42	13-15	4,000-5,200	3.50-3.90
Cigarettes, American 20	35-45	15-16	3,900-5,100	3.50-3.90

1 Kilogram - 2.204 lbs. 1 Litre - 1.759 pints. Exchange rate with sterling at the time of going to press:- Austria:15.97. A.S. France: 7.68 Francs. Italy: 2,333 Lire. Switzerland: 1.86 S. Francs.

SOME OF YOUR EXTRAS

Country/Resort	Mountain Restaurants			Night Clubs and Discothèques	
	Snack Lunch	Full Lunch	Litre Wine	First Drink*	Litre Wine
Austria	*A.S.*	*A.S.*	*A.S.*	*A.S.*	*A.S.*
Alpbach	60-90	150	140	30-80	200
Badgastein	40-60	130-180	160	40-110	200-350
Bad Goisern	60	150	120	—	—
Bad Hofgastein	50	100-150	140	80	300
Berwang	50-100	120	150	60-80	190
Brand	50	120	160	60	200
Dienten	50	130	140	30	160
Dorfgastein	90	130	150	70	250
Ellmau	50	120	150	40	250
Fieberbrunn	60	100	150	50	300
Filzmoos	50	100	120	50	120-180
Finkenberg	40-80	80-150	120	50	150-300
Fulpmes	40-70	80-140	180	60	230
Galtür	70	160	175	60	180-250
Gargellen	50	100-160	120	50	150-300
Gaschurn	45-75	80-140	160	30	150-250
Gosau	50-100	100	150	60	120-150
Hinterstoder	50	80	160	50	150
Hintertux	60	130	200	50	300
Ischgl	75	120-200	160	50	230-350
Kaprun	75	150	150-200	70	200-400
Kirchberg	60	120	150	40	160
Kitzbühel	60	130-150	150	50-80	150-200
Lanersbach	60-70	80-100	150	50	200
Lech	80-100	120-150	250-280	100	350-400
Lermoos	60-100	100-180	150	40	200
Mayrhofen	40-80	120	200	40	200
Obergurgl	70-110	100-150	100-250	25-95	130-400
Obertauern	70	150	120	50-130	200-350
Obertraun	90	160	140	-	-
Saalbach/Hinterglemm	80-100	120-200	160	120	150-400
St. Anton	100	180	200	90	160-350
Seefeld	80	150	160	80	260
Serfaus	100	200	100	70	240
Sölden	70-150	120-200	120-200	50-120	200-320

* In some cases, particularly in France and Italy, the following drinks are cheaper.

SOME OF YOUR EXTRAS

Country/Resort		Mountain Restaurants		Night Clubs and Discothèques	
	Snack Lunch	Full Lunch	Litre Wine	First Drink*	Litre Wine
Austria	*A.S.*	*A.S.*	*A.S.*	*A.S.*	*A.S.*
Westendorf	80-90	130-150	160	25-50	160-250
Wildschönau	60	120	160	45	180-250
Zell am See	60	150	160	50-90	200-300
Zell am Ziller	60	120	150	40	150-200
Zürs	100	200	250-280	100	350-400
France	*Francs*	*Francs*	*Francs*	*Francs*	*Francs*
Alpe d'Huez	70	120	50	25-50	-
Avoriaz	50-70	100	50	70	-
Barèges	50	80	30	45	-
Chamonix	90	150	50	80	-
Chatel	70	100	40	50	-
Courchevel	90	120	80	80	-
Flaine	50	110	80	25-50	-
Isola 2000	60	90	50	60	-
La Plagne	45	75	60	70	-
La Toussuire	50	80	40	60	-
Les Arcs	50	150	80	50	-
Les Deux Alpes	60	120	60	80	-
Les Gets	70	90	30	60	-
Les Houches	70	90	40	40	-
Les Menuires	65-70	85-105	45	60	-
Megève	80	130-170	70-100	90-120	-
Morzine	70	90	60	80	-
St. Lary	60	120	30-50	60	-
Serre Chevalier	60	100	70	60	-
Tignes	65	140	80	70	-
Val d'Isère	90	140	80	70	-
Italy	*Lire*	*Lire*	*Lire*	*Lire*	*Lire*
Arabba	8,000	20,000	10,000	15,000	-
Bardonecchia	8,000	20,000	9,000	10,000	-
Cavalese	10,000	28,000	12,000	15,000	40,000
Cortina	9,000	28,000	12,000	25,000	-
Corvara/Colfosco	12,000	25,000	10,000	20,000	35,000
Foppolo	12,000	25,000	6,000	5,000	15,000
La Villa	12,000	25,000	8,000	20,000	30,000
Limone	15,000	25,000	8,000	20,000	-
Livigno	10,000	25,000	12,000	8,000	15,000
Madonna	15,000	30,000	9,000	30,000	-
Piancavallo	12,000	25,000	10,000	20,000	-
Pila	8,000	20,000	9,000	10,000	-
Santa Caterina	–	25,000	7,000	–	-
San Martino	10,000	20,000	8,000	15,000	-
San Vigilio	15,000	28,000	15,000	15,000	25,000
Selva	15,000	15-30,000	7-10,000	6-15,000	25,000
Sestriere	20,000	40,000	15,000	15,000	20,000
Switzerland	*S. Francs*	*S. Francs*	*S. Francs*	*S. Francs*	*S. Francs*
Adelboden	11	18	32	8-16	46
Andermatt	11	22	27	8	36
Anzère	10	15	25	12	35
Arosa	10	18	30	20	30-50
Barboleusaz	8	15	24	8	30
Braunwald	10	20	25	9	30
Champéry	10	20	28	10	40
Chateau d'Oex	11	16	27	15	45
Crans/Montana	10	20	30	20	60
Davos	12	25	30	16	68
Engelberg	15	25	30	15	45
Flims	15	18	32	12	45
Flumserberg	8	25	30	12	40
Grächen	8	12	28	10	40
Grindelwald	13	20	30	12	40
Gstaad	16	30	30	10	60
Haute-Nendaz	10	16	27	10	45-50
Klosters	10-12	15-25	30-35	15	50
Lenzerheide	12	25	30	10	50
Les Diablerets	15	25	25	10-15	50
Leysin	6-10	16-20	15	6	25
Morgins	12	17	21	11	40
Pontresina	16	23	28	15	40
Saas Fee	10	20-25	21	12	40
St. Moritz	10-20	15-30	30-40	18-38	80
Verbier	12	18	29	15	40
Veysonnaz	8	15-20	24	15	40
Villars	15	23	28	19	-
Wengen	15	25	30	15	-
Wildhaus	9-10	25	30	8	50
Zermatt	10-15	20-30	25-30	15	40-80
Malbun (Liechtenstein)	12	17	18	5	21

* In some cases, particularly France and Italy, the following drinks are cheaper.

ARTIFICIAL SKI SLOPES - U.K.

We list below some of the Artificial Ski Slopes in the UK. Due to a greater number of Ski Slopes being included in this edition it is regretted that we have not been able to include footnotes on the additional facilities at each Centre. If you require this information and cannot get through by telephone to any of the Ski Slopes listed, please ring our Editorial Office 0171.937.1595 • Denotes discounts for members of the Skier's Holiday Guide Club. See Club Section.

CITY/TOWN	ADDRESS & TELEPHONE NO.	Main Slope Measurements length metres	width metres	Ski Tow	Floodlit	Equipment Hire	Refreshments Facilities	Open all year	Additional Slopes
Aldershot	• Alpine Ski Centre, Gallwey Road, Hants, GU11 2DD Tel: 01252 25889	110	10	yes 3	yes	yes	yes	yes	2
Alford	Greystone Road, Aberdeenshire, AB33 8TY Tel: 019755 63024	86	50	yes	yes	yes	yes	yes	1
Bracknell	Bracknell Ski Slope, John Nike Leisuresport Ltd., John Nike Way, RG12 8TN Tel: 01344 860033	150	20	yes 2	yes	yes	yes	yes	2
Brentwood	• Warley Gap, Little Warley, CM13 3DP Tel: 01277 211994	160	20	yes 2	yes	yes	yes	yes	3
Calshot	Calshot Activities Centre, Calshot Road, Southampton, SO45 1BR Tel: 01703 892077	30	13	yes	yes	yes	yes	yes	2
Cardiff	Ski Centre Cardiff, Fairwater Park, Fairwater, CF5 3JR Tel: 01222 561793	100	25	yes	yes	yes	yes	yes	–
Chatham	John Nike Leisuresport Ltd, Chatham Ski Centre, Capston Road, ME7 3JH Tel: 01634 827979	200	35	yes 2	yes	yes	yes	yes	1
Churchill	• Avon Ski Centre, Lyncombe Lodge, Avon, BS19 5PQ Tel: 01934 852335	165	10-30	yes 2	yes	yes	yes	yes	3
Edinburgh	• Hillend Ski Centre, Biggar Road, EH10 7DU Tel: 0131 445 4433	400	20	yes 3	yes	yes	yes	yes	3
Esher	• Sandown Ski Club, More Lane, KT10 8AN Tel: 01372 467132	120	50	yes	yes	yes	yes	yes	1
Glasgow	Bearsden Ski Club, The Mound, Stockiemuir Road, Bearsden, G61 3RS Tel: 0141 9431500	120	20-35	yes 2	yes	yes	yes	yes	1
Gloucester	Gloucester Ski Centre, Matson Lane, GL4 6EA Tel: 01452 414300	240	7	4	yes	yes	yes	yes	3
Halifax	Halifax Ski Centre, Sportsman Leisure, Bradford, Old Road, Swalesmoor, HX3 6UG Tel: 01422 340760	90	6-30	yes 2	yes	yes	yes	yes	–
Harlow	Harlow Snowboard & Ski School, Hammarksjold Road, CM20 2JF	160	30	–	–	yes	yes	yes	–
Hemel Hempstead	• Hemel Ski Centre, St. Albans Hill, HP3 9NH Tel: 01442 241321	180	18	yes 3	yes	yes	yes	yes	3
London	• Crystal Palace Ski School, PO Box 676, Upper Norwood SE19 2BL Tel: 0181 778 9876	30	20	no	yes	yes	yes	yes	–
London	Beckton Alpine Centre, Alpine Way, Beckton, E6 4LA Tel: 0171 5110351	250	30	yes	yes	yes	yes	yes	–

ARTIFICIAL SKI SLOPES - U.K.

CITY/TOWN		ADDRESS & TELEPHONE NO.	Main Slope Measurements length metres	width metres	Ski Tow	Floodlit	Equipment Hire	Refreshments Facilities	Open all year	Additional Slopes
Newhaven		Borowski Ski and Snowboard Centre, New Road, East Sussex, EN9 OEH Tel: 01273 515402	40	10	yes	yes	yes	yes	yes	–
Newmilns	•	Newmilns Ski Slope, High Street, KA16 9EB Tel: 01560 322320	100	6-7	yes	yes	yes	yes	yes	–
Nottingham		Richard Herrud Leisure Centre, Foxhill Road, Carlton, NG41 1RL Tel: 0115 9612949	60	25	yes	yes	yes	yes	yes	no
Orpington		Bromley Ski Centre, Sancy Lane, St. Pauls Cray, BR5 3HY Tel: 01689 876812	120	30	yes 3	yes	yes	yes	yes	1
Plymouth		Plymouth Ski Centre, John Nike Leisure Sport, Marchmills, PL6 8[illegible]Q Tel: 01752 600220	160	22	yes 2	yes	yes	yes	yes	2
Polmont		Polmonthill Ski Centre, Polmont Farm, Falkirk, FK2 OYE Tel: 01324 503835	100	16	yes	yes	yes	yes	yes	–
Rossendale		Ski Rossendale, Haslingden Old Road, Rawtenstall, Lancs., BB4 8RR Tel: 01706 226457	200	25	yes 5	yes	yes	yes	yes	4
Sheffield		Sheffield Ski Village, Vale Road, Parkwood Springs, S3 9SJ Tel: 0114 2769459	330m. of runs		yes 3	yes	yes	yes	yes	8
Southampton		Southampton Ski Centre, Sports Centre, Bassett, S016 7AY Tel: 01703 790970	110	varies	yes 2	yes	yes	machines	yes	2
Sunderland		Sunderland Ski Centre, Silksworth Lane Sunderland, SR3 2AN Tel: 0191 5535785	165	18	yes 3	yes	yes	yes	yes	2
Swadlincote		John Nike Leisure Sport, Hill Street, Swadlincote Derbyshire DE11 8LP Tel: 01283 217200	160	22	yes 4	yes	yes	yes	yes	1
Tallington	•	Tallington Ski & Snowboard Centre, Tallington Lakes, Nr. Stamford, Lincs. PE9 4RJ Tel: 01778 344990	120	20	yes	yes	yes	yes	no	2
Tamworth		Tamworth Snowdome, Leisure Island River Drive, B79 7ND Tel: 0990 000011 **Note:** An indoor centre with real snow	150	30	travelators	yes	yes	yes	yes	–
Telford		Telford Ski Centre, Court Street, Madeley, TF7 5DZ Tel: 01952 586862	85	12	yes 2	yes	yes	yes	yes	–
Tunbridge Wells	•	Bowles Ski Centre, Eridge Green, TW3 9LW Tel: 01892 665665	76	11	yes	yes	yes	yes	yes	–
Uxbridge	•	Hillingdon Ski & Snowboard Centre, Gatting Way, Park Road, UB8 1NR Tel: 01895 255609	195	14	yes 3	yes	yes	yes	yes	3
Welwyn Garden City	•	Gosling Ski Centre, Stanborough Road, AL8 6XE Tel 01707 391039	160	22	yes 2	yes	yes	yes	yes	1
Willington		Spectrum Ski School, Spectrum Leisure Centre, Hunwick Lane, Crook, Co. Durham DL15 OJA Tel: 01388 747000	70	20	yes	yes	yes	yes	yes	–

SPORTS SHOPS

We give below a list of Sports Shops in the U.K. showing if they stock ski clothing for adults and children, whether they stock children's skis and boots and whether they provide a hire service for skis, boots and clothing and a ski maintenance service; also if they stock snowboards and boots.

● Denotes discounts for members of the Skier's Holiday Guide Club, see Club Section.

		Ski Clothing		Children's		Hire Services			Ski Main- tenance	Snowboards and boots for sale
CITY/TOWN	ADDRESS & TELEPHONE NO.	Adults	Children	Skis	Boots	Skis	Boots	Clothing		
Aberdeen	• Anne Robb Sports Studio, 61 St. Swithin St. AB1 6KL. Tel: 01224 323254	*	*	*	*				*	
Altrincham	Nick Estcourt Ski & Climb, 53 Stamford New Road, WA14 1DS. Tel: 0161-928 6613	*	*	*	*				*	*
Aviemore	Ellis Brigham, 9-10 Grampian Road. Tel: 01479 810175	*	*	*	*	*	*	*	*	*
	• Ski Road Skis, Inverdruie Visitor Centre, PH22 1QH. Tel: 01479 810922	*	*	*	*	*	*	*	*	*
	• Speyside Sports, 64 Grampian Road, PH22 1PD. Tel: 01479 810656	*	*	*	*	*	*	*	*	*
Barnet	• John Pollock, 67 High Street, EN5 5UR Tel: 0181-440 3994	*	*	*	*	*	*	*	*	*
Bedford	• Two Seasons, 42 Harpur Street, MK40 2QT. Tel: 01234 350720	*	*	*	*	*	*	*	*	*
Bicester	• Beans, 86 Sheep Street, Oxfordshire OX6 7LP. Tel: 018692 46451	*	*	*	*	*	*	*	*	*
Birmingham	Snow & Rock, 14 Priory, Queensway, B4 6BS. Tel: 0121 236 8280	*	*	*	*				*	*
Blackpool	• The Alpine Centre Ltd., 193/5 Church Street, FY1 3NY. Tel: 01253 24307	*	*	*	*	*	*		*	*
Bournemouth	Snow Togs, 6 St. Michael's Road. Tel: 01202 557690	*	*	*	*	*	*	*	*	*
Bowness-on-Windermere	• Ski Treks-Lakeland Leisure, Lake Road, Cumbria, LA23 3BJ. Tel: 015394 44786					*	*	*	*	*
Brighton	• Eurosport Ltd., 67 North Road, BN1 1YD. Tel: 01273 688258	*	*			*	*	*	*	*
Bristol	Ellis Brigham, 160 Whiteladies Road, Clifton BS8 2XZ. Tel: 0117 9741157	*	*	*	*	*	*		*	*
Broughton-in-Furness	• Mountain Centre, Market Street, Tel: 01229 716461	*	*	*	*	*	*	*	*	Boots Only
Burnley	• Sportak Ltd, 25 Hammerton Street, BB11 1NA. Tel: 01282 436816	*	*						*	
Buxton	• Jo Royle, 6 Market Place, SK17 6EB. Tel: 01298 25824	*	*	*	*	*	*	*	*	
Cardiff	Ski Dreams, 490 Coudbridge Road East, Victoria Park CF5 1BL. Tel: 01222 569355	*	*	*	*	*	*	*	*	*
Canterbury	• Captain's Cabin, 19 Wincheap, CT1 3TB. Tel: 01227 457906	*	*	*	*	*	*	*	*	*

SPORTS SHOPS

We give below a list of Sports Shops in the U.K. showing if they stock ski clothing for adults and children, whether they stock children's skis and boots and whether they provide a hire service for skis, boots and clothing and a ski maintenance service; also if they stock snowboards and boots.

- Denotes discounts for members of the Skier's Holiday Guide Club, see Club Section.

		Ski Clothing		Children's		Hire Services			Ski Main-tenance	Snowboards and boots for sale
CITY/TOWN	ADDRESS & TELEPHONE NO.	Adults	Children	Skis	Boots	Skis	Boots	Clothing		
Catterick	• Ski Slope Shop, Horne Road, Richmond, DL9 4LE. Tel: 01748 833788	*	*	*	*	*	*		*	
Chatham	• Captain's Cabin Ltd., 93 High Street, ME4 4DL Tel: 01634 819777	*	*	*	*	*	*	*	*	*
Chelmsford	• Ski Plus, International House, Navigation Road CM2 6HX. Tel: 01245 264143	*	*	*	*	*	*	*	*	*
Cheltenham	• Horace Barton & Son, Cheltenham Ski Centre, 12 Regent St. Tel: 01242 516772	*	*	*	*	*	*	*	*	*
Chester	Ellis Brigham, 7 Northgate Street. Tel: 01244 318311	*	*	*	*	*	*		*	*
	• Sail & Ski, 9 Pepper Street, CH1 1EA Tel: 01244 344580	*	*	*	*	*	*	*	*	*
Colchester	Harpers Sports, 7-9 Head St., CO1 1NX Tel: 01206 765451	*	*						*	
Derby	Prestidge Ski & Climbing, 47 Queen St., DE1 3DE. Tel: 01332 342245	*	*	*	*				*	
Eastbourne	• Outdoor Life, 3 High Street, Old Town, BN21 1HG Tel: 01323 725372	*	*					*	*	
Edinburgh	Blues The Ski Shop, 1 Wemyss Place, EH3 6DH. Tel: 0131 2258369	*	*	*	*	*			*	*
	Nevisport Ltd., 81 Shandwick Place. Tel: 0131 229 1197	*	*	*	*	*	*	*	*	*
Elland	• BAC Outdoor Leisure, Central Hall, Coronation Street, Halifax HX5 0DF. Tel: 01422 371146	*	*	*	*	*		*	*	*
Esher	• Europa Ski Lodge, The Ski Centre, More Lane, Surrey. Tel: 01372 467131	*	*	*	*				*	
Glasgow	Blues The Ski Shop, 129 Buchanan Street, G1 2JA. Tel: 0141 204 0686	*	*	*	*	*			*	*
	Nevisport Ltd., 261 Sauchiehall St., G2 3E2. Tel: 0141 332 4814	*	*	*	*	*	*	*	*	*
Grantown-on-Spey	• Speyside Sports, 47 High St., PH26 3EG Tel: 01479 872946	*	*	*	*	*	*	*	*	
Gloucester	• Barton Ski Shop, Ski Centre, Robinswood. Tel: 01452 414300	*	*	*					*	
Hanley (Stoke on Trent)	• Mountain Fever, 25 Brunswick Street, ST1 1DR. Tel: 01782 266137	*	*	*	*	*	*	*	*	*
Harlow	• John Pollock, Harlow Sports Centre, Hammarskjold Road, CM20 2JF Tel: 01279 425009	*	*	*	*	*	*	*	*	*
Havant	• Filarwskis, 26-28 East Street, Hants PO9 1AQ. Tel: 01705 499599	*	*	*	*	*	*	*	*	*

SPORTS SHOPS

We give below a list of Sports Shops in the U.K. showing if they stock ski clothing for adults and children, whether they stock children's skis and boots and whether they provide a hire service for skis, boots and clothing and a ski maintenance service; also if they stock snowboards and boots.

• Denotes discounts for members of the Skier's Holiday Guide Club, see Club Section.

		Ski Clothing		Children's		Hire Services			Ski Main-tenance	Snowboards and boots for sale
CITY/TOWN	ADDRESS & TELEPHONE NO.	Adults	Children	Skis	Boots	Skis	Boots	Clothing		
Hemel Hempstead	Snowcap, 22-24 Lawn Lane, Herts HP3 9NH. Tel: 01442 242911	*	*	*	*	*	*		*	
Keswick	George Fisher, 2 Borrowdale Road, CA12 5DA. Tel: 017687 72178	*	*						*	
Kingston upon Thames	• Snowbusiness Ltd, 35 London Road. Tel: 0181 541 4857	*	*	*	*	*	*	*	*	*
Leeds	• Severn Sports, 80 Town Street, Armley, LS12 3AA. Tel: 0113 2791618	*	*	*	*	*	*	*	*	*
Leicester	• Roger Turner, 52A London Road, LE2 OQD. Tel: 0116 2551952	*	*	*	*			*	*	
Lincoln	Linsports, 21-23 Silver Street LN2 1EX Tel: 01522 524674	*	*		*				*	
Liverpool	• Ellis Brigham, 73 Bold Street, L1 4EZ. Tel: 0151 709 6912	*	*	*	*	*	*	*	*	*
London	Ellis Brigham Ltd., 30-32 Southampton Street, WC2E 7HE. Tel: 0171-240 9577	*	*	*	*	*	*		*	*
	• Don Farrell, 14/15 Holmstall Parade, Edgware, HA8 5HX. Tel: 0181 205 6693	*	*	*	*	*	*		*	
	Lillywhites Ltd, 24-36 Regent Street, SW1Y 4QF. Tel: 0171 915 4000	*	*						*	*
	Snow & Rock, 188 Kensisngton High Street, W8 7RG.C Tel: 0171 937 0872	*	*	*	*				*	*
	Snow & Rock, 150 Holborn, EC1N 2LC Tel: 0171 831 8545	*	*	*	*				*	*
Loughton	• John Pollock Ltd, 157 High Road, Essex IG10 4LF. Tel 0181 508 6626	*	*	*	*	*	*	*	*	*
Manchester	Ellis Brigham Mountain Sports, 211 Deansgate, M3 3NW Tel: 0161 834 7278	*	*	*	*	*	*	*	*	*
	Ellis Brigham, Wellington Mill, 211 Duke Street (off Liverpool Road), M3 4NF Tel: 0161 834 5555	*	*	*	*	*	*	*	*	
Milton Keynes	• The Outdoor Shop, 27-31 High Street, Stony Stratford, MK11 1AA. Tel: 01908 568 913	*	*					*	*	
Newcastle-upon-Tyne	• LD Mountain Centre Ltd, 34 Dean Street NE1 1PG. Tel: 0191 232 3561			*	*	*	*		*	*
Northampton	• Two Seasons, 203 Wellingborough Road, NN1 4ED. Tel: 01604 36941	*	*	*	*	*	*	*	*	*
Norwich	• R. G. Pilch, 1 Brigg Street, NR2 1QW Tel: 01603 628224	*	*		*	*	*	*	*	
Nottingham	• Roger Turner Mountain Sports, 120 Derby Road, NG1 5FB. Tel: 01159 417 230	*	*	*	*			*	*	
Oldham	• Paul Braithwaite Outdoor Sports, Rhodes Bank, OL1 1TA. Tel: 01616 202 863	*	*	*	*	*	*	*	*	*

SPORTS SHOPS

We give below a list of Sports Shops in the U.K. showing if they stock ski clothing for adults and children, whether they stock children's skis and boots and whether they provide a hire service for skis, boots and clothing and a ski maintenance service; also if they stock snowboards and boots.

● Denotes discounts for members of the Skier's Holiday Guide Club, see Club Section.

		Ski Clothing		Children's		Hire Services			Ski Main-	Snowboards and boots
CITY/TOWN	ADDRESS & TELEPHONE NO.	Adults	Children	Skis	Boots	Skis	Boots	Clothing	tenance	for sale
Oxford	● Westsports, 274 Banbury Road, Summertown. Tel: 01865 510453	*	*	*	*	*	*	*	*	*
Peterborough	● Hereward Ski & Walk, 14 Fenlake Business Centre, Fengate. Tel: 01733 893647	*	*		*		*	*	*	*
	Wrights Ski Chalet, 5-7 Lincoln Road, PE1 2RJ Tel. 01733 312184	*	*	*	*	*	*	*	*	
Pontefract	● Mr. T. Crossley Tordoff, Jubilee Way, W. Yorks, WF8 1DB. Tel: 01977 702002	*	*	*	*	*	*	*	*	*
Pontypool	1A Torfaen Business Centre, New Inn, NP4 OLS. Tel: 01495 752650	*	*	*	*	*	*	*	*	*
Portsmouth	● Peter Anderson Sports Ltd, 48-52 Elm Grove, Southsea, PO5 1JG. Tel: 01705 820611	*	*	*	*	*	*	*	*	*
Reading	● Pro-Activ, 90-96 Queens Road, RG10 0GU. Tel: 01734 591008	*				*		*	*	
Reigate	Surf & Ski Sports Ltd, 41 Bell Street, Surrey, RH2 7AQ. Tel: 017372 22218	*	*	*	*				*	*
Richmond	● The Snowball Ski Co., 1 George Street, Surrey,TW9 1JY. Tel: 0181 940 6293	*	*						*	*
Southampton	Snow Togs, 431 Millbrook Road. Tel: 01703 773925	*	*	*	*	*	*	*	*	*
Stockport	● Alpenstock, 35 St. Petersgate, SK1 1DH Tel: 0161 480 3660	*	*	*	*	*	*	*	*	*
	● Base Camp, 89 Lower Hillgate, SK1 3AW. Tel: 0161 480 2945	*				*	*		*	*
Sunderland	● Reynolds Outdoor Centre, 6 Derwent Street. Tel: 0191 565 7945	*						*	*	*
Swindon	● Westsports Ski Shop, 18 Fleet Street, SN1 1RQ. Tel: 01793 532588	*	*	*	*	*	*	*	*	*
Yeadon (Leeds)	● The Great Outdoors, 1 Ivegate, W. Yorks. LS19 7RE. Tel: 0113 2504686	*	*	*	*	*	*		*	*

SPORTS SHOPS

We give below a list of Sports Shops in the U.K. showing the main type of skis, bindings and boots stocked.

• Denotes discounts for members of the Skier's Holiday Guide Club – see Club Section.

		SKIS											BINDINGS					BOOTS					
CITY/TOWN	ADDRESS & TELEPHONE NO.	KASTLE	K2	SALOMON	VOLKL	ATOMIC	BLIZZARD	DYNASTAR	FISCHER	HEAD	ROSSIGNOL	OTHER MAKES	LOOK	MARKER	SALOMON	TYROLIA	OTHER MAKES	DYNAFIT	KOFLACH	NORDICA	RAICHLE	SALOMON	OTHER MAKES
Aberdeen	• Anne Robb Sports Studio, 61 St. Swithin St.,AB1 6XL Tel: 01224 323254			*				*	*				*		*		*			*		*	
Altrincham	Nick Estcourt Ski & Climb, 53 Stamford New Road, WA14 1DS. Tel: 0161-928 6613		*	*							*				*					*		*	
Aviemore	Ellis Brigham, 9-10 Grampian Road. Tel: 01479 810175		*	*	*						*			*	*					*		*	*
	• Ski Road Skis, Inverdruie Visitor Centre, PH22 1QH Tel: 01479 810922			*		*		*		*	*				*					*		*	*
	• Speyside Sports, 64 Grampian Road, PH22 1PD Tel: 01479 810656			*	*	*		*		*	*		*	*	*	*			*	*		*	
Barnet	• John Pollock, 67 High Street, EN5 5UR Tel: 0181-440 3994	*		*							*			*	*					*		*	
Bedford	• Two Seasons, 42 Harpur Street, MK40 2QT Tel: 01234 350720		*	*	*			*	*		*			*	*					*		*	*
Bicester	• Beans, 88 Sheep Street, Oxfordshire OX6 7LP Tel: 018692 46451	*	*						*	*						*		*			*		*
Birmingham	Snow & Rock, 14 Priory, Queensway, B4 6BS. Tel: 0121 236 8280	*	*	*					*	*	*	*		*	*	*	*			*	*	*	*
Blackpool	• The Alpine Centre Ltd., 193/5 Church Street, FY1 3NY. Tel: 01253 24307		*	*	*				*	*	*	*		*	*	*		*			*	*	
Bournemouth	Snow Togs, 6 St. Michael's Road. Tel: 01202 557690		*	*					*	*	*			*	*	*	*			*		*	*
Brighton	• Eurosport Ltd., 67 North Road, BN1 1YD. Tel: 01273 688258								*	*						*					*		*
Bristol	• Ellis Brigham, 160 Whiteladies Road, Clifton, . BS8 2XZ. Tel: 0117 974 1157		*	*	*				*	*	*	*		*	*		*			*		*	*
Broughton-in-Furness	• Mountain Centre, Market Street, Tel: 01229 716461			*	*	*	*	*		*	*		*	*	*	*	*		*	*		*	*
Burnley	• Sportak Ltd, 25 Hammerton Street, BB11 1NA. Tel: 01282 436816			*											*							*	
Buxton	• Jo Royle, 6 Market Place, SK17 6EB. Tel: 01298 25824			*	*					*	*	*		*	*		*			*		*	
Cardiff	Ski Dreams, 490 Cowbridge Road East, Victoria Park, CF5 1BL. Tel: 01222 569355		*	*						*					*							*	
Canterbury	• Captain's Cabin, 19 Wincheap, CT1 3TB. Tel: 01227 457906	*	*	*	*	*		*	*	*	*			*	*	*	*	*		*	*	*	*
Catterick	• Ski Slope Shop, Horne Road, Richmond, DL9 4LE. Tel: 01748 833788			*				*			*				*		*			*		*	*
Chatham	• Captain's Cabin Ltd., 93 High Street, ME4 4DL. Tel: 01634 819777	*	*	*	*	*		*	*	*	*			*	*	*	*			*	*	*	*
Chelmsford	• Ski Plus, International House, Navigation Road, CM2 6HX. Tel: 01245 264143	*		*				*	*	*	*			*	*	*	*			*	*	*	*
Cheltenham	• Horace Barton & Son, Cheltenham Ski Centre, 12, Regent Street. Tel: 01242 516772			*					*	*	*				*	*				*		*	

SPORTS SHOPS

We give below a list of Sports Shops in the U.K. showing the main type of skis, bindings and boots stocked.

● Denotes discounts for members of the Skier's Holiday Guide Club - see Club Section.

		SKIS											BINDINGS					BOOTS					
CITY/TOWN	ADDRESS & TELEPHONE NO.	KASTLE	K2	SALOMON	VOLKL	ATOMIC	BLIZZARD	DYNASTAR	FISCHER	HEAD	ROSSIGNOL	OTHER MAKES	LOOK	MARKER	SALOMON	TYROLIA	OTHER MAKES	DYNAFIT	KOFLACH	NORDICA	RAICHLE	SALOMON	OTHER MAKES
Chester	Ellis Brigham, 7 Northgate Street. Tel: 01244 318311		*	*	*						*			*	*					*		*	*
	● Sail & Ski, 9 Pepper Street, CH1 1EA Tel: 01244 344580	*	*	*							*			*	*		*			*		*	
Colchester	Harpers Sports, 7-9 Head Street, C01 1NX Tel: 01206 765451									*				*						*	*		
Derby	Prestidge Ski & Climbing, 47 Queen Street, DE1 3DE. Tel: 01332 3-2245	*		*										*	*					*		*	*
Edinburgh	Blues The Ski Shop, 1 Wemyss Place, EH3 6DH Tel: 0131 2258369	*	*	*						*	*			*	*					*		*	*
	Nevisport Ltd., 81 Shandwick Place. Tel: 0131 229 1197	*		*	*			*	*		*			*	*		*			*		*	*
Elland	● BAC Outdoor Leisure, Central Hall, Coronation Street, Halifax HX5 0DF. Tel: 01422 371146	*	*	*					*		*			*	*	*		*		*			*
Esher	Europa Ski Lodge, The Ski Centre, More Lane, Surrey Tel: 01372 467131	*		*					*					*	*	*				*	*	*	
Glasgow	Blues The Ski Shop, 129 Buchanan Street, G1 2JA. Tel: 0141 204 0686	*	*	*						*	*			*	*					*		*	*
	Nevisport Ltd., 261 Sauchiehall Street, G2 3E2 Tel: 0141 332 4814	*	*	*					*		*			*	*		*			*		*	*
Grantown-on-Spey	● Speyside Sports, 47 High Street, PH26 3EG Tel: 01479 872946			*	*	*				*	*		*	*	*	*			*	*		*	
Gloucester	● Barton Ski Shop, Ski Centre, Robinswood. Tel: 01452 414300	*		*						*	*				*	*				*		*	
Hanley (Stoke on Trent)	● Mountain Fever, 25 Brunswick Street, ST1 1DR Tel: 01782 266137	*		*										*	*					*		*	
Harlow	● John Pollock, Harlow Sports Centre, Hammarskjold Road, CM20 2JF. Tel: 01279 425009	*		*							*			*	*					*		*	
Havant	● Filarinski, 26-28 East Street, Hants. PO9 1AQ. Tel: 01705 499599		*	*	*	*			*	*	*	*		*	*	*	*		*	*	*	*	*
Hemel Hempstead	● Snowcap, 22-24 Lawn Lane, Herts. HP3 9NH. Tel: 01442 242911	*	*	*					*		*			*	*	*		*		*	*	*	
Keswick	George Fisher, 2 Borrowdale Road, CA12 5DA. Tel: 017687 72178	*		*	*									*	*					*		*	
Kingston upon Thames	● Snowbusiness Ltd, 35 London Road. Tel: 0181 541 4857		*					*			*		*	*	*	*			*	*			*
Leeds	● Severn Sports, 80 Town Street, Armley, LS12 3AA Tel: 0113 2791618	*	*	*					*	*	*			*	*	*		*		*		*	*
Leicester	● Roger Turner, 52A London Road, LE2 0QD Tel: 0116 2551952	*		*											*					*		*	
Lincoln	Linsports, 21-23 Silver Street, LN2 1EX Tel: 01522 524674	*												*						*			

SPORTS SHOPS

We give below a list of Sports Shops in the U.K. showing the main type of skis, bindings and boots stocked.

• Denotes discounts for members of the Skier's Holiday Guide Club – see Club Section.

		SKIS											BINDINGS					BOOTS					
CITY/TOWN	ADDRESS & TELEPHONE NO.	KASTLE	K2	SALOMON	VOLKL	ATOMIC	BLIZZARD	DYNASTAR	FISCHER	HEAD	ROSSIGNOL	OTHER MAKES	LOOK	MARKER	SALOMON	TYROLIA	OTHER MAKES	DYNAFIT	KOFLACH	NORDICA	RAICHLE	SALOMON	OTHER MAKES
Liverpool	• Ellis Brigham, 73 Bold Street, L1 4EZ. Tel: 0151 709 6912		*	*	*						*			*	*			*		*		*	*
London	Ellis Brigham Ltd., 30-32 Southampton Street, WC2E 7HE Tel: 0171 240 9577	*	*	*	*						*			*	*		*			*		*	*
	• Don Farrell, 14/15 Holmstall Parade, Edgware, HA8 5HX. Tel: 0181 205 6693	*	*	*					*		*			*	*	*		*		*	*	*	
	Lillywhites Ltd, 24-36 Regent Street, SW1Y 4QF. Tel: 0171 915 4000	*	*	*						*				*	*	*				*	*	*	*
	Snow & Rock, 188 Kensington High Street, W8 7RG. Tel: 0171 937 0872	*	*	*					*	*	*	*		*	*	*	*			*	*	*	*
	Snow & Rock, 150 Holborn, EC1N 2LC. Tel: 0171 831 8545	*	*	*					*	*	*	*		*	*	*	*			*	*	*	*
Loughton	• John Pollock Ltd, 157 High Road, Essex IG10 4LF. Tel 0181 508 6626	*		*							*			*	*					*		*	
Manchester	Ellis Brigham Mountain Sports, 211 Deansgate, M3 3NW. Tel: 0161 834 7278	*	*	*	*				*	*	*	*		*	*					*		*	*
	Ellis Brigham , Wellington Mill, Duke Street, (off Wellington Road) M3 4NF. Tel: 0161 834 5555	*	*	*	*				*	*	*			*	*					*		*	*
Newcastle-upon-Tyne	• LD Mountain Centre Ltd, 34 Dean Street NE1 1PG. Tel: 0191 232 3561	*		*	*									*	*			*		*	*	*	*
Northampton	• Two Seasons, 203 Wellingborough Road, NN1 4ED. Tel: 01604 36941		*	*	*			*	*		*			*	*					*		*	*
Norwich	• R. G. Pilch, 1 Brigg Street, NR2 1QW Tel: 01603 628224	*	*	*											*					*		*	
Nottingham	• Roger Turner Mountain Sports, 120 Derby Road, NG1 5FB. Tel: 01559 417230	*		*						*				*	*					*		*	
Oldham	Paul Braithwaite Outdoor Sports, Rhodes Bank, OL1 1TA. Tel: 0161 620 2863			*	*			*							*							*	
Oxford	• Westsports, 274 Banbury Road, Summertown. Tel: 01865 510453		*	*					*	*	*			*	*	*				*		*	*
Peterborough	• Hereward Ski & Walk, 14 Fenlake Business Centre, Fengate. Tel: 01733 893647								*	*						*		*	*		*		*
	Wrights Ski Chalet, 5-7 Lincoln Road, PE1 2RJ. Tel. 01733 312184		*	*	*			*			*				*					*		*	*
Pontefract	• Mr. T. Crossley Tordoff, Jubilee Way, W. Yorks., WF8 1DB. Tel: 01977 702002		*	*	*				*		*				*	*		*			*	*	*
Pontypool	• Ski Dreams, 1A Torfaen Business Centre, New Inn, NP4 0LS. Tel: 01495 752650		*	*						*					*							*	
Portsmouth	• Peter Anderson Sports Ltd, 48-50 Elm Grove, Southsea, PO5 1JG Tel: 01705 820611			*					*		*				*	*	*	*			*	*	*
Reading	• Pro-Activ, 90-96 Queens Road, RG10 0GU. Tel: 01734 591008			*					*	*					*	*	*				*	*	
Reigate	• Surf & Ski Sports Ltd, 41 Bell Street, Surrey, RH2 7AQ. Tel: 017372 22218		*	*							*			*	*					*		*	*

SPORTS SHOPS

We give below a list of Sports Shops in the U.K. showing the main type of skis, bindings and boots stocked.

• Denotes discounts for members of the Skier's Holiday Guide Club - see Club Section.

		SKIS											BINDINGS					BOOTS					
CITY/TOWN	ADDRESS & TELEPHONE NO.	KASTLE	K2	SALOMON	VOLKL	ATOMIC	BLIZZARD	DYNASTAR	FISCHER	HEAD	ROSSIGNOL	OTHER MAKES	LOOK	MARKER	SALOMON	TYROLIA	OTHER MAKES	DYNAFIT	KOFLACH	NORDICA	RAICHLE	SALOMON	OTHER MAKES
Richmond	• The Snowball Ski Co., 1 George Street, Surrey, TW9 1JY. Tel: 0181 940 6293		*	*					*	*	*			*	*	*				*	*	*	*
Southampton	Snow Togs, 429-431 Millbrook Road. Tel: 01703 773925		*	*					*	*	*				*	*	*			*		*	*
Stockport	• Alpenstock, 35 St. Petersgate, SK1 1DH Tel: 0161 480 3660		*	*					*					*	*	*		*		*	*	*	
	• Base Camp, 89 Lower Hillgate, SK1 3AW. Tel: 0161 480 2945							*					*							*			
Sunderland	• Reynolds Outdoor Centre, 6 Derwent Street. Tel: 0191 565 7945			*							*				*		*			*		*	*
Swindon	• Westsports Ski Shop, 18 Fleet Street, SN1 1RQ. Tel: 01793 532588		*	*					*	*	*			*	*	*				*		*	*
Yeadon (Leeds)	• The Great Outdoors, 1 Ivegate, W. Yorks LS19 7RE. Tel: 01132 504686		*	*	*				*	*	*			*	*	*		*		*	*	*	*

WINTER SPORTS INSURANCE

Whilst not wishing to sound alarmist, it would be extremely foolhardy to embark on your ski holiday without adequate insurance.

Despite being an active sport with an element of risk, the accident rate is low in comparison to the vast numbers participating. But you should not regard these facts as an argument against not taking out insurance. Never feel smug telling yourself you have been skiing for years and never had an accident so insurance is a waste of money. Or, that you are going to ski for a couple of days to see if you like it. Even if you are not going to ski, you will still need accident and medical cover. So be prepared, be insured.

Studies carried out by both resorts and insurance companies give no true indication to who is most likely to have an accident nor at what stage of their skiing life. So it could happen to beginner or expert alike although the greater number of minor injuries occur with the beginner to intermediate group, possibly through over-reaching themselves.

MAKING SURE

If you are booking your holiday through a tour operator the chances are that wintersports insurance will be included in your invoice and be payable at the time of booking. This is to cover both you and them against the eventuality of your cancelling and almost without exception is mandatory.

Should you not wish to be covered by the tour operators' umbrella insurance scheme you must indicate this on the booking form and most companies ask you to provide proof that you are adequately covered on some alternative scheme and may insist on your having their 'Cancellation Cover'.

It is also wise to read through the cover offered and see if it is adequate for your needs, you may wish to add to it or prefer to insure elsewhere with a company specialising in Wintersports Insurance with a policy especially designed for skiers. Obviously no-one wishes to dwell too much on the less favourable aspects of any holiday but it is better to be safe than sorry. And although having insurance won't prevent you from breaking your leg it won't be quite so painful if you don't have a large medical or special transportation bill added to your already considerable chagrin.

GETTING THE BEST COVER

A good policy should cover many eventualities from cancellation, loss of baggage en route, belongings in the resort and in your accommodation, skis etc., on the slopes, breakage of equipment, illness, personal accident, (check carefully as some policies cover you on the slopes but not if you break a leg getting on the plane or fall down the escalator at the airport).

And then there is the expensive follow on to your accident. Some resorts charge for getting you off the mountain and even if the injury is slight, a bandage and a bit of heat treatment can be expensive. You may have to take taxis to and from treatments or simply to move around the resort. Also, some policies ask you to pay an initial sum before their cover becomes effective. So, we urge you again to read the policy very carefully and know in advance just what cover is given and under what conditions.

Whatever the extent of cover, it is always advisable to have a cash fund available, as more often than not injured parties have some outlay before financial assistance arrives, such as a taxi back from the clinic. Should the accident be more severe you may need a helicopter lift off the mountain, private ambulance to the nearest hospital not to mention all the specialist care required when you get there.

Check that this is all covered – the cost can be horrendous. Check too for a 'Get you Home' service, should the injuries be very severe the airline may insist on the unfortunate patient being accompanied by a nurse or a doctor or even be flown by special ambulance plane. It is at this point that the whole business of any 'holiday' insurance becomes a five or even six figure exercise and insurers call on the funds raised through all the thousands they insure who don't have an accident. Think less then when you buy your insurance of it being an expensive extra and more of an investment, if you don't need it this year you may at some time in the future.

Check too to see if it allows for a friend or relative to stay with you either longer in the resort if you can't travel immediately or accompany you on a flight other than the one intended on your package deal.

THE OTHER SIDE OF THE ACCIDENT

So far we have looked at the Personal Accident cover but you must also have Third Party. You are familiar enough with this with your motoring insurance and perhaps wonder what it has to do with skiing. This will cover you against damages should you crash into another skier or skiers causing them injury, breaking their equipment or worse still having legal charges brought against you which is possible in some countries.

Finally a good policy will provide you with loss of earnings due to the effects of an injury resulting from your ski accident. There are some provisos here so check the small print. Usually it has to be proved that the treatment you are receiving prevents you from working.

Or, inability to work because of the nature of the injury, such as immobility in the case of a broken leg. It may be more difficult to effect payment should complications arise after you return home, or you become ill as a result of your accident. Policies vary so read the small print carefully.

A COMPLEX BUSINESS

Well, as you can see Wintersports insurance is not simple or without expensive implications to the insurer. It is vital that insurers understand and are fully aware of all these implications because inadequate cover is almost as bad as no cover at all. Read through the details of the policy carefully before buying and make sure that you will be fully covered in any eventuality. If you are skiing in the United States then the cover has to be even greater and you should ask your insurers about this. Skiing is an expensive sport and maybe you think of wintersports insurance as yet another overpriced extra. But think again, can you afford to be without it?

NATIONAL TOURIST OFFICES IN THE U.K.

THE ANDORRAN DELEGATION
63 Westover Road, London SW18 2RF
Tel: 0181 874 4806

ARGENTINIAN CONSULATE
Trevor House, 100 Brompton Road, London SW3
Tel: 0171 318 1340

AUSTRALIAN TOURIST COMMISSION
Gemini House, 10-18 Putney Hill, London SW15 6AA. Tel: 0181 780 2227 (Aussie Helpline)

AUSTRIAN NATIONAL TOURIST OFFICE
30 St Georges Street, London W1R 0AL
Tel: 0171 629 0461

BOLIVIA TOURS & TRAVEL
120 Wilton Road, London SW1.
Tel: 0171-233 5384

BULGARIA: BALKAN HOLIDAYS
19 Conduit Street, London W1R 9TT
Tel: 0171 491 4499

CANADIAN GOVERNMENT OFFICE OF TOURISM
62-65 Trafalgar Square, London SW1Y 5BJ
Tel: 0171 930 8540

CHILE TOURIST SERVICE
47 Causton Street, London SW1. Tel: 0171-976 5511

FRENCH GOVERNMENT TOURIST OFFICE
178 Piccadilly, London W1V OAL
Tel: 071 491 7622
0171 499 6911 (recorded messages)

GERMAN NATIONAL TOURIST OFFICE
65 Curzon Street, London W1Y 7PE
Tel: 0171 495 3990

ITALIAN STATE TOURIST OFFICE
(E.N.I.T.) 1 Princes Street, London W1R 8AY
Tel: 0171 408 1254

JAPANESE TOURIST OFFICE
Heathcote House, 20 Savile Row, London W1X 1AE. Tel: 0171 734 9638

KOREAN NATIONAL TOURISM CORP.
1 Hanover Square, London W1. Tel: 0171-408 1591

NEW ZEALAND TOURISM BOARD
New Zealand House, Haymarket, London SW1Y 4TQ. Tel: 0839-300900

NORWEGIAN TOURIST BOARD
5 Lower Regent Street, London SW1Y 4LR
Tel: 0171 839 6255

POLISH NATIONAL TOURIST OFFICE
310 Regent Street, London W1. Tel: 0171-580 8811

ROMANIAN NATIONAL TOURIST OFFICE
83 Marylebone High Street, London W1M 3DE
Tel: 0171 224 3692

SCOTTISH TOURIST BOARD – TOURIST INFORMATION CENTRE
19 Cockspur Street, London SW1Y 5BL
Tel: 0171 930 8661

SPANISH NATIONAL TOURIST OFFICE
57-58 St. James's Street, London SW1A 1LD
Tel: 0171 499 0901

SWEDISH TOURIST OFFICE
73 Welbeck Street, London W1M 8AN
Tel: 0171 935 9784

SWISS NATIONAL TOURIST OFFICE
Swiss Centre, 1 New Coventry Street, London W1V 8EE. Tel: 0171 734 1921

UNITED STATES TRAVEL AND TOURISM
The American Embassy, PO Box 1, 124 Grosvenor Square, London W1A 1EN
Tel: 0171 495 4466

SKI ORGANISATIONS

BRITISH ASSOCIATON OF SKI INSTRUCTORS (BASI)
Grampian Road, Aviemore,
Invernesshire PH22 1RL.
Tel: 0479 810 407

BRITISH SKI CLUB FOR THE DISABLED
Springmount,
Berwick St. John,
Shaftesbury SP7 0HQ
Tel: 0747 828515

BRITISH SKI FEDERATION
258 Main Street, East Calder,
West Lothian EH53 0EE
Tel: 0506 884343

ENGLISH SKI COUNCIL
6th Floor, Area Library Building,
The Precinct, Halesowen, West
Midlands. B63 4AJ Tel: 021 501 2314

SCOTTISH NATIONAL SKI COUNCIL
Caledonia House, South Gyle,
Edinburgh EH12 9DQ
Tel: 031 317 7280

SKI CLUB OF GREAT BRITAIN
118 Eaton Square, London SW1W 9AF
Tel: 071 245 1033

SKI COUNCIL OF WALES
240 Whitchurch Road,
Cardiff CF4 3ND
Tel: 0222 619637

ULSTER SKI COUNCIL
8 Abercorn Park, Hillsborough
County Down BT26 6HA
Tel: 0846 683243 (evenings only)

CHECK LIST

PHOTCOPY BEFORE USING VOUCHERS

DOCUMENTS CHECK

- [ ] Passport - check expiry date
- [ ] Have passport pictures taken for lift pass
- [ ] Arrange Eurocheques
- [ ] Check expiry dates on Credit Cards
- [ ] If you have not taken automatic wintersports Insurance with holiday booking apply for cover with Skiers Holiday Guide Club
- [ ] Pay bills that will fall due
- [ ] Check credit on charge accounts
- [ ] If driving to the slopes check all motoring documents
- [ ] Driving Licence
- [ ] Insurance (Motoring contingency)
- [ ] Green Card
- [ ] Road Fund Licence

THINGS TO DO AND ARRANGE

- [ ] Cancel milk and papers
- [ ] Arrange for animals to be looked after
- [ ] Inform the Police of your absence if your home is to be left empty
- [ ] Have car serviced if driving to the resort
- [ ] If car is to be left at the airport book off-perimeter parking
- [ ] Check emergency pack (hired from motoring organisation)
- [ ] Emergency windscreen
- [ ] Spares Kit
- [ ] Continental lighting kit
- [ ] Hazard warning triangle (compulsory in some countries)
- [ ] First Aid Kit (compulsory in some countries)
- [ ] Arrange hire or purchase of roof box or roof rack (Vouchers in Guide)
- [ ] Snowchains (Vouchers in Guide)
- [ ] Check spare wheel

PACKING LIST

Skiwear

- [ ] Ski suit, pants and anorak
- [ ] Roll or zip neck sweatshirts
- [ ] Thermal underwear
- [ ] Liner gloves & socks
- [ ] Suncream & lipsalve
- [ ] Sweaters
- [ ] Ski hats & gloves
- [ ] Plenty of socks
- [ ] Goggles & Sunglasses

Personal

- [ ] Sensible après ski boots
- [ ] Casual clothing
- [ ] Toilet items
- [ ] Hand cream
- [ ] Foot powder
- [ ] Moisturiser, eye cream etc
- [ ] Analgesics
- [ ] Warm coat or anorak
- [ ] Underwear
- [ ] Night clothes
- [ ] Nail scissors
- [ ] Deodorant
- [ ] Elastic bandage, heat rub

Travel Wallet

- [ ] Passport
- [ ] Tickets
- [ ] Sterling
- [ ] Passport size photographs for lift pass
- [ ] Travel details
- [ ] Currency
- [ ] Eurocheques
- [ ] Credit Cards
- [ ] Address & telephone book

SKIER'S HOLIDAY GUIDE CLUB VOUCHER

To: **SKIER'S HOLIDAY GUIDE CLUB,**
8 St. Albans Grove,
London W8 5PN

Self-Catering Holidays by Air or Rail

This is to confirm that the undermentioned is a member of the Skier's Holiday Guide Club and, as agreed, is entitled to a reduction of £5 per person.

David G. Ross

Surname...Init........................Mr/Mrs/Miss

Address..

....

....Tel.No...

Please note: This voucher which is valid for 12 months from 1st October 1997, should be completed and signed and forwarded with your booking form. The appropriate reduction will be made from your account.

SKIER'S HOLIDAY GUIDE CLUB VOUCHER

To: **SKIER'S HOLIDAY GUIDE CLUB,**
8 St. Albans Grove,
London W8 5P

Hotel Holidays by Air or Rail

This is to confirm that the undermentioned is a member of the Skier's Holiday Guide Club and, as agreed, is entitled to a reduction of £10 per person.

David G. Ross

Surname..Init.................................Mr/Mrs/Miss

Address..

....

....Tel.No..

Please note: This voucher which is valid for 12 months from 1st October 1997, should be completed and signed and forwarded with your booking form. The appropriate reduction will be made from your account.

SKIER'S HOLIDAY GUIDE CLUB VOUCHER

To: **SKIER'S HOLIDAY GUIDE CLUB,**
8 St. Albans Grove,
London W8 5P

Staffed Chalet Holidays by Air or Rail

This is to confirm that the undermentioned is a member of the Skier's Holiday Guide Club and, as agreed, is entitled to a reduction of £10 per person.

David G. Ross

Surname..Init.................................Mr/Mrs/Miss

Address..

....

....Tel.No..

Please note: This voucher which is valid for 12 months from 1st October 1997, should be completed and signed and forwarded with your booking form. The appropriate reduction will be made from your account.

SKIER'S HOLIDAY GUIDE CLUB VOUCHER

To: **SNOW-CHAINS EURO PRODUCTS**
The Bourne End Enterprise Centre
Borough Green, Kent, TN15 8DG. Tel: 0732 884408

Snow-Chains for Cars

This is to confirm that the undermentioned is a member of the Skier's Holiday Guide Club and, as agreed, is entitled to a 10% reduction on the purchase of snow-chains for cars.

David G. Ross

Surname..Init..............................Mr/Mrs/Miss

Address..

....

....Tel No...

Please note: This voucher which is valid for 12 months from 1st October 1997, should be completed and signed and presented to Snow-Chains Euro Products when making your purchase.

All correspondence should be direct with Snow-Chains Euro Products and not with the Club.

SKIER'S HOLIDAY GUIDE CLUB VOUCHER

To: **SKIER'S HOLIDAY GUIDE CLUB,**
8 St. Albans Grove,
London W8 5PN

'Car Skiing' & Self-Catering Holidays

This is to confirm that the undermentioned is a member of the Skier's Holiday Guide Club and, as agreed, is entitled to a reduction of £20 per car.

David G. Ross

Surname.. .Init.................................Mr/Mrs/Miss

Address..

....

....Tel.No..

Please note: This voucher which is valid for 12 months from 1st October 1997, should be completed and signed and forwarded with your booking form. The appropriate reduction will be made from your account.

SKIER'S HOLIDAY GUIDE CLUB VOUCHER

To: **SNOW-CHAINS EURO PRODUCTS**
The Bourne End Enterprise Centre
Borough Green, Kent, TN15 8DG. Tel: 0732 884408

Car Roof Boxes

This is to confirm that the undermentioned is a member of the Skier's Holiday Guide Club and, as agreed, is entitled to a 10% reduction on the purchase of Car Roof Boxes.

David G. Ross

Surname..Init..............................Mr/Mrs/Miss

Address..

....

....Tel No...

Please note: This voucher which is valid for 12 months from 1st October 1997, should be completed and signed and presented to Snow-Chains Euro Products when making your purchase.

All correspondence should be direct with Snow-Chains Euro Products and not with the Club.

CONCESSIONS FOR MEMBERS

UK SPORTS SHOPS

Country/Resort	Name of Sports Shop	Percentage Discount to Members On Hire	On Purchases
Aberdeen	Ann Robb Sports Studio	–	10
Aviemore	Ski Road Skis	15	10
	Speyside Sports	10	10
Barnet	John Pollock	-	5
Bedford	Two Seasons	10	10
Bicester	Beans	–	10
Blackpool	Alpine Centre	–	10
Bowness-on-Windermere	Ski Treks/Lakeland Leisure	10	12
Brighton	Eurosport Ltd	10	10
Bristol	Ellis Brigham	5	–
Broughton-in-Furness	Mountain Centre	–	10
Burnley	Sportak Ltd	–	10++****
Buxton	Jo Royle	–	10
Canterbury	Captain's Cabin Ld.	10***	10***
Catterick	Ski Slope Shop	10	10
Chatham	Captain's Cabin	10***	10***
Chelmsford	Ski Plus	–	10
Cheltenham	Horace Barton & Son	–	10
Chester	Sail & Ski	–	10
Eastbourne	Outdoor Life	–	10+
Elland	BAC Ski Shop	10	10
Esher	Europa Ski Lodge	–	5
Gloucester	Horace Barton	–	10
Grantown-on-Spey	Speyside Sports	10	10****
Hanley	Mountain Fever	–	10
Harlow	John Pollock	–	5
Havant	Filarinskis	5	10
Hemel Hempstead	Snowcap	–	5
Kingston Upon Thames	Snowbusiness Ltd	10***	10***
Leeds	Severn Sports	–	10
Leicester	Roger Turner Mountain Sports	–	10
Liverpool	Ellis Brigham	10	–
London	Don Farrell	–	10***
Loughton	John Pollock	–	5
Milton Keynes	The Outdoor Shop	–	20
Newcastle-upon-Tyne	LD Mountain Centre	–	10
Northampton	Two Seasons	10	10
Norwich	R. G. Pilch	–	10***
Nottingham	Roger Turner Mountain Sports	–	10
Oldham	Paul Braithwaite	10	10
Oxford	Westsports	–	10
Peterborough	Hereward Ski & Walk	–	20****
Pontefract	Crossley Tordoff	–	10
Portsmouth	Peter Anderson Sports	–	10
Reading	Pro Activ	5	5
Richmond	Snowball Ski Company	–	Varies
Stockport	Alpenstock	–	10
	Base Camp	–	10
Sunderland	Reynolds Outdoor Centre	–	5
Swindon	Westsports Ski Shop	–	10
Yeadon (Leeds)	The Great Outdoors	–	10

***Credit Cards 5% ****Not on special offers +On Purchases of £100 or over
++Cash/Cheque sales only

CONCESSIONS FOR MEMBERS

ARTIFICIAL SKI SLOPES

City Town	Name of Slope	Percentage Discount to Members
Aldershot	Alpine Ski Centre	10++
Churchill	Avon Ski Centre	10*
Edinburgh	Hillend Ski Centre	10++
Halifax	Halifax Ski Centre	10
Hemel Hempstead	Hemel Ski Centre	5++
London	Crystal Palace Ski School	10
Newmilns	Newmilns Ski Slope	10
Tallington	Ski & Snowboard Centre	10
Tunbridge Wells	Bowls Ski Centre	10*
Uxbridge	Hillingdon Ski & Snowboard Centre	10
Welwyn Garden City	Gosling Ski Centre	10++

*On Ski Lessons ++ Recreational skiing

GLOBAL SKI GUIDE

SKI HOTLINE

Latest reports for 180+ ski resorts throughout Europe and North America. For full details of snow and weather conditions by voice or fax dial:

0891 654 625
For a voice forecast

0897 500 625
For a fax forecast

Please ensure you use a fax handset if accessing a fax report. Calls cost 50p/min at all times (as at 8/97). SKI Hotline is a product of Newstel Information Ltd, 203 Pentagon Centre, Glasgow G3 8AZ. Helpline: 0990 133 345

SKIER'S HOLIDAY GUIDE CLUB

MEMBERSHIP CARD
1997/98

The holder of this card is a member of the Club from 1st October 1997 for a period of one year. It is only valid when a passport photograph of the member has been inserted and signed.
Aim of Club: To promote skiing in co-operation with interested organistions in the U.K. and overseas.
Service to Members: U.K. or Overseas members are entitlted to:

- *Free Advisory service on all aspects of skiing holidays
- *Discounts at 51 sports shops in the U.K.
- *Discounts at 162 Resort sports shops
- *Discounts at 11 artificial ski slopes in the U.K.
- *Discounts on package holidays by car, rail or by air*
- *Discount for Car Roof Boxes*
- *Discounts for Car Snow chains*
- *Comprehensive Winter Sports Insurance Service
- *Booking service air travel only
- *Booking service for apartments, chalets and hotels

Passport photo of Member

*Vouchers in Guide

Signature...

CONCESSIONS FOR MEMBERS

RESORT SPORTS SHOPS

Country/Resort	Name of Sports Shop	Percentage Discount to Members On Hire	OnPurchases
ANDORRA			
Arsinal	Sports Rossel	20	5
La Massana	Sports Rossel	20	5
Pal	Sports Rossel	20	5
Pas de la Casa	Ski Calbo	20	5
Soldeu	Ski Calbo	20	5
AUSTRIA			
Fieberbrunn	Widmann Sport	10	–
Gargellen	Madrisa–Skiverleih	10	–
Hochgurgl	Intersport Riml	10	5
Lermoos	Sport Mader	10	–
Obergurgl	Intersport Riml	10	–
Obertauern	Sporthaus Gloria	10	5
St. Anton	Sport Pangratz	10	5
Seefeld	Sport Christian	15	–
Söll	Ski Centre Stoll Söll	15	10
Steinach	Sport Messner	10	10
Westendorf	Dieter's Sport Shop	15++	10++
Zell am Ziller	Schuh u Sport Pendl	5	5
	++Cash		
FRANCE			
Alpe D'Huez	Henri Sports (Les Bergers)	20	5
	Henri Sports (Chamois d'Or)	20	5
	Man Sport (Les Bergers)	20	5
Argentière	Les Grands Montets Sports	20	5
Avoriaz	Superski (Place Central)	20	5
	Mir-Famose (Place Central)	20	5
	Skiland (Falaise)	20	5
	SkiFun (Falaise)	20	5
	Sport Espace (Falaise)	20	5
Chamonix	Ogier Sports	20	5
Chatel	Intersport	15	10
	Francis Sport (Les Névés)	20	5
	Francis Sport (Chamois d'Or)	20	5
	Le Linga	20	5
Courchevel 1650	Serge Sport (Ourse Bleue)	20	5
Courchevel 1850	Ski Service (Club Hotel)	20	5
	Ski Service (Chabichou)	20	5
	Ski Service (Chamois)	20	5
	Ski Service (Tovets)	20	5
	Ski Service (New Solarium)	20	5
	Ski Service (Bellecôte)	20	5
Flaine	Flaine Sport (Forêt)	20	5
	Général Sport (Hameau)	20	5
	La Boutique (Forum)	20	5
Isola 200	Morisset Sport	20	5
La Clusaz	Guy Perillat Shop (Le Portillo)	20	5
Belle Plagne	Belle Plan Sports	20	5
Plagne Centre	Allais Ski Service	20	5
Plagne Bellecôte	Skiteam	20	5
Plagne 1800	Plagne 1800 Sports	20	5
Champagny	In'Sport	20	5
Aime 200	Skiteam	20	5
Montabert	Sport Passion	20	5
Les Coches	La Godille	20	5
La Rosière	Ski Boutique La Poudre	20	5
La Tania	Ski Wave	20	5

CONCESSIONS FOR MEMBERS

RESORT SPORTS SHOPS

Country/Resort	Name of Sports Shop	Percentage Discount to Members On Hire	On Purchases
FRANCE			
Le Corbier	Noel Sports	20	5
Les Arcs	Ski Shop (Arc 1600)	20	5
	Ski Shop (Arc 1800)	20	5
	Ski Shop (Arc 2000)	20	5
Les Carroz	Ski 2000	20	5
Les Coches	La Poudreuse	20	5
Les Deux Alpes	Brun Sport (Centre)	20	5
	Hibernatus (Vénosc)	20	5
	J M Sports	20	5
	La Datcha	20	5
Les Menuires	Léo Lacroix Sports (La Croisette)	20	5
	Léo Lacroix Sports (Réberty)	20	5
	Skiloc CC Sports (Preyerand)	20	5
Mégève	Duvillard et Lafforgue	20	5
Méribel	Sport Boutique (Les Carlines)	20	5
	Sport Boutique (Centre)	20	5
	Germain Sport (Centre)	20	5
	Sport Tecnik (La Chaudanne)	20	5
	Chamois Sports (1600)	15	10
Méribel Mottaret	Ski Espace (Res. Olympia)	20	5
	Superski (Res. Le Pralin)	20	5
	Surf Machine (Res. Plan du Lac)	20	5
	Sport Boutique (Hameau)	20	5
Morzine	La Caribou Sports	20	5
Risoul	Evasion Sport (Front de Neige)	20	5
	Evasion Sport (Res. Mélèzes A)	20	5
	Free Ride (Mélèzes)	20	5
St Lary	Rodriguez Sport (Pla d'Adet)	20	5
Serre Chevalier	Régis Sport (1350)	20	5
	Régis Sport (1400)	20	5
	Régis Sport (1400)	20	5
Tignes	Point Service Ski (Val Claret)	20	5
	Point Service Ski (Lavachet)	20	5
	Point Service Ski (Le Borsat)	20	5
	Point Service Ski (Chalet Club)	20	5
	Point Service Ski (Rd Point Pistes)	20	5
	Point Service Ski (Le Lac)	20	5
	Sport Glisse (Val Claret)	20	10
Val Cenis	Sports Vanoise	20	5
	La Poudre	20	5
Val d'Isére	Skiset (La Daille)	20	5
	Point Service Ski (Centre)	20	5
Valfréjus	Ski Pro	20	5
Valloire	Val d'Auréa Sport	20	5
Valmorel	Claude Sport	20	5
Val Thorens	Goitschel Sports (Péclet)	20	5
	Goitschel Sports (Caron)	20	5
	Goitschel Sports (Espace Goitschel)	20	5
	Skiloc CC Sports (Altineige)	20	5
Vaujany	Sami Ski	20	5
Villars de Lans	Nouvelles Glisses	20	5
ITALY			
Foppolo	Mode Sport F. Berera	5	10
Limone	Bottero Ski	10	10
Macugnaga	Rabogliatti Sport	10	10

CONCESSIONS FOR MEMBERS

RESORT SPORTS SHOPS

Country/Resort	Name of Sports Shop	Percentage Discount to Members On Hire	On Purchases
NORWAY			
Nordseter	Aktivitets & Skisenter	10	–
Wadahl	Wadahl Sports	10	10
SPAIN			
Sierra Nevada	Veleta Ski	10	10
SWEDEN			
Duved	Duveds Skiduthyrning	10	10
SWITZERLAND			
Adelboden	Hari Sport	10	–
Andermatt	Meyer's Sporthaus	10	10
	Alpina Sport	10	–
Anzere	Jacky Sports	10	–
	Crazy Corner Sports	10	–
Arosa	Carmenna Sport	10	–
	Bananas Snowboard Centre	10	–
Bettmeralp	Mattig Sport	10	–
Braunwald	Kessler Sport	10	–
Celerina	Testa Sport	10	10
Champery	Berra Sports	10	10*
	Borgeat Sports	10	–
Crans-Montana	Galeries Bouby Sports	10	–
Davos-Dorf	Ettinger Sport	10	5
	PaarSenn Sport	10	–
Davos-Platz	Ettinger Sport	10	5
	Grischetta Sport	10	–
Disentis	Bergbahnen Disentis AG	10	–
Engelberg	Quattro Sport	10	–
	Titlis-Sport	10	10
Flims-Dorf	Bundi Sport	10	–
Flims-Waldhaus	Bundi Sport	10	–
Flumserberg	Gubser Sport	10	
Grindelwald	Graf Sport	10	–
Gstaad	Hermenjat Sports	10	–
	Hermenjat Boutiques	10	–
Klosters	Gotschna Sport	10	–
	Albeina Sport	10	–
Laax	Meini Sport Mode	10	–
Lenzerheide	Pesco Sport	10	–
Les Diablerets	Jacky Sports	10	–
Leysin	Hefti Sports	10	–
Morgins	Morgins-Sports	10	–
Riederalp	Krüger Sport	10	–
Rougemont	Duperrex Sport	10++	10++
Saas-Fee	Anthamatten Sport	10	–
Samnaun	Hangl Sport	10	–
Samedan	Luthi Sport	10	–
Savognin	Wasescha Sport AG	10	–
Schönreid	Frautschi Sports AG	10	–
Scuol	Hanin Conradin Sport	10	–
Silvaplana	Skiservice Corvatsch	10	–
St. Moritz-Bad	Corviglia Sport Shop	10	–
St. Moritz	Corviglia Sport Shop	10	–
Verbier	Danni Sports	20	10
	La Vallée Sport	10	–
	Ski Service SA	10	–
Villars	Dätwyler Sport	10	–
Wildhaus	Steiner Sport	10	–
Zermatt	Bayard Sport	10	–
Zuoz	Willy Sport	10	–
	* Over SF 100 ++ Cash	–	